WITHDRAWN

NORTH DAKOTA
STATE UNIVERSITY
MAY 3 0 1980
SERIALS DEPT.
LIBRARY

THE BOWKER ANNUAL

THE BOWKER ANNUAL OF LIBRARY & BOOK TRADE INFORMATION

25TH EDITION
1980

Edited and Compiled by Filomena Simora

Consulting Editors
Frank L. Schick and Carolyn Forsman

Sponsored by
The Council of National Library and Information Associations Inc.

R. R. BOWKER COMPANY
New York & London, 1980

Published by R. R. Bowker Co.
1180 Avenue of the Americas, New York, N.Y. 10036
Copyright © 1980 by Xerox Corporation
All rights reserved
International Standard Book Number 0-8352-1273-4
International Standard Serial Number 0068-0540
Library of Congress Catalog Card Number 55-12434
Printed and Bound in the United States of America

No copyright is claimed for articles in this volume prepared by U.S. Government employees as part of their official duties. Such articles are in the public domain and can be reproduced at will.

Contents

Preface xi

PART 1
REPORTS FROM THE FIELD

NEWS REPORTS
LJ News Report, 1979. *Noël Savage* 3
SLJ News Report, 1979. *Bertha M. Cheatham* 28
PW News Report, 1979. *Chandler B. Grannis* 37

SPECIAL REPORTS
The White House Conference on Library and Information Services.
 Marilyn K. Gell and *Vera Hirschberg* 43
The WHCOLIS Preconferences. *Alice B. Ihrig* 47
Library Service to Disabled People: A State of the Art Report for the 1970s.
 Ruth A. Velleman 53
On-Demand Information Services. *Renée Schick* and *Alix C. Levy* 66

FEDERAL AGENCIES
The Copyright Office: Developments in Copyright Law, 1979.
 Marybeth Peters 70
Federal Information Centers. *Donald R. Knenlein* 73
National Commission on Libraries and Information Science.
 Alphonse F. Trezza 80
National Technical Information Service. *Ted Ryerson* 83
National Telecommunications and Information Administration.
 William Garrison 86
U.S. Government Information Clearinghouses: A Directory 92

FEDERAL LIBRARIES
Library of Congress. *James W. McClung* 94
National Library Service for the Blind and Physically Handicapped.
 Frank Kurt Cylke and *Eunice Lovejoy* 99
National Library of Medicine. *Robert B. Mehnert* 105
Technical Information Systems/National Agricultural Library.
 Eugene M. Farkas 109

NATIONAL ASSOCIATIONS

American Booksellers Association. *G. Roysce Smith* 112

American Library Association. *Thomas J. Galvin* 115

American National Standards Committee Z-39 and International Organization for Standardization Technical Committee 46.
Robert W. Frase and *James L. Wood* 124

Association of American Publishers. *Mary McNulty* 132

Association of Research Libraries: A Five-Year Review, 1975-1979.
John G. Lorenz 140

Council for Computerized Library Networks. *James G. Schoenung* 145

Information Industry Association. *Paul G. Zurkowski* 149

National Librarians Association: A Forum for Librarians. *Peter Dollard* 156

OCLC, Inc. *Philip Schieber* 162

Special Libraries Association, 1977-1980.
David R. Bender and *Richard E. Griffin* 167

PART 2
LEGISLATION, FUNDING, AND GRANTS

Legislation Affecting Librarianship in 1979.
Eileen D. Cooke and *Carol C. Henderson* 175

Legislation Affecting Publishing in 1979. *Washington Staff, AAP* 187

Legislation Affecting the Information Industry, 1979. *Robert S. Willard* 195

FEDERALLY FUNDED PROGRAMS AND GRANT-MAKING AGENCIES

Library Services and Construction Act (LSCA). *Elizabeth H. Hughey* 204

Elementary and Secondary Education Act, Title IV, Part B—Instructional Materials and School Library Resources. *Beatrice Simmons* 218

Higher Education Act, Title II-A, College Library Resources.
Sheldon Z. Fisher and *Frank A. Stevens* 221

Higher Education Act, Title II-B, Library Education.
Frank A. Stevens and *Babetta Norwood* 223

Higher Education Act, Title II-B, Library Research and Demonstration Program. *Henry T. Drennan* 232

Higher Education Act, Title II-C, Strengthening Research Library Resources. *Frank A. Stevens* 239

General Revenue Sharing Support for Libraries. *Frank Wm. Goudy* 242

National Endowment for the Humanities Support for Libraries, 1979 246

National Science Foundation Support for Information Science Research.
Sarah N. Rhodes 251

National Historical Publications and Records Commission 258

FOUNDATION AND OTHER GRANTS

Council on Library Resources, Inc. *Nancy E. Gwinn* 264

The Foundation Center as a Resource 271

Analysis of Foundation Grants to Libraries, 1979.
Robin M. Klor and *Janis Witkins* 277

Foundation Grants to Libraries, 1979. *Compiled by The Foundation Center* . 285

PART 3
LIBRARY EDUCATION, PLACEMENT, AND SALARIES

Guide to Library Placement Sources. *Margaret Myers* 307

Placements and Salaries, 1978: New Directions.
Carol L. Learmont and *Richard Troiano* 321

Sex, Salaries, and Library Support, 1979.
Kathleen M. Heim and *Carolyn Kacena* 334

Accredited Library Schools 345

Library Scholarship Sources 347

Library Scholarship and Award Recipients 349

PART 4
RESEARCH AND STATISTICS

LIBRARY RESEARCH AND STATISTICS

Research on Libraries and Librarianship in 1979: An Overview.
Mary Jo Lynch 359

Recent Developments in Library Statistical Activities. *Eugene T. Neely* 363

Characteristics of the U.S. Population Served by Libraries. *Nadine Edles* ... 371

Number of Libraries in the United States and Canada 373

Public and Academic Library Acquisition Expenditures 375

Urban-Suburban Public Library Statistics. *Joseph Green* 380

Special Libraries Serving State Government Agencies.
Herbert Goldhor and *Linda C. Smith* 392

Public School Library Media Centers. *Robert David Little* 395

Surveys of Law Libraries, 1973–1979. *Alfred J. Lewis* 401

Public Library Buildings in 1979.
Karl Nyren, *Barbara Livingston*, and *Bette-Lee Fox* 410

Academic Library Buildings in 1979.
Karl Nyren, *Barbara Livingston*, and *Bette-Lee Fox* 431

Two-Year College Learning Resource Center Buildings in 1979.
D. Joleen Bock 441

BOOK TRADE RESEARCH AND STATISTICS

Book Industry Study Group, Inc. *John P. Dessauer* 443
Book Title Output and Average Prices, 1978-1979. *Chandler B. Grannis* 446
Prices of U.S. and Foreign Published Materials. *Sally F. Williams* 454
U.S. Census of Book Publishing, 1977. *John P. Dessauer* 467
U.S. Consumer Expenditures on Books in 1978. *John P. Dessauer* 473
Number of Book Outlets in the United States and Canada 476
Book Review Media Statistics 477

PART 5
INTERNATIONAL REPORTS AND STATISTICAL ANALYSES

INTERNATIONAL REPORTS

Frankfurt Book Fair, 1979. *Herbert R. Lottman* 481
International Librarianship. *Naimuddin Qureshi* 490
International Publishers Association. *J. A. Koutchoumow* 495
Library and Information Services in Egypt, 1979. *Mohamed M. El Hadi* 501
The Parliamentary Library: Present and Future. *Erik J. Spicer* 507

INTERNATIONAL STATISTICS

American Exports and Imports and International Title Output.
    Chandler B. Grannis 510
British Book Production, 1979 514

PART 6
REFERENCE INFORMATION

BIBLIOGRAPHIES

The Librarian's Bookshelf. *Carol S. Nielsen* 521
Basic Publications for the Publisher and the Book Trade. *Jean R. Peters* 532

DISTINGUISHED BOOKS

Literary Prizes, 1979 539
Notable Books of 1979 549
Best Young Adult Books of 1979 550
Best Children's Books of 1979 552
Best Sellers of 1979: Hardcover Fiction and Nonfiction. *Daisy Maryles* 554

PART 7
DIRECTORY OF ORGANIZATIONS

DIRECTORY OF LIBRARY AND RELATED ORGANIZATIONS

National Library and Information-Industry Associations, United States and Canada	563
State, Provincial, and Regional Library Associations	631
State Library Agencies	642
State School Library and Media Associations	646
State Supervisors of School Library/Media Services	652
International Library Associations	656
Foreign Library Associations	666

DIRECTORY OF BOOK TRADE AND RELATED ORGANIZATIONS

Book Trade Associations, United States and Canada	676
International and Foreign Book Trade Associations	682
U.S. Book Distribution and Exchange Programs	689

CALENDAR, 1980–1981 695

INDEX 699

DIRECTORY OF U.S. AND CANADIAN LIBRARIES 725

Preface

With the publication of the twenty-fifth anniversary edition of the *Bowker Annual*, coverage has been expanded to include the information industry as well as libraries and the book trade.

In the newly created Special Reports section of Part 1, there are a number of reports that reflect the increasing importance of information services in the United States: a report on the White House Conference on Library and Information Services, another on the pre-White House conferences, and a brief overview of on-demand information services.

In the Federal Agencies section of Part 1, there are reports from the National Technical Information Service and the National Telecommunications and Information Administration. Two very useful directories are also included in this section: "U.S. Government Information Clearinghouses" and "Federal Information Centers" (the latter directory appears at the end of the report on the Federal Information Centers program).

Of interest on the national level, representing the information industry, is the report from the Information Industry Association, and in the area of networks there are reports from OCLC, Inc., and the Council for Computerized Library Networks.

Rounding out the coverage of 1979 legislative activity in Part 2, and offering a new perspective to this coverage, is the article "Legislation Affecting the Information Industry, 1979."

And, in Part 7, the directory of "National Library Associations, United States and Canada" has been expanded to include information-industry associations.

Going beyond the 1980 edition's focus on the information industry, there are many other informative articles reflecting important issues and activities of 1979.

Recent developments in library services to the handicapped is the subject of two separate articles: "Library Service to Disabled People: A State of the Art Report for the 1970s" (a Part 1 Special Report) and a report from the National Library Service for the Blind and Physically Handicapped in the Federal Libraries section of Part 1.

Complementing annual reports from a selected group of national associations in Part 1 are a five-year review of the activities of the Association of Research Libraries and a three-year review of the activities of the Special Libraries Association.

Added this year to the comprehensive coverage of funding to libraries in Part 2 is the report "General Revenue Sharing Support for Libraries."

As in last year's edition, library education, placement, and salary information has been gathered in Part 3. New this year to this group of articles is the report "Sex, Salaries, and Library Support, 1979." Also new to Part 3 is "Library Scholarship and Award Recipients," which appeared in Part 6 of previous editions.

New this year in Part 4 are reports on the results of several recently completed surveys, an overview of law library surveys from 1973 to 1979, a report on recent developments in library statistical activities, and a special report on the Book Industry Study Group, Inc. Also in Part 4 is the overview article by Mary Jo Lynch "Research on Libraries and Librarianship in 1979," which last year appeared in Part 1. Information on 1979 book trade mergers is included in "*PW* News Report, 1979," in Part 1.

In Part 5, the reader finds a wide range of subject coverage with an international frame of reference—from the annual report on the Frankfurt Book Fair, to a report on the activities of the International Publishers Association, to an overview of the status of the parliamentary library in the world. Please note that prices of foreign published materials are included in Part 4, together with U.S. price information, for the convenience of librarians.

Reference and Directory Information, Part 6 of previous editions, has been divided this year into Parts 6 and 7 to separate the two very distinct types of information it contained. Included this year under Reference Information (Part 6) are all of the articles on distinguished books, together with "The Librarian's Bookshelf" and "Basic Publications for the Publisher and the Book Trade." Part 7 contains all of the organizational directory information.

Following this year's index (at the back of the book) is a considerably expanded "Directory of U.S. and Canadian Libraries."

We wish to gratefully acknowledge all those who contributed articles and information for the *Bowker Annual* this year. Special thanks go to Nancy L. Leff for her dedication to the editorial and production quality of this edition.

As always, we welcome your comments on this volume and suggestions for articles for future editions.

Part 1
Reports from the Field

News Reports

LJ NEWS REPORT, 1979

Noël Savage
Associate News Editor, *Library Journal*

The White House Conference on Libraries and Information Services was the main event in 1979, a year dominated by the uncertainties of a shaky economy. Close to 900 delegates and alternates, ranging in age from 10 to 80, came to Washington to chart—and influence—the destinies of libraries in the years ahead. Some were chosen to speak for librarians, but the majority were there as the voice of the people—all the people. The 105 at-large delegates were specifically chosen to make the assembly a "microcosm of society." The delegates had a clear task in sight: saving the library from the economic neglect that is jeopardizing its survival today and from the obsolescence that threatens to make it irrelevant in the future.

The delegates asked for federal money, with no strings, to build better facilities, utilize new technology, create and strengthen networks, and help people enrich their lives and alter their destinies in a world where the options for nearly everyone are narrowing. They showed special concern that libraries assume their rightful moral obligation in taking up the cause of the illiterate, the handicapped, the poor, and the disadvantaged. The traditional task of providing books was mentioned, but in itself drew little interest.

The WHCOLIS delegates learned something about the democratic process—its shortcomings and its advantages—as they tried to adapt to the regimen of the conference. Five days running, morning until night, were filled with meetings for the debate of issues in large- and small-group workshops, speeches, actual voting, and courtesy calls from the president and congressmen. Over a dozen caucuses were formed to defend regional and group concerns, but they ended up working together even before the ground rules were agreed upon. Roadblocks to a smooth running conference looked formidable at first, but a threatened donnybrook over rules didn't happen thanks in part to the late hour when debate started.

The conference was so structured that delegates broke off into small groups to prepare resolutions for review in larger Theme Groups. The themes selected in advance by WHC staff (Library and Information Services for . . . Meeting Personal Needs; for Lifelong Learning; for Improving Organizations and Professions; for Effectively Governing Society; and for Increasing International Cooperation) were not—to many delegates—clearly representative of the priorities pegged at pre-WHC meetings. No procedures were provided for interchange among the five parallel Theme Groups prior to voting on issues. The upshot: Theme Groups spent a lot of time drafting resolutions asking for many of the same things, as if there were five separate White House Conferences.

Note: Reprinted from *Library Journal*, January 15, 1980.

Delegates working in small groups had to make concessions as they fought for the adoption of their carefully worded resolutions. More concessions—and the elimination of cherished language and meanings—were to come as the resolutions were stripped down to the bare bones by debate in Theme Groups and rewriting in resolution committees that had to work against the clock and almost around the clock. Delegates in one Theme Group mutinied against their moderator, who had to be replaced. Two Theme Groups walked out on Saturday night because WHC staff couldn't move paper fast enough to provide them with needed information. But somehow it all came together in the last grueling hours: delegates, skillfully manipulated into getting down to basics by moderator Edmund Reggie, voted at last on a set of pared down resolutions.

The upshot was that the president, Congress, and the nation would get only a bare outline of the concerns articulated behind the closed doors watched over by security guards. But what they got was cast in near-concrete consensus.

What was lost in the shuffle was the delegates' great concern for issues—such as access and free information—that in the past have been generally taken for granted. The WHCOLIS deliberations indicated unmistakably that people see a need for constitutional guarantees assuring free access; that they're greatly concerned with defense of local control; that they want the federal government to help, but they fear government control and they are confused about what its role in the dissemination of information should be. They're not sure whether new technology will expand or restrict (by virtue of fees) access. There's great ambivalence towards a National Periodicals Center, coolness towards making the Library of Congress the national library, and opposition to almost any organization of national scope—including ALA, taking a leadership role.

Discussion in the international cooperation group got snagged thanks to a speech by Canadian Bernard Ospry, who warned that small nations could lose their national identity and much more by sharing data with a suprapower, even one as seemingly altruistic as the United States. There was fierce debate about the wisdom of censoring Russia for violating the Helsinki agreement—a proposal that was scratched in the end, after it was pointed out that all nations, including the United States, practice censorship.

The question of money to support libraries came up again and again. One panacea—a national per capita aid formula—didn't seem to be such a hot idea to states that have high per capita aid now, and would stand to gain nothing. The delegates ended up endorsing numerous aid packages. But after having worked out their own funding proposals, they were angered by the clout of Whitney North Seymour, Jr., who used a combination of political savvy and moonie-like promotion gimmicks to muster the support he needed to win endorsement of what had seemingly become his National Library Act proposal.

The 34 top resolutions to emerge out of the five Theme Groups included concerns which came up again and again: equal (but not necessarily free) access to all information for all the people; representation on library boards for the handicapped and increased accessibility for the handicapped; literacy; cooperative approaches to lifelong learning; access to libraries and instruction in their use for children; access to resources through networks; mandated school libraries; a national information policy; a new Office of Library and Information Service in the DOE; involvement of libraries in public issues and government; steps to improve international cooperation—reducing U.S. costs, exchanging personnel; and developing standards for information in machine-readable form.

Other resolutions voted: support for access under First Amendment guarantees; federal funding for network planning at all levels including the local level; more federal aid instead of the cutbacks proposed now for the 1981 budget; new federal support for research and development, cultural awareness programs, youth incentives, and elementary and school libraries; and a nationwide campaign to improve "public awareness of libraries." Also: a new White House Conference every decade; a National Indian Omnibus Library Bill; youth representation on the National Commission on Libraries and Information Science (NCLIS); and the establishment of a planning body to be appointed from the delegates by NCLIS.

Delegates came down on the side of innovation, local autonomy, and service to people who are excluded from society. They seemed ready to go home and continue the fight for these priorities at city hall and at the state capital. They got tips on strategy from Ralph Nader, who warned that government and corporations preserve the status quo by making sure communications are dull. He warned that if the library message is dull, it too will not get across. TV consumer advocate Nicholas Johnson warned that TV is a totalitarian system ruled by a few; the revolution to overcome it, he urged, could start in libraries. New York State Senator Major Owens said that libraries get "pitiful pennies" and deserve much more.

The delegates heard the governor of Arkansas and the mayors of Dallas and the District of Columbia back libraries, knowing that these leaders put their money where their mouth is. They saw President Carter deliver a speech—all smiles—but make no promises or recollect any promises made to libraries in 1975. And at the congressional hearing concluding WHC, they saw the kind of gimlet-eyed and knowledgeable scrutiny their agenda for the 1980s would get when it gets to Capitol Hill. [See the Special Reports section of Part 1 for a summary of the preconference activities by Alice B. Ihrig and an overview article on the White House Conference by Marilyn Gell and Vera Hirschberg—*Ed.*]

THE FUTURE IN FUNDING

Despite high hopes at WHC, prospects are slim for major increases in federal library aid. Delegates were reminded that President Carter's "lean and austere" budget for 1980 proposes a $388 million reduction in federal aid to schools and libraries. It urges zero funding for Higher Education Act Title II programs (College Library Resources, Training, and Demonstrations) as well as a major reduction in LSCA (for Library Services and Interlibrary Cooperation) and especially drastic cuts in Elementary and Secondary Education Act money for library materials. Congress may go along with White House austerity; there is a growing consensus that fiscal restraint is imperative.

Legislation ahead: The Ninety-sixth Congress will review renewal of HEA; it will consider potentially sweeping revision of legislation (Title 44) governing the way government disseminates (or bars access to) information; and it will have brought before it a National Library Act "study bill" proposing a whole new approach to federal aid. NLA proposes direct federal aid to libraries, more LSCA money for cooperation and for buildings, and the creation of a National Library Agency. Chief sponsor of NLA, the Urban Libraries Council, was seeking originally to improve the lot of big urban libraries. ULC had sought, with meager success, a special claim on LSCA money, but failed to win exclusive rights to new LSCA Title I funds over the $60 million "trigger." The NLA proposal also raised early opposition; it did not get the endorsement of COSLA (Chief Officers of State Library Agencies), which is most concerned that state libraries retain responsibility for programs and funds. In response, COSLA developed its own legislative blueprint.

When Congress examines proposals for new library legislation and funding, this lack of consensus in the field will not be lost on legislators. [For detailed reports on federal funding, see the articles in Part 2 under Federally Funded Programs and Grant-Making Agencies—*Ed.*]

The future for library funding appears to be in state aid, where growth has been strong and steady: 42 states now support their public libraries, while 21 help their public library systems. All together these states gave close to $155 million in 1979. New York was the biggest giver ($34 million), while Maryland was tops in per capita aid ($2.42).

Dramatic gains were logged in 1979: North Dakota and Oregon launched state aid programs; Minnesota and Oklahoma doubled library support. Illinois legislators overrode the governor's veto to bring about "full library funding" of $16 million, with much of it earmarked for library systems hard hit by three years of state level austerity. Many other states are giving more too: Michigan, Colorado, Connecticut, Florida, Maryland, Rhode Island, South Carolina, and West Virginia.

State library clout can be quite critical to funding prospects. Aggressive leadership at the state agency level has been bringing home the bacon in such states as Illinois, New York, Ohio, Louisiana, West Virginia, Maryland, and Washington.

State library associations have become adept at building grass-roots support for libraries and getting the library message across to legislators. In 1979, the New York Library Association again stepped up its traditionally vigorous lobbying program.

The vulnerability of the state library agency to the existing political machine became apparent again in 1979. Pennsylvania "politicized" its library agency by removing from Civil Service the positions of state librarian and bureau chief. And at year's end it looked as if Georgia's top library post would become a political appointment too. On the other hand, Michigan's state library challenged Civil Service "reform" starting with the demotion of MSL staffers; it won out when Michigan's pre-WHC backed its cause.

State aid prospects could improve dramatically thanks to the citizen power which was brought out by the WHCOLIS preconferences. Arkansas, Connecticut, the District of Columbia, Louisiana, and Michigan conferences spawned citizen groups that have pledged to pressure politicians for more library money. Florida's spinoff group launched a two-year PR blitz to bring more dollars to that state's libraries. In striking contrast with this fighting spirit was the action of Vermont delegates following their governor's rousing speech on the evils of state and federal aid; they promised to abandon the unholy pursuit of outside aid and dig instead for local gold (even from private sources).

Public libraries still count on local funding for a good 82 percent of their revenue. Despite the recession, the majority of America's libraries have been logging small but steady gains. But most library budgets are being outpaced by inflation.

The tight economy helped make tax reform a popular political tactic again in 1979. But few states and localities opted to jeopardize vital municipal services with as drastic a reform as California's Proposition 13. Had the tax revolt spread across the nation as had been feared at first, libraries would have lost the mainstay of their funding. At year's end things were looking up even in Proposition 13 country, with the promise of direct state aid for California libraries.

THE CALIFORNIA STORY

But 1979 was a very difficult year for them. Proposition 13 tax losses forced the layoff of more than 1,200 library staffers, eliminated nearly 11,000 hours of service weekly, cut book budgets 20 percent, and reduced or eliminated both "inreach" and outreach programs. Interlibrary loan traffic dropped 50 percent.

Very little of California's $4 billion in "bail out aid" found its way to libraries. But when the state saw fit to give extra emergency aid to "special districts" (which rely on property tax revenue for all of their income, and were consequently devastated by Proposition 13) libraries were specifically mentioned as a priority; Los Angeles County was one pulled back from the brink. The aid provided special districts was woefully inadequate, however, and their funding shortage hurt the majority of California's county libraries, which provide library service to the districts and count on them for revenue.

Libraries came up with different strategies for survival. Palm Springs sold two of its four branches and then convinced city fathers to up its book budget 65 percent and provide money for an OCLC connection. San Diego Library Director Kenneth Wilson saved the book budget, but lost the support of his dwindling staff, and finally resigned. Some libraries (Contra Costa) braced for a lean future by consolidating administration and investing in automation.

But library unions won their fight for pay increases when the state high court ordered California to lift a Proposition 13-linked wage freeze. Unfortunately, this victory killed a $5 billion state aid package that was to have been doled out on the condition that city employees get raises no higher than those of state employees.

The Proposition 13 climate spawned a bill aimed at ending "free" library service, but legislators wouldn't okay it. The Attorney General nixed fees for basic library service, but urged libraries to charge for such extra services as meeting room use. The California State Library had earlier decreed what is basic in library service, "free loans, free reference assistance, and the acquisition of current materials."

The California Library Association urged the state to take up responsibility for its libraries, taking care to assure "a minimum of state control and the preservation of local autonomy in the administration of library service."

California assumed long-range funding responsibility for all locally supported services with the passage of AB 8, which shifted property tax revenue formerly earmarked for schools (funded now direct) to cities ($207 million); counties ($312 million); and special districts ($200 million). With AB 8, libraries have more of a chance at winning more of the take because no particular service (such as police or fire protection) gets priority. And prospects for California's ailing county libraries improved when they were given a shot at both special district and county money for the first time.

If libraries do fare poorly in the stiff competition for AB 8 dollars, California will weigh anew direct library aid.

SURVIVING IN THE LEAN YEARS

Fighting against Proposition 13-type tax cutting, government bodies across the land have turned to highly visible efforts to decrease waste and inefficiency in government. Zero-base budgeting, requiring that all funding be justified, has become a common practice. In the case of the Memphis Shelby County Library, zero-base budgeting won a much needed budget boost.

Seeking assurance that tax dollars are being properly spent, New York City ordered "performance audits" for all departments, including libraries. NYPL trustees balked at first, invoking their "private" status, but then thought better of it.

In cases of extreme hardship, counties sought to relieve cities of a portion of their funding burden. This didn't work out for Rochester, New York, where the city reduced library funding more when the county stepped in. Tight budgets have stimulated interest in the merging of public and county library systems in places like Rochester and Genessee County, Michigan.

To win out in the battle of the budget, libraries have had to develop the political savvy to compete for funds, enlist their communities for their budget wars, and become more adept at PR.

Indications are that libraries have achieved the kind of visibility that can count heavily. In dramatizing NYPL's fiscal plight, the news media for the first time consistently mentioned libraries along with police and fire protection as "the basic services that the city has a duty to finance." NYPL's branch libraries won the restoration of over $2 million in funding and escaped a major cutback ordered by the mayor. A Bel Air, Maryland, survey found that the vast majority not only oppose cutbacks in library support, but are willing to pay more taxes to enable libraries to do more.

Building strong alliances with the ruling political structure can be critical to a library's survival. Aurora, Colorado's library won ground when it moved its administrative offices into city hall; its close proximity with government helped bring Aurora's budget up 27 percent. Quincy, Illinois, has consistently racked up bigger budgets by giving city hall up-to-date statistics to show how much it's doing with the taxpayer's money. Tucson Public showed its appreciation for its 17 percent funding boost by telling city fathers its plan for saving money with automation and for expanding information service.

Coming to grips with big tax losses better than any other county agency similarly afflicted, the Prince George's County Memorial Library System (Maryland) won the respect of county government with its bold plan for opening two branches and installing automated circulation despite staff and dollar losses. The Free Library of Philadelphia faced the fact that it will have to devise new approaches to library service if it is to get along with permanently reduced funding. Philadelphia Friends pulled out all the stops—rallies, motorcades, petitions—in a desperate fight to win back a 23 percent funding loss, but less than half was restored.

Community support has in many other cases given libraries the muscle to fight off assaults on their bugdets. Irate phone calls in the wee hours of the morning prodded county government to move quickly to restore funding to New York's Ramapo Catskill Library System. Public outcry saved Baltimore's Enoch Pratt Free Library from a $350,000 cutback; the mayor now wants the people to pressure the state to give the central library the money it "deserves as a valuable state resource."

People are often coming down on the side of libraries when they go to the polls. Voters prodded Osceola County, Florida, to restore library funding. The majority opted to put more dollars into libraries in places like Cuyahoga County, Ohio; Dauphin County, Pennsylvania; and Colorado Springs. But a library bond issue in Oklahoma City got thumbs down as did everything else proposed in a recent referendum.

Many communities came out strongly for new libraries. Phoenix voted the money to build a new branch and buy more books. Aurora, Colorado; Pawtucket, Rhode Island; and Omaha, Nebraska were among the many communities to vote for new libraries. Iowa City disregarded the objections of the Chamber of Commerce and the media by putting its vote behind a new downtown library. But in Kenosha, Wisconsin, city fathers had to put up the money for a library that voters consistently turned down.

There's a growing debate over local versus state or federal responsibility for building libraries. A growing number of states now offer help to communities, but Florida was the latest to cut off construction aid, and LSCA Title II hasn't provided construction dollars for years.

Federal aid still flows in other channels, however. Conceiving of libraries as an essential component of "neighborhood improvement," Community Development Act people awarded funding to restore New York's historic Solvay Public Library. A combination of county money and revenue sharing built a new facility for the First Regional

Library, serving five counties in Mississippi. An Appalachian Regional Commission grant helped bring a library to the Rural Hall/Stanleyville area of North Carolina. CETA money was used to hire an artist in residence to spruce up Seattle branches.

THE ACQUISITIONS CRUNCH

The acquisitions budgets of American public and academic libraries have for the most part been growing steadily. Some libraries (Hennepin County and Nobles County, Minnesota; Dallas, and Louisville) racked up stunning gains. Others (Knoxville-Knox) were hurt by lean budgets. But libraries today are finding more varied ways to cope with tight budgets, and are not automatically choosing the unpopular option of cutting the book budget. Some, in fact, are even putting more money into books as a kind of earnest of good fiscal intentions.

The Association of Research Libraries pegged shrinkage in buying power for its prestigious members: budgets are going up 11 percent, but actual buying is up only 3 percent. Canada pegged lost buying power stemming from its shaky dollar at 25 percent.

But high book prices are starting to meet with "meaningful price resistance"—possibly the first stage of a recession-linked buying slowdown. Publishers weren't hurt by the stock market crash of 50 years ago, but they're bigger and far more vulnerable to the nation's economy now. They're starting to experiment with lower prices for the bookstore consumer.

Academic libraries with little hope of new construction money have sought out ways to cope with soaring costs and a shortage of space for books and people. The University of Oregon complained that its future would be one of "continued reductions in library services and collections." ARL looked for relief in national library programs (like the National Periodicals Center it backed so strongly) designed to help everyone "use limited resources to maximum effect." But there is still a minority opinion favoring continued growth: Stanford's David Weber held that in 50 years the most prestigious libraries would house up to 20 million volumes and not just 10. And top libraries like Yale and Harvard kept buying as if the now controversial University of Pittsburgh study never pointed a finger at academe's "wildly wasteful ways." But studies at Cornell and Carnegie-Mellon sought to determine if the acquisitions practices at these libraries are indeed out of touch with user need.

Many academic libraries moved decisively—at last—to stem the flow of acquisitions money into periodicals. Often backed with new quota systems, they cancelled more subscriptions to save money for books. The Interuniversity Library Council (Fort Worth-Dallas) was only one consortium which went into cooperative purchasing to stimulate the elimination of expensive subscriptions.

Academic libraries of all sizes are turning increasingly to cooperative acquisitions programs to keep pace with the surge in published information and the prices charged for it. Houston research libraries formed a consortium for sharing in 1979. Seeking to make libraries more efficient, ARL has long been helping big institutions develop "self-study" expertise to improve collection development, management, and services; last year it extended its guidance to the small academic library too. The Universal Serials and Book Exchange has a warehouse of periodical retreads (many of them high demand items) which could be the answer for libraries with small budgets and gaps in their collections. But USBE is not getting enough traffic to support its operations, and libraries are in danger of losing this low-cost-efficient source of materials.

As another answer, some states are helping build up the collections of their academic libraries. Florida has committed itself to a five-year investment of $10 million annually. Foundation aid is helping too: Catholic University got close to $2 million from the National Endowment to buy books and otherwise "enhance the study of the humanities." The University of Tennessee's collection will grow thanks to a generous Lyndhurst grant. NYPL's Research Libraries got their annual NEH challenge grant, which seems to generate the kind of good publicity that stimulates perennial giving.

And federal money available under HEA Title II-C strengthened the resources of 25 chosen research libraries: the $6 million they share will help buy 40,000 books, preserve another 20,000, and open access to their resources nationally. The older HEA II-A program still helps institutions large and small buy books, and in its revised form is designed to channel a little more aid to needier libraries.

Urban public libraries serving over 750,000 made unexpectedly strong gains in funding during the 1977-1979 biennium—41 percent in per capita support. Steps being taken to shore up the urban library stem in part from the recognition that these facilities are the people's university as well as statewide resources. Dallas got an NEH challenge grant to stock its new main library.

There's been a shift in thinking about the proper use of LSCA, which is now buying books as well as fueling innovative projects. Chicago Public got $438,016 in LSCA money for book buying. New York State got $1.5 million in LSCA to put more books in all its libraries. And LSCA can now be used both to buy and stock kiosk libraries. Richmond, Virginia, was the first to win LSCA for this kind of neighborhood improvement.

Louisiana put its first state aid (over $1.5 million) into books in 1978. One indication of its impact: the book budget of the New Orleans Public Library tripled.

Libraries, both public and academic, have tried to stretch the library dollar by using discount lease packages. Brodart's McNaughton lease plan has become the only show in town, however. In 1979 Brodart bought the businesses of such firms as Josten's, H. R. Huntting, and Clark's. In 1980, McNaughton book prices will be increased drastically.

While the budget crunch has turned some libraries off approval plans, others are investing more in plans that promise to harness new technology to help cut their clerical costs and get books to the shelves faster. U.S. firms such as Baker & Taylor are starting to offer keen competition to British approval plans (Blackwell's Oxford) now that they have more British titles in stock. The first reports on B&T's LIBRIS automated acquisitions system gave it points for improving book ordering productivity and for speedy book delivery.

WEATHERING THE ENERGY CRUNCH

Libraries today have had to budget for an energy-scarce future and the likelihood of steeper fuel bills. Libraries are planning for long-range energy saving, and some have benefited from new federal and state funding to make facilities energy efficient. Milwaukee's Atkinson branch library became the first building in Wisconsin to win money for energy conversion—to be followed by three more Milwaukee branches.

The Tulsa City-County Library System found that storm windows and insulation curbed energy costs significantly at certain of its branches. Even totally electric libraries are finding ways to beat the energy crunch. The Schaumburg Township Library in Illinois did it with a Honeywell computerized electrical control system, an approach which hasn't worked for all. New York's North Tonawanda Public Library cut energy use 25 percent, and will save more when it switches from electrical heating to gas.

More libraries being built today are designed to save energy. Idaho State University's new library did it with heavy insulation, minimum window-to-wall area ratio, and an unusual heating system. Earth berms helped make Connecticut's Groton Public Library the most energy efficient building in town.

Libraries in places as different as Santa Fe, New Mexico, and Rochester, New York, are counting on solar energy to help them conserve energy. Wheaton College (Norton, Massachusetts) plans for low energy use with an underground library addition.

The energy crunch, coupled with dwindling usage, has fueled the belief in some quarters that the time of the bookmobile has come and gone. Baltimore County and the Connecticut State Library took their bookmobiles off the road permanently. Other libraries are thinking smaller: Washington's King County Library System replaced its big trucks with smaller Travelling Library Centers that go direct to the homebound instead of following a route.

But bookmobile boosters contend that bookmobiles save energy if you consider the number of patron trips they save. Bookmobiles are trying to build a case for their own survival by doing more than ever before. Not uncommon are such varied services as blood pressure and diabetes screenings, plant clinics, skin care demonstrations, puppet shows, films, and clowns.

Bookmobiles are still important in some communities. Rockland County, New York, proved that sidelining the bookmobile can be the best way of driving home the impact of budget cuts; public protest prodded the county to restore library funding.

THE FUTURE IN NETWORKS

The year just past has been the start of a new era in networking as the major contenders for national and regional dominance staked out new claims for territory and as pious pronouncements about cooperation were elbowed roughly by territorial growls. At the same time, current thinking about networking and what it can mean for the future of the library has taken on new clarity. Library planners are now eyeing options among which they will have to choose. The conception of a highly sophisticated national network that would supersede existing network structures is an idea whose time has clearly passed. Today's consensus holds that network development should be evolutionary and "built on strength"—allowing libraries to survive in their present forms as they move into the future.

Competition among stakeholders for network territory is now viewed by many as healthy and in the best interests of national network development: components that can't do what is expected of them will simply fail without jeopardizing the total structure. That coexistence among disparate network components is possible is reflected in current practice: libraries today are tapping data base vendors for bibliographic search; OCLC, RLIN, or WLN (Washington Library Network) for shared cataloging; OCLC for interlibrary loan; and the RLIN network for subject search and reference.

A key element in current thinking about network governance is opposition to the idea of centralization; a national coordinating agency for networking gets thumbs down. There was fast fading support in 1979 for having the Council on Library Resources, the Library of Congress, or NCLIS take the driver's seat in network development. And there was a serious questioning of CLR's efforts to forge a network structure, making LC the "keystone of the nation's bibliographic structure"—one apparently designed with the needs of the research libraries most in mind. CLR has achieved little progress so far in its goal of bringing about an interface between the two major bibliographic utilities, OCLC and RLIN/WLN. The utilities say they're all for interface (Battelle will study the possibilities), but they're also making much of their "responsibility towards their members." Meanwhile, there's suspicion about CLR's real priorities; some people concerned for the future of OCLC feel CLR has only RLG interests at heart.

Hostility towards centralization has also helped fuel resistance to the proposed National Periodicals Center—something that seemed a sure thing in 1978, and still being urged by NCLIS and ARL, but now under attack from many sides. At year's end, the Pacific Northwest Bibliographic Center nixed NPC as incompatible with its "regional concerns." [For reports on the recent activities of OCLC, Inc., and the Council for Computerized Library Networks, see the National Associations section of Part 1—*Ed.*]

THE RLG CHALLENGE

Clearly seeking the commanding position on the network scene, RLG aligned itself in 1979 with the regionally successful Washington Library Network and agreed to share data bases and jointly develop products and services. It offered a "partnership" to the California Library Authority for Systems and Services (CLASS) to broker RLG/WLN services to all kinds of libraries in California and neighboring states—an arrangement that could appeal to regional organizations should it work for CLASS. And RLG spent the year seeking out members (measuring up to ARL's high standards), winning over from the OCLC camp such heavies as state universities in Iowa, Michigan, and Colorado as well as Cornell, Princeton, Dartmouth, Rutgers, the University of Pennsylvania, Brown, and Brigham Young. The defection of a few state universities, coupled with RLG's promise that members would get preferential treatment in ILL, caused some regional network planners to express alarm at the possible loss of access to resources of libraries joining RLIN, but RLG reaffirmed its continuing loyalty and good faith.

RLG is building an image as a prestigious research library club taking responsibility for national network services to all research libraries, and therein lies some of its appeal. But some academic libraries have remained fiercely loyal to OCLC, claiming it to be a proven system, improving every day, and far less expensive than its unproven competitor. But the exodus of OCLC members to RLG raised fears that OCLC could lose major sources of shared cataloging, and with its volume of business reduced, would be forced to hike its prices.

OCLC is seeking to discourage defection by demanding that its members buy all their English-language monographic cataloging from OCLC and by selling members on new contract provisions that would bar "third party access" to OCLC records. This could lead to a court challenge since it involves the very institutions that helped make OCLC what it is today.

But the new competition has also prompted OCLC to sharpen its performance: it's working to develop a circulation control system by acquiring and adapting an already developed system; it has an ILL subsystem up and running and its acquisitions system will be ready to go in 1980. In evident response to the "membership" appeal of RLG, it is also talking about "repersonalizing" bibliographic service.

One show of faith in the future of OCLC made big news in 1979: its $38.5 million construction bond issue sold out in a mere five days. OCLC clearly sees itself as the nationwide computerized library network with over 2,100 terminals in over 1,500 libraries in 46 states. At year's end, pressing hard against the competition, OCLC sought out CLASS just as RLG had—waving a proposal for a 100-member resource-sharing network based on OCLC.

REGIONALS ON THE MOVE

Regional organizations (that depend on OCLC for survival) are taking bold initiatives. One by one, the regionals (AMIGOS was the latest) have severed their ties with the educational bodies that nurtured them in their early years; they're now charting their own destinies. SOLINET, AMIGOS, and the Midwest Region Library Network (MIDLNET) came out with specific plans for network development in their regions. And looking to the day when they could possibly interface with each other, nine of the regionals last year decided to identify areas and activities where more cooperation would be profitable to all.

The regionals are apparently eager to broker RLIN as well as OCLC services. Members of the Southeastern Library Network openly expressed interest in being a middleman for RLIN, while SOLINET staff were pushing for "more flexibility" in their contract with OCLC. AMIGOS had BCR (Bibliographic Center for Research) create a private file of catalog records from AMIGOS/OCLC tapes in what looks like an attempt to create a regional alternative to OCLC's subject search system. With the new clout given them within OCLC governance structure (as the OCLC Users Group), the regionals fought on both sides of the issue of "third party use" of OCLC records, something OCLC is not willing to give up now.

RLG seems to be wary of the ambitions of the regionals too: it cut off the brokering of RLIN cataloging information being handled by BCR when two clients for RLIN services joined the network; RLG evidently wants to provide shared cataloging directly to its members, with no broker or middleman. RLG has hedged on just how much of its business it will allow regionals, acting as its broker, to provide nonmembers in the market for RLIN/WLN services, mentioning only search access thus far. But RLG is evidently still going ahead with plans to provide bibliographic services to libraries in California and other western states through CLASS.

The regionals may be entering a new phase where they will be coming into competition with state or multistate organizations too: the State University of New York/OCLC user group (SUNY/OCLC is a state-based broker) has challenged the propriety of putting major state funding into NYSILL, New York's present hierarchical interloan network, when OCLC's promising new ILL subsystem could—they claim—do a better and far less expensive job of connecting people with resources.

The network territorial maneuverings of 1979 resemble the copyright wars of the early 1970s in some ways. OCLC, Inc., very much a business enterprise despite the nonprofit flag of convenience it sports, is trying to harden its boundaries both against the research libraries community and to contain its ambitious vassal states, the regional networks. The issue of "third party access," much argued toward the year's end, found OCLC in the awkward position of trying to restrict its members' use of their own bibliographic records, a situation analogous to the publisher who attempts to restrict or levy a tariff on a purchaser's sharing of an article in a periodical he has bought. While OCLC was mired in this problem, its chief rival utility, RLIN, announced that it wouldn't consider placing such restrictions on *its* members.

As for copyright, the furor has died down considerably, becoming a hot issue only when the private sector saw fit to fight off the copyright threat it saw in the proposed National Periodicals Center. Towards year's end, music publishers announced a new "get tough" policy aimed at the likes of larcenous choirs who had been photocopying their scores.

The Copyright Clearance Center set up by publishers to collect royalties continued to run in the red in 1979 and had to use most of the fees it collected to subsidize its own operations. But CCC, in turn, forced the National Technical Information Service's new Journal Article Copy Service out of business.

Libraries that charge patrons for photocopying came under fire from an unexpected quarter: the New York Chemists' Club got hit with a sizable bill for back payment of sales tax plus penalties. But Iowa exempted its libraries from sales tax liability.

THE WAY OF THE MULTITYPE

Federal money has to a large extent fueled state level library system development, but more states are seeing the wisdom of putting money into cooperation, particularly multitype cooperation. Minnesota amended its legislation to allow multitypes to share the $365,000 appropriated for cooperation. New York moved into a significant new stage of network development with two big regional projects linking school cooperative agencies (BOCES) with that state's strong systems of public and academic libraries. At question, however, is whether New York has wasted time and money in uncoordinated, top heavy system development, while other states, later developing, will get much better results with less outlay thanks to proper, well-coordinated planning.

There are other indications that multitype cooperation is the wave of the future. Ten states (Colorado, Indiana, Illinois, Kansas, Kentucky, Maine, North Dakota, Rhode Island, Vermont, and Washington) put all their money into multitype cooperation. New on the multitype scene is the Consortium of Rhode Island Academic and Research Libraries, which has 13 public and academic libraries as members and is trying out a reciprocal borrowing plan for faculty members.

NEW TECHNOLOGY

Skepticism about the promise of the technology dwindled in 1979. The rapid rise in resource sharing that came about thanks to OCLC and the on-line circulation systems brought into sharper focus what technology could do for libraries. And many of 1979's pioneering ventures gave hint of the future for technology in libraries. Among them: a CATV and circulation system hookup that will transform TV sets into terminals for an on-line catalog (Lexington, Virginia); an on-line interface linking OCLC and CLSI (Innovative Interfaces, Inc.), thereby allowing libraries to combine cataloging and circulation file building; access to DIALOG's 75 data bases via CLSI terminals; and OCLC's "home book club" allowing for audience participation in a TV book discussion program. But the pitfalls of new technology were evident at what was to have been a showcase production for it: at the White House Conference information center. Many of the data bases on display did not work, and it was the print collection at the information center that caught the eye of White House staffers who expressed a desire to duplicate it for the executive staff.

New successes and the waning memory of old failures made predicting the future of technology a popular pastime again. One crystal ball gazer held that by 2001 there would be little need for libraries and librarians in a nation wired to provide low cost electronic access to information for all the people, direct in their homes and offices. But other gazers into electronic entrails held out hope for libraries, pointing to the growth of big library consortia, with more to come; more heterogeneity in higher education offerings; and more interlocking of libraries, government, and business. But some people felt that new technology would not be the great equalizer after all; differences in the living conditions and education of the people would vary more markedly than ever before.

People monitoring developments today find that the engineering of governance and not technology to be the chief concern: "The technology we can handle. But our institutions are getting so complex that we're getting into trouble." Meanwhile libraries of all types began to look to consortia and regional cooperative organizations to provide them with stronger support for their automation programs.

Library advances in technology have been hampered by funding shortages and the lack of research that could help libraries modify direction as needed, observed Barbara Markuson of INCOLSA. But some promising investigations were launched: Carnegie-Mellon University will see if the technology of big libraries could also automate small libraries. EDUCOM will seek out barriers holding back computer-based sharing in academic libraries.

The rapid advance of technology has prompted most—but not all—libraries to abandon efforts to maintain in-house expertise. This leads to a potential problem of overdependence on the vendors of systems such as OCLC and CLSI. In response, online user groups have come to the fore to articulate the voice of the individual librarian in discourse with the vendor.

The training and retraining of librarians has been a weak link in library exploitation of data bases; BCR is exploring the use of a microcomputer to train a number of students simultaneously in data-base use. The University of Pittsburgh is taking the lead among library schools with an intensive on-line training project.

Librarians want the know-how to be smarter shoppers. The Special Library Association's previews of automation systems played to packed houses in New York, Washington, D.C., and Columbus EDUCOM ran seminars comparing the merits of BRS, Lockheed, and the System Development Corporation.

Fees remained a hot question, but there was growing acceptance of charging for sophisticated technology and specialized library expertise. But the feeling is strong that fees could price libraries—and too many people—out of the information marketplace. California State College, Stanislaus, showed how to provide free, and superior, data-base access with money saved by eliminating certain print reference tools. New York and South Dakota state funding helps bring free on-line searches within everyone's reach. But increased demand (including soaring ILL requests) have forced South Dakota to try to curb use. Some public libraries are experimenting with free public access to technology: Minneapolis launched a now thriving on-line reference service. But many other libraries are charging for such frills.

The fuss the Bibliographic Retrieval Services User Group put up when *Psychological Abstracts* boosted prices for on-line access points to new watchfulness by information consumers; the pricing practices of OCLC and RLG's RLIN are also expected to come under scrutiny.

THE CATALOGING REVOLUTION

The closing of the catalog will be costly, complex, and disruptive, but most major libraries will have little choice but to follow suit when LC closes its catalog. Many card catalogs ceased to function over a decade ago, and now impede access. 1978's debate about the *Anglo-American Cataloguing Rules* revision prompted LC to delay until 1981 the date for closing its catalog and switching to *AACR II*. But the adoption of the new code is now more widely viewed as both inevitable and desirable. The University of Illinois is one of the first to switch to *AACR II* for its new cataloging. But OCLC won't be ready to handle *AACR II* records until 1981.

New thinking about cataloging holds that COM—Computer Output Microfilm —is only a short-term solution to be superseded eventually by the on-line catalog. But COM can be cost effective if you consider that the major expense is in converting data to a master tape, which can be the basis for either form of catalog as well as other automated systems for circulation, acquisitions, and resource sharing. And COM tape can be used to provide economical access to lesser used files.

The COM revolution is going strong. Chicago Public, Dallas Public, and Los Angeles County are among those to have made the switch. Cuyahoga County expects to save up to $235,000 a year with COM. Alabama created an ALICAT to open statewide access to the resources of its major libraries. SOLINET went into the business of producing COM CATS at prices that are hard to beat. Its customers have included Florida State University, the Joint University Libraries of Nashville (now Vanderbilt University Libraries), and the Memphis and Shelby County Library. AMIGOS is going into COM business too.

There are other options in cataloging other than COM and OCLC. Ramapo Catskill, New York, and a school system in Montgomery County, Maryland, opted for the relatively inexpensive Mini Marc system that relies on regularly updated MARC microform records of LC cataloging rather than on-line access to a databank. Warner Eddison Associates is marketing a software package (INMAGIC) developed by them to enable small libraries to build a data base of their holdings and produce anything from library cards to bibliographies and billing and ordering printouts. MARCFICHE is still another option.

ON-LINE CIRCULATION

The majority of libraries serving populations of 25,000 and up (70 percent according to one estimate) are expected to automate their circulation systems. On-line circulation is increasing resource sharing and boosting circulation, while decreasing staff hours on circulation tasks. It's saving libraries money too: San Jose's SCI (Systems Control, Inc.) system saved $170,000 in one year and brought in fines revenue faster too.

Competition for circulation business hasn't let up, but there's greater receptivity among vendors to the idea of interfacing. AMIGOS aims to develop a protocol to allow libraries in different states to interconnect their diverse systems, home builts as well as shelf models. Wyoming tried to get all its libraries to buy the same system—a plan was set back, but not irretrievably when Natrona County jumped the gun in opting for CLSI. But other vendors suddenly became eager to interface with CLSI, although when polled by the Metropolitan Washington Council of Governments as late as 1978, the vendors were more hesitant, voicing concern about third party use of their software.

A growing number of libraries planned for the linkage of data bases for circulation, cataloging, and other functions. Atlanta plans to integrate its Dataphase system with its OCLC cataloging subsystem and the COM catalog it gets from Baker & Taylor. Montgomery County, Maryland, will hook its SCI circulation system into data bases developed for its book catalog and its BATAB acquisitions system.

Money for on-line circulation is coming from a variety of sources. State money, LSCA, foundation grants, and gifts will pay for a 100-terminal system linking all types of libraries in one Connecticut region. Revenue sharing enabled Tulsa City-County to go into Dataphase. Chula Vista, California, got a local lending institution to back its

Dataphase connection. And Natrona County sold the city its parking lot to get money for its CLSI.

More libraries are sharing their circulation systems both to economize and open up access to area resources. The Spokane County Library system is sharing its Dataphase system with both public and university libraries. Gaylord has a mini-network going in Long Island, New York. CLSI has piggy-back arrangements in Detroit; Napa, California; and southeast Connecticut. The North Suburban Library System's CLSI now taps into the collection of the University of Illinois. Clark County, Nevada's LIBS 100 is the hub of an expanding network that now includes the state library. The University of Illinois went on-line with its Library Computer System and plans to extend the system to other universities in Illinois.

Circulation system vendors developed new capabilities aimed at attracting customers. Gaylord came out with an inexpensive Micro Mini I, and also upgraded its software to do a better job with interlibrary loan. CLSI modified its system to handle more terminals, and then proceeded to rack up such big contracts as Hennepin County, California State University, Rice University, Michigan State, and Florida's state university system. SCI claimed to be cost competitive on smaller systems like the one it developed for Anaheim as well as bigger systems it is primarily designed for.

New contenders for automation business entered the packed field in 1979. Canada's Geac, which started in banking automation, branched out to libraries (London, Ontario Public, and the University of Guelph, Yale, and Connecticut's Southwestern Regional Library Council and Capitol Region Library Area). And IBM's multifunction DOBIS/LIBIS system attracted attention in both Canada and the United States.

A FUTURE IN THE PROFESSION?

The job crunch worsened in 1979 as libraries continued to fight against rising personnel costs by freezing vacancies, consolidating positions, sharing staff, and making more use of paraprofessionals and volunteers. The reallocation of people became a common means of dealing with staff shortages; the University of Hawaii has put its collection development people at public service posts. In California, a rash of early retirements, sudden dismissals of library directors, and a migration out of state of top talent made it clear that Proposition 13 would have far broader ramifications than the first wave of staff layoffs and library closings had indicated.

The steadily worsening job market in the public sector gave impetus to the exodus of librarians to the private sector.

Job prospects for the beginning librarian did not improve substantially. New graduates found jobs scarcest in school and public libraries, and consequently migrated to academe or to "other library organizations." Many had to accept a nonprofessional position if they wanted to work in a library. The State University of New York at Buffalo tried to help; it launched a high powered placement service to tell employers exactly what its grads have to offer. Meanwhile joblines and conference placement services tried to match growing numbers of job seekers with increasingly selective employers.

The competition for jobs was stiffer than ever and promising beginners often had an edge because they would start with a lower salary. Contra Costa County, California, filled many of its vacancies with beginners and also made more use of students and nonprofessionals.

For the seasoned professional, the easy job mobility of years past has ended. There's a new reluctance to switch jobs or even to take a leave of absence to upgrade one's competencies. A lack of applicants prompted the Council on Library Resources to scuttle its fellowship program, and similarly threatens CLR's internship program.

Keeping personnel costs down has become a top priority. Some libraries are complying most strictly with federal anti-inflation wage guidelines. Four Baltimore area libraries put a lion's share of their hard-won budget increases into books instead of salaries. Wisconsin's Beloit College put some staffers on "involuntary leave" to save money.

Efforts to hold salaries down have adversely affected the slow, but up until now, steady progress in improving the wages and mobility of women. The threat of reverse discrimination lawsuits has chilled efforts to undo the damage of historic discrimination practiced against blacks and other minority groups. And belt-tightening has indirectly hurt efforts to bring faculty status benefits to librarians.

Staff and money shortages have prompted new thinking about librarianship ranging from expecting librarians to handle any job in the small shop to performing only the most professional duties in the larger one. Coming down on the side of flexibility, Baltimore County retrained staffers to better serve everyone from kids to seniors.

In the years ahead, the number of professionals to be found in libraries is expected to dwindle substantially as support staff and computers replace them. The question most libraries will have to face is how best to redeploy their professionals. One approach is to make the expertise of librarians more accessible to people by stationing them in more public service areas. White Plains, New York, has almost its whole team of reference librarians at a counter by the front door—making the patron's first library encounter a quite professional one.

GOVERNING TODAY'S LIBRARY

In 1979 there was new receptivity to the old idea that the director must be the driving force in the library. People at the helm of today's libraries are expected to be skillful managers capable of coping with change, allocating resources properly, and handling interpersonal relations with staff, trustees, and city hall. An MBA degree is probably the most desirable addition to the MLS especially for the female administrator. And today's library director needs expertise in politics to deal effectively with city fathers, who often want to shape the library's destiny themselves. Summing up what it takes to manage, Lillian Bradshaw of Dallas said "you've got to be an active manipulator" to get what you want. Robert Rohlf of Hennipin said that "personality" is what it takes to lead a library system.

Today's library trustee also needs to be adept in the art of governance. Recognizing this, state libraries in New York and Illinois held workshops to provide trustees with the basics in political and economic survival. Illinois gave more intensive training to its most promising trustee leaders and sent them back to the front lines to help trustees everywhere cope.

Trustees have become more concerned about their legal liability: the New York State Association of Library Boards has launched an investigation into the question. Meanwhile ALA's legal adviser Newton Minow told the Executive Board those areas where boards could be held legally responsible for their action (or inaction): "obedience, diligence [in preventing negligent mismanagement by administrators or board members]; and loyalty" (avoidance of personal conflict of interest).

NEW THINKING IN EDUCATION

Educators are looking to the future with an eye towards charting a course that will ensure their long-term survival in the hard years ahead. Library schools are developing new curricula, beefing up their MLS fare, and going after nonpros in efforts to fill classrooms.

Fully expecting libraries to become just another component in the information marketplace, some schools are specializing in training students to function throughout the whole information environment and not in libraries alone. Noting that 35 percent of its grads don't want to work in a library today, Syracuse University has taken an extreme stand, holding that library school must sever its umbilical cord to the library.

Drexel and Queens College, New York, changed the names of their library schools in the past year to emphasize their new stress on "modern librarianship" and information science. Others are trying to attract students with new sixth-year programs, double degrees, and courses expected to count heavily with prospective employers.

A growing number of schools aim to keep MLS candidates in school longer with a two-year degree program. Indiana University developed a special degree program that stops short of the Ph.D. And Columbia has scheduled a meeting in March of all ALA deans to examine the questions raised by the two-year program.

And library schools are also seeking out the nonpro. The University of Pittsburgh launched a BA program in information science. The University of Maryland went after foreign students with an international program ranging in scope from individual courses all the way up to the MLS.

Intensified recruitment efforts stimulated new criticism that library schools are flooding a glutted market with people who can't find jobs. Meanwhile, ALA's Committee on Accreditation quietly practiced a form of birth control by withholding first-time site visits. But it reaccredited the degree programs at Rhode Island, Oklahoma, and San Jose, California, and gave Alberta's new MLS program its blessing.

Despite some disappointment that continuing education is not paying off for many library schools, some are still trying. At year's end, the University of Michigan named a coordinator to its new statewide continuing education venture.

The University of Pittsburgh has been earning prestige as well as extra revenue with annual year-end seminars that bring together top library leaders, educators, and librarians for discussion of topics of national interest. And East Carolina University broke new ground in staff education with a high level seminar on new technology, featuring top leaders in the field.

Library associations have been moving aggressively into continuing education too—posing what might turn out to be unbeatable competition for schools. Indications are that librarians prefer the format and price of workshop-type continuing education fare offered by state and national associations. The Special Libraries Association has invested heavily in continuing education with a five-year program of integrated courses and a full-time educational director. ALA's Standing Committee on Library Education is concerned with a stronger educational role for the association. The Medical Library Association has developed a series of courses to recertify MLA librarians.

Interest in providing certification for library continuing education proceeded in 1979. Michigan started evaluating programs for certification status. The Continuing Library Education Network Exchange (CLENE) continued to work for the establishment of a national voluntary continuing education recognition system, but its first proposals drew criticism for being too liberal in their definition of learning experiences.

One clear indication of the need for keeping the line staffer au courant with new developments is the appalling lack of information on major library concerns such as the closing of the catalog, the National Periodicals Center, or the national library network when these come up for discussion at association meetings. One prescription for learning in the area of new technology suggested to New England librarians last year by Susan Martin (Johns Hopkins): a lifetime of homework, including periodic reviews of the library literature, enrollment in seminars, and attention to exhibits at conferences.

New approaches to inservice training were tried in 1979. The Tacoma Public Library had a consultant design a "portable" reference skills training packet for eventual use in all of Washington's libraries. Michigan's Grand Rapids Public Library hired a historian who helped school and library personnel in archive building.

Staff exchange has been praised as a means of expanding the horizons of librarians. Wisconsin developed a promising statewide interchange involving personnel from all types of libraries. Columbus, Ohio, and Gloucestershire, England, swapped librarians. And Indiana University faculty members changed places with librarians from the Monroe County Public Library for a day. The Illinois Regional Library Council tried a low-key approach to exchange; it published a human resources directory and encouraged librarians to swap their know-how. Meanwhile the Bibliographic Center for Research established a people resources bank, offering to provide special expertise "for a price."

VOLUNTEERS AND CETA STAFF

Federal programs have helped staff libraries, but no one knows how long this aid will last. In 1979, Congress slated the termination of hundreds of thousands of Comprehensive Employment and Training Act (CETA) employees, but at the last minute offered waivers in case of "extreme hardship." Some of the big urban libraries will be hurt badly if CETA ends. New York Public relies on CETA for one-third of its branch system work force. But NYPL has been losing CETA people steadily (some are filling its vacancies), and the city won't replace them because of the uncertain future of the CETA program. The upshot: NYPL's staff and hours are steadily shrinking.

Volunteers have become important to the nation's economy: Congress saluted them in 1977 for providing $68 billion in services. Volunteers are vital to libraries too: they're doing highly specialized curatorial work (Chicago's Newberry Library) and running kiosks (Baltimore County and Huntsville, Alabama) as well as handling programming, circulation desk duty, and behind the scenes work in many more traditional libraries.

Volunteers enabled some of California's libraries (Ventura, Kern County, Stanislaus) stay afloat after Proposition 13 hit, but their use stirred union opposition.

On the whole, volunteers have found a niche in libraries and have won respect for their contribution. Oklahoma's Tulsa City-County Library brought in high ranking government and library people to thank its volunteers at a ceremony held last year.

Volunteer work is starting to be recognized as job experience by major employers. In some states, volunteers are even eligible for workmen's compensation.

Libraries now realize that it takes time and money to make a volunteer program work. More of them are hiring full-time volunteer coordinators; Chicago Public Library is one. The Public Library of Columbus and Franklin County stepped up recruitment in 1979; its volunteer corps doubled and provided 11,375 hours of service.

Friends organizations are growing in stature too. ALA's Library Administration and Management Association spurred the creation of a national Friends organization.

THE QUESTION OF UNION CLOUT

The recession has made unions more appealing to the embattled staffer, but it has also made it harder for unions to follow through on their promises. And opposition by administrations is tougher than ever. Boston University asked the courts to disband its new library union after the National Labor Relations Board refused to do it. The union representing employees at LC's Copyright Office narrowly escaped decertification stemming from LC's charge of encouraging a "work slowdown."

Having less luck in winning big salary increases, unions are trying to improve the lot of library employees in other ways. The union at Metro Toronto added improved working conditions and better job security to its list of priorities. A strike action at Springfield, Massachusetts, forced a contract settlement that involved not only salaries, but also liability for injuries sustained at work.

The validity of the MLS as a job requirement became an issue in Norwalk, Connecticut. Union action forced the library to give to a nonprofessional a job it had created for an MLS grad who came to Norwalk under CETA. And the union then took up the cause of the professional involved when the library tried (unsuccessfully) to fire her.

THE WOMEN'S RIGHTS ISSUE

The Equal Rights Amendment became a highly charged issue in 1979. By the slender majority of one vote, Council prodded ALA to take Midwinter out of Chicago. The Palmer House promptly threatened to sue. At the urging of ALA headquarters, the membership reconsidered its obligations to Palmer House and ERA and in the largest mail vote in ALA history, it voted overwhelmingly to return Midwinter to Chicago even if Illinois doesn't ratify ERA.

ALA remains on record for boycott. And at its Dallas conference, the association committed itself anew to ERA by establishing a $10,000 kitty to help its chapters to continue the ERA fight. The Chicago boycott question is still very much alive: ALA's Task Force on Women will boycott Chicago in the name of ERA this month.

The Special Libraries Association nixed an ERA boycott at first, but in 1979 a big mail vote put SLA squarely in the militant ERA camp. The Medical Library Association and the National Librarians Association are also for boycott as are some 500 or so other organizations. NOW (National Organization of Women) got the courts to sanction boycott as a legitimate political tactic just before the critical ALA vote on Midwinter.

Nationwide recruiting efforts to get more women to the top haven't had much effect. But the University of Washington (Seattle) is developing a model Career Project for Women Librarians that aims to show how proper counseling and training can help women get ahead.

NEW INTERNATIONALISM

Renewed relations between China and the United States paved the way for an exchange of people and ideas. A delegation of high ranking American librarians went to China to forge new alliances; the Special Libraries Association invited Chinese librarians to the United States. Meanwhile, China started to rebuild libraries and collections that had been neglected during that nation's repressive Cultural Revolution. And in 1979, China sought access to many U.S. data banks.

Progress in strengthening ties with the Russian library community was achieved with the long awaited First Soviet American Library Seminar. But the revelation of Russia's big investment in library development prompted some White House Conference planners to try to resurrect Sputnik-like competition in the hope that Congress would pump dollars into libraries just as it had done with NASA years ago. More hostility towards Russia was generated when publishers drew attention to Russian censorship (and their own titles) by trying (unsuccessfully) to get the books of Soviet dissidents into the Moscow Book Fair.

The demand for information and materials from countries behind the Iron Curtain grew. The Slavic Reference Service at the University of Illinois reported business booming. Columbia is helping its Iron Curtain "exchange partners" get USBE materials.

In a year proclaimed International Year of the Child libraries saluted kids from all over the world with such things as international story phone service (Cambridge, Massachusetts), pen pal matching (Albany, New York), and ethnic festivals (Salt Lake County).

IYC brought out a stress on the rights of children. Salt Lake County focused on child abuse, foster care, and the emotional pressures borne by society's child; Chicago Public brought in specialists to define children's legal, medical, and social rights. The California Library Association endorsed free library service for children.

THE QUESTION OF OUTREACH

The White House Conference delegates came out strongly for outreach, although the economy crunch spurred new speculation in 1979 on whether it is wise and appropriate for financially ailing libraries to channel money into outreach services that often fail to reach the nonuser. The library community is clearly split on the issue, but the majority backs special services to nonusers and groups otherwise denied access to information.

"Traditionalists' argue that libraries shortchange the people who actually use libraries by diverting staff and money to outreach. They oppose efforts by libraries to address society's ills or to do the job that schools have failed to do. In 1979, they challenged some of the ideas that undergird outreach.

"Back to basics" advocates contend that libraries cannot change disparities in the distribution of wealth and education in American society, and should thus concentrate on the people who have always used libraries most—the educated elite.

Opposition to outreach was strongest in Proposition 13 country. California State Librarian Ethel Crockett urged cutbacks in outreach to bring about a better "balancing" of priorities, presumably to benefit active library users. But her stance, denounced by some Californians, helped fuel an effort to oust her from office before her announced retirement. But there was also strong hostility to putting major state funding into two multilingual I&R services for California's varied ethnic communities. In the end, only one such service was set up.

1979's anti-outreach sentiment was vigorously countered by proponents of the belief that libraries have a social and ethical obligation to reach out. One forceful reason given: minority groups are becoming the majority population in many American cities. Also: libraries can't afford to ignore illiteracy if they want to have a place in tomorrow's world; half the nation will be functionally illiterate by 1990 unless schools improve dramatically.

Government and foundations have been providing libraries with funding for experiments in education, I&R, and most recently, the humanities. This outside support has been especially critical to libraries in the inner city and in poor rural areas that get much sparser tax support than do well-heeled communities. But the long pursued goal of equalization—correcting disparities in the level of services communities with different resources can provide—has yet to be brought in sight.

Meanwhile, enriching cultural opportunities has become an important target area for libraries. Humanities programming is a relatively new area of involvement for libraries, growing every day. NEH seeded an Akron Summit, Ohio, project to get "hard-to-involve" people into humanities projects as well as a Cumberland County, North Carolina, library/museum venture. Alabama set up a state humanities resource center and hired a traveling humanist-in-residence. Minneapolis and Seattle in 1979 became the newest "NEH Learning Libraries." Thanks to the Kellogg Foundation, an "educational brokering" experiment in career development for "working class adults" was launched by New York's Westchester Library System, while New York State developed an educational counseling service. Alabama's Selma County has been reaching the illiterate via its bookmobile.

In some cases, local government will step in when federal funding for projects that have proven themselves runs out. In 1979, Forsyth County, North Carolina, took up responsibility for the library's thriving Adult Continuing Education Program.

Wake County, North Carolina, took over the library's popular I&R service two years ago, but it pulled out stakes when the economy crunch really hit.

MARKETING THE LIBRARY

The idea that the library's survival is inextricably linked to its marketing ability has caught on. Among urban public libraries trying to "sell themselves" to their communities: Cleveland Public bought a radio station in 1979 "to enable it to share its cultural wealth with a much larger audience." Dallas Public is long embarked on a course to make itself a name by developing extensive research resources.

California's Huntington Beach Library went on TV to tell of the impact of Proposition 13 and to show people what libraries have to offer them in the way of innovative programs and services.

Academic libraries began to show keen new interest in PR; an ALA-Dallas workshop on the topic was mobbed. Aggressive marketing worked for the Business Library at the UCLA Management School, and it looks as if the big surge in use will bring library funding up.

ETHNIC OUTREACH

That service to varied ethnic communities remains a priority concern is evidenced in such endeavors as the Houston Metropolitan Research Center's work in documenting the history of Mexico-Americans and the Fairfax County, Virginia, County Library's efforts to help Vietnamese refugees become more "assertive consumers."

Ethnic communities appreciate their libraries: blacks and Hispanics polled in Ohio gave libraries top grades as information sources. Maryland's Harford County Library found that black families use libraries more often than do whites, although they're harder to reach at first.

Improving library service to minorities has started appealling to politicians too. Despite the dollar crunch, San Bernardino, California, okayed a new branch to serve a Mexican-American community. Colorado amended legislation to make Indian tribes eligible for state library money for the first time.

SERVING THE HANDICAPPED

Growing recognition of the special access problems of the handicapped spurred action again in 1979. Improving building access became one target area as libraries added ramps, elevators, and automated doors primarily for the benefit of the handicapped.

New York put Kurzweil Reading Machines in every public library system, hoping to prod localities to buy more machines. New Jersey moved to upgrade its Library for the Blind and Handicapped by okaying much needed expansion in a new building.

Libraries reached out to the deaf community by training staffers in sign language techniques and by installing TTY machines in public service areas. Ontario's Midwestern Library System produced video book reviews for broadcast to the deaf. Indiana's Lake County Public Library published a newsletter for the deaf community. And attacking the problem of staff insensitivity, the Public Library of Columbus and Franklin County held a workshop to acquaint librarians with the special problems of the handicapped. [See "Library Service to Disabled People: A State of the Art Report for the 1970s" in the Special Reports section of Part 1. Also see the report from the National Library Service for the Blind and Physically Handicapped in the Federal Libraries section of Part 1—*Ed.*]

MEDICAL AND LAW INFORMATION

Just in recent years, new ground has been broken in opening up access to medical information. One forward looking step taken in 1979: Case Western Reserve's pioneering program to transform area public libraries into health information dissemination centers —complete with both resources and trained staff.

New York eyed a proposal to upgrade hospital libraries with the end goal of bringing them into that state's powerful network. Orange County, California, established a Nursing Information Consortium (NICOC) to improve hospital collections for nurses countywide. The Clinical Medical Librarian (CML) program at the University of Texas Medical Center in Galveston reported encouraging progress with this new specialty in its second year. And in more and more libraries, people are growing accustomed to and using medical reference works formerly reserved for the eyes of physicians.

The need for better access to law materials was a recurring theme at WHC, where there were calls for a National Law Library as well as the development of law collections at public libraries. The American Association of Law Libraries announced its budding law network (LAWNET) which it sees as having a future in the evolving national network.

WORKING ON "INREACH"

Libraries are developing new sensitivity to the "traditional" library user too. One target area: doing something about the noise problem. Many libraries now being built have glassed-in reference areas or quiet lounges. The State University of New York-Oswego designated silent study areas as well as semiquiet areas, installed new carpeting, and put sound-absorbent panels around its copying machines.

Public libraries in 1979 were also reevaluating priorities in collection development. Giving people the kind of books they (and not librarians) seem to want prompted libraries to buy more best-sellers in quantity, order more paperbacks, and increase their rotating rental (McNaughton) collections. More of them are weeding their collections periodically, something that automatically brings circulation up. Some (New York and San Francisco) are expanding AV holdings to include videotapes.

Libraries are also working their way into the hearts of the traditional patron by speeding up research queries with economically priced computerized reference service (Chicago Public); making it easier to browse with portable subject guides (Orlando, Florida); and fighting the energy shortage by mailing reserves out to patrons (King County, Washington).

Libraries are experimenting in highly specialized information delivery, but the private sector has been swift to oppose library involvement in any service an entrepreneur could turn a profit on.

New sensitivity to the library user (instead of the employer) is reflected in the new ethnic statement for librarians now being developed by ALA.

SECURITY IN LIBRARIES

New crime statistics show an unexpected surge in violence of all kinds. For libraries, the problem of protecting the people and books in both suburban and urban library facilities has grown worse. Guards and electronic security systems have become a basic line of defense for most libraries.

The theft of library materials has become of growing concern. Automated circulation systems can pinpoint losses; at Tucson branches, the ripoff rate is 17 percent for books, and well over 50 percent for AV.

A Carnegie study found theft and mutilation of library materials on the upswing in America's universities, particularly its medical schools where students often practice surgery in the stacks. The University of California at Berkeley has to put 10 percent of its acquisitions budget into replacement copies.

Library treasures have become the target of the professional thief. Pros were prime suspects in the last year's theft of 153 rare books on the New World (Minnesota's Carleton College) and Melville memorabilia (in New Bedford, Massachusetts). Yale lost $20,000 in valuable maps to a visiting professor. And a San Francisco amateur art collector swiped hundreds of valuable art books before police nailed him.

Many libraries, especially small ones, can't afford to insure or adequately protect their valuables. The high cost of security prompted Maine's Rockport Library to sell a valuable Eastman painting. The Rockford Public Library in Illinois tried to build a case for expensive electronic security by quoting alarming book losses, but it was then assailed for allowing the problem to happen.

People are stealing anything in libraries that isn't tied down. In Noe Valley, California, it was a piano; in Oklahoma City, a bunch of no smoking signs; and in New York's City College, an OCLC terminal.

But libraries are starting to get the legal support they need in their battle against crime. A new Iowa statute gives staffers in that state liability protection should he or she see fit to detain a suspected thief.

More libraries are taking the hard line with delinquent patrons. The Carnegie Public Library became one of the first in Mississippi to go after delinquents with the law after its softer tactics failed to work. Knoxville-Knox County Public made the first real dent in its $26,000 annual loss rate by sending out mailgrams and following up with house calls. Spokane County found steeper fines, coupled with backup from a collection agency, to be most effective in persuading delinquents to come clean.

Chicago Public is going after delinquents with fines of up to $500 and arrest warrants. Robeson, North Carolina, does a thorough job of screening potential library patrons by requiring up-to-date IDs.

Seeking to foil delinquents who take advantage of reciprocal borrowing privileges, the Central Massachusetts Regional Library System (Worcester) set up "Central Delinquency File" to keep track of offenders.

Libraries have had to concern themselves increasingly with protecting people. A New York Public guard had to deal with an unprovoked stabbing assault in the library's Main Reading Room.

Besides adding police to their work force, libraries are doing more to train staff to cope with life in the combat zone that a library can become. New York's METRO cooperative brought in library administrators as well as specialists in mental health, law enforcement, and police work for a high level treatment of library security problems. The Library Council of Metropolitan Milwaukee developed a portable multimedia workshop kit to help libraries everywhere take a crack at learning to deal with problem situations ranging from theft to deviant behavior.

That library security has become an emotionally charged issue became apparent at the METRO security workshop: staffer after staffer stood up to voice in strident tones their resentment, anger, and fear of the problem patron. One consensus reached was that library administrators too often dodge the problem and refuse to give embattled staffers the support they need.

And an *LJ* editorial urging librarians to deal more compassionately with the harmless "Crazy Willies" in libraries triggered scores of angry letters telling of the senseless brutality and violence that can be a part of life in the library war zone. But a few letters poignantly told of important lessons learned in reaching out to the walking wounded.

Some libraries are trying to help the troubled individual adapt. Orange, New Jersey, has a library-based program aimed at bringing the mentally disabled back into the community. The library in Berkeley Heights, New Jersey, has been working successfully with the severely psychologically disabled. And New York's Rochester Public Library has for years quietly been helping them reenter the workforce.

Vandalism remains an unsettling problem for many libraries. To get a volatile situation in control, libraries need support from the community, including the neighborhood cop. More youngsters are dropping out of school than ever before, and vandalism problems are expected to mount.

Youngsters in Somerset County, England, scaled a rooftop to set a fire that ruined almost everything in the Bridgewater library. In the United States, arsonists torched the libraries of California's Concord High School and San Diego's St. Augustine's Boy's High School.

In Massachusetts, a fire of unknown origin swept through the 160-year-old Norfolk County prison, taking with it a pioneering jail library, just established by three cooperating public libraries.

The dangers of propane gas were pointed up by a fiery explosion that wrecked Enoch Pratt's 30-year-old bookmobile.

Human error can also figure in accidents. Faulty building design was blamed for the hazard of bricks falling from the facade of the University of Massachusetts' Amherst Library; the building had to be closed. In Ohio, a backhoe operator accidentally slashed OCLC cables, shutting down the system for a day or so.

Natural disasters can exact a heavy toll. Hurricanes peeled off roofs and soaked books at libraries in Alabama and Mississippi. Mobile's hurricane emergency plan was foiled by 150-mile-an-hour winds, driving rain, and downed telephone lines. Undaunted, Mobile's heroic staff started tarring rooftops when the wind died down. Connecticut's Windsor Public Library helped three communities pick up the pieces after a tornado hit by setting up a disaster information center.

Last year the Wyoming State Library sought to help libraries cope with all kinds of disasters by offering advice and assistance via its Disaster Recovery Assistance Team (DRAT).

The preservation of library materials got new attention in 1979. The Western Council of State Libraries launched a major effort to establish conservation programs in all 17 states in the region. ARL set to devising "self-study" procedures to help academic libraries come up to grips with their preservation problems.

Preservation is an expensive proposition. New England's Document Conservation Center announced efforts to bring down its costs, while noting it had no shortage of customers.

The lack of trained personnel has greatly hampered the development of preservation programs in academe. But Columbia is developing curricula to train both conservators and library administrators.

INTELLECTUAL FREEDOM

In recent years, the courts have been more sensitive to the First Amendment rights of students and less in sympathy with school boards that remove books from library collections. A Massachusetts district court ordered the Chelsea school board to bring *Male and Female under 18* back to the library. In New Hampshire, court action forced the Nashua school board to rescind its ban on *Ms.* magazine. But the courts backed a 1976 ban imposed by the Island Trees, New York, school board, which promptly celebrated by cancelling subscriptions to several UN publications and to *LJ*.

The privacy rights of prisoners became an issue in Maryland, where the Montgomery County Library won backing both from prison authorities and the county attorney in its refusal to give the prosecution the reading records of an inmate up on a murder rap. At issue was "the loss of credibility with the entire inmate population."

ALA's Freedom to Read Foundation celebrated its tenth anniversary in 1979, hailing the victorious conclusions of three FTRF-backed court battles: the voiding of a wide-ranging antiobscenity statute in Tennessee, the rehiring of embattled Fair Lawn, Alabama, Librarian Claire Oaks, who fought a tenacious battle against city fathers (who wanted to prune the collection and at one point actually dissolved the library to oust her); and the reopening of a bookstore that had been shut down for trafficking in porn. But long simmering opposition to FTRF's relatively new concern for pornographers (rather than for librarians and libraries) was expressed in a demand for an "investigation" of the relationship between FTRF and ALA.

ALA's 1977 film, *The Speaker*, continued to spark dissent. Virginia Lacy Jones scorned it as a "glowing example of subtle and vicious prejudice." But Columbia's Richard Darling blasted the film's critics (especially the library press) for paying short shrift to the *Library Bill of Rights*. Meanwhile the price of the film went up to $545.

Work proceeded on the revision of the *Library Bill of Rights*. Concern was expressed on how to best assure the protection of the rights of the individual; the consensus was for a "laundry list" approach to assure library access for all individuals regardless of sex, age, race, religion, national origin, political viewpoint, lifestyle, economic background, handicap, and the like. The bill's provisions for liberalizing use of library meeting rooms stirred concern that certain locally active groups would overuse library facilities. North Carolina's Forsyth County Library revamped its meeting room policy following a melee that disrupted a KKK exhibit at the library; its new policy clearly endorses "free expression and free access," but it guards against disruption and overuse.

From Iran came a report of the fate of libraries and librarians following the fall of the Shah: many libraries have been closed, some were torched by "townspeople fighting campus communism," and collections are being purged.

THE AGENDA FOR THE 1980s

As libraries of all types face the 1980s, they will be aware of the agenda which the White House Conference has set for them. To the best of our knowledge now, the library history of the coming decade will be written in terms of the priorities identified at state and national conferences; all of them, in one way or another, call for action to improve the accessibility of information to people: literacy, networking, international data flow, serving the unserved. The tools we will use to implement these will be varied and will include legislation, creative institutional initiatives, devotion to the resource-sharing way of life, and development of the informational skills of both libraries and their patrons —people of all ages and from all walks of life. As 1979 fades into the past, we can see the agenda was there all the time; the White House Conference wrote it large for us.

SLJ NEWS REPORT, 1979

Bertha M. Cheatham

Associate Editor, *School Library Journal*

Once again, it's time for a roundup of the library news events of the year, particularly the trends, programs, issues, and legislation affecting librarians and library services to children and young people. The year marked a number of special events— the International Year of the Child focused worldwide attention on the rights of children; the creation of a new cabinet, a Department of Education; the convening of the White House Conference on Library and Information Services; the visit of Pope John Paul; a visit by an American library delegation to the People's Republic of China; and last but not least, *School Library Journal* reached its twenty-fifth year.

IYC AND SPECIAL PROGRAMS

Children's librarians had a slow start on planning programs for the International Year of the Child (IYC) which publicized the rights of children. But at year's end there were many reports of exciting IYC programs for both children and parents. One of the most unusual conferences held during the IYC year was the "Books and Broadcasting for Children." This 36-day symposium drew together 34 librarians, television producers, children's book authors, and magazine editors from 32 countries to discuss the present and future impact of print and electronic media on children, the relationship between books and TV, the role of governments in policymaking for television, and the processes in developing books and radio and TV programs for children.

The symposium, administered jointly by WPBT-TV, the Community Television Foundation of South Florida, and the Association for Library Service to Children (ALSC), was an experiment in international communications and was a unique opportunity for foreign and U.S. professionals to see and discuss books, TV, and library programs designed specifically for children.

Elizabeth Huntoon, coordinator of children's services at the Chicago Public Library, who with Martha Barnes, children's coordinator of Westchester Library System, represented the Association for Library Service to Children (ALSC), said the problem of getting kids to read is universal. Although some countries have very few

Note: Reprinted from *School Library Journal*, January 1980, where the article was entitled "Library News of the Year in Retrospect."

books published each year (Venezuela publishes about 10 or 12 titles; some East African countries can only afford to publish paperbacks), television or radio reached a wide segment of the literate and nonliterate population of most countries.

Cecily Truett, project director of WPBT-TV, in assessing the symposium, said that, in general, the participants noted a lack of priority was given to children's media at the administrative and funding levels in their countries; children's programming took second place to the development of adult materials. All symposium participants agreed there had to be an interconnection between the various types of media—TV, for instance, should and could lead children to books. Truett remarked that a great deal of emphasis was placed on the importance of radio—a medium often taken for granted in the United States. In illiterate societies, radios are a prime and mobile source (often taken into the field by laborers) for teaching the illiterate.

Another topic of discussion involved advances in technology such as video disks which are more readily available to worldwide markets and will change the emphases in children's library services and extend the availability of children's media programming.

The participants made several recommendations to stimulate continued international communication and cooperation: the establishment of an international newsletter on children's media and an international program exchange in children's radio and television.

The joint symposium (a first) served as a beginning for worldwide cooperation in promoting literacy and reading.

The year of the child received wide recognition in the United States as children's problems and children's rights dominated the library programming in children's rooms across the country. However, throughout the year, the press carried news of children in other countries who were deprived of library services and basic needs. Children's library services and librarians in embattled Iran felt the impact of the political crisis in which students seized Americans and held 50 hostages.

According to a report in the June 15 *Library Journal*, the Teheran American School, connected with the U.S. Embassy, was shut down and the Community School, connected with the U.S. Presbyterian Church, was closed temporarily. The report stated that "children and young adults play new war games now, and many use real guns looted from army posts. A few children's libraries were burned in Teheran to protest their royal connections. At the time, Lila Ponzrand, librarian of a slum branch children's library, had been called before a revolutionary committee for questioning about alleged collaboration with the ousted shah's regime."

The anonymous writer of the *LJ* report also spoke of a "new censorship" in which children's book collections were under scrutiny and books that were not "Islamically inspired" were banned. The writer also said that Western ideas in the eight Iranian library schools and Iranian life are now deemphasized since the students' determination to "de-Westernalize" Iran according to Ayatollah Ruhollah Khomeini's dictates.

While the U.S. press and TV carried heartrending reports about the fate of starving Cambodian children who were a large part of the "boat people" who fled that country, U.S. librarians were reaching out to help better prepare parents of pre-school-age children for the complexities of life in a highly inflated economy of a free society.

One unusual program at the Dallas Public Library, designed to enhance service for children from infancy to age eight, called for the creation of a new position—that of Librarian for Early Childhood Services. Frances Smardo, the librarian who holds this title, arranged a series of 36 IYC programs which involved authors, child psychologists, child development center directors, and consumers services to speak to parents, teachers, librarians, and others who work with youngsters. An "Ap*PARENT*ly Speaking" section of materials about topics such as child development and home learning activities has been set up in the library.

Evidence that the IYC year caught on with libraries was also seen in the many different programs held throughout New York State. When word of UNICEF's offer to send a list of Pen Pal offices went out to librarians (Albany Public Library recruited some 2,000 letter writers who contacted an equal number of pen pals), the UNICEF office in New York was swamped with over 5,000 requests and had a difficult time trying to catch up with the heavy demand.

The Wayne County/Ontario Cooperative System geared their IYC program toward providing first book experiences for infants; the Mid-York Library System (and others) promoted a statewide Parents as Reading Partners campaign in which parents were urged to read to their children at least 15 minutes a day; the Mid-Hudson Library System conducted a survey of agencies concerned with children's reading to serve as a model for interagency cooperation, information exchange, and which were included in a guide for interested parents.

Brooklyn Public Library set up "The Child's Place," a multiservice area for two-and-a-half to six-year-olds at their New Lots branch. Free workshops for "caregivers" and parents focused on reading readiness, toys, and storytelling. A "non-sexist childrearing" program was another feature of the IYC year.

SCHOOL LIBRARIES

As a result of the strong insistence in January 1977 by directors of the American Association of School Librarians, the National Commission on Libraries and Information Science (NCLIS) and AASL came up with a 21-member task force to determine how to integrate school library media programs into a proposed national network. In 1979, the Task Force published their recommendations in a report titled *The Role of the School Library Media Program in Networking*. The report detailed five major stumbling blocks to the full acceptance of schools which need the resources a national network can offer: psychological barriers, political and legal factors, funding factors, communication factors, and planning processes. The report was a landmark, but school libraries and librarians are still overlooked by major networks. However, now questions were being asked about upgrading schools' services with advanced technology, and AASL began to take a more active role in communicating the import of a national network to allied groups such as the Association of School Administrators and the Association for Educational Communications and Technology. (School needs were included in the November White House Conference on Library and Information Services and all state pre-WHCLIS conferences listed many recommendations for school library services.)

Although the involvement of schools in the proposed National Library Network is still a future possibility, the year saw a quantum leap in incorporating schools in one state network structure. New York State has set up two regional projects to eventually bring schools into existing library networks. Six library cooperation projects to link school libraries with public and academic libraries will be channeled through BOCES (Board of Cooperative Services) agencies.

Another three-year pilot project, METRO, was also initiated in 1979. The goal of METRO is to build four independent school library systems. Improved interlibrary loan, access to regional resources, and improved cooperation between district libraries are expected end results.

Cooperative library efforts in various parts of the country also paid dividends.

The Timberland (Washington) Regional Library received an award for maintaining a long-term liaison with the educational community. The library, which serves five counties, furnished the schools with facilities, equipment, staff, and expertise to back their educational programs.

The Purcell (Oklahoma) Public Schools received a grant from Oklahoma's department of education to provide a school/library cooperation demonstration project.

FUNDING ISN'T WHAT IT USED TO BE

School library media professionals, long dissatisfied with the guidance, counseling, and testing section tacked on to Title IV-B of the Elementary and Secondary Act (ESEA), breathed a collective sigh of relief when this section was pulled out to become Title IV-D last year. But now it seems their troubles are far from over as other educational groups clamor for their share of federal funds. The music educators raised a ruckus about being eliminated from the "instructional equipment" definition (which bars the purchase of such items as gym mats, parallel bars, and refrigerators). Apparently several sympathetic legislators felt the music teachers needed such funds and introduced two separate bills (H.R. 5569 and H.R. 5772) which called for Title IV-B to be amended to include a third category for the band people. AASL and school library media specialists are fighting the amendments to prevent further fragmentation of ESEA Title IV-B by other specialized groups.

The news, late in the year, that the proposed 1981 funds for school library resources will be cut drastically (from $171 million to $90 million) if HEW's recommendations are accepted by the Office of Management and Budget brought ALA, AASL, and others together to work out strategies for reaching legislators to block such a move. Such an extensive cut in funds could set school media programs back to the pre-1960 era. [For detailed reports on federal funding, see the articles in Part 2 under Federally Funded Programs and Grant-Making Agencies—*Ed.*]

INTELLECTUAL FREEDOM

The three-year battle over the book-banning fracas in Island Trees, New York, ended with "a body blow to the First Amendment," in the words of Richard D. Emery, New York Civil Liberties Union counsel who represented the five students who sued the board. Judge George C. Pratt, in his decision, said the board's action did not restrict the student's right to read; the book removal did not "sharply and directly implicate basic First Amendment values." It's not over yet—the case is under appeal, and many IF supporters have filed amicus briefs in support of the students.

Chief Judge Shane Divine of the U.S. District Court in Nashua, New Hampshire, came down on the side of students who filed suit against the Nashua Board of Education for banning *Ms.* magazine, withdrawing copies from the high-school library, and cancelling the library's subscription. He ordered the board to replace the banned numbers and to resubscribe to the magazine.

In his decision, Divine chided the board for its "high-handed, unconstitutional, and educationally unsound" action. He felt the political content of *Ms.* magazine influenced the board more than sexual overtones (mainly in advertising) that they had cited.

In another IF conflict, the librarian of the Vergennes (Vermont) Union High School was forced to resign her job because she actively opposed the school board's decision to ban *The Wanderers* by Richard Price (Houghton Mifflin, 1974) from the high school library and restrict access to *Dog Day Afternoon* by Patrick Mann (Delacorte, 1974; Dell, 1975) and *Carrie* by Stephen King (Doubleday, 1974). Librarian Elizabeth Phillips, a plaintiff in the suit brought against the school board, alleges violations of her First Amendments rights and that of students. School board Chairperson Larry Gebo claimed *The Wanderers* was more obscene than *Playboy* magazine.

Phillips, who did not fight to reinstate her position, is still a plaintiff in the suit filed by the Vermont Chapter of the American Civil Liberties Union on behalf of several teachers and students. She opposed and asked for a reversal of the school board's decision to ban purchases of paperback books and its plan to color code or number cards to determine which students could have access to "objectionable" books, one of which was *Forever* by Judy Blume (Bradbury, 1975).

U.S. District Court Judge Albert W. Coffrin dismissed the complaint and upheld the school board's book acquisition and removal policy: the case is under appeal.

Under fire for inserting pink warning bookmarks in books that have attracted customer complaints, Follett Library Book Company of Crystal Lake, Illinois, chose to ignore all protests from publishers and ALA's IF Committee. Follett continues to insert bookmarks suggesting that purchasers examine the books before distributing them "to assure yourself that the subject matter and vocabulary meets your standards." According to Follett, only 9 percent of the 1,923 comments received as a result of a survey claimed the bookmark was a form of censorship. However, Follett's managers indicated that the bookmarks would not be sent to any librarians among their clientele who asked to have them left out.

This year, the Canadian Library Association voted to make their Intellectual Freedom Fund the top program priority for budget allocation. One item of concern is a new obscenity legislation which they are opposing.

One of the more interesting incidents receiving media attention in 1979, was the melee which broke out when blacks, members of the American Nazi party, and other anti-Ku Klux Klan groups attempted to bar the KKK for staging an exhibit of Klan paraphernalia in the Forsyth (North Carolina) Public Library. From all reports it would appear that the library administration was taken by surprise by the violent response to a group (pledged to secrecy) which excludes and preys on ethnic and racial groups.

Library Director William H. Robert, who received hundreds of negative calls, maintained that the library's policy does not mean that it endorses the exhibit. All exhibit and meeting space is "available on equal terms for the lawful activities of all groups and persons, regardless of their beliefs and affiliations." Missing from Forsyth PL's revised policy was a statement contained in ALA's *Library Bill of Rights* to the effect that meeting rooms be open for "socially useful and cultural activities and discussion of current public questions." While community groups, regardless of beliefs and affiliations had equal access, the LBR specifies "that meetings be open to the public."

ALA, ERA, AND MEMBERSHIP

Two hotly debated issues of the American Library Association this year were eventually decided in mail votes. One was the repeal of the Association's decision to boycott Chicago for the 1980 Midwinter Meeting; the other, a proposed dues increase.

Council had a difficult time arriving at its decision to bypass Chicago in view of the fact that ALA had long had an agreement to use the Palmer House hotel for its mid-year meetings. President Russell Shank's vote broke a dramatic tie in favor of the ERA advocates' proposal to stop holding ALA meetings in Chicago until, or unless, Illinois ratifies the Equal Rights Amendment. Then a petition was introduced calling for a mail vote by the entire membership in which the ballot would have the pros and cons of holding Midwinter '80 in Chicago, risking the possibility of fighting a costly breach-of-contract suit with Palmer House. Members voted overwhelmingly for Midwinter '80's return to Chicago. Whether ALA members voted in favor of honoring a quasi-contract or against ERA is still a matter of debate.

ALA has made a financial commitment toward aiding in the ERA ratification fight to the tune of $10,000. It is reported that some members of the SRRT Task Force on Women expect to revive plans calling for the relocation of ALA headquarters. This group also asked its members to refuse to attend 1980 Midwinter Meeting. They are also stepping up a push for boycotting Chicago for all future Midwinter meetings, backed by other groups such as the Women in Libraries Caucus of the Florida Library Association.

Sixty-nine percent of the Special Library Association's ballots mailed out to members approved SLA's plan to boycott states which have not ratified ERA. No winter meetings will be scheduled in non-ERA states after 1980; no annual conferences will be held in states that have not ratified the ERA or passed their own statewide equal rights legislation after 1984.

Far fewer ALA members returned the ballot authorizing an increase in membership dues. Less than half of the 32,478 ballots mailed out were returned (13,174) and the increase passed with 7,282 "yes" votes. Beginning this year, personal members will have to pay $50 (a $15 increase); foreign librarians $30 (a $10 increase); unsalaried librarians' dues were upped from $10 to $15; it still costs $15 to join a division.

BUDGETS AND FUNDS

Shock waves from Proposition 13 were still reverberating in California through the year. The controversial measure to reduce property taxes caused 1979 cutbacks in libraries that weren't directly affected immediately following the passage of the Jarvis-Ganns initiative. The San Francisco Public Library planned for service reductions at the main library and branches and library closings to cope with an expected loss in operating revenue due to budget cutbacks in all city departments.

Sacramento City-County Public Library campaigned for community support to ward off another budget cutback of 33 percent; the library was hit with a budget cut of 23 percent in 1978. One hundred and sixty-two volunteers of Ventura County Library pitched in to help the strapped library continue to maintain an acceptable level of service after 37 staff positions were eliminated. They were trained to mend the shelf books, aid in circulation, tell stories, and assist with film programs.

Emergency state aid, $623,000, temporarily bailed out the Los Angeles Public Library. The library had suffered a 43 percent loss in revenue and had to close 90 branches, shut down all branches on Sundays and Mondays, and put a freeze on hiring staff. And in San Diego, City Librarian L. Kenneth Wilson resigned his position in the midst of staff dissatisfaction about his failure to get funding to restore positions. (Many of SDPL's minorities staff were eliminated through job cutbacks.) Wilson summed up the situation as one of the library's failures to reach citizens who pay taxes "but don't really have access to their libraries. Our pleas for money and explanations of our budget plight went over like a lead balloon. . . . Libraries must do a better job of getting information to the people and telling government representatives what libraries are all about or they won't survive."

To prevent a total breakdown of libraries in the state, the California legislature voted to grant $35.7 million in emergency 1979–1980 aid to go to county and special districts which lost property tax revenue support. And Senator James Nielsen is drafting a long-range funding proposal for the state's libraries.

LSCA (Library Services and Construction Act) funds supported many library programs. Twenty-two New York Public Library systems were allotted $1.5 million to provide more books. Chicago Public Library received a grant of $438,016 for books (including easy books) and audiovisual material and equipment.

FINES AND FEES

The high cost of books, materials, and salaries has forced libraries to reexamine the costs of services and the loss of materials. A perpetual problem with overdues has libraries experimenting with tougher procedures of dealing with overdue materials. Spokane (Washington) County Library reported that fines of up to $10 and the threat of a collection agency resulted in a significant drop in overdues.

For a while, California flirted with the idea of imposing fees for basic library services until attorneys advised state librarian, Ethel Crockett, that fees for nonresident taxpayers are not legitimate since they have already paid for library services, but county-free libraries could charge fees to nonresidents users. Knoxville-Knox County Public Library (Tennessee) has a terminal hooked up to a Western Union mailgram computer which it uses to notify patrons of overdues with information as to the cost of replacing the materials and fines involved. This notice is followed up by a home visit after 72 hours. Although return rates rose, the library still has a serious book loss problem at the main branch. Carnegie (Mississippi) Public Library posts a list of delinquent borrowers in the library and in the town newspaper and threatens to issue arrest warrants if a final deadline is ignored. At its inception, the library witnessed a higher rate of return. Chicago and Tucson, Arizona, have legislation on the books to increase overdue and vandalism fines; the Iowa legislature passed a law which made the theft of library materials a criminal offense.

YOUTH SERVICES

The ALA Youth Services Divisions are in various stages of redefining goals and priorities and future directions. The American Association of School Librarians got ALA's Executive Board's okay to hold a national conference apart from ALA's annual conference. The first ever to be conducted by an ALA youth division is set for the Commonwealth Convention Center in Louisville, Kentucky, September 25-28, 1980. It's a bold undertaking since to make it a financial success, AASL must draw at least 3,000 plus conferees. Their constituency, school library media specialists, are just settling back in school routines at that time of the year.

AASL's activities indicate they are on the move to attract members from media groups and independent schools. Membership voted to add a nonpublic schools section this year, and with the very active and expanding Affiliate Assembly (now in its third year), AASL stands to regain its standing as one of the largest ALA divisions. The fact that AASL is reexamining the structure and functions of unit groups and a joint AASL/ AECT Committee is working to keep lines of communication open between the two groups points out that they are headed in a more positive direction than was exhibited in the not-too-distant past.

The Association of Library Services for Children pushed for more support for school and public library services to children in the White House Conference on Library and Information Services recommendations. An ALSC resolution presented to WHCOLIS reflected two prominent concerns among librarians serving children. ALSC recommended the employment of a children's library specialist in every public and school facility and at all state levels.

The ALA *Library Bill of Rights* drew much attention since the Intellectual

Freedom Committee was considering dropping "age" from any designation of barriers to library access. (It was retained.)

Also, the prestigious Newbery/Caldecott banquet is being reevaluated. Some members pointed out the cost of staging the N/C dinner and the use of ALSC staff and related expenses. Alternatives will be explored and a decision as to any changes will be made before Midwinter 1983.

Concerned children's librarians read about the transformation of librarians into generalists at the Baltimore County Public Library. In the Woodlawn branch, every staff professional undergoes retraining to aid patrons of all ages in many library service areas. Although this BCPL trend does not signal the end of age-level specialists throughout the country, it does interest those who train specifically for working with and knowing about the psychology and abilities of children from preschool to high school age and feel that children are a special group with special needs and problems.

The Young Adult Services division, which also supported the retention of "age" in the *Library Bill of Rights* (although it refused to set its own age limitations in defining YA patrons), is backing broad support for youth rights under the First Amendment. YASDs 1979 emphasis was on youth advocacy and free access to all information young adults need and request (including legal rights, and controversial materials such as birth control).

The division is also following the lead of others in sponsoring workshops or mini-conferences apart from regularly scheduled ALA meetings. An institute on Intellectual Freedom and the Rights of Youth was held in 1979 at Rutgers; a two-day workshop on adolescent needs is set for March 21 and 22, in Arlington, Virginia.

LIBRARY EVENTS AND SERVICES

Virginia Beach Public Library and public libraries in New York State and Massachusetts all had Kurzweil Reading Machines (KRM) installed this year. The machine, invented by Raymond Kurzweil while he was a student at the Massachusetts Institute of Technology, is becoming more available since the market price, once $50,000, dropped to around $20,000. Through the use of an optical scanner, the machine transforms print into a computer voice.

The threat of a nuclear disaster at the Three Mile Island (Pennsylvania) nuclear plant was largely responsible for one of the more unusual library services of the year. During the period when women and children were evacuated to Hershey, due to the threat of radioactivity, the Dauphin County Library came to the rescue and handed out books to occupy preschoolers and paperbacks for mothers who had to wait until it was determined that the nuclear reactor was safe.

Meanwhile, in Canada it's the age of the computer. Preschoolers at the Oakville (Ontario) Public Library were introduced to computers designed to improve their prereading skills. A single home computer attracted up to 160 children for one half-hour session each week. The library reported that it's fun for the children as they work at a keyboard and match up their answers on a video monitor to determine the correct one. Parents pay $12 to enroll their child in the program which proved so popular that Oakville is acquiring more home computers and hiring part-time supervisors to help out.

Libraries held a series of fund-raising events involving kids. A program at the Free Library of Philadelphia, a fund-raising Reader's Marathon, boosted funds for children's services. The cooperative effort of the school district—teachers, archdiocese, and the friends of the library—drew over 100,000 schoolchildren, who had friends and relatives pledge 10 cents or more for every book read in one month. And the Scranton

Public Library and the Osterhout Free Library benefited from a two-day basketball marathon sponsored by the Johnson School of Technology.

Humanities programs, backed by grants from the National Endowment for the Humanities, added another emphasis to library programming. The Seattle Public Library's grant of $308,475 from NEH supports an ongoing series of programs about Seattle's history and ethnic neighborhoods.

In Ohio, the State Library has guided libraries in planning programs centering around five program areas: Literature and Ohio's Children, Trans-Ohio, Ethnic Ohio, Ohio Authors, and one titled InventOhio.

High school dropouts and adult patrons are the target of the Kaskaskia Library System (Illinois) which received a $105,564 LSCA grant to devise a method of preparing those who have not completed high school for the high school equivalency exam.

Libraries are becoming more involved in television and the media as a means of getting people and books together. The CBS/Broadcast Group and the Library of Congress launched a joint "Read More about It" book project to reach a nationwide audience. Viewers watching selected CBS broadcasts, will hear several book titles (suggested by LC) on the subject of the program mentioned. Also, a list of titles on various perspectives of the topic is available to libraries, the book trade press, newspapers, and CBS affiliate stations.

Public TV aired a series of Shakespeare programs which were widely advertised in free materials sent to school librarians to stimulate students' interest and supplement English teachers' assignments. The New York State Library produced and distributed a free Shakespeare broadside ("Turn on to Shakespeare at your public library") to New York libraries and provided extra copies for handouts.

Librarians who are members of the Roundtable of Children's Literature (Boston) participate in a weekly cable-TV show "New England Today" aired over channel 56. The show's producer has allowed them to decide on topics and they tell stories, interview children, inform parents on ways of selecting suitable books, and plan programs around holiday themes.

THE END OF A DECADE

The year 1979 drew to a close with the library issues and concerns of laypersons and professionals discussed in more than 57 state conferences in advance of the White House Conference on Library and Information Services held in November. These concerns led to the 25 resolutions, decided on (by more than 900 delegates) at the WHCOLIS conference, which will go on to the president and Congress for consideration. Readers who want to get an idea of what the major issues will be in the next decade can examine the summary prepared by WHCOLIS (1717 K St. N.W., Washington, DC 20036). [See the Special Reports section of Part 1 for a summary of preconference activities by Alice B. Ihrig and an overview article on the White House Conference by Marilyn Gell and Vera Hirschberg—*Ed.*]

The conference deliberations did stress public awareness programs to make taxpayers and legislators knowledgeable of the many library services and librarys' potentials in meeting the needs of citizens in this era of technological advances. The WHCOLIS resolutions may well forecast new directions for libraries in the 1980s.

PW NEWS REPORT, 1979

Chandler B. Grannis
Contributing Editor, *Publishers Weekly*

TRENDS IN THE INDUSTRY

U.S. statistics of book publishers' sales, adjusted to reflect Census Bureau reports, 1972–1978, showed receipts for 1972 of $3,017,800; for 1977 of $5,127,800; and for 1978 of $5,772,200—dollar increases of 91 percent between 1972 and 1978 and 12.6 percent between 1977 and 1978. The rate of unit sales increase evidently has dropped.

A recent *PW* survey cited ongoing growth in output of mass market paperback originals, now estimated at 40 percent to 50 percent of each month's releases.

A P.E.N. American Center survey of 358 writers, in midyear, showed their average annual income from writing to be $21,192; 65 percent earned $10,000 or less; 55 percent earned income as teachers.

President Carter's budget last January called for reductions in a wide range of book and library programs.

Publishers engaged in much self-analysis. In January, at Yale seminars, publishers assessed the "revolution" in the industry, referring to paperback expansion, conglomerate ownership, and electronic technology. Later, they examined "responsibilities" at an AAP symposium, and offered five-year projections at the spring Pubmart.

B'nai B'rith in August released a sharp critique of negligible treatment or omission of the holocaust in modern history texts. *PW*'s October education survey reviewed problems of readability, ultraconservative pressures, the expanding adult education market, and vocational vs. scholarly trends in colleges. An AAP school division seminar featured Frances FitzGerald (*America Revised*, Little, Brown), who said many social studies texts make history dull and sidestep the how and why of events.

Automatic ordering systems were promoted by R. R. Bowker and others. With advice by the Book Industry Systems Advisory Committee, Bowker set up a Standard Address Numbering Agency to assign SAN numbers to book buying and selling organizations.

Henry E. Taylor, Dallas bookseller, and colleagues studied retail cost ratios, the question of passing along cost of freight to consumers, and some publishers' failure to control costs and waste in shipping.

A *PW* survey showed shift away from San Francisco emphasis solely on small publishers, as major eastern publishers expand in the Bay Area.

Interviews by *PW* in late spring explored the subsidiary rights function in trade publishing and total company income.

Summer gasoline shortages upset book travelers' schedules and augured ill for shopping center business.

PW released what is probably the most extensive study ever made of backlist selling, stressing its importance and unrealized potential (*PW*, April 9).

Scholarly Communication (Johns Hopkins), the National Enquiry report, was released and widely discussed. Regarding university presses' needs, it emphasized cooperative activities and more aggressive expansion of markets; concerning needs of re-

---

Note: Adapted from *Publishers Weekly*, February 22, 1980, where the article was entitled "News Highlights and Trends."

search libraries, it emphasized fostering of unified information systems under central public authorities.

A White House Library Conference on Library and Information Science, several years in preparation, was held in November and brought to a head debates about centralizing of information. Need for integrated research systems was asserted, without consensus on central bureaucracies or their forms.

In this connection, a House-passed measure, part of the Higher Education Act extension, would authorize a National Periodicals Center (or system), provided other programs first were funded to 1979 levels.

MERGERS AND NONMERGERS

Mattel, Inc., agreed in January with Western Publishing Co. to acquire the latter for a reported $120.8 million.

McGraw-Hill executives and employees, in January, denounced as "illegal," "improper," and "reckless" the American Express Co. procedure in its bid to take over the publishing firm. A House banking group considered probing Amex conduct. The Authors Guild asked FTC or the Justice Department to bar the takeover. McGraw-Hill board rejected the "sweetened" Amex offer of $40 a share; some investors started suit against the publisher to recover alleged losses. In May, a majority of McGraw-Hill shares were voted to support the board.

In February and July, McGraw-Hill purchased two firms pertinent to its operations, Pre Test Service, Inc., and Data Resources, Inc.

Harcourt Brace Jovanovich sold its mass market paperback publishing company, Jove Publications, in January to MCA, Inc. Also in January, Simon & Schuster bought a remainder house, Bookthrift, Inc., and in a shift among major retailers, Bill Martindale sold his Santa Monica, California, bookstore to the A. C. Vroman, Inc., chain.

The trade departments of J. B. Lippincott and T. Y. Crowell combined as a single unit within Harper & Row (which had acquired Crowell in 1977, Lippincott in 1978).

American Broadcasting Co. agreed to buy 51.6 percent of Chilton Co., the latter to retain its identity, publications, and market services.

Meanwhile debate went on in the Association of American Publishers about mergers, and Lawrence Hill & Co. resigned, charging small publishers' interests were in conflict with AAP policies, despite AAP programs for small firms.

An antitrust warning from the U.S. Justice Department in February deterred Harlequin Enterprises, Toronto, from purchasing Pinnacle Books from Michigan General Corporation.

Elsevier, the Netherlands, controller of Dutton, American Elsevier, and Nelson trade books, reported in February it had merged with Nederlanse Dagbladunie, major Dutch periodicals publisher-printer.

Broadman Press, Southern Baptist publisher, bought A. J. Holman Co., oldest U.S. Bible publisher, from Harper & Row in May.

Via a 100-year lease, Ohio University Press (a state university unit) in effect acquired Swallow Press (an independent publisher) in June.

Kluwer N.V., the Netherlands, agreed in August to buy Stein and Day, but withdrew after about six weeks.

Intext offered in August to merge with a subsidiary of National Education Corporation superseding an agreement with Cohen-Hatfield Industries.

Macmillan considered purchase by Mattel, Inc., but shelved the proposal in favor of one from American Broadcasting Co., which later withdrew. In November Macmillan announced determination to stick to its "principal fields of expertise" in publishing.

RCA announced in September its intention to sell Random House, Inc. (including Knopf, Pantheon, and Ballantine); no sale has yet been reported. Meanwhile, Ballantine and Independent News (Warner) "melded" their distribution, dividing the operational functions.

In a cooperative arrangement rather than a merger, two university presses, Wesleyan and Columbia, combined many noneditorial functions, in the fall.

In September, American Elsevier bought Congressional Information Service, Inc., and purchased Hawthorn Books' publishing assets from Howard & Wyndham Co., the Hawthorn titles to be "folded into" Dutton's backlist operation.

A leading western house, Howell-North Books, was acquired by Leisure Dynamics (which had bought A. S. Barnes and Oak Tree Press in 1978).

Houghton Mifflin offered in December to buy J. P. Tarcher, Inc., Los Angeles paperback nonfiction publisher, as an independent division.

BOOK TRADE ORGANIZATIONS

National Association of College Stores' annual meeting, New York, showed stores affected by college enrollment drops; resentment of publishers' 20 percent discounts; disappointment by publishers over exhibition facilities.

Association of American Publishers held a four-day New England conference in March for 63 "small publishers" (under $500,000 in annual sales).

AAP annual meeting focused on: responsibilities of publishing; Supreme Court trends threatening freedom to publish and to read; and increases in copyright violations.

American Booksellers Association held its biggest annual meeting and trade show, 18,500 attending; also the saddest of its conventions because of loss of 27 persons in the crash of a Chicago to Los Angeles flight. The first ABA Philadelphia regional was held in October.

In June the new Society for Scholarly Publishing, made up of persons who produce, publish, and use scholarly publications, held its first meeting.

The Association of American University Presses stressed greater contacts with professions, national and local foundations and government resources, and examined the China market. The AAUP annual convention was marked by presentation and discussion of the report of the National Enquiry into the Production and Dissemination of Scholarly Knowledge, under way since 1973.

A new group, Women in Scholarly Publishing, was formed by individuals attending the AAUP convention.

The Information Industry Association, studying government information policy, defended profit-centered units as against nearly all public or governmental activity.

The Educational Paperback Association pressed for increased use of UPC (Universal Product Code) on book covers, to aid in wholesaling and inventory work.

The thirtieth and last National Book Award ceremonies took place in April, under AAP. In June AAP announced a new plan, The American Book Awards (TABA), to form an "Academy" for nominating and voting on "best" books; the total of possible winners will be 29. Principal trade organizations decided to take part, but not some groups of authors and critics. Farrar, Straus & Giroux decided not to submit entries; publishers' opinions seemed divided; 44 former winners and judges of NBA called for boycott of TABA, fearing domination of commercial over critical criteria.

A group of top sales promotion people brightened the pre-Christmas period with a "Remainder Ball" in New York, at which guests dined on turkey hash; remainder awards were given.

A midsummer review of courses and programs for education for, about, and in publishing showed strong growth in offerings. AAP set up a reference center under its office for education.

VARIETIES OF BOOK FAIRS

The Montreal fair was cancelled, partly over policy difference (French cultural vs. general Canadian promotion).

Future U.S. participation in the Moscow Book Fair was thrown into doubt by confiscation of 40-odd American books, last-minute cancellation of a visa for Random House's president, and other restrictions.

Nevertheless, AAP and a Soviet trade agency agreed to four trade arrangements in December on sales, translations, and display and book fair procedure—all before the Afghanistan crisis.

Among numerous other book fairs, Bologna (children's books) was the largest so far; Jerusalem had increased foreign representation; Frankfurt, in its thirty-first year, had a record 3,533 individual exhibits.

In the United States, publishers and booksellers organized a mid-Manhattan street fair, "New York Is Book Country," attracting 200,000 people, September 15; 50 D.C. publishers displayed their variety in December at a Washington Book Fair; increased sales and attendance marked annual antiquarian book fairs in several cities.

INTERNATIONAL BOOK TRADE

The major event in the world book scene in 1979, aside from disputes over the Moscow Book Fair, was doubtless the visit of the first delegation of American publishers to the People's Republic of China in the spring. The two sides exchanged information about opportunities, procedures, copyright, translation, and other matters.

The year 1979, declared by UNESCO the International Year of the Child, inspired focus on combating illiteracy and on studies of childhood.

Reports in the winter from the World Bank showed it significant in aid to third world education and the purchase and production of teaching materials.

A new French government rule forbidding the setting of suggested prices for books caused international as well as domestic confusion.

An international survey report (*PW*, July 16) showed extensive book piracy—unauthorized reprinting of U.S. and U.K. books in at least 20 countries.

NOTES FROM THE COMPANIES

In February, William Morrow and Bantam Books formed a joint imprint, Perigord Press, for acquiring hardcover and paperback rights.

Novelist J. B. Donleavy reported having bought Olympia Press in a 1977 bankruptcy sale—thus settling an old breach-of-contract dispute.

Harcourt Brace Jovanovich announced plans in April to begin publishing a 50-volume America's Library of Classics by American authors.

In September, Literary Classics of the U.S., Inc., was formed with National Endowment for the Humanities and Ford Foundation aid to prepare a series of heavy volumes of "central texts"—for distribution by others.

HBJ in midyear, having found Senator Barry Goldwater's memoirs unsuitable for the firm, sought an injunction against their publication by Morrow until Goldwater returned HBJ's $65,000 advance; but Morrow did publish.

In October a maverick author showed anger at HBJ by buzzing its New York building in a small airplane.

Chester Kerr, retiring as director of Yale University Press, announced formation of a new Houghton Mifflin subsidiary, reviving the name Ticknor & Fields.

New American Library, which had had a hardcover list for a short time after its sale to Times-Mirror, planned to renew hardcover publishing in 1980.

The *New York Review of Books* launched the *London Book Review* during the shutdown of the *Times* papers and planned to continue after it was over.

W. B. Saunders Co. announced two trade imprints, Saunders Press and Saunders Paperbacks; distribution by Holt.

Bantam Books paid a record $3,208,875 in Crown's September auction of paperback rights to *Princess Daisy* by Judith Krantz.

CBS-TV, with cooperation by the Library of Congress, began a program series in November, "Read More About," tying in books with major movies and TV shows.

The famous Eighth Street bookstore in New York City was suddenly closed in October by its owner, Eli Wilentz.

In November, Crown Publishers paid a probable record price—over $100,000—for a hardcover first novel, *The Clan of the Cave Bear* by Jean Auel.

Thomas Congdon left his imprint operation at Dutton late in the year to form his own house, Congdon and Lattès, with a French partner.

Simon & Schuster—which had added a fourth imprint publisher, Linden Press, in July—announced a major expansion, in November, appointing several top executives from other firms and from within, and adding a fifth hardcover imprint, Kenan Press.

FREEDOM TO PUBLISH AND READ

U.S. Supreme Court barred use of an "open-end warrant" in voiding a 1976 police seizure of a Goshen, New York, bookstore's stock; the store was backed by six book industry and related associations.

The six-group anticensorship coalition asked the Supreme Court to affirm a U.S. Court of Appeals decision overturning a Texas obscenity statute that could bar materials not yet judged obscene.

Tennessee's supreme court voided a 1978 state antiobscenity act as specifying "no recognizable offense and no identifiable parties to charge."

Progressive magazine challenged a federal injunction against printing an article (prior restraint) on hydrogen bomb technology; book publishers, writers, and news media supported the *Progressive*. Publication elsewhere ended the case.

A U.S. Court of Appeals upheld the CIA's rule that employees sign lifetime secrecy agreements, but reversed a lower court order confiscating Frank Snepp's royalties on *Decent Intervals* (Random) for alleged violation of such an agreement.

Publishers, authors, and libraries protested the practice of Follett Library Book Co. in tagging books it considers "possibly objectionable."

In August, a federal District Court upheld the Island Trees, Long Island, New York, school board that had required a school librarian to remove from shelves certain widely respected books, including Kurt Vonnegut's *Slaughterhouse Five*.

Members of P.E.N. American Center protested at the Czech UN mission in New York in October against human rights violations in the conviction of five writers and others.

The Authors Guild and others asked New York's legislature in November to strengthen the state's "shield law" to protect not only journalists but book authors as well.

In a move considered "chilling" by many religious writers and publishers, Rome's Sacred Congregation for the Doctrine of the Faith, and Pope John Paul II, declared December 18 that the Reverend Hans Kung "can no longer be considered a Catholic theologian" because of various writings, including *On Being a Christian* (Doubleday, Pocket) and the forthcoming *The Church—Maintained in Truth?* (Seabury).

Earlier, Vatican authorities directed critical interrogation toward other leading Catholic theologians and their books, including: Edward Schillebeeckx, *Jesus* (Seabury); Charles Curran *Transition and Tradition in Moral Theology* (Notre Dame); Leonardo Boff, *Jesus Christ, Liberator* (Orbis); Anthony Kosnik, *Human Sexuality*, written for Catholic Theological Society of America (Paulist Press and Doubleday).

SOME OTHER LEGAL MATTERS

Ashley Books sued CBS in February, claiming the network falsely portrayed it as a "vanity" publisher in a "60 Minutes" segment.

The Nation printed excerpts from ex-President Ford's *A Time to Heal* before publication by Harper & Row; Harper charged "theft"; the magazine said it was only using public property.

Grosset & Dunlap sued the Stratemeyer Syndicate and Simon & Schuster in May to stop transfer of publishing rights in Stratemeyer series books to S&S.

U.S. Supreme Court rulings in two cases on June 26 made it harder for publishers and authors to defend against libel suits by people who claim they are not "public figures."

A threat to all creative writing was seen in the Supreme Court's refusal in December to review a California award to a psychologist claiming defamation through a character in a work of fiction (*Touching* by Gwen Davis Mitchell, Doubleday).

Book publishing executives protested an Internal Revenue Service proposal for compulsory withholding from income of commissioned salespeople.

In the summer, the Copyright Clearance Center began partial distribution of royalty fees received in 1978 for photocopying.

A suit by Allyn & Bacon charged a 1976 Wiley book, *Organic Chemistry*, infringed A&B's *Organic Chemistry*, 1959–1973.

The House of Representatives voted partial restoration of Postal Service subsidies; Senate passage is in doubt.

The ABA protested that postage rate increases would threaten bookstore profits so far as to endanger the free flow of information.

Special Reports

THE WHITE HOUSE CONFERENCE ON LIBRARY AND INFORMATION SERVICES

1717 K St. N.W., Suite 601, Washington, DC 20036
202-634-1527

Marilyn K. Gell
Director

Vera Hirschberg
Public Relations Director

Twenty-three years ago, when a library trustee from Greenfield, Massachusetts, named Channing Bete, Sr., first proposed the idea of a White House Conference on Library and Information Services, the nation was still in the Industrial Age. The mighty industrial machine of America had converted from a wartime to a peacetime footing and was churning out a steady stream of consumer goods ranging from gas-guzzling, fish-tailed Cadillac convertibles to so-called Danish modern armchairs.

By November 1979, on the eve of the first White House Conference on Library and Information Services, the gas-guzzlers and the clumsy Scandinavian adaptations were gone. In their place were new products born of a new age, the Information Age. Christmas 1979 saw a boom in computerized toys. Americans were beginning to erect satellite receivers in their backyards. Information technology had made it possible to send a letter in 30 seconds across the United States. New developments in communications and computer technology had made possible the development of new industries such as cable television, fiber optics, minicomputers, and microchips. Government reports now estimate that more than 50 percent of the gross national product is devoted to the storage, retrieval, and dissemination of information.

The impact of these changes on American society has affected every American's daily life and is an increasing concern to public policymakers. And it is beginning to affect the public's traditional view of libraries as passive purveyors of information drawn from musty stacks. Just as technology enables society to better disseminate, retrieve, and store information, so, too, does it present libraries with new problems. In the light of inflation and dwindling tax bases, how can they afford to install new equipment? Indeed, in today's society, will they survive at all?

These are among the many issues some 3,500 conference participants faced when they convened in Washington, D.C., November 15–19, 1979, to consider the future role of library and information services in a rapidly changing society.

The conference was the culmination of 22 years of grass-roots participation and active public interest in Bete's proposal resulting in the support of four presidents: Lyndon B. Johnson, Richard M. Nixon, Gerald R. Ford, and Jimmy Carter, who addressed the conferees. The conference stemmed directly from congressional passage of

Note: For further information on the White House Conference, see the report in the January 15, 1980 issue of *Library Journal—Ed.*

a joint resolution in December 1974 signed into PL 93-568 by President Ford on December 31 of that year. The law directed that the National Commission on Libraries and Information Science, a permanent, independent federal agency established in 1970, plan and conduct the conference. The goal was "to develop recommendations for the further improvement of the nation's libraries and information centers and their use by the public consistent with the following seven policies:

1. Access to information and ideas is indispensable to the development of human potential, the advancement of civilization, and the continuance of enlightened self-government.
2. The preservation and the dissemination of information and ideas are the primary purpose and function of libraries and information centers.
3. The growth and augmentation of the Nation's libraries and information centers are essential if all Americans are to have reasonable access to adequate services of libraries and information centers.
4. New achievements in technology offer a potential for enabling libraries and information centers to serve the public more fully, expeditiously, and economically.
5. Maximum realization of the potential inherent in the use of advanced technology by libraries and information centers requires cooperation through planning for, and coordination of, the services of libraries and information centers.
6. The National Commission on Libraries and Information Science is developing plans for meeting national needs for library and information services and for coordinating activities to meet those needs.
7. Productive recommendations for expanding access to libraries and information centers will require public understanding and support as well as that of public and private libraries and information centers.

In 1975 an Advisory Committee to the White House Conference was organized and in May 1977, President Carter signed a Supplemental Appropriations Bill that included $3.5 million to fund the conference.

In September 1977 the National Commission on Libraries and Information Science (NCLIS) hired a small consulting staff to begin planning the conference and to assist the states and territories to hold Pre-White House conferences. In the fall of 1978 a new chairman, Charles Benton, was appointed; and in early 1979 a reconstituted Advisory Committee was established and a new director, Marilyn Gell, was appointed.

In all, between September 1977 and April 1979, 57 state and territorial conferences were held throughout the nation, including conferences held in the District of Columbia and by Indians living on or near reservations. An additional Pre-White House conference was held in July 1979 by the Federal Library Committee. These meetings involved more than 100,000 people, including professional and community representatives. The Pre-White House conferences served as the springboard for the national conference by developing a full range of issues and electing 568 delegates and 238 alternates to the White House Conference. An additional 105 delegates-at-large were chosen by the White House Conference Advisory Committee.

NCLIS rules required that delegates to both the preconferences and the national conference be proportionately one-third professional and two-thirds lay or community representatives. Delegates thus came from a rich diversity of backgrounds and included teachers, students, farmers, businesspeople, secretaries, retirees, public officials, as well as members of the library and information services community. As a true cross section of the population, the delegates were eminently qualified to approach the conferences as a workshop in participatory democracy.

They were assisted in this task not only by the structure of the conference itself, which was user-oriented, but by preconference mechanisms that helped to provide the broadest possible representation of views from the library and information services community and the public. These included input from the official 28-member Advisory Committee to the conference, and from a new body, the Information Community Advisory Committee (ICAC), which NCLIS Chairman Charles Benton established in the spring of 1979. The ICAC, which included representatives of the top echelons of the media, the communications industry, and the publishing industry, met three times before the conference and brought support, assistance, and a clearly defined private sector viewpoint to the planning of the conference.

In addition, five theme conferences and several preconference meetings, coordinated by the staff, helped to further broaden input to the planning process. The theme conferences were Federal Funding Alternatives; The Structure and Governance of Library Networks; Libraries and Literacy; International Information Exchange; and New Communication and Information Technology. Further information was developed by two substantive meetings of more than 50 leaders of information and library community associations and by a meeting of the Federal Library Committee's Federal Libraries and Information Services Pre-White House Conference, July 19–20, 1979.

The issues articulated in the 3,000 resolutions passed at all of these meetings and at the Pre-White House conferences in the states and territories were grouped into five user-oriented themes to structure the conference. Under the umbrella theme of "Bringing Information to People," the five theme areas were Library and Information Services for Personal Needs; Lifelong Learning; Governing Society; Business and the Professions; and International Cooperation and Understanding.

The conference was conceived to filter as many important concerns as possible into the final resolutions. Consequently, delegates were assigned to one of 34 small work groups within the theme area of their choice at the outset. In nine hours of discussion, the work groups hammered out drafts of resolutions. These in turn were further refined during many more hours of debates in the larger theme sessions. Finally, when the delegates met during the last two days in general sessions, they continued the process by further refining and voting on the final resolutions.

During this process the delegates were assisted by the resources of the Conference Information Center, which was planned and designed by the Library of Congress. In addition to traditional reference sources, such as books and vertical files, the center was an amalgam of data bases and computer terminals through which delegates could retrieve any information they needed to help them in their work, including the texts of the resolutions passed at the state and territorial conferences and the proceedings of each of the theme conferences.

Delegates were also given an opportunity to air their views at three separate open hearings, chaired by members of NCLIS and at a joint congressional hearing cochaired by Senator Claiborne Pell (D–R.I.) and Representative William Ford (D–Mich.). The two legislators are chairmen, respectively, of the Senate Subcommittee on Education, the Arts and the Humanities, and of the House Subcommittee on Postsecondary Education. The two subcommittees have jurisdiction over most federal library and information services programs. Ten senators and representatives heard testimony from the delegates at the hearing.

President Carter headed the long list of political and other notables who addressed the conference. Recalling that his love of books and libraries stemmed from his childhood days, the president stressed that "instant access to information and the calm reasoned guidance of a qualified librarian can make the difference between the success or failure even of a life." The president drew perhaps his greatest applause when he said he was convinced that the new U.S. Department of Education "will have a greater expanded and much more effective role in emphasizing the importance of books, of learning, and particularly of libraries." A second ovation came when he concluded his remarks by telling the delegates: "You can remember that you've got a friend in the White House."

Among the others who addressed the conference were Marilyn Gell, its director; NCLIS Chairman Charles Benton; Senator Pell; Senator Jacob K. Javits (R.-N.Y.), cosponsor with Senator Edward Kennedy (D.-Mass.) of the National Library Study Act; Representative John Brademas (D.-Ind.); Representative Ford; Richard M. Neustadt, assistant director of the domestic policy staff, White House; Daniel Boorstin, Librarian of Congress; and Ralph Nader, the consumer activist.

Stuart E. Eizenstat, assistant to the president for domestic affairs and policy, had assured NCLIS and conference planners at a meeting on March 9, 1979, that the White House takes the conference "seriously." At the conference he followed up on this commitment by announcing that a new intergovernmental task force will be formed specifically to study conference resolutions following presentation of the conference's final report to the president in March 1980.

During the final voting sessions, delegates passed 25 resolutions by two-thirds vote following debate. Fifteen of these were a product of the workshop process, while 10 were generated by petition. Forty-five of 49 resolutions on a paper ballot were passed by majority vote without debate.

While the delegates showed they strongly believe in local choice of program and materials and greater state funding for library and information services, a great many resolutions urged centralized planning and coordination to streamline services and facilities. This concern was reflected in resolutions calling for "a comprehensive approach . . . to the planning and development of multi-type library and information networks" at all levels of government, guaranteeing "access by all individuals to such networks and programs," and for "international communications and sharing to be included within the framework of the networks" to be created.

Strong support for an assistant secretary position within the new Department of Education to coordinate such library and information services programs was also evident.

Delegates also voted for a national public awareness program to be coordinated at the federal level to promote active use of libraries and information services by individuals and communities; and for "free access, without charge or fee to the individual, and information to all public and publicly supported libraries for all persons."

Concern for the functionally illiterate, the physically handicapped, and the incarcerated was evidenced in votes for literacy training, and new programs in libraries to deal with the problems of these individuals.

In the area of technology, delegates urged that national and international standards be developed for producing, publishing, transmitting, and storing information with special emphasis to be given to standards dealing with computer communications network protocols, machine-readable information, and compatibility of hardware and software. Although conferees urged federal development of such standards, they also stressed the need to encourage the private sector to participate "and support the development of such standards."

There was also considerable sentiment for the development of a national information policy to ensure that government agencies at all levels work together to make available new and existing library and information services to the maximum extent possible; to guarantee all citizens "equal and full access" to publicly funded library and information services programs; and to protect personal and economic privacy and national security.

As many conference participants noted, libraries and information services in the nation are at crossroads; the conference, they felt, clearly established a new agenda for the decade of the 1980s. In effect, the conference amounted to a call for a new reordering of institutional roles, priorities, and relationships. It is still too early to tell whether the enthusiasm and interest generated in Washington can be translated over the long term into substantive new realities. However, a beginning has been made. Among the developments several states and regional meetings have been held throughout the country to assess the conference results:

NCLIS devoted its entire two-day December meeting to discussing the conference resolutions as a basis for its national program for the 1980s.

The secretary of education, Shirley M. Hufstedler, has received and is reviewing the conference recommendation to create a position of assistant secretary for library and information services.

Following the White House Conference, its staff began work on the conference's final report, which was due on President Carter's desk in mid-March.

Inquiries from members of Congress, state officials, and the press show that the conference succeeded in building greater public awareness of the issues facing library and information services now and in the future.

NCLIS has begun to develop plans for an ad hoc follow-up committee composed of delegates elected by each state and territorial delegation to the conference, as specified in a conference resolution.

If one overriding conclusion were to be drawn from the experience of the White House Conference, it would be that democracy works. The conference did in fact bring together a microcosm of the people of the United States to discuss a multitude of complex and controversial issues. The process was intense. It involved negotiation and compromise. The result however is a tribute to the many dedicated participants. The recommendations passed are substantive and deal with significant and far-reaching issues. If the momentum for involvement generated by the conference continues, many of these resolutions are sure to find their way into the machinery of government and the fabric of our society.

THE WHCOLIS PRECONFERENCES

Alice B. Ihrig

Director, Civic and Cultural Programs, Moraine Valley Community College, Palos Hills, IL 60465

In an era when the device of a White House conference is overused and little noticed, the White House Conference on Library and Information Services, held in November 1979, is an exception to the experience of such conferences. It has received good grades for its organization, has been offered a White House Task Force as an avenue for its recommendations, and has provided the benchmark for activities of individuals, localities, states, and the federal government in promoting library and information services.

At the root of the apparent success of the national conference are the 57 state and territorial preconferences that, in varying degrees, provided the basis for a productive, practical, and predictive national meeting. Further, the preconferences had a life of their own—an emphasis on state and local recommendations and activity that will buttress national programs and stimulate library services at many governmental levels.

Congress authorized the calling of a White House Conference on Library and Information Services based on public participation at the preconference level. Two-thirds of the delegates to state conferences were to be non-library-related, a category that turned out to be somewhat difficult to interpret, but that was worked out to protect the concept of greater input from laypeople.

In many states the library profession felt itself underrepresented, a possible target for the "uninformed" citizens who could control the conference. This fear rarely materialized. Librarians found comforting support for their ideas on better service from the public. One of the most satisfying products of the preconferences was the commitment made by the public to work for libraries. There is a challenge to the library community in each state to build and maintain this public interest—to develop organizations and events to stay in touch with and mobilize the resources of enthusiastic delegates well informed on the problems of providing library and information services. A risk is that follow-up may be neglected, prepared delegates lost through failure to mount the effort needed to make use of laypersons with their considerable influence.

All the preconferences produced piles of recommendations, many reaffirming public support for the library in positive demand for more funds, better attention to the many kinds of libraries, expanded cooperative ventures from interlibrary loan through the spectrum of technological marvels, and legislation at all levels. Most of the resolutions were directed to local and state solutions. However, King Research, Inc., culled some 3,000 resolutions directed to the national conference from the reports of the preconferences (*Issues and Resolutions: A Summary of Pre-Conference Activities*, National Commission on Libraries and Information Science, September 1979).

The preconferences elected more than 600 official delegates to the White House Conference. Swelled by alternates attending at their own or state expense, observers, volunteers, and staff, the attendee count came to about 4,000, the largest White House Conference to date. The participation level was unusually high, caused partly by the need to cover as many of the 3,000 "ideas" as possible, plus the need to allow for new ideas and to winnow resolutions down to a manageable prioritized number.

The translation from the original recommendations from the preconferences to the somewhat controversial categories assigned to the discussion groups at the White House Conference is a process bearing on the final resolutions. In a graphic presentation published in September 1979, King Associates, Inc., first grouped the state and territory outcomes into the following implementation categories:

Funding and taxation
Legislation
Governance
Policies
Planning and evaluation
Research and development

Technology
Resource sharing and networking
Personnel development, staff support
Public relations and public awareness
Standards and guidelines
Physical access
Copyright
Censorship
Materials, holdings, and services
Preservation and storage

Even reduced to similarities, the categories seemed uneven in weight, overlapping, of mixed value in terms of federal solutions, and probably productive of an enormous number of resolutions to handle in the four days of the national conference. For example, the section on Public Relations and Public Awareness had five sections—libraries, information services, government, educational institutions, and public sector—each with a minimum of two substantial resolutions. The resolutions so listed tended to the specific, however. Under libraries, the preconferences contributed this list: expend funds and disseminate information; public awareness unit; public relations director; volunteer; library-related persons; state plant to implement; state consultant to assist locally; state workshops and seminars; and statewide locator file. Clearly, this function was seen as essentially local. Even those suggestions listed under government tended toward state participation.

Facing a limit on discussion group space, a limit on time for debate, and a problem in training discussion leaders, the White House Conference developed "theme" areas and then spent a great deal of time defending them. The themes were Personal Needs, Lifelong Learning, Organizations and Professions, Governing Our Society and International Cooperation. Now the preconference recommendations were resorted into the five areas. The list of 16 became "implementation concerns." The five themes took on goals. Issue papers were prepared around these themes to focus the thinking of delegates on library and information services for each of the theme areas.

This conversion trail is important in assessing the role and influence of the preconferences. Early in the process, many states asked that the final details of the national conference be held off until the preconference results were in. There had been fear that the National Commission would preempt the content, possibly tailoring it to the goals of the commission. "Local autonomy," whether applied to states or localities, was a strong concern throughout the conference process. State planners were ruffled by guidelines put out by the National Commission and its Advisory Committee. The costs of preconferences concerned many states. There had been mixed support for the idea of a White House Conference at all. Given this unrest, there was remarkable cooperation and professionalism in the preconferences.

No two preconferences were alike, even when the liaison from the national staff was the same. States applied their prior experience to the planning and format of the meetings. Generally, there was a planning committee, carefully balanced with the required two-thirds lay element. Generally, there were regional and areas hearings—small conferences inviting participation by the public and the professionals in stating problems and concerns. In some cases the preconference delegates rose from these meetings; in others the mix of delegates was carefully selected by committee. Geographical considerations were important in every case; age, sex, race, economic status, and profession or employment were considerations. Librarians vied for the one-third component. It was difficult to decide the appropriate configuration, given the need to represent the public, school, academic, special and private library, and information services. States tended to try to increase the involvement of librarians by using them as conference observers, volunteers, resource persons, and discussion leaders and recorders.

Preconference formats varied, but generally consumed at least two full days. Although speakers were used, they were secondary to the discussion groups, which pounded out recommendations for scrutiny by the delegate bodies. In every case, the discussion technique was central to the planning. Most states chose issues around which to discuss. Identification of issues was done by reviewing those arising at area meetings, by committee identification, and by compiling suggestions from many sources. While resolutions varied state to state, topics were more often similar. For example, these topics from a random selection of states:

Mississippi
Services, facilities, and materials
Personnel
Information network and library cooperation
Finance and governance
Evaluation and accountability
Value of libraries and information services

North Carolina
Access
Advocacy
Finance
Legislation
Library facilities
Library personnel
Planning and policy
Resource sharing and networks
Service to special groups
Technology

Nevada
Organization/basic structure and authority
Funding
Basic services, program, personnel
Special services, program, personnel
Community relations, publicity
Organizing for action/implementing change

Missouri
Purpose of libraries
Access to information
Governance of libraries

Technology and libraries
Financing of libraries

Connecticut
Improve access to available library resources
Strengthening existing state, regional, and local systems services
Develop new resources and services
Ensure a basic minimum of library and information service to Connecticut citizens
How to identify and respond to community needs?

Delaware
Are library services available to all?
What should a library do?
Who pays and who controls?
Libraries and machines?

Although all states emphasized "libraries," there was considerable attention to other sources of information, including that marketed through commercial avenues. Most conferences featured exhibits demonstrating technology already in use. Many recognized future problems, such as copyright, in their resolutions. Some were criticized for overemphasis on the public library. A number converted the common knowledge of public libraries into a broader background for their lay delegates.

It was natural that the states and territories should produce mainly state and local resolutions. It was a purpose of many preconferences to obtain support for state and local programs, hence encouragement of understanding of state and local problems. State library agencies and state library associations are recognizing the plethora of "local" resolutions as a breeding ground for better state legislation, better relationships with local funding bodies, and stimulation of citizen action in support of local libraries.

Every preconference set future aims. Many urged regular conferences. Some set the beginnings for state Friends of the Library (Pennsylvania), a statewide citizen support group (Washington), or an implementation committee named from the conference. Most expect the national delegates to serve as an implementation committee. In some cases, delegates from an area or region pledged to organize.

As the states and territories worked through their preconferences, they found ways to cooperate with other states and with groups within the state not usually involved in library matters. States that held early conferences (Georgia, Pennsylvania, Virginia, Oklahoma, Idaho, Massachusetts, New York, Colorado) were consulted and even copied. Pennsylvania's "Speak Out" title for regional meetings was widely used. The library press analyzed each effort. Interested organizations began to build position papers. Public interest groups began to take notice and to join in. Major public relations efforts foundered at the national level, but many states reported good "coverage" about their activities.

What were the outcomes of the preconferences in the states and territories? Were the efforts productive and funds well spent? The states answered these questions in the evaluations they submitted as part of their conference reporting. Generally, states and the territories felt that:

> The preconferences were successful in focusing attention on the problems current to library and information services and in setting out these problems to

52 / SPECIAL REPORTS

an appropriate audience: general public, media, preconference participants, library and information community, and, in a preparatory sense, the national conference.

The preconferences, with the White House label, secured considerable interest among legislators and policymakers and laid groundwork for legislative drives and greater funding.

The preconferences, held across the country, carried more weight than ordinary conferences.

The preconferences forced the library and information communities to work together and set the stage for greater cooperation between these two branches of the information business.

The preconferences raised the consciousness of a substantial number of citizens who are in a position to help as libraries fight for greater recognition and fulfillment of their roles.

The preconferences placed a stamp of approval on the work that librarians have been doing and emphasized the need for librarians to work more closely with the public if professional objectives are to be realized.

The preconferences brought to a head the problems libraries face and provide direction for planning and implementation.

The preconferences opened communication between the library community and the public and drew out commitments on both sides to work together more frequently and continuously.

The preconferences told the library community that it has a public relations job to do; the public delegates demanded more information on what libraries do.

The preconferences made distinctions between what should be done locally and what should be done nationally and generally rejected total reliance on the federal government. State and local involvement in federal decisions was demanded.

The preconferences produced intelligent and progressive recommendations that can be used as the basis for building a better library system.

What the preconferences did not do is also told in the reports. White House spotlight and all, the preconferences did not light up the skies for the public at large. Winning friends and workers for libraries is not a goal achieved by one successful conference.

The preconferences smoothed some paths, but did not offer much that is new about how to get things done. They added volunteers to legislative lobbying teams; they made converts out of light users; they found new supporters in old settings; they discovered leaders. But they confirmed what is known: library support is hard work and demands perseverance.

The preconferences reaffirmed some old assignments. Even the public expects the state library agency to perform miracles. Perhaps more people now understand the realities of state budgets and the limitations placed on agencies.

No one expected the White House preconferences to make an instant difference. Yet some did. In Minnesota, an exuberant legislative package from the preconference spurred legislative action. In Pennsylvania, the conference demanded and got a statewide Friends group. State libraries all over the country rushed the conference results to their funding sources.

Most persons left with the implementation of preconference results feel that there is a solid citizen plank under the needs of libraries. They see a long and productive relationship with the public delegates if efforts are made to continue the friendships developed during the preconferences.

Because the preconferences were local, because the people involved can be reached, and because it is easier to fight for the libraries from a home base, for these reasons, knowledgeable librarians predict greater immediate results from the preconference attention to local matters. They see the national conference as more difficult to implement. And they are not waiting for libraries at the national level to catch fire with Congress or the White House.

The 57 preconferences (49 states, U.S. territories, the District of Columbia) made possible the White House Conference. In a federation like the United States, success comes from the two levels—state and national—that together solve problems.

The preconferences, including the special American Indian gathering, provided skilled and interested delegates, who overrode the small inconveniences of a national conference to pull together sensible and workable recommendations for the library and information services of this country.

LIBRARY SERVICE TO DISABLED PEOPLE: A STATE OF THE ART REPORT FOR THE 1970s

Ruth A. Velleman

Library Director, Human Resources School, Albertson, New York 11507

The decade of the 1980s opens auspiciously for disabled people. Many segments of our society are now attempting to be of service to this very important group in our population, after centuries of neglect. A resolution, adopted by the United Nations General Assembly, has proclaimed 1981 the "International Year of Disabled Persons." How has this change come about?

BACKGROUND

Before the nineteenth century there was little or no interest in the disabled. Originally considered to be the responsibility of their families, disabled persons became the early nineteenth-century inhabitants of asylums and poor houses. Those services that developed were a mixture of social welfare programs and some medical and physical restoration. The first two groups to be served with educational programs were the blind and visually impaired and the deaf and hard of hearing.

During the first part of the twentieth century the foundations were laid for current rehabilitation and special education programs for the disabled. In 1918 the federal government established a National Vocational Rehabilitation program for physically

Note: Sources for filling all of the special information needs referred to later in this article, and much more, will be found in *Serving Physically Disabled People: An Information Handbook for All Libraries* by Ruth A. Velleman, which was published by R. R. Bowker in December 1979.

disabled veterans consisting mainly of prosthetic appliances and job assistance. In 1919 the Easter Seal Society for Crippled Children and Adults was established and it still functions today as one of the oldest institutions serving all disabled people with a national network of centers for education and rehabilitation. Through its central rehabilitation library in the head office in Chicago, its journal *Rehabilitation Literature*, and its other publications, the Easter Seal Society carries on an active program of information and education.

In the early 1920s public attitudes changed considerably. Parents began to form organizations to foster education and care for their disabled children, and the United States established a division of special education in the Federal Bureau of Education, with Elise Martens as its first director.[1] Under the influence of Franklin D. Roosevelt, the Social Security laws of 1935 included funds to develop programs for physically handicapped children and adults.

World War II gave new impetus for education and vocational training of the handicapped. Rehabilitation counseling emerged as a new profession, and the Office of Vocational Rehabilitation was established through the Barden-LaFollette Act of 1943.[2] This act extended vocational rehabilitation to adults of work age, and in many states this service is also available to young adults prior to the legal work age, with vocational rehabilitation counselors working with the schools in this area.

In 1945 Congress passed a joint resolution that established the President's Committee on Employment of the Handicapped, and many states followed suit by forming governor's committees. Promotional materials developed by these organizations were aimed at fostering positive attitudes toward the education and employment of disabled people.

The Vocational Rehabilitation Amendments of 1954 provided for expansion in all areas of professional service to the handicapped.[3] The 1960s and 1970s have been years of great progress in the fields of education and vocational rehabilitation of the disabled, progress that has been encouraged by several pieces of landmark legislation.

CURRENT LEGISLATION

In 1973, Congress passed the Rehabilitation Act of 1973 (PL 93-112).[4] In Title V of this act, Section 501 provides for the employment of the disabled in the federal government; Section 502 created the Architectural and Transportation Barriers Compliance Board; Section 503, the affirmative action clause, states that private businesses receiving $2,500 or more in federal funds must take "affirmative action" to search out and employ the disabled; and Section 504, known as the "equal access" clause, states that the disabled shall have equal access to all programs that receive federal funds.

A parallel development was PL 94-142, the Education for all Handicapped Children Act, which states that all disabled children in the United States are entitled to a free education in the most appropriate and least restrictive environment.[5] Somewhat inaccurately called the "mainstreaming act," PL 94-142, together with Section 504, encourages large numbers of disabled people to enter the mainstream of American life.

In 1978, the Rehabilitation Act of 1973 was amended with PL 95-602, the Rehabilitation, Comprehensive Services and Developmental Disabilities Amendments of 1978.[6] A redefinition of developmental disabilities is an important feature of the law, major provisions of which include the establishment of a National Institute of Handicapped Research, a program to increase the fostering of employment opportunities for the handicapped, a comprehensive service plan to encourage independent living for the severely disabled, and a significant strengthening of the enforcement possibilities of Section 504 of the Rehabilitation Act of 1973.

Included in the 1978 amendment is a reiteration of the need, expressed in the Rehabilitation Act of 1973, for a central clearinghouse of information for the handicapped. Thus Congress, in the decade of the 1970s, officially recognized that the provision of information is an important component in the education and rehabilitation of the disabled.

DISABILITIES DEFINED

Many programs and services use their own definitions of handicap or handicapping conditions. Some of these definitions are contained within enabling legislation (federal or state) or regulatory language. The definition used in the Rehabilitation Act of 1973 is: "Anyone who . . . has a physical or mental impairment which substantially limits one or more of the person's major life activities . . . has a record of such impairment . . . is regarded as having such an impairment." The term "handicapped" includes orthopedic disorders, mental retardation, mental illness, speech and hearing disorders, perceptual dysfunction, visual impairment, specific learning disabilities, and other diseases and conditions.

Physical disabilities are very diversified. They fall into three basic anatomical categories: those involving the skeletal structure, the muscular system, and the neuromuscular system. Special health problems are also included in the physical disability groupings. They include cerebral palsy, quadriplegia or paraplegia due to spinal cord injury, postpolio, muscular dystrophy, and related muscle diseases, multiple sclerosis, osteogenesis imperfecta, familial dysautonomia, arthrogryposis, spina bifida, and others. Special health problems include hemophilia, epilepsy, sickle cell anemia, diabetes, cardiac conditions, and others.

STATISTICS

It is difficult to estimate the numbers of disabled members of the population as there is often double reporting through organizations and institutions. It is estimated, however, that over 36 million people in the United States are disabled in some way. The 1980 census will ask more specific questions than ever before in this area in order to determine these numbers more accurately.

CHANGING ATTITUDES

The changing social condition of the disabled population has required that old stereotypes be discarded and new attitudes brought to bear on the nature of this special group. New educational opportunity, offered at an early age and extending through college or vocational training programs, as well as independent living projects begun by severely physically disabled people to help themselves, has resulted in greater social and economic independence for all segments of the disabled population. The development of special hand controls for private automobiles and the acquisition by many communities of ramped buses have resulted in greater mobility for orthopedically disabled people. As they emerge from their homes and institutions, it has become apparent that, given opportunities for education, socialization, and work experience, disabled people will develop the same similarities and differences as those of able-bodied individuals. For further reading I would recommend Beatrice Wright's *Physical Disability: A Psychological Approach* (New York: Harper & Row, 1960), Frank Bowe's *Handi-*

capping America: Barriers to Disabled People (New York: Harper & Row, 1978), and an excellent set of pamphlets on attitudes published by the Regional Rehabilitation Research Institute on Attitudinal, Legal and Leisure Barriers, George Washington University, Washington, D.C. 20036.

ARCHITECTURAL AND TECHNICAL NEEDS

Architectural barriers used to prevent many physically disabled people from being able to utilize libraries. Although federal and state laws already on the books had mandated that new public buildings must be made accessible to the disabled, it was Section 504 of the Rehabilitation Act of 1973 that made it necessary for libraries to begin making adaptations to existing buildings. The American National Standards Institute in 1961 published basic standards for building adaptation, known as ANSI Standards. These were distributed through the National Easter Seal Society, and were adapted and restated to suit special needs by many states, colleges, and other institutions. The revised Standards have been published and will be available by spring 1980.

Generally accepted measurements and standards have also been set forth in several recent issues of the newsletter *Report*, published by the National Center for a Barrier Free Environment, Washington, D.C. The National Center, formed in 1974, is a coalition of the major advocacy organizations in this field and works to carry out the mandate of the Architectural and Transportation Barriers Compliance Board. It is in the process of establishing a library of materials in the area of access.

None of the standards mentions libraries, per se, except for a General Services Administration report, *Design Criteria: New Public Building Accessibility* (December 1977), which provides several pages of recommendations for libraries. Additional library adaptations were described by this author in an article in *School Library Journal* (October 1974).

The following includes some general principles to be considered when making adaptations for the physically disabled.

Standard wheelchairs are 25 inches wide, 42 inches long, and have a turning radius of 60 × 60 inches. Doors should be 32 inches wide, lightweight, with see-through panels, and lever handles. There should be at least one ground level entrance where possible with thresholds consisting of metal strips with gripper edges. Ramp grades should not exceed a 1-foot rise for every 12 feet. Reserved parking spaces for the disabled require an extra 4 feet of space next to each car, and curb cuts must be supplied where needed.

Special library adaptations would include perimeter wall shelving when possible, or stacks 5 feet apart, card catalog on a 16-inch base, and apronless tables without pedestals at a preferred height of 29 inches. Where study carrels are used in school, public, or special libraries, a 48-inch width is recommended. Cabinets and bins for media and vertical files can be made accessible by the use of cabinets on low bases without cross bars, and by the use of side files. Tile floors should be nonskid for crutch walkers. Carpeting should be institution grade, tackless, acrylic with a tight weave and no padding, if possible, and cemented to the floor. Adapted toilet stalls, lowered public telephones, and audible and visible warning signals for the visually handicapped and hearing impaired should, of course, be standard in all public buildings.

Modification in equipment is minimal in cases where the disabled person has hand control. For persons with hand and arm disabilities, automatic page turners (not usually too effective) or reading stands may be acquired. Publications of the American Heart Association and the British Red Cross Society include descriptions of inexpensive ways of constructing page turning equipment. More expensive models are listed in *Reading, Writing, and Other Communication Aids for Visually and Physically Handicapped Persons*, prepared by the National Library Service for the Blind and Physically Handicapped. This publication also lists reading aids such as large print books and magnifiers, as well as recorded books.[7] [See the report by Frank Kurt Cylke and Eunice Lovejoy on the National Library Service for the Blind and Physically Handicapped in the Federal Libraries section of Part 1—*Ed.*]

READING INTERESTS

Handicapped individuals for the most part have the same variety of interests as members of the able-bodied population. This means that their tastes in leisure reading will reflect very closely the tastes of the general public. Disabled children also take delight in the same books that able-bodied children enjoy. There are, however, a few differences. Disabled children, contrary to popular belief, do not choose to read about the handicapped and are quick to find inaccuracies in such literature. On the other hand they do appreciate seeing the disabled portrayed in literature as part of the general population. Many handicapped children suffer reading lags because of developmental disabilities, or long periods of hospitalization with resultant interruption of schooling. In addition, severe hearing impairment may cause language and reading difficulties. Many disabled children, therefore, require high-interest, low-vocabulary material. Some need concrete rather than abstract concepts in their literature.

SPECIAL INFORMATION NEEDS

Physically disabled people have certain special informational needs, deriving from their physical limitations. These include information about architectural specifications for housing such as bathroom and kitchen modifications for wheelchair users. Knowledge about prosthetics and orthotics, where to find specialized equipment for one-handed or quadriplegic users, specially designed clothing for people who are congenitally incontinent or have had colostomies, special communication devices, travel information, including adapted public accommodations, airlines, bus and rail regulations, and information about recreational activities for the disabled are all of great importance. Also much needed by all disabled people is information about legal rights and financial aid, referral information to service agencies such as special schools, offices of vocational rehabilitation, and other rehabilitation training facilities. Disabled people are also in great need of sexual information. Until recently there was not too much material available in this important area, but now there is a great deal.

PUBLIC LIBRARY SERVICES

Public libraries are the backbone of library and information services in the United States and they have always led the way in providing special patrons such as the blind, the homebound and the institutionalized with basic reader services. [See the report on the National Library Service for the Blind and Physically Handicapped in the Federal Libraries section of Part 1—*Ed.*] There are, however, an increasing number of public libraries around the country now reaching out to the community to offer services to the handicapped wherever they are, and to encourage them to come to the library. Generally, this service tends to vary in effectiveness from state to state, depending on the level of leadership offered by the state library as well as on grass-roots movements by some local public libraries.

The state of Ohio has long been in the forefront in library service to the disabled. The newsletter *Ohio Libraries Reach Out*, issued by Eunice Lovejoy, Library Development Consultant, Services to the Handicapped, keeps all libraries in the state abreast of new developments in the field of the disabled. The public library of Cincinnati and Hamilton County has a highly developed outreach program of library service to disabled children. The long standing outreach service program of the public library of Columbus and Franklin County has been implemented with CETA funds for the purpose of expansion. Some staff members are being trained to communicate via sign language with deaf patrons.[8]

Public library service to the deaf is a developing field and the decade of the 1980s will see exciting new developments. A prototype for library service to deaf patrons is the program developed by Alice Hagemeyer in her position as librarian for the deaf at the Washington, D.C., Public Library. Washington, D.C., is the home of many agencies working with deaf people and has the largest deaf population in the United States.[9] Hagemeyer serves this population with a very active program. She has the cooperation of Gallaudet College in the development of her program.

Alice Hagemeyer, who has written a great deal about library service to the deaf, makes the following recommendations based on her goals for her own program.

Since most of the materials on deafness used to be on the medical and technical aspects of deafness, it is important to assemble a collection of materials on the cultural realities of deafness, as well as on deaf heritage. A collection of videotapes and captioned or signed films that provide information to deaf persons would be worthwhile. Funding can be sought through the Library Services Construction Act, as well as from private sources such as Quota International or Lions International. Service should include the ownership of a teletypewriter for use in information service in lieu of a telephone. The hiring of deaf employees would facilitate reaching the deaf community as well as make it possible to offer classes in signing and fingerspelling. Such classes are now being offered in greater and ever increasing numbers. Library resources on deafness need to be made known to the community through visits, brochures, annual Deaf Awareness Weeks, and other methods of publicity. During that week events for each day might include displays of special devices for the hearing impaired, book readings, posters, and a lecture series by deaf authors or authorities on hearing and noise pollution. Free hearing tests by a local clinic and free mini-classes on sign language will increase interest. Hagemeyer also maintains a list of local interpreters to the deaf with their phone numbers.[10]

Some programs that emulate the Washington, D.C., Public Library's program have been funded by LSCA in recent years. One notable example is the program at the Metropolitan Cooperative Library System in the greater Los Angeles area, which attempts to bring deaf people into the mainstream of library service by helping them use libraries as information and social centers and sensitizing the hearing population to the problems of deafness. A model plan of service is being implemented within each of the 25 MCLS member libraries.[11]

AMERICAN LIBRARY ASSOCIATION

During the late 1970s the American Library Association (ALA) became actively involved in the provision of library service to the deaf, as its structure went through several changes. Early involvement of the ALA in library service to the handicapped centered in the Committee on Library Service to the Blind and in the Association for Hospital and Institution Libraries (AHIL). In 1973, the Health and Rehabilitative Library Services Division (HRLSD) was organized when AHIL and the ALA Round

Table on Library Service to the Blind joined to form a new service division. This new division grew directly out of concern for the changing needs of the disabled population. The Round Table was originally limited to service to the blind, whereas by 1976 Congress had expanded this service to include all print-handicapped people. In addition, there was growing awareness in AHIL that service to the disabled needed to be expanded beyond hospitals and institutions, to all types of libraries and agencies servicing persons with special needs. Many of these people were now becoming members of the general population.

At the 1975 ALA annual conference in San Francisco, the new division cosponsored with the Public Library Division two programs for Library Service to Special Patrons, which were extremely well attended. At the annual conference in Chicago in 1976 this division cosponsored a preconference Institute on Mainstreaming the Exceptional Child in the Library. The annual meeting in June 1977 brought a proposal for a merger between HRLSD and the Association of State Library Agencies, this merger becoming effective in 1979 and resulting in the formation of the Association of Specialized and Cooperative Library Agencies (ASCLA).

As early as July 1976, at the annual meeting of ALA in Chicago, a group of librarians from the Washington, D.C., Public Library led an effort to have the organization officially recognize the needs of deaf persons. An ad hoc committee was established that recommended, in 1978, the formation of a permanent unit on Library Service to the Deaf within the newly constituted ASCLA. In September 1978 the new Library Service to the Deaf Section officially came into existence. Before the midwinter 1980 ALA conference in Chicago, this new section set up seven standing committees. In addition a subcommittee, chaired by Alice Hagemeyer, was charged with studying how to provide interpreting services for all conference programs as well as in exhibit areas. Program possibilities for the future include a joint preconference program with YASD for 1981 on working with deaf young adults. Immediate plans for the LSD Section are to cosponsor programs, encouraging other divisions to recognize their responsibility to the deaf in their own program plans.[12]

THE PRESIDENT'S COMMITTEE ON EMPLOYMENT OF THE HANDICAPPED: LIBRARY COMMITTEE

In 1959 a committee on libraries was established as one of the 16 standing committees of the President's Committee on Employment of the Handicapped. Emerson Greenaway, former President of ALA and former director of the Free Library of Philadelphia, was its first chairman. The committee, which continues today, is made up of members of the library profession who are involved in some aspect of library service to the handicapped. Its goal is to encourage libraries to serve persons with handicaps by acting as resource centers for community education and vocational information, and by performing as model employers of handicapped persons.[13]

In recent years the Library Committee has cosponsored programs with ALA on a wide range of subjects concerning library service to the handicapped. It has been instrumental in encouraging ALA to adopt a policy statement encouraging the employment of handicapped people in libraries, and continues to work closely with ALA on matters pertaining to policies and regulations relating to employment of handicapped people. The Library Committee also encourages library schools to establish courses on library service to the handicapped and promotes workshops and institutes in this area. It has published a brochure, for the use of the library profession, on the final regulations of Section 504.[14]

SPECIAL EDUCATION LIBRARIANSHIP

During the decade of the 1970s two special fields began to emerge and become more visible in the area of library service to the disabled, one in the field of special education and the other in the health science field of rehabilitation.

The field of school librarianship offers a unique challenge in today's educational picture. As the emphasis shifts toward more instructional materials to enrich the teaching program, the expanded school library media center becomes indispensable to the complete academic development of the student. With this change in curriculum methods has come the realization that the child who, for physical reasons, has been educated on a home instructional program or in a special class without access to such a center has been deprived of a vital part of his or her educational experience.

The school library media specialist has a triple role in service to the physically disabled student. The traditional functions of reading guidance, teaching library skills, and creative media work with students are supplemented by important information services to teachers to aid them in understanding student disabilities and acquaint them with sources for any special curriculum materials needed for classroom work. The third role, and a significant one, is that of information specialist for the parents of disabled students to help them locate the information they need to cope with daily living requirements, educational expectations, and the vocational futures of their children.

Background

School library service to exceptional children was not reported on before the 1950s. By 1957, however, some areas of the country were reporting on the establishment of special school library services for handicapped children. Most of these services were in elementary schools where modified classes had been provided. The groups first to be served for the most part were the deaf and the blind, and not the orthopedically handicapped.[15]

During this time, in regular school programs new instructional materials in programmed format, nonprint materials such as realia, recordings, filmstrips, sound filmstrips, cassettes and tapes (video and audio), microforms, film loops and films, and the hardware to accommodate all of the new software made it necessary for school libraries to become school library media centers or instructional materials centers. Earliest efforts toward use of these new media in the education of disabled children was in the education of the deaf. Blind children, too, began to benefit from new types of recorded formats for their text materials.

Orthopedically and mentally handicapped children were the last to be served by the library media field. Until recently, children in special classes continued to be deprived of school library services and many special schools did not have library media centers. This picture is changing slowly. A full account of a prototype program, at the Human Resources School in Albertson, New York, can be found in *Serving Physically Disabled People: An Information Handbook for All Libraries*, by Ruth A. Velleman (R. R. Bowker, 1979).

During the 1970s sophistication of educational technology has resulted in the development of new methods of dealing with children with varying types of disabilities. At the same time, because of PL 94-142, more disabled children than ever before are entering regular classrooms. Teaching staff and other professionals concerned with the education of exceptional children, as well as parents, have become cognizant of the fact that the trained library media specialist, aware of where special materials can be obtained, is an indispensable member of the educational team.

Fortunately for school librarians, the 1970s saw the growth of many educationally related data bases in the United States. As one of the 16 clearinghouses in the ERIC (Educational Resources Information Center) network, the Clearinghouse on Handicapped and Gifted Children operates under the sponsorship of the Council for Exceptional Children, the professional educational organization in the field. This clearinghouse has gone beyond the scope of ERIC to develop the ECER data base, with more extensive coverage than any of the other clearinghouses. *Exceptional Child Education Resources* is the print index and abstract for the ECER data base. It includes all citations on exceptional children submitted to ERIC as well as additional dissertations, nonprint media, and other documents dealing with the education of exceptional children.

Closer Look is an organization, funded by the Bureau of Education of the Handicapped, which operates as a national information center to help parents of handicapped children and young adults locate special services. A newsletter is published free of charge.

During the 1960s, through the U.S. Office of Education, Bureau of Education of the Handicapped, a network of national centers was set up to increase instructional options for the education of handicapped children. These offices were established in 13 regions in the United States, Puerto Rico, and the Virgin Islands. Parallel offices, called regional resource centers, provided diagnostic assessment and prescriptive services. At the end of September 1977, the Learning Resource Centers were phased out and merged into the Regional Resource Centers, with emphasis on the implementation of PL 94-142.

A National Center on Educational Media and Materials for the Handicapped, located at Ohio State University, had developed a data base relating to child-directed instructional materials, which was accessed through the regional offices. As a result of the 1977 reorganization, the contract for the Ohio center was not renewed by the federal government. However, it continues to operate out of Ohio State University. The task of continuing and updating the data base (NIMIS) was taken over by the National Information Clearinghouse for Special Education Materials (NICSEM) at the University of Southern California. Two newsletters, *The Program Tree* and *Frankly Speaking*, are issued by this center. Materials in the data base are still accessed through local regional resource centers.

Special materials for blind and visually impaired children have always been available through the American Printing House for the Blind, in Louisville, Kentucky, which was designated a national center in the late 1800s by Congress. Local school districts receive materials for visually impaired students on a quota system, through local sources of distribution. School librarians should inform themselves of this service and provide information to teachers. Valuable publications offering guidelines for mainstreaming visually impaired students are available from the American Foundation for the Blind in New York City.

Deaf and hearing-impaired students who enter regular school programs will represent a very great challenge to librarians. The schools for the deaf pioneered in the use of a great deal of media, and good media centers are maintained by almost all of these special facilities. There was, until quite recently, little use of print materials in library media centers. Deaf children do benefit, however, from high-interest, low-vocabulary books. Because deaf children learn primarily by sight, concepts must be presented in visual format; abstract concepts and words with multiple meanings are difficult for them to comprehend, and library books with simple syntax and clear pictures are most effective.

Captioned films for the deaf is a service of the federal government and information can be obtained from Captioned Films and Telecommunications Branch, Bureau of Education of the Handicapped, Washington, D.C. 20202.

College Library Service

According to a survey by the Kansas State Teachers College in 1964, updated by the Office of Education in 1967, 200 colleges across the nation had modified their campuses or buildings in various ways and to varying degrees to accommodate physically disabled students.[16]

In 1976 a new directory entitled *The College Guide for Students with Disabilities*, published jointly by ABT Publications in Massachusetts and Westview Press in Colorado, and based on a study funded by the Bureau of the Education for the Handicapped, reported new findings that illustrate the progress that has been made in a decade. The 3,038 colleges listed in the *Higher Education Directory* of the National Center on Educational Statistics were surveyed. Approximately 1,000 positive responses were received, indicating that almost a third of the colleges in the country now have some sort of architectural adaptations and/or special programs for the disabled, no matter how minimal. Adaptations range from minor accommodations such as curb cuts and reserved parking spaces, to total architectural accessibility to all classrooms, dormitories, and special buildings such as libraries, as well as physical assistance where necessary for severely disabled students.[17]

Many of the colleges surveyed indicated accessible library buildings. In 1976, the State Library of Ohio published a study on the accessibility and services of the college libraries in the state.[18] One hundred and fifteen librarians of postsecondary educational institutions were surveyed. Of this number, close to 100 reported that their libraries were accessible to the disabled. Special equipment such as audiovisual aids, electric typewriters, and tape recorders were available at almost all libraries. Magnifiers and braille typewriters were available at some of the libraries. Others indicated that they borrowed materials for their students from the state regional libraries for the blind and physically handicapped.

An outstanding program for disabled students at Wright State University in Fairborn, Ohio, provides physical attendant care when necessary in cases of severe disability. All buildings are completely adapted. A director of handicapped student services attends to all needs of students. The Wright State University Library includes a Tape Center for the Handicapped administered by the head of the department of library media production and instructional laboratories. This center provides audiotapes of required textbooks for handicapped students, as well as other books. The office is staffed at all times to provide accessibility as requested by instructors and students. In addition, the Regional Library for the Blind and Physically Handicapped is utilized for loan materials, as well as Recording for the Blind, with head offices in New York City, which records text materials.[19]

REHABILITATION LIBRARIANSHIP

Most disabled people need a variety of services from birth to adulthood. This is generally called rehabilitation, the process through which a disabled person is restored to his or her highest level of self-sufficiency. It might better be defined as "habilitation" in the case of the congenitally disabled. It is achieved through a combination of medicine and therapy and education and vocational training, the ultimate goal being a life of dignity and independence on whatever level possible, whether through competitive employment, a form of sheltered work, or simply an independent living situation. It calls for a team approach, and librarians only now are becoming part of that team.

Rehabilitation librarians do not need to become rehabilitation counselors. Part of their training, however, must be to become acquainted with the goals of the professionals in the rehabilitation field, with the structure of the field itself, and with the body of existing rehabilitation literature so that they will be able to retrieve the information being generated in ever-increasing quantities and deal with these materials in an organized fashion.

During the 1970s the field of rehabilitation grew rapidly. In addition to private agencies, old ones as well as some new ones, Veterans Administration offices, and state offices of vocational rehabilitation, a network of research centers was established, funded by the Rehabilitation Services Administration of the Department of Health, Education, and Welfare and now placed under the new National Institute of Handicapped Research. These centers are nationwide, located in ten regions, each specializing in some area of rehabilitation—some in medical rehabilitation such as spinal cord injury, some in rehabilitation engineering (inventing new and exciting devices for the disabled), and some in work evaluation and training. Some specialize in only one or two disabilities such as deafness research or mental retardation. All of these centers are producing and disseminating information in both print and nonprint form. The magazine *The Informer*, published by the Information Exchange at the Arkansas Research and Training Center in Region IV, reports quarterly on the work of the centers.

The Rehabilitation Act of 1973 made provision for the establishment of a National Center for Deaf-Blind Youths and Adults to be called the Helen Keller Center, with the goal of identifying the deaf-blind population in the country and setting up training programs in independent living and employment skills. The Helen Keller Center established a library in the fall of 1976 at its headquarters in Sands Point, Long Island.

In December 1976 the Office for Handicapped Individuals in Washington, D.C., published a *Directory of National Information Sources on Handicapping Conditions and Related Services*, which lists over 280 national organizations, all of which publish pamphlet and/or audiovisual materials in the field of rehabilitation. These materials are a very important part of the body of rehabilitation information; however, much of it is ephemeral and difficult to track down.

It became apparent, during the information explosion of the 1970s, that information networking was going to be necessary in the fields of medical and vocational information. Ultimately, one computerized data base in this area will be a reality. Some data bases now exist. The editor of the magazine *Accent on Living* operates a computerized retrieval system called Accent on Information (AOI) in the area of activities of daily living (ADL). The American Alliance for Health, Physical Education and Recreation (AAHPER) operates an information and research information center (IRUC) in the area of adapted physical education and recreation. This is a computerized data base. A therapeutic recreation information center called TRIC, operates out of California State University in Sacramento, where it also has a computerized data base. There is also a National Clearinghouse of Rehabilitation Training Materials at Oklahoma State University in Stillwater that maintains materials in the broad area of rehabilitation training. Information is publicized in bibliographical form through the *Clearinghouse Memorandum*, which is sent out at approximately three-month intervals to professionals in the field of rehabilitation.

In October 1977, the Rehabilitation Services Administration made a five-year grant to establish a National Rehabilitation Information center. The center, known as NARIC, is located at the graduate department of library science at Catholic University in Washington, D.C., and its director, Judith J. Senkevitch, is a librarian. Its basic goal is to improve information delivery to the rehabilitation community. For a start it will house all RSA-generated research reports, as well as other materials relevant to the area of vocational rehabilitation. At the present time, NARIC's computerized system is available to a limited number of organizations through BRS (Bibliographic Retrieval Services, Inc.). They will generate bibliographies on request. In the future, hopefully all materials, including the indexing of rehabilitation periodicals (not yet fully indexed in a central way), will come under the NARIC umbrella. The address is: NARIC, Box 136, Catholic University of America, Washington, D.C. 20064.

LIBRARY EDUCATION

In June 1976 the National Library Service to the Blind and Physically Handicapped conducted a survey to determine which ALA-accredited library school programs offered special courses, institutes, seminars, or workshops to prepare librarians to serve the disabled.[20] Fifty-nine out of 67 accredited schools in the United States and Canada, or 88 percent, responded. At present, 76 percent do not offer any preparation to students in this field; however, 54 schools indicated willingness to consider such programs in the future. Many of the schools stated that service to disabled readers is included in more general courses. Fifteen library schools offer courses in related areas such as hospital and institution libraries, general health science libraries, bibliotherapy, or library service to all disadvantaged groups, including the aged. Some schools offer opportunity to do independent study in this field.

Catholic University Library School offered the first comprehensive program in library service to the handicapped. This program provides a postmaster's certificate for 24 credit hours of study in a variety of situations, including media for handicapped readers, library services to the hearing impaired, aging, and institutionalized, prison librarianship, and bibliotherapy. Medical literature may also be studied and practicums are available offering work experience in appropriate areas. Recently, Florida State University at Tallahassee has instituted a program offering two courses plus a practicum.

During the 1977-1978 school year, the Palmer Graduate Library School of Long Island University initiated a course, taught by the author in library service to the disabled, as part of the regular master's degree program, as well as for continuing education. This course offers students training in all aspects of library service to the disabled. Its objectives are to identify the disabled and explore physical and psychological characteristics, to develop insights into reasons for negative attitudes, to explore information needs, to review the literature of medical and vocational rehabilitation, to explore the learning problems and potential of exceptional children, and to determine the responsibility of the librarian in the field. Because this course is, of necessity, a survey course, plans for the future include its expansion into more intensive work in specific areas.

During the summer of 1975, Case Western Reserve University, in Cleveland, Ohio, in cooperation with the State Library of Ohio, offered a one-week institute in all aspects of library service to the handicapped. In the summer of 1976 the Palmer Graduate Library offered a one-week institute for the training of school library media specialists to work with disabled children. This institute was planned and directed by the author. In the fall of 1977 the State University at Albany, Library School, offered a one-week institute in library service to the adult disabled. All of these institutes were federally funded.

The University of New Orleans, which does not have a library school, offers courses in library service to exceptional children within the curriculum of the department of education. Between 1974 and 1979 New York, Louisiana, Massachusetts, Rhode Island, North Carolina, Mississippi, and Michigan, among others, have held workshops and institutes in library service to the disabled. These workshops were either state or federally funded for public, institution, or school librarians.

CONCLUSION

The past ten years have witnessed great changes in the lives of disabled people who are entering the mainstream of life in greater numbers than ever before. This has required that old stereotypes be discarded and new attitudes developed toward this special group.

The new fields of special education and rehabilitation librarianship have been developed with the goal of serving this population. This requires a knowledge of special informational and educational needs as well as of architectural modifications of buildings and equipment. To accomplish these goals, a variety of informational resources have been made available to public, school, and institution librarians.

Networks of rehabilitation research centers, special education regional resource centers, as well as special institutes and the initiating of a few library school courses on library services to the special patron, have reflected the growing interest in this area. Data bases, including the newly formed NARIC, will help librarians better serve the disabled by making available to them all of the information needed to help them achieve independent living, education, and realistic career goals.

NOTES

1. C. Esco Obermann, *A History of Vocational Rehabilitation in America* (Minneapolis: Denison, 1965), p. 270.
2. PL 113, 78th Congress, Washington, D.C., 1943.
3. PL 565, 83rd Congress, Washington, D.C., August 3, 1954.
4. PL 93112, 93rd Congress, Washington, D.C., September 26, 1973.
5. PL 94-142, 94th Congress, Washington, D.C., November 29, 1975.
6. PL 95-602, 95th Congress, Washington, D.C., November 6, 1978.
7. National Library Service for the Blind and Physically Handicapped, *Reading, Writing, and Other Communication Aids for Visually and Physically Handicapped Persons*, Washington, D.C., 1978.
8. *Library Journal* 102 (August 1977): 1552.
9. Alice Hagemeyer, *The Deaf American*, October 1978.
10. Ibid.
11. U.S. Office of Education and Chief Officers of State Library Agencies, *Library Programs Worth Knowing About*, September 1977, p. 7.
12. Association of State Library Agencies, *Interface*, Fall 1979, p. 4.
13. President's Committee on Employment of the Handicapped, *Projects Completed under Management by Objective* (Washington, D.C., April 30, 1975).
14. _____, *A Librarian's Guide to 504* (Washington, D.C., 1979).
15. Ruth A. Velleman, *Serving Physically Disabled People: An Information Handbook for All Libraries* (R. R. Bowker, 1979), p. 274.
16. U.S. Department of Health, Education, and Welfare, *Mobility for Handicapped Students* (Washington, D.C., August 1968).
17. Elinor Gollay and Alwina Bennett, *The College Guide for Students with Disabilities: A Detailed Directory of Higher Education Services, Programs and Facilities Accessible to Handicapped Students in the U.S.* Cambridge, Mass.: ABT Publications and Boulder, Colo.: Westview Press, 1976).
18. *Libraries for College Students with Handicaps: A Directory of Academic Library Resources and Services in Ohio* (Columbus, Ohio: State Library, 1976).

19. Patricia Marx with Ralph Carder, "Merging Handicapped Student Services with Library Media Services at Wright State University," *HRLSD Journal* 2 (Fall 1976), p. 7.
20. National Library Service for the Blind and Physically Handicapped, "Survey of Accredited Library School Programs to Prepare Librarians to Serve Handicapped Individuals" (Washington, D.C., June 1976).

ON-DEMAND INFORMATION SERVICES

Renée Schick

Senior Information Specialist, Capital Systems Group, Inc., Rockville, Maryland

Alix C. Levy

InfoQuest Manager, Capital Systems Group, Inc., Rockville, Maryland

During the past few years, on-demand fee-based information-gathering services have mushroomed across the country in tandem with the increased use of on-line information retrieval. Researchers, policymakers, and planners are acutely aware of the need for information and the complexity of obtaining it—and they are increasingly willing to pay for fast and accurate services.

Information brokers provide a link between information users and resources that complements rather than replaces traditional library services. The information broker's area of specialization lies in the skill of getting information to the user in all fields of knowledge; few brokers specialize in particular subject fields.

Information service companies in the private sector range from small operations to extensive networks. Some large academic and public libraries also have set up separate fee-for-service departments for requests that cannot be filled due to the time and budget restraints of their own reference staffs.

TYPES OF SERVICES

Information brokers generally offer a combination of the following services: data base searching, document delivery, information research and analysis, and information management.

Data Base Searching

Publicly available on-line data bases from a variety of sources are today's most important information resource. The majority of files provide references to bibliographic citations, usually accompanied by abstracts. During the last two years, ever increasing numbers of nonbibliographic files have become available; these data bases contain dictionary, patent, or statistical information, refer the user to contracts, grants, and research in progress, or contain full texts of legal cases, statutes, legislative proceedings, or news articles.

As of the fall of 1979, the three major on-line data base vendors—BRS (Bibliographic Retrieval Services), Lockheed, and SDC (Systems Development Corporation)

—provided access to over 130 data bases containing information in all fields of science, technology, law, medicine, and the humanities. While there is considerable overlap beteen vendors, analysis shows a significant number of files that are unique to each:

	Lockheed	SDC	BRS
Total number of files offered by vendor	93	59	27
Files uniquely available from vendor	51	37	7

Source: *Directory of On-Line Information Services*, 4th ed. Rockville, MD: CSG Press, September 1979.

Information brokers usually maintain access to more than one of the three large vendors as well as to other suppliers of specialized data bases; they frequently make special arrangements with vendors requiring subscription or minimal use fees such as the Source, Technotec, or legal and patent files. Some brokers are MEDLARS centers and can search all National Library of Medicine files, not just MEDLINE.

Searchers at information service companies have extensive on-line experience and keep abreast of constantly changing software capabilities developed by the major vendors. In addition, they have the special training necessary to access such files as the New York Times Information Bank. This expertise results in accurate, fast, and cost-effective information collection.

Document Delivery

As more and more citations are being identified by on-line searching, there is an ever-increasing need to locate and reproduce copies of journal articles and other documents. Information brokers answer these needs. Many are located near major library centers or have runners in large special libraries across the country. They maintain publishers files and have contacts with government agencies and book dealers that save time and effort in obtaining unusual, out-of-print, or unpublished items. Clients can call, write, telex, or cable their requests. Some information brokers specialize in document delivery and do little else; others provide the service as a convenience to their search customers.

Documents are often ordered on-line by the broker through SDC's Electronic Mailbox and Lockheed's Dialorder Service. Telefax service speeds document delivery from libraries to brokers and from brokers to users; the increasing popularity and rapidly lowering costs of this technology should revolutionize document delivery within the next year or two. Most brokers also provide special rush service and handle any copyright paperwork and fees.

Information Research and Analysis

Information research can range from a simple reference question to a full report on a specific topic. In order to make full use of data retrieved by on-line searching, many customers ask the broker to sift and analyze the search yield, eliminate duplicate entries retrieved from different data bases, arrange the materials in logical subject clusters, and provide indexes. The difference between a full report and a raw computer printout is worth a great deal to the busy client. Other searches may be supplemented by library research or statistical analysis of retrieved data. Surveys, state-of-the-art reports, and regular SDI (Selective Dissemination of Information) services based on specific customer information need profiles may also be supplied by the information broker. Some companies specialize in business information, and others cover medicine, the sciences, humanities, or legal research.

Information Management

Many businesses are beset by information management problems and need consultant services to arrange and organize their files and data. Services may consist of setting up a filing system, organizing and maintaining a library, designing and operating an automated management information system, etc. Information service firms may provide one-time or intermittent consulting services or may actually provide the personnel to do the complete task.

WHY BUY INFORMATION SERVICES

Individuals or companies who have only an occasional need for on-line data base searches find information broker services satisfactory and cost effective. To set up access to information services means, at the very least, rental of a computer terminal, making arrangements with a data base vendor, and investing in training a staff person to do searches. Unless a user consistently has used the required skills, he will not be an effective searcher. The yield will be unsatisfactory, and solving the inevitable equipment and service problems will result in frustrating experiences.

A surprising number of users of information-on-demand services are libraries and other organizations that already have access to information-gathering technology. Libraries are now experiencing budget and personnel cuts and can no longer handle all their information activities in-house; industrial concerns specializing in a particular subject area or temporarily overloaded with information requests find that a call to an information broker is a quick and inexpensive way to fill certain needs.

Advantages of buying information services include:

Fast turnaround: Most brokers will answer requests quickly, often within 24 hours.

Expertise: Knowing the fastest channels for getting information and being aware of the most efficient searching techniques are the information broker's livelihood, but often a sideline for his client.

Confidentiality: The information broker acts as an agent for a client and need not reveal his client's name or affiliation in seeking information.

Scope of coverage: For one-time questions, many libraries will go "outside" for the answer. This is particularly true if specialized on-line data bases that are not normally accessed need to be searched.

Personnel: Information gathering is labor intensive for both professional and clerical staff. The client's staff time can remain dedicated to regular tasks while the broker handles fact finding and document delivery.

Geography: Information broker services, and in particular document delivery services, are often very advantageous to clients in isolated U.S. areas or abroad. On-demand companies in the Washington area, for example, can locate U.S. government documents quickly and easily or search government data bases at the appropriate agency if they are not accessible through remote terminals or public vendor services. Developing countries can take advantage of U.S. technology without heavy investment.

COSTS

Rates for providing information services vary greatly, but several generalizations can be made:

Data base searching: In early 1980, a service charge of $25 for a single data base search is fairly typical; to this are added computer and telecommunication charges, which average $15 for a simple search. Multiple and comprehensive searches are often billed by professional man-hour.

Document delivery: Fees range from $4 to $25 per document, depending on source and turnaround time. Xerographic copying, telephone, telefax, postage, computer charges, and copyright fees are charged at cost. Many firms quote minimum billing charges, and some add special fees if source verification is necessary.

Information research, analysis and management: Services are usually billed by professional man-hour, ranging from $30 to $50, with a two- to three-hour minimum per task. Computer, telephone, postage, and other direct charges are billed at cost. Large projects are usually negotiated individually.

HOW TO FIND OUT ABOUT ON-DEMAND INFORMATION SERVICES

The *Directory of Fee-Based Information Services*, available from Information Alternative, Box 657, Woodstock, New York 12498, is a listing of information brokers. It is arranged by state and includes the key individuals, addresses, phone numbers, rates, areas of specialization, and types of services offered by several hundred individuals and organizations.

Another source of descriptive information is the *Information Industry Market Place*, published by R. R. Bowker Company, 1180 Avenue of the Americas, New York, New York 10036. This extensive directory of information industry products, services, and suppliers in the United States and abroad contains a chapter on information brokers.

Federal Agencies

THE COPYRIGHT OFFICE: DEVELOPMENTS IN COPYRIGHT LAW, 1979

Library of Congress, Washington, DC 20559
703-557-8700

Marybeth Peters
Chief, Information and Reference Division

The Copyright Office, a department of the Library of Congress, is essentially an office or record; its main function is to register claims to copyright and record documents pertaining to copyright claims. The new copyright law, however, has considerably enlarged the responsibilities of the office.

The law has preempted virtually all state common law and statutory law that was equivalent to copyright and created in its place a single federal system of copyright protection that attaches from the creation of the work and lasts in most instances for the life of the author plus 50 years after the author's death. Thus, all works now receive federal statutory copyright protection from the moment they are created, without regard to when or whether they are ever published, and all of these works are eligible for registration in the Copyright Office.

The new copyright law generally makes registration voluntary rather than mandatory; there are, however, a substantial number of advantages attached to registration. Many are availing themselves of these advantages; and, in 1979, more than 10,000 applications were received each week.

Although registration is voluntary, the law does contain a mandatory deposit requirement for all works published with a notice of copyright in the United States. Throughout 1979 the Copyright Office vigorously enforced these requirements so that the collections of the Library of Congress would be enriched. Indeed the Copyright Office was thrust into more active acquisitions activity due to the decreasing budgets for libraries, which is becoming a national fact of life.

Two of the compulsory licenses established in the new copyright law are administered by the Licensing Division of the Copyright Office: secondary transmissions by cable television and public performances on jukeboxes. The office collected and invested in interest-bearing accounts approximately $1 million from jukebox receipts and $12 million from cable systems. This money is to be distributed to copyright owners by the Copyright Royalty Tribunal.

The Copyright Office also maintains a national copyright information service. Answers to questions, informational circulars and copies of the law, regulations, and application forms may be obtained free of charge by writing to the Copyright Office, Library of Congress, Washington, D.C. 20559 or by calling 703-557-8700 between 8:00 A.M. and 7:00 P.M. (Eastern Time) on weekdays.

The new law gives the Copyright Office several special projects that take the form of reports to Congress. The Register of Copyrights has already delivered two of these reports: one containing recommendations on whether the law should provide performance rights in sound recordings; the other on the voluntary licensing arrangements that were reached with respect to the use of nondramatic literary works by public broadcast stations. In 1982 the Register must report on the law's library reproduction provisions. Section 108(i) provides that "Five years from the effective date of this Act, and at five-year intervals thereafter, the Register of Copyrights, after consulting with representatives of authors, book and periodical publishers, and other owners of copyrighted materials, and with representatives of library users and librarians, shall submit to Congress a report setting forth the extent to which this section has achieved the intended statutory balancing of the rights of creators, and the needs of users." The law states that the report should also describe any problems that may have arisen and should include recommendations or suggested legislation.

The Register of Copyrights began this consultation in 1978, first in separate meetings with representatives of the library and user communities and with representatives of copyright proprietors and authors. Subsequently, an advisory committee was formed to assist the Copyright Office in fulfilling this responsibility. The committee, the membership of which is representative of all interests involved, first met on December 19, 1978 and continues to meet several times a year. An internal Copyright Office planning group met frequently throughout 1979 under the guidance of Ivan Bender, then special legal consultant to the general counsel. (Mr. Bender left the Copyright Office in December 1979 to return to private industry.)

So far the study of the Copyright Office has been directed at defining the most pervasive and controversial problems experienced in applying the new law to the reproduction of copyright materials. The office has also surveyed existing literature on any photocopying studies that have already been completed or initiated to avoid any duplication of effort.

The Copyright Office is now planning a series of regional hearings. The first was scheduled for January 19, 1980 to coincide with the midwinter meeting of the American Library Association. Additional hearings are planned for Houston, Texas, Los Angeles, California, and Washington, D.C.

OFF-THE-AIR TAPING

One of the most difficult problems that was left unresolved by the new copyright law concerns off-the-air taping. Educators and librarians have been particularly concerned about this. On March 2, 1979 a conference on off-the-air taping for educational use was held under the auspices of the House Judiciary Subcommittee on Courts, Civil Liberties, and the Administration of Justice. To help resolve the differences among the various interests Robert W. Kastenmeier, the subcommittee chairman, invited 18 representatives of the concerned groups to serve as an ad hoc committee. The goal of this committee is to come up with proposed guidelines on fair use for broadcast audiovisual works. The counsel to the subcommittee and a representative from the Copyright Office were designated as monitors to the group.

Since March the committee has been meeting monthly, alternating between Washington and New York. It was originally hoped that a compromise could be reached by December 1979; the issues, however, are most complex and an easy solution has not been possible. At this time there continue to be some differences in view, but it is hoped that a continued spirit of cooperation and desire to find reasonable compromises will eventually lead to agreement.

An important case in the noneducational area was decided in 1979. On October 2 Judge Ferguson issued a 102 page ruling in *Universal City Studios, Inc.* v. *Sony Cor-*

poration of America, 203 U.S.P.Q. 656 (C.D. Cal. 1979), commonly known as the Betamax case. He made five specific findings, one of which concerned home use. Judge Ferguson found that neither the old nor the new copyright law gave copyright owners a monopoly power over an individual's off-the-air copying in his or her home for private, noncommercial use. Only one defendant was an individual who made copies at home; the primary defendants were the manufacturer, distributor, wholesaler, advertiser, and retailer of the videotape recorders. However, most of these defendants could not have been liable unless the court found home copying to be an infringement.

Using the four factors found in Section 107 of the new law, the judge concluded that home copying is fair use. He placed great emphasis on the fact that the plaintiffs, motion picture producers, had not introduced any concrete evidence on any harm that could be attributable to the marketing of the Betamax. The defendants have indicated that they will vigorously pursue an appeal.

LEGISLATIVE DEVELOPMENTS

Despite enactment of the new copyright law in 1976, there continues to be substantial congressional activity in the copyright field. While several proposals involve matters that might be considered part of the unfinished business of copyright revisions, others reflect new concerns. Bills that are currently before Congress include establishing a limited performance right in sound recordings through a compulsory license that would require payments to performers and producers of copyrighted works (H.R. 997, S. 1552); establishing protection for ornamental designs of useful articles (H.R. 4530); creating protection of the moral rights of artists in their works by preventing distortion, mutilation, alteration, and destruction (H.R. 288); and creating protection for imprinted design patterns on semiconductor chips (H.R. 14293). Several bills that would exempt certain groups from liability for public performances of music were introduced in the House of Representatives (H.R. 2487, H.R. 4264, H.R. 5183). Other bills that were introduced proposed tax incentives for the arts and humanities (H.R. 1847, H.R. 2113, H.R. 2498, S. 1078, S. 397).

Finally, the administration of public printing services and the distribution of public documents were the subjects of H.R. 4572 and S. 1435. (These bills would revise Title 44 of the United States Code.) The bills' stated purpose is to enact amendments necessitated by the technological advances that are changing the way government information is generated, produced, and disseminated. Change is also required because of a growing demand for improved and increased access to this information. The Librarian of Congress has alerted the sponsors of these bills of certain copyright concerns that are implicit in the bills.

INTERNATIONAL COPYRIGHT

The year 1979 brought renewed and revitalized interest in the possibility of the United States joining the Berne Union, the world's first major multilateral treaty on copyright. Since its inception, it has fostered the establishment and maintenance of a high level of international protection. The United States has never adhered to the Berne Union. In recent years one of the major reasons for its failure to join was the requirement in U.S. law of certain formal conditions of protection, particularly registration in the Copyright Office and use of the copyright notice on published copies of a work.

The question now is how close does the new U.S. law come to meeting the minimal standards needed to accede to this convention. Several international meetings were held on the subject; and in May 1979 Arpad Bogsch, director general of the World Intellectual Property Organization (the organization that administers the Berne Union), visited the United States to ascertain the attitude of various groups toward adherence to the Berne Convention. In Washington, D.C., he met with the International Copyright Advisory Panel of the U.S. Department of State. Discussion indicated a strong measure of support for Berne membership. It now appears, however, that the notice provisions of the new U.S. copyright law would have to be eliminated before the United States could join the Berne Union.

FEDERAL INFORMATION CENTERS

Office of Consumer Affairs, Office of External Affairs,
General Services Administration, Washington, DC 20405
202-566-1937

Donald R. Knenlein

Coordinator, Federal Information Centers Program

Federal Information Centers (FIC) are a focal point in the community for information about the federal government. Centers assist people who have questions about federal services, programs, and regulations but do not know where to turn for an answer. FIC information specialists either answer an inquirer's questions directly or perform the necessary research to locate and put the inquirer in touch with the expert best able to help. However, the program is not intended to discourage the public from directly approaching a federal agency or department. FICs operate as a part of a much larger and diversified network of information programs devoted to providing information to the public on services available to them. While all centers develop a capacity to respond to a significant volume of inquiries related to state, local, and private services available in the community, FICs have a particular advantage and responsibility in providing detailed information on federal activities.

Currently there are 38 FICs with an additional 47 cities connected to the nearest center by toll-free telephone tielines. The first pilot FIC opened to Atlanta in July 1966. The purpose of the experiment was to test the feasibility of providing the public with easy access to federal information and assistance through an efficient data and referral source, which would work in conjunction with other major federal information services. In October 1969, President Richard Nixon directed that the pilot project be expanded to other major metropolitan areas, and that the cost of the project be shared by all benefiting agencies. Consequently, the number of centers increased to the present 38, with operating costs being shared equally by 17 executive departments and agencies.

Simultaneously, in an effort to test another method of expanding this service to more of the population, toll-free telephone tielines were made available to the citizens of 47 highly populated areas in close proximity to FIC cities. Together, the centers and the tielines provide service to approximately half of the U.S. population on a toll-free basis.

In 1972, an experimental federal-state-local government information center opened in San Diego, California. The San Diego center has been testing procedures for centralizing research and referral services for all levels of government in one jointly funded facility.

Shortly after taking office, President Jimmy Carter directed the Office of Management and Budget (OMB) to study the effectiveness of the FIC program. The study team presented its findings to the president in March 1977. The OMB report praised the high degree of responsiveness to the substantial volume and wide diversity of questions received by the FICs. The team perceived the FIC information specialists as highly competent in terms of dealing with the public, generally knowledgeable of government programs and services, and resourceful in seeking answers to complex questions and problems.

The OMB study suggested several enhancements to the FIC program. The three major recommendations were obtain legislative authority to elevate the FICs from pilot to full program status; establish at least one FIC in each of the 22 states currently without a center; and expand toll-free service so that all U.S. residents may contact an FIC on a local call basis.

The first recommendation was carried out in October 1978, when President Carter signed PL 95-491, the Federal Information Centers Act. The act authorizes and directs the Administrator of General Services to establish within the General Services Administration (GSA) a nationwide network of FICs based on the currently operating centers, for the purpose of responding to requests from the public about the rules, programs, and benefits of the federal government. The bill also authorizes GSA to receive direct appropriation from Congress to fund the program, instead of distributing the costs among the benefiting agencies.

Plans are underway to implement the second and third OMB study recommendations. In Florida, statewide service will be offered by the Miami and St. Petersburg centers in early 1980, making the FIC only a toll-free telephone call away for all Florida residents. Using Florida as a model, in mid-1980, the Omaha, Kansas City, and St. Louis FICs will provide toll-free telephone service to residents of Nebraska and Missouri. In addition, new FICs will be established in Des Moines and Topeka and will offer statewide toll-free service to residents of Iowa and Kansas. A new center will also be established in Anchorage, Alaska.

OPERATIONS

FIC operational guidelines are outlined in the *GSA Handbook* (Federal Information Center [FIC] Operations, ADM P 1035.8, May 30, 1979). Reference copies of this handbook are available in all FICs and in government depository libraries. Within GSA, the FIC coordinator's office is a division of the Office of Consumer Affairs, located in the Office of the Assistant Administrator for External Affairs. In the GSA regions, the FICs are located in the Office of the Assistant Regional Administrator for External Affairs. The FIC manager is responsible for the day-to-day operation of the center and is supervised by the assistant regional administrator for external affairs. Policy direction and management oversight are provided by the FIC coordinator's office in Washington, D.C.

FICs are located near the main public areas of federal buildings, offering high visibility and easy access for the public. The hours of operation are generally the same as those of the major federal agencies in the area. Nationwide the program has 163 staff members. Staff size varies from center to center, but the average staff complement is four. FICs located in cities that are bilingual to a significant degree have staff members who speak the appropriate language. FICs also maintain a list of local interpreters who can assist in serving foreign-speaking inquirers. Seventy percent of the $4,294,000 budget for FY 1980 covers salaries and associated personnel costs. Another 10 percent covers communications costs, with the remainder slated for resource and reference materials, supplies, training, and travel.

The number of inquiries received by the centers has increased as the number of centers and tieline cities has grown. During FY 1979, 38 FICs answered over seven million inquiries. Seventy-five percent of these inquiries were by telephone with the remainder from visitors to the centers. Letter inquiries accounted for less than 1 percent of the total inquiry volume. Currently, the centers nationwide receive about 30,000 inquiries per working day.

The range of inquiry by subject matter is broad and diverse. About 10 percent of the questions pertain to state and local government or private organizations. Questions relate to all of the more than 120 agencies of the executive branch, as well as the judicial and legislative branches of the federal government. To answer inquiries, FIC staff members must have extensive knowledge and comprehension of the functions, activities, organization, interrelationships, and overlapping jurisdictions of agencies and levels of government. FIC staff members must also be able to investigate, interpret, and analyze current events, legislation, and government regulations to anticipate and respond to the information needs of the public.

Both the coordinator's office and the FIC managers publicize the services provided by the centers. Periodically the coordinator's office develops a national public service campaign consisting of public service announcements for airing on radio and television stations in FIC and tieline cities. Articles describing the FIC program are placed in national publications. In addition, the FIC brochure, available in both English and Spanish, is widely distributed. Copies may be requested from any FIC or by writing the Consumer Information Center, Pueblo, Colorado 81009.

The FIC data base is entirely manual and consists of a wide variety of resource and reference materials. The cornerstone of this data base is a functional index of the programs and areas of responsibility of all federal, state, and local government and private agencies. The functional subjects are listed alphabetically by key words, followed by reference to the name, address, and telephone number of the local, regional, and/or national office that has the greatest knowledge about the subject. The functional index is comprehensive enough to serve as a direct referral source in some cases, but more frequently serves as a search aid for investigating lengthier, more complex inquiries.

In addition to the functional index, the FIC uses reference publications to meet the information needs of the community. The coordinator's office supplies each center with national reference materials, brochures, fact sheets, and news releases. Each FIC obtains useful state and local government and appropriate community and private publications. FICs subscribe to at least one major newspaper and extract information useful in anticipating and answering questions. All information, regardless of the source, is verified before it is given to an inquirer.

Both the FIC managers and the coordinator's staff meet with government and private organizations that share the responsibility for providing information, advice, and assistance to the public. Through personal visits and telephone contacts, they obtain information about new resources, progams, or changes in agency organization, policy, or procedures, and encourage other organizations to contact the FICs when new information is received. FIC managers visit tieline cities twice a year to meet with government and private groups to update the information resources for those cities.

SPECIAL PROJECTS

In addition to responding to inquiries from the public, the FIC program has been involved in numerous projects to improve service to the public. In a cooperative effort to increase the usefulness of commercial telephone directories, last year the FICs worked with American Telephone and Telegraph Company (AT&T) to develop a "blue pages" supplement to the telephone directories in Little Rock, Chicago, Boston, and Sacramento. Government telephone numbers are listed in the blue pages by subject as well as by organization name. Blue pages have been so well received by the public that AT&T plans to include blue pages in more city directories. FICs will continue to cooperate with local telephone companies on the development of future blue pages.

Dial-a-Reg is a project being tested in Chicago and Los Angeles in conjunction with the Office of the Federal Register. This is a daily recorded announcement in the test FICs that highlights and summarizes the most important items in that day's *Federal Register*. Daily issues of the *Federal Register* and the *Code of Federal Regulations* are available to the public for their use, and complex inquiries on actions mentioned in that day's announcement can be handled by the information specialists in the Chicago and Los Angeles FICs.

FEDERAL INFORMATION CENTERS

For more information about the FIC program, please telephone, visit, or write the center nearest you:

Alabama
Birmingham
800-322-8591 (toll-free to Atlanta, GA)
Mobile
800-438-1421 (toll-free to New Orleans, LA)

Alaska
Federal Bldg. and U.S. Courthouse, 701 C St., *Anchorage* 99513
907-271-3650

Arizona
Phoenix
Federal Bldg., 230 North First Ave., *Phoenix* 85025
602-261-3313
Tucson
800-622-1511 (toll-free to Phoenix, AZ)

Arkansas
Little Rock
800-378-6177 (toll-free to Memphis, TN)

California
Los Angeles
Federal Bldg., 300 North Los Angeles St., *Los Angeles* 90012
213-688-3800

Sacramento
Federal Bldg. and U.S. Courthouse, 650 Capitol Mall, *Sacramento* 95814
916-440-3344
San Diego
Federal Bldg., 880 Front St., Rm. 1S11, *San Diego* 92188
714-293-6030
San Francisco
Federal Bldg. and U.S. Courthouse, 450 Golden Gate Ave., P.O. Box 36082, *San Francisco* 94102
415-556-6600
San Jose
800-275-7422 (toll-free to San Francisco, CA)
Santa Ana
800-836-2386 (toll-free to Los Angeles, CA)

Colorado
Colorado Springs
800-471-9491 (toll-free to Denver, CO)
Denver
Federal Bldg., 1961 Stout St., *Denver* 80294
303-837-3602

Pueblo
800-544-9523 (toll-free to Denver, CO)
Connecticut
Hartford
800-527-2617 (toll-free to New York, NY)
New Haven
800-624-4720 (toll-free to New York, NY)
District of Columbia
Seventh and D Sts. S.W., Rm. 5716, *Washington* 20407
202-755-8660
Florida
Fort Lauderdale
800-522-8531 (toll-free to Miami, FL)
Jacksonville
800-354-4756 (toll-free to St. Petersburg, FL)
Miami
Federal Bldg., 51 S.W. First Ave., *Miami* 33130
305-350-4155
Orlando
800-422-1800 (toll-free to St. Petersburg, FL)
St. Petersburg
William C. Cramer Federal Bldg., 144 First Ave. S., *St. Petersburg* 33701
813-893-3495
Tampa
800-229-7911 (toll-free to St. Petersburg, FL)
West Palm Beach
800-833-7566 (toll-free to Miami, FL)
Florida, North
Sarasota, Manatee, Polk, Osceola, Orange, Seminole, and Volusia counties and north
800-282-8556 (toll-free to St. Petersburg, FL)
Florida, South
Charlotte, De Soto, Hardee, Highlands, Okeechobee, Indian River, and Brevard counties and south
800-432-6668 (toll-free to Miami, FL)
Georgia
Federal Bldg. and U.S. Courthouse, 75 Spring St., *Atlanta* 30303
404-221-6891

Hawaii
Federal Bldg., 300 Ala Moana Blvd., P.O. Box 50091, *Honolulu* 96850
808-546-8620
Illinois
Everett McKinley Dirksen Bldg., 219 S. Dearborn St., Rm. 250, *Chicago* 60604
312-353-4242
Indiana
Gary/Hammond
800-883-4110 (toll-free to Indianapolis, IN)
Indianapolis
Federal Bldg., 575 N. Pennsylvania, *Indianapolis* 46204
317-269-7373
Iowa
Des Moines
Federal Bldg., 210 Walnut St., *Des Moines* 50309
515-284-4448
Other Iowa Locations
800-532-1556
Kansas
Topeka
Federal Bldg. and U.S. Courthouse, 444 S.E. Quincy, *Topeka* 66683
913-295-2866
Other Kansas Locations
800-432-2934
Kentucky
Federal Bldg., 600 Federal Place, *Louisville* 40202
502-582-6261
Louisiana
U.S. Postal Service Bldg., 701 Loyola Ave., Rm. 1210, *New Orleans* 70113
504-589-6696
Maryland
Federal Bldg., 31 Hopkins Plaza, *Baltimore* 21201
301-962-4980
Massachusetts
J.F.K. Federal Bldg., Cambridge St., Rm. E-130, *Boston* 02203
617-223-7121

78 / FEDERAL AGENCIES

Michigan
Detroit
McNamara Federal Bldg., 477 Michigan Ave., Rm. 103, *Detroit* 48226
313-226-7016
Grand Rapids
800-451-2628 (toll-free to Detroit, MI)
Minnesota
Federal Bldg. and U.S. Courthouse, 110 S. Fourth St., *Minneapolis* 55401
612-725-2073
Missouri
Kansas City
Federal Bldg., 601 E. 12 St., *Kansas City* 64106
816-374-2466
St. Louis
Federal Bldg., 1520 Market St., *St. Louis* 63103
314-425-4106
Other Missouri Locations
800-392-7711 (for residents with 314 area code)
800-892-5808 (for residents with 417 or 816 area code)
Nebraska
Omaha
U.S. Post Office and Courthouse, 215 N. 17 St., *Omaha* 68102
402-221-3353
Other Nebraska Locations
800-642-8383
New Jersey
Newark
Federal Bldg., 970 Broad St., *Newark* 07102
201-645-3600
Paterson/Passaic
800-523-0717 (toll-free to Newark, NJ)
Trenton
800-396-4400 (toll-free to Newark, NJ)
New Mexico
Albuquerque
Federal Bldg. and U.S. Courthouse, 500 Gold Ave. S.W., *Albuquerque* 87102
505-766-3091

Santa Fe
800-983-7743 (toll-free to Albuquerque, NM)
New York
Albany
800-463-4421 (toll-free to New York, NY)
Buffalo
Federal Bldg., 111 W. Huron St., *Buffalo* 14202
716-846-4010
New York
Federal Bldg., 26 Federal Plaza, Rm. 1-114, *New York* 10007
212-264-4464
Rochester
800-546-5075 (toll-free to Buffalo, NY)
Syracuse
800-476-8545 (toll-free to Buffalo, NY)
North Carolina
Charlotte
800-376-3600 (toll-free to Atlanta, GA)
Ohio
Akron
800-375-5638 (toll-free to Cleveland, OH)
Cincinnati
Federal Bldg., 550 Main St., *Cincinnati* 45202
513-684-2801
Cleveland
Federal Bldg., 1240 E. Ninth St., *Cleveland* 44199
216-522-4040
Columbus
800-221-1014 (toll-free to Cincinnati, OH)
Dayton
800-223-7377 (toll-free to Cincinnati, OH)
Toledo
800-241-3223 (toll-free to Cleveland, OH)
Oklahoma
Oklahoma City
U.S. Post Office and Courthouse, 201 N.W. Third St., *Oklahoma City* 73102
405-231-4868
Tulsa
800-584-4193 (toll-free to Oklahoma City, OK)

Oregon
Federal Bldg., 1220 S.W. Third Ave., Rm. 109, *Portland* 97204
503-221-2222

Pennsylvania
Allentown/Bethlehem
800-821-7785 (toll-free to Philadelphia, PA)

Philadelphia
Federal Bldg., 600 Arch St., *Philadelphia* 19106
215-597-7042

Pittsburgh
Federal Bldg., 1000 Liberty Ave., *Pittsburgh* 15222
412-644-3456

Scranton
800-346-7081 (toll-free to Philadelphia, PA)

Rhode Island
Providence
800-331-5565 (toll-free to Boston, MA)

Tennessee
Chattanooga
800-265-8231 (toll-free to Memphis, TN)

Memphis
Clifford Davis Federal Bldg., 167 N. Main St., *Memphis* 38103
910-521-3285

Nashville
800-242-5056 (toll-free to Memphis, TN)

Texas
Austin
800-472-5494 (toll-free to Houston, TX)

Dallas
800-767-8585 (toll-free to Forth Worth, TX)

Fort Worth
Lanham Federal Bldg., 819 Taylor St., *Fort Worth* 76102
817-334-3624

Houston
Federal Bldg. and U.S. Courthouse, 515 Rusk Ave., *Houston* 77208
713-226-5711

San Antonio
800-224-4471 (toll-free to Houston, TX)

Utah
Ogden
800-399-1347 (toll-free to Salt Lake City, UT)

Salt Lake City
Federal Bldg., 125 S. State St., Rm. 1205, *Salt Lake City* 84138
801-524-5353

Virginia
Newport News
800-244-0480 (toll-free to Norfolk, VA)

Federal Bldg., 200 Granby Mall, Rm. 120, *Norfolk* 23510
804-441-3101

Richmond
800-643-4928 (toll-free to Norfolk, VA)

Roanoke
800-982-8591 (toll-free to Norfolk, VA)

Washington
Seattle
Federal Bldg., 915 Second Ave., *Seattle* 98174
206-442-0570

Tacoma
800-383-5230 (toll-free to Seattle, WA)

Wisconsin
Milwaukee
800-271-2273 (toll-free to Chicago, IL)

THE NATIONAL COMMISSION ON LIBRARIES AND INFORMATION SCIENCE

1717 K St. N.W., Suite 601, Washington, DC 20036
202-653-6252

Alphonse F. Trezza
Executive Director

The enabling legislation for the National Commission on Libraries and Information Science (NCLIS) is PL 91-345, which was passed in 1970. This law charges NCLIS with the responsibility to appraise the adequacies and deficiencies of current library/information service; study library/information needs and analyze the means by which these needs may be met; promote research and development activities to improve library and information services; develop overall plans for meeting library/information needs of the nation; advise all levels of government and private agencies on library and information sciences; and advise the president and Congress on the implementation of national information policy.

The commission's first order of business was the establishment of a framework for meeting the current and foreseeable information needs of the nation's citizens. This framework was published in mid-1975 as *Toward a National Program for Library and Information Services: Goals for Action*. This document, built around five assumptions and eight objectives, is the product of extensive communication with concerned parties —librarians, legislators, scholars, schoolchildren, technologists, teachers, and citizens from every walk of life and every part of the country. This communication took place at public hearings and at meetings of both providers and users of information, and included not only public hearings but one-on-one discussions and voluminous correspondence. As a result, the Program Document received almost universal support for its principles and concept and was almost immediately endorsed by the major library and information science professional associations.

Even before the Program Document was completed, NCLIS had begun its implementation activities in areas where there was a clear need. However, with the support of the Program Document by the community assured, these implementation activities expanded into more areas. Implementation of a nationwide program for library and information resources is—must be—a very long term, evolutionary process, and the commission must operate with very limited resources. Therefore NCLIS has concentrated its efforts on approaches that combine solving a problem and developing consensus at the same time. These are exemplified by NCLIS task forces, consisting of representatives from various concerned constituencies, which have met periodically to address such problems as effective access to the periodical literature, new directions for American National Standards Committee Z39, computer network protocols, the role of school library media centers in networking, etc. Previous editions of the *Annual* have noted earlier activities of this sort. This article discusses some of these activities in progress during 1979 and what is, perhaps, the most significant event for library and information services in 1979, the White House Conference held late in the year.

The White House Conference on Library and Information Services, which took place November 15 through 19, 1979, was the culmination of a 22-year effort by the library and information community and of two years of preconference activities involving

57 states and territories and tens of thousands of citizens from all walks of life. It was organized around five theme areas derived from the state and territorial preconferences, as follows: Library and Information Services for: Meeting Personal Needs, Enhancing Lifelong Learning, Improving Organizations and Professions, Effectively Governing Society, and Increasing International Cooperation. At a packed conference (in terms of both attendance and activities), the delegates, in small working groups, theme sessions, and plenary sessions, developed, discussed, and passed 15 of 17 priority resolutions and 10 of 32 petition resolutions. In a paper ballot vote on 49 lower priority resolutions not discussed and debated at the conference, 45 more resolutions were passed.

Space does not permit more than a cursory glance at this output, but some of the key resolutions included call for: an assistant secretary for library and information services in the new Department of Education; a national information policy to maximize the provision of library and information services; a combined effort by local, state, and federal governments to identify and train the functionally illiterate; a program to eliminate barriers separating special groups (e.g., children, aged, minorities, handicapped, etc.) from library and information services; and a new federal program for international training and free exchange of both personnel and materials. The complete set of resolutions will be included in the final report of the conference, which will be available in the spring of 1980.

An accurate assessment of the White House Conference may be years—if not decades—away, since a great deal depends upon how effectively the commission and the library information community are in achieving implementation of its recommendations, but it has undoubtedly given a great deal of visibility to library and information services, heightened awareness of their importance and problems among legislators, government officials, and citizenry, and provided a strong impetus for greater efforts to improve the provision of such services.

In the meantime, 1979 was also a year of great activity in the commission's continuing effort to establish a means of providing prompt and assured access to the periodical literature through a National Periodicals System. At an NCLIS-sponsored open forum in early spring, some 200 interested persons gathered to discuss the concept of and plans for a National Periodicals Center. The need for this open forum arose from the controversy engendered by the publication of *A National Periodicals Center: Technical Development Plan* (the burgundy book) produced by the Council on Library Resources (CLR) at the behest of the Library of Congress (LC). This, in turn, grew out of the recommendations of *Effective Access to the Periodical Literature: A National Program* (the green book), which was the final report of an NCLIS task force, that recommended a three-level system, of which a National Periodicals Center operated by LC would be Level II. While the open forum did not achieve a consensus, there was a clear majority favoring the establishment of such a center. The commission-sponsored National Periodicals System Advisory Committee (NPSAC) immediately endorsed the recommendations of the open forum and established a team to draft appropriate legislation and documentation. While this team was developing its material, NCLIS, to ensure that all reasonable alternatives were explored, commissioned Arthur D. Little, Inc., to perform a study of the alternatives and costs. However, before either the NPSAC or A. D. Little could complete its work, legislation closely resembling the final draft of the legislative drafting team was introduced as Part D of Title II of the reauthorization of the Higher Education Act (HEA). At its regular meeting the following week, NCLIS, based on the recommendations of the NPSAC and the contractor report entitled *A Comparative Evaluation of Alternative Systems for the Provision of Effective*

Access to Periodical Literature, adopted resolutions affirming its support of the concept of a National Periodicals Center, supporting legislation to that end, and requesting the opportunity to testify at scheduled Senate hearings. The chairman and representatives of several library and publisher organizations did testify in support of establishing a National Periodicals Center and indicating that in its final form, it should include the essence of the legislative draft approved by NCLIS and reflect the implications of the A. D. Little report. A meeting to discuss the next steps to be taken is scheduled for January 1980.

Another milestone in NCLIS activities was reached after several years of planning and preparation, with the first meeting of the NCLIS Task Force on Public/Private Sector Relations. This group has the difficult task of examining the tenuous—and sometimes, tense—relations between the public and private sectors of the economy in the area of information products and services, seeking ways to improve the definitions of their respective roles, and developing recommendations for ameliorating the unavoidable tensions between the two sectors. By its second meeting, the task force had initiated a Delphi study and formed subcommittee working groups to examine specific pieces of the many-sided problem. The third meeting is scheduled for January 1980.

The reports of two earlier task forces were published during 1979. The first of these, *The Role of the School Library Media Program in Networking*, was followed almost immediately by the establishment, under NCLIS sponsorship, of a broadly based implementation committee, which has been working actively, and with considerable success, to promote implementation of the recommendations of the report by various concerned organizations. During the year, the Council of Chief State School Officers adopted a policy statement supporting the active participation of school library media programs in the development of a nationwide network, and official support by other educational organizations is expected during 1980. The second report, *Problems of Bibliographic Access to Nonprint Media: Final Report*, was the long awaited report of Project Mediabase, a joint effort by NCLIS and the Association for Educational Communications and Technology (AECT). When an inventory of existing bibliographic files on nonprint media disclosed the fact that the only data element common to all files was the title, a set of preliminary specifications for bibliographic records on nonprint media was developed and subsequently discussed extensively at meetings of three major professional associations. In addition to the specifications, the report discusses attitudinal problems, as well as operational impediments that deter the inclusion of records for nonprint media in network files and activities. It suggests the use of recognized cataloging standards and further study of the economic and management implications of integration of nonprint media in networking efforts.

In the international arena, NCLIS supported the efforts of the International Federation of Library Associations (IFLA) and the United Nations Educational, Scientific and Cultural Organization (UNESCO) to establish an office that will develop standards for and promote Universal Availability of Publications (UAP), regardless of the source or destination of the publication. NCLIS is proud to have a part in the initiation of this critical first step of an effort to make all knowledge resources available to the entire world.

On the home front, NCLIS continued its support of an LC project aimed at the design of a configuration for a national bibliographic data base. The current phase of the study focuses on the provision of authority control in a fashion that will permit distribution of authority control and processing across many different institutions to improve both efficiency and interinstitutional communications.

NCLIS also provided valuable assistance to the Joint Committee on Printing (JCP) in its examination of possible changes to Title 44 of the U.S. Code (which deals with the Government Printing Office, GPO, and the Depository Library Program) by providing the members of the JCP-appointed Advisory Committee with advance copies of an NCLIS-commissioned report, *Government Publications: Their Role in the National Program for Library and Information Services*, by participating in the deliberations of the Advisory Committee, and by providing briefings on library and information community concerns for the JCP staff. As the year closed, bills to change at least some of the provisions of Title 44 had been introduced and were being considered by both houses of Congress.

The commission's plans for 1980 include continuation of ongoing projects, which are the Public/Private Sector Task Force, the National Periodicals System Advisory Committee, and the School Library Media Program Implementation Committee. In addition, the commission has authorized initial efforts of a task force on International Relations and another on the Needs of Cultural Minorities. Of course, follow-up and implementation of the recommendations of the White House Conference loom large on the horizon and will occupy a good deal of the commission's attention during 1980 and for many years to come. Fortunately, major restructuring of the NCLIS program does not appear necessary, since virtually all of the resolutions of the White House Conference address concerns that are discussed in the Program Document cited above. However, the resolutions do provide a sharper focus for NCLIS activities and a sense of the perceived priorities of the community at large, both of which are valuable input.

With the impetus, heightened awareness, and widened support provided by the White House Conference, it is hoped that the commission will, with the help of the rest of the library information community, legislators, administrators, and citizens at large, be able to hasten the nation's progress toward the ideal stated in its National Program Document: "To eventually provide every individual in the United States with equal opportunity of access to that part of the total information resource which will satisfy the individual's educational, working, cultural and leisure-time needs and interests, regardless of the individual's location, social or physical condition or level of intellectual achievement."

NATIONAL TECHNICAL INFORMATION SERVICE

U.S. Department of Commerce
5285 Port Royal Rd., Springfield, VA 22161
703-557-4600

Ted Ryerson

Special Assistant to the Director

Publications of the U.S. government are a principal source of information and knowledge for practically every field of endeavor. They are used extensively within the United States and throughout the world by small businesses, large corporations, governments, libraries, individual researchers and scientists, and the general public.

84 / FEDERAL AGENCIES

Each agency of the U.S. government is obliged by law to make available to the public and private sector the information it gathers and the knowledge it produces. Taken as a whole, the agencies provide authoritative and timely information on almost every conceivable subject, and their information is used continually as a reference source for decision makers, policymakers, and problem solvers. Within the past half century, however, the volume and diversity of U.S. government publications have expanded dramatically, challenging the world's ability to organize, retrieve, and manipulate them to solve problems.

The National Technical Information Service (NTIS) and its predecessor organizations, for more than 30 years, have served as a focal point for the collection, announcement, and dissemination of unclassified U.S. government-sponsored research and development reports and translations of foreign technical literature to the scientific and technical and industrial communities. The ontogeny of the organization can be summarized as follows:

> An executive order established the Publications Board in 1945 to collect and declassify World War II technical data for dissemination to industry.
>
> The U.S. Department of Commerce established the Office of Technical Services in 1946 to consolidate the activities of the board and other organizations.
>
> Public Law enacted in 1950 directed the Commerce Department to set up and maintain a national clearinghouse for scientific and technical information to be implemented through the Office of Technical Services.
>
> The Federal Council for Science and Technology recommended expansion of the Department's clearinghouse function in 1964. The Clearinghouse for Federal Scientific and Technical Information was organized on the foundations of the Office of Technical Services.
>
> On September 2, 1970, the National Technical Information Service (NTIS) was established as a primary operating unit of the U.S. Department of Commerce. The order abolished the Clearinghouse for Federal Scientific and Technical Information (CFSTI) and transferred its functions from CFSTI to NTIS with full authority to establish and monitor a clearinghouse of scientific, technical, and engineering information and to assist operating units in the dissemination of business and statistical information.

The NTIS mission is to collect research publications containing scientific and technical information produced or funded by federal, state, and local government sources; and to promote the use of these information products by organizing them for easy access and by publishing news bulletins and catalogs, by exhibits and speeches, by mail promotion, and by utilizing other public and private mechanisms, such as marketing dealers. NTIS directs its services to private businesses, individuals, universities, federal agencies, state and local governments, and international customers.

NTIS sells its products and services under provisions of Title 15, U.S. Code 1151-1157. This statute obligates NTIS to recover its costs and it has become self-sustaining.

The NTIS report collection includes reports acquisitioned from the National Aeronautics and Space Administration, the Departments of Defense, Energy, Commerce, Health, and Human Resources, and more than 200 other federal agencies. It makes over 1 million publications available, none of which is ever out of print. In 1978 it sold nearly 6 million copies to some 100,000 customers in the United States and abroad.

When government agencies make their technical reports available, NTIS in turn catalogs, indexes, and abstracts them, keyboards them to its computer, and microfilms the report. The indexes are maintained under computer control and the data base can be accessed by the public either directly or through any one of several commercial computerized bibliographic utilities. After reviewing the computer results, a customer may request a copy of the particular report(s) needed either in microform or hard copy. NTIS serves and then bills the customer accordingly.

NTIS's coverage is very broad. Its vast data base contains information on almost any conceivable subject. NTIS was founded to provide bibliographic control and physical availability for a class of documents rather than for a subject area; and yet NTIS is not simply an archive but a publisher whose products are meant to be actively used and to be sold at a price that will recover their cost. In order to meet Congress's requirement that it be self-sustaining, NTIS markets its services aggressively through various products and services.

From the 270 new reports collected and processed daily and from the record made of them, a number of current awareness periodicals are created. Abstract newsletters are created in 26 different subject areas such as chemistry, physics, energy, behavior and society, and the environment. A comprehensive journal called *Government Reports Announcements and Index (GRA&I)* is published biweekly for librarians, technical information specialists, and others requiring all the summaries in a single volume. A cumulative index is produced at the end of each year to assist those using the journals.

Many federal agencies and some nonprofit organizations utilize NTIS as the public promoter and sales agent for many of their periodicals. More than 20,000 subscribers buy copies of over 70 different periodicals sold by NTIS. These subscriptions range in subject matter from solar energy bibliographies to monthly energy statistics to the Environmental Protection Agency's quarterly bibliography.

As a result of the many awareness services, NTIS fills orders for about 12,000 reports daily in addition to 7,000 standing orders for periodicals. Each year it supplies customers with about 6 million research reports, which are generally available in both paper copy and microfiche.

NTIS has a specialized packaging service called Selected Research in Microfiche (SRIM) that automatically provides subscribers with full text microfiche copies of research reports in special interest subject areas they select. NTIS analysts help subscribers choose from among 500 different subject categories and 200,000 unique descriptive terms. For example, if a subscriber's area of interest is "energy" or "energy use, supply and demand," he would receive about 140 complete report texts over a 12-month period at about one-fourth the cost if purchased individually. The reports are sorted automatically and distributed to subscribers every two weeks as a standing order service.

Information about licensable technology is also acquisitioned and made available. NTIS obtains foreign patent protection on selected government inventions and negotiates directly for licenses utilizing these inventions. The availability of licensable government technology is brought to customers' attention by a special abstract newsletter, *Government Inventions for Licensing*.

NTIS also makes available government-generated machine-readable data products and the related computer software that is available to process the data. There has been a phenomenal increase in both the number and types of machine-readable data bases established by and for the U.S. government primarily for its own use. At the same time, the many users and potential users are finding that machine-readable data gathered, organized, and presented for one purpose can be reorganized and reformatted and used just as effectively for other purposes. They are also finding that a number of data bases, or parts of a number of data bases, can be merged into more comprehensive data bases of great value that will permit extensive new and different analyses and correlations.

NTIS plans to increase substantially the effort devoted to developing a publicly available machine-readable products and services program during the 1980s. Major program objectives include:

Increasing coverage by NTIS of government machine-readable products.

Providing reference services to all government machine-readable products.

Providing custom reports prepared from government machine-readable data files where appropriate.

In addition, General Services Administration (GSA) selected NTIS to organize and manage a Federal Software Exchange Center. Federal Property Management Regulations require all agencies, other than defense, to report common-use software to the exchange. Although the primary GSA market is other federal agencies, NTIS will also sell copies of the software to the public, with GSA's permission.

The value of the NTIS to information practitioners is impossible to exaggerate. For the researcher it is a source of information that greatly reduces the possibility of "reinventing the wheel"; for the manager it can go a long way in helping to solve the problems of funding and autonomy; and for the librarian it is a source of verification and guide to unpublished government reports.

NATIONAL TELECOMMUNICATIONS AND INFORMATION ADMINISTRATION

U.S. Department of Commerce
1800 G St. N.W., Rm. 774, Washington, DC 20504
202-377-1832

William Garrison

Public Information Officer

The National Telecommunications and Information Administration's (NTIA) establishment was a Commerce Department response to the president's Reorganization Plan No. 1 of 1977. NTIA, as an arm of the Commerce Department, is the principal federal agency for the development and implementation of our national and international policy on virtually the entire range of private, commercial, and governmental electronic communications. The head of the agency is the assistant secretary for communications and information. In addition to serving as administrator of NTIA, he is also the principal adviser to the president on telecommunications policies pertaining to the nation's economic and technological advancements and to the regulation of the telecommunications industry.

The newly created NTIA inherited most of the functions of the two agencies abolished in the reorganization: the Office of Telecommunications Policy in the Executive Office of the President and the Office of Telecommunications in the Commerce Department.

In the domestic area, NTIA helps manage the federal government's use of telecommunications resources. For example, it specifies what frequencies federal radio stations can operate on, and it establishes policies affecting the government's use of the radio frequency spectrum. The agency also analyzes issues within the communications industries, especially those issues pertinent to common carrier and broadcasting. NTIA coordinates the federal government's assistance to state and local governments in their planning and use of telecommunications systems.

With respect to international telecommunications, NTIA coordinates U.S. government positions for international conferences and advises the State Department on international communications policy.

Additionally, NTIA examines potential applications of telecommunications systems and conducts scientific and engineering research to enlarge our understanding of telecommunications technology.

Nine offices make up the agency, of which the following four carry out the bulk of NTIA's program activities:

The Office of Telecommunications applications, which assesses and serves the needs of public service agencies and other telecommunications users.

The Office of Federal Systems and Spectrum Management, which assigns federal radio frequencies; that is, it specifies which radio frequencies government stations can operate on. This office does engineering and administrative work for federal spectrum management, and also works with government communications systems.

The Institute for Telecommunications Sciences, which conducts NTIA's telecommunications technology research programs. The Institute consists of four divisions: Spectrum Utilization, System Technology and Standards, Applied Electromagnetic Science, and Advanced Communications Networks.

The Office of Policy Analysis and Development, which is responsible for NTIA's analysis and formulation of domestic and international telecommunications and information policies.

Supporting these four offices are the Office of Planning and Policy Coordination, the Office of the Chief Counsel, the Office of International Affairs, the Office of Administration, and the Office of Congressional Relations and Public Affairs.

In 1979, NTIA representatives produced many publications and reports, testified extensively before the House and Senate on diverse legislation, and filed over 30 pleadings to the Federal Communications Commission. And, through its Public Telecommunications Facilities Program, NTIA distributed over $18 million to eligible telecommunications users.

In addition to its three offices in Washington, D.C., NTIA has a center dedicated to spectrum management in Annapolis, Maryland, and another office in Frostburg, Maryland. NTIA's Institute for Telecommunications Sciences and a policy research and analysis division are located in Boulder, Colorado.

WORKING WITH TELECOMMUNICATIONS INDUSTRIES

Broadcasting. NTIA is working to provide more diversity in the ownership of broadcast stations and in the programming choices offered to the public, primarily by finding ways to increase the number of radio and television broadcast outlets. Reduction of the frequency spacing between stations on the AM radio band, for example, would allow more stations to use the limited AM radio frequencies; NTIA is performing research to determine the feasibility of this reduction. Moreover, NTIA has suggested how directional antennas might be used in commercial FM broadcasting. The antennas transmit a more precise beam and cause less interference with neighboring signals; consequently, their use would enable more stations to operate on existing frequencies.

Encouraging greater minority ownership and control of broadcasting stations is another way to increase diversity in station ownership. To do this, NTIA identifies possible sources of loans—both government and private—that would assist minorities. It also suggests regulatory policies conducive to minority ownership. With these efforts, NTIA, by August of 1979, helped to more than double the number of new minority outlets by working with the Federal Communications Commission, the Small Business Administration, and the Economic Development Administration.

Common Carrier. Common carrier regulation, particularly possible deregulation of the telephone industry, is a major NTIA concern. Modern technology has challenged the assumption that the telephone industry is a "natural" monopoly. NTIA researchers are examining the implications of competition in the telephone industry at the national, state, local, and international levels. What effects will competition have on local and intercity rates, and to what extent will competition change services available to consumers in both urban and rural areas? These are just two of the many questions that must be explored in light of new technologies and growing competition in the common carrier field.

Cable Television. Studying the deregulation of cable television—what it would entail and whom it would affect—is another NTIA activity. NTIA looks at the possible impact such deregulation would have on local broadcast stations and weighs its advantages and disadvantages for cable operators, local broadcasters, and the general public.

Land Mobile Radio. To aid planning for land mobile radio use, NTIA provides computerized techniques constructed to inform mobile radio users about such conditions as weather, terrain, transmitter and receiver design, and operational patterns. Any U.S. land mobile radio user can use this information via a computer terminal and a telephone line to the NTIA computer at the Institute for Telecommunications Sciences in Boulder.

International Telecommunications. NTIA promoted the establishment of a new international organization, the International Maritime Satellite Organization (INMARSAT), which provides satellite communications to and from ships at sea. Also, after helping to establish a procedure for the integrated planning of international satellite and underseas cable facilities in the North Atlantic region, NTIA will conduct research on future technologies and international services.

In addition, NTIA, along with the Department of State, exercises presidential oversight responsibilities for the Communications Satellite Corporation (Comsat). Comsat acts as this country's representative to the International Telecommunications Satellite consortium (INTELSAT) and to the newly established INMARSAT.

WORKING WITH TELECOMMUNICATIONS USERS

For program purposes, NTIA divides telecommunications users into two categories: nonfederal and governmental.

Nonfederal Users

Rural Telecommunications. NTIA works to hasten the process of bringing to rural areas telecommunications services that are commonplace in the cities. Relatively higher cost of delivering some communications services to rural areas makes federal cooperation in this effort highly desirable.

The focal point of this federal participation is a rural telecommunications subcommittee within the Interagency Committee on Telecommunications Applications that NTIA chairs. In addition, NTIA helped develop a set of Rural Telecommunications Initiatives, which the White House announced in February 1979. NTIA also submits expert analysis on rural telecommunications in regulatory and legislative proceedings, and publishes special studies on the communications needs of rural communities.

Public Telecommunications Facilities Program. NTIA awards matching grants to noncommercial telecommunications systems for the planning and construction of telecommunications facilities. Through this Public Telecommunications Facilities Program (PTFP), NTIA works to extend the delivery of public broadcasting services to unserved areas of the country and to improve present services.

In FY 1980, the program will distribute $23.7 million. Eligible applicants for these grants include:

A public broadcasting station

A noncommercial telecommunications entity

A system of public telecommunications entities

A nonprofit foundation, corporation, institution, or association organized primarily for educational or cultural purposes

A state or local government, or any agency thereof, or political or special subdivision of a state

Government Users

NTIA's second major user category is composed of government agencies—federal, state, and local.

Federal Government. The value of the federal government's telecommunications inventory has been estimated at $60 billion. And the range of federal telecommunications users is vast. Aircraft radio navigation, communications for maritime safety, intelligence gathering by satellite, and nationwide record-retrieval systems are just a few examples.

To ensure that duplication of systems is kept to a minimum, NTIA evaluates federal agencies' telecommunications procurement plans and recommends policy changes to the Office of Management and Budget. Similarly, NTIA is helping to coordinate federal funding of emergency medical service programs in an effort to harmonize policies and funding.

NTIA also provides scientific and engineering advice to federal agencies through its Institute for Telecommunications Sciences in Boulder, Colorado.

State and Local Governments. With regard to telecommunications issues involving state and local governments, NTIA's role is primarily one of coordinator. For example, NTIA coordinates activities relating to the emergency telephone number 911. In this effort, it assists states and communities that wish to implement a 911 system, and provides model state 911 legislation.

Public Service Agencies. In his Civilian Space Policy, President Carter assigned to NTIA the responsibility for pulling together the communications needs of public service agencies—such as health, education, and law enforcement institutions—with the aim of creating a market force for communications satellite use. To satisfy another aspect of this White House assignment, NTIA is working with the Department of Interior and the Agency for International Development in setting up satellite applications for remote areas overseas.

WORKING WITH TELECOMMUNICATIONS RESOURCES

NTIA's resource activities largely revolve around the management of the federal government's share of the frequency spectrum. Federal and nongovernmental users share 40 percent of the radio frequency spectrum, with the federal government maintaining exclusive use of 25 percent. NTIA manages the federal spectrum use, while the Federal Communications Commission is responsible for nonfederal use.

Assignment of Frequencies. NTIA assigns radio frequencies to federal agencies. Currently, 48 agencies use the spectrum, the largest being the navy, air force, army, and the Federal Aviation Administration.

Systems Review. NTIA reviews proposed federal telecommunications systems before they are built to ensure interference-free performance of essential communications systems and save the government hundreds of millions of dollars.

And, using mobile equipment with receiving antennas hooked up to a computerized signal processor, NTIA checks to see that spectrum users are utilizing their frequencies properly.

Protection Efforts. Many government telecommunications systems are vulnerable to unauthorized eavesdropping through the monitoring of microwave transmissions. NTIA and the Defense Department share responsibility for protecting government transmission of valuable but unclassified information from interception by a foreign nation. This effort includes policy development, technical evaluation of protection techniques, and the taking of surveys in federal agencies to identify vulnerable telecommunications systems and to specify information that should be protected.

International Spectrum Management. Since radio waves do not respect international boundaries, all nations must agree on worldwide spectrum allocations. These agreements are made during international negotiations sponsored by the International Telecommunication Union (ITU), a UN agency with 154 member nations.

ITU's most significant international negotiations involving spectrum management—the World Administrative Radio Conference '79 (WARC '79)—took place during the final three months of 1979 at ITU headquarters in Geneva. At this conference, worldwide radio frequency bands were allocated by service. In preparation for the conference, the United States conducted hundreds of committee meetings, held numerous discussions with other countries, and submitted over 300 pages of proposals, including many for new allocations in various services.

NTIA played a major role in the conference preparations as the agency responsible for coordinating the federal government's position on conference issues and in joining with the Federal Communications Commission in preparing the final U.S. national position.

INFORMATION POLICY AND TECHNOLOGY

The widespread use of new information technologies, especially small computers linked to modern communications systems, has brought about many changes in relationships among nations, institutions, industries, and individuals. NTIA is developing national policies to resolve the problems arising from these new electronic methods of handling information. This NTIA activity is twofold: the development of information policy and the enhancement of information technology. NTIA's information policy program concentrates on privacy and information industry issues.

Information Policy

Privacy. To protect the individual's rights to privacy in the applications of electronic technology, President Carter, in April 1979, announced a major Privacy Initiative. NTIA helped provide the foundation for this initiative and is serving as the Executive Branch's "lead agency."

To implement the initiative, NTIA drafted or helped draft several congressional bills concerning the use, collection, and dissemination of personal information gathered by the credit, banking, insurance, and research industries and transmitted via electronic systems. And it assisted the Department of Health, Education, and Welfare in drafting a medical records privacy bill and the Department of Justice in preparing two bills pertaining to financial privacy and police access to reporters' notes.

Issues within Information Industries. NTIA is composing a collection of essays that will explain the broad aspects of information policy. Two, for example, center on electronic mail and electronic funds transfer services. The latter currently consists of services provided by electronic banking cards. In the future, however, electronic funds transfer is expected to include more diverse services.

Information Technology

NTIA coordinates federal government activities involving new information technologies such as viewdata and teletext. The term "viewdata" refers to a group of electronic services that can transform the everyday television set into a computer display terminal via the telephone. Teletext is a means of broadcasting information over unused portions of the television signal. The generic term "videotext" encompasses both viewdata and teletext.

NTIA works to reduce the cost and improve the delivery of public and federal information videotext services. It also explores the policy issues and regulatory barriers that inhibit the progress of U.S. videotext development. For example, NTIA is part of an Interagency Policy Steering Committee to identify applications, policy issues, and evaluation guidelines of Green Thumb, a pilot videotext service sponsored by the U.S. National Weather Service and the U.S. Department of Agriculture.

Green Thumb's goal is to develop a videotext service that will provide farmers with up-to-the-minute agriculture information. With Green Thumb, farmers would use their telephones to dial into a state computer data base. A device connecting their television sets to their telephones would then allow farmers to select from among various categories of information stored in the state data base and have that information displayed on their television screens.

As the principal adviser to the president on issues pertaining to the U.S. communications industries and to the regulation of those industries, the National Telecommunications and Information Administration has become a primary element in the movement of this nation toward an era of electronic communications that will revolutionize our lives, both public and private. NTIA continues to develop innovative governmental policies that will bring a cohesive foundation to our electronic future.

U.S. GOVERNMENT INFORMATION CLEARINGHOUSES: A DIRECTORY

The following list of clearinghouses has been compiled to provide access to sources of information, most of which are in the human services field. The name, address, telephone number, and contact person, when known, are listed for each clearinghouse.

Adult Education

Clearinghouse on Adult Education and Lifelong Learning (ADELL), 6011 Executive Blvd., Rockville, MD 20852. *Contact.* Jerry Walker. Tel. 301-770-3300; 800-638-6628.

Aging

National Clearinghouse on Aging, 330 Independence Ave. S.W., Rm. 4255, Washington, DC 20201. *Contact.* Kris Pappajohn. Tel. 202-245-0995.

Alcohol

National Clearinghouse for Alcohol Information, 1776 E. Jefferson St., Rockville, MD 20852. Mailing address: Box 2345, Rockville, MD 20852. Tel. 301-468-2600; 301-770-3000.

Bilingual Education

National Clearinghouse for Bilingual Education, 1500 Wilson Blvd., Rosslyn, VA 22209. *Contact.* Joel Gomez. Tel. 703-522-0710.

Child Abuse

National Center on Child Abuse and Neglect, 400 Sixth St. S.W., Rm. 5847, Washington, DC 20013. *Contact.* Frances Bynoe. Tel. 202-755-0587.

Drug Abuse

National Clearinghouse for Drug Abuse Information, 5600 Fishers La., Rm. 10A-56, Rockville, MD 20857. Tel. 301-443-6500.

Education

ERIC Processing and Reference Facility, 4833 Rugby Ave., Bethesda, MD 20014. *Contact.* Dorothy Slawsky, Reference Libn. Tel. 301-656-9723.

Federal Community Education Clearinghouse, 6011 Executive Blvd., Rockville, MD 20852. *Contact.* Larry Reitz. Tel. 301-770-3000; 800-638-6698.

Elections

National Clearinghouse for Information on the Administration of Elections, Federal Election Commission, 1325 K St. N.W., Washington, DC 20463. Tel. 202-523-4183; 800-424-9530.

Environment

Environmental Science Information Center, Commerce Dept. D-8 NOAA, Rockville, MD 20852. Tel. 301-443-8137.

U.S. International Environmental Referral Center, 401 M St. S.W., Rm. 2903, Washington, DC 20460. Tel. 202-755-1836.

Family Planning

Family Planning Information Clearinghouse, 6110 Executive Blvd., Suite 250, Rockville, MD 20852. Tel. 301-881-9400.

Federal Government*

Federal Information Center, General Services Admin., F St. between 18 and 19 Sts. N.W., Washington, DC 20402. Tel. 202-566-1937.

---

*For the Federal Information Center that serves your city, see the directory of Federal Information Centers at the end of the report on the Federal Information Centers Division of the Office of Consumer Affairs earlier in this section of Part 1—*Ed.*

U.S. GOVERNMENT INFORMATION CLEARINGHOUSES / 93

Food and Nutrition

Food and Nutrition Information and Educational Material Center, National Agricultural Lib., Beltsville, MD 20801. Tel. 301-344-3719.

Maps

National Cartographic Information Center, Dept. of the Interior, 12201 Sunrise Valley Dr., Reston, VA 22092. Tel. 703-860-6187.

Mental Health

Clearinghouse for Mental Health Information, Parklawn Bldg., 5600 Fishers La., Rm. 11A-21, Rockville, MD 20857. *Contact.* Joan Abell. Tel. 301-443-4515.

Organizations

National Referral Center, Science and Technology Div., Lib. of Congress, Washington, DC 20540. Tel. 202-426-5670.

Rehabilitation

National Rehabilitation Information Center, 308 Mullen Lib., Catholic Univ., Washington, DC 20064. *Contact.* Judith J. Senkevitch. Tel. 202-635-5826.

Smoking

National Clearinghouse on Smoking and Health, 5600 Fishers La., Rm. 158, Rockville, MD 20852. Tel: 301-443-1690.

Solar Energy

National Solar Heating and Cooling Information Center, Box 1607, Rockville, MD 20850. WATS. 800-523-2929; in Pennsylvania: 800-462-4983.

Science

Smithsonian Science Information Exchange, 1730 M St. N.W., Rm. 300, Washington, DC 20036. Tel. 202-381-4211.

Law Enforcement

National Criminal Justice Information & Statistics Service, 4340 E. West Hwy., Bethesda, MD 20531. Tel. 301-492-9050.

Technology†

National Technical Information Service (NTIS), 5258 Port Royal Rd., Springfield, VA 22161. Tel. 703-557-4600.

†See the report on the National Technical Information Service in the Federal Agencies section of Part 1—*Ed.*

Federal Libraries

THE LIBRARY OF CONGRESS

Washington, D.C. 20540
202-287-5000

James W. McClung
Public Information Specialist, Information Office

In 1979, the Library of Congress moved its first office unit into the long-awaited James Madison Memorial Library of Congress Building, opened a Performing Arts Library at the John F. Kennedy Center, led a delegation of American librarians on a tour of the People's Republic of China, and carried forth many active programs of service to the Congress, to the creative artist through copyright, to the scholar and the public at large, and to the library community.

JAMES MADISON MEMORIAL BUILDING

Long planned to relieve crowded conditions and to allow many divisions relocated to other areas in the city to return to Capitol Hill, the James Madison Memorial Building—20 years in the planning and construction—opened its doors to the first Library of Congress (LC) staff members in December when a unit of the American Law Division of the Congressional Research Service (CRS) moved into the modern facility. Two other divisions of CRS moved in January and the rest of the department is to follow closely in early 1980. The first research division and collections to move will be the Geography and Map Division, also scheduled for the spring. The building will be opened to the public, in part, in April 1980. The Madison Building will eventually house the Copyright Office, CRS, the Law Library, much of Processing Services, and most of the special collections in Research Services, with office space for over 4,000 LC employees.

PERFORMING ARTS LIBRARY

The Performing Arts Library, a joint project of the Library of Congress and the John F. Kennedy Center for the Performing Arts, opened on March 8, 1979, after more than two years of planning. During its first seven months of operations, more than 13,000 readers used its 4,000-volume book collection, 319 periodicals, listening and viewing facilities, computer terminal offering direct on-line access to LC data bases, and other services. The library was the host at several special programs—a panel discussion on the American musical, the opening session of the annual meeting of the American Dance Guild, and briefings for visitors sponsored by the Alliance for Arts Education, a joint project of the Kennedy Center and the U.S. Office of Education. Special exhibits mounted in conjunction with Kennedy Center programs—a festival entitled "Paris: The Romantic Epoch" and the visit of the Vienna State Opera—provided a wider audience an opportunity to view items from several Library of Congress special collections, including maps, music, photographs, prints, and rare books.

CENTER FOR THE BOOK

Created in October 1977, the Library's Center for the Book completed a second full year of activities noted for their diversity. Toward the end of 1979, the center published *Reading in America 1978*, a 98-page volume devoted primarily to selected findings from the Book Industry Study Group's 1978 research survey of the reading habits of American adults—presented and discussed in a 1978 center program. The book is a companion volume to *Television, the Book, and the Classroom* (announced last year); they are available for $4.95 each, prepaid, from the Information Office, Library of Congress, Washington, D.C. 20540.

More than a dozen major programs sponsored by the Center for the Book, or cosponsored with other LC divisions and outside organizations, took place in 1979, involving hundreds of people and dozens of institutions. These included lectures by Anthony Hobson on bookbinding, Elaine Moss and Barbara Rollock on children's literature, Ian Willison on "Libraries and Scholarship," Barbara W. Tuchman on "The Book," Elaine L. Konigsburg in observance of National Children's Book Week, and Robert Darnton on "The Encyclopédie and the Working Class." There were symposia on "The Responsibilities of the American Publisher," "The Textbook in American Education," "Japanese Literature in Translation," and "The International Flow of Information: A Trans-Pacific Perspective," which consisted of a seminar in Hawaii and programs in Los Angeles, New York City, Washington, D.C., and Corsicana and Dallas, Texas.

The Center for the Book also appointed its first resident consultant in 1979, Elizabeth L. Eisenstein, who served from January to June, during which time she continued her own studies, advised the center about the future of its historical program, attended center meetings, and worked on papers to be presented during the next year to the scholarly community. Supported entirely by gifts, the center received several generous donations during 1979, allowing it to pursue its work in programs and publications and to hold meetings for its National Advisory Board and the five committees that advise the center on such matters as the international role of the book and reading development.

Capping the year's activities was the launching of a joint Library of Congress/Columbia Broadcasting System project entitled "Read More about It" that grew out of the center's 1978 seminar on "Television, the Book, and the Classroom." The project offers reading lists to libraries and bookstores to accompany selected CBS specials, at the end of which three or four specific titles are recommended for further reading by one of the performers. The project officially got under way with a reading list to accompany "All Quiet on the Western Front," aired on November 14, 1979.

NATIONAL REFERRAL CENTER

The National Referral Center, established in 1962 to handle referrals in the area of science and technology, today makes referrals in virtually all subject areas, including the arts and humanities. It is a free service of LC that directs those who have questions on any subject to organizations that can provide the answers. The service uses a subject-indexed computerized file of approximately 13,000 organizations or information resources. The referral center is not equipped to furnish answers to specific questions or to provide bibliographic assistance.

In FY 1979 the center answered nearly 5,000 requests for referral services; additional requests were answered by pre-prepared materials or publications issued under the series title NRC Switchboard, which are informal lists of resources of information on specific topics such as hazardous materials, population, or environmental education. At the end of FY 1979, the National Referral Center inventory contained 12,715 active information resources; 798 new resources were added and 5,918 were updated. Subject indexing was provided or revised for 1,934 resources, and 2,361 new cross-references were established.

Inquiries regarding the center should be addressed to the Library of Congress, National Referral Center, Washington, D.C. 20540, 202-287-5670 (for referral services) and 202-287-5680 (for registration of information resources).

AMERICAN FOLKLIFE CENTER

Mandated by PL 94-201 to engage in the preservation, presentation, and dissemination of American folk cultural traditions, the American Folklife Center pursued these goals in 1979 through its publications, field projects, programs and workshops, exhibits, concerts, and other professional activities. Publications included a redesigned brochure containing basic information on the center, a pamphlet entitled "Where to Turn for Help in Folklore and Folklife," and *Folklife and Fieldwork*, a layman's guide to folk cultural materials. Commemorating the fiftieth anniversary of the Archive of Folk Song was a long-playing recording *Folk-Songs of America: The Robert Winslow Gordon Collection, 1922-1932*, with an accompanying 29-page illustrated brochure about the work of the archive and its first head, Robert W. Gordon. The Chicago Museum of Contemporary Art published a 24-page catalog, *Inside Our Homes, outside Our Windows*, to accompany an exhibition of the same name jointly presented by the museum, the center, and photographer Jonas Dovydenas. The photographs in the catalog, and the larger selection in the exhibit, were produced during the center's Chicago Ethnic Arts Project of 1977. The Rhode Island Folklife Project, begun in August 1979, also resulted in an exhibition of photographs by Henry Horenstein, on view at year's end at the Museum of Rhode Island History in Providence.

Other new or continuing field projects included the Montana Folklife Survey, designed to assist the Montana Arts Council in inaugurating a state folklife program, and the Paradise Valley (Nevada) and Blue Ridge Parkway (Virginia and North Carolina) Folklife projects, both begun in 1978. The center organized the Ethnic Heritage Workshop in Seattle, Washington, conducted a National Maritime Folklife Survey, and presented a series of two-day discussion workshops on media issues at seven universities with graduate programs in folklore. The center also held its usual series of outdoor summer concerts, now an established tradition on LC's Neptune Plaza.

The Federal Cylinder Project, coordinated by the center with financial assistance from the Bureau of Indian Affairs, got underway in June 1979. The goal of the project is to preserve several thousand cylinder recordings, principally of Native American songs and stories, found in the collections of the Library of Congress, the Smithsonian Institution, and other federal agencies. The early recordings will be transferred to magnetic tape and an accompanying catalog will be prepared.

STAFF, BUDGET, AND SERVICES

For FY 1980, LC is operating on a budget of $177,491,000, and there were over 5,000 full- and part-time staff members at year's end. In late summer, LC management officials and labor representatives signed a labor contract covering employees in the Congressional Research Service. There are now labor contracts covering eligible staff members in seven of LC's eight departments; over 98 percent of LC staff works in those seven departments.

In FY 1979, more than 739,000 readers used the various Research Services reading rooms, and 1,683,045 volumes were circulated to readers; 220,457 volumes were loaned outside LC. The Law Library had 121,401 readers who used 356,295 items; 3,746 items were loaned from the law collections. The Congressional Research Service responded in 1979 more than 300,000 times to the legislative, oversight, and representational needs of the Congress, made significant progress in cooperation with other support agencies, and consolidated its structure to improve its service. To inform members, committees, and their staffs of the information and analytical capabilities available to them, CRS offered institutes, seminars, slide/sound and cassette briefings, and personal visits to congressional offices. The Copyright Office, feeling the impact of the new copyright law that went into effect January 1, 1978, received registrations at the rate of 10,000 per week, and completed more than 429,000 registrations—a sizable increase over 1978. The number of cases requiring correspondence decreased as registrants became more experienced in completing the new application forms.

COLLECTIONS

The collections of the Library of Congress increased by 1,297,481 items in FY 1979, bringing the total to more than 75,600,000. Notable acquisitions augmented LC's collections in music, recordings, private papers, architectural drawings, and photographs. The Motion Picture, Broadcasting and Recorded Sound Division acquired the audio portion of the videotapes of the proceedings of the U.S. House of Representatives—the first audio "Congressional Record"—and took the first steps in off-the-air archival recording of television programs authorized under the American Television and Radio Archive created by the new copyright law. The Manuscript Division received the papers of the late Margaret Mead.

The notable acquisition of 1979—and one of the great acquisitions of LC's 180-year history—was the transfer to the Library of Congress of the unrivaled Lessing J. Rosenwald Collection of illustrated books and manuscripts. Rosenwald, who died last June at the age of 88, had spent most of his life assembling an incomparable collection of books (which he donated to the LC a number of years ago) and prints (which he gave to the National Gallery of Art). But the bulk of Rosenwald's book collection remained at Alverthorpe Gallery, the Rosenwald facility in Jenkintown, Pennsylvania, during his lifetime, and only in the fall of 1979 was the collection transferred to LC in Washington, D.C., to a specially refurbished bookstack in the Rare Book and Special Collections Division. In 1978 the Library of Congress had published a catalog to the Rosenwald collection (see the 1979 *Bowker Annual*, p. 64).

CATALOGING, NETWORKING, ACQUISITIONS

Cooperation characterized LC's cataloging activity in FY 1979. It expanded its work with the Government Printing Office to include the establishment of personal as well as corporate name authorities. It began its first venture with a state library, agreeing to initiate a cooperative name authority project with the Texas State Library. The Africana cooperative cataloging project with Northwestern University went into its second year, and discussions were held with the National Library of Medicine, the National Agricultural Library, and several large academic libraries to explore cataloging cooperation in the area of name authorities and in other areas of mutual concern. The national library of Norway and the Library of Congress entered into an agreement to exchange MARC tapes similar to those already established with the National Library of Canada, the Bibliothèque Nationale, the National Library of Australia, and the British Library.

Many new alphabets were added to the romanized cataloging program, including Amharic, Armenian, Burmese, Georgian, Greek, Ottoman Turkish, Thai, and the Cyrillic and South Asian language groups. The effect will be to advance LC's goal of providing the broadest possible scope for its automated system, based on the firm conviction that adequate bibliographic control of information will become increasingly difficult if comprehensive machine-readable data files are not available.

Nationwide network activities were in a transition state in 1979. Emphasis on technical aspects, such as the development of a message delivery system, shifted to a concern for the economic considerations of library networking. Efforts to develop LC's networking capabilities have been suspended pending congressional action on a feasibility study the Congress requested to analyze alternatives for the exchange of machine-readable bibliographic data.

PRESERVATION

Promising developments in the preservation area were the indications in 1979 of commercial interest in supplying the library community with the deacidification (diethyl zinc, DEZ vapor phase) treatment developed and patented by the Library of Congress and the increasing receptiveness of the paper industry to the manufacture of acid-free papers, a development that would have important long-range consequences for library preservation programs. The Preservation Office fills its national obligation for dissemination of information about techniques, methods, and new developments in restoration and preservation by talks, workshops, lectures, and presentations by the staff and also by publication of a series of pamphlets on preservation problems. Late in the year the first issue of *National Preservation Report* appeared, superseding the former *Newspaper and Gazette Report*. The new publication is designed to bridge the information gap between the librarian and the conservator and the scientist.

EXHIBITS AND PUBLICATIONS HIGHLIGHTS

Major exhibits of the year were "Tales, Rhymes and Riddles in the Spirit of Childhood," some 60 notable children's books displayed in observance of UNESCO's International Year of the Child, 1979, and "'We Have a Sporting Chance...' The Decision to Go to the Moon," an exhibition and accompanying catalog commemorating the tenth anniversary of the first successful landing by man on the moon on July 20, 1969. "Posada's Mexico," a major exhibition dealing with printmaker José Guadalupe Posada (1852–1913), went on view during the last two months of 1979 and will travel in 1980 to the Amon Carter Museum in Fort Worth, Texas, and elsewhere. A profusely illustrated 316-page exhibit catalog, also entitled *Posada's Mexico*, is available for $16 from the Superintendent of Documents, U.S. Government Printing Office, Washington, D.C. 20402 (Stock No. 030-014-00004-9). A major exhibition at year's end was "The Circle of Knowledge," a sampling of 38 from the more than 3,000 encyclopedias in LC's collections ranging from the fifteenth century to the present; a catalog also accompanies this exhibit (available for $2.50 prepaid from the Information Office, Library of Congress, Washington, D.C. 20540).

Other LC publications in 1979, in addition to bibliographies and technical works, included a facsimile of Brahms's Violin Concerto, Op. 77, described as "absolutely beautiful!" by distinguished violinist Yehudi Menuhin, who wrote the introduction. The 128-page work (106 pages of it the facsimile itself) is available for $50 prepaid from the Information Office, Library of Congress, Washington, D.C. 20540. During the year, LC also issued, through the Superintendent of Documents, the third, fourth, and fifth volumes of *Letters of Delegates to Congress, 1774–1789*. These volumes cover the period from January 1 through December 31, 1776. Volumes III, IV, and V sell for $10.25, $11.25, and $16, respectively. Their publication marks the completion of about 20 percent of the projected 25-volume series designed to fill a conspicuous gap in the knowledge of the American Revolution.

NATIONAL LIBRARY SERVICE FOR THE BLIND AND PHYSICALLY HANDICAPPED

1291 Taylor St. N.W.
Washington, DC 20542
202-882-5500

Frank Kurt Cylke
Director

Eunice Lovejoy
Library Consultant, Services to the Handicapped, The State Library of Ohio, Columbus, Ohio

A free national library program of braille and recorded materials for blind and physically handicapped persons is administered by the National Library Service for the Blind and Physically Handicapped (NLS), Library of Congress. With the cooperation of authors and publishers who grant permission to use copyrighted works, NLS selects and produces full-length books and magazines in braille and on recorded disc and cassette. Reading materials are distributed to a cooperating network of regional and subregional (local) libraries where they are circulated to eligible borrowers. Reading materials are sent to borrowers and returned to libraries by postage-free mail. Established by an act of Congress in 1931 to serve blind adults, the program was expanded in 1952 to include children, in 1962 to provide music materials, and again in 1966 by PL 89-522 to include individuals with other physical impairments that prevent the reading of standard print.

FUNDING

The NLS program is funded annually by Congress. The FY 1979 appropriation was $34,130,000. Regional and subregional libraries receive funding from federal, state, and local sources. In FY 1978, the combined federal, state, and local expenditure for the program was more than $41,000,000.

LIBRARY SERVICES

Eligibility

Anyone who is unable to read or use standard printed materials as a result of temporary or permanent visual or physical limitations may receive service. A recent survey indicates that as many as 2 million persons with some type of visual impairment are eligible and another million with physical conditions such as paralysis, missing arms or hands, lack of muscle coordination, or prolonged weakness could benefit from the use of reading materials in recorded form.

Readers and Circulation

Network libraries reported a total readership of 720,030 adults and children for FY 1979 (Table 1). About 22,000 readers borrowed braille materials, and 697,670 borrowed materials in recorded formats. Nearly 16 million books and magazines were circulated to readers in the United States and its territories, and to American citizens living abroad. Many regional and subregional libraries also have collections of large-type books for circulation to handicapped readers.

TABLE 1 USE OF LIBRARY SERVICES, 1979

Type of Service	Volume of Use
READERS	
Recorded cassette	272,430
Recorded disc	424,240
Open reel tape	1,000
Braille	22,360
Total	720,030
CIRCULATION	
Recorded Cassette	
Individuals	3,550,900
Deposit collections	186,500
Direct circulation magazines	10,200
Interlibrary loan	19,600
Total	3,767,200
Recorded Disc	
Individuals	5,786,000
Deposit collections	274,300
Direct circulation magazines	5,363,300
Interlibrary loan	58,000
Total	11,481,600
Open Reel Tape	
Individuals	4,100
Deposit collections	—
Direct circulation magazines	—
Interlibrary loan	100
Total	4,200
Braille	
Individuals	268,400
Deposit collections	10,900
Direct circulation magazines	352,200
Interlibrary loan	12,600
Total	644,100
GRAND TOTAL CIRCULATION	
Individuals	9,609,400
Deposit collections	471,700
Direct circulation magazines	5,725,700
Interlibrary loan	90,300
Total	15,897,100

Book Collection

Books are selected on the basis of their appeal to a wide range of interests. Bestsellers, biographies, fiction, and how-to-do-it books are in greatest demand. The national book collection currently contains more than 25,000 titles. Each year about 1,900 titles are mass-produced for distribution through network libraries. Another 700 titles recorded on tape or transcribed into braille by volunteers are circulated in more limited quantities. Titles expected to be extremely popular are produced on flexible disc in several thousand copies and circulated to borrowers within several months of their publication in print form.

Magazines

Seventy magazines on disc, cassette, and in braille are offered through the program. Readers may request free subscriptions to *Harper's, U.S. News, National Geographic, Consumer Reports, Good Housekeeping, Sports Illustrated, Jack and Jill,* and many other popular magazines. Current issues are mailed to readers at the same time the print issues appear, or shortly thereafter.

Special Equipment

Playback equipment is loaned free to readers for as long as library materials are being borrowed. Talking book machines are designed to play disc-recorded books and magazines in 8 rpm and 16 rpm; cassette book machines are designed for cassettes recorded at $^{15}/_{16}$ ips and the standard speed of $1\frac{7}{8}$ ips as well as on two tracks and four tracks. Available accessories for playback equipment include earphones and pillowphones. An auxiliary amplifier for hearing-impaired persons is available from NLS on special request.

Music Services

Persons interested in music materials may receive them directly from the Music Section of NLS. The collection consists of scores in braille and large type; textbooks and books about music in braille, large type, and in recorded form; elementary instruction for piano, organ, and guitar on cassette; and other instructional materials in recorded form.

Volunteer Services

Free correspondence courses leading to certification in braille transcribing (literary, music, and math braille) and braille proofreading are offered. Voice auditions and informal training are given to volunteer tape narrators. During FY 1978, nearly 500 volunteers became braillists, braille proofreaders, or tape narrators through the NLS program. Thousands of volunteers throughout the United States produce books for libraries and readers. Approximately 3,000 Telephone Pioneers, senior or retired telephone industry workers, contribute their time and skills to the maintenance and repair of playback equipment. Volunteers repaired 75,000 talking book and cassette book machines in 1978.

Information Services

Questions on various aspects of blindness and physical handicaps may be sent to NLS or to any network library. This service is available without charge to individuals, organizations, and libraries.

Research and Development Projects

Research efforts are directed toward reducing costs for books and equipment, speeding delivery of reading materials to borrowers, and improving the quality of materials and services. Current research projects involve application of the most advanced computer technology to rapid and economical braille production; design of a single unit (called a combination machine) to play both cassette and disc recordings; and development of a braille output capability for the Kurzweil Machine, a reading aid that scans a printed page and automatically converts it to speech.

THE NETWORK OF LIBRARIES

Historical Perspective

When President Herbert Hoover signed into law the Pratt-Smoot Act, which created a national library service for the blind, he could not have anticipated the thriving network that it has become today. In 1931, the Library of Congress began operating this program under an annual appropriation of $100,000. Eighteen libraries were selected as regional distribution centers for braille books. With a budget of $34,130,000 in FY 1979, the Library of Congress utilized a network of 56 regional libraries (see Table 2) and 102 subregional libraries for the distribution of braille and recorded books and magazines (both discs and cassettes). The machines on which to play the recorded materials are distributed by these same libraries as well as 62 machine lending agencies, and the machines are repaired by 3,000 Telephone Pioneers.

The original regional libraries, chosen by the Library of Congress after consultation with the American Library Association and the American Foundation for the Blind, had actively responded to the reading needs of blind persons since the early 1900s. One major problem that the libraries faced was the lack of a standard form of embossed printing. In 1932, a common form of braille was adopted in all English-speaking countries. In 1933, library service to blind people was revolutionized when the American Foundation for the Blind developed the first talking book. This breakthrough, a long playing, unbreakable disc and a machine on which to play it, made books and magazines available to persons who had never learned to read braille.

TABLE 2 ORGANIZATIONAL LOCATION OF REGIONAL LIBRARIES
IN THE NATIONAL LIBRARY SERVICE NETWORK
(as of July 1979)

City and State	Organizational Location
Montgomery, AL	Alabama Public Library Service
Anchorage, AK	Alaska State Library, Department of Education
Phoenix, AZ	Arizona State Department of Library and Archives
Little Rock, AR	Arkansas Library Commission
Los Angeles, CA	Braille Institute of America, Inc.
Sacramento, CA	California State Library
Denver, CO	Colorado State Library, Department of Education
Hartford, CT	Connecticut State Library
Dover, DE	Delaware Division of Libraries, Department of Community Affairs
Washington, DC	D.C. Public Library
Daytona Beach, FL	Division of Blind Services, Department of Education
Atlanta, GA	Division of Public Libraries, Department of Education
Honolulu, HI	Office of Library Services, Department of Education

TABLE 2 ORGANIZATIONAL LOCATION OF REGIONAL LIBRARIES IN THE NATIONAL LIBRARY SERVICE NETWORK (cont.)

City and State	Organizational Location
Boise, ID	Idaho State Library
Chicago, IL	Chicago Public Library
Indianapolis, IN	Indiana State Library
Des Moines, IA	Iowa Commission for the Blind
Topeka, KS	Kansas State Library
Frankfort, KY	Kentucky Department of Library and Archives
Baton Rouge, LA	Louisiana State Library
Augusta, ME	Maine State Library
Watertown, MA	Perkins School for the Blind
Baltimore, MD	Maryland State Department of Education, Division of Library Development and Services
Lansing, MI	Michigan State Library Services, Department of Education
Wayne, MI	Wayne County Federated Library Systems
Faribault, MN	Office of Public Libraries, Department of Education
Jackson, MS	Mississippi Library Commission
St. Louis, MO	Missouri State Library
Helena, MT	Montana State Library
Lincoln, NE	Nebraska Library Commission
Carson City, NV	Nevada State Library
Concord, NH	New Hampshire State Library
Trenton, NJ	New Jersey State Library, Department of Education
Santa Fe, NM	New Mexico State Library
Albany, NY	New York State Library, Department of Education
New York, NY	New York Public Library
Raleigh, NC	North Carolina State Library, Department of Cultural Resources
Cleveland, OH	Cleveland Public Library
Cincinnati, OH	Public Library of Cincinnati and Hamilton County
Oklahoma City, OK	Oklahoma Department of Institutions, Social and Rehabilitative Services
Salem, OR	Oregon State Library
Philadelphia, PA	Free Library of Philadelphia
Pittsburgh, PA	Carnegie Library of Pittsburgh
San Juan, PR	Puerto Rico Department of Education, Public Library Services
Providence, RI	Rhode Island Department of State Library Services
Columbia, SC	South Carolina State Library
Pierre, SD	South Dakota State Library
Nashville, TN	Tennessee State Library and Archives
Austin, TX	Texas State Library
Salt Lake City, UT	Utah State Library Commission
Montpelier, VT	Vermont Department of Libraries
Richmond, VA	Virginia Commission for the Visually Handicapped
St. Thomas, VI	St. Thomas Bureau of Libraries, Department of Cultural Affairs
Seattle, WA	Seattle Public Library
Charleston, WV	West Virginia Library Commission
Milwaukee, WI	Milwaukee Public Library

Summary

Regional libraries in state libraries of library commissions	29
Regional libraries in state departments of education	11
Regional libraries in other state organizations	4
Regional libraries in local public library systems	10
Regional libraries in private organizations	1
Regional libraries in schools for the blind	1
Total	56

Growth was steady as changes in legislation opened up the service to more people. Initially, use was limited to adults who were blind. In 1952, blind children became eligible for the service. In 1966, service was extended to other physically impaired persons who could not use normal printed materials. The 1966 amendments to the Library Services and Construction Act made federal funds available to state library agencies for establishing or improving library services to blind and handicapped persons. The 1966 changes in the laws promoted a dramatic increase in the use of the service and expansion of the national network to its present size.

The Library of Congress has encouraged the development of "subregional libraries" since the early 1970s, when the Kansas and Illinois regional libraries placed collections of materials in local public libraries and arranged for them to serve all the readers in a specific geographical area. While many public libraries have acted as a referral source for the service, and some have had deposit collections of talking books, the subregional library acts as a branch of the regional library. This trend toward decentralization is consistent with the provision of the Rehabilitation Act of 1973, which specified that recipients of federal funds must take care not to isolate or concentrate handicapped persons in settings away from nonhandicapped program participants. Today there are 102 subregional libraries in 21 states.

Problems Facing Regional Libraries

Two problems plagued the regional libraries who were pioneers in the 1930s, and they continue to be matters of concern: financing and storage and distribution of materials. While the Library of Congress provides a basic collection of reading materials, it does not provide money for staffing and housing the collection or for producing additional materials. That is the responsibility of the state, local, or private agency that administers the service. Funding has come from all levels of the public and private sectors. Twenty states and territories used Library Services and Construction Act funds for at least a third of their operating budgets for regional libraries in FY 1978, while only nine were totally funded by state money. Many subregionals are dependent on LSCA money as well as local funds. Volunteers have played an active role in producing materials and supporting the day-to-day operation of the libraries.

Standards for the service, which could serve as a basis for realistic financing, were first developed in 1966 by a subcommittee of the Commission on Standards and Accreditation of Services for the Blind (COMSTAC) created by the American Foundation for the Blind. In 1978-1979, a subcommittee of the Association of State and Cooperative Library Agencies, American Library Association, prepared a new draft of standards to be published by the American Library Association in 1980. Even before these are published, plans are already underway for testing and updating them within the next five years.

Some of the problems resulting from the distribution of materials to thousands of people are being resolved through the computerization of record keeping and processing at 20 regional libraries. New technology, in the form of recorded books and magazines on cassettes and equipment for duplicating books as they are needed, has played an important part in reducing the amount of space required for storing the reading materials. The creation of multistate centers, where less used materials are kept, relieves regional libraries of the responsibility for keeping material for which there is limited use.

The Library of Congress is not unmindful of the problems. Since 1951, it has held national meetings of representatives of groups that provide the reading materials—

both the producers and the distributors. In the last 13 years such national meetings have been held biennially, with meetings of regional groups (Northeast, Southeast, Midlands, and Far West) scheduled on alternate years. These meetings inform the library network of proposed changes and solicit their input into the decision-making process at the national level. Other techniques that the Library of Congress uses to enhance communication with the network are special-purpose committees to advise it at the national level. Such committees are composed of representatives of the regional groups of librarians, consumers, and producers of materials and equipment.

NATIONAL LIBRARY OF MEDICINE

8600 Rockville Pike, Bethesda, MD 20209
301-496-6308

Robert B. Mehnert

Public Information Officer

The year 1979 marked the centenary of *Index Medicus*, the Library's monthly compilation of references to biomedical journal articles. The event, widely noted throughout the medical community, was celebrated at a special meeting of the Board of Regents of the National Library of Medicine (NLM) in May. The proceedings are in press.

Also noteworthy in 1979 was completion of the construction of the Lister Hill Center building. The center's specialized computer and communications laboratories, conference facilities, and audiovisual capabilities will allow the Library to develop new communications systems for the benefit of the entire health community.

A number of the Library's major programs will be moved into the new building in 1980. These will include the Lister Hill National Center for Biomedical Communications (NLM's research and development component), Specialized Information Services (responsible for the Library's Toxicology Information Program), NLM's National Medical Audiovisual Center (now located in Atlanta), and the Extramural Programs (NLM's grant assistance activity).

When the move to the new building is accomplished, all the divisions of the Library will be located at one site for the first time. This will greatly facilitate the integration of various NLM programs and will lead to improved library services to the health community. The new building will be formally dedicated in May 1980.

Another significant event in 1979 was the beginning of planning for MEDLARS III. MEDLARS (Medical Literature Analysis and Retrieval System) is NLM's computer-based bibliographic system, operational since 1964. MEDLARS III is intended to improve, extend, and integrate both internal operations (such as technical processing of books and journals) and external network responsibilities. In this latter category, MEDLARS III will provide new capabilities to assist the nation's health-science libraries in the creation of bibliographic records, retrieval of bibliographic and text

Note: The National Library of Medicine is a part of the National Institutes of Health, one of the six agencies that make up the Department of Health, Education, and Welfare's (HEW) U.S. Public Health Service.

information, access to national holdings and location information, and ordering and delivery of documents.

The three national libraries—Library of Congress, National Agricultural Library, and NLM—have begun a series of meetings to increase cooperation and resolve differences in their procedures. Principal topics at the meetings have been cooperation in building an on-line name authority file, cooperative acquisitions, and cataloging.

On the international scene, NLM and the World Health Organization (WHO) have entered into an experimental arrangement for one year under which the Library will provide MEDLARS computer searches and photocopies of journal articles to the developing countries of the WHO regions of Africa, Southeast Asia, the eastern Mediterranian, and the western Pacific.

There were several important appointments to the NLM staff in 1979: Kent A. Smith, deputy director; Charles N. Farmer, Jr., director of the Library's National Medical Audiovisual Center, Atlanta; Philip D. Amoruso, executive officer; Tamas Doszkocs, Ph.D., chief, Technical Services Division (Library Operations); A. D. Merritt, M.D., chief, Health Professions Applications Branch (Lister Hill Center); and Phyllis Mirsky, head, Reference Section (Library Operations).

LIBRARY OPERATIONS

The nationwide MEDLARS network through which the Library provides computerized on-line access to the biomedical literature continues to expand. Over 1.4 million searches were performed in 1979, a remarkable increase of almost 30 percent over last year. There are almost 20 data bases available for searching on the network, but the majority of searches are done on MEDLINE (MEDLARS on-line) and its backfiles. MEDLINE contains some 600,000 references to journal articles from the last two to three years; the backfiles go back to 1966.

The number of institutions in the United States that belong to the MEDLARS network rose to slightly over 1,000. The attempts by NLM and the Regional Medical Libraries to increase participation by hospitals and health care institutions have been successful; some 350 now are members of the network. A new foreign partner was added to increase MEDLARS' international scope: the Ministry of Health in Rome, Italy.

Figures at the end of the fiscal year (September 30, 1979) show that the Library's public services continue at the high levels of recent years. (See Table 1.) Assistance for onsite users reached new peaks in 1979—32,000 inquiries answered and 168,000 reader requests for literature. The demand for interlibrary loans continues strong, almost 250,000 requests being received in 1979. This figure may be compared with 180,000 requests as recently as five years ago. Throughput time for photocopied interlibrary loans has improved to the extent that 83 percent are filled within four days of receipt and up to 90 percent within ten days. These high levels have been maintained despite serious reductions in manpower experienced during the year.

Related to the planning for MEDLARS III, described earlier, was the Library's decision to put all cataloging information on-line and to close the card catalog. Cataloging records from 1965 to present (about 40 percent of the general collection) are already computerized and available on-line through the CATLINE data base. The project to convert 1801-1965 cataloging records to a computerized format was begun in late 1979.

Several new bibliographic works of interest to the scholarly and library community were published this year. They are available from the Government Printing Office. The first is *A Short Title Catalogue of Eighteenth Century Printed Books in*

TABLE 1 SELECTED NLM SERVICE STATISTICS, 1979*

Service	Number
Collection (book and nonbook)	2,574,140
Serial titles received	22,172
Titles cataloged	16,319
Articles indexed for MEDLARS	246,210
Circulation requests filled	333,148
For interlibrary loan	188,279
For readers	144,869
Reference requests	48,651
Computerized searches (all data bases)	1,403,655
On-line	1,005,379
Off-line	398,276

*For the year ending September 30, 1979.

the National Library of Medicine. It lists some 25,000 titles of books and journals in NLM's historical collections, between 30 and 40 percent of which are not listed in previous catalogs or in the *National Union Catalog.* In addition there were two new works dealing with serials: a two-volume *Index of NLM Serial Titles* and *Health Science Serials,* a quarterly microfiche publication.

The title "Editor, *Index Medicus,*" which was carried on early volumes of this publication, was revived in 1979. Clifford A. Bachrach has been appointed editor and is responsible for the quality of format and content of *Index Medicus.*

TOXICOLOGY INFORMATION PROGRAM

NLM's Toxicology Information Program has as its objectives to create computer-based toxicology data banks and to establish and operate toxicology information services for the scientific community. TOXLINE, the largest and most frequently used data base developed by the program, contains over 600,000 references (with an additional 400,000 references in a backfile). Almost 65,000 on-line searches were done by TOXLINE users in 1979, involving over 10,000 hours of computer connect time. Another large file, CHEMLINE (chemical dictionary on-line), almost doubled in size in 1979. It now contains more than 425,000 records for chemical substances known by some 800,000 different names. Two other files also grew in size this year: RTECS (Registry of Toxic Effects of Chemical Substances), which contains acute toxicity data for almost 37,000 substances, and the Toxicology Data Bank, which contains evaluated data extracted from textbooks and handbooks on over 1,500 substances. A new on-line service will be introduced in 1980, the Laboratory Animal Data Bank. This data base will provide comparative data on laboratory animals used as experiment controls in research.

In addition to the data bases in operation and under development, the Toxicology Information Program sponsors the Toxicology Information Response Center at the Oak Ridge National Laboratory in Tennessee. This center answers questions and performs specialized literature searches, for a fee. In 1979, the center began a new service to provide rapid (48-hour) literature searches for federal agencies confronted with a crisis related to a toxic substance.

The National Toxicology Program (NTP), an HEW-wide effort to strengthen the department's activities in testing chemicals, was established by the secretary in 1979. NLM's Toxicology Information Program provides basic information support for the NTP.

LISTER HILL NATIONAL CENTER
FOR BIOMEDICAL COMMUNICATIONS

The Lister Hill Center is the Library's research and development component. In 1979 the center phased out the experimental Public Health Service/Communications Technology Satellite nationwide network that had successfully demonstrated the potential of high-quality interactive television for health-sciences education and teleconferencing. During its 818 days of operation the network had logged 2,082.7 broadcast hours; over 16,000 people had appeared before the cameras. Summary evaluations of the network's experience have been published and are available from the National Technical Information Service.

The prototype hepatitis data base, described in the 1978 and 1979 editions of the *Bowker Annual*, has been successfully demonstrated and has led to the establishment of a "Knowledge Base Program" within the center. A Knowledge Base is one in which information is selected, reviewed, compacted, and synthesized to form a package of "knowledge" in a subject for use by medical practitioners. These packages present a mass of useful information and are designed to improve the practitioner's ability to solve day-to-day problems of diagnosis, prognosis, and treatment of illness. The Hepatitis Knowledge Base is being field-tested at nine major medical centers and biomedical libraries. Its feasibility demonstrated, the Lister Hill Center is now extending the concept with two additional subjects—peptic ulcer and human genetics.

The center is continuing to investigate the application of optical videodisc technology to biomedical communication. In addition to its obvious uses related to graphics —computer-based education, on-line medical encyclopedias, etc.—there is an exciting potential for encoding textual information and storing up to 5 billion characters per side on a videodisc. It would thus be possible to store all of MEDLINE (about 3 million citations) on one side of one disc. The discs could be duplicated at less than $10 each in quantities of 1,000. The Lister Hill Center presently has two videodisc players, and computer protocols are being developed to allow storage and retrieval of text rather than video information.

NATIONAL MEDICAL AUDIOVISUAL CENTER

The National Medical Audiovisual Center (NMAC) is the component of NLM responsible for planning and administering a national program to improve the quality and use of audiovisual learning materials in health professional education. Located in Atlanta, Georgia, the center will be moving in March 1980 to the new Lister Hill Center building in Bethesda, Maryland.

The center completed 101 audiovisual productions in 1979, including videotape and film programs and slide/audiotape units. Because moving to the new building will require the dismantling, shipping, and reinstallation of much equipment, audiovisual production will be disrupted for several months in 1980. Similarly, the film and videotape loan program is being temporarily suspended so that the units may be recovered, repaired, packed, and shipped. Over 45,000 motion pictures and videotapes were lent to health-science institutions in the year ending September 30, 1979.

A wide range of research and evaluation projects were completed or carried forward in 1979 by NMAC. Included were studies concerned with analyzing and validating instructional design and audiovisual development models, cost effective techniques in medical photography, and experimental visual excerpts for existing audiovisual materials.

Nine new lesson plans are being developed for use in NMAC's workshop and training programs. The regional training centers supported by NMAC continue to be popular with those involved in health-science education; 766 participants attended the 35 workshops conducted in 1979.

GRANT PROGRAMS

Under the Medical Library Assistance Act, NLM administers grants for improving biomedical library resources; research in information sciences related to health; training to integrate clinical practice, health research, and education with appropriate computerized techniques; and support of biomedical scientific publications. In fiscal year 1979 the Library, through its Extramural Programs, awarded 154 grants and 9 Regional Medical Library contracts totaling $8,986,000.

The Regional Medical Library (RML) Program, funded under contract by the Extramural Program, is a nationwide network of 11 Regional Medical Libraries and more than 100 Resource Libraries coordinated by NLM. Beginning this year, NLM will make renewal of the RML contracts competitive. Three Regional Medical Library contracts were open to competitive bidding in 1979, the results to be announced early in 1980. Contracts for the remaining regions will be open to proposals in 1980 and 1981.

This year NLM funded library consortia representing 150 local health institutions, primarily hospitals. Support for consortia, begun in 1977, is aimed at helping groups of cooperating health institutions so that coordinated information services can be developed in large geographic areas. In just three years NLM has achieved its five-year goal to support 250 new institutions. In the entire Regional Medical Library network there are an estimated 2 million interlibrary loan transactions each year.

Three new grant programs related to research in biomedical communications were begun in 1979. New Investigator Awards provide funding for researchers who are, for the first time, seeking support for research projects of their own design. Research Career Development Awards, on the other hand, support more established researchers who have shown outstanding potential for contributions to health-related information science. The third new program supports studies of computer applications in health-science communication.

TECHNICAL INFORMATION SYSTEMS/NATIONAL AGRICULTURAL LIBRARY

U.S. Dept. of Agriculture
Beltsville, MD 20705
301-344-3778

Eugene M. Farkas

Chief, Educational Resources Division

The acute national need to develop alternate sources of energy in the new decade led to the publication of an energy research directory and a companion bibliography by Technical Information Systems/National Agricultural Library (TIS/NAL) in 1979.

Solar Energy and Non-Fossil Fuel Research: A Directory of Projects Related to Agriculture, 1976-79, prepared by TIS in response to recent federal legislation, includes 814 federal, state, private, and foreign projects. It is the first in a series of planned energy research compilations with most projects accessible through the TIS Current Research Information System (CRIS) data base. The bibliography on the subject was *Energy for Agriculture: A Computerized Retrieval System* compiled by B. A. Stout and C. A. Myers of the Agriculture Engineering Department, Michigan State University.

These two volumes symbolize the central role in society's decision-making processes that libraries and their modern information systems are destined to play in the years ahead. The books—one produced federally and the other prepared by a state university—also illustrate the close cooperation at all levels essential to effective technical information programs.

NEW STRUCTURE

Technical Information Systems was created two years ago as part of the Science and Education Administration (SEA), U.S. Department of Agriculture. Three divisions have been set up under a new TIS functional structure. The Library Operations Division administers the NAL; the Information Systems Division is responsible for the numerous computer systems necessary to large-scale, modern technical information operations; and Educational Resources Division reaches out to new users both inside and outside the agricultural community, making them aware of the technical information services available, and coordinating delivery of these services by TIS and cooperating institutions.

The major accomplishments of SEA/TIS in 1979 involved new initiatives, expansion of existing resources and services, and modernization of established activities.

NATIONAL MARKET STUDY

In support of its outreach efforts, TIS launched an extended nationwide marketing study, "Agricultural Information Users and Their Needs." The study, due to be completed by the end of 1980, is expected to provide a comprehensive assessment of the need for scientific and technical information in both the public and private sectors.

The Food and Nutrition Information Center (FNIC) met with representatives from six state educational agencies to plan ways by which FNIC could work more effectively with states in disseminating nutrition education information and materials. The number of persons served by the center increased 66 percent over 1978 to a total of 11,467. Lending requests went up 36 percent, including almost 10,000 loans of audiovisual items. A new catalog, *Audiovisual Resources in Food and Nutrition*, was published with increased emphasis placed on the human nutrition research and education areas.

SERVICE TO STATES

The Current Awareness Literature Service (CALS), a computer-based literature search system, was expanded to serve a number of new groups, including state agricultural experiment stations and state extension specialists. CALS presently has more than 4,000 federal and 1,000 state researcher profiles. FAMULUS, a personal documentation system for research workers, has been installed at the University of California's Riverside Computer Center, making it possible for local scientists to access their files directly.

An electronic mail network designed to provide rapid, effective communication between and among the states and SEA is being pilot-tested in 22 states in cooperation with the extension service. TIS helped plan and conduct four regional agriculture computer workshops attended by 275 extension specialists in Pittsburgh, Pennsylvania, Kansas City, Missouri, Atlanta, Georgia, and Reno, Nevada.

AGRICOLA DATA BASE

The TIS bibliographic data base (AGRICOLA), which is commercially available through on-line vendors, grew by 140,000 citations to journal articles and monographs. The AGRICOLA file, beginning with 1970, now has grown to 1.4 million citations, and is the largest agricultural bibliographic compilation in machine-readable form in the world. At the present time, this file is undergoing a major conversion to a new bibliographic format known as SAMANTHA, which has extensive publishing and compilation capabilities, and is MARC compatible.

The Regional Document Delivery System, a cooperative effort with land-grant libraries to get literature to USDA field personnel, was expanded from 25 to 27 states plus Puerto Rico. The regional structure was changed from five to six for greater equalization of requests received and for efficiency of operation. Regional centers now are the land-grant libraries in the states of California (Davis), Georgia, Iowa, Minnesota, Texas, and Washington.

The microfilming of land-grant agricultural publications from the inception of the state institutions through 1969 has been completed for 23 states in the South, Southwest, and New England. This program, in its seventh year, is jointly funded and organized by TIS in conjunction with the land-grant libraries. Eight additional states in the Great Plains and Mountain areas were in the process of filming in 1979.

NEW PUBLICATIONS SERIES

A new publication series, *Bibliographies and Literature of Agriculture (BLA)*, was established by the Department of Agriculture to provide a centralized source for bibliographic and related information for the department. All bibliographic manuscripts must be approved by the library before issuance. Publications prepared by TIS/NAL and available through USDA include the *Guide to Manuscripts in the National Agricultural Library*; *Aquaculture and Hydroponics, A Bibliography*; *Sorghums and Millets Bibliography, April 1976–August 1978*; *Agriculture of the American Indian, A Selected Bibliography*; *International Symposium on Animal Health and Disease Data Banks, Dec. 4–5, 1978—Proceedings*; *AGRICOLA Users Guide*; *TIS Guide to Services*; and three volumes of the *Inventory of Agricultural Research (CRIS)*.

In cooperation with USDA's Animal and Plant Health Inspection Service, the first International Symposium on Animal Health and Disease Data Banks was held with 120 persons attending from 15 countries. A *Proceedings* volume offers the first major summarization of the state of the art and problems in animal health information gathering and use.

Fifty-nine separate tours of TIS operations in the NAL building were conducted for 295 visitors, including 139 from foreign countries. Tours and briefings were arranged for the Library of Congress, the National Technical Information Service, Georgetown University, university graduate library schools, National Library of Medicine, U.S. State Department, USDA Graduate School, and other institutions.

TIS/NAL OFFICERS

Richard A. Farley, deputy director for technical information systems, science and education administration; Samuel T. Waters, associate deputy director; Chester E. Swank, liaison officer for extension; Wallace C. Olsen, chief, Library Operations Division; John M. Myers, chief, Information Systems Division; Eugene M. Farkas, Chief, Educational Resources Division.

National Associations

AMERICAN BOOKSELLERS ASSOCIATION

122 E. 42 St., New York, NY 10017
212-867-9060

G. Roysce Smith
Executive Director

The American Booksellers Association (ABA), Inc., was organized in 1900 to bring together in one organization, for their mutual benefit, bookstores of all sizes and philosophies. On December 31, 1979, the association recorded 4,589 main stores and 1,276 branch stores as regular members. Publishers, wholesalers, sidelines manufacturers, and suppliers of goods and services are accepted as associate members, of which there are 728 recorded.

The ABA achieves its purpose in many ways—through publications, workshops, and seminars, liaison with other segments of the industry, surveys and studies, national and regional meetings, and other related activities. It is governed by an elected board of four officers, 16 directors, and the immediate past president. Current officers, who will serve through June 8, 1980, are as follows: president, Charles S. Haslam, Haslam's Book Store, St. Petersburg, Florida; vice-president, Ethel Stevenson, Macy's California, San Francisco, California; treasurer, Adrien (Bud) Lorentz, Peninsula Book Shop, Palo Alto, California; and secretary, J. C. Boyd, Boyd's Lovelace Book Store, Wichita Falls, Texas.

The board employs a staff of 25, including G. Roysce Smith, executive director; Robert D. Hale, associate executive director; and Victoria M. Stanley, assistant executive director.

PUBLICATIONS

The ABA Book Buyer's Handbook, revised annually, lists publishers' addresses, key personnel, and the terms under which publishers do business with booksellers, e.g., discounts, co-op ad policies, and returns policies. It also contains a useful collection of supplementary information in its 672 pages. Edited by Mary Ann Tennenhouse, it is an indispensable bookselling tool. It is available *only* to ABA bookseller members. A copy of each of ABA's other publications is sent free to all bookseller and associate members and they are available to nonmembers at established rates.

American Bookseller, a monthly magazine, began publication in September 1977 after several decades of gestation. It had long been felt that existing publications did not address themselves specifically or urgently enough to the day-to-day challenges and problems of retail bookselling. Specialized bibliographies have been a regular feature. Under the editorship of Ann S. Haslam, the magazine continues to be provocative and helpful.

ABA Newswire, a weekly publication first issued in February 1973, lists advance information on author tours, book reviews, and advertising and promotion. The author listings include lectures as well as television, radio, and in-store appearances. Librarians and booksellers find this a valuable aid in ensuring that they have books on hand when demand is greatest. Also included are brief reports of the latest information on matters of vital interest to retail booksellers. Allen Kimbrell is *Newswire*'s editor.

The *ABA Basic Book List* is issued annually. A highly selective list of titles chosen by a committee of booksellers from actual sales records of member stores, it is intended as a guide for the neophyte bookseller or the established bookseller who may want to review what others find salable. It is also edited by Mary Ann Tennenhouse, as is the biennial *ABA Sidelines Directory*, which contains brief articles by booksellers about sidelines and lists sources for both sidelines and store supplies and fixtures.

A Manual on Bookselling, a comprehensive textbook about establishing and maintaining a bookstore, has over 30,000 copies in print since the revised edition was published in 1974. A copy is supplied free by ABA to each member store, and a trade edition for resale is published by Harmony Books, an imprint of Crown Publishers. A second revised edition will be published in the summer of 1980, and it is planned that a Spanish-language edition will follow shortly.

WORKSHOPS AND SEMINARS

A major function of ABA is promoting professional competence through continuing bookseller education. While part of this goal can be attained through publications and through national and regional meetings, ABA is committed to a series of highly successful training sessions, which are more intensive and which provide input and participation by those attending. The Booksellers School, now in its fifteenth year, is sponsored jointly by ABA and the National Association of College Stores (NACS). Nearly 5,500 established and aspiring booksellers have attended the school. Six schools are scheduled for 1980. Four sessions are basic bookselling and two are prospective bookselling. The basic schools are set for Savannah, Georgia (February); Portland, Oregon (March); Kansas City, Missouri (April); and Salt Lake City, Utah (August). Prospective schools will be held in Southfield, Michigan (March), and Denver, Colorado (August). Enrollment is limited to 80 at each four-day school.

One-day workshops in specialized subjects will be held in Rochester, New York (general); Stockbridge, Massachusetts (general); Washington, D.C. (children's books); Richmond, Virginia (general); Los Angeles (children's books); and Seattle (children's books).

BOOK PROMOTION

The long-contemplated Give-a-Book-Certificate program, a joint project of ABA and NACS, got off the drawing boards in November 1978 and into the stores. By the end of 1979, 700 stores were participating in this program, which allows customers to buy a gift certificate in one store and redeem it in any participating store in the country. In order to focus nationwide attention on the program, this year saw the design of a new logo, new window decals and streamers, headers for the display racks and production of 800 taped radio interviews, news releases for 900 newspapers, and camera-ready ad mats for use by publishers and booksellers.

ABA joined with other national organizations within the industry to support the American Book Awards, designed to replace the National Book Awards.

CONVENTIONS AND REGIONAL MEETINGS

ABA participated in regional meetings with regional bookselling associations in Philadelphia, New Orleans, and Hyannis during the fall.

The annual national ABA Convention and Trade Exhibit was held in Los Angeles, May 26–29, 1979. Some 18,000 people attended; and 800 exhibitors filled 1,247 exhibits, 7 percent more exhibit space than was used in 1978 in Atlanta. International interest in the meeting continued to rise.

Authors addressing the convention were Arnold Lobel, David Macaulay, Ellen Raskin, Alvin Toffler, Daniel Boorstin, Barbara Sher, James Baldwin, Ray Bradbury, Steve Martin, Daniel Curzon, Adele Scheele, Maya Angelou, Gerald Ford, Michael Korda, Robin Cook, Margot Zemach, and George T. Simon. Another 130 authors met booksellers in the autograph areas and at parties.

The 1980 convention will be held in Chicago, June 7–10.

FINANCIAL CRISIS IN BOOKSELLING

ABA, along with the Postal Committee of the Association of American Publishers, continued the battle to convince the Postal Rate Commission and Congress to review the postage rate increases that went into effect in 1978 and 1979. Indeed, coping with the insensitive increases continued to be the single most urgent factor affecting the survival of retail bookselling in the United States. Book post rates had increased 350 percent since 1970, with booksellers reporting incoming transportation as high as 5 to 8 percent, as opposed to 3.1 percent in 1977.

At the ABA annual membership meeting, held during the Los Angeles convention, a petition devised by the Southern California Booksellers Association was circulated for signing and was mailed to all ABA members immediately following the convention, asking that they gather signatures from their customers. In all, 60,600 signatures were collected and copies were sent to President Jimmy Carter and to key members of Congress along with a letter urging a rollback to 1975 rates.

Booksellers were urged to write to their congressmen, citing statistics from their own experience and asking for their support of the Senate's bill, S. 1096, and the House bill, H.R. 79. In addition, booksellers were to ask for a thorough and realistic reappraisal of the Postal Reorganization Act of 1970. As 1979 came to a close, H.R. 79 resoundingly passed the House of Representatives. S. 1096 was not reported out of the Senate committee.

On another front, not totally unrelated to the postal rate problem, the members present at the Los Angeles annual meeting drafted a resolution and mandated that it be sent to the top management of the publishing houses. Publishers were ". . . encouraged to take any reasonable steps necessary to preserve the existence of the independent bookstore in America." Specifically, publishers were asked to rethink their terms of sale to small and medium-sized firms; and to escalate their efforts to consolidate back orders and limit the number of publication dates per month, thereby, lessening the inbound shipping costs to booksellers. At the close of the year, no moves toward the solution of these problems seemed forthcoming, other than some tentative attempts at consolidation.

AMERICAN LIBRARY ASSOCIATION

50 E. Huron St., Chicago, IL 60611
312-944-6780

Thomas J. Galvin
President

International cooperation, the White House Conference on Library and Information Services, and continuing education were the focus of many of the American Library Association's (ALA's) activities in 1979. ALA grew increasingly involved in jointly sponsored programs with foreign countries and played host to visitors from many nations. ALA Executive Director Robert Wedgeworth traveled to Australia to deliver the keynote address at the Twentieth Biennial Conference of the Library Association of Australia, August 26-29, at the National University of Canberra. Wedgeworth was greeted by a capacity audience of over 3,000 librarians. He visited major cities throughout the continent and found Australians most impressed with ALA's public relations and legislative activities.

ALA Past President Russell Shank, President-Elect Peggy Sullivan, and Councilor Alice Ihrig went to China, September 10-30, as part of a 12-member library delegation invited by National Library of Beijing Director Liu Jiping. Although the ALA delegation was impressed by the strength of the library collections, they found the librarians were using techniques from 30 years ago.

The first Soviet-American Library Seminar, jointly sponsored by the American Library Association, the Library of Congress, and the U.S. International Communication Agency, was held in Washington, D.C., May 4-6. The seminar's theme, "Library Service for an Informed Society: Planning for Library Services, Library Education, Library Statistics, and Information Needs and Uses in the Soviet Union," attracted more than 100 persons. Following the seminar, seven visiting Soviet librarians toured libraries and other institutions in Columbus, Ohio, Albany, New York, New York City, and ALA headquarters in Chicago.

President Thomas J. Galvin served as ALA's voting delegate at the Forty-fifth IFLA Council Meeting held August 1979 in Copenhagen, Denmark. Over 1,000 delegates from 61 countries attended the conference, where former ALA President Jean Lowrie was elected to the executive board of the International Federation of Library Associations and Institutions (IFLA). Lowrie, current chairperson of the International Relations Committee and director of the Western Michigan (Kalamazoo) University School of Librarianship, is the only executive board member from the western hemisphere. ALA, through the efforts of International Relations Committee (IRC) Officer Jane Wilson, was active in organizing the U.S. institutional members' proxy vote at this meeting, and during the year, the IRC sponsored two meetings of the U.S. institutional members of IFLA.

At the 1979 ALA annual conference in Dallas, the International Relations Round Table sponsored a program on "Professional Work at the International Level," which featured presentations on many aspects of IFLA's professional activities, including the Office for Universal Bibliographic Control and the International Board of Books for Young People. A second IRC-sponsored international relations policy statement, "Guidelines for Selection of Representatives to International Conferences, Meetings and Assignments," was approved by the ALA Council in June.

After 22 years of anticipation and hard work, the White House Conference on Library and Information Services was held November 15–19, 1979, in Washington, D.C. There, 675 official delegates met to develop recommendations on the nation's libraries and information centers and their use by the public. President Thomas J. Galvin represented ALA as its at-large delegate. ALA had played a crucial role in obtaining necessary presidential approval and congressional funding for the conference to take place. Of the many individuals who worked to obtain this support, Eileen Cooke, associate executive director of ALA and director of its Washington office, deserves much of the credit.

Early in the year, ALA distributed *A Perspective on Libraries* to White House Conference delegates. This booklet, prepared particularly for the delegates by the Public Information Office, is a summary of the 1978 Gallup Study on Reading and Library Usage, funded by the Baker & Taylor Company.

Six weeks before the conference, ALA distributed a special information packet to delegates that included "Information and the American Citizen," a statement of ALA's goals for consideration at the White House Conference, along with a number of position statements prepared by ALA units.

ALA sent 19 volunteer staff members to the conference to work in a variety of capacities from group facilitators to clerical assistants. ALA also hosted a reception at the Library of Congress in honor of the delegates. Baker & Taylor Company and the Xerox Publishing Group helped support the gala celebration.

As a follow-up to the White House Conference, ALA will sponsor a special invitational colloquium on America's information needs for the next decade in conjunction with the association's June 1980 New York annual conference. Twenty-five leaders from government, education, industry, communications, publishing, librarianship, and the information professions will meet, under the leadership of former Federal Communications Commission chair, Newton N. Minow, to address the theme "An Information Agenda for the 1980's." The colloquium reflects ALA's continuing concern for the identification and discussion of national issues relating to information and public policy.

A $200,000 grant from the National Endowment for the Humanities made it possible for the association to demonstrate its strong commitment to continuing education. The grant funded a special project to demonstrate the effectiveness of public library programming using Courses by Newspaper. The project continues through the fall of 1980.

In December 1979, with grant support from the Kellogg Foundation, some 60 ALA members and staff participated in a three-day policy development forum, held in Madison, Wisconsin, to review the current state of continuing education for librarianship and to define an optimal role for the association in continuing education. Forum participants recommended that ALA begin immediately to design, develop, communicate, implement, and continuously evaluate a national comprehensive long-range plan for continuing education to improve the quality of library service, and that staffing be expanded in this area at ALA headquarters.

ALA personal membership grew in 1979 by almost 1,000, bringing the total number of association members to 35,798, a healthy increase over last year. Organizational membership decreased slightly from 3,241 in 1978 to 3,075 in 1979. The Association of College and Research Libraries remained the largest ALA division with 8,904 members, and the Government Documents Round Table increased its membership by almost 1,000 for a total of 1,468, making it the largest round table in ALA.

The 1979 annual conference, ALA's ninety-eighth, was held June 23–29, in

Dallas. The conference attracted 10,650 registrants who attended 1,906 meetings. There were 2,700 registered exhibitors and 683 booths. The 1979 conference theme, "The Library in American Society," was highlighted by a number of notable speakers, including Nobel Laureate Isaac Bashevis Singer, economist John Kenneth Galbraith, author James Michener, and author/commentator Shana Alexander. Lowell A. Martin was named an honorary member of the association.

The midwinter meeting, held January 7-12 in Washington, D.C., had a total registration of 4,243, an all-time attendance record for an ALA midwinter meeting. The total includes 839 exhibitors.

ALA completed FY 1979 with revenues and expenditures as budgeted. In order to maintain a balanced budget in 1980, the membership voted to increase personal members' dues by $15, from $35 to $50. Nonsalaried librarians' dues increased from $10 to $15, foreign members' dues increased $20 to $30, and student dues remained at $10. This was the first dues increase since 1970. During its spring meeting, the ALA executive board approved the use of credit cards for dues payment.

PUBLISHING SERVICES

In 1979, ALA Publishing Services published 34 ALA books and accepted four more for distribution. Best-sellers included the *Anglo-American Cataloging Rules*, 2nd ed.; the *ALA Year Book 1979; Instruction in School Media Center Use; Book Bait*, 3rd ed.; *Books that Changed the World;* and *Handbook for Storytellers*. Among new basic expositions are *From Press to People*, a primer of U.S. government documents management and use, and *Children's Faces Looking Up*, a handbook for long-term story programs. At the end of the year, the Canadian Library Association delivered *Nonbook Materials* for ALA distribution. It promises to become a popular textbook in teaching the cataloging of nonbook materials.

Videocassettes have been added to materials offered by ALA Publishing Services. Programs include the "ALA Satellite Seminar on Copyright," produced in collaboration with the Maryland Center for Public Broadcasting; "Creative Storytelling Techniques," related to the successful *Handbook for Storytellers;* and a four-part program entitled "An Introduction to the *Anglo-American Cataloging Rules*, Second Edition," produced by the Resources and Technical Services Division.

Two new appointments were made in the publishing program during 1979. Arthur Plotnik, editor of *American Libraries* since 1975, took on additional responsibilities as editorial development director for general ALA publishing programs. Joel Lee, ALA headquarters librarian since 1977, assumed new duties as associate editorial development officer.

American Libraries, ALA's monthly news magazine, completed its tenth year in its magazine format (previously titled *ALA Bulletin*) with a circulation of 39,000, the largest of any general library periodical. The magazine's "Leads" section, the profession's largest monthly guide to library jobs, grew by 10 percent and will include a new section, beginning in January 1980, called "Consultants Clearinghouse." Janice Warren Grey became the new "Leads" editor.

A November article on newspaper indexing by staff writer Susan Cherry initiated a new policy to publish major staff-written reports. A special June issue, devoted to 10 years of change in the profession, explored major social changes in the library world and reviewed technological advances during the decade. Other articles included special reports on the effects of Proposition 13 in California, user studies, and major cataloging issues. The October issue featured a preview of the White House Conference on

Library and Information Services with a focus on the people involved. The magazine also initiated new feature profiles of ALA units and published Round V of the Prize Articles Competition, sponsored by the J. Morris Jones-Bailey K. Howard-World Book Encyclopedia-ALA Goal Awards.

Library Technology Reports (LTR), the association's testing service that issues special reports to subscribers six times a year, featured a report on circulation control systems—a segment of library technology that LTR has monitored for more than a decade—in the January–February issue. Microfiche reader-printers were covered in the March–April issue. Nancy H. Knight reconsidered theft detection systems in the May–June issue and by 1979, LTR had published four surveys on such systems.

WOMEN'S ISSUES

The Equal Rights Amendment was the focus of much ALA activity and some controversy in 1979. In the second largest mail ballot in ALA history, 15,434 out of 35,297 members cast ballots on whether the executive board should reaffirm the ALA contract with the Palmer House for the association's 1980 midwinter meeting in Chicago. Sixty-two percent voted to reaffirm the contract. It had been feared that the Palmer House might sue ALA after the association cancelled its 1979 midwinter meeting. However, the hotel wrote last October that in light of the association's reconfirmation of the Palmer House for midwinter 1980, the hotel would not seek redress for cancellation of the 1979 meeting.

ALA reaffirmed its support of the ERA through the formation of a nine-member ERA task force charged with assisting ALA chapters in their efforts to secure passage of ERA in their states. During the annual conference in Dallas, Council voted to provide $10,000 to support local action in ALA state chapters on behalf of ERA ratification. The task force has sent a questionnaire to all chapters to survey the status of ERA in each state and produced a brochure, *ALA's for ERA*, that explains why ALA is for ERA. Several hundred brochures have already been distributed to state library agencies and chapters, as well as to ALA councilors and executive board members. The task force's midwinter meeting activities will include a general information session on what ALA and other agencies are doing to support ERA. The task force is also planning a program for the 1980 annual conference in New York that will serve as a fund raiser for ERA and a kickoff for efforts in the states in 1980 and 1981.

INTELLECTUAL FREEDOM

The Office for Intellectual Freedom's (OIF's) 1979 activities included a special celebration of the Freedom to Read Foundation's (FTRF's) tenth anniversary. FTRF President Kathleen Molz reviewed the foundation's progress over the past 10 years and attorney Robert O'Neil and author Jessica Mitford gave their prognosis for the First Amendment for the next decade. O'Neil praised decisions giving new protection to commercial speech, speech of public employees, and symbolic speech. He said that the progress in the law had been striking in the case of litigation in the lower courts over censorship of school libraries. Mitford focused on the difficulties of muckraking authors and warned that the shrinking number of publishers will pose problems for "subversive" authors.

Pressures on schools and libraries to censor library collections continued to grow. The OIF renewed its efforts with workshops in Dallas and Atlanta presented by the Academic Freedom Group. The OIF also mailed a special brochure designed to address the problem, "Censorship in the Schools, What Is It, How Do You Cope," to 35,000 school librarians.

In 1979, the FTRF authorized grants to assist Jean Layton to file suit in U.S. District Court to regain her job. Layton, who had worked at the Davis County (Utah) Library for 20 years, and been director for the past nine, refused to comply with a board member's request to remove a book from her libraries. A dispute ensued and Layton was subsequently fired.

ALA and the New York Library Association filed an amicus brief in the U.S. Court of Appeals, Second Circuit, in *Pico* vs. *Board of Education*. This case challenges the right of the Island Trees school board to remove books from the district's libraries.

The Intellectual Freedom Committee devoted much of its time in 1979 to preparing a revision of the "Library Bill of Rights," to be presented to the ALA Council at the 1980 midwinter meeting for approval.

ACCREDITATION

The Committee on Accreditation began revisiting programs holding accredited status under the "Standards for Accreditation, 1972," and at the same time has been considering applications received from programs not currently accredited under the 1972 standards. There are now 67 programs of graduate library education accredited by the ALA, 60 in the United States and 7 in Canada.

DIVISIONS

American Association of School Librarians (AASL)

AASL has spent much of the year planning for its first national conference, scheduled for September 1980. The conference, "'80 and Beyond," will examine issues and trends facing school librarianship during the next decade. Program "strands" dealing with legislation and funding, networking and resource sharing, education and accountability, automation and information, public relations and progress, and freedom and access will be addressed in forums, theme sessions, and minisessions.

AASL has been identified by the National Institute of Education (NIE) as the agency responsible for selecting 16 building-level library media specialists to participate as interns in three dissemination workshops to be held at NIE during 1980.

Four titles are now available in the AASL series of 12 monographs "School Media Centers: Focus on Issues and Trends." The series is designed to examine the problems and opportunities that define the professional functions of the media specialist. Current titles include *Cultural Pluralism and Children's Media*, *Projecting a Positive Image through Public Relations*, *The Teaching Role of the School Media Specialist*, and *A Place for Caring and Celebration*.

AASL has also formed a new Promotion and Recognition of Secondary School Media Programs Committee. The committee will present a proposal at ALA midwinter 1980 to review the possibilities for identifying exemplary programs on the secondary level either through an award or other means of recognition.

American Library Trustee Association (ALTA)

At the 1979 ALA annual conference, ALTA conducted trustee workshops and programs on these priority topics: Nonthreatening Networks, Breaking Architectural Barriers, Should I Automate, Community Analysis, Innovative Public Relations, and

Innovative Library Financing. ALTA also sponsored an autograph party to celebrate the newly revised edition of *The Library Trustee* by Virginia Young.

ALTA's major publication of 1979 was *Securing a New Library Director* by Andrew Geddes and James A. Hess.

Association of College and Research Libraries (ACRL)

ACRL's first national conference (Boston 1978) met with such success that the division sought and received approval for a second conference, scheduled for 1981 in Minneapolis.

ACRL's interest in providing more continuing education opportunities has resulted in the formation of a new continuing education office and the appointment of a continuing education program officer.

The division devoted much of its time in 1979 to revising its constitution and bylaws and establishing three new chapters, bringing the total number of ACRL chapters to 21.

Association for Library Service to Children (ALSC)

A delegation of four ALSC members arrived in the Soviet Union on January 23, 1979, for an 18-day observation tour of library service to children in the USSR. A slide presentation of the tour was given at the ALA annual conference.

ALSC also cosponsored a major international symposium on "Books and Broadcasting for Children," a special program for the International Year of the Child. The program involved children's literature and television specialists from 30 nations and was a joint project of ALSC, WPBT-TV (Miami, Florida), and the International Communications Agency.

Association of Specialized and Cooperative Library Agencies (ASCLA)

The merger of the Association of State Library Agencies and the Health and Rehabilitative Library Services Division has resulted in a new division with a long list of accomplishments for the year.

Two grants totaling $110,000 from the U.S. Office of Education were used to underwrite a two-part project designed to improve jail library services. The first part of the project includes a three-day institute, scheduled for March 10–12, 1980, in Texas. The institute will train 100 participants—library and jail staff—in improving jail library services. The participants will then return to their respective states to share the institute information.

The second part of the project will be the development of curriculum material containing planning and implementation of jail library service information.

ASCLA publications in 1979 included the biennial *State Library Agencies: A Survey Project Report*, an important reference tool for anyone interested in state library agency activities, funding, etc. In April, ASCLA published *Equal Access: A Manual of Procedures for Initiating a Public Library Home Service Program*. This is a step-by-step booklet on providing library service to shut-ins. *Standards of Services for the Library of Congress Network of Libraries for the Blind and Physically Handicapped* received final approval and was published. In addition, the State Library Agency Section conducted and published a survey of the administration of LSCA funds/projects within state library agencies.

The ASCLA board adopted a statement outlining the responsibilities of libraries in distributing and providing health care information.

Library Administration and Management Association (LAMA)

LAMA appointed Roger Parent its new full-time executive secretary. Parent replaces Donald Hammer, who had served as part-time executive secretary for both LAMA and the Library and Information Technology Association.

During the ALA annual conference in Dallas, a new organization, Friends of Libraries U.S.A., was formed. This new group will be devoted to the formation and support of friends of library groups across the country. It is estimated that there are already 2,000 Friends of Library groups with roughly half a million members.

Other conference activities included a two-day workshop on "Sexism: Monitor Awareness—Review Thinking Sessions." The workshop was designed to make men and women more aware of the nature, causes, and consequences of sex role stereotyping as well as to increase sensitivity to the way in which sexism affects libraries and the people who use them. This is the second workshop sponsored by the newly formed Committee on Sexism and Racism Awareness. The committee is interested in raising the consciousness of library personnel from all types of libraries.

LAMA's new Statistics Section held its first meeting at the annual conference where more than 400 persons attended its program "Recent Studies in Measurement for Better Decisions and Service in Public Libraries."

LAMA's 1979 publications include The Personnel Administration Section's *The Personnel Performance Appraisal;* the third edition of *Certification of Public Libraries in the United States; Guidelines for Writing an Effective Resume; Automated Circulation: A Selected Annotated Bibliography;* and *The Collection and Use of Public Library Statistics by State Agencies: A Compilation of Forms,* a 654-page volume that includes how and what statistics are collected by each of the 50 state library agencies, and how the statistics are used.

Library Information and Technology (LITA)

LITA Executive Secretary Donald Hammer became the division's full-time program officer this year. LITA began to publish a newsletter during 1979, and other new developments include the appointment of the International Mechanization and Consultation Committee, an ad hoc group that will cooperate with other international organizations in the library and information fields. The Video Cable Communications Section appointed regional representatives who are on call for those in their region needing advice, information, or consultation on video in libraries. A list of these representatives is contained in a newly developed information packet on video and libraries that includes the 1977 Survey on Library Video Resources, available from the LITA office. The division also sponsored four institutes in different parts of the country on topics from automated acquisitions to closing the catalog.

Public Library Association (PLA)

After years of research and testing, PLA is ready to publish "A Planning Process for Public Libraries," a reworking of the entire standards concept that will allow libraries to respond to the individual needs of their communities. PLA has been working on this ambitious and far-reaching project with a grant from the U.S. Office of Education. A testing phase, with three libraries serving as pilot projects, was completed this year. The "Planning Process" will be available in spring 1980.

PLA's conference programs in 1979 focused on activities including budgeting for small and medium-sized libraries, alternative education programs, the role of the library in providing consumer information, and library service to the developmentally disabled.

PLA's conference activities were highlighted by presentation of the first Allie Beth Martin Award. The award honors the late Mrs. Martin, former director of the Tulsa (Oklahoma) City-County Library System and past president of ALA. Author James Michener, the featured speaker, donated his honorarium to award recipient Harriet Bard to buy books for her library.

Reference and Adult Services Division (RASD)

The fully revised third edition of *Reference Works for Small and Medium-Sized Libraries* was completed in 1979 by an RASD ad hoc committee. It contains 1,048 entries—a 36 percent increase over the 770 entries in the 1973 edition. The committee worked 18 months compiling and revising entries. Copies are available from the ALA Order Department.

RASD's Local History Committee of the History Section completed new guidelines for establishing local history collections. The committee spent several years researching and surveying local history collections and services. The complete guidelines were published in the Fall 1979 issue of *RQ*. And in 1979, *RQ*, RASD's quarterly publication, was redesigned. Helen Josephine was appointed its new editor.

Resources and Technical Services Division (RTSD)

RTSD's 1979 activities reflect the division's strong commitment to the education of librarians across the country in the practice and use of *The Anglo-American Cataloging Rules*, 2nd ed. A preconference at the ALA annual conference trained 380 participants in the use of AACR II. These persons will return to their regions and train others. Over the next two years, RTSD will conduct more than 30 regional workshops designed to train librarians in the historical perspective and application of AACR II as well as in how to interpret the rules for use under the guidelines currently available. RTSD will also hold 12 additional workshops with the Library of Congress (LC) on how LC will interpret and apply AACR II.

RTSD was also able to publish *Guidelines for Collection Development* in 1979 and redesign and increase the publication schedule of its newsletter to six times a year. The RTSD board approved the formation of a Preservation Section.

Young Adults Services Division (YASD)

In 1979, YASD completed *Bibliography of Bibliographies*, a booklet co-authored with the Association of Library Service to Children on selecting material for children and young adults. During the year, YASD has been working on revising several of its outstanding book lists for the college bound: Fiction, Biographies, and the Performing Arts.

YASD's "High Interest/Low Reading Level Information Packet" has been a strong and steady seller throughout the year. The packet was developed for a 1978 preconference "Dispelling the High/Low Blues," and focuses on the problems of evaluating, locating, selecting, and using high interest/low reading materials for junior and senior high school students. YASD also plans to make a high/low reading list available with its annually revised collection of "notable" books lists and other selection tools.

OTHER UNIT ACTIVITIES

Library History Round Table (LHRT)

This round table voted during the ALA annual conference to change its name from American Library History Round Table to Library History Round Table.

Office for Library Personnel Resources (OLPR)

The Office for Library Personnel Resources Advisory Committee Minimum Standards Qualifications for Librarians Task Force won the 1979 J. Morris Jones-World Book Encyclopedia ALA Goal Award. The $5,000 grant was made to support an immediate and intensive effort to identify clearly, describe, and assess the potential impact of the laws, regulations, and guidelines related to equal employment opportunity that are influencing traditional practices in recruiting, selecting, hiring, and promoting librarians. This issues was addressed during a three-day retreat in the fall of 1979, funded by the grant. The consultants at the retreat unanimously agreed that carefully developed, job-related, employee selection systems are essential. The task force will be making recommendations during 1980 on what ALA should do to assist libraries in the employee selection procedures.

OLPR continued to operate the midwinter meeting and annual conference Placement Center and give job advice.

Office for Library Service to the Disadvantaged (OLSD)

Illiteracy continued to be the prime target of OLSD activities in 1979. A $132,000 grant from the Lilly Endowment, Inc., made it possible for OLSD to conduct three regional workshops across the country. The workshops were designed to train 123 librarians in the techniques of establishing literacy programs in libraries. The workshop participants then returned to their states to counsel librarians in establishing literacy programs in the library. OLSD also developed three demonstration collections of books and films designed to help and encourage beginning collections for the new adult reader. The collections are available to any library in the United States and can be obtained through interlibrary loan from ALA headquarters library.

OLSD also published the *Directory of Literacy and Adult Learning Programs*, 91 descriptive profiles of library literacy programs offered in 1978 by public libraries. The office was represented on an advisory board with Literacy Volunteers of America for development of a *Bibliography of Humanistic Reading for Grade Levels 1-8*, funded by the National Endowment for the Humanities. OLSD also produced a brochure, "Literacy, Libraries Can Make It Happen," that focuses on the library's role in the national effort to combat illiteracy, what ALA is doing to help, and a list of important contacts for materials, information on local programs, training, and collaboration. And in an effort to create better cooperation between literacy organizations, OLSD won the approval of the Literacy Volunteers of America and Laubach Literacy International as new ALA affiliates.

The Subcommittee on Library Service for American Indian People launched an important new project to help develop libraries and/or library linkages for Indians living in semiurban or urban areas. Consultants visited two sites in 1979 at the request of the individual communities.

Public Information Office (PIO)

"The Library Is Filled with Success Stories" was the theme of 1979's National Library Week (NLW) campaign. Four new posters were developed, but the best illustration of the theme came from a second-grader from Eureka, Missouri, Brenda Bitsch, who was the grand prize winner in the ALA-American Association of School Librarians-Scholastic Magazines National Student Poster Contest, "What My Library Means to Me." The young artist made a presentation of her poster at the White House to Rosalynn and Amy Carter in honor of National Library Week. National Library Week was given further recognition in 1979 thanks to McDonald's Corporation, which sponsored a special salute to NLW. Libraries in more than 26 states cooperated with local McDonald's restaurants to develop cooperative NLW programs.

PIO Director Peggy Barber and NLW Committee Member Mona Garvey have initiated work on a clip art book, scheduled to be published in 1980. "About Books," PIO's nationally syndicated weekly book column, is now in its third year. Accompanying the reviews, "What Americans Are Reading" is the only library best-seller list.

AMERICAN NATIONAL STANDARDS COMMITTEE Z39: LIBRARY AND INFORMATION SCIENCES AND RELATED PUBLISHING PRACTICES
AND
INTERNATIONAL ORGANIZATION FOR STANDARDIZATION TECHNICAL COMMITTEE 46—DOCUMENTATION

U.S. Department of Commerce, National Bureau of Standards
Admin. E-120, Washington, DC 20234
301-921-3402

Robert W. Frase
Executive Director

James L. Wood
Chairman

In the United States, the principal responsibility for developing and promoting standards for information systems, products, and services rests with the American National Standards Committee Z39: Library and Information Sciences, and Related Publishing Practices. Z39 is a standards-developing committee created in 1939 by the American Standards Association (predecessor to ANSI, the American National Standards Institute) at the request of the American Library Association, the American Association of Law Libraries, the Medical Library Association, and the Special Libraries Association. The secretariat, responsible to ANSI for the work of Z39, is the Council of National Library and Information Associations.

Z39 develops standards relevant to information systems, products, and services as they relate to libraries, information services, and publishing. The committee also encourages the use of these standards in library, publishing, document delivery, information dissemination, and information and data handling systems. Z39 functions to ensure that American National Standards within its scope remain dynamic, that duplication of work is minimized, that promulgation of conflicting standards is avoided, and that individual enterprise and initiative are encouraged.

Internationally, Z39 participates in the development of International Organization for Standardization (ISO) standards for librarianship, documentation, and related information handling, including information systems and interchange networks as applied to documentation. Many current ISO standards are adaptations of ANSC Z39 standards.

The American National Standards Institute has set formal procedures for the development and approval of American National Standards. In Z39, a subcommittee is appointed that develops the proposed standard, which is then submitted to the Z39 member organizational representatives (presently 58) for comment and vote. If there are negative votes, the subcommittee tries to resolve them, and this may lead to changing the text of the proposed standard and reballoting. At the same time, comment from interested persons outside Z39 is solicited through a notice in the ANSI biweekly publication *Standards Action*. Z39 responds in writing to any negative comments that are received. Once this public review is complete, the proposed standard is submitted to the ANSI Board of Standards Review (BSR), along with the record of the voting, any other pertinent documentation, and a certification that the ANSI procedural requirements have been met. If the BSR approves the standard, that fact is also published in *Standards Action*, after which the standard is prepared for publication by ANSI.

ANSI requires that all published standards be reconsidered every five years for possible reaffirmation, revision, or discontinuance. Each of these alternatives follows the same procedures as used when developing a new standard.

Z39 ACTIVITIES DURING 1979

The year 1979 was the most productive in the history of Z39 in terms of standards approved. Five new standards were published and two others approved for publication. In addition, five revised standards were published and two others approved for publication.

New Standards Approved in 1979

Z39.35-1979 Romanization of Lau, Khmer, and Pali, $4.50.
Z39.37-1979 Romanization of Armenian, $3.50.
Z39.39-1979 Newspaper and Journal Publishing Statistics, $3.50.
Z39.40-1979 Microform Publishing Statistics, $3.50.
Z39.41-1979 Book Spine Formats, $3.50.
Z39.42-1980 Reporting Serial Holdings (not yet published).
Z39.43-1980 Standard Account Number (not yet published).

Revised Standards Approved in 1979

Z39.2-1979 Bibliographic Information Interchange on Magnetic Tape, $4.
Z39.9-1979 Identification Number for Serial Publications, $3.50.
Z39.13-1979 Advertising of Books, $4.50.
Z39.14-1979 Writing Abstracts, $4.50.
Z39.15-1980 Title Leaves of a Book (not yet published).
Z39.16-1979 Preparation of Scientific Papers for Written or Oral Presentation, $4.50.
Z39.21-1980 Book Numbering (not yet published).

Standards Submitted for Public Review

In addition, at the end of the year the following three revisions of published standards and two proposed new standards had been submitted to the Board of Standards Review for public review concurrent with balloting in Z39:

Z39.19-1974 Guidelines for Thesaurus Structure, Construction, and Use, $5.

Z39.22-1974 Proof Corrections, $5.50.
Z39.23-1974 Standard Technical Report Number, $3.50.
Z39.30- Standard Order Form—Single Copy (New).
Z39.38- Romanization of Yiddish (New).

Standards in Subcommittee

The following four standards published in 1974 and one new standard were still in subcommittee:

Z39.4-1974 Basic Criteria for Indexes (Revision), $4.
Z39.7-1974 Library Statistics (Revision), $6.50.
Z39.18-1974 Guidelines for the Format and Production of Scientific and Technical Reports (Revision), $4.50.
Z39.20-1974 Criteria for Price Indexes for Library Materials (Revision), $4.
SC 42 Serial Claim Form (New).

1975 Published Standards Requiring Review in 1980

The following Z39 standards published in 1975 will require review in 1980 for reaffirmation, revision, or withdrawal:

Z39.25-1975 Romanization of Hebrew, $4.50.
Z39.26-1975 Advertising of Micropublications, $2.

Other Published Standards

The following are other published Z39 standards not listed above:

Z39.1-1977 Periodicals: Format and Arrangement, $4.50.
Z39.5-1969 (R1974) Abbreviation of Titles of Periodicals, $4.
Z39.6-1965 (R1977) Trade Catalogs, $3.50.
Z39.8-1977 Compiling Book Publishing Statistics, $4.
Z39.10-1971 (R1977) Directories of Libraries and Information Centers, $4.
Z39.11-1972 (R1978) System for the Romanization of Japanese, $4.
Z39.12-1972 (R1978) System for the Romanization of Arabic, $3.50.
Z39.24-1976 System for the Romanization of Slavic Cyrillic Characters, $4.
Z39.27-1976 Structure for the Identification of Countries of the World for Information Interchange, $2.
Z39.29-1977 Bibliographic References, $12.75.
Z39.31-1976 Format for Scientific and Technical Translations, $4.
Z39.33-1977 Development of Identification Codes for Use by the Bibliographic Community, $3.50.

All Z39 standards are published by the American National Standards Institute and must be purchased from ANSI, 1430 Broadway, New York, New York 10018.

CHANGES IN MEMBERSHIP

During the year two members resigned from the committee and the following three new members were approved: U.S. Board on Geographic Names, U.S. Department of Commerce, Printing and Publishing Division, and National Commission on Libraries and Information Services. The following additional organizations were approved for membership by the secretariat on December 7, 1979, but except where noted had not yet accepted membership: Aztex Corporation (membership accepted), CBS/Publishing Group, Pelican Publishing Company, Society for Scholarly Publishing, Westminster Press, and U.S. Department of Energy.

An information membership (nonvoting) was established, but as of the end of 1979 there were as yet no information members.

OTHER ACTIVITIES

The annual meeting of Z39 was held at the Library of Congress on May 9, 1979. The Z39 Executive Council met four times during the year.

A set of bylaws (the first for Z39) was approved by a nearly unanimous vote of the membership and ratified by the Z39 secretariat on December 7, 1979. These bylaws, which include a change of name for Z39 and a change in scope, have been submitted for approval at the ISSMB meeting schedueld for March 4, 1980. A handbook of subcommittees has been prepared and is in process of duplication and distribution to Z39 members and subcommittee chairpersons.

A Z39 liaison with the new American National Standards Committee X12—Business Data Interchange—was established.

Several steps were taken during the year to increase the awareness of Z39 activities and the use of Z39 standards:

1. The National Technical Information Service of the U.S. Department of Commerce has agreed to place a bibliographic reference to all published Z39 standards on the tapes that it distributes so that information on Z39 standards and instructions on ordering them from ANSI can be retrieved electronically through such systems as Lockheed DIALOG.
2. A proposal has been made to the publications department of ANSI to include newly published Z39 standards in the Library of Congress Cataloging in Publication program. Under this arrangement the Library of Congress cataloging information on these standards would be included in the preliminary and final MARC tapes that are distributed by the Library of Congress and used in several thousand libraries in the United States and other countries as selection and ordering tools.
3. The R. R. Bowker Company has expressed an interest in publishing a collection of Z39 standards in somewhat reduced format similar to the *ISO Standards Handbook 1—Information Transfer* published in 1977.
4. A small descriptive brochure on Z39 is being printed.
5. Four issues of the Z39 quarterly newsletter, *VOICE of Z39*, were published in January, April, July, and October and distributed to a mailing list that has grown to about a thousand names.
6. Mailing labels for the Z39 mailing list were furnished to the sales department of ANSI for a mailing of the June 1979 sales brochure on Z39 published standards.

FUNDING

Financially, Z39 during the year received grants or was assured of grants from the U.S. National Science Foundation, the U.S. National Commission on Libraries and Information Services (two grants), and the Council on Library Resources (two grants). The National Bureau of Standards has provided office space and supporting services for the Z39 office in Gaithersburg, Maryland. A fund-raising campaign soliciting voluntary contributions to Z39 for the support of Z39 activities was undertaken with the support of several national organizations in the fields of libraries, information services, indexing and abstracting services, and publishing. This campaign was still under way at the end of the year; some contributions have been received and others were in prospect.

128 / NATIONAL ASSOCIATIONS

In summary, 1979 was one of the most productive years in the history of Z39. The coming year should be equally if not more productive in developing new and revised standards as indicated by the work program described above; and new ground should be broken in bringing Z39 standards into use in the library, information services, and publishing communities.

Z39 OFFICERS AND SUBCOMMITTEES

Officers (Executive Council)

Chmn. James L. Wood, Dir., Chemical Abstracts Service, Box 3012, Columbus, OH 43210. 614-421-6949, ext. 6062; *V.-Chair.* Sally H. McCallum, Network Development Office, Lib. of Congress, Washington, DC 20540. 202-287-5137; *Councilors Representing Libraries.* Glyn T. Evans, Dir. of Lib. Services, State Univ. of New York, Central Admin., State Univ. Plaza, Albany, NY 12246. 518-474-1430; James E. Rush, Dir., R & D Div., OCLC, Inc., 1125 Kinnear Rd., Columbus, OH 43212. 614-486-3661; *Councilors Representing Information Services.* Ben-Ami Lipetz, Dean, School of Lib. and Info. Science, State Univ. of New York at Albany, 1400 Washington Ave., Albany, NY 12222. 518-455-6288; Robert S. Tannehill, Jr., Lib. Mgr., Chemical Abstracts Service, Box 3012, Columbus, OH 43210. 614-421-6940, ext. 2028; *Councilors Representing Publishing.* Robert F. Asleson, Pres., R. R. Bowker Co., 1180 Ave. of the Americas, New York, NY 10036. 212-764-5102; Sandra K. Paul, SKP Associates, 565 Fifth Ave., New York, NY 10017. 212-687-3145; *Secretariat Rep.* John T. Corrigan, C.F.X., Council of National Lib. and Info. Assns., Catholic Lib. Assn., 461 W. Lancaster Ave., Haverford, PA 19041. 215-649-5251; *Exec. Dir.* Robert W. Frase, ANSC Z39, National Bureau of Standards, Admin. Rm. E-120, Washington, DC 20234. 301-921-3402; *ANSI Staff.* Helen Stefanakis, American National Standards Institute, 1430 Broadway, New York, NY 10018. 212-354-3345.

Numbered Subcommittees

Machine Input Records (SC-2). Chpn. Henriette D. Avram, Network Development Office, Lib. of Congress, Washington, DC 20540. 202-287-5137.

Romanization of Hebrew and Yiddish (SC-5). Chpn. Herbert C. Zafren, Dir. of Libs., Hebrew Union College-Jewish Institute of Religion, 3101 Clifton Ave., Cincinnati, OH 45220. 513-221-1875.

Library Statistics (SC-7). Chpn. Katherine Emerson, Lib., Univ. of Massachusetts, Amherst, MA 01002. 413-545-2780.

Bibliographic Entries for Microfiche Headers (SC-33). Chpn. Francis Spreitzer, Dept. of Micrographics and Reprography, Univ. Lib., University Park, Univ. of Southern California, Los Angeles, CA 90007. 213-741-6077.

Standard Order Form (SC-36). Chpn. Peter Jacobs, V.P. in Charge of Sales, Bro-Dart, Inc., 1609 Memorial Ave., Williamsport, PA 17701. 717-326-2461.

Serial Claim Forms (SC-42). Chpn. Lois Upham, School of Lib. and Info. Services, North Texas Univ., Denton, TX 76203. 817-788-2078.

Letter-Designated Subcommittees Appointed in 1979

Abbreviation of Titles of Periodicals (SC-A). Chpn. Robert S. Tannehill, Jr., Lib. Mgr., Chemical Abstracts Service, Box 3012, Columbus, OH 43210. 614-421-6940.

Language Codes (SC-C). Chpn. Lillian Kozuma, Head, Cataloging Sec., National Lib. of Medicine, 8600 Rockville Pike, Bethesda, MD 20014. 301-496-3497.

Computer-to-Computer Protocol (SC-D). Chpn. David C. Hartmann, Network Development Office, Lib. of Congress, Washington, DC 20540. 202-287-5137.

Serial Holdings Statement at the Detailed Level (SC-E). Chpn. Susan Brynteson, Univ. of Delaware Lib., Newark, DE 19711.

Serial Publication Patterns (SC-F). Chpn. Ann Ekstrom, Dir., Lib. Services Div., OCLC, Inc., 1125 Kinnear Rd., Columbus, OH 43212. 614-486-3661.

Terms and Symbols Used in Form Functional Areas of Interactive Retrieval Systems (SC-G). Chpn. Pauline Atherton, Assoc. Dir., ERIC Clearinghouse on Information Resources, Syracuse Univ., School of Education, Syracuse, NY 13210. 315-423-3640.

Pattern Data Element Identification and Application Numbering (SC-H). Chpn. Philip J. Pollick, Senior Info. Scientist, Chemical Abstracts Service, Box 3012, Columbus, OH 43210. 614-421-6940.

Price Indexes for Library Materials (SC-I). Chpn. Fred C. Lynden, Asst., Univ. Lib. for Technical Services, Brown Univ. Lib., Providence, RI 02912. 401-863-2162.

Bibliographic Data Source File Identification (SC-J). Chpn. John G. Mulvilhill, Mgr., GeoRef, American Geological Institute, 5205 Leesburg Pike, Falls Church, VA 22041. 703-379-2480.

Basic Criteria for Indexes (SC-K). Chpn. Jessica L. Milstead, 875 Marion Rd., Cheshire, CT 06410. 203-397-3893.

Transliteration (SC-L). Chpn. Charles Husbands, Harvard Univ. Lib., Cambridge, MA 02138. 617-830-3724.

Serial Publication Page Margins (SC-M). Chpn. Larry X. Besant, Asst. Dir., Ohio State Univ. Libs., 1858 Neil Avenue Mall, Columbus, OH 43210. 614-422-6152.

Coded Character Sets for Bibliographic Information Interchange (SC-N). Chpn. Charles T. Payne, Univ. of Chicago Lib., Chicago, IL 60637. 312-753-2908.

Library Item and Patron Identification Codes (SC-O). Chpn. Howard Harris, Maryland State Bd. for Higher Educ., 16 Francis St., Annapolis, MD 21401. 301-269-2971.

INTERNATIONAL STANDARDIZATION ACTIVITIES

Z39 participates in the development of international standards for libraries, documentation and information centers, indexing and abstracting services, and publishing through its membership in the International Organization for Standardization, Technical Committee 46: Documentation (ISO/TC 46). ISO/TC 46 is one of 1,940 technical bodies within ISO engaged in developing international standards to facilitate the exchange of goods and services and to develop mutual cooperation in the sphere of intellectual, scientific, technological, and economic activities. Since its establishment in 1947, TC 46 has produced 25 ISO standards.

Decisional powers governing the work of TC 46 reside with the Plenary Assembly, the delegates representing member bodies, i.e., national standards organizations, which actively participate in the program of TC 46. The secretariat of TC 46, held by DIN (Deutsches Institut für Normung), is responsible to the ISO Council and to the members of the technical committee for all TC 46 activities. A steering committee assists the secretariat to plan and program the work of the TC 46 subcommittee and working groups between meetings of the Plenary Assembly.

The program of work of TC 46 is conducted by six subcommittees: SC 2—Conversion of Written Languages; SC 3—Terminology of Documentation; SC 4—Automation in Documentation; SC 5—Monolingual and Multilingual Thessauri and Related

Indexing Practices; SC 6—Bibliographic Data Elements in Manual and Machine Applications; and SC 7—Presentation of Publications. TC 46 Working Group 1—Numbering Systems in Documentation is now Working Group 2 under Subcommittee 6, entitled "Codes and Numbering Systems for the Representation of Bibliographic Data Elements." Subcommittees 2, 4, and 6 are subdivided into working groups. Henriette D. Avram (Library of Congress) is the convenor of Subcommittee 4/Working Group 1, which deals with character sets for documentation and bibliographic use, and James L. Wood (Chemical Abstracts Service) is the convenor of the new SC 6/Working Group 2.

During 1979, the Plenary Assembly met on April 24-25 in Warsaw, Poland, and the Steering Committee twice, on April 23 in Warsaw and December 3-4 in Columbus, Ohio. Numerous meetings of the TC 46 subcommittees and working groups were held.

Plenary Assembly Meeting

Seventy-four delegates from 17 countries attended the Eighteenth Plenary Assembly meeting of TC 46 in Warsaw, Poland, on April 24-25. The United States was represented by Henriette D. Avram (Library of Congress) and James L. Wood (Chemical Abstracts Service). Wood served as head of the U.S. delegation. The hosts for the meetings were the Polish Standards Institute and the Polish Institute for Scientific, Technical and Economic Information.

At this meeting, the TC 46 secretariat reported on the status of voting on various TC 46 drafts, requests from the International Federation of Library Associations and Institutions for new subcommittees, and the need to improve liaison with other ISO technical committees. Persons chairing the six TC 46 subcommittees and Working Group 1 reported on their groups' activities. Immediately following each report, the chair of the steering committee reported on the actions taken by the steering committee as they related to the subcommittees' programs of work and the priorities to be given to each work item. The need for TC 46 to develop standards dealing with new products, services, and information techniques required for the utilization of information was discussed.

The next item of business was the election of a new steering committee. There was much discussion about the need to elect members for staggered terms to ensure continuity, the need to limit individuals serving on the steering committee to the chairs of subcommittees, and the need for a steering committee at all. The chair called for nominations from the floor. Only Italy responded, bringing the number of candidate member countries to nine. Of the 17 delegations present only 15 cast votes. The People's Republic of China and Japan abstained.

The result of the election was 15 votes for the United States, 11 votes each for France, the Federal Republic of Germany, and Hungary, and 10 votes each for Poland and Sweden. Thus the country representation in the steering committee remained the same with the exception of Poland, which replaced the United Kingdom.

Steering Committee Meetings

At the April 23 Warsaw meeting, the steering committee reviewed the work of all subcommittees and working groups. Subcommittee 2 was asked to maintain as a priority the revision of ISO/R9-1968 *International System for the Transliteration of Cyrillic Characters* and to accelerate the working procedure concerning Greek, Arabic, and Hebrew characters. Subcommittee 3 was urged to give priority to the *Vocabulary of Information and Documentation*. The revision of ISO 2709-1973 *Format Exchange for Bibliographic Information on Magnetic Tape* and the work on the principles for bibliographic filing and application level protocols were given top priority for Subcommittee 4. Subcommittee 5 was requested to maintain as priority items work on the guidelines for the establishment of multilingual thessauri, the general methods for the analysis of documents, and the identification of subjects and the revision of ISO 2788-1974 *Guidelines for the Establishment and Development of Monolingual Thessauri.* Subcommittee 6 was asked to maintain as a priority the revisions of ISO 690-1975 *Bibliographical References. Essential and Supplementary Elements* and ISO 832-1975 *Bibliographical References. Abbreviations of Typical Words.* Subcommittee 6 was requested to include in its priorities the directory of data elements in bibliographic records. The replacement of ISO/R30-1956 *Bibliographical Strip* by a new ISO standard covering bibliographical identification of publications in series was identified as priority work for Subcommittee 7. Working Group 1 was asked to maintain as priority the numbering systems in documentation.

The steering committee requested the secretariat to maintain the liaison established with IFLA and UNESCO concerning library statistics and statistics of book and periodical production.

Recommendations emanating from the December 3-4 Columbus meeting included improving the format and content of the status reports issued by the TC 46 secretariat and subcommittee secretaries; a review of the use of ad hoc groups in lieu of working groups; the need for ISO standards covering language codes and transliteration systems for languages of the developing countries; the publication of the chapters of the *Vocabulary of Information and Documentation* as separate ISO standards; clarification of the scope of Subcommittee 6/Working Group 1; the transformation of Subcommittee 6/Working Group 2 into a subcommittee; improving the procedures for introducing new items of work to TC 46; and the need for establishing and maintaining liaison with other international groups working in the area of standardization. The steering committee also discussed the need for alignment of the Plenary Assembly and steering committee meetings with the terms of office of the steering committee members, the procedures for the election of steering committee members, and the role of the steering committee.

Owing to a lack of a quorum at the Columbus meeting, these recommendations must be approved by a majority of the steering committee members before they can be acted upon.

Z39 Actions

During 1979, Z39 reviewed and voted or commented on over 50 TC 46 working papers, draft proposals, and draft international standards. Several of these documents related to revisions of existing ISO standards, for example, ISO 4-1972 *International Code for the Abbreviation of Titles of Periodicals;* ISO/R30-1956 *Bibliographic Strip;* ISO 690-1975 *Bibliographic References, Essential and Supplementary Elements;* ISO 832-1975 *Bibliographic References, Abbreviations of Typical Words;* ISO 2146-1972 *Directories of Libraries, Information, and Documentation Centers;* ISO 2709-1973 *Format for Bibliographic Information Interchange on Magnetic Tape;* and ISO 2788-1974 *Guidelines for the Establishment and Development of Monolingual Thessauri.* The draft proposals voted on included a micrographic vocabulary; mathematic, Cyrillic, and bibliographic character sets; and headers for microfiche. Draft international standards reviewed and voted upon included *Codes for the Representation of Names of Countries* and *Spine Titles on Books and Other Publications.* Z39 also voted for the withdrawal of ISO 833-1974 *International List of Periodical Title Word Abbreviations* and to assign the maintenance of this list to the International Serials Data System, International Center, Paris, France.

ISO/TC 46 published standards are sold in the United States by the American National Standards Institute, 1430 Broadway, New York, New York 10018. In addition to the individual ISO/TC 46 published standards, ANSI also has for sale a 500-page compilation of the texts of 56 ISO/TC 46 and related ISO standards covering the fields of bibliographic references and descriptions, abstracts and indexing; presentation of documents; conversion of written languages; document copying; microforms; bibliographic control; libraries and information systems; mechanization and automation in documentation; classifications and controlled language for information storage and retrieval; and terminology (principles): *ISO Standards Handbook 1—Information Transfer* (1977).

Participation in the work of ISO/TC 46 is an important aspect of the overall standards program of Z39. The Z39 Executive Council voted at its December 11, 1979 meeting to establish an International Standards Advisory Board to assist the Executive Council make decisions relevant to TC 46 matters. It is the intention of the Executive Council to have the votes it casts on international standards and the delegates selected to attend TC 46 meetings represent the desires of the U.S. library, information service, and publishing communities.

ASSOCIATION OF AMERICAN PUBLISHERS

One Park Ave., New York, NY 10016
212-689-8920

1707 L St. N.W., Washington, DC 20036
202-293-2585

Mary McNulty
Staff Director, Public Relations Division

During 1979, the Association of American Publishers (AAP) developed some important new initiatives and reinforced continuing ones. The American Book Awards (TABA) were created as an industrywide awards program to be conducted under the auspices of the AAP, and to replace the National Book Awards, which lacked broad-based industry support. TABA will recognize the best books written, translated, or designed by U.S. citizens and published during 1979 by U.S. publishers. The goals of the awards program are to recognize and reward literary merit; generate greater public awareness of books, their authors, and the book community; increase interest in reading generally; and reach new audiences for books. Members of the TABA Academy (which is made up of national, nonprofit membership organizations within the book community) include AAP, the American Booksellers Association (ABA), the American Library Association (ALA), the Children's Book Council, the Association of American University Presses, the National Association of College Stores, and the Council of Writers Organizations. The National Medal for Literature, one of the nation's most prestigious literary awards, will also be presented under TABA auspices at ceremonies in the spring of 1980.

In the international area, AAP undertook new ventures in China and the Soviet Union. A delegation of 19 AAP members visited the People's Republic of China in April at the invitation of the China National Publications Import Corporation. In return, a 15-member delegation of Chinese publishers will visit the United States this spring. Further follow-up may include a large U.S. exhibition of books in 1980 to be held simultaneously in several Chinese cities.

The Second International Moscow Book Fair was the occasion for two exhibits organized by the association. One, a central exhibit of some 3,500 American books, was the largest collection of U.S. books ever assembled in the USSR. The centerpiece of this exhibit was a special book display entitled "America through American Eyes," which attempted to portray the quality of life in the United States today through 321 recent books written by Americans about America. Selections from the exhibit were made by a committee of distinguished writers.

As part of the recommendation of a Management Audit Team, appointed to assess the association's performance during its first decade, a "technology watch" will be instituted in the *AAP Newsletter* on subjects such as data base publishing, tele-ordering, and computer composition. European development in these areas will also be reported.

The Smaller Publishers Group of the AAP established a scholarship fund in memory of Stephen Greene, who was killed in a plane crash in May. A stipend from this scholarship fund will be provided to a native-born New England college graduate to be applied to tuition costs at an approved book publishing institute. The fund is administered by the Education for Publishing Committee of AAP.

AAP witnesses—publishers and staff—appeared before Senate and House committees as well as federal administrative bodies testifying on such matters as economic concentration in the publishing industry, education funding, postal rates, literacy and basic skills, testing, the National Periodical Center, and federal el-hi and college programs. In addition, four members of the association's Washington staff were registered as lobbyists for the publishing industry.

ORGANIZATION

The association, whose membership comprises some 350 companies, is the major voice of the book publishing industry in the United States. AAP was founded in 1970 as the result of the merger of the American Book Publishers Council and the American Educational Publishers Institute.

AAP members publish the great majority of printed materials sold to American schools, colleges, libraries, bookstores, and by direct mail to homes. All regions of the country are represented. Member firms publish hardcover and paperback books: textbooks, general trade, reference, religious and technical, scientific and medical, professional and scholarly, and journals. AAP members also produce a range of other educational materials, including classroom periodicals, maps, globes, films and filmstrips, audio- and videotapes, records, slides, transparencies, and test materials.

Association policies are established by an elected 29-member board of directors representing large and small firms from many geographic locations. Alexander Hoffman (Doubleday) is chairman of the board for FY 1979 to 1980. AAP President Townsend Hoopes, chief operating officer, is responsible for managing the AAP within the framework of basic policies set by the board. A staff of approximately 35 professional and nonprofessional personnel is located in two offices, New York and Washington.

The AAP operates under an organizational plan that ensures central direction of association affairs as "core" activities and gives important initiatives to the seven AAP divisions, each covering a major product line or distinct method of distribution of the industry. Each AAP division annually elects a chairperson and establishes committees to plan and implement independent projects. Marketing, promotion, research projects, and relations with other associations concerned with mutual problems are central features of divisional programs.

CORE COMMITTEES

Core activities include matters related to copyright, freedom to read, postal rates and regulations, statistical surveys, book distribution, public information, press relations, communications, international freedom to publish, and education for publishing.

The Copyright Committee safeguards and promotes the proprietary rights of authors and publishers domestically and internationally. It closely monitors copyright activity in the United States and abroad. It prepares congressional testimony for appropriate AAP spokespersons, assigns representatives to attend national and international copyright meetings, and sponsors seminars on copyright matters. Charles Butts (Houghton Mifflin) chairs this committee, which has been reorganized to include representatives from each AAP division.

The committee plays an active role in disseminating information about the 1978 copyright law. This function includes providing speakers to address publisher, librarian, and educator groups and preparing and distributing printed information. Over 2,000 copies of its publication *Photocopying by Academic, Public and Non-Profit Research Libraries* have been distributed. The Copyright Committee maintains liaison with the U.S. Copyright Office and informs publishers of new and proposed regulations that relate to their activities. It participates in negotiations concerning copyright-related policy to be followed by users of copyrighted material. The Copyright Committee is actively studying the extent of photocopying violations by corporate libraries and college campus copy mills and is laying the groundwork for enforcement cases in the courts in both areas.

The Freedom to Read Committee is concerned with protecting freedoms guaranteed by the First Amendment. It analyzes individual cases of attempted censorship by Congress, or by state legislatures, federal, state, or municipal governments, local school boards, or any other institution. Its action may take the form of a legal brief in support of a position against censorship, testimony before appropriate legislative committees, or public statements and communications protesting any attempt to limit freedom of communication. The committee works closely with other organizations that support its goals. During the year the committee worked closely with the AAP School Division to formulate an appropriate national study aimed at providing information about how to anticipate and counter censorship, and also to develop guidelines useful to publishers, educators, and librarians. Anthony Schulte (Random House/ Knopf) is chairman.

The Postal Committee monitors the activities of the U.S. Postal Service, the Postal Rate Commission, and congressional committees having responsibility for postal matters. It presents the publisher's point of view to those in policymaking positions through direct testimony, by economic analyses of proposed postal programs, and through a variety of other means. George Larie (Doubleday) is chairman.

The International Freedom to Publish Committee is the only body formed by a major group of publishers in any country for the specific purpose of protecting and expanding the freedom of written communication. The committee monitors the general status of freedom to publish, and discusses problems of restriction with our own government, other governments, and international organizations. As may be appropriate, it makes recommendations to these organizations and issues public statements. During the year the committee has acted as unofficial host to visiting dissident writers such as Dr. Gholamhossein Sa'edi from Iran and Mihajlov Mihajlov from Yugoslavia. The committee, together with Fund for Free Expression, assumed responsibility for organizing the AAP centerpiece exhibit "America through American Eyes" at the Moscow Book Fair. Lawrence Hughes (William Morrow) chairs this committee.

The Book Distribution Task Force was formed by the Association of American Publishers in 1976 to foster the development and implementation of more efficient book distribution systems for all book publishers. During the year the task force surveyed publishers' base line book distribution costs and also the current usage in the industry of computers and computer software programs.

A white paper on *The Role of Publishers in the National Library Network* prepared by the Task Force and the AAP Libraries Committee stimulated the Network Advisory Committee to the Library of Congress to establish a private sector subcommittee to determine the appropriate role for publishers, wholesalers, retailers, and indexing and abstracting services in the development and maintenance of a national network of bibliographic information. The Task Force assumed the responsibility for finalizing a standardized format for publisher invoices and implementing a monthly microfiche service, both projects initiated by the College Division. The Task Force investigated the question of a computerized data base of all book title information, and requested proposals to study the question. Publishers and other concerned individuals and organizations are kept informed of technological and standardization developments by periodic bulletins. Robert Follett (Follett) chairs the Book Distribution Task Force.

The Education for Publishing Program was implemented by AAP in 1978 after a three-year exploration and study of the education and training needs of the book publishing industry. The goals of the Education for Publishing Committee, chaired by Werner Mark Linz (Seabury), are to promote and advance the continuing education development of employees already in the industry; to help attract, prepare, and educate new talent to enter the industry; and to help inform the public about the book publishing industry. This mission is being carried out by informing and guiding educational and training institutions in providing authoritative and useful courses on book publishing; initiating and sponsoring professional development courses on book publishing for industry employees; encouraging and assisting in the development and improvement of in-house training programs conducted by member companies; and by creating and providing career and other information about the industry. A Publishing Education Information Service has been established within the Education for Publishing program. The new service is envisioned as a research, referral, and communication service for publishers, educators and serious students seeking information about book publishing.

A new core committee, the Communications Task Force, was established at the recommendation of AAP chairman Alexander Hoffman. Chaired by Byron Hollinshead (Oxford University Press), the committee's primary aim is to devise means of achieving better understanding of the basic facts about book publishing by various publics: the publishing community itself; its immediate constituencies—authors, booksellers, librarians, educators, and book reviewers and reporters assigned to the publishing industry; suppliers—printers, binders, paper manufacturers, and financiers;

government in its various manifestations—legislatures, regulatory bodies, executive agencies, and the Library of Congress, and its Copyright Office; the book reading public; and the public at large.

DIVISIONS

General Publishing Division

The General Publishing Division (GPD), chaired by A. Dale Timpe, represents publishers of fiction and nonfiction, children's literature, reference, and religious books. It maintains close cooperation with members of the AAP's Mass Market Paperback and Professional and Scholarly Publishing divisions on areas of mutual concern.

Among the division's responsibilities, in cooperation with the Mass Market Paperback Division, is the sponsorship of The American Book Awards program. As noted earlier, the awards, which debut in the spring of 1980, will be given annually for books in categories reflecting the major areas of interest of the book-reading public.

Through its committee structure, the GPD sponsors seminars, conferences, research, and publications on a wide range of subjects of interest to its members. It maintains active liaison (through joint committees) with the ABA, ALA, and Special Libraries Association and cosponsors with them activities of interest to the members of those organizations.

Through its Libraries Committee, the division was closely involved in the first White House Conference on Library and Information Services. Two members of the AAP staff were voting delegates to the conference. A program for publishers on the future of books in libraries was held in April.

An active group of smaller publishers is focused within the GPD. It plans programs and publications of particular interest to the growing number of smaller publishers within all divisions of AAP. The group sponsored two successful regional seminars in 1979, one in upstate New York and one in Chicago.

A program for librarians on the selection and acquisition of materials produced by smaller publishers was held in Dallas at the 1979 ALA convention.

The Marketing Group cosponsored with *Publishers Weekly* a major study of backlist booksales and promotions and presented a full-day program on the changing role of the trade sales representative.

Mass Market Paperback Division

The Mass Market Paperback Division, chaired by William Sarnoff (Warner Books), is concerned with making the paperback book an integral part of the educational and leisure reading of Americans today. Through the media, book fairs, and exhibits, the industry makes every effort possible to emphasize that paperback books provide easy accessibility to all kinds of personal and professional reading. The division worked closely with the General Publishing Division to establish The American Book Awards program.

In addition, the division is concerned with the mass paperback industry's marketing, production, and distribution problems. Its focus is on problems on the national and international levels. Separate divisional committees address themselves to the problems of financial planning, industry statistics, operational management, advertising and promotion, production, and freight and postal concerns. The division represents the industry at both the ABA and the National Association of College Stores (NACS) annual meetings. The division implemented a Rack Clearance Center in January. This is a clearinghouse for requests from wholesalers, jobbers, distributors, and rack manufacturers for financial reimbursement for rack installations.

The division launched a public relations campaign to the book trade in an effort to counteract the growing problem of stripped mass paperback books. A "Campus Paperback Best-Seller List," initiated last year, was compiled monthly by the *Chronicle of Higher Education* and distributed to college bookstores and newspapers.

College Division

The College Division, chaired by David Amerman (Prentice-Hall), is directly concerned with all aspects of the marketing, production, and distribution of textbooks to the postsecondary education field. It pays special attention to maintaining good relations between the publishing industry and college faculty, bookstore managers, and college students. In order to develop and maintain strong relations with the college student, the division has established the AAP Student Service, a public relations program featuring a series of publications specifically directed to the college student. They include *How to Get the Most Out of Your Textbook*, *How to Prepare Successfully for Examinations*, *How to Improve Your Reading Skills*, and *How to Build Your Writing Skills*. A new study skills publication, *How to Get the Most Out of a College Education*, was recently published. The division has developed several publications directed to college faculty, including this year a new audiovisual slide show and the pamphlet "An Author's Guide to Academic Publishing."

The division maintains close relations with college bookstores through the NACS-College Division Liaison Committee. The committee recently has updated a publication for college bookstore managers on *Textbook Questions and Answers*. The committee cosponsors annually an Advanced Financial Management Seminar for college store managers in the spring.

The College Division marketing committee has sponsored a Rely on Your Textbook advertising program with posters and news releases to campus newspapers and college bookstores. The division published in November the first in-depth wholesale textbook industry survey, which was undertaken to shed light on marketing practices within the industry and to help publishers improve their marketing techniques in response to distribution patterns.

Professional and Scholarly Publishing Division

The Technical, Scientific and Medical Division, chaired by Frank Urbanowski (MIT Press), polled its membership in the fall and approved a change of name to the Professional and Scholarly Publishing Division, the consensus being that this identification better reflects the various types of publishing the members represent. The division is concerned with production, marketing, and distribution of technical, scientific, medical, and scholarly books and journals. Many of these publications are aimed, essentially although not exclusively, at the practicing engineer, scientist, and businessperson. To this end, the division monitors relevant government activity, including in this past year proposals for a national periodicals system and revisions to Title 44, that part of the U.S. Code that controls government printing activity as well as policies, levels of funding, and related matters. The division provides for a continuous exchange of information and experience through seminars covering developments in marketing, sales, new technologies, and copyright; and maintains relations with other professional associations, including STM (International Group of Scientific, Technical and Medical Publishers), the National Science Foundation, other government agencies, and industrial research groups.

In the past year, the division formed a government relations committee that will seek to increase government awareness of the professional and scholarly publishers' needs and interest. A Public Relations Committee was also formed to improve the recognition and understanding of professional and scholarly publishing. Other standing committees include marketing, statistics, and journals. The division often sponsors informal workshops and holds an annual spring seminar.

School Division

The School Division is governed by a nine-member executive committee who serve three-year rotating terms. Its current chairman is Gary Eisenberger (Charles Merrill). The work of the division is concerned with the production, marketing, and distribution of textbooks and instructional materials, grades K through 12. The division also sponsors timely seminars and conferences on topics of interest to educators and publishers. It works to improve textbook selection procedures and purchasing patterns, to improve instructional programs, and to seek increased levels of funding for programs of education. The division operates out of the AAP Washington office under Robert T. Rasmussen, vice president, School Division.

Activities in the 50 state legislatures relative to schools and educational publishing are very important to school publishers. The division retains legislative advocates in key states to monitor more closely legislative activities and to represent the interests of educational publishers at educational conferences. Liaison committees have also been organized to meet at least annually with state boards of education and members of the state legislatures in the 22 adoption states as well as selected open territory states to review laws and regulations concerning the selection and adoption of instructional materials.

Other standing committees of the division include Social Issues, Research, Order Flow Improvement, Standards and Specifications, Depositories, Public Relations, Statistics Review, Testing, and Right to Read.

Through the work of the Public Relations Committee, a grass-roots public information campaign has been undertaken by the division to acquaint parents and school board members with some of the issues of concern to educational publishers, especially the declining portion of the educational dollar being spent for instructional materials. The publication *Parents' Guide to More Effective Schools* was issued to encourage more parental involvement in school activities. Public service ads and public service radio spots are widely distributed.

International Division

The International Division, formed to recognize the rising importance of foreign markets for U.S. books, focuses on those issues that affect marketing of books to other countries, and the ever-growing complexities of the international marketplace. Kenneth T. Hurst (Prentice-Hall International) chairs this division, which represents the entire spectrum of publishing in both size of firm and product line.

Among the priorities of the division are improving trade relations with the third world and sharing professional skills via workshops; developing a strong relationship with U.S. government agencies (U.S. International Communication Agency and the State and Commerce departments) interested in promoting the book abroad through national fairs and exhibits; promoting respect for international copyright; professional development of members through a variety of seminars and workshops; the development of international sales statistics; and promoting attendance and active participation in international book fairs.

The division was actively involved in organizing a major U.S. exhibit for the Moscow Book Fair this year. It also was responsible for a large International Visitors Center during the 1979 ABA convention, which served as a meeting place for the international staffs of both U.S. and foreign publishing houses.

Direct Marketing/Book Club Division

The Direct Marketing/Book Club Division, led by chairman Carl Jaeger (Time-Life Books) and vice chairman L. William Black (Walter J. Black), is actively concerned with the marketing and distribution of books through direct response and book clubs. It works closely with the AAP Postal Committee to study the effects of new postal rates and regulations and monitors new developments. The division's marketing committee sponsored seminars during the year: International Direct Marketing, Success Stories in Direct Book Marketing, The Role of the Product Manager, Credit and Collections, and Broadcast. A bibliography of direct marketing resource material was developed for use in responding to requests for information from AAP members and the public.

AWARDS

In 1979, AAP sponsored the thirtieth celebration of the National Book Awards. The awards ceremony, which took place at Carnegie Hall on April 25, was presided over by Dick Cavett as master of ceremonies and Senator Daniel P. Moynihan as guest speaker.

In addition, the association presented the fourth annual Curtis G. Benjamin Award for Creative Publishing given during the AAP annual meeting banquet in May. This year's recipient, Stuart Brewster (Addison-Wesley), was cited for the book *Fundamentals of the American Free Enterprise System*. The Professional and Scholarly Publishing Division completed the third year of its awards program, recognizing the best books and journals in its field.

LIAISON WITH OTHER ASSOCIATIONS

The AAP has effective working relations with a large number of professional associations and agencies having allied interests. These include the American Booksellers Association, American Council on Education, American Library Association, Book Industry Study Group, Book Manufacturers Institute, Children's Book Council, Council of the Great Cities Schools, Association of Media Producers, Information Industry Association, International Publishers Association, International Reading Association, National Association of College Stores, National Association of Teachers of English, National Education Association, P.E.N. American Center, Publishers Publicity Association, Publishers Library Promotion Group, Special Libraries Association, and UNESCO.

PUBLICATIONS

While some AAP publications are circulated to members only, many are available to nonmembers.

The *AAP Newsletter* provides a periodic report to members on issues of concern to the publishing industry. The *Capital Letter*, issued monthly, offers news of federal government actions relating to the book community. Newsletters are prepared by the College Division, International Division, School Division, General Publishing

Division, Mass Market Paperback Division, and Professional and Scholarly Publishing Division. Periodic bulletins are published by the Book Distribution Task Force and the Education for Publishing Program. The AAP also publishes annual industry statistics, an exhibits directory listing, etc. A publications list is available from the association on request.

THE ASSOCIATION OF RESEARCH LIBRARIES: A FIVE-YEAR REVIEW, 1975–1979

1527 New Hampshire Ave. N.W., Washington, DC 20036
202-232-2466

John G. Lorenz
Former Executive Director

The Association of Research Libraries (ARL) experienced a period of significant growth and change during the years 1975–1979. Following eight years of service as executive director by Stephen A. McCarthy (1967–1974), John P. McDonald of the University of Connecticut served as executive director from 1975 to May 1976 and John G. Lorenz, former deputy Librarian of Congress, was executive director from 1976 through 1979.

In the five-year period 1975–1979, the number of institutional members increased from 94 to 111. From 1975 to 1979, total volumes in member university libraries increased from approximately 180 million volumes to over 206 million. Microform holdings increased from 74 million to 106 million. Expenditures for materials increased from $106 million to $147 million and total expenditures from $364 million to $483 million. However, professional staff only increased from 6,946 to 7,265 and total staff from 26,054 to 27,883. This brief summary gives some concept of the dimensions of the holdings and expenditures of ARL university libraries, their growth over a five-year period, and some indication of the effects of inflation on major university libraries in a period in which the average price of U.S. books increased from about $14 to over $20 and the average price of U.S. periodicals from about $17 to $27.

MAJOR LEGISLATION AND GRANTS

Two major pieces of legislation important to research libraries came to fruition during this five-year period. The first was the Copyright Revision Act in 1976, which established the principle of "fair use" in federal legislation, made specific provisions for library photocopying, and established a study Commission on New Technological Uses of Copyrighted Works. The association expended a considerable amount of time and effort on copyright issues. An early observation of the results of the legislation after two years seems to be that a good balance has been achieved to date between copyright owners and the users of copyrighted materials.

A second piece of legislation even more important to research libraries was the new Title II-C of the Higher Education Act (Education Amendments of 1976), which authorized federal grants for strengthening research library resources and to assist them in making their collections available to other libraries. In 1976, for example, ARL libraries had loaned 2.4 million items from their collections to other libraries on interlibrary loan. With the rising costs of service, several ARL libraries had already found it necessary to institute charges to cover, at least partially, the cost of such loans.

The new law authorized grants of $10 million for 1977, $15 million for 1978, and $20 million for 1979, and defined a major research library as a "public or private nonprofit institution, including the library resources of an institution of higher education, an independent research library, or a State or other public library, having library collections which are available to qualified users and which—(1) make a significant contribution to higher education and research; (2) are broadly based and are recognized as having national or international significance for scholarly research; (3) are of a unique nature, and contain material not widely available; and (4) are in substantial demand by researchers and scholars not connected with that institution."

The first appropriation under HEA, Title II-C, was $5 million for 1978. This was achieved by action initially in the Senate appropriations subcommittee and the particular assistance of Senator Eagleton of Missouri. The Commissioner of Education's regulations indicated that about 20 grants should be made and provided criteria for evaluating applications for grants, including consideration of geographic distribution. In the first year under the program, grants were made to 20 research libraries. (For a detailed analysis, see the 1979 edition of the *Bowker Annual*, pp. 164–166.)

For 1979, $6 million was appropriated by the Congress and grants were made to the University of Alaska, Fairbanks ($150,000); University of California, Berkeley ($750,000); University of Southern California, Los Angeles ($200,000); Henry E. Huntington Library & Art Gallery, San Marino ($225,000); Colorado State University, Fort Collins ($215,000); Yale University, New Haven ($160,000); University of Chicago ($69,000); Northwestern University, Evanston ($250,000); University of Illinois, Urbana ($125,000); University of Indiana, Bloomington ($200,000); University of Kansas, Lawrence ($115,000); Harvard University, Cambridge ($300,000); University of Michigan, Ann Arbor ($351,438); Missouri Botanical Garden ($200,000); Rutgers University, New Brunswick ($200,000); Princeton University ($250,000); New York State Education Department, Albany ($250,000); Cornell University, Ithaca ($194,897); American Museum of Natural History, New York City ($242,165); Columbia University, New York City ($250,000); New York Public Library ($300,000); University of North Carolina, Chapel Hill ($220,500); University of Texas, Austin ($150,000); University of Virginia, Charlottesville ($300,000); and University of Wisconsin, Madison ($182,000).

For 1980, the administration's budget requested $6 million and this amount was appropriated by the Congress. These grants will not be made until later in 1980. Early information on the recommendations of the Department of Health, Education, and Welfare for the 1981 budget request reflect the favorable evaluation of the Title II-C program by including a substantial increase in the amount requested. This is in contrast to requests for other library grant programs that unfortunately show decreases.

THE NATIONAL PERIODICALS CENTER

Another major development and legislative effort over the past five years has been for a National Periodicals Center (NPC). Several of the basic studies were done by and for the Association of Research Libraries, and ARL representatives participated in the other committees and task force efforts, including those of the National Commission on Libraries and Information Science (NCLIS), that provided the basis for the development of draft legislation by a representative group in 1979. The idea for introducing National Periodical Center legislation into the reauthorization of the Higher

Education Act was developed in discussions between the ARL executive director and the dean of libraries at New York University when he was preparing testimony for the House subcommittee.

Despite the fact that an NCLIS open forum of about 200 representatives in March 1979 clearly recommended approval of a NPC and urged that legislation be promptly drafted, NCLIS also contracted for a study by A. D. Little to provide a "Technical Economic Analysis of Alternatives for Access to Periodical Literature." Its report in September 1979 was essentially negative, giving the impression that in five years the new technology linking library systems would be able to meet the objectives of a NPC. However, the report did leave the door open for further study of a national system such as prescribed in the draft legislation. At the NCLIS meeting in September 1979, after hearing reports, including one by an ARL representative, the commission voted unanimously to support the establishment of the NPC, and the specific legislation that by that time had become Title II-D of the HEA reauthorization bill passed by the House.

The principal provisions of Title II-D of H.R. 5192, fully supported by ARL and other library and educational organizations are as follows:

> From funds appropriated to carry out this part, there shall be established a National Periodical Center to serve as a national periodical resource by contributing to the preservation of periodical materials and by providing access to a comprehensive collection of periodical literature to public and private libraries throughout the United States.
>
> There is established a nonprofit corporation, to be known as the National Periodical Center Corporation which shall not be considered an agency or establishment of the United States Government.
>
> The Corporation shall seek to establish a national system to provide reliable and timely document delivery from a comprehensive collection of periodical literature.
>
> For the purposes of establishing the system described in subsection (a) the Corporation shall have the authority—
>
> (1) to acquire current and retrospective periodicals, and to preserve and maintain a dedicated collection of such documents;
>
> (2) to provide information on periodicals to which the corporation can insure access, including those circulated from private sector sources, and cooperate in efforts to improve bibliographic and physical access to periodicals;
>
> (3) to make such periodicals available, on a cost reimbursable or other basis as determined by the Board, through libraries by loan or by photoreproduction or other means; and when required by the copyright owner, reasonable and appropriate reimbursement shall be made to copyright owners for the copying of material under copyright;
>
> (4) to cooperate with and participate in international borrowing and lending activities as may be appropriate for such purposes;
>
> (5) to enter into cooperative agreements with the Library of Congress, the National Library of Medicine, the National Agricultural Library, other Federal agencies, State and local agencies and instrumentalities, and private libraries and other organizations for such purposes;
>
> (6) to establish regional offices of the Corporation to the extent necessary and appropriate; and
>
> (7) to coordinate the training of librarians and other users in the use of the Corporation's services.
>
> The corporation shall have a Board of Directors consisting of fifteen members, including fourteen members appointed by the President, by and with the advice and consent of the Senate, and the Executive Director of the Corporation.
>
> The members of the Board appointed by the President shall be representatives of

the needs and interests of the Government, academic and research communities, libraries, publishers, the information community, authors, and the public. Except for the initial Board of Directors, the members shall be appointed after consultation with the Board.

The members of the initial Board of Directors shall serve as incorporators and shall take whatever actions are necessary to establish the Corporation under the laws of the jurisdiction in which it is incorporated.

The term of office of each member of the Board shall be six years.

The Corporation shall have a Director, and such other officers as may be named and appointed by the Board. The Director shall have authority with respect to the management of the operations of the Corporation, subject to such rules as many be prescribed by the Board.

ARL PROGRAMS AND PROJECTS

In addition to advances in federal legislation and appropriations for research libraries over the past five years, the ARL office has also improved its communication and publications program. A full-time information officer position was added to the staff in 1976. As a result, the ARL *Newsletter* is now published regularly five times a year, a new brochure on the association was published, and publications such as *Association Proceedings* have been expanded and speeded up. Some of the major programs on which ARL has published proceedings in the last five years have included The Library of Congress as the National Bibliographic Center; Research Libraries and Cooperative Systems; National Library Planning; Changing Environment for Research Library Development; Collection Analysis in Research Libraries; National Planning for Bibliographic Control; and The Future of Scholarly Communication.

The statistics gathering, analysis, and publishing program of the association has also been expanded over the past five years. Now included is more information on average salaries of ARL librarians by position, sex, size and type of institution, and geographic location. The ARL Task Force on Statistics also prepared a special supplementary report using regression techniques to analyze the operations of individual libraries and improve comparisons with other libraries.

Other task forces consisting primarily of ARL directors were established during the five years and reflect some of the major concerns and objectives of the association. They include Bibliographic Control, Network Development, and National Periodical Center. A new task force that reflects concern for library education was approved at the October 1979 meeting of the association.

Two significant projects were undertaken by the ARL staff late in the five-year period. The first was the development of a Library Catalog Cost Model Project under which King Research, Inc., in collaboration with ARL staff, developed and tested a cost model that would assist libraries in comparing the costs of alternatives to present card catalogs. The project included two workshops with representatives of more than 70 libraries participating. A final report will be published in early 1980 by ARL.

The second project is based on the award of a grant of $50,000 by the National Endowment for the Humanities in support of a project to plan and coordinate North American efforts toward building a machine-readable data base of catalog records for materials in microform. The project, entitled "Bibliographic Control of Materials in Microform," will involve librarians, micropublishers, representatives of bibliographic utilities, and others in working together to develop the agreements, standards, and mechanisms required for the cooperative development of a widely accessible cataloging data base. Particular emphasis will be given to facilitating the production and dissemination of analytics for titles published in large microform sets.

In addition to the central ARL Office, two other administrative units are directly under ARL, the Office of Management Studies (formerly Office of University Library Management Studies) and the Center for Chinese Research Materials. Both programs are primarily supported by outside funding and both have had considerable increases in funding over the past five years.

The Office of Management Studies (OMS), in 1975, with the assistance of the Council on Library Resources, expanded its Management Review and Analysis Program for research libraries to include self-study procedures for small and medium-sized academic libraries under an Academic Library Development Program. An added new operation also used the self-study process and applied it to the development and maintenance of research collections. This project is supported primarily by the Andrew W. Mellon Foundation and is known as the Collections Analysis Project (CAP).

In 1978, OMS received new and additional financial support from the Council on Library Resources and the Andrew W. Mellon Foundation, plus a five-year commitment from ARL to begin a new Academic Library Program incorporating the existing self-study programs and extending opportunities for participation to all types of academic libraries. One important part of the new program is the training of outstanding mid-career librarians in the consultation process to help libraries in their own development and problem-solving work. The goal is to so train 100 librarians over a five-year period.

One further grant has been from the Lilly Endowment to assist small academic libraries in their planning and development procedures. Ongoing operations that have increased in size and quality over the past five years have been the Systems and Procedures Exchange Center and the Management Skills Institute Operation. Participation in both services is available to all libraries and librarians.

The ARL Center for Chinese Research Materials (CCRM) was established in May 1968, upon the recommendation of the Joint Committee on Contemporary China of the American Council of Learned Societies and the Social Science Research Council. Since its founding, the center has served primarily as a publishing house that reproduces newspapers, periodicals, monographs, government documents, and research tools focusing on twentieth-century China.

By obtaining materials through loan arrangements with libraries and private collections throughout the world, the center has been highly successful in completing runs of widely scattered, rare, and highly significant periodicals. By subsidizing its costs with foundation grants, the center has been able to offer reproductions of these materials at prices so low that libraries of every size can now acquire resources that even the most heavily endowed libraries would never have been able to collect on their own.

CCRM has been supported by grants from the Ford Foundation, the Andrew W. Mellon Foundation, and the National Endowment for the Humanities and by the sale of publications. Increased funding from the Mellon Foundation and the National Endowment on a matching loan basis for three-year period has been achieved and fruitful contacts have been established with the USSR and the People's Republic of China.

Useful relationships have been established over the last five years with other organizations concerned with research libraries. These have included particularly the Association of American Universities, along with the Association of Graduate Schools, both of which have established committees on research libraries that have been particularly helpful in supporting action toward a National Periodical Center. The American Council on Education has also been helpful in supporting legislation and appropriations useful to research libraries.

IN CONCLUSION

Through efforts of ARL, both direct and indirect, the last five years have seen a heightened awareness and understanding of research libraries as essential and irreplaceable resources for scholarship, research, and needed information for the support of science, technology, and the humanities. This heightened awareness was assisted and evidenced in 1977 with the publication of a report of 15 distinguished university presidents, *Research Universities and the National Interest*, which included an important chapter on "The Major Research Libraries: Strengthening a National Heritage."

Although the two years since the publication of the report have seen both achievement and progress on some of the recommendations, it is worth noting all of the recommendations here:

1. Appropriations be made to carry out HEA Title II-C.
2. A national lending library be established with support of the federal government, the Library of Congress, ARL, NCLIS, and the Center for Research Libraries.
3. Establish a permanent body to assess the quality of national library resources and help shape national policy.
4. Improve national bibliographic services under Library of Congress operation and assistance of ARL and other representatives of libraries, the scholarly community, and users.
5. ARL should establish a research and analysis unit to develop information to improve library management.
6. Federal government attention and support of the Library of Congress to ensure an effective national preservation program.

In concluding the review of the five-year period, it is interesting to examine the resolutions that were approved by the delegates to the White House Conference on Library and Information Services in November 1979. It is gratifying to note that most of the objectives and concerns expressed above have been included in some form in these resolutions, particularly the resolution on networking, which includes the provision that "plans be developed at the national, regional and local level to include specific plans for a National Periodicals System and include the concept of a National lending library for print and non-print materials."

COUNCIL FOR COMPUTERIZED LIBRARY NETWORKS

1875 I St. N.W., Washington, DC 20006
202-223-6800, ext. 456

James G. Schoenung

Executive Director, PALINET/ULC
Secretary, Council for Computerized Library Networks

The Council for Computerized Library Networks (CCLN) is a nonprofit corporation made up of library networks that provide on-line services to libraries and information centers in North America. CCLN network members, which make use of state-of-the-art computer and telecommunications equipment, are located across the

United States and Canada and, collectively, provide on-line library and information services to over 3,000 public, academic, special, federal, and school libraries—including both nonprofit and for-profit institutions. Services offered by CCLN members include on-line shared cataloging and union catalog systems available through bibliographic utilities such as OCLC, Inc., the Research Libraries Group's RLIN network (formerly known as BALLOTS), the Washington Library Network (WLN), and the University of Toronto Library Automation Systems (UTLAS), as well as on-line interlibrary loan, serials control, acquisitions, circulation, and machine-assisted search services. In addition to their ongoing activities relating to research, development, marketing, implementation, and maintenance of computerized products and services, network members also offer training and consulting services to aid libraries in making optimal use of new technologies. Some network members are intrastate (e.g., INCOLSA in Indiana), some are regional (e.g., SOLINET covers 11 southern states), and some are national or international in scope (e.g., OCLC, Inc., now has member libraries in Canada as well as every state in the United States).

PURPOSES

CCLN serves several purposes. It collects, packages, and distributes information concerning on-line library networks; it serves as a forum for information exchange among network users regarding questions of governance, management, staffing, and finances; and it organizes and coordinates professional development activities. It also acts as a change agent by promoting dialogue within the library community and among other professional groups working in allied fields. It participates in planning the emerging national library and information network, informs the private sector of members' problems with existing technologies and services and suggests new products and solutions, and makes research and development recommendations to the federal government and foundations to facilitate support of state, regional, national, and international networking efforts. It is the only organization devoted solely to promoting networking issues and concerns and allows suppliers and users of library and information services a voice in influencing the development of these services.

MEMBER SERVICES

CCLN member services fall into four major areas: information dissemination on networking itself, information collection of CCLN's membership, training and professional development, and information exchange.

The difficulty of staying abreast of changes in technology, new services, funding sources, relevant legislation, and a host of similar topics is eased by the council's existing and planned publications program. The first issue of the *CCLN News* was distributed in the summer of 1979. This quarterly is devoted to news of CCLN activities; technical development announcements; information regarding grants, RFPs (Requests for Proposals), and contracts; updates covering regional, national, and international networking and automation events; reports about regulations, tariffs, rulings, etc.; announcements and summaries of educational and professional meetings, conferences, workshops, and related continuing education events; and discussion of other news of immediate value to the on-line network users. CCLN issues a "News Flash Current Awareness Service" to supplement its newsletter in providing timely information. Future council publications include "Network Technology Reports" and "Resource Surveys."

Computerized networks have grown so rapidly throughout the 1970s that even network staffs encounter problems in tracking their colleagues' activities. CCLN fills this need for up-to-date information by providing a clearinghouse for files of members' newsletters and publications. It also prepares a membership directory and conducts periodic surveys of network fees, services, organizational structure, operations, and the like.

Apart from training provided by the networks and some vendors, there is little concerted effort to educate librarians in preparing for and using computerized network services. To overcome this lack, CCLN offers a variety of professional development opportunities for network staff, participating libraries, and library and information science educators and students. This is done on a routine basis by means of program meetings that follow regular CCLN board meetings; special colloquia targeted for national and international audiences are planned for 1980 on topics such as "The On-Line Catalog" and "International Library Networking."

Finally, CCLN provides a forum for exchanging ideas within the library profession by inviting observers from the following groups to attend its meetings: the Library of Congress, the National Commission on Libraries and Information Science, the National Library of Canada, and the Council on Library Resources. The council, in turn, serves as a member of the Library of Congress's Network Advisory Committee, which is discussing plans for the evolution of a national library network, and represents library networks and their users perspective in many professional groups, such as the American Library Association's Policy Development Forum on Continuing Education. The expansion of CCLN services is beyond the reach of any single network member and presents a coherent range of services to an important sector of the library community.

CCLN MEMBERSHIP

The council offers two types of membership: network members and associate members. On-line computerized library networks that provide services on a nonprofit basis to administratively independent libraries for a state, region, or multistate area in North America may apply for network membership. During the 1979–1980 fiscal year there were 23 agencies in this category: AMIGOS Bibliographic Council; Bibliographical Center for Research, Rocky Mountain Region, Inc.; California Library Authority for Systems and Services (CLASS); Cooperative College Library Center (CCLC); Five Associated University Libraries (FAUL); Illinois Library and Information Network (ILLINET); Indiana Cooperative Library Services Authority (INCOLSA); Michigan Library Consortium (MLC); Midwest Region Library Network (MIDLNET); Minnesota Interlibrary Telecommunications Exchange (MINITEX); New England Library Information Network (NELINET); New York State Interlibrary Loan Network (NYSILL); OCLC, Inc.; OHIONET; PALINET and Union Library Catalogue of Pennsylvania; Pittsburgh Regional Library Center (PRLC); Research Libraries Group (RLG); Southeastern Library Network (SOLINET); State University of New York (SUNY); University of Toronto Library Automation Systems (UTLAS); Washington Library Network (WLN); and Wisconsin Library Consortium (WLC). New applicants are admitted to membership upon a two-thirds vote of current network members. Each network member has one representative with one vote at business meetings who is eligible to serve on the executive committee. Network members represent their own local constituencies at CCLN meetings.

Associate members are individual libraries that make use of services supplied by a council network member. Associate members may not attend CCLN business meetings (unless they are the designated representative of a council network member);

however, they may attend CCLN program meetings, receive the *CCLN News* and "News Flash Service," and attend CCLN conferences and colloquia at member rates. During the 1979–1980 fiscal year, the council had over 200 associate members.

The council is currently studying two other types of membership: affiliate members and educational members. The former applies to those providers of services, systems, or data bases that are of interest or use to network members. Educational members would include accredited institutions offering advanced degrees in library, information, or computer science.

ORGANIZATION AND STAFF

Network members elect four officers: president, vice-president/president-elect, secretary, and treasurer. These officers and the past president serve on the CCLN executive committee. The council's affairs are conducted at regularly scheduled business meetings, which are generally held in conjunction with a program meeting. As the need arises, special committees are appointed, such as the Legislative Committee. During FY 1979–1980, the council's operating budget was $28,000.

Throughout 1979 CCLN maintained a secretariat with an office located in Washington, D.C. The secretariat was responsible for carrying out a membership drive, accounting and financial reports, editing the *CCLN News*, and increasing public awareness of CCLN services and activities.

RECENT DEVELOPMENTS

CCLN grew out of a group of OCLC-affiliated regional networks known as the Council of Regions (COR), which had its first informal meeting in 1973. The council's history up to mid-1977 is well documented in an article by James T. Dodson that appeared in the 1977 edition of the *Bowker Annual*. CCLN's development from mid-1977 up to the present (i.e., January 1980) represents a period of reexamination of the council's role followed by a strong effort to develop programs that support library networking. An important step in CCLN's growth was the acceptance by the membership of a program plan in April 1978. This planning document called for the council to play an increasingly active role over the next five years. One recommendation, which has since been accomplished, involved the council's incorporation; CCLN is now seeking tax-exempt status under Title 501C, which will allow it to receive grants and pursue an active research program.

While not all of the program plan's recommendations have been implemented, many have, and CCLN's achievements over the past several years are notable. These include recruitment of a greatly increased membership base, recognition by and representation on various national library organizations, establishment of a secretariat in Washington, D.C., publication of a newsletter, and sponsorship of important colloquia.

THE FUTURE

Over the past few years the council has moved to a position of acceptance by other groups. It clearly has a significant role to play in presenting the viewpoint of on-line networks in regional and national developments and in providing a neutral environment in which different, sometimes competitive, networks can discuss the broader issues involved in planning for the future. It is worth noting that networks are dynamic organizations and change is the rule rather than the exception. It is likely that CCLN will continue to respond to changing conditions, implement additional services programs, and offer increased leadership in linking together the disparate parts that will form the national network.

INFORMATION INDUSTRY ASSOCIATION

316 Pennsylvania Ave. S.E., Washington, DC 20003
202-544-1969

Paul G. Zurkowski
President

As information and communication technologies expand our information handling capacities, the information industry will naturally expand and grow. Just what is the information industry? For members of the Information Industry Association (IIA), the common denominator is information content: multiple applications and multiple markets for information content. A business is primarily information if:

It is being impacted by technological changes in information production, distribution, and marketing.

It is focusing more on information content (utilizing all media appropriate to various markets) than on a specific delivery medium.

It is looking beyond its primary medium to electronic and other forms of production, distribution, and marketing for use.

The information business faces unprecedented opportunities arising from entrepreneurial applications of new technological capabilities. Companies of all kinds need the support of a trade group exclusively devoted to their business. IIA, created 11 years ago to be just that trade group, is now "home" for a broadly based group of leading information companies serving business and industry with information-age capabilities. IIA grew out of three major factors coming together in the 1960s:

1. Following the launching of Sputnik, the U.S. government, led by the efforts of Senator Hubert H. Humphrey, addressed the nation's scientific and technical information-handling capabilities. The decision was made to rely essentially on the professional societies, which traditionally maintain the record of achievement in their respective disciplines, to develop information systems to support the further development of science and technology. This involved subsidizing the development of what we now call professional society data bases such as Chemical Abstracts, Engineering Index, BIOSIS, and others. Private companies that were engaged or becoming engaged in these areas of activity began agitating for the creation of a trade group to represent their interests and to get government to deal equitably with information activities in both the for-profit and not-for-profit sectors.

2. In the mid-1960s, William T. Knox, an executive from ESSO Research, came into government as an assistant to the president's science adviser and, among other duties, served as secretary to a government coordinating committee called COSATI, the Committee on Scientific and Technical Information. In trying to relate government information activities to counterparts in the private sector,

Knox identified a void. He found there was no national focal point for the interests of private sector information companies. Later, when he moved to McGraw-Hill Book Company, Inc., he took a leadership role in bringing the industry together. Subsequently, he was elected first president of the board of directors of the Information Industry Association in November 1968.

3. Another dimension of the history of the founding of IIA involves the copyright revision process that was just getting under way in the 1960s. Many of the industry companies were beginning to see that information in electronic media faced serious copyright problems. This focal point for industry interest ultimately brought industry activists together with Paul G. Zurkowski, who was to become the association's first executive director. At that time Zurkowski served as legislative assistant to Congressman Robert W. Kastenmeier, chairman of the Judiciary Committee subcommittee revising the copyright law.

In the spring of 1968 a group of industry executives met and decided to put up money to incorporate a trade group. The charter was adopted at a meeting in Philadelphia on November 2, 1968. A board of directors was elected with Knox being elected president, a title subsequently changed to chairman. A search committee interviewed candidates to head the staff and selected Zurkowski. Offices were opened in Washington, D.C., in February 1969 and the first annual meeting of the association was held in New York City in March 1969.

The association has been involved in many issues and has firmly established the concept of the information industry as a separate and identifiable industry. The advent of on-line information services since 1976-1977 has stimulated a ground swell of interest in the business of information based on the recognition that information is the core business, regardless of how it is delivered and used. By bringing information executives together, the association has identified common interests for a large and growing list of companies. Counting subsidiaries such as Standard and Poors of McGraw-Hill and Greenwood Press of Congressional Information Service, more than 150 companies are active members of the association.

HIGHLIGHTS OF 1979 ACTIVITIES

A brief review of the highlights of the association's activities in 1979 provides an insight into the interests of IIA and its members.

Membership

The IIA launched a new membership campaign—Join the Information Revolution—in the spring of 1979, and offered special rates to small information companies. In joining the association, major corporations such as A. C. Nielsen Company and J. Walter Thompson testify to the diversity in the industry.

The IIA board of directors adopted a definition of "information industry revenues" for membership dues purposes.

> The information industry consists of concerns that create, assemble, organize, manage, or distribute information products and services through any medium appropriate to the client or customer.
>
> For the purposes of this definition, "information" represents the resulting intellectual work product when data elements are organized and communicated in a useful form (e.g., to help answer a question, solve a problem, or form the basis for action).
>
> Excluded from the Information Industry Revenues, as defined, is the production of materials purely for entertainment, such as movies, television, games, trade books and paper-

backs, as well as the production of materials only used in formal education such as textbooks for elementary, high school, and college.

The production of certain controlled circulation magazines and consumer publications, depending on their content and purpose, may be included.

Major new categories of membership were adopted by the IIA membership at its 1979 annual meeting.

Observer members. Membership is now available to companies engaged in closely related businesses that are interested in information industry activities, but not yet actively marketing information products and services. Dues for observers are set at $500 for companies with total revenues under $50 million, and $1,000 for companies with over $50 million in annual gross receipts. Observer status is also available to sister trade associations on a separate dues schedule.

Government and nonprofit members. For the first time, membership is now available to nonprofit organizations and government agencies engaged in the information business and information activities, which, if organized for profit, would entitle a society or an agency to corporate voting membership. Associate dues levels are approximately 50 percent of corporate voting member rates.

Publications

The third edition of *Information Sources*, the directory of members of the IIA, was published early in 1979. It provides one or more pages describing the services of each of the member companies, and also includes telephone numbers of key executives in each company. It has proved a very popular reference tool for information managers and others with a need for immediate contact with the industry. Because of the diversity of products and services offered by this industry, *Information Sources* is the single best definition of the industry.

In 1979 IIA also published *The Information Resource: Policy, Background and Issues—An Infostructure Handbook*, edited by Forest Horton, noted information and systems expert. The handbook contains nine chapters outlining major issue areas, the subissues involved, agencies and initiatives concerned, the private sector interests, national and international meetings, and publications and major literature available on each. The book literally describes the nation's information infostructure.

Other Highlights

IIA approved the launching of an industry survey designed to define clearly the information industry universe and its contributions to the gross national product and to enable the industry to better measure itself. Phil Nielsen (A. C. Nielsen) chairs the steering committee managing the survey. IIA is also launching a salary survey in 1980 (to be performed by the A. S. Hansen Company) to identify the types of employees active in the industry and their respective job descriptions and pay levels. Jim Petersen (Aspen Systems Corp.) chairs the steering committee on the salary survey.

John Rothman, director of information, New York Times Company, received the 1979 Hall of Fame Award for his professional contributions to the field and particularly for his role in the development of the New York Times Information Bank. Rothman, in accepting the award, warned against succumbing to the dictates of the information technology "machines" and urged the industry to assume responsibility for the flow of content through the technology. He urged that technology be made to fit human beings rather than the reverse. And he warned against the industry becoming the "sorcerer's apprentice" to information technology.

IIA joined the following organizations in 1979 (representatives are named): National Council of Professional Service Organizations, Bill Creager (Capital Systems Group) and Herb Brinberg (Aspen Systems); American Society for Information Science (institutional member), Helena M. Strauch (IIA); Library of Congress Network Advisory Committee, Robert S. Willard (IIA).

ASSOCIATED INFORMATION MANAGERS

AIM, formerly known as the Program for Information Managers, is a program of services to assist in the development of an executive position devoted to the management of information resources in government agencies, corporations, and universities. During 1979 a variety of services were provided to its membership, which grew from 250 to 750.

In 1979, AIM initiated publication of *AIM Network*, a biweekly newsletter (23 issues were published). *Network* includes industry and product news as well as AIM member news and legislative updates. The AIM Career Clearinghouse listed over 40 position openings in *AIM Network* and reported good responses to its effort to connect information workers with position openings. Nearly 200 applicants and 20 employers participated in the AIM Clearinghouse, which operated during the National Information Conference and Exposition.

The 1979–1980 *AIM Membership Roster* published the results of the AIM membership survey, indicating salary level, education level, percent of information use, and type of information used for over 650 information managers.

Over 300 information managers attended the AIM caucus to hear Richard Harden, special assistant to the president for information management.

Current articles and public documents were distributed through the AIM Microlibrary, a microfiche current-article service for members.

A policy council was formed to respond to policy issues impacting information managers.

AIM sponsored nine regional meetings: three in New York City, one each in Chicago, Atlanta, Philadelphia, and San Francisco, and two in Washington, D.C. (Five more informal regional meetings were held in conjunction with the National Information Conference and Exposition III.)

NATIONAL INFORMATION CONFERENCE AND EXPOSITION (NICE)

IIA sponsors NICE once a year to bring together everyone concerned with information content to discuss how to manage it, how to distribute it using information technologies, and how to maximize its application to the basic purpose of specific organizations and activities. NICE constitutes a complete marketplace for information.

NICE III, held at the Sheraton Washington Hotel in April 1979, attracted over 1,600 registrants and 70 exhibit booths. Chairman Andy Garvin (FIND/SVP) concluded that the concept of the information manager and the need for a broadly based seminar program and trade show about information has "jelled." The NICE III exhibit promotion brochure was honored by *Association Trends* for "Excellence in Association Publications." The 1979 Information Product of the Year Award was shared by "Checklist of State Publications," a product of Information Handling Services, and "The Silent 700" terminals produced by Texas Instruments. IIA formed an awards committee chaired by Ronald Henderson (Information and Publishing Systems) to set criteria for future product awards programs.

1979 COMMITTEE ACTIVITIES

Education and Marketing Committee

Phil Nielsen chaired IIA's eleventh annual meeting, held in October at the Sheraton Washington Hotel. Attendance was the largest ever at an IIA annual meeting. Ithiel de Sola Pool (Massachusetts Institute of Technology) spoke on the real challenges to First Amendment protections for information transmitted electronically. Managing Growth and Change, the theme of the working sessions, dealt with many aspects of the business of information. Chris Burns (Washington Post Company) chaired the preconference town meeting, which launched the effort to identify information policy discussion agenda.

Government Relations Committee

The Information Policy Discussion Group breakfasts became a monthly event in Washington, D.C., on Capitol Hill in 1979, a Legislative Fly-In was held in March, and industry executives involved with Congress, the White House, and executive agencies met on pending information-related issues.

IIA participated in the national debate on the National Periodicals Center proposal. Bob Willard (IIA), chairman of the Information Policy Discussion Group, participated in the legislative drafting committee to seek a common ground on problems of document delivery. He also attended the NCLIS meeting in Denver to pursue IIA's position and testified before the Senate Committee on the National Periodicals Center urging that full hearings be held on the proposal before it is authorized. Griff McDonald (UMI) was instrumental in shaping IIA's position, which is similar to the one reflected in the Arthur D. Little report on the NPC proposal.

IIA staff and members participated in the planning for the Congressional Chautaugua on Information, part of a series of special activities by the Congressional Clearinghouse on the Future. IIA's legislative program to revise Title 44 (government publications law) received strong support from industry executives. James B. Adler (CIS) and James McCain (IHS) worked long hours on the Advisory Committee and with industry representatives. Major progress was made in revising the law to serve the public interest. IIA testified before the joint House-Senate hearings on the bill.

IIA sponsored a reception in the U.S. Capitol on the one hundred and thirty-fifth anniversary of Alexander Graham Bell's first telegraph message, commemorating the opening of the electronic information age.

WITS (Worldwide Information and Trade System) was a major target of the association in 1979. The U.S. House reduced appropriations from $5 million to $1 million as a signal to the Commerce Department to involve the private sector. The Senate restored funding to the $4 million level, but added key language urging cooperation with the private sector.

IIA members testified at a Small Business Administration hearing in Iowa on the problems small businesses face from government competition. Sue Rugge (IOD) testified about the difficulties her information search and document fulfillment company faces from subsidized government information services provided to business by the Department of Commerce.

A dozen IIA members representing information retailers met with Assistant Secretary of Commerce R. DePaulo on the Commerce Information Retrieval Service.

IIA participated on the NCLIS Public/Private Sector task force. The association also joined in on the Information Community Advisory Committee to the White House Conference on Libraries and Information Services (WHCOLIS). The IIA staff participated at WHCOLIS as volunteers and facilitators. Board Chairman Bob Asleson (R. R. Bowker) testified at open hearings at WHCOLIS. Bob Asleson and Sam Wolpert (Predicasts) were voting delegates to WHCOLIS.

The House Administration Committee announced it would make LEGIS (legislative status system) available for distribution. Bob Willard covered the policy implications of this move in an article for *Information World*.

An IIA Committee of Members was asked to review an information policy statement prepared by the National Telecommunications and Information Administration. And Paul Zurkowski (IIA) was asked to review a National Science Foundation funding proposal.

In 1979, the IIA Proprietary Rights Committee renewed its activities under the chairmanship of Peyton Neal (Bureau of National Affairs). The General Accounting Office published a report calling for better management of information resources in government. There was strong IIA involvement in shaping this report.

Herb Brinberg (Aspen Systems) participated as a member of the National Technical Information Service Advisory Committee, a recently formed group. He also served on a Commerce Department sponsored Innovation Committee. His participation focused on information's role in industrial innovation. (This group was formed in 1978 and continued work in 1979.)

IIA members continued active participation on the Board of the Copyright Clearance Center (CCC) and on its Advisory Committee. Agreement on revision of the CCC bylaws to separate Advisory Committee participation from board meetings was reached.

International Committee

IIA's International Committee produced a policy statement on the international flow of information. It urges the elimination of trade and other barriers to the flow of information needed for cultural, commercial, and economic development.

In 1979, problems developed over applications for authority to extend public data network service to Japan. Data-base distribution firms argued that the network is needed immediately to open the Japanese market to U.S. data-base producers, just as packet switching created a large European market for American data-base services. IIA entered FCC proceedings and filed supporting pleadings.

IIA launched a European committee to involve IIA European members and employees of U.S. firms located in Europe in IIA activities.

A Netherlands Information Industry Association was formed, consisting of relevant companies, publishers, and electronic industry firms in the "primary information sector."

Three IIA board members visited China: Ted Lee (IHS) accompanied Commerce Secretary Juanita Kreps; IIA Board Chairman Bob Asleson joined a publisher group on their visit; and Isaac Auerbach (Auerbach Publishers) explored information technology issues.

West Coast Committee

IIA launched the West Coast Committee at a "Discover the Information Industry" membership development luncheon in Los Angeles with speaker Paul Zurkowski. Also the West Coast Committee has made plans to host the 1980 IIA annual conference, to be held in San Francisco, October 7-10, 1980. Tom Collins (SDC) is conference chairman.

INDUSTRY MOMENTUM BUILDING

The industry was given some definition in the 1979 *Information Market Place* (R. R. Bowker Company), indicating the dynamic growth of the industry. *Business Week* began a regular "Information Processing" department. On-line, Inc., sponsored its first major On-line Conference in the United States. And IIA Board Member Bob Riley (Chase) was named to the National Micrographics Association Productivity Council.

Throughout the year the IIA staff was invited to speak to various groups, participate in their meetings, or contribute articles to industry publications. Here is a sample of some of the major activities of 1979.

Paul Zurkowski spoke to the Communications Networks Conference in Washington in January, addressed a session on Marketing of Information Services in March, and ran a panel on New Concepts in Business Information in London in April. Zurkowski also participated on the Transborder Data Flow Advisory Committee and attended the NFAIS annual meeting and the Third International On-line Meeting in London. Zurkowski's article on "First Amendment Implications of Secondary Information Services" was published in the Spring issue of *Communications and the Law*, and his keynote address at the third NICE was reprinted in the September 15, 1979 issue of *Library Journal*, which was published in conjunction with the White House Conference.

In addition to a variety of government relations activities, Bob Willard participated on the NCLIS Open Forum on the National Periodicals Center. He attended the National Association of Broadcasters national conference and the National Computer Conference in New York City, and addressed the local Washington, D.C., chapter of the Data Processing Management Association and an International Communication Agency seminar among other groups in the information community. Willard writes a monthly column for *Information World*, covering information policy issues.

Representing IIA and AIM, Helena Strauch attended the Library Association of the City University of New York spring seminar, cosponsored by NYSLA and other library organizations, and the On-line '79 Conference in Atlanta. She writes a three- to four-page information industry AIM section for the bimonthly magazine *The Information Manager* and contributes articles to the special conference edition (NICE) of *Information World*.

FUTURE PLANS

The association plans an intensive effort to involve all active U.S. information companies in its programs. Major efforts are planned to provide member companies assistance in dealing with the day-to-day management problems unique to the information industry. This will involve member-only activities such as strategic planning sessions, technology interchange programs, developing new sources of knowledgeable information workers, and more.

For further information contact the appropriate IIA staff member at 316 Pennsylvania Ave. S.E., Washington, D.C. 20003, Tel. 202-544-1969. [A listing of IIA staff members, board members, and committee chairpersons is included in Part 7 under "National Library and Information-Industry Associations, U.S. and Canada"—*Ed.*]

NATIONAL LIBRARIANS ASSOCIATION: A FORUM FOR LIBRARIANS

Box 586, Alma, MI 48801

Peter Dollard
Past President

John Thomas founded the National Librarians Association (NLA) in May 1975. He outlined his reasons for doing so in the very first issue of the NLA *Newsletter*. The NLA, he said, was "formed to provide an association dedicated specifically to the professional needs of librarians—to protect the interests of librarians, to initiate legislative action aimed at maintaining minimum levels of competence, to raise the dignity and status of the profession, to focus attention on the career concerns of librarians, to remove the barriers now separating the different kinds of librarianship, to involve the total membership in the governing process, ... to bargain for rights and privileges, and, in short, to create a strong, dynamic, truly professional organization."

Thomas pointed out that other library associations served a different function: they promoted libraries and librarianship, but not, per se, the professional interests of librarians. Many NLA members state that point with considerable heat. Ellis Hodgin, for example, one of the members of NLA's first executive board, asserted, in the third issue of the NLA *Newsletter*, that ALA, "the one organization which could have ... been a strong national voice ... [that could have] ... defined, protected, and promoted the welfare or status of the individual librarian ... [had shown] ... a devastating lack of professional advocacy" by failing to do so.

Thomas, who left the profession altogether only 18 months after founding NLA, practiced law in India before emigrating to Canada in the late 1960s. He earned his MLS and entered the profession in 1970, when he became university bibliographer at North Carolina A&T University. Dismayed by the low status of American librarianship, and after considerable exploration of alternative solutions, he announced his intention to form a National Librarians Association in *American Libraries* (March 1975). He wrote a constitution and bylaws, appointed NLA's first executive board, and, on May 22, 1975, succeeded in having NLA incorporated in North Carolina. In April 1976, the Internal Revenue Service granted NLA tax-exempt status.

From the very beginning, most American librarians have viewed NLA with a considerable degree of skepticism. For example, Thomas received only several dozen responses to the *American Libraries* letter in which he called upon colleagues to join with him in founding NLA. He wrote to every responder, asking if they were willing to work for NLA. Many of those people never answered; those who did were appointed to various NLA offices. NLA's first executive board was constituted by that self-selection process. Those willing to serve were appointed. Thomas appointed himself NLA's first president. Peter Dollard, director of the Alma College (Michigan) Library, was appointed vice-president/president-elect. Robert Burr, then circulation librarian at William and Mary College Library, was appointed secretary. Bynum Crews, a colleague of Thomas at North Carolina A&T, was appointed treasurer. Thomas also announced three at-large appointments to NLA's executive board: Roy Fry, Loyola University of Chicago; Richard Miller, Arcadia (California) Public Library; and Susan Vaughn, Brooklyn College Library. NLA's first executive board had a **broad** geographic representation, though it was overburdened by academic librarians. At that time, in the fall of 1975, NLA had only 20 or 25 members.

PROMOTIONAL ACTIVITIES BEGIN

NLA's executive board took upon itself responsibility for being the active leadership core that NLA would need if it hoped to thrive. In 1975 and early 1976, board members began to become acquainted with each other through letters and phone calls. Those methods of communication are difficult in any case, but are particularly so in a situation in which all efforts are voluntary. Nevertheless, NLA began to plan for the future.

The first executive board meeting was held in Greensboro, North Carolina, on April 2 and 3, 1976. Present at that meeting were Thomas, Burr, Crews, Dollard, and Ellis Hodgin from the College of Charleston (South Carolina) Library, who by that time had been appointed to the executive board in place of Richard Miller. That first board meeting, a most productive one, resulted in extensive revision and refinement of the bylaws as well as completion of plans for NLA's first business meeting to be held three months later in Chicago.

A major concern of the executive board was the need to let the profession know that NLA existed and that members were wanted. One important decision that was made was to establish a *Newsletter*. It was decided that NLA's *Newsletter* could serve not only as an organ for communication with the membership but also as a means of demonstrating NLA's seriousness of intent. It was therefore decided that a commercially printed format would be used rather than a mimeographed typewritten publication. Peter Dollard was appointed editor of the *Newsletter*. The first issue, published in January 1976, included NLA's constitution and bylaws as well as an article by John Thomas on "The Birth of the NLA." Only 500 copies were printed, since NLA's membership was still extremely limited. Announcements were sent to the library media about the *Newsletter* and subscriptions were solicited.

A second vital part of NLA's early efforts was the establishment of several standing committees that could hammer out position statements for NLA. At the beginning, anyone who expressed a strong concern about a particular issue was offered the opportunity to chair an NLA committee on that particular issue. The first two issues of the *Newsletter* record the creation of committees on membership, education, placement, job security, remuneration, and employment practices, status, programs, legislation, and ethics. One consequence of NLA's first annual conference, held in the summer of 1976, was that those eight committees were consolidated into the three standing committees that continue to be the core of NLA committee activity: certification standards, professional welfare, and professional education.

Those three committees were charged with the very difficult task of coming to terms with questions raised again and again, especially by those who perceived NLA's battle to be of dubious value: What does NLA stand for other than for commiseration with one's fellow librarians? The executive board recognized an obligation to answer that question speedily. After all, if there was in fact a need for NLA, then it should be possible to spell out with some degree of specificity what NLA could do for librarians. At the same time, a clear statement of goals and objectives would be invaluable for recruitment purposes. The standing committees were therefore perceived to be primarily a midrange means of articulating NLA philosophy, while, at the same time, the very appointment of working committees was perceived to be a spur to further membership growth.

A third area identified as a priority of high importance was the need to publicize

NLA's existence as widely as possible. That area has continued to be NLA's most problematic one. There was, first of all, the need to write down what NLA was doing and then to transmit that information to the appropriate media. The media proved in general to be rather indifferent to NLA. Most items were ignored altogether; on the few occasions when they were published, there was normally a high response rate from readers.

Clearly, there was no anti-NLA conspiracy. Instead, it was apparent that NLA simply lacked credibility. It was so misunderstood that it was referred to in such a way as, on one occasion, to suggest that it was a southern-based reactionary group, while, on another occasion, it was dismissed as some sort of fanatical left-wing organization.

In addition to these only slightly successful attempts to inform the profession about NLA by means of news releases to the media, several flyers were mailed bulk-rate to thousands of libraries across the country. It turned out that these flyers were very helpful. Each one generated enough new memberships and new subscribers to justify the considerable cost of duplicating and mailing the flyer. Every one of the flyers also generated many letters asking what NLA was up to.

PROGRAMS PRESENTED

At the time of NLA's first business meeting in 1976, total membership had not yet reached 50. That first business meeting was held, through the courtesy of the ALA Social Responsibilities Round Table (SRRT), in the SRRT suite at the Palmer House Hotel in Chicago. For the most part it was a get-acquainted session. It was also a sort of archetypal NLA meeting in that NLA's members showed themselves to be representative of almost every part of the spectrum on any issue.

The meeting focused for the most part on a paper prepared by Thomas, Dollard, Hodgin, and Burr that attempted to spell out some ideas about NLA concerns, goals, and priorities. On nearly every issue, NLA's members disagreed. Should librarians be certified? Yes, said some, it's the only way to assure that the profession has minimal levels of competency. It's why I joined NLA! No, said others, it's not necessary since the library schools in effect play that role. I joined NLA in order to help fight against this move toward certification! So it ran on every issue. The only clear picture of an NLA "world view" that emerged was that people who joined NLA evidenced a very strong conviction that certain kinds of ideas relating to professional issues had to be discussed more widely. It became clear that, in effect, a major role for NLA would be to provide a forum for the discussion of such ideas.

The enthusiasm generated by that noisy and crowded first business meeting dissipated over the next few months. Several board members found it necessary to resign and, by the time of NLA's 1977 midwinter conference in Washington in 1977, it had become doubtful that NLA itself would survive beyond its first 18 months.

The minimum number needed for a quorum was present at that 1977 meeting: Dollard, Vaughn, June Stratton, who had been appointed NLA treasurer, and Ron Johnson, who had been appointed NLA secretary. John Thomas had indicated his intention to resign his presidency and there seemed little hope that NLA would hold together. Those four board members, however, demonstrating an unusual sort of tenacity of conviction, proceeded to plan NLA's future. Dollard was appointed acting president, Gerald R. Shields, an ALA councilor and former editor of the ALA *Bulletin*, was invited to join NLA's executive board, and plans were laid for NLA's very first program.

As plans for that first program were made, it became more and more clear that a series of well-publicized programs of substance might themselves very well prove to be one of the best services that NLA could offer to the profession at large. Such programs could help focus discussion on issues important to all librarians. Needless to say, they might also help NLA recruit members and continue its growth.

The first of NLA's programs was held in Detroit in 1977. The program included presentations by four distinguished speakers: Gerald R. Shields; Richard Dougherty, editor of the *Journal of Academic Librarianship;* Gail Schlachter, from the University of California at Davis; and Martin Erlich, from the Orange (California) Public Library. These four speakers addressed the general question of what it is that librarians should expect from their professional associations. *Library Journal* described the program as one of the best of the conference.

NLA's second program was held in Chicago in 1978. A nationwide call for papers on topics of interest was issued. The program was titled "Speaking Up for Librarians: A Forum on Professional Concerns." A large crowd heard John Berry, editor of *Library Journal*, moderate a program that included three speakers: Indra David, Oakland (Michigan) University Library, spoke on "Concerning Library Education"; David Bernstein, Bloomfield Hills Township (Michigan) Public Library, delivered a paper on "The Reference Interview"; and Ronald Wyllys, a teacher at the University of Texas at Austin Library School, spoke on "Augmented Librarianship." Susan Vaughn chaired the group that solicited, read, and selected the papers.

The third in NLA's series of annual programs was held in Dallas in 1979. Labeled a "Participatory Speak-Up," the program was developed out of a nationwide call for papers. Fran Hopkins, NLA's secretary, coordinated the call for papers. The speakers were Keith Cottam, who reported on the work of the ALA Task Force on Minimum Qualifications for Librarians; Kenneth Hedman, University of Texas at El Paso Library, argued that the second master's was a legitimate requirement for academic librarians; Gerald Shields, SUNY-Buffalo Library School, reported the results of a survey of his school's graduates of the past decade. This program was also well attended.

NLA's fourth annual program will be held in New York in 1980. In addition to sponsoring programs at the annual conference, NLA also sponsors programs held at state and regional library conferences, including the California, Michigan, Washington, Illinois, and Midwest Federation of Library Associations conferences. Such programs have proven to be so popular that they continue to be a high action priority for NLA. Joseph Rine, chief librarian at the Metropolitan Community College in Minneapolis, was appointed NLA's conference planner in late 1979.

DIFFICULTIES CONFRONTED

These many activities succeeded in bringing NLA membership to a total of 578 by June 30, 1979. In addition, 220 libraries were subscribing to the NLA *Newsletter*. On the one hand, such a membership total is miniscule when compared, for example, to that of such associations as the American Library Association, the Special Libraries Association, or the Association of College and Research Libraries. On the other hand, this total membership size was reached against considerable odds. Communication is costly and incomplete since NLA members are scattered from one end of the country to the other; NLA has a credibility problem since most librarians assume there already *is* a professional association for American librarians; NLA's low dues limit what it can do for its members; NLA's raison d'etre continues to evolve and that frustrates people who want all their answers yesterday; NLA is a bit overloaded with academic librarians and badly underrepresented by school librarians; all of NLA's work is done by volunteers in their spare time.

Despite these problems, NLA has continued to show a slow but steady growth. In

1977, the goal was to reach 100 members; by 1978 the goal was 500; the goal is now 1,000 members. The steady growth rate has been accompanied by a steady increase in the association's maturity. The original committee structure evolved into the present structure of three standing committees that have made substantial progress in articulating NLA goals and philosophies. NLA's Certification Standards Committee completed its third draft of a position statement in December 1979. NLA's Professional Welfare Committee has completed the second draft of its position paper. NLA's Professional Education Committee completed its first draft in early 1980.

Other activities have also emerged. For example, the November 1978 issue of the *Newsletter* included the first installment in NLA's serial Bibliography on Professionalism. This annotated bibliography, initiated by Donald Krueger, now at the Ontario Legislative Library, identifies studies dealing with all aspects of professionalism. A total of 79 citations had been listed by November 1979. Irene Godden, Colorado State University Library, assumed responsibility for this serial bibliography late in 1979.

In the summer of 1978, NLA formed an ad hoc Grievance Referrals Committee in order to meet the need caused by the fact that NLA periodically receives requests for advice and assistance in cases of employment grievances. Since the membership has not yet approved the mechanism being developed by NLA's Professional Welfare Committee, and since NLA's limited income precludes substantial amounts of investigative time, the ad hoc Grievance Referrals Committee responds by suggesting appropriate courses of action, whether through the American Library Association, the courts, union organizations, etc. The committee's members are selected on the basis of their expertise in this area. Elaine Clever, Temple University Library, chairs this committee.

The steadily increasing maturity of NLA is also epitomized by the gradual introduction of the democratic governing process. NLA's constitution stipulated that its initial executive board, which was self-appointive, would serve through June 30, 1978. On July 1, 1978, the first three members elected to NLA's executive board took office: Julio Martinez, at-large, San Diego State University Library; Fran Hopkins, secretary, Franklin and Marshall College Library; and June Stratton, vice-president/president-elect, then of the South Bend (Indiana) Public Library. On July 1, 1979, three additional members were elected to NLA's executive board: Mary-Elinor Kennedy, treasurer, Methuen (Massachusetts) Public Library; Bonnie Jackson Clemens, at-large, University of Georgia Libraries; and Norman Tanis, vice-president/president-elect, California State University at Northridge Library. Peter Dollard, the last nonelected member of NLA's executive board will rotate off the board on June 30, 1980.

Yet another sign of increased maturity has been the emergence of state chapters of NLA. By 1980, there were five: Hawaii, California, Washington, Illinois, and Michigan. It is hoped that these state chapters will eventually provide a mechanism for meaningful grass-roots involvement in NLA across the country.

GOALS EMERGE

NLA came into being in response to a long-felt need. Many librarians had long wanted a true professional association that would articulate, advocate, and defend the professional role of librarians. The American Library Association had for decades denied that it could play such a role. There were hopes by its founders and by most of those who joined that NLA would at last meet the long-perceived need. It has turned out, however, that NLA is coming to play a role that is even more complex than was at first foreseen. In the beginning were some ideas about improving the quality of graduate library school education, about removing the incompetent from the profession, about raising the status and salaries of librarians. Though such concerns certainly persist, NLA's role has come to be more catholic than was at first envisioned.

Most important, it has come to see itself not as the oracular fount of answers but, instead, as a forum in which questions are raised. If "the incompetents are to be removed," for example, then who are they and how are they to be identified? Indeed, what *is* competency? Will the identification of what competency is help librarians validate their standing as professionals? How does the MLS degree relate to the question of competency?

All the original assertions have branched out, making it more clear that the road NLA is to follow in the future is not a neatly paved highway but a multileveled roadway cluttered with obstructions. Some general tendencies seem to be emerging however. Most fundamental is the conviction that the profession has failed dismally in its responsibility to identify the core knowledge that binds all librarians into a single profession. Indeed, even many NLA members deny that such a core exists. The consensus among NLA's members, however, seems to be that librarians would be better if they were all required to be knowledgeable about the history of libraries, the social context in which libraries function, the philosophical nature of knowledge, the complex interactions between the information seeker and the mediator, the management requirements in libraries, the possibilities of computer applications, the very real challenges of identifying which materials are most suitable for one's clientele, the application of bibliometric analysis to library operations, the need to encourage among librarians the love for books as artifacts as well as information sources, the librarian as entrepreneur, and so on.

These goals have evolved into support for the extension of the MLS program to two years, with an extended internship sandwiched in the middle. There is also considerable interest in imposing a thesis requirement as a means of emphasizing the intellectual and scholarly aspects of the graduate program. There is also concern for tougher admissions and grading standards.

NLA's Certification Standards Committee has developed a lengthy document that, among other things, advocates a nationwide certification for librarians. Such a program would also involve periodic recertification as well as decertification of librarians who do not maintain their skills. The intent of such a program is not to pile up mountains of paper and red tape. Instead, the intention is to make it less possible for practicing professionals to sit on the laurels of their MLS. NLA would like to see pressure brought to bear on those colleagues who do not keep current, so that library users will meet librarians with rusty skills less frequently. NLA believes that this sort of across the board enhancement of the typical librarian's skill levels will make library users more cognizant of the value of the contribution made by librarians.

The third major thrust of NLA's developing ideas of the role it will play lies in the areas being discussed by NLA's Professional Welfare Committee. Though, like NLA's other committees, there has not yet been any stamp of approval given to this committee's ideas, certain fundamental ideas will certainly remain intact. First, the professional must be permitted to function in the library in a truly professional way. That is, there must be an absolute minimum of bureaucratic stratification and a maximum of participation by professionals in establishing and implementing the goals of the library. NLA will develop model statements of appropriate management systems for all kinds of libraries. NLA will also develop model procedures for remedying situations in which professional participation is not sufficiently realized.

It is also essential that NLA develop mechanisms for the speedy investigation of professional grievances and, in cases where it is justified, NLA intends to be the advocate of the librarian. NLA members perceive it to be the case that the American Library

Association has attempted to serve the needs of all—library, board of trustees, users, professionals, and support staff—to such an extent that the professional concerns of librarians are too often relegated to the rear. Since users and governing boards have their own independent means of promoting their self-interest, NLA will represent only the librarian, so that professional concerns can be clearly articulated and advocated within the context of the adversary nature of American litigation.

NLA'S FUTURE

NLA's founders at the beginning contended that there should be no need for an NLA. For more than a century, after all, American librarians have had the American Library Association. At the beginning, there was some hope that, if nothing else, NLA might be some sort of gadfly to ALA, helping to push it more toward an advocacy role for librarians. As events have developed, however, it has become more obvious that the library profession may well be of the type that requires both individual and institutional branches, somewhat in the manner of medicine, which has one organization for physicians and another for hospitals. It has become more and more clear to NLA's members that our society should have an organization strongly committed to working for the goals of American libraries as institutions. Indeed, many NLA members are also members of ALA and support ALA's institutional goals.

By the same token, NLA members have come to accept the idea that concern for the professional interests of librarians may not be, as ALA has long contended, consistent with what ALA is. If that is the case, then it is the case that NLA, born to be a gadfly, may well transform over the next decade into a truly strong and independent professional association with quite a substantial contribution to make to American librarianship.

As we enter the 1980s with inflation, declining revenues for libraries, high unemployment, and increased reliance on competitive information resources, it is likely that the status and image of librarians will suffer more than ever. It may well be the case that such factors will persuade MLS holders that their self-interest is better served by a librarian association than by a library association. Should librarians come to perceive that to be the case, then it is quite possible that, by the end of the 1980s, NLA will be as influential and significant a voice on the American library scene as those associations now dedicated to American libraries.

OCLC, INC.

1125 Kinnear Rd., Columbus, OH 43212
614-486-3661

Philip Schieber

Public Relations Manager

Last spring a group of 75 children in the fourth grade took turns searching the world's largest data base of bibliographic information. On a tour of the facilities of the Ohio College Library Center (OCLC) in Columbus, ten-year-old boys and girls browsed through 5.5 million catalog records from more than 2,000 libraries that ranged in size from large research libraries to small public libraries. They sat at OCLC terminals and looked for information about books, and they found what they were looking for.

For OCLC and its member libraries, teaching a child to do an author/title search on a computerized catalog may be largely symbolic, but it is an important symbol. The next generation of library users will have grown up with the idea that computers and libraries can actually bring information to people when and where they need it. By the time those children who visited OCLC are in college or working, the role of libraries in their lives may be different from what it was when OCLC first came into being, just about the time they were born.

HISTORY AND GOVERNANCE

From its founding in 1967 as the Ohio College Library Center, a nonprofit corporation, OCLC grew from an intrastate network of Ohio academic libraries to an international network that welcomes libraries of all types and sizes. The role of Ohio libraries in OCLC's early years is well known: They provided both believers in the cause and financial support for an experiment called the on-line union catalog and shared cataloging system. After four years of development, in August 1971, the on-line system came up, and Ohio University in Athens, Ohio, was the first institution to do on-line cataloging. The rest, as they say, is history.

By the end of 1971, 54 Ohio libraries were on-line. In 1972, libraries outside Ohio began coming on-line via regional library networks such as PALINET. By 1975, there were 20 regional networks and about 600 libraries in 37 states participating in OCLC's network system. And yet only Ohio libraries could participate in OCLC's governance, for only these institutions' representatives could elect from among themselves the nine-member Board of Trustees of the Ohio College Library Center.

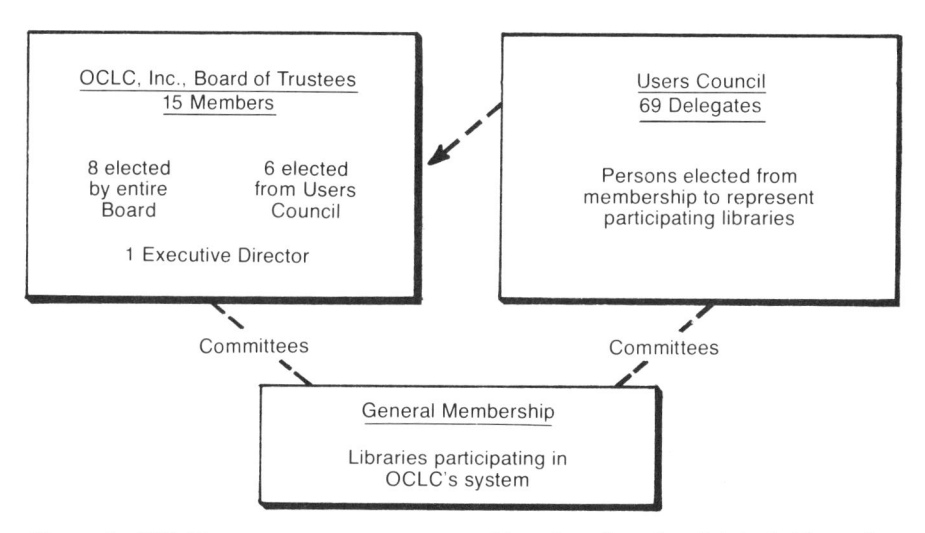

```
┌─────────────────────────────────────┐      ┌─────────────────────────────────┐
│   OCLC, Inc., Board of Trustees     │      │       Users Council             │
│         15 Members                  │◄-- --│       69 Delegates              │
│                                     │      │                                 │
│   8 elected         6 elected       │      │   Persons elected from          │
│   by entire         from Users      │      │   membership to represent       │
│     Board            Council        │      │   participating libraries       │
│                                     │      │                                 │
│        1 Executive Director         │      │                                 │
└─────────────────────────────────────┘      └─────────────────────────────────┘
              Committees  --        ┌──────────────────────┐   -- Committees
                            ────────│  General Membership  │────
                                    │                      │
                                    │ Libraries participating in │
                                    │    OCLC's system     │
                                    └──────────────────────┘
```

Figure 1. OCLC's governance structure combines benefits of a tightly held not-for-profit corporation and a network cooperative. Libraries participating in organizations contracting with OCLC, Inc., are members of OCLC, Inc. Decision-making powers with regard to replacement of management and approval of policy and budgets reside in a Board of Trustees. The Users Council provides a formal institutional means for participating libraries in networks and other direct contractors of OCLC, Inc., to participate in election of trustees, and thus in policy decisions.

At the annual meeting in December 1975, the Ohio membership passed a resolution directing the Board of Trustees to "study the advisability of extending membership to libraries outside the State of Ohio." An Advisory Council appointed by the board retained the consulting firm of Arthur D. Little, Inc., to develop recommendations for a new governance structure for the Ohio College Library Center. On December 20, 1977, the Ohio representatives amended the Articles of Incorporation and Code of Regulations of the Ohio College Library Center, reconstituting it as OCLC, Inc. With the new name came an extended base for membership and an expanded structure for governance (Figure 1).

The overwhelming majority of libraries participating in the OCLC system are members of regional networks with which OCLC has contracts for supplying library processes and products to their member libraries. These regional networks provide the basic means by which OCLC furnishes support services to users of the OCLC system. Regional networks participating in OCLC are AMIGOS Bibliographic Council (AMIGOS), Bibliographical Center for Research (BCR), Consortium of Universities of the Washington Metropolitan Area (CAPCON), Cooperative College Library Center (CCLC), Five Associated University Libraries (FAUL), Federal Library Committee (FEDLINK), ILLINET Bibliographic Data Base Service (ILLINET), Indiana Cooperative Library Services (INCOLSA), Midwest Region Library Network (MIDLNET), Minnesota Interlibrary Telecommunication Exchange (MINITEX), Michigan Library Consortium (MLC), Nebraska Library Commission (NEBASE), NELINET, OHIONET, PALINET, Pittsburgh Regional Library Center (PRLC), Southeastern Library Network (SOLINET), State University of New York (SUNY), OCLC Western Service Center (Western/OCLC), and Wisconsin Library Consortium (WLC).

THE OCLC SYSTEM

Since its founding, OCLC has pursued two objectives: to increase availability of library resources to library patrons and to lower the rate of rise for library per-unit costs.

OCLC and its member libraries are achieving these objectives via the OCLC on-line system—a nationwide network of specially designed, synchronous OCLC cathode-ray tube terminals connected via multiple-party telephone circuits to OCLC's computer system in Columbus.

In January 1980, there were approximately 3,200 synchronous terminals operating on the system; moreover, there were 400 additional libraries authorized to use the OCLC shared cataloging system via direct dial-up telephone communication or the TYMNET network.

From these terminals more than 2,000 libraries were using the OCLC system to catalog books, order custom-printed catalog cards, maintain location information (5.5 million bibliographic records in the on-line union catalog, with more than 45 million listings of locations), and arrange for interlibrary lending of these materials. Libraries were also using a serials control subsystem to check in journals and periodicals.

In the autumn of 1979 participating libraries were cataloging on-line over 300,000 books each week, for which OCLC was printing more than 2 million catalog cards. The number of records in the on-line union catalog was growing at a rate of about 20,000 records a week, of which 80 percent were input by participating libraries and the remainder contributed by the Library of Congress via tapes from its LC-MARC II Subscription Service. The OCLC system supports cataloging of books, serials, and every form of nonprint material for which there is a MARC format, in addition to realia, for which there is not yet a Library of Congress MARC format.

TABLE 1 ON-LINE CATALOGING ACTIVITY, 1977–1979

	Total Titles Cataloged 1977/78	Total Titles Cataloged 1978/79	Chargeable First-Time Uses 1977/78	Chargeable First-Time Uses 1978/79	Input Cataloging 1977/78	Input Cataloging 1978/79	Percent Cataloging Using Existing Records 1977/78	Percent Cataloging Using Existing Records 1978/79
AMIGOS Bibliographic Council	1,302,717	1,502,619	972,171	1,128,746	71,729	79,208	93.1	93.4
Bibliographical Center for Research (BCR)	548,448	829,249	405,974	578,325	16,423	22,466	96.1	96.3
Consortium of Universities of the Washington Metropolitan Area (CAPCON)	140,910	188,157	119,273	159,778	7,227	6,250	94.3	96.2
Cooperative College Library Center (CCLC)	50,509	47,074	23,556	22,928	181	770	99.2	96.8
Federal Library Committee (FEDLINK)	280,510	398,007	163,526	211,363	39,240	44,309	80.6	82.7
Five Associated University Libraries (FAUL)	177,541	201,027	134,295	146,784	18,877	27,057	87.7	84.4
ILLINET Bibliographic Data Base Service	512,829	631,961	415,926	495,822	20,408	32,352	95.3	93.8
Independent Organizations	32,280	22,460	26,648	17,025	1,074	344	96.1	98.0
Indiana Cooperative Library Services (INCOLSA)	362,071	454,607	279,345	345,549	17,786	23,680	94.0	93.6
Michigan Library Consortium (MLC)	517,546	582,907	407,291	423,553	20,924	17,603	95.1	96.0
Midwest Region Library Network (MIDLNET)	205,556	244,579	149,274	191,624	9,267	8,330	94.2	95.9
Minnesota Interlibrary Telecommunication Exchange (MINITEX)	211,485	316,220	176,689	252,102	10,426	15,105	94.4	94.3
Nebraska Library Commission (NEBASE)	89,106	99,923	69,622	77,123	7,178	6,273	90.7	92.5
NELINET	790,668	851,688	610,043	648,410	50,590	47,362	92.3	93.2
OHIONET	925,136	963,696	615,214	643,524	52,204	43,537	92.2	93.7
PALINET	704,198	796,693	597,464	664,953	38,306	33,284	94.0	95.2
Pittsburgh Regional Library Center (PRLC)	244,977	292,117	190,516	226,009	7,689	8,278	96.1	97.5
Southeastern Library Network (SOLINET)	1,975,104	2,276,755	1,485,207	1,702,726	88,883	90,615	94.4	94.9
State University of New York (SUNY)	815,073	954,109	615,365	688,010	26,691	29,461	95.8	95.9
Western/OCLC	447,892	810,972	369,585	668,405	16,272	36,125	95.8	94.9
Wisconsin Library Consortium (WLC)	282,534	389,846	228,271	308,044	15,369	17,416	93.7	94.7
Total	10,617,090	12,854,666	8,055,255	9,600,803	536,744	589,825		
Average							93.8	94.2

The OCLC on-line system presently operates 87 hours a week: 7 A.M. to 10 P.M. Eastern Time, Monday through Friday, and from 8 A.M. to 8 P.M. on Saturdays. One of OCLC's long-range goals is to make the system available during a library's normal hours of operation, whether the library be in London, England, or Honolulu, Hawaii —two locations, by the way, that happen to have libraries with OCLC holding symbols.

For the year ending June 30, 1979, participating libraries cataloged 12.8 million titles on-line, for which OCLC produced 101,601,268 catalog cards. (In the OCLC, Inc., *1978/79 Annual Report*, OCLC President and Executive Director Frederick G. Kilgour pointed out that it was "a matter of concern, however, that participating libraries had to spend at least $2.4 million for catalog card storage cabinets to house these cards on increasingly expensive floor space. Needless to say, this expenditure, which will increase annually, points up one of the major savings that will be accomplished when on-line local catalogs terminate the growth of card catalogs.") Participants in the on-line Serials Control Subsystem checked in 401,573 issues of serials.

Table 1 provides a breakdown of on-line cataloging activity by participating networks. The principal charge for using the OCLC system is the first-time use charge, which is defined as the first time a library uses a record in the data base for catalog production that it did not input. As can be seen from the table, participating libraries are enjoying a "hit rate"—percent cataloging using existing records—of 94.2 percent.

In July 1979, OCLC began charging for transactions on its Interlibrary Loan Subsystem. Use of the new subsystem continued to rise in 1979 as shown by the following monthly totals of on-line interlibrary loan transactions: July, 31,022; August, 33,699; September, 38,740; and October, 56,355.

The Interlibrary Loan Subsystem, as stated in OCLC's *1978/79 Annual Report*, "provides for verification of bibliographic information and of patron requests for interlibrary loans, locations for four-fifths of requested items by use of on-line catalog, automatic transmission of interlibrary loan requests and resulting responses, automatic forwarding of interlibrary loan requests to potential lenders, as well as immediate access to an institution's interlibrary loan records and automatic updating of those records."

At the end of 1979, three subsystems—On-line Union Catalog and Shared Cataloging Subsystem, Interlibrary Loan, and Serials Control—were operational. Three additional major subsystems—acquisitions, circulation, and public service—are under development.

In addition to developing new subsystems, there is a considerable amount of development activity devoted to improving or enhancing existing subsystems. In one three-month period in 1979, for example, OCLC staff successfully completed 40 of 42 attempted software installations. These were enhancements to existing subsystems, and whether major or minor, they all point to the dynamism of the OCLC system and OCLC's continuing efforts to improve service to users.

ORGANIZATION

OCLC's organization consists of the following divisions under the Office of President and Executive Director: Administrative Services, Computer Facilities, Development, Finance, and User Services. There is also an Office of Planning and Research, and a Research Department conducts mission-oriented research on human/computer interaction, delivery of library services to the home, and improved access techniques.

FUTURE PLANS

As OCLC enters the 1980s, there seems to be a gathering momentum that will propel the OCLC network into innovative and exciting ways to help libraries provide information to patrons. In the immediate future are improvements in the on-line shared cataloging process that OCLC expects to implement, including support of AACR 2, the ability to catalog on-line in nonroman alphabets using a new OCLC terminal, a shelf-listing process for current cataloging, and on-line authority files. In 1980, OCLC expects to bring up its Acquisitions Subsystem. OCLC is also actively exploring development of an original-equipment-manufacturer type of arrangement whereby OCLC could make available in the near future a circulation system integrated into the OCLC on-line system.

According to OCLC's *1978/79 Annual Report*, "the major event of the year was the successful sale of a $38.5 million industrial revenue bond issue that included $25.7 million for a new building, $8.6 million for refinancing existing debt, and $3.8 million for acquisition of new equipment." Ground was broken on June 5, 1979 for the new building, which will have four stories and contain 126,400 square feet of office space and a three-story, 44,000 square-foot computer room. The building is scheduled to be completed in January 1981.

When OCLC begins to move its personnel and equipment into the new building in 1981, it will have a staff of about 500 persons and an organization with assets in excess of $50 million. In 1967, OCLC had a staff of two persons and assets of $62,000.

As for those schoolchildren at the beginning of this article, what might they see from OCLC libraries in the next ten years? OCLC has a number of research projects under way to study ways that libraries can use information and communication technologies such as cable television and mini- and microcomputers to provide information to library patrons when and where they need it. As library users the young adults might be able to access their libraries' catalogs via television sets and "magic boxes" designed and developed by OCLC, or they might consult electronic encyclopedias, or any number of new processes and products that emerge from OCLC's efforts to promote the evolution of library use, of libraries themselves, and of librarianship.

SPECIAL LIBRARIES ASSOCIATION, 1977–1980

235 Park Ave. S., New York, NY 10003
212-477-9250

David R. Bender
Executive Director

Richard E. Griffin
Assistant Executive Director

The Special Libraries Association (SLA) enters the 1980s after experiencing a decade of unprecedented growth in the 1970s. Since 1969, the association's membership has increased by more than 63 percent, and its income before expenses has more than doubled (from $380,000 in 1969 to over $800,000 in 1979). In the three years since the last *Bowker Annual* report on SLA, the association's membership has grown by more than 15 percent, and there are reasonable indications that the average annual growth trend of 6 percent since 1969 will continue in future years.

NEW EXECUTIVE DIRECTOR

Following the sudden and untimely death of Executive Director Frank E. McKenna, in November 1978, the board of directors designated a search committee to choose his successor. In June 1979 the board unanimously approved the appointment of David R. Bender as executive director, effective July 30, 1979.

Bender holds a doctorate in the field of educational technology. He comes to SLA from the School Library Media Services Branch of the Maryland Department of Education, where his responsibilities included supervision of the agency's library. He is an experienced administrator with interests in continuing education and publications. Bender is concerned that there be more participative management in the association through association-member communication and interaction. He is also concerned that SLA monitor and react to proposals for new government programs and legislation that will affect special libraries.

CHAPTER AND DIVISION GROWTH

A unique feature of SLA is its organization of active chapters and divisions. The chapters hold meetings throughout the year and enable SLA members to become active locally in the affairs of SLA. The divisions, on the other hand, provide members with a means of direct communication with others who share a common subject interest or information format (e.g., photographic slides, engineering drawings, maps and charts, newspaper clippings) in their libraries. The chapters and divisions serve as an informal information network, and it is this information network that is frequently cited by SLA members as their single most important reason for joining SLA.

SLA is a unique association in its direct per capita financial support of chapters and divisions through the granting of an annual allotment to each unit. The minimum annual allotment is $400. In 1979 the largest allotment granted to an SLA unit was in excess of $5,500.

Since 1977, the association has added three new chapters: Arizona Chapter (1978), Central Pennsylvania Chapter (1979), and Rhode Island Chapter (1977); and one new division has been formed: Telecommunications/Communications Division (1977). The number of chapters now totals 49. The chapters are located in the United States (46), Canada (2), and Europe (1). There are 29 divisions. During the 1970s, 12 new chapters and 6 new divisions were established.

STUDENT GROUPS

The association also fosters the establishment of student groups at schools of library and information science in the United States and Canada. These units are independent of SLA chapters; however, cooperative programs are undertaken and student members are encouraged to participate in chapter activities as well as student group activities. There are currently 31 SLA student groups, three of which have been established since 1977. Each group serves as a focus for special library activities in the library school, and through its programs and activities encourages students to consider special librarianship as a career. Many groups have sponsored workshops, panel discussions with invited speakers, programs at SLA annual conferences, and tours of local special libraries. SLA subsidizes the expenses of each group through granting a modest annual allotment.

PROFESSIONAL DEVELOPMENT ACTIVITIES

In the mid-1970s the SLA board of directors authorized a pilot program of regional continuing education courses for members and other interested persons who could not take advantage of the continuing education courses held during SLA's annual conferences. The success of the pilot program led the association in 1977 to employ a manager for professional development. The responsibilities of the position include the planning and coordination of continuing education programs and all other association activities pertaining to the professional development of SLA members.

The increased staff support has resulted in an expansion of SLA's education activities both at annual conferences and on a regional basis throughout the United States and Canada. Sequences of courses have been developed in four areas: management, communications, technology, and information science. In addition, courses on issues and problems of special interest are offered. As a participant in the Council on the Continuing Education Unit, the association is authorized to award continuing education units to course registrants.

To meet better the educational requirements of the association's membership, funds are being sought for a comprehensive continuing education needs assessment that will be undertaken during 1980.

Another responsibility of the Professional Development Department is the triennial SLA salary survey and its annual updates. The 1979 "SLA Salary Survey Report," published in the December 1979 issue of *Special Libraries*, is the association's fifth triennial survey since 1967 and the sixth survey of the salaries of SLA members undertaken since 1959. The 1979 survey includes several new features, among which are comparison of salaries by type of institution within each standard metropolitan statistical area; comparison of salaries and primary responsibility with type of institution; and comparison of male and female salaries as a function of years of experience, supervisory responsibility, and type of organization.

WHITE HOUSE CONFERENCE

The White House Conference on Library and Information Services was undoubtedly the most significant event of 1979 for all components of the library, publishing, and other information-related professions. Several SLA members were chosen to represent their states as delegates or alternates to the conference. The executive director represented SLA interests and concerns as a delegate-at-large, and the 1979 president-elect, James Dodd, served as an official observer.

A special committee prepared a brochure, "Issues for Delegate Consideration," for distribution to delegates and alternates prior to the conference. The booklet discusses the issues under the eight program objectives developed by the National Commission on Libraries and Information Science for formulating and implementing a national program for library service.

Immediately following the conference, the special committee began studying the conference resolutions in order to advise the SLA board on how the association can contribute to the implementation of resolutions that will have an effect upon special libraries.

GOVERNMENT RELATIONS

The leadership of the late SLA executive director, Frank E. McKenna, in representing the interest of American libraries in the drafting of the U.S. Copyright Law of 1976 culminated in 1978 with the preparation and publication by SLA of *Library Photocopying and the U.S. Copyright Law of 1976*. Copies of this analysis of the new statute were distributed to every SLA member in January 1978. The association keeps informed of developments in the copyright area through the chairman of its Copyright Committee, who also serves as chairman of the Copyright Committee of the Council of National Library and Information Associations and as a member of the Register of Copyrights' Advisory Committee for the five-year review mandated by the new law.

As an international association with 10 percent of its membership in Canada, SLA has assisted the Canadian chapters with counsel and staff support as the Canadian government prepares to enact new copyright legislation.

The staff, officers, and members of SLA are active on several other fronts affecting the future of special libraries in the information age. These include networking and expanded networking involvement; support of legislation for a National Periodicals Center as the first step toward establishing a national library agency; and monitoring the revision of Title 44 of the U.S. Code. To keep the members, officers, and staff informed of issues of national concern and to represent the interests of SLA in the seat of the U.S. government, the executive director makes bimonthly visits to Washington, D.C., to meet with congressmen and members of the staffs of the various departments of the federal government.

ANNUAL CONFERENCES

In November 1978, after several months of pro and con discussion concerning the selection of conference sites in states that have not ratified the Equal Rights Amendment, the SLA board of directors voted to submit the question to a mail vote of the membership. Results of the balloting were tabulated in December 1978. Over two-thirds of the voting members approved the action:

> That the Special Libraries Association shall hold no Winter Meetings after 1980 and no Annual Conferences after 1984 in states of the United States that have not ratified the Equal Rights Amendment, or passed their own statewide equal rights legislation, or until such time as the ratification of the present proposed Equal Rights Amendment has occurred; and further that this action not extend beyond June 30, 1982, the terminal date of the E.R.A. Extension Resolution (HJS 638).

So as not to be punitive in perpetuity, the action of SLA's members would cease to be effective after the terminal date of the ERA Extension Resolution. Winter meeting sites through 1980 and annual conference sites through 1984 are not affected because the association has already negotiated legally binding contracts for these meetings. Directly affected are states to be considered by SLA as winter meeting sites for the years 1981-1985 and annual conference sites for the years 1985-1988. The association will select sites for these meetings before June 1982.

SLA conferences have grown in size and complexity during recent years. The employment of a full-time staff person to handle conference arrangements, the discontinuance of chapter-hosted conferences, and the capability of selecting the conference program committees from SLA's entire membership have given the association greater flexibility and more continuity in the planning and coordination of annual conference activities.

The 1977 annual conference, the last to be hosted by an SLA chapter, broke all attendance records for SLA. More than 4,100 librarians, information experts, and exhibitors gathered in New York City under the international theme "Worldwide Information Sources." Distinguished guests included Preben Kirkegaard, president of the International Federation of Library Associations and Institutions (IFLA) and Margreet Wijnstroom, secretary-general of the federation.

Internationalism was carried one step further at the 1979 SLA conference. The conference was designated by the SLA board of directors as the First Worldwide Conference on Special Libraries. SLA sponsored the conference in cooperation with the Japan Special Libraries Association (SENTOKYO) and the Special Libraries Division of the International Federation. Honolulu was selected as the conference site because of its accessibility from both the U.S. mainland and Japan.

In spite of a strike that affected 60 percent of the airline service between the U.S. mainland and Hawaii and that was further compounded by the grounding of all DC-10 aircraft, more than 1,800 persons from 18 countries and Hong Kong attended the Honolulu conference. Simultaneous translation equipment and personnel and Japanese-English interpreters were available at the plenary sessions and other selected programs. Generous grants from the H. W. Wilson Foundation, the Xerox Corporation, and the Exxon Education Foundation assisted SLA in meeting the extraordinary expenses of this particular conference.

Librarians and information scientists from several participating countries delivered papers at the plenary and contributed paper sessions, and many participated in programs of SLA divisions as speakers or panelists.

Following the conference, several SLA chapters hosted members of the SENTOKYO delegation during their study tour of selected U.S. libraries in southern California, New York, New Jersey, Boston, and Washington, D.C.

OTHER INTERNATIONAL ACTIVITIES

In 1976 SLA promoted the formation of the Special Libraries Division (SLD) in the new structure of IFLA. Frank McKenna was instrumental in organizing the new division, and at the time of his death, he was serving as chairman of the Science and Technology Libraries Section of SLD. Under the new IFLA structure, several of the existing IFLA sections and round tables (Geography and Map Libraries Section, Astronomical and Geophysical Librarians Round Table, Administrative Libraries Section and Social Science Libraries Section) were reorganized under the umbrella of the Special Libraries Division; and several new sections and round tables were established: Art Librarians Round Table, Music Librarians Round Table, Science and Technology Libraries Section, and Biological and Medical Sciences Libraries Section. SLA supports the expansion in IFLA of opportunities for participation by special librarians, and has designated official representatives to each SLD section and round table, many of which correspond to existing SLA divisions.

It is hoped that SLA and the People's Republic of China can jointly sponsor an exchange program in 1980. Toward this end, SLA established the China Fund, and generous contributions have been received already in support of an exchange of visiting delegations. However, plans for the exchange are tentative at this date and will not be finalized until the association is sure that it can secure adequate funding for the project.

IMPROVING SERVICES TO MEMBERS

SLA staff has been reorganized and augmented with the goal of improved services to members. The benefits to the membership of hiring a conference and exhibits coordinator and a manager for professional development have been discussed earlier in this article. In addition, a new position, assistant executive director, has been created and filled through promotion of a staff member.

The division of responsibilities in the executive office between the executive director and the assistant executive director has enabled the executive director to devote more of his efforts to programming, research and planning, and government and public relations activities. The assistant executive director has assumed the responsibilities of internal association affairs, including membership services, chapter and division relations, and personnel services.

The information services emanating from the association office have improved markedly as a result of the completion of the cataloging of the SLA library and a thorough weeding and reorganization of the association's archives. Hence, the manager for information services has improved resources for responding to inquiries about special librarianship and the history and development of SLA. Since completion of the cataloging and reorganization of the archives, there has been increased usage of the association's Information Services Department by members, staff, and nonmember librarians.

Other efforts have been made to improve the association's responsiveness to the membership. These include the leasing of word processing equipment; the updating of SLA's in-house computer system; and the installation of modern yet economical mailroom, photocopying, and collating equipment. Additional means of improving member services are being studied, such as an expanded publications program and a revamping of *Special Libraries*, SLA's official journal, in both content and design.

The association's mission for the future is clear: to make a better product for the membership. That product is a package of services that will continue to meet the professional needs of information specialists in an era when continued and frequent changes in technology are expected to influence dramatically the creation of information and its subsequent storage and retrieval. The SLA staff will devote its major efforts to providing the members with services to assist them in coping with these anticipated advances in information technology. After all, service to the membership is the ultimate goal of SLA and indeed its reason for existence.

Part 2
Legislation, Funding, and Grants

Note: For an overview of library-related research in 1979, see the article by Mary Jo Lynch in Part 4—*Ed.*

LEGISLATION AFFECTING LIBRARIANSHIP IN 1979

Eileen D. Cooke
Director, ALA Washington Office

Carol C. Henderson
Deputy Director, ALA Washington Office

Members of Congress in 1979, keenly aware of the state of the economy and sensitive to the taxpayers' plight, scaled back both the quantity of legislation and the level of funding. New measures received increasingly close scrutiny, and tended to succeed only if they addressed national priorities or helped to solve urgent national problems. Library legislation in the first session of the ninety-sixth Congress did not escape this intense scrutiny, although there were a few bright spots on the horizon. All in all, not an auspicious year for the first White House Conference on Library and Information Services, but on the other hand, a statement of priorities by library users was never more needed.

The House began the year by transferring jurisdiction over public library and arts and humanities programs from the Select Education Subcommittee to the Postsecondary Subcommittee under Representative William Ford (D-Mich.). Although funding for college library and library training and demonstration programs was reduced, a House-passed extension of the Higher Education Act would increase the authorization for both, as well as establish a National Periodicals Center. A separate Department of Education became a reality, and White House Conference delegates recommended an Assistant Secretary of Education for Library and Information Services. WHCOLIS delegates also approved the principles embodied in S. 1124, a national library act study bill. The House but not the Senate passed a postal reorganization bill (H.R. 79), and revision of Title 44 covering government printing and document distribution advanced to a second version (H.R. 5424). There were regulatory developments in the areas of copyright and emergency building temperature restrictions.

CONGRESSIONAL BUDGET PROCESS

The congressional budget process, in place now for four years, has gradually become effective in giving Congress better control of federal spending. With the growing pressure to restrain federal spending, the process bears special attention because it can affect education and library funding. Until 1974, budget and spending priorities were determined by the executive branch or by piecemeal congressional actions. The Congressional Budget and Impoundment Control Act of 1974 set a timetable and procedures for the budget process, established House and Senate budget committees, and a Congressional Budget Office as an alternate source of economic forecasts and analysis.

Specific programs are not mentioned in the congressional budget resolutions, but the budget committees determine functional levels for broad categories of government activity based on certain assumptions about the economy and likely congressional action. Most federal library programs form a tiny part of Function 500, Education, Training, Employment and Social Services. The first budget resolution sets spending and revenue targets; the second sets an absolute spending ceiling and revenue floor. Proposals that would exceed the limits in the second budget resolution are subject to points of order and concomitant cuts or rescissions.

Congress was supposed to approve the first budget resolution by May 15, a deadline not quite reached in 1979 because of a controversy over levels for education program funding. David Obey (D–Wis.), a member of both the House Budget Committee and the Labor-HEW Appropriations Subcommittee, led a successful move to defeat the conference measure on the grounds that it contained too little for education and too much for defense. Extra spending authority for Function 500 was added to House Concurrent Resolution 107, which then served as an overall budget target for Congress.

Congress also missed the September 15 deadline for the second budget resolution. It took until November 28 to reach agreement on Senate Concurrent Resolution 53, which became a binding budget ceiling for FY 1980. House-Senate conferees agreed on budget figures in an earlier version of the second budget resolution (S. Con. Res. 36), but split on whether or not to invoke the reconciliation provisions of the budget act.

If approved, reconciliation would direct appropriations and authorizing committees to go back to spending bills already passed and recommend legislation making specified cuts to bring congressional spending in line with the budget ceilings. Library and education programs could be affected. The budget finally adopted did not contain formal reconciliation instructions but did include compromise language stating Congress's intent to stay within the ceiling and avoid a third budget resolution.

FUNDING

Although President Carter told WHCOLIS delegates in November that they had "a friend in the White House," he had begun the year by transmitting a "lean and austere" budget to Congress, including reduction or elimination of major library grant programs for FY 1980 (October 1, 1979 through September 30, 1980). In most but not all cases Congress restored funding to the previous year's level.

For the Library Services and Construction Act Titles I and III, the Carter budget proposed $56.9 and $3.3 million, respectively. Congress restored LSCA to the FY 1979 levels of $62.5 million for Title I and $5 million for Title III. For the Elementary and Secondary Education Act IV-B school library program, which received $180 million in 1979, the budget figure was $149.6 million and Congress appropriated $171 million. However, both the FY 1980 amounts reflect a transfer of $18 million to the new ESEA IV-D guidance, counseling, and testing program, which was formerly part of IV-B.

The budget proposed elimination of the Higher Education Act II-A college library resources program and the II-B library training and demonstration program. For college libraries the House approved $9,975,000, equal to the previous year's level, but the Senate provided no funding, just an admonition that the program should be changed to target on the neediest colleges. House-Senate conferees split the difference and $4,987,500 was appropriated. The II-B training and demonstration program was funded at $1 million, down from the previous level of $3 million, and the II-C research library program received $6 million, the same as the budget and previous year's figure.

These programs, together with the Medical Library Assistance Act, which received $10,625,000, approximately $2 million more than both the budget and last year's level, were included in the Labor-HEW Appropriations Bill (H.R. 4389). Although H.R. 4389 never became law because of a dispute over federal funding for abortion, the program amounts were agreed to and included in a continuing resolution (H. J. Res. 440). Continuing resolutions are usually temporary measures, but this one (now PL 96-123) continues funding for library and other programs through the entire 1980 fiscal year.

The Library of Congress (LC), the National Agricultural Library, and the National Library of Medicine all received small increases over the previous year, but in the case of LC, the $177.5 million appropriated was far less than the $193 million requested. The lower amount for FY 1980 will mean fewer books purchased, a reduction in services to the blind and handicapped, and no growth for the Copyright Office—all areas hit particularly hard by Congress's action on the complex LC budget.

Funding levels for these and other library and related programs are shown in Table 1, while the status of legislation of interest to librarians is detailed in Table 2.

HIGHER EDUCATION ACT EXTENSION

The major piece of education and library legislation pending as the year ended was extension and revision of the Higher Education Act. The House passed a five-year extension bill, H.R. 5192, on November 7 by a vote of 385 to 15, continuing the Title II library programs and authorizing a National Periodicals Center. The Senate has held hearings and is expected to develop its own bill in February. Meanwhile, both House and Senate passed a one-year HEA extension bill on July 31 (H.R. 4476, now PL 96-49), so that the FY 1981 appropriations schedule could be met while the reauthorization process was underway.

The House-passed measure would make several changes to the II-A college library resources program. The basic grant to college libraries would be renamed "resource development grant" and would be increased from the present $5,000 to $10,000. Supplemental grants would be deleted, and revised special-purpose grants transferred to Title II-B. Although both the administration and the Senate Appropriations Committee had suggested targeting the grants to the neediest institutions, H.R. 5192 does not include need criteria. Maintenance-of-effort provisions would be strengthened and authorization levels set at $60 million per year for FY 1981 through 1985.

Authorization for II-B programs would also be $60 million per year, to be divided one-third for library training, one-third for research and demonstrations, and one-third for special purpose grants. Training programs could include new techniques of information transfer and communication technology. The special-purpose grants, currently unfunded in II-A, would provide assistance to meet special national or regional needs, for consortium projects, or to other library institutions to improve library services to higher education institutions.

No major change would be made in the II-C research library program. H.R. 5192 would add a new II-D, a National Periodicals Center, authorized at $15 million, but to be funded only if Parts A, B, and C were funded at FY 1979 levels. (See "National Periodicals Center" later in this article for further details.)

In other provisions of H.R. 5192, Title I, Education Outreach Programs, would consolidate continuing education from the existing Title I Education Information Centers from Title IV, and the comprehensive state planning function from Title XII. Title VI, International Foreign Language Studies, would replace Title VI of the National Defense Education Act and Title I of the International Education Act. The House Education and Labor Committee's report (H. Rept. 96-520) on the bill states that particular attention should be paid to the library holdings of the international studies graduate centers. The current Title VI, Improvement of Undergraduate Instruction, would be repealed.

Title VII, Construction, Reconstruction and Renovation of Academic Facilities, would be amended to provide assistance to economize on use of energy; comply with handicapped accessibility requirements or environmental protection or health and

178 / LEGISLATION, FUNDING, AND GRANTS

TABLE 1 FUNDS FOR LIBRARY AND RELATED PROGRAMS

Programs	FY 1979 Appropriation	FY 1980 Authorization	Carter FY 1980 Budget	FY 1980 Appropriation
Library Programs				
ESEA Title IV-B: School Libraries	$180,000,000[a]	Necessary sums	$149,600,000[a,b]	$171,000,000[a,b]
GPO Superintendent of Documents	23,613,000	44 USC 301	23,037,000	23,000,000
HEA Title VI-A: Undergraduate Equipment	(0)	$ 70,000,000	(0)	(0)
Higher Education Act: Title II	18,975,000	140,000,000	6,000,000	11,987,500
Title II-A: College Library Resources	9,975,000	84,000,000	(0)	4,987,500
Title II-B: Training	2,000,000	23,976,000	(0)	666,700
Title II-B: Demonstrations	1,000,000	12,024,000	(0)	333,300
Title II-C: Research Libraries	6,000,000	20,000,000	6,000,000	6,000,000
Library of Congress	174,646,300	2 USC 131-167	192,900,000	177,491,000
Library Services and Construction Act	67,500,000	170,000,000	60,237,000	67,500,000
Title I: Library Services	62,500,000	150,000,000	56,900,000	62,500,000
Title II: Public Library Construction	(0)	Necessary sums	(0)	(0)
Title III: Interlibrary Cooperation	5,000,000	20,000,000	3,337,000	5,000,000
Medical Library Assistance Act	8,987,000	16,500,000	8,625,000	10,625,000
National Commission on Libraries and Information Service	660,000	750,000	668,000	668,000
National Library of Medicine	32,444,000	40 USC 275	32,806,000	33,375,000
USDA SEA Technical Information Systems[c]	7,527,000	7 USC 2204	7,835,000	7,835,000
Library-Related Programs				
Adult Education Act	100,000,000[a]	250,000,000	90,750,000[a]	100,000,000[a]
Community Education	3,190,000	42,000,000	3,138,000	3,138,000
Consumers Education	3,601,000	5,000,000	3,135,000	3,617,000
Corporation for Public Broadcasting	162,000,000[d]	Formula-based	172,000,000[d]	172,000,000[d]
Education for Handicapped Children (state grants)	804,000,000[a]	Formula-based	862,000,000[a]	874,500,000[a]
Education Information Centers	3,000,000	40,000,000	(0)	3,000,000
Educational TV and Radio Programming	6,000,000	Necessary sums	6,000,000	6,000,000
ESEA Title I: Educationally Disadvantaged Children	3,078,382,000[a]	Formula-based	3,078,382,000[a]	3,115,593,000[a]
ESEA Title II: Basic Skills Improvement	27,750,000	Necessary sums	35,000,000	35,000,000
ESEA Title IV-C: Educational Innovation and Support	197,400,000[a]	Necessary sums	197,000,000[a]	197,400,000[a]
ESEA Title VII: Bilingual Education	158,600,000	299,000,000	173,600,000	166,963,000
ESEA Title IX: Ethnic Heritage Studies	2,000,000	15,000,000	(0)	3,000,000

LEGISLATION AFFECTING LIBRARIANSHIP IN 1979 / 179

Gifted and Talented Children	3,780,000	Necessary sums	3,780,000	6,280,000
HEA Title I-A: Community Service	16,000,000	40,000,000	(0)	10,000,000
HEA Title I-B: Lifelong Learning	(0)	40,000,000	(0)	(0)
HEA Title III: Developing Institutions	120,000,000	120,000,000	120,000,000	110,000,000
HEA Title VII: Construction and Renovation	29,000,000	580,000,000	29,000,000	54,000,000
Indian Education Act	71,735,000	Necessary sums	76,875,000	In conference
Metric Education	1,840,000	20,000,000	1,840,000	1,840,000
National Center for Educational Statistics	10,561,000	30,000,00	10,893,000	9,947,000
National Endowment for the Arts	149,640,000	Necessary sums	154,400,000	In conference
National Endowment for the Humanities	145,293,000	Necessary sums	150,100,000	In conference
National Historical Publications and Records Committee	4,000,000	4,000,000	3,500,000	4,000,000
National Institute of Education	96,614,000	210,500,000	98,285,000	91,172,000
NDEA Title VI: Foreign Language Development	17,000,000	75,000,000	18,000,000	17,000,000
Postsecondary Education Improvement Fund	13,000,000	75,000,000	14,000,000	13,500,000
Public Telecommunications Facilities	18,000,000	40,000,000	23,705,000	23,705,000
Teacher Centers	12,625,000	100,000,000	13,000,000	13,000,000
Telecommunications Demonstrations	1,000,000	1,000,000	1,000,000	1,000,000
Women's Educational Equity	9,000,000	80,000,000	10,000,000	10,000,000

[a]Advance funded program.
[b]Reflects transfer of $18 million to new ESEA IV-D guidance, counseling, and testing, a program previously included in IV-B.
[c]Formerly National Agricultural Library.
[d]CPB funded two years in advance.

TABLE 2 STATUS OF LEGISLATION OF INTEREST TO LIBRARIANS
(96th Congress, 1st Session, Convened January 15, 1979, Recessed January 3, 1980)

Legislation	House Introduced	House Hearings	House Reported by Subcommittee	House Committee Report Number	House Floor Action	Senate Introduced	Senate Hearings	Senate Reported by Subcommittee	Senate Committee Report Number	Senate Floor Action	Conference Report	Final Passage	Public Law
Arts and Humanities Endowments Extension	HR 3333, 6121	X				S 1386	X						
Communications Act Revision	H. Con. Res. 186	X		435		S 611, 622	X	X	311	X	582		
Congressional Budget Ceilings, FY 1980		X				S. Con. Res. 53	X						
Criminal Code Revision	HR 2444	X		143	X	S 1722, 1723	X			X			
Department of Education	HR 4591	X		338	X	S 210	X		49	X	459	X	96-88
Education Amendments of 1978, technical amendments						HR 4591							
ESEA IV-B Amendment, Band Instruments	HR 5569, 5772	X											
Federal Redtape Reduction Act	HR 3570					S 1411	X						
Higher Education Act Extension	HR 5192	X	X	520	X	S 1839	X						
HEA, one-year extension and technical amendments	HR 4476	X	X	318	X	S 1350				X		X	96-49
Literacy Commission	H. J. Res. 316	X				S. J. Res. 70							
Lobbying Disclosure	HR 4395	X		590		S 1564	X						
LSCA, Maintenance of Effort	HR 4271	X											
Natl. Commission, Info. Tech. in Educ.	HR 4326	X											
NHPRC extension	HR 3923	X	X	141	X	HR 3923	X		283	X		X	96-98
National Library Act						S 1124							
National Science Foundation Authorization						S 527	X	X	106	X	321	X	96-44
Postal, Children's Magazine Rates	HR 2729	X		61	X	S 1110	X	X	282	X			

Postal, Phased Rate Extension	HR 79	X			S 1096	X	X			
Postal Service Act of 1979		X				X			
Privacy Legislation	HR 2465 et al.		126	X	S 865, 867				
Public Works and Economic Development Amendments	HR 2063	X			S 914	X	270	X		
Revenue Sharing Extension	HR 2291	X	180	X	S 513, 263	X				
Small Community Library Services Assistance Act	HR 4234				S 1078	X				
Tax Incentive, Manuscript Donations	HR 2498				S 1436	X				
Title 44 Revision	HR 5424	X								
Appropriations FY 1980										
Agriculture	HR 4387	X	242	X	HR 4387	X	246	X	553	X	96-108
Continuing Resolution (including Labor-HEW)	H. J. Res. 440		609	X		X		X	646	X	96-123
Continuing Resolution (including Legislative Branch)	H. J. Res. 412		500	X	H. J. Res. 412	X			513	X	96-86
HUD and Independent Agencies	HR 4394	X	249	X	HR 4394	X	258	X	409	X	96-103
Interior and Related Agencies	HR 4930	X	374	X	HR 4930	X	363	X	604	X	96-126
Labor-HEW	HR 4389	X	244	X	HR 4389	X	247	X	400	X	
Legislative Branch	HR 4390	X	245	X	HR 4390	X					
State, Justice, Commerce	HR 4392	X	247	X	HR 4392	X	251	X	402	X	96-68
Treasury, Postal Service	HR 4393	X	248	X	HR 4393	X	299	X	471	X	96-74

For bills, reports, and laws write: House and Senate Documents Rooms, U.S. Capitol, Washington, DC 20515 and 20510, respectively.

safety laws; assist research facilities, including libraries, and to acquire special research equipment; and assist institutions with unusual increases in enrollment. A new Title XI, Urban Grant University Program, would aid urban universities (in SMSAs over 500,000) to help find answers to urban problems and to make their resources more readily and effectively available to the urban communities in which they are located.

NATIONAL PERIODICALS CENTER

Legislation that would create a National Periodicals Center (NPC) was included in the Higher Education Act extension bill introduced September 6 by Bill Ford (D–Mich.), chairman of the House Postsecondary Education Subcommittee, and passed by the House on November 7 by a vote of 385–15. The NPC authorization would be a new Part D of Title II of the Higher Education Act, and would be funded only if Parts A, B, and C of Title II were funded at the FY 1979 levels. These levels are $9.975 million for II-A college library resources, $3 million for II-B library training and demonstrations, and $6 million for the II-C research library program.

The NPC would be organized as a nonprofit corporation (which would not be a part of the U.S. government) with a 15-member board of directors appointed by the president with the advice and consent of the Senate. Members of the board would serve six-year terms, and are to be "representative of the needs and interests of the Government, academic and research communities, libraries, publishers and information community, authors, and the public." The NPC would have authority

> To acquire current and retrospective periodicals, and to preserve and maintain a dedicated collection of such documents
>
> To provide information on periodicals to which the corporation can insure access, including those circulated from private sector sources, and cooperate in efforts to improve bibliographic and physical access to periodicals
>
> To make such periodicals available, on a cost reimbursable or other basis as determined by the board, through libraries by loan or by photoreproduction or other means; and to assure that all fees set by the copyright owners will be paid by the borrowing library for each such reproduction of a document under copyright delivered by or through the corporation with the consent of the copyright owner
>
> To cooperate with and participate in international borrowing and lending activities as may be appropriate for such purposes
>
> To enter into cooperative agreements with the Library of Congress, the National Library of Medicine, the National Agricultural Library, other federal agencies, state and local agencies and instrumentalities, and private libraries and other organizations for such purposes
>
> To establish regional offices of the corporation to the extent necessary and appropriate
>
> To coordinate the training of librarians and other users in the use of the corporation's services.

Part D is almost identical in substance to the draft NPC legislation developed by a legislative drafting team assembled by the National Commission on Libraries and Information Science on the recommendation of its Advisory Committee on a National Periodical System. The drafting team included representatives of the library, higher education, and private publishing communities.

DEPARTMENT OF EDUCATION

Judge Shirley M. Hufstedler was sworn in as the first secretary of education on December 6 after confirmation by the Senate by a vote of 81-2 on November 30. Signed into law on October 17 (PL 96-88), the cabinet-level Department of Education will take effect no later than six months after the first secretary takes office. The new department transfers and consolidates some 170 federal education programs and contains strong provisions prohibiting federal control of education and limiting staff growth of the department.

The law does not mandate a library unit, and the status of the current Office of Libraries and Learning Resources within the new department is not yet clear. One of the strongest recommendations of the White House Conference on Library and Information Services was for establishment of an Assistant Secretary for Library and Information Services in the Department of Education.

NATIONAL LIBRARY ACT

The National Library Act, a legislative proposal initiated by the National Citizens Emergency Committee to Save Our Public Libraries, was introduced May 14 as a study bill, S. 1124, by Senators Jacob Javits (R-N.Y.) and Edward Kennedy (D-Mass.). The National Citizens Emergency Committee was founded in 1976 in response to the crisis in library funding; Whitney North Seymour, Jr., a former New York Public Library trustee, is secretary. The proposal is also endorsed by the Urban Libraries Council. Introduced "to provide a focal point for debating the key issues for proposed new library legislation in connection with the White House Conference on Library and Information Services," S. 1124 would replace the Library Services and Construction Act with an expanded program of aid to public libraries administered by a new National Library Agency with a presidentially appointed director and board.

The bill would provide for direct financial assistance to public libraries for operating expenses on a matching 20 percent federal, 50 percent state, 30 percent local basis. In additional titles of the bill it would continue public library construction assistance, establish grants for services to special constituencies, assist interlibrary cooperation including development and maintenance of library and information networks, and fund special training programs for library personnel to supplement HEA II-B programs.

White House Conference delegates endorsed and supported enactment of a national library act incorporating the general principles of S. 1124 with such modifications as shall appear desirable after full congressional hearings.

TITLE 44 U.S. CODE REVISION
(GOVERNMENT PRINTING AND DOCUMENT DISTRIBUTION)

The Public Printing Reorganization Act of 1979 (H.R. 4572 and S. 1436), which was introduced on June 21, was replaced by a new version entitled the National Publications Act of 1979 (H.R. 5424) on September 27. Frank Thompson (D-N.J.) introduced the substitute bill in order to clarify the intent of several sections of the initiative which is designed to "help bring about greater economy and efficient management in the provision of a wide variety of printing and information distribution services for the Congress and the executive agencies." Markup of the bill was scheduled for early in 1980.

The key elements of the proposed revision can be summarized as follows:

The Joint Committee on Printing (JCP) is to be replaced by a presidentially appointed seven-voting member National Publications Committee—three members chosen from the general public, including the chairman, and a member representing each of the following groups: the printing industries, the publishing and information industries, the library community and labor unions.

The commission will develop and implement a central, comprehensive, and unified policy for printing and distributing government publications and will issue regulations which are subject to presidential and legislative veto, as well as public comment prior to their final promulgation.

The board will appoint three managers of equal status: a director of administration, a director of production services, and a director of distribution services, who will be responsible respectively for the delivery of administrative services, printing services and the distribution of government publications (sales, depository, and exchange).

As an independent agency, National Publications Agency (NPA) budget requests will be subject to scrutiny by the Office of Management and Budget.

Each executive agency will be required to appoint someone to oversee all printing services in compliance with Title 44 and maintain a comprehensive index of that agency's publications.

Additional reponsibilities of the director of distribution services (formerly the superintendent of documents) will include the authority to prescribe bibliographic and indexing standards for the government and to establish a national documents center.

POSTAL LEGISLATION

The House passed H.R. 79, the Postal Service Act of 1979, on September 7 by a vote of 350–14. A less comprehensive reorganization bill than last year's H.R. 7700, H.R. 79 nevertheless calls for appointment of the postmaster general by the president with confirmation by the Senate. The bill would also increase the public service subsidy and extend phased rate increases for fourth-class mail over a longer period of time—four more years for the library rate or until 1991, and two more years for the book rate or until 1981.

H.R. 79 would extend the fourth-class library rate to books sent from libraries and educational institutions, as well as books sent to them. It would make clear that all libraries and not just public libraries are eligible for the library rate. Finally it would enable nonprofit institutions such as libraries to send and receive additional materials, including book catalogs, teaching aids, and science kits under the library rate.

In the Senate, no action was taken on a postal reorganization bill, but a measure (S. 1096) extending phasing for the library and book rates for two additional years was approved by the Senate Subcommittee on Energy, Nuclear Proliferation, and Federal Services. The Senate passed on October 30 a bill (S. 1110) that would provide a lower postal rate for the smallest circulation newspapers and magazines, and would extend the current second-class classroom rate to include children's magazines without paid advertising designed specifically for use at home as supplemental educational reading.

NATIONAL HISTORICAL PUBLICATIONS AND RECORDS COMMISSION

Congress approved on October 19 a bill (H.R. 3923, now PL 96-98) extending the authorization for the National Historical Publications and Records Commission

(NHPRC) through FY 1981 at the current level of $4 million per year. The NHPRC is a small grant-making unit within the National Archives and Records Service that provides assistance for projects for the preservation and use of historical records, and for documentary publications projects. Libraries of all types have received grants for conservation and preservation activities under the NHPRC records program.

TAX INCENTIVE FOR MANUSCRIPT DONATIONS

Senate hearings were held October 22 on the Artists Tax Equity Act of 1979 (S. 1078), introduced May 7 by Senator Jacob Javits (R-N.Y.). The bill would make several changes to the Internal Revenue Code of 1954, including a tax credit of 30 percent of the fair market value of a literary, musical, or artistic composition donated by the author or artist to a library or museum. Prior to 1969 an author or artist who donated literary, musical, or artistic compositions or papers to a library or museum could take a tax deduction equal to the fair market value of the items. The 1969 Tax Reform Act (PL 91-172) limited such deductions to the cost of materials used to produce the composition. In the House, a measure (H.R. 2498) introduced in February by William Brodhead (D-Mich.) would restore the pre-1969 tax deduction, but no hearings have yet been scheduled.

COPYRIGHT

The advisory committee appointed by the Register of Copyrights to assist the Copyright Office in the five-year review of library photocopying provisions mandated by Section 108(i) of the copyright law (PL 94-553) has been meeting periodically since its first meeting in December 1978. The Copyright Office completed a bibliography of existing surveys of library photocopying on the effect of the 1976 copyright law on libraries, with the intent of using existing data whenever possible. In addition, a further survey will probably be conducted in 1981. The Copyright Office also plans several regional hearings during 1980 to get input for the review from librarians and library users as well as all interested parties. Announcement of the first hearing (held in Chicago on January 19 preceding ALA's midwinter meeting) and issues for possible consideration appeared in the December 17 *Federal Register* (pp. 73168-73170).

A copyright Off-Air Taping Conference was held March 2 by the House Judiciary Subcommittee on Courts, Civil Liberties, and the Administration of Justice with the cooperation of the Register of Copyrights. Following up on this meeting, Robert Kastenmeier, subcommittee chair, asked 19 individuals representing a cross section of affected groups to constitute an ad hoc negotiating committee to develop guidelines on fair use for broadcast audiovisual works. The committee's first meeting was held April 27, and meetings are continuing under cochairs Eileen Cooke of ALA and Leonard Wasser of the Writers Guild of America, East.

The Copyright Office is considering regulations allowing copyright of the graphic design elements of printed publications, and of the arrangement or "formating" of factual data not copyrightable in itself. An advance notice of proposed rule making was published in the August 14 *Federal Register* (pp. 47555-47556) and a public hearing was held on October 10.

EMERGENCY BUILDING TEMPERATURE RESTRICTIONS

The Emergency Building Temperature Restrictions Regulations, effective July 16, place temporary restrictions on nonresidential building temperatures. Building owners and operators are required to post a "Certificate of Building Compliance" in a prominent location in their buildings. Civil penalties of up to $5,000 and criminal penalties of up to $10,000 are provided for violations. The regulations will remain in effect until April 16, 1980 unless rescinded earlier by the president.

The regulations generally require thermostat settings of 65° F maximum for heating and 78° F minimum for cooling except to lower the room dewpoint temperature to 65° F. ("Dewpoint temperature" means the temperature at which condensation of water vapor begins as the temperature of the air-vapor mixture is reduced.) The American Library Association was among many organizations and individuals protesting the potential damage to library materials posed by the upper temperature and humidity limits. In response, the introduction to the final regulations, published in the July 5 *Federal Register* (pp. 39354–39369), states:

> Comments were received from museums, libraries, art preservation associations and archival institutions strongly urging exemption from the heating and cooling restrictions where necessary to protect museum collections, library and archival collections and historical collections and structures. An express exemption has not been included, since Sec. 490.31(a)(4), which provides for exemptions where special environmental conditions are required to protect "materials," is intended to make available exemptions when necessary to preserve such collections and structures.

Such a general exemption is deemed effective when claimed, but a written statement describing and justifying a claimed exemption must be available for review in the event of a building inspection. Department of Energy officials suggest that any generally accepted standard in the library and archival community would be sufficient. The ALA response to the proposed regulations may prove helpful in this regard; the text is attached to the July 17 *ALA Washington Newsletter.*

A Department of Energy manual, *How to Comply with the Emergency Building Temperature Restrictions*, was published in the September 26 *Federal Register* (pp. 55504–55515). The manual contains the regulations and required forms and is also available from: Emergency Building Temperature Restrictions, Rm. GE-004A (CS-39), Forrestal Bldg., U.S. Dept. of Energy, Washington, DC 20585. Or call toll free, 9:00–5:30 Eastern time, Monday–Friday; Continental U.S., 800-424-9122; AK, HI, PR, Virgin Islands, 800-424-9088; Metropolitan Washington, DC, 252-4950.

WHITE HOUSE CONFERENCE ON LIBRARY AND INFORMATION SERVICES

No chronicle of legislative activity during 1979 would be complete without reference to the first White House Conference on Library and Information Services held November 15–19 in Washington, D.C. Over 900 delegates and alternates (two-thirds of that number "lay" delegates) adopted 25 resolutions dealing with the future of library and information services. Many of the WHCOLIS recommendations would require new or amended federal legislation.

Speakers at the conference included President Carter, Presidential Assistant for Domestic Affairs and Policy Stuart Eizenstat, and several members of Congress. The WHCOLIS ended with a congressional hearing sponsored jointly by the House and Senate subcommittees with jurisdiction over federal library programs. Presiding were Claiborne Pell (D-R.I.), chair of the Senate Education, Arts and Humanities Subcommittee, and William Ford, chair of the House Postsecondary Education Subcommittee.

OTHER LEGISLATIVE ACTIVITIY

There were other congressional hearings on federal library programs during the year. April 3 was the date for an oversight hearing on the major LSCA, ESEA, and HEA federal library programs. Sponsored by the House Elementary, Secondary and Vocational Education Subcommittee, chaired by Carl Perkins (D-Ky.), and the House Postsecondary Education Subcommittee, chaired by William Ford (D-Mich.), the hearing focused on the need for funding for major federal library programs.

A hearing was held November 28 by the House Elementary, Secondary and Vocational Education Subcommittee on two bills (H.R. 5569 and H.R. 5772) that would add school band instruments as a third eligible category in addition to school library resources and instructional equipment as uses of Elementary and Secondary Education Act IV-B funds. Following up on congressional comments on the use and misuse of IV-B funds, the U.S. Office of Education had proposed regulations for ESEA IV specifying that band instruments would not qualify as instructional equipment. Resolution of this problem and publications of final regulations were still pending as the year ended.

Other measures on which action was not completed during the first session of Congress included reauthorization of the National Endowment for the Arts and the National Endowment for the Humanities (S. 1386), major criminal code revision including antiobscenity provisions (S. 1722), and revision of the Communications Act of 1934. In the communications area, major revision bills were introduced in the House (H.R. 3333) and the Senate (S. 611 and S. 612). House Communications Subcommittee Chair Lionel Van Deerlin (D-Calif.) dropped the House bill for lack of support in the subcommittee, but introduced a revision of the common carrier portion of the Communications Act on December 13 (H.R. 6121).

LEGISLATION AFFECTING PUBLISHING IN 1979

Washington Staff, AAP*

Perhaps even more than usual for the first half of a regular two-year congressional session, the Ninety-sixth Congress left major issues unsettled as it reached its midway point. A combination of searing domestic issues—energy, inflation, abortion, to name but three—plus international crises (principally Iran), along with the forthcoming congressional and presidential elections of 1980, seemed to conspire to prevent the lawmakers from confronting and resolving major issues. As might be expected, this near-paralysis held both welcome and unwelcome implications for the book publishing industry.

CRIMINAL CODE

As never before the auspices seemed to favor enactment of a recodification of federal criminal laws by the Ninety-sixth Congress—if indeed the project was ever to

---

*The general Washington staff of the AAP (Association of American Publishers) includes Richard P. Kleeman, Roy H. Millenson, Diane Rennert, and Carol A. Risher, all of whom contributed to this article.

come to pass after more than a dozen years of incubation. Book publishers and others in the press therefore kept close watch on First Amendment aspects of this awesome legislative undertaking, which remained far from conclusion as the Congress began its Christmas 1979 recess.

The factors favoring enactment of a new criminal code were both personal and political. Senator Edward M. Kennedy (D-Mass.) assumed the chair of the Senate Judiciary Committee, and his longtime determination to see the criminal code project through was certainly not diminished by his presidential ambitions. In the House, while the Judiciary Committee chair did not change, that committee's Criminal Justice Subcommittee was newly headed by Congressman Robert F. Drinan (D-Mass.) both a geographical and philosophical kinsman of Kennedy. The subcommittee, which in the previous Congress had concluded that wholesale, "omnibus" revamping of the criminal laws was not practicable, came around—by virtue of an almost entirely new membership —to the view that the right kind of recodification could be accomplished.

By the beginning of the second session of the Ninety-sixth Congress, in January 1980, the Senate Committee had voted out a criminal code bill (S. 1722) that was almost a carbon copy of the mammoth S. 1437, which the Senate had passed (but the House allowed to languish) in 1978. The House subcommittee had labored all year on producing its counterpart, but had not yet sent a measure to the full Judiciary Committee. The reconciling of Senate and House versions promised to be a task of major proportions and, with both congressional and presidential elections approaching, members of Congress were hoping to get the code—with its many controversial aspects—out of the way early in 1980, or recognize that once again the job had proved too much for them.

In representations to both legislative houses and to the Department of Justice, the organized publishing industry, through AAP, sought to minimize the code's tendency to involve the federal government in the affairs of a free press while pragmatically recognizing that Congress was not to be deterred from enacting restrictions on hardcore obscenity and pornography. In some considerable measure, AAP appeared to have been persuasive with the congressional committees and the administration, but in both houses the prospects for irresponsible amendments, in committee and on the floor, were imminent and not reassuring, especially in an election year.

Despite widespread sentiment for overruling the 1978 Supreme Court decision, in *Zurcher* v. *Stanford Daily*, that unannounced searches of the premises of a newspaper not suspected of any criminal activity were allowable, there was no consensus among lawmakers or lobbying groups as to what sort of legislation should accomplish this. The differences arose between those favoring a pure press protection measure, including book publishers in its coverage, and those seeking broader guarantees against unannounced searches of the premises of all "innocent third parties." As a result, no legislation appeared even close to enactment by the conclusion of the first session of the Ninety-sixth Congress.

EDUCATION AND LIBRARY AFFAIRS

Funding

As in previous years, the Carter budget requested decreases in most library programs. And, as in previous years, Congress enacted increases over the president's requests, although in several instances appropriations showed no increases over the previous year's funding.

For Library Services (LSCA I), the president asked $56.9 million for FY 1980 (the fiscal year beginning October 1, 1979). This was the same amount he had requested in each of the two previous years. Congress raised Library Services to $62.5 million, the same amount as had been appropriated the last year. This means that, as was the case in FY 1979, money will once more be available for the urban library program authorized by the Library Services and Construction Act Amendments of 1977 (PL 95-123), which provide that urban libraries receive a portion of any funds appropriated over the $60 million level.

Congress also ignored the presidential request to cut the ESEA IV-B (Instructional Materials and School Library Resources) program. Funding was increased by $9 million to $171 million, which fell short of inflationary increases in the price of books, other instructional materials, and instructional equipment.

Of all library programs, the severest blow was dealt to College Library Resources (HEA II-A), which received $4.988 million. While this was greater than the zero requested by the administration, it remains the lowest amount ever appropriated for the program since its enactment in 1965 and is half the funding of every previous year dating back to 1964.

Congress also rejected the presidential request to cut the program for assistance to medical libraries (Title III-J of the Public Health Service Act), increasing its funding to $10.6 million. Last year's appropriation was $8.967 million.

Research libraries (II-C, HEA) received $6 million; the same amount was received last year.

Enjoying a modest increase was the Inexpensive Book Distribution Program conducted by Reading Is FUNdamental, raised by $500,000 over the budget and last year to $6.5 million.

Outside of the Department of Health, Education, and Welfare, the National Agricultural Library advanced slightly over last year to $7.835 million, the budget figure.

The National Library of Medicine received $44 million, an increase of $2.569 million over the previous year and the president's budget. A large portion of the increase will be used to permit the library to continue to acquire literature for its expanded collection of materials concerning health planning, health care financing, health professionals, and other topics of growing interest to health practitioners, administrators, and the public.

New Legislation

The House of Representatives on November 7, 1979, by a 385-15 vote, approved the Education Amendments of 1980 (H.R. 5192), sending the bill to the Senate where action is scheduled for the spring of 1980. This measure revises and extends higher education programs through FY 1985.

The House bill, in extending Title II (College and Research Library Assistance and Library Training and Research) of the Higher Education Act, increased the basic grants under Part A (College Library Resources) from $5,000 to $10,000, redefining them as "Resource Development Grants." Institutions may use these funds for books, materials, and networking; $60 million annually was authorized. Special Grants were transferred from Part A to Part B (Library Training; Research and Development), which part was authorized at $60 million annually. Part C (Strengthening Research Libraries) was continued with a $20 million annual authorization.

The House added a new, and controversial, Part D to Title II that would establish a National Periodicals Center, a nonprofit corporation funded at $15 million annually to provide access to periodicals for all public and private libraries. The bill further stipulates that Part D shall not be funded unless all the other parts of Title II receive appropriations at the FY 1979 level. It is anticipated that the proposal for a National Periodicals Center will be subject to careful scrutiny in the Senate where it runs the risk of being eliminated from the bill.

In another area, a House subcommittee held hearings in November on a proposal (H.R. 5569 and H.R. 5572) to permit ESEA IV-B (Instructional Materials and School Library Resources) to be used to acquire band instruments "for such purposes as the school administration considers desirable." The Association of American Publishers (AAP) was joined by the Association of Media Producers and the American Library Association in opposing this legislation. No further action was taken on it in 1979.

The bill to create a Department of Education (PL 96-88) contains the Section 103(b) language urged by AAP that would bar any Department of Education official from exercising "any direction, administration, or control" over the "selection or content of library resources, textbooks, or other instructional materials by any educational institution or school system, except to the extent authorized by law."

Senator Jacob K. Javits (R–N.Y.) was joined by Senator Edward M. Kennedy (D–Mass.) in sponsoring legislation, "The National Library Act" (S. 1124), suggested by the Urban Libraries Council and the National Citizens Emergency Committee to Save Our Public Libraries. Joint Senate-House hearings were held on the bill at the White House Conference on Library and Information Services. A conference resolution indicated general support of the proposal, although not endorsing its specific provisions.

Other Activities

A highlight of 1979 was the first White House Conference on Library and Information Services (November 15–19) attended by over 900 delegates from the United States and its territories. Publishers were active both in planning the conference and in participating in it.

A stack of resolutions was adopted, with an emphasis on access, including information and consumer services. Technology was cited as a means of extending services to greater populations, including special constituencies such as the handicapped, the disadvantaged, Indians, and those living in underdeveloped areas. Arrangements were made both for a citizens' follow-up and a follow-up within the federal government on the resolutions adopted.

In the Senate, a series of ten Education Subcommittee hearings, chaired by Senator Thomas Eagleton (D–Mo.), was held in Washington and elsewhere in the country on basic skills and literacy. On July 24, three AAP education publishers testified. David Amerman (Prentice-Hall), chairman of the AAP College Division, and Lawrence Jackel (Litton Educational) and Richard Gladstone (Houghton Mifflin), both from the School Division, told the committee of the special role of textbooks in basic skills instruction and discussed educational issues of concern to the committee. The publishers also responded to committee questioning, which concentrated on school and college texts being pitched to a lower readability level than that of the pupil's grade.

More than 300 publishers furnished books for distribution at the October 11 Reading Is Fun Day sponsored by Reading Is FUNdamental.

Publishers were featured at the conference on the textbook in American education cosponsored by the Center for the Book in the Library of Congress and the National Institute of Education held at the Library on May 2–3.

Government Printing Reorganization Act

Identical bills, H.R. 4572 and S. 1436, were introduced in June 1979 by Representatives Frank Thompson (D-N.J.) and Senator Claiborne Pell (D-R.I.), respectively, in an attempt to amend Title 44, U.S. Code. The bills sought to centralize control over all printing done on behalf of the U.S. government. Unfortunately, the language of the legislation was too all-encompassing and brought within its ambit any works funded wholly or partially by the government. This created an uproar in the private sector because this language meant the Government Printing Office (GPO) would control the dissemination of any information generated under government grants to private sector researchers and scholars.

Among the national organizations testifying at the four days of hearings before a joint session of the Committee on House Administration and the Senate Committee on Rules and Administration in July were the American Library Association (ALA), the Association of American Publishers (AAP), the Information Industry Association (IIA), and the Printing Industry of America (PIA). All of these groups spoke in opposition to the bills.

Subsequent to the hearings and following the August congressional recess, Congressman Thompson introduced a new bill, H.R. 5425. The new bill was a great improvement over the earlier version and, in fact, specifically excluded works done under U.S. government grants. The "National Publications Act," H.R. 5424, creates a National Publications Agency (NPA) that will replace the Government Printing Office. The new NPA will be an independent establishment located in the executive branch of the government rather than the legislative branch where the GPO now falls. There was an additional day of hearings held after H.R. 5424 was introduced. This enabled executive branch agencies to testify. The Department of Defense, the General Services Administration, the Office of Personnel Management, and the National Aeronautics and Space Administration all testified in opposition to H.R. 5424. With several substantial amendments, H.R. 5424 was scheduled for committee action in late January 1980. At this writing, it was expected that the House would complete action in February 1980 and the Senate would begin its consideration of the issue shortly thereafter.

National Periodicals Center

The House of Representatives, during consideration of amendments to the Higher Education Act, H.R. 5192, added a new Part D to Title II establishing a National Periodicals Center (NPC). The $15 million NPC, as proposed, would provide a centralized access point for journal articles and other short works. Libraries would be able to sue the NPC in lieu of interlibrary loan. The introduction of NPC legislation in the House bill occurred without any specific hearings on the topic. This fact created great concern in various private sector industries involved.

On October 4, 1979, during Senate consideration of amendments to the Higher Education Act, opportunity was provided for four organizations to testify concerning the National Periodicals Center. The four organizations testifying on the NPC were the Association of American Publishers, the American Library Association, the Information Industry Association, and the National Commission on Libraries and Information Science (NCLIS). During the White House Conference on Libraries and Information Services, discussion of the issue revealed that there was no unanimity among conference delegates. NPC was clearly an issue fraught with controversy. The Senate subcommittee is scheduled to consider this bill in February 1980. There is some speculation concerning whether an NPC proposal will be included in the Senate bill and also whether it will be accepted in the final legislation voted upon during the meeting of the conference committee.

COPYRIGHT ISSUES AFFECTING PUBLISHING

Off-Air Videotaping

In March 1979, the Subcommittee on Courts, Civil Liberties and the Administration of Justice of the Judiciary Committee of the House of Representatives held an open forum on copyright, inviting witnesses to testify on the fair uses of copyrighted materials when applying the law to off-air videotaping of broadcast materials. Following the full-day hearing, the subcommittee, in conjunction with the Copyright Office, appointed an ad hoc committee to attempt to negotiate guidelines for what constitutes fair use when it comes to off-air videotaping by educational institutions. The ad hoc committee has met on a monthly basis since April. If the committee is successful in negotiating guidelines, these will be printed and distributed by the Judiciary Committee of the House of Representatives. Represented on the ad hoc committee are the Association of American Publishers, the Authors League of America, the American Library Association, and several school groups as well as broadcast, guild, and union interests.

Five-Year Review

The Copyright Act of 1976 (PL 94-553) requires that the Register of Copyrights perform a review of the library photocopying section of the copyright law. The completion of the review is scheduled for 1983. The Register of Copyrights appointed a ten-person advisory committee to assist her in ascertaining the information to be gathered and analyzed in her efforts to comply with this five-year review. The Copyright Office will be sponsoring a series of open hearings to enable librarian and copyright proprietors to testify concerning the adequacy of the new copyright law and whether or not it is achieving the statutory balance of the rights of copyright holders and the needs of copyright users. The first hearing is scheduled for January 1980 in Chicago directly preceding the American Library Association midwinter meeting.

CONCENTRATION

The Competition Review Act of 1979 was once again introduced in the Ninety-sixth Congress. Senator Gary Hart (D-Colo.) is principal Senate author of the measure, and Representative Morris Udall (D-Ariz.) lists some 23 House cosponsors of his bill, unveiled at a July 19, 1979 press conference.

Essentially the same as the previous year's version, the bill would mandate a commission study of competition and concentration in various basic industries, and of federal policies promoting or inhibiting competition. In the present bill, the study would last five years, rather than three, as in earlier versions.

Book publishing again is not singled out for study, but is presumed included under the category of "communications."

No action was taken on the legislation during 1979.

LOBBY LEGISLATION

Since 1976, Congress has been considering amendments to the 1946 Regulation of Lobbying Act. In the Ninety-fifth Congress, the House passed what was considered a strong lobby disclosure bill, but the Senate Governmental Affairs Committee failed to approve a measure, and the legislation died at the end of 1978.

A strong lobby bill was once again introduced in 1979, which, among other things, would require disclosure of the dues paid by each individual member of a trade association if a certain fraction of association funds is used for lobbying activities. Additionally, the original bill called for the disclosure of grass-roots solicitation of support for or opposition to legislation. Both of these provisions were subsequently knocked out when the bill was considered by the full House Judiciary Committee.

No further action was taken on the measure during the first session and it is expected that it will go to the full House for debate in early 1980.

In the Senate, Senator Lawton Chiles (D-Fla.) introduced his lobbying bill on July 24. It is generally far more restrictive than the House bill. Hearings were held on it and other measures with no other action taken by the end of the first session.

POSTAL LEGISLATION

On the first day of the Ninety-sixth Congress, Congressman Charles Wilson (D-Calif.), chairman of the House Subcommittee on Postal Operations and Services, introduced H.R. 79, the Postal Service Act of 1979. It subsequently passed the House by an overwhelming vote of 350-14. Following are highlights of the bill.

An increase in public service appropriation from $920 million to $1.1 billion for FY 1980 with additional increments through FY 1982. Under present law, the $920 million public service appropriation terminated in July 1979 with 10 percent reduction of that amount through 1985 when it ends permanently.

The phasing of postal rates for Special Rate Fourth Class (books and records) and all other classes with the exception of first and parcel post, would be extended an additional two years. Phasing for special rate fourth class ended July 6, 1979.

Teaching aids, catalogs of books, and eligible education materials would be allowed to be shipped *to* and *from* qualifying institutions at the preferred library rate.

The bill languished in the Senate and no action was taken by the end of 1979 by Senator John Glenn's (D-Ohio) Subcommittee on Energy, Nuclear Proliferation and Federal Services, despite the fact that a large number of important union and user groups petitioned Glenn urging that he take a more positive and active role on postal matters in his position as chairman of the responsible Senate subcommittee. Among those critical of the lack of progress in the Senate were AAP, most of the various press associations, the third-class mailing groups, and numerous nonprofit organizations.

A separate bill was introduced by Senator Ted Stevens (R-Alaska), S. 1096, to extend the phase-in period by two years for second, third, special rate fourth class, and the library rate.

Fourth Class Postal Rates

The last rate increase granted to the Postal Service took effect in May 1978. No rate requests were made in 1979, although it is anticipated that the Postal Service will seek a further rate increase early in 1980 from the Postal Rate Commission with new rates to take effect ten months later. The phased rates for special rate fourth class expired July 6, 1979.

Alternate Delivery

A number of publishers are engaged in an experiment in California and other locations involving delivery of books by other than the U.S. Postal Service. The books are trucked and then delivered door-to-door from a drop point by a private carrier. The experiment is also being carried out in cooperation with a number of magazines.

Most of the book publishers involved sponsor book clubs. The real question is whether sufficient density can be reached to make the operation cost-effective.

Uniform Rate Threat

Serious consideration continues to be given by the Postal Rate Commission, some elements of the Congress, and the Postal Service itself to elimination of the uniform book rate. The theory is that the uniform rate is an average rate and that long haul shipments drive up the price, in turn forcing short haul shipments out of the mail system. The solution being suggested for this problem is zoned rate, similar to that for parcel post. Such a rate would compound mailers' administrative problems and have serious social implications because publishers' plants tend to be concentrated in the East and zoned rate would discriminate against West Coast consumers.

Court of Appeals Case

The Court of Appeals has effectively held that the cost methodology previously employed by the Postal Service prior to 1976 put an undue burden on first-class mail. In the last rate case, following the Court of Appeals decision, the Postal Rate Commission shifted its methodology and placed a much greater cost burden on the parcel classes, including books. An appeal to the Supreme Court attacking the methodology mandated by the Court of Appeals is pending.

Classification

The Postal Reorganization Act of 1970 required the Postal Service to submit proposals for modifying classifications and the structure of mail classes and subclasses upon which postal rates are set. The preceding was initiated before the Postal Rate Commission in January 1978. The initial proposals of the Postal Service were of a relatively minor nature; among the six reclassification proposals put forth were two discounts for special rate fourth class mail presorted to certain specifications. Because of the priority given to successive postal rate cases, the classification preceding was pursued only sporadically between 1973 and 1976. In April 1976, a settlement agreement was reached providing for, among other things, adoption of a discount for presorted special rate fourth class mail. The proposal was originally implemented in June 1976. The schedule has also been amended to include maps as eligible for special rate fourth class treatment. Other relatively minor classification changes resulting from the Postal Service task forces have been made.

Although the classification proceeding was initially confined to minor proposals of the Postal Service, it has, at the initiative of the Postal Rate Commission, expanded to encompass other classification changes, including a complete overhaul of the classification system. In 1978, the Postal Rate Commission issued a Recommended Decision that liberalized advertising and other materials that may be included in a special rate fourth class mail shipment. Among proposals made in 1978 and still pending are those that relate to special discounts for bulk parcel post, discount for presorted third-class mailing, and a proposal for a new electronics-originated computer mail service. In addition, the mail classification case relating to basic reform is still pending. Issues in that case range from the Postal Service's position that the existing fourth-class mail system should be preserved essentially intact to proposals for a radical restructuring that would base the classification system on considerations such as weight and shape.

The issues also include a dispute concerning the extent to which the Postal Rate Commission has jurisdiction over classification matters. This issue was, however, mooted to a great extent by the stipulated domestic mail classification system that was approved by the parties to the mail classification case. At the request of the Postal Rate Commission, the Postal Service has issued a series of contracts to independent marketing and economic consultants that are intended to provide the function, cost, and marketing data necessary for a determination of the various proposals for the basic reform. These economic analyses are not expected to be concluded until the early 1980s. It is highly unlikely that fundamental changes in the mail classification system will be made until the conclusion of these studies.

LEGISLATION AFFECTING THE INFORMATION INDUSTRY, 1979

Robert S. Willard

Vice President, Government Relations, Information Industry Association

It was said so often that it almost came to be a cliché. There were even some resolutions introduced in the first days of the Congress that would have formally ratified the name. The Ninety-sixth Congress was going to be an "oversight Congress."

The mood of the country was such that the federal legislators felt the better part of valor would be to analyze how well old laws were working rather than to create new ones. Indeed, at the end of the first session, House Majority Whip John Brademas quoted a Congressional Research Service report that described a 25 percent increase in oversight activities by congressional committees when compared to the Ninety-fifth Congress.

However, other numbers do not indicate any marked departure from a "business as usual" Congress. For example, in the first session of the Ninety-sixth Congress (1979), 230 public and private laws were enacted, only 20 less than the 250 of the first session of the Ninety-fifth (1977). Numeric comparisons of course are risky. Congress devotes much more attention and energy to a bill such as the $100 billion plus Defense Department appropriations (PL 96-154) than to one authorizing a gold medal for John Wayne (PL 96-15); both are included in the 230 laws passed in 1979. Also the first session of a biennial Congress is not a good yardstick for measuring the output of the two-year period; in the Ninety-fifth Congress, more than twice as many bills became law in the second session than did in the first. Congress, like most other organizations, is apt to put off its business until the last minute: in 1979, nearly 30 percent of the public laws passed were completed in the last month of the year.

One significant area of decreased activity is in the number of measures introduced in the House—only 7,459 in the first session of the Ninety-sixth compared to 12,490 in the similar part of the Ninety-fifth. However, this decrease is more likely a reflection of a House rule change that allows an unlimited number of cosponsors of a given bill or resolution. In the past, if more than 25 Members wished to sponsor a measure, an identical bill or resolution had to be introduced for each 25 Members. In the Senate, where no such rule existed, there is only a slight drop in the number of introduced measures, from 2,796 in 1977 to 2,712 in 1979.

Note: The opinions expressed in this article are those of the author and do not necessarily represent those of the Information Industry Association.

INFORMATION POLICY LEGISLATION

For those concerned with information, its use within the government, and the public policies affecting it, the task of tracking legislative developments in the area is staggering. A congressional report entitled *Information Policy: Public Laws from the 95th Congress*, was issued in January 1979 and it identified about 75 laws concerned with "gathering and distributing information." It also stated that more than 1,500 such measures had been introduced.

There is nothing to indicate that the pace has slackened in the Ninety-sixth Congress. In a year-end wrap up in the January 1980 issue of *Information World*, it is reported that a Library of Congress SCORPIO search identified more than 1,000 bills having to do with such topics as "information storage and retrieval systems, data banks, information networks, libraries, archives, privacy, communications, broadcasting, technology transfer and freedom of information." (Thirteen of these measures had become law.)

Obviously, this article cannot discuss these 1,000 or so measures affecting information policy. Rather, the litmus test for inclusion here is the author's determination that some legislative action such as hearings or lobbying activity has focused attention on the measure. Further, although substantial research has been devoted to this article, no claim to exhaustive coverage is made; the legislation referred to in this article will simply serve as examples of the myriad concerns that come under the "information policy" rubric.

ADMINISTRATION INVOLVEMENT

Before turning to specific legislative proposals, it is valuable to discuss executive branch involvement in information policy legislation. Bits and pieces of information policy responsibility are strewn throughout the executive branch; a partial list of players would include the Domestic Policy Staff, the Office of Management and Budget, the Office of Science and Technology Policy, all within the Executive Office of the President; the General Services Administration, the Department of State; the Department of Commerce, including such agencies as the National Telecommunications and Information Agency, the Patent and Trademark Office, the National Technical Information Service, and the National Bureau of Standards; the Federal Communications Commission; the National Commission on Libraries and Information Science; and the National Science Foundation, among many others.

Studies in the past (such as those by the Commission on Federal Paperwork) have recommended the focusing of much information policy activity in a single entity; but so far the Carter administration has greeted these proposals with unbridled disinterest. Nevertheless, a substantial amount of attention has been paid to information policy issues by the administration. In 1979 alone, eight messages to Congress and three addresses to national meetings demonstrated the president's concern with these issues. The messages to Congress are as follows:

International Communications Policy and International Journalistic Freedom (January 19)

Rural Telecommunications (February 14)

Science and Technology (March 27)

Privacy (April 2)

Electronic Mail (July 19)

Common Carrier Reform (September 21)

Industrial Innovation (October 31)

Paperwork Reduction (November 30)

The three national meetings were the National Association of Broadcasters in Dallas (March 25), where President Carter unveiled his regulatory reform program; the National Cable Television Association in Las Vegas (May 23), which the president addressed by two-way satellite TV and discussed the role of cable TV and other technologies in increasing citizen participation in their government; and in Washington, the White House Conference on Library and Information Services (November 16).

Unfortunately absent from any of these presentations is an explicit statement of the unifying information policy thread that binds these various issues together. Yet it is clear that, despite the understandable pull of such competing issues as energy, inflation, and defense, the White House is not ignoring information policy.

CONGRESSIONAL ACTIVITY

Information policy legislation in 1979 can be analyzed in five categories. First, there are those proposals which mandate or encourage the government to become involved in the information marketplace, thus possibly competing with other providers in that marketplace. Second, there are a number of measures aimed at protecting the economic value of information resources. Government rules affecting the transport of information, or communications, comprise the third category. Fourth are those legislative items that address civil liberty issues in the information arena, specifically privacy and First Amendment rights. Finally, the fifth category contains those proposals that assign a regulatory role to the government that may be an incentive or an impediment to flows of information. Sometimes, of course, a particular bill may fit in more than one category; however, for simplicity, none of the legislation discussed will appear more than once.

Government Competition

Perhaps no issue is of greater concern to the rapidly growing information industry than that posed by the potential competition of subsidized government information activities. In a Congressional Joint Committee on Printing (JCP) report, *Federal Government Printing and Publishing: Policy Issues*, this issue was described as follows:

> On the one hand, there is the principle that, "In a democratic free-enterprise system, the government should not compete with its citizens." (OMB Circular No. A-76 Revised, March 29, 1979). On the other hand, there is a strong obligation on the part of the government to insure that all citizens are as well informed as possible about government activities. While private publishers can be helpful in this regard, the final responsibility is that of the government, which may find it necessary to act in cases where private publishers have failed to do a job which the government considers essential to the public welfare. Balancing these two conflicting principles is a difficult task. . . .

This quotation is from a report of an advisory committee established by the JCP to examine the issues that would be involved in a rewrite of Title 44 of the United States Code, the statutory charter of the Government Printing Office and the Federal Depository Library program. Although its context is that of government publication, the conflict it describes is wide spread.

Legislation to rewrite Title 44 was introduced in both the House and Senate in June: H.R. 4572 was introduced by JCP Chairman, Representative Frank Thompson, Jr. and 17 cosponsors; Senator Claiborne Pell, Vice Chairman of the JCP, introduced an identical bill in the Senate (S. 1436). Four days of joint (House/Senate) hearings were held in July with a wide range of witnesses. In late September, Thompson introduced a new version of the Title 44 rewrite (H.R. 5424) that sought to address the concerns raised by various witnesses.

The bill establishes a new, independent executive branch agency, the National Publications Agency, with policy direction coming from a board consisting of seven presidential appointees and one nonvoting representative from the House of Representatives, the Senate, and the Office of Management and Budget. Policy and regulations would have to be adopted openly according to federal administrative procedures, although they would be subject to congressional or presidential vetoes. The Joint Committee on Printing would be abolished. Production and distribution functions would be put on an equal footing. Finally, no special advantage would be given to either the government or the private sector in the production or distribution of government information; rather, fair competition among all interested participants would be the rule.

One problem with the bill, however, is present in the sweeping definition of "public document." In addition to traditional ink-on-paper products and new microfilm products, the definition would also include audiovisual presentations and computer data bases. The full implications of including these media remain to be examined. (In late January, the House Administration Committeee voted to report H.R. 5424 to the full House; however, the new agency has been taken out of the executive branch and returned to the legislative.)

Title 44 revision may be one of the most significant pieces of legislation in the government competition area, but it is not unique. Another important bill is one attempting to establish a National Periodicals Center (NPC), a federal lending library for journal articles. This activity would threaten to compete both with major microfilm republishers as well as with existing document delivery services.

The NPC is authorized in a new section II-D of the Higher Education Amendments. This section appeared in H.R. 5192 when it was introduced in the House in early September as a "clean bill," that is, a new version of legislation already discussed by committee. No hearings were held on NPC on the House side, although at least one library witness testifying on all Title II programs stated the need for an NPC. It was not until the Senate began hearings on the Higher Education Act that some time was devoted to the NPC, but it quickly became clear that a number of unresolved questions are held by the Senate, and it is unclear what action the Senate will take in 1980. (The full House passed H.R. 5192 with the NPC included in early November 1979.)

A third potential government competition issue was contained in H.R. 4392, Appropriations for Departments of State, Justice, Commerce, the Judiciary, and Related Agencies. The matter at hand was the funding of a Commerce Department data base known as the Worldwide Information and Trade System (WITS). The justification for this system, according to Commerce, is that many small and medium-size businesses could be exporting and thus helping to decrease this country's trade deficit, but these companies don't have information about overseas markets. Conversely, potential customers overseas don't have information on U.S. vendors with needed products. Therefore, Commerce asked Congress for $5 million to begin building an information system to meet these information needs. Meanwhile, the information industry contended that these needs could be met using existing products and services in the marketplace and that WITS would damage the capabilities of this industry. After numerous meetings between Congressional personnel and industry members, the WITS budget was reduced 20 percent and clear instructions were given that Commerce should "fully involve the private information industry in the development of WITS" and that the department should "not duplicate or compete with the private sector." This legislation became PL 96-68 on September 24.

These three proposals, Title 44 revision, the National Periodicals Center, and the Worldwide Information and Trade System, were considered vitally important by the Information Industry Association and much time and energy was spent attempting to shape these proposals to the interests of the industry. Meanwhile, other legislative activities that could have profound effects on the information marketplace were taking place.

For example, H.R. 4537, a nearly 400-page bill to approve and implement the trade agreements negotiated in the Tokyo Round of Multilateral Trade Negotiations, was signed into law (PL 96-39) on July 26, 1979, a scant 37 days after it was introduced. A number of information aspects were included in the bill. It establishes a "library of information relating to foreign subsidy practices and countervailing measures" within the International Trade Commission; it directs the U.S. Trade Representative to make information available to persons who ask about foreign trade practices and trade agreements; and it creates within the Department of Commerce a "Standards Information Center" to serve as the central national collection facility and as the inquiry point for requests for information related to standards.

It is unclear what the marketplace effects of this law will be. There are, for example, companies that provide standards-related information; how will these companies be affected by the new standards information center? The law requires the center to "use its best efforts" to rely on privately available information but it allows the Secretary of Commerce to prescribe "reasonable fees." How will this pricing compare to market-determined pricing and what will the competitive results be? These issues were not analyzed fully by the Congress in the 37 days it dealt with the bill.

Another example of this type of legislation is S. 918, the Small Business Development Center Act of 1979 which was introduced in early April and which, by the time it had passed both houses in slightly different versions, had come to include a number of additional provisions affecting small business. Still part of the bill is the establishment of small business development centers (SBDC), which would be public or educational entities that would receive federal matching funds to provide business assistance to small firms. On the staff there would be "information specialists to assist in providing information searches and referrals." Among the services of the SBDC would be "furnishing one-to-one individual counseling," "maintaining current information concerning Federal, state and local regulations," "providing and maintaining a comprehensive library that contains current information and statistical data," and "conducting in-depth surveys for local small business groups in order to develop general information regarding the local economy. . . ." These services are now offered by components of the information industry, many of which are small businesses themselves, and it is not easily apparent how these firms will be affected by the SBDCs. (At the end of 1979, there was still disagreement between the House and Senate although a conference committee of the two bodies was working to iron out the differences. These differences are unrelated to the information policy aspects of the bill.)

One additional feature of the bill as shaped by the conference serves as an example of how information policy provisions are incorporated into legislation without full consideration. Title IV of S. 918 calls for the head of the Small Business Administration to establish and maintain "an external small business economic data base for the purpose of providing the Congress and the Administration information on the economic condition and the expansion or contraction of the small business sector." It further requires regular publication of various economic indexes. Here again there appears to be no discussion of the impact on those information industry firms whose businesses are to collect, package, and disseminate economic information on business establishments.

Data Protection

Turning from the issue of government competition, a second area of concern to the information community are those legislative activities aimed at protecting the economic value of information resources. Two separate issues come to bear here, copyright protection and computer security.

Oversight hearings and other nonlegislative action with regard to copyright occurred in 1979. Hearings on the operation of the Patent Office and the Copyright Royalty Tribunal, an examination of the retransmission consent proposition in cable TV, and the initiation of a stakeholders' committee to look at off-the-air video recording for educational purposes all took place in 1979. No major legislation affecting copyright law was introduced, but two bills introduced in the House offer some indication of the complexity of proprietary rights issues. The first, H.R. 288, was introduced on the first day of the Ninety-sixth Congress and is cited as the "Visual Artists Moral Rights Amendments of 1979." No hearings have been held on this bill which would give to owners of copyright in a pictorial, graphic, or sculptural work the additional right to object to any distortion, mutilation, or other alteration of the work. What effect this provision would have on editorial cartoonists and satirists is certainly unclear and would raise some fundamental First Amendment questions that will have to be addressed if this legislation moves forward.

A second bill concerns itself with the protection of computer software. This subject was discussed by the National Commission on New Technological Uses of Copyrighted Works (CONTU) but so far (despite rumors about an impending bill) no legislation to afford copyright protection to computer programs and data bases has been introduced. One area, however, that CONTU did not address is the protection of computer software that is physically embedded in an integrated circuit, semiconductor chip. However, H.R. 1007, introduced in January, attempts to provide this protection. Hearings were held in April, but support for this concept was not unanimous. Some felt that patents offer better protection for the underlying process involved in a computer program. Many of the same arguments debated by CONTU were made in the hearing. In short, the hearing, and the introduction of the bill, point up the difficulty the Congress has in dealing with the information proprietary issues forced by the new technologies.

In the area of computer security, there is one bill before the Senate that is a reintroduced version of a bill first introduced in both Houses in the Ninety-fifth Congress. S. 240, the Federal Computer Systems Protection Act of 1979, was introduced in late January; however, hearings were held on the predecessor bill during the Ninety-fifth Congress. In November, the bill was unanimously approved by a Senate subcommittee and passage in early 1980 was predicted. The bill would make it a federal offense to use or attempt to use a computer to obtain property through fraudulent means or damage a computer, when such a computer is owned by or operated for the government or is operated in interstate commerce. Home computers are specifically exempted. What is especially significant about this bill is the definition of "property," which means "anything of value, and includes tangible and intangible personal property, information in the form of electronically processed, produced, or stored data, or any electronic data processing representations thereof, and services." Therefore, under this bill, any unauthorized access to data bases could risk federal prosecution.

Communications

Without the ability to put information where it is needed at the time it is needed, the information loses its value. One of the keys to the rapid growth of information services in this country is the high quality communications infrastructure to move information around. Much of this communications infrastructure has grown under the 45-year-old Communications Act of 1934, but in 1979 the pressure to update this act built up, and before the year was out a number of legislative proposals were receiving critical attention on both sides of Capitol Hill.

The most ambitious of these proposals was a complete rewrite of the 1934 act. This "attic to basement" revision, H.R. 3333, was introduced by Congressman Lionel Van Deerlin in late March and it was based on a bill that had been introduced in June the prior year. Numerous witnesses had testified both before and after the introduction of both bills. H.R. 3333 would have removed much regulation from various broadcasting and common carrier services; it would have abolished the Federal Communications Commission and restructured the National Telecommunications and Information Agency (taking away the "Information" component); and it would have charged a fee to broadcasters for the use of the electromagnetic spectrum. (The fee would have been based on economic utility in each market area.)

However, by July, it was clear that support for an attic to basement rewrite was not present. Instead the House decided to concentrate on the rooms where the telephones were and ignore the rooms with radio and TV. Meanwhile attention focused on the Senate where two bills, S. 611, introduced by Senator Ernest Hollings and characterized as a Communications Act "renovation," and S. 622, introduced by Senator Barry Goldwater, were under consideration. Although these latter bills contained some broadcast implications, it quickly became clear that the major concern of the Congress was on the common carrier aspects of communications law. The National Telecommunications and Information Agency (NTIA) focused its policymaking energies on the issue and at about the same time the president was sending his common carrier message to Congress, NTIA issued a "primer" on common carrier. Many of the concepts in that document eventually worked their way into the substitute legislation that Congressman Van Deerlin introduced to replace his earlier, more ambitious total rewrite.

A major information concern of the Communications Act amendments is the role of the "dominant carrier" (a legal euphemism for AT&T) in providing "information services." The NTIA primer, which generally supports AT&T activity in the marketplace through separate subsidies, recommended against AT&T providing "mass media services," which include broadcasting, cable and pay television, printed or electronic publishing, and similar electronic services. NTIA took this position "because diversity in mass media services enhances the flow of information to the American public." It felt the size and wealth of AT&T would discourage other firms from entering the information marketplace. It appeared that this concept would be incorporated in the House legislation.

Another aspect of communications is electronic mail. No legislation authorizing a role for the U.S. Postal Service in this area was handled by Congress in 1979. H.R. 79, the Postal Service Reform Act, remains silent on the issue, unlike similar legislation considered in the Ninety-fifth Congress. However, there was a brief skirmish in the Senate in relation to the appropriation for the Postal Service; in subcommittee, language was added to the bill to sharply limit the Postal Service role in electronic mail. This event triggered a full-scale lobbying and letter writing assault by individuals and organizations on both sides of the issue. Before the matter reached the floor, the sponsors of the restrictive amendment pulled it from the bill. It seems certain that 1980 will see major consideration of the electronic mail issue in both the House and Senate.

Civil Liberties

Legislation affecting the relationship between information and individual rights is a fourth category for looking at information policy developments in the first session of the Ninety-sixth Congress. Very little legislation in this area actually passed either the House or the Senate but a significant amount of attention was paid to the subject in preparation for possible passage before the Ninety-sixth Congress adjourns.

An exception, however, is S. 37, one of the earliest bills signed into law by the president in 1979 (PL 96-3). This bill was a one-sentence amendment to the Right to Financial Privacy Act which had been passed by both the House and Senate in the last 24 hours of the Ninety-fifth Congress. One provision of that law was that financial institutions had to notify all customers of their new rights under the law. These institutions pointed out the large expense of such notice, especially in the case of inactive accounts, and argued that notices could be sent to account holders with the next regular statement or other scheduled mailing, or at the time the privacy right could be exercised.

Numerous other privacy bills were introduced. Congressman Barry Goldwater, Jr., a member of the Privacy Protection Study Commission which issued its final report in the summer of 1978, introduced a number of bills implementing the commission's recommendations. In April, the administration sent Congress two bills affecting personal privacy, one having to do with medical records, the other federally funded research records. These were followed up by a third bill to provide privacy protection for insurance, consumer credit, and banking records, and for Electronic Funds Transfer systems. These bills were the subject of hearings during 1979, and the administration's efforts will be directed toward their early enactment.

In April, President Carter also sent Congress a bill designed to reverse the effects of the Supreme Court decision in 1978 allowing newsroom searches by law enforcement officials (*Zurcher* v. *Stanford Daily*). The administration bill, H.R. 3486, would restrict police searches for materials held by the press and "others involved in the dissemination of information to the public."

Regulation of Information Flows

The final area of information policy legislation during the Ninety-sixth Congress, first session, encompassed those measures that impede or that encourage the flows of information. One of the foremost examples deals with the paperwork burden the government puts on its citizens and the effect this has on the flow of information from the citizens back to the government. H.R. 3570, the Paperwork and Redtape Reduction Act, was introduced by Congressman Frank Horton who earlier had been chairman of the Commission on Federal Paperwork. This bill would establish responsibility for information management in the Office of Management and Budget and would require the coordination of information requests by various agencies in order to prevent unnecessary duplication of requests. The president, in his message on paperwork reduction, supported this legislation and similar legislation introduced in the Senate by Senator Lawton Chiles.

Another example of legislation affecting information flows is the area of such flows across international boundaries. Very little legislation has been introduced in this area, and that which has been, along with other congressional activity, has focused on mechanisms to develop policy affecting international information flows rather than the policy itself. For example, Congressman Barry Goldwater introduced House Joint

Resolution 36 authorizing the president to convene an international conference on communication and information to discuss these issues. Also, both the Government Information and the Communications subcommittees in the House have focused attention on "transborder data flow." The latter committee also considered during 1979 a proposal to bring together within the State Department all the elements involved in this issue into an Agency of International Telecommunications Policy.

Another aspect of international information flow is scientific and technical information for development of Third World countries. The International Development Cooperation Act, which was signed into law on August 14, contained a section establishing an Institute for Scientific and Technological Cooperation. This institute would be a principal technology transfer agent between the United States and less developed countries and would have specific information dissemination functions. (Toward the end of 1979, it was still undetermined when the institute would be activated.)

CONCLUSION

The breadth and amount of information policy legislation, as indicated at the beginning of this article, is staggering. This article has had to leave a number of 1979 events affecting information either ignored or glossed over. There is no mention of the new Department of Education; no reference to the appropriations for such activities as the Library of Congress, the GPO, the Federal Communications Commission, etc.; no reference to space, communications satellites, and remote sensing; no discussion of the television broadcasting of the House proceedings, nor of the unwillingness of the House to make available the computer data base of legislative status information. These and many other items came before the Congress in 1979.

Clearly, both the administration and the Congress are frequently being asked to address information policy issues. This trend is certain to continue into the 1980s as the government must come to grips with the public policy of the information age.

Federally Funded Programs and Grant-Making Agencies

LIBRARY SERVICES AND CONSTRUCTION ACT (LSCA)

Elizabeth H. Hughey

Chief, State and Public Library Services Branch, Division of Library Programs, Office of Libraries and Learning Resources, USOE

The Library Services and Construction Act (LSCA), originally enacted as the Library Services Act in 1956 (PL 84-597), has been amended and extended through 1982 by the 1977 amendments (PL 95-123) that were signed into law on October 7, 1977. Under these amendments, LSCA continues as a state formula grant program with four titles and matching requirements for Titles I and II. The titles are I, Library Services; II, Public Library Construction; III, Interlibrary Cooperation; and IV, Older Readers Services.

Emphases in Title I are on (1) providing library services to disadvantaged persons in both rural and urban areas; (2) extending library services to the state's institutionalized residents and to the physically handicapped, including the blind; (3) strengthening metropolitan public libraries that serve as national or regional resource centers; (4) improving and strengthening the capacity of the state library administrative agencies to meet the needs of all the people in a given state; and (5) serving persons with limited English-speaking ability. Title I also provides funds for many of the activities authorized under Title IV, Older Readers Services, which was added to LSCA by the Older Americans Comprehensive Services Amendments of 1973 but not funded to date.

The 1977 amendments incorporated several changes in the act, two of which were implemented in FY 1978: Any federal funds expended for the administration of the act must be equally matched by state or other nonfederal funds; and funds available for expenditure in the current fiscal year for library services to the physically handicapped and to persons in institutions substantially supported by the state must be not less than the amount expended from all sources in the second preceding fiscal year. Under previous legislation the maintenance of effort had been established at FY 1971 expenditures level.

A third change legislated at the same time was not implemented until FY 1979, when Congress appropriated an amount for Title I that exceeded $60 million. A priority was added to Title I to focus attention on the needs of major urban resource libraries. This provision provides that when appropriations for Title I exceed $60 million, a portion (not more than 50 percent) of the money beyond that figure will be reserved for major urban resource libraries. "Major urban resource library" is defined as "any public library located in a city having a population of 100,000 or more individuals, as deter-

Note: Written in collaboration with branch staff: Shirley A. Brother, Nathan M. Cohen, Clarence Foglestrom (on detail), Dorothy A. Kittel, Lawrence E. Leonard, Evaline B. Neff, and Pauline Winnick.

mined by the U.S. Commissioner of Education," and that has collections of value and provides services to individual users and other libraries throughout the defined regional area in which such library is located. The portion of funds from the excess over $60 million to be reserved for major urban resource libraries is based on the ratio of the state's urban population to the state's entire population.

It is the responsibility of state library administrative agencies to designate and support one or more major urban resource libraries within each state that meet defined criteria. Congress further stipulates that states not reduce the level of support previously received by participating major urban resource libraries. In those states where a qualified major urban resource library does not exist, all funds, including those covered by this provision, are to be expended following Title I priorities. This added Title I priority, first activated for FY 1979 with an appropriation of $62.5 million, continues at the same level, thus causing $2.5 million to be subject to the major urban resource library provision in FY 1980.

All programs funded under LSCA are administered by the 57 state and territorial library administrative agencies, each of which submitted a three-year basic state plan for FY 1980, 1981, and 1982 and annually submits a long-range program for library development based on the state's assessed needs and an annual program. These documents outline a state's goals, objectives, priorities, and activities for specified periods of time. Furthermore, they provide to the U.S. Commissioner of Education assurances that specific requirements will be met annually as stated in the three-year (FY 1980, 1981, 1982) state-federal agreement signed by both parties.

All qualifying documents are developed by the state in consultation with the appropriate representatives of the U.S. Commissioner of Education. A statewide advisory council assists the state library administrative agency in developing and reviewing the documents. The council must be broadly representative of all types of libraries and of library user groups. Each council must have a minimum of one-third of its members who are consumers, thereby continuing an effective liaison with the statewide community of users and potential users.

To ensure efficient management of the LSCA programs at all government levels, a cooperative management review program was initiated during FY 1975 by the regional and central staff responsible for administering the act. The administration of this program delegated to the Office of Education regions in FY 1967 was returned to the Office of Education headquarters in FY 1978. Subsequently, new state and subject specialty assignments were made to the administrative librarians. State management reviews and project monitoring continued according to an established procedure, with a team that includes two representatives from the Office of Libraries and Learning Resources staff and state library representation. At the discretion of the state librarian, a member of the LSCA Statewide Advisory Council also participates.

TITLE I—LIBRARY SERVICES

Title I of the act expresses a national concern for groups of citizens who may be out of the mainstream of public library services and thus underserved. The legislative concern that these citizens shall derive the benefits of good library services is matched by the parallel concern that the state and local agencies, which have the responsibility for improvement of the users' services, be given the capability to perform their administrative tasks. The state library agencies, in planning for the productive use of funds for statewide library development, have interfaced LSCA priorities with the identified informational and library needs of the people within their states.

TABLE 1 LSCA TITLE I, LIBRARY SERVICES, STATE ALLOTMENTS AND MATCHING REQUIREMENTS, FY 1980

States and Outlying Areas	Total Federal Allotment	Total State and Local Matching	$60 Million Level	Excess of $60 Million
Alabama	$1,070,997	$ 711,621	$1,029,041	$ 41,956
Alaska	297,460	603,934	292,765	4,695
Arizona	743,930	640,641	717,729	26,201
Arkansas	707,826	449,131	683,364	24,462
California	5,364,859	6,906,090	5,116,070	248,789
Colorado	819,443	853,231	789,605	29,838
Connecticut	933,185	1,262,028	897,868	35,317
Delaware	337,340	418,350	330,724	6,616
District of Columbia	361,645	621,621	353,859	7,786
Florida	2,197,793	2,009,315	2,101,560	96,233
Georgia	1,389,567	1,047,415	1,332,266	57,301
Hawaii	410,257	520,453	400,129	10,128
Idaho	401,997	311,396	392,267	9,730
Illinois	2,849,565	3,717,767	2,721,937	127,628
Indiana	1,462,484	1,389,474	1,401,671	60,813
Iowa	881,506	851,013	848,678	32,828
Kansas	747,469	772,395	721,098	26,371
Kentucky	1,018,373	741,083	978,952	39,421
Louisiana	1,127,395	803,737	1,082,723	44,672
Maine	455,801	318,580	443,479	12,322
Maryland	1,176,242	1,401,540	1,129,217	47,025
Massachusetts	1,563,247	1,677,987	1,497,580	65,667
Michigan	2,358,730	2,641,758	2,254,745	103,985
Minnesota	1,139,194	1,122,907	1,093,953	45,241
Mississippi	763,045	416,496	735,923	27,122
Missouri	1,337,888	1,183,099	1,283,076	54,812
Montana	380,759	305,912	372,052	8,707
Nebraska	566,947	534,349	549,271	17,676
Nevada	350,318	455,938	343,077	7,241
New Hampshire	400,582	347,889	390,920	9,662
New Jersey	1,931,609	2,592,066	1,848,199	83,410
New Mexico	482,230	341,813	468,635	13,595
New York	4,431, 565	5,288,911	4,227,732	203,833
North Carolina	1,501,421	1,105,213	1,438,732	62,689
North Dakota	353,386	304,443	345,997	7,389
Ohio	2,724,025	2,718,582	2,602,444	121,581
Oklahoma	864,751	705,810	832,730	32,021
Oregon	762,808	751,602	735,698	27,110
Pennsylvania	2,983,601	2,974,069	2,849,516	134,085
Rhode Island	421,112	395,154	410,461	10,651
South Carolina	879,146	590,015	846,432	32,714
South Dakota	362,353	258,646	354,533	7,820
Tennessee	1,212,819	850,149	1,164,032	48,787
Texas	3,221,939	2,986,036	3,076,374	145,565
Utah	499,692	363,632	485,256	14,436
Vermont	313,742	226,261	308,263	5,479
Virginia	1,402,310	1,354,886	1,344,395	57,915
Washington	1,068,636	1,238,437	1,026,795	41,841
West Virginia	637,268	472,762	616,205	21,063
Wisconsin	1,295,883	1,212,601	1,243,095	52,788
Wyoming	295,807	333,838	291,192	4,615
American Samoa	47,103	24,265	46,761	342
Guam	62,630	32,264	61,540	1,090

TABLE 1 LSCA TITLE I, LIBRARY SERVICES, STATE ALLOTMENTS AND MATCHING REQUIREMENTS, FY 1980 (cont.)

States and Outlying Areas	Total Federal Allotment	Total State and Local Matching	$60 Million Level	Excess of $60 Million
Puerto Rico	956,311	492,645	919,880	36,431
Trust Territory	65,910	—	64,662	1,248
Virgin Islands	62,395	32,143	61,316	1,079
Northern Mariana Islands	43,704	22,514	43,526	178
Total	$62,500,000	$62,705,907	$60,000,000	$2,500,000

Estimated distribution of $62,500,000 with a minimum allotment of $200,000 to the 50 states, District of Columbia, and Puerto Rico and $40,000 to the other outlying areas; the remainder distributed on the basis of the total resident population, July 1, 1977. Required matching expenditures computed on the basis of FY 1980–1981 "federal share" percentages.

As priority areas are discussed, an overlap of project types will become evident. It should be noted, too, that all titles of LSCA can and do converge for expanded program advantages. Services for handicapped and elderly persons (Title I) have been furthered by the construction and remodeling of library facilities (Title II) to free them from physical barriers. Access to materials from state, public, school, academic, and special libraries through interlibrary cooperation (Title III) enlarges the library and information resources available to all persons served by the various programs under Title I.

See Table 1 for an overview of federal allotments and state and local matching requirements under LSCA, Title I, Library Services, for FY 1980.

Services to the Disadvantaged

A significant portion of Title I funds is used to encourage the development and delivery of innovative library programs to disadvantaged persons. Libraries are directing their efforts toward ameliorating the causes and effects of poverty by providing a variety of educational services geared for all age groups. For adults, such services include basic literacy and adult education courses, independent learning with the library giving guidance through specially trained learner's advisers, consumer and health education, and parenting classes. Children and youth benefit from such group and individualized library experiences as storytelling, reading guidance and tutoring, arts and crafts, and preschool and reading readiness programs that stimulate learning. Such library programs not only supplement and expand existing school-based learning but also offer creative alternatives to formal education in an environment that allows for individual growth and personalized study goals.

For the economically and educationally disadvantaged population, library services are supplied both in and outside the actual library facility. Outreach services to isolated rural areas are accomplished through extensive use of bookmobiles and books-by-mail delivery. Books, magazines, and wide selection of materials, including art prints, sculptures, and educational games, are thereby distributed to geographically isolated persons and to individuals homebound through illness, age, and/or other handicaps. Linkage with information services is provided as well.

Migrants are also served wherever they may be located. One LSCA program seasonally takes its diverse services to the top of a mountain to reach more than 600

Mexican-American migrant workers planting and harvesting crops. Special children's programs offering stories, music, and films and adult programs, including nutrition information, adult basic education, and how-to-do-it skills, are presented bilingually.

Use of advanced communications technology, including cable television, video, and specialized radio receivers, has furthered the libraries' capabilities to supply needed information in a timely manner. In one Appalachian state, bookmobiles equipped with two-way radio communications systems cross the countryside bringing rural residents the "instant" information they need to deal with the crises of daily life.

Coping and survival information/skills are also provided to the urban disadvantaged through special library information and referral (I&R) centers. These I&R services link persons in need with the appropriate community and social agencies that can provide help and, increasingly, job information. The library's follow-up component ensures that the services thus identified have actually been received by the client.

Economically disadvantaged Americans of diverse ethnic backgrounds are served by and featured in Title I-supported library programs. These build on recognizing and highlighting various cultural identities and strengths, and promote participation of the ethnic group in designing programs and selecting materials for their specific needs.

Native Americans participate in library activities both in urban library centers and on reservations. Activities include presentations of films that use Indian tribal dialects, cultural heritage programs, classes on Indian handicrafts, and instruction in native languages and tutoring for schoolchildren to reduce the extremely high dropout rate. Library training for Indians that enables them later to serve their own communities is another important aspect of LSCA programs.

The community library's response to the dilemmas of its disadvantaged residents has proved to be creative and supportive in human terms.

Services to the Institutionalized

By definition in the act, state institutional library services means "the providing of books and other library services" to residents of institutions operated or substantially supported by the state. Eligible institutions run the gamut from correctional institutions (penitentiaries, prison farms and road camps, reformatories, vocational and rehabilitation facilities, and youth training centers and schools) to health and custodial facilities (mental hospitals, sanatoriums, and old-age homes) to residential schools for the developmentally disabled and physically handicapped. This wide variance in the types of institutions served necessitates an equally large diversity of library services.

Title I funds are used to establish and upgrade institutional libraries, enabling them to demonstrate the benefits of good library service and make a more meaningful contribution to the overall rehabilitation program of the institution. Strengthening an institution library is partly accomplished through purchase of equipment and materials, contracts with local public libraries for services (for example, bookmobile visits), and provision of centralized ordering and processing. Additionally, institutional libraries are upgraded through improved staffing, which includes both the hiring of qualified personnel and the development of existing staff through in-service training.

In correctional institutions, the emphasis is on socialization and educational rehabilitation programs. Library services offer residents opportunities to engage in independent learning programs and formal academic work, including college and correspondence courses. Book deposits in recreational areas and organized reading and discussion groups stimulate inmates to increase their reading and communication skills. Projects designed to support prerelease information and counseling programs have been recently developed by libraries in response to the demonstrated need for improved services in these areas. Libraries also initiate creative writing experiences that sometimes result in publications. Drug and alcohol educational materials, films, and programs are made available, along with special bilingual/bicultural presentations for those institutionalized persons of different cultural and ethnic backgrounds. Inmates who exhibit interest and competence in library work are also given on-the-job training working as library aides. These aides and other personnel are often given introductory training in the provision of specialized library service, including legal reference work required for prison clientele.

Residents of noncorrectional institutions receive parallel services, with emphasis on recreation and rehabilitation to help overcome mental and physical handicaps. Specially trained librarians, working with hospital staff, conduct bibliotherapy sessions for patients in mental hospitals to help clarify their perception of reality. Bibliotherapy in schools for the handicapped assists the residents in adjusting to their physical conditions and in relating to the world around them. Recreational reading, crafts and music programs, and personal visits from the librarians and volunteers are important factors in providing library service beneficial to the institutionalized.

The intensified interest of the community in persons shut out from society and the attempt to "mainstream" these persons (return them to productive community living at an early date) has produced innovative LSCA projects for the institutionalized.

Services to the Handicapped

The definition of services to the physically handicapped as described in the act is "the providing of library services, through public or other nonprofit libraries, agencies, or organizations, to physically handicapped persons (including the blind and other visually handicapped) certified by competent authority as unable to read or to use conventional printed materials as a result of physical limitations." In actual practice, the services of libraries to handicapped persons are of a broader nature and encompass the entire "handicapped community," i.e., the parents, relatives, teachers, and laypersons who are in contact and deal with the handicapped. One important achievement of library programs in this field is the increased public awareness of the needs and problems of handicapped people.

Because serving the handicapped is an unfamiliar area for many librarians, state library agencies sponsor statewide and regional workshops to promote recognition of and training for such services. From these extensive in-service training efforts, worthy projects result on a local level.

The majority of library projects for the handicapped are directed at the blind and visually impaired, who comprise the greatest percentage of persons eligible for special-service programs. Services are frequently provided by mail delivery or personal visits by outreach librarians and volunteers who bring talking books and related equipment, special print magnifiers, braille magazines, books and bookmarks, recordings, and large-print materials.

Some projects serving the blind are even more specialized and can supplement the regular services with talking books in many languages (including Vietnamese) and foreign-language magazines. Sculpture designed to be enjoyed through touch is also loaned to the blind. Many libraries sponsor taping projects in order to supply up-to-date materials to handicapped persons, including students with special textbook requirements. Others, working in cooperation with local associations for the blind, sponsor programs to demonstrate new aids and appliances and publicize services and resources available to the handicapped.

Public libraries are also taking note of advances in technology that can facilitate a blind person's access to printed materials. One recent and exciting technological advance is the Kurzweil Reading Machine, a reading device that scans ordinary printed materials and reads aloud in synthetic English speech. This innovative instrument, easily operated by push button controls, enables a blind person to "read" the printed word independently for the first time. The availability of such a machine in a public library allows a blind patron access to virtually anything in printed form.

Special radio reading for the blind is another vital service made possible with LSCA support. This service entails the use of library-loaned, specially adapted receivers that pick up daily library-produced broadcasts. These broadcasts consist of readings of local and city newspapers, book discussion programs, and announcements of interest, and are jointly programmed by media and library personnel and representatives of the handicapped consumers.

Children with visual handicaps can often be mainstreamed into summer reading programs or can take advantage of special summer library activities geared to their individual needs. These reading programs even offer award certificates in braille and large print.

Library projects also reach out to those with physical handicaps other than blindness. The deaf are another group of underserved persons. Although they can read traditional materials, many other programs and services that libraries offer require verbal communication and are thus inaccessible to them. To alleviate the barriers to full service, some libraries have installed TTY (Teletypewriter) machines by which the deaf can communicate their reference needs and receive information not only on weather, sports, and news but also emergency warnings and job opportunities. Other libraries have trained personnel to speak in sign language and do finger spelling. Thus, library programs, such as children's story hours, public forums, book discussions, and captioned films, are made available to all persons regardless of physical impairments.

Developmentally disabled children and their parents receive help from the library in dealing with their problems. Instructional materials centers supply educational toys, games, and realia to help parents develop specific skills in their handicapped children.

Mentally retarded persons of all ages can benefit from library programs even though their use of books is limited. Projects utilizing audiovisual materials are often successful in reaching these persons. One such project involved the library, in conjunction with hospital staff, in the production of a videotape series to help retarded adults acquire such daily life skills as shopping, meal preparation, riding public transportation, etc. The eventual outcome of such efforts is handicapped adults capable of independent living.

The growing visibility and determination of handicapped persons to be included in learning, employment, and contributing roles in the society act positively on library program plans for this targeted use of LSCA support.

Services to Persons of Limited English-Speaking Ability

Spanning the entire country, Title I-supported services are addressing the objectives of bilingual/bicultural education on a statewide basis and locally in rural and urban settings. With the 1974 Education Amendments, states were required to add criteria in their annual needs assessment and planning to ensure that priority would be given to programs and projects serving areas with high concentrations of persons of limited English-speaking ability.

Library services for Americans disadvantaged by language are offered in many areas and illustrate library responsiveness to a wide range of ages and corresponding needs. Library preschool programs for Spanish-speaking children help prepare them for entry into formalized education by fostering the development of bilingual reading and listening skills, preception skills, language expression, etc. Concurrent parenting classes also assist parents as "the children's first teachers" in creating a proper home learning environment. Other bilingual programs for children include story hours in different languages, media mobiles with bilingual staff and materials, and bilingual Dial-a-Story program.

Young adults participate in library programs, among them those that emphasize their ethnic backgrounds through artistic and literary expression. Adult basic education classes enroll many participants lacking the ability to speak English. In one statewide adult education program where the participants were mainly Spanish-speaking, the state library agency added LSCA support to select and place bilingual materials in public libraries that the newly literate adults would be able to read and enjoy. One library's 24-hour information and referral service is operated by bilingual staff to connect persons of limited English-speaking ability with local community agencies.

Those population groups doubly disadvantaged by their limited ability to speak English and who have handicaps or are totally isolated are reached with very specialized services. Books-by-mail catalogs offer rural residents bilingual book selection, and handicapped persons can receive talking books in their mother tongue. Bilingual programs and large-print books serve the elderly who would otherwise be unable to participate in library services. The talents of the aging are also incorporated into oral history projects that aim to preserve the cultural heritage of ethnic groups and geographic locales.

On the state level, statewide workshops are conducted, followed by book grants, to train participants in the selection of foreign-language books and transmit the skills of bilingual storytelling. Studies are conducted to identify ethnic populations and their needs and guidelines for planning services to ethnic groups have been developed. Minority recruitment and training programs provide scholarships to attend graduate library school, producing multilingual librarians of ethnic backgrounds who will advance the quality, kind, and number of bilingual library programs nationally. In-depth circulating book and film collections are provided by the state for cooperative use by public libraries. Such collections include reading and audiovisual materials that reflect the cultural heritage and mother tongues of the population groups in the state.

Services to the Aging

Service to older readers is one of the emphases of LSCA, but such programs have always been an integral part of public library service. Special recognition and program development are resulting from the growth of the "aging" age group, the increasing assessment of community needs by libraries, the expanding activities of other agencies, and the greater involvement of libraries as cooperating agencies among those providing specialized services to senior citizens. A partnership with the increasing number of older persons brings the realization of the types of library activities that make libraries more beneficial to aging persons in groups and as individuals.

As increased numbers of retired persons or senior citizens came to the libraries, the number of programs within the library increased, then expanded to programs reaching those who did not or could not come to the library. Special programs on consumer education, literacy, job counseling, volunteerism, and personal reading interests and special programs designed for those in nursing homes are created to meet particular needs. The use of volunteers is a recognized part of special programs.

With special programs and intensified service came the need to train personnel in libraries and the program-related agencies, i.e., continuing education as well as less structured orientation for those taking part in the provision of services. Book and materials collections are feeling the change of increased emphasis both for the library user and the persons providing services. Professional materials in the gerontological fields is a contribution that the library provides to its coworkers in other agencies as well as the large-print books for senior citizens' easier reading.

One aspect of service to the aging that is receiving increasing attention as a service provider is that of information and referral. In some library systems, it is one element in a comprehensive information and referral service (I&R) and in others it takes the project form with "outreach services" as a spin-off.

In addition to the service given this specific age group, there is the increased interrelation and integration of library service with different governmental levels and public and private agencies to a stronger degree.

Strengthening the State Library Administrative Agencies

Strengthening the state library administrative agencies has impact on all library services rendered throughout the states. For this reason, LSCA emphasizes upgrading the agencies' capabilities to carry out their administrative responsibilities.

Consultants operating on a statewide basis can achieve significant advances in library development and interlibrary cooperation. Approaches to school-public library cooperation have broadened in recent years, largely due to liaison consultants who train personnel and coordinate library activities to ensure maximum user services from both types of libraries.

Some resources, services, and programs are most economically and effectively administered from the state library agencies. One important example is a quality film collection selected, purchased, and shared with all participating libraries. Packaged programs, circulating art collections, and other services are also provided from state to local libraries. Bookmobile and books-by-mail services, often supplied locally, are also delivered from the state level to those rural areas without public libraries and to persons in migrant camps, Indian reservations, and training schools, among others.

Because the statewide improvement of library services depends on the caliber of personnel in the community as well as on the state level, LSCA supports statewide efforts to advance the professional growth of all staff members. In order to create competent and motivated people-oriented librarians and support staff, the state library agencies carry out a sustained program of in-service training through workshops, institutes, and scholarships. (For the addresses of state library agencies and the names of their directors, see the Directory of Library Organizations in Part 6—*Ed.*)

Major Urban Resource Libraries (MURL)

A new priority was added to Title I in the 1977 amendments to improve the capability of public libraries in densely populated areas (cities with 100,000 population) to serve as major resource libraries that, because of the value of their collections to individual users and to other libraries, need special assistance to furnish services at a level required to meet the demands for such services. This amendment is applicable only when the annual appropriation for Title I exceeds $60 million (*Federal Register*, vol. 43, no. 108, Monday, June 5, 1978). This provision was activated for FY 1979 when the annual LSCA Title I appropriation exceeded $60 million by $2.5 million.

For purposes of strengthening major urban resource libraries, the Commissioner of Education issued a list of cities of over 100,000 population (1976 U.S. Bureau of the Census estimated) with 169 cities and the District of Columbia qualifying.

The state's share of the amount in excess of $60 million ($2.5 million) subject to the major urban resource libraries provision, is computed separately (see Table 1) and subject to one of the following:

> For a State in which the total population of the cities with 100,000 population or more exceeds 50% of the allocation for strengthening major urban resource libraries;
>
> or
>
> For a State in which the total population of the cities with 100,000 population or more does not exceed 50% of the State's total population, the State shall reserve a percentage of the allocation equal to the ratio of the combined population of these cities to the State's total population;
>
> or
>
> For a State without cities with 100,000 population, the provision for strengthening major urban resource libraries is not applicable. However, such State is allotted its proportionate share of the $2.5 million to use for purposes consistent with Title I of the Act and the State's State Plan.

For FY 1979, the following states (13) allocated the minimum amount for MURL: Alabama, Arizona, California, Louisiana, Minnesota, Mississippi, New Jersey, Oklahoma, Rhode Island, Tennessee, Texas, Utah, and Washington. States (28) exceeding the minimum amount were Alaska, Arkansas, Connecticut, Florida, Georgia, Hawaii, Idaho, Illinois, Indiana, Iowa, Kansas, Kentucky, Maryland, Massachusetts, Michigan, Nebraska, Nevada, New Mexico, New York, North Carolina, Ohio, Oregon, Pennsylvania, South Carolina, Virginia, Puerto Rico, Missouri, and Wisconsin. States (9) not having cities with over 100,000 were Delaware, Maine, Montana, New Hampshire, North Dakota, South Dakota, Vermont, West Virginia, and Wyoming. Territories not having cities over 100,000 were American Samoa, Guam, Trust Territory, Virgin Islands, and the Northern Mariana Islands.

One hundred and fifty cities actually received funds through meeting the established criteria developed by their respective states for activities and services to strengthen libraries. Activities most frequently mentioned were interlibrary loan, strengthening reference collection, purchasing audiovisual materials, purchasing government publications, strengthening periodical and monograph collections, materials for the limited English-speaking, enrichment of special collections, services to the elderly and homebound, and services to the public libraries and individual users of the region.

Note: Federal Programs for Libraries, 2nd ed. (U.S. Office of Education) is a funding sources directory supplying program information on nine federal library programs and 76 federal library-related programs. Programs are indexed by applicant eligibility, program authorization, Catalog of Federal Domestic Assistance number, federal agency, and subject. An annotated listing of 20 directories and other recent publications relevant to library-related funding sources and a selected bibliography of publications on the grants process are also included. Single copies are available from USOE Office of Libraries and Learning Resources as long as supply lasts.

TITLE II—PUBLIC LIBRARY CONSTRUCTION

Title II funds for public library construction were last appropriated in 1973. The administration did not request nor did the Congress appropriate funds for this program from FY 1974 to 1980. During this six-year period, however, 202 public libraries have been awarded construction grants under Title II authorization, utilizing monies carried over from previous fiscal years and/or funds from other federal programs.

In FY 1979, nine public library construction projects were administered under LSCA Title II authority and received $2,281,370 in federal aid. All of this funding was supplied by the Appalachian Regional Development Act. Local funds contributed $1,765,696 and state funds were $750,425 for a total amount of $4,797,491.

During the 15-year period that public library construction has been administered under LSCA (FY 1965-1979), 2,064 projects have been approved by the states for a total obligation of $685.4 million. The federal share of this obligation is $195.7 million of which $174.5 million has been provided by LSCA and $21.1 million from other federal sources. Approximately $489.8 million has been forthcoming from state and local sources to support library construction projects. This figure represents an overall support level of 71 percent from nonfederal sources and testifies to the effectiveness of the LSCA program in stimulating matching support. (See Table 2.)

Various federal funding sources have supported library construction projects

TABLE 2 LSCA TITLE II, CONSTRUCTION, FUNDING FOR FY 1965-1979

Fiscal Year	Number Library Projects Approved	Federal	Local and State[a]	Total
1965	363	$ 29,864	$ 62,851	$ 92,715
1966	364	29,778	62,483	92,261
1967	278	24,583	52,107	76,690
1968	284	27,429	66,137	93,566
1969	211	22,257	69,500	91,757
1970	65	5,095	16,989	22,084
1971	114	8,571	34,427	42,998
1972	131	9,533	30,646	40,179
1973	52	2,606	15,360	17,966
1974	99	10,787[b]	44,570	55,357
1975	65	4,048[c]	26,776	30,824
Total LSCA	2,026	174,551	481,846	656,397
Appalachia	0	14,300[d]	0	14,300
Subtotal	2,026	$188,851	$481,846	$670,697
1976[e]	11	1,606	938	2,544
1977[e]	5	851	3,432	4,283
1978[e]	13	2,094	1,021	3,115
1979[e]	9	2,281	2,516	4,797
Total	2,064	$195,683	$489,753	$685,436

[a]Budgeted amounts as reported by states.
[b]1973 appropriation released in FY 1974.
[c]Carryover funds from FY 1973 appropriation not obligated in FY 1974.
[d]Funds from the Appalachian Regional Development Act that were allocated to LSCA-administered projects are listed separately from LSCA funds. Since projects also included LSCA funds, the number of projects and local/state matching funds for these projects are included above.
[e]Although LSCA federal funds were not available for projects after FY 1975, all projects for FY 1976-1979 were administered under the LSCA administrative authority, but funded from other federal programs as follows: FY 1976—Appalachian Regional Development Act, 7 projects, $1,029,678; Public Works and Economic Development Act, Title X, Job Opportunities, 3 projects, $546,000; and Urban Growth and New Community Development Act, 1 project, $30,000; FY 1977 —Appalachian Regional Development Act, 4 projects, $768,000; and Local Public Works, 1 project, $82,500; FY 1978—Appalachian Regional Development Act, 9 projects, $1,166,105; Department of Defense, Trident Project, 2 projects, $350,000; and Local Public Works, 2 projects, $578,000; FY 1979—Appalachian Regional Development Act, 9 projects, $2,281,370.

administered under the authority of LSCA Title II. Currently these include Appalachian Regional Development Act, General Revenue Sharing program (Title I of the State and Local Fiscal Assistance Act of 1972), and the Community Development block grant program (Title I of the Housing and Community Development Act of 1974). For FY 1979, a new source of funding was made available by the National Energy Conservation Policy Act 1978, PL 95-619, which provided small amounts of assistance for energy conservation activities for buildings owned by public care institutions and units of local government, including libraries. Funds were authorized through FY 1979 at $15 million for energy audits and $50 million for technical assistance to prepare engineering plans. Funds will remain available until expended.

In addition to these grant programs, community facility loans at 5 percent interest are available from the Farmers Home Administration for library construction in communities of under 10,000 in population.

Along with the national concern for energy conservation, recent legislation has also dealt with the issue of accessibility of public agencies and their services to handicapped persons. A new federal requirement applicable to public libraries was instituted in FY 1977 under Section 504 of the Rehabilitation Act of 1973. It requires that any agency benefiting from federal assistance have nondiscriminatory practices toward the handicapped. This affects personnel practices and the provision of services, which must be made available through any means necessary, including removal of physical barriers.

The Office of Civil Rights, Department of Health, Education, and Welfare, which has been designated to administer Section 504, offers a clarification of the requirements for public libraries in Policy Interpretation Number 3 (45 FR 36034, August 14, 1978). It states:

> The Section 504 regulation was carefully written to require "program accessibility" not "building accessibility," thus allowing recipients flexibility in selecting the means of compliance. For example, they may arrange for the delivery of their services at alternative sites that are accessible or use aides to deliver services to persons at their homes. The regulation does not require that all existing facitilies or every part of an existing facility be made accessible; structural changes are not necessary if other methods are effective in making the recipient's services available to mobility impaired persons. For example, a library building in a rural area with one room and an entrance with several steps can make its services accessible in several ways. It may construct a simple wooden ramp quickly and at relatively low cost. Mobility impaired persons may be provided access to the library's services through a bookmobile or by special messenger service or clerical aide or any other method that makes the resources of the library "readily accessible." However, recipients are required to give priority to methods that offer handicapped and nonhandicapped persons programs and activities in the same setting.

Since the inception of the LSCA construction program, all building projects funded have been required to be accessible to the handicapped. Additionally, Title II projects have been subject to the provisions of the Architectural Barriers Act of 1968, which stipulates that construction assisted with federal funds meet the requirements of the "American Standard Specifications for Making Buildings and Facilities Accessible to, and Usable by, the Physically Handicapped" issued by the American National Standards Institute.

Consideration for ease of access is one of many factors LSCA Title II construction projects have been concerned with. "Public Library Construction 1965-1978" provides insight into other pertinent concerns of library construction projects and presents an overview of federally supported library construction efforts. National data, along with state breakouts, are examined in the areas of costs, population served, number and type of project, floor area, seating capacity, and book volume capacity. Copies are available upon request from USOE Office of Libraries and Learning Resources.

TITLE III—INTERLIBRARY COOPERATION

In FY 1979 the appropriation for Title III was $5 million, an increase of $1,663,000. (See Tables 3 and 4.) This enabled the states to maintain their interlibrary loan networks, their continuing education projects, their efforts to identify special resources within the state, and to coordinate the acquisition of specialized materials. In Massachusetts, for example, the Hampshire Inter-Library Center received a grant to publish and distribute a new edition of *The Pioneer Valley Union List of Serials*, which includes the holdings of 40,000 titles in the libraries of the University of Massachusetts, four colleges, the Hampshire Inter-Library Center, and the Northampton Public Library. In Wisconsin the state library agency contracted with the University of Wisconsin-

TABLE 3 LSCA TITLE III, INTERLIBRARY COOPERATION, STATE ALLOTMENTS, FY 1980

States and Outlying Areas	Federal Allotment	States and Outlying Areas	Federal Allotment
Alabama	$ 88,165	New Jersey	$135,756
Alaska	45,389	New Mexico	55,607
Arizona	70,079	New York	274,000
Arkansas	68,082	North Carolina	111,967
California	325,609	North Dakota	48,482
Colorado	74,254	Ohio	179,575
Connecticut	80,544	Oklahoma	76,760
Delaware	47,595	Oregon	71,123
Florida	150,475	Pennsylvania	193,929
Georgia	105,781	Rhode Island	52,227
Hawaii	51,627	South Carolina	77,556
Idaho	51,170	South Dakota	48,978
Illinois	186,517	Tennessee	96,008
Indiana	109,814	Texas	207,109
Iowa	77,686	Utah	56,573
Kansas	70,274	Vermont	46,290
Kentucky	85,255	Virginia	106,486
Louisiana	91,284	Washington	88,034
Maine	54,145	West Virginia	64,180
Maryland	93,985	Wisconsin	100,601
Massachusetts	115,386	Wyoming	45,298
Michigan	159,375	District of Columbia	48,939
Minnesota	91,936	Puerto Rico	81,823
Mississippi	71,136	American Samoa	10,393
Missouri	102,924	Northern Mariana Islands	10,205
Montana	49,996	Guam	11,251
Nebraska	60,292	Virgin Islands	11,238
Nevada	48,312	Trust Territory	11,433
New Hampshire	51,092		
	Total		$5,000,000[a]

[a]Distribution of $5,000,000 with a federal "minimum" allotment of $40,000 to the 50 states, District of Columbia, and Puerto Rico; $10,000 to the other outlying areas and the balance distributed on the basis of total resident population, July 1, 1977.

TABLE 4 LSCA TITLE III EXPENDITURE PATTERNS, FY 1980
(Based on Latest LSCA Annual Reports)

Category	No. of States	Percent of Total Expenditures
Telecommunications networks for reference and bibliographic services and interlibrary loan	46	59
Centralized acquisition and processing materials	8	5
Centralized listings of holdings of periodicals in institutions	22	4
Comprehensive statewide planning	6	1
Training of specialists in interlibrary cooperation	9	1
Networking among states	16	1
Combinations of above categories	28	29

Madison to study and explore the need for a cooperative media examination center, to recommend the scope of such a program and its appropriate relationship to existing multitype library organizations. The project resulted in a comprehensive report, including wide-range citizen input and specific recommendations for establishing regional centers. Interlibrary cooperative activities have changed in emphasis and focus. From single-purpose projects involving more than one type of library (e.g., the expansion or establishment of telecommunications networks for interlibrary loan and reference services, the development of centralized technical processing centers, the development of union catalogs and lists, and surveys of library resources and needs), states have moved to projects that require different types of libraries within a geographic area to assess needs cooperatively, jointly develop plans and programs to meet needs, and jointly evaluate their efforts. Such projects require a commitment from each library represented on the council to see itself in relation to the total community and to the larger world of library and information services.

Interstate library activities are also increasing in number. States affiliated with regional library associations have used some Title III funds to give partial support to such activities as the Pacific Northwest Bibliographic Center, which serves Alaska, Idaho, Montana, Oregon, and Washington; and the Rocky Mountain Center for Bibliographical Research, which has received support from Arizona, Colorado, Nebraska, New Mexico, North Dakota, South Dakota, Utah, and Wyoming. The states in the Southwestern Library Association (Arkansas, Louisiana, New Mexico, Oklahoma, and Texas) established the Southwestern Library Interstate Cooperative Endeavor, which provides a formal structure for developing activities in the areas of continuing education for library personnel and in the use of modern technology for bibliographic control of library materials. In the southeastern region, some states used Title III funds to support the Southeastern Library Association's intensive study of libraries in each of the states as a preliminary step to identifying needs that might be met more effectively by multistate, regional cooperative activities. The New England Library Information Network serves the six New England states and is in the process of reassessing its goals, purposes, and activities. A group of states in the upper Midwest has formed a network to meet the needs of Indiana, Illinois, Wisconsin, Minnesota, and North Dakota libraries. The multistate regional networks are currently grappling with the as yet unanswered problems of interface and their role in what might become a national network.

ELEMENTARY AND SECONDARY EDUCATION ACT TITLE IV, PART B—INSTRUCTIONAL MATERIALS AND SCHOOL LIBRARY RESOURCES

Beatrice Simmons

Education Program Specialist, School Media Resources Branch, Division of Library Programs, Office of Libraries and Learning Resources, USOE

The name of the program funded under Title IV, Part B, of the Elementary and Secondary Education Act, known formerly as Libraries and Learning Resources, has been changed to Instructional Materials and School Library Resources by the Education Amendments of 1978, PL 95-561. In addition, the Education Amendments eliminated minor remodeling and transferred testing, counseling, and guidance to a new program, Part D of Title IV. Federal regulations have been written to address the changes made in the program.

ESEA Title IV, Part B, as amended, provides funds to states, seven extrastate jurisdictions, and to the Bureau of Indian Affairs, Department of Interior, for the acquisition of school library resources, textbooks, and other printed and published materials; and for the acquisition of instructional equipment to be used in providing education in academic subjects. These benefits are for the use of children in public and private nonprofit elementary and secondary schools. Funds are also provided to state educational agencies for program administration.

Amounts alloted to states and other jurisdictions for FY 1977, 1978, and 1979 were $147,333,000, $154,497,324, and $167,500,000, respectively. Table 1 shows the allotments for FY 1980. Funds are alloted to the states, Puerto Rico, and the District of Columbia on the basis of the number of children aged five to seventeen as compared with total number of children in all states and jurisdictions. One percent of the amount available under Title IV-B is reserved for American Samoa, Guam, the Virgin Islands, the Trust Territory of the Pacific Islands, the Northern Mariana Islands, and for schools conducted for Indian children.

Title IV, Part B, is administered cooperatively in the Office of Education with Part C and Part D of Title IV. Staff in the programs review the state plans and annual amendments submitted by their states and other jurisdictions, prepare regulations and administrative memoranda, conduct conferences, review state and local Title IV programs, and provide technical assistance. The review and monitoring of state and local programs for Part B is on a triennial cycle.

Part B funds are distributed among local educational agencies according to the enrollments in public and private schools within the school districts of those agencies, except that higher per pupil allotments are provided to local educational agencies whose tax effort for education is substantially greater than the state average tax effort for education but whose per pupil expenditures (excluding ESEA Title I funds) are no greater than the state average per pupil expenditure and to local educational agencies with the largest numbers of percentages of children whose education imposes a higher than average cost per child. Examples of children whose education imposes a higher than average cost per child are children from low-income families, children from families in which English is not the dominant language, and children living in sparsely populated areas. Table 2 shows the number of states and the various types of high-cost children identified in FY 1978 and 1979.

TABLE 1 ALLOTMENTS UNDER ESEA TITLE IV-B, AS AMENDED (PL 95-561) FOR PROGRAM YEAR 1980

State or Area	Amount	State or Area	Amount
Alabama	$3,094,097	New Jersey	$ 5,905,937
Alaska	393,015	New Mexico	1,086,149
Arizona	1,911,480	New York	14,066,349
Arkansas	1,739,983	North Carolina	4,476,793
California	16,949,647	North Dakota	546,648
Colorado	2,115,133	Ohio	8,814,245
Connecticut	2,483,138	Oklahoma	2,175,872
Delaware	482,336	Oregon	1,840,023
District of Columbia	500,200	Pennsylvania	9,139,375
Florida	6,041,706	Puerto Rico	3,101,242
Georgia	4,276,713	Rhode Island	739,582
Hawaii	732,436	South Carolina	2,465,273
Idaho	725,291	South Dakota	571,658
Illinois	9,171,531	Tennessee	3,433,518
Indiana	4,480,366	Texas	10,693,570
Iowa	2,368,806	Utah	1,139,742
Kansas	1,786,430	Vermont	407,306
Kentucky	2,847,569	Virginia	4,105,216
Louisiana	3,529,986	Washington	2,944,037
Maine	903,934	West Virginia	1,454,154
Maryland	3,440,664	Wisconsin	3,908,709
Massachusetts	4,587,552	Wyoming	335,849
Michigan	7,856,719	American Samoa	126,480
Minnesota	3,358,488	Guam	377,166
Mississippi	2,154,434	Northern Marianas	53,545
Missouri	3,797,950	Trust Territory	387,000
Montana	646,688	Virgin Islands	357,014
Nebraska	1,254,074	Bureau of Indian Affairs	
Nevada	528,783	(Department of the Interior)	480,973
New Hampshire	707,426		
	Total	$180,000,000[a]	

[a]Distribution of $180,000,000 with 1 percent ($1,782,178) reserved for the outlying areas and the balance distributed on the basis of the 5–17 population, July 1, 1977, for the 50 states, District of Columbia, and Puerto Rico, with distribution made on the total public and nonpublic elementary and secondary school enrollment, fall 1977, for the areas.

Staff of participating local education agencies, in consultation with appropriate private school officials, choose the program purpose or purposes for which they wish to use their allocation. Table 3 shows the purposes for which funds were expended in FY 1977 and 1978.

Instructional materials and equipment have been used in a consolidated fashion to develop alternative teaching programs that impact on learning in reading, oral and written communication, and other basic skills. Additionally, a variety of instructional equipment such as calculators, computer terminals, and video recorders have promoted individualized teaching and learning and generally improved the quality of instruction. Part B funds have also been used by local educational agencies to expand guidance and counseling programs with emphasis upon the infusion of guidance into regular classroom activity and the involvement of parents in counseling plans. New techniques have been employed to help students identify with changing societal roles and careers, open-

TABLE 2   ESEA TITLE IV, PART B: HIGH-COST CHILDREN FACTORS SELECTED BY STATES, FY 1977, 1978, 1979

	Number of States		
	1977	1978	1979
Aid for dependent children	5	2	2
Basic skills (reading, mathematics)	2	7	3
Bilingual (cultural isolation)	26	26	25
Critical subjects (other than reading and mathematics)	2	1	2
Free lunch	2	2	1
Gifted and talented	10	16	12
Guidance	1	3	3
Handicapped, exceptional children, special education	10	20	19
Hawaiian English program	1	1	—
Institutionalized program (includes foster homes, neglected and delinquents, and institutionalized)	10	10	10
Low achievers	—	1	5
Low income (economically and educationally disadvantaged)	38	35	34
Migrant (including immigrant children in American Samoa)	3	3	2
Minorities	1	1	2
Reading difficulties	2	—	—
Small schools	10	9	16
Sparsity (isolation, sparsity, transportation)	26	29	28
Special needs	4	1	2
Vocational education	3	1	1

TABLE 3   ESEA TITLE IV-B FUNDS, BY PROGRAM PURPOSE, FY 1978 AND 1979

Purpose	1978	1979
Administration	$ 4,513,772	$ 4,860,876
School library resources/other instructional materials	66,004,262	65,965,586
Textbooks	4,983,354	3,344,559
Instructional equipment	40,428,691	41,233,644
Minor remodeling	608,992	1,085,799
Testing	2,540,286	2,524,768
Counseling and guidance	11,678,142	12,578,592
Total	$130,757,499	$131,593,824

ing career opportunities, especially among young men and women who are potential dropouts.

Certain publications that may be of interest to teachers and librarians are the newly revised *Aids to Media Selection for Students and Teachers*, the revised *Questions and Answers about Title IV, Part B of the Elementary and Secondary Education Act*, a *Fact Sheet on ESEA*, and the federal regulations interpreting the amended ESEA Title IV. Requests for these publications should be directed to: School Media Resources Branch, Division of Library Programs, Office of Libraries and Learning Resources, U.S. Office of Education, 400 Maryland Ave. S.W., ROB no. 3, Rm. 3125 B, Washington, D.C. 20202. Only single copies of *Aids to Media Selection for Students and Teachers* can be issued.

HIGHER EDUCATION ACT, TITLE II-A, COLLEGE LIBRARY RESOURCES

Sheldon Z. Fisher
Education Program Specialist

Frank A. Stevens
Chief, Library Education and Postsecondary Resources Branch, Division of Library Programs, USOE

The College Library Resources Program under Title II-A of the Higher Education Act of 1965, as amended, is targeted to support the improvement of library resources in academic institutions and certain other eligible library agencies. Since the inception of the program in 1966, approximately 2,600 institutions of higher education have participated annually, and 36,471 awards for basic, supplemental, and special-purpose grants totaling $185.62 million have been made.

The Title II-A program authorizes grants to eligible applicants to assist in the acquisition for library purposes of books, periodicals, documents, magnetic tapes, phonograph records, audiovisual materials, and other related library materials, including initial binding. Costs of library and audiovisual equipment and general operating supplies and services are not eligible. Grant funds may be used to a limited extent for the cataloging and processing of materials purchased with grant funds. Eligible applicants are limited to public and private nonprofit institutions of higher education (individually or in combination); branches of institutions in communities other than that of the parent institutions; and other public and/or private nonprofit library agencies whose primary function is to provide library and information services to students, faculty, and researchers of higher education on a formal, cooperative basis.

The authorizing legislation provides for three types of grants: basic grants of up to $5,000 for each eligible institution; supplemental grants related to enrollment, programs, and demonstrated needs; and special-purpose grants (on a matching basis). Funds available under Title II-A must first be used to satisfy all eligible requests for basic grants, and then funds remaining (if any) may be used for supplemental grants. Funds still remaining (if any) up to 25 percent of the total appropriation may be reserved by the Commissioner of Education for special-purpose grants. The appropriation history for Title II-A since 1973 has been such that only basic grants have been funded.

Funding for FY 1979 provided a grant for $3,963 for each eligible institution unless a lesser amount was requested (due to an inability to "match"). Eligible recipients were located in every state, the District of Columbia, Guam, Puerto Rico, the Virgin Islands, and Trust Territory. In all, 2,520 grant awards were made to institutions of higher education, including 23 public and private nonprofit library institutions and 23 combinations of institutions.

In connection with basic grants, the Commissioner has the authority to waive the requirement for maintenance of effort in those instances where the institution can show special or unusual circumstances. The criteria for waiver and other program regulations for Title II-A were last published in the November 18, 1974 *Federal Register*, pp. 40491–40566.

In the Education Amendments of 1976, the Congress authorized a new Title

TABLE 1   HIGHER EDUCATION ACT, TITLE II-A,
COLLEGE LIBRARY RESOURCES, FY 1979

State or Area	No. of Grants	1979 Obligations	State or Area	No. of Grants	1979 Obligations
Alabama	55	$215,980	Nevada	8	$ 31,641
Alaska	11	43,593	New Hampshire	21	79,860
Arizona	27	104,538	New Jersey	43	170,409
Arkansas	26	103,038	New Mexico	23	84,377
California	193	757,835	New York	197	771,825
Colorado	29	113,064	North Carolina	93	368,496
Connecticut	38	147,831	North Dakota	15	58,482
Delaware	9	35,667	Ohio	105	416,115
District of Columbia	16	62,882	Oklahoma	36	142,668
Florida	77	302,308	Oregon	31	121,390
Georgia	69	271,968	Pennsylvania	139	547,292
Hawaii	11	43,530	Rhode Island	14	53,619
Idaho	9	35,667	South Carolina	49	194,187
Illinois	108	428,004	South Dakota	17	67,308
Indiana	47	184,975	Tennessee	46	181,935
Iowa	54	213,750	Texas	109	431,967
Kansas	41	162,483	Utah	10	39,630
Kentucky	35	137,279	Vermont	21	79,684
Louisiana	28	109,001	Virginia	67	265,058
Maine	22	87,066	Washington	42	165,283
Maryland	40	156,557	West Virginia	24	92,486
Massachusetts	91	352,581	Wisconsin	78	306,958
Michigan	71	280,784	Wyoming	7	27,741
Minnesota	50	195,187	Guam	1	3,963
Mississippi	41	162,372	Puerto Rico	33	128,253
Missouri	50	197,461	Trust Territories	2	7,926
Montana	15	56,209	Virgin Islands	2	7,926
Nebraska	24	95,112			
	Total		2,520	$9,903,201	

TABLE 2   HISTORY OF GRANTS UNDER HEA, TITLE II-A,
COLLEGE LIBRARY RESOURCES PROGRAM, FY 1966–1979

FY	Appropriation	Basic	Supplemental	Special Purpose	Obligations
1966	$10,000,000	1,830	—	—	$ 8,400,000
1967	25,000,000	1,983	1,266	132	24,500,000
1968	25,000,000	2,111	1,524	60	24,900,000
1969	25,000,000	2,224	1,747	77	24,900,000
1970	12,500,000	2,201	1,783	—	9,816,000
1971	9,900,000	548	531	115	9,900,000
1972	11,000,000	504	494	21	10,993,000
1973	12,500,000	2,061	—	65	12,500,000
1974	9,975,000	2,377	—	—	9,960,000
1975	9,975,000	2,569	—	—	9,957,416
1976	9,975,000	2,560	—	—	9,958,754
1977	9,975,000	2,600	—	—	9,946,484
1978	9,975,000	2,568	—	—	9,963,611
1979	9,975,000	2,520	—	—	9,903,201

II-C Strengthening Research Library Resources Program. This act is designed for major research libraries to help them in the collection and dissemination of research materials. Legislation specifically prohibits a library from receiving funding from both Title II-A and Title II-C during the same fiscal year.

For FY 1979, $9.9 million was distributed to 2520 institutions. Notification of grant award for the FY 1979 Title II-A program was made on December 27, 1978. Table 1 lists the number of grants and total funds by state. Table 2 traces the funding history of Title II-A by fiscal year from 1966 to date.

HIGHER EDUCATION ACT, TITLE II-B, LIBRARY EDUCATION

Frank A. Stevens

*Chief, Library Education and Postsecondary Resources Branch,
Division of Library Programs,
Office of Libraries and Learning Resources, USOE*

Babetta Norwood

*Program Specialist, Library Education and
Postsecondary Resources Branch*

Title II-B (Library Training) of the Higher Education Act of 1965, as amended (20 U.S.C. 1021, 1031, and 1033), authorizes a program of federal financial assistance to institutions of higher education and other library organizations and agencies to assist in training persons in librarianship. Grants are made for fellowships and traineeships at the associate, bachelor, master, post-master, and doctoral levels for training in librarianship and information science. Grants may also be used to assist in covering the costs of institutes or courses of training or study to upgrade the competencies of persons serving in all types of libraries, information centers, or instructional materials centers offering library and information services, and those serving as educators.

In FY 1974, the Title II-B Training Program Regulations were revised primarily for the purpose of establishing explicitly the evaluation criteria and the corresponding point-scoring system governing the selection and rejection of proposals. The regulations were published in final form in the *Federal Register* on May 17, 1974 (45 CFR 132). These revised regulations are a part of the application package that is provided upon request to all interested parties at the time of the annual program announcement.

FELLOWSHIP/TRAINEESHIP PROGRAM

For the academic year 1979–1980, a total of 162 (19 doctoral, 4 post-master, 134 master, 2 bachelor, and 3 associate) fellowships were awarded to 36 library and information science education programs under the Higher Education Act, Title II-B, as amended. Table 1 represents a review of the fellowship/traineeship program. Grants were awarded consistent with the statutory mandate of the Education Amendments of 1972 that at least 50 percent of any Title II-B library training appropriation be used for fellowships or traineeships. With an appropriation of $2 million in FY 1979, $1,054,550 was awarded for fellowships.

TABLE 1 LIBRARY EDUCATION FELLOWSHIP/TRAINEESHIP PROGRAM, FY 1966–1979

Academic Year	Institutions	Doctoral	Post-master	Master	Bachelor	Assoc.	Total	FY
1966/67	24	52	25	62	—	—	139	1966
1967/68	38	116	58	327	—	—	501	1967
1968/69	51	168	47	494	—	—	709	1968
1969/70	56	193	30	379	—	—	602	1969
1970/71	48	171	15	200	+ 20[a]	—	406	1970
1971/72	20	116	6	—	+ 20[a]	—	142	1971
1972/73	15	39	3	+ 20[a]	—	—	62	1972
1973/74	34	21	4	145 + 14[a]	—	20	204	1973
1974/75	50	21	3	168 + 3[a]	—	5	200	1974
1975/76	22	27	6	94	—	—	127	1975
1976/77	12	5	3	43	—	—	51	1976
1977/78	37	18	3	134	—	5	160	1977
1978/79	33	25	9	139	10	5	188	1978
1979/80	36	19	4	134	2	3	162	1979
Total		991	216	2,319 + 37[a]	12 + 40[a]	38	3,653	

[a]Indicates traineeships.

Stipend levels varied, depending on the level of study, length of program, and degree of related prior experience, within a range of $2,500 to $4,700 per fellow/trainee, plus dependency allowance as permitted. Additionally, grantee institutions received an institutional allowance of up to $3,000 per fellow/trainee.

The order of priorities for training levels for the fellowship program in FY 1979 was as follows: master, associate, post-master, doctoral, and bachelor. Key factors given substantial consideration in the review process were the extent to which the fellowship program award would increase opportunities for minority groups and/or economically disadvantaged persons to enter the library profession and the extent to which the fellowship program award could prepare librarians to work more responsively with the disadvantaged and develop viable alternatives to traditional library service patterns.

The selection of persons as fellowship/traineeship recipients was, and has been throughout the history of the program, entirely the responsibility of the grantee institution. However, such selection and program operation must be consistent with the contents of the grant application.

Fellowship grants were awarded in FY 1979 to the institutions shown in Table 2.

INSTITUTE PROGRAM

The institute program provides long- and short-term training and retraining opportunities for librarians, media specialists, information scientists, and for persons desiring to enter these professions. Many institutes have given experienced practitioners the opportunity to update their skills and to advance themselves in a given subject. Institute programs have been supported since FY 1968 under the Higher Education Act of 1965 and since FY 1973 under further amendments included in the Education Amendments of 1972.

TABLE 2 FELLOWSHIPS FOR TRAINING IN LIBRARY AND INFORMATION SCIENCE, ACADEMIC YEAR 1979–1980

Institution	Project Director	No.	Level*	Amount
Alabama Alabama A&M University, Normal 35762	Howard G. Ball	4	M	$25,200
Arizona University of Arizona, 1515 E. First St., Tucson 85719	Donald C. Dickinson	5	M	31,800
California University of California, M-11 Wheeler Hall, Berkeley 94720	Michael K. Buckland	2	M	12,600
Colorado University of Denver, Denver 80208	G. Travis White	8	P (2) M (6)	54,400
District of Columbia Catholic University of America, Washington 20064	Elizabeth Stone	4	M	24,600
Florida Florida State University, Tallahassee 32306	Harold Goldstein	4	M	25,200
University of South Florida 4202 E. Fowler, Tampa 33620	John A. McCrossan	2	M	12,600
Illinois University of Illinois, Urbana 61801	Roger G. Clark	7	D (3) M (4)	50,100
Kentucky University of Kentucky, Lexington 40506	Timothy Sineath	2	M	12,600
Maryland University of Maryland, College Park 20742	Kieth C. Wright	5	M	31,800
Massachusetts Simmons College, 300 The Fenway, Boston 02115	Ching-Chih Chen	2	P	16,600
Michigan University of Michigan, 508 Union Dr., Ann Arbor 48109	Russell E. Bidlack	12	D (4) M (8)	84,200
Mississippi Coahoma Junior College, Rte. 1, Box 616, Clarksdale 38614	McKinley C. Martin	3	AA	14,850
University of Southern Mississippi, Southern Sta., Box 5146, Hattiesburg 39401	Onva K. Boshears	6	M	37,800
New Jersey Rutgers University, 4 Huntington St., New Brunswick 08903	Esther R. Dyer	10	M	63,000
New York Columbia University, Box 20, Low Memorial Library, New York 10024	Richard L. Darling	4	M	25,200

TABLE 2 FELLOWSHIPS FOR TRAINING IN LIBRARY AND INFORMATION SCIENCE, ACADEMIC YEAR 1979–1980 (cont.)

Institution	Project Director	No.	Level*	Amount
Long Island University, C. W. Post Center, Greenvale 11548	Mohammed M. Aman	2	M	12,600
Pratt Institute, Brooklyn 11205	Rhoda Garoogian	2	M	12,600
Queens College, 65-30 Kissena Blvd., Flushing 10022	Richard J. Hyman	2	M	12,600
St. John's University, Grand Central & Utopia Pkwys., Jamaica 11439	Antonio Rodriguez-Buckingham	3	M	19,200
SUNY at Albany, 1400 Washington Ave., Albany 12222	Lucille Whalen	5	M	31,800
SUNY at Buffalo, Buffalo 14260	George S. Bobinski	6	D (3) M (3)	44,100
North Carolina				
North Carolina Central University, 1805 Fayetteville, Durham 27707	Annette L. Phinazee	2	M	12,600
North Dakota				
University of North Dakota, Grand Forks 58202	Darell Evanson	2	BS	10,100
Ohio				
Case Western Reserve University, 10950 Euclid Ave., Cleveland 44106	James E. Rogers	4	M	25,200
Kent State University, Kent 44242	Lubomyr R. Wynar	4	M	25,200
Pennsylvania				
Drexel University, 32 and Chestnut Sts., Philadelphia 19104	Guy Garrison	6	M	37,800
University of Pittsburgh, 3500 Victoria St., Pittsburgh 15261	Thomas J. Galvin	8	D (3) M (5)	56,700
Tennessee				
George Peabody College for Teachers, 21 Ave. S., Nashville 37203	Edwin S. Gleaves	4	M	25,200
University of Tennessee, 804 Volunteer Blvd., Knoxville 37916	Ann E. Prentice	2	M	12,600
Texas				
North Texas State University, N.T. Box 13796, Denton 76203	James L. Thomas	3	M	19,200
Texas Woman's University, Box 22905, T.W.U. Sta., Denton 76204	Brooke E. Sheldon	9	D (3) M (6)	62,700
University of Texas at Austin, Box 7576, University Sta., Austin 78712	C. G. Sparks	4	M	25,200
Washington				
University of Washington, Seattle 98195	Peter Hiatt	8	M	42,500

TABLE 2 FELLOWSHIPS FOR TRAINING IN LIBRARY AND INFORMATION SCIENCE, ACADEMIC YEAR 1979–1980 (cont.)

Institution	Project Director	No.	Level*	Amount
Wisconsin				
University of Wisconsin-Madison, Madison 53706	Charles A. Bunge	3	D	24,900
University of Wisconsin-Oshkosh, 800 Algoma Blvd., Oshkosh 54901	Eugenia Schmitz	3	M	19,200

*D = doctoral, P = post-master, M = master, BS = bachelor of science, A = associate of arts.

In FY 1971, the program was redirected dramatically to permit the Office of Education to focus on certain critical and priority areas. The priorities through FY 1979 are:

1. To attract minority and/or economically deprived persons into the library, media, and information science fields as professionals and paraprofessionals.
2. To train professionals in service to the disadvantaged, including the aged and the handicapped.
3. To present alternatives for recruitment, training, and utilization of library personnel and manpower.
4. To foster and develop innovative practice to reform and revitalize the traditional system of library and information service.
5. To retrain librarians to master new skills needed to support key areas, such as the Right to Read campaign, drug abuse education, environmental and ecological education, early childhood education, career education, management (planning, evaluation, and needs assessment), human relations and social interaction, service to the institutionalized, community learning center programs, service to foster the quality of life, intellectual freedom, and institute planning.

TABLE 3 LIBRARY TRAINING INSTITUTE PROGRAM ENROLLMENT DATA, FY 1968–1979

Academic Year	Participants	Institutes	FY
1968/69	2,084	66	1968
1969/70	3,101	91	1969
1970/71	1,347	46	1970
1971/72	1,557	38	1971
1972/73	684	17	1972
1973/74	1,301 + 45[a]	26 + 3[a]	1973
1974/75	1,339 + 35[a]	30 + 2[a]	1974
1975/76	1,244 + 35[a]	26 + 2[a]	1975
1976/77	120	5	1976
1977/78	802 + 112[a]	22 + 3[a]	1977
1978/79	1,101 + 100[a]	24 + 1[a]	1978
1979/80	1,081	24	1979
Total	16,088	426	

[a]Traineeship program.

TABLE 4 INSTITUTES SUPPORTED WITH HEA, TITLE II-B, LIBRARY EDUCATION FUNDING, FY 1979

Institute	Program Director	Award Amount	No. of Participants	Level[a]/ Eligibility Requirements[b]	Geographic Area
Arizona University of Arizona, Tucson, 85719 Graduate Library Institute for Spanish-Speaking Americans August 14, 1979–August 13, 1980	Arnulfo D. Trejo	$84,147	15	13/A	Southwest
California Foothill College, Los Altos Hills, 94022 Library Aide Training Institute October 1, 1979–June 30, 1980	Betty Nevin	57,229	25	4/E	Santa Clara County
Colorado University of Denver, Denver 80208 Training for Library Change in Rural Areas August 5–11, 1979 and December 2–8, 1979	Anne J. Mathews	39,576	30	2/E	Colorado, Montana, Utah, Idaho, Wyoming, New Mexico
University of Denver, Denver 80208 Institute in Law Librarianship Spring 1980 (3 days)	Alfred J. Coco	8,000	100	4/E	National
Connecticut University of Connecticut, Storrs 06268 Implementing Media Services in Schools for Librarians with No Audiovisual Skills July 2–August 10, 1979	Suleiman D. Zalatimo	25,057	40	5/A	New England
District of Columbia Books for the People Fund, Inc., Washington, D.C. 20009 In-service Training Institutes on Library Collections for the Spanish-Speaking, March 1980 (one week) in conjunction with Rutgers University April 1980; (one week) in conjunction with Miami-Dade Community College	Ana Divino Cleveland Annette Lopez	30,000	100	2, 3, 4, 5/A, E	National

HIGHER EDUCATION ACT, TITLE II-B, LIBRARY EDUCATION / 229

Catholic University of America, Washington, D.C. 20064 Statewide Systems of Continuing Education: New Directions November 1979 (5 days), January 1980 (2 days), June 1980 (2 days)	Elizabeth W. Stone	55,000	36	8/D	National
Georgia Atlanta University, Atlanta 30314 Training of Minority Information Professionals to Deliver Effective Services in an Information Environment September 1, 1979–August 31, 1980	Lorene B. Brown	80,000	10	13/A	National
Illinois Northern Illinois University, DeKalb 60115 Services and Materials for the Handicapped: An Institute for School Library Media Professionals August 12–17, 1979	Henry C. Dequin	14,000	30	5/C	National
American Library Association, Chicago 60611 National Institute on Library Service to Jail Populations March 10–12, 1980	Connie House	70,000	100	2, 8, 9/E	National
Indiana Ball State University, Muncie 47306 Improving School Library Services through Management for Mainstreaming June 17–22, 1979	Patricia F. Beilke	24,100	60	5, 6/A	Indiana and adjacent states
Michigan University of Michigan, Ann Arbor 48109 School Library Media Services for Handicapped Students in a Mainstreamed Environment July 8–20, 1979 (conducted at Jackson State University, Miss.) July 29–August 10, 1979 (conducted at University of Michigan)	Helen Lloyd	44,000	60	5/A	Southeast and Midwest

230 / FEDERALLY FUNDED PROGRAMS AND GRANT-MAKING AGENCIES

TABLE 4 INSTITUTES SUPPORTED WITH HEA, TITLE II-B, LIBRARY EDUCATION FUNDING, FY 1979 (cont.)

Institute	Program Director	Award Amount	No. of Participants	Level[a] / Eligibility Requirements[b]	Geographic Area
Minnesota Mankato State University, Mankato 56001 Basic Audiovisual Skills for Public Librarians from Rural and Culturally Deprived Areas of Minnesota and Adjacent States September 1, 1979–August 31, 1980	Frank Birmingham	35,000	20	2, 4/E	Minnesota and adjacent states
Mississippi University of Mississippi, University 38677 Training School Library and Media Specialists to Service the Handicapped Student July 30–August 10, 1979	Myra Macon	17,000	30	5/A	Mississippi
New York Queens College of CUNY, Flushing 11367 Ethnicity and Librarianship—Services to Multi-ethnic Groups in the Neighborhoods of the New York Area September 1, 1979–August 31, 1980 (30 days)	David Cohen	29,036	30	2/D	New York City
State University of New York at Buffalo, Amherst 14260 Coping with the Rising Cost of Media and Declining Library Budgets June 2–6, 1980	John W. Ellison	10,027	50	1/A	National
North Dakota University of North Dakota, Grand Forks 58202 Library Training of Media Aids and Support Personnel September 1, 1979–August 31, 1980	Donald K. Lemon	82,000	12	4/E	North Dakota
Oklahoma Central State University, Edmond 73034 Special Programming in Correctional Libraries August 5–11, 1979	Annetta J. Clark	19,100	30	9/A	Southwest

HIGHER EDUCATION ACT, TITLE II-B, LIBRARY EDUCATION / 231

Oklahoma State Department of Education, Oklahoma City 73105 Library Media Model In-service Demonstration Project July 1, 1979–June 30, 1980	LeRoy Ireton	51,110	100	5, 6/E	Oklahoma
Pennsylvania Edinboro Foundation, Edinboro 16412 The Handicapped Child in the School Library Media Center July 9–20, 1979	Virginia M. Crowe	13,965	25	5, 6/D	National
Pennsylvania Department of Education, Harrisburg 17126 School/Public Library Regional Cooperation September 11–14, 1979	John Christopher	15,000	49	2, 5, 6, 8/A	Pennsylvania and 6 other states
South Dakota Black Hills State College, Spearfish 57783 A Competency Based Training Program in Library Science for American Indians June 1, 1979–September 1, 1980	Lowell Amiotte	72,000	10	4/E	South Dakota
Tennessee Austin Peay State University, Clarksville 37040 Training Disadvantaged Students as Library Paraprofessionals to Serve all Types of Libraries July 1, 1979–June 30, 1980	Mildred G. Wallace	45,000	19	4/E	Tennessee, Kentucky
Utah Utah State University, Logan 84322 National Videodisc/Microcomputer Institute for Library Media Professionals June 11–15, 1979	R. Kent Wood	25,103	100	1/A	National

[a] 1 = professional librarian; 2 = public librarian; 3 = academic librarian; 4 = paraprofessional; 5 = school librarian; 6 = administrative or supervisory librarian; 7 = library educator; 8 = state librarian; 9 = institutional librarian; 10 = special librarian; 11 = trustee; 12 = community information specialist; 13 = graduate student.
[b] A = Baccalaureate or equiv.; D = MLS or equiv.; E = HS diploma or equiv.

6. To train those who teach other trainers.
7. To train library trustees, school administrators, and other persons with administrative, supervisory, and advisory responsibility for library, media, and information services, such as boards of education, state advisory councils, etc.
8. To train and retrain persons in law librarianship.

In FY 1979, 68 institute proposals were received requesting over $2 million in Title II-B support. Of these, 24 were selected for a total of $945,450. The 24 institute programs authorized training for 1,081 participants. Table 3 provides a summary of the institute program since its inception in FY 1968.

Institute participants enrolled in short-term programs are provided a weekly stipend of up to $75 and an allowance of $15 per week for each dependent. In some instances, travel allowances are also made where severe economic hardship so justifies. Participants in year-long institute programs are given stipends based on those described above under the fellowship/traineeship program.

Of special note again in the institute programs was the eligibility of library agencies other than institutions of higher education. Twelve such agencies made application, of which four were supported.

Table 4 is a list of institutes supported with FY 1979 grant funding ($945,450) including information on the duration of the institute, the program director, number of participants, level of interest, eligibility requirements, and amount awarded. A more complete project description is contained in the publication *FY 79/Abstracts*, Library Training Programs, which is available upon request from USOE, Bureau of Elementary and Secondary Education, Office of Libraries and Learning Resources, Library Education and Postsecondary Resources Branch, 400 Maryland Ave. S.W., Washington, D.C. 20202.

HIGHER EDUCATION ACT, TITLE II-B, LIBRARY RESEARCH AND DEMONSTRATION PROGRAM

Henry T. Drennan

Program Officer
Library Research and Demonstration Branch
Division of Library Programs
Office of Libraries and Learning Resources, USOE

Although this article marks the end of the decade of the 1970s, a summary statement would be premature on the progress and implications of research and demonstration projects conducted in the past 10 years under the Higher Education Act, Title II-B, Library Research and Demonstration. One resource that could greatly assist such a summary perspective published by the Office of Libraries and Learning Resources, *The Directory of Library Research and Demonstrations Projects, 1966-1975*, appeared in 1978. The *Directory* and subsequent annual *Abstracts* are available upon request to USOE, Bureau of Elementary and Secondary Education, Office of Libraries and Learning Resources, Library Research and Demonstration, 400 Maryland Ave. S.W., ROB no. 3, Rm. 3319A, Washington, D.C. 20202.

The ten years' activities included in the *Directory* identified 249 funding actions in the period. Table 1 identifies the subject category (in broad groupings) for which federal funds were funished for FY 1967-1977.

The Library Research and Demonstration Program is authorized under the Higher Education Act (as amended) Title II-B to provide financial assistance to eligible parties to support research and demonstration projects relating to the improvement of libraries or the improvement of training in librarianship. The funds obligated annually for selected years are presented in Table 2.

Lawrence W. Papier, former program officer for Library Research and Demonstration, presented in his paper in the 1979 *Bowker Annual* a conceptual framework that grouped library and information science objectives. Using Papier's conceptual grouping, one can illustrate selectively the program's response to library needs as proposed by the library research community and as determined for the program by federal administrators. Some sense of trends developed in libraries and information science can be grasped from these illustrations of projects operated with federal funds.

Describing the impact of research and of demonstrations of promising practice is more difficult. Some of the research ventures or demonstration projects result in immediate replication. Some have continuing long-range development. One demonstration project commenced on January 1, 1970, at the beginning of this closing decade, with an overall grant of $215,000 continues to transform library management and services. The proposal to develop a computerized regional shared cataloging system made by the Ohio College Library Center has evolved into a national initiative in networking, fostering continuing experimentation in services at the end of the decade.

Recent initiatives assisted by the Higher Education Act, Title II-B, research program can be described under the conceptual cluster mentioned above. A major concept the Research and Demonstration Program has followed since its creation is the promotion of research and design in experimental activities that assemble the knowledge resources of communities and organizations into more effective patterns of service. Emphasis is given as well to special target groups that can be described as underemployed, undereducated, culturally or geographically isolated groups with others who have been unserved or minimally served in the past.

Illustrative of this trend is the commencement of an inquiry into the nature and extent of libraries' participation in literacy education. In late September 1979, Education and Human Development, Inc., a subsidiary of Contract Research Corporation, received a contract to examine and describe literacy activities in public school libraries, community libraries, community college libraries, and state institutional libraries nationally. State library agencies are asked to participate for their planning and policymaking role in this national survey. The strong research interest in the role of libraries in literacy that eventuated in this survey grew from the interest of the Commissioner of Education, from the advocacy of state meetings of the White House Conference on Libraries and Information, from the leadership of the American Library Association, and from the record of earlier surveys and demonstrations in the area of literacy supported by the Office of Libraries and Learning Resources. The national literacy survey scheduled to end in the fall of 1980 is thought to be a difficult task with its multiplicity of concerned agencies and a relatively undeveloped data base—the problem of any first-time survey. Its product will be a comprehensive description of the role selected libraries play in support of literacy.

An illustration of redesigned services to meet new responsibilities is the object of the grant made to the South Dakota State Department of Education to plan a curriculum for assisting school library/media specialists in providing optimal library ser-

TABLE 1 SUBJECT CATEGORIES OF FUNDING ACTIONS, HEA, TITLE II-B, LIBRARY RESEARCH AND DEMONSTRATION PROGRAM, FY 1967–1979

Subject Category	FY/67	FY/68	FY/69	FY/70	FY/71	FY/72	FY/73	FY/74	FY/75	FY/76	FY/77	FY/78	FY/79	Total
Education and training	10	3	7	3	0	2	3	5	5	6	4	0	1	49
Functional development reader services, processing (including acquisitions, cataloging, classification, etc.)	10	7	10	8	0	0	4	5	7	4	3	4	3	65
Institutional cooperation to serve special target groups	0	0	4	5	5	15	10	8	2	4	2	6	4	65
Planning and development	10	4	8	4	10	12	6	2	4	3	4	4	3	74
Technology: ADP, microfilm, hardware, etc.	8	7	10	10	3	2	1	0	1	2	5	3	1	53
Total	38	21	39	30	18	31	24	20	19	19	18	17	12	306

TABLE 2 TOTAL OBLIGATIONS AND NUMBER OF PROJECTS FUNDED, HEA, TITLE II-B, LIBRARY RESEARCH AND DEMONSTRATION, FY 1967–1979

FY	Obligation	No. of Projects
1967	$ 3,381,052	38
1968	2,020,942	21
1969	2,986,264	39
1970	2,160,622	30
1971	2,170,274	18
1972	2,748,953	31
1973	1,784,741	24
1974	1,418,433	20
1975	999,338	19
1976	999,918	19
1977	995,193	18
1978	998,904	17
1979	980,563	12
Total	$23,645,197	306

vices for handicapped children. South Dakota is one of the 18 substantially rural states in the United States. In the role it chose to develop library instruction supporting handicapped services, the state department can be viewed as providing appropriate services in a rural setting or as providing answers on a stubborn staffing topic to rural America. The project was completed in the summer of 1979.

Appropriate rural library service development, as well, is the objective of design activities for the community of Olney, Texas. This rural community employed basic planning to create a comprehensive library serving persons of all ages with knowledge needs. North Texas State University is presently evaluating the Olney Community Library since its establishment in 1973. The evaluators will identify the problems and solutions of an administrative, legal, social, and financial nature encountered in operating a comprehensive library delivering services to a community of interest formerly designated "school" or "public." In seeking the solution of concentrated services, the library is changing a former diffuse pattern of organization to one that now calls for conserving designs.

In these two projects school library media curricula in South Dakota and Texas, library research deals with a rural society that, unrecognized to most of us, is one of the fastest growing sectors of our nation. The provision of comprehensive information to users and the concept of efficient use of resources development of a comprehensive library/media center continue to call for research within the library community. A recent demonstration project designed by the Dallas Public Library sought with important results to determine the feasibility of providing enhanced services to the gerontological community of the Dallas metropolitan area. In this case the target group was a body of highly specialized individuals whose common theme is the development of varied support services to the elderly. In a sense, the library created this group as a public library constituency through promoting the group's ability and confidence to make demands upon the library and ensured that continuing demand by designing a response program that provided perceived access to the library's ordinary resources.

Conceptually, the efficient use of academic resources has been examined in two projects through research of the State University of New York-Albany. In a project completed in 1978, the university research team sought to develop a series of library material collection analysis reports by discipline and form utilizing Ohio College Library Center archival tapes. Reports resulted in a paradigmatic analytical set of holdings by institutional level and rank order listings designed for the formation of logical acquisition policies.

In 1978-1979, SUNY conducted further policy research for the development of a responsive acquisitions formula to ensure an adequate flow of current library materials into academic libraries. This concept, of great interest to academic librarians, resulted in a study completed early in 1979 that aimed to validate and modify the generalized formula drawn up earlier and to establish a feedback mechanism that would maintain the formula by accommodating additional factors and changing values.

Assessment research, structured inquiry, that appraises the need for new answers and designs is basic to a developing society. Such study may be difficult to separate from topical research because knowledge is a continuum. A topic that has been dealt with fairly extensively is that of "information." The primary study sponsored by the Library Research and Demonstration Program appeared under the title of *Information Needs of Urban Residents* completed by the Regional Planning Council (of Maryland) and Westat, Inc. Previous information need studies had been performed, but the Regional Planning Council Study had the merit of examining a complete metropolitan area, that of Baltimore. Too, it queried persons at all socioeconomic levels on their information sources and needs.

A current example of assessment research employed to ascertain the need for establishment or redesign of services occurs in New England. Simmons College in Boston is the grantee conducting a six-state regional investigation of citizens' information needs in New England. The present study, like the one cited above, concerns information but from a different perspective. The study employs a major geographic region as its field and seeks ultimately to evaluate networking as a mechanism for optimum access to information.

Grants and contracts whose purpose is the development of new techniques and technological innovation complete the model by which the Research and Demonstration Program endeavors to satisfy its obligation to the varied field of library and information science. The sponsorship of the Ohio College Library Center demonstration begun in 1969 is illustrative of that developmental concept. More recent ones are the work performed by the University of California-Los Angeles on the use of an on-line microfiche catalog for technical service and retrieval of bibliographic data, by the University of North Carolina-Greensboro, applying information science techniques to augment access to school media center material, and by the Washington State Library by the employment of computer simulation to assist network planners in the design, implementation, and evaluation stages of network development.

Projects conducted with the assistance of HEA II-B, Research and Demonstration Program, are thus performed by a variety of agencies. Although universities and colleges numerically are the largest grouping of grantees, assistance is available to many different types of agencies. Table 3 reports the kinds of sponsoring organizations by type.

During FY 1979, 12 projects were funded. A list of the projects is included in Table 4. The list includes the grantee or contractor, principal investigator or project director, title of the project, and the dollar amount of the award.

Reports resulting from each project are made available to the Educational Re-

TABLE 3 LIBRARY RESEARCH AND DEMONSTRATION PROGRAM, HEA, TITLE II-B, SPONSORING ORGANIZATIONS

	FY/67	FY/68	FY/69	FY/70	FY/71	FY/72	FY/73	FY/74	FY/75	FY/76	FY/77	FY/78	FY/79	Total
Universities and colleges	25	10	22	11	7	13	13	9	8	11	11	11	10	161
Nonprofit organizations	9	7	9	8	3	6	1	7	6	4	3	3	1	67
Profit organizations	2	2	5	5	0	2	0	0	0	1	0	0	1	18
Public libraries	1	0	0	0	1	2	3	3	1	0	0	1	0	12
Government agencies	1	0	1	2	3	3	0	0	0	0	0	0	0	10
Local school districts	0	2	1	2	2	2	4	1	0	0	0	0	0	14
State and municipal governments	0	0	1	2	2	3	3	0	4	3	4	2	0	24
Total	38	21	39	30	18	31	24	20	19	19	18	17	12	306

TABLE 4   FUNDED PROJECTS, FY 1979, HEA, TITLE II-B,
LIBRARY RESEARCH AND DEMONSTRATION

Institution and Principal Investigator	Project Title	Funds Awarded
American Library Association Sandra Cooper	Curriculum Materials for Library Service to Jail Populations	$ 41,000
California, University of, Los Angeles Nathaniel Davis	A Survey of and Guide to Abstracting and Indexing Services for Current Black Periodical Literature	55,040
Catholic University of America Elizabeth W. Stone	Development and Demonstration of Criteria and Guidelines for Quality Control in Continuing Education for Library/Information/Media Personnel: A Provider Evaluation and Approval Program	90,000
Contract Research Corporation Ester G. Smith	Libraries in Literacy	189,193
Drexel University Thomas A. Childers	Survey of Public Library Information and Referral Service: Phase II—Organizational Context and User Reactions	61,000
Elgin Community College Jack Weiss	Research and Demonstration for a Comprehensive Package of Computer Programs to Serve Community College Learning Resource Centers, Phase II	145,000
Gallaudet College Elaine Costello	Development of a National Information Center on Deafness	39,368
North Texas State University James A. Kitchens	Evaluation and Assessment of the Olney Community Library	42,499
Portland State University Joyce Petrie	Educational Media for Handicapped Children in Regular K-12 Schools	80,200
Seattle University Linda Fitzpatrick	Information for Community Action: A Demonstration of University/Public Library Cooperation in Meeting Community Groups' Informational Needs	82,457
Simmons College Ching-chih Chen	A Regional Investigation of Citizens' Information Needs in New England	99,806
Temple University Elliott Shore	Alternative Publications in College Libraries: An Evaluative Model	55,000

sources Information Center (ERIC). As the material becomes available, it is announced in ERIC's monthly *Resources in Education* (Washington, D.C.: Superintendent of Documents, U.S. Government Printing Office). The announcement includes an abstract, price of the report in hard copy or microfiche, and order instructions.

HIGHER EDUCATION ACT, TITLE II-C, STRENGTHENING RESEARCH LIBRARY RESOURCES

Frank A. Stevens

Chief, Library Education and Postsecondary Resources Branch, Division of Library Programs, USOE

Title II-C of the Higher Education Act of 1965, as amended, Strengthening Research Library Resources Program, authorizes federal financial assistance to major research libraries for the purpose of promoting research and education of higher quality by providing financial aid to help maintain and strengthen their collections, and to make these collections available to researchers and scholars beyond their primary users and to other libraries whose users have need for research materials.

The Title II-C program was enacted through the Education Amendments of 1976 on October 12, 1976 in recognition of the fact that the major research libraries of the nation represent the bibliographic foundation of our research resources and that financial stringency and increased costs have severely reduced their capabilities for resource sharing.

Major research libraries are those whose collections make a significant contribution to higher education and research, are broadly based, are recognized as having national or international significance for scholarly research, are of a unique nature, are not widely held, and are of such importance that substantial demands are made upon the institution by researchers and scholars outside its primary clientele. They include institutions of higher education, public libraries, state libraries, and private nonprofit independent research libraries.

It is estimated that approximately 200 libraries fall within this definition, and the Title II-C program is authorized to make up to 150 grants annually to assist them. Specific criteria have been established by regulation, published in the *Federal Register* on December 28, 1977, measuring significance as a major research library and measuring appropriateness of projects. Additionally, criteria were also established in the regulation to ensure reasonable regional allocation of grant funds throughout the nation.

The authorizing legislation prohibits any institution from receiving a grant under the HEA, Title II-A, College Library Resources Program, and Title II-C during the same fiscal year.

Announcement of the closing date for receipt of applications is published annually in the *Federal Register*. Application packages are available upon request to all interested parties at the time of program announcement.

TABLE 1 PROGRAM FUNDING RECORD, HEA, TITLE II-C, STRENGTHENING RESEARCH LIBRARY RESOURCES, FY 1977–1979

Fiscal Year	Authorization	Appropriation	Expenditures
1977	$10,000,000	0	0
1978	15,000,000	$5,000,000	$4,999,996
1979	20,000,000	6,000,000	6,000,000

TABLE 2 ANALYSIS OF APPLICATIONS,
HEA, TITLE II-C, FY 1979

Category	Amount
Number of proposals received	87
Amount of funds requested	$25,000,000
Number of proposals supported	26[a]
Applicants by type of library	
Institutions of higher education	58
Independent research libraries	8
Public libraries	7
State libraries	4
Historical societies	1
Museums	5
Medical libraries	2
Other	2

[a]Four of these proposals were jointly sponsored, directly benefiting eight additional institutions.

Funds provided may be used for the acquisition of books and other library materials; binding, repairing, and preserving books and other library materials; cataloging, abstracting, and making available guides of library collections; distributing materials and bibliographic information to users beyond primary clientele; acquisition of equipment, supplies, and communication expenses; and hiring necessary additional staff to

TABLE 3 NUMBER OF APPLICATIONS AND AWARDS, BY REGION,
HEA, TITLE II-C, FY 1979

Region No.	Geographic Description	No. of Applications	No. of Awards
I	New England (Connecticut, Maine, Massachusetts, New Hampshire, Rhode Island, Vermont)	7	3
II	New York, Puerto Rico, Virgin Islands	9	5
III	Middle Atlantic (Delaware, District of Columbia, Maryland, New Jersey, Pennsylvania, West Virginia)	16	3
IV	Southeast (Alabama, Florida, Georgia, Kentucky, Mississippi, North Carolina, South Carolina, Tennessee, Virginia)	5	1
V	Great Lakes (Indiana, Michigan, Ohio)	8	2
VI	Midwest (Illinois, Iowa, Minnesota, Missouri, Wisconsin)	17	5
VII	Southwest (Arizona, Arkansas, Louisiana, New Mexico, Oklahoma, Texas)	9	1
VIII	Mountain Plains (Colorado, Kansas, Montana, Nebraska, Nevada, North Dakota, South Dakota, Utah, Wyoming)	5	2
IX	Pacific Northwest (Alaska, Idaho, Oregon, Washington)	5	1
X	California, Hawaii, American Samoa, Guam	6	3

carry out funded activities. Each institution is limited to one application, which may include more than one project. The length of a project cannot exceed three years.

Fiscal year 1979 was the second year of program operations. Table 1 provides the program funding record. Eighty-seven applications were received in FY 1979 requesting over $25 million. Table 2 provides an analysis of the FY 1979 applications by type of applicant. Table 3 indicates the Title II-C designated regional areas and the number of applications and awards for each region.

Six million dollars was available for award in FY 1979. In order to achieve maximum program impact, 26 grants were awarded—the highest being $750,000 and the lowest being $70,000. Twenty grants were awarded to institutions of higher education, four were awarded to independent research libraries, one was awarded to a public library, and one was awarded to a state library. Table 4 lists the institutions that received

TABLE 4   ANALYSIS OF GRANT AWARDS BY MAJOR ACTIVITY, HEA, TITLE II-C, FY 1979

Institution	Collection Development	Preservation	Bibliographic Control and Access
University of Alaska	—	$ 111,145	$ 38,855
American Museum of Natural History	$117,980	—	124,185
Boston Public Library	—	—	150,000
University of California, Berkeley	—	—	750,000
University of Chicago	1,050	4,000	63,699
Colorado State University	—	—	215,000
Columbia University	—	250,000	—
Cornell University	194,897	—	—
Harvard University	—	300,000	—
Henry E. Huntington Library and Art Gallery	—	225,000	—
University of Illinois	125,000	—	—
Indiana University	—	—	200,000
University of Kansas	—	—	116,689
University of Michigan	—	—	350,000
Missouri Botanical Garden	—	—	200,000
New York Public Library	—	300,000	—
New York State Education Department	—	—	250,000
University of North Carolina, Chapel Hill	—	—	220,500
Northwestern University	160,948	—	89,052
Princeton University	—	—	250,000
Rutgers University	—	43,056	156,944
University of Southern California	—	—	200,000
University of Texas, Austin	28,558	—	121,442
University of Virginia	—	—	300,000
University of Wisconsin, Madison	—	—	182,000
Yale University	—	160,000	—
Total	$628,433	$1,393,201	$3,978,366

Note: The nature of the Title II-C program is such that the grants do not conveniently break down into detailed categories of program activities. Further, some grants include more than one project. Therefore, the table analyzes each grant by the amount of funding for three general program activities: collection development, preservation, and bibliographic control and access.

FY 1979 grant awards and the major program activities to be undertaken. A more complete project description is contained in the publication *FY/79 Abstracts: Strengthening Research Library Resources Program*, which is available upon request from the Office of Libraries and Learning Resources, Division of Library Programs, Library Education and Postsecondary Resources Branch, 400 Maryland Ave. S.W., Washington, D.C. 20202. Like the initial slate of grants awarded in FY 1978, this second slate indicates a wide range of activities and subject matter emphasizing collection development, preservation, and resource sharing.

GENERAL REVENUE SHARING SUPPORT FOR LIBRARIES

Frank Wm. Goudy

Assistant Professor, Western Illinois University Libraries, Macomb, IL 61455

With the passage of the State and Local Fiscal Assistance Act of 1972 (general revenue sharing), a trust fund of $30.2 billion was established for a five-year period to run from January 1972 through December 1976. However, because the legislation was not actually passed until October 1972, payments were not authorized until FY 1973.

The philosophy behind general revenue sharing was that it would decentralize power by providing funding not directly controlled by the federal government as were most categorical grants. Through this decentralization, states and localities could assume a greater self-control for ideas and projects deemed necessary for state and community development. This concept was particularly embraced by the Republican party during the 1968 presidential elections. Presidential candidate Richard Nixon was enthusiastic over the idea of some form of revenue sharing, as he felt it could potentially limit the expanding power of the federal government, assist in abolishing many wasteful categorical grants, and place much of the decision making for programs at the state and local levels where they originally and more properly belonged.

Enactment of the State and Local Fiscal Assistance Act of 1972 comprised the entire Ninety-second Congress with substantial compromise involved between the Republican president and the Democratic Congress. It was finally agreed upon that all 50 states and more than 39,000 local governments would be eligible to receive funding based upon an established formula. Especially important was Section 103 of Title I of the bill, which listed libraries as one of eight "priority items" that were to receive special consideration in the allocation of general revenue-sharing dollars. However, the impact of this priority status was significantly weakened by language that excluded the state government portion from any priority considerations as well as all capital outlays at the local level.

Through June 30, 1976, expenditures for general revenue sharing totaled nearly $23.675 billion with 1.24 percent of that amount ($293.8 million) allocated to libraries. The $293.8 million was received as follows: FY 1973, $18.5 million; FY 1974, $82.3 million; FY 1975, $95 million; and FY 1976, $98 million. Of the 14 specific categories reported by the Office of Revenue Sharing, libraries came in tenth.

General revenue sharing has been continued through FY 1980 with the passage

TABLE 1 GENERAL REVENUE-SHARING FUND EXPENDITURES AND GOVERNMENT ALLOCATIONS TO LIBRARIES (BY STATE), 1976–1977

(In Thousands of Dollars)

State	Total GRS Expended	Total GRS Expended on Libraries	Percent of GRS Expended on Libraries	GRS Allocated to Libraries by Type of Government			
				State Government	Counties	Municipalities	Townships
Alabama	$102,462	$ 1,331	1.30	—	$ 520	$ 811	—
Alaska	10,314	81	.79	—	2	79	—
Arizona	63,189	704	1.11	—	109	595	—
Arkansas	77,428	342	.44	—	238	104	—
California	712,708	12,881	1.81	—	2,314	10,567	—
Colorado	88,737	3,655	4.12	—	167	348	—
Connecticut	85,605	1,403	1.64	$3,140	—	808	$ 595
Delaware	15,249	617	4.05	—	612	5	—
District of Columbia	27,875	499	1.79	—	—	499	—
Florida	263,453	3,455	1.31	—	2,700	755	—
Georgia	95,226	791	.83	—	360	431	—
Hawaii	30,541	—	—	—	—	—	—
Idaho	26,739	114	.43	—	17	97	—
Illinois	309,399	1,356	.44	—	6	1,224	126
Indiana	210,468	66	.03	—	7	—	59
Iowa	87,812	724	.82	—	233	491	—
Kansas	49,912	395	.79	—	134	261	—
Kentucky	108,617	981	.90	—	393	588	—
Louisiana	140,193	565	.40	—	327	238	—
Maine	39,549	337	.85	—	24	139	174
Maryland	79,343	1,177	1.48	—	662	515	—
Massachusetts	191,922	1,641	.86	—	—	481	1,160
Michigan	266,824	2,103	.79	—	596	1,147	360
Minnesota	133,707	924	.69	44	538	342	—
Mississippi	105,327	3,155	3.00	1,987	533	635	—
Missouri	116,316	689	.59	536	11	142	—
Montana	28,060	330	1.18	—	213	117	—
Nebraska	40,066	339	.85	230	59	50	—

244 / FEDERALLY FUNDED PROGRAMS AND GRANT-MAKING AGENCIES

TABLE 1 GENERAL REVENUE-SHARING FUND EXPENDITURES AND GOVERNMENT ALLOCATIONS TO LIBRARIES (BY STATE), 1976–1977 (cont.)

State	Total GRS Expended	Total GRS Expended on Libraries	Percent of GRS Expended on Libraries	GRS Allocated to Libraries by Type of Government			
				State Government	Counties	Municipalities	Townships
Nevada	17,893	43	.24	—	35	8	—
New Hampshire	20,357	182	.89	—	—	146	36
New Jersey	207,355	1,120	.54	—	—	758	362
New Mexico	36,695	44	.12	—	21	23	—
New York	762,759	9,118	1.20	—	7,379	773	966
North Carolina	210,045	2,310	1.10	—	1,666	644	—
North Dakota	23,930	86	.36	—	17	69	—
Ohio	287,684	367	.13	94	94	171	8
Oklahoma	68,418	186	.27	—	79	107	—
Oregon	67,083	2,773	4.13	—	2,278	495	250
Pennsylvania	353,336	8,510	2.41	—	3,895	4,365	219
Rhode Island	27,746	228	.82	—	—	9	—
South Carolina	70,069	382	.55	—	365	17	—
South Dakota	24,135	143	.59	—	77	66	—
Tennessee	92,620	2,089	2.26	—	738	1,351	—
Texas	295,064	4,843	1.64	—	2,035	2,808	—
Utah	36,436	190	.52	—	89	101	—
Vermont	18,966	75	.40	—	1	20	54
Virginia	134,599	1,689	1.25	—	522	1,167	—
Washington	66,099	1,670	2.53	—	6	1,664	—
West Virginia	53,462	1,083	2.03	—	785	298	—
Wisconsin	161,585	1,811	1.12	—	633	1,151	27
Wyoming	11,317	125	1.10	—	125	—	—
Total	$6,554,694	$79,722	1.22	$6,031	$31,615	$37,680	$4,396

Source: U.S. Department of Commerce and U.S. Department of Treasury, *Expenditures of General Revenue Sharing and Antirecession Fiscal Assistance Funds 1976–1977* (Washington, D.C.: Government Printing Office, 1979).

TABLE 2 GENERAL REVENUE-SHARING FUND EXPENDITURE CATEGORIES, 1976–1977
(In Thousands of Dollars)

Category	Amount Expended	Percent of GRS Expended
Education	$1,248,437	19.05
Police protection	942,809	14.38
Highways	799,024	12.19
Fire protection	523,467	7.99
Health	476,732	7.27
Finance and general administration	327,675	5.00
Sanitation	292,096	4.45
General public buildings	261,719	3.99
Parks and recreation	247,588	3.78
Correction	166,652	2.54
Public welfare	165,699	2.53
Hospitals	138,542	2.11
Debt redemption	90,214	1.38
LIBRARIES	79,722	1.22
Utility systems	79,281	1.21
Sewerage	78,781	1.20
Interest on debt	55,811	.85
Natural resources	27,455	.42
Housing and urban renewal	17,627	.27
Airports	7,963	.12
Other	527,400	8.05
Total	$6,554,694	100.00

Source: U.S. Department of Commerce and U.S. Department of Treasury. *Expenditures of General Revenue Sharing and Antirecession Fiscal Assistance Funds 1976–1977* (Washington, D.C.: Government Printing Office, 1979).

of the State and Local Fiscal Assistance Amendments of 1976 (PL 94-488). This new act provided an additional $25.5 billion with all priority items being deleted.

The data in the following tables were obtained from a report sponsored jointly by the Bureau of the Census and the Office of Revenue Sharing. Because the original legislation ended in December 1976 and the amended act began in January 1977, the information presented overlaps these two laws.

The data in Table 1 indicate that libraries received $79.722 million in FY 1977, or 1.22 percent of the total general revenue-sharing funds available. As both a percentage and a dollar amount, this is less than the 1.41 percent, or $98 million, received in FY 1976. However, it is very close to the 1.24 percent average received during the first four years of general revenue-sharing funding. In comparison to other listed expenditure categories, libraries ranked only fourteenth out of the 20 reported areas (Table 2).

NATIONAL ENDOWMENT FOR THE HUMANITIES SUPPORT FOR LIBRARIES, 1979

806 15 Street N.W.,
Washington, DC 20506
202-724-0386

The National Endowment for the Humanities (NEH) is an independent federal grant-making agency created by Congress in 1965 to support projects of research, education, and public activity in the humanities. According to the legislation that established the Endowment, the humanities include, but are not limited to, the following fields: history, philosophy, languages, literature, linguistics, archaeology, jurisprudence, history and criticism of the arts, ethics, comparative religion, and those aspects of the social sciences employing historical or philosophical approaches. This last category includes cultural anthropology, sociology, political theory, international relations, and other subjects concerned with questions of value.

The Endowment's grant-making operations are conducted through five major divisions. The Division of Research Grants provides support for group projects of research in the humanities, for research resources, for the preparation of important research tools, and for the editing of significant humanistic texts. The Division of Fellowships, through several programs, provides stipends that enable individual scholars, teachers, and members of nonacademic professions to study areas of the humanities that may be directly and fruitfully related to the work they characteristically perform. The Division of Education Programs supports projects and programs through which institutions endeavor to renew and strengthen the impact of teaching in the humanities at all levels. The Division of Public Programs—through projects in the media, projects involving individual academic humanists, and projects of nonacademic public institutions such as libraries, museums, and historical organizations—seeks to encourage broad national dissemination and increased understanding of the humanities. The Division of Special Programs is designed to fund innovative projects that do not fall into specific categories established in the existing divisions. Finally, there is the Division of State Programs, which makes grants to citizens' committees in each state to provide support for local humanities projects.

Other projects are eligible for support through the Office of Planning and Policy Assessment and through a program of Challenge Grants.

CATEGORIES OF SUPPORT

The NEH seeks to cooperate with libraries in strengthening the general public's knowledge and use of the humanities through its various programs. These programs are:

Division of Public Programs

Libraries Humanities Projects awards grants for projects that draw upon those humanistic resources in libraries that are designed to serve the general adult public. The specific goals of the library program are to strengthen programs that stimulate and respond to public interest in the humanities; to enhance the ability of library staff to plan and implement these programs, and to increase the public's awareness and use of a library's existing humanities resources.

A few project ideas that are eligible for support are listed below. Librarians are encouraged to replicate, combine formats, or create entirely new approaches to humanities programming.

A library can sponsor programs on humanities themes that draw on the library's book, magazine, audiovisual, and staff resources. The theme may be related directly to the humanities disciplines or provide a humanistic perspective on a popular community topic or issue.

Libraries could work with community groups to plan and present programs for the public using and publicizing the library's humanities resources. Such projects could include humanities workshops for community and group leaders or the preparation of special print materials or displays on library holdings.

A library can attempt to increase the use of humanities resources by planning programs in conjunction with television programs or exhibitions developed by other community institutions.

A library may plan projects that strengthen professional staff expertise in the humanities as well as provide humanities programming for the public. These could include workshops on the humanities disciplines, reference training, or programming ideas in preparation for a public humanities program.

A state library, library association, or large library system could produce "packaged" programs that would include specially prepared humanities materials, scholars and experts in the humanities as speakers, and special activities designed for use in local public libraries.

A library can plan a formal or informal sequential educational program for the adult public on a humanities topic or issue of interest to the community.

A library may develop a new concept or theme for public programming: investigating the history of a community's people and institutions; exploring the relationship between a community's values and the technology of an advanced society; relating the humanities to library services and human needs; reaching audiences who do not normally use the library or the humanities; or combining humanities programming with new trends in library service.

Any nonprofit library may apply. Libraries may submit proposals individually or in cooperation with other community organizations. Academic and school libraries are also eligible if the proposed project is aimed at the adult public.

Division of Education Programs

Libraries are among those institutions that may receive support through a number of programs in this division for projects aimed at improving the teaching of the humanities or developing new humanities curricula. The division's Cultural Institutions Program, which assisted libraries and museums in providing formal and systematic educational programs designed for both the students and the general public, has been transferred to the Libraries Humanities Projects in the Division of Public Programs.

Division of Fellowships

Through its program of Fellowships Support to Centers for Advanced Study, this division provides funds to independent research libraries for stipends to resident scholars. In 1979, the Newberry Library, the Huntington Library, and the American Antiquarian Society each housed NEH fellows.

Division of Research Grants

The Research Resources Program focuses on making raw research materials more accessible to scholars. It increases access to materials through projects that address national problems in the archival and library field, through projects that serve as models in systems development and library automation, and through processing grants that are used to catalog, inventory, or otherwise gain bibliographic control of significant research collections.

The Resources Program also helps to develop collections by providing funds either to microfilm materials in foreign repositories so that they will be available in the United States or to collect data through oral history techniques. Responsibility for applications to prepare bibliographies, indexes, guides to various kinds of source materials, and similar finding aids has been transferred from the Research Tools to the Research Resources Program. The latter also has a small additional amount of funding available to support projects in the area of conservation and preservation that will benefit more than a single institution.

Division of Special Programs

In order to promote innovative programming, the Endowment supports a selected number of special projects designed to develop and test new applications of humanistic knowledge or new ways of disseminating it—especially to sectors of the society not normally involved in humanistic study. Libraries and library organizations, either working alone or in conjunction with other institutions, are among those who may receive support for such projects.

Challenge Grants

Libraries are also eligible for support under the Endowment's program of Challenge Grants, now in its third year of funding. Challenge Grants are designed to stimulate increased support for humanities institutions from private citizens, business and labor organizations, state and local governments, and civic and other groups by offering one federal dollar for every three raised in the private sector. Challenge Grants are intended to be a means by which institutions can better finance their humanities operations and more effectively serve their respective clientele; they should help secure long-term financial stability and economic independence. To those ends, funds may cover a variety of costs: to help in fund-raising plans and development efforts; for general expenses; to defray deficits; to cover increased costs and the renovation of facilities; for acquisition of equipment and materials; for maintenance, preservation, and conservation of collections; and for other management and administrative expenses.

Office of Planning and Policy Assessment

As an aid in understanding national needs in the humanities and designing new or improved programs to meet such needs, this office of the Endowment supports projects in the following areas: collection and analysis of data assessing the status and effectiveness of important sectors of humanistic activity; research into and development of more efficient and less expensive ways of organizing and disseminating humanistic knowledge; and testing and demonstration of improved management and administrative systems for humanities organizations, including libraries.

LIBRARY GRANTS AWARDED IN 1979

Division of Public Programs

Library Humanities Projects

Oklahoma Department of Libraries, Oklahoma City, $400,000: to improve library services and promote quality humanities programs stressing Oklahoma's multicultural heritage.

Chicago Public Library, Chicago, $100,300: a year-long program designed to give out-of-school adults the opportunity to learn more about the literature of the many foreign cultures represented in the ethnic populations of Chicago.

Library Council of Metropolitan Milwaukee, Milwaukee, $18,000: to plan a series of learning experiences that will relate the Milwaukee area libraries' humanities collections to the interests of the Milwaukee community.

Santiago Library System, Orange, CA, $61,000: four workshops will be planned stressing the importance and scope of local historical reference sources.

Regents of the University of California, Berkeley, $8,994: the School of Library and Information Studies will design a program of bibliographic instruction for the nonstudent adult in order to stimulate and enable more sophisticated use of public library resources.

San Joaquin Valley Library System, Fresno, CA, $83,161: to increase the involvement of the San Joaquin Valley Japanese-American community with the libraries in the area.

Southwestern Library Association, Denton, TX, $177,982: to present public programming in oral history in southwestern communities.

Cincinnati Historical Society, Cincinnati, $106,446: Cincinnati neighborhood studies project.

Alpha Regional Library, Spencer, WV, $2,692: to involve the general adult public of three West Virginia counties in local history and cultural heritage.

Seattle Public Library, Seattle, WA, $308,475: the project will consist of five series of public programs on local history.

Portsmouth Public Library, Portsmouth, VA, $20,000: to plan a program of the history of black and white interrelationships during the last 200 years in lower Tidewater, Virginia.

Department of Conservation and Cultural Affairs, St. Thomas, Virgin Islands, $108,324: a series of lecture/discussions on the emancipation of the slaves (1848) and the Fireburn revolt against near-slavery conditions 30 years later.

Maryland State Department of Education, Baltimore, $145,260: to increase the use of the humanities collection in the Maryland Department of Public Safety and Correctional Services libraries.

Cumberland County Public Library, Fayetteville, NC, $20,362: to plan a series of six public humanities programs in the development of Western civilization.

Marymount College, Tarrytown, NY, $11,000: Marymount College Library will be made available to local residents for their private research projects.

New York State Education Department, Albany, NY, $22,995: New York State: its history and social and cultural development as reflected in humanities resources of public libraries.

Division of Education Programs

Higher Education

Franklin and Marshall College, Lancaster, PA, $50,000: to integrate the use of both online bibliographic retrieval services and traditional reference sources and search strategies in selected humanities curricula.

Lake Forest College, Lake Forest, IL, $73,975: faculty-centered library instruction in the humanities.

Tusculum College, Greeneville, TN, $25,545: to develop a comprehensive program designed to enlarge the library's role in the college's teaching process.

Research Foundation of SUNY for and in Conjunction with SUNY at Stony Brook, Stony Brook, NY, $26,642: to create a new type of academic resource.

University of Massachusetts, Boston, $16,500: center to support activities for the John F. Kennedy Library.

Education Institutes

Newberry Library, Chicago, $317,894: institutes in Renaissance studies.

Folger Shakespeare Library, Washington, DC, $334,452: a three-year plan for development of the Folger Institute of Renaissance and Eighteenth-Century Studies.

Newberry Library, Chicago, $384,320: teaching new social history.

Research Division

Conferences

Boston Public Library, Boston, $8,897: a two-day conference to assess the Sacco-Vanzetti case: developments and reconsiderations, 1979.

Folger Shakespeare Library, Washington, DC, $9,581: a symposium about contemporary poetry.

Newberry Library, Chicago, $14,193: Renaissance rhetoric conference.

Research Publications

Henry E. Huntington Library, San Marino, CA, $4,000: to study the concepts of property law brought by pioneers settling in the West in the years of the gold rush.

Henry E. Huntington Library, Art Gallery, San Marino, CA, $4,000: a study of Milton.

Research Resources

Ohio College Library Center, Columbus, OH, $60,000: development of non-Roman alphabet capability for library processes.

New York Public Library, New York, $150,000: Schomburg vertical file and manuscript project.

New York Public Library, New York, $4,800,000: financing on the national level for the research libraries of the New York Public Library.

Association of Research Libraries, Washington, DC, $50,000: bibliographic control of materials in microform.

Association of Research Libraries, Washington, DC, $151,924: design and test a self-study procedure to enable academic libraries to identify and address preservation problems.

Newberry Library, Chicago, $900,000: library operations grant.

Municipal Library Department, Dallas, TX, $41,747: to process and develop finding aids for archival material in the performing arts accumulated by the Dallas Public Library during the past 25 years.

Free Library of Philadelphia, Philadelphia, $39,830: a basic catalog of the John Frederick Lewis Collection of Cuneiform Tablets.

Spruance Library of the Bucks County Historical Society, Doylestown, PA, $450.00: to hire two consultants, a librarian, and an archivist for organizing the library and papers of Henry C. Mercer.

Council on Library Resources, Washington, DC, $200,000: computerized bibliographic network for libraries.

Research Tools

Newberry Library, Chicago, $77,140: to compile old Northwest historical boundary data file.

Newberry Library, Chicago, $20,000: to prepare for publication a catalog of maps of the west North Central states printed before 1900.

Folger Shakespeare Library, Washington, DC, $29,451: Shakespeare film resource inventory.

American Theological Library Association, c/o Lutheran Theological Seminary, Philadelphia, $97,922: an in-depth index of multiauthor religious publications.

Henry E. Huntington Library and Art Gallery, San Marino, CA, $105,740: to provide as complete a listing as possible of the extant English verse that was printed or transcribed during the years 1501-1558.

Division of Special Programs

Program Development

Council of the Southern Mountains, Clintwood, VA, $37,900: the Council of the Southern Mountains Appalachian mobile bookstore.

National Consumers League, Washington, DC, $16,497: to inventory historic records, letters, and documents in the Consumers League's office files, the Library of Congress, and university libraries.

Science, Values, and Human Technology

Knox College—National Science Foundation, Washington, DC, $12,000: value presuppositions in scientific textbooks.

Youth Programs

Wichita Public Library, Wichita, KS, $7,510: development of a model for rural youth involvement in the humanities: dramatic interpretations and discussions of literature.

NATIONAL SCIENCE FOUNDATION SUPPORT FOR INFORMATION SCIENCE RESEARCH

1800 G St. N.W., Washington, DC 20550
202-632-5800

Sarah N. Rhodes

Division of Information Science and Technology

The National Science Foundation (NSF) is an independent agency of the federal government, established by Congress in 1950 to promote the progress of science. Along with other responsibilities, the foundation is directed to foster the interchange of scientific information among U.S. and foreign scientists and to develop new or improved methods for makng scientific information available. From 1958 to 1978 support for these activities was provided through the Office of Science Information Service. In 1978 the decision was made to return responsibility for supporting the dissemination of scientific information to the research divisions for the various scientific disciplines supported by the foundation. At the same time, the foundation established the Division of Information Science and Technology as a new research division in the Directorate for Scientific, Technological, and International Affairs.

RESEARCH IN INFORMATION SCIENCE

The foundation, through the Division of Information Science and Technology (IST), supports basic and applied research to advance understanding of the properties and structure of information and information transfer, and to contribute to the store of scientific and technical knowledge that can be applied in the design of information systems. Research proposals in five specific categories are considered.

Standards and Measures

Progress in information science depends on improved measures and more accurate standards for assessing the predictions of theory, comparing the results of experiments, and evaluating the effectiveness of information processing algorithms and systems. The continued development and refinement of such tools is, therefore, the first concern of this category. Major research questions include:

How can the essential properties of information systems be formally characterized? Work that applies to combined human and machine-based systems is particularly encouraged.

How can objective and quantitative measures of the attributes of information such as complexity, meaning, utility, and value be defined?

How can measures of complexity, meaning, and utility be related to characteristics of information systems and to design for organization, transfer, interpretation, and utilization of information collections?

How can standard experimental environments and test collections be designed to control variability and enhance the comparability of experimental results?

Structure of Information

Information systems involve data files, or other types of information stored in some physical form, and users. This category is concerned with the structural properties of information as organizing principles, as well as with structures that govern information systems and access collections. Its major objectives are characterizing information bearing structures and obtaining a better understanding of the relationship between form and content. The first of these two objectives is important because it leads to an understanding of which information structures are the most efficient in given circumstances; it may also suggest how human beings organize or should organize the information they use. The second objective is important because computers and other information processing machines operate directly on the *form* of a statement, not on its content, or *meaning*. The extent to which meaning can be conveyed by form determines how effective a machine, or information system, can be in answering the more complicated kinds of questions people ask. Illustrative research questions are:

How are existing collections of information organized and how should they be organized for maximum benefit?

What relationships exist between information and the structure of language?

How can patterns of information in text, image, and numerical archives or files be identified and recognized automatically?

Behavioral Aspects of Information Transfer

Some of the most interesting information systems are biological ones. They exhibit many features that still cannot be efficiently duplicated by physical systems, such as the extraction of meaning from text materials, complex object identification, language translation, coping with imprecise directions or discussions, and associative memory. Research in this category is concerned with the abilities and limitations of people as information processors. The main directions for study include:

> Investigations of human information processing, including those aspects of learning, memory, problem solving, and pattern recognition that are relevant to information processing principles.
>
> Investigations of the interface between human beings as information processors and the inanimate information systems and sources with which they interact, such as printed material, computer terminals, and video or microform displays.
>
> Investigations of those aspects of information representation that admit some generalization and abstraction from specific biological mechanisms. Problem areas include organization of information by the sensory system, the nature of categorical representations, and information filtering and rejection of nonessential content.

Infometrics

The creation, transmission, and use of scientific and technical information play an increasingly important role in the economy. Research studies of these processes are the subject matter of this category. They will involve conceptual tools and data-gathering techniques originating in such disciplines as economics, information science, computer science, management science, and psychology. The objective of this category is to strengthen understanding of the role of information in the economy and to assess and predict the impact of technological, regulatory, and policy changes on the information system. Important research questions are:

> What is the role of scientific and technical information as an input to production? What is the nature of information as a product? How can such concepts as complementarity and substitution, economies of scale, and public goods be applied to information goods and services?
>
> What is the comparative flexibility and substitutability of informational and noninformational parts of the labor force? What are the possible trade-offs between the information labor and information capital?
>
> How can one solve the aggregation problems encountered in modeling information flow? How can one relate information flow in firms to information flow in industries and to information flow in the economy as a whole?
>
> What criteria should be used in validating information models?

Information Technology

This category is primarily concerned with two issues: identifying and supporting research needed to best utilize existing information technology and examining the potential use of promising new systems and ideas that are not being pursued in the private sector; and to promote the development and use of more effective instrumentation for information science research.

Regarding the second concern, special instruments such as microscopes and telescopes, which extend normal human abilities to observe and measure physical properties, have been essential to the advance of the physical and biological sciences. Information science is similarly dependent on instruments that make it possible to observe and measure properties of information and information transfer in a way that extends immediate individual perception. This category will capitalize on the rapid advance of microelectronic, telecommunications, and other technologies to promote the development of instrumentation for information science research. Major research questions include:

> What advanced systems are technologically feasible over the next five to ten years? What are the social and economic implications of such technology?
>
> What is the impact of information technology advances on information science research? In particular, which research directions hold greater opportunity and which are made less essential by technological change?
>
> What instruments to assist information science research are now practical or feasible as a result of advances in technology?

In order to enhance the development of information science and contribute to the scientific vitality of the field, the division has established Special Research Initiation Awards for New Investigators as part of its program of research support. These awards are offered only to principal investigators who have earned a doctoral degree in a field related to information science, including the information, computer, cognitive, and mathematical sciences, linguistics, and electrical engineering, and have held the doctorate for no more than five years.

SUBMISSION AND REVIEW OF PROPOSALS

Proposals may be submitted by academic institutions, nonprofit and profit-making organizations, units of government (federal, state, or local), or by groups of such organizations. Joint proposals that bring a coordinated range of expertise and research skills to bear on complex problems are particularly encouraged. In the selection of projects to be supported, preference is given to research that is fundamental and general and to applied research concerned with scientific and technical information rather than, for example, business information or mass communication. The development of hardware is beyond the scope of this program, as are projects to develop, implement, or evaluate information systems except for the purpose of generalizations beyond the particular information systems involved.

A program announcement, *Research in Information Science* (NSF-79-68), which also provides information on how to submit a proposal, is available from the Division of Information Science and Technology. Potential applicants are encouraged to discuss their research ideas with division staff, in person, or by letter or telephone.

Except for proposals for Special Research Initiation Awards, for which the deadline is the first Wednesday in February, research proposals may be submitted at any time. Review generally requires six to eight months, and proposed activities should be scheduled with that in mind. Proposals are reviewed by foundation staff and external reviewers selected for their knowledge and expertise in topics addressed by the proposals. The award of NSF grants is discretionary. In general, projects are supported in order of merit to the extent permitted by available funds. The principal criteria by which a research proposal is evaluated are the technical adequacy of the investigators and their institutional base, the adequacy of the research design, the scientific significance of the proposed project, its utility or relevance, and its implications for the scientific potential of the field.

The foundation plans to award approximately $5.2 million for information science research in FY 1980.

DISSEMINATION OF RESULTS

The foundation encourages grantees and contractors to present their research results at appropriate professional meetings and to publish in scientific journals. Copies of final technical reports are made available through the National Technical Information Service of the U.S. Department of Commerce. In addition, summaries of awards are available through the Smithsonian Science Information Exchange. Annual lists of awards and bibliographies of reports from completed projects are available from the division.

Table 1 lists the grants and contracts for research in information science awarded by the foundation in FY 1979. Most of these awards were supported entirely by the Division of Information Science and Technology, but a few were funded jointly by IST and other NSF divisions, including the Division of Mathematical and Computer Sciences and the Division of Social Sciences.

TABLE 1   NSF AWARDS FOR INFORMATION SCIENCE RESEARCH, FY 1979

Investigator(s)/ Award No.	Institution/Title	Amount ($)	Duration (months)
Dharma P. Agrawal*	Wayne State University Subgraph Identification Using Associative Techniques with Applications to Information Science and Chemical Structure Investigation	61,470	24
Beth Elaine Allen*	University of Pennsylvania Alternative Representations of Information in Microeconomic Systems	77,987	24
Yale Braunstein	Brandeis University Economics of Market Structure in Scientific and Technical Information	156,523	24
Alphonse Chapanis and Gerald Weeks	Johns Hopkins University Human Requirements in Information Retrieval	195,841	24
Franklin Cooper	Haskins Laboratories Verification of Syllable Hypotheses in Automatic Phonetic Analysis of Spoken English	109,475	12
William Cooper	University of California, Berkeley Baysian Retrieval System Design	97,125	24
Susan E. Cozzens	Institute for Scientific Information User Requirements for Scientific Reviews	31,421	12
Anthony Debons	University of Pittsburgh A Survey of Manpower Requirements for Scientific and Technical Communication	147,314	12
Martha Evens*	Illinois Institute of Technology Structuring the Lexicon and the Thesaurus with Lexical-Semantic Relations	43,575	24

TABLE 1   NSF AWARDS FOR INFORMATION SCIENCE RESEARCH,
FY 1979 (cont.)

Investigator(s)/ Award No.	Institution/Title	Amount ($)	Duration (months)
John Flowers	University of Nebraska Human Attention and Performance Limitations in Processing Visual Information	34,672	18
Joyce Friedman	University of Michigan Computer Studies in Formal Linguistics	87,508	24
Marilyn Gell	National Commission on Libraries and Information Science Electronic Information Exchange in Planning for White House Conference on Library and Information Services	40,335	7
A. Gerstenfield and Richard H. Franke	Worcester Polytechnic Institute The Critical Review Process: Impact upon Scientific and Technological Information	147,255	24
Kenneth R. Hammond, Richard L. Cook, and Robert Taylor	University of Colorado Designing Information Systems for More Effective Use in Decision Making	105,531	12
Robert Hayes and Harold Borko	University of California, Los Angeles Mathematical Models of Information System Use	196,640	24
Thomas B. Hickey*	OCLC, Inc. Probabilistic Matching and Control of Author Names in Automated Library Systems	42,321	12
Aravind K. Joshi	University of Pennsylvania Computer Science and Computer Engineering Research Equipment	175,100	12
Allen Kent	University of Pittsburgh Economics of Information Transfer Using Resource Sharing Networks—Network Modeling Simulation	233,496	30
Jerry S. Kidd	University of Maryland Research on Behavioral Variables Related to Information Systems	163,011	18
Patrick W. Langley*	Carnegie-Mellon University An Information Processing Theory of Procedural Learning	53,715	24
Wendy G. Lehnert, Roger C. Schank, and Robert P. Abelson	Yale University Text Processing Effects and Memory Recall	291,988	24
James E. Loy	National Bureau of Standards Support of the Numerical Data Advisory Board	12,300	12
David Maier*	SUNY, Stony Brook Relational Theory of Databases	89,655	24

TABLE 1   NSF AWARDS FOR INFORMATION SCIENCE RESEARCH, FY 1979 (cont.)

Investigator(s)/ Award No.	Institution/Title	Amount ($)	Duration (months)
Jane H. McCarroll	Innovative Systems Research, Inc. Electronic Information Exchange in Research on Devices for the Disabled	20,275	12
Robert T. Niehoff	Battelle Columbus Laboratories Advanced Concepts and Studies of a Vocabulary Switching System	148,900	12
Charles D. Parsons and Isaac Levi	Columbia University Normal Sentence Forms and Information Structure	354,377	24
Judea Pearl	University of California, Los Angeles Investigating Computational Gains using Partial Information	68,751	30
Jane Perlmutter*	University of Texas, Austin Representation, Retrieval, and Reorganization of Conceptual Information	63,952	24
Joseph J. Pollock	American Chemical Society Automatic Spelling Error Detection and Correction for Large Data Bases	153,160	30
J. Francis Reintjes	Massachusetts Institute of Technology A Research Program on Electronic Document-Delivery Systems for Interlibrary Loans	83,725	12
Nancy K. Roderer and Robert R. V. Wiederkehr	King Research, Inc. Evaluation Measures and Methods for On-Line Bibliographic Systems	143,864	15
Gerard Salton	Cornell University Mathematical Modelling in Automatic Information Retrieval	145,040	24
Gerard Salton	Cornell University Fast Computational Processes in Information Retrieval	29,605	12
Vladimir Slamecka	Georgia Institute of Technology Syntactic Structure of Information and Information Processes	137,790	24
Pasquale Sullo and William A. Wallace	Rensselaer Polytechnic Institute A Reliability Theoretic Construct for Document Usage and Information Flow	72,800	12
Aaron Tenenbaum*	Brooklyn College Efficiency of Sequential Search Algorithms	38,378	12
Julius T. Tou	University of Florida Development of Theory and Techniques for Automated Knowledge Utilization, Transfer, and Extension	166,740	24
Yao-chung Tsao*	Rensselaer Polytechnic Institute Information Processing of Logographic and Alphabetic Writing Symbols	27,850	12

TABLE 1   NSF AWARDS FOR INFORMATION SCIENCE RESEARCH, FY 1979 (cont.)

Investigator(s)/ Award No.	Institution/Title	Amount ($)	Duration (month)
Bonnie L. Webber*	University of Pennsylvania Research in Natural Language Man-Machine Interaction	83,598	24
Judith A. Werdel	National Academy of Sciences International Scientific and Technical Information Programs	96,500	12
James L. Wood and Robert W. Fraze	Council of National Library Association ANSI Committee Z39	20,000	12
Marshall C. Yovits	Ohio State University Extension and Applications of a Theory of Information Flow and Analysis: The Use of Information in a Decision-Making Environment	105,670	24
Lotfi A. Zadeh	University of California, Berkeley A Theory of Approximate Reasoning	29,000	12
Pranas Zunde	Georgia Institute of Technology Study of Potential New Applications of Information Theory to Problems of Information Science	82,449	12

*Special Research Initiation Award.

NATIONAL HISTORICAL PUBLICATIONS AND RECORDS COMMISSION

General Services Administration
National Archives and Records Service
Washington, DC 20408
202-724-1616

In 1934, the Congress established the National Historical Publications Commission to make plans, estimates, and recommendations for the publication of important historical documents and to work with various public and private institutions in gathering, annotating, and publishing papers and records of national historical significance.

The commission was inactive until 1950 when, at the urging of President Truman, the Congress provided funds for a small professional staff. In 1964, the commission's publications program was strengthened by the enactment of PL 88-383, which allows the Administrator of General Services, upon recommendation of the commission, to make allocations to federal agencies and grants to state and local agencies as well as to nonprofit organizations and institutions for collecting, editing, and publishing significant historical documents.

On December 22, 1974, President Gerald R. Ford signed PL 93536, which changed the commission's name to the National Historical Publications and Records

Commission (NHPRC). With new funds—the annual authorization was increased from $2,000,000 to the present level of $4,000,000—the commission was to assist agencies and institutions in all states and territories in gathering, arranging, describing, and preserving significant papers and records.

The commission has also sponsored publication of the *Guide to Archives and Manuscripts in the United States* (1961), and has published a *Directory of Archives and Manuscript Repositories in the United States* (1978), the first publication from the commission's national automated data base on repositories and their holdings; the bibliographic volumes, *Writings on American History;* an important survey by Walter Rundell, Jr., *In Pursuit of American History: Research and Training in the United States;* and an analysis of historical editing, *The Publication of American Historical Manuscripts*, edited by Fred Shelley and Leslie Dunlap.

Representation on the commission is fixed by law to include a member of the federal judiciary, one member from each house of Congress, two presidential appointees, the Librarian of Congress or an alternate, the secretary of defense or an alternate, the secretary of state or an alternate, and two members each of the American Historical Association, the Organization of American Historians, the American Association for State and Local History, and the Society of American Archivists. The Archivist of the United States serves as chairperson.

The commission's grants for both the publications and records programs usually require the contribution of nonfederal funds in a matching or cost-sharing plan.

PUBLICATIONS PROGRAM

The commission has always been more than a grant-making agency. For 14 years before the start of its grant program in 1964, the commission made recommendations and undertook studies on the publication of documentary materials, worked with public and private organizations to inaugurate projects, and offered advice and assistance on documentary editing to the scholarly community. Its fellowship program and editing institutes provide training; its conferences and seminars of editors provide forums for debate and discussion.

At commission-sponsored conferences in Washington, D.C., in December 1978, and in New Orleans in April 1979, editors met to examine the use of microforms in the field of documentary preservation and publication and to discuss other mutual concerns. The commission's research staff continues to provide photocopies from the National Archives, the Library of Congress, and other institutions to editors of sponsored projects and to offer guidance and advice on a wide range of research questions.

In FY 1979, the commission recommended 84 publication grants, averaging $23,810 each, to institutions and organizations in 26 states and the District of Columbia. Many of these went to support continuing projects such as *The Adams Papers* ($86,500 grant to the Massachusetts Historical Society), *The Papers of Thomas Jefferson* ($99,152 to Princeton University), *The Papers of Booker T. Washington* ($26,347 to the University of Maryland), *The Papers of Samuel Gompers* ($51,400 to the University of Maryland and Pace University), and *The Papers of Jane Addams* ($29,500 to the University of Illinois at Chicago Circle).

Volumes from commission-sponsored projects that were published during the year include volume 1 of the *Frederick Douglass Papers* (Yale University Press), volume 12 of the *Papers of James Madison* (University Press of Virginia), volumes 27–31 of *The Papers of Woodrow Wilson* (Princeton University Press), and volume 26—the final volume—of *The Papers of Alexander Hamilton* (Columbia University

Press). Among microform publications completed during the year were *The Horatio Gates Papers* (20 reels, New-York Historical Society), *The Isabella Beecher Hooker Papers* (145 microfiche, Stowe-Day Foundation), and *The Frank B. Kellogg Papers* (54 reels, Minnesota Historical Society).

New publication grants included a two-year $16,753 grant to Eastern Michigan University for a book edition of the naval journals of Edward Baker, written (1848–1861) at the end of the age of sail; $33,470 to Indiana State University for a book and microform edition of the papers of the twentieth-century socialist leader and frequent presidential candidate Eugene V. Debs; and $5,339 to the University of Massachusetts for a study to determine the feasibility of publishing the papers of Elizabeth Cady Stanton and Susan B. Anthony, principal leaders of the woman suffrage movement.

RECORDS PROGRAM

The records grant program supports a variety of activities relating to preservation of historical records and their preparation for use by researchers. Survey and accessioning, appraisal, arrangement and description, preparation of guides and other finding aids, microfilming, and training are among the items that regularly appear in proposals to the commission. The records program does not at this time support projects relating to newspapers, rare books or published items (except where these are incidental parts of collections of historical records), or oral history interviewing or transcribing. Emphasis is on the information in records rather than on the artifact value of the items; thus microfilming or other means of copying fragile records is usually preferred to the much more expensive restoration of individual documents.

The commission strongly endorses standard archival techniques, especially in arrangement and description of historical records, and has supported several projects that foster the awareness of these techniques, including the Basic Manual Series of the Society of American Archivists and H. G. Jones, *Local Government Records: An Introduction to Their Management, Preservation and Use,* published in late 1979 by the American Association for State and Local History. Finally, the commission has supported several workshops on archival techniques and on conservation methods.

To carry out the historical records program, the commission relies heavily on the advice of State Historical Records Advisory Boards, made up of archivists, historical program administrators, and others interested in historical records within the state. These advisory boards, chaired by a historical records coordinator, develop priorities and preferred approaches and review records grant proposals from the states prior to commission consideration. The head of the state's archival program is usually the state coordinator; the director of the state-funded historical society, where one exists, is also a member of the board. Many advisory boards, which have been appointed in every state except Maine and Mississippi, have placed local needs, especially local government records programs, among their highest priorities. State records are also often a high priority.

Although the commission wishes to respond as effectively to the needs of small and local repositories as it does to large ones, it hopes that small repositories will consider forming cooperative projects when possible. Often a cooperative program involving several institutions with common problems can be cost-effective and can more readily justify the level of resources necessary to support a professional approach.

Suggestions for Applicants

The records program distributes an introductory pamphlet, detailed "Suggestions for Applicants" that should be read by all applicants, *Annotation* (a newsletter), lists of grant projects funded in the past, and special guidelines for microform projects. At present there are three records program application deadlines each year: February 1, June 1, and October 1.

Historical Records Grant Proposals Invited

This list describes types of projects that the commission wishes to particularly encourage because of the lack of applications in these areas of need.

Conservation. The development of national, regional, statewide, or intrastate conservation programs providing training, consulting, and other services for the conservation of historical records.

Appraisal. The development of guidelines for appraisal of the archival value of records, especially for the records of types of institutions that play a major continuing role in American life. The development of general schedules is particularly encouraged.

Institutional Models. The development of archival programs, especially those linked to ongoing records management programs, which may serve as models for similar institutions, particularly the following types: hospitals; religious bodies; local governments; social service, voluntary, trade, labor, business, professional, cultural, and nonprofit organizations. Projects that demonstrate substantial interest by national, regional, or other levels above the custodial level are strongly encouraged, so that the model programs may be endorsed and made known to members with similar needs.

Training. Workshops, manuals, consultation, and other approaches directed toward custodians of records of archival value who are not themselves archivists. This includes programs directed at upper-level administrators of organizations that create or hold records of archival value as well as those directly in charge of the records.

Repository Cooperation. Cooperative programs among repositories in a geographic area, special subject field, or in similar institutional settings. Such projects might be designed to share information; provide or obtain special training; develop state of the art methods; establish working agreements or more formal relationships; adopt cooperative acquisition policies; undertake joint surveys; or other cooperative approaches that are more effective than is possible by repositories acting individually.

Note: In these and in other types of projects supported by the records program, the NHPRC encourages increased involvement by national, regional, and state professional organizations, particularly archival groups. This may include direct administration of a project or indirect involvement through sponsorship, guidance, evaluation, or endorsement for a project administered by an institution or institutions working with the professional organization.

National Data Base for Archives and Manuscripts

In addition to its grants function, the records program administers the development of a national automated data base of information on historical records repositories and their holdings. The first publication of this program is a *Directory of Archives and Manuscript Repositories in the United States* (1978) listing basic information about the holdings of over 3,200 repositories. The *Directory* is arranged by state and city, and as special features includes separate lists of 18 types of repositories such as local historical societies, museums, religious institutions, corporate archives, and public libraries. The commission has also developed information standards, field and tag assignments, selection codes, and editorial and indexing formats that are being used by survey projects in several states using the SPINDEX program for archival description and the production of guides. These projects, sponsored by the commission, are identifying and describing repository holdings to the collection level or below. Information about its data base design and sponsored projects is available from the commission.

New Projects

In FY 1979 the commission recommended 85 records grants totaling $1,693,879 for projects in 34 states. The average grant was $19,928. Grants were made to colleges and universities (19), private historical societies, museums, and archives (21), state agencies (18), cities and counties (11), public and special libraries (6), and to nine other institutions. The commission received 180 requests totaling $5,679,328. Many projects received reduced outright grants or offers of reduced grants conditional upon increased nonfederal funding.

The following grants are representative of those recommended during FY 1979:

Grants to Cities and Counties

Baltimore Bureau of Records Management, Maryland: $24,624 to arrange and describe the records of the mayor and the city council of Baltimore from 1797 to 1971, and to identify conservation needs for these records.

City of Portland, Oregon: $64,377 for the second year of a program to develop a model municipal archives and records program. During the first year the project produced a comprehensive city records manual, accessioned and described many city records of archival value, and established an automated system for archives and records management.

Grants to State Agencies

California Historical Records Advisory Board, Sacramento: $73,396 in support of the board's historical records educational and consultant service to develop improved archival and manuscript programs throughout the state and to prepare detailed recommendations to meet future needs of the archival community in California.

Mississippi Department of Archives and History, Jackson: $30,932 for a project, in conjunction with the State Legislative Audit Committee, to survey and report on historical records in executive agencies, boards, and commissions, and to prepare recommendations for legislation and other action necessary to improve archival and records programs for the state government.

Washington State Historical Records Advisory Board, Olympia: $55,095 for preparation and publication of a guide to records and papers in Washington historical records repositories and, in computer output microfiche, to active public records in the state.

Grants to Colleges and Universities

St. Cloud State University, St. Cloud, MN: $3,600 for the development of an automated data base for its archival program.

Atlanta University, GA: $26,177 for the second and final year of a project to arrange and describe the archives of the Southern Regional Council. The records relate to economic and social developments in the South during the years 1944–1966.

Auburn University Archives, Auburn, AL: $10,050 to preserve and make available historically significant glass plate negatives from the J. F. Knox collection. The photos relate primarily to the history of Birmingham from 1890 to the 1940s. A previous small grant of $2,000 supported preservation of nitrate negatives in the Knox collection.

Grants to Private Historical Societies, Museums, and Archives

YIVO Institute, New York: $87,675 to survey, collect, and process the records of the Landsmanshaftn organizations in the New York City area. The Landsmanshaftn are mutual aid societies formed by Jewish immigrants and organized largely around the city or town (mostly European) of origin of the members.

United Negro College Fund, New York: $15,222 (matching) for arrangement and description of records of the United Negro College Fund and for planning for future programs to preserve and make available to research historical records in member colleges and universities.

Grants to Public and Special Libraries

Library Council of Metropolitan Milwaukee, Wisconsin: $29,067 for a historical records assistance and awareness project, a program whereby established Milwaukee area repositories assist other records custodians in the preservation and administration of historical records.

Dallas Public Library, Dallas: $13,934 (matching) to preserve and make accessible to researchers selected photographs in the library's Rogers and Hayes photo collections, which document the history of Dallas from 1917 to 1955.

YMCA Historical Library, New York: $2,000 for consultation in planning a comprehensive YMCA archival and records management program.

Other Records Project Grants

Archdiocese of Boston, MA: $24,620 (mostly matching) for the second year of a project to arrange and describe the archives of the archdiocese, to publish a guide to its holdings, and to refine policies and procedures for an ongoing archival program.

History of Science Society, Syracuse, NY: $5,280 for a study, report, and project proposals relating to problems in the documentation of science and technology in the United States. This is a cooperative project of the Society of American Archivists, the Society for the History of Technology, and the History of Science Society.

Massachusetts Committee for the Preservation of Architectural Records, Cambridge: $5,880 for a pilot project to survey architectural records in private hands and in architectural offices in the greater Boston area, and to lay the groundwork for additional surveying and accessioning.

PUBLICATIONS OF THE COMMISSION

Annotation (the commission's triannual newsletter).
Fact Sheet: The National Historical Publications and Records Commission and Its Work.
Publications Catalog, 1976.
Report to the President, 1978.
Publications Program Guidelines and Procedures: Applications and Grants.
National Historical Publications and Records Commission Subvention Program Guidelines.
Records Program Guidelines and Procedures: Applications and Grants.
Suggestions for Records Program Applicants.
The State Historical Records Coordinator and the State Historical Records Advisory Board: Suggested Roles and Procedures.
Microform Guidelines.
SPINDEX and Guide/Data Base: Introductory Materials.
Directory of Archives and Manuscript Repositories in the United States.
Annual Report.

Foundation and Other Grants

COUNCIL ON LIBRARY RESOURCES, INC.

One Dupont Circle, Suite 620, Washington, DC 20036
202-296-4757

Nancy E. Gwinn
Program Officer

The Council on Library Resources, Inc. (CLR), both funds and undertakes activities that hold promise of solving some of the generic problems of libraries and the interests of those they serve. Support for CLR operations and programs is provided by a number of foundations, including, for FY 1979, the following: the Carnegie Corporation of New York, the Commonwealth Fund, the Exxon Education Foundation, the Ford Foundation, the William and Flora Hewlett Foundation, the Lilly Endowment, Inc., the Andrew W. Mellon Foundation, the Rockefeller Foundation, the Alfred P. Sloan Foundation, and the National Endowment for the Humanities.

The council's special concern is with academic and research libraries because they are a fundamental component of the entire system. The content of their comprehensive collections, taken together, is an essential part of the foundation of our civilization. Their staffs of distinctively trained subject bibliographers, information specialists, and administrators contribute in significant ways to the work of scholars and the performance of libraries of all kinds.

To help identify problems that appear to be most pressing, the council periodically poses certain key questions. How can a national bibliographic structure be built so that anyone requiring information can identify and locate what is required with reasonable ease and at an acceptable cost? How can the management and internal operations of libraries be improved so that the library patron can make efficient use of collections and human resources? How can the nation's library collections be preserved as a national resource and yet be made widely available? What is needed in terms of professional education and training for academic and research librarians and library managers? What is the role of the academic library in higher education and how can that partnership be enhanced? What kinds of basic information and analysis do we need about library economics, library relationships to other components of the information community, library staffing and collections, etc., that will help libraries improve their performance in support of research and instruction?

While the answers to such questions may be uncertain, the simple process of asking them helps to identify problem categories needing attention. Certain of these topics become focal points of CLR program priorities. At present these include bibliographic services, library resources and their preservation, library operations and services, and professional education and training. In addressing these concerns, the council will support developmental and analytical work undertaken by a variety of institutions and individuals.

The following paragraphs discuss highlights of the council's program activity for the 1979 fiscal year (July 1, 1978 to June 30, 1979) in the context of the council's concerns. Warren J. Haas is president of the council, and Mary Agnes Thompson is CLR secretary and treasurer.

BIBLIOGRAPHIC SERVICES

The principal event of the year was the beginning, in November 1978, of CLR's Bibliographic Service Development Program (BSDP), under the guidance of CLR Program Officer C. Lee Jones. The program works toward the provision of effective bibliographic services that will meet existing and future needs of scholarship and research, toward the improvement of bibliographic products, and toward the purposeful control of costs of bibliographic processes in individual libraries. Seven private foundations and the National Endowment for the Humanities are supporting the CLR venture with funds exceeding $5 million. The project is scheduled to last at least five years.

In the first eight months of the program, CLR staff identified and began bringing together the parties likely to be most concerned with bibliographic services in order to determine the most fruitful areas for the application of resources. The BSDP management and program committees, composed of the chief executive officers of three major bibliographic networks and others with particular competence in bibliographic matters, have advised CLR staff to concentrate on the creation of a bibliographic records service. Issues for consideration will include data-base generation and control, communication between data bases, and promulgation of standards to facilitate information exchange. The BSDP planners are also turning their attention to the problems of individual libraries and their potential capacity to use the products of a nationwide bibliographic record service.

At the end of this report year, for example, a request for proposal had been prepared that will result in a detailed assessment of the consequences and requirements of various options associated with the linking of bibliographic networks. In particular, the study will focus on the impact of such linkages on three major library functions: cooperative cataloging, interlibrary loan, and on-line reference searching. It will consider the effects on libraries, library users, brokers of bibliographic services, and the bibliographic networks themselves.

In October 1979, CLR announced that Battelle-Columbus Laboratories, Inc., had been selected to carry out the work. Battelle will consult over 260 libraries of all types to gather data for the study. OCLC, Inc., the Research Libraries Group, the Washington Library Network, and the Library of Congress will also provide information. The study is expected to last six months.

The BSDP is particularly concerned with the lack of standards needed if bibliographic records are to be exchanged within a machine environment. Even the second edition of the *Anglo-American Cataloging Rules* (*AACR-2*), an important force for standardization, contains options on rules such as those governing choices of entry or entry style. If libraries and networks with machine-readable data bases and catalogs do not select the same options, they will have difficulty sharing data.

To ensure that the Library of Congress and the major bibliographic networks select the same options for implementation in 1981, the BSDP created a Joint Committee on Bibliographic Standards. Members of the committee include technical experts from the networks, as well as from research libraries, the Library of Congress, the National Library of Medicine, and CLR. The committee has reached a number of decisions on options and is currently awaiting final approval of the balance.

If the various present efforts to establish a system of national bibliographic control are successful, it may be possible for library users to have freely available access to records of nearly the entire publishing output of the nation. The records would have been generated in a variety of ways by a large number of agencies. Ideally, each record would have been prepared only once and then shared by all who need it.

If this concept of access, whether created through machine-readable or manual means, is carried forward by other countries, then each nation will have established bibliographic control over its own publications. If suitable standards are used in the generation of records, they can be exchanged among nations to the benefit of all societies involved. This concept is the basis of the program of the International Office for Universal Bibliographic Control (UBC), administered by the International Federation of Library Associations and Institutions. The council has supported this office, which is located within the British Library, since its establishment in 1974. One of its major activities is the promulgation, publication, and monitoring of use of the numerous International Standards Bibliographic Descriptions. Acceptance of the ISBDs as standards will ensure uniformity in bibliographic record and facilitate their exchange across national boundaries.

In the United States, the agency responsible for the voluntary development of standards relevant to information systems, products, and services as they relate to libraries, information services, and publishing is the American National Standards Committee Z39. CLR has supported the committee since 1961 and in FY 1979 awarded two successive one-year grants to assist the committee while it seeks other funds for its continuing program.

Although CLR is no longer responsible for the management of the CONSER (Conversion of Serials) project, the council still has an active interest in it, particularly as it relates to the overall goals of the BSDP. In September 1978, CLR awarded a grant to the National Library of Canada to enable the library to publish, in computer output microfiche (COM), bibliographic records contained in the CONSER file. The CONSER project is a cooperative file-building effort initiated five years ago to develop a national data base of serials records. Production of CONSER/COM allows libraries that are not members of OCLC, Inc., which manages the data base, to have access to all the authenticated records in the file. The Library of Congress will distribute CONSER microfiche, and eventually the entire CONSER file, in the United States.

LIBRARY OPERATIONS AND SERVICES

The central effort of the past year in this grant category is the Academic Library Program administered by the Office of Management Studies (OMS) in the Association of Research Libraries. CLR (drawing on funds from the Carnegie Corporation), the Andrew W. Mellon Foundation, the Lilly Endowment, and ARL itself have joined in support of the office. Recently, the National Endowment for the Humanities also provided a grant to OMS for work in the area of preservation.

CLR has funded OMS since 1970. The OMS has applied a kind of self-help methodology to library operations through such programs as the Management Review and Analysis Program, the Academic Library Development Program, and the Collection Analysis Project. The OMS is also preparing a Planning Program for Small Libraries and will shortly begin work on a services development program. Each program provides guidance to academic libraries in the form of manuals, procedures, and personal consultation to help the libraries examine themselves, analyze their operations, identify strengths and weaknesses, and outline areas and methods for change.

The five-year project will be advanced by the training of up to 100 librarians as consultants to assist libraries in conducting their self-investigations. During the year the first 20 librarians to receive the training were chosen from a field of over 250 applicants and participated in a two-week consultation skills workshop.

Of increasing importance to the library profession is the work of the International Federation of Library Associations and Institutions (IFLA). CLR has awarded a new grant, the fourth since 1971, to the IFLA secretariat to enable the organization to develop further its professional programs. IFLA has had consultative status with UNESCO for many years and provides an important international forum for the discussion of library problems.

IFLA's expansion of its professional activities began in 1976 following a restructuring of the association. The revised statutes created a professional organization composed of divisions by type of library, by library activity, and by region. Within the divisions are 35 sections and round tables that engage the energies of school, public, special, academic, and national librarians from 106 countries. The CLR grant supports the work of a deputy secretary-general who acts as secretary to a new professional board and coordinates the divisional and sectional programs.

LIBRARY RESOURCES AND THEIR PRESERVATION

Preservation has always been high on the list of CLR priorities, even though CLR has not been able to support preservation programs or collection development at individual libraries. In May 1979, CLR and the Andrew W. Mellon Foundation invited about 20 individuals with knowledge of paper manufacturing, publishing, and library book preservation programs to discuss book paper and its use and to identify ways to address propsective aspects of the collection preservation problem.

Examples of questions raised at the meeting were: Is book paper that meets reasonable specifications for permanence and durability readily available in sufficient variety and at acceptable cost? If appropriate paper is available, why is it not more generally or universally used for publication of books and journals? If it is not available, or if other obstacles exist, what action is required, and by whom?

At the conclusion of the discussion, those present formed a committee that will propose procedures for identifying preservation objectives and options for action, recommend ways to arrive at acceptable standards, and attempt to extend understanding and wider recognition of the preservation problem itself. CLR has set aside a small sum to support the activities of the committee.

Preservation is only one aspect of the library resource problem; collection building and assessment are also primary issues. Numerous questions require an analytic approach. Assessing the concept of "national collections," understanding better the relationship between proximity of materials and their use, and improving methods for assessing collection strength are only a few of the issues that must be addressed. Specific action to be taken in the future is not yet certain, but the past year has seen some progress. A small step was taken when a CLR grant was awarded to support a summer 1979 conference of book selection officers from academic libraries to discuss the problem of retrospective collection development.

Last year's report described the preparation by council staff of *A National Periodicals Center Technical Development Plan* (Washington, D.C.: Council on Library Resources, 1978). Such a center would contain a comprehensive periodical collection for national use. Although CLR's official role in this effort was concluded when the report was turned over to the Library of Congress, CLR staff received numerous requests to explain the intent of the plan to library users, scholars, publishers, the for-profit information sector, and librarians. Program staff therefore prepared a slide show illustrating the concept of an NPC. The show has been presented at meetings, workshops, and conferences from coast to coast.

Finally, the University of California, Berkeley, has published a compilation of statistical data on the holdings of 27 research libraries, including the Library of Congress. The report's preparation was supported by a CLR grant awarded in January 1978. Entitled "Titles Classified by the Library of Congress Classification: National Shelflist Count," the 64-page document represents the third phase in a study of the distribution of holdings among research libraries that was undertaken by the Chief Collection Development Officers of Large Research Libraries, an ALA-affiliated group. The project director believes that the project "provides the beginnings of a national program for the evaluation and coordination of research library collections."

PROFESSIONAL EDUCATION AND TRAINING

In his editorial in the November 1979 issue of the *Journal of Academic Librarianship*, Richard M. Dougherty muses on the suitability of current professional library education curricula for preparing students for jobs in large contemporary libraries. "How many schools prepare students to cope with the problems of collection development, preservation, computer management, or managing rare book and manuscript collections?" he queries. Even if, as he suspects, a few schools do offer organized instruction in each of these specialties, declining enrollments, with corresponding declines in the ranks of teaching faculty, will make it ever more difficult to sustain.

The council is also concerned with the quality of professional education and in particular how it relates to the staffing needs of large academic and research libraries. The council has been discussing these issues with a variety of individuals in the past year. Although a specific program has yet to be defined, the conviction persists that professional education is an area that deserves concentrated attention.

As in former years, the council's interest in professional development of individual working librarians has continued by awarding fellowships and internships. Rebecca D. Dixon and Susan K. Nutter were chosen as the Academic Library Management Interns for the 1979–1980 academic year. Dixon, director of the Library Services Division of the Center for the Study of Youth Development, has moved to Cambridge, Massachusetts, to intern with Jay K. Lucker, director of libraries at the Massachusetts Institute of Technology (MIT). Nutter, associate head of the Engineering Libraries at MIT, went to Chapel Hill, North Carolina, in September to begin her internship with James F. Govan, director of the University of North Carolina Libraries.

Following a review of the program, CLR announced that the period of internship would be reduced to ten months for the 1980–1981 academic year. Council advisers agreed that the shortened period would not significantly dilute the experience and would free funds for additional internships. Following an expanded publicity campaign for the program, the council received 102 applications for the 1980–1981 academic year by its October deadline. Up to five interns will be chosen for the seventh year of the program.

Like its predecessor above, the Health Sciences Library Management Intern Program is designed to increase the number of librarians who, in addition to having the intellect, personality, and character required for director-level positions, also have a firm grounding in management processes and techniques. The program is funded by the National Library of Medicine and administered by the council.

Three women emerged successfully from a field of 19 applicants for the 1979–1980 academic year. June E. Bandemer, assistant director of the Falk Library of the Health Professions, University of Pittsburgh, is interning with C. K. Huang, director of the Health Sciences Library, State University of New York at Buffalo. Eleanor Goodchild, director of library services at the Los Angeles County Harbor General Hospital, has moved to Texas to work with Richard A. Lyders, executive director of the Houston Academy of Medicine, Texas Medical Center Library. Leonoor S. Ingraham, coordinator of collection development and head of public services at the Health Sciences Library, University of Oregon, is interning with Gerald S. Oppenheimer, director of the University of Washington Health Sciences Library.

The oldest of the council's professional development programs, the CLR Fellowship Program, was suspended following the selection of ten fellows for the 1979-1980 academic year. However, the council continues to entertain research proposals from individuals and two such grants were awarded in the past year. Robert B. Downs, dean of library administration emeritus, University of Illinois, will prepare a second edition of his *British Library Resources* with the aid of a small CLR grant. Wayne A. Wiegand, assistant professor in the College of Library Science, University of Kentucky, will edit a series of essays to be entitled "Leaders in American Academic Librarianship, 1925-1975." Some of the 12 to 15 essays will be published in the *Journal of Academic Librarianship* prior to their collective appearance as a monograph.

The recipients of the final round of fellowship awards, for academic year 1979-1980, and their projects follow:

Judith S. Braunagel, assistant professor, SUNY at Buffalo Library School, and *Rao Aluri*, research assistant, OCLC, Inc. To compile a guide to U.S. government scientific and technical information sources.

Boyd Childress, periodicals librarian, Western Kentucky University. To study the history and development of the libraries of the eight state universities in the South from 1860 to 1880 in order to determine their relationship to their parent institutions.

Sheila D. Creth, assistant director, University of Connecticut Library. To investigate current approaches and methodologies in the area of manpower planning and job analysis as reflected in selected academic libraries and private industry.

George S Grossman, director of the Law Library, University of Minnesota. To study the historical development of legal literature and legal research tools in England.

William E. Hannaford, Jr., acquisitions librarian, Middlebury College. To study collection development in ten small college libraries.

Mary E. Pensyl, head, NASIC Search Service, Massachusetts Institute of Technology. To study the impact of user demands on the reference departments of academic and research libraries that have offered online bibliographic services for several years.

Anne B. Piternick, professor, School of Librarianship, University of British Columbia. To investigate sources of support for bibliographic activities in the United States with emphasis on public and private funding and the economics of publishing.

Patricia Ann Polansky, Russian bibliographer, University of Hawaii. To work for three months at the Scott Polar Research Institute Library in Cambridge, England, and to attend the fourteenth Pacific Science Congress.

Suzanne Striedieck, chief, Serials Department, Pennsylvania State University. To study the effectiveness of technical services operations from the point of view of general reference librarians.

In FY 1979, 20 new grants and appropriations were approved for a total of $500,808.

NEW GRANTS AND AUTHORIZATIONS, 1978-1979

Council-Administered Projects
Academic Library Management Intern Program $ 58,234
Bibliographic Service Development Program
  Preparation of request for proposal on analyzing the linking of
    bibliographic utilities 6,434
  Position paper on standards 2,500
  Travel grant for U.S. representative at meeting in Copenhagen on
    international authority system 1,105
  Partial support for U.S. representative at ISBD(AN) meeting in Sweden 579
Fellowship Program 24,437
Health Sciences Library Management Intern Program
  1978-1979 83,751
  1979-1980 86,730
Council of National Library and Information Associations, Inc.
  Continued support of American National Standards Institute Committee Z39
    Through September 1979 20,000
    Through September 1980 30,000
Robert B. Downs
  Preparation of second edition of *British Library Resources* 3,000
International Federation of Library Associations and Institutions
  Professional activities of the secretariat through February 1981 75,000
Library of Congress
  Meeting on MARC format for *AACR-2* 805
National Endowment for the Humanities
  Continuation of College Library Program 41,058
National Library of Canada
  Production of CONSER/COM 23,000
OCLC, Inc.
  Development of non-Roman alphabet capability for library processes 15,000
Carl M. Spaulding
  Travel grant to chair meetings of new standards group 2,000
State University of New York at Binghamton
  Meeting on retrospective collection development 2,675
University of California, Los Angeles
  Preparation of third edition of *Handbook of Data Processing for Libraries* 14,500
University of Kentucky, Lexington
  Preparation of "Leaders in American Academic Librarianship, 1925-75" 10,000
    Total $500,808

ONGOING GRANTS, 1978-1979

American Association of Law Libraries
  Survey of U.S. and Canadian law library resources ($20,000—1968)
American Library Association
  Ethnic and sexual composition/salary survey for librarians ($13,856—1977)
  Secretariat for the U.S. National Committee for the UNESCO General Information
    Program (USNC/UNESCO-PGI) ($2,500—1978)

Association of Research Libraries
  Academic Library Program ($326,500—1978)
  Office of Management Studies ($81,136—1974; $210,000—1975)
Earlham College
  Periodical list for CHOICE ($7,500—1975)
International Federation of Library Associations and Institutions
  International Office for Universal Bibliographic Control ($70,000—1974; $144,200—1975; $150,000—1977)
Iowa State University
  Mechanized indexing procedures applied to production of subject-enhanced keyword index ($1,926—1977)
Library of Congress
  Use of the ISSN by the U.S. Postal Service ($14,231—1978)
MIDLNET
  Toward salary of a technical adviser ($22,778—1977)
National Association of State University and Land Grant Colleges,
Office for Advancement of Public Negro Colleges
  Status report on libraries of black public colleges ($4,000—1978)
New York Public Library, on behalf of the National Citizens Emergency Committee to Save Our Public Libraries
  Research on future role of public libraries in preparation for White House Conference on Libraries and Information Services ($15,000—1978)
Princeton University
  Microform service development program ($10,000—1976)
Stockton State College
  Innovative use of Books for College Libraries II ($5,150—1977)
University of California, Berkeley
  National shelflist measurement project ($20,000—1978)
University of Connecticut
  New England Academic Librarians' Writing Seminar ($20,610—1976)
University of North Carolina, Chapel Hill
  Administration of ANSI Committee Z39 through June 1978 ($23,719—1976)

CLR PUBLICATIONS AVAILABLE FREE UPON REQUEST

23rd Annual Report (Washington, D.C., 1979).
CLR Recent Developments (Washington, D.C., 1973-   ).
CLR Program Guidelines (brochure).

THE FOUNDATION CENTER AS A RESOURCE

888 Seventh Ave., New York, NY 10019
212-975-1120

The Foundation Center is the only independent nonprofit organization in the United States that gathers and disseminates factual information on philanthropic foundations and the grants they make. Two equally important concerns of the center have been to compile reliable descriptive data and statistics on the field of foundations for trustees and officers of foundations to use and to be a useful resource for the grant-seeking public.

At the center's headquarters in New York City, staff members gather information from government reports, foundation reports, and other sources for the center's computerized data banks. Computer storage of data makes it possible to retrieve quickly foundation facts and studies. The center offers comprehensive, current information through its printed and microfiche publications, its reference library collections, and the special services of the Associates Program. The Associates Program provides assistance to organizations or individuals that need constant access to foundation information. For an annual fee, associates gain access to mail and telephone reference service, photocopying, computer searching, and library research assistance.

The center operates its headquarters in New York, with field offices in Washington, D.C., Cleveland, and San Francisco. The center has also established a network of cooperating collections in public, academic, and foundation libraries in all 50 states, Mexico, Puerto Rico, and the Virgin Islands. The libraries are free and are open for the public to use.

REFERENCE COLLECTIONS

California

The Foundation Center, 312 Sutter St., San Francisco 94108. 415-397-0902.

District of Columbia

The Foundation Center, 1001 Connecticut Ave. N.W., Washington 20036. 202-331-1400.

New York

The Foundation Center, 888 Seventh Ave., New York 10019. 212-975-1120.

Ohio

The Foundation Center, Kent H. Smith Lib., 739 National City Bank Bldg., Cleveland 44114. 216-861-1933.

COOPERATING COLLECTIONS

Alabama

Birmingham Public Lib., 2020 Park Place, Birmingham 35203. 205-254-2541.

Auburn Univ. at Montgomery Lib., Montgomery 36117. 205-279-9110.

Alaska

Univ. of Alaska, Anchorage Lib., 3211 Providence Dr., Anchorage 99504. 907-263-1848.

Arizona

Tucson Public Lib., Main Lib., 200 S. Sixth Ave., Tucson 85701. 602-791-4393.

Arkansas

Westark Community College Lib., Grand Ave. at Waldron Rd., Fort Smith 72913. 501-785-4241.

Little Rock Public Lib., Reference Dept., 700 Louisiana St., Little Rock 72201. 501-374-7546.

California

Edward L. Doheny Memorial Lib., Univ. of Southern California, Los Angeles 90007. 213-741-2540.

San Diego Public Lib., 820 E. St., San Diego 92101. 714-236-5816.

Colorado

Denver Public Lib., Sociology Div., 1357 Broadway, Denver 80203. 303-573-5152.

Connecticut

Hartford Public Lib., Reference Dept., 500 Main St., Hartford 06103. 203-525-9121.

Delaware

Hugh Morris Lib., Univ. of Delaware, Newark 19711. 302-738-2965.

Florida

Jacksonville Public Lib., Business, Science, and Industry Dept., 122 N. Ocean St., Jacksonville 32202. 904-633-3926.

Miami-Dade Public Lib., Florida Collection, One Biscayne Blvd., Miami 33132. 305-579-5001.

Georgia

Atlanta Public Lib., 10 Pryor St. S.W., Atlanta 30303. 404-688-4636.

Hawaii

Thomas Hale Hamilton Lib., Univ. of Hawaii, Humanities and Social Sciences Div., 2550 The Mall, Honolulu 96822. 808-948-8568.

Idaho

Caldwell Public Lib., 1010 Dearborn St., Caldwell 83605. 208-459-3242.

Illinois

Donors Forum of Chicago, 208 S. La Salle St., Chicago 60604. 312-726-4882.

Sangamon State Univ. Lib., Shepherd Rd., Springfield 62708. 217-786-6633.

Indiana

Indianapolis-Marion County Public Lib., 40 E. St. Clair St., Indianapolis 46204. 317-635-5662.

Iowa

Des Moines Public Lib., 100 Locust St., Des Moines 50309. 515-283-4259.

Kansas

Topeka Public Lib., Adult Services Dept., 1515 W. Tenth St., Topeka 66604. 913-233-2040.

Kentucky

Louisville Free Public Lib., Fourth and York Sts., Louisville 40203. 502-584-4154.

Louisiana

East Baton Rouge Parish Lib., Centroplex Lib., 120 St. Louis St., Baton Rouge 70802. 504-344-5291.

New Orleans Public Lib., Business and Science Div., 219 Loyola Ave., New Orleans 70140. 504-586-4919.

Maine

Univ. of Southern Maine, Center for Research and Advanced Study, 246 Deering Ave., Portland 04102. 207-780-4411.

Maryland

Enoch Pratt Free Lib., Social Science and History Dept., 400 Cathedral St., Baltimore 21201. 301-396-5320.

Massachusetts

Associated Foundation of Greater Boston, 294 Washington St., Suite 501, Boston 02108. 617-426-2608.

Boston Public Lib., Copley Sq., Boston 02117. 617-536-5400.

Michigan

Alpena County Lib., 211 N. First Ave., Alpena 49707. 517-356-6188.

Henry Ford Centennial Lib., 16301 Michigan Ave., Dearborn 48126. 313-271-1000.

Purdy Lib., Wayne State Univ., Detroit 48202. 313-577-4040.

Michigan State Univ. Libs., Reference Lib., East Lansing 48824. 517-353-8816.

University of Michigan-Flint, UM-F Lib., Reference Dept., Flint 48503. 313-762-3408.

Grand Rapids Public Lib., Sociology and Education Dept., Library Plaza, Grand Rapids 49502. 616-456-4411.

Michigan Technological Univ. Lib., Hwy. U.S. 41, Houghton 49931. 906-487-2507.

Minnesota

Minneapolis Public Lib., Sociology Dept., 300 Nicollet Mall, Minneapolis 55401. 612-372-6555.

Mississippi

Jackson Metropolitan Lib., 301 N. State St., Jackson 39201. 601-944-1120.

Missouri

Clearinghouse for Midcontinent Foundations, Univ. of Missouri, Kansas City, School of Education Bldg., 52 St. and Holmes, Kansas City 64110. 816-276-1176.

Kansas City Public Lib., 311 E. 12 St., Kansas City 64106. 816-221-2685.

Metropolitan Assn. for Philanthropy, Inc., 5600 Oakland, G-324, St. Louis 63110. 314-647-2290.

Springfield-Greene County Lib., 397 E. Central St., Springfield 65801. 417-869-4621.

Montana

Eastern Montana College Lib., Reference Dept., Billings 59101. 406-657-2320.

Nebraska

W. Dale Clark Lib., Social Sciences Dept., 215 S. 15 St., Omaha 68102. 402-444-4822.

Nevada

Clark County Lib., 1401 E. Flamingo Rd., Las Vegas 89109. 702-733-7810.

Washoe County Lib., 301 S. Center St., Reno 89505. 702-785-4190.

New Hampshire

New Hampshire Charitable Fund, One South St., Box 1335, Concord 03301. 603-225-6641.

New Jersey

New Jersey State Lib., Governmental Reference, 185 W. State St., Box 1898, Trenton 08625. 609-292-6220.

New Mexico

New Mexico State Lib., 300 Don Gaspar St., Santa Fe 87501. 505-827-2033.

New York

New York State Lib., Cultural Education Center, Humanities Sec., Empire State Plaza, Albany 12230. 518-474-7645.

Buffalo and Erie County Public Lib., Lafayette Sq., Buffalo 14203. 716-856-7525.

Levittown Public Lib., Reference Dept., One Bluegrass La., Levittown 11756. 516-731-5728.

Plattsburgh Public Lib., Reference Dept., 15 Oak St., Plattsburgh 12901. 518-563-0921.

Rochester Public Lib., Business and Social Sciences Div., 115 South Ave., Rochester 14604. 716-428-7328.

Onondaga County Public Lib., 335 Montgomery St., Syracuse 13202. 315-473-4491.

North Carolina

North Carolina State Lib., 109 E. Jones St., Raleigh 27611. 919-733-3270.

Winston-Salem Foundation, 229 First Union National Bank Bldg., Winston-Salem 27101. 919-725-2382.

North Dakota

Lib., North Dakota State Univ., Fargo 58105. 701-237-8876.

Ohio

Public Lib. of Cincinnati and Hamilton County, Education Dept., 800 Vine St., Cincinnati 45202. 513-369-6940.

Oklahoma

Oklahoma City Community Foundation, 1300 N. Broadway, Oklahoma City 73103. 405-235-5621.

Tulsa City-County Lib. System, 400 Civic Center, Tulsa 74103. 918-581-5144.

Oregon

Lib. Assn. of Portland, Education and Documents Rm., 801 S.W. Tenth Ave., Portland 97205. 503-223-7201.

Pennsylvania

Free Lib. of Philadelphia, Logan Sq., Philadelphia 19103. 215-686-5423.

Hillman Lib., Univ. of Pittsburgh, Pittsburgh 15260. 412-624-4528.

Rhode Island

Providence Public Lib., Reference Dept., 150 Empire St., Providence 02903. 401-521-7722.

South Carolina

South Carolina State Lib., Reader Services Dept., 1500 Senate St., Columbia 29211. 803-758-3181.

South Dakota

South Dakota State Lib., State Library Bldg., 322 S. Fort St., Pierre 57501. 605-773-3131.

Tennessee

Memphis Public Lib., 1850 Peabody Ave., Memphis 38104. 901-528-2957.

Texas

Hogg Foundation for Mental Health, Univ. of Texas, Austin 78712. 512-471-5041.

Dallas Public Lib., History and Social Sciences Div., 1954 Commerce St., Dallas 75201. 214-748-9071.

El Paso Community Foundation, El Paso National Bank Bldg., Suite 1616, El Paso 79901. 915-533-4020.

Houston Public Lib., Bibliographic and Info. Center, 500 McKinney Ave., Houston 77002. 713-224-5441, ext. 265.

Funding Info. Lib., Minnie Stevens Piper Foundation, 201 N. St. Mary's St., Suite 100, San Antonio 78205. 512-227-8119.

Utah

Salt Lake City Public Lib., Info. and Adult Services, 209 E. Fifth St., Salt Lake City 84111. 801-363-5733.

Vermont

State of Vermont Dept. of Libs., Reference Services Unit, 111 State St., Montpelier 05602. 802-828-3261.

Virginia

Richmond Public Lib., Business, Science, and Technology Dept., 101 E. Franklin St., Richmond 23219. 804-780-8223.

Washington

Seattle Public Lib., 1000 Fourth Ave., Seattle 98104. 206-625-4881.

Spokane Public Lib., Reference Dept., W. 906 Main Ave., Spokane 99201. 509-838-3361.

West Virginia

Kanawha County Public Lib., 123 Capitol St., Charleston 25301. 304-343-4646.

Wisconsin

Marquette Univ. Memorial Lib., 1415 W. Wisconsin Ave., Milwaukee 53233. 414-224-1515.

Wyoming

Laramie County Community College Lib., 1400 E. College Dr., Cheyenne 82001. 307-634-5853.

Puerto Rico

Consumer Education and Service Center, Dept. of Consumer Affairs, Minillas Central Government Bldg. N., Santurce 00908.

Virgin Islands

College of the Virgin Islands Lib., St. Thomas, U.S. Virgin Islands 00801. 809-774-1252.

Mexico

Biblioteca Benjamin Franklin, Londres 16, Mexico City 6, D.F.

FOUNDATION CENTER PUBLICATIONS

The Foundation Directory, Edition 7, Marianna O. Lewis, ed. 1979. 594 pp. The standard reference guide to the field. *Edition 7* covers 3,138 foundations. The foundation included must have assets of more than $1 million or award grants in excess of $100,000 annually. $40. Available from Columbia University Press, 136 S. Broadway, Irvington, N.Y. 10533.

Foundation Center Source Book Profiles, Sherry Goldstein, ed. Annual looseleaf subscription provides analytical profiles of the 1,000 largest grant-making U.S. foundations. Subscribers receive about 85 totally new foundation profiles every other month. In each subscription year, subscribers receive new profiles for 500 foundations. Information included provides breakdowns of foundation giving, background on grant-making patterns, board of trustees, publications, and grant procedures. $200 annual subscription. Order from The Foundation Center.

The Foundation Grants Index, Lee Noe, ed. Bimonthly listing included as a section of *Foundation News*. The annual volume provides a detailed listing of over 15,000 grants of $5,000 or more reported by nearly 500 major foundations. Annual. $20 plus $1 postage and handling. Order from Columbia University Press, 136 S. Broadway, Irvington, N.Y. 10533.

COMSEARCH Printouts. Computer printouts in 59 subject areas listing grants of $5,000 and more awarded to nonprofit organizations by about 500 major foundations. Request complete list of available subjects from The Foundation Center. Available as microfiche, $3 per subject prepaid; and in a paper printout, $11 per subject prepaid. Order from The Foundation Center.

Foundation Grants to Individuals, Edition 2. 1979. 236 pp. Profiles the programs of 1,000 foundations that make grants to individuals, with application information. Arranged by broad program areas, with detailed subject index. $15 prepaid. Order from The Foundation Center.

The Foundation Center National Data Book, Edition 4. 1979. The only directory that includes information on the more than 21,000 private foundations that are currently active grant makers. Volume 1 is arranged alphabetically by state and within each state in descending order of annual grant amounts. Volume 2, the index, provides alphabetical access to the foundations included in the *Data Book*. 2 vols. $45 prepaid. Order from The Foundation Center.

Free materials available on request: *What Makes a Good Proposal?* F. Lee Jacquette and Barbara L. Jacquette. *What Will a Foundation Look for When You Submit a Grant Proposal?* Robert A. Mayer. *How to Find the Information You Need on an Aperture Card—A Guide to IRS Information Returns on Film. Foundation Center Libraries Description of Resources Available.*

Bibliographies include *A Basic Guide to Information on Foundations and Other Nonprofit Funding Sources; Grants to Individuals; Scholarships, Fellowships and Loans to Individuals; Proposal Writing;* and *Area Foundation Directories.*

ANALYSIS OF FOUNDATION GRANTS TO LIBRARIES, 1979

Robin M. Klor

Librarian, The Foundation Center

Janis Witkins

Retrieval Specialist, The Foundation Center

In 1979, private foundations reported to The Foundation Center nearly $37 million in grants for library services. These grants to libraries included support for a wide variety of projects undertaken by many different types of libraries in 39 states and 9 foreign countries. Total reported foundation support to libraries increased $13 million in 1979, although the number of grants actually decreased from 564 in 1978 to 403 in 1979. The large number of grants reported in 1978 was due to a major effort by the W. K. Kellogg Foundation of Michigan in support of individual library participation in a computerized national library network.

FOUNDATION CENTER DATA BASES

The analysis of private foundation grants to libraries that follows is based on entries to The Foundation Center's Grants Index Data Base in 1979. This data base supplies information on foundation grants of $5,000 or more in many subject areas. About 400 foundations are included and most of these are the larger foundations in the United States. The Foundation Grants Index Data Base generates the bimonthly installments of the Foundation Grants Index that are published in the magazine *Foundation News*. There is also an annual cumulation in *The Foundation Grants Index*. In both of these publications, a key word and phrase index is provided that allows the grants researcher easy access to the program interests of each foundation listed. The Foundation Center also publishes *COMSEARCH Printouts*. These are computer printouts in 59 subject areas that provide the researcher aid in determining which foundations have made grants in their area of interest. There is a printout available on Libraries and Information Services. The Foundation Grants Index Data Base is also available through the Lockheed/DIALOG Information Retrieval Service, and copies of all printed indexes from this data base are available at The Foundation Center's regional collections. (A list of the regional collections is included in the preceding article, "The Foundation Center as a Resource.")

The reporting of grants to The Foundation Center by foundations is done on a voluntary basis. The 400 to 500 foundations included in the Index (out of a universe of 21,500 active grant-making foundations in the United States) generally represent the largest private foundations in the nation.

The Foundation Grants Index is a basic tool in researching foundations and the grants that they make. In conducting a thorough search for sources of funding, the researcher should also examine the smaller foundations, which generally provide support projects on a local level.

The Foundation Center's *National Data Book* is a useful reference work in helping to identify the smaller foundations in a particular area, by city or by zip code. There

TABLE 1   LIBRARY GRANTS BY TYPE OF LIBRARY

Type of Library	Amount	Percent	Number of Grants
Academic	$20,532,012	56	189
Special	8,385,191	23	79
Library networks and associations	3,410,387	9	13
Public	2,424,764	7	74
Other (nonprofit organizations, etc.)	847,967	2	16
Government agencies	440,208	1	9
School	422,327	1	20
Library of Congress	38,448	less than 1	3
Total	$36,501,304	100	403

are also many state directories of foundations, published by a variety of sources, that provide information on the program interests of foundations in their state. Not all states have directories, and those that do vary in content and quality. The Foundation Center will provide a bibliography of area directories upon request.

COMPUTER ANALYSIS OF 1979 GRANTS TO LIBRARIES*

In 1979, The Foundation Center data bases included information on grants made by 398 foundations, which reported 19,487 grants amounting to $1,088,714,024. Of this total, 150 foundations reported making grants to 403 libraries and information centers for a total of $36,501,304 (Tables 1 and 2).

In reviewing the trends in foundation grants to libraries, it becomes clear that the same patterns that apply to foundation funding in general also apply in part to the grants that foundations make to libraries. For example, academic institutions are a leading recipient of foundation grants, and this tendency is again viewed in foundation grants to libraries, where academic libraries were the recipients of 56 percent of the total giving.

The average grant size increased in the past year. Grants in the $100,000 and $499,999 range accounted for 40 percent of the total giving. This was followed by grants made in the $500,000 to $999,999 range (25 percent). In the past, grants had traditionally been small and numerous.

Foundation grants were awarded for a wide range of projects aiding libraries and information centers. The Helene Fuld Health Trust of New York made the largest number of grants (25) for the acquisition of library-related materials in nursing schools and hospitals. The foundation granted $585,777 for the purchase of library books, audiovisual hardware and software, and library furniture. The foundation states: "A major project has been, and continues to be, the furnishing of funds for the acquisition of the grantee schools of various types of audio-visual hardware and software and the formulation of an educational closed circuit television network."

The type of support that received the largest share of the grant dollar was for buildings and equipment. These grants were received by all types of libraries and were used for a wide range of projects, from major library building programs to minor library renovation projects (Table 3).

In 1979, foundations supported library projects in 39 states, with New York leading the recipients (Tables 4, 5, and 6). A large amount of the over $7 million received

---

*For the purpose of this analysis, foundation grants to library information services and learning resource centers have been included.

TABLE 2 LIBRARY GRANTS PROFILE

Range	Amount	Percent	Number of Grants
$5,000–$49,000	$ 4,247,683	11	262
$50,000–$99,999	2,895,818	8	49
$100,000–$499,999	14,643,449	40	73
$500,000–$999,999	9,016,666	25	16
$1 million or over	5,697,688	16	3
Total	$36,501,304	100	403

by libraries in New York was awarded to the New York Public Library, which received $1,080,246 from 24 different foundations. The New York Public Library is perennially a leading library recipient, although foundation grants received by the library in 1979 were considerably less than in years past.

The largest gift to a library in 1979 was a $3,207,688 grant by the Heineman Foundation for Research, Educational, Charitable and Scientific Purposes. This was a grant made to the Pierpont Morgan Library of New York for the acquisition of rare books, manuscripts, letters, and autographs. The amount of the grant represents the value of the material that was actually given.

Other large grants in 1979 included a grant made by the Andrew W. Mellon Foundation for $1 million to the Research Libraries Group to help meet the operation and development costs of the Research Libraries Information Network. This is a national information and technical services network primarily for the use of research libraries. The Andrew W. Mellon Foundation also made five other grants related to the Research Libraries Information Network. The Kresge Foundation made grants of $750,000 (for a second and final payment of a $1,500,000 grant) and $750,000 (for the first installment of an intended $1,500,000 grant) to the University of Michigan (Ann Arbor). These grants were toward the construction of the law school library.

Not all grants recorded were for such large amounts of money, and the purposes of grants varied widely, including support for special collections, expansion and renovation, and, to a lesser extent, the continuation of existing services threatened by cutbacks of public funds.

TABLE 3 LIBRARY GRANTS BY GRANT PURPOSE

Purpose	Amount	Percent	Number of Grants
Buildings and equipment	$ 9,529,629	26	51
General support	8,123,886	22	131
Acquisitions and materials	6,133,502	17	79
Renovation and expansion	6,587,376	18	57
Special projects	2,626,646	7	46
Computer-related projects	2,299,563	6	12
Endowment	415,000	1	4
Publications and research	412,635	1	12
Evaluations and studies	318,419	less than 1	6
Other	33,148	less than 1	2
Fellowships and scholarships	16,500	less than 1	2
Conferences	5,000	less than 1	1
Total	$36,501,304	100	403

TABLE 4 FOUNDATION FUNDING OF LIBRARIES BY STATE

	Amount Given		Amount Received	
State	Dollars	No.	Dollars	No.
Alabama	—	—	—	—
Alaska	—	—	—	—
Arizona	—	—	$ 55,000	2
Arkansas	—	—	—	—
California	$ 3,666,468	33	6,394,635	46
Colorado	10,000	2	49,026	3
Connecticut	1,159,164	7	2,547,980	10
Delaware	—	—	—	—
District of Columbia	690,906	19	2,748,406	23
Florida	442,682	10	499,682	10
Georgia	350,000	2	967,778	12
Hawaii	—	—	—	—
Idaho	—	—	30,000	1
Illinois	468,560	12	998,571	17
Indiana	911,221	6	554,000	3
Iowa	—	—	34,000	2
Kansas	—	—	95,434	3
Kentucky	—	—	53,800	3
Louisiana	—	—	—	—
Maine	—	—	83,000	1
Maryland	—	—	25,000	1
Massachusetts	75,000	1	2,317,445	20
Michigan	7,217,846	42	2,872,798	21
Minnesota	248,000	8	150,000	5
Mississippi	—	—	—	—
Missouri	5,000	1	15,000	1
Montana	—	—	—	—
Nebraska	—	—	50,882	1
Nevada	430,000	2	390,000	1
New Hampshire	—	—	10,000	1
New Jersey	126,000	7	187,000	7
New Mexico	—	—	15,000	1
New York	13,562,165	158	7,731,207	79
North Carolina	—	—	533,090	10
North Dakota	—	—	—	—
Ohio	85,000	4	200,000	8
Oklahoma	1,061,400	3	500,000	1
Oregon	—	—	—	—
Pennsylvania	3,440,073	48	2,082,204	44
Rhode Island	5,000	1	30,000	3
South Carolina	—	—	—	—
South Dakota	—	—	30,000	2
Tennessee	—	—	15,000	2
Texas	2,434,319	32	2,874,319	30
Utah	—	—	49,731	2
Vermont	—	—	100,000	1
Virginia	—	—	373,500	8
Washington	30,000	2	350,316	4
West Virginia	—	—	10,000	2
Wisconsin	82,500	3	7,500	1
Wyoming	—	—	—	—
Total	$36,501,304	403	$36,031,304	392

TABLE 5   LEADING LIBRARY RECIPIENTS OF FOUNDATION GRANTS

Institution	Grant Amount	Number of Grants
New York Public Library		
Astor (Vincent) Foundation	$ 10,000	1
Booth Ferris Foundation	100,000	1
Calder (Louis) Foundation	25,000	1
Carnegie Corporation of New York	15,000	1
Clark (Edna McConnell) Foundation	30,000	1
Commonwealth Fund	400,000	1
Corning Glass Works Foundation	26,500	1
Culpeper (Charles E.) Foundation	40,880	1
Davis (Arthur Vining) Foundation	50,000	1
Dodge (Cleveland H.) Foundation	5,000	1
Fairchild (Sherman) Foundation	50,000	1
General Motors Foundation	5,000	1
Irving One Wall Street Foundation	14,000	2
Manufacturers Hanover Foundation	43,500	2
Merck Company Foundation	5,000	1
Mobil Foundation	57,500	1
New York Times Company Foundation	22,866	1
Rubinstein (Helena) Foundation	15,000	1
S & H Foundation	20,000	1
Scherman Foundation	75,000	1
Shell Companies Foundation	5,000	1
Shubert Foundation	10,000	1
United States Steel Foundation	5,000	1
Weatherhead Foundation	50,000	1
Subtotal	$1,080,246	26
Pierpont Morgan Library		
Cary (Mary Flagler) Charitable Trust	$ 50,000	1
Heineman Foundation for Research, Educational, Charitable and Scientific Purposes	3,207,688	2
Kresge Foundation	150,000	1
Kress (Samuel H.) Foundation	50,000	1
Teagle Foundation	10,000	1
United States Steel Foundation	25,000	1
Subtotal	$3,492,688	7
University of Michigan		
Aeroquip Foundation	$ 5,000	1
Benedum (Claude Worthington) Foundation	250,000	1
Kellogg, (W. K.) Foundation	500,000	1
Kresge Foundation	1,500,000	2
McGregor Fund	65,000	3
Mellon (Andrew W.) Foundation	83,000	1
Pew (J. Howard) Freedom Trust	100,000	1
Subtotal	$2,503,000	10
Research Libraries Group		
Carnegie Corporation of New York	$ 500,000	1
Hewlett (William and Flora) Foundation	300,000	1
Mellon (Andrew W.) Foundation	1,000,000	1
Sloan (Alfred P.) Foundation	500,000	1
Subtotal	$2,300,000	4

TABLE 5 LEADING LIBRARY RECIPIENTS OF FOUNDATION GRANTS (cont.)

Institution	Grant Amount	Number of Grants
Stanford University		
Ahmanson Foundation	$ 200,000	1
Amoco Foundation	10,000	1
Calder (Louis) Foundation	50,000	1
Kresge Foundation	500,000	1
Merrill (Charles E.) Trust	100,000	2
Pew (J. Howard) Freedom Trust	500,000	1
Scaife (Sarah) Foundation	150,000	1
Subtotal	$1,510,000	8
Trinity University		
Brown Foundation	$ 666,666	1
Clark Foundation, The	5,000	1
Houston Endowment	500,000	1
Mabee (J. E. and L. E.) Foundation	500,000	1
Subtotal	$1,671,666	4
Yale University		
Booth Ferris Foundation	$ 50,000	1
Cary (Mary Flagler) Charitable Trust	63,000	2
Mudd (Seeley G.) Fund	1,500,000	1
Subtotal	$1,613,000	4

Foundation grants were not limited to support of libraries in the United States, as eleven grants distributed in nine countries were reported in 1979 (Tables 7 and 8).

SEEKING FOUNDATION FUNDING

The totals for library funding in 1979 present interesting and diverse patterns of foundation support. Equally important is the role of libraries in the competition for available funding. Table 9 lists private foundations whose statements of purpose note a specific interest in libraries. But as a "prospect list" or guide to the foundation world

TABLE 6 MAJOR LIBRARY GRANT MAKERS (IN DOLLAR AMOUNTS)

Name	State	Amount	Number of Grants
Kresge Foundation	Michigan	$5,250,000	19
Mellon (Andrew W.) Foundation	New York	3,581,500	14
Heineman Foundation for Research, Education, Charitable and Scientific Purposes	New York	3,212,688	3
Pew Memorial Trust	Pennsylvania	1,791,500	21
Rockefeller Foundation	New York	1,162,420	10
Kellogg (W. K.) Foundation	Michigan	1,503,048	4
Mudd (Seeley G.) Fund	California	1,500,000	1

TABLE 7 FOREIGN LIBRARY GRANTS

Foundation	State	Amount Authorized	Recipient
Ford Foundation	New York	$200,000	India
Council on Library Resources	District of Columbia	75,000	Netherlands
Tinker Foundation	New York	70,000	Chile
Lilly Endowment	Indiana	25,000	England
Merrill (Charles E.) Trust	New York	20,000	England
Rockefeller Brothers Fund	New York	25,000	Philippines
Council on Library Resources	District of Columbia	23,000	Canada
Merrill (Charles E.) Trust	New York	10,000	France
Dodge (Cleveland H.) Foundation	New York	5,000	France
Fuld (Helen) Health Trust	New York	10,000	Turkey
Ford Foundation	New York	7,000	Uruguay

it is severely limited. The grant-seeking librarian whose search is confined to foundations with an established interest in libraries may be investigating only the most obvious prospects.

Because library programs often cut across the entire range of foundation interests, it is essential that search techniques include a review of grants in a broad spectrum of areas. A librarian who is seeking, for example, to establish a program for handicapped persons will want to investigate foundations with an established interest in community services to the handicapped, whether or not the foundations have ever supported library programming. A foundation with an established interest in funding services to youth, the handicapped, or the aged may not be aware that libraries operate special programs for these population groups until the grant-seeking librarian presents a proposal in one of the areas of special interest.

The key to successful fund raising and an increase in support for libraries is initiative. The sources are available to help the researcher identify and evaluate foundations as funding sources. What the fund-seeking librarian must remember is that it is important to use imagination and creativity in matching particular needs to a foundation's interests.

TABLE 8 FOREIGN LIBRARY GRANTS BY RECIPIENT COUNTRIES

Recipient	Amount	Number of Grants
Canada	$ 23,000	1
Chile	70,000	1
England	45,000	2
France	15,000	2
India	200,000	1
Netherlands	75,000	1
Philippines	25,000	1
Turkey	10,000	1
Uruguay	7,000	1
Total	$470,000	11

TABLE 9   FOUNDATIONS WITH A STATED INTEREST IN LIBRARIES
(From *The Foundation Directory*, Edition 7)

Foundation	State
Bacon (The Francis) Foundation	California
Bell (James F.) Foundation	Minnesota
Boinsteel Foundation	Michigan
Braun Foundation	California
Callaway Foundation, Inc.	Georgia
Camp (Apollos) and Bennet Humiston Trust	Illinois
Camp Foundation	Virginia
Congdon (Edward E.) Foundation	Minnesota
Consolidated's Civic Foundation, Inc.	Wisconsin
Council on Library Resources, Inc.	District of Columbia
Dover Foundation, Inc.	North Carolina
Eccles (Ralph M. and Ella M.) Foundation	Pennsylvania
Eleutherian Mills-Hasley Foundation, Inc.	Delaware
Emerson (Fred L.) Foundation, Inc.	New York
Favrot Fund, The	Texas
Ferre (The Louis A.) Foundation	Puerto Rico
Foundation for Biblical Research and Preservation of Primitive Christianity, The	New Hampshire
Fremont Area Foundation, The	Michigan
Frick (Helen Clay) Foundation	Pennsylvania
Gebbie Foundation, Inc.	New York
Glosser (David A.) Foundation	Pennsylvania
Goddard (The Charles B.) Foundation	Texas
Grainger Foundation, Inc.	Illinois
Grolier Foundation, Inc.	New York
Grundy Foundation	Pennsylvania
Harnischfeser Foundation	Wisconsin
Hartz Foundation	Minnesota
Harvard-Yenching Institute	Massachusetts
Heineman Foundation for Research, Educational, Charitable and Scientific Purposes, Inc.	New York
Interlake Foundation	Illinois
Justus (Edith C.) Trust	Pennsylvania
Kelley (Edward Bangs) and Elze Kelley Foundation, Inc.	Massachusetts
Kempner (Harris and Eliza) Fund	Texas
Kinney-Lindstrom Foundation	Iowa
Knapp Foundation, Inc.	Maryland
Larsen Fund	New York
Lesher (Margaret and Irvin) Foundation	Pennsylvania
Lincoln National Life Foundation, Inc.	Indiana
Longwood Foundation, Inc.	Delaware
Loutit Foundation	Michigan
Lumpkin Foundation	Illinois
Markey (The John C.) Charitable Fund	Ohio
Marshall (Mattie H.) Foundation	Georgia
Martin Foundation, Inc.	Indiana
Milbank (The Dunleavy) Foundation, Inc.	New York
Morgan City Fund, The	Louisiana
Morrison Charitable Trust	North Carolina
Mudd (The Seeley G.) Fund	California
Mulford (The Clarence E.) Trust	Maine
Munson (W. B.) Foundation	Texas
National Home Library Foundation	District of Columbia
O'Conner (A. Lindsay and Olive B.) Foundation	New York
Ohrstrom Foundation, Inc., The	Virginia

TABLE 9   FOUNDATIONS WITH A STATED INTEREST IN LIBRARIES (cont.)

Foundation	State
Patterson (W. I.) Charitable Fund	Pennsylvania
Pforzheimer (The Carl and Lily) Foundation, Inc.	North Carolina
Piper (Minnie Stevens) Foundation	Texas
Pitts (William I. H. and Lula E.) Foundation	Georgia
Price-Waterhouse Foundation	New York
Reynolds (Z. Smith) Foundation, The	North Carolina
Rhode Island Foundation	Rhode Island
Sherman Foundation	California
Slemp Foundation	Virginia
Snow (The John Ben) Foundation, Inc.	New York
Sprause (The Seth) Educational and Charitable Foundation	New York
Stevens (The Abbot and Dorothy H.) Foundation	Massachusetts
Temple (T. L. L.) Foundation	Texas
Tenzler Foundation, The	Washington
Walter (The Rosalind P.) Foundation	New York
Warren Memorial Foundation	Maine
Whittenberger (Claude R. and Ethel B.) Foundation	Idaho
Williams (John D.) Charitable Trust	Pennsylvania
Wilson (The H. W.) Foundation	New York

FOUNDATION GRANTS TO LIBRARIES, 1979

Compiled by The Foundation Center

Ahmanson Foundation, CA

$5,000 to Allentown College of Saint Francis, Center Valley, PA, for library expansion and equipment.

$75,000 to Atlanta University Center, Atlanta, GA, for new center library (continuing support).

$25,000 to Hoover Institution, Stanford, CA, for special acquisition fund.

$25,000 to Southwestern University, School of Law, Los Angeles, CA, for furnishings and fixtures for expansion of library.

$200,000 to Stanford University, Graduate School of Business, Stanford, CA, for addition to J. Hugh Jackson Library.

$300,000 to UCLA Foundation, Los Angeles, CA, for books for biomedical library.

$22,000 to UCLA Foundation, Los Angeles, CA, for books and program support for Clark Library.

$100,000 to UCLA Foundation, Los Angeles, CA, for Department of Special Book Collections at Research Library.

$5,000 to UCLA Foundation, Los Angeles, CA, for library special collection (continuing support).

$25,000 to United States International University, San Diego, CA, for library resource materials.

$150,000 to University of California (Los Angeles), Center for Health Sciences, Los Angeles, CA, for biomedical library expansion.

$100,000 to University of California (San Diego), Medical School, La Jolla, CA, for building fund, cancer center facility, and medical library.

$100,000 to University of Southern California, Los Angeles, CA, for library book acquisitions.

Atlantic Richfield Foundation, CA

$25,000 to Athenaeum of Philadelphia, Philadelphia, PA, for foundation's humanities and arts program.

$62,000 to Atlanta University Center, Atlanta, GA, for dual degree program with Georgia Tech and for science and engineering section of new library.

$5,000 to Los Angeles Public Library, Los Angeles, CA.

Bankamerica Foundation, CA

$5,000 to Saint Helena Public Library, Saint Helena, CA.

Hewlett (William and Flora) Foundation, CA

$47,000 to Florida State University, Center for the study of Population, Tallahassee, FL, (three-year grant; world population).

$200,000 to Folger Shakespeare Library, DC, to match challenge grant for library renovation, including installation of modern electrical and mechanical equipment and climate controls (three-year grant).

$300,000 to Research Libraries Group, Stanford, CA, to provide joint cataloging, shared resources, and other services to research libraries (three-year grant).

Humboldt Area Foundation, CA

$8,000 to Loleta Union School District, Loleta, CA, toward construction of library-media center.

Irvine (James) Foundation, CA

$250,000 to Graduate Theological Union, Berkeley, CA, for construction of combined library facility (continuing support).

$50,000 to San Francisco Conservatory of Music, San Francisco, CA, for renovation and refurbishing of library.

Kaiser (Henry J.) Family Foundation, CA

$8,500 to Foundation Center, New York, NY, for general support and for San Francisco branch library.

Mudd (Seeley G.) Fund, CA

$1,500,000 to Yale University, New Haven, CT, toward construction of library for social sciences.

Packard (David and Lucile) Foundation, CA

$5,000 to Peninsula Conservation Foundation, Palo Alto, CA, to improve library facilities and conservation education program.

Rosenberg Foundation, CA

$7,833 to Foundation Center, New York, NY, for program support and toward operations of the Foundation Center Bay Area Library in San Francisco (continuing support).

San Francisco Foundation, CA

$18,500 to Eighty Langton Street, San Francisco, CA, to strengthen administration and improve library for gallery center in San Francisco.

San Mateo Foundation, CA

$7,635 to Peninsula Library System of San Mateo County, San Mateo, CA, for countywide directory of human services providers.

Skaggs (L. J.) and Mary C. Skaggs Foundation, CA

$5,000 to International Human Assistance Programs, New York, NY, for rural mobile library in Davao del Sur, Philippine Islands, to make books, pamphlets, and educational aids available to residents for use in improving farming and other skills.

Steele (Harry G.) Foundation, CA

$15,000 to Father Garrett's Boys, Acton, CA, for construction of library and classroom building.

Strauss (Levi) Foundation, CA

$5,000 to California Center for Research and Education in Government, Sacramento, CA, for subscriptions to *California Journal for Selected Libraries in California*.

$10,000 to Midwestern State University, Wichita Falls, TX, to expand history collection at Moffet Library.

Coors (Adolph) Foundation, CO

$5,000 to Denver Public Library Foundation, Denver, CO, to underwrite Reading Is Fundamental Program.

Denver Foundation, CO

$5,000 to Denver Public Library Foundation, Denver, CO, for Reading Is Fundamental Program.

Dana (Charles A.) Foundation, CT

$200,000 to Babson College, Wellesley, MA, toward renovation of Sir Isaac Newton Library building to serve as modern teaching facility (challenge grant).

$300,000 to Boston College, Chestnut Hill, MA, toward construction of central research library (challenge grant).

$500,000 to Connecticut College, New London, CT, toward cost of renovation of Palmer Library building to serve as new Academic Center for the Humanities (challenge grant).

$95,000 to Recording for the Blind, New York, NY, toward startup cost of a standby library.

Fairchild (Sherman) Foundation, CT

$50,000 to New York Public Library, New York, NY, for general support.

General Electric Foundation, CT

$7,500 to Hoover Institution, Stanford, CA, for study, prospects for the 1980s: Overview of Problems Facing the United States.

New Haven Foundation, CT

$6,664 to Orange, Treasurer of the Town of, Orange, CT, for library fund (continuing support).

Cafritz (Morris and Gwendolyn) Foundation, DC

$26,800 to Library of Congress, DC, for series of seminars to commemorate or celebrate important persons or events.

$5,000 to New Educational Ways, DC, for remedial reading program and purchase of reading materials for Alley Library.

Council on Library Resources, DC

$326,500 to Association of Research Libraries, Office of Management Studies, DC, to train librarians as consultants to libraries in academic institutions to help them improve service to users (five-year grant).

$20,000 to Council of National Library Associations, American National Standards Committee Z39, Haverford, PA, for activities to develop standards in fields of library and information science and related publishing practices (Washington, DC).

$75,000 to International Federation of Library Associations and Institutions, Professional Coordination Office, The Hague, Netherlands, for professional coordination activities (two-year grant; continuing support).

$6,648 to Library of Congress, DC, for meeting attended by representatives of Library of Congress, National Library of Canada, American Library Association, and Canadian Committee on MARC, for the purpose of identifying format changes required to implement the Anglo-American Cataloguing Rules 2 in 1980.

$41,058 to National Endowment for the Humanities, College Library Program, DC, for grants to Franklin and Marshall College, Lake Forest College, and Tusculum College to improve student ability to make use of library resources as part of course-related work (five-year grant; National Endowment will add to grant funds).

$37,400 to National Endowment for the Humanities, College Library Program, DC, for grant to Salem State College, MA, to improve student ability to make use of library resources (three-year grant; National Endowment will add to grant funds).

$23,000 to National Library of Canada, Cataloguing Branch, Ottawa, Canada, for computer output microform service listing authenticated bibliographic records created in the CONSER project (Conversion of Serials) which is expected to be valuable source of standard bibliographic data about serials for Canadian and American libraries.

$15,000 to OCLC, Columbus, OH, to develop a non-Roman alphabet capability for computerized input, processing, storage, and display of bibliographic and related information, to increase availability of information in non-Roman languages, and decrease cost of processing such information.

$14,500 to University of California (Los Angeles), Graduate School of Library and Information Science, Los Angeles, CA, for revision of second edition of *Handbook of Data Processing for Libraries*.

$10,000 to University of Kentucky Research Foundation, College of Library Science, Lexington, KY, toward editorial expenses of essays on leaders in American academic librarianship, 1925–1975, for publication.

Folger Fund, DC

$5,000 to Folger Shakespeare Library, DC (continuing support).

National Home Library Foundation, DC

$5,000 to Alderson-Broaddus College, Pickett Library, Philippi, WV, to improve humanities-related holdings.

$15,000 to Corcoran Gallery of Art, DC, to strengthen resources of two libraries that serve the gallery and the school of art.

$5,000 to Highlander Research and Education Center, New Market, TN, to purchase books for Highlander Library.

$30,000 to John F. Kennedy Center for the Performing Arts, DC, for reference works for Performing Arts Library.

$5,000 to Planned Parenthood of Metropolitan Washington, DC, for purchase of materials for Library-Resources Center.

$25,000 to University of Minnesota (Minneapolis), Hubert H. Humphrey Institute of Public Affairs, Minneapolis, MN, for library resources in area of public service.

Bush (Edyth) Charitable Foundation, FL

$5,000 to Lutheran High School Association of Central Florida, Orlando, FL, for library materials (matching grant).

$15,235 to Stetson University, College of Law, Saint Petersburg, FL, to purchase books, periodicals, and equipment for Law Library (matching grant).

$133,247 to Winter Park Memorial Hospital, Winter Park, FL, for medical library and lounge.

Conn Memorial Foundation, FL

$39,200 to University of Tampa, Tampa, FL, for Forward Fund, library, and new classroom.

$5,000 to Webber College, Babson Park, FL, for furniture for new library.

Davis (Arthur Vining) Foundations, FL

$35,000 to Adelphi University, Garden City, NY, toward costs of projected major library addition (two-year grant).

$35,000 to Dropsie University, Philadelphia, PA, for library acquisitions and scholarship fund (two-year grant).

$100,000 to Harvard University, Harvard-Yenching Library, Cambridge, MA, to endow Memorial Book Fund (two-year grant).

$50,000 to New York Public Library, New York, NY, for special contribution in memory of Morris Hadley (two-year grant).

$25,000 to Westminster Theological Seminary Center, Miami, FL, for library acquisitions.

Callaway Foundation, GA

$100,000 to Atlanta University Center, Atlanta, GA, for joint library fund.

$250,000 to Mercer University, Walter F. George School of Law, Macon, GA, to construct and equip law library.

Amoco Foundation, IL

$5,000 to Newberry Library, Chicago, IL.

$5,000 to Satilla Regional Library, Douglas, GA.

$10,000 to Stanford University, Stanford, CA, for Hoover Institution, International Research Library.

Chicago Community Trust, IL

$15,000 to Chicago City-wide College, Chicago, IL, to implement series of discussion groups for senior citizens in neighborhood libraries and nutrition sites.

Field Foundation of Illinois, IL

$20,000 to Newberry Library, Chicago, IL, to help meet challenge grant from National Endowment for the Humanities for renovation.

Joyce Foundation, IL

$100,000 to Newberry Library, Chicago, IL, to match grant from National Endowment for the Humanities.

McCormick (Robert R.) Charitable Trust, IL

$30,000 to Newberry Library, Chicago, IL (continuing support).

Monticello College Foundation, IL

$6,500 to Newberry Library, Chicago, IL, for Monticello College Foundation Fellowship for postdoctoral research at Newberry Library.

Regenstein (Joseph and Helen) Foundation, IL

$69,560 to University of Chicago, Joseph Regenstein Library, Chicago, IL, to purchase three rare books.

$100,000 to University of Chicago, Joseph Regenstein Library, Chicago, IL, for library maintenance program.

Woods Charitable Fund, IL

$7,500 to Donors Forum of Chicago, Chicago, IL, to operate Forum's library (renewal grant).

$100,000 to National Endowment for the Humanities, DC, for the Center for the History of the American Indian at the Newberry Library in Chicago, IL (renewal grant/Native Americans).

Indianapolis Foundation, IN

$60,000 to Flanner House, Indianapolis, IN, toward construction of library wing in new building (two-year grant).

Lilly Endowment, IN

$132,221 to American Library Association, Chicago, IL, for programs to teach basic literacy skills to disadvantaged adults.

$200,000 to Association of Research Libraries, DC, to enable 20 Indiana college and university libraries to improve their services and management (two-year grant).

$250,000 to Indiana University Foundation, Bloomington, IN, for acquisitions for Lilly Library.

$244,000 to Indianapolis-Marion County Public Library, Indianapolis, IN, for purchase of additional land and relocation of Meridian Street parking lot.

$25,000 to Oxford University, Lincoln

College, Oxford, England, for support of Lincoln College Library.

Permanent Charity Fund, Committee of the, MA

$75,000 to Public Library of the City of Boston, Boston, MA, to develop Outreach programs for Boston Schoolchildren and teachers (three-year grant).

Aeroquip Foundation, MI

$5,000 to University of Michigan (Ann Arbor), Ann Arbor, MI, for Ford Library.

Dewaters Charitable Trust, MI

$19,327 to Goodrich Schools, Goodrich, MI, for purchase of library collection for Goodrich Elementary School.

Ford Motor Company Fund, MI

$5,000 to Detroit Public Library, Friends of, Detroit, MI.

$40,000 to Folger Shakespeare Library, DC.

$10,000 to Thessalonica Agricultural and Industrial Institute, New York, NY, for special programs.

Fremont Area Foundation, MI

$35,671 to Fremont, City of, Fremont, MI, for public library fund (continuing support).

General Motors Foundation, MI

$8,333 to Gerald R. Ford Commemorative Committee, Grand Rapids, MI, for capital support for President Ford Library/Museum Fund.

$5,000 to New York Public Library, New York, NY, for unrestricted operating support.

Gerstacker (Rollin M.) Foundation, MI

$100,000 to President Ford Library-Museum Fund, Ann Arbor, MI.

Grand Rapids Foundation, MI

$30,000 to Aquinas College, Learning Resource Center, Grand Rapids, MI.

Kellogg (W. K.) Foundation, MI

$321,982 to Cornell University, Ithaca, NY, to establish comprehensive library educational information and referral networks for adult learners (two-year grant).

$500,000 to University of Michigan, Ann Arbor, MI, to help construct Gerald R. Ford Presidential Library.

$365,750 to University of the State of New York, Albany, NY, to establish comprehensive library educational information and referral networks for adult learners (two-year grant).

$315,316 to University of Washington, Seattle, WA, to implement model continuing professional education program for public librarians (three-year grant).

Kresge Foundation, MI

$250,000 to American University, DC, for construction of library.

$150,000 to Azusa Pacific College, Azusa, CA, toward renovation and expansion of library.

$150,000 to Calvin College, Grand Rapids, MI, to construct addition to library-classroom building.

$150,000 to College of the Holy Cross, Worcester, MA, for expansion and renovation of Dinand Library.

$15,000 to Covenant Theological Seminary, Saint Louis, MO, to remodel library.

$150,000 to Dickinson School of Law, Carlisle, PA, for construction of library-advocacy center.

$500,000 to Folger Shakespeare Library, DC, to renovate and expand facilities.

$500,000 to Huntington Library, Art Gallery and Botanical Gardens, San Marino, CA, to construct new wing, roads, and parking area, and renovate library space.

$10,000 to Peterborough Town Library, Peterborough, NH, for expansion.

$150,000 to Pierpont Morgan Library, New York, NY, toward renovation of library's roof and fence.

$500,000 to Stanford University, Stanford, CA, toward construction of library (second and final payment on grant of $1,000,000).

$250,000 to Trinity College, Hartford, CT, for addition to library.

$375,000 to University of California (Berkeley), Berkeley, CA, toward construction of library in engineering center (second and final payment on grant of $750,000).

$150,000 to University of California (Los Angeles), Los Angeles, CA, toward expansion of Biomedical Library as part of new Health Sciences Building.

$750,000 to University of Michigan (Ann Arbor), Ann Arbor, MI, toward construction of library for law school (second and final payment of $1,500,000 grant).

$750,000 to University of Michigan (Ann Arbor), Ann Arbor, MI, toward construction of library for law school (first installment of intended $1,500,000 grant).

$100,000 to University of Pittsburgh, Pittsburgh, PA, toward expansion of library facilities at Western Psychiatric Institute and Clinic.

$100,000 to University of Vermont, Burlington, VT, toward construction of library addition.

$250,000 to Washington and Lee University, Lexington, VA, toward construction of library building.

McGregor Fund, MI

$5,000 to Detroit Public Library, Friends of the, Detroit, MI, for operating costs.

$50,000 to Hiram College, Hiram, OH, for Library Endowment.

$6,467 to Jefferson-Chalmers Non-Profit Housing Corporation, Detroit, MI, for community redevelopment library.

$50,000 to Oberlin College, Oberlin, OH, for library acquisitions.

$25,000 to University of Michigan (Ann Arbor), William L. Clements Library, Ann Arbor, MI, for accessions.

$20,000 to University of Michigan (Ann Arbor), Ann Arbor, MI, for Medical Library and Learning Resource Center.

$20,000 to University of Michigan (Ann Arbor), Ann Arbor, MI, for President Gerald R. Ford Library and Museum.

Mott (Charles Stewart) Foundation, MI

$25,000 to Foundation Center, New York, NY, to support general objectives of the center, which provides information on philanthropic agencies through library services, publications, and research.

Steelcase Foundation, MI

$5,000 to President Ford Library-Museum Fund, Ann Arbor, MI.

Bremer (Otto) Foundation, MN

$5,000 to Correctional Services of Minnesota, Law Enforcement Resource Center, Saint Paul, MN, for expansion of film library as part of police training program.

Bush Foundation, MN

$49,000 to Newberry Library, Chicago, IL, toward development of atlas of Great Lakes Indian history (Native Americans).

Davis (Edwin W. and Catherine M.) Foundation, MN

$5,000 to Saint John's University, Collegeville, MN, for Malta microfilm project of Hill Monastic Manuscript Library.

General Mills Foundation, MN

$5,000 to Gerald R. Ford Commemorative Committee, Grand Rapids, MI, for presidential library and museum.

$5,000 to Providence Athenaeum, Providence, RI, for remodeling.

Jerome Foundation, MN

$64,000 to International Foundation for Art Research, New York, NY, to establish international archive for records of stolen art (continuing support).

McKnight Foundation, MN

$100,000 to Owen Wangensteen Historical Library of Biology and Medicine, Minneapolis, MN, to purchase rare books.

Saint Paul Foundation, MN

$15,000 to University of Minnesota (Saint Paul), Library School, Saint Paul, MN, to catalog the Hench Collection of Sherlock Holmes Literature (two-year grant).

Monsanto Fund, MO

$5,000 to Friends of the Musser Public Library, Muscatine, IA.

Bunbury Company, NJ

$25,000 to Princeton University, Library, Princeton, NJ, for general purposes.

Edison (Charles) Fund, NJ

$26,000 to Chautauqua Institution, Chautauqua, NY, toward maintenance of institution and park, for library exhibit, lecture series, scholarship awards, and live regional auditions.

Merck Company Foundation, NJ

$5,000 to New York Public Library, New York, NY, for capital development.

Schering-Plough Foundation, NJ

$25,000 to Massachusetts Institute of Technology, Whitaker College of Health Sciences and Technology, Cambridge, MA, for library-reading room.

Schumann (Florence and John) Foundation, NJ

$25,000 to Newark Public Library, Children's and Schools' Department, Newark, NJ, to support bilingual program for Hispanic children in neighborhood communities (two-year grant).

Victoria Foundation, NJ

$5,000 to New Jersey Committee for the Humanities, Newark, NJ, for conference on urban literature held at Rutgers University, Newark Museum, and Newark Public Library.

$15,000 to Newark Public Library, Newark, NJ, for operating grant, matched by Schumann Foundation, to launch programs aimed at Newark's Hispanic community.

Fleischmann (Max C.) Foundation, NV

$40,000 to Anza-Borrego Desert Natural History Association, Borrego Springs, CA, for visitors' center, library shelving, and display cabinets.

$390,000 to University of Nevada, National Judicial College, Reno, NV, for program support and for law library fund.

Astor (Vincent) Foundation, NY

$10,000 to New York Public Library, Astor, Lenox, and Tilden Foundations, New York, NY, for general support.

Biddle (Mary Duke) Foundation, NY

$5,000 to Catawba College, Salisbury, NC, for library materials.

$5,000 to Duke University Medical Center, Durham, NC, for Seeley Mudd Medical Library acquisitions.

$5,000 to Duke University Medical Center, Durham, NC, for Seeley Mudd Medical Library acquisitions (continuing support).

Booth Ferris Foundation, NY

$100,000 to Campbell College, Law School, Buies Creek, NC, for library.

$100,000 to New York Public Library, New York, NY, for document preservation and other purposes.

$50,000 to Yale University, School of Music, New Haven, CT, for purchase of the Virgil Thomson Library.

Burden (Florence V.) Foundation, NY

$18,692 to Brooklyn Public Library, Office of Services to the Aging, Brooklyn, NY, for stipends and related costs for 12 senior assistants who will work in branch libraries. To enrich and expand resources for the elderly in these libraries by organizing educational programs and other events.

Calder (Louis) Foundation, NY

$50,000 to Lenox Hill Hospital, New York, NY, to expand and improve Health Science Library and related educational facilities.

$25,000 to New York Public Library, New York, NY, for general support.

$20,000 to Recording for the Blind, New York, NY, for Recording for the Blind Duplicate Master Tape Library.

$50,000 to Stanford University, Hoover Institution, Stanford, CA, to acquire materials for Louis Calder Memorial Collection on Latin American Affairs (two-year grant).

$200,000 to University of Miami, Coral Gables, FL, to improve and complete basement of Louis Calder Memorial Medical Library.

Carnegie Corporation of New York, NY

$15,000 to New York Public Library, New York, NY, toward support of National Citizens Emergency Committee to Save Our Public Libraries.

$129,000 to New York University, Research Library Association of South Manhattan, New York, NY, toward development of computerized bibliographic system for members (two-year grant).

$15,000 to Ohio College Library Center, Research and Development Division, Columbus, OH, toward development of non-Roman alphabet capability for computerized library systems.

$500,000 to Research Libraries Group, Stanford, CA, toward development of research library information network.

Cary (Mary Flagler) Charitable Trust, NY

$50,000 to Pierpont Morgan Library, New York, NY, for replenishment of purchase fund for Mary Flagler Cary Music Collection (continuing support).

$51,476 to Rochester Institute of Technology, Rochester, NY, for renovation of Cary Memorial Library.

$30,000 to Yale University, Library, New Haven, CT, for publication of catalog of Cary Playing Card Collection (continuing support).

$33,000 to Yale University, Library, New Haven, CT, for publication of catalog of Cary Playing Card Collection (continuing support).

Clark (Edna McConnell) Foundation, NY

$30,000 to New York Public Library, New York, NY, for general support.

Commonwealth Fund, NY

$25,000 to Atlanta University Center, Atlanta, GA, toward construction of library shared by the six center institutions.

$400,000 to New York Public Library, New York, NY, for general support of research libraries (three-year grant).

Corning Glass Works Foundation, NY

$26,500 to New York Public Library, New York, NY, for general support.

Culpeper (Charles E.) Foundation, NY

$40,880 to New York Public Library, New York, NY, to purchase two Kurzweil Machines and necessary miscellaneous supplies needed for the use of blind persons.

$10,000 to Ransom-Everglades School, Miami, FL, for library needs.

$10,000 to University of Richmond, Law School, Richmond, VA, for modernization of Law Library.

Dodge (Cleveland H.) Foundation, NY

$5,000 to American Library in Paris, Paris, France, for endowment.

$5,000 to New York Public Library, New York, NY (continuing annual support).

Ford (Edward E.) Foundation, NY

$25,000 to Holton-Arms School, Bethesda, MD, to support expansion and renovation of library (matching grant).

$25,000 to Westlake School for Girls, Los Angeles, CA, toward construction of library (matching grant).

Ford Foundation, NY

$16,000 to American Council of Learned Societies, New York, NY, to support committee of scholars and librarians who are organizing national system of East Asian library materials.

$21,166 to Center for Research Libraries, Chicago, IL, to study cost of producing National Union Catalog of Books on the Far East.

$19,500 to Center for Research Libraries, Chicago, IL, for committee to plan centralized acquisition of international studies material for cooperative use by research libraries.

$7,000 to Center of Information and Studies of Uruguay, Montevideo, Uruguay, to purchase library collection of the late Professor Carlos Real de Azua.

$7,500 to International Piano Archives, Ivor, VA, for expenses related to recording pianist Ervin Nyiregyhazi (continuing support).

$35,000 to National Endowment for the Humanities, DC, for directory of regional archives and manuscript repositories in the Soviet Union.

$200,000 to National Institute of Public Finance and Policy, New Delhi, India, for staff development, research, library and equipment acquisitions (two-year grant).

Frueauff (Charles A.) Foundation, NY

$5,000 to Hofstra University, School of Law, Hempstead, NY, for library fund.

$5,000 to Lenox Hill Hospital, New York, NY, for Health Sciences Library.

Fuld (Helene) Health Trust, NY

$10,000 to American Hospital of Istanbul, School of Nursing, Istanbul, Turkey, for audiovisual equipment, software, and library books.

$30,000 to Boise State University, School of Practical Nursing, Boise, ID, for audiovisual equipment and library books.

$20,000 to Burbank Hospital, School of Nursing, Fitchburg, MA, for audiovisual equipment, software, library books, and transfer of equipment from Mt. Auburn Hospital School of Nursing.

$30,000 to Conemaugh Valley Memorial Hospital, School of Nursing, Johnstown, PA, for audiovisual equipment and library books.

$30,000 to Duke University Medical Center, School of Nursing, Durham, NC, for audiovisual equipment and library books.

$18,390 to Fletcher Hospital, School of Nursing, Fletcher, NC, for visual aids, library books, and equipment.

$10,640 to Flushing Hospital and Medical Center, School of Nursing, Flushing, NY, for hardware, library books, and equipment (continuing support).

$38,908 to Grady Memorial Hospital, School of Nursing, Atlanta, GA, for renovations, library books, and audiovisual software.

$9,840 to Haskell Indian Junior College, School of Practical Nursing, Lawrence, KS, for office and classroom equipment, library books, and software.

$37,500 to Keuka College, School of Nursing, Keuka Park, NY, for equipment and furnishings, hardware and software, library books, and patient care unit (continuing support).

$15,415 to Lawrence Memorial Hospital, School of Nursing, Medford, MA, for furnishings, smoke detectors, library books, and software (continuing support).

$10,380 to Lowell General Hospital, School of Nursing, Lowell, MA, for library books, furnishings, and renovations.

$22,316 to Mattatuck Community College, School of Nursing, Waterbury, CT, for library books, minibus, and health equipment.

$39,026 to Memorial Hospital Beth-El School of Nursing, Colorado Springs, CO, for library equipment and furnishings, student lounge, media and study center, and faculty offices.

$29,510 to Memorial Hospital of Roxborough, School of Nursing, Philadelphia, PA, for minibus, hardware, software, equipment, renovations, and library books.

$25,624 to Mennonite Hospital School of Nursing, Bloomington, IL, for library and residence hall furnishings, library books, and equipment (continuing support).

$10,000 to Misericordia Hospital Medical Center, School of Nursing, Bronx, NY, for library books and software.

$50,882 to Nebraska Methodist Hospital School of Nursing, Omaha, NE, for audiovisual equipment, library books, and software (continuing support).

$10,000 to Norfolk General Hospital School of Practical Nursing, Norfolk, VA, for library books, software, furnishings, and equipment (continuing support).

$15,000 to Presbyterian Hospital Center School of Nursing, Albuquerque, NM, for library books and equipment (continuing support).

$25,000 to Presentation College, School of Nursing, Aberdeen, SD, for software, minibus, learning resource center, library books, and humidifier (continuing support).

$10,000 to Saint Elizabeth Hospital School of Nursing, Utica, NY, for library books and software (continuing support).

$27,121 to Saint Joseph's Hospital, School of Nursing, Reading, PA, for library books, software, and equipment.

$24,194 to Wesley Medical Center, School of Nursing, Wichita, KS, for audiovisual equipment, security system, air conditioning, library books, and expansion of media center.

$36,031 to Westminster College, Saint Mark's Hospital School of Nursing, Salt Lake City, UT, for equipment, software, and library books.

Fund for the City of New York, NY

$12,500 to Citizens Committee for New York City, Self-Help Neighborhood Awards Program, New York, NY, to stimulate self-help and volunteer activities related to libraries, block associations, and clean-up campaigns through cash awards program.

$10,000 to Citizens Committee for New York City, Self-Help Neighborhood Awards Program, New York, NY, to stimulate self-help and volunteer activities related to libraries, block associations, and clean-up campaigns through cash awards program (continuing support).

Gannett (Frank E.) Newspaper Foundation, NY

$5,000 to Augustana College, Sioux Falls, SD, toward expansion of Mikkelsen Library.

$5,000 to Friends of the Tucson Public

Library, Tucson, AZ, for Reading Is Fundamental program to distribute free books to preschool children.

$5,000 to Grinnell Library, Poughkeepsie, NY, for campaign to expand community library in Wappingers Falls, Dutchess County.

$5,000 to Marshall University, Huntington, WV, toward purchase of rare books in medicine and allied health professions for Marshall University Library.

$10,000 to Oakmont Carnegie Library, Tarentum, PA, toward renovation and restoration of landmark library.

Gifford (Rosamond) Charitable Corporation, NY

$125,000 to Lemoyne College, Syracuse, NY, toward construction of library.

Hayden (Charles) Foundation, NY

$75,000 to Adelphi University, Garden City, NY, toward expansion of Swirbul Library.

$25,000 to Brooklyn Law School, Brooklyn, NY, toward expansion of library facilities.

$25,000 to Buckingham Browne and Nichols School, Cambridge, MA, toward library and school center for the upper school.

$50,000 to Seton Hall University, South Orange, NJ, toward library expansion.

Hearst (William Randolph) Foundation, NY

$20,000 to Hoover Institution of War, Revolution, and Peace, Stanford, CA.

$10,000 to University of California (Berkeley), Bancroft Library, Berkeley, CA.

Heineman Foundation for Research, Educational, Charitable and Scientific Purposes, NY

$5,000 to Library of Congress, DC.

$10,000 to Pierpont Morgan Library, New York, NY.

$3,197,688 to Pierpont Morgan Library, New York, NY, for rare books, manuscripts, letters, and autographs (grant represents the value of material actually given).

Hyde (Lillia Babbitt) Foundation, NY

$15,000 to Historic Deerfield, Deerfield, MA, for restoration of historic buildings and their contents and for library acquisitions.

$6,000 to National Schools Committee for Economic Education, Old Greenwich, CT, to distribute copies of *The American Ideal of 1776* by Hamilton Long to public libraries to familiarize more people with the Constitution and U.S. founding principles.

$10,000 to University High School, Newark, NJ, for facilities at Rutgers University Campus.

Irving One Wall Street Foundation, NY

$7,000 to New York Public Library, New York, NY.

$7,000 to New York Public Library, New York, NY (continuing support).

J. M. Foundation, NY

$29,000 to Hoover Presidential Library Association, West Branch, IA, toward definitive biography of President Herbert Hoover (renewal grant).

Kaplan (J. M.) Fund, NY

$10,000 to New York, City of, New York, NY, for municipal archives project to conserve original drawings and blueprints of Brooklyn Bridge.

Kress (Samuel H.) Foundation, NY

$250,000 to Columbia University, New York, NY, for East Asian Library (five-year grant).

$250,000 to Harvard University, Cambridge, MA, for expansion of Fogg Art Museum and Art History Library (four-year grant).

$100,000 to National Gallery of Art, Center for Advanced Study in the Visual

Arts, DC, for general support of photographic archive (two-year grant; continuing support).

$50,000 to Pierpont Morgan Library, New York, NY, to improve and enlarge prints and drawings department (two-year grant).

Manufacturers Hanover Foundation, NY

$35,500 to New York Public Library, New York, NY.

$8,000 to New York Public Library, New York, NY (continuing support).

McDonald (J. M.) Foundation, NY

$20,000 to Paleontological Research Institute, Ithaca, NY, to catalog research library of fossil collections.

$15,000 to Philadelphia College of Textiles and Science, Philadelphia, PA, toward library book collection.

$20,000 to Providence Athenaeum, Providence, RI, for repairs and improvement of oldest library in United States.

Mellon (Andrew W.) Foundation, NY

$35,000 to Art Institute of Chicago, Chicago, IL, to assist the affiliation of its art library with Research Libraries Information Network (similar awards made to two other museum libraries).

$270,000 to Asia Society, New York, NY, to assist publication activity of Asia House Gallery by supporting exhibition catalogs and its scholarly journal, *Archives of American Art*, and to support performing arts program.

$300,000 to Association of Research Libraries, Center for Chinese Research Materials, DC, for general support (three-year grant; matching grant).

$10,000 to Atlanta University Center, Atlanta, GA, for preliminary investigations for planning of the new library.

$35,000 to Cleveland Museum of Art, Cleveland, OH, to assist the affiliation of its art library with Research Libraries Information Network (similar awards made to two other museum libraries).

$350,000 to Georgetown University, DC, toward salaries of two new senior faculty appointments in the humanities and social sciences at schools of law and medicine, and toward expenses for seminars and library acquisitions (three-year grant).

$800,000 to Marine Biological Laboratory, Woods Hole, MA, to reorganize, rehabilitate, and expand library services and to further develop research and education programs of its Ecosystems Center.

$41,000 to Metropolitan Museum of Art, New York, NY, to assist the affiliation of its art library with the Research Libraries Information Network (similar awards made to two other museum libraries).

$165,000 to National Archives Trust Fund Board, DC, for use by National Historical Publications and Records Commission in renewed support of its educational and training programs for historical editors.

$350,000 to Newberry Library, Center for the History of the American Indian, Chicago, IL, for program support and for partial endowment for position of director of the center (Native Americans).

$1,000,000 to Research Libraries Group, Stanford, CA, to help meet operation and development costs of Research Libraries Information Network, a proposed national information and technical services network primarily for the use of research libraries (three-year grant).

$12,500 to University of Chicago Press, Chicago, IL, to continue development of Chicago Visual Library.

$83,000 to University of Michigan (Ann Arbor), Library, Ann Arbor, MI, to install and test technical processing methods that would improve use of Research Libraries Information Network.

$130,000 to University of Pennsylvania, Philadelphia, PA, to assist the affiliation of its library with Research Libraries Group.

Merrill (Charles E.) Trust, NY

$10,000 to American Library in Paris, Paris, France, for general purposes.

$75,000 to Atlanta University Center, Atlanta, GA, toward construction of Library.

$10,000 to Bancroft Library, Berkeley, CA, to edit Mark Twain papers.

$20,000 to Barry College, Miami Shores, FL, to establish library collection in administration and management.

$20,000 to London School of Economics and Political Science, London, England, toward completion of move of British Library.

$25,000 to Monterey Institute of Foreign Studies, Monterey, CA, for library expansion.

$20,000 to Oglethorpe University, Atlanta, GA, for library acquisitions.

$10,000 to Rugby Restoration Association, Rugby, TN, to construct Rugby Library Building, and to start or strengthen libraries in Cabbage-Town, Del Rio, and Highlander Center.

$50,000 to Stanford University, Graduate School of Business, Stanford, CA, for library expansion.

$50,000 to Stanford University, Stanford, CA, for library expansion.

$15,000 to Union Theological Seminary in Virginia, Richmond, VA, to expand library resources.

$25,000 to Wake Forest University, Winston-Salem, NC, for Z. Smith Reynolds Library.

$25,000 to Washington and Lee University, Lexington, VA, for library construction.

$25,000 to Williston Academy, Easthampton, MA, for library campaign.

Mobil Foundation, NY

$57,500 to New York Public Library, New York, NY (continuing support).

New York Times Company Foundation, NY

$22,866 to New York Public Library, New York, NY.

Rockefeller Brothers Fund, NY

$57,000 to Princeton Theological Seminary, Committee for Theological Library Development, Princeton, NJ, to train personnel and improve operating procedures in libraries of accredited theological schools.

$25,000 to Ramon Magsaysay Award Foundation, Manila, Philippines, toward capital fund of foundation's Asian library.

Rockefeller Foundation, NY

$18,800 to Alice Lloyd College, Pippa Passes, KY, for development of photographic archive for oral history project.

$11,650 to Amherst College, Amherst, MA, to establish film and videotape archive at Folger Shakespeare Memorial Library in Washington, DC.

$12,000 to Artnews Archive Foundation, New York, NY, to develop archive of contemporary coverage of information relating to the visual arts.

$5,500 to Association for Population/Family Planning Libraries and Information Centers International, Clarion, PA, to compile information sources (world population).

$31,500 to California State College, Sonoma, CA, for regional ethnic archive project focusing on northern San Francisco Bay area.

$7,500 to Columbia University, New York, NY, for library development center.

$6,870 to Foxfire Fund, Rabun Gap, GA, for archive of Foxfire Collection.

$550,000 to New World Records, New York, NY, for record collection tracing social and cultural history of the United States through its music for distribution to music schools, libraries, and FM and public broadcasting stations.

$264,900 to Rockefeller University, New York, NY, for operation of foundation's archives at Rockefeller Archive Center.

$253,700 to University of North Carolina (Chapel Hill), Southeastern Black Press Institute, Chapel Hill, NC, for workshops, internships, and apprenticeships and to establish Black Press Archive.

Rubinstein (Helena) Foundation, NY

$15,000 to French Library in Boston, Boston, MA, for general support.
$5,000 to National Citizens Emergency Committee to Save Our Public Libraries, DC, toward funding goal.
$15,000 to New York Public Library, New York, NY, for general support of research libraries.
$10,000 to Recording for the Blind, New York, NY, for expansion of Master Tape Library.

S & H Foundation, NY

$20,000 to New York Public Library, New York, NY.

Scherman Foundation, NY

$75,000 to New York Public Library, New York, NY (continuing support).

Shubert Foundation, NY

$10,000 to New York Public Library, Astor, Lenox and Tilden Foundations, New York, NY, for Lincoln Center Library of the Performing Arts.

Sloan (Alfred P.) Foundation, NY

$13,700 to Associated Western Universities, Salt Lake City, UT, to expand circulation of and fields covered by *Videocourse Bibliograph the Catalog* (three-year grant).
$500,000 to Research Libraries Group, Stanford, CA, toward establishment of Research Libraries Information Network, which will provide research libraries with automated services to control costs and expand access to information (two-year grant).

Surdna Foundation, NY

$30,000 to Amherst College, Amherst, MA, for Folger Shakespeare Memorial Library.

Teagle Foundation, NY

$10,000 to Pierpont Morgan Library, New York, NY, for scholarships.

Tinker Foundation, NY

$23,000 to Spanish Institute, New York, NY, for program support, including literary lectures and acquisitions for Tinker Library (final grant of three-year commitment).
$70,000 to Universidad de Chile, Institute of International Studies, Santiago, Chile, to support activities and for publications, library acquisitions, study groups, and international conference on Latin America and the South Pacific.

Watertown Foundation, NY

$10,000 to Carthage Free Library, Carthage, NY.

Watson (John Jay and Eliza Jane) Foundation, NY

$15,000 to Pratt Institute, Brooklyn, NY, for library resources and services (matching grant).
$10,000 to Recording for the Blind, New York, NY, for Duplication of Master Tape Library.

Weatherhead Foundation, NY

$50,000 to New York Public Library, New York, NY, for Weatherhead Foundation Southwest Fund (continuing support).

Bingham (William) Foundation, OH

$50,000 to Radcliffe College, Schlesinger Library, Cambridge, MA, for support of library.

Cleveland Foundation, OH

$5,000 to Lake County Historical Society, Mentor, OH, to expand research library.

Gund (George) Foundation, OH

$5,000 to Cleveland Public Library, Cleveland, OH, to commission sculpture by Harry Bertoia.

$25,000 to Cleveland State University, Cleveland-Marshall College of Law, Cleveland, OH, for library campaign.

Mabee (J. E. and L. E.) Foundation, OK

$61,400 to Bethel College, Newton, KS, for library renovation.

$500,000 to Oral Roberts University, Tulsa, OK, for library expansion.

$500,000 to Trinity University, San Antonio, TX, for library project building fund.

Alcoa Foundation, PA

$5,000 to People's Library, New Kensington, PA.

Annenberg Fund, PA

$10,000 to Episcopal Academy, Merion, PA, for Roger Annenberg Memorial Library-Learning Center.

Benedum (Claude Worthington) Foundation, PA

$250,000 to University of Michigan, Law School, Ann Arbor, MI, for construction of addition to library.

Gulf Oil Foundation of Delaware, PA

$5,000 to Friends of LBJ Library, Austin, TX.

Hillman Foundation, PA

$20,000 to Pittsburgh Learning Laboratory Center, Pittsburgh, PA, toward purchase of office-classroom building.

$30,000 to University of Pittsburgh, Western Psychiatric Institute and Clinic, Pittsburgh, PA, toward expansion of library facilities and services.

$18,800 to University of Pittsburgh, Hillman Library, Pittsburgh, PA, to purchase microform reader-printer equipment and shelving attachments to store microfilm containers.

Justus (Samuel) Charitable Trust, PA

$35,720 to Oil City, City of, Oil City, PA, for library support.

Penn (William) Foundation, PA

$35,000 to Free Library of Philadelphia, Philadelphia, PA, for study of future library functions in this region and development of program to accomplish the library's goals.

$50,000 to Library Company of Philadelphia, Philadelphia, PA, to assist in meeting costs of its 1981 celebration of a quarter of a millennium of continuous service (two-year grant).

Pew (J. Howard) Freedom Trust, PA

$25,000 to Asbury Theological Seminary, Wilmore, KY, for library cataloging project (continuing support).

$500,000 to Stanford University, Hoover Institution on War, Revolution and Peace, Stanford, CA, for domestic studies program and fellows program.

$100,000 to University of Michigan, Ann Arbor, MI, toward construction of President Ford Library.

$66,000 to Warren Wilson College, Swannanoa, NC, for renovation of Carson Hall and expansion of library facility.

$108,500 to Westminster Theological Seminary, Philadelphia, PA, for library renovations and acquisitions, development program, and faculty salary program (continuing support).

Pew Memorial Trust, PA

$70,000 to Academy of Vocal Arts, Philadelphia, PA, for opera theater program and for matching grant for production materials and library addition.

$100,000 to Amherst College, Amherst, MA, for Folger Shakespeare Library Building Fund.

$23,500 to Athenaeum of Philadelphia, Philadelphia, PA, for installation and operation of computer-based library catalog system.

$300,000 to Atlanta University Center, Atlanta, GA, for new library facility.

$83,000 to Bowdoin College, Brunswick, ME, for purchase and installation of compact shelving and study stations for library.

$6,000 to Braille Circulating Library, Richmond, VA, for book recording project.

$200,000 to Bryn Mawr College, Bryn Mawr, PA, for library acquisition and related costs and for science equipment (continuing support).

$20,000 to Delaware County Christian School Society, Newtown Square, PA, for high school library acquisitions and equipment.

$50,000 to Dickinson School of Law, Carlisle, PA, for construction of library-advocacy center.

$44,000 to Dropsie University, College for Hebrew and Cognate Learning, Philadelphia, PA, for library maintenance and preservation.

$75,000 to Friends Central School, Philadelphia, PA, for library resources center.

$10,000 to George School, Newtown, PA, for construction and furnishing of multimedia center in library.

$100,000 to Gettysburg College, Gettysburg, PA, toward library learning resources center (challenge grant).

$50,000 to Juniata College, Huntingdon, PA, for equipment for library and natural sciences department.

$25,000 to Pratt Institute, Brooklyn, NY, for library renovations.

$50,000 to Protestant Episcopal Theological Seminary in Virginia, Alexandria, VA, for construction of library addition.

$250,000 to Saint Joseph's University, Philadelphia, PA, for library-learning center.

$100,000 to Smith College, Northampton, MA, for modernization and expansion of Neilson Library.

$150,000 to Trinity College, Hartford, CT, for expansion of library.

$25,000 to Wake Forest University, Winston-Salem, NC, for library improvements.

$60,000 to Widener College, Chester, PA, for library acquisitions (matching grant).

Pitcairn-Crabbe Foundation, PA

$15,000 to Allegheny College, Meadville, PA, for renovation and conversion of Reis Library.

Pittsburgh Foundation, PA

$10,000 to New Castle Free Public Library, New Castle, PA, for building fund.

$12,000 to Peoples Library, New Kensington, PA, to increase reference collection.

$23,750 to State Correctional Institution of Pittsburgh, Pittsburgh, PA, for furnishings and equipment, and for library improvements at Western Penitentiary.

Scaife (Sarah) Foundation, PA

$150,000 to Stanford University, Hoover Institution on War, Revolution and Peace, Stanford, CA (continuing support).

Trexler Foundation, PA

$100,000 to Allentown Public Library, Allentown, PA, toward new library building.

United States Steel Foundation, PA

$5,000 to New York Public Library, New York, NY, for operating support (continuing support).

$25,000 to Pierpont Morgan Library, New York, NY, for capital support.

Whitaker Foundation, PA

$10,000 to Dickinson School of Law, Carlisle, PA, toward construction of library-advocacy center.

$15,000 to Harrisburg Public Library, Harrisburg, PA, for renovation of central branch.

Williamsport Foundation, PA

$8,803 to James V. Brown Library, Williamsport, PA.

$15,000 to James V. Brown Library, Williamsport, PA (continuing support).

Rhode Island Foundation, RI

$5,000 to New School, Middletown, RI, for acquisitions and library furnishings.

Anderson (M. D.) Foundation, TX

$50,000 to Texas Medical Center, Houston, TX, for library.

$10,000 to Wimberly, Village Library of, Wimberly, TX.

Brown Foundation, TX

$25,000 to Columbus, City of, Columbus, TX, for library building.

$50,000 to Lyndon Baines Johnson Foundation, Friends of the LBJ Library, Austin, TX, for endowment fund.

$50,000 to President Ford Library-Museum Fund, New York, NY, for library and museum.

$666,666 to Trinity University, San Antonio, TX, for new library building.

Burkitt Foundation, TX

$5,000 to Catholic Archives of Texas, Austin, TX, for purchase of microfilm camera.

$5,000 to Saint Terese School, Seattle, WA, for librarian compensation (matching grant/minority students).

Carter (Amon G.) Foundation, TX

$20,000 to Fort Worth Public Library, Fort Worth, TX, for general support.

$5,000 to Friends of the LBJ Library, Austin, TX, for general support.

Clark Foundation, The, TX

$5,000 to Austin College, Library, Sherman, TX, for learning resources support in the sciences.

$5,000 to Southern Methodist University, Library, Dallas, TX, for library support in field of urban problems.

$5,000 to Texas Christian University, Library, Fort Worth, TX, for library support in the fields of law enforcement and airport management.

$5,000 to Trinity University, Library, San Antonio, TX, for library support in field of solar energy.

$5,000 to University of Dallas, Library, Dallas, TX, for library support in classical languages.

Cullen Foundation, TX

$60,000 to Houston, City of, Houston, TX, for library board and for historical photograph collection in public library.

Fikes (Leland) Foundation, TX

$333,333 to Friends of Dallas Public Library, Dallas, TX, toward new library (challenge grant).

$14,600 to University of Texas, Richardson, TX, for geological library (challenge grant).

Hoblitzelle Foundation, TX

$50,000 to Hockaday School, Dallas, TX, for library expansion.

Houston Endowment, TX

$15,000 to Elsa, City of, Elsa, TX, toward library construction.

$410,000 to Lyndon Baines Johnson Foundation, Austin, TX, for endowment funds for LBJ Presidential Library.

$500,000 to Trinity University, San Antonio, TX, toward construction of library (continuing support).

Moody Foundation, TX

$5,000 to Lytle Public Library, Lytle, TX, for expansion and to furnish library shelving and furniture for new addition.

$5,000 to Mount Calm Library, Mount Calm, TX, toward construction of library-community center to serve surrounding towns and rural communities in Hill County.

$44,720 to Rosenberg Library, Galveston, TX, to assist in conducting phase I of the history of Galveston since 1900 project.

Richardson (Sid W.) Foundation, TX

$10,000 to Archives of American Art, New York, NY, for collection of data related to area of northern Texas.

$5,000 to Mount Calm, City of, Mount Calm, TX, for construction of library facility.

$50,000 to Olney Community Library Board, Olney, TX, for equipment for library facility.

Shell Companies Foundation, TX

$5,000 to Hoover Institution, Stanford, CA.

$5,000 to Houston Public Library, Houston, TX.

$5,000 to Lyndon Baines Johnson Foundation, Austin, TX, for library.

$5,000 to New York Public Library, New York, NY.

Seattle Foundation, WA

$5,000 to Cornish Institute of Allied Arts, Seattle, WA, for acquisitions for school library.

Weyerhaeuser Company Foundation, WA

$25,000 to University of Washington, Law Library, Seattle, WA, to acquire Indonesian law materials.

De Rance, Inc., WI

$50,000 to Friends of Our Little Brothers, Phoenix, AZ, toward construction of administrative buildings, a library, and student cooperative.

$25,000 to Sisters of the Blessed Sacrament, Fund for American Indian Education, Cornwells Heights, PA, for library building at Saint Catherine's Indian School in Santa Fe, NM (Native Americans).

Stiemke (Walter and Olive) Foundation, WI

$7,500 to Riveredge Nature Center, Newburg, WI, for construction of library dormer.

Part 3
Library Education, Placement, and Salaries

GUIDE TO LIBRARY PLACEMENT SOURCES

Margaret Myers
Director, Office for Library Personnel Resources
American Library Association

This year's guide updates the listing in the 1979 *Bowker Annual* with information on new joblines, new services, and changes in contacts and groups listed previously. The sources listed primarily give assistance in obtaining professional positions, although a few indicate assistance for paraprofessionals. The latter tend to be recruited primarily through local sources.

GENERAL SOURCES OF LIBRARY JOBS

Library Literature. Classified ads of library vacancies and positions wanted are carried in many of the national, regional, and state library journals and newsletters. Members of associations can sometimes list "position wanted" ads free of charge in their membership publications. Listings of positions available are regularly found in *American Libraries, College & Research Libraries Newsletter, Journal of Academic Librarianship, Library Journal, LJ/SLJ Hotline, Special Libraries,* and *Wilson Library Bulletin.* Newsletters such as the *Acquisitive Librarian, Black Caucus Newsletter,* and *American Indian Libraries* are beginning to carry some job ads. State and regional library association newsletters, state library journals, and foreign library periodicals carrying such ads are listed in later sections.

Newspapers. The *New York Times* Sunday Week in Review section carries a special section of ads for librarian jobs in addition to the regular classifieds. Local newspapers, particularly the larger city Sunday editions, often carry job vacancy listings in libraries, both professional and paraprofessional.

National Registry for Librarians. 40 W. Adams St., Chicago, IL 60603, 312-793-4904. Established as a professional placement service in 1965, the Registry is a centralized nationwide clearinghouse for professional librarians and employers. There are no registration, referral, or placement fees for this service. Librarians seeking professional employment complete an application form. Employers also complete job order forms, which describe their vacancies. Copies of all applications meeting the employer's selection criteria are forwarded to allow the employer to contact the applicant directly. The Registry does not maintain a file of school credits or personal references, nor does it make any recommendations. The Registry does not maintain or distribute vacancy lists.

Theresa M. Burke Employment Agency. 25 W. 39 St., New York, NY 10018, 212-398-9250. A licensed professional employment agency that has specialized for over 30 years in the recruitment of library and information personnel for academic, public, and special libraries. Staffed by employment counselors who have training and experience in both library service and personnel recruitment. Presently the majority of openings are in special libraries in the Northeast and require subject backgrounds and/or specific kinds of experience. Fees are paid by the employer.

LIBRARY JOBLINES

Library joblines or job "hotlines" give recorded telephone messages of job openings in a specific geographical area. Most tapes are changed once a week on Friday afternoon, although individual listings may sometimes be carried for several weeks. The classified section of *American Libraries* carries jobline numbers in each issue. Although the information is fairly brief and the cost of calling is borne by the individual job seeker, a jobline provides a quick and up-to-date listing of vacancies that is not usually possible with printed listings or journal ads.

Most joblines carry listings for their state or region only, although some will occasionally accept out-of-state positions if there is room on the tape. While a few will list technician and other paraprofessional positions, the majority are for professional jobs only. When calling the joblines, one might occasionally find a time when the telephone keeps ringing without any answer; this will usually mean that the tape is being changed or there are no new jobs for that period.

The following are in operation: American Society for Information Science, 202-659-8132; Arizona State Library/JAM, 602-278-1327; British Columbia Library Association, 604-263-0014 (B.C. listings only); California Library Association, 916-443-1222 for northern California and 213-629-5627 for southern California (identical lists); California Media and Library Educators Association, 415-697-8832; Colorado State Library, 303-839-2210 (Colorado jobs only, includes paraprofessional); Florida State Library, 904-488-5232 (in-state listings only); Georgia Library Association/JMRT, 404-634-5726 (5 P.M.–8 A.M. Monday through Friday; 12 noon Saturday through 8 A.M. Monday); Illinois Library Job Hotline, 312-828-0930 (cosponsored by the Special Libraries Association Illinois Chapter and Illinois Regional Library Council—all types of jobs listed); Maryland Library Association, 301-685-5760; Metropolitan Washington Council of Governments (D.C.), 202-223-2272; Midwest Federation of Library Associations, 517-487-5617 (also includes paraprofessional and out-of-state if room on tape) (cosponsored by six state library associations—Illinois, Indiana, Michigan, Minnesota, Ohio, Wisconsin); New England Library Board, 203-525-9647 (New England area jobs only); New Jersey State Library Association/State Library, 609-695-2121; New York Library Association, 212-687-1352; North Carolina State Library, 919-733-6410 (professional jobs in North Carolina only); Oregon Library Association, 503-585-2232 (cosponsored by Oregon Educational Media Association); Pacific Northwest Library Association, 206-543-2890 (Alaska, Alberta, British Columbia, Idaho, Montana, Oregon, Washington; includes both professional and paraprofessional and other library-related jobs); Pennsylvania Cooperative Jobline, 412-362-5627 (cosponsored by the Pennsylvania Library Association, Pennsylvania Learning Resources Association, Pittsburgh Regional Library Center, Special Libraries Association-Philadelphia Chapter, Medical Library Association, Philadelphia and Pittsburgh groups, American Society for Information Science-Delaware Valley Chapter; Pennsylvania School Librarians Association (also accepts paraprofessional and out-of-state listings); Special Libraries Association, Southern California Chapter, 213-795-2145; University of South Carolina College of Librarianship, 803-777-8443; Virginia Library Association Jobline, 804-355-0384. A new jobline was added during 1979 in New England, and another was scheduled to start in Illinois in spring 1980.

For those employers who wish to place vacancy listings on the jobline recordings, the following numbers can be called: Arizona, 602-269-2535; ASIS, 202-659-3644; California, 916-447-8541; Colorado, 303-839-2174; Washington, DC, 202-223-6800, ext. 344; Florida, 904-487-2651; Georgia, 404-329-6872; New Jersey, 609-292-6237; New York, 212-687-6625; North Carolina, 919-733-2570; Pennsylvania Library Association, 412-362-6400; Virginia, 804-770-5572; New England, 203-525-2681.

Write: British Columbia Library Association, Box 46378, Sta. G, Vancouver, B.C.

V6R 4G6, Canada; California Media and Library Educators Association, 1575 Old Bayshore Hwy., Suite 204, Burlingame, CA 94010; Maryland Library Association, 115 W. Franklin St., Baltimore, MD 21201; Oregon Library Association JOBLINE, Oregon State Library, Salem, OR 97310; PLNA Jobline, c/o Pacific Northwest Bibliographic Center, University of Washington, 253 Suzzalo Library FM-25, Seattle, WA 98195; University of South Carolina, College of Librarianship Placement, Columbia, SC 29208, (no geographical restrictions).

For the Midwest Federation Jobline, employers should send listings to their own state association executive secretary, who will refer these to the Michigan Library Association where the recording equipment is housed. There is a $5 fee to be paid by the employer for each listing. Paraprofessional positions are also accepted.

For the Illinois Library Job Hotline, contact Illinois Regional Library Council, 425 N. Michigan Ave., Chicago, IL 60611. An employer fee will be charged.

SPECIALIZED LIBRARY ASSOCIATIONS AND GROUPS

American Association of Law Libraries, c/o Albert Brecht, 53 W. Jackson Blvd., Chicago, IL 60604, 312-939-4764. Placement service is available without charge. Lists of openings and personnel available are published several times per year in a newsletter distributed to membership. Applicants are referred to placement officers for employment counseling.

American Chemical Society, Division of Chemical Information, c/o Bruno M. Vasta, National Library of Medicine, 8600 Rockville Pike, Bethesda, MD 20014. The division sponsors a referral service for unemployed literature chemists (knowledgeable of chemistry reference works, indexing, abstracting). Lists of positions available are sent on request at no charge, although no resumes or credentials are handled through the service.

American Libraries, c/o J. W. Grey, 50 E. Huron St., Chicago, IL 60611. "Career LEADS EXPRESS": advance galleys (three to four weeks) of job listings to be published in next issue of *American Libraries*. Early notice of some 40 to 60 "Positions Open" sent about the fourteenth of each month; does not include editorial corrections, late changes, and the majority of "Late Job Notices," as they appear in the regular *AL* LEADS section. For each month, send $2 check made out to *AL* EXPRESS; self-addressed, standard business-size envelope (4 × 9), and 15¢ postage on envelope.

Consultants Keyword Clearinghouse (CKC). A new *American Libraries* service that helps match professionals offering library/information expertise with institutions seeking it. Published quarterly, CKC appears in the Career LEADS section of the January, April, June, and October issues of *AL*. Rates: $3/line—classified; $30/inch—display. Inquiries should be made to J. W. Grey, LEADS editor, *American Libraries*, 50 E. Huron St., Chicago, IL 60611; 312-944-6780, ext. 326.

American Library Association, 50 E. Huron St., Chicago, IL 60611, 312-944-6780. A placement service is provided at each annual conference (June or July) and midwinter meeting (January). Handouts on interviewing, preparing a résumé, and other job-seeking information are available from the ALA Office for Library Personnel Resources.

American Library Association, Association of College and Research Libraries, Fast Job Listing Service, 50 E. Huron St., Chicago, IL 60611. Monthly circular listing job openings received in ACRL office during previous four weeks (supplements listings that will continue to appear in *C&RL News*). $5 to ACRL members requesting service (indicate ALA/ACRL membership number); $10 to nonmembers. Renewable each six months.

American Library Association (ALA) Black Caucus, c/o Dean Virginia Lacy Jones, Atlanta University School of Library Service, Atlanta, GA 30314. Although not a placement service, a Data Bank of black librarians is maintained, and employers do request information on possible candidates.

ALA Social Responsibilities Round Table, Rhode Island Affiliate, c/o Marcia Hershoff, 228 W. School St., Woonsocket, RI 02895. SRRT Jobline appears monthly in *Rhode Island Library Association Bulletin*, listing positions in southeast New England, including paraprofessional jobs. Job seekers desiring copy of most recent monthly Jobline send self-addressed, stamped envelope. Groups of envelopes may also be sent. To post a notice, contact Barbara Cohen, Adams Library, Rhode Island College, Providence, RI 02908.

American Society for Information Science, 1155 16 St. N.W., Suite 210, Washington, DC 20036, 202-659-3644. There is an active placement service operated at ASIS annual meetings (usually October) and midyear meetings (usually May) (locales change). All conference attendees (both ASIS members and nonmembers), as well as ASIS members who cannot attend the conference, are eligible to use the service to list or find jobs. Job listings are also accepted from employers who cannot attend the conference; interviews are arranged and special seminars are given. During the rest of the year, current job openings are listed on the ASIS Jobline. Seventeen of the ASIS chapters have placement officers who further assist members in finding jobs.

The ASIS Jobline operates 24 hours a day, seven days a week. Brief descriptions, including contact information, of current job openings around the country are recorded every Friday noon. New jobs are listed first, starting with overseas or West Coast jobs and working back toward jobs in the Washington, DC, area. Thereafter, jobs still available from the preceding week's recordings are listed. The average tape length is 7 minutes. The number to call is 202-659-8132.

American Theological Library Association, c/o Office of the Executive Secretary, Lutheran Theological Seminary, 7301 Germantown Ave., Philadelphia, PA 19119. Free to members; $5 filing fee for nonmembers for listing up to two years or until employment is secured. Application forms should be requested. Referrals are made throughout the year. Although not large in numbers, openings are representative of the size of the association.

Art Libraries Society/North America (ARLIS/NA), c/o Executive Secretary, Suite 4444, 7735 Old Georgetown Rd., Washington, DC 20014. Art librarian jobs are listed in the newsletter (five times a year).

Association for Educational Communication & Technology Placement Service, 1126 16 St. N.W., Washington, DC 20036, 202-833-4180. Positions available are listed in the monthly *AECT Bulletin* by code number and state; responses to ads are forwarded by the association to the appropriate employer/employee. A placement center operates at annual conferences. Available also to nonmembers; request application.

Council of Library/Media Technical Assistants, c/o Richard Taylor, Editor, Wilbur Wright College, 3400 N. Austin Ave., Chicago, IL 60634. *COLT Newsletter* appears 11 times a year and will accept listings for library media technical assistant positions. However, correspondence relating to jobs cannot be handled.

Information Exchange System for Minority Personnel (IESMP, Inc.), Box 91, Raleigh, NC 22602. Nonprofit organization designed to recruit minority librarians for EEO/AA employers. *Informer*, quarterly newsletter. Write for membership categories, services, and fees.

Medical Library Association, 919 N. Michigan Ave., Suite 3208, Chicago, IL

60611, 312-266-2456. Placement service is free to MLA members and $25 for nonmembers. Registration period is six months. Lists of all available positions are sent to registrants monthly by first-class mail; enrollees also have the option of placing position wanted or available ads in the *MLA News* for two months. Also offers placement service at annual conference each summer.

Music Library Association, Placement Officer, Karen K. Miller, The Cleveland Institute of Music, 11021 East Boulevard, Cleveland, OH 44106. Registration fee of $7 per year (September through August). MLA members who register receive the *Job List*. Employers are sent information about candidates matching their requirements.

Reforma, National Association of Spanish Speaking Librarians in the U.S., Editor, Arnulfo D. Trejo, Graduate Library School, College of Education, University of Arizona, 1515 E. First St., Tucson, AZ 85719. Quarterly newsletter lists and invites listings especially those for bilingual and minority librarians. For listing of Spanish speaking/Spanish-surnamed professionals, request: "Quien Es Quien: A "Who's Who of Spanish-Heritage Librarians in the U.S." for $3 from Arizona Center for Educational Research & Development, College of Education, Rm. 311, University of Arizona, Tucson, AZ 85721. Revised edition due spring 1980. The *Amoxcalli* quarterly newsletter of the Reforma El Paso Chapter lists job openings also. Contact chapter at Box 2064, El Paso, TX 79951.

Special Libraries Association, 235 Park Ave. S., New York, NY 10003, 212-477-9250. In addition to the Conference Employment Clearing House, a monthly listing of positions wanted and available, *Employment Opportunities*, is available free for six months to SLA members who request this in writing. Most SLA chapters also have employment chairpersons who act as referral persons for employers and job seekers. The official journal of the association, *Special Libraries*, carries classified advertising ten times a year.

STATE LIBRARY AGENCIES

In addition to the joblines mentioned previously, some of the state library agencies issue lists of job openings within their areas. These include Indiana (on request); Iowa (*Iowa Jobline*, mo., sent to all accredited library education programs and interested individuals); Minnesota (*Position Openings in Minnesota and Adjoining States*, mo., sent to public and academic libraries); Mississippi (job vacancy list, mo.); North Carolina (*News Flash*, irreg. newsletter lists available positions in North Carolina public libraries); Ohio (*Library Opportunities in Ohio*, mo., sent to all accredited library education programs and interested individuals upon request); Pennsylvania ("positions open"); Texas (Texas Placement News, bi-mo., free).

On occasion, when vacancy postings are available, state library newsletters or journals will list these, such as Alabama (*Cottonboll*, mo.); Indiana (updated list from *Extension Division Bulletin*, upon request); (*Library Occurrent*, q.); Missouri (*Show-Me Libraries*, mo.); Nebraska (*Overtones*, 13 times a year); New Mexico (*Hitchhiker*, w., newsletter); New Hampshire (*Granite State Libraries*, bi-mo.); Oklahoma (*Source*, mo.); Utah (*Horsefeathers*, mo.); Wyoming (*Outrider*, mo.); and American Samoa (Office of Samoan Information, Pago Pago, *News Bulletin*, daily). When vacancies are known at the Michigan State Library, these are listed in the *State Library Newsletter*, particularly for public library directors, but not necessarily for general staff members.

Many state library agencies will refer applicants informally when vacancies are known to exist, but do not have formal placement services. The following states primarily make referrals to public libraries only: Alabama, Arkansas, Connecticut, Georgia, Idaho, Kansas, Kentucky, Louisiana, Maryland, Maine, North Carolina, Oklahoma, South Carolina (institutional also), Tennessee, Vermont, and Wyoming. Those who refer applicants to all types of libraries are Arizona, Florida, Guam, Indiana, Kansas, Maine, Maryland, Massachusetts, Mississippi, Missouri, Montana, Nebraska, Nevada (largely public and academic), New Hampshire, New Mexico, North Carolina, North Dakota, Ohio, Oklahoma, Rhode Island, South Dakota, Utah, Virginia, West Virginia (public, academic, special), and Wyoming. The Missouri State Library offers a formal placement service, matching interests and qualifications of registered job applicants with positions available in Missouri libraries. For the addresses of the state agencies, see "State Library Agencies" in Part 7.

STATE AND REGIONAL LIBRARY ASSOCIATIONS

State and regional library associations will often make referrals, run ads in association newsletters, or operate a placement service at annual conferences, in addition to the joblines sponsored by some groups. Referral of applicants when jobs are known is done by the following associations: Arkansas, Delaware (also for Delaware listings, call the Maryland, New Jersey, or Pennsylvania joblines), Hawaii, Louisiana, Michigan, Nevada, South Dakota, Tennessee, Texas, and Wisconsin. Although listings are infrequent, job vacancies are placed in the following association newsletters or journals when available: Alaska (*Sourdough*, 6 times a year); Arizona (*ASLA Newsletter*, mo.); Connecticut (*CLA Memo*, 10 times a year); District of Columbia (*Intercom*, 11 issues); Georgia (*Georgia Librarian*); Iowa (*Catalyst*, 6 times a year); Kansas (*KLA Newsletter*, 3 times a year); Minnesota (*MLA Newsletter*, 11 issues a year); Missouri (*MLA Newsletter*, bi-mo.); Mountain Plains Library Association (newsletter lists vacancies and position wanted ads for individual and institutional members or area library school students); New Mexico (shares notices via State Library's *Hitchhiker*, w.); Nevada (*Highroller*, 6 times a year); New Hampshire (*NHLA Newsletter*, 6 times a year; *Granite State Libraries*); *New Jersey Libraries* (8 times a year); North Carolina (q.); Oklahoma (*The Oklahoma Librarian; President's Newsletter*); Pennsylvania (*PLA Bulletin*, mo.); Rhode Island Library Association (*Bulletin*, mo.); Vermont (*VLA News*, Box 803 Burlington, VT 05402, 10 issues a year); *Virginia Librarian* (q.); *West Virginia Libraries*. The *Southeastern Librarian* lists joblines in that geographical area.

At their annual conference the following associations have indicated some type of placement service, although it may only consist of bulletin board postings: Alabama, Arkansas, Connecticut, California, Illinois, Kansas, Maryland, Mountain Plains, New England, New Jersey, New Mexico, New York, Texas, and Vermont.

The following associations have indicated they have no placement service at this time: Florida, Indiana, Kentucky, Minnesota, Mississippi, North Dakota, Oklahoma, Pacific Northwest, South Carolina, Southwest, Washington, and Wyoming. State and regional association addresses are found in the *Bowker Annual*.

LIBRARY EDUCATION PROGRAMS

Library education programs offer some type of service for their current students as well as alumni. Of the ALA-accredited programs, the following handle placement activities through the library school: Atlanta, British Columbia, Columbia, Dalhousie, Denver, Drexel, Emory, Geneseo, Hawaii, Illinois, Long Island, Louisiana, Michigan, Minnesota, Missouri, Pittsburgh, Pratt, Queens, Rosary, Rutgers, Texas-Austin, Toronto, UCLA, Western Ontario, and Wisconsin-Madison.

The central university placement center handles activities for the following schools: Alabama A&M, Arizona, Brigham Young, California-Berkeley, Case Western, McGill, North Carolina, Peabody/Vanderbilt, St. John's, Southern California, and South Florida. However, in most cases, faculty in the library school will still do informal counseling regarding job seeking.

In some schools, the placement services are handled in a cooperative manner; in most cases the university placement center sends out credentials while the library school posts or compiles the job listings. Schools utilizing both sources include Alabama, Albany, Buffalo, Catholic, Chicago, Clarion State, Denver, Emporia, Florida State, Geneseo, Indiana, Iowa, Kent, Kentucky, Maryland, Montreal, North Carolina Central, North Texas, Northern Illinois, Oklahoma, Peabody/Vanderbilt, Pratt, Queens, Simmons, South Carolina, South Florida, Southern Connecticut, Syracuse, Tennessee, Texas Woman's, Washington, Wayne State, Western Michigan, and Wisconsin-Milwaukee.

In sending out placement credentials, schools vary as to whether they distribute these free, charge a general registration fee, or request a fee for each file or credentials sent out.

Those schools that have indicated that they post job vacancy notices for review but do not issue printed lists are: Alabama, Alabama A&M, Albany, Atlanta, British Columbia, Catholic, Chicago, Drexel, Emory, Emporia, Florida State, Hawaii, Kent, Louisiana, McGill, Maryland, Montreal, North Carolina Central, Northern Illinois, Peabody/Vanderbilt, Queens, Simmons, South Carolina, South Florida, Southern California, Syracuse, Tennessee, Texas-Austin, Texas Woman's, Toronto, Washington, Wayne State, Western Michigan, and Western Ontario. (Notices of positions open are sent to graduates on the school's Placement Mailing List as they are received.)

In addition to job vacancy postings, some schools issue a printed listing of positions open that is distributed primarily to students and alumni and only occasionally available to others. The following schools issue listings free to students and alumni *only* unless indicated otherwise: Albany; Arizona (every two weeks, $6 per year for alumni, $12 per year for nonalumni); Brigham Young; Buffalo (bi-mo. newsletter; service to all area professionals upon request for academic year); California-Berkeley (alumni receive 10 a year out-of-state listings if registered; $20 fee for service, also a jobline, call 415-642-1716 to list positions); Case Western (alumni $10 for six lists); Clarion State (free to students and alumni); Columbia (alumni six issues, $2); Dalhousie ($5 per year for students, alumni, and others); Denver (alumni $5 per year); Geneseo (free in office; by mail only to students and alumni who send self-addressed, stamped envelopes); Illinois (free in office; by mail to anyone who sends No. 10 self-addressed, stamped envelopes); Indiana (others may send self-addressed, stamped envelopes); Iowa (students and alumni as part of $10 registration fee); Kentucky; Long Island (no charge); Michigan (free for one year following graduation, all other graduates $5 per year, 12 issues); Minnesota (if 28¢ self-addressed envelopes are supplied); Missouri (Library Vacancy Roster, tri-w. printout, 50¢ an issue, with minimum of 10 issues, to anyone); North Carolina (subscription fee of $10 per year); North Texas State ($5 for six months, students and alumni); Peabody/Vanderbilt (students and alumni if registered for fee); Pittsburgh (others for $3 for six months); Rhode Island ($2.50 for 6 issues); Rosary ($10 per year, every other week); Pratt (alumni, weekly during spring, fall, and summer sessions; others, renew every three months); Rutgers (alumni and others $4 for six months); St. John's (students and alumni, $5 per year); Southern Connecticut; Syracuse (listings sent out by university service twice a month, 8 mo./yr. 50¢ per month; available to anyone requesting); UCLA (alumni need to renew every three months); Western Michigan ($7.50 for 26 weeks to anyone, issued by

University Placement Services); Wisconsin-Madison (subscription $5 per year for 12 issues, to anyone); Wisconsin-Milwaukee (monthly to SLS graduates registering with Department of Placement & Career Development).

As the job market has tightened, a number of schools are providing job-hunting seminars and short courses or more actively trying to help graduates obtain positions. Most schools will offer at least an annual or semiannual discussion on placement, often with outside speakers representing different types of libraries or recent graduates relating experiences. Some additional programs offered by schools include Atlanta (job-hunting seminar); Berkeley, California (career awareness workshops on resumes, interview, and job search); Brigham Young (students write resume that is critiqued in basic administration class); British Columbia ("Employment Week" in spring term with employers invited to interview); Buffalo (assists laid-off local employees; sends list of graduates to major libraries in the United States; operates SDI service; resume seminar and follow-up critique, strategy sessions for conference job seeking; "Put a Buffalo in Your Library" buttons); Columbia (alumni/student career day; sessions on resume writing, interviewing, job counseling, during the spring; edge-notched card service); Dalhousie (sessions on job searching, etc. with critiquing of resumes); Denver (resume writing in administration course, interview workshop, profile of students so job listings can be sent matching interests); Drexel (job search workshops; resumes, cover letters, interviewing, employers present for questions and answers; job applicant matching service using edge-notched cards available to recent graduates and alumni who register for service; individual job counseling by appointment available to graduates and alumni); Emory (job strategy meeting each term, resume assistance and job counseling); Hawaii (workshop each semester, computer-based placement file); Illinois (resume writing, interview role playing in library administration class counseling/critiquing for individuals in library school placement office; computer-based placement profiles for students and alumni; job search workshops by university-wide placement service); Iowa (job strategy and resume-writing session each term; individual counseling); Kentucky (runs SDI service for students and alumni completing interest profile); McGill (special committee investigates ways to bring employers/students together, monitors opportunities in the province, seeks information about careers of graduates; "Get-Acquainted Day" held each year for potential employers/second-year students; colloquium series includes employment-related subjects); Michigan (a student committee scans and clips newspapers and periodicals for vacancy notices to post); Montreal (telephone service in cooperation with graduates); North Carolina (workshop on resume preparation, job-seeking strategy, interview techniques; students may do mock interview on videotape with critique); North Carolina Central (seminars, counseling); Peabody/Vanderbilt (regular seminars on library marketplace, resume preparation, interviews, etc.); Pittsburgh (individual counseling, preconference strategy sessions, placement colloquium sessions, day-long workshops covering search strategy, resumes, and other means of access; interview techniques); Pratt (job clinics throughout the year, book of resumes sent to employers); Rhode Island (resumes critiqued in library administration course, jobs seminar annually); Rutgers (workshops on search strategy, interviewing, placement booths at local and state conferences); Simmons (series of four programs each semester); South Carolina (seminars on job search and resume writing offered as part of curriculum); South Florida (part-time administrative assistant recruits minority students and identifies placement possibilities); Southern Connecticut (five sessions in one Annual Job Workshop Week); Syracuse (annual "Career Survival Day"); Texas-Austin (series of sessions on career development); Toronto (publishes annual placement and salary survey in Canadian Library Association's *Feliciter*); UCLA (compiles "Job Hunting Handbook"); Washington (job-search strategy and interviewing discussions; postings); Western Ontario (maintains vertical file of information about specific libraries and geographical areas, conducting research project to identify job vacancies); Wisconsin-Madison (job-finding programs, résumé writing); Wisconsin-Milwaukee (Job Fair with interview role playing and résumé writing).

Employers will often list jobs with schools only in their particular geographical area; some library schools will give information to nonalumni regarding their specific locales, but are *not* staffed to handle mail requests and advice is usually given in person. Schools that have indicated they will allow librarians in their areas to view listings are Alabama, Alabama A&M, Albany, Arizona, Brigham Young, British Columbia, Buffalo, Case Western, Catholic, Chicago, Dalhousie, Denver, Emory, Emporia, Florida State, Geneseo, Illinois, Indiana, Iowa, Kent, Kentucky, Louisiana, Peabody/Vanderbilt, Pittsburgh, Pratt, Queens, Rutgers, Rhode Island, St. John's, South Carolina, Southern California, Southern Connecticut, Syracuse, Tennessee, Texas-Austin, Texas Woman's, Toronto, UCLA, Washington, Wayne State, Western Michigan, Western Ontario, Wisconsin-Madison, and Wisconsin-Milwaukee.

A list of accredited program addresses appears later in this section of Part 3 of the *Bowker Annual*. Individuals interested in placement services of other library education programs should contact the schools directly.

FEDERAL LIBRARY JOBS

The first step in obtaining employment in a federal library is to become listed in the Librarian's Register, which is a subset of files maintained by the U.S. Office of Personnel Management in order to match federal job applicants with federal job vacancies (1900 E St. N.W., Washington, DC 20415). Applicants must have forms SF-171 and 1170/34 (the latter replaces form CS-1143) on file in order to be considered for a position. Also of great help is a photocopy of the applicant's library school transcript or a typed list of relevant courses. Form CS-226 may be used for this purpose if desired. Forms may be obtained from local Federal Job Information Centers in major metropolitan areas listed in the telephone book under "U.S. Government."

One is considered for all grades for which one is qualified and indicate one will accept. As vacancies occur, applications will be evaluated in relation to an agency's specific requirements, and names are referred for consideration. Eligibility will remain in effect for one year; updated information must be submitted to remain eligible after this time.

Applications are accepted only when the register is "open." The frequency with which, and the length of time, the register is open depend on the size of the inventory. The inventory is judged to be too low when a significant proportion of applicants who are qualified for positions decline them. This so-called declination rate is reversed by opening the register, thereby expanding the applicant pool.

In recent years the register has been opened once each year, usually in the spring. It was open April 16–27 in 1979. It generally remains open approximately two weeks, with advance notice going to all local Federal Job Information Centers. Prospective applicants can expect the circumstances in 1980 to be similar to those in 1979. Applicants who are most likely to be successful are those with training and experience in the fields of medical librarianship, law librarianship, and the sciences. Most vacancies occur in the Washington area, with New York and California trailing far behind.

The examiner does not select those to be hired, but does play the crucial role in weighing the relative experience of those on the register. When selecting the most qualified candidates, whose forms are then forwarded to the hiring agency, the examiner must consider many factors simultaneously: work experience, education (formal and informal), geographic preference, etc. Any information that should be considered must be on these forms and must not be left for someone to discover during the interview stage. Chances are that the applicant may never reach the interview stage if pertinent experience or education is not explained at the outset.

In addition to filing the appropriate forms, applicants also can attempt to make personal contact directly with federal agencies in which they are interested. The *Federal Times* and the Sunday *Washington Post* sometimes list federal library openings. In addition, there are some "excepted" agencies, which are not required to hire through the usual OPM channels. While these agencies may require the SF-171 or other standard forms, they maintain their own employee selection policies and procedures. Government establishments with positions outside the competitive civil service include Energy Research and Development Administration; Board of Governors of the Federal Reserve System; Central Intelligence Agency; Department of Medicine and Surgery; Federal Bureau of Investigation; Foreign Service of the United States; National Science Foundation; National Security Agency; Central Examining Office; Tennessee Valley Authority; U.S. Nuclear Regulatory Commission; U.S. Postal Service; Judicial Branch of the Government; Legislative Branch of the Government; U.S. Mission to the United Nations; World Bank and IFC; International Monetary Fund; Organization of American States; Pan American Health Organization; and United Nations Secretariat.

In addition, the Library of Congress operates its own independent merit selection system. Thus, applicants for positions at the library should submit an SF-171, Personal Qualifications Statement, to the Library of Congress, Employment Office, Washington, DC 20540. Persons who apply for specific vacancies by Posting Number enhance their prospects for consideration.

General information on applying for federal jobs can be found in the *Occupational Outlook Quarterly*, Winter 1977, pp. 2–9 ("Working for U.S."), and pp. 17–23 ("Standard Form 171"); also see *The Uncle Sam Connection* by James E. Hawkins (Follett, 1978, 168 pp., $4.95). See also "Professional Careers for Librarians," announcement No. 422, April 1977 (GPO 1977/779-322).

ADDITIONAL GENERAL AND SPECIALIZED JOB SOURCES

School Libraries. School librarians often find that the channels for locating positions in education are of more value than the usual library ones. However, the National Center for Information on Careers in Education is no longer in operation. A list of commercial teacher agencies may be obtained from the National Association of Teachers Agencies, c/o Elwood Q. Taylor, 1825 K St., N.W., Suite 706, Washington, DC 20006.

The Chronicle of Higher Education (published weekly during the academic year, 1717 Massachusetts Ave. N.W., Washington, DC) is receiving more classified ads for library openings than previously, although many are at the administrative level; *Academe* (newsletter of the American Association of University Professors, One Dupont Circle, Washington, DC 20036) also lists librarian jobs at times, as well as *Change: The Magazine of Learning* (NBW Tower, New Rochelle, NY 10801).

American Association of Junior Colleges Career Staffing Center, 621 Duke St., Box 298, Alexandria, VA 22314, 703-548-8020. Persons interested in junior or community college positions complete a registration form and submit with a $20 yearly fee.

Condensed personnel information is sent to deans who make direct contact with individuals in whom they are interested; in addition, vacancy listings are distributed to registrants in the spring.

Affirmative Action Register, 8356 Olive Blvd., St. Louis, MO 63132. The goal is to "provide female, minority and handicapped candidates with an opportunity to learn of professional and managerial positions throughout the nation and to assist employers in implementing their Affirmative Action Programs." Free distribution of monthly bulletin is made to leading businesses, industrial and academic institutions, and over 4,000 agencies that recruit qualified minorities and women, as well as to all known female, minority, and handicapped professional organizations, placement offices, newspapers, magazines, rehabilitation facilities, and over 8,000 federal, state, and local governmental employment units. Individual mail subscriptions are available for $15 per year. Librarian listings are in most every issue. Sent free to libraries on request.

Catalyst, 14 E. 60 St., New York, NY 10022. A national nonprofit organization dedicated to expanding career opportunities for women, through publications, local resource center listings, and library, which serves as a clearinghouse for all information concerning women and work, careers, and career education.

Cooperative College Register, 621 Duke St., Alexandria, VA 22314. Reestablished in 1977, the register served persons seeking positions in higher education. However, there has not been sufficient interest to continue this clearinghouse function and it is not accepting new registrations.

Educational Information Service, Box 662, Newton Lower Falls, MA 02162. Instant Alert service for $24 sends individual 12 notices of openings on same day EIS hears of job. Publishes lists of faculty and administrative education openings (library jobs only a small portion, however). Send for list of other services and fees.

Federal Research Service, Box 1059, Vienna, VA 22180, 703-281-0200. Published every other Wednesday, the *FRS Report* is a compilation of current vacancies in federal government agencies. Subscription rates are $21 for six biweekly reports; send for information on rates for longer periods. Since this includes all types of positions in the government, it is likely that only a small percentage are librarian vacancies.

OVERSEAS

Opportunities for employment in foreign countries are limited and immigration policies of individual countries should be investigated. Employment for Americans is virtually limited to U.S. Government libraries, libraries of U.S. firms doing worldwide business, and American schools abroad. Library journals from other countries will sometimes list vacancy notices (e.g., *Quidunc* [Australia], *British Columbia Library Association Reporter, Ontario Library Review, Canadian Library Journal, Feliciter, Library Association Record, Times Literary Supplement,* and *Times Higher Education Supplement*). Some persons have obtained jobs by contacting foreign publishers or vendors directly.

Although they do not specifically discuss librarian positions, several general brochures may be of help in providing further addresses: "American Students and Teachers Abroad: Sources of Information about Overseas Study, Teaching, Work, Travel" and "Federal Jobs Overseas" from Superintendent of Documents, U.S. Government Printing Office, Washington, DC 20402, for $1 and 30¢ respectively. "How to Get a Job Overseas" is available for $3 from International Publications, Indianapolis, IN 46229.

Action. Office of Recruitment and Communications, 812 Connecticut Ave. N.W., Washington, DC 20525. An umbrella agency that includes the Peace Corps and Vista. Will sometimes need librarians in developing nations and host communities in the United States. For further information, call toll-free 800-424-8580 and ask for Recruitment. Recruiting offices in many large cities.

Council for International Exchange of Scholars, Suite 300, 11 Dupont Circle, Washington, DC 20036, 202-833-4950. Administers U.S. government Fulbright awards for university lecturing and advanced research abroad; usually six to eight awards per year are made to specialists in library science. Open to U.S. citizens with university or college teaching experience. Request registration forms to receive spring announcement for academic year to start 12 to 18 months later.

Department of Defense, c/o Director, Department of Defense Dependents Schools, OAS (M&RA), Rm. 152, Hoffman I, 2461 Eisenhower Ave., Alexandria, VA 22331. Overall management and operational responsibilities for the education of dependents of active duty military personnel and DOD civilians who are stationed overseas, including recruitment of teaching personnel, are assigned to this agency. For application brochures, write to the above address specifying "Attention: Recruitment."

Educational Information Service, Box 662, Newton Lower Falls, MA 02162. Instant Alert services for $24 will send individual 12 notices of overseas openings on same day EIS learns of opening (library jobs small portion, however). Send for free details of other services.

Home Country Employment Registry, National Association for Foreign Student Affairs, 1860 19 St. N.W., Washington, DC 20009. Services are offered to U.S.-educated foreign students to assist them in locating employment in their home countries following completion of their studies.

International Association of School Librarianship, c/o School of Librarianship, Western Michigan University, Kalamazoo, MI 49008. Informal contacts might be established through this group.

International School Services, Box 5910, Princeton, NJ 08540. Private, nonprofit organization established to provide educational services for American schools overseas, other than Department of Defense schools. These are American elementary and secondary schools enrolling children of business and diplomatic families living away from their homeland. ISS seeks to register men and women interested in working abroad in education who meet basic professional standards of training and experience. Specialists, guidance counselors, department heads, librarians, supervisors, and administrators normally will need one or more advanced degrees in the appropriate field as well as professional experience commensurate with positions sought.

U.S. International Communication Agency (formerly USIA). Will occasionally seek librarians with MLS, four years' experience for regional library consultant positions. Candidates must have proven administrative ability and skills to coordinate the overseas USICA library program with the other information functions of USICA in various cities worldwide. Relevant experience might include cooperative library program development, community outreach, public affairs, project management, and personnel training. USICA maintains more than 139 libraries in over 82 countries with 1 million books and 660 local library staff worldwide. Libraries provide reference service and materials about the United States for foreign audiences. Five-year U.S. citizenship; entering salary $18,179 to $27,453, depending upon qualifications. Overseas allowances and differentials where applicable, vacation leave, term life insurance, medical and retirement programs. Send standard U.S. Government Form 171 to Employment Branch, ICA, Washington, DC 20547.

Overseas—Special Programs

ALA Black Caucus. Has a librarian exchange program with Africa. Contact E. J. Josey, New York State Education Department, Cultural Education Center, Rm. 10C47, Empire State Plaza, Albany, NY 12230.

International Exchanges. Most exchanges are handled by direct negotiation between interested parties. In order to facilitate such arrangements, the *IFLA Journal* (issued February, May, August, and November) now provides a listing of persons wishing to exchange positions *outside* their own country. All listings must include the following information: full name, address, present position, qualifications (with year of obtaining), language, abilities, preferred country/city/library, and type of position. Send to IFLA Secretariat, Netherlands Congress Building, Box 82128, 2508 EC, The Hague, Netherlands.

USING INFORMATION SKILLS IN NONLIBRARY SETTINGS

Many librarians are using their information skills in a variety of ways in nonlibrary settings. These jobs are not usually found through the regular library placement sources, although many library schools are trying to generate such listings for their students and alumni. Job listings that do exist may not call specifically for "librarians" by that title, so ingenuity may be needed to search out jobs where information management skills are desired. Some librarians are working on a free-lance basis by offering services to business, alternative schools, community agencies, legislators, etc; these opportunities are usually not found in advertisements but created by developing contacts and publicity over a period of time. A number of information-brokering business firms have developed from individual free-lance experiences. Small companies or other organizations often need one-time service for organizing files or collections, bibliographic research for special projects, indexing or abstracting, compilation of directories, and consulting services. Bibliographic networks and on-line data base companies are using librarians as trainers, researchers, systems analysts, etc. Jobs in this area are sometimes found in library network newsletters, the *Online* journal, or other data processing journals. (The first Online conference held in 1979 included a placement center.)

Librarians can be found working in law firms as litigation case supervisors (organizing and analyzing records needed for specific legal cases); with publishers as sales representatives, marketing directors, editors, and computer services experts; with community agencies as adult education coordinators, volunteer administrators, grants writers; etc.

Information on existing information services or methods for using information skills in nonlibrary settings can be found in: *Wilson Library Bulletin* (49) 440–445, February 1975; *Special Libraries* (67) 243–250, May/June 1976; *ASIS Bulletin* (2): 10–20, February 1976; *RQ* (18): 177–179, Winter 1978; and *New York Times*, December 12, 1979, "Careers" Section. *The Canadian Library Journal* (34), no. 2, April 1977, has an entire issue on alternative librarianship. Syracuse University, School of Information Studies, 113 Euclid Ave., Syracuse, NY 13210, has available *Proceedings of the Information Broker/Free-Lance Librarian Workshop*, April 1976, for $5, and *Alternative Careers in Information/Library Services: Summary of Proceedings of a Workshop*, July 1977, for $5.50. *The Directory of Fee-Based Information Services* lists information brokers, free-lance librarians, independent information specialists, and public and institutional libraries. Individuals do not need to pay to have listing; directory is available for $6.95 from Information Alternative, Box 657, Woodstock, NY 12498. It is supplemented by *The Journal of Fee-Based Information Services* (bi-mo.; $11 one-year subscription to institutions, $9 to others). Issues include new listings, changes of address, announcements, feature articles, and an exchange column. *What Else Can You Do with a Library Degree*, edited by Betty Carol Sellen, is published by Neal-Schuman Publishers and Gaylord Brothers, Inc. (Box 4901, Syracuse, NY 13221) for $14.95 plus 25¢ postage.

JOB HUNTING IN GENERAL

Wherever information needs to be organized and presented to patrons in an effective, efficient, and service-oriented fashion, the skills of professional librarians can be applied, whether or not they are in traditional library settings. However, it will take considerable investment of time, energy, imagination, and money on the part of an individual before a satisfying position is created or obtained, in a conventional library or another type of information service. Usually, no one method or source of job hunting can be used alone. Public and school library certification requirements often vary from state to state; contact the state library agency for such information in a particular state. Certification requirements are summarized in *Certification of Public Libraries in the U.S.*, 3rd ed., 1979, from the ALA Library Administration and Management Association ($3). A summary of school library/media certification requirements by state is found in *School Library Journal* (24): 38-50, April 1978. Civil service requirements either on a local, county, or state level often add another layer of procedures to the job search. Some civil service jurisdictions require written and/or oral examinations; others assign a ranking based on a review of credentials. Jobs are usually filled from the top candidates on a qualified list of applicants. Since the exams are held only at certain time periods and a variety of jobs can be filled from a single list of applicants (e.g., all Librarian I positions regardless of type of function), it is important to check whether a library in which one is interested falls under civil service procedures.

If one wishes a position in a specific subject area or in a particular geographical location, remember those reference skills to ferret information from directories and other tools regarding local industries, schools, subject collections, etc. Working as a substitute librarian or in temporary positions while looking for a regular job can provide valuable contacts and experience. Part-time jobs are not always advertised, but often found by canvassing local libraries and leaving applications.

For information on other job-hunting and personnel matters, request a checklist of personnel materials available from the ALA, Office for Library Personnel Resources, 50 E. Huron St., Chicago, IL 60611.

PLACEMENTS AND SALARIES, 1978: NEW DIRECTIONS

Carol L. Learmont
Assistant Dean, School of Library Service, Columbia University

Richard Troiano
Placement Assistant, School of Library Service, Columbia University

This is the twenty-eighth annual report on placements and salaries of graduates of American Library Association (ALA) accredited library schools. This year there were 63 eligible schools, and 62 schools completed the questionnaire in whole or in part. All geographical areas except the West are fully represented. Never before have we had such an excellent response. We thank all of you for your efforts to help make this a useful tool for the profession.

THE JOB MARKET

Forty-two schools reported no major difficulties in placing 1978 graduates. Thirteen schools reported major or some difficulty, as against 22 that reported major difficulty in 1977. California's Proposition 13 seems to have affected some of the western schools adversely, but one school reported no change, although it braced for one. A majority of placement officers mentioned the large number of openings available for people with science and math backgrounds, and the scarcity of such people coming into the profession. They also stressed that coursework in computerized information retrieval systems enhanced marketability. More and more schools are posting library-related opportunities along with the traditional library positions.

Salaries for 1978 graduates improved over those offered to 1977 graduates, but did not keep up with the increase in the cost of living. The 1978 salaries increased at the rate of 5.3 percent, compared to 6.5 percent in 1977, 5.2 percent in 1976, and 6 percent in 1975. In 1978 the average (mean) beginning salary for all graduates was $12,527; for women, $12,368 (increased by 6.1 percent from 1977); and for men, $12,525 (a 6.3 percent increase). Median salaries were $12,120 for all graduates; $12,079 for women and $12,112 for men (Tables 2 and 7). For new graduates with prior experience in a form relevant for salary purposes, the average beginning salary was $13,856 (up from $12,468 in 1977); without experience, $11,513 (up from $11,002 in 1977) (Table 12).

PLACEMENTS

The 62 schools responding in the survey awarded first professional degrees to 5,442 graduates in 1978 (Table 1). This was 25 fewer than the 5,467 awarded by 53 schools in 1977. In 1974, 52 schools reported awards to 6,370, an average of 123 graduates per school; in 1977 the average number of graduates was 103; for 1978 the average number was 88. Even taking into account the increased reportage, this appears to be a significant drop in the number of graduates. It seems clear that fewer beginning librarians are in the job market.

Note: Adapted from *Library Journal*, July 1979.

322 / LIBRARY EDUCATION, PLACEMENT, AND SALARIES

TABLE 1 STATUS OF 1978 GRADUATES, SPRING 1979

	No. of Graduates			Not in Lib. Positions			Empl. Not Known			Permanent Prof. Placements/			Temp. Prof. Placements/			Nonprof. Library Placements			Total in Lib. Positions		
	Women	Men	Total	Women	Men	Total	Women	Men	Total	Women	Men	Total	Women	Men	Total	Women	Men	Total	Women	Men	Total
United States	3,680	996	4,971*	538	166	714*	842	208	1,193*	2,127	587	2,756*	110	14	132*	137	34	176*	2,374	635	3,064
Northeast	1,297	330	1,852*	166	54	220	384	90	612*	742	187	929	37	4	41	42	8	50	821	199	1,020
Southeast	601	184	785	75	25	100	174	51	225	335	102	437	10	2	12	7	4	11	352	108	460
Midwest	1,125	299	1,424	169	58	227	164	38	202	710	188	898	42	3	45	40	12	52	792	203	995
Southwest	243	74	387*	34	9	53*	40	13	58*	155	48	245*	2	1	11*	12	3	20*	169	52	276*
West	414	109	523	94	20	114	80	16	96	185	62	247	19	4	23	36	7	43	240	73	313
Canada	343	128	471	43	29	72	54	16	70	215	75	290	30	7	37	1	1	2	246	83	329
All Schools	4,023	1,124	5,442*	581	195	786*	896	224	1,263*	2,342	662	3,046*	140	21	169*	138	35	178*	2,620	718	3,393*

*Includes figures undifferentiated by sex

TABLE 2 PLACEMENT AND SALARIES OF 1978 GRADUATES

	Place-ments	Salaries			Low Salary			High Salary			Average Salary			Median Salary		
		Women	Men	Total	Women	Men	Total	Women	Men	Total	Women	Men	Total	Women	Men	Total
Alabama	37	17	9	26	10300	10946	10300	13131	15700	15700	12001	11954	11984	12000	11500	12000
Alabama A&M	10	8	1	9	8300	9100	8300	16200	0	16200	12500	9100	10800	11900	9100	11900
New York (Albany)	45	21	6	27	7500	1080	7500	13150	14000	14000	11274	12680	11586	11800	12750	11801
Arizona	46	21	7	28	8000	1020	8000	17800	13000	17800	11789	11828	11799	11130	11800	11450
Atlanta	38	26	12	38	8300	9288	8508	16000	14657	16000	11742	11886	12472	11550	13200	12000
Brigham Young	24	9	7	16	8508	9600	8508	17000	20905	20905	12114	13672	13327	11550	13200	12354
British Columbia	55	2	2	4	15000	12000	12000	19000	27000	27000	17000	19750	18375	17000	19750	17000
Buffalo	36	4	36	8800	12000	8800	21000	13650	21000	12933	12587	13207	12800	12000	12500	
California (LA)	46	32	10	42	9900	11300	9900	16656	14600	16656	12359	12352	12358	12180	12000	12060
Case Western	62	25	5	30	8195	9492	8195	17410	15432	17410	11670	11064	11586	11500	9666	11250
Catholic	45	32	13	45	7500	11400	7500	27000	27000	27000	15119	16148	15417	14476	14000	14192
Chicago	24	0	0	0	0	0	0	0	0	0	0	0	0	0	0	0
Clarion	32	21	7	28	8500	8500	8500	12000	12000	12000	9500	10500	10500	9500	10500	10500
Columbia	100	53	13	66	8000	9000	8000	21000	16500	21000	11700	12100	11800	11800	12000	11950
Dalhousie	26	6	5	11	10500	8900	8900	15632	14100	15632	13795	11858	12915	14145	13000	13000
Denver	35	16	10	26	10000	10500	10000	14721	15000	15000	12011	12807	12317	11942	12284	12000
Drexel	70	48	16	64	8000	10000	8000	25600	23000	25600	12472	11907	12395	11598	11668	11600
Emory	37	28	7	35	9600	10500	9600	17497	12900	17497	11881	11429	11791	10969	11000	11000
Emporia	38	30	6	36	8200	6300	6300	34000	14081	34000	11654	11226	11440	10857	12000	11166
Florida State	10	5	3	8	9700	10800	9700	12500	13500	13500	10740	12000	11212	10500	10800	10800
Geneseo	50	26	6	32	8800	9200	8800	13250	13660	13660	11157	11960	11308	11000	12000	11000
Hawaii	22	16	4	20	7500	13488	7500	26400	21000	26400	15274	17372	15715	14000	17500	15000
Illinois	89	51	14	65	8400	10274	8400	19200	15750	19200	11542	12279	11701	11000	12150	11300
Indiana	85	43	9	52	7000	8652	7000	16827	14000	16827	11438	10450	11267	11000	10000	11000
Iowa	35	13	6	19	10000	9000	9000	15090	15686	15686	11912	11831	11886	11700	11000	12000
Kent State	76	46	14	60	8000	8000	8000	18757	21000	21000	11721	12147	11820	11653	10900	11500

School	Placements	Salaries Women	Salaries Men	Salaries All	Low Salary Women	Low Salary Men	Low Salary All	High Salary Women	High Salary Men	High Salary All	Average Salary Women	Average Salary Men	Average Salary All	Median Salary Women	Median Salary Men	Median Salary All
Kentucky	71	16	3	19	7064	9750	7064	15000	12000	15000	11542	11150	11480	11650	11700	11700
Louisiana State	57	26	10	36	8000	9600	8000	14500	17000	17000	10542	11920	10936	11000	11258	11000
Long Island	54	38	5	43	5000	8000	5000	22000	22000	22000	10800	14600	12700	11450	11400	11400
McGill	50	15	0	15	13127		13127	20000		20000	14500		14500	6700		16700
Michigan	144	84	19	103	8300	9400	8300	19500	20000	22000	12440	12000	12370	13548	11600	12000
Minnesota	20	15	1	16	9500	11600	9500	16750	11600	19500	13846	11600	13706		12300	13374
Missouri	44	35	7	42	7860	10200	7860	18500	16350	16750	11345	12048	11462	11720	14900	11500
Montreal	45	22	13	37	12000	12000	12000	16596	20000	20000	15367	14964	15241	11500	12425	14905
North Carolina	67	48	19	67	7420	8400	7420	16000	17000	18500	11824	12351	11977	11650	11276	11960
North Carolina Central	20	17	3	20	9000	5500	9000	14000	12300	16596	11630	11692	11648	1989	10000	11500
Northern Illinois	12	11	1	12	9550	10000	9550	17000	10000	16000	12040	10000	11020	11200	10640	10750
North Texas State	47	6	6	12	10300	10300	10800	16000	16000	16000	11690	11813	11934	12000	11500	11100
Peabody	39	21	3	24	6000	10600	6000	14500	16700	17000	12056	12733	11748	12324	12336	11859
Pittsburgh	99	32	3	35	7020	7020	8000	16000	15600	16000	11690	11942	11395	11500	14300	11700
Pratt	23	20	5	25	9200	13500	9200	17900	28000	28000	11601	18600	15200	11700	12000	12500
Queens	22	17	15	32	9500	11200	9500	18500	17000	17000	11800	13056	12321	1232	11600	12000
Rosary	97	44	6	50	6000	6000	8510	16000	25500	25500	12137	12079	12475	10346	11330	11500
Rutgers	86	23	4	27	8000	9500	8000	18000	16700	18500	12611	11755	11682	12576	11700	11500
St. Johns	21	7	26	33	10500	11000	10500	17000	15000	16000	11662	12380	12300	11500	11130	11500
Simmons	135	70	6	76	7100	9300	7100	18000	16800	18000	12242	11625	11647	10680	10500	11232
South Carolina	22	16	7	23	7200	8500	7200	16150	12300	15841	11654	10633	10851	12000	5144	10330
Southern California	84	37	4	44	7680	12000	7680	9000	16500	17000	10956	14249	12781	11690	10600	12576
Southern Connecticut	44	40	0	40	8089	10000	8089	18000		18000	12503	12137	12005	12590		11500
South Florida	22	17	10	27	7680		7680	17000	19200	9000	12189		10946	13900	12100	10680
Syracuse		24	4	28	9000	9500	9000		18811	19200	10946	12729	12250	11886	10000	12000
Tennessee	59	8	17	25	8500	9168	8500	15180	17100	18811	12485	11970	12021	13041	3050	11290
Texas (Austin)	48	31	0	31	9000	9000	9000	24135	25000	17100	12390	12325	11429	12135	13500	13050
Texas Woman's	55	53		53				19900		16812	11858		11858	13500	14500	10800
Toronto	76	29	16	69	9800	10400	9800	23000	14700	25000	13994	14888	14136	11400	12250	13690
Washington	52	12	2	63	8543	9500	8543	23358	13000	19900	12843	13049	12684	12500	13500	12167
Wayne State	19	21	2	45	10000	14328	10000	30000	27000	23000	15517	14500	15362	11886	11500	14000
Western Michigan	39	37	15	14	8320	11500	8320	20800	14000	23358	12426	12250	12410	13041	10500	12135
Western Ontario	58	25	16	23	9000	9000	9000	30000	27000	30000	14430	10613	13329	12135		14500
Wisconsin (Madison)	57	25	3	52	10000	10000	10000	20800	14000	20800	12034	11597	11864			11500
Wisconsin (Milwaukee)	25	20		41	7000	9000	7000	30000	16000	30000	13531	11833	13310	12500	10500	12500

SUMMARY BY REGION

	Placements	Salaries Women	Salaries Men	Salaries All	Low Salary Women	Low Salary Men	Low Salary All	High Salary Women	High Salary Men	High Salary All	Average Salary Women	Average Salary Men	Average Salary All	Median Salary Women	Median Salary Men	Median Salary All
United States	2,676	1,429	423	1,870*	6,000	6,000	5,000	34,000	28,000	34,000	12,087	12,344	12,281	11,732	11,832	11,804
Northeast	862	504	139	643	5,000	7,020	5,000	27,000	28,000	28,000	11,920	12,919	12,689	11,722	11,988	11,804
Southeast	432	227	70	297	6,000	8,400	6,000	19,000	18,811	19,000	11,737	11,536	11,597	11,370	11,073	11,418
Midwest	866	475	120	595	7,000	6,000	6,000	34,000	25,500	34,000	12,382	11,794	12,245	11,821	11,497	11,864
Southwest	253	84	40	142*	8,000	9,000	8,000	17,800	17,100	17,800	11,561	11,971	11,623	11,592	11,685	11,479
West	263	139	54	193	7,500	9,500	7,500	26,400	21,000	26,400	12,851	13,916	13,197	12,355	13,744	12,693
Canada	310	135	45	182*	9,800	8,900	8,900	30,000	27,000	30,000	14,847	14,415	14,749	15,140	15,030	14,966
All Schools	2,986	1,564	468	2,052*	5,000	6,000	5,000	34,000	28,000	34,000	12,368	12,526	12,528	12,079	12,113	12,120

*Includes figures undifferentiated by sex

Table 1 shows permanent and temporary professional placements, as well as nonprofessional library placements and totals for the three. Table 1 also indicates the number of graduates reported who were not in library positions or whose employment status was unknown at the beginning of April 1979. Fourteen percent were not in library positions, compared to 18 percent reported at the beginning of April 1978 for 1977 graduates. In April 1979 the whereabouts of 23 percent were unknown, compared to 21 percent in April 1978. Sixty-two percent of the 1978 graduates were known to be employed either in professional or nonprofessional positions in libraries or library-related work, compared to 61 percent of the 1977 graduates. Fifty-six percent of the 1978 graduates were employed in permanent professional positions, the same percentage as the 1977 graduates. Employment distribution for 2,986 of the 5,442 graduates is shown in Table 3 and Table 11.

Some placement officers were able to estimate the number of graduates unemployed after three months, four months, and six months. Forty schools recorded at least some figures. The median for those unplaced after three months was 28 percent; after four months, 19 percent; and after six months, 13 percent.

In 1978, 5 percent of all known library placements were in nonprofessional positions (Table 1). In 1977, 3 percent were in that category, and in 1976, 6 percent. About 5 percent of the women and 5 percent of the men were in nonprofessional positions compared to 3 percent of the women and 2 percent of the men in 1977 and 6 percent of the women and 5 percent of the men in 1976.

Public and school library placements continued to drop in 1978. College and university libraries increased slightly. Other library agencies showed a marked increase (Table 4).

U.S. and Canadian placement comparisons appear in Table 5. Table 6, showing special placements, is self-explanatory.

DEMAND AND SUPPLY

Forty-five schools indicated a total of 36,902 vacant positions reported to them. These were at all levels, and most of the positions were no doubt listed simultaneously at several of the schools. In 1977, 44 schools reported a total of 39,642 positions. The average number reported per school in 1978 was 820, compared to 900 in 1977, and 698 in 1976.

Fifteen schools reported increases in vacancy listings ranging from 3 to 45 percent; the median was 15 percent. Fifteen schools reported no significant changes from 1977. Six schools reported a decline, ranging from 10 to 44 percent. Nine placement officers reported major difficulty in placing 1978 graduates; four reported some difficulty; and 42 reported no major difficulty. Seven placement officers felt that they had more difficulty placing graduates in 1978 than in 1977; 18 felt they had less difficulty; and 31 felt they had about the same amount of difficulty both years.

Library and library-related positions are still difficult to find. No significant improvement was noted over last year, with the exception of the increase in the other libraries and library agency category, which reflects not only special libraries but nontraditional areas in which more graduates are finding jobs. This is clearly an important growth area.

SALARIES

The salary statistics reported here include only full-time annual salaries, excluding such variables as vacations and other fringe benefits, which are part of the total compensation. In addition, they do not reflect differences in hours worked per week. Although such information would provide more precise comparability, such data are probably beyond most needs of library schools and of the profession. In any case, the validity of the analysis presented here rests on comparable statistics collected annually since 1951.

Of the 62 schools reporting, 62 supplied some salary data. Not every school could provide all the information requested, nor could they supply it for all their employed graduates. The schools were asked to exclude atypical salaries, such as those for which the stipend includes both compensation and living allowances, those for graduates from outside North America who return to employment in their home countries, and all salaries for part-time employment. With these exclusions added to the number of salaries not known or reported, we have known salary information for 2,054 of the 1978 graduates (1,566 women and 468 men). This represents 51 percent of known placements and 37.7 percent of all graduates reported, a smaller percent of known placements than in 1977 (56 percent), and a fractionally larger proportion of total graduates (37.6 percent) in 1977. Salary data as reported by the 62 schools are given in Table 2 and summarized in Table 7.

Average (Mean) Salaries

The 1978 average salary for all graduates was $12,527, an increase of $633 (5.3 percent) over the 1977 average of $11,894. Annual changes in average salaries since 1967 are shown in Table 8, which also includes a beginning salary index figure that may be compared with the Annual Cost of Living Index (COL) reports issued by the U.S. government.

The COL index for 1978 was 195.3, an increase of 13.8 points over the 1977 figure of 181.5, a gain of 7.6 percent. The comparable increase in the beginning salary index is 5.5 percent, two full points below the increase in the cost of living.

The difference in the range reported average salaries of 1978 graduates is $7,875. For women the range was $7500; for men $10,650. The women's average salary for all schools is $158 less than the men's average salary, but is higher in one of the five U.S. regions and in Canada. Of the 58 schools that reported salaries for both men and women, average salaries for women were higher in 30 schools and higher for men in 28 schools. Table 11 compares the salaries offered to men and women in different types of libraries. It shows that women are earning $312 less than men in overall average salary.

Median Salaries

In 1978 the median salary for all graduates was $12,120, an increase of $1,079 over 1977's median salary of $11,041. The median salary for women was $12,233 and for men $12,270. In 27 of the 62 schools the median salary for women was higher than that for men, and in two additional schools it was the same.

Salary Range

The 1978 range of individual salaries offered to newly graduated librarians displays the usual large gap between lowest and highest because of such variables as education and experience (see Tables 9, 10, 11, and 12). The range in 1978 (Table 7) was from a low of $5,000 to a high of $34,000, a difference of $29,000. The low salary was received by a woman in reference in a public library and the highest by a woman in a junior college library.

326 / LIBRARY EDUCATION, PLACEMENT, AND SALARIES

TABLE 3 PLACEMENTS BY TYPE OF LIBRARY

Schools	Public			Elementary & Secondary			College & University			Other			Total		
	Women	Men	Total	Women	Men	Total	Women	Men	Total	Women	Men	Total	Women	Men	Total
Alabama	5	3	8	13	2	15	8	5	13	0	1	1	26	11	37
Alabama A&M	0	0	0	7	2	9	1	0	1	0	0	0	8	2	10
New York (Albany)	4	2	6	14	0	14	10	3	13	10	2	12	38	7	45
Arizona	10	2	12	9	0	9	8	5	13	9	3	12	36	10	46
Atlanta	5	4	9	6	3	9	9	4	13	6	1	7	26	12	38
Brigham Young	8	1	9	2	0	2	2	2	4	4	5	9	16	8	24
British Columbia	12	3	15	5	5	10	12	4	16	12	2	14	41	14	55
Buffalo	6	2	8	11	1	12	10	1	11	5	0	5	32	4	36
California (LA)	3	3	6	0	0	0	13	7	20	17	3	20	33	13	46
Case Western	10	3	13	7	0	7	10	6	16	20	6	26	47	15	62
Catholic	5	1	6	3	1	4	3	2	5	21	9	30	32	13	45
Chicago	4	0	4	0	0	0	4	7	11	7	2	9	15	9	24
Clarion	5	5	10	13	2	15	2	0	2	4	1	5	14	8	32
Columbia	16	4	20	0	0	0	20	6	26	34	11	45	79	21	100
Dalhousie	2	2	4	3	0	3	0	0	0	9	1	10	20	6	26
Denver	11	1	12	3	0	3	6	3	9	8	0	9	25	10	35
Drexel	14	6	20	11	1	12	3	8	11	22	5	27	54	16	70
Emory	11	1	12	4	1	5	9	3	12	6	2	8	30	7	37
Emporia	4	1	5	19	2	21	8	2	11	1	0	1	32	6	38
Florida State	2	0	2	4	1	5	1	2	3	0	0	0	7	3	10
Geneseo	11	2	13	11	0	11	14	6	20	5	1	6	41	9	50
Hawaii	4	0	4	7	2	9	3	1	4	4	1	5	18	4	22
Illinois	25	4	29	6	0	6	22	16	38	13	3	16	66	23	89
Indiana	24	8	32	13	0	13	28	7	35	4	1	5	69	16	85
Iowa	4	3	7	10	4	14	8	2	10	3	1	4	25	10	35
Kent State	17	6	23	24	2	26	9	7	16	7	4	11	57	19	76
Kentucky	11	3	14	14	0	14	22	10	32	6	5	11	53	18	71
Louisiana State	18	5	23	15	0	15	7	5	12	7	0	7	47	10	57
Long Island	13	3	16	12	1	13	13	2	15	9	1	10	47	7	54
McGill	2	0	2	3	0	3	11	2	13	26	6	32	42	8	50
Michigan	33	5	38	26	1	27	31	11	42	31	6	37	121	23	144
Minnesota	3	1	4	3	0	3	3	1	4	9	0	9	18	2	20
Missouri	15	1	16	8	0	8	7	5	12	7	1	8	37	7	44
Montreal	7	5	12	0	0	0	9	4	13	11	7	18	27	16	45
North Carolina	13	3	16	3	1	4	22	11	33	10	4	14	48	19	67
North Carolina Central	1	3	4	9	0	9	7	0	7	0	0	0	17	3	20
Northern Illinois	6	0	6	2	0	2	2	0	2	1	2	2	11	1	12
North Texas State	6	4	10	12	0	12	6	4	10	11	4	15	35	12	47
Peabody	7	2	9	15	0	15	8	2	10	3	2	5	33	6	39
Pittsburgh	18	7	25	22	2	24	15	4	19	18	13	31	73	26	99
Pratt	1	0	1	3	0	3	6	0	6	10	3	13	20	3	23

TABLE 4 PLACEMENTS BY TYPE OF LIBRARY, 1951-1978

Year	Public	School	College & Universities	Other Library Agencies*	Total
1951-1955**	2076 (33%)	1424 (23%)	1774 (28%)	1000 (16%)	6264
1956-1960***	2057 (33%)	1287 (20%)	1878 (30%)	1105 (17%)	6327
1961-1965	2876 (30%)	1979 (20%)	3167 (33%)	1600 (17%)	9622
1966-1970	4773 (28%)	3969 (23%)	5834 (34%)	2456 (15%)	17032
1971	999 (29%)	924 (26%)	1067 (30%)	513 (15%)	3503
1972	1117 (30%)	987 (26%)	1073 (29%)	574 (15%)	3751
1973	1180 (31%)	969 (25%)	1017 (26%)	712 (18%)	3878
1974	1132 (31%)	893 (24%)	952 (26%)	691 (19%)	3668
1975	994 (30%)	813 (24%)	847 (25%)	714 (21%)	3368
1976	764 (27.1%)	655 (23.2%)	741 (26.3%)	657 (23.2%)	2817
1977	846 (28.4%)	673 (22.6%)	771 (25.9%)	687 (23.1%)	2977
1978	779 (26.1%)	590 (19.9%)	819 (27.4%)	798 (26.7%)	2986

*From 1951 through 1966 these tabulations were for "special and other placements" in all kinds of libraries. Beginning with 1967, these figures include only placements in library agencies that do not clearly belong to one of the other three groups.
**Figures for individual years are reported in preceding articles in this series.

TABLE 5 U.S. AND CANADIAN PLACEMENTS COMPARED
(Percentages May Not Total 100 Because of Rounding)

	Placements	Public Libraries	School Libraries	College & University Libraries	Other Lib. & Library Agencies
All Schools	2986	779 (26.1%)	590 (19.7%)	819 (27.4%)	798 (26.7%)
Women	2281	595 (26.1%)	516 (22.6%)	559 (24.5%)	611 (26.8%)
Men	648	167 (25.8%)	58 (8.9%)	246 (27.9%)	177 (27.3%)
U.S. Schools	2676	711 (26.6%)	566 (21.2%)	740 (27.7%)	659 (24.6%)
Women	2046	544 (26.6%)	499 (24.4%)	501 (24.5%)	502 (24.5%)
Men	575	150 (26.1%)	51 (8.9%)	226 (39.3%)	148 (25.7%)
Canadian Schools	310	68 (21.9%)	24 (7.7%)	78 (25.2%)	138 (44.5%)
Women	235	51 (21.7%)	17 (7.2%)	58 (24.7%)	109 (46.4%)
Men	73	17 (23.3%)	7 (9.6%)	20 (27.4%)	29 (39.7%)

High Salaries

In 1978 the range of high salaries was from $12,000 to $34,000, a difference of $22,000. There is a considerable overlap between the lowest high salaries and the highest low salaries reported. Twenty-eight salaries were at $20,000 or over (15 women, 13 men). The median high salary for all graduates was $18,000. For women it was $17,454; for men, $16,000, continuing the reversal of pattern for the fifth consecutive year. Distribution of high salaries by type of library is outlined in Table 9 and in a different context in Table 11.

School and special libraries accounted for the majority of high salaries reported with 36 percent each. School libraries were up from 33 percent in 1977. Special libraries were also up from 27 percent of the posts in 1977. Academic libraries accounted for 22 percent, down from 24 percent in 1977. Public libraries dropped sharply from 16 percent in 1977 to under 7 percent in 1978. Media specialists, especially in school libraries; information specialists, especially in special libraries; and administrative positions were most commonly mentioned. The high salary positions were scattered geographically so that no significant or discernible pattern emerged. Most of the positions were located in the major population centers except for the West coast, especially California. As usual the primary reasons given for high salaries were special knowledge, background and skills, civil service appointments, and particularly prior service in the hiring organizations.

Low Salaries

Lowest beginning salaries offered to 1978 graduates ranged from $5,000 to $15,000, with $8,500 as the median low for all graduates, a remarkable 11.8 percent, or $900 more than in 1977. The highest low salaries overlap with the lowest high salaries. Of the 59 schools reporting low salaries for both men and women, 44 reported higher low salaries for men and three report the same.

Public libraries once again accounted for the majority of low salaries reported (41 percent). This was a decrease from 45 percent in 1977. Academic and special libraries followed with 22 percent each. Academic libraries remained unchanged from the 22 percent of reported low salaries in 1977, and 22 percent represented an increase of 5 percent for special libraries over the 17 percent figure for 1977. School libraries accounted for 15.5 percent of the total, fractionally smaller than the 16 percent figure for 1977. Again there was no significant pattern in the geographical locations of the positions. Most of the positions seem to be beginning-level posts in reader or technical services. The primary reason given for the low salaries was geographical preference.

TABLE 6 SPECIAL PLACEMENT*

	Women	Men	Total
Government Jurisdiction (U.S. and Canada)			
Other government agencies (except USVA hospitals)	132	15	147
State and Provincial libraries	36	19	55
National libraries	38	18	56
Armed Services libraries (domestic)	4	1	5
Total Government Jurisdiction	210	53	263
Library Science			
Advanced Study	17	8	25
Teaching	16	8	24
Total Library Science	33	16	49
Children's Services—School libraries	182	17	199
Children's Services—Public libraries	131	13	144
Law	97	35	132
Audiovisual and media centers	89	31	120
Youth Services (school)	80	14	94
Science and Technology	72	19	91
Business and Finance (banking, business administration)	64	15	79
Medicine (inc. Nursing schools)	63	11	74
Rare Books, manuscripts, archives	27	33	60
Communications Industry (advertising, newspaper, publishing, radio & TV, etc.)	31	20	51
Research & Development	35	7	42
Information science services	35	15	50
Outreach activities and services	30	10	40
Systems analysis; automation	22	18	40
Hospitals (inc. USVA hospitals)	35	2	37
Social sciences	22	12	34
Youth services (public libraries)	30	3	33
Art and Museum	23	8	31
Music	21	9	30
Religion (seminaries, theological schools)	14	12	26
Professional associations	8	12	20
Historical agencies	10	6	16
Free lance	10	3	13
Networks and consortia	4	9	13
Library services for the blind	9	2	11
Centers for Spanish-speaking	7	4	11
Bookstore	6	3	9
Geneological	5	4	9
Maps	5	4	9
Children's services—other	6	2	8
Correctional institutions	4	3	7
International relations	2	4	6
Youth services—other	4	1	5
International agencies	1	3	4
Architecture	3	—	3
Theatre & motion pictures	1	1	2
Women's organizations	1	—	1
Total Special Placements	**1432**	**434**	**1866**

*Includes special placements in all types of libraries, not limited to the "other libraries and library agencies" shown in Table III.

TABLE 7 SALARY DATA SUMMARIZED

	Women	Men	Total
Average (Mean Salary)	12,368	12,525	12,527
Median Salary	12,079	12,112	12,120
Individual Salary Range	5,000–34,000	6,000–28,000	5,000–34,000

330 / LIBRARY EDUCATION, PLACEMENT, AND SALARIES

TABLE 8 AVERAGE SALARY INDEX FOR STARTING LIBRARY POSITIONS, 1967–1978

Year	Library Schools	Fifth-Year Graduates	Average Beginning Salary	Increase in Average	Beginning Index
1967	40	4030	$ 7305	—	105
1968	42	4625	7650	$355	112
1969	45	4970	8161	501	118
1970	48	5569	8611	450	121
1971	47	5670	8846	235	126
1972	48	6079	9248	402	128
1973	53	6336	9423	175	135
1974	52	6370	10000	617	145
1975	51	6010	10594	554	153
1976	53	5415	11149	555	153
1977	53	5467	11894	745	163
1978	62	5442	12527	633	171

TABLE 9 HIGH SALARIES BY TYPE OF LIBRARY

	Public			School			College & University			Other Libraries & Lib. Agencies		
	Women	Men	Total	Women	Men	Total	Women	Men	Total	Women	Men	Total
$ 7,000							1		1			
$ 8,000	1	1			1	1						
$ 9,000			1		2	3	1		1	2	2	3
$10,000		1	9	1	3	3	1	2	3	1	4	5
$11,000	4	5	16		4	12	2		6	1	3	4
$12,000	10	6	20	1		6	5	4	15	4	7	11
$13,000	7	13	15	8	4	10	10	10	16	5	3	8
$14,000	3	6	6	6	4	5	9	6	17	7	2	9
$15,000	7	3	8	2	3	11	5	8	10	6	7	13
$16,000	6	1	6	8	3	6	7	5	11	5	3	8
$17,000	1	3	4	5	1	3	2	4	4	4	2	6
$18,000	1	1	2	3		2		2	1	5	2	6
$19,000				2		1	2	1	2	3	1	3
$20,000				1	2	2		3	3			
$21,000					1	3			4			4
$22,000	1		1									
$23,000						1	1		1		1	1
$24,000				1	2	3						
$25,000				1		1						
$26,000					2	2				1	1	2
$27,000											1	1
$28,000												
$29,000												
$30,000				1		1	1		1			
$31,000												
$32,000												
$33,000												
$34,000							1		1			

NEXT YEAR?

Twenty-nine placement officers see no change in the number of vacancies reported so far in 1979; eight predict a decrease; and twelve feel there is an increase. Forty-one schools expect that 1979 graduates will have the same difficulty finding professional positions as did the 1978 graduates. Five expect less difficulty, and ten expect more difficulty.

The responses to a question about types of libraries that are noticeably increasing or decreasing in the number of vacancies are summarized as follows:

Number of schools that think positions are:

	Increasing	Decreasing
Public libraries	4	4
School libraries	3	17
Academic libraries	8	7
Other libraries and library agencies	12	2

Decreases are again attributed to tight budgets and budget cutbacks, declining school enrollments, and loss of federal funding. It is speculated that fewer new jobs are opening up and there is less movement among those who have jobs. Several schools report a trend toward use of paraprofessionals instead of professionals, and a few reported that new graduates seem to be taking paraprofessional positions. The brightest note is the general feeling that special libraries and library-related work will continue to gain unless there is a severe recession. The whole area now referred to as "information management" is seen as an excellent source of placement opportunities.

Thirty schools expect that salaries being offered in 1979 are stronger than 1978. Estimates range from $150 to $1,700, with most estimates in the $500 to $1,000 range. Sixteen schools do not see any change in 1979.

Graduates with undergraduate backgrounds in math, computer science, engineering, and the natural and physical sciences are in great demand and very short supply. Thirty schools reported difficulty in filling vacancies requiring such backgrounds and mentioned the desirability of recruiting new students specializing in these fields.

It is still a buyer's market in the library field, with the possible exception of those with a background in science and technology. The number of graduates has decreased, and it is impossible to tell how many beginning-level positions are really available. Many people do seem to be finding opportunities where they have previously worked in a full-time, part-time, or volunteer position. No statistics are kept on this, but many placement officers seem to feel that intern programs or fieldwork has opened many doors.

Once again the authors would like to thank all who contributed to the splendid response this year. Most of the questionnaires were completed fully and accurately. We know what a time-consuming process it can be. We hope the information gathered will make the effort worthwhile to the schools, the graduates, and to prospective students.

TABLE 10 LOW SALARIES BY TYPE OF LIBRARY

	Public			School			College & University			Other Libraries & Lib. Agencies		
	Women	Men	Total	Women	Men	Total	Women	Men	Total	Women	Men	Total
$ 5,000	1			2		2						
$ 6,000			1	2		2					1	1
$ 7,000	4	1	5	9	1	10						2
$ 8,000	14	7	21	10	3	13	5		5	2		14
$ 9,000	13	7	20	9	5	14	6		6	12	2	15
$10,000	11	14	25	10	1	11	11	10	21	11	4	23
$11,000	5	3	8		4	4	12	6	18	5	12	11
$12,000	1	7	8	4		4	9	16	25	5	6	12
$13,000		1	1		2	2	4	4	8	1	7	12
$14,000	1		1		4	4		5	5		2	3
$15,000	1		1	1	1	2	2	1	3			
$16,000					1	1				1		
$17,000				1	1	2	2		2		2	3
$18,000								1	1			
$19,000					1	1						
$20,000												
$21,000	1		1									
$22,000				1	1	2						
$23,000												
$24,000					1	1						
$25,000												
$26,000				1		1						
$27,000					1	1						
Totals	**52**	**40**	**92**	**49**	**26**	**75**	**50**	**45**	**95**	**48**	**26**	**74**

TABLE 11 COMPARISON OF SALARIES BY TYPE OF LIBRARY

	Place-ments	Salaries Known			Low Salary			High Salary			Average Salary			Median Salary		
		Women	Men	Total	Women	Men	Total	Women	Men	Total	Women	Men	Total	Women	Men	Total
Public Libraries																
United States	711	359	109	473*	5,000	7,020	5,000	23,491	18,811	23,491	11,291	11,182	11,382	11,321	11,205	11,273
Northeast	215	115	42	157	5,000	7,020	5,000	18,263	14,400	18,263	10,756	11,017	10,923	10,764	11,068	11,026
Southeast	100	56	19	75	9,000	8,500	8,500	15,649	18,811	18,811	11,040	11,744	11,190	10,955	11,507	10,991
Midwest	255	139	33	172	7,000	8,000	7,000	16,000	15,000	16,000	10,971	10,848	10,880	11,175	11,083	10,732
Southwest	71	16	8	29*	9,000	10,000	9,000	15,180	13,000	15,180	11,481	10,888	11,765	11,395	10,657	11,151
West	70	33	7	40	8,543	9,600	8,543	23,491	14,280	23,491	13,723	11,498	13,780	13,679	11,669	13,637

PLACEMENTS AND SALARIES, 1978 / 333

TABLE 12 EFFECTS OF EXPERIENCE ON SALARIES

	Salaries without Previous Experience (44 Schools)			Salaries with Previous Experience (44 Schools)		
	Women	Men	All	Women	Men	All
Number of Positions	661	196	865	499	138	647
Range of Low Salaries	6,000-12,000	8,000-13,488	6,000-13,488	5,000-19,000	6,000-25,000	5,000-25,000
Mean (Average)	8,856	10,284	8,816	10,199	11,766	10,016
Median	8,802	10,140	8,802	9,893	11,506	9,888
Range of High Salaries	9,800-23,358	10,000-21,831	9,800-23,358	8,500-30,000	10,000-28,000	8,500-30,000
Mean (Average)	14,529	13,499	14,978	18,256	17,637	18,974
Median	14,003	13,000	15,038	17,000	16,500	17,005
Range of Average Salaries	8,625-15,199	9,100-14,833	8,625-15,241	8,200-21,646	10,000-25,000	8,200-25,000
Mean (Average)	11,438	11,742	11,513	13,796	14,349	13,856
Median	11,336	11,600	11,464	13,063	13,411	13,036

SEX, SALARIES, AND LIBRARY SUPPORT, 1979

Kathleen M. Heim
Faculty Member, Graduate School of Library Science, University of Illinois

Carolyn Kacena
Head, Catalog Department, University of Arizona

This report continues and updates the analyses of the relationships between sex of director and per capita support in large public libraries initiated in 1972 by Carpenter and Shearer.[1] The data utilized come from the 1979 survey of public libraries conducted by the Public Library of Fort Wayne and Allen County, Indiana.[2] [The data-gathering technique is explained in Note 2 at the end of this article—*Ed.*]

Several trends have been noted in the previous four reports: fewer female librarians are administrators than the percentage of the qualified pool would predict; lower compensation for those women who *do* become library administrators than for their male counterparts; and lower per capita support and lower compensation for entry level professionals in libraries administered by women than in those which are administered by men.

The raw data from the Indiana survey have again been analyzed via the *SPSS-Statistical Package for the Social Sciences* and the same analyses made as in the prior four reports. Tables 1 to 3 provide comparisons with the availability of data in the earlier reports, so readers have supportive data against which to measure our interpretations and comparisons.

CURRENT LIBRARY SUPPORT

In 1979 per capita support of large public libraries in the United States and Canada was up $0.50 per person to a total mean per capita support figure of $6.96 (Table 4). Comparable figures in the earlier reports were $6.46 in 1977; $5.80 in 1975; $4.50 in 1973; and $3.70 in 1971. This is up only 8 percent over the two-year period of 1977–1979, but 88 percent for the eight-year period of analyzed data, 1971–1979. General inflation in 1977 was 6.5 percent; in 1978, 7.6 percent; and projected in 1979, 13 percent.[3] Thus from 1977 to 1979 the rate of inflation was 27.1 percent compared to the 8 percent increase of per capita support for libraries.

While the early 1970s promised significant gains for public libraries, with support exceeding general economic growth, the latter half of the decade is rather dismal: from 1975 to 1979 general inflation was 42 percent, yet libraries gained only 19 percent in overall support.

REGIONAL SUPPORT

Previous reports have analyzed the data according to the census regions. The 1979 data continue to demonstrate regional differences in support and growth of support. In Table 4 observe that the increases in per capita support from 1977 to 1979 ranged from 2 percent in Canada to 14 percent in the North Central region. In 1977 there was spectacular

Note: Adapted from *Library Journal,* January 1, 1980.

TABLE 1 DISTRIBUTION OF RESPONDENTS BY GEOGRAPHIC REGIONS

U.S. Regions & Canada	1971 Number of Responses	1971 Percent of Total Responses	1973 Number of Responses	1973 Percent of Total Responses	1975 Number of Responses	1975 Percent of Total Responses	1977 Number of Responses	1977 Percent of Total Responses	1979 Number of Responses	1979 Percent of Total Responses
Northeast	43	16%	43	16%	31	13%	40	14%	47	15%
South	93	34%	93	34%	78	32%	98	34%	116	37%
North Central	65	24%	63	23%	65	27%	69	24%	73	23%
West	56	20%	58	21%	51	21%	62	21%	57	18%
Canada	18	6%	19	7%	17	7%	21	7%	24	8%
TOTAL	275	100%	276	101%*	242	100%	290	100%	317	101%*

*Total is greater than 100% because of rounding.

TABLE 2 DISTRIBUTION OF RESPONDENTS BY SIZE OF POPULATION SERVED

Size of Population Served	1971 Number of Respondents	1971 Percent of Total	1973 Number of Respondents	1973 Percent of Total	1975 Number of Respondents	1975 Percent of Total	1977 Number of Respondents	1977 Percent of Total	1979 Number of Respondents	1979 Percent of Total
100,000–199,999	131	48%	139	50%	107	44%	152	52%	171	54%
200,000–399,999	80	29%	79	29%	72	30%	78	27%	81	26%
400,000–749,999	43	16%	37	13%	41	17%	41	14%	46	14%
750,000 and over	20	7%	21	8%	22	9%	19	7%	19	6%
TOTAL	274*	100%	276	100%	242	100%	290	100%	317	100%

*One respondent did not report population size. Since this library offers service by contract, the size of the population is unknown to us.

TABLE 3   DISTRIBUTION OF RESPONDENTS BY SEX OF DIRECTOR

Sex of Director	1973* Number of Respondents	Percent of Total	1975 Number of Respondents	Percent of Total	1977 Number of Respondents	Percent of Total	1979 Number of Respondents	Percent of Total
Male	175	66%	166	72%	199	69%	204	66%
Female	89	34%	63	28%	88	31%	105	34%
TOTAL**	264	100%	229	100%	287	100%	309	100%

*Data was not provided for 1971.
**Totals differ from those in Tables 1 and 2 because some directorships were vacant.

growth in Canada (28 percent), but there was an actual decrease in the Northeast United States. The data for 1979 show a slight growth in the Northeast, but no region exhibits growth greater than or equal to the current inflation rates. The South continues to show the lowest dollar support per capita (24 percent below the Northeast), but also shows one of the highest percentages of increase. The West shows the greatest decrease in support growth within the United States: from 18 percent increase in the 1975–1977 years to 7 percent in the 1977–1979 period; however, it continues to be 9 percent ahead of the next closest U.S. region with the absolute difference in per capita support between the West and North Central regions at the $1.10 level of 1977 (Table 5).

SUPPORT BY POPULATION

The 1977 report saw libraries and library systems serving 200,00 to 399,999 as best holding the line against inflation, while the largest libraries (750,000+) had lost considerable ground. This time larger library support has taken a phenomenal leap forward: 41 percent growth in per capita support. The overall average growth was a mere 8 percent in spite of this (Table 6).

TABLE 4   CHANGES IN THE MEAN PER CAPITA PUBLIC LIBRARY EXPENDITURE, 1977–1979, BY REGION

U.S. Regions & Canada	Per Capita Support (Number of Reporting Libraries) 1977	1979	Change: 1977-1979 (Percent)
Northeast	$6.38 (40)	$6.61 (47)	0.23 (3%)
South	$4.71 (98)	$5.32 (116)	0.61 (13%)
North Central	$6.83 (69)	$7.76 (73)	0.93 (14%)
West	$7.93 (62)	$8.48 (57)	0.55 (7%)
Canada	$9.32 (20)	$9.48 (24)	0.16 (2%)
All	$6.46 (289)	$6.96 (317)	0.50 (8%)
Range	$4.71 to $9.32	$5.32 to $9.48	0.16 to 0.93 (2% to 14%)

TABLE 5   CHANGES IN THE MEAN PER CAPITA PUBLIC LIBRARY EXPENDITURE, 1971-1979, BY REGION

U.S. Regions & Canada	Per Capita Support (Number of Responses)		Change: 1971-1979 (Percent)
	1971	*1979*	
Northeast	$3.90 (40)	$6.61 (47)	$2.71 (69%)
South	$2.60 (92)	$5.32 (116)	$2.72 (105%)
North Central	$4.40 (61)	$7.76 (73)	$3.36 (76%)
West	$4.60 (55)	$8.48 (57)	$3.88 (84%)
Canada	$4.40 (18)	$9.48 (24)	$5.08 (115%)
All	$3.70 (266)	$6.96 (317)	$3.26 (88%)
Range	$2.60 to $4.60	$5.32 to $9.48	$2.71 to $5.08 (69% to 115%)

SEX AND SUPPORT

Female public library directors continued to receive less per capita support than male directors in 1979. The mean support for male directors was $7.37, and for the female directors, $6.05. As shown in Table 7, the proportionate change decreased to 22 percent advantage to the men. For comparative purposes, in 1971 the differential was 30 percent; 1973, 23 percent; 1975, 19 percent; and 1977, 23 percent.

While miniscule in comparison to the data on overall advantage, three of the regions have reversed the trend of financial advantage to men. The Canadians have increased the female advantage from 19 percent to 29 percent; both the North Central and the West have shifted slightly, with 3 percent advantages to the female directors. Both the South and Northeast, however, continue budgetary discrepancies between male and female directors that are close to 50 percent (Table 7).

DIRECTORS' SALARIES

The median salary for directors in 1979 was $27,540, discounting the two vacant positions reported. This contrasts to $24,620 in 1977, $23,000 in 1975, $18,000 in 1973,

TABLE 6   CHANGES IN THE MEAN PER CAPITA PUBLIC LIBRARY EXPENDITURE, 1977-1979, BY SIZE OF POPULATION SERVED

Size of Population Served	Per Capita Support (Number of Responses)		Change: 1977-1979 (Percent)
	1977	*1979*	
100,000-199,999	$6.43 (152)	$6.74 (171)	$0.31 (5%)
200,000-399,999	$6.02 (78)	$6.28 (81)	$0.26 (4%)
400,000-749,999	$7.58 (40)	$8.33 (46)	$0.75 (10%)
750,000+	$6.04 (19)	$8.52 (19)	$2.48 (41%)
All	$6.46 (289)	$6.96 (317)	$0.50 (8%)
Range of Means	$6.02 to $7.58	$6.28 to $8.52	$0.26 to $2.48 (4% to 41%)

TABLE 7   FINANCIAL ADVANTAGE OF MEN TO WOMEN BY REGION, 1979, IN PER CAPITA SUPPORT

U.S. Regions & Canada	Female (Number of Responses)	Male (Number of Responses)	Percentage of Advantage* to Males
Northeast	$ 4.75 (13)	$7.33 (34)	54%
South	$ 4.33 (54)	$6.27 (59)	45%
North Central	$ 7.94 (13)	$7.72 (60)	− 3%
West	$ 8.62 (17)	$8.37 (37)	− 3%
Canada	$11.18 (8)	$7.94 (14)	−29%
ALL	$ 6.05 (105)	$7.37 (204)	22%

*Advantage figured by $\frac{\text{Men} - \text{Women}}{\text{Women}}$ as in earlier reports.

TABLE 8   DIRECTORS' MEDIAN SALARY, BY REGION, 1979

U.S. Regions & Canada	Median	Salary of Director Minimum − Maximum	Number of Responses
Northeast	$24,310	$14,500 − $40,210	46
South	$24,080	$11,400 − $47,500	115
North Central	$27,800	$15,225 − $49,500	73
West	$30,520	$20,400 − $51,820	57
Canada	$34,957	$20,140 − $42,250	24
TOTALS	$27,540	$11,400 − $51,820	315

and $17,160 in 1971. The lowest director's salary was $11,400—below the median beginning salary of $11,648—and the highest was $51,820 (Table 8).

The adequacy of directors' compensation may be tested by using the U.S. Department of Labor's "higher living standard" for an urban family of four, which finds that the directors overall are losing ground to inflation (Table 9).[4] The latest comparison shows less than 0.5 percent difference in the standard and the directors' median salary.

Tables 8, 9, and 10 update the male/female salary differences in public libraries at the director level. The median salary for male directors was $28,881; for female directors, $23,451. In absolute dollars, the difference is $5,430, or 23 percent less for females than males. In terms of the higher living standard (Table 9), the male directors have remained above the standard (5 percent above), while the female directors face a 14 percent deficit.

TABLE 9   PERCENTAGE OF DIFFERENCE BETWEEN DIRECTORS' MEAN SALARY AND HIGHER LIVING STANDARD

Year	Directors' Median Salary	Dept. of Labor Standard	Difference (Percent)
1972/73	$18,900	$16,558	$2,342 (14%)
1974/75	$23,000 (+21%)	$20,777 (+25%)	$2,223 (11%)
1976/77	$24,620 (+ 7%)	$23,759 (+14%)	$ 861 (4%)
1978/79	$27,540	$27,420 (+15%)	$ 120 (0.4%)

TABLE 10 MEDIAN, MINIMUM, AND MAXIMUM OF DIRECTORS' SALARY, BY SEX, BY REGION, 1979

U.S. Regions & Canada	Median	Male Minimum-Maximum	Median	Female Minimum-Maximum	Difference (Male-Female)
Northeast	$26,400 (33)	$14,500-$40,210	$23,451 (13)	$16,620-$30,860	$ 2,949 (13%)
South	$27,605 (58)	$15,870-$47,500	$21,105 (54)	$11,400-$45,090	$ 6,500 (31%)
North Central	$27,802 (60)	$21,110-$49,500	$25,800 (13)	$15,225-$48,500	$ 2,002 (8%)
West	$31,376 (37)	$20,400-$51,820	$28,710 (17)	$21,800-$37,490	$ 2,666 (9%)
Canada	$35,000 (14)	$23,800-$42,250	$28,359 (8)	$20,140-$37,180	$ 6,641 (23%)
ALL	$28,881 (202)	$14,500-$51,820	$23,451 (105)	$11,400-$48,500	$ 5,430 (23%)

The lowest salary of a female director was $11,400, and the lowest male salary was $14,500. While the actual dollar difference at the low end remains circa $3,000, the greatest change is at the top: from a difference in 1977 of over $10,000, in 1979 the highest paid male was only $3,200 above the highest paid female director. A further note of optimism is that the lowest paid director is no longer paid less than the median beginning salary for her region: $11,400 for the director and $10,982 for the median Southern salary for beginners. Unfortunately, she is below the median beginner's salary across all regions: $11,648.

The sex of the director still appears to have standard impact on his/her salary, and women are still substantially below the higher living standard used to measure executive salaries.

SEX AND REGION

There is a continued trend in most of the regions to narrow the differential between salaries paid male and female directors. The Northeast has moved from 19 percent difference in 1977 to only 13 percent in 1979. The North Central and West regions made the greatest change, to 8 percent and 9 percent, respectively, from the 1977 highs of 26 percent and 20 percent each. Both the South and Canada appear to have slipped: the South from 23 percent to 31 percent and Canada from 19 percent to 23 percent. The overall difference remains 23 percent as it was in 1977. Only in the North Central and the West are the mean tenure of female directors significantly less than the mean tenure of the males. Since the library boards in the other areas seem satisfied with their directors in terms of contract renewal, the differentials in salaries remain difficult to justify (Table 11).

SEX AND POPULATION

Perhaps because of the small sample of female directors for large systems—only three respondents in the libraries serving populations of 750,000+ were women—the library directors serving large areas are now better paid when female. The librarians serving populations of 400,000 to 749,999 have continued to show the worst differential: 9 percent in 1973, 7 percent in 1975, 29 percent in 1977, and 31 percent in 1979. The difference in the length of tenure, although greater than in smaller institutions, does not seem sufficient to explain the differential in salary (Tables 12 and 13).

While the distribution of salaries for male and female directors shown in Table 14 illustrates movement upward, there remain anomalies of sex. For example, 43 percent of the men earn $30,000 or more, while female directors earn over $30,000 in only 18 percent

TABLE 11   MEAN TENURE OF DIRECTORS, BY SEX AND REGION, 1979

U.S. Regions & Canada	Male	(Number of Responses)	Female	(Number of Responses)
Northeast	6.14	(34)	7.52	(13)
South	8.30	(59)	8.25	(53)
North Central	8.35	(58)	3.65	(13)
West	8.38	(37)	7.88	(17)
Canada	6.71	(14)	9.84	(8)
ALL	7.86	(202)	7.65	(104)

TABLE 12 DIRECTORS' MEDIAN SALARIES IN 1979, BY SEX OF DIRECTOR AND SIZE OF POPULATION SERVED

Population Served	Male	(Number of Responses)	Female	(Number of Responses)	Difference (Male-Female)
100,000-199,999	$26,252	(100)	$22,190	(67)	4,062 (18%)
200,000-399,999	$29,390	(51)	$24,830	(27)	4,560 (18%)
400,000-749,999	$38,845	(36)	$29,650	(8)	9,195 (13%)
750,000 and over	$37,830	(15)	$45,090	(3)	−7,260 (−16%)
ALL	$28,881	(202)	$23,451	(105)	5,430 (23%)

TABLE 13 MEAN TENURE OF DIRECTORS, BY SEX AND POPULATION SERVED, 1979

Size of Population Served	Male	(Number of Responses)	Female	(Number of Responses)
100,000-199,999	7.54	(102)	7.46	(67)
200,000-399,999	7.23	(51)	9.03	(26)
400,000-749,000	8.96	(35)	5.09	(8)
750,000 +	9.64	(14)	6.58	(3)
ALL	7.86	(202)	7.65	(104)

TABLE 14 CHANGES IN THE DISTRIBUTION OF THE DIRECTORS' SALARIES, 1977-1979, BY SEX OF DIRECTOR

	Male 1977	Male 1979	Change	Female 1977	Female 1979	Change
Less than $15,000	0.5%	0.5%	0	9%	5%	−4%
$15,000-19,999	12.0%	4.0%	−8%	26%	20%	−6%
$20,000-24,999	29.0%	20.0%	−9%	41%	34%	−7%
$25,000-29,999	29.0%	32.0%	3%	13%	22%	9%
$30,000-39,999	26.0%	35.0%	9%	11%	16%	5%
$40,000 plus	4.0%	8.0%	4%	0%	2%	2%
TOTAL*	101.5%	100.5%		100%	99%	

*Total varies from 100% because of rounding.

TABLE 15 INCREASE IN 1979 MEDIAN BEGINNING PROFESSIONAL SALARIES OVER 1977, BY REGION

U.S. Regions & Canada	Median Salary 1977	1979	Change: 1977-1979 (Percent)
Northeast	$10,005	$10,650	$ 645 (6%)
South	$10,165	$10,982	$ 817 (8%)
North Central	$10,510	$11,825	$1,315 (13%)
West	$11,340	$12,480	$1,140 (10%)
Canada	$12,210	$14,265	$2,055 (17%)
ALL	$10,575	$11,648	$1,073 (10%)

of the cases reported. Twenty-five percent of the women continue to earn less than $20,000, while only 4.5 percent of the male directors fall into this salary level. However, 52 percent of the men and 56 percent of the women earn $20,000 to $29,999.

BEGINNERS' COMPENSATION

Beginning librarians continue to lose the battle against inflation. Although general inflation was 27.1 percent, median starting salaries overall were raised only 10 percent during this two-year period. [See Table 15.] In the Northeast and South the median continues to rise very slowly (6 and 8 percent, respectively). When compared with the lower standard of living figure for an urban family of four ($11,546), the median beginning salary overall of $11,648 is uncomfortably close.[5]

Canada has doubled its advantage to 14 percent more in beginning compensation than is offered in the West, which continues to be the highest paid region in the United States. The lowest salary offered in 1979 was $7,440 in the Northeast, and the highest was $20,776, in the West. The difference was $13,336, or almost twice the lowest reported.

The size of population served continues to have a positive effect on beginners' compensation: the smallest libraries continue to offer the lowest median salary and tie for the lowest increase over 1977; the largest libraries continue to pay better but also show only an 11 percent (tie for lowest) increase over 1977 (Table 16).

TABLE 16 INCREASE IN 1979 MEDIAN BEGINNING PROFESSIONAL SALARIES OVER 1977, BY SIZE OF POPULATION SERVED

Size of Population Served	1977	Median Salary (Number of Responses)	1979	(Number of Responses)	Change: 1977-1979 (Increase Percent)
100,000-199,999	$10,280	(143)	$11,380	(169)	$1,100 (11%)
200,000-399,999	$10,445	(78)	$11,900	(81)	$1,455 (14%)
400,000-749,999	$11,025	(40)	$12,456	(45)	$1,431 (13%)
750,000 +	$11,610	(19)	$12,887	(19)	$1,277 (11%)
ALL	$10,575	(280)	$11,648	(314)	$1,073 (10%)

TABLE 17 CHANGES IN THE DISTRIBUTION OF BEGINNING PROFESSIONAL SALARIES, 1975-1977, BY SEX OF DIRECTOR

Beginning Prof. Salary	Male Director 1977	1979	Change	Female Director 1977	1979	Change
Less than $8,000	3%	1%	−2%	5%	3%	−2%
$ 8,000-8,999	6%	1%	−5%	12%	4%	−8%
$ 9,000-9,999	20%	12%	−8%	28%	21%	−7%
$10,000-10,999	25%	19%	−6%	24%	23%	−1%
$11,000-11,999	29%	22%	−7%	11%	14%	+3%
$12,000-12,999	10%	23%	+13%	12%	16%	+4%
$13,000-13,999	4%	11%	+7%	5%	12%	+7%
$14,000 +	4%	11%	+7%	2%	7%	+5%
TOTAL*	101%	100%		99%	100%	

*Total varies from 100% because of rounding.

SEX AND BEGINNERS

None of the libraries reports salaries based on the sex of the entry-level librarian, but the salaries remain lowest for those beginners who choose to work for a female director: 14 percent of the beginners under male directors versus 28 percent of those under female directors earn less than $10,000. While the percentage of those earning $10,000 to $10,999 report to females as often as to males, the disparity also shows in starting salaries above $11,000. When one looks at the $13,000+ category, however, some changes also occur, with 22 percent of those reporting to male directors and 19 percent of those reporting to female directors in this salary range (Table 17). While the upper levels of the starting salary range appear to be gaining in equity, the median beginning salary for those reporting to females is $11,160, $386 below the "lower living standard." The male directors' median beginners' salary is $11,784 for a 6 percent differential/disadvantage in buying power in the recruitment market for female directors (Table 18).

SUMMARY

Per capita library support continues to lose ground to inflation, with the differential between male and female directors remaining at 22 percent. Beginning librarians show a 10 percent increase in median salary, compared to 9.5 percent for female

TABLE 18 RANGE OF MEDIAN BEGINNING PROFESSIONAL SALARIES, BY SEX OF DIRECTOR, 1979

Sex of Director	Median Beginning Salary	Minimum/Maximum Beginning Salary
Female	$11,160	$7,500-$14,815
Male	$11,784	$7,440-$20,776
Differential	$ 624 (6%)	−1% to 40%

directors and 9.7 percent for male directors. In spite of comparable percentages of increase, female directors earn 23 percent less on the average than their male counterparts. Female directors also remain 14 percent below the higher living standard while the male directors earn an average of 5 percent more than the BLS standard.

Per capita support of public libraries gained only 8 percent from 1977 to 1979. The inflationary rate, however, for the same two years was 27.1 percent, so the race to keep ahead of inflation continues to be a losing one. Since the proportionate per capita support to female directors is 22 percent less than for male directors, there is, it follows, less adequate support for new or continued services in their libraries. Competition for beginning librarians continues to favor male-administered public libraries. While all libraries face problems with inflation, the female director and her staff continue to face the toughest battle.

NOTES

1. Raymond L. Carpenter and Kenneth D. Shearer, "Sex and Salary Survey: Selected Statistics of Large Public Libraries in the United States and Canada," *Library Journal*, November 15, 1972, pp. 3682–3685. (Reprinted in the *Bowker Annual of Library and Book Trade Information, 1973*. Bowker, 1973, pp. 406–414.)
———. "Sex and Salary Update," *Library Journal*, January 15, 1974, pp. 101–107. (Reprinted in the *Bowker Annual of Library and Book Trade Information, 1974*. Bowker, 1974, pp. 310–322.)
———. "Public Library Support and Salaries in the Seventies," *Library Journal*, March 15, 1976, pp. 777–783. (Reprinted in the *Bowker Annual of Library and Book Trade Information, 1976*. Bowker, 1976, pp. 360–370.) Kathleen M. Heim and Carolyn Kacena, "Sex, Salaries, and Library Support," *Library Journal*, March 15, 1979, pp. 675–680.

2. *Statistics of Public Libraries in the United States and Canada Serving 100,000 Population or More* (Fort Wayne Public Library, Indiana, 1979).
As a service to the libraries of North America, the Public Library of Fort Wayne and Allen County has, for a number of years, conducted a biennial survey of public libraries serving populations exceeding 100,000. This article is an adaptation of the findings of the most recent survey, conducted in February and March 1979.
From the *American Library Directory* (31st ed., 1978) the compilers selected all public library agencies whose entries indicated the appropriate population. In many cases it was impossible to determine whether an agency was a library performing direct service to the public or the headquarters of a cooperative. Rather than exclude any library unintentionally, many doubtful cases were included in the survey. This procedure produced a list of 519 agencies to which questionnaires were sent. Of that total, 317 libraries returned usable responses and 49 disqualified themselves from consideration. The responses, arranged in tabular form, allow for full comparison and contrast, and for further analysis of the data.
Abla M. Shaheen handled the mailing, tabulated the data, and proofread the final product. She was assisted by Susan Knuth and Sharon Rigdon. Earlean C. Brooks typed the final copy. Don B. Rust and Carolyn Thomas performed the printing. Rick J. Ashton, assistant director of the library, coordinated the entire project. The Public Library of Fort Wayne and Allen County expects to repeat this survey in January 1981. Suggestions which will make it more informative or more useful to its readers are most welcome.

3. "Current Labor Statistics: Consumer Price Indexes, 1967–78," *Monthly Labor Review*, July, p. 73.

4. "Financial and Business Statistics," *Federal Reserve Bulletin,* June 1979, p. A51.

5. U.S. Bureau of Labor Statistics. "Autumn 1978 Urban Family Budgets and Comparative Indexes for Selected Urban Areas," *News Release,* April 29, 1979.

ACCREDITED LIBRARY SCHOOLS

This list of graduate schools accredited by the American Library Association was issued in October 1979. A list of more than 400 institutions offering both accredited and nonaccredited programs in librarianship appears in the thirty-second edition of the *American Library Directory* (Bowker, 1979).

NORTHEAST: CT; DC; MA; MD; NJ; NY; PA

Catholic University of America, Grad. Dept. of Lib. and Info. Science, Washington, DC 20064. Elizabeth W. Stone, Chpn. 202-635-5085.

Clarion State College, School of Lib. Science, Clarion, PA 16214. Elizabeth A. Rupert, Dean, 814-226-2271.

Columbia University, School of Lib. Service, New York, NY 10027. Richard L. Darling, Dean. 212-280-2291.

Drexel University, School of Lib. and Info. Science, Philadelphia, PA 19104. Guy Garrison, Dean. 215-895-2474.

Long Island University, C. W. Post Center, Palmer Grad. Lib. School, Greenvale, NY 11548. Ralph J. Folcarelli, Acting Dean. 516-299-2855/2856.

Pratt Institute, Grad. School of Lib. and Info. Science, Brooklyn, NY 11205. Nasser Sharify, Dean. 212-636-3702.

Queens College, City University of New York, Grad. School of Lib. and Info. Studies, Flushing, NY 11367. Richard J. Hyman, Dir. 212-520-7194.

Rutgers University, Grad. School of Lib. and Info. Studies, New Brunswick, NJ 08903. Thomas H. Mott, Jr., Dean. 201-932-7500.

St. John's University, Div. of Lib. and Info. Science, Jamaica, NY 11439. Mildred Lowe, Dir. 212-969-8000, ext. 200.

Simmons College, School of Lib. Science, Boston, MA 02115. Robert D. Stueart, Dean. 617-738-2225.

Southern Connecticut State College, Div. of Lib. Science and Instructional Technology, New Haven, CT 06515. Emanuel T. Prostano, Dir. 203-397-4532.

State University of New York at Albany, School of Lib. and Info. Science, Albany, NY 12222. Ben-Ami Lipetz, Dean. 518-455-6288.

State University of New York at Buffalo, School of Info. and Lib. Studies, Buffalo, NY 14260. George S. Bobinski, Dean. 716-636-2411.

State University of New York, College of Arts and Science, Geneseo, School of Lib. and Info. Science, Geneseo, NY 14454. Ivan L. Kaldor, Dean. 716-245-5322.

Syracuse University, School of Info. Studies, Syracuse, NY 13210. Robert S. Taylor, Dean. 315-423-2911.

University of Maryland, College of Lib. and Info. Services, College Park, MD 20742. Kieth C. Wright, Dean. 301-454-5441.

University of Pittsburgh, School of Lib. and Info. Sciences, Pittsburgh, PA 15260. Thomas J. Galvin, Dean 412-624-5230.

University of Rhode Island, Grad. Lib. School, Kingston, RI 02881. Bernard S. Schlessinger, Dean. 401-792-2878/2947.

SOUTHEAST: AL; FL; GA; KY; NC; SC; TN

Alabama Agricultural and Mechanical University, School of Lib. Media, Normal, AL 35762. Howard G. Ball, Dean. 205-859-7216.

Atlanta University, School of Lib. and Info. Studies, Atlanta, GA 30314. Virginia Lacy Jones, Dean. 404-681-0251, ext. 311/312.

Emory University, Div. of Libnshp., Atlanta, GA 30322. A. Venable Lawson, Dir. 404-329-6840.

Florida State University, School of Lib. Science, Tallahassee, FL 32306. Harold Goldstein, Dean. 904-644-5775.

North Carolina Central University, School of Lib. Science, Durham, NC 27707. Annette L. Phinazee, Dean. 919-683-6485.

University of Alabama, Grad. School of Lib. Service, University, AL 35486. James D. Ramer, Dean. 205-348-4610.

University of Kentucky, College of Lib. Science, Lexington, KY 40506. Timothy W. Sineath, Dean. 606-258-8876.

University of North Carolina, School of Lib. Science, Chapel Hill, NC 27514. Edward G. Holley, Dean. 919-933-8366.

University of South Carolina, College of Libnshp., Columbia, SC 29208. F. William Summers, Dean. 803-777-3858.

University of South Florida, Grad. Dept. of Lib., Media, and Info. Studies, Tampa, FL 33620. John A. McCrossan, Chpn. 813-974-2557 or 2100.

University of Tennessee, Knoxville, Grad. School of Lib. and Info. Science, Knoxville, TN 37916. Ann E. Prentice, Dir. 615-974-2148.

Vanderbilt University, George Peabody College for Teachers, Dept of Lib. Science, Nashville, TN 37203. Edwin S. Gleaves, Chpn. 615-327-8037.

MIDWEST: IA; IL; IN; KS; MI; MN; MO; OH; WI

Case Western Reserve University, School of Lib. Science, Cleveland, OH 44106. Conrad H. Rawski, Dean. 216-368-3500.

Emporia State University, School of Lib. Science, Emporia, KS 66801. Charles Bolles, Dir. 316-343-1200, ext. 203/204.

Indiana University, Grad. Lib. School, Bloomington, IN 47401. Bernard M. Fry, Dean. 812-337-2848.

Kent State University, School of Lib. Science, Kent, OH 44242. A. Robert Rogers, Dean. 216-672-2782/7988.

Northern Illinois University, Dept. of Lib. Science, DeKalb, IL 60115. Sylvia G. Faibisoff, Chpn. 815-753-1735.

Rosary College, Grad. School of Lib. Science, River Forest, IL 60305. Sister M. Lauretta McCusker, O.P., Dean. 312-366-2490.

University of Chicago, Grad. Lib. School, Chicago, IL 60637. Don R. Swanson, Dean. 312-753-3482.

University of Illinois, Grad. School of Lib. Science, Urbana, IL 61801. Roger Clark, Dean. 217-333-3280.

University of Iowa, School of Lib. Science, Iowa City, IA 52242. Frederick Wezeman, Dir. 319-353-3644.

University of Michigan, School of Lib. Science, Ann Arbor, MI 48109. Russell E. Bidlack, Dean. 313-764-9376.

University of Minnesota, Lib. School, 117 Pleasant St. S.E., Minneapolis, MN 55455. Wesley C. Simonton, Dir. 612-373-3100.

University of Missouri, Columbia, School of Lib. and Info. Science, Columbia, MO 65211. Edward P. Miller, Dean. 314-882-4546.

University of Wisconsin—Madison, Lib. School, Madison, WI 53706. Charles A. Bunge, Dir. 608-263-2900.

University of Wisconsin—Milwaukee, School of Lib. Science, Milwaukee, WI 53201. Mohammed M. Aman, Dean. 414-963-4707.

Wayne State University, Div. of Lib. Science, Detroit, MI 48202. Robert E. Booth, Dir. 313-577-1825.

Western Michigan University, School of Libnshp., Kalamazoo, MI 49008. Jean Lowrie, Dir. 616-383-1849.

SOUTHWEST: AZ; LA; OK; TX

Louisiana State University, Grad. School of Lib. Science, Baton Rouge, LA 70803. Jane R. Carter, Dean. 504-388-3158.

North Texas State University, School of Lib. and Info. Sciences, Denton, TX

76203. Dewey E. Carroll, Dean. 817-788-2445.

Texas Woman's University, School of Lib. Science, Denton, TX 76204. Brooke E. Sheldon, Dir. 817-387-2418.

University of Arizona, Grad. Lib. School, Tucson, AZ 85721. Ellen Altman, Dir. 602-626-3565.

University of Oklahoma, School of Lib. Science, Norman, OK 73019. James S. Healey, Dir. 405-325-3921.

University of Texas at Austin, Grad. School of Lib. Science, Austin, TX 78712. C. Glenn Sparks, Dean. 512-471-3821.

WEST: CA; CO; HI; UT; WA

Brigham Young University, School of Lib. and Info. Sciences, Provo, UT 84602. Maurice P. Marchant, Dir. 801-374-1211, ext. 2976.

San Jose University, Div. of Lib. Science, San Jose, CA 95192. Leslie H. Janke, Dir. 408-277-2292.

University of California, Berkeley, School of Lib. and Info. Studies, Berkeley, CA 94720. Michael K. Buckland, Dean. 415-642-1464.

University of California, Los Angeles, Grad. School of Lib. and Info. Science, Los Angeles, CA 90024. Robert M. Hayes, Dean. 213-825-4351.

University of Denver, Grad. School of Libnshp., Denver, CO 80208, Margaret Knox Goggin, Dean. 303-753-2557.

University of Hawaii, Grad. School of Lib. Studies, Honolulu, HI 96822. Ira W. Harris, Dean. 808-948-7321.

University of Southern California, School of Lib. Science, University Park, Los Angeles, CA 90007. Roger C. Greer, Dean. 213-741-2548.

University of Washington, School of Libnshp., Seattle, WA 98195. Peter Hiatt, Dir. 206-543-1794.

CANADA

Dalhousie University, School of Lib. Service, Halifax, N.S. B3H 4H8. Norman Horrocks, Dir. 902-424-3656.

McGill University, Grad. School of Lib. Science, Montreal, P.Q. H3A 1Y1. Vivian Sessions, Dir. 514-392-5947.

Université de Montréal, Ecole de bibliothéconomie, Montreal, P.Q. H3C 3J7. Daniel Reicher, Dir. 514-343-6044.

University of Alberta, Faculty of Lib. Science, Edmonton, Alta. T6G 2J4. William Kurmey, Dean. 403-432-4578.

University of British Columbia, School of Libnshp., Vancouver, B.C. V6T 1W5. Roy B. Stokes, Dir. 604-228-2404.

University of Toronto, Faculty of Lib. Science, Toronto, Ont. M5S 1A1. Katherine H. Packer, Dean. 416-978-3234.

University of Western Ontario, School of Lib. and Info. Science, London, Ont. N6A 5B9. William J. Cameron, Dean. 519-679-3542.

LIBRARY SCHOLARSHIP SOURCES

For a more complete list of the scholarships, fellowships, and assistantships offered for library study, see *Financial Assistance for Library Education* published biannually by the American Library Association.

American Library Association. Two scholarships of $3,000. The David H. Clift Scholarship is given to a varying number of U.S. or Canadian citizens who have been admitted to an accredited library school. For information, write to: Staff Liaison, David H. Clift Scholarship Jury, ALA, 50 E. Huron St., Chicago, IL 60611; the Louise Giles Minority Scholarship is given to a varying number of minority students who are U.S. or Canadian citizens and have been admitted to an accredited library school. For information, write to: Staff Liaison, Louise Giles Minority Scholarship Jury, ALA, 50 E. Huron St., Chicago, IL 60611.

American-Scandinavian Foundation. Fellowships and grants for 25 to 30 students, in amounts from $500 to $5,000, for advanced study in Denmark, Finland, Iceland, Norway, or Sweden. For information, write to: Exchange Division, American-Scandinavian Foundation, 127 E. 73 St., New York, NY 10021.

Beta Phi Mu. Three scholarships: (1) $1,500 each for a varying number of persons accepted in an ALA-accredited library program; (2) $750 each for a varying number of Beta Phi Mu members for continuing education; (3) the Harold Lancour Scholarship for Foreign Study, $750 each for a varying number of students for graduate study in a foreign country related to the applicant's work or schooling. For information, write to: Exec. Secy., Beta Phi Mu, Graduate School of Library and Information Science, University of Pittsburgh, Pittsburgh, PA 15260.

Canadian Library Association. Howard V. Phalin-World Book Graduate Scholarship in Library Science. A $2,500 maximum scholarship for a Canadian citizen or landed immigrant to attend an accredited library school in Canada or the United States. H. W. Wilson Scholarship of $2,000 and Elizabeth Dafoe Scholarship of $1,750 for a Canadian citizen or landed immigrant to attend an accredited Canadian library school. For information, write to: Scholarships and Awards Committee, Canadian Library Association, 151 Sparks St., Ottawa, Ont. K1P 5E3, Canada.

Catholic Library Association. Rev. Andrew L. Bouwhuis Scholarship of $1,500 for a person with a B.A. degree who has been accepted in an accredited library school. (Award based on financial need and proficiency.) World Book-Childcraft Awards. One scholarship of a total of $1,000 to be distributed among no more than four recipients for a program of continuing education. Open to CLA members only. For information, write to: Scholarship Committee, Catholic Library Association, 461 W. Lancaster Ave., Haverford, PA 19041.

Fulbright-Hays Awards. Fellowships and grants of varying amounts for university lecturing or advanced research abroad to candidates with a Ph.D. and library and teaching or research experience. Foreign language proficiency required in some instances. For information, write to: Council for International Exchange of Scholars, Suite 300, 11 Dupont Circle, Washington, DC 20036.

Information Exchange System for Minority Personnel. Scholarship of $500, intended for minority students, for graduate study. For information, write to: Dorothy M. Haith, Chpn., Clara Stanton Jones School, Box 91, Raleigh, NC 27602.

Medical Library Association. Varying number of scholarships of $2,000 each for minority students, for graduate study in medical librarianship. Grants of varying amounts for continuing education for medical librarians with an M.L.S. and two years' professional experience. Open to MLA members only. For information, write to: Scholarship Committee, Medical Library Association, Suite 3208, 919 N. Michigan Ave., Chicago, IL 60611.

The Frederic G. Melcher Scholarship (administered by Association of Library

Service to Children, ALA). Scholarship of $4,000 for a U.S. or Canadian citizen admitted to an accredited library school who plans to work with children in school or public libraries. For information, write to: Exec. Secy., Association of Library Service to Children, ALA, 50 E. Huron St., Chicago, IL 60611.

Mountain Plains Library Association. Four grants of $500 each for residents of the association area. Open only to MPLA members with at least two years of membership. For information, write to: Joseph R. Edelen, Jr., MPLA Exec. Secy., University of South Dakota Library, Vermillion, SD 57069.

Natural Sciences and Engineering Research Council. Ten scholarships of $7,000 each for postgraduate study in science librarianship and documentation for a Canadian citizen or landed immigrant with a bachelor's degree in science or engineering. For information, write to: J. H. Danis, Scholarships Officer, Natural Sciences and Engineering Research Council, Ottawa, Ont. K1A OR6 Canada.

Special Libraries Association. Four $3,000 scholarships for U.S. or Canadian citizens, accepted by an ALA-accredited library education program who show an aptitude for and interest in special libraries. For information, write to: Scholarship Committee, SLA, 235 Park Ave. S., New York, NY 10003. Three scholarships of $1,500 each for minority students with an interest in special libraries. Open to U.S. or Canadian citizens only. For information, write to: Positive Action Program for Minority Groups, c/o SLA.

LIBRARY SCHOLARSHIP AND AWARD RECIPIENTS

AALS Research Grant Award—$1,500. For a project that reflects the goals and objectives of the Association of American Library Schools (AALS). *Offered by:* AALS. *Winner:* James S. Healey, Dir., School of Lib. Science, Univ. of Oklahoma, Norman, OK, for "Effects of the Loss of Accreditation on Three Library Schools."

AASL/Encyclopaedia Britannica School Library Media Program of the Year Award—$5,000. For outstanding school media programs. *Offered by:* ALA American Association of School Librarians and the Encyclopaedia Britannica Co. *Winner:* Greenwich Public Schools, Greenwich, CT.

AASL President's Award—$2,000. For demonstrating excellence and providing an outstanding national or international contribution to school librarianship and school library development. *Offered by:* ALA, American Association of School Librarians. *Donor:* Baker & Taylor. *Winner:* Frances E. Henney.

ACRL Academic/Research Librarian of the Year Award—$2,000 (equally divided). For an outstanding national or international contribution to academic and research librarianship and library development. *Offered by:* ALA, Association of College and Research Libraries. *Donor:* Baker & Taylor. *Winners:* Frederick G. Kilgour, Pres. & Exec. Dir., OCLC, Inc., and Henriette D. Avram, Dir., Network Development Office, Lib. of Congress.

AIA/ALA-LAMA Library Buildings Award. For excellence in the architectural design and planning of libraries. *Offered by:* American Institute of Architects and ALA Library Administration and Management Association. *Winner:* Not awarded in 1979.

ALA Honorary Life Membership Award. *Offered by:* American Library Association. *Winner:* Lowell Martin.

ASCLA Exceptional Service Award. For exceptional service to ASCLA or any of its component areas of service, namely, services to patients, the home-bound, medical, nursing, and other professional staff in hospitals, and inmates, demonstrating professional leadership, effective interpretation of program, pioneering activity, or significant research or experimental projects. *Offered by:* Association of Specialized & Cooperative Library Agencies. *Winner:* Genevieve M. Casey, Wayne State Univ.

Alabama Public Library Service Graduate Scholarships (Full-Time)—$4,000. For Alabama residents admitted to an ALA-accredited library school and interested in a career in public librarianship. *Offered by:* Alabama Public Lib. Service. *Winners:* Marianne S. Lovell, Prattville, AL, and George Willis Vickery, Jr., Dothan, AL.

Alabama Public Library Service Graduate Scholarships (Part-Time)—$500. For an Alabama public librarian admitted to an ALA-accredited library school program and demonstrating a commitment to public library service. *Winners:* Becky Cothran, Selma, AL; George David Lilly, Huntsville, AL; Mary Sue Mitchell, Huntsville, AL; and James Douglas Pate, Birmingham, AL.

American Library History Round Table Essay Award—$300. For an essay which demonstrates excellence in research in library history. *Offered by:* ALA American Library History Round Table. *Winner:* Dennis Thomison for *The Private Wars of Chicago's Big Bill Thompson.*

Joseph L. Andrews Bibliographic Award. For a contribution, either in single work or as a career product, that is particularly noteworthy and of value to law librarians and to the legal profession. *Offered by:* American Association of Law Libraries. *Winner:* Beatrice J. Kalisch for *Child Abuse: An Annotated Bibliography.*

Armed Forces Librarians Achievement Citation. For significant contributions to the development of armed forces library service and to organizations encouraging an interest in libraries and reading. *Offered by:* Armed Forces Librarians Section, ALA Public Library Association. *Winner:* Mariana J. Thurber.

Beta Phi Mu Award—$500. For distinguished service to education for librarianship. *Offered by:* ALA Awards Committee. *Donor:* Beta Phi Mu Library Science Honorary Association. *Winner:* Conrad Rawski, Dean, Case Western Reserve School of Lib. Science.

Beta Phi Mu Continuing Education Scholarship—$750. For a varying number of Beta Phi Mu members for continuing education. *Offered by:* Beta Phi Mu. *Winner:* Ann Carlson, Reference Libn., Orlando (FL) Public Lib.

Black Caucus Awards. For distinguished service to librarianship. *Offered by:* ALA Black Caucus. *Winners:* Lucille C. Thomas, New York City Board of Education, and E. J. Josey, New York State Library.

Rev. Andrew L. Bouwhuis Scholarship—$1,500. For a student in financial need, for graduate study in library science. *Offered by:* Catholic Library Association. *Winner:* Karen Sinkule, Uniontown, PA.

John Brubaker Memorial Award. For an outstanding work of significant interest to the library profession published in the *Catholic Library World. Offered by:* Catholic Library Association. *Winner:* Mary Margrabe, Library Consultant, Frederick, MD.

CIS/GODORT/ALA Documents to the People Award—$1,000. For effectively encouraging the use of federal documents in support of library services.

Offered by: ALA Government Documents Round Table. *Donor:* Congressional Information Service, Inc. *Winner:* Yuri Nakata, Univ. of Illinois at Chicago Circle.

CLA Outstanding Service to Librarianship Award. *Offered by:* Canadian Library Association. *Winner:* Jack E. Brown, Prof. of Lib. Science, McGill Univ., Montreal, P.Q., Canada.

CLR Fellowships. For a list of the recipients for the 1979-1980 academic year, see the report from the Council on Library Resources, Inc., in the Foundation and Other Grants section of Part 2.

CSLA Award for Outstanding Congregational Librarian. For distinguished service to the congregation and/or community through devotion to the congregational library. *Offered by:* Church and Synagogue Library Association. *Winner:* Anita Dalton, Libn., Forward Baptist Church, Cambridge, Ont., Canada.

CSLA Award for Outstanding Congregational Library. For responding in creative and innovative ways to the library's mission of reaching and serving the congregation and/or the wider community. *Offered by:* Church and Synagogue Library Association. *Winner:* United Presbyterian Church of the Atonement Lib., Silver Spring, MD.

CSLA Award for Outstanding Contribution to Librarianship. For providing inspiration, guidance, leadership, or resources to enrich the field of church or synagogue librarianship. *Offered by:* Church and Synagogue Library Association. *Winner:* NETWORK, the Media Center of the Episcopal Diocese of Alaska.

Francis Joseph Campbell Citation. For an outstanding contribution to the advancement of library service to the blind. *Offered by:* Section on Library Service to the Blind and Physically Handicapped of the Association of Specialized and Cooperative Library Agencies. *Winners:* Jenny M. Beck and Volunteer Sevices for the Blind.

James Bennett Childs Awards. For distinguished contributions to document librarianship. *Offered by:* ALA Government Documents Round Table. *Winner:* Catharine Reynolds, Univ. of Colorado-Boulder.

Chinese-American Librarians Association Distinguished Service Award. For a member of the Chinese-American Librarians Association with a record of distinction in service. *Offered by:* Chinese-American Librarians Association. *Winner:* Ernst Wolff.

David H. Clift Scholarship—$3,000. For a worthy student to begin a program of library education at the graduate level. *Offerd by:* ALA Awards Committee, Standing Committee on Library Education. *Winners:* Pete Giacoma, Salt Lake City, and Sheila L. Nollen, Macomb, IL.

Eileen R. Cunningham International Scholarship. For an outstanding foreign medical librarian. *Offered by:* Medical Library Association. *Winners:* Margaret Okeke and K. S. Yeung.

Elizabeth Dafoe Scholarship—$1,750. For a Canadian citizen or landed immigrant to attend an accredited Canadian library school. *Offered by:* Canadian Library Association. *Winner:* Donald Meakins, Vancouver, B.C., Canada.

John Cotton Dana Award (formerly SLA Special Citation). For exceptional support and encouragement of special librarianship. *Offered by:* Special Libraries Association. *Winners:* Ruth S. Smith and Jessie C. Wheelwright.

John Cotton Dana Library Public Relations Award. For an outstanding public relations program. *Offered by:* Public Relations Section of the ALA Library Administration and Management Association. *Donor:* H. W. Wilson Co. *Winners:* Houston (TX) Public Lib., Milwaukee (WI) Public Lib., and Timberland Regional Lib., Olympia, WA.

Dartmouth Medal. For achievement in creating reference works outstanding in quality and significance. *Offered by:* Reference and Adult Services Division of American Library Association. *Winner: The Encyclopedia of Bioethics*, ed. by Warren T. Reich, published by Free Press, a division of Macmillan.

Melvil Dewey Medal. For recent creative professional achievement of a high order, particularly in library management, library training, cataloging and classification, and the tools and techniques of librarianship. *Offered by:* ALA Awards Committee. *Donor:* Forest Press. *Winner:* Russell E. Bidlack.

Distinguished Library Service Award for School Administrators. For a unique and sustained contribution toward furthering the role of the library and its development in elementary and/or secondary education. *Offered by:* ALA American Association of School Librarians. *Winner:* Richard C. Hunter, Supt., Richmond (VA) City Schools.

Janet Doe Lectureship Honor. For the individual who presents the Janet Doe Lecture on an aspect of the history or philosophy of medical librarianship at the annual meeting. *Offered by:* Medical Library Assocation. *Winner:* Gwendolyn S. Cruzat.

Robert B. Downs Award. *Offered by:* University of Illinois Graduate School. For an outstanding contribution to intellectual freedom in libraries. *Winner:* Ralph E. McCoy, Dean Emeritus of Lib. Affairs, Southern Illinois Univ., Carbondale.

Ida and George Eliot Prize—$100. For the publication issued in the preceding calendar year which has been judged most effective in furthering medical librarianship. *Offered by:* Medical Library Association. *Winner:* Ursula Poland for "The Medical Library Association's International Fellowship Program."

Louise Giles Minority Scholarship—$3,000. For a worthy student who is a U.S. or Canadian citizen and is also a member of a principal minority group. *Offered by:* ALA Awards Committee, Office for Library Personnel Resources Advisory Committee. *Winners:* Mercedes Mendoza, College Park, MD, and Frances Lynn Smith, Chicago, IL.

Murray Gottlieb Prize—$100. For the best unpublished essay submitted by a medical librarian on the history of some aspect of health sciences or a detailed description of a library exhibit. *Offered by:* Medical Library Association. *Winner:* Georgia Walter for "Osteopathic Medicine: Past and Present."

Grolier Foundation Award—$1,000. For an unusual contribution to the stimulation and guidance of reading by children and young people through high school age, for continuing service, or one particular contribution of lasting value. *Offered by:* ALA Awards Committee. *Donor:* Grolier Foundation. *Winner:* Anne Pellowski, Dir.-Libn., Info. Center on Children's Cultures, U.S. Committee for UNICEF.

Grolier National Library Week Award—$1,000. For the best plan for a public relations program. *Awarded by:* National Library Week Committee of the American Library Association. *Donor:* Grolier Educational Corp. *Winner:* Utah State Lib. Assn.

Philip M. Hamer Award. For high quality work in a documentary publication by an associate or assisting editor on publications projects sponsored or endorsed by the National Historical Publications and Records Commission. *Offered by:* Society of American Archivists. *Winner:* Raymond W. Smock, Booker T. Washington Papers.

Oliver Wendell Holmes Award. For a foreign archivist to facilitate supplementary travel while in the United States or Canada for training. *Offered by:* Society of American Archivists. *Winner:* Steve Mwiyeriwa, Archivist of Malawi.

Bailey K. Howard-World Book Encyclopedia-ALA Goal Award—$5,000. To support programs that recognize, advance, and implement the goals and objectives of the American Library Association. *Donor:* World Book-Childcraft International, Inc. *Winner:* Committee on the Status of Women in Librarianship.

Hubbard Scholarship—$2,000 given biennially. For a senior in an accredited college or university to do graduate study in the field of library science. *Offered by:* Georgia Library Assn. *Winner:* Not awarded in 1979.

John Phillip Imroth Memorial Award for Intellectual Freedom—$500. For a notable contribution to intellectual freedom and remarkable personal courage. *Offered by:* ALA Intellectual Freedom Round Table. *Donor:* Intellectual Freedom Round Table. *Winner:* Alex Allain, St. Mary Parish Lib., Franklin, LA.

Information Industry Association Hall of Fame Award. For leadership and innovation in furthering the progress of the information industry. *Offered by:* Information Industry Association. *Winner:* John Rotham, Director of Information, The New York Times Company.

Information Product of the Year Award. For excellence in product innovations and development of a product introduced within the past five years. *Offered by:* Information Industry Association. *Winners:* Information Handling Services for "Checklist of State Publications" and Texas Instruments for "The Silent 700."

JMRT Professional Development Grant. *See* 3M Company Professional Development Grant.

J. Morris Jones-World Book Encyclopedia-ALA Goal Award—$5,000. To support programs that recognize, advance, and implement the goals and objectives of the American Library Association. *Donor:* World Book-Childcraft International, Inc. *Winner:* ALA Office for Lib. Personnel Resources Advisory Committee, Minimum Qualifications for Libns. Task Force.

Kohlstedt Exhibit Award. For the best single and multiple booth displays at the annual ALA conference. *Offered by:* Kohlstedt Committee of the ALA Exhibits Round Table. *Winners:* Society for Visual Education, Inc. (best single booth), and the 3M Company (best multiple booth).

LITA Award for Achievement in Library and Information Technology. For distinguished leadership, notable development or application of technology, superior accomplishments in research or education, or original contributions to the literature of the field. *Offered by:* Library and Information Technology Association. *Winner:* Frederick G. Kilgour, OCLC, Inc.

LRRT Research Award—$500. To encourage excellence in library research. *Offered by:* ALA Library Research Round Table. *Winners:* Charles R. McClure, Univ. of Oklahoma, Graduate Lib. School, for "Perceived Values of Information Sources for Library Decision-Making"; and Pauline Wilson, Univ. of Tennessee Graduate School for Lib. and Info. Science, for "Librarians and Their Stereotype."

Harold Lancour Scholarship for Foreign Study—$750. For a varying number of students for graduate study in a foreign country related to the applicant's work or schooling. *Offered by:* Beta Phi Mu. *Winner:* Judy Komor, Lib. Media Specialist, Ithaca H.S., Ithaca, NY.

M. Claude Lane Award. For an individual who has made significant contributions in the field of religious archives. *Offered by:* Society of American Archivists. *Winner:* Sister M. Felicitas Powers, Sisters of Mercy National Office.

Waldo Gifford Leland Prize. For the author of an outstanding contribution in the field of archival history, theory, or practice. *Offered by:* Society of

American Archivists. *Funded by:* Waldo Gifford Leland Prize Fund. *Winner:* Donald R. McCoy for *The National Archives: America's Ministry of Documents.*

Joseph W. Lippincott Award—$1,000. For distinguished service to the profession of librarianship, such service to include outstanding participation in the activities of professional library associations, notable published professional writing, or other significant activity on behalf of the profession and its aims. *Offered by:* ALA Awards Committee. *Donor:* Joseph W. Lippincott. *Winner:* Helen Lyman, Prof. Emeritus, Univ. of Wisconsin.

Margaret Mann Citation. For outstanding professional achievement in the area of cataloging and classification. *Offered by:* ALA Resources and Technical Services Division/Cataloging and Classification Section. *Winners:* Michael Gorman, Univ. of Illinois, and Paul Winkler, Lib. of Congress.

Allie Beth Martin Award—$2,000. For an outstanding librarian. *Offered by:* ALA Public Library Association. *Donor:* Baker & Taylor Co. *Winner:* Harriet E. Bard, Head Libn., Morrisson-Reeves Lib., Richmond, IN.

Medical Library Association Scholarship Awards—$2,000. For individuals interested in the field of medical librarianship with at least one year remaining for an M.L.S. in an ALA-approved graduate library school. *Offered by:* Medical Library Association. *Winners:* Paul Brederman and Elaine M. Russo.

Frederic G. Melcher Scholarship—$4,000. For young people who wish to enter the field of library service to children. *Offered by:* ALA Association for Library Service to Children. *Winners:* Dianne Albers, Louisville, KY, and Linda Halas Papajcik, Lakewood, OH.

Isadore Gilbert Mudge Citation. For a distinguished contribution to reference librarianship. *Offered by:* Reference and Adult Services Division of American Library Association. *Winner:* Henry J. Dubester, Bethesda, MD (formerly of the Lib. of Congress).

Music Library Association Prizes—$50. For the best book-length bibliography or research tool and for the best review of a book or score published in *Notes. Offered by:* Music Library Association. *Winners:* Rita Benton (best book) and Christopher Rouse (best review).

National Library Service Resources Section Scholarship Award—$1,200. Presented to the author/authors of an outstanding monograph, published article, or original paper on acquisitions pertaining to college or university libraries. *Offered by:* ALA Resources and Technical Services Division, Resources Section. *Donor:* Arnold Santos and National Library Service, Inc. *Winners:* Mona East and Rose Mary Magrill for "Collection Development in Libraries," *Advances in Librarianship* 8 (1978).

Marcia C. Noyes Award. For lasting, outstanding contribution to medical librarianship. *Offered by:* Medical Library Association. *Winner:* Not awarded in 1979.

Eunice Rockwell Oberly Award for Bibliography in the Agricultural Sciences—$145. For the best bibliography in the field of agriculture or one of the related sciences. *Offered by:* ALA Association of College and Research Libraries, Agriculture and Biological Sciences Section. *Winners:* James B. Beard, Harriet Beard, and D. P. Martin for *Turfgrass: A Bibliography from 1672 to 1972.*

Shirley Olofson Memorial Award. For individuals to attend their second annual conference of ALA. *Offered by:* ALA Junior Members Round Table. *Winners:* Robert Heriard, Univ. of New Orleans; Charlene Hurt, Washburn Univ., Topeka, KS; Marilyn Kaye, Univ. of Chicago Grad. Lib. School; Wayne Mullin, Univ. of Arizona, Tucson; Paul Weber, Adams-Brown Counties Bookmobile, Winchester, OH; and Lisa Whyte, Brooklyn Public Lib.

Howard V. Phalin-World Book Graduate Scholarship in Library Science—$2,500 (maximum). For a Canadian citizen or landed immigrant to attend an accredited library school in Canada or the United States. *Offered by:* Canadian Library Association. *Winner:* Richard Hopkins, Calgary, Alta., Canada.

Esther J. Piercy Award. For contribution to librarianship in the field of technical services by younger members of the profession. *Offered by:* ALA Resources and Technical Services Division. *Winner:* Pamela W. Darling.

Herbert W. Putnam Award—$500. For outstanding ability, for travel, writing, or any other use that might improve service to the library profession or to society. *Awarded by:* ALA Awards Committee. *Winner:* Isabel Schon.

RTSD Resources Section Scholarship—$1,000. *Offered by:* ALA Resources and Technical Services Division. *Winners:* Mona East and Rose Mary Magrill.

Sarah Rebecca Reed Scholarship—$1,500. For a varying number of beginning students accepted in an ALA-accredited library program. *Offered by:* Beta Phi Mu. *Winners:* Jo Ann Fisher and Karen Leigh Sinkule.

Rittenhouse Award—$200. For the best unpublished paper on medical librarianship submitted by a student enrolled in, or having been enrolled in, a course for credit in an ALA-accredited library school, or a trainee in an internship program in medical librarianship. *Offered by:* Medical Library Association. *Winner:* Lonnie J. Spotts for "Independent Study-Guidelines for Conversion of Subject Headings for the FDA Medical Library Methodology Using Drug Class Terms as a Model."

John R. Rowe Memorial Award—$500. To aid or improve some particular aspect of librarianship or library service on the basis of need in the profession or in the operation of professional library associations. *Offered by:* ALA Exhibits Round Table. *Winner:* Pennsylvania Lib. Assn.

SLA Hall of Fame. For an extended and sustained period of distinguished service to the Special Libraries Association in all spheres of its activities. *Offered by:* Special Libraries Association. *Winners:* Gretchen Little and Frank E. McKenna.

SLA Honorary Member. In recognition of contribution to or support of librarianship. *Offered by:* Special Libraries Association. *Winner:* Helen F. Spencer, Pres., Kenneth and Helen F. Spencer Foundation.

SLA Minority Stipends—$500. For students with financial need who show potential for special librarianship. *Offered by:* Special Libraries Association. *Winners:* Kirk Gregory, St. Louis, MO; Hiawatha Norris, Claremont, CA; Thu-Thuy Thi Trinh, Austin, TX; and Kieth Martin West, Flushing, NY.

SLA Professional Award. For a significant achievement or contribution to librarianship which advances the stated objectives of the Special Libraries Association. *Offered by:* Special Libraries Association. *Winner:* Not awarded in 1979.

SLA Scholarships—$2,500. For students with financial need who show potential for special librarianship. *Offered by:* Special Libraries Association. *Winners:* Wendolyn Clark, Florence, AL; Donna Harnden, St. Paul, MN; and Mary S. Williams, Berkeley, CA.

Charles Scribner's Sons Award—$250. To attend ALA's annual conference. *Offered by:* ALA Association for Library Service to Children. *Donor:* Charles Scribner's Sons. *Winners:* Penny S. Markey, Iaconboni Lib., Los Angeles County (CA) Public Lib. System, and Rita Auerbach, Connetquot (NY) Public Lib.

Ralph R. Shaw Award for Library Literature—$500. For an outstanding contribution to library literature issued during the three years preceding the presentation. *Offered by:* ALA Awards Committee. *Donor:* Scarecrow Press. *Winner:* Joan K. Marshall for *On Equal Terms: A Thesaurus for Nonsexist Indexing and Cataloging* (Neal-Schuman, 1977).

Society of American Archivists Distinguished Service Award. For an organization or archival institution that has made an exemplary contribution to the profession. *Offered by:* Society of American Archivists. *Winner:* Not awarded in 1979.

3M Company Professional Development Grant—$5,000. To encourage professional development and participation of new librarians in ALA and JMRT activities. To cover expenses for recipients attending the ALA San Francisco conference. *Offered by:* ALA Junior Members Round Table. *Winners:* Erlene Mae Bishop, Reference Libn./Media Specialist, Mt. Vernon College, Washington, DC; Mary Bride Bayer, Libn., Churchland Branch Lib., Portsmouth, VA; Jerald Andrew Merrick, Head of Adult Services, Salina Public Lib., Salina, KS; and Vivian Jean Williams, Dir., Pearl River County Lib. System, Picayune, MS.

Trustee Citations. For distinguished service to library development whether on the local, state, or national level. *Offered by:* ALA American Library Trustee Association. *Donor:* ALA. *Winners:* Jean M. Coleman, Dayton & Montgomery County (OH) Public Lib., and Ella Pretty, Fraser Valley Regional Lib., Abbotsford, B.C., Canada.

H. W. Wilson Co. Award—$250. For the best paper published in *Special Libraries* in 1977. *Offered by:* Special Libraries Association. *Winner:* Not awarded in 1979.

H. W. Wilson Education Foundation Scholarship—$2,000. For a Canadian citizen or landed immigrant to attend an accredited Canadian library school. *Offered by:* Canadian Library Association. *Winner:* Karen Wiandt, Waterloo, Ont., Canada.

H. W. Wilson Library Periodical Award—$500. To a periodical published by a local, state, or regional library, library group, or library association in the United States or Canada which has made an outstanding contribution to librarianship. *Offered by:* ALA Awards Committee. *Donor:* H. W. Wilson Co. *Winner: The Southeastern Librarian,* ed. by Leland Park of Davidson (NC) College.

H. W. Wilson Library Recruitment Award—$1,000. Presented to any local, state, or regional library association, any library school, or any other appropriate group concerned with recruitment to the profession. *Offered by:* ALA Awards Committee. *Donor:* H. W. Wilson Co. *Winner:* Not awarded in 1979.

World Book-Childcraft Award—$1,000 divided among no more than four recipients. For a specific program of study. *Offered by:* Catholic Library Association. *Winners:* Mary A. Grant, Brooklyn, NY; Gloria Fischer, Lansdale, PA; and Patricia Ann LeClercq, Poughkeepsie, NY.

Part 4
Research and Statistics

Library Research and Statistics

RESEARCH ON LIBRARIES AND LIBRARIANSHIP IN 1979: AN OVERVIEW

Mary Jo Lynch
Director, ALA Office for Research

For some time it looked as if 1979 would be the year that saw the end of federal funds specifically earmarked for library research and development. First the president's budget recommended zero funding for the Higher Education Act, Title II-B, which includes the Library Research and Demonstration Program as well as the Library Training Program. Then Congress restored $1 million for Title II-B but said it could be used only for fellowships and institutes. Just in time, Senator Javits reminded his colleagues that, according to the original authorization, at least one-third of the funds must be spent on the research and demonstration program, and $330,000 was made available for this purpose. That amount is miniscule in the face of what needs to be done but something is better than nothing.

The importance of the HEA II-B Library Research and Demonstration Program in the public library field was made obvious by the dean of Drexel University, Guy Garrison, in a paper he presented to the Library Research Round Table at the Dallas Conference of the American Library Association. Covering "Trends in Public Library Research in the 1970s," Garrison described not the results, but the demographics—"who did the work, where was it done, who paid, what subjects were covered, what format did the end products take, and how well were the results disseminated." Table 1, based on

TABLE 1 RESEARCH PROJECTS LISTED BY TYPE, NUMBER, AND DOLLAR VALUE

Type	Number	Percent of Total	Dollar Value	Percent of Dollar Value
Dissertations	90	47	$ 2,250,000 (est.)	17
Title II-B projects	40	21	7,918,000	60
Other projects	63	32	3,045,000 (est.)	23
Total	193		$13,213,000	

a table in Garrison's paper, tells part of the story. If dissertations are removed from the total, HEA II-B funded 39 percent of the projects and provided 72 percent of the funds for public library research. Garrison's paper was published in the April 1980 issue of *Public Libraries*.

RESEARCH AND THE WHITE HOUSE CONFERENCE

The White House Conference on Library and Information Services played a significant role in focusing research efforts during 1979. Early in the year, the California State Library sponsored a statewide survey of information needs in order to provide data that could be used in the state pre-White House conference. The study of California citizens conducted by King Research, Inc., with the assistance of Brenda Dervin, sought "to identify their needs for information, the ways they seek to satisfy those needs, and how well these needs are met." The uniqueness of this survey was explained in an introduction to the report:

> Needs for information arise out of the current situations in which individuals find themselves. Consequently, in this survey it was necessary to allow the people being interviewed the opportunity to recall recent situations they had encountered. It was then possible to discuss their resulting information needs in terms of the questions they asked themselves in these situations.

A similar study was conducted later in the year by Simmons College with funds from the HEA II-B Research and Demonstration Program. An executive summary of "Citizen Information Seeking Patterns: A New England Study" directed by Ching-Chih Chen was distributed to delegates at WHCOLIS. Based on telephone interviews in 2,400 New England households, the data from this study will provide:

> Insights into the behavior of information seekers (e.g., their source awareness and problem articulation), source providers consulted, perceived level of satisfaction with information source providers, institutional and environmental barriers to effective information seeking, and reasons for use and non-use of libraries.

A final report will be available from Ching-Chih Chen in the summer of 1980.

Also distributed to delegates at the White House Conference were the results of Gerald Jahoda's national survey of "Public Library Service to Physically Handicapped Persons." This study is another supported by the HEA II-B Library Research and Demonstration Program.

Before the National White House Conference on Library and Information Services took place in November, there were 57 state, territorial, and topical pre-White House conferences that produced close to 3,000 resolutions. *Issues and Resolutions: A Summary of Pre-Conference Activities*, prepared by King Research, Inc., organizes the results of those activities into five theme areas and notes 16 "information issues" that cut across all five. "Research and development" is one of those issues; it was summarized in the report as follows: "Generally, resolutions reflected views that both Federal and State governments should sponsor demonstration projects, develop research methods, and establish procedures that can be employed by local libraries."

Resolutions on another implementation issue, "new technology," also involved research, since "most resolutions in this area called for support of research or evaluation dealing with video and computer technology."

RESEARCH AND THE CATALOG

Another motivating force for research efforts in 1979 was the advent of the second edition of the *Anglo-American Cataloging Rules*, known as AACR2. A column of "News about AACR2 Implementation Studies" was started in the *RTSD Newsletter* in order to communicate information about studies done in individual libraries to estimate the impact of AACR2 on their technical services so that appropriate plans could be made by management. Although few such studies were done, the column has functioned as a useful source of information related to this important topic.

One large-scale study undertaken to assist library managers in making AACR2-related decisions was sponsored by the Association of Research Libraries (ARL). Some 70 university libraries (58 ARL members plus 13 other Ph.D.-granting institutions) participated in the project, supplying funds and data that enabled researchers Gene Palmour, Bob Weiderkehr, and Richard Boss to develop a model that can be used to estimate the cost of various forms of a library catalog. The results were to be published by ARL in the spring of 1980.

Two reviews of research regarding catalog use may be helpful to librarians struggling with decisions about future catalogs: *Library Research* published "The Performance of Card Catalogs: A Review of Research" by Ruth F. Hafter in the Fall 1979 issue. Also appearing in fall 1979 was Kathryn Weintraub's survey of "The Essentials or Desiderata of the Bibliographic Record as Discovered by Research," published in *Library Resources and Technical Services.*

RESEARCH AND THE COLLECTION

The results of the National Enquiry on Scholarly Communication were published by Johns Hopkins University in a monograph called *Scholarly Communication.* The report was short on original data, although a list of "Principal Studies Commissioned by the National Enquiry" indicates that some original work was done. The chapter on "Research Libraries and Scholarly Communication" includes a summary of the study by Hugh Cline and Lorraine Sinnot of the Educational Testing Service, which was financed by the Enquiry and by the National Endowment for the Humanities. In *Organizational Case Studies of Collection Development Policies and Practices,* which will probably be published commercially in 1980, Cline and Sinnot examined collection development in seven well-known academic libraries using methods employed in anthropological field research. They hoped to contribute to both social scientific study of complex organizations and the discussion of policy issues currently facing academic libraries. The report will be interesting to librarians for the light it sheds on how social scientists view academic libraries.

A major issue in the area of collection development—the difficulty of designing, executing, and interpreting studies of collection use—was emphasized by the "Report on the Study of Library Use at Pitt by Allen Kent et al.," a response by the Senate Library Committee of the University of Pittsburgh to the report described in this article last year and now available from Marcel Dekker (*The Use of Library Materials: The University of Pittsburgh Study*). According to the report's abstract, the faculty, librarians, and administration of the University of Pittsburgh asked the Senate Library Committee to "undertake an evaluation" of the Kent study. The report of that effort criticizes the Kent study on numerous matters "in particular, its structure in text and footnotes, which makes careful investigation and reporting on it a difficult matter, and its experimental design, execution, and manipulation of data, in terms of holdings, use and costs." The Senate Committee reports that the Kent study "consistently overestimates the number of books, monographs and journals *available for use* and consistently underestimates their *usage.*" For these reasons the Senate report concludes that the Kent study "fails to support the validity of its root hypotheses that 'much of the material purchased for research libraries' is 'little or never used' and that when costs are assigned to uses, the costs of use are 'unexpectedly high.'"

The report will soon be available through the ERIC system. It merits close study as does the work it criticizes. Perhaps the study of both will help academic librarians formulate ways to study collection use that will be accepted as valid and reliable by all members of the academic and library community.

Another perspective on academic library collection development is provided by Charles Osburn's *Academic Research and Library Resources* (Greenwood). Based on Osburn's doctoral dissertation at Michigan, the book presents a lucid and erudite analysis of post-World War II changes in university research caused by changes in federal government policy. Chapters on new patterns of research in the sciences, the social sciences, and the humanities are followed by a chapter analyzing the response of academic librarians. Osburn concludes that academic librarians need to be much more sensitive than they have been in the recent past to what researchers really want from the collections supposedly developed to support their work.

RESEARCH AND LITERACY

The year 1979 also saw action at the other end of the literacy spectrum. In July the Office of Education issued a Request for Proposal for a study of "Libraries and Literacy." The study is to produce a state-of-the-art report on the role of libraries of all types in literacy education. An award was made in September to Contract Research Corporation of Belmont, Massachusetts. The results of this study may help to correct the impression left by a report made to the Ford Foundation in 1979 by Carmen St. John Hunter and David Harman. *Adult Illiteracy in the United States* (McGraw-Hill) mentions libraries as one of the places where literacy activities take place, but implies that libraries are totally uninterested in reaching out to people in the community who do not automatically seek their services.

RESEARCH AND INFORMATION PROFESSIONALS

A *Progress Report on the Occupational Survey of Information Professionals*, directed by Anthony Debons of the University of Pittsburgh, was released in March covering the first phase of this National Science Foundation financed effort. The project as a whole was designed "to determine which information functions are performed in all sectors of the U.S. economy, and the number of professionals involved in performing each function." Phase 1 sought (1) to formulate an outline classification of functions by the performance of which information professionals could be identified; and (2) to carry out a pilot survey to test (a) whether data could be collected on the basis of the functions established in the outline classification; and (b) an operational approach for implementation of the full-scale survey to be undertaken in Phase 2.

According to the *Progress Report*, Phase 1 was successful in identifying nine information functions: systems analysis; systems design; data/information preparation; data/information analysis; searching for information on behalf of others; other operational information functions exclusive of management; managing information programs, services, or data bases; educating or training information workers; and information research and development. Phase 2 will involve a national survey of organizations employing information professionals in order to establish how many are performing each of the nine functions.

Studying librarians more specifically were the two papers that won the Library Research Round Table research awards in 1979: Charles McClure's "Perceived Values of Information Sources for Library Decision-Making" and Pauline Wilson's "Librarians and Their Stereotype." Another paper reporting research on the library profession won the top award in round five of the *American Libraries* Prize Article Competition—Judith S. Braunagel's "Job Mobility of Men and Women Librarians and How it Affects Career Advancement."

RECENT DEVELOPMENTS IN LIBRARY STATISTICAL ACTIVITIES

Eugene T. Neely

*Chairperson, Statistics Section,
ALA Library Administration and Management Association
and
Coordinator of Public Services, General Library,
University of Missouri-Kansas City*

Library statistics have traditionally been viewed by many librarians as a pedestrian area of endeavor, or, at best, a necessary evil. In recent years, however, there has been an appreciable increase in both interest and activity in library statistics. There are many reasons for these new nods of approbation: Library administrators are becoming more aware of the need for data as an aid to making internal management decisions and as an instrument for local accountability. In these years of inflation and financial constraints, comparative statistics of similar libraries, as well as longitudinal data on an individual institution, can be strong allies in justifying budget requests, or, perhaps more often, useful weapons in forestalling budget cuts. Also, research in library and information science has become more sophisticated. Librarians today are generally better trained in statistical methods; and they are more comfortable, and sometimes truly imaginative, in their collection and analysis of data.

The following will attempt to highlight some of the more significant recent developments in the area of library statistical activities.

AMERICAN LIBRARY ASSOCIATION

The collection, analysis, and publication of library statistics have long been a concern of the American Library Association (ALA). For many years, and until quite recently, a growing number of individual statistics committees (representing different types of libraries, functional activities, and formats of material) were located within the Library Organization and Management Section (LOMS) of the Library Administration and Management Association (LAMA), formerly the Library Administration Division (LAD) of ALA. The Statistics Coordinating Committee, composed of the chairpersons of the various statistics committees plus a number of ex-officio and liaison members, served as an umbrella body, coordinating the work of the individual committees. An early product of the LAD Statistics Coordinating Committee was the publication, by ALA in 1961, of *Definitions for Library Statistics: A Preliminary Draft*. This led to the Coordinating Committee's proposal, submitted to and funded by the Council on Library Resources, for creating the ALA Statistics Coordinating Project. The principal objective of this project was the development of a handbook on library statistics (*Library Statistics: A Handbook of Concepts, Definitions, and Terminology*, published by ALA in 1966), which is still used today as an authoritative source.

The 1970s brought increased interest in various aspects of library statistics—

collection and analysis of data, basic statistical methods, state and national statistical surveys, publication of statistics. Librarians have been particularly concerned over the absence of statistical data in many areas of librarianship, by the lack of standard definitions of terms, and by inconsistencies in the collection and reporting of statistics, making meaningful comparisons among individual libraries virtually an impossibility. Interest in library statistics has been dramatically demonstrated by the overflow crowds at programs presented by the statistics committees at ALA annual conferences and by the enthusiastic response to the ALA preconferences sponsored by the Committee on Statistics for Reference Services in 1977 and 1979.

The advisory role that the statistics committees serve for the Learning Resources Branch of the National Center for Education Statistics (NCES) in the design and related activities of its Library General Information Surveys (LIBGIS) has been strengthened. The committees have been responsible for formulating a number of definitions, which have been adopted by NCES and which, therefore, approach being what might be called "standard terminology." Included among these would be the definitions for "Reference Transaction," "Directional Transaction," and "Group Presentation" provided by the Reference Committee. Definitions of "periodicals" and "government publications" were formulated by the Technical Services Committee, in conjunction with appropriate committees from the Government Documents Round Table (GODORT) and the Resources and Technical Services Division (RTSD) of ALA. For the past two years, the statistics committees have been actively engaged in reviewing drafts of the *Handbook of Standard Terminology for Reporting Information about Libraries*, prepared for NCES by the National Center for Higher Education Management Systems. (This handbook will be discussed in greater detail below.)

The work of the committees and of individual committee members have resulted in a number of publications. The official proceedings of programs and symposia are available in print and/or on cassette.[1] The Public Libraries Committee sponsored a compilation of forms used by state library agencies in each of the 50 states to collect statistics on public libraries. This publication was edited by Kenneth Shearer, who interpreted and summarized the practices of each state.[2] As a project of the Reference Committee, Marcella Ciucki reviewed and analyzed forms collected from libraries across the nation for recording reference and information service activities.[3] Encouraged by their work on the statistics committees, others have conducted research and/or contributed articles to the literature. Of particular value is Katherine Emerson's article on "National Reporting on Reference Transactions, 1976-78."[4] Aside from the detailed information that it provides on reference statistics, the article presents an interesting case history of the process involved in the formulation of definitions and the standardization of statistical reporting in one area of librarianship.

In 1979, upon the recommendation of a Special Committee to Study the Role of the Library Organization and Management Section, the LAMA board approved a reorganization of the statistical committees by which they have been removed from LOMS and elevated to full section status within LAMA. This separation reflects the importance and major role that the statistics committees have in LAMA and ALA as a whole; and it will allow LOMS to direct its attention to other equally important areas of management concern, which had become overshadowed by statistics. The new Statistics Section (SS) elected its first officers last spring; and it has written a set of bylaws, which, pending approval by the LAMA board, will be voted upon by the SS membership this spring.

The objectives of the Statistics Section, as stated in its bylaws, are as follows:

1. To exercise overall responsibility within ALA for all matters pertaining to needs

for and uses of statistical measurement of library resources, services, and facilities —regardless of type of library or functional activity.
2. To work with other organizations, agencies, and associations in planning and advising in areas of library statistical concerns; to recommend and/or conduct research into statistical needs; to conduct educational programs for the profession regarding statistical needs, activities, and programs; to recommend, sponsor, and/or prepare guidelines, standards, and tools to be used in statistical activities; and to recommend inclusions, definitions, procedures, and policies concerning library statistics.

The section has preserved much of its former structure and content. In addition to a seven-person Executive Committee charged with the general oversight and direction of the section, the much larger Coordinating Committee has been retained to provide a forum for communication and exchange of ideas among the various other standing committees of the section. It has been charged specifically with coordinating the work of the standing committees in order to ensure that there will be minimal duplication of effort and maximum uniformity in offering recommendations to the profession concerning library statistics. The Coordinating Committee is composed of all members of the Executive Committee, all chairpersons of the individual standing committees, and up to 15 ex-officio liaison members.

Somewhat elaborate provisions for liaison representation have been made in consideration of the fact that all of the statistical concerns of ALA are centralized in the Statistics Section. Ex-officio liaison representation between the committees of the section (especially the Coordinating Committee) and other units of ALA, as well as outside agencies, can and should be established whenever such representation seems desirable in order to initiate or to further communication and cooperation. Outside agencies represented by liaison committee appointments may include other major library organizations, agencies of the federal government concerned with libraries and library statistics, and other groups involved in the planning for or implementation of guidelines, standards, and tools to be used in library statistical activities.

The Statistics Section is presently composed of the following standing statistics committees. The current (1979–1980) chairperson for each committee is listed as a contact for further information.

Committee	*Chairperson*
Coordinating	Eugene T. Neely University of Missouri–Kansas City
Development, Organization, Planning, and Programming	Janis C. Keene Tulsa City–County Library
Circulation	Mary Frances Collins University of Illinois
College and University Libraries	Harold A. Olsen San Jose State University
Library Education	Robert D. Stueart School of Library Science, Simmons College
Nonprint Media	Evelyn H. Daniel School of Information Studies, Syracuse University
Personnel	Mary Lou Harkness University of South Florida

Committee	Chairperson
Public Libraries	Galen E. Rike Department of Library Science, Ball State University
Reference	Florence J. Wilson George Mason University
School Library Media Centers	Noreen R. Michaud Simsbury (CT) High School
State Library Agencies	Janice Feye-Stukas Office of Public Libraries, St. Paul, MN
Technical Services	Carolyn Kacena University of Arizona

NATIONAL CENTER FOR EDUCATION STATISTICS

The following shows the status of Library General Information Surveys (LIBGIS) of the National Center for Education Statistics (NCES) from 1976 to the present, as of January 15, 1980.

LIBGIS II (Initiated during 1976)

Survey of State Library Agencies	Completed. Published by the University of Illinois Graduate School of Library Science in January 1980.
Survey of Special Libraries in State Governments	Nearing completion. To be completed and published by the University of Illinois Graduate School of Library Science in late summer of 1980.
College and University Library Survey, 1976	Completed. Published by the University of Illinois Graduate School of Library Science in summer of 1979.

LIBGIS III (Initiated during 1977)

Federal Library Survey, 1978	Will be completed in spring of 1980. To be published by the Federal Library Committee (Library of Congress).
Public Library Survey, 1977–1978	Completed. Manuscript and data to be sent to Government Printing Office in spring of 1980.
College and University Library Survey, 1977	Completed. Manuscript and data to be published by the University of Illinois Graduate School of Library Science in fall of 1980.

LIBGIS IV (Initiated during 1978)

Public School Library Media Survey, 1977	Completed. Manuscript and data to be sent to Government Printing Office in spring of 1980.
Handbook of Standard Terminology for	Completed by the original contractor, the

Reporting and Recording Information about Libraries	National Center for Higher Education Management Systems. To be reviewed, edited, and updated by the ALA Office for Research and to be completed in May of 1980. (More detailed information follows later in this article.)
Survey of Library Consortia, Cooperatives and Networks, 1978	Completed. Manuscript and data to be sent to Government Printing Office in spring of 1980.
Feasibility Study of Public Library Users	Completed. Will not be separately published.

LIBGIS V (Initiated during 1979)

Survey of Nonpublic School Library Media Centers, 1979	Survey forms to be mailed spring 1980.
	Survey forms mailed in summer of 1979.
College and University Libraries, 1979	To be completed by fall of 1980.

LIBGIS VI, to be initiated during 1980, will consider initiating the following surveys: Library Personnel Resources, Research Libraries, Special Libraries in Commerce and Industry. More detailed information on the projected library personnel resources survey follows later in this article.

There is a growing concern throughout the library community over the lengthening delays in the availability of the results of library surveys conducted by NCES in printed or other easily accessible form. As can be seen from the information given above on the status of LIBGIS surveys, although survey data seem to be collected and tabulated and the manuscripts "completed" in a reasonable amount of time, there are unreasonable delays in publication—sometimes as much as four years. NCES, despairing of necessary clearance and budgeting for publication by the Government Printing Office, has begun to seek outside publishers for its surveys. In view of the pressing needs of individual libraries and of local, state, and national government agencies for current statistical information, the Coordinating and Executive committees of the Statistics Section, meeting in joint session at the ALA Dallas conference last June, resolved: "Whereas the Statistics Section of LAMA recognizes the great value of up-to-date information about libraries as collected in the National Center for Education Statistics' LIBGIS surveys, the Statistics Section strongly recommends that NCES give top priority to reducing the delays between the collection of library survey data and the publication of those data to make them quickly accessible and useful." Another area of concern has been the decreasing number of library surveys that NCES has had approved and funded each year.

The chairperson of the ALA/LAMA Statistics Section was granted a five-minute testimony at one of the open hearing sessions held by the National Commission on Libraries and Information Science during the White House Conference on Libraries and Information Services, November 16–17, 1979. After a few introductory remarks, the following resolution was read and filed, becoming a part of the official minutes of the open hearings. While this resolution was written by the SS chairperson as an individual and not as an official position of the section, he feels confident that it represents the consensus of the Executive and Coordinating committees and at least a majority viewpoint of the membership as a whole.

RESOLUTION ON LIBRARY STATISTICAL SURVEYS BY THE FEDERAL GOVERNMENT

The resolution presented below is an expansion and amplification of the resolution included in *Issues and Resolutions: An Analysis of Pre-White House Conference Activities* (Theme 4, Goal 2, page 60), which reads as follows:

> The Federal Government should provide for the collection and dissemination of library statistics, using standard terminology. A minimum three-year production cycle should be maintained for all types of libraries.

Expanded Resolution

Whereas national library statistical surveys have been conducted since the 1870s by the U.S. Office of Education, and since 1966 by the National Center for Education Statistics, and are now being transferred to the Department of Education; and

Whereas national library statistics have been used as a basic method for describing the characteristics of all types of libraries; and

Whereas library statistics have provided primary data for evaluating library services, performance, and needs; and

Whereas library statistics have been used by Congress and various Presidential administrations to improve legislation in support of libraries, such as the Library Services and Construction Act (1956), the Elementary and Secondary Education Act (1965) and the Higher Education Act (1965);

Therefore, be it resolved that the Secretary of Education be requested to retain *at least* the three-year cycle for basic library surveys (public, academic, and school), and that other surveys of libraries be conducted *at least* every six years and that this schedule be maintained by the National Library Agency, should such agency be established by Congress; and

Be it further resolved that new or repeated surveys on critical issues be regularly conducted in support of developing legislation such as that for the National Library Act, the National Periodicals Center, and the Library Manpower Study; and

Be it further resolved that the results of library surveys conducted by the federal government be released in printed or other easily accessible form within twelve months after the deadline for return of survey forms by respondents; and

Finally, be it further resolved that the responsibility for library statistical surveys be placed under that office of the Department of Education responsible for administering other federally supported library programs and that it be placed under the National Library Agency if and when such agency is established.

NCHEMS *HANDBOOK OF STANDARD TERMINOLOGY*

In 1977, the National Center for Educational Statistics (NCES) contracted with the National Center for Higher Education Management Systems (NCHEMS) to produce a document that would identify the types of information useful for communicating data about library resources and library programs. In its Introduction, the purpose of the *Handbook* is described as follows:

> The structure of information and related terminology are intended to provide a sound basis for management and planning; to enhance information exchange; and to facilitate reporting to external agencies and organizations. This *Handbook* provides library managers, boards of trustees, and other library decisionmakers with guidance in identifying items of information from which to obtain factual and comparative data for developing policies and decisions; for communications with constituencies, legislative bodies, and governing organizations; and for fulfilling information requests of external agencies. Ideally, the items and use of data elements defined in this *Handbook* will enhance the comparability and compatibility of data collected for a variety of reasons and by a variety

of organizations; and will reduce duplication and response burden associated with these diverse data-collection activities. In this context, it is hoped that the terminology and data definitions included in this *Handbook* will evolve into a standard language for inter- and intra-organizational communications.

During the 1979 ALA midwinter meeting, the statistics committees devoted an entire day to a careful review and critique of the penultimate draft of the NCHEMS *Handbook*. In summary, while the committees were pleased that the document had been produced and believed that it enabled them to discuss definitions of library statistical terms, as well as the collection of data about library resources and programs in a more productive way than had been possible earlier, they were dissatisfied with many aspects of the *Handbook*. The specific criticisms of the document were discussed, summarized, and recorded—especially weaknesses and omissions in the glossary itself. At the 1979 ALA annual conference in Dallas, the Executive and Coordinating committees of the Statistics Section, in a joint meeting, voted on several recommendations concerning the *Handbook*. One of these specified that NCES appoint an editorial coordinator to revise the final draft submitted by NCHEMS. Later in the summer, Mary Jo Lynch, director of the ALA Office of Research (OFR), submitted to NCES an unsolicited proposal to edit and update the NCHEMS *Handbook*. The Office of Research was awarded the contract in late fall. Lynch will coordinate the project, assisted by consultants who will focus on particular subject areas. All will work closely with the committees of the Statistics Section, which will continue in its advisory and reviewing roles. The projected date for completing the final manuscript of the revised *Handbook* was May 1980.

AMERICAN NATIONAL STANDARDS COMMITTEE Z39

The American National Standards Committee on Library and Information Science and Related Publishing Practices (ANSC Z39) appointed a subcommittee at the end of 1977 to revise the 1968 Standard on Library Statistics (Z39.7). Chaired by Katherine Emerson, who at the time of appointment was chair of the ALA Statistics Coordinating Committee, it includes Ellen Altman, Evelyn Daniel, Janice Feye-Stukas, Glenn Miller, and C. James Schmidt, with Helen Eckard representing the National Center for Education Statistics. Working with revisions of the previous standard discussed by the ALA statistics committees and those of other library associations, it presented a draft for discussion at the 1978 ALA annual conference and a revised draft of the personnel and financial sections at the 1979 annual conference. A second full draft of the principles for library statistical reporting and the items selected as most useful for both individual libraries and national statistical reporting will be presented for public discussion at the 1980 ALA annual conference. Because of the long involvement of the ALA statistics committees, the National Center for Education Statistics, and several research projects (including now the ALA Office for Research's project to edit and update the NCHEMS *Handbook*) in the revision of definitions for statistical reporting, the Z39.7 Subcommittee has focused largely on content and structure. It is expected that the definitions, as they emerge from the ALA/OFR revision, will be compatible with this reporting structure and that the definitions and structure will be mutually supportive.

The goals of the revised standard are to provide figures for accountability both within the library and to funding agencies, for an understanding of collections as intellectual resources that transcend format differences, and for understanding and analysis of library performance and outputs as goals and products of inputs. A major goal is widespread adoption of the same categories and definitions by the many different agencies that now impose an excessive burden on libraries by requesting statistics based on different definitions and aggregations.

Also recently appointed by ANSC Z39 is a subcommittee to revise the 1974 Standard for Price Indexes for Library Materials (ANSC Z39.20), which provides criteria for developing price indexes. The objective of this standard was to enable the measurement of periodic changes in the average list price of certain library materials, divided into categories such as hardcover trade and technical books, paperback books, periodicals, serial services, and library-produced microfilm. In addition to reviewing the existing standard, the new subcommittee, chaired by Fred Lynden of Brown University, is charged with developing price indexes for nonprint media and other types of materials not included in the 1974 standard. The subcommittee hopes to have the proposed revisions completed by the spring of 1980.

SURVEYS ON LIBRARY AND INFORMATION PERSONNEL RESOURCES

The National Science Foundation has awarded a research grant to the University of Pittsburgh for an Occupational Survey of Information Professionals. [See the preceding article, "Research on Libraries and Librarianship in 1979: An Overview," by Mary Jo Lynch for a report on the progress of this survey—*Ed.*] It is hoped that the Library Personnel Resources Survey proposed by NCES for initiation in 1980 will be funded, so that it can supplement the Pittsburgh project. This survey will update the 1972 library manpower study conducted jointly by NCES and the Bureau of Labor Statistics. It will focus on library personnel as distinct from information professionals, so that there will be minimal duplication, yet parallel data, between the two studies. Both the Pittsburgh and the proposed NCES surveys will provide valuable and vital data for planning in library and information science education and for training and utilization of library and information professionals.

NOTES

1. *Proceedings of the Symposium on Measurement of Reference, July 8, 1974, Waldorf-Astoria Hotel, New York City*, ed. by Katherine Emerson. Sponsored by the Committee on Statistics for Reference Services of the American Library Association, Library Administration Division, Library Organization and Management Section. Chicago: Library Administration Division, American Library Association, 1974. The papers from the proceedings are summarized in *RQ* 14 (Fall 1974): 7-19. *The Purposes of Reference Measurement, July 19, 1976, Hyatt Regency Hotel, Chicago, Illinois: A Program*, ed. by Candace Morgan. Sponsored by the Committee on Statistics for Reference Services of the American Library Association, Library Administration Division, Library Organization and Management Section. Chicago: Library Administration Division, American Library Association, 1978.
2. *The Collection and Use of Public Library Statistics by State Library Agencies: A Compilation of Forms*, ed., with an analysis, by Kenneth D. Shearer, and a "Guide to State Publications" by David Nickell. Sponsored by LAMA/LOMS Statistics for Public Libraries Committee. Chicago: Library Administration and Management Association, American Library Association, 1978.
3. Marcella Ciucki, "Recording of Reference/Information Service Activities: A Study of Forms Currently Used." *RQ* 16 (Summer 1977): 273-283.
4. Katherine Emerson, "National Reporting on Reference Transactions, 1976-78." *RQ* 16 (Spring 1977): 199-207.

CHARACTERISTICS OF THE U.S. POPULATION SERVED BY LIBRARIES

Nadine Edles

*Division of Statistical Services, Statistical Information Branch,
National Center for Education Statistics,
U.S. Department of Health, Education, and Welfare*

	Number	Percent
Total U.S. population (July 1, 1979)[a]	220,415,000	100.0
Resident population of 50 states and D.C.	219,930,000	99.8
Armed forces overseas	485,000	0.2
Resident population of U.S. outlying areas (1970)[b]	3,022,000	—
U.S. population, five years and over, including armed forces abroad (July 1, 1979)[c]	204,618,000	100.0
5–9 years	16,493,000	8.1
10–14 years	18,063,000	8.8
15–19 years	20,919,000	10.2
20–24 years	20,738,000	10.1
25–64 years	103,972,000	50.8
Age 65 and over	24,433,000	11.9
Public and nonpublic school enrollment (Fall 1979)[d]	58,395,000	100.0
Kindergarten through grade 8	31,695,000	54.3
Grades 9–12	15,300,000	26.2
Higher education, total enrollment	11,400,000	19.5
Nonpublic school enrollment[e]	7,560,000	12.6
Kindergarten through grade 8	3,625,000	6.0
Grades 9–12	1,435,000	2.4
Higher education, total enrollment	2,500,000	4.2
Educational status of population aged 25 and over		
Total aged 25 and over (March 1979)[f]	123,019,000	—
With four or more years of college	19,332,000	15.7
With one to three years of college	17,379,000	14.1
With four years of high school or more	81,092,000	65.9
With less than four years of high school	41,928,000	34.1
Residence in and outside metropolitan areas		
Total noninstitutional population (April 1978)[g]	213,500,000	100.0
Nonmetropolitan areas	70,400,000	33.0
Metropolitan areas	143,000,000	67.0
In central cities	59,700,000	28.0
Outside central areas	83,300,000	39.0

CHARACTERISTICS OF THE U.S. POPULATION SERVED BY LIBRARIES (cont.)

	Number	Percent
Employment status		
Total civilian noninstitutional population 16 years old and over (October 1979)[h]	162,375,000	—
Civilian labor force, total	103,474,000	100.0
Employed	97,293,000	94.0
Unemployed	6,182,000	6.0
Occupational groups		
Employed persons, 16 years old and over (October 1979)[h]	97,293,000	100.0
Professional and technical workers	14,929,000	15.3
Managers and administrators, except farm	10,648,000	10.9
Clerical workers	17,825,000	18.3
Sales workers	6,247,000	6.4
Craftsmen and kindred workers	12,974,000	13.3
Operatives	14,550,000	14.9
Service workers	12,977,000	13.3
Farm workers and nonfarm laborers	7,369,000	7.6
Total faculty and students served by college and university libraries (Fall 1978)	12,230,000	100.0
Faculty	830,000	6.8
Students, total enrollment	11,400,000	93.2

[a] As of July 1, 1978, estimates of the Bureau of the Census, U.S. Department of Commerce. Armed forces overseas includes forces stationed in outlying areas of the United States. *Current Population Reports*, Series P-25, September 1979.

[b] As of April 1, 1970, Puerto Rico, Guam, Virgin Islands, American Samoa, Canal Zone, and the Trust Territory of the Pacific Islands. Includes members of the armed forces overseas stationed in these outlying areas. U.S. Census of Population, *Number of Inhabitants*, PC(1), 1970, A53-A58.

[c] As of July 1, 1978, age data are Series II estimates by the Bureau of the Census, U.S. Department of Commerce. *Current Population Reports*, P-25, no. 704, July 1977, *Projections of the Population of the United States: 1977 to 2050*.

[d] As of Fall 1978, estimates of the U.S. Department of Health, Education, and Welfare, National Center for Education Statistics, Back-to-School press release, August 30, 1979.

[e] A segment of public and nonpublic school enrollment reported above. Percentages for nonpublic school enrollment are based on the total figure for public and nonpublic school enrollment.

[f] As of March 1977, Bureau of the Census, U.S. Department of Commerce. Unpublished data.

[g] Bureau of the Census, U.S. Department of Commerce, *Statistical Abstract of the United States*, 1979 edition in process. Due to rounding, details will not add up to total.

[h] U.S. Department of Labor, Bureau of Labor Statistics, "The Employment Situation: October 1979" (press release). Details will not add to total because of independent seasonal adjustment.

As of Fall 1979, estimates of the U.S. Department of Health, Education, and Welfare, National Center for Education Statistics, Back-to-School press release, August 30, 1979. Faculty includes full-time and part-time staff with the rank of instructor or above and junior staff, such as graduate assistants, who provide instruction in colleges, universities, and professional schools.

NUMBER OF LIBRARIES IN THE UNITED STATES AND CANADA

Statistics are from the thirty-second edition of the *American Library Directory*, edited by Jaques Cattell Press (Bowker, 1979). Data are exclusive of elementary and secondary school libraries. The directory does not list small public libraries. Law libraries with fewer than 10,000 volumes are included only if they specialize in a specific field. The count of these libraries, shown separately under the Summary section below, is from the Bowker Company's mailing lists. In addition to listing and describing some 32,300 individual libraries, the thirty-second edition of the *ALD* lists over 350 library consortia, including processing and purchasing centers and other specialized organizations.

LIBRARIES IN THE UNITED STATES

A. Public libraries	8,601
Public libraries with branches	1,212
Public library branches	5,789
Total public libraries (including branches)	14,390*
B. Junior college libraries	1,135
Departmental	80
Departmental medicine	8
Departmental religious	3
University and college	1,912
Departmental	1,549
Departmental law	176
Departmental medicine	233
Departmental religious	92
Total academic libraries	4,676*
C. Armed forces	
Air Force	129
Law	1
Medical	13
Army	179
Law	2
Medical	26
Navy	181
Law	3
Medical	20
Total armed forces libraries	489*
D. Government libraries	1,451
Law	397
Medical	238
Total government libraries	1,451*
E. Special libraries	5,294*
F. Law libraries	429*
G. Medical libraries	1,705*
H. Religious libraries	1,012*
Total law (including academic, armed forces, and government)	1,008
Total medical (including academic, armed forces, and government)	2,243
Total religious (including academic)	1,107
Total special (including all law, medical, and religious)	9,652
Total libraries counted (*)	29,446

LIBRARIES IN REGIONS ADMINISTERED BY THE UNITED STATES

A. Public libraries	15
Public libraries with branches	4
Public library branches	18
Total public libraries (including branches)	33*
B. Junior college libraries	8
University and college libraries	26
Departmental	16
Departmental law	3
Total academic libraries	50*
C. Armed forces	
Air Force	2
Army	6
Navy	4
Total armed forces	12*

D. Government libraries 14
   Law 7
   Medical 2
   Total government libraries 14*
E. Special libraries 24*
F. Medical libraries 7*
G. Religious libraries 1*
Total libraries counted (*) ... 141

LIBRARIES IN CANADA

A. Public libraries 666
   Public libraries with
      branches 113
   Public library branches .. 778
   Total public libraries
      (including branches) ... 1,444*
B. Junior college libraries ... 82
   Departmental 37
   Departmental medicine . 4
   University and college ... 128
   Departmental 218
   Departmental law 17
   Departmental medicine . 29
   Departmental religious . 11
   Total academic libraries .. 465*
C. Government libraries 217*
D. Special libraries 463*
E. Law libraries 42*
F. Medical libraries 109*
G. Religious libraries 50*
Total libraries counted (*) ... 2,790

SUMMARY

Total U.S. libraries 29,446
Total libraries administered by
   the United States 141
Total Canadian libraries 2,790
Grand total libraries listed ... 32,377

Note: Numbers followed by an asterisk are added to find "Total libraries counted" for each of the three geographic areas (United States, U.S.-administered regions, and Canada). The sum of the three totals is the "Grand total libraries listed" in the *ALD* (shown in the Summary). For details on the count of libraries, see the preface to the thirty-second edition of the *ALD—Ed.*

PUBLIC AND ACADEMIC LIBRARY ACQUISITION EXPENDITURES

Every two years the R. R. Bowker Company compiles statistics on library acquisition expenditures from information reported in the *American Library Directory*. The statistics given here are based on information from the 31st edition of the directory (1978), which was compiled from questionnaire responses received between fall 1977 and spring 1978. In most cases the statistics reflect expenditures for the 1976–1977 period.

The total number of public libraries listed in the 31st edition of the *ALD* is 8,455, while the total for academic libraries is 4,129. Not included in the *ALD* are public libraries with annual incomes of less than $2,000 or book funds of less than $500 (of which there are an estimated 2,500 libraries) or law libraries of less than 10,000 volumes (of which there are approximately 330).

UNDERSTANDING THE TABLES

Number of Libraries includes only those libraries in the *ALD* that reported either annual income or acquisition expenditures (7,635 public libraries; 2,347 academic libraries). Those libraries that did not report acquisition expenditures but did report annual income are included in the count, although they are not reflected in the columns of acquisition expenditure figures.

Total Acquisition Expenditures for a given state is almost always greater than (in a few cases equal to) the sum of the Categories of Expenditure. This is because the Total Acquisition Expenditures amount also includes the expenditures of libraries that did not itemize by category.

Categories of Expenditure. Figures in these columns represent only those libraries that itemized expenditures. Libraries that reported a total acquisition expenditure amount but did not itemize are only represented in the Total Acquisition Expenditures column.

Unspecified includes monies reported as not specifically books, periodicals, AV, microform, or binding (e.g., library materials) or any of the categories in combination. When libraries report only Total Acquisition Expenditures without itemizing by category, the total amount is *not* reflected as unspecified.

Estimated Percent of Acquisitions is based on a comparison of the budgets that included specific expenditures for each of the categories and the national totals for each category, i.e., the total amount spent on books in the United States was compared with the sum of all budgets that reported detail about book expenditures. The reader should note, therefore, that the percentages are not based on the figures in the Total Acquisition Expenditures column.

Note: This is a reprint of the article that appeared in the 1979 *Bowker Annual*.

376 / LIBRARY RESEARCH AND STATISTICS

TABLE 1 PUBLIC LIBRARY ACQUISITION EXPENDITURES

State	Number of Libraries	Total Acquisition Expenditures	Books	Periodicals	Audiovisual	Microform	Binding	Unspecified
Alabama	85	$ 4,653,000	$ 552,713	$ 154,079	$ 115,745	$ 46,293	$ 37,702	$880,237
Alaska	17	936,673	552,632	35,095	102,600	136,000	20,290	—
Arizona	77	3,205,166	1,265,792	151,480	88,454	26,600	53,600	11,123
Arkansas	42	725,244	486,844	66,983	8,219	2,997	11,473	—
California	171	43,369,684	19,719,341	2,473,879	1,341,894	260,236	430,718	499,227
Colorado	116	6,640,115	2,115,856	242,332	79,000	17,366	68,920	3,213
Connecticut	145	3,923,625	2,409,796	200,660	140,701	17,431	50,101	160,219
Delaware	10	487,478	369,965	70,400	36,345	1,500	—	—
District of Columbia[1]	2	782,233	617,001	104,000	50,000	—	—	—
Florida	83	6,984,558	4,407,925	339,136	442,483	182,582	184,027	195,327
Georgia	52	6,007,989	2,216,381	207,406	218,826	55,769	70,882	6,273
Hawaii[2]	—	—	—	—	—	—	—	—
Idaho	99	1,360,327	940,325	41,683	63,912	7,953	12,660	420
Illinois	556	31,660,032	5,287,092	1,378,006	—	959,455	322,874	43,770
Indiana	214	11,029,065	3,510,562	349,949	410,279	101,069	159,815	44,827
Iowa	456	2,675,694	924,639	137,287	165,016	37,515	23,586	1,084
Kansas	286	2,805,683	1,834,813	218,845	61,662	48,294	45,866	4,233
Kentucky	100	4,613,421	1,460,465	113,649	117,700	6,511	48,566	19,311
Louisiana	67	4,110,516	967,424	174,817	111,540	9,281	50,829	129,060
Maine	159	2,050,510	604,517	91,077	46,663	14,808	13,729	10,090
Maryland	30	6,723,763	3,729,286	224,569	429,795	16,069	52,190	907,157
Massachusetts	336	12,980,455	5,807,244	766,105	463,321	250,856	110,791	231,658
Michigan	352	14,033,959	6,539,792	657,195	525,754	139,716	145,306	52,473
Minnesota	135	6,222,181	3,170,864	345,677	448,501	35,762	150,836	3,074
Mississippi	48	2,916,105	766,394	74,833	46,668	10,437	12,960	40,000
Missouri	121	9,083,991	3,073,079	338,087	375,028	73,531	95,977	202,046
Montana	62	1,832,574	373,888	36,190	14,833	5,150	2,654	71,690
Nebraska	234	3,185,884	758,894	77,711	85,725	9,418	16,099	18,958

Nevada	18	795,062	233,584	21,919	9,400	4,950	210,568
New Hampshire	211	2,735,110	883,136	21,818	3,234	7,800	7,399
New Jersey	288	11,908,711	5,342,992	639,719	169,254	112,648	139,274
New Mexico	42	$ 577,255	$ 244,376	$ 15,678	$ 1,424	$ 6,902	$ 24,720
New York	724	21,747,874	12,440,348	516,300	141,209	289,053	204,230
North Carolina	107	4,771,123	2,372,935	306,915	31,587	63,185	148,760
North Dakota	60	931,973	342,145	56,558	4,407	2,137	2,543
Ohio	247	30,296,011	9,042,118	1,256,718	84,240	320,914	45,176
Oklahoma	81	2,716,169	1,086,832	99,193	52,620	40,696	22,200
Oregon	88	3,924,587	1,031,267	70,424	11,096	11,577	116,050
Pennsylvania	395	9,008,768	3,326,867	237,809	127,989	64,468	3,127,310
Rhode Island	41	2,243,028	402,396	13,837	5,751	11,344	20,658
South Carolina	40	2,603,327	1,499,621	167,246	8,100	78,002	208,521
South Dakota	71	800,184	316,494	71,691	40,846	8,006	2,866
Tennessee	68	3,706,843	1,334,448	243,662	20,419	46,518	187,498
Texas	340	11,748,133	6,432,706	445,051	59,506	299,132	1,126,016
Utah	46	4,315,279	956,309	204,269	4,143	27,588	2,780
Vermont	163	632,758	326,360	17,412	3,724	4,607	11,192
Virginia	77	5,668,572	2,819,567	227,345	79,638	77,563	170,421
Washington	66	6,683,127	3,820,320	304,495	23,659	108,785	141,630
West Virginia	74	1,710,470	586,106	63,124	1,171	10,821	157,783
Wisconsin	308	10,912,508	2,684,800	300,647	60,099	58,720	127,934
Wyoming	21	599,502	182,080	21,490	1,800	—	8,000
Canal Zone	1	53,355	33,140	—	3,909	4,000	225
Pacific Islands	2	200,859	143,046	28,460	1,000	1,500	—
Puerto Rico	1	500	—	—	—	—	—
Total U.S.	7,635	$336,291,461	$132,347,517	$11,270,918	$3,422,824	$3,864,599	$9,749,224
Estimated % of Acquisitions			74.8	6.4	1.9	2.2	5.5

[1]Does not include the Library of Congress.
[2]The Hawaiian public libraries failed to report any acquisition expenditures.

378 / LIBRARY RESEARCH AND STATISTICS

TABLE 2 JUNIOR COLLEGE, COLLEGE, AND UNIVERSITY LIBRARY ACQUISITION EXPENDITURES

State	Number of Libraries	Total Acquisition Expenditures	Books	Periodicals	Audiovisual	Microform	Binding	Unspecified
Alabama	47	$ 5,188,412	$ 2,359,624	$1,269,418	$ 122,070	$294,821	$ 188,206	$ 53,237
Alaska	6	624,338	436,094	110,659	32,202	26,619	16,906	—
Arizona	17	3,933,541	1,245,350	729,435	76,240	79,811	129,128	140,000
Arkansas	21	2,624,349	1,028,903	414,189	34,396	56,388	72,551	—
California	164	44,657,896	12,869,766	8,308,118	2,562,059	839,646	2,608,098	4,196,483
Colorado	32	5,919,668	2,236,069	1,837,378	297,100	169,445	210,951	—
Connecticut	39	6,087,023	1,808,304	1,078,596	87,118	50,379	161,717	2,513,917
Delaware	8	1,176,715	33,020	432,444	2,746	3,416	89,068	602,616
District of Columbia	14	5,808,316	1,490,864	847,373	31,830	38,630	194,137	1,612,014
Florida	74	8,561,817	4,679,386	2,938,032	294,523	317,598	423,778	13,311
Georgia	58	7,600,757	3,368,877	2,492,716	137,216	257,562	421,016	200,645
Hawaii	14	1,693,303	556,292	75,802	98,728	202,837	109,681	551,465
Idaho	9	1,478,481	692,589	487,166	68,509	27,668	52,426	—
Illinois	104	16,024,827	5,883,836	4,057,003	548,127	220,682	848,880	436,561
Indiana	49	9,742,069	2,721,285	1,698,925	119,097	55,644	482,076	721,161
Iowa	48	5,554,794	2,331,972	1,860,429	82,499	211,729	291,497	88,969
Kansas	47	3,656,938	2,059,569	1,108,357	134,598	100,061	163,303	3,000
Kentucky	35	5,258,850	2,281,809	1,322,939	75,938	91,892	221,395	97,617
Louisiana	25	5,204,984	1,847,179	1,363,808	18,557	163,361	317,744	807,304
Maine	28	1,980,700	719,390	348,487	28,243	19,600	47,630	193,650
Maryland	40	5,443,595	1,562,604	1,059,889	182,666	94,961	246,224	—
Massachusetts	76	12,954,928	4,284,434	2,255,391	264,408	224,417	823,307	3,275,036
Michigan	69	11,144,997	2,742,148	2,037,413	264,062	211,881	593,326	3,919,057
Minnesota	40	5,481,681	1,643,012	830,290	159,807	58,655	144,516	92,534
Mississippi	36	3,337,281	801,511	662,439	75,236	60,139	117,068	400
Missouri	56	10,137,995	3,252,632	1,863,333	187,086	67,617	311,891	30,816

PUBLIC AND ACADEMIC LIBRARY ACQUISITION EXPENDITURES / 379

Montana	11	968,333	296,589	335,984		23,150	
Nebraska	23	3,472,271	1,757,501	1,018,934	1,187	139,864	
Nevada	5	748,166	363,064	274,128	104,825	44,138	
New Hampshire	19	2,044,902	872,590	958,014	800	65,300	
New Jersey	49	9,670,944	2,902,531	945,066	77,406	288,923	2,084,276
New Mexico	19	3,187,185	1,048,455	592,388	331,268	157,598	33,460
New York	167	29,529,537	8,203,079	5,659,042	11,064	983,768	2,406,525
North Carolina	103	1,984,111	4,311,368	3,041,182	516,685	558,495	1,701,941
North Dakota	13	1,197,558	656,185	347,078	296,269	12,238	30,471
Ohio	92	13,590,286	5,331,686	4,123,260	10,018	580,811	1,022,253
Oklahoma	40	4,121,302	479,229	566,002	122,332	89,850	77,338
Oregon	36	3,823,306	1,059,882	1,164,940	59,018	162,506	
Pennsylvania	134	18,385,631	6,830,968	4,842,724	50,971	920,824	72,041
Rhode Island	11	2,253,583	542,796	559,011	742,990	102,651	17,550
South Carolina	50	5,658,539	2,267,621	1,324,177	9,499	198,181	30,157
South Dakota	15	785,973	328,548	280,478	156,243	31,777	
Tennessee	48	12,541,277	3,458,254	1,825,161	12,649	389,867	335,940
Texas	115	23,620,009	9,862,235	4,829,262	240,055	859,747	2,041,617
Utah	11	1,409,952	41,020	399,800	264,047	63,200	
Vermont	18	1,540,149	772,090	491,888		53,562	35,794
Virginia	65	7,443,106	3,725,402	1,590,080	37,445	221,322	108,819
Washington	40	6,903,351	1,675,580	1,933,583	173,148	361,742	190,764
West Virginia	23	2,808,089	591,373	281,969	33,563	34,175	
Wisconsin	54	6,999,828	2,806,045	2,371,191	59,476	292,070	82,435
Wyoming	7	832,624	447,091	321,935	119,561	42,390	4,382
Canal Zone	1	5,150	2,000	2,100	2,306	500	
Pacific Islands	2	143,953	138,282	3,480			
Puerto Rico	20	1,407,351	548,791	203,781	577		28,000
Total U.S.	2,347	$358,354,721	$126,256,774	$81,776,667	5,097	38,994	
					$7,383,958	$16,004,163	$29,761,022
Estimated % of Acquisitions			46.5	30.1	2.7	5.9	11.0

URBAN-SUBURBAN PUBLIC LIBRARY STATISTICS

Joseph Green
Director, Atlantic County Library, Pleasantville, NJ

The year 1979 is the seventh year of this compilation but the second year as a joint venture between the Montgomery County (Maryland) Department of Public Libraries and Joseph Green. The collection of pertinent data for comparison of urban libraries with surrounding suburban libraries continues to be the primary goal of the survey. However, comparisons between urban libraries (or suburban libraries) on a national basis can also be made.

For the purposes of this survey, a library system is defined as one that is centrally funded and uses a common policy for controlling the basic operation of public libraries within a particular jurisdiction. This strict definition makes it difficult to survey many suburban libraries that are either cooperatives or federations, among them those in the suburbs of New York, Chicago, and Philadelphia.

Of the 52 libraries questioned, 48 answered the survey for a 92 percent response rate. Some earlier respondents did not participate this year while earlier nonparticipants chose this year to send information. This situation, of course, causes inconsistency in the survey. (Figures for 1969 to 1978 can be found in corresponding editions of the *Bowker Annual*.)

Another source of inconsistency is the reporting year used by libraries. Those using a calendar year have a six-month lag behind those that use the fiscal year. Nevertheless, the response rate for the 1979 survey represents one of the best in the history of the survey.

In Tables 1, 2, and 3 libraries are arranged by reported population, largest to smallest. The data in Tables 4 and 5 are arranged in order of performance, highest to lowest. The following abbreviations are used in the tables: "F" for fiscal year, "C" for calendar year, "U" for urban libraries, "S" for suburban libraries, and "U-S" for urban-suburban libraries. The abbreviation "N/A" indicates data not available; either the respondent does not gather information in that category or the information was not sent.

Once again, we issue our annual caveat to anyone using the data in budget work, annual reports, or local or national publicity. Because the survey participants use the data to meet their own local priorities, it is difficult to draw anything greater than informal comparisons between libraries.

TABLE 1 PUBLIC LIBRARY TOTAL OPERATING EXPENSES, STATE AID, AND EXPENDITURES FOR LIBRARY MATERIALS, 1978 AND 1979

Library	Population 1978	Population 1979	Total Operating Expenses $ 1978	Total Operating Expenses $ 1979	State Aid $ 1978	State Aid $ 1979	Library Materials Expenses $ 1978	Library Materials Expenses $ 1979
Chicago Public Lib., IL (C) (U)	3,362,947	—	31,157,539	—	4,270,171	—	3,267,622	—
New York Public Lib., NY (F) (U)	3,306,377	3,306,377	27,567,000	29,861,000	3,891,000	4,524,000	3,867,000	3,948,000
Brooklyn Public Lib., NY (F) (U)	2,345,493	2,345,493	16,725,645	16,981,575	2,227,495	2,227,495	2,095,978	2,328,975
Los Angeles Public Lib., CA (F) (U)	2,787,900	2,801,900	17,727,058	16,875,565	—	—	2,959,388	2,373,337
Queens Borough Public Lib., NY (F) (U)	1,986,174	1,986,174	18,195,604	18,249,872	1,884,456	1,884,456	2,095,831	2,255,102
Free Lib. of Philadelphia, PA (F) (U)	1,950,098	1,950,098	19,745,736	18,852,264	1,691,516	1,618,535	2,069,181	1,800,698
Detroit Public Lib., MI (F) (U)	1,514,063	1,514,063	12,778,620	14,442,090	383,375	696,893	1,071,770	1,241,803
Houston Public Lib., TX (C) (U)	1,455,046	—	10,693,778	—	525,337	—	1,691,600	—
Miami-Dade County Lib. System, FL (F) (U-S)	1,165,111	1,165,111	10,004,150	10,572,000	598,894	822,002	1,725,000	1,608,650
Buffalo-Erie County Public Lib., NY (C) (U-S)	1,113,491	—	10,031,848	—	1,274,972	—	1,234,565	—
Milwaukee Public Lib., WI (C) (U)	953,133	—	8,967,633	—	284,675	—	899,752	—
San Antonio Public Lib., TX (F) (U)	922,904	935,960	3,178,888	3,132,827	118,152	105,995	649,475	613,159
Cincinnati-Hamilton County Public Lib., OH (C) (U-S)	924,018	—	8,156,495	—	103,587	—	1,171,035	—
Orange County Public Lib., CA (F) (S)	887,375	913,825	6,452,484	6,495,671	—	2,602,778	881,594	1,108,829
Dallas Public Lib., TX (F) (U)	887,500	898,000	7,141,594	7,515,565	77,372	90,339	1,103,168	1,161,229
Enoch Pratt Free Lib., Baltimore, MD (F) (U)	850,000	850,000	9,316,805	9,394,144	3,403,380	3,758,056	1,266,127	1,215,909
San Diego Public Lib., CA (F) (U)	783,000	817,000	5,306,605	4,471,089	—	—	761,640	886,189
Memphis-Shelby County Public Lib., TX (F) (U-S)	744,200	799,329	4,943,889	5,765,861	248,691	295,662	601,455	733,573
Indianapolis-Marion County Public Lib., IN (C) (U-S)	765,687	—	6,188,778	—	125,870	—	914,806	—
St. Louis County Public Lib., MO (F) (S)	752,250	—	5,346,966	—	253,454	—	936,036	—
District of Columbia Public Lib. (F) (U)	691,500	691,500	9,949,500	10,404,400	—	—	793,100	904,100
King County Lib. System, WA (C) (S)	672,604	—	4,914,396	—	—	—	592,321	—
Prince George's County Memorial Lib., MD (F) (S)	685,000	662,500	7,411,384	8,270,913	1,002,049	974,577	914,220	864,957
San Francisco Public Lib., CA (F) (U)	666,500	657,200	8,983,562	7,856,124	16,015	42,480	983,326	891,664
Baltimore County Public Lib., MD (F) (S)	645,100	647,800	8,310,617	8,593,374	761,463	756,541	1,515,572	1,674,567
Cuyahoga County Public Lib., OH (C) (S)	644,500	—	10,177,499	—	—	—	1,055,220	—
Boston Public Lib., MA (F) (U)	641,071	641,071	10,983,108	11,611,977	240,000	240,000	2,246,458	2,239,929

TABLE 1 PUBLIC LIBRARY TOTAL OPERATING EXPENSES, STATE AID, AND EXPENDITURES FOR LIBRARY MATERIALS, 1978 AND 1979 (cont.)

Library	Population 1978	Population 1979	Total Operating Expenses $ 1978	Total Operating Expenses $ 1979	State Aid $ 1978	State Aid $ 1979	Library Materials Expenses $ 1978	Library Materials Expenses $ 1979
Cleveland Public Lib., OH (C) (U)	629,176	—	14,983,233	—	299,509	—	2,014,570	—
St. Louis Public Lib., MO (C) (U)	622,236	622,236	4,671,220	5,002,857	469,758	243,267	544,351	597,185
Fairfax County Public Lib., VA (F) (S)	605,600	628,580	5,370,450	5,695,320	96,421	153,822	1,105,346	1,076,755
San Diego County Public Lib., CA (F) (S)	600,425	626,425	3,946,164	3,650,205	—	1,044,610	778,543	605,986
Atlanta Public Lib., GA (C) (U)	607,592	—	4,761,148	—	439,539	—	939,911	—
Jacksonville Public Lib. System, FL (F) (U-S)	604,286	605,690	2,891,007	3,257,253	197,249	265,961	487,239	444,537
Dayton-Montgomery County Public Lib., OH (C) (U-S)	600,000	—	3,991,151	—	4,021	—	819,834	—
New Orleans Public Lib., LA (C) (U)	599,129	—	2,942,135	—	114,595	—	216,370	—
Montgomery County Dept. of Public Libs., MD (F) (S)	593,500	596,800	5,876,948	7,659,459	474,080	471,760	826,015	863,258
Hennepin County Lib. System, MN (C) (S)	567,900	—	7,128,043	—	203,616	—	994,485	—
Contra Costa County Lib. System, CA (F) (S)	542,100	549,970	5,155,890	5,124,778	—	—	655,002	523,375
Carnegie Lib. of Pittsburgh, PA (C) (U)	520,117	—	6,574,685	—	1,501,229	—	610,612	—
San Bernardino County Free Lib., CA (F) (S)	483,535	505,675	3,376,127	3,450,343	—	928,127	417,879	679,512
Seattle Public Lib., WA (F) (U)	490,000	497,300	6,352,228	7,367,699	383,900	538,498	890,617	918,483
Fresno County Public Lib., CA (F) (U-S)	462,050	468,700	3,887,535	3,613,631	—	42,068	425,608	410,880
Tulsa City-County Lib., OK (F) (U-S)	425,000	425,000	2,865,107	2,920,291	—	19,546	300,400	377,000
Omaha Public Lib., NE (C) (U)	364,446	—	2,209,976	—	35,839	—	432,730	—
Alameda County Lib., CA (F) (S)	359,000	360,000	3,990,556	3,148,269	156,615	1,497,009	681,869	456,277
Annapolis and Anne Arundel County Public Lib., MD (F) (U-S)	344,500	359,500	2,548,983	3,205,160	494,650	551,610	434,999	642,487
Oakland Public Lib., CA (F) (U)	342,790	344,780	3,595,026	3,789,053	9,189	10,000	510,410	533,270
San Mateo County Public Lib., CA (F) (S)	237,205	238,015	3,427,576	2,312,604	306,258	703,006	452,556	313,555

TABLE 2 PUBLIC LIBRARY CIRCULATION, REFERENCE, AND STAFF FIGURES, 1978 AND 1979

Library	Circulation 1978	Circulation 1979	Reference Questions 1978	Reference Questions 1979	Total Staff (FTE) 1978	Total Staff (FTE) 1979	Professional Staff (FTE) 1978	Professional Staff (FTE) 1979
Chicago Public Lib., IL (C) (U)	6,789,001	—	3,770,859	—	1,514.50	—	383.00	—
New York Public Lib., NY (F) (U)	9,027,596	9,164,156	3,972,598	4,006,146	1,204.50	1,228.00	468.00	477.00
Brooklyn Public Lib., NY (F) (U)	6,432,524	6,902,037	2,401,494	2,521,034	788.00	747.00	259.00	266.00
Los Angeles Public Lib., CA (F) (U)	11,887,441	11,129,823	17,787,181	17,215,742	1,094.25	1,112.25	376.00	374.50
Queens Borough Public Lib., NY (F) (U)	6,225,518	6,228,500	7,020,059	7,331,394	—	884.25	—	315.00
Free Lib. of Philadelphia, PA (F) (U)	5,279,455	4,840,059	816,042	792,081	871.00	815.00	307.00	291.00
Detroit Public Lib., MI (F) (U)	1,957,977	2,022,007	2,287,206	1,487,927	509.00	519.00	215.00	221.00
Houston Public Lib., TX (C) (U)	5,323,615	—	1,840,838	—	517.00	—	204.00	—
Miami-Dade County Lib. System, FL (F) (U-S)	2,957,268	2,942,937	1,153,536	1,179,233	301.00	345.00	103.00	117.00
Buffalo-Erie County Public Lib., NY (C) (U-S)	5,319,587	—	N/A	—	531.00	—	168.00	—
Milwaukee Public Lib., WI (C) (U)	3,302,356	—	1,344,450	—	368.00	—	138.00	—
San Antonio Public Lib., TX (F) (U)	2,375,444	2,361,041	N/A	N/A	168.00	167.00	78.00	78.00
Cincinnati-Hamilton County Public Lib., OH (C) (U-S)	5,569,000	—	1,752,419	—	420.80	—	150.00	—
Orange County Public Lib., CA (F) (S)	4,878,513	4,435,790	552,188	505,790	241.50	242.50	77.00	79.00
Dallas Public Lib., TX (F) (U)	3,752,120	3,573,391	2,648,061	2,736,112	418.36	426.24	132.00	135.00
Enoch Pratt Free Lib., Baltimore, MD (F) (U)	2,315,823	2,410,374	108,403	110,640	428.00	414.00	137.00	143.00
San Diego Public Lib., CA (F) (U)	4,475,482	3,937,174	1,221,991	1,061,232	283.40	214.95	99.78	79.78
Memphis-Shelby County Public Lib., TX (F) (U-S)	2,585,509	2,568,506	1,165,937	1,302,984	327.00	328.00	96.00	101.00
Indianapolis-Marion County Public Lib., IN (C) (U-S)	3,540,248	—	1,080,479	—	312.78	—	127.10	—
St. Louis County Public Lib., MO (F) (S)	6,897,237	—	N/A	N/A	352.00	—	37.00	—
District of Columbia Public Lib. (F) (U)	1,592,900	1,432,125	N/A	N/A	334.00	341.00	148.00	142.00
King County Lib. System, WA (C) (S)	3,838,995	—	N/A	N/A	242.00	—	69.00	—
Prince George's County Memorial Lib., MD (F) (S)	3,684,341	3,607,199	636,678	607,176	370.00	363.00	126.00	118.00
San Francisco Public Lib., CA (F) (U)	2,494,858	2,362,851	1,425,499	998,216	252.00	250.00	136.00	135.00
Baltimore County Public Lib., MD (F) (S)	7,558,042	7,939,642	N/A	N/A	426.00	463.00	164.00	159.00
Cuyahoga County Public Lib., OH (C) (S)	4,048,766	—	808,656	—	520.95	—	149.00	—
Boston Public Lib., MA (F) (U)	2,118,222	2,138,112	N/A	N/A	547.00	564.00	204.00	211.00
Cleveland Public Lib., OH (C) (U)	2,661,798	—	2,133,977	—	495.00	—	145.00	—

TABLE 2 PUBLIC LIBRARY CIRCULATION, REFERENCE, AND STAFF FIGURES, 1978 AND 1979 (cont.)

Library	Circulation 1978	Circulation 1979	Reference Questions 1978	Reference Questions 1979	Total Staff (FTE) 1978	Total Staff (FTE) 1979	Professional Staff (FTE) 1978	Professional Staff (FTE) 1979
St. Louis Public Lib., MO (C) (U)	1,770,031	1,792,646	506,436	568,599	254.00	259.00	62.00	61.00
Fairfax County Public Lib., VA (F) (S)	5,063,676	4,955,633	1,359,076	1,568,813	319.00	319.00	85.00	85.00
San Diego County Public Lib., CA (F) (S)	3,114,606	3,051,061	481,633	421,675	203.92	173.00	33.00	33.00
Atlanta Public Lib., GA (C) (U)	2,354,402	—	104,862	—	264.00	—	95.00	—
Jacksonville Public Lib. System, FL (F) (U-S)	2,021,340	1,882,257	451,616	432,951	183.50	191.50	49.50	54.00
Dayton-Montgomery County Public Lib., OH (C) (U-S)	4,182,878	—	518,988	—	220.00	—	41.00	—
New Orleans Public Lib., LA (C) (U)	1,227,682	—	735,382	—	187.66	—	46.00	—
Montgomery County Dept. of Public Libs., MD (F) (S)	5,558,754	5,667,985	N/A	N/A	328.00	339.40	165.00	158.00
Contra Costa County Lib. System, CA (F) (S)	3,145,559	3,015,286	366,331	360,611	215.10	209.60	70.00	71.00
Hennepin County Lib. System, MN (C) (S)	4,538,581	—	—	—	321.00	—	101.60	—
Carnegie Lib. of Pittsburgh, PA (C) (U)	3,108,830	—	503,282	—	372.00	—	96.00	—
San Bernardino County Free Lib., CA (F) (S)	1,958,673	1,861,101	247,462	253,620	116.90	111.90	28.10	22.50
Seattle Public Lib., WA (F) (U)	4,391,104	4,279,251	849,601	913,430	320.88	335.98	107.02	90.50
Fresno County Public Lib., CA (F) (U-S)	2,046,664	2,069,496	513,842	502,737	176.20	141.90	45.50	51.00
Tulsa City-County Lib., OK (F) (U-S)	1,672,242	1,655,357	755,215	647,868	196.00	200.00	28.00	26.00
Omaha Public Lib., NE (C) (U)	1,691,598	—	236,454	—	116.30	—	N/A	N/A
Alameda County Lib., CA (F) (S)	2,234,016	1,497,009	353,729	N/A	213.97	135.60	53.75	45.50
Annapolis and Anne Arundel County Public Lib., MD (F) (U-S)	2,627,560	3,063,780	188,730	125,702	172.00	168.00	39.00	37.00
Oakland Public Lib., CA (F) (U)	1,729,217	1,571,202	339,238	263,315	155.22	147.85	46.65	47.65
San Mateo County Public Lib., CA (F) (S)	1,423,328	980,457	166,641	84,616	165.00	101.00	24.50	20.50

URBAN-SUBURBAN PUBLIC LIBRARY STATISTICS / 385

TABLE 3 PUBLIC LIBRARY PER CAPITA SUPPORT AND CIRCULATION, LIBRARY MATERIAL SUPPORT, AND WORKLOAD PER STAFF MEMBER, 1978 AND 1979

Library	Per Capita Support $ 1978	Per Capita Support $ 1979	Library Material Support $ 1978	Library Material Support $ 1979	Per Capita Circulation 1978	Per Capita Circulation 1979	Workload per Staff Member 1978	Workload per Staff Member 1979
Chicago Public Lib., IL (C) (U)	9.26	—	.97	—	2.00	—	4,483	—
New York Public Lib., NY (F) (U)	8.34	9.03	1.17	1.19	2.70	2.80	7,495	7,463
Los Angeles Public Lib., CA (F) (U)	6.36	6.02	1.06	.85	4.30	4.00	10,864	10,007
Brooklyn Public Lib., NY (F) (U)	7.13	7.24	.89	.99	2.70	2.90	8,163	9,237
Queens Borough Public Lib., NY (F) (U)	9.16	9.19	1.06	1.14	3.10	3.10	7,074	7,044
Detroit Public Lib., MI (F) (U)	8.44	9.54	.71	.82	1.30	1.30	3,847	3,896
Houston Public Lib., TX (C) (U)	7.35	—	1.16	—	3.70	—	10,297	—
Buffalo-Erie County Public Lib., NY (C) (U-S)	9.00	—	1.11	—	4.80	—	10,018	—
Milwaukee Public Lib., WI (C) (U)	9.41	—	.94	—	3.50	—	8,974	—
San Antonio Public Lib., TX (F) (U)	3.44	3.35	.70	.66	2.60	2.50	14,140	14,138
Cincinnati-Hamilton County Public Lib., OH (C) (U-S)	8.82	—	1.27	—	6.00	—	13,260	—
Orange County Public Lib., CA (F) (S)	7.27	7.11	.99	1.21	5.50	4.90	20,201	18,292
Dallas Public Lib., TX (F) (U)	8.05	8.37	1.24	1.29	4.20	4.00	8,969	8,384
Enoch Pratt Free Lib., Baltimore, MD (F) (U)	10.96	11.05	1.49	1.43	2.70	2.80	5,387	5,822
San Diego Public Lib., CA (F) (U)	6.78	5.47	.97	1.09	5.70	4.80	15,792	18,317
Memphis-Shelby County Public Lib., TX (F) (U-S)	6.64	7.21	.81	.92	3.50	3.20	7,907	7,830
Indianapolis-Marion County Public Lib., IN (C) (U-S)	8.08	—	1.19	—	4.60	—	11,319	—
District of Columbia Public Lib. (F) (U)	14.39	15.04	1.15	1.31	2.30	2.10	4,769	4,199
King County Lib. System, WA (C) (S)	7.30	—	.88	—	5.70	—	20,307	—
Prince George's County Memorial Lib., MD (F) (S)	10.81	12.48	1.33	1.30	5.40	5.40	9,958	9,937
San Francisco Public Lib., CA (F) (U)	13.48	11.95	1.48	1.37	3.70	3.60	9,900	9,451
Baltimore County Public Lib., MD (F) (S)	12.88	13.26	2.35	2.59	11.70	12.20	17,741	17,148
Cuyahoga County Public Lib., OH (C) (S)	15.79	—	1.64	—	6.30	—	7,772	—
Cleveland Public Lib., OH (C) (U)	23.81	—	3.20	—	4.20	—	5,377	—
Fairfax County Public Lib., VA (F) (S)	8.87	9.06	1.83	1.71	8.40	7.90	15,842	15,534
San Diego County Public Lib., CA (F) (S)	6.57	5.83	1.30	.97	5.20	4.90	15,274	17,636

TABLE 3 PUBLIC LIBRARY PER CAPITA SUPPORT AND CIRCULATION, LIBRARY MATERIAL SUPPORT, AND WORKLOAD PER STAFF MEMBER, 1978 AND 1979 (cont.)

Library	Per Capita Support $ 1978	Per Capita Support $ 1979	Library Material Support $ 1978	Library Material Support $ 1979	Per Capita Circulation 1978	Per Capita Circulation 1979	Workload per Staff Member 1978	Workload per Staff Member 1979
St. Louis Public Lib., MO (C) (U)	7.51	8.04	.87	.96	2.80	2.90	6,969	6,921
Atlanta Public Lib., GA (C) (U)	7.84	—	1.55	—	3.90	—	8,918	—
Jacksonville Public Lib. System, FL (F) (U-S)	4.78	5.38	.81	.73	3.30	3.10	11,015	9,829
Dayton-Montgomery County Public Lib., OH (C) (U-S)	6.65	—	1.37	—	6.90	—	19,013	—
Montgomery County Dept. of Public Libs., MD (F) (S)	9.90	12.83	1.39	1.47	9.40	9.50	16,947	16,700
New Orleans Public Lib., LA (C) (U)	4.91	—	.36	—	2.00	—	6,542	—
Hennepin County Lib. System, MN (C) (S)	12.55	—	1.75	—	8.00	—	14,139	—
Carnegie Lib. of Pittsburgh, PA (C) (U)	12.64	—	1.19	—	6.00	—	8,357	—
Contra Costa County Public Lib., PA (C) (U)	9.51	9.32	1.21	.95	5.80	5.50	14,624	14,386
San Bernardino County Free Lib., CA (F) (S)	6.98	6.82	.86	1.34	4.00	3.70	16,755	16,632
Seattle Public Lib., WA (C) (U)	12.96	14.82	1.82	1.85	9.00	8.60	13,685	12,737
Fresno County Public Lib., CA (F) (U-S)	8.41	7.71	1.00	.88	4.40	4.40	11,616	14,584
Tulsa City-County Lib., OK (F) (U-S)	6.74	6.87	.71	.89	3.90	3.90	8,532	8,361
Omaha Public Lib., NE (C) (U)	6.06	—	1.19	—	4.60	—	14,545	—
Annapolis and Anne Arundel County Public Lib., MD (F) (U-S)	7.40	8.92	1.26	1.79	7.60	8.50	15,277	18,237
Oakland Public Lib., CA (F) (U)	10.49	10.99	1.49	1.54	5.00	4.60	11,546	10,627
San Mateo County Public Lib., CA (F) (S)	14.45	9.72	1.91	1.32	6.00	4.10	8,626	9,707
Free Lib. of Philadelphia, PA (F) (U)	10.13	9.67	1.06	.92	2.70	2.50	6,061	5,938
St. Louis County Public Lib., MO (F) (S)	7.11	—	1.24	—	9.20	—	19,594	—
Boston Public Lib., MA (F) (U)	17.13	18.11	3.50	3.49	3.30	3.30	3,872	3,791
Alameda County Lib., CA (F) (S)	11.11	8.75	1.90	1.27	6.20	4.20	10,441	11,040
Miami-Dade County Lib. System, FL (F) (U-S)	8.57	9.07	1.48	1.38	2.50	2.50	9,825	8,530

URBAN-SUBURBAN PUBLIC LIBRARY STATISTICS / 387

TABLE 4 URBAN AND SUBURBAN PUBLIC LIBRARY PERFORMANCE RANKED BY VOLUME, 1978

	Per Capita Support $		Per Capita Library Material Support $		Per Capita Circulation		Workload per Staff Member
1.	Cleveland Public Lib., OH (U)	23.81	1. Boston Public Lib., MA (U)	3.50	1. Baltimore County Public Lib., MD (S)	11.2	1. King County Lib. System, WA (S)	20,307
2.	Boston Public Lib., MA (U)	17.30	2. Cleveland Public Lib., OH (U)	3.20	2. Montgomery County Dept. of Public Libs., MD (S)	9.4	2. Orange County Public Lib., CA (S)	20,201
3.	Cuyahoga County Public Lib., OH (S)	15.79	3. Baltimore County Public Lib., MD (S)	2.35	3. St. Louis County Public Lib., MO (S)	9.2	3. St. Louis County Public Lib., MO (S)	19,594
4.	San Mateo County Public Lib., CA (S)	14.45	4. San Mateo County Public Lib., CA (S)	1.91	4. Seattle Public Lib., WA (U)	9.0	4. Dayton-Montgomery County Public Lib., OH (U-S)	19,013
5.	District of Columbia Public Lib. (U)	14.39	5. Alameda County Public Lib., CA (S)	1.90	5. Fairfax County Public Lib., VA (S)	8.4	5. Baltimore County Public Lib., MD (S)	17,741
6.	San Francisco Public Lib., CA (U)	13.48	6. Fairfax County Public Lib., VA (S)	1.83	6. Hennepin County Lib. System, MN (S)	8.0	6. Montgomery County Dept. of Public Libs., MD (S)	16,947
7.	Seattle Public Lib., WA (U)	12.96	7. Seattle Public Lib., WA (U)	1.82	7. Annapolis and Anne Arundel County Public Lib., MD (U-S)	7.6	7. San Bernardino County Free Lib., CA (S)	16,755
8.	Baltimore County Public Lib., MD (S)	12.88	8. Hennepin County Lib. System, MN (S)	1.75	8. Cuyahoga County Public Lib., OH (S)	6.3	8. Fairfax County Public Lib., CA (S)	15,842
9.	Carnegie Lib. of Pittsburgh, PA (U)	12.64	9. Cuyahoga County Public Lib., OH (S)	1.64	9. Alameda County Public Lib., CA (S)	6.2	9. San Diego Public Lib., CA (U)	15,792
10.	Hennepin County Lib. System, MN (S)	12.55	10. Atlanta Public Lib., GA (U)	1.55	10. San Mateo County Public Lib., CA (S)	6.0	10. Annapolis and Anne Arundel County Public Lib., MD (U-S)	15,277
11.	Alameda County Public Lib., CA (S)	11.11	11. Oakland Public Lib., CA (U)	1.49	10a. Carnegie Lib. of Pittsburgh, PA (U)	6.0	11. San Diego County Public Lib., CA (S)	15,274
12.	Enoch Pratt Free Lib., Baltimore, MD (U)	10.96	11a. Enoch Pratt Free Lib., Baltimore, MD (U)	1.49	10b. Cincinnati-Hamilton County Public Lib., OH (U-S)	6.0	12. Contra Costa County Lib. System, CA (S)	14,624
13.	Prince George's County Memorial Lib., MD (S)	10.81	12. San Francisco Public Lib., CA (U)	1.48	11. Contra Costa County Lib. System, CA (S)	5.8	13. Omaha Public Lib., NE (U)	14,545
14.	Oakland Public Lib., CA (U)	10.49	13. Montgomery County Dept. of Public Libs., MS (S)	1.39	12. King County Public Lib. System, WA (S)	5.7	14. San Antonio Public Lib., TX (U-S)	14,140
15.	Free Lib. of Philadelphia, PA (U)	10.13	14. Dayton-Montgomery County Public Lib., OH (U-S)	1.37	12a. San Diego Public Lib., CA (U)	5.7	15. Hennepin County Lib. System, MN (S)	14,139
16.	Montgomery County Dept. of Public Libs., MD (S)	9.90						

388 / LIBRARY RESEARCH AND STATISTICS

TABLE 4   URBAN AND SUBURBAN PUBLIC LIBRARY PERFORMANCE RANKED BY VOLUME, 1978 (cont.)

Per Capita Support $	Per Capita Library Material Support $	Per Capita Circulation	Workload per Staff Member
17. Contra Costa County Lib. System, CA (S) 9.51	15. Prince George's County Memorial Lib., MD (S) 1.33	13. Orange County Public Lib., CA (S) 5.5	16. Seattle Public Lib., WA (U) 13,685
18. Milwaukee Public Lib., WI (U) 9.41	16. San Diego County Public Lib., CA (S) 1.30	14. Prince George's County Memorial Lib., MD (S) 5.4	17. Cincinnati-Hamilton County Public Lib., OH (U-S) 13,260
19. Chicago Public Lib., IL (U) 9.26	17. Cincinnati-Hamilton County Public Lib., OH (U-S) 1.27	15. San Diego County Public Lib., CA (S) 5.2	18. Fresno County Public Lib., CA (U-S) 11,616
20. Queens Borough Public Lib., NY (U) 9.16	18. Annapolis and Anne Arundel County Public Lib., MD (U-S) 1.26	16. Oakland Public Lib., CA (U) 5.0	19. Oakland Public Lib., CA (U) 11,546
21. Buffalo-Erie County Public Lib., NY (U-S) 9.00	19. Dallas Public Lib., TX (U) 1.24	17. Buffalo-Erie County Public Lib., NY (U-S) 4.8	20. Indianapolis-Marion County Public Lib., IN (U-S) 11,319
22. Fairfax County Public Lib., VA (S) 8.87	19a. St. Louis County Public Lib., MO (S) 1.24	18. Omaha Public Lib., NE (U) 4.6	21. Jacksonville Public Lib. System, FL (U-S) 11,015
23. Cincinnati-Hamilton County Public Lib., OH (U-S) 8.82	20. Contra Costa County Lib. System, CA (S) 1.21	18a. Indianapolis-Marion County Public Lib., IN (U-S) 4.6	22. Los Angeles Public Lib., CA (U) 10,864
24. Miami-Dade County Public Lib. System, FL (U-S) 8.57	21. Indianapolis-Marion County Public Lib., IN (U-S) 1.19	19. Fresno County Public Lib., CA (U-S) 4.4	23. Alameda County Public Lib., CA (S) 10,441
25. Detroit Public Lib., MI (U) 8.44	21a. Carnegie Lib. of Pittsburgh, PA (U) 1.19	20. Los Angeles Public Lib., CA (U) 4.3	24. Houston Public Lib., TX (U) 10,297
26. Fresno County Public Lib., CA (U-S) 8.41	21b. Omaha Public Lib., NE (U) 1.19	21. Dallas Public Lib., TX (U) 4.2	25. Buffalo-Erie County Public Lib., NY (U-S) 10,018
27. New York Public Lib., NY (U) 8.34	22. New York Public Lib., NY (U) 1.17	21a. Cleveland Public Lib., OH (U) 4.2	26. Prince George's County Memorial Lib., MD (S) 9,958
28. Indianapolis-Marion County Public Lib., IN (U-S) 8.08	23. Houston Public Lib., TX (U) 1.16	22. San Bernardino County Free Lib., CA (S) 4.0	27. San Francisco Public Lib., CA (U) 9,900
29. Dallas Public Lib., TX (U) 8.05	24. District of Columbia Public Lib. (U) 1.15	23. Tulsa City-County Public Lib., OK (U-S) 3.9	28. Miami-Dade County Lib. System, FL (U-S) 9,825
30. Atlanta Public Lib., GA (U) 7.84	25. Buffalo-Erie County Public Lib., NY (U-S) 1.11	23a. Atlanta Public Lib., GA (U) 3.9	29. Milwaukee Public Lib., WI (U) 8,974
31. St. Louis Public Lib., MO (U) 7.51	26. Free Lib. of Philadelphia, PA (U) 1.06	24. San Francisco Public Lib., CA (U) 3.7	30. Dallas Public Lib., TX (U) 8,969
			31. Atlanta Public Lib., GA (U) 8,918

URBAN-SUBURBAN PUBLIC LIBRARY STATISTICS / 389

32.	Annapolis and Anne Arundel County Public Lib., MD (U-S)	7.40	26a.	Queens Borough Public Lib., NY (U)	1.06	24a.	Houston Public Lib., TX (U)
33.	Houston Public Lib., TX (U)	7.35	26b.	Los Angeles Public Lib., CA (U)	1.06	25.	Milwaukee Public Lib., WI (U)
34.	King County Lib. System, WA (S)	7.30	27.	Fresno County Public Lib., CA (U-S)	1.00	25a.	Memphis-Shelby County Public Lib., TN (U-S)
35.	Orange County Public Lib., CA (S)	7.27	28.	Orange County Public Lib., CA (S)	.99	26.	Jacksonville Public Lib. System, FL (U-S)
36.	Brooklyn Public Lib., NY (U)	7.13	29.	Chicago Public Lib., IL (U)	.97	26a.	Boston Public Lib., MA (U)
37.	St. Louis County Public Lib., MO (S)	7.11	29a.	San Diego Public Lib., CA (U)	.97	27.	Queens Borough Public Lib., NY (U)
38.	San Bernardino County Free Lib., CA (S)	6.98	30.	Milwaukee Public Lib., WI (U)	.94	28.	St. Louis Public Lib., MO (U)
39.	San Diego Public Lib., CA (U)	6.78	31.	Brooklyn Public Lib., NY (U)	.89	29.	Free Lib. of Philadelphia, PA (U)
40.	Tulsa City-County Public Lib., OK (U-S)	6.74	32.	King County Lib. System, WA (S)	.88	29a.	New York Public Lib., NY (U)
41.	Dayton-Montgomery County Public Lib., OH (U-S)	6.65	33.	St. Louis Public Lib., MO (U)	.87	29b.	Brooklyn Public Lib., NY (U)
42.	Memphis-Shelby County Public Lib., TN (U-S)	6.64	34.	San Bernardino County Free Lib., CA (S)	.86	29c.	Enoch Pratt Free Lib., Baltimore, MD (U)
43.	San Diego County Public Lib., CA (S)	6.57	35.	Memphis-Shelby County Public Lib., TN (U-S)	.81	30.	San Antonio Public Lib., TX (U-S)
44.	Los Angeles Public Lib., CA (U)	6.36	35a.	Jacksonville Public Lib. System, FL (U-S)	.81	31.	Miami-Dade County Lib. System, FL (U-S)
45.	Omaha Public Lib., NE (U)	6.06	36.	Detroit Public Lib., MI (U)	.71	32.	District of Columbia Public Lib. (U)
46.	New Orleans Public Lib., LA (U)	4.91	37.	San Antonio Public Lib., TX (U-S)	.70	33.	Chicago Public Lib., IL (U)
47.	Jacksonville Public Lib. System, FL (U-S)	4.78	38.	New Orleans Public Lib., LA (U)	.36	33a.	Jefferson-Parish Lib., LA (S)
48.	San Antonio Public Lib., TX (U-S)	3.44				34.	Detroit Public Lib., MI (U)

32.	San Mateo County Public Lib., CA (S)	8,626
33.	Tulsa City-County Public Lib., OK (U-S)	8,532
34.	Carnegie Lib. of Pittsburgh, PA (U)	8,357
35.	Brooklyn Public Lib., NY (U)	8,163
36.	Memphis-Shelby County Public Lib., TN (U-S)	7,907
37.	Cuyahoga County Public Lib., OH (S)	7,772
38.	New York Public Lib., NY (U)	7,495
39.	Queens Borough Public Lib., NY (U)	7,074 (est.)
40.	St. Louis Public Lib., MO (U)	6,969
41.	New Orleans Public Lib., LA (U)	6,542
42.	Free Lib. of Philadelphia, PA (U)	6,061
43.	Enoch Pratt Free Lib., Baltimore, MD (U)	5,387
44.	Cleveland Public Lib., OH (U)	5,377
45.	District of Columbia Public Lib. (U)	4,769
46.	Chicago Public Lib., IL (U)	4,483
47.	Boston Public Lib., MA (U)	3,872
48.	Detroit Public Lib., MI (U)	3,847

3.7	
3.5	
3.5	
3.3	
3.3	
3.1	
2.8	
2.7	
2.7	
2.7	
2.7	
2.6	
2.5	
2.3	
2.0	
2.0	
1.3	

TABLE 5 URBAN AND SUBURBAN PUBLIC LIBRARY PERFORMANCE RANKED BY VOLUME, 1979

Per Capita Support $		Per Capita Library Material Support $		Per Capita Circulation		Workload per Staff Member	
1. Boston Public Lib., MA (U)	18.11	1. Boston Public Lib., MA (U)	3.49	1. Baltimore County Public Lib., MD (S)	12.2	1. San Diego County Public Lib., CA (S)	18,317
2. District of Columbia Public Lib. (U)	15.04	2. Baltimore County Public Lib., MD (S)	2.59	2. Montgomery County Dept. of Public Libs., MD (S)	9.5	2. Orange County Public Lib., CA (S)	18,292
3. Seattle Public Lib., WA (U)	14.82	3. Seattle Public Lib., WA (U)	1.85	3. Seattle Public Lib., WA (U)	8.6	3. Annapolis and Anne Arundel County Public Lib., MD (U-S)	18,237
4. Baltimore County Public Lib., MD (S)	13.26	4. Annapolis and Anne Arundel County Public Lib., MD (U-S)	1.79	4. Annapolis and Anne Arundel County Public Lib., MD (U-S)	8.5	4. San Diego Public Lib., CA (U)	17,636
5. Montgomery County Dept. of Public Libs., MD (S)	12.83	5. Fairfax County Public Lib., VA (S)	1.71	5. Fairfax County Public Lib., VA (S)	7.9	5. Baltimore County Public Lib., MD (S)	17,148
6. Prince George's County Memorial Lib., MD (S)	12.48	6. Oakland Public Lib., CA (U)	1.54	6. Contra Costa County Lib. System, CA (S)	5.5	6. Montgomery County Dept. of Public Libs., MD (S)	16,700
7. San Francisco Public Lib., CA (U)	11.95	7. Montgomery County Dept. of Public Libs., MD (S)	1.47	7. Prince George's County Memorial Lib., MD (S)	5.4	7. San Bernardino County Free Lib., CA (S)	16,632
8. Enoch Pratt Free Lib., Baltimore, MD (U)	11.05	8. Enoch Pratt Free Lib., Baltimore, MD (U)	1.43	8. Orange County Public Lib., CA (S)	4.9	8. Fairfax County Public Lib., VA (S)	15,534
9. Oakland Public Lib., CA (U)	10.99	9. Miami-Dade County Lib. System, FL (U-S)	1.38	8a. San Diego Public Lib., CA (U)	4.9	9. Fresno County Public Lib., CA (U-S)	14,584
10. San Mateo County Public Lib., CA (S)	9.72	10. San Francisco Public Lib., CA (U)	1.37	9. San Diego County Public Lib., CA (S)	4.8	10. Contra Costa County Lib. System, CA	14,386
11. Free Lib. of Philadelphia, PA (U)	9.67	11. San Bernardino County Free Lib., CA (S)	1.34	10. Oakland Public Lib., CA (U)	4.6	11. San Antonio Public Lib., TX (U-S)	14,136
12. Detroit Public Lib., MI (U)	9.54	12. San Mateo County Public Lib., CA (S)	1.32	11. Fresno County Public Lib., CA (U-S)	4.4	12. Seattle Public Lib., WA (U)	12,737
13. Contra Costa County Lib. System, CA (S)	9.32	13. District of Columbia Public Lib. (U)	1.31	12. Alameda County Public Lib., CA (S)	4.2	13. Alameda County Public Lib., CA (S)	11,040
14. Queens Borough Public Lib., NY (U)	9.19	14. Prince George's County Memorial Lib., MD (S)	1.30	13. San Mateo County Public Lib., CA (S)	4.1	14. Oakland Public Lib., CA (U)	10,627
15. Miami-Dade County Lib. System, FL (U-S)	9.07			14. Los Angeles Public Lib., CA (U)	4.0	15. Los Angeles Public Lib., CA (U)	10,007
16. Fairfax County Public Lib., VA (S)	9.06						

URBAN-SUBURBAN PUBLIC LIBRARY STATISTICS / 391

17.	New York Public Lib., NY (U)	9.03	15.	Dallas Public Lib., TX (U)	1.29
18.	Annapolis and Anne Arundel County Public Lib., MD (U-S)	8.92	16.	Alameda County Public Lib., CA (S)	1.27
19.	Alameda County Public Lib., CA (S)	8.75	17.	Orange County Public Lib., CA (S)	1.21
20.	Dallas Public Lib., TX (U)	8.37	18.	New York Public Lib., NY (U)	1.19
21.	St. Louis Public Lib., MO (U)	8.04	19.	Queens Borough Public lib Lib., NY (U)	1.14
22.	Fresno County Public Lib., CA (U-S)	7.71	20.	San Diego County Public Lib., CA (S)	1.09
23.	Brooklyn Public Lib., NY (U)	7.24	21.	Brooklyn Public Lib., NY (U)	.99
24.	Memphis-Shelby County Public Lib., TN (U-S)	7.21	22.	San Diego Public Lib., CA (U)	.97
25.	Orange County Public Lib., CA (S)	7.11	23.	St. Louis Public Lib., MO (U)	.96
26.	Tulsa City-County Public Lib., OK (U-S)	6.87	24.	Contra Costa County Lib. System, CA (S)	.95
27.	San Bernardino County Free Lib., CA (S)	6.82	25.	Free Lib. of Philadelphia, PA (U)	.92
28.	Los Angeles Public Lib., CA (U)	6.02	25a.	Memphis-Shelby County Public Lib., TN (U-S)	.92
29.	San Diego County Public Lib., CA (U)	5.83	26.	Tulsa City-County Public Lib., OK (U-S)	.92
30.	San Diego Public Lib., CA (U)	5.47	27.	Fresno County Public Lib., CA (U-S)	.88
31.	Jacksonville Public Lib. System, FL (U-S)	5.38	28.	Los Angeles Public Lib., CA (U)	.85
32.	San Antonio Public Lib., TX (U-S)	3.35	29.	Detroit Public Lib., MI (U)	.82
			30.	Jacksonville Public Lib. System, FL (U-S)	.73
			31.	San Antonio Public Lib., TX (U-S)	.66

16.	Prince George's County Memorial Lib., MD (S)	4.0	9,937
17.	Jacksonville Public Lib. System, FL (U-S)	3.9	9,829
18.	San Mateo County Public Lib., CA (S)	3.7	9,707
19.	San Francisco Public Lib., CA (U)	3.6	9,451
20.	Brooklyn Public Lib., NY (U)	3.3	9,237
21.	Miami-Dade County Lib. System, FL (U-S)	3.2	8,530
22.	Dallas Public Lib., TX (U)		8,384
23.	Tulsa City-County Public Lib., OK (U-S)	3.1	8,361
24.	Memphis-Shelby County Public Lib., TN (U-S)	3.1	7,830
25.	New York Public Lib., NY (U)	2.9	7,463
26.	Queens Borough Public Lib., NY (U)	2.9	7,044
27.	St. Louis Public Lib., MO (U)	2.8	6,921
28.	Free Lib. of Philadelphia, PA (U)	2.5	5,938
29.	Enoch Pratt Free Lib., Baltimore, MD (U)	2.5	5,822
30.	District of Columbia Public Lib. (U)	2.5	4,199
31.	Detroit Public Lib., MI (U)	2.1	3,896
32.	Boston Public Lib., MA (U)	1.3	3,791

SPECIAL LIBRARIES SERVING STATE GOVERNMENT AGENCIES

Herbert Goldhor
Director, Library Research Center, Graduate School of Library Science, University of Illinois at Urbana-Champaign

Linda C. Smith
Assistant Professor, Graduate School of Library Science, University of Illinois at Urbana-Champaign

In 1977, the Learning Resources Branch of the National Center for Education Statistics (NCES) sent a 73-item, 5-page questionnaire (plus 5 pages of definitions and instructions) to 1,400 special libraries that had been identified in various sources as serving state government agencies. The survey form was part of LIBGIS II. Data were requested for FY 1977, and usable responses were received from 1,134 libraries (81% of those polled) in 49 states and the District of Columbia. This is the first such survey ever done of these libraries, and the results fill yet another gap in the statistics on American librarianship. NCES arranged to code the responses, enter them onto a computer tape, and produce frequency counts of most of the data elements. We at the University of Illinois are planning to analyze the data from this survey, and to prepare a full report within the year. This present summary is based on tables provided by NCES.

The 1,134 special libraries represent a mean average of 23 per state, the median average is 19, and the range is from 3 (in the District of Columbia and in Rhode Island) to 74 (in Illinois). The survey form asked each respondent to classify its library in one or another of 15 categories, and the results are shown in Table 1. In number of respondents, special libraries in three fields (education, health science, and law and legislation) constitute 37% of the total; and libraries serving persons in various types of state institutions are another 35%. Libraries in the other 8 of the 15 types make up slightly less than 28% of the total.

When one examines the data on these 1,134 libraries, the grouping that makes sense consists of (A) the libraries in the state institutions, (B) the comprehensive reference and law and legislation libraries, and (C) all other libraries in this sample. Table 2 shows the data for each of a dozen or so main aspects of the services and resources of these libraries, for all 1,134 libraries, and for each of the three groups just named. Thus Table 2 indicates that these libraries had 1,714 service outlets, an overall ratio of one to 1.5. The institutional libraries had measurably fewer outlets per library than did the others, and Group B libraries had measurably more outlets per library than did the special libraries in Group C.

In all the measures of resources in Table 2, the state law and general reference libraries dominate the picture with 40% to over 80% of the totals. Thus, for example, of almost 19,000,000 volumes held by all 1,134 libraries, almost two-thirds are in the 141 libraries of Group B (but note that Group A libraries added 11% of their total books in 1976/77, Group C 5%, but Group B only 3%). In regard to the number of government documents held, Group B has its highest percentage of the total, for any measure on Table 2, and Group A its lowest. In this and other ways, the institutional libraries (Group A) resemble small public libraries, e.g., on the average they had 6,100 volumes

TABLE 1   DISTRIBUTION OF THE LIBRARIES
IN THE SURVEY SAMPLE, BY TYPE

Type or Category of Library	No.	Percent of Total
A. Specialized technical libraries in the field of		
Education	159	14.0
Health science	152	13.4
Law and legislation	107	9.4
Engineering, science, and transportation	62	5.5
Environment	40	3.5
Commerce and industry	38	3.4
History	31	2.7
Welfare	22	1.9
Agriculture and forestry	12	1.1
All other subject fields	77	6.8
Subtotal	700	61.7
B. Institution libraries serving residents of		
Hospitals	151	13.3
Adult correction agencies	136	12.0
Juvenile correction agencies	104	9.2
Other institutions	9	0.8
Subtotal	400	35.3
C. Comprehensive reference libraries serving several state departments or agencies (including state libraries)	34	3.0
Total	1,134	100.0

and 50 current periodical subscriptions. Group C libraries are most like pure special libraries, e.g., they spent the highest percentage of all expenditures on library materials.

Clearly these 1,134 libraries constitute an important source of materials. Besides the more than 29,000,000 books, government documents, and bound periodical volumes, they held 1,300,000 volumes of unbound noncurrent periodicals, almost 6,000,000 microforms, over 800,000 audiovisual titles, and almost 3,500,000 other materials (60% of which were in state historical libraries, presumably manuscripts). The importance of these collections is shown by the fact that all 1,134 libraries loaned 740,000 items to other libraries in 1976/77 but borrowed only 253,000 (a ratio of almost three to one).

As will be seen from Table 2, these libraries had a total staff of 4,415 persons in full-time equivalents, of whom 41% were librarians and other professionals and 53% were clerical employees (an overall ratio of 1:1.1). Almost one-third of the librarians were men, and they outnumbered women librarians only in adult correctional institution libraries. The highest ratio of professional to clerical staff was found in this type of library (1:2.1), and the lowest (1:0.3) in juvenile correctional agency libraries. The general state comprehensive reference libraries had 32% of all the professional librarians, the education libraries 11%, and the law and legislation libraries another 11%.

Of the persons in charge of these 1,134 libraries, 41% had no more than a four-year college education (7% no more than high school), and the largest group of these (about one-third) were in the health science and hospital libraries. Another 36% held the master's degree in library science as the highest earned degree, and 4% more the five-year BSLS; the other 19% held a subject master's or had completed programs of study beyond a master's degree.

TABLE 2 ANALYSIS OF SURVEY DATA ON SERVICES AND RESOURCES

Group[1]	Respondents No.	%	Service Outlets No.	Ratio	Average No. of Hours per Week	Average No. of Seats for Readers	Volumes[2] Held No.	%	Volumes[2] Added No.	%	Titles Held[2] No.	%
A	400	35	585	1:1.5	38.6	37	2,442	13	260	30	1,922	24
B	141	13	325	1:2.3	45.7	35	12,192	64	385	44	3,572	44
C	593	52	804	1:1.4	41.1	19	4,277	23	232	26	2,620	32
Total	1,134	100	1,714	1:1.5	40.8	27	18,911	100	877	100	8,114	100

Group	Documents[2] No.	%	Bound Periodicals Held[2] Volumes No.	%	Titles No.	%	Current Periodical Subscriptions[2] No.	%	Microforms Held[2] Physical Units No.	%	Periodical Titles No.	%
A	13	0.2	66	3	24	15	19	14	61	1	3	1
B	7,127	87	1,424	74	64	41	58	44	4,116	70	244	86
C	1,064	13	435	23	70	44	56	42	1,745	29	36	13
Total	8,204	100	1,925	100	158	100	133	100	5,922	100	283	100

Group	Total Staff (FTE)[3] Librarians and Other Professionals No.	%	Average per Library	Clerical Employees No.	%	Average per Library	Operating Expenditures Total[2] No.	%	Salaries %	Materials %
A	401	19	1.0	419	18	1.0	$14,500	15	58	14
B	873	42	6.2	1,294	55	9.2	58,948	63	40	16
C	790	38	1.3	638	27	1.1	20,222	22	68	17
Total	2,064	99	1.8	2,351	100	2.1	$93,670	100	48	16

[1]Group A consists of libraries in state institutions, B of comprehensive reference and law and legislation libraries, and C of all other special libraries serving state government agencies.
[2]Number in thousands.
[3]FTE = Full-Time Equivalent.

Total operating expenditures were $93,670,000 (see Table 2), of which 48% was for salaries (other than for building staff), 16% for library materials of all kinds and for binding and rebinding, and 36% for equipment, plant operation, utilities, and all other expenses (including fringe benefits). As might be expected, the comprehensive reference libraries accounted for over half of all expenditures, law and legislation libraries for 10% of the total, and adult correctional institution libraries for another 10%. Comprehensive reference libraries devoted 39% of all expenditures to salaries, while the mean average for all other groups of libraries in this sample was 61%. Law and legislation libraries spent more than a quarter of their funds for books, more than twice as large a percentage as any other group of libraries; agriculture and forestry libraries spent almost 30% of their funds for periodicals, almost three times the percentage of any other group. The mean average salary of all 4,415 professional and clerical employees in these libraries in 1976/77 was over $10,000.

There are many other possible approaches to the analysis of these data, and we plan to incorporate some of them in the final report along with some figures for each of the 1,134 libraries by name. This was a benchmark survey that captured many quantifiable aspects of the situation of these libraries at one point in time, and will provide a basis for comparison and for measurement of future progress.

PUBLIC SCHOOL LIBRARY MEDIA CENTERS

Robert David Little

Department of Library Science, Indiana State University

A survey of U.S. public schools by the Learning Resources Branch of the National Center for Education Statistics in the fall of 1978 found that 83.5% of the 85,063 public schools have school library media centers. Almost 95% of the students enrolled in public schools attended schools with library media centers. The survey was conducted as a part of the Library General Information Survey (LIBGIS IV) program. Statistics on public school library media centers were also collected in 1974 as a part of the LIBGIS I program. A comparison of data from the two surveys shows that, although the number of schools with library media centers (LMCs) and the enrollment of students in schools with LMCs have declined (see Table 1), the percentages of schools with LMCs and students enrolled in schools with LMCs remained fairly consistent. The differences appear to be a result of the reduction in the total number of public schools during the period, the decline in the total student enrollment, and sampling error.

METHODOLOGY

For both surveys a representative sample of 3,500 schools was selected to gather the data. The design was a one-stage stratified simple random sample. The schools were stratified by region (a. North Atlantic, b. Great Lakes and Plains, c. Southeast, and d. West and Southwest); by location (a. Standard Metropolitan Statistical Area (SMSA) —central city, b. SMSA—outside central city, and c. outside SMSA); by school grade (secondary, or elementary/combined); and by enrollment (a. 2,000 or more, b. 1,000–

TABLE 1 NUMBER OF PUBLIC SCHOOLS WITH LMCs AND NUMBER OF STUDENTS ENROLLED, FALL 1974 AND FALL 1978

	Fall 1974		Fall 1978	
Level	No. of Schools	Students Enrolled	No. of Schools	Students Enrolled*
All schools	74,625	43,929,000	71,037	40,406,000
Secondary schools	22,315	18,099,000	17,975	16,040,000
Elementary and combined schools	52,310	25,830,000	53,062	24,365,000

*Numbers have been rounded.
Source: Learning Resources Branch of the National Center for Education Statistics.

1,999, c. 700–999, d. 500–699, e. 300–499, and f. under 300). For both surveys, information was collected on the availability of school library media services, resources, expenditures, staff, and facilities.

RESOURCES

As expected, the total number of books, periodical subscriptions, and audiovisual materials available in LMCs increased between the spring of 1974 and the spring of 1978 (see Table 2). Over the four-year period the total number of books available increased by 34,278,000, or 6.8%, the number of periodical subscriptions increased by 990,000, or 34.2%, and the number of titles of audiovisual materials increased by 8,915,000, or 13.1%.

These increases in total resources available, along with the decline in the number of students enrolled, resulted in increases in the number of items available per student. The number of books per student increased by 1.9, or 16.5%, the number of periodical subscriptions per student increased by 0.03, or 42.9%, and the number of titles of audiovisual materials per student increased by 0.4, or 26.7%. While the per student resources available have increased, they are still less than the minimum recommendations in *Media Programs: District and School* (Chicago: American Library Association, 1975).

Although the total of resources available increased during the four-year period, the number of volumes of books added per year decreased. For the 1977–1978 school year 8,318,000 fewer books were purchased than during the 1973–1974 school year.

EXPENDITURES

Total operating expenditures for public school library media centers increased by almost $227,000,000, or 19.2%, between the 1973–1974 school year and the 1977–1978 school year (see Table 3). Expenditures increased for salaries and wages by 23.9%, for books by 8%, for periodicals by 22.5%, and for equipment by 8.5%. Expenditures decreased for audiovisual materials by 18.8%.

Over the four-year period total per student expenditures increased $7.97 per student, or 29.6% (see Table 4). While during the 1973–1974 school year per student expenditures in secondary schools were substantially greater than in elementary/combined schools, in the 1977–1978 school year per student expenditures for secondary schools and elementary/combined schools were virtually identical. Per student expenditures increased for salaries and wages by 34.7%, for books by 17.5%, for periodicals by 31.6%, and for equipment by 18.5%. Per student expenditures for audiovisual materials decreased by 11.7%.

TABLE 2 MATERIALS AVAILABLE IN PUBLIC SCHOOL LMCs AT THE END OF SCHOOL YEARS, 1973–1974 AND 1977–1978

Materials	All Schools 1973–1974	All Schools 1977–1978	Secondary Schools 1973–1974	Secondary Schools 1977–1978	Elementary and Combined Schools 1973–1974	Elementary and Combined Schools 1977–1978
Books						
Volumes held						
Total number	506,965,000	541,243,000	198,733,000	190,970,000	308,232,000	350,273,000
Per student	11.5	13.4	11.0	11.9	11.9	14.4
Volumes added						
Total number	37,487,000	29,169,000	15,281,000	10,745,000	22,206,000	18,424,000
Per student	0.9	0.7	0.8	0.7	0.9	0.8
Periodical subscriptions						
Total number	2,892,000	3,882,000	1,573,000	1,531,000	1,319,000	2,351,000
Per student	0.07	0.1	0.09	0.1	0.05	0.1
Audiovisual materials						
Total number of titles	68,024,000	76,939,000	24,305,000	26,731,000	43,719,000	50,208,000
Per student	1.5	1.9	1.3	1.7	1.7	2.1

Source: Total numbers from the Learning Resources Branch of the National Center for Education Statistics.

TABLE 3 TOTAL EXPENDITURES FOR PUBLIC SCHOOL LMCs BY EXPENDITURE CATEGORY AND BY LEVEL, SCHOOL YEARS 1973–1974 AND 1977–1978

Expenditure Categories	All Schools 1973–1974	All Schools 1977–1978	Secondary Schools 1973–1974	Secondary Schools 1977–1978	Elementary and Combined Schools 1973–1974	Elementary and Combined Schools 1977–1978
Total operating expenditures	$1,182,280,000	$1,409,087,000	$545,890,000	$558,862,000	$636,390,000	$850,225,000
Salaries and wages	818,320,000	1,013,828,000	376,660,000	393,995,000	441,660,000	619,833,000
Books	162,960,000	176,015,000	76,100,000	67,910,000	86,860,000	108,105,000
Periodicals	24,870,000	30,463,000	14,310,000	16,135,000	10,560,000	14,328,000
Audiovisual materials	90,440,000	73,440,000	42,570,000	30,998,000	47,870,000	42,442,000
Equipment	66,450,000	72,110,000	28,010,000	29,947,000	38,440,000	42,163,000
Other operating expenditures	19,240,000	43,231,000	8,240,000	19,877,000	11,000,000	23,354,000

Source: Learning Resources Branch of the National Center for Education Statistics.

TABLE 4   PER STUDENT EXPENDITURES FOR PUBLIC SCHOOL LMCs
BY EXPENDITURE CATEGORY AND BY LEVEL,
SCHOOL YEARS 1973–1974 AND 1977–1978

Expenditure Categories	All Schools 1973–1974	All Schools 1977–1978	Secondary Schools 1973–1974	Secondary Schools 1977–1978	Elementary and Combined Schools 1973–1974	Elementary and Combined Schools 1977–1978
Total operating expenditures	$26.91	$34.88	$30.16	$34.84	$24.64	$34.90
Salaries and wages	18.63	25.09	20.81	24.56	17.10	25.44
Books	3.71	4.36	4.20	4.23	3.36	4.44
Periodicals	0.57	0.75	0.79	1.01	0.41	0.59
Audiovisual materials	2.06	1.82	2.35	1.93	1.85	1.74
Equipment	1.51	1.79	1.55	1.87	1.49	1.73
Other operating expenses	0.44	1.07	0.46	1.24	0.43	0.96

There were only small changes in the distribution of the expenditures for public school library media centers by expenditure category (see Table 5). Salaries and wages continued to account for the greater part (71.9% during the 1977–1978 school year) of the expenditures. The differences between the expenditure categories for secondary schools and elementary schools continued to be minor.

STAFF

The number of certified staff members (certified as librarians, audiovisual specialists, media specialists, or classroom teachers) in LMCs as measured in full-time equivalents increased by 19,100, or 30.5%, between the fall of 1974 and the fall of 1978 (see Table 6). The ratio of certified staff members to students declined from 1 to 701 in 1974 to 1 to 494 in 1978. Although in 1974 there was less than 1 certified staff member for every public school LMC, by 1978 there were 1.15 certified staff members for every LMC.

TABLE 5   PERCENT DISTRIBUTION OF EXPENDITURES FOR PUBLIC SCHOOL
LMCs BY EXPENDITURE CATEGORY AND BY LEVEL,
SCHOOL YEARS 1973–1974 AND 1977–1978

Expenditure Categories	All Schools 1973–1974	All Schools 1977–1978	Secondary Schools 1973–1974	Secondary Schools 1977–1978	Elementary and Combined Schools 1973–1974	Elementary and Combined Schools 1977–1978
Salaries and wages	69.2%	71.9%	69.0%	70.5%	69.4%	72.9%
Books	13.8	12.5	13.9	12.1	13.6	12.7
Periodicals	2.1	2.2	2.6	2.9	1.7	1.7
Audiovisual materials	7.7	5.2	7.8	5.5	7.5	5.0
Equipment	5.6	5.1	5.1	5.4	6.0	5.0
Other operating expenses	1.6	3.1	1.5	3.6	1.7	2.7

TABLE 6 NUMBER OF CERTIFIED EMPLOYEES IN PUBLIC SCHOOL LMCs BY LEVEL AND BY SEX, FALL 1974 AND FALL 1978 SEMESTERS*

Level	Fall 1974 Men	Fall 1974 Women	Fall 1974 Total	Fall 1978 Men	Fall 1978 Women	Fall 1978 Total
All schools	7,378	55,281	62,659	6,263	75,496	81,759
Secondary schools	4,629	22,985	27,614	3,934	27,456	31,390
Elementary and combined schools	2,749	32,296	35,045	2,329	48,040	50,369

*The category of certified employees includes staff certified as librarians, audiovisual specialists, media specialists, or classroom teachers. Number is in full-time equivalents.

Source: Learning Resources Branch of the National Center for Education Statistics.

Women continue to comprise the largest percentage of LMC staff members. In fact the actual number of men employed in LMCs declined. The percentage of women staff members increased from 88% in 1974 to 92% in 1978.

IN SUMMARY

During the four-year period between surveys, declining enrollments have resulted in more resources per student and improved ratios between students and certified staff members in library media centers. Total expenditures in actual dollars have increased substantially; however, the number of volumes added per student has declined. Actual expenditures for audiovisual materials have also declined. Statistics on LMC facilities from the 1978 survey were not yet available at the time this summary was being prepared.

PLANS FOR NONPUBLIC SCHOOL SURVEY

Although statistics for public school LMCs have been collected periodically since 1876, statistics on LMCs in nonpublic schools have not been collected and published by the federal government. In order to eliminate this gap in data, the Learning Resources Branch of the National Center for Education Statistics plans to survey nonpublic LMCs in the spring of 1980. The survey will sample over 1,600 of the 16,000 nonpublic schools in the United States. The statistics to be collected will follow the LIBGIS format and provide information on the availability of school library media services, resources, expenditures, staff, and facilities for nonpublic schools. When completed, data for all elementary and secondary schools in the United States will be available for the first time.

SURVEYS OF LAW LIBRARIES, 1973-1979

Alfred J. Lewis

Statistics Coordinator, American Association of Law Libraries (through June 1979)
Assistant Law Librarian, University of California, Davis

It has always been clear to law librarians that it is reasonable to divide law libraries according to type. Certainly, for example, there are significant qualitative differences between law firm libraries and law school libraries. But law librarians have not been able to agree on *how* to divide and what to name these divisions. Categories are, therefore, not used uniformly in statistical surveys.

The primary source of law library statistics has been the annual surveys of the various types of law libraries that have been conducted with varying degrees of success for the past 11 years. This effort has been partially funded by the Council on Library Resources.

Law school library surveys[1] have been the most successful. They have been a joint project of the American Association of Law Libraries, the American Bar Association (ABA), and the American Association of Law Schools (AALS). Only ABA- and AALS-approved law schools are included (approximately 179 schools). The response rate each year has been close to 100 percent. This survey reports high, median, and low figures for salaries and fringe benefits, broken down according to size. The bulk of the report is a very full, school-by-school tabulation of data on collection size (book stock, microforms, AV, and serial subscriptions by volumes, volume equivalents, and titles), staffing (librarians, supporting staff, and students), expenditures and budget (salaries, library materials, equipment, etc.), physical facilities (area, shelving, seating, etc.), hours, students, faculty, and book dollars per student. In addition, there has been sporadic reporting on special topics.

The survey of law libraries that serve a local bar has also been successful for the past four years.[2] It currently reports responses from over 100 law libraries that serve local attorneys as their primary clientele. Such libraries are generally called "county law libraries," some are called "bar association libraries," and a few go under other names. Approximately 60 to 70 percent of all such libraries respond, which is a good rate of return considering that many of these libraries are quite small and often without permanent staff. These libraries range in size from 5,000 volumes in rural counties to over 600,000 volumes in the large cities. Gonzalez's reports cover salaries (starting, high, low, and average) of librarians broken down by size of library. Collection size, staffing, and expenditures are reported in a manner similar to the law school library reports mentioned above. The tabulation is again library by library. In addition, this report also covers "sources of funds" and "categories of clientele served," plus occasional reporting of schedule of hours, branches, nonmonetary contributions to library support, bar dues, percentages of court fees and bar income allocated to library support, and other subjects of particular interest to county/bar librarians.

The third category in the series noted above is the survey of governmental law libraries. Only one report has been published,[3] possibly because of a low rate of return (40 percent). It is interesting that the significant differences among law libraries forced

Note: See the 1973 edition of the *Bowker Annual* for a report on law library surveys prior to 1973—*Ed.*

the compiler to further subdivide this category into state law libraries, state and local court libraries, federal court libraries, state and local government agency libraries, and federal government agency and legislative libraries. Salaries, collection, expenditures, and staffing are covered in a manner similar to the law school and bar library series. In addition, the report covers some facets of each library's position within the administrative hierarchy and its primary functions.

The fourth category in the series is law firm libraries. Because of the traditional confidentiality desired by these private institutions and certain price-fixing legal problems, it has been difficult to survey these libraries. Only one report has been published.[4] Unlike prior reports in this series, individual libraries are not named. Percentages and numerical distributions by size of library are provided. The report covers salaries, professional degrees, expenditures, volumes, services, and staffing.

The American Association of Law Libraries has recently divided itself into a number of "Special Interest Sections." This has generated a greater sense of identity and has provided the leadership and organization that may lead to greater success in statistical surveying of the various categories of law libraries. For future statistical information, the reader is advised to contact one of these sections: Academic Law Libraries, Private Law Libraries, or State, Court, and County Law Libraries.[5]

A partial update to Roalfe's 1953, in-depth survey of law libraries[6] was conducted in 1973-1974. The results are reported in the May 1974 issue of the *Law Library Journal*. These surveys were, for the most part, quite detailed. The report does not name individual libraries. The categories of libraries included are county law libraries,[7] state law libraries (or supreme court law libraries where they serve as *the* government's law library),[8] corporate law libraries (not including law firm libraries),[9] federal court libraries,[10] and the Library of Congress Law Library.[11]

Law librarians have found that the standard sources of information on price increases for book and other library materials have not been specific enough for their purposes. Five years ago an annual compilation of averages and indexes of prices for legal publications was initiated.[12] It currently provides mean cost per title, percentage increase over the prior year, and an index (1973-1974 base) for legal monographs, periodicals, looseleaf services, court reporters, continuations, and "all serials." Each category of material is defined and the titles included within each are also listed.

In addition to the annual surveys, a large number of one-time surveys have been conducted. The results of these have been reported in the following list of articles. All references are to the *Law Library Journal*.

Law School Libraries

Allen, C. "Whom We Shall Serve: Secondary Patrons of the University Law School Library." May 1973, p. 160.

Bailey, J., and Dee, M. "Law School Libraries: Survey Relating to Autonomy and Faculty Status." February 1974, p. 3.

Bailey, J., and Trelles, O. "Autonomy, Librarian Status and Librarian Tenure in Law School Libraries." August 1978, p. 425.

Brock, C., and Edelman, G. "Teaching Practices of Academic Law Librarians." February 1978, p. 96.

Cogswell, R., and Wolfe, B. "Hours of Opening and After-Hours Access in University Law Libraries." February 1973, p. 88.

Dee, M., and Kessler, R. "The Impact of Computerized Methods on Legal Research Courses." May 1976, p. 164.

Grossman, G. "Clinical Legal Education and the Law Library." February 1974, p. 60.

Levy, C. "In Re Law Library Miscellany." February 1974, p. 32.

Sadow, S., and Beede, B. "Library Instruction in American Law Schools." February 1975, p. 27.

Schlueter, K. "Selection of Government Documents in Law School Libraries." August 1978, p. 477.

Tanguay, G. "The Case for the Special Status of the University Law Library." February 1973, p. 12.

Law Firm Libraries

Carter, A. "Budgeting in Private Law Firm Libraries." February 1978, p. 187.

Meyers, M. "The Impact of LEXIS on the Law Firm Library." February 1978, p. 158.

Shediac, M. "The Greater Philadelphia Law Library Association's 1977 Salary Survey." February 1978, p. 170.

State Law Libraries

Poe, E. "State Law Libraries 'Weight of Fatigue.'" February 1973, p. 81.

Wolfe, C. "Current Problems Facing State Law Libraries." February 1978, p. 108.

Miscellaneous Law Libraries

Moreland, C. "Private Libraries for the Legal Profession." August 1974, p. 387.

Werner, O. J. "The Present Legal Status and Conditions of Prison Law Libraries." August 1973, p. 259.

Automation

Rogers, E., and Cooper, W. "Survey of Professional Attitudes toward Research Retrieval Systems." Winter 1979, p. 130.

Schulte, L. "A Survey of Computerized Legislative Information Systems." Winter 1979, p. 99.

Cataloging and Classification

Enyingi, P. "Subject Cataloging Practices in American Law Libraries." February 1975, p. 11.

Kwan, C. "Classification Policies in Law Libraries Using Subclass KF." February 1973, p. 34.

Piper, P., and Kwan, C. "Cataloging and Classification Practices in Law Libraries." August 1978, p. 481.

Circulation

Magavero, G. "Circulation Policy in Law Libraries." February 1976, p. 15.

Richmond, M. "Attitudes of Law Librarians to Theft and Mutilation Control Methods." February 1975, p. 60.

Continuing Education

Gasaway, L., and Margeton, S. "Continuing Education for Law Librarianship." February 1977, p. 39.

TABLE 1 NUMBER AND SIZE (VOLUME COUNT) OF U.S. LAW LIBRARIES BY STATE AND TYPE OF LIBRARY

State	Law School No.	Law School Size[a]	Local Bar/County No.	Local Bar/County Size[b]	Law Firm No.	Law Firm Size[c]	Government No.	Government Size[b]	Miscellaneous No.	Miscellaneous Size[b]
Alabama	1	100,000	3	25,000	1	10,000	1	125,000		
	1	150,000	1	50,000	3	20,000				
Alaska					1	10,000	1	50,000		
Arizona	2	150,000	4	25,000	3	10,000	1	100,000		
			1	50,000						
			1	125,000						
Arkansas	1	50,000	2	25,000			1	75,000		
	1	100,000								
California	10	50,000	26	25,000	29	10,000	16	25,000	11	25,000
	7	100,000	4	50,000	15	20,000	2	50,000	1	50,000
	4	150,000	1	100,000	6	30,000	1	125,000		
	2	200,000	2	150,000	2	40,000	1	175,000		
	2	250,000	1	250,000	1	50,000				
	1	400,000	1	600,000						
Colorado	1	100,000	11	25,000	5	10,000	3	25,000	7	25,000
	1	150,000			1	20,000	1	100,000		
Connecticut	1	50,000	8	25,000	2	10,000	1	200,000	3	25,000
	1	150,000	2	50,000					1	50,000
	1	600,000	1	100,000						
Delaware	1	100,000	3	25,000			1	25,000	1	25,000
District of Columbia	2	50,000	1	50,000	30	10,000	30	25,000	13	25,000
	2	100,000			5	20,000	16	50,000	1	50,000
	1	150,000			3	30,000	3	75,000		
	2	200,000			1	40,000	3	100,000		
							1	150,000		
							1	175,000		
							1	200,000		
							2	225,000		
							1	250,000		
							1	275,000		
							1	1,600,000		

Florida	2 1 1 2	50,000 100,000 150,000 250,000	9 2	25,000 50,000	4 2	10,000 30,000	2 1	25,000 75,000	2	25,000
Georgia	1 1 1 1	50,000 100,000 150,000 250,000	2	25,000	7 3 1	10,000 20,000 30,000	1 1	25,000 125,000		
Hawaii	1	100,000			1 1	10,000 20,000				
Idaho	1	50,000	1	25,000			3 2	25,000 75,000		
							1	100,000		
Illinois	2 3 2 1 2	50,000 100,000 150,000 300,000 350,000	3 1 1	25,000 150,000 175,000	8 9 6	10,000 20,000 30,000	3 1 2 1	25,000 50,000 75,000 100,000	13 1	25,000 50,000
Indiana	2 1 1	100,000 200,000 250,000	6	25,000	3 1	10,000 20,000	1 1	25,000 75,000	1	25,000
Iowa	1 1	100,000 300,000	3	25,000	1	10,000	1	175,000		
Kansas	1 1	50,000 150,000	3	25,000			1	175,000	1	25,000
Kentucky	2 1	100,000 150,000	1	25,000			1	75,000	2	25,000
Louisiana	1 1 1 1	50,000 100,000 150,000 250,000			1 1	10,000 30,000	1 1	50,000 100,000		
Maine	1	100,000	6	25,000	1 1	10,000 30,000	1	75,000	1	25,000
Maryland	1 1	100,000 150,000	8 1	25,000 125,000	5 2	10,000 20,000	4 1	25,000 125,000		

TABLE 1 NUMBER AND SIZE (VOLUME COUNT) OF U.S. LAW LIBRARIES BY STATE AND TYPE OF LIBRARY (cont.)

State	Law School No.	Law School Size[a]	Local Bar/County No.	Local Bar/County Size[b]	Law Firm No.	Law Firm Size[c]	Government No.	Government Size[b]	Miscellaneous No.	Miscellaneous Size[b]
Massachusetts	7	100,000	12	25,000	15	10,000	4	25,000	1	25,000
	1	1,300,000	1	50,000	1	20,000	1	100,000		
			2	75,000						
			1	100,000						
			1	175,000						
Michigan	1	50,000	3	25,000	3	10,000	1	25,000	2	25,000
	3	100,000	1	50,000	2	20,000	1	100,000	1	50,000
	1	200,000	1	100,000						
	1	500,000								
Minnesota	2	100,000	2	25,000	5	10,000	1	50,000	4	25,000
	1	400,000	1	50,000	2	20,000	1	250,000		
					1	30,000				
Mississippi	1	50,000	2	25,000			1	100,000		
	1	100,000								
Missouri	1	100,000	2	25,000	3	10,000	4	25,000	2	25,000
	3	150,000	1	50,000	1	20,000	1	100,000		
			1	75,000						
Montana	1	100,000					1	50,000	1	25,000
Nebraska	1	100,000	1	25,000	1	10,000	1	125,000		
	1	150,000			1	20,000				
Nevada			1	25,000			1	50,000	1	25,000
			1	75,000					1	50,000
New Hampshire	1	50,000					1	75,000		
New Jersey	1	100,000	7	25,000	5	10,000	3	25,000	1	25,000
	1	200,000	1	50,000	2	20,000	1	100,000		
	1	250,000								

New Mexico	1	150,000			2	10,000	1	100,000
New York	1	50,000	1	10,000				
	3	100,000	1	20,000				
	4	150,000	16	25,000	42	10,000	19	25,000	23	25,000
	2	200,000	4	50,000	33	20,000	2	50,000	1	50,000
	1	300,000	1	75,000	5	30,000	1	75,000	1	200,000
	1	500,000	3	100,000	2	40,000	3	100,000		
	1	550,000	1	125,000	3	50,000	1	150,000		
			2	150,000			1	250,000		
			1	400,000			2			
North Carolina	2	50,000	1	25,000			2	25,000		
	1	200,000					1	100,000		
	1	250,000								
North Dakota	1	200,000					1	100,000		
Ohio	5	100,000	1	25,000						
	3	150,000	36	25,000	4	10,000	1	25,000	2	25,000
	1	300,000	3	50,000	5	20,000	1	50,000		
			3	75,000	1	30,000	1	175,000		
			1	125,000	1	40,000				
			1	150,000	1	50,000				
Oklahoma	1	50,000	3	25,000	1	10,000	1	100,000	2	25,000
	2	100,000								
Oregon	3	100,000	3	25,000	1	10,000	1	50,000		
			1	150,000	1	20,000	1	125,000		
Pennsylvania	2	50,000	29	25,000	13	10,000	9	25,000	9	25,000
	1	100,000	1	125,000	6	20,000	1	50,000		
	1	200,000	1	200,000	1	30,000	1	125,000		
	1	250,000								
	1	300,000								
Puerto Rico	1	50,000					3	25,000		
	2	100,000					1	50,000		
							1	75,000		
Rhode Island					1	10,000	1	25,000	1	25,000
							1	100,000		
South Carolina	1	200,000					1	50,000		

TABLE 1 NUMBER AND SIZE (VOLUME COUNT) OF U.S. LAW LIBRARIES BY STATE AND TYPE OF LIBRARY (cont.)

State	Law School No.	Law School Size[a]	Local Bar/County No.	Local Bar/County Size[b]	Law Firm No.	Law Firm Size[c]	Government No.	Government Size[b]	Miscellaneous No.	Miscellaneous Size[b]
South Dakota	1	100,000					1	50,000		
Tennessee	2	100,000	1	50,000	1	10,000	3	25,000		
	1	150,000					1	50,000		
Texas	1	50,000	6	25,000	9	10,000	3	25,000	6	25,000
	3	100,000	1	50,000	3	30,000	2	75,000		
	1	150,000			2	50,000				
	2	200,000			1	70,000				
	1	400,000								
Utah	1	150,000	2	25,000			1	50,000		
	1	200,000								
Vermont	1	50,000	1	25,000			1	100,000	2	25,000
Virginia	3	100,000	3	25,000	3	10,000	3	25,000	2	25,000
	1	150,000			1	30,000	1	75,000		
	1	400,000								
Washington	2	100,000	7	25,000	4	10,000	2	25,000	1	25,000
	1	300,000	1	75,000	4	20,000	1	175,000		
West Virginia	1	100,000	1	25,000	1	20,000	1	75,000	1	25,000
Wisconsin	1	100,000	4	25,000	2	10,000	1	25,000	2	25,000
	1	150,000	1	50,000	1	40,000	1	125,000		
Wyoming	1	100,000					1	50,000		

[a] Rounded to 50,000s.
[b] Rounded to 25,000s.
[c] Rounded to 10,000s.

Minority Employment

Brecht, A., and Mills, R. "Minorities Employed in Law Libraries." May 1978, p. 283.

A final source of statistics on law libraries is the latest *Directory of Law Libraries*.[13] It can supply information on location, number, size, and kinds of law libraries in the United States, Canada, and some other foreign countries. Table 1 is an arrangement of data from the *Directory*. The volume counts have been rounded off considerably in order to keep the table at an appropriate size. This has especially affected the counting of the very small (e.g., 10,000 volumes and less) local bar and miscellaneous law libraries.

NOTES

1. A. Lewis, "Statistical Survey of Law School Libraries and Librarians." These annual surveys have been published in the May issue of the *Law Library Journal* from 1970 through 1978. In 1979 it is in the Spring issue.
2. S. Gonzalez, "Statistical Survey of Law Libraries Serving a Local Bar." This annual survey has been published in the May issue of the *Law Library Journal* from 1976 through 1978. In 1979 it is in the Summer issue.
3. S. Gonzalez, "Statistical Survey of Governmental Law Libraries," *Law Library Journal*, August 1973, p. 290.
4. A. Head, "1972 Statistical Survey of Law Firm Libraries and Librarians," *Law Library Journal*, August 1974, p. 389.
5. The address for all the Special Interest Sections is American Association of Law Libraries, 53 W. Jackson Blvd., Chicago, IL 60604.
6. William R. Roalfe, *The Libraries of the Legal Profession* (St. Paul, MN: West Publishing Co., 1953).
7. B. Ochal, "County Law Libraries," *Law Library Journal*, May 1974, p. 177.
8. W. Pershing and L. Pershing, "State Law Libraries and Supreme Court Law Libraries," *Law Library Journal*, May 1974, p. 235.
9. L. Kulpa, "Corporate Law Libraries," *Law Library Journal*, May 1974, p. 244.
10. R. Hecht, "Survey of Federal Court Libraries," *Law Library Journal*, May 1974, p. 259.
11. C. Kenyon, "Library of Congress Law Library," *Law Library Journal*, May 1974, p. 276.
12. B. Scott, "Price Index for Legal Publications." These annual indexes have been published in the February issues of the *Law Library Journal* from 1976 through 1978. In 1979 it is in the Winter issue.
13. American Association of Law Libraries, *Directory of Law Libraries*, 1978 ed. Available from the association headquarters, 53 W. Jackson Blvd., Chicago, IL 60604 for $10.

PUBLIC LIBRARY BUILDINGS IN 1979

Karl Nyren
Senior Editor, *Library Journal*

Barbara Livingston
Assistant Editor, *Library Journal*

Bette-Lee Fox
Associate Editor, *Library Journal*

This year's report of new library construction is an encouraging one, indicating that Americans have not by any means given up building libraries, even though in some places they have been putting them on exceedingly short rations. The total of 165 projects tops last year's tally by 30 projects.

Among this year's crop there were at least four public libraries built to serve also as school libraries for their communities. Many of the new libraries share buildings or building complexes with city offices, community centers, civic centers (which may be the same thing), fire stations, and at least one each is bedded down with an ambulance corps, a senior center, or a swimming pool.

Many library reports noted that their new buildings are completely accessible to the handicapped—and highspots in this area are two big libraries built for service to the handicapped—in Chicago and in Montgomery, Alabama.

Energy saving was mentioned frequently, and in a wide variety of ways. Our newest libraries are saving energy in some of the newest ways (solar heat, heat pumps) and in some of the oldest ways, too (a screened porch, tree shading, below-grade construction, and earth berms).

Among new features mentioned were drive-in windows, computers, a full-sized tree in a children's room and playground equipment outside, wiring for future video and other new technology, bookstore type shelving, and out in Terre Haute, the minor marvel of a self-furling flagpole.

Reading the future in the annual report of new public library buildings is something like measuring the moss on the north sides of trees or the length of the fur on woolly caterpillars. But if thoroughly unreliable, it can be encouraging as we move down into the fiscal winter that threatens to last throughout the 1980s. First, one cannot deny that vigorous figure of 165 new libraries built in the same year that Proposition 13 scorched the library earth in California. Then there is the good news that, in at least two communities, the new library is the first library they've had. In Orange, Texas, the new library is the first to be housed in a building not handed down from some other use. And in West Paterson, New Jersey, the new one-story library is designed to receive a second story in a future that West Paterson clearly believes is going to happen.

A new feature this year, and one we have hoped to launch for some time, is an apparently fragmentary report of new Canadian public libraries. Alberta was well represented, but not the other provinces; next year we hope to do better. It seems obvious that leaving out the entire Canadian experience hardly contributes to our endeavor of drawing a yearly cross section of North American library building activity.

Note: Reprinted from *Library Journal*, December 1, 1979.

TABLE 1   NEW PUBLIC LIBRARY BUILDINGS CONSTRUCTED DURING YEAR ENDING JUNE 30, 1979

Symbol Code: B—Branch Library; BS—Branch & System Headquarters; M—Main Library; MS—Main & System Headquarters; S—System Headquarters; Sc—School District
NA—Not Available

Community	Pop in M	Code	Project Cost	Gross Sq. Ft.	Const. Cost	Sq. Ft. Cost	Equip. Cost	Site Cost	Other Costs	Vols.	Reader Seats	Fed. Funds	State Funds	Local Govt. Funds	Gift/Other Funds	Notes
ALABAMA																
Ashland	12	M	149,000	2,400	132,000	62.00	21,500	NA	0	10,000	21	149,000	none	500	1,225	Library for Blind & Physically Handicapped
Montgomery	7	B	1,357,040	50,000	1,000,375	20.00	356,665	NA	NA	275,000	50	1,213,040	144,000	0	0	
Oxford	15	B	156,300	6,338	125,191	19.75	31,109	NA	NA	25,000	NA	0	10,000	146,300	NA	5 AV listening rooms
Sylacauga	25	M	810,314	21,500	667,184	37.30	82,439	NA	60,241	75,000	84	592,000	0	143,314	75,000	
Tuscaloosa	116	M	2,362,292	56,519	2,303,914	36.24	173,400	0	130,010	250,000	491	560,000	0	1,500,000	334,476	Parent browsing/waiting rooms adjacent children's area
ALASKA																
Galena	1	Sc	5,800,000	34,800	4,200,000	121.00	600,000	NA	1,000,000	12,000	60	1,500,000	3,750,000	500,000	0	Public/school facility
Homer	5	M	300,000	3,500	232,600	66.45	38,110	NA	29,289	12,000	26	0	70,000	27,000	3,000	Stained-glass window by local artist
Nome	3	M	376,352	1,740	325,444	187.00	10,604	NA	10,182	20,000	10	0	225,000	166,059	0	Seaside south windows
Seldovia	.5	M	175,175	4,672	150,625	32.24	20,300	NA	4,250	10,000	30	0	150,000	25,000	0	
Skagway	1	M	225,000	NA	189,350	NA	17,650	25,000	18,000	NA	NA	0	225,000	25,000	0	
CALIFORNIA																
Brentwood	8	B	259,226	4,074	195,552	48.00	20,434	43,240	NA	18,000	36	251,726	0	0	7,500	Part of community center
Dublin	25	B	1,578,168	14,400	860,100	58.00	125,000	239,580	133,080	75,000	136	0	0	0	0	
Lodi	33	M	2,498,000	30,750	1,800,000	60.16	292,000	200,000	156,000	150,000	184	1,907,360	0	600,000	2,000	Decorative tile mural; graffiti-resistant exterior walls
Los Angeles	24	B	863,349	7,500	730,620	97.42	39,882	NA	NA	30,000	52	863,349	0	0	0	

TABLE 1 NEW PUBLIC LIBRARY BUILDINGS CONSTRUCTED DURING YEAR ENDING JUNE 30, 1979 (cont.)

Community	Pop in M	Code	Project Cost	Gross Sq. Ft.	Const. Cost	Sq. Ft. Cost	Equip. Cost	Site Cost	Other Costs	Vols.	Reader Seats	Fed. Funds	State Funds	Local Govt. Funds	Gift/Other Funds	Notes
North Fork (firehouse included)	4	B	232,547	4,777	212,440	44.47	20,107	NA	NA	18,000	33	209,600	0	22,947	0	Library/firehouse with library on top
Orange	10	B	62,000	10,000	484,000	48.00	88,000	54	94,000	40,000	152	320,000	NA	NA	NA	Utilizes north light for energy conservation
Placerville	50	M	2,086,000	37,800	1,789,000	47.57	152,000	NA	136,000	164,000	165	1,050,000	0	1,036,000	0	23,000 sq. ft. nonlibrary
Ridgecrest	21	B	504,684	7,465	482,188	65.62	182,251	NA	NA	27,500	130	503,964	0	0	0	Similar construction as in 2 Bakersfield branches
Rowland Heights	40	B	1,281,042	15,000	1,231,273	82.08	101,331	NA	NA	55,000	56	209,000	0	1,072,042	0	Museum wing paid for separately
St. Helena	20	M	730,000	10,000	558,187	55.82	58,948	0	139,046	NA	NA	100,000	0	259,046	340,000	
San Bernadino	6	B	480,837	5,602	414,000	73.90	31,607	NA	35,230	42,180	31	349,961	0	130,876	0	Slump stone exterior matches civic center
Simi Valley	75	B	3,228,000	32,000	1,800,000	56.25	438,000	NA	NA	200,000	216	5,000	0	300,000	NA	Life-size tree in children's area; broadcasting system and AV alcoves
Stockton	50	B	1,278,180	14,000	1,088,800	77.77	135,080	NA	54,300	60,000	79	952,350	0	325,840	225,000	Energy-saving: insulation, fluorescent lighting, earth berms, tree shading
Union City (Civic Ctr)	35	B	4,982,462*	13,798	855,476	62.00	5,000	NA	0	50,000	50	4,980,462	0	0	2,000	*Includes civic center

PUBLIC LIBRARY BUILDINGS IN 1979 / 413

CONNECTICUT														
South Windsor	16	M	874,329	15,000	730,410	48.69	43,079	NA	NA	90,000	65	390,000	0	303,550	180,779	
FLORIDA															
Jacksonville	100	B	1,432,800	23,000	1,051,368	45.71	156,312	NA	225,020	100,000	137	0	300,000	1,132,700	0	Arched portico acts as energy efficient sunscreen and minimizes glare
GEORGIA															
Baxley	13	B	284,500	6,683	221,900	33.20	41,900	NA	20,700	20,000	49	0	140,000	140,000	4,500	
Dallas	15	B	328,722	7,500	274,058	36.54	33,067	NA	21,596	30,000	50	0	164,386	150,000	14,386	
Douglas	23	S	189,500	12,600	163,808	15.00	20,000	NA	5,692	84,000	150	0	10,000	135,000	50,000	
Hawkinsville	8	B	247,258	5,500	203,290	44.79	34,000	23,500	0	21,500	58	180,000	10,000	32,000	25,258	
Hazlehurst	9	B	70,000	3,000	51,000	17.00	15,000	NA	350	10,000	80	0	7,500	25,000	46,315	All utilities underground
Lithia Springs	9	B	320,000	7,000	277,838	39.66	20,782	NA	21,379	20,000	40	0	157,500	162,500	0	
Savannah	72	B	893,814	15,000	545,408	36.36	116,360	NA	231,045	61,250	85	0	250,000	642,884	2,500	
Vienna	10	B	242,432	6,000	177,860	40.40	43,116	20,000	1,449	50,000	54	162,000	21,739	49,246	9,447	
GUAM															
Agana	54	M	1,370,295	18,000	1,185,000	76.13	46,000	NA	139,295	101,100+	126	1,250,000	74,295	NA	NA	
HAWAII															
Waimea	3	Sc	852,500	10,000	695,000	64.50	118	NA	30,500	27,300	121	0	852,500	0	0	Serves community, students, and teachers
IDAHO															
Idaho Falls	40	M	2,862,179	62,925	2,028,624	32.00	337,010	257,476	95,000	200,000	277	0	0	2,677,000	0	Totally accessible to handicapped; interior garden atrium under large glass dome; 10,000 sq. ft. designed as lease space
Rexburg	12	M	496,649	11,452	441,365	34.08	54,401	NA	884	50,000	60	351,413	100,000	NA	NA	Children's, Young Adult, adult on 1 floor handled with circulation desk

TABLE 1 NEW PUBLIC LIBRARY BUILDINGS CONSTRUCTED DURING YEAR ENDING JUNE 30, 1979 (cont.)

Community	Pop in M	Code	Project Cost	Gross Sq. Ft.	Const. Cost	Sq. Ft. Cost	Equip. Cost	Site Cost	Other Costs	Vols.	Reader Seats	Fed. Funds	State Funds	Local Govt. Funds	Gift/Other Funds	Notes
ILLINOIS																
Bensenville	19	M	1,086,000	18,500	825,000	44.60	147,000	NA	114,000	100,000	120	NA	NA	790,000	161,000	
Chicago (Blind population of Illinois)		B	2,500,000	32,000*	2,500,000	78.12	NA	NA	NA	150,000	16	0	1,000,000	1,500,000	0	*The Illinois Regional Library for the Blind and Physically Handicapped has allotted 3,300 sq. ft. to community library service with 55 reader seats and 23,000 vol.
Coal Valley	5	M	75,000	1,460	60,000	51.37	15,000	NA	NA	10,000	12	NA	NA	NA	40,000	
Frankfort	11	M	1,041,209	14,800	721,938	48.78	96,983	82,555	139,733	60,120	76	0	0	1,041,209	0	
Glen Ellyn	25	M	900,000	15,000	707,594	47.17	128,685	NA	70,000	148,000	140	0	0	900,000	NA	
Mokena	8	B	333,937	7,913	288,499	36.46	31,308	NA	14,130	26,750	42	0	0	333,937	0	
Streamwood	37	M	2,200,000	46,000	1,811,480	39.38	140,076	NA	285,087	210,000	240	0	NA	2,000,000	211,500	Large exterior sunken courtyards; electric heat and AC.
INDIANA																
Terre Haute	115	M	4,551,117	69,600	3,533,394	50.76	458,322	463,639	55,762	240,000	600	0	0	4,551,117	0	Closed-circuit video surveillance
IOWA																
Ackley	4	M	135,000	5,300	120,000	NA	15,000	NA	NA	30,000	50	0	0	120,000	15,650	
Charles City	10	M	528,393	9,400	472,367	50.25	56,026	NA	NA	55,000	80	472,367	0	0	56,026	
Duncombe	1	M	27,088	1,500	21,688	15.80	3,800	NA	7,600	NA	6	0	0	18,133	8,955	New building in conjunction with fire station; figures are for library portion only

PUBLIC LIBRARY BUILDINGS IN 1979 / 415

Garner	3	M	269,000	6,916	209,910	30.35	25,000	NA	34,090	25,000	30	9,600	0	205,333	55,000	Senior citizen area built next to library
George	2	M	82,166	3,125	62,678	26.29	20,500	NA	NA	35,000	40	32,000	0	25,000	41,000	Remaining funds used to purchase books
Hanlontown	.5	M	46,000	1,170	40,000	35.00	6,000	NA	NA	4,000	8	0	0	15,000	25,000	Library is part of community building: fire station, city hall, community room. Entire complex $120,000
Le Grand	2	B	38,000	18,000	30,442	NA	7,119	NA	NA	2,389	5	0	0	0	38,000	All labor was volunteered; log structure
Mitchellville	2	M	50,995	1,540	38,947	25.83	3,861	3,000	13,393	10,000	20	7,931	NA	5,139	36,153	
Plainfield	3	B	92,000	2,700	90,000	34.00	2,000	NA	NA	NA	12	0	0	1,000	92,000	
Rock Rapids	3	M	330,000	5,500	253,000	23.00	26,000	NA	51,000	26,000	46	0	0	217,000	113,000	
KANSAS																
Emporia	36	M	1,462,297	25,685	1,168,900	45.50	126,625	NA	166,772	120,000	130	0	0	1,250,000	212,297	Screened porch; energy efficient
Syracuse	3	M	238,000	3,906	178,000	45.00	60,000	NA	NA	25,000	50	NA	NA	178,000	NA	Moved from courthouse basement
LOUISIANA																
Belle Chasse	10	B	302,999	5,320	264,220	47.76	12,042	NA	26,737	15,000	25	0	0	302,999	0	Fully-equipped sound studio and darkroom
Crowley	52	M	708,409	14,976	534,824	35.71	119,846	NA	53,737	65,000	58	0	0	NA	NA	
Plaquemine	30	M	1,271,150	19,971	957,713	47.96	137,068	NA	76,368	70,000	91	0	0	1,271,150	0	
MARYLAND																
Annapolis	25	B	1,617,106	12,671	858,048	67.71	55,494	NA	66,300*	40,000	64	1,478,000	0	139,106	0	*Library's share of community storm drainage system cost
Glenarden	13	B	707,407	9,445	562,933	59.60	76,466	36,363	31,645	40,000	45	NA	259,939	447,468	NA	Cathedral ceiling; natural light through slit windows

TABLE 1 NEW PUBLIC LIBRARY BUILDINGS CONSTRUCTED DURING YEAR ENDING JUNE 30, 1979 (cont.)

Community	Pop in M	Code	Project Cost	Gross Sq. Ft.	Const. Cost	Sq. Ft. Cost	Equip. Cost	Site Cost	Other Costs	Vols.	Reader Seats	Fed. Funds	State Funds	Local Govt. Funds	Gift/ Other Funds	Notes
Towson	8	B	96,583	1,250	81,078	77.27	15,505	NA	NA	15,000	2	0	0	96,583	0	Bookstore-type shelving; located in shopping center
Edgemere minilibrary																
Towson	10	B	16,028	1,600	1,276	10.02	14,752	NA	NA	23,000	2	0	0	16,028	0	
Wellwood minilibrary																
MICHIGAN																
Caro	11	M	692,321	14,500	501,022	35.00	76,699	NA	114,599	50,000	54	200,000	0	492,321	22,381	Drive-up window; lower level theater; upstairs balcony
Grand Rapids	10	B	575,155	9,720	464,884	58.90	45,000	NA	65,271	15,050	48	NA	NA	533,101	28,000	
Grand Rapids	20	B	329,791	6,250	255,645	40.90	26,830	30,000	17,316	30,000	52	161,000	0	168,791	0	
Saginaw	30	B	700,000	15,600	601,172	38.54	59,428	NA	39,398	45,000	35	500,000	0	200,000	0	
MINNESOTA																
Longville	2	B	36,500	1,440	33,700	23.40	2,800	10,000	0	9,000	14	0	0	2,000	34,500	Multi-purpose municipal building, includes ambulance and city council and clerk offices
Mankato	2	MS	1,348,082	38,400	1,153,082	35.10	195,000	NA	NA	150,000	163	139,500	0	300,000	0	
Pine City		B	94,400	2,047	81,875	40.00	11,900	0	625	10,000	20	71,750	0	22,650	site	Library combined with city hall
MISSISSIPPI																
Brookhaven	45	S	120,454	2,290	104,050	45.44	8,600	NA	7,804	NA	NA	0	60,227	60,227	0	
Collins	2	B	222,980	4,140	165,678	40.01	22,261	NA	35,041	12,150	22	0	107,740	107,740	7,500	
Crenshaw	1	B	113,200	2,856	89,092	31.19	17,820	NA	6,288	11,000	24	0	56,600	18,656	37,944	
D'Iberville	7	B	156,600	3,256	99,931	30.69	33,466	NA	7,403	NA	23	0	78,300	78,300	0	
Gulfport	41	B	200,000	3,830	115,672	30.20	38,150	NA	8,678	NA	30	0	100,000	100,000	0	
Hazlehurst	34	S	160,000	4,646	219,645	47.27	25,468	NA	14,887	27,000	40	0	130,000	42,000	88,000	

PUBLIC LIBRARY BUILDINGS IN 1979 / 417

Holly Springs	24	S		292,904	7,169	228,922	31.93	25,848	NA	38,134	23,000	42	0	146,452	143,610	2,842	
Laurel	56	S		721,114	24,353	453,954	18.64	56,343	NA	35,876	100,000	100	0	200,000	521,114	0	
New Albany	19	S		220,000	4,557	153,657	40.65	52,626	NA	13,717	50,775	40	0	110,000	102,000	8,000	
Rolling Fork	2	B		56,258	1,250	42,232	33.78	10,954	NA	3,072	NA	0	0	27,650	28,608	0	
Southaven	9	B		400,000	9,000	249,880	27.76	72,128	NA	77,992	35,000	62	0	200,000	200,000	0	
Vicksburg	25	B		1,571,873	36,660	1,134,940	30.96	123,186	NA	313,747	114,000	150	0	200,000	1,360,643	11,230	
MISSOURI																	
Bridgeton	75	B		966,809	17,600	672,000	38.18	150,846	90,289	64,831	90,000	150	0	0	0	0	One level
Farmington	8	M		188,000	4,200	168,000	45.00	30,000	NA	NA	28,000	45	0	0	188,000	0	
St. Louis	50	B		1,246,168	20,500	922,464	45.00	158,036	51,017	83,088	100,000	168	0	0	0	0	
NEBRASKA																	
Alma	2	M		155,000	3,400	132,000	38.80	17,000	1,000	NA	13,000	60	0	0	5,000	150,000	In city park
NEW JERSEY																	
Allendale	6	M		NA	7,800	NA	NA	42,000	NA	NA	50,000	64	NA	NA	NA	NA	
Elmwood Park	22	M		946,000	12,600	NA	NA	85,000	NA	NA	65,000	93	821,000	NA	NA	125,000	
Hanover Twp.	11	M		333,000	5,175	293,000	56.62	40,000	NA	NA	40,000	42	0	0	293,000	1,000	
Manville	13	M		906,000	14,500	90,000	64.41	90,000	NA	NA	75,000	90	906,000	0	28,000	0	
South River	15	M		808,000	8,000	718,000	89.00	40,000	NA	28,000	30,000	44	718,000	0	50,000	40,000	
W. Paterson	12	M		422,267	7,180	335,000	46.65	29,898	87,267	50,000	45,000	55	338,000	0	162,000	32,000	Structured to receive second floor expansion in future
NEW MEXICO																	
Jal	3	M	1,270,000	15,300	1,100,000	71.00	90,000	NA	NA	35,000	112	0	0	1,270,000	Recessed below grade for energy savings.
Las Cruces	85	M	2,166,787	28,000	1,552,608	55.45	141,000	322,420	150,757	140,000	207	2,166,787	0	0	0	Recessed; adjacent outdoor amphitheater; 2 meeting rooms for 200
Roswell	60	M	1,250,000	22,500	937,519	41.67	211,635	17,846	83,000	110,000	182	0	0	1,250,000	0	Glass enclosed circulation area; children's courtyard
Santa Fe	20	B	1,166,140	22,070	1,080,067	48.94	91,000	NA	NA	40,000	95	1,166,140	0	0	0	Solar heated; shares building with swimming pool and juvenile division of police dept.

TABLE 1   NEW PUBLIC LIBRARY BUILDINGS CONSTRUCTED DURING YEAR ENDING JUNE 30, 1979 (cont.)

Community	Pop in M	Code	Project Cost	Gross Sq. Ft.	Const. Cost	Sq. Ft. Cost	Equip. Cost	Site Cost	Other Costs	Vols.	Reader Seats	Fed. Funds	State Funds	Local Govt. Funds	Gift/Other Funds	Notes
NEW YORK																
Camden	5	B	57,972	784	NA	NA	NA	NA	NA	14,000	NA	0	0	10,000	47,000	Maypole structure for column-free space
Chappaqua	13	M/Sc	2,257,000	25,440	1,406,000	55.26	195,000	227,000	202,000	70,000	100	0	0	0	2,257,000	
Chittenango	12	M	196,000	2,400	155,000	NA	20,000	NA	NA	20,000	20	NA	0	0	5,000	Skylight; heat and A/C by heat pump
Ellenburg Ctr.	1	B	48,720	1,350	1,920	36.09	NA	NA	NA	3,500	36	48,720	0	0	0	First library in town, this reading center, includes a classroom area.
Henrietta	33	M	1,360,435	20,000	1,152,274	57.61	106,665	NA	101,496	66,000	109	1,360,435	0	0	0	Solar heated.
Howard Beach (Queens, NYC)	36	B	668,218	7,500	423,218	56.00	50,000	45,000	150,000	40,000	100	0	0	668,218	0	
New York	NA	NA	4,000,000	40,000	3,000,000	90.00	350,000	NA	NA	300,000	NA	4,000,000	0	0	0	Schomburg Center for Research on Black Culture, open to all researchers; multi-media collection
NORTH CAROLINA																
Bayboro	9	M/Sc	421,594	10,557	421,594	40.00	51,500	NA	NA	15,000	90	20,000	381,594	41,500	0	First library in North Carolina built as joint school-public library
Gastonia	157	MS	2,158,391	60,000	1,803,134	35.97	241,000	*	114,257	250,000	240	2,158,391	0	0	*	*Gift of city
Mayodan	10	B	348,146	5,500	313,261	63.29	33,424	NA	1,460	25,000	32	235,518	0	94,898	17,730	
Shallotte	13	B	94,396	2,300	82,430	35.84	9,399	NA	2,566	7,500	28	0	0	50,503	43,893	

PUBLIC LIBRARY BUILDINGS IN 1979 / 419

Walnut Cove	1	B	211,371	4,692	170,000	45.05	20,000	NA	21,371	25,000	30	108,000	0	60,000	43,371	Landscaped grounds include picnic tables
OHIO															
Cleveland	629	B	681,999	10,400	577,657	66.33	58,226	NA	46,116	20,000	62	NA	NA	NA	NA	Reading garden
Cleveland	629	B	620,711	8,300	507,463	61.50	63,100	NA	50,068	20,000	67	NA	NA	NA	NA	Exterior reading court
Gallipolis	27	M	448,236	8,000	333,013	41.82	53,990	NA	61,233	75,000	32	0	0	NA	325,000	
Marion	65	M	1,642,724	27,444	1,305,419	47.57	203,772	102,251	30,951	111,000	150	25,000	1,642,393	0	0	First in community center complex
N. Royalton	19	B	879,000	15,641	672,000	56.20	109,820	NA	83,711	60,000	87	0	0	879,000	NA	
West Milton	9	Sc	350,000	7,800	315,000	44.00	6,000	25,000	NA	45,000	117	10,000	0	250,000	90,000	
OREGON															
Shady Grove	4	B	125,000	3,000	102,000	34.00	5,416	NA	17,584	10,000	44	0	0	125,000	0	
Sutherlin	6	B	180,000	3,700	158,000	40.00	7,000	20,000	NA	18,000	42	0	3,000	58,000	100,000	
PENNSYLVANIA															
Martinsburg	2	B	1,100,000	NA	176,000	NA	15,000	7,500	NA	17,000	75	0	0	NA	NA	
Philadelphia	325	B	1,744,922	23,800	1,422,285	60.60	79,235	85,075	138,397	100,000	342	86,167	0	1,658,825	0	
Pittsburgh	67	M	1,772,026	30,000	1,276,302	59.04	365,725	NA	130,000*	185,000	190	NA	NA	NA	18,000	*Computer. Drive-up window and reading patio/deck are included
Warminster	438	M	645,484	15,488	480,444	31.02	109,654	NA	55,186	64,000	151	0	0	643,768	1,716	
SOUTH CAROLINA															
Bennettsville	27	M	519,990	8,500	387,297	45.56	57,703	30,000	44,990	60,000	52	482,590	0	37,400	0	Multi-colored lighting in interior
Charleston	27	B	291,335	6,091	217,703	35.74	32,298	35,000	6,334	30,000	45	256,335	0	35,000	0	
Salem	.5	B	25,500*	1,000	18,000	NA	7,500	NA	548	10,000	25	25,500	0	0	0	*For total project; city hall is 2,900 sq. ft., library is 1,000 sq. ft.
Walhalla	41	M	916,646	23,540	739,600	31.42	98,271	0		150,000	100	916,646	0	0	0	Solar heated; north skylights
Westminster	3	B	326,019	326,019	5,000	295,863	59.17	NA	10,156	25,000	50	326,019	0	0	0	Solar heated; north skylights

TABLE 1 NEW PUBLIC LIBRARY BUILDINGS CONSTRUCTED DURING YEAR ENDING JUNE 30, 1979 (cont.)

Community	Pop in M	Code	Project Cost	Gross Sq. Ft.	Const. Cost	Sq. Ft. Cost	Equip. Cost	Site Cost	Other Costs	Vols.	Reader Seats	Fed. Funds	State Funds	Local Govt. Funds	Gift/Other Funds	Notes
SOUTH DAKOTA																
Vermillion	13	M	710,182	11,000	NA	64.56	56,000	NA	NA	60,000	56	550,000	0	84182	42,678	
TENNESSEE																
Memphis	30	B	171,500	5,000	146,500	29.30	16,000	NA	8,500	18,000	50	0	150,000	21,500	0	Part of community center
Paris	27		377,021	8,364	295,685	35.35	42,153	34,350	4,833	25,000	64	0	0	250,000	127,021	
TEXAS																
Angleton	133	M	1,145,086	22,000	787,568	35.62	180,988	NA	NA	109,320	96	1,145,086	0	0	21,000*	*Raised by Friends
Austin	367	M	5,523,428	110,633	4,960,058	44.83	563,370	NA	NA	400,000	592	0	0	5,523,428	0	One of two U.S. libraries using Mosler Telelift System
Lake Jackson	20	B	350,000	10,000	350,000	33.65	70,000	NA	NA	35,000	58	0	0	350,000	0	
Orange	NA	M	1,138,034	20,062	911,600	45.44	57,622	60,000	108,812	75,000	120	0	0	1,000,000	138,034	First building in Orange specifically for library; previous sites were post office and woman's club
Plano	66	B	1,027,763	26,246	785,000	29.91	76,313	NA	166,450	65,000	114	0	0	990,000	45,000	
Texarkana	59	M	1,303,762	20,516	1,079,493	52.62	104,500	NA	119,769	100,000	100	1,303,762	0	0	0	At the Texas-Arkansas border, designed with few windows on west and south sides
Woodlands	18	B	210,435	5,000	133,720	42.08	18,000	NA	76,715	50,000	150	105,000	0	51,603	53,832	Built in cruciform
VIRGINIA																
Arlington	167	B	1,104,000	10,000	961,811	96.18	77,189	NA	65,000	35,000	90	0	0	1,100,000	4,000	Houses fire station, recreation center

PUBLIC LIBRARY BUILDINGS IN 1979 / 421

Chesapeake	18	B	314,265	6,300	253,300	40.20	30,000	NA	30,965	35,000	68	314,265	0	0	0	Inner court
Roanoke	63	B	278,017	5,115	231,000	45.00	27,838	NA	19,179	18,000	86	0	0	278,017	0	
Virginia Beach	269	B	7,578	8,067	352,824	43.74	59,786	NA	NA	45,000	120	0	0	447,578	0	
Wytheville	23	B	313,903	8,500	198,863	NA	59,500	35,000	20,540	50,000	80	138,903	0	60,000	115,000	Constructed by CETA personnel
WASHINGTON																
Bremerton	129		2,112,648	38,752	1,521,571	39.26	370,821		311,250	120,000	223	0	0	2,108,290	4,358	Emphasis on energy efficiency
Burlington	4	M	241,025	3,880	NA	62.12	32,000	NA	NA	20,000	28	565,000	NA	345,000	NA	Complex also contains city offices and police dept.
Centralia	62	B	1,182,200	13,510	760,600	56.00	170,000	NA	251,600	40,000	88	1,182,200	0	0	0	Playground equip.
Olympia	27	B	1,691,480	20,840	1,226,664	58.86	100,000	NA	364,816	75,000	100	175,000	0	1,500,000	198,014	Designed around central reading room
Seattle	28	B	1,138,900	9,000	638,595	71.00	76,631	90,000	6,386	30,000	90	NA	NA	NA	NA	
WEST VIRGINIA																
Barrett	2	B	46,095	1,250	38,980	36.88	5,615	NA	1,500	6,000	24	0	30,350	15,745	NA	Unattached addition also included
Branchland	1	B	20,000	480	17,750	36.98	2,100	NA	150	4,500	12	0	18,000	2,000	0	Heat pump
Brandywine	2	B	20,000	480	17,750	36.98	2,100	NA	150	4,500	12	0	18,000	2,000	0	Heat pump
Center Point	6	B	20,000	480	17,750	36.98	2,100	NA	150	4,500	12	0	18,000	2,000	0	Heat pump
Circleville	2	B	20,000	480	17,750	36.98	2,100	NA	150	4,500	12	0	18,000	2,000	0	Heat pump
Cowen	3	B	49,941	1,250	41,127	39.95	7,214	NA	1,600	6,000	24	0	49,941	0	0	
Eleanor	1	B	20,000	480	17,750	36.98	2,100	NA	150	4,500	12	0	18,000	2,000	0	Heat pump
Gilbert	1	B	20,000	480	17,750	36.98	2,100	NA	150	4,500	12	0	18,000	2,000	0	Heat pump
Glenville	4	B	58,646	1,250	50,000	46.92	7,146	NA	1,500	6,000	24	0	52,500	6,146	0	
Hundred	1	B	20,000	480	17,750	36.98	2,100	NA	150	4,500	12	0	18,000	2,000	0	Heat pump
Matewan	1	B	20,000	480	17,750	36.98	2,100	NA	150	4,500	12	0	18,000	2,000	0	Heat pump
Mt. Hope	5	B	57,437	1,250	42,815	45.51	7,122	6,000	1,500	6,000	24	0	50,050	7,387	0	
Oak Hill	52	S	286,179	5,366	243,765	53.33	27,606	NA	14,808	30,000	NA	0	203,022	15,000	68,157	Also unattached addition
Ronceverte	2	B	20,000	480	17,750	36.98	2,100	NA	150	4,500	12	0	18,000	2,000	0	Heat pump
Thomas	2	B	20,000	480	17,750	36.98	2,100	NA	150	4,500	12	0	18,000	2,000	0	Heat pump
WISCONSIN																
Brown Deer	15	M	745,000	15,000	581,000	50.00	108,000		56,139	50,000	60	745,000	0	0	0	Skylight and patio/garden
Chilton	3	M	237,438	6,152	237,411	NA	27,719	NA	NA	NA	40	0	0	137,411	100,000	
WYOMING																
Pine Bluffs	3	B	151,000	NA	132,000	NA	9,000	10,000	NA	8,000	20	136,000	0	11,000	4,000	
Ten Sleep	1	B	65,274	3,200	65,274	NA	0	NA	NA	30,000	25	65,274	0	0	0	School library also in building

TABLE 2 PUBLIC LIBRARY BUILDING ADDITIONS, REMODELINGS, AND RENOVATIONS

Community	Pop in M	Code	Project Cost	Gross Sq. Ft.	Const. Cost	Sq. Ft. Cost	Equip. Cost	Other Costs	Vols.	Reader Seats	Fed. Funds	State Funds	Local Govt. Funds	Gift/Other Funds	Notes
CALIFORNIA Hayward	100	M	1,797	25,400	1,436,684	74.00	225,000	135,000	120,000	142	1,715,000	0	82,000	0	Proximity to Hayward earthquake required special foundation & construction
Los Alamitos	33	B	440,000	5,000	380,000	38.00	16,778	NA	50,000	84	0	0	440,000	1,000	
Manteca	23	B	704,604	9,228	593,715	64.34	44,589	66,300	60,000	63	704,604	0	0	0	
Pacific Grove	18	M	347,171	6,050	301,362	36.85	20,000	25,865	75,000	117	228,140	0	85,105	33,926	
Santa Barbara	175	M	4,096,627	52,000	3,080,000	57.88	569,000	464,662	300,000	300	3,378,000	0	250,000	40,000	Existing building unsound, requiring new structure
CONNECTICUT New Milford	17	M	709,000	18,684	664,000	3,050	45,000	17,000	90,000	57	664,000	0	0	62,000	Renovation and addition to 1896 English Gothic building and Federal period clapboard house structure with modern wing
COLORADO Aurora	180	B	18,000	2,500	10,000	NA	8,000	0	10,000	16	0	0	18,000	0	
Englewood	35	M	194,796	6,300	NA	NA	NA	NA	150,000	16	0	0	194,796	0	Includes price of new bookmobile garage
FLORIDA Bradenton	35	B	96,285	1,000	87,000	NA	5,285	2,000	25,000	20	56,000	0	35,000	1,285	CETA labor used
GEORGIA Lavonia	3	B	117,768	3,378	92,224	27.30	17,078	8,526	15,000	18	100,000	15,000	1,068	1,700	

PUBLIC LIBRARY BUILDINGS IN 1979 / 423

Willacoochee	3	B	5,000	1,064	NA	4.00	NA	NA	NA	15	0	0	5,000	0	Remodeled building was formerly an old log cabin belonging to the Woman's Club
IDAHO															
Council	2	M	9,374	2,810	78,550	28.24	5,600	NA	30,000	80	0	0	32,000	48,000	2 pre-built classrooms connected in "L" shape
Gooding	3	M	320,000	NA	301,581	27.12	13,915	362	30,000	38	333,348	5,000	0	9,278	Remodeled supermarket
ILLINOIS															
Chicago	11	B	201,575	5,800*	161,375	27.82	40,200	NA	28,000	102	0	0	201,575	0	Store front library *Garage/storage area = 1,370 sq. ft.: Public service area = 4,330 sq. ft.
DeKalb	32	M	342,195	4,934	287,785	58.33	16,831	37,579	17,976	60	0	0	342,195	0	
Dunlap	4	M	37,486	1,500	29,447	19.63	7,212	826	15,000	18	0	0	37,486	0	
Knoxville	3	M	NA	3,155	NA	NA	0	NA	NA	34	0	0	13,746	4,638	Building gift of First Farmers National Bank of Knoxville
Lombard	40	M	1,728,538	34,300	1,277,737	50.39	290,750	160,051	192,500	171	0	0	1,728,538	0	Remodeling on ground level
Orion	3	M	135,000	2,808	119,439	48.00	10,221	NA	20,000	110	0	0	2,000	88,200	
Park Ridge	43	M	1,100,000	17,848	770,000	43.14	180,000	102,000	168,000	220	0	0	1,100,000	0	
Prairie View	9	M	538,716	11,196	487,241	43.28	51,475	40,000	40,000	43	NA	NA	NA	500,000	Property was former nursery with many trees
Wheaton	40,846	M	1,750,000	71,918	1,550,000	34.25	200,000	NA	270,000	380	0	0	1,550,000	200,000	
INDIANA															
Flora	5	M	16,650	896	8,658	9.66	7,992	NA	8,436	15	NA	NA	NA	16,650	Children's room bookstacks can be moved to the side for movies and story hours
Mishawaka	55	M	38,813	70	35,285	504.08	0	3,528	0	0	0	38,813	0	0	Passenger elevator

424 / LIBRARY RESEARCH AND STATISTICS

TABLE 2   PUBLIC LIBRARY BUILDING ADDITIONS, REMODELINGS, AND RENOVATIONS (cont.)

Community	Pop in M	Code	Project Cost	Gross Sq. Ft.	Const. Cost	Sq. Ft. Cost	Equip. Cost	Other Costs	Vols.	Reader Seats	Fed. Funds	State Funds	Local Govt. Funds	Gift/ Other Funds	Notes
IOWA																
Corydon	2	M	106,212	4,824	72,950	15.12	21,262	NA	9,852	40	0	0	0	106,212	No tax money used, all gift funds
Garnaville	1	M	23,053	2,820	13,000	5.57	10,053	NA	15,000	30	2,000	NA	NA	21,000	Former theater
Ottumwa	42	M	43,401	NA	34,401	NA	NA	NA	NA	NA	34,401	0	0	0	Passenger elevator
Pella	10	M	229,489	9,568	197,724	24.00	17,917	13,848	31,000	75	0	0	149,000	79,000	Serves 3 counties and 2 school system
Summer	NA	M	2,523	NA	800	NA	500	1200	500	NA	350	0	1,673	500	
West Bend	1	M	60,571	1,728	53,571	31.00	7,000	NA	4,954	27	0	0	0	60,571*	*Donated by community member
Winterset	16	M	47,110	2,900	37,355	12.88	7,513	2,241	5,000	48	NA	NA	24,672	22,437	
KANSAS																
Girard	3	M	NA	3,838	NA	NA	NA	NA	13,525	96	0	0	NA	NA	
MAINE																
Augusta	22	M	770,000	13,141	644,225	49.02	33,209	NA	50,000	60	550,000	0	220,000	0	Preservation & restoration of 1896 historic building
Orrington	3	Sc	105,320	3,281	98,430	30.00	10,944	NA	14,000	68	105,320	0	0	2895	School/public library; solar dome
Wells	4	M	249,900	3,640	208,226	57.20	24,102	17,572	30,000	55	249,900	0	0	0	
MARYLAND																
Bladensburg	16	B	40,000	5,500	25,766	4.68	14,234	NA	20,000	27	0	0	0	40,000*	*From newly instituted overdue fines system
Maryland City	12	B	150,000	3,700	15,397	4.16	30,905	103,698	12,000	30	0	0	150,000	0	Bookstore atmosphere; 2 shopping center stores renovated
Williamsport	5	B	356,000	7,600	305,590	40.21	27,002	22,408	26,500	33	354,000	2,000	0	0	

PUBLIC LIBRARY BUILDINGS IN 1979 / 425

MICHIGAN												
Adrian	20	M	490,430	34,000	176,941	9.31	66,724	246,765	100,000	104	306,016	0	0	184,414	Purchased existing J.C. Penny store
Coldwater	39	S	1,008,740	15,000	781,000	52.00	106,110	11,500	60,000	73	721,000	0	280,300	0	
Mason	530	S	257,130	7,000	249,488	36.73	0	0	NA	NA	240,000	0	17,129	0	Addition was a community room
Norton Shores	23	B	215,300	3,100	191,000	61.61	7,300	17,000	NA	NA	210,000	0	5,300	0	
Oxford	11	M	100,467	2,000	85,089	50.00	7,186	8,192	10,000	60	0	0	100,467	0	
MISSOURI												
Marionville	2	B	37,449	2,310	17,488	7.57	2,200	NA	15,000	25	0	0	19,500	18,449	
Van Buren	NA	S	NA	NA	NA	NA	NA	1,500	NA	40	0	0	1,500	250	Paid for with overdue fines
West Plains	10	M	10,000	NA	5,000	NA	5,000	NA	15,000	NA	0	0	0	0	
MONTANA												
Livingston	13	M	231,355	3,420	209,128	61.15	NA	NA	60,000	50	0	0	231,355	0	
NEBRASKA												
Axtell	1	M	3,754	300	3,078	10.26	676	1,775	5,200	18	505	500	211	529	
Lincoln	184	MS	711,595	10,000	598,308	59.83	97,600	15,687	NA	NA	711,595	0	0	0	
Ravenna	1	B	8,555	840	5,524	6.58	803	2,229	2,000	25	281	794	2,003	5,476	Drab basement turned into children's reading room
NEW HAMPSHIRE												
Salem	26	M	548,421	9,150	399,610	60.00	88,184	47,605	64,300	127	534,880	0	3,720	0	
NEW JERSEY												
Wayne	20	B	168,480	9,000	128,410	21.00	25,095	14,975	30,000	36	0	146,623	0	21,857	A converted elementary school
West Orange	45	M	954,286	29,000	792,286	27.32	90,000	72,000	147,000	110	400,000	0	554,000	0	
NEW YORK												
Blue Point	13	M	288,580	7,000	256,081	36.58	NA	32,499	45,000	NA	200,000	0	88,580	0	
Dundee	2	M	80,000	2,596	72,318	55.00	NA	NA	NA	20	0	0	0	80,000	
Ellenburg Depot	1	B	1,627	444	NA	3.67	NA	NA	NA	8	NA	NA	900	176	
Greece	75	B	201,800	4,085	177,000	43.33	15,000	22,300	12,000	20	NA	NA	NA	NA	Renovation of former grocery store into library/community center
Greenlawn	20	Sc	45,406	2,400	28,635	12.00	13,771	3,000	15,000	20	NA	NA	NA	NA	
Malone	15	M	208,000	1,024	171,000	166.99	2,977	0	12,000	0	208,000	0	2,977	0	
Mt. Kisco	8	M	497,000	3,579	386,849	108.09	30,000	80,151	50,000	190	160,000	0	307,000	30,000	

426 / LIBRARY RESEARCH AND STATISTICS

TABLE 2 PUBLIC LIBRARY BUILDING ADDITIONS, REMODELINGS, AND RENOVATIONS (cont.)

Community	Pop in M	Code	Project Cost	Gross Sq. Ft.	Const. Cost	Sq. Ft. Cost	Equip. Cost	Other Costs	Vols.	Reader Seats	Fed. Funds	State Funds	Local Govt. Funds	Gift/Other Funds	Notes
Orwell	1	M	6,018	567	5,033	10.52	985	NA	5,750	14	0	0	1,518	4,500	Renovated rooms in town hall
Pittsford	25	B	70,874	1,550	45,889	29.61	22,093	2,892	4,000	15	NA	NA	NA	NA	Remodeled
Plattsburgh	19	M	16,500	4,800	6,500	3.43	9,500	NA	14,000	26	0	0	3,600	12,900	Interior construction done by inmates of Clinton Correctional Facility
Port Jervis	13	M	75,000	7,400	NA	NA	21,500	NA	40,000	70	0	0	75,000	0	
Tarrytown	20	M	1,302,000	14,000	1,080,000	62.00	70,000	151,800	80,000	78	1,302,000	0	0	0	
Uniondale	1,429	S	1,051,049	33,300	525,550	32.76	53,000	495,000	100,000	NA	0	0	0	NA	Former supermarket plus 6 stores
NORTH CAROLINA														
Asheville	60	M	2,486,480	52,000	1,788,668	34.40	219,338	NA	193,000	152	1,428,000	0	45,480	13,000	Indoor access to 750 car garage
Boone	25	M	49,630	7,000	44,630	6.80	5,000	0	60,000	30	48,000	47,630	2,000	NA	Library is on ground floor of rock building from 1930s WPA
Spring Lake	6	B	68,000	4,516	61,000	NA	7,000	NA	20,000	25	56,000	0	12,000	NA	Renovation of former city hall
Troy	19	B	292,217	6,300	236,404	4,638	22,904	33,719	43,748	107	286,000	0	6,217	0	
OHIO														
Cleveland (E. 131 St.)	629	B	84,715	13,700	378,333	47.00	30,695	16,186	20,000	42	NA	NA	NA	NA	Historic landmark building
Cleveland (Carnegie-West)	629	B	1,046,582	28,000	807,379	69.00	93,040	146,163	22,000	61	NA	NA	NA	NA	A single-story addition
Painesville	40	M	545,909	10,000	392,054	54.59	105,812	48,042	100,000	156	0	0	0	545,909	
OREGON														
Canyonville	5	B	6,103	302	6,103	20.20	0	NA	9,000	5	0	3,000	1,453	1,650	

PUBLIC LIBRARY BUILDINGS IN 1979 / 427

PENNSYLVANIA													
Indiana	25	M	240,946	6,428	178,005	37.48	42,818	20,147	68,000	64	0	0	13,000	241,117	
Lancaster	320	MS	50,000	3,502	45,000	12.86	3,000	2,000	60,000	63	0	0	0	50,000	
TENNESSEE															
Clarksville	75	MS	418,000	16,075	361,310	22.50	25,190	31,500	40,000	78	350,000	0	71,800	18,000	
TEXAS															
Bellville	5	B	108,337	4,500	72,992	24.30	24,000	0	25,000	38	0	0	0	108,337	
VIRGINIA															
Hampton	4	B	48,177	1,870	42,217	22.58	5,960	NA	25,000	20	47,182	0	995	0	Moved from store front to cafeteria in school building
Waynesboro	NA	M	871,000	14,500	861,000	NA	10,000	NA	NA	NA	711,000	NA	150,000	10,000	
WASHINGTON															
Kirkland	30	B	325,913	10,502	221,853	21.12	47,207	NA	60,000	52	0	0	320,913	5,000	In conjunction with Senior Citizen's Center; 2 stained glass windows
Marysville	251	S	358,195	6,400	292,142	45.46	47,159	NA	NA	0	0	0	358,195	0	
Mukilteo	1	B	NA	660	NA	NA	NA	NA	10,000	23	NA	NA	NA	5,000	Part of community center
North Bend	3	B	46,782	3,036	44,385	14.62	NA	2,397	17,000	20	12,385	0	24,000	8,000	Now connected to Museum
Seattle	2,000	MS	2,315,649	197,000	1,822,176	18.00	239,473	254,000	900,000	817	2,315,649	0	0	0	
Tacoma	35	B	95,000	1,629	79,700	48.93	NA	NA	NA	NA	95,000	0	0	0	
West Richard	3	B	NA	960	NA	NA	NA	5,600	8	NA	NA	NA	NA	200	Renovated city hall; before library service was by bookmobile only
WISCONSIN															
Dorchester	1	M	2,160	NA	NA	NA	NA	NA	NA	NA	0	0	2,160	0	
Sun Prairie	20	NA	113,500	4,451	110,000	21.00	3,500	NA	60,000	65	0	0	50,000	63,500	

TABLE 3 LEASED PUBLIC LIBRARY BUILDING SPACE NEWLY OCCUPIED DURING YEAR ENDING JUNE 30, 1977

Symbol code: B—Branch Library; BS—Branch & System Headquarters; M—Main Library; MS—Main & System Headquarters; S—System Headquarters; NA—Not Available

Community	Pop in M	Code	Gross Cost	Const. Sq. Ft.	Sq. Ft. Cost	Equip. Cost	Site Cost	Other Costs	Vols.	Reader Seats	Fed. Funds	State Funds	Local Govt. Funds	Gift/Other Funds
Kalispell, Mont.	48	M	764,700	14,715	43.81	0	NA	65,800	150,000	100	764,000	0	700	0
Lemon Grove, Calif.	21	B	NA	9,000	NA	24,300	NA	NA	55,000	140	0	0	NA	0
Littleton, Colo.	37	M	NA	12,000	NA	3,000	8.70/sq. Ft.	2,000	50,000	140	0	0	NA	0
Mt. Zion, Ill.	6	M	7,100	608	11.68	0	NA	0	2,500	26	0	0	7,100	0
Santa Clara, Calif.	NA	B	NA	6,890	NA	NA	2,790.45/mo.	NA	75,000	84	0	0	NA	0

TABLE 4 SIX-YEAR COST SUMMARY—PUBLIC LIBRARY BUILDINGS

(For 1969 thru 1973 data, see p. 3518 of December 1, 1973 *Library Journal*, or p. 263 of 1974 *Bowker Annual*)

	Fiscal 1974	Fiscal 1975	Fiscal 1976	Fiscal 1977	Fiscal 1978	Fiscal 1979
Number of new bldgs.	121	125	187	142	135	165
Number of ARR's (1)	74	87	90	69	83	99
Sq. ft., new bldgs.	1,649,962	1,474,751	1,817,272	2,100,016	1,355,130	2,794,667
Sq. ft., ARR's	514,393	586,854	980,338	585,635	624,755	853,875
New bldgs:						
Construction cost	$51,427,583	$47,860,591	$66,374,466	$85,986,538	$54,508,361	92,015,718
Equipment cost	5,410,499	5,982,891	8,212,051	10,727,160	7,433,541	12,672,493
Site cost	6,574,522	4,364,214	5,266,693	8,401,254	5,508,018	2,816,422
Other costs	5,458,811	5,417,981	7,858,816	9,442,938	6,712,240	8,106,465
Total—Project cost	68,871,415	63,625,677	87,712,026	114,557,890	74,162,160	115,611,098
ARR's—Project cost	13,918,096	17,220,607	36,966,911	17,144,009	16,773,136	28,877,686
New & ARR Project cost	$82,789,511	$80,846,284	$124,678,937	$131,701,899	$90,935,296	$144,488,784
Fund Sources:						
Federal, new bldgs.	$6,152,183	$8,599,789	$23,030,416	$19,226,511	$13,304,652	62,713,111
Federal, ARR's	1,414,257	2,924,804	4,323,509	1,149,718	4,046,901	18,107,556
Federal, total	$7,566,440	$11,524,593	$27,353,925	$20,376,229	$17,351,553	$80,820,667

PUBLIC LIBRARY BUILDINGS IN 1979 / 429

State, new bldgs.	$1,483,444	$1,955,815	$5,241,537	$5,757,047	$5,803,920	13,797,410
State, ARR's	282,739	823,164	2,264,815	1,381,725	1,095,665	1,282,911
State, total	$1,766,183	$2,778,979	$7,506,352	$7,138,772	$6,899,585	$15,080,321
Local, new bldgs.	$56,225,651	$46,813,074	$50,501,926	$82,266,956	$47,193,528	69,244,923
Local, ARR's	11,172,752	12,049,376	26,900,408	13,286,234	10,364,429	9,299,527
Local, total	$67,398,403	$58,862,450	$77,402,334	$95,553,190	$57,557,957	78,544,450
Gift, new bldgs.	$5,010,137	$6,256,999	$8,938,147	$7,307,376	$7,860,060	11,390,586
Gift, ARR's	1,048,348	1,423,263	3,478,179	1,326,332	1,266,141	1,282,911
Gift, total	$6,058,485	$7,680,262	$12,416,326	$8,633,708	$9,126,201	$12,763,497
Total funds used	$82,789,511	$80,846,284	$124,678,937	$131,701,899	$90,935,296	$106,298,268

(1) Additions, Remodelings and Renovations

TABLE 5 CANADA—PUBLIC LIBRARY BUILDINGS

Community	Pop in M	Code	Project Cost	Gross Sq. Ft.	Const. Cost	Sq. Ft. Cost	Equip. Cost	Site Cost	Other Costs	Vols.	Reader Seats	Fed. Funds	State Funds	Local Govt. Funds	Gifts Funds	Notes
ALBERTA																
Camrose	11	M	555,000*	6,233	470,000	75.00	32,000	NA	40,000	NA	NA	0	250,000	300,000	5,000	*Plus land
Claresholm	4	M	217,927	4,000	206,066	51.52	9,402	NA	2,459	15,000	30	0	98,045	95,452	24,200	
Drumheller	6	M	575,000	5,400	NA	55.00	NA	NA	NA	NA	32	150,000		200,000	200,000	
															25,000	
Ft. Saskatchewan	10	M	1,430,000	20,000	1,149,815	57.49	230,000	NA	50,000	47,611	90	0		570,000	860,000	Basement for town recreation dept.
Ft. McMurray	30	M	NA	20,000	NA	NA	NA	NA	NA	50,000	NA	NA	NA	NA	NA	
Red Deer	38	M	593,000	8,625	593,000	69.00	NA	NA	NA	100,000	70	0		296,500	29,650	
															266,850	
Whitecourt	5	M	350,000	5,000	350,000	61.00	14,000	NA	NA	25,000	21	NA	NA	NA	NA	2nd floor addition
BRITISH COLUMBIA																
West Vancouver	37	M	1,244,215	26,000	1,2367,631	48.00	35,750	NA	NA	150,000	160	0	333,333	995,182	15,700	

Once again this year, *LJ* extends thanks to the state and territorial library agencies which collected and delivered the architectural issue questionnaires which provide the information for this annual tabulation. Their efforts were supplemented by *LJ* staffers, who followed up every fleeting reference found to a new or remodeled building and, for the first time, did the massive job of tabulation in-house. As ever, there will be some projects that have been missed; reports on these are still welcome and will be both added to next year's report and used to correct this year's statistical results.

This year's tally of additions, remodelings, and renovations totaled 99.

An impressive array of buildings not originally designed to house books and libraries found themselves entering new lives as local public libraries. These ranged from a log cabin to two former supermarkets and 11 stores, two city halls, a theater, a basement, an elementary school, a school cafeteria, and a house.

The taut financial character of the year was reflected in many instances, among them two projects—for $40,000 and $10,000—fully paid for out of overdue fines, and another in which free labor contributed by jail inmates was a vital element. And as with wholly new buildings reported this year, there were several examples of space sharing with other organizations either in a building or a complex. Among these were a senior center, a community center, and a museum.

The growing, if reluctant, edging of school and public libraries into cooperative action could be seen in reports of space being refurbished and provided for joint school/public use in Pella, Iowa, and Orrington, Maine. Orrington also provided the sole mention in this group of a solar component.

It seemed noteworthy that the report of the Maryland City project included the proud observation that their new space has a "bookstore atmosphere." There speaks the voice of 1979, loud and clear.

ACADEMIC LIBRARY BUILDINGS IN 1979

Karl Nyren
Senior Editor, *Library Journal*

Barbara Livingston
Assistant Editor, *Library Journal*

Bette-Lee Fox
Associate Editor, *Library Journal*

After a one-year hiatus, *Library Journal* again continues the series of compilations of academic library construction and remodeling which had been produced annually by Jerrold Orne until 1977. In 1978, the apparent scarcity of academic library construction led to the decision to skip a year; the few projects announced seemed unlikely to yield statistical results of significance. The disappearance of the academic library feature from the Architectural Issue, however, alarmed many who have come to depend upon it.

The extensive work of locating and getting reports on new projects was handled this year by the staff of *LJ*. The resumption of the academic library feature was widely publicized and questionnaires were mailed to all 1,792 college and university libraries on the R. R. Bowker mailing list. In addition, the pages of *Library Journal, LJ/SLJ Hotline,* and other publications were scoured and libraries which had not already reported were contacted. Inevitably, there will be projects which, in spite of these efforts, will have been missed; as in former years, if and when late news is received of such projects, their reports will be used to correct the statistical tables next year.

This year, we are reporting on projects which were completed between July 1, 1977 and June 30, 1979. Reports of projects which were completed after the closing date for this issue will be filed for the next architectural issue. This will probably be in 1980; the one-year interval seems to have more than statistical value, and readers look forward to it as a report on the year past in library construction and remodeling.

A trend which has grown markedly in the past two years involves the construction of libraries as parts of larger academic buildings. This has in too many cases made it impossible to determine when nonlibrary areas are being reported along with those used solely for libraries. This has made a meaningful tally of square foot costs impossible.

In the two-year reporting period, we have been able to identify a total of 92 projects; 38 of these were all new construction; 8 were additions; 22 were additions and renovations; and 18 were renovations only. Outside of this tabulation for general academic libraries, there were six law library projects reported.

Note: Reprinted from *Library Journal,* December 1, 1979.

TABLE 1   ACADEMIC LIBRARIES, 1969-1979

	1969	1970	1971	1972	1973	1974	1975	1976	1977	1978-1979
New Libraries	47	41	33	17	17	21	18	15	6	38
Additions	3	9	6	2	1	9	2	5	5	8
Additions plus Renovation	16	16	10	3	3	10	5	8	7	22
TOTALS	66	66	49	22	21	40	25	28	18	66
Combined Additions and Addition plus Renovation	19	25	16	5	4	19	7	13	12	30
Percentage of Combined A and A & R	28.78	37.87	32.65	22.72	19.04	47.50	28.00	46.42	66.63	32

TABLE 2   NEW LIBRARIES

Name of Institution	Project Cost	Gross Area	Assignable	Non-Assignable	Sq. Ft. Cost	Building Costs	Equipment Cost	Book Capacity	Seating Capacity	Notes
Univ. of Louisville, Belknap campus, Ky.	14,000,000	250,000	185,000	65,000	46.02	11,506,957	2,100,000	1,250,000	2,600	
Univ. of Cincinnati, Central Library, Ohio	13,750,000	216,000	180,000		63.66	14,954,000*	1,350,000	700,000	1,949	*Includes a Garage area costing $4.3 million with 350,000 gross sq. ft. A joint library of UGL Library, SEL Library & Special Collections
State Univ. of New York at Buffalo, Amherst, N.Y. (Capen Hall-Joint Library)	11,431,155	225,663	137,090	88,573	83.38	9,922,100	1,509,055	565,000	2,210	
State Univ. of New York at Buffalo, Amherst, N.Y. (Lockwood Memorial Library)	10,674,000	233,680	152,571	81,109	69.96	9,374,000	1,300,000	1,000,000	2,100	
Washington & Lee Univ., Lexington, Va.	9,200,000	130,000	115,000	15,000				500,000	800	Largest building on campus

ACADEMIC LIBRARY BUILDINGS IN 1979 / 433

Institution									
State Univ. of New York, College at Plattsburgh	7,382,609	133,036	102,095	31,941	43.03	5,990,609	810,000	425,000	1,452	
Northeastern Illinois Univ. Chicago	7,217,025	149,815	104,871	4,944	48.17	6,042,000	907,775	450,000	1,505	
California State College, Pa.	7,100,000	143,976	137,855	6,121	37.00	5,323,500	724,900	500,000	2,500	
Univ. of Northern Colorado, Greeley	5,253,208	221,887	154,742	67,105	20.52	4,553,058	317,338	525,000	2,500	
Texas Tech Univ., Lubbock	4,800,000	181,413	165,936	15,477	23.11	4,193,485	102,000	3,000,000	500	
Pan American Univ., Edinburg, Tex.	5,757,591*	132,502	102,137	30,365	35.11	4,652,539	1,105,052	200,000	1,717	*estimated. LRC
Trinity Univ., San Antonio, Tex.	5,282,524	164,653	NA	NA	61.51	3,547,786	1,269,531	1,200,000	2,000	
Clarkson College, Potsdam, N.Y.	4,300,000	55,000	40,000	15,000	63.00	3,400,000	450,000	160,000	600	LRC
Lassen College, Susanville, Calif.	4,000,000	25,000	21,000	4,000		3,500,000	498,909	16,000	90	LRC
Indiana Central Univ., Indianapolis	4,000,000	93,000	70,865*	2,135	38.39	3,570,000	49,700	200,000	600	*estimated
South Dakota State Univ., Brookings	3,800,000	116,200	104,500	11,700	31.00	2,910,945	642,967	600,000	1,084	
Millikin Univ., Decatur, Ill.	3,500,000	60,000	42,475	7,525	48.33	2,900,000	380,000	300,000	550	
Ramapo College of New Jersey, Mahwah	3,400,000	63,520	47,270	16,250	53.50	3,100,000	270,000	160,000	1,077	
Albion College, Mich.	2,700,000	41,000	30,000	11,000	56.00	2,300,000	400,000	200,000	350	LRC
Lander College, Greenwood, S.C.	2,652,375	35,985	26,468	9,517	32.14	2,025,000	290,964	113,000	258	Includes a 3rd floor not used for library
Miami Univ., Oxford, Ohio	2,480,000	53,000	42,500	10,500	40.75	2,160,000	320,000	200,000	700	Science library
Morris College, Sumter, S.C.	2,300,000	53,450	39,064		35.52	1,899,000	150,000	100,000	450*	Library & Fine Arts Center *Plus 600 auditorium
Los Angeles Pierce College, Woodland Hills, Calif.	1,944,099	17,121	12,625	4,496	63.44	1,358,473	154,277	50,000	246	
Washburn Univ. of Topeka, Kan.	1,837,981	52,568	43,858	8,710	34.96	1,649,366	188,615	300,000	357	
Miles College, Birmingham, Ala.	1,661,358	39,760	32,830	6,930	30.77	1,223,360	225,000	200,000	750	

TABLE 2 NEW LIBRARIES (cont.)

Name of Institution	Project Cost	Gross Area	Assignable	Non-Assignable	Sq. Ft. Cost	Building Costs	Equipment Cost	Book Capacity	Seating Capacity	Notes
Coastal Carolina College of the Univ. of South Carolina, Conway	1,300,000	47,000	40,000		30.00		150,000	200,000	500	
Univ. of Louisville, Belknap campus, Ky.	1,300,000	15,740	12,312	3,428	38.56	1,064,000	124,200	77,250	140	Speed School Engineering Library
East Texas Baptist College, Marshall	1,219,350	29,580	25,447	4,133	33.78	999,350	220,000	150,000	300	
Philadelphia College of Pharmacy and Science, Pa.	1,100,100	24,000	19,960	4,040	39.20	940,500	159,600	76,375	245	
Atlantic Christian College, Wilson, N.C.	1,100,000	27,000	25,000	2,000	40.00	NA	53,000	175,000	300	
Univ. of Texas at El Paso	1,053,000	28,628	23,294	5,334	26.76	766,045	215,000	160,375	236	A major branch library, Library Annex, housing science, engineering and math, gov't. documents & maps
Florida State Univ., Tallahassee	866,500	18,000	15,509	4,491	42.00	756,000	49,964	23,344	250	
Univ. of Maryland, College Park	589,263	11,354	7,071	4,283	48.26	547,973	41,290	50,000	85	Art Library in Art-Sociology Building Architecture & fine arts library
Auburn Univ., Ala.	408,407	8,820	6,702	2,118	39.05	344,421	48,280	20,000	95	
New Mexico State Univ., Grants	395,000*	6,800	NA	NA	NA	395,000*	20,000	23,000	60	*Part of larger construction project; solar heated
Northwest Bible College, Minot, N.D.	354,235	10,449	NA	NA	33.90	334,235	20,000	60,000	125	
Univ. of South Carolina, Beaufort	148,138	7,290*	4,070	540	20.32	133,138	15,000	45,000	56	*Part of larger building, gross library area 4610 sq. ft.
Sinte Gleska College, Mission, S.D.	100,000	6,000	NA	NA	17.00	75,000	25,000	30,000	50	Includes television studio

ACADEMIC LIBRARY BUILDINGS IN 1979 / 435

TABLE 3 ADDITIONS

Name of Institution	Project Cost	Gross Area	Assignable	Non-Assignable	Sq. Ft. Cost	Building Cost	Equipment Cost	Book Capacity	Seating Capacity	Notes
Augustana College, Sioux Falls, S.D.	1,460,000	30,000	27,000	3,000	43.00	1,298,000	162,000	100,000	150	
Northeast Louisiana Univ., Monroe	1,100,875	30,443	27,924	2,519	36.16	815,582	200,171	117,000*	200	*Bound volumes of serials are all that will be housed in this 3rd fl. addition
Friends Bible College, Haviland, Kan.	300,000	12,600	NA	NA	27.00	NA	NA	50,000	200	
Pennsylvania Univ., Middletown (Capitol campus)	180,000	5,000	NA	NA	30.00	150,000	30,000	50,000	NA	Annex for additional stack space only
Southern Utah State College, Cedar City	50,000*	NA	NA	NA	NA	NA	NA	NA	NA	*This is a west entrance-exit for handicapped
Univ. of Tennessee, Knoxville	NA	16,000	15,474	526	NA	NA	37,165*	110,000	326	Agriculture-Veterinary Medicine Library. *Shelving only
Mercy College, White Plains, N.Y.	22,784	1,200	NA	NA	6.00	7,200	15,584	8,000	42	
San Diego State Univ. Calif.	13,600	NA	16,093	NA	NA	*	4,000	62,740	126	*Project done by campus personnel

436 / LIBRARY RESEARCH AND STATISTICS

TABLE 4   ADDITION PLUS RENOVATION

Name of Institution	Project Cost	Gross Area	Assignable	Non-Assignable	Sq. Ft. Cost	Building Cost	Equipment Cost	Book Capacity	Seating Capacity	Notes
Univ. of Hawaii, Honolulu	Total	12,500,000	280,448	223,265	57,183	NA	11,300,000	1,200,000	1,700,000 1,700	Costs combined by contractor
	New	NA	173,540	135,639	37,901	NA				
	Renovated	NA	106,908	87,626	19,282	NA				
Texas A & M Univ. College Station	Total	12,235,210	469,650	376,398	93,252		9,833,385	1,100,000	2,032,520 4,470	
	New	NA	234,146	186,308	47,838	40.37	9,454,060	1,100,000	1,032,520 2,670	
	Renovated	NA	235,504	190,090	45,414	NA	894,900	NA	1,000,000 1,800	
Univ. of California, Santa Barbara	Total	10,496,000	332,110	237,902	94,208		8,188,000	447,000	1,508,430 3,266	
	New	8,271,000	122,500	91,000	31,500	51.46	6,446,000	444,000	535,176 1,387	
	Renovated	2,225,000	209,610	146,000	62,708	10.61	1,742,000	33,000	973,254 1,879	
Loma Linda Univ., Calif.	Total	6,080,250	81,959	72,567	9,392		NA	NA	381,081 875	
	New	5,906,250	52,500	49,000	3,500	60.00	NA	NA	181,081 625	
	Renovated	175,000	29,459	23,567	5,892	NA	NA	NA	200,000 250	
Columbia Univ., New York, N.Y.	Total	5,500,000*	27,800	21,800	6,000	62.00	1,723,600	200,000	300,000 375	*Avery Architectural and Fine Arts Library
	New	NA	12,800	10,800	2,000	NA	793,600	150,000	200,000 200	
	Renovated	NA	15,000	11,000	4,000	NA	930,000	50,000	100,000 175	
Ohio State Univ., Columbus	Total	4,500,000	179,028	165,184	13,844	61.52	3,497,437	495,000	2,100	
	New	2,430,040	39,500	34,399	5,101	14.82	1,890,075		500,000	
	Renovated	2,067,804	139,528	130,785	8,743	33.25	1,607,362			
Univ. of Wyoming, Laramie	Total	3,431,490	86,206	NA	31,652		2,866,490	565,000	650,000 528	
North Carolina Central Univ., Durham	Total	2,243,698	102,876	82,304	20,572	22.00	1,986,156	240,900	500,000 1,200	
	New		51,150	40,920	10,230	NA	NA	NA	NA 560	
	Renovated		51,726	41,384	10,342	NA	NA	NA	NA 640	
Messiah College, Grantham, Pa.	Total	2,101,575	540,627	NA	NA	NA	1,814,060	287,515	300,000 582	
	New		40,413	NA	NA	33.20	NA	NA	NA NA	
	Renovated		14,214	NA	NA	NA				
Morehead State Univ., Ky.	Total	2,405,000	47,500	39,000	8,500		2,100,000	375,000	350,000 450	
	New	2,375,000	37,500	34,000	3,500	62.00	2,000,000	375,000	300,000 400	
	Renovated	100,000	10,000	5,000	5,000	10.00	100,000	0	50,000 50	
St. Norbert College, De Pere, Wis.	Total	1,636,000	59,000	45,268	13,732	38.30	1,434,000	202,000	203,000 550	
	New	1,299,000	30,000	27,804	2,196	9.38	1,149,000	150,000	200,000 211	
	Renovated	337,000	29,000	17,464	11,536		285,000	52,000	3,000 339	

ACADEMIC LIBRARY BUILDINGS IN 1979 / 437

Institution									
Univ. of Montana, Missoula	Total New Renovated	1,615,116	94,600 82,800 11,800	NA 79,400 NA	NA 3,400 NA	17.27 NA	NA 1,460,000 NA	NA NA NA	NA 980,000 NA	NA 1,900 NA
Univ. of Portland, Ore.	Total New Renovated	1,271,100 1,087,100 194,000	49,126 23,550 25,576	47,606 22,978 24,628	1,520 572 948	42.85 NA	1,183,100 1,009,100 174,000	88,000 78,000 20,000	350,000 175,000 175,000	425 200 225
Univ. of Minnesota, Technical College, Crookston	Total New Renovated	1,118,150	17,759 10,250 7,509	12,648 6,660 5,988	5,111 3,590 1,521	93.00 63.00 30.00	815,390 645,750 169,640	145,000 NA NA	40,000 22,000 18,000	132 112 20
Elizabeth City State Univ., N.C.	Total New Renovated	1,247,000	20,000	16,000	4,000	50.00	1,000,000	247,000	150,000	500
Nazareth College of Rochester, N.Y.	Total New Renovated	794,000 NA NA	27,000 11,000 16,000	25,400 11,000 14,400	1,600 0 1,600	29.41 NA NA	699,000 NA NA	50,000* NA NA	140,000 110,000 30,000	235 35 200
Mercy College, Yonkers Extension Center,	Total New Renovated	493,992 479,732 14,260	20,125 19,165 960	NA NA NA	NA NA NA	24.00 6.00	465,720 459,960 5,760	28,272 19,772 8,500	24,170 11,970 12,200	59 43 16
Univ. of Southwestern Louisiana, Lafayette	Total New Renovated	415,970	29,000 27,000 2,000	1,375 NA 1,375	NA NA 625	14.32 NA NA	382,500 NA NA	NA NA NA	900,000 250,000 NA	2,000 108 NA
Alfred Univ., N.Y.	Total New Renovated	400,000 395,000 5,000	9,275 7,200 2,075	8,347 6,480 1,867	928 720 208	45.00 2.00	332,345 329,345 3,000	30,301 25,042 5,259	60,000 50,000 10,000	88 76 12
Queens College Charlotte, N.C.	Total New Renovated	150,000 80,000 70,000	3,500 2,000 1,500	NA NA NA	NA NA NA	40.00 46.00	128,000 58,000 709,000	22,000 22,000 0	16,000 15,000 1,000	40 20 20
Delta State Univ., Cleveland, Miss.	Total New Renovated	* 35,000***	18,000 6,000 12,000	NA NA NA	NA NA NA	NA 2.92	NA NA 35,000	250,000 250,000 NA	40,000 ** 40,000	250 200 50
St. Cloud State Univ., Minn.	Total New Renovated		1,215			NA	1,500*	3,566	8,000*	NA

*Stacks included in construction cost; other furnishings budgeted outside project cost

*Within $4 million Education Building
**Media Center
***Classroom space renovated by campus carpenters
*Excludes labor

438 / LIBRARY RESEARCH AND STATISTICS

TABLE 5 RENOVATION ONLY

Name of Institution	Project Cost	Gross Area	Assignable	Non-Assignable	Sq. Ft. Cost	Building Cost	Equipment Cost	Book Capacity	Seating Capacity	Notes
Univ. of Houston (downtown), Tex.	639,000	42,000	34,000	8,000	15.21	389,000	250,000	140,000	420	
Northern State College, Aberdeen, S.D.	490,000	29,852	22,478	7,374	14.04	419,164	700,836	146,250	365	
Kent State Univ., Ohio	400,000	21,000	NA	NA	14.69	400,000	0	*	*	*Most of area in this audiovisual facility is for production and film storage
Case Western Reserve Univ., Cleveland, Ohio	340,000	6,500	NA	NA	22.30	145,000	180,000	100,000	NA	Electrically operable compact stacks
Univ. of Alaska, Fairbanks*	289,861	8,959	8,270	325	35.05	219,361	16,000	NA	20	*Expand and secure rare books, archives, manuscripts
Univ. of Toledo, Ohio	224,647	9,055	8,800	NA	21.05	190,655	NA	NA	NA	The Ward M. Canaday Center for Research and Use of Rare Books and Special Collections
Eastern New Mexico Univ. at Roswell	220,000	10,626	NA	NA	14.12	150,000	70,000	35,000	82	A branch campus library with 1500 students
Jersey City State College, N.J.	200,000	10,000	8,000	2,000	20.00	165,000	NA	10,000	120	
Univ. of Wisconsin, Platteville	145,720	5,400	5,000	400	21.76	117,506	10,500	30,000	100	All figures estimated

ACADEMIC LIBRARY BUILDINGS IN 1979 / 439

Univ. of California, Riverside	142,000		6,000	NA	23.67	61,600	80,400	100,000	NA	
Montana State Univ., Bozeman	124,000	6,215	5,720	465	15.50	96,000	28,000	80,000	40	Public facility for health sciences
Furman Univ., Greenville, S.C.	122,171	4,032	3,864	168	21.34	86,059	33,559	45,000	38	
Boston Univ., Mass	101,086	2,658	2,658	0	38.03	35,000	66,086	1,300,000*	58	*Only holds microforms
Colgate Rochester Divinity School, Rochester, N.Y.	100,000*	NA	NA	NA	NA	NA	NA	24,000		*Multi-tier deck, new entrance, reading room redecoration
Univ. of South Dakota, School of Medicine, Vermillion	80,000	1,200	NA	NA	NA	NA	NA	15,000	14	Health Science Library
Univ. of Wisconsin, River Falls	71,300	9,828	9,596	232	28,650	42,650	46,464	112	
Carnegie-Mellon Univ., Pittsburgh, Pa.	45,000	1,454	1,454	0	30.95	25,000	20,000	NA	NA	
Abilene Christian Univ., Abilene, Tex.	43,615	2,709	1,753	956	16.10	NA	NA	0	*	*35 work stations
Center for Biblical Studies, Modesto, Calif.	4,030	1,000	NA	NA	4.03	2,500	1,530	20,000	40	

TABLE 6   NEW LAW LIBRARIES

Name of Institution	Project Cost	Gross Area	Assignable	Non-Assignable	Sq. Ft. Cost	Building Cost	Equipment Cost	Book Capacity	Seating Capacity	Notes
College of William & Mary, Williamsburg, Va.	5,569,963*	43,620	65,757*	NA	46.61*	4,100,000*	769,000*	178,164	443	*Includes figures for nonlibrary area (44,334 sq. ft.; 8,064 book cap.)
Univ. of Arizona, Tucson	4,662,661	NA	39,132	NA	47.59	NA	410,000	194,385	475	
Pace University, White Plains, N.Y.	4,000,000	55,000	31,000	24,000	69.00	3,387,000	138,000	200,000	260	
Cleveland State Univ., Ohio (Cleveland-Marshall College of Law)	3,075,000	45,000	31,537	13,463	98.65	2,911,000	200,000	170,000	410	
Hamline Univ., St. Paul, Minn.	4,250,000	80,000	67,000*	NA	50.00	4,000,000	250,000	140,000	325	*Net library area: 28,000 (all figures are for entire law school)
Univ. of Louisville, (Belknap Campus), Ky.	77,000	51,500	25,500	55.00*	4,235,000	NA	230,000	360**		*based on p.s.f. cost of law complex **stations

TWO-YEAR COLLEGE LEARNING RESOURCE CENTER BUILDINGS IN 1979

D. Joleen Bock

Professor, Department of Educational Media, Appalachian State University, Boone, North Carolina

Only 1 percent of the two-year institutions reported new LRC facilities completed in 1978–1979, slightly less than the 1.2 percent in 1977–1978, and considerably less than the 3 percent reported in 1976–1977. The small number of new LRC buildings reported reflects general enrollment trends in two-year colleges. Fall 1978 data (*1979 College, Junior, and Technical College Directory*, AACJC, 1979) show a net increase of only one two-year institution over 1977 and an enrollment decrease of 3.2 percent.

	Number of Colleges		Enrollment	
	Public	Independent	Public	Independent
1977	1,037	198	4,160,611	149,373
1978	1,047	187	3,159,456	144,602

Our survey shows 12 new LRC buildings and one remodeled (Maysville, Ky.). Costs per square foot for new buildings ranged from $35 to $61.88. The central tendency was the $40–$45 range, approximately the same as in 1977–1978.

The percent of FTE allowed for seating ranged from 2 percent at Maricopa (Ariz.) to 58 percent at remodeled Maysville (Ky.).

TABLE 1 FACILITIES IN 13 LRC'S, BUILT JULY 1, 1978–JUNE 30, 1979

Services	Number of Colleges
Library	13
AV Distribution	12
Graphic/Photographic Production	10
Audio-Video Production	11
Reprographic Production	5
Audio/Video Learning Laboratory	9
Learning Assistance Center	6
Career Information Center	5
CAI Terminals	3

Nonbuilding questions asked included the following topics:

1. *Automated Circulation:* Spokane (Wash.) and Brookhaven and North Lake (Dallas) installed Dataphase systems.

2. *Public Catalog:* All were card catalogs except on the Dallas campuses, where microfiche catalogs are a systemwide operation. Aiken (S.C.) will have a book catalog by 1980.

3. *Intershelving Book and AV Materials:* Only Southeast (Nebr.) had integrated shelving. Aiken (S.C.) uses book blocks to indicate cataloged AV materials which are located separately from the stacks.

Note: Reprinted from *Library Journal*, December 1, 1979.

TABLE 2 TWO-YEAR COLLEGE LRC BUILDING CONSTRUCTION, JULY 1, 1978–JUNE 30, 1979

College	FTE	Gross Area	Total ASF	Sq. Ft. Cost	Furn & Equip. Cost	Seats	Percent of FTE Fall 78	Key to Facilities
ARIZONA								
Maricopa Tech.	3,377	1,500	500	$38	$8,700	55	2	ABFG
CALIFORNIA								
Sierra	8,000	27,000	NA	NA	NA	550	7	ABCDF
FLORIDA								
JC at Jacksonville—								
Kent Campus	3,500	35,655	NA	40	300,000	424	13	ABCDFHI
KENTUCKY								
Henderson	488	20,000	18,000	42.50	50,000	200	41	ABCDEF
Hopkinsville	645	23,400	21,490	NA	NA	280	44	ABCDEFG
Maysville	260	NA	10,208	7	NA	150	58	ABDEFGH
NEBRASKA								
Southeast—								
Milford Campus	1,350	NA	NA	NA	NA	100	8	ABCDH
NEW YORK								
Schenectady County	1,417	35,990	26,910	16.88	126,052	450	32	ABCDFG
SOUTH CAROLINA								
Aiken Tech	876	7,000	7,000	45	50,000	105	12	ABCDH
TEXAS								
Bee County	1,557	23,667	18,067	42	70,000	279	18	AH
Dallas County								
Brookhaven	1,700	22,000	18,270	NA	300,000	200	12	ABCDEFGI*
North Lake	1,991	NA	11,100	NA	NA	NA	NA	ABDEFI*
WASHINGTON								
Spokane	5,250	20,000	18,000	35	100,000	215	4	ABCDEGI

Key to Facilities: A = Library   B = AV Distribution   C = Graphic/Photographic Production   D = Audio/Video Production   E = Reprographic Production   F = Audio/Video Learning Laboratory   G = Learning Assistance Center   H = Career Information Center   I = CAI Terminals.
*Also reported Testing Centers.

Book Trade Research and Statistics

BOOK INDUSTRY STUDY GROUP, INC.

Box 2062, Darien, CT 06820
203-655-2473

John P. Dessauer
Managing Agent

The Book Industry Study Group (BISG) is a voluntary research organization composed of some 150 individuals, firms, and trade associations from the various sectors of the book industry: publishers, manufacturers, suppliers, wholesalers, retailers, librarians, and others engaged professionally in the development, production, and dissemination of books.

The first informal organizational meeting of BISG was held in November 1975, when a group of publishers, manufacturers, and trade association representatives met during the annual conference of the Book Manufacturers Institute to discuss the urgent need to improve the industry's research capability. Encouraged by the interest of participants, this small group invited other industry firms and organizations to join it in sponsoring a feasibility study for establishing a permanent research organization. The group was incorporated as a not-for-profit corporation in New York in February 1976, and its first *Report on Book Industry Information Needs* was completed in April. This report, written by Paul D. Doebler, summarized the findings of a study team headed by John P. Dessauer, which included Doebler, E. Wayne Nordberg, and Barbara O. Slanker. The report confirmed the feasibility of a program of major research studies by and about the book industry.

From the beginning, the group enjoyed the support of the major trade associations: the Association of American Publishers (AAP), the Association of American University Presses (AAUP), the American Booksellers Association (ABA), the Book Manufacturers Institute (BMI), and the National Association of College Stores (NACS). In addition, the group has enrolled leading publishing and book manufacturing firms, paper manufacturers, retailers, wholesalers, and libraries. In seeking support from and representing every sector of the industry, the group has affirmed its belief in the interdependence of all segments and their need to find common ways to study and resolve their problems.

The group's officers and directors have similarly hailed from the various constituencies of the group. The officials elected for 1979–1980 include Andrew H. Neilly, Jr. (John Wiley & Sons), chairman (who was founding chairman and has been twice reelected to head BISG); DeWitt C. Baker (Elsevier/Dutton), vice chairman; Howard Willets, Jr. (Great Northern Paper Company), treasurer; JoAnn McGreevy (New York University Book Centers), secretary; and Alexander J. Burke, Jr. (McGraw-Hill Book Company), Martin P. Levin (Times Mirror Company), George Q. Nichols (National

Publishing Company), and Sandra K. Paul (SKP Associates), members of the executive committee. Others serving on the board of directors include Robert F. Asleson (R. R. Bowker Company), William C. Becker (Princeton University Press), Arthur Brody (Brodart), Jerry D. Butler (R. R. Donnelley & Sons), Hendrik Edelman (Rutgers University Library), Ranald P. Hobbs (BCMA Associates), Harold T. Miller (Houghton Mifflin Company), Charles F. Myers (Simon & Schuster), and John U. Wisotzkey (Maple Press). The group maintains offices on the premises of its managing agent, John P. Dessauer, Inc., at 25 Dubois Street, Darien, Connecticut 06820.

PUBLICATIONS, 1976–1979

The first research report launched by the group (after the publication of its original feasibility study) was a *Paper Availability Study* by E. Wayne Nordberg and Kazi Hasan. This volume, which was released in 1976, probed into the nature and causes of the paper shortage of 1974 and projected the future availability of book papers based on analyses of raw materials, cost, demand, and worldwide supply factors. The authors' forecast, which has proved to be remarkably accurate, has been updated yearly in the BISG annual publication, *Book Industry Trends*.

Research Report No. 3 was *Library Acquisitions: A Look into the Future* by John P. Dessauer, an extensive revision of a study that had originally appeared in *Publishers Weekly* in 1975, and that estimated and forecast the value and volume of materials acquisitions by U.S. libraries for five years in the past and five years in the future. Now out of print, the study has been updated and incorporated for the past two years in *Book Industry Trends*.

Book Industry Trends first appeared in 1977 as Research Report No. 4. *Book Industry Trends-1977* by John P. Dessauer, Paul D. Doebler, and E. Wayne Nordberg examined developments in technology, consumer tastes, and industry growth in book manufacturing, publishing, wholesaling, retailing, and libraries; analyzed the economic outlook for the various sectors; and provided estimates and forecasts for the markets enjoyed by various types of books in over 100 pages of tables.

Book Industry Trends-1978 by the same authors (Research Report No. 5) included articles by Paul D. Doebler on "Growth and Development of Consumer Bookstores since 1954," on "Current Events, Trends and Emerging Priorities in Library Management," and on "The Economics of In-House Composition." E. Wayne Nordberg contributed an extensive analysis of "Economic Trends and the Book Industry" and joined with Kazi Hasan in updating "Trends in Printing-Writing Papers." John P. Dessauer again produced sales estimates and projections at publisher, wholesaler, manufacturer, and consumer levels, including, in addition, an update of his earlier study on library acquisitions.

The most significant and extensive of the group's projects to date appeared next: *The 1978 Consumer Research Study on Reading and Book Purchasing* (Research Report No. 6). Prepared for BISG by the research firm Yankelovich, Skelly and White, Inc., this $100,000 study was based on interviews with a randomly chosen sample of 1,450 U.S. consumers—1,250 book readers and buyers and 200 nonreaders. Under the supervision of a BISG committee chaired by Martin P. Levin (Times-Mirror), assisted by Carol Gold (John Wiley), the researchers inquired into the leisure-time habits and preferences of consumers, the demographics of readers and nonreaders, the motivations and criteria for choices of buyers, the efficacy of distribution channels, and the impact of promotional devices. The results of the study, which were presented initially in October 1978 at the Center of the Book of the Library of Congress, received extensive press coverage and broad national attention.

Also in 1978, the group published the first issue of the *BISG Bulletin*, an occasional newsletter (expanded to regular, semimonthly publication in 1980).

In *Book Industry Trends-1979* (Research Report No. 7), J. Kendrick Noble, Jr., joined the team of authors and contributed estimates and forecasts of the school and college textbook markets. Paul Doebler prepared "A Scenario for the Development of Book Production Technology, 1980-1990," as well as an essay on "The Office of the Future: Technological Evolution of the Work-Place Environment for Books and Other Information Media." Wayne Nordberg updated his analysis of economic trends and his forecast of paper availability. John Dessauer brought his dollar and unit estimates and projections of industry sales into conformity with the 1977 U.S. Census of Manufactures, which had been released in spring 1979.

Also in 1979 the group launched two of its Alert Services—listings in the *BISG Bulletin* of important information of interest to book industry planners. The *Book Industry Studies Alert*, which contains significant publications and sources of information about the industry, is compiled for BISG by Jean Peters (R. R. Bowker). The *Book Industry Distribution Systems Alert*, a compilation of information about book distribution systems and related matters, is conducted by Sandra K. Paul (SKP Associates).

THE OUTLOOK FOR 1980

As 1980 approached, the group was working on a number of continuing projects. In cooperation with AAP, BISG was managing a college market study that would update and expand earlier inquiries conducted under AAP auspices—with support from NACS—into the reading and book-buying habits of college faculty and students and the efficacy of the college store delivery system. Carol Gold (John Wiley) was acting for the BISG Consumer Study Committee in this effort, which was under contract to Crossley Surveys, Inc.

A committee chaired by Alexander J. Burke, Jr. (McGraw-Hill) was concluding preparations for a quarterly survey of publishers' inventory and manufacturers' capacity data designed to inquire into loading/capacity relationships in the industry.

A BISG committee on machine readable codes, working under the chairmanship of Sandra K. Paul, was developing guidelines for the printing of International Standard Book Numbers in OCR-A book jackets and covers.

A distinguished panel chaired by Arthur Brody (Brodart) was preparing for a comprehensive in-depth study of book distribution and its multifaceted problems. This will be a major undertaking, comparable in scope and commitment to the BISG consumer study. A number of internationally recognized research organizations will be asked to make proposals for conducting what is likely to become one of the group's landmark inquiries.

The entire BISG effort is under constant review by the group's Planning Committee chaired by DeWitt C. Baker (Elsevier/Dutton). During 1980, this committee, which proposes long-term goals and short-term priorities for BISG, will concentrate in particular on the possible restructuring and expansion of the annual *Book Industry Trends*.

Early in 1980, the *BISG Bulletin* was expanded to semimonthly publication. Edited by John P. Dessauer, the *Bulletin* is updating *Book Industry Trends* throughout the year, featuring monthly industry sales estimates as well as articles by the *Trends* authors and by guest contributors. A third Alert Service—on Information Technology, conducted for BISG by Robert C. Badger (John Wiley)—has been incorporated in the new *Bulletin*.

The group is also working to expand its membership in 1980, hoping in particular to attract small publishers and book manufacturers through a special dues plan for small firms. The group currently provides six membership categories; three regular—commercial, nonprofit institutional, and personal; and three special—retailers, university presses, and non-profit libraries. The BISG membership prospectus points out that while "the immediate purpose of the Group is to promote and support research in and about the Industry, so that the various sectors will be better able to realize their professional and business plans, the Group's ultimate goal is to increase readership, improve distribution of books of all kinds, and expand the market for them." These are goals all book professionals obviously share. As the industry's awareness of the importance of research grows, people in the field are likely to look increasingly to the Book Industry Study Group for the information necessary to achieve their common objectives.

BOOK TITLE OUTPUT AND AVERAGE PRICES, 1978–1979

Chandler B. Grannis
Contributing Editor, *Publishers Weekly*

According to preliminary figures compiled by R. R. Bowker for 1979, the year's output of American book titles in hardcover increased about 9.7% over that of 1978 (Table 1) and paperback output (mass market and trade combined) rose over 8% from the 1978 figures (Table 2).

The overall average prices of hardcover volumes increased about 13.4% (Table A), according to Bowker's preliminary tabulations, although, when works costing over $80 a volume are omitted, the increase in average price appears to be about 6.6% (Table A-1).

A hand count of certain books advertised in *PW*'s Fall Announcements issues shows that median prices of novels, biographies, and books of history increased by about $1 per volume, comparing 1978 with 1979.

The title counts are given in Tables 1 through 6; the price averages, in Tables A–D. Tables 1–6 and A–C are based on computer analyses of information that appears also as listings in Bowker's current bibliographic publication *Weekly Record*. Table D, however, represents (as noted above) a manual computation from advertisements.

All the data shown here, except in Table D, include preliminary and final figures for 1978 and preliminary figures only for 1979. Preliminary figures are those derived from 12 months—i.e., the calendar year—of work in recording books for the *Weekly Record*. Final figures represent six additional months of work in recording books of the same year. The final figures for 1979 will be computed after the end of June and published in *Publishers Weekly* later in the summer; the most recent final figures appeared in the September 3, 1979, issue of *PW*. Final price average figures, representing a larger base than those given here, will surely be somewhat different, but the 12-month figures now presented are at least indicative of trends.

Note: Reprinted from *Publishers Weekly*, February 22, 1980, where the article was entitled "1979 Title Output and Average Prices: Preliminary Figures."

TABLE 1 AMERICAN BOOK TITLE OUTPUT, 1978 AND 1979
(From *Weekly Record* Listings of Domestic and Imported Hardbound and Paperbound Books)

Categories with Dewey Decimal Numbers	1978 titles (preliminary) New Books	1978 titles (preliminary) New Editions	1978 titles (preliminary) Totals	1978 titles (final) New Books	1978 titles (final) New Editions	1978 titles (final) Totals	1979 titles (preliminary) New Books	1979 titles (preliminary) New Editions	1979 titles (preliminary) Totals
Agriculture (630-639; 712-719)	350	108	458	408	144	552	340	92	432
Art (700-711; 720-779)	1,056	221	1,277	1,229	254	1,483	1,369	243	1,612
*Biography	1,208	352	1,560	1,454	437	1,891	1,281	396	1,677
Business (650-659)	705	262	967	925	323	1,248	912	260	1,172
Education (370-379)	733	155	888	871	192	1,063	802	154	956
Fiction	1,936	903	2,839	2,455	1,238	3,693	2,065	786	2,851
General Works (000-099)	904	213	1,117	1,047	263	1,310	953	185	1,138
History (900-909; 930-999)	1,147	516	1,663	1,361	655	2,016	1,245	502	1,747
Home Economics (640-649)	587	100	687	717	128	845	607	109	716
Juveniles	2,100	221	2,321	2,617	292	2,909	2,337	286	2,623
Language (400-499)	264	127	391	303	155	458	333	110	443
Law (340-349)	681	244	925	786	279	1,065	726	274	1,000
Literature (800-810; 813-820; 823-899)	1,029	418	1,447	1,254	546	1,800	1,084	381	1,465
Medicine (610-619)	1,818	492	2,310	2,177	611	2,788	2,123	533	2,656
Music (780-789)	187	164	351	231	208	439	173	138	311
Philosophy, Psychology (100-199)	842	230	1,072	1,048	319	1,367	899	248	1,147
Poetry, Drama (811; 812; 821; 822)	833	271	1,104	972	325	1,297	875	218	1,093
Religion (200-299)	1,461	356	1,817	1,750	430	2,180	1,555	392	1,947
Science (500-599)	1,811	539	2,350	2,155	722	2,877	2,082	521	2,603
Sociology, Economics (300-339; 350-369; 380-399)	4,425	935	5,360	5,259	1,206	6,465	5,165	1,069	6,234
Sports, Recreation (790-799)	790	174	964	948	212	1,160	780	167	947
Technology (600-609; 620-629; 660-699)	1,294	320	1,614	1,511	385	1,896	1,530	399	1,929
Travel (910-919)	278	81	359	324	90	414	421	102	523
Total	26,439	7,402	33,841	31,802	9,414	41,216	29,657	7,565	37,222

*Dewey Decimal Numbers omitted because biographies counted here come from many Dewey classifications.

TABLE 2 PAPERBACK TITLES AT ALL PRICE LEVELS, 1978 AND 1979
(From *Weekly Record* Listings of Domestic and Imported Hardbound and Paperbound Books)

Categories	1978 titles (prelim.) New Bks.	New Eds.	Totals	1978 titles (final) New Bks.	New Eds.	Totals	1979 titles (prelim.) New Bks.	New Eds.	Totals
Fiction	578	496	1,074	732	720	1,452	622	509	1,131
Nonfiction	6,396	1,678	8,074	7,620	2,196	9,816	6,939	1,863	8,802
Total	**6,974**	**2,174**	**9,148**	**8,352**	**2,916**	**11,268**	**7,561**	**2,372**	**9,933**

TABLE 3 MASS MARKET PAPERBACKS, 1978 AND 1979
(From *Weekly Record* Listings of Domestic and Imported Books)

Categories	1978 titles (prelim.) New Bks.	New Eds.	Totals	1978 titles (final) New Bks.	New Eds.	Totals	1979 titles (prelim.) New Bks.	New Eds.	Totals
Fiction	429	375	804	554	546	1,100	417	397	814
Nonfiction	24	147	171	26	212	226	38	206	244
Total	**453**	**522**	**975**	**580**	**758**	**1,326**	**455**	**603**	**1,058**

TABLE 4 PAPERBACKS OTHER THAN MASS MARKET, 1978 AND 1979
(From *Weekly Record* Listings of Domestic and Imported Books)

Categories	1978 titles (prelim.) New Bks.	New Eds.	Totals	1978 titles (final) New Bks.	New Eds.	Totals	1979 titles (prelim.) New Bks.	New Eds.	Totals
Fiction	149	121	270	178	174	352	205	112	317
Nonfiction	6,372	1,531	7,903	7,594	1,984	9,578	6,901	1,657	8,558
Total	**6,521**	**1,652**	**8,173**	**7,772**	**2,158**	**9,930**	**7,106**	**1,769**	**8,875**

TABLE 5 ENGLISH TRANSLATIONS, 1978 AND 1979
(From *Weekly Record* Listings of Domestic and Imported Hardbound and Paperbound Books)

Original Language	1978 titles (prelim.) Totals	1978 titles (final) Totals	1979 titles (prelim.) Totals
French	242	286	272
German	196	237	241
Italian	50	62	51
Oriental	57	70	61
Russian	84	102	131
Scandinavian	28	34	27
Spanish	45	60	54
Other	426	494	531
Total	1,128	1,345	1,368

TABLE 6 BOOK IMPORTS, 1978 AND 1979
(From *Weekly Record* Listings of Domestic and Imported Hardbound and Paperbound Books)

Category	1978 titles (prelim.) New Books	New Editions	Totals	1978 titles (final) New Books	New Editions	Totals	1979 titles (prelim.) New Books	New Editions	Totals
Agriculture	61	12	73	63	14	77	84	7	91
Art	110	19	129	117	20	137	149	21	170
Biography	117	11	128	115	15	130	126	14	140
Business	40	9	49	42	9	51	44	13	57
Education	110	4	114	114	3	117	131	4	135
Fiction	69	14	83	68	13	81	44	9	53
General Works	92	11	103	95	12	107	113	8	121
History	168	30	198	171	32	203	196	24	220
Home Economics	39	2	41	43	2	45	30	3	33
Juveniles	29	3	32	30	3	33	28	1	29
Language	63	11	74	64	10	74	91	11	102
Law	50	9	59	46	11	57	61	13	74
Literature	125	11	136	127	14	141	139	13	152
Medicine	318	85	403	353	93	446	325	52	377
Music	13	3	16	14	3	17	19	8	27
Philosophy, Psychology	91	4	95	96	5	101	97	9	106
Poetry, Drama	130	6	136	129	6	135	97	9	106
Religion	77	9	86	77	10	87	109	6	115
Science	599	50	649	648	62	710	613	51	664
Sociology, Economics	729	40	769	760	46	806	861	50	911
Sports, Recreation	62	7	69	65	6	71	91	10	101
Technology	155	26	181	165	28	193	209	37	246
Travel	41	6	47	43	8	51	50	6	56
Total	3,288	382	3,670	3,445	425	3,870	3,707	379	4,086

TABLE A AVERAGE PER-VOLUME PRICES OF HARDCOVER BOOKS, 1978 AND 1979*
(From Weekly Record Listings of Domestic and Imported Books)

Categories with Dewey Decimal Numbers	1978 volumes (preliminary) Total volumes	1978 volumes (preliminary) Total prices	1978 volumes (preliminary) Average prices	1978 volumes (final) Total volumes	1978 volumes (final) Total prices	1978 volumes (final) Average prices	1979 volumes (preliminary) Total volumes	1979 volumes (preliminary) Total prices	1979 volumes (preliminary) Average prices
Agriculture (630-639; 712-719)	348	$ 5,886.21	$16.91	416	$ 7,171.51	$17.24	332	$ 6,586.31	$19.84
Art (700-711; 720-779)	889	18,884.09	21.24	1,017	21,465.66	21.11	1,110	23,832.23	21.47
†Biography	1,297	20,385.99	15.72	1,574	24,811.58	15.76	1,376	23,448.68	17.04
Business (650-659)	747	14,828.98	19.85	956	18,424.87	19.27	930	21,494.78	23.11
Education (370-379)	538	7,431.47	13.81	657	9,103.77	13.86	613	9,112.04	14.86
Fiction	1,778	19,677.29	11.07	2,254	25,397.16	11.27	1,722	19,495.18	11.32
General Works (000-099)	956	25,986.18	27.18	1,140	29,081.02	25.51	783	21,920.07	27.99
History (900-909; 930-999)	1,373	23,472.12	17.10	1,661	28,564.49	17.20	1,362	25,816.69	18.95
Home Economics (640-649)	414	4,652.18	11.24	495	5,577.75	11.27	441	5,248.36	11.90
Juveniles	2,347	15,472.16	6.59	2,961	19,492.20	6.58	2,605	18,583.88	7.13
Language (400-499)	224	3,812.81	17.02	256	4,266.81	16.67	290	5,455.01	18.81
Law (340-349)	637	17,359.41	27.25	713	17,294.98	24.26	733	20,241.68	27.61
Literature (800-810; 813-820; 823-899)	1,105	19,640.04	17.77	1,354	24,338.84	17.98	1,060	17,910.49	16.90
Medicine (610-619)	1,830	46,956.74	25.66	2,199	54,995.74	25.01	2,045	56,702.58	27.73
Music (780-789)	286	7,101.87	24.83	361	8,909.37	24.68	228	4,220.39	18.51
Philosophy, Psychology (100-199)	768	11,473.78	14.94	968	14,277.90	14.75	851	14,422.04	16.95
Poetry, Drama (811; 812; 821; 822)	739	10,664.53	14.43	878	13,050.86	14.86	708	11,118.69	15.70
Religion (200-299)	914	12,116.18	13.26	1,077	14,039.62	13.04	1,078	14,850.53	13.78
Science (500-599)	1,914	51,293.89	26.80	2,331	61,066.06	26.20	2,067	59,143.98	28.61
Sociology, Economics (300-339; 350-369; 380-399)	3,870	125,639.38	32.46	4,663	138,284.66	29.66	4,606	192,187.97	41.73
Sports, Recreation (790-799)	620	8,165.56	13.17	732	9,488.38	12.96	634	8,616.80	13.59
Technology (600-609; 620-629; 660-699)	1,184	27,748.53	23.44	1,384	31,336.77	22.64	1,475	38,454.17	26.07
Travel (910-919)	217	3,655.75	16.85	250	4,279.95	17.12	288	4,342.34	15.08
Total	24,995	$502,305.14	$20.10	30,297	$584,719.95	$19.30	27,337	$623,204.89	$22.80

*See Table A-1.
†Dewey Decimal Numbers omitted because biographies counted here come from many Dewey classifications.

TABLE A-1 AVERAGE PER-VOLUME PRICES OF HARDCOVER
BOOKS, ELIMINATING ALL VOLUMES PRICED AT $81 OR MORE*

Dewey Classifications	1978 (prelim.)	1978 (final)	1979 (prelim.)
General Works (000-099)	$20.26	$20.34	$19.83
Philos., Psychol. (100-199)	14.70	15.10	16.62
Religion (200-299)	13.06	13.29	12.90
Soc., Econ., Law, Educ. (300-399)	16.75	16.95	18.15
Languages (400-499)	17.02	17.01	18.25
Science (500-599)	24.43	25.21	26.61
All Classifications (000-999)	$17.78	$18..01	$18.95

*Compare indicated categories with Table A.

As detailed in the September 3 issue, certain classes of books are underreported in the *Weekly Record* and therefore in these statistics. This point applies notably to mass market paperbacks, especially fiction, and to elementary and high school textbooks. Publications of units of government and university theses—two categories that are regularly cited by the Department of Commerce as publishing roughly 40,000 titles a year between them—are omitted from *Weekly Record* listings.

It is also important to remember that distortion of price averages may occur in a few categories in which extremely costly special reports are published, bearing prices from $85 to $300, $400, and more. Table A-1 shows what the price averages would be in certain broad Dewey classifications, and in all of them together, if prices over $80 were eliminated from the hardcover price computations.

Table D, based on ads in *PW*'s Fall Announcements issues, indicates increases in the average prices of general novels of about 8.2%; volumes of biography, memoirs, and letters, 17.6%; and volumes of history (including pictorial history) about 8.3%.

The most important statistical report of the year was undoubtedly that of the Census of Manufactures for 1977, published by the Department of Commerce. It provided extensive new information that expanded the book industry's own studies. The book publishing and manufacturing census data in full, together with the AAP 1977 and 1978 sales totals, all presented and analyzed by John P. Dessauer, are reprinted in this volume under the title "The U.S. Census of Book Publishing, 1977" in the Book Trade Research and Statistics section of Part 4. In a further use of the Census and AAP data, Dessauer has also edited the massive annual study "Book Industry Trends 1979," recently issued by the Book Industry Study Group, Inc.

TABLE B AVERAGE PER-VOLUME PRICES OF MASS MARKET PAPERBACKS, 1978 AND 1979*
(From Weekly Record Listings of Domestic and Imported Books)

Category	1978 Total volumes	1978 Total prices	1978 Average prices	1978 Total volumes (final)	1978 Total prices (final)	1978 Average prices (final)	1979 Total volumes	1979 Total prices	1979 Average prices
Biography	19	$37.95	$2.00	28	57.00	2.04	46	$107.05	$2.61
Fiction	804	1,518.70	1.89	1,100	2,064.90	1.88	814	1,634.75	2.01
History	11	22.40	2.04	15	30.75	2.05	13	30.60	2.35
Juveniles	27	39.60	1.47	38	52.60	1.38	76	112.85	1.48
Medicine	25	50.70	2.03	32	65.40	2.04	31	74.15	2.39
Philosophy, Psychology	20	40.00	2.00	31	61.50	1.98	15	38.35	2.56
Sociology, Economics	41	89.25	2.18	56	121.45	2.17	46	106.00	2.30
Sports, Recreation	15	32.32	2.15	17	37.07	2.18	18	40.35	2.24
Total, all categories, including the above	1,001	$1,914.92	$1.91	1,374	$2,614.17	$1.90	1,131	$2,327.10	$2.06

*Limited to categories in which at least 15 titles were tabulated for 1978 final report.

TABLE C AVERAGE PER-VOLUME PRICES OF TRADE PAPERBACKS, 1978 AND 1979
(From Weekly Record Listings of Domestic and Imported Books)

Category	1978 Total volumes	1978 Total prices	1978 Average prices	1978 Total volumes (final)	1978 Total prices (final)	1978 Average prices (final)	1979 Total volumes	1979 Total prices	1979 Average prices
Agriculture	113	$ 657.81	$5.82	139	$ 815.00	$5.86	95	$ 623.62	$6.56
Art	390	2,649.68	6.79	471	3,209.53	6.81	511	4,282.10	8.38
Biography	242	1,157.05	4.78	286	1,350.90	4.72	253	1,448.10	5.72
Business	211	1,660.88	7.87	280	2,237.86	7.99	232	1,985.06	8.56

BOOK TITLE OUTPUT AND AVERAGE PRICES, 1978-1979 / 453

Category				
Education	352	2,290.63	6.51	6.68
Fiction	271	1,241.84	4.58	4.63
General Works	311	1,993.03	6.41	6.67
History	303	1,828.56	6.03	5.99
Home Economics	290	1,449.49	5.00	4.98
Juveniles	282	803.06	2.85	2.82
Language	168	1,059.29	6.31	6.18
Law	303	3,373.47	11.13	10.97
Literature	358	1,978.96	5.53	5.48
Medicine	454	3,836.43	8.45	8.31
Music	68	462.15	6.80	6.91
Philosophy, Psychology	294	1,933.40	6.58	6.60
Poetry, Drama	374	1,759.24	4.70	4.62
Religion	896	3,762.65	4.20	4.22
Science	438	4,140.41	9.45	9.49
Sociology, Economics	1,465	9,538.65	6.51	6.52
Sports, Recreation	333	1,778.32	5.34	5.42
Technology	433	3,366.90	7.78	7.55
Travel	142	875.15	6.16	6.02
Total	**8,491**	**$53,597.05**	**$6.31**	**$6.31**

410	2,737.28	6.68	6.92
353	1,633.69	4.63	4.21
342	2,281.58	6.67	6.66
368	2,202.51	5.99	6.54
365	1,819.48	4.98	5.37
340	957.56	2.82	3.16
203	1,254.86	6.18	7.54
361	3,961.17	10.97	11.53
458	2,508.33	5.48	6.40
556	4,618.61	8.31	9.46
81	559.65	6.91	8.65
379	2,501.70	6.60	6.49
428	1,977.69	4.62	4.19
1,093	4,617.30	4.22	4.53
550	5,218.92	9.49	11.22
1,764	11,493.79	6.52	7.64
413	2,239.28	5.42	6.08
518	3,912.23	7.55	8.81
164	987.75	6.02	5.89
10,322	**$65,096.67**	**$6.31**	**$7.05**

TABLE D AVERAGE AND MEDIAN PRICES, THREE CATEGORIES, PW FALL ANNOUNCEMENT ADS, 1972–1979

Novels, except Mystery, Western, SF, Gothic: Average & Median Prices			Biography, Memoirs, Letters: Average & Median Prices			History, including Pictorial, but not Art books: Average & Median Prices		
	Avg.	Med.		Avg.	Med.		Avg.	Med.
1979—291 vols./43 pubs.	$10.42	$9.95	1979—160 vols./67 pubs.	$15.92	$13.95	1979—219 vols./67 pubs.	$16.88	$15.95
1978—282 vols./43 pubs.	$9.63	$8.95	1978—213 vols./73 pubs.	$13.54	$12.95	1978—207 vols./85 pubs.	$15.59	$15.00
1977—233 vols./37 pubs.	$9.18	$8.95	1977—169 vols./62 pubs.	$13.12	$12.50	1977—241 vols./72 pubs.	$15.83	$15.00
1976—150 vols./34 pubs.	$8.74	$8.95	1976—130 vols./61 pubs.	$12.87	$11.95	1976—151 vols./63 pubs.	$13.96	$14.95
1975—150 vols./35 pubs.	$8.51	$7.95	1975—128 vols./53 pubs.	$12.50	$10.95	1975—178 vols./74 pubs.	$15.32	$13.95
1974—212 vols./38 pubs.	$7.68	$7.95	1974—190 vols./80 pubs.	$12.31	$10.95	1974—219 vols./74 pubs.	$12.91	$12.50
1973—225 vols./40 pubs.	$7.34	$6.95	1973—190 vols./78 pubs.	$10.67	$8.95	1973—228 vols./73 pubs.	$13.38	$12.50
1972—171 vols./37 pubs.	$6.95	$6.95	1972—170 vols./61 pubs.	$10.12	$8.95	1972—262 vols./89 pubs.	$12.30	$12.30

PRICES OF U.S. AND FOREIGN PUBLISHED MATERIALS

Sally F. Williams
Budget and Planning Officer, Harvard College Library,
Harvard University, Cambridge, MA. Tel. 617-495-2400

As expected, prices of library materials in 1979 continued to rise. The only comforting note is that at first glance it appears that this year's price increases have not exceeded the increase in the general cost of living as measured by the Consumer Price Index. (See Tables 1-12.) Whereas the average 1979 price for a U.S. hardcover book increased 13.4 percent over that of 1978 (Table 3), the prices of U.S. periodicals and serial services (Tables 1 & 2) showed increases of only 10.1 and 11.1 percent respectively. Furthermore, a sample survey of 1980 subscription prices of U.S. periodicals showed the price increases holding at 10.1 percent.

International price information is typically late in being reported and this handicaps U.S. libraries who need up-to-date facts for sensible budgeting. Preliminary findings indicate that the international price picture is even worse than the domestic outlook.

After steep increases of 18 and 22 percent in 1975 and 1976, British book prices stabilized in 1977 and 1978 with two consecutive increases of only 3 percent (Tables 9 & 10). But preliminary reports for 1979 in the *Library Association Record* indicate that British book prices are on the rise again at a 14 percent rate. The prices for British periodicals have increased more dramatically. Prices paid in 1978 for 1979 subscriptions rose 9.2 percent over the previous year. The estimate for 1980 subscriptions is that prices paid in 1979 will be 17 percent higher than those paid in 1978 for 1979 subscriptions.

For academic books, as reported in *LMRU Report No. 14* (Alan Cooper, "Average Prices of British Academic Books 1978," Library Management Research Unit, Loughborough University, 1979, p. 9), the rises in 1975 and 1976 were 21 percent and 35 percent respectively. There was another large increase of 23 percent in 1977 and a relatively modest 8 percent increase in 1978. There seems to be no correlation between overall increases in prices for all British books and British academic books except that they have both been increasing each year with the academic books increasing at a higher rate. While it is difficult to predict future price trends, it would seem safe to say that the average British academic book in 1979 will cost at least 14 percent more than in 1978, and probably 17 to 20 percent more.

The average price of a German book in 1978 increased 6.5 percent over the 1977 price (Table 11). While books in the areas of geography, anthropology, and travel had a substantial decrease in price, books in the natural sciences and technology had substantial price increases. The German book index continues to reflect a large number of inexpensive titles: of the 33,715 books published, 26.7 percent cost less than 5 DM and 45.3 percent cost less than 10 DM. Table 11 includes both cloth and paper editions. If paperbacks are not counted, the average price of a German cloth book in 1978 was 30.54 DM, up 10.3 percent over the 1977 prices.

Illustrating the zany range of price increases are the prices paid by eight libraries for Latin American books (Table 12). The low was a decrease of 39.5 percent (Jamaica) and the high was an increase of 203.5 percent of 1979 prices over 1978. The overall price increase was 8.7 percent. The nine countries with the highest number of book purchases by the eight libraries studied showed an overall increase of 6.85 percent.

But as long as the dollar continues to decline in value against foreign currencies, libraries purchasing materials from abroad get little comfort from figures that show inflation in foreign countries increasing more slowly than U.S. inflation. The dollar has declined the most in the European countries that supply the bulk of library materials. Comparing the value of the dollar in seven European countries at the close of 1979 with the dollar value in 1970, one sees the following: one-third the value in Switzerland, one-half the value in the Netherlands and West Germany, three-fourths the value in France and Italy. In Spain the dollar lost only 5 percent of its value. Only in Great Britain was the dollar worth more in 1979 than in 1970.

Library budgets are being stretched to the limit due to double-digit library materials inflation, decreased value of the dollar abroad, and increased volume of publishing worldwide. Therefore, materials budgets need to be carefully allocated. For just this purpose the Library Materials Price Index Committee of the Resources Section of the ALA Resources and Technical Services Division has sponsored the preparation and publication of the accompanying tables.

The price indexes were designed to measure the rate of price changes of newly published materials against those of earlier years. They reflect retail price trends at the national level, not the cost to a particular library, and are useful for comparing with local purchasing patterns. The price indexes were never intended to be a substitute for information that a library might collect about its own purchases. The prices on which the indexes are based do not include discounts, vendor service charges, or taxes paid. These variables naturally affect the average price for library materials paid by a particular library. However, as recent studies have shown, this does not necessarily mean that the rate of increase in prices paid by a particular library is significantly different from the rate of increase shown by the price indexes. The Library Materials Price Index Committee is very interested in pursuing correlations of individual library's prices with national prices and would like to be informed of any studies undertaken.

This year the Library Materials Price Index Committee is pleased to present a new index of selected U.S. daily newspaper subscription prices (Table 8). This index, updated every three years, shows the average annual subscription rate since 1969, the index value using 1969 as the base year and the increase in index points. It shows a 31 percent increase in the annual subscription rate from 1975 to 1978.

As in previous years, readers are cautioned to use the indexes with care and note the particulars of each index. Be aware, for example, of the categories "preliminary" and "final" in the U.S. book prices tables. Take note that the German book price index includes both paperback and hardcover books and this affects the price, as noted earlier. Also note that this year the U.S. nonprint media price index (Table 6) omits black and white 16mm films because of the paucity of production of this type.

In addition to the indexes presented here there are two other published price indexes not sponsored by the Library Materials Price Index Committee that are of interest. These are: G. R. Hill and J. M. Boonin, "Price Indexes, Foreign and Domestic Music," *Music Library Association Notes* 35 (March 1979): 593–609; and B. Scott, "Price Index for Legal Publications," *Law Library Journal* 72 (Winter 1979): 144–145.

The current members of the Library Materials Price Index Committee are Sally F. Williams (chairperson), Peter Graham, Nelson A. Piper, Thomas W. Leonhardt, and William Z. Schenck. Consultants to the Committee are Noreen G. Alldredge, Hugh C. Atkinson, Norman B. Brown, Frank Clasquin, Imre T. Jarmy, Jane F. Pulis, and David B. Walch.

TABLE 1 U.S. PERIODICALS: AVERAGE PRICES AND PRICE INDEXES, 1975–1979
(Index of 100.0 Equivalent to Average Price for 1967–1969)

Subject Area	1967–1969 Average Price	1975 Average Price	1975 Index	1976 Average Price	1976 Index	1977 Average Price	1977 Index	1978 Average Price	1978 Index	1979 Average Price	1979 Index
U.S. periodicals (based on the total group of titles included in the indexes which follow)	$8.66	$19.94	230.3	$22.52	260.0	$24.59	283.9	$27.58	318.5	$30.37	350.7
Agriculture	4.68	9.70	207.3	10.75	229.7	11.58	247.4	12.48	266.7	14.16	302.6
Business and economics	7.54	15.26	202.4	16.98	225.2	18.62	246.9	21.09	279.7	22.97	304.6
Chemistry and physics	24.48	76.84	313.9	86.72	354.3	93.76	383.0	108.22	442.1	118.33	483.4
Children's periodicals	2.60	4.69	180.4	5.32	204.6	5.82	223.8	6.34	243.8	6.70	257.7
Education	6.34	14.72	232.2	16.00	252.4	17.54	276.7	19.49	307.4	21.61	340.9
Engineering	10.03	26.64	265.6	31.87	317.7	35.77	356.6	39.77	396.5	42.95	428.2
Fine and applied arts	6.71	11.09	165.3	12.42	185.1	13.72	204.5	14.82	220.9	17.42	259.6
General interest periodicals	7.28	14.36	197.3	15.24	209.3	16.19	222.4	17.26	237.1	18.28	251.1
History	6.04	11.14	184.4	11.94	197.7	12.64	209.3	13.71	227.0	14.67	242.9
Home economics	6.45	14.24	220.8	17.86	276.9	18.73	290.4	21.67	336.0	23.21	359.8
Industrial arts	6.87	10.59	154.2	12.51	182.1	14.37	209.2	15.48	225.3	17.65	256.9
Journalism and communications	5.72	14.70	257.0	15.90	278.0	16.97	296.7	19.95	348.8	23.86	417.1
Labor and industrial relations	3.01	7.40	245.9	10.33	343.2	11.24	373.4	13.24	439.9	15.74	522.9
Law	8.71	15.00	172.2	16.21	186.1	17.36	199.3	18.74	215.2	20.98	240.9
Library science	6.27	14.18	226.2	15.96	254.5	16.97	270.7	19.34	308.5	20.82	332.1
Literature and language	5.38	10.41	193.5	11.60	215.6	11.82	219.7	12.84	238.7	13.84	257.2
Math, botany, geology and general science	15.30	35.95	235.0	42.51	277.8	47.13	308.0	54.16	354.0	58.84	384.6
Medicine	19.38	42.38	218.7	47.47	244.9	51.31	264.8	57.06	294.4	63.31	326.7
Philosophy and religion	5.27	9.05	171.7	9.94	188.6	10.89	206.6	11.66	221.3	13.25	251.4
Physical education and recreation	4.89	7.80	159.5	9.27	189.6	10.00	204.5	10.79	220.7	12.27	250.9
Political science	6.18	12.79	207.0	13.09	211.8	14.83	240.0	15.62	252.8	17.47	282.7
Psychology	14.55	27.51	189.1	29.39	202.0	31.74	218.1	34.21	235.1	38.10	261.9
Sociology and anthropology	6.11	14.85	243.0	17.11	280.0	19.68	322.1	21.58	353.2	23.70	387.9
Zoology	13.39	27.37	204.1	31.34	234.1	33.69	251.6	37.05	276.7	40.15	299.9
Total number of periodicals	6,944	3,075		3,151		3,218		3,255		3,314	

*Compiled by Norman B. Brown. For further comments see Library Journal, September 1, 1979, "Price Indexes for 1979: U.S. Periodicals and Serial Services," by Norman B. Brown. For average prices for years prior to 1975, see previous editions of the Bowker Annual.

TABLE 2 U.S. SERIAL SERVICE: AVERAGE PRICES AND PRICE INDEXES, 1975–1979*
(Index Base 1967–1969 = 100)

	1967–1969 Average Price	1975 Average Price	1975 Index	1976 Average Price	1976 Index	1977 Average Price	1977 Index	1978 Average Price	1978 Index	1979 Average Price	1979 Index
Business	$119.76	$166.60	139.1	$192.25	160.5	$216.28	180.6	$222.45	185.7	$249.05	208.0
General and humanities	28.23	76.82	272.1	86.60	306.8	90.44	320.4	94.88	336.1	118.83	420.9
Law	60.87	99.10	162.8	113.37	186.2	126.74	208.2	137.91	226.6	158.65	260.6
Science and technology	65.23	120.78	185.2	122.69	188.1	141.16	216.4	160.61	246.2	173.96	266.7
Social sciences (excluding business and law)	65.63	126.13	192.2	136.40	207.8	145.50	221.7	153.94	234.6	169.55	258.3
Soviet translations	90.82	147.95	162.9	161.84	178.2	175.41	193.1	187.44	206.4	201.89	222.3
U.S. documents	18.37	53.48	291.1	60.36	328.6	62.88	342.3	72.52	394.8	75.87	413.0
"Wilson Index"	253.33	348.92	137.7	406.50	160.6	438.00	172.9	467.17	184.4	487.75	192.5
Combined†	$ 72.42	$118.03	163.0	$129.47	178.6	$142.27	196.5	$153.95	212.6	171.06	236.5

*The definition of a serial service has been taken from the American National Standard Criteria for Price Indexes for Library Materials (ANSI 239.20–1974). For further comments see *Library Journal*, September 1, 1979, "Price Indexes for 1979: U.S. Periodicals and Serial Services," by Norman B. Brown. For average prices for years prior to 1975, see previous editions of the *Bowker Annual*.
†Excludes "Wilson Index."

TABLE 3 U.S. HARDCOVER BOOKS: AVERAGE PRICES AND PRICE INDEXES, 1977–1979*
(Index of 100.0 Equivalent to Average Prices for 1967–1969)

	1967–1969 Average Price	1977 (Final) Vols.	1977 (Final) Average Price	1977 (Final) Index	1978 (Prelim.) Vols.	1978 (Prelim.) Average Price	1978 (Prelim.) Index	1978 (Final) Vols.	1978 (Final) Average Price	1978 (Final) Index	1979 (Prelim.) Vols.	1979 (Prelim.) Average Price	1979 (Prelim.) Index
Agriculture	$9.71	434	$16.24	167.3	348	$16.91	174.2	416	$17.24	177.5	332	$19.84	204.3
Art	12.44	1,285	21.24	170.7	889	21.24	170.7	1,017	21.11	169.7	1,110	21.47	172.6
Biography[1]	9.71	1,732	15.34	158.0	1,297	15.72	161.9	1,574	15.76	162.3	1,376	17.04	175.5
Business	10.41	800	18.00	173.0	747	19.85	190.7	956	19.27	185.1	930	23.11	222.0
Education	6.58	720	12.95	196.8	538	13.81	209.9	657	13.86	210.6	613	14.86	225.8
Fiction	4.96	1,920	10.09	219.7	1,778	11.07	223.2	2,254	11.27	227.2	1,722	11.32	228.2
General works[2]	15.28	1,238	30.99	202.8	956	27.18	177.9	1,140	25.51	167.0	783	27.99	183.2
History	9.95	1,588	17.12	172.1	1,373	17.10	171.9	1,661	17.20	172.9	1,362	18.95	190.4
Home economics[2]	6.55	480	11.16	170.4	414	11.24	171.6	495	11.27	172.1	441	11.90	181.7
Juveniles	3.53	2,850	6.65	188.4	2,347	6.59	186.7	2,961	6.58	186.4	2,605	7.13	202.0
Language[2]	10.13	337	14.96	147.7	224	17.02	168.0	256	16.67	164.6	290	18.81	185.7
Law	13.22	623	25.04	189.4	637	27.25	206.1	713	24.26	183.5	733	27.61	208.8
Literature	8.04	1,372	15.78	196.3	1,105	17.77	221.0	1,354	17.98	223.6	1,060	16.90	210.2
Medicine	13.41	2,196	24.00	179.0	1,830	25.66	191.4	2,199	25.01	186.5	2,045	27.73	206.8
Music	9.08	279	20.13	221.7	286	24.83	273.5	361	24.68	271.8	228	18.51	203.8
Philosophy, psychology[2]	8.41	934	14.43	171.6	768	14.94	177.7	968	14.75	175.4	851	16.95	201.5
Poetry, drama	6.69	999	13.63	203.7	739	14.43	215.7	878	14.86	222.1	708	15.70	234.7
Religion	6.29	1,040	12.26	194.9	914	13.26	210.9	1,077	13.04	207.3	1,078	13.78	219.1
Science	12.67	2,419	24.88	196.4	1,914	26.80	211.5	2,331	26.20	206.8	2,067	28.61	225.8
Sociology, economics[2]	9.35	4,751	29.88	319.6	3,870	32.46	347.2	4,663	29.66	317.2	4,606	41.73	446.3
Sports, recreation	7.91	722	12.28	155.3	620	13.17	166.5	732	12.96	163.8	634	13.59	171.8
Technology	13.03	1,583	23.61	181.2	1,184	23.44	179.9	1,384	22.64	173.8	1,475	26.07	200.1
Travel[2]	9.34	298	18.44	197.4	217	16.85	180.4	250	17.12	183.3	288	15.08	161.4
Totals	$8.77	30,600	$19.22	219.2	24,995	$20.10	229.2	30,297	$19.30	220.0	27,337	$22.80	260.0

*Price indexes are based on the books recorded in the "Weekly Record" of *Publishers Weekly*. 1979 (preliminary) includes items listed during 1979 with an imprint of 1979; 1978 (final) includes items listed January 1978–June 1979 with an imprint date of 1978; 1978 (preliminary) includes items listed during 1978 with an imprint of 1978; 1977 (final) includes items listed January 1, 1977–June 30, 1978 with an imprint date of 1977. (See "Book Title Output and Average Prices, 1978–1979" by Chandler B. Grannis, earlier in this section of Part 4.)

[1] Includes biographies placed in other classes by the Library of Congress.
[2] New category. Index base is 1967 and 1969, rather than 1967 through 1969.

TABLE 4 U.S. MASS MARKET PAPERBACK BOOKS: AVERAGE PRICES AND PRICE INDEXES, 1977-1979*
(Index Base, 1967-1969 = 100)

	1967-1969	1977 (Final)			1978 (Prelim.)			1978 (Final)			1979 (Prelim.)		
	Average Price	No. of Books	Average Price	Index	No. of Books	Average Price	Index	No. of Books	Average Price	Index	No. of Books	Average Price	Index
Agriculture	$ .88	5	$1.55	176.1	3	$1.80	204.6	—	—	—	—	—	—
Art	.86	4	2.78	323.3	2	2.60	302.3	—	—	—	—	—	—
Biography	.93	33	1.84	197.9	19	2.00	215.1	88	$2.04	237.2	46	$2.61	303.5
Business	1.06	7	2.06	194.3	5	2.53	238.7	—	—	—	—	—	—
Education	1.33	2	1.73	130.1	0	0.00	—	—	—	—	—	—	—
Fiction	.75	1,386	1.66	221.3	804	1.89	252.0	1,100	1.88	250.7	814	2.01	268.0
General works†		20	1.88	—	6	2.07	—	—	—	—	—	—	—
History	.98	35	2.06	210.2	11	2.04	208.2	15	2.05	209.2	13	2.35	239.8
Home economics†		15	1.93	—	6	2.11	—	—	—	—	—	—	—
Juveniles	.71	42	1.40	197.2	27	1.47	207.0	38	1.38	194.4	76	1.48	208.5
Language†		1	1.50	—	0	0.00	—	—	—	—	—	—	—
Law	.86	6	1.98	230.2	0	0.00	—	—	—	—	—	—	—
Literature	.96	10	1.98	206.3	4	1.93	201.0	—	—	—	—	—	—
Medicine	.87	51	2.04	234.5	25	2.03	233.3	32	2.04	234.5	31	2.39	274.7
Music	.83	4	2.29	276.0	1	1.95	235.0	—	—	—	—	—	—
Philosophy, psychology†		55	1.87	—	20	2.00	—	31	1.98	—	15	2.56	—
Poetry, drama	.92	6	2.10	228.3	1	1.95	212.0	—	—	—	—	—	—
Religion	.85	15	1.73	203.5	4	2.03	238.8	—	—	—	—	—	—
Science	.96	10	1.92	200.0	4	1.95	203.1	—	—	—	—	—	—
Sociology, economics†		71	1.90	—	41	2.18	—	—	—	—	—	—	—
Sports, recreation	.87	51	1.86	213.8	15	2.15	247.1	56	2.17	250.6	46	2.30	257.5
Technology	1.04	15	2.07	199.0	3	2.73	262.5	17	2.18		18	2.24	
Travel†		9	2.07	—	0	0.00	—	—	—	—	—	—	—
All‡	$0.79	1,853	$1.72	217.7	1,001	$1.91	241.8	1,374	$1.90	240.5	1,131	$2.06	260.8

*See footnote to Table 3. Figures for 1978 (Final) and 1979 (Prelim.) are limited to categories in which at least 15 titles were tabulated for 1978.
†No base for calculation of index has been established.
‡"All" includes all items listed in "Weekly Record" including categories in which fewer than 15 titles were tabulated.

TABLE 5 U.S. TRADE (HIGHER PRICED) PAPERBACK BOOKS: AVERAGE PRICES AND PRICE INDEXES, 1977–1979*
(Index Base, 1967–1969 = 100)

Category	1967–1969 Average Price	1977 (Final) No. of Books	1977 Average Price	1977 Index	1978 (Prelim.) No. of Books	1978 Average Price	1978 Index	1978 (Final) No. of Books	1978 Average Price	1978 Index	1979 (Prelim.) No. of Books	1979 Average Price	1979 Index
Agriculture	$3.13	164	$5.01	160.1	113	$5.82	185.9	139	$5.86	187.2	95	$6.56	209.6
Art	3.48	527	6.27	180.2	390	6.79	195.1	471	6.81	195.7	511	8.38	240.8
Biography	2.25	340	4.91	218.2	242	4.78	212.4	286	4.72	209.8	253	5.72	254.2
Business	5.10	288	7.09	135.0	211	7.87	149.9	280	7.99	156.7	232	8.56	167.8
Education	2.91	487	5.72	196.6	352	6.51	223.7	410	6.68	229.5	333	6.92	237.8
Fiction	1.66	385	4.20	253.0	271	4.58	275.9	353	4.63	278.9	322	4.21	253.6
General works†	—	344	6.18	—	311	6.41	—	342	6.67	—	353	6.66	—
History	2.87	420	5.81	202.4	303	6.03	210.1	368	5.99	208.7	379	6.54	227.9
Home economics†	—	300	4.77	—	290	5.00	—	365	4.98	—	267	5.37	—
Juveniles	1.23	407	2.68	217.0	282	2.85	231.7	340	2.82	229.3	348	3.16	256.9
Language†	—	230	7.79	—	168	6.31	—	203	6.18	—	153	7.54	—
Law	4.11	348	10.66	259.4	303	11.13	270.8	361	10.97	266.9	288	11.53	280.5
Literature	2.44	517	5.18	212.3	358	5.53	226.6	458	5.48	224.6	387	6.40	262.3
Medicine	4.61	598	7.63	165.5	454	8.45	183.3	556	8.31	180.3	570	9.46	205.2
Music	3.19	89	6.36	199.4	68	6.80	213.2	81	6.91	216.6	79	8.65	271.2
Philosophy, psychology†	—	421	5.57	—	294	6.58	—	379	6.60	—	279	6.49	—
Poetry, drama	1.81	483	4.71	260.2	374	4.70	259.7	428	4.62	255.3	396	4.19	231.5
Religion	1.96	1,063	3.68	187.8	896	4.20	214.3	1,093	4.22	215.3	867	4.53	231.1
Science	4.06	635	8.81	217.0	438	9.45	232.8	550	9.49	233.7	516	11.22	276.4
Sociology, economics†	—	2,029	6.03	—	1,465	6.51	—	1,764	6.52	—	1,590	7.64	—
Sports, recreation	2.11	354	4.87	230.8	333	5.54	253.1	413	5.42	256.8	300	6.08	288.2
Technology	8.84	630	7.97	90.2	433	7.78	88.0	518	7.55	85.4	456	8.81	99.7
Travel	—	187	5.21	—	142	6.16	—	164	6.02	—	235	5.89	—
Totals	$3.24	11,246	$5.93	183.0	8,491	$5.31	163.9	10,322	$6.31	195.8	9,209	$7.05	217.6

*See footnote to Table 3.
†New category. No base for calculation of index has been established. Average prices reported.

TABLE 6 U.S. NONPRINT MEDIA: AVERAGE PRICES AND PRICE INDEXES, 1974–1979*
(Index Base, 1972 = 100)

Category	1972 Average Quantity	1972 Index	1974 Average Quantity	1974 Index	1975 Average Quantity	1975 Index	1976 Average Quantity	1976 Index	1977 Average Quantity	1977 Index	1978 Average Quantity	1978 Index	1979 Average Quantity	1979 Index
16mm Films														
Average rental cost per minute	$1.15	100	$1.15	100	$1.18	102.6	$1.16	100.9	$1.23	107	$1.22	106.1	$135.00	117.3
Average b & w purchase cost per minute	7.32	100	7.44	101.6	7.10	97.0	—	—	—	—	9.70	132.5	—	—
Average color purchase cost per minute	11.95	100	11.55	96.7	12.85	107.5	12.93	108.2	13.95	116.7	12.56	105.1	13.62	113.9
Average length per film	241.39	100	277.20	114.8	282.70	117.1	253.43	105	308.85	127.9	350.42	145.1	328.24	135.9
Average length per film (min.)	20.2	100	24		22		19.6		22.14		27.9		24.1	
Filmstrips														
Average cost of filmstrip with cassette	$12.95	100	$15.94	123.1	$17.19	132.7	$17.18	132.7	$18.60	143.6	$17.43	134.6	$21.42	165.4
Average cost of filmstrip set (cassette)	37.56	100	63.76	169.8	73.91	196.8	58.41	155.5	76.26	203.0	62.31	165.9	65.97	175.6
Average number of filmstrips per set	2.9	100	4.0		4.3		3.4		4.1		3.6		3.08	
Average number of frames per filmstrip	63.3	100	57.6		66.3		62.8		64.2		58.0		71.8	
Multimedia Kits														
Average cost per kit	$51.33	100	$100.00	194.82	$140.25	273.2	$93.63	182.4	$93.65	182.4	$117.38	228.7	$85.70	166.9
Sound Recordings														
Average cost per disc	$6.10	100	$6.63	108.7	$6.88	112.8	$5.85	95.9	$6.72	110.2	$7.06	115.8	$7.21	118.2
Average cost per cassette	7.81	100	10.76	137.8	10.32	132.1	12.08	157.7	10.63	136.1	12.57	161.1	12.58	161.1
Average cost per cassette set	19.53	100	24.75	126.7	30.96	158.5	44.70	228.9	31.89	163.3	66.00	337.9	32.70	167.4
Average number of cassettes per set	2.5	100	2.3		3.0		3.7		3.0		5.3		2.6	

*Compiled by David B. Walch. Cost analysis for the nonprint media shown in this table was based on information derived from selected issues of *Previews* and *Booklist*. It should be noted that the years listed do not necessarily reflect the year of production. For example, the majority of films reviewed by *Previews* in 1979 were actually produced in 1978.

TABLE 7 U.S. LIBRARY MICROFILM: AVERAGE RATES AND INDEX VALUES, 1969–1978

Negative Microfilm[1] (35mm per exposure)	1969	1972	1975	1978
Average rate	$ .0493	$ .0621	$ .0707	$ .0836
Index value	100.0	125.9	143.4	169.7
Percent + or −	0	+25.9	+17.3	+26.3
Positive Microfilm[2] (35mm per foot)				
Average rate	$ .0960	$ .0839	$ .1190	$ .1612
Index value	100.0	87.4	123.9	168.0
Percent + or −	0	−12.6	+36.6	+44.0

*Compiled by Imre T. Jarmy, Library Materials Price Index Committee, Resources Section, Resources and Technical Services Division, American Library Association, from the *Directory of Library Reprographic Services: A World Guide*, 7th edition (Microform Review, Westport, Conn., 1978), supplemented by data secured by correspondence and by telephone interviews with the staffs of the indexed libraries. These libraries are listed in the "Library Microfilm Rates" articles in the following issues of *Library Resources and Technical Services:* Winter 1967 (11:1), Summer 1969 (13:3), Summer 1970 (14:3), Winter 1974 (18:1), Fall 1977 (21:4), and Summer 1979 (23:3); in the *Newspaper and Gazette Report*, April 1978 (6:1); and in the *National Preservation Report*, April 1979 (1:1). The rates listed in the fourth edition of the *Directory* are used as base prices with an index value of 100 in computing subsequent index values.

[1] Includes 49 selected libraries for 1969; 48 for 1972; 46 for 1975; and 48 for 1978.
[2] Includes 22 selected libraries for 1969; 20 for 1972; 19 for 1975; and 19 for 1978.

TABLE 8 SELECTED U.S. DAILY NEWSPAPERS: AVERAGE SUBSCRIPTION RATES AND INDEX VALUES, 1969–1978*

Year	Average Rate	Index Value	% (+ or −)
1969	$34.1592	100.0	0
1972	42.7647	125.2	+25.2
1975	58.4120	171.0	+45.8
1978	76.4391	223.8	+52.8

*Compiled by Imre T. Jarmy, Library Materials Price Index Committee, Resources Section, Resources and Technical Services Division, American Library Association, from data secured by correspondence and by telephone interviews with the circulation managers and publishers of the indexed newspapers and, when necessary, by examination of the pertinent year end editions of individual issues. Data for 95 of the 133 titles indexed were available at press time. The complete list will be published in the Summer 1980 edition of *Library Resources and Technical Services*.

TABLE 9 BRITISH BOOKS BY MAJOR CATEGORIES: AVERAGE PRICES AND PRICE INDEXES, 1974–1978*
(1966/1967 Average Price = 100)

	1966/1967 Average Price £ p	1974/1975 Average Price £ p	1974/1975 Index	1976 Average Price £ p	1976 Index	1977 No. of Books	1977 Average Price £ p	1977 Index	1978 No. of Books	1978 Average Price £ p	1978 Index
Adult fiction	.85	1.68	197.6	2.27½	267.6	3,806	2.55	300.0	4,137	2.76	324.71
Adult nonfiction[1]	2.19	4.53	206.8	5.14½	234.9	22,806	6.40	292.2	25,826	6.54	298.63
Reference books[2]	2.66	4.75	178.6	5.16½	194.2	1,968	7.30	274.4	2,248	7.59	285.34
Children's fiction	.54	1.17	216.7	1.36½	252.8	1,204	1.44	266.7	1,337	1.54	285.19
Children's nonfiction	.67½	1.17½	174.1	1.32½	196.3	1,055	1.19	176.3	1,211	1.20	177.78
All categories combined	1.84½	3.83	207.6	4.51	244.4	28,871	5.49	297.6	32,511	5.65	306.23

*Data compiled by Thomas Leonhardt from the *British National Bibliography*. See *Library Association Record*, February 1979.
[1] See Table 10 for breakdown by Dewey classes.
[2] Reference books are included in the total for nonfiction.

TABLE 10 BRITISH ADULT NONFICTION BOOKS: AVERAGE PRICES AND PRICE INDEXES, 1974–1978*
(Index Base 1966/1967 = 100)

Classes	1966–1967 Average Price £ p	1974/1975 Average Price £ p	1974/1975 Index	1976 Average Price £ p	1976 Index	1977 No. of Books	1977 Average Price £ p	1977 Index	1978 No. of Books	1978 Average Price £ p	1978 Index
000	5.21	6.40	122.8	6.23½	119.7	724	8.18	157.0	938	8.44	162.00
100	1.86½	3.91	209.7	5.22	279.9	654	5.61	300.8	698	6.38	342.09
200	1.29½	2.93	226.2	3.06	236.3	890	3.18	245.6	1,169	2.86	220.85
300	1.47	4.39	298.6	4.88	332.0	6,125	6.28	427.2	6,598	6.24	424.49
400	.66	2.34	357.2	2.99½	453.8	479	3.63	550.0	796	2.75	416.67
500	2.99	6.26	209.4	9.04	302.3	2,159	10.95	366.2	2,244	11.72	391.97
600	2.47½	4.71	190.7	6.14	248.1	4,718	7.94	320.8	5,412	8.59	347.07
700	2.38½	3.71	155.9	4.68	196.2	2,444	5.57	233.5	2,797	5.52	231.45
800	1.03½	2.75	265.7	3.09½	299.0	2,193	3.44	332.4	2,287	3.51	339.13
900	1.69½	4.73	279.1	4.53½	267.6	2,420	4.54	267.8	2,887	4.67	275.52

*Data compiled by Thomas Leonhardt from *Library Association Record*, February 1979.
000 General works; Bibliographies; Librarianship
100 Philosophy; Psychology; Occultism, etc.
200 Not subdivided
300 Social Science; Politics; Economics; Law; Public Administration; Social Welfare; Education; Social Customs, etc.
400 Language; School Readers
500 General Science; Mathematics; Astronomy; Physics; Chemistry; Geology; Meteorology; Pre-history; Anthropology; General Biology; Botany; Zoology
600 Medicine; Public Safety; Engineering/Technology; Agriculture; Domestic Economy; Business Management; Printing and Book Trade; Manufactures; Building
700 Architecture; Fine Arts; Photography; Music; Entertainment; Sports; Amusements
800 General and Foreign Literature; English Literature
900 Geography; Travel; Biography; History

TABLE 11 GERMAN BOOKS: AVERAGE PRICES AND PRICE INDEXES, 1975–1978*
(Index Base 1966/1967 = 100)

	1967–1969 Average Price	1975 Average Price	1975 Index	1976 Average Price	1976 Index	1977 Average Price	1977 Index	1978 Average Price	1978 Index
General, library science, college level textbooks	DM32.66	DM45.10	138.0	DM54.03	165.4	DM68.47	209.6	DM61.93	189.6
Religion	16.33	23.48	143.8	22.33	136.7	23.21	142.1	24.57	150.4
Philosophy, psychology	26.45	24.03	90.9	23.21	87.8	26.67	100.8	27.28	103.1
Law, administration	23.57	33.46	142.0	35.19	149.3	33.92	143.9	36.92	156.6
Social sciences, economics, statistics	20.07	24.70	123.1	25.72	128.2	25.97	129.4	29.13	145.1
Political and military science	16.47	19.81	120.3	24.37	147.9	—	—	21.64	131.4
Literature and linguistics	28.97	36.37	125.5	25.83	89.2	27.79	95.9	29.43	101.6
Belles lettres	5.83	6.50	111.5	6.98	109.4	6.57	112.7	7.44	127.6
Juveniles	6.09	8.24	135.3	8.24	135.3	9.07	149.4	9.26	152.1
Education	10.65	16.76	157.4	17.03	159.9	16.50	154.9	17.54	164.7
School textbooks	5.66	9.31	164.5	10.10	178.5	10.88	192.2	11.44	196.9
Fine arts	30.18	51.15	169.5	51.85	171.8	49.70	164.7	46.81	155.1
Music, dance, theatre, film, radio	23.79	36.65	154.1	27.07	113.8	28.04	117.9	28.76	120.9
History, folklore	31.24	49.92	159.8	36.99	118.4	39.79	124.2	39.75	127.2
Geography, anthropology, travel	16.26	30.60	188.2	31.20	191.9	32.20	198.0	27.46	168.9
Medicine	40.60	49.06	120.8	52.57	129.5	50.29	123.9	50.82	125.2
Natural sciences	34.73	69.07	198.9	81.77	235.4	93.45	269.1	97.02	279.4
Mathematics	25.40	29.70	116.9	32.50	127.9	28.98	114.1	30.22	119.0
Technology	21.89	34.04	155.5	42.66	194.9	42.45	193.9	57.85	264.3
Touring guides and directories	18.43	19.27	104.6	23.08	125.2	21.78	118.2	34.56	187.5
Home economics and agriculture	12.31	19.86	161.3	24.60	199.8	25.10	203.9	21.75	176.7
Sports and recreation	12.00	17.22	143.5	19.93	166.1	18.99	158.3	20.13	167.8
Miscellaneous	11.18	7.65	68.4	—	—	—	—	—	—
Totals	DM18.60	DM23.67	127.3	DM20.52	110.3	DM21.87	117.6	DM23.28	125.2

*Indexes are tentative and based on average prices *unadjusted* for title production. Figures for 1978 were compiled by William Z. Schenck from *Buch und Buchhandel in Zahlen*, Frankfurt, 1979.

TABLE 12 LATIN AMERICAN BOOKS: NUMBER OF COPIES AND AVERAGE COST, FY 1977, 1978, AND 1979*

Country	1977 No. of Books	1977 Average Cost	1977 % (+ or −) over 1976	1978 No. of Books	1978 Average Cost	1978 % (+ or −) over 1977	1979 No. of Books	1979 Average Cost	1979 % (+ or −) over 1978
Argentina	8,615	$6.45†	+10.3	6,208	$ 9.16†	+42.0	4,753	$ 9.10†	−0.7
Bolivia	1,071	6.30†	−7.2	1,441	7.91	+25.5	1,302	9.61†	+21.5
Brazil	8,115	7.43	+14.0	7,061	8.45	+13.7	7,882	8.63	+2.1
Chile	1,348	8.14†	+26.4	1,019	11.94	+46.6	1,684	10.52†	−11.9
Colombia	2,338	6.51†	+21.7	2,510	7.09†	+8.9	2,320	9.42†	+32.9
Costa Rica	56	4.10	−48.4	133	5.22	+27.3	94	4.05	−22.4
Cuba	—	—	—	1	12.66	—	1	15.00	+18.5
Dominican Republic	232	7.33	+35.5	263	6.13	−16.3	501	6.86	+11.9
Ecuador	366	4.96	+18.9	576	6.79	+36.8	739	5.74	−15.5
Guatemala	54	7.28	+16.9	128	5.91	−18.8	80	6.13	+3.7
Guyana	48	7.45	+69.3	328	2.26	−69.6	62	4.60	+203.5
Haiti	66	5.74	+26.7	220	5.77	+.5	278	6.86	+18.9
Honduras	262	5.37	−4.3	638	4.56	−15.0	216	6.01	+31.8
Jamaica	37	8.06	+54.1	164	6.56	−18.6	257	3.97	−39.5
Mexico	2,932	4.42	−4.7	3,042	5.43	+22.8	3,197	6.39†	+17.7
Nicaragua	20	6.93	+0.3	5	11.50	+65.9	13	12.54	+9.0
Panama	142	4.10	+2.8	160	5.72	+39.5	38	4.16	−27.3
Paraguay	328	6.78	+15.7	365	6.63†	−2.2	322	8.77†	+32.3
Peru	2,338	5.23	−18.3	2,230	5.93	+13.3	3,251	6.29†	+6.1
Puerto Rico	139	5.75	+5.5	408	5.29	−8.0	487	5.95	+12.5
El Salvador	69	4.58	+1.6	49	4.94	+7.8	71	7.45	+50.8
Trinidad	10	7.40	+68.9	24	4.87	−34.1	55	4.22	−13.3
Uruguay	991	7.14†	+55.9	2,226	7.36	+3.0	2,165	8.55†	+16.2
Venezuela	1,534	7.47	+13.9	1,831	7.25	−2.9	1,552	8.98	+23.9

*Compiled by Robert C. Sullivan, Seminar on the Acquisition of Latin American Library Materials (SALALM), Subcommittee on Cost Statistics, from reports on the number and cost of current monographs purchased by the libraries of Cornell University, University of Florida, University of Illinois, Library of Congress, University of Minnesota, New York Public Library, University of Texas, and University of Wisconsin. A full explanation of the methodology employed is contained in the SALALM XXI Working Paper No. A-4 dated May 1976.
†Includes some binding costs.

U.S. CENSUS OF BOOK PUBLISHING, 1977

John P. Dessauer
Book Industry Statistician

As it has at regular intervals since the earliest days of the Republic, the U.S. government last year conducted a Census of Manufactures. Included in this program, covering the year 1977 and carried out by the Bureau of the Census of the Department of Commerce, was a survey of book publishing (Standard Industrial Code 2731), extending a series that had last been updated for 1972.

Census surveys are the backbone of the industry's sales statistics. The estimates released by the Association of American Publishers (AAP) are based on census findings, and although as the AAP statisticians we estimate industry sales for the years between census surveys, these estimates are revised and brought into conformity with census data every five years.

Extensive revisions in the 1977 AAP estimates have become necessary as the result of the 1977 census. After adjustments, the 1977 census total amounts to $4914.3 million. Our earlier estimates had placed that total at $4400.6 million. Differences for some publishing categories are even more substantial, as for adult trade hardbound books, where the adjusted census figure amounts to $807.0 million compared to our earlier estimates of $631.8 million.

Table 1 shows the preliminary 1977 sales data, including 1972 figures for comparison purposes, released by the Census Bureau. Dollar values are shown for all categories; unit data are given for some classifications. (Because the availability of unit data has always been limited, AAP estimates have confined themselves to dollars. Since 1977, however, unit estimates have appeared in the annual publication *Book Industry Trends*, published by the Book Industry Study Group.) Table 2 contains revised AAP estimates for 1977 brought into conformity with the census data. In addition, 1972 estimates, already aligned with the 1972 census, are provided, as well as the AAP estimates for 1978. (These data, appearing in a current AAP release, are extracted from the AAP's "1978 Industry Statistics Report.")

In developing the 1977 AAP estimates, substantial adjustment had to be made in the census figures in recognition of the following differences between the two programs:

Inclusions and Exclusions. The Census of Manufactures is the most complete survey of U.S. book publishing in existence. Respondents are required to reply to questionnaires under penalty of law, and questionnaires are sent to all firms whose employer identification number classifies them as a book publisher. Some publishing entities are not surveyed, however, because their employer number does not identify them as book publishers: certain societal and university presses and religious houses, for example, operating as departments of churches, scholarly associations, or universities. Recently, Allen H. Foreman, chief of the Printing and Publishing Section of the Industry Division of the Bureau of the Census and his staff have been making progress in improving coverage, but some gaps inevitably remain.

While AAP estimates have not been able to repair most of the above omissions either, the AAP coverage of university presses is more inclusive than that of the census

Note: Adapted from *Publishers Weekly*, July 9, 1979, where the article was entitled "The 1977 U.S. Census of Book Publishing Reveals Significant Industry Expansion."

TABLE 1 1977 CENSUS OF MANUFACTURES (INDUSTRY SERIES)
Book Publishing (SIC 2731) Preliminary Report
Products and Product Classes—Quantity Sold and Value of Receipts of All Producers, 1977 and 1972

1977 Product Code	Product	Unit of measure	Number of companies with receipts of $100,000 or more	1977 Quantity sold[1][2]	1977 Value of receipts[1] ($ million)	1972 Quantity sold[1][2]	1972 Value of receipts[1] ($ million)
2731- --	BOOK PUBLISHING—TOTAL	.....	(NA)	(X)	4975.5	(X)	2915.4
27311 --	**Textbooks, including teachers' editions**		(NA)	(X)	1410.2	(X)	809.6
	Elementary textbooks (grades k-8):	Million					
27311 11	Hardbound, including teachers' editions		27	**64.3	246.9	65.8	162.4
27311 12	Paperbound, including teachers' editions		32	**44.8	96.9	44.5	57.5
	High school textbooks (grades 9-12):						
27311 13	Hardbound, including teachers' editions		27	**32.5	174.7	40.5	132.4
27311 14	Paperbound, including teachers' editions		27	**9.8	28.4	7.3	12.8
	College textbooks, grades 13 and over, including private business, institutes, and training courses of college-grade:						
27311 15	Hardbound		47	*57.4	468.1	57.1	277.3
27311 16	Paperbound		42	*24.7	121.2	(S)	45.1
	Workbooks, objective tests, manuals, etc., paperbound:						
27311 21	Elementary (grades k-8)		29	*79.3	160.5	69.7	53.8
27311 23	High school (grades 9-12)		21	(S)	46.0	21.3	23.4
27311 25	College		14	5.6	16.4	6.1	11.5
	Standardized tests, including both tests and answer sheets, but excluding textbook-related objective tests and manuals,						
27311 31	paperbound	Million	6	(S)	27.1	24.1	14.2
27311 00	Textbooks, n.s.k.	.....	(NA)	(X)	24.0	(X)	19.2
27313 --	**Technical, scientific, and professional books**	.....	(NA)	(X)	685.0	(X)	403.0
	Law books, including supplements (designed for the profession):	Million					
27313 15	Hardbound		20	10.3	210.1	8.6	114.9
27313 17	Paperbound		13	*4.9	56.2	(S)	32.0
	Medical books, including nursing and dental subjects (designed for the profession):						
27313 25	Hardbound		20	*9.6	123.1	6.6	55.9
27313 27	Paperbound		11	*1.6	15.8	(S)	3.2
	Business books (nonfiction books on business for adult readers in the profession):						
27313 35	Hardbound		16	2.5	30.3	4.2	37.9
27313 37	Paperbound		6	2.2	5.2	1.1	4.1
	Other technical, scientific, and professional books:						
27313 45	Hardbound		56	**10.8	154.4	(S)	80.2

U.S. CENSUS OF BOOK PUBLISHING, 1977 / 469

27313 47	Paperbound	Million	36	18.6	56.6	25.0	54.9
27313 00	Technical, scientific, and professional books, n.s.k.	......	(NA)	(X)	33.3	(X)	19.9
27314 --	**Religious books**						
	Bibles and testaments:		(NA)	(X)	234.2	(X)	131.2
27314 11	Hardbound, including flexible	Million	22	14.7	75.1	29.3	52.6
27314 13	Paperbound		9	4.7	7.7		
27314 23	Hymnals and devotionals, including prayer books and missals, hardbound and paperbound		14	*9.2	21.0	6.6	9.0
	Other religious books, including books of fiction or nonfiction dealing with religious subjects for adult and juvenile reading:						
27314 25	Hardbound		36	*22.8	66.8	18.3	30.0
27314 27	Paperbound	Million	36	*48.3	52.2	39.7	28.3
27314 00	Religious books, n.s.k.	......	(NA)	(X)	11.4	(X)	11.3
27315 --	**General books (trade, etc.)**		(NA)	(X)	1864.0	(X)	1006.7
	Adult trade books (fiction or nonfiction sold primarily through retail or wholesale booksellers at trade discounts):						
27315 41	Hardbound	Million	70	*86.8	365.1	(S)	232.1
27315 43	Paperbound[3]		59	74.0	144.0	³385.8	³220.5
	Book club books:						
27315 15	Hardbound		17	146.1	340.1	31.0	98.0
27315 17	Paperbound		8			81.2	33.3
27315 71	Mail order books, hardbound and paperbound		30	37.4	362.3	44.9	198.2
27315 31	Mass market paperbound books, usually of rack size, distributed predominantly to mass market outlets[3]		21	566.7	460.1	159.8	³90.3
	Juvenile books, fiction and nonfiction, excluding toy and coloring books:						
27315 51	Hardbound[4]		39	45.3	113.0	449.0	479.8
27315 53	Paperbound[4]	Million	17	60.4	36.7	414.8	48.4
27315 00	General books (trade, etc.), n.s.k.[4]	......	(NA)	(X)	42.7	(X)	46.1
27317 --	**General reference books**		(NA)	(X)	310.1	(X)	235.3
	Subscription reference books:						
27317 21	Encyclopedias	Million	15	(S)	202.2	12.7	166.9
27317 23	Religious	↔	4	(S)	5.1	(S)	3.6
27317 25	Other	Million	9	(S)	25.1	12.6	28.0
	Other reference books:						
27317 41	Dictionaries and thesauruses	Million	14	5.6	32.1	5.7	12.7
27317 43	Atlases	↔	3	1.4	1.4	(S)	1.2
27317 49	Other	Million	27	(S)	38.6	(S)	19.5
27317 00	General reference books, n.s.k.	......	(NA)	(X)	5.6	(X)	3.4
27318 --	**Other books, excluding pamphlets**		(NA)	(X)	113.8	(X)	125.4
	Music books:						
27318 12	Hardbound	Million	5	1.7	2.3	(S)	2.9
27318 14	Paperbound	↔	17	12.2	21.2	15.4	10.3

TABLE 1 1977 CENSUS OF MANUFACTURES (INDUSTRY SERIES) (cont.)

1977 Product Code	Product	Unit of measure	Number of companies with receipts of $100,000 or more	1977 Quantity sold[1][2]	1977 Value of receipts[1] ($ million)	1972 Quantity sold[1][2]	1972 Value of receipts[1] ($ million)
27318 11	University press books, hardbound and paperbound		6	1.5	10.7	⁵28.8	⁵87.0
	Other books, n.e.c.:				63.7		
27318 17	Hardbound	Million	13	14.2	9.8	(X)	25.2
27318 19	Paperbound		14	(S)	6.1	(X)	48.7
27318 00	Other books, excluding pamphlets, n.s.k.		(NA)	(X)		(X)	6.2
29319 --	Pamphlets (5-48 pages)		(NA)	(X)	44.1	(X)	42.5
27319 43	Music	Million	10	*29.2	25.8	20.1	
27319 59	Other, including religious and text	Million	11	**156.0	13.7	444.2	—
27319 00	Pamphlets, n.s.k.		(NA)	(X)	4.6	(X)	
27310 00	Book publishing, n.s.k., typically for establishments with 5 employees or more (see NOTE 2)		(NA)	(X)	191.4	(X)	94.8
27310 02	Book publishing, n.s.k., typically for establishments with fewer than 5 employees (see NOTE 2)		(NA)	(X)	122.7	(X)	60.7

Source: Reprinted, with slight changes in format, from U.S. Department of Commerce, Bureau of the Census; U.S. Census of Manufactures: 1977, Table 3.
Note: Includes quantity and value of products of this industry produced by (1) establishments classified in this industry (primary) and (2) establishments classified in other industries (secondary). Transfers of the products of this industry from one establishment of a company to another establishment of the same company (interplant transfers) are also included.
²Note 2: In 1977 Census of Manufactures, shipments data for establishments of small companies, typically those with fewer than five employees, were estimated from administrative records data rather than collected from respondents. These shipments figures are included in code ending with "002." In both 1977 and 1972 Census of Manufactures, products not completely identified on standard forms were coded to appropriate product class (5 digits) followed by "00." or in some cases to appropriate product group (4 digits) followed by "000."
— Represents zero. n.s.k. Not specified by kind. (S) Withheld because estimate did not meet publication standards. (X) Not collected. (NA) Not available. n.e.c. Not elsewhere classified.
¹For some establishments, data have been estimated from central unit values, which are based on quantity-value relationships of reported data. The following symbols are used when percentage of each quantity figure estimated in this manner equals or exceeds 10% of published figure: * indicates 10–19% estimated; ** indicates 20–29% estimated. If 30% or more is estimated, figure is replaced by (S).
²Quantity and value reported by all producers of product, not just those with shipments of $100,000 or more.
³For 1977, the term "mass market paperbound books" was introduced, replacing the 1972 term "wholesale paperbound books." The old term appears to have caused a misclassification of books between adult trade paperbound books and wholesale paperbound books in 1972.
⁴For 1972, data for mass merchandised juvenile books were collected separately, but included with data for "general books (trade, etc.), n.s.k.," to avoid disclosing operations of individual companies. For 1977, data for mass merchandising juvenile books were included with "juvenile books, fiction and nonfiction, excluding toy and coloring books."
⁵For 1972, data for university press books were not collected separately, but were included with data for "other books, n.e.c."

TABLE 2 ESTIMATED BOOK PUBLISHING INDUSTRY SALES, 1972–1978
Millions of Dollars

	1972 $	1977 $	1977 % Increase over 1972	1978 $	1978 % Change from 1977	1978 % Increase over 1972
Trade (Total)	442.0	807.0	82.6	940.5	16.5	112.8
Adult Hardbound	251.5	484.3	92.6	564.7	16.6	124.5
Adult Paperbound	79.6	171.6	115.6	205.4	19.7	158.0
Juvenile Hardbound	106.5	126.5	18.8	134.6	6.4	26.4
Juvenile Paperbound	4.4	24.6	459.1	35.8	45.7	713.6
Religious (Total)	117.5	249.0	111.9	273.8	10.0	133.0
Bibles, Testaments, Hymnals & Prayerbooks	61.6	116.5	89.1	134.8	15.7	118.8
Other Religious	55.9	132.5	137.0	139.0	4.9	148.7
Professional (Total)	381.0	701.0	84.0	807.9	15.2	212.0
Technical & Scientific	131.8	248.9	88.8	277.0	11.3	110.2
Business & Other Professional	192.2	288.8	50.3	336.2	16.4	74.9
Medical	57.0	163.3	186.5	194.7	19.2	241.6
Book Clubs	240.5	404.3	68.1	460.1	13.8	91.3
Mail Order Publications	198.9	397.3	99.7	441.4	11.1	121.9
Mass Market Paperback (Total)	252.8	541.9	114.4	608.1	12.2	140.5
Rack-Sized	250.0	488.4	95.4	544.9	11.6	118.0
Nonrack-Sized	2.8	53.5	1810.7	63.2	18.1	2157.1
University Presses	41.4	56.1	35.5	62.2	10.9	50.2
Elementary & Secondary Text	497.6	747.3	50.2	823.5	10.2	65.5
College Text	375.3	662.4	76.5	749.2	13.1	99.6
Standardized Tests	26.5	44.7	68.7	52.0	16.3	96.2
Subscription Reference	278.9	303.3	8.7	351.5	15.9	26.0
AV & Other Media (Total)	116.2	151.3	30.2	151.2	– 0.1	30.1
Elhi	101.2	131.4	29.8	130.5	– 0.7	29.0
College	9.2	11.6	26.1	12.2	5.2	32.6
Other	5.8	8.3	43.1	8.5	2.4	46.6
Other Sales	49.2	62.2	4.9	50.8	–18.3	3.3
Total	**3017.8**	**5127.8**	**69.9**	**5772.2**	**12.6**	**91.3**

SOURCE: Association of American Publishers

because of the Association of American Publishers–American Association of University Presses sponsored annual statistical survey which enjoys extensive participation by presses.

AAP estimates, on the other hand, exclude pamphlets and Sunday school materials that are incorporated in the census.

Classifications and Definitions. The Census Bureau and industry associations have cooperated for decades with the objective of keeping differences in product classification, definition, and nomenclature to a minimum. Generally, therefore, there is more agreement than disagreement regarding these matters, which greatly facilitates comparison between the two programs. Still, there are differences. The census, for example, classifies General Reference Books and Music Books together, whereas AAP estimates include these books under other umbrella categories, such as trade, elhi, text, college text, etc.

Of course, any industry survey may become contaminated with error when respondents misclassify data or misinterpret directions. However, since AAP canvasses are conducted with greater regularity and in more extensive detail than census surveys, AAP data have occasionally proved very effective in detecting and correcting errors in census reports, particularly when the categories in question were well represented in AAP samples.

Yet another difference looms large between the two programs, however: the unclassified or partially classified categories in census reports. Most of these categories result from the failure of publishers to break down their sales into brackets specified by the census (e.g., 27315 00—General Books, not specified by kind, or 27310 00—Book Publishing, not specified by kind). Furthermore, "in 1977 Census of Manufactures, shipments data for establishment of small companies, typically those with fewer than 5 employees, were estimated from administrative records data rather than collected from respondents." The category so estimated (27310 02) is also not classified by type of book.

Since all sales in AAP estimates are segregated by category, substantial allocations had to be made in restating the census findings in AAP terms. The most important of these included:

Sales in umbrella sections not specified by kind were allocated within their sections in the same proportion as data specifically reported.

Industry sales not specified by kind (categories 27310 00 and 27310 02) were also allocated in proportion to specified data. Somewhat more weight, however, was given to consumer-oriented categories in allocating data from section 27310 02 on the assumption that more small publishers are consumer rather than educationally or professionally oriented.

An estimated $70.5 million in audiovisual and other nonbook revenues was extracted from textbook sales ($65 million from elhi and $5.5 million from college).

An estimated $35 million in revenues was transferred from professional to book club sales.

An estimated $35 million in adult trade paperbound and $18.5 million in juvenile paperbound sales were reclassified as nonrack-sized mass market paperbound revenues.

$36.1 million in pamphlet sales (category 27319) was eliminated.

An estimated $45.4 million in university press book sales was added.

(Similar adjustments, particularly with regard to mass market paperbacks, trade paperbound books, and book club sales, had been necessary to reconcile the 1972 census with the AAP matrix.)

Since the census, as the master survey of book publishing, provides a quintennial measurement of the industry's progress by which other measurements must be judged, we must ask why our earlier estimates had fallen short of the mark. The answer lies largely in the number of establishments reporting to the 1972 and 1977 census. In 1972 the total number of these establishments was 1,205 of which 307 employed 20 or more people; by 1977 the total had risen to 1,750, with 348 employing 20 or more. Total establishments had risen by 45%; larger establishments by 13%.

Significantly, the activities of this sizable number of new entrants had remained largely unmeasured until the 1977 census. Relatively few of the new publishers joined existing trade associations; even fewer reported to industry surveys. Unknown, and to a large degree undetected, these new enterprises could not be provided for in our estimates of industry sales. Now that the 1977 Census Report has given dimensions to an expanding publishing universe, future sales estimates will be able to make allowances for any additional growth.

This is already the case with the 1978 estimates shown in Table 2. Based, as in the past, on sample surveys of publishers in AAP statistical reports, the 1978 estimate makes additional allowances for industry expansion. According to records maintained by the R. R. Bowker Company, new publishing houses continued to come into existence at a lusty pace during 1978, so that this allowance is amply justified.

The value of the 1977 census for the industry has been far from exhausted. Much remains to be extracted from it, including estimates of unit sales and dollar and unit estimates for the interim years 1973 through 1976. (Both of these features appeared in "Book Industry Trends—1979," published by BISG at the end of 1979.) In the meantime, the census has alerted us to a significant new development: the substantial impact on industry sales of a sizable number of small new publishing ventures. Each if the pace of expansion were now to slacken, even if some of the new imprints were ultimately to fail, a safe assumption is that the existence of so many small independent publishers is bound to affect the future of the book field profoundly and lastingly.

U.S. CONSUMER EXPENDITURES ON BOOKS IN 1978

John P. Dessauer

Book Industry Statistician

Expenditures on books by U.S. individuals and institutions increased by 14.1% in 1978 to $6.5 billion. The rate of increase was the same as that posted in 1977 when expenditures totaled $5.7 billion. However, the number of books (units) purchased in 1978 increased by only 5.3% to nearly 1.6 billion compared to an 8.8% increase in 1977 when units totaled 1.5 billion.

Note: Reprinted from *Publishers Weekly*, February 1, 1980.

TABLE 1 U.S. DOMESTIC CONSUMER EXPENDITURES ON BOOKS, 1977 AND 1978
(Millions of Dollars and Units)

	1978 Dollars	1978 Units	1977 Dollars	1977 Units	% Change Dollars	% Change Units	Dollars per Unit 1978	Dollars per Unit 1977	% Change
Trade	1,448	372	1,228	277	17.3	12.7	4.62	4.43	4.3
Adult Hardbound	866	123	737	108	17.5	14.4	7.04	6.82	3.2
Adult Paperbound	329	90	274	84	19.9	7.5	3.66	3.26	12.3
Juvenile Hardbound	185	50	175	48	5.9	6.0	3.70	3.65	1.4
Juvenile Paperbound	61	48	42	38	46.3	27.9	1.27	1.11	14.4
Religious	425	112	399	106	6.7	5.4	3.79	3.76	0.8
Hardbound	295	44	279	44	5.6	0.2	6.70	6.34	5.7
Paperbound	131	68	120	62	9.2	9.0	1.93	1.94	−0.5
Professional	777	50	648	50	19.9	0.5	15.54	12.96	19.9
Hardbound	615	28	511	28	20.3	0.8	21.96	18.25	20.3
Paperbound	162	22	137	22	18.6	0.1	7.36	6.23	18.1
Book Clubs	452	230	394	211	14.6	9.2	1.97	1.87	5.4
Hardbound	324	60	285	57	13.8	5.4	5.40	5.00	8.0
Paperbound	128	170	109	154	16.8	10.6	0.75	0.71	5.6
Mail Order Publications	453	44	406	40	11.7	8.6	10.30	10.15	1.5
Mass Market Paperback	959	499	859	492	11.6	1.4	1.92	1.72	11.6
University Presses	67	8	59	7	12.5	7.9	8.38	8.01	4.6
Hardbound	49	4	44	3	11.6	3.3	13.75	12.75	7.8
Paperbound	17	4	15	4	15.2	12.0	3.96	3.85	2.9
Elhi Text	808	249	732	245	10.4	1.5	3.24	2.99	8.4
Hardbound	435	91	401	91	8.6	−0.2	4.78	4.41	8.4
Paperbound	373	158	331	154	12.6	2.5	2.36	2.15	9.8
College Text	830	89	724	84	14.6	5.3	9.33	8.62	8.2
Hardbound	632	56	555	55	14.0	2.9	11.29	10.09	11.9
Paperbound	197	32	169	30	16.8	9.9	6.16	5.63	9.4
Subscription Reference	327	1	281	1	16.1	8.2	291.52	270.48	7.8
Total	6,537	1,594	5,729	1,514	14.1	5.3	4.10	3.78	8.5

Note: Dollar and unit data have been rounded to millions. Change percentages, however, are based on unrounded data. Source subtotals and totals may not add exactly due to rounding.

Source: Book Industry Trends, 1979.

TABLE 2 CHANNELS OF U.S. DOMESTIC BOOK DISTRIBUTION,
1977 AND 1978
(Estimated Consumer Expenditures—Millions of Dollars and Units)

	1978 Dollars	1978 Units	1977 Dollars	1977 Units	% Change Dollars	% Change Units
General retailers	2,163	641	1,867	595	15.8	7.8
College stores	1,196	197	1,049	194	14.1	1.7
Libraries and institutions	550	84	481	79	14.5	6.0
Schools	1,038	320	940	316	10.5	1.5
Direct to consumer	1,496	317	1,313	299	14.0	6.0
Other	94	34	80	31	16.4	8.9
Total	6,537	1,594	5,729	1,514	14.1	5.3

The data are excerpted from estimates and projections of industry sales in *Book Industry Trends, 1979*, which was published recently by the Book Industry Study Group. These estimates have been completely revised from earlier versions to bring them into conformity with the 1977 U.S. Census of Manufactures released earlier in 1979. [See the article "The U.S. Census of Book Publishing, 1977" that appears earlier in this section of Part 4—*Ed.*]

Table 1 shows consumer expenditures by type of book. Apparently, 1978, like 1977 before it, was a good year for tradebooks, which scored a 17.3% dollar and 12.7% unit increase. Most remarkable was a unit gain of 14.4% by adult trade hardbounds, which compared very favorably with the 7.5% unit growth shown by adult trade paperbounds and the 1.4% unit increase posted by mass market paperbacks. On the other hand, juvenile paperbounds were the most successful category of all, with a 46.3% dollar and a 27.9% unit gain.

The dollar expenditures per unit listed in the table provide an indication of the price inflation at work in the various categories. There appears to be some correlation between substantial price increases and lower unit sales, as in the case of adult trade paperbounds, professional books, and mass market paperbacks. The juvenile paperbound figures also reflect sizable price increases; however, changes in the type and age level of titles released during 1978 probably had a greater impact on the averages than did inflation in this instance.

Expenditures by channel of distribution are estimated in Table 2. General retailers had a good year, although they did not match the 19.0% dollar and 15.3% unit gains established in 1977. Libraries and institutions performed slightly better than in 1977 as did consumers buying directly from publishers and book clubs. The pace of increase for college stores and schools fell off compared to 1977, although any growth was bound to be impressive in view of declining enrollments and tight budgets in many localities.

Overall, 1978 was a year of solid growth for the industry in which favorable general economic conditions, increased consumer interest in books, and the continued, if modest, recovery of institutional markets worked together to produce not only expectable dollar increases but encouraging unit gains as well.

NUMBER OF BOOK OUTLETS IN THE UNITED STATES AND CANADA

The *American Book Trade Directory* has been published by the R. R. Bowker Company since 1915. Revised biennially, it features lists of booksellers, publishers, wholesalers, periodicals, reference tools, and other information about the U.S. book market as well as markets in Great Britain and Canada. The data provided in Tables 1 and 2 for the United States and Canada, the most current available, are from the 1979 edition of the directory.

The 17,159 stores of various types shown in Table 1 are located in approximately 4,533 cities in the United States, Canada, and regions administered by the United States. All "general" bookstores are assumed to carry hardbound (trade) books, paperbacks, and children's books; special effort has been made to apply this category only to bookstores for which this term can properly be applied. All "college" stores are assumed to carry college-level textbooks. The term "educational" is used for outlets handling school textbooks up to and including the high school level. The category "mail order" has been confined to those outlets that sell general trade books by mail and are not books clubs; all others operating by mail have been classified according to the kinds of books carried. The term "antiquarian" covers dealers in old and rare books. Stores handling only secondhand books are classified by the category "used." The category "paperbacks" represents stores with stock consisting of more than an 80% holding of paperbound books. Other stores with paperback departments are listed under the

TABLE 1 BOOKSTORES IN THE UNITED STATES (AND CANADA)

Antiquarian	835 (56)	Museum store and art gallery	159 (9)
Mail order-antiquarian	476 (11)	Newsdealer	116 (5)
College	2,442 (137)	Office supply	69 (2)
Department store	1,276 (111)	Paperback*	731 (26)
Drugstore	16 (2)	Religious	2,751 (182)
Educational	104 (11)	Rental	4 (0)
Exporter-importer	24 (1)	Science-technology	49 (4)
Foreign language	87 (19)	Special†	605 (185)
General	4,638 (1,170)	Stationer	151 (22)
Gift shop	91 (9)	Used	311 (10)
Juvenile	83 (12)		
Law	57 (1)	Total listed in the United States	15,163
Mail order (general)	172 (10)		
Medical	103 (3)	Total listed in Canada	1,996

*This figure does not include paperback departments of general bookstores, department stores, stationers, drugstores, or wholesalers handling paperbacks.
†This indicates stores specializing in subjects other than those specifically given in the list.

TABLE 2 WHOLESALERS IN THE UNITED STATES (AND CANADA)

General wholesalers	695 (98)	Total listed in the United States	1,019
Paperback wholesalers	324 (13)	Total listed in Canada	111

Note: In Tables 1 and 2, the Canadian figure for each category is in parentheses following the U.S. figure.

major classification ("general," "department store," "stationers," etc.), with the fact that paperbacks are carried given in the entry. A bookstore that specializes in a subject to the extent of 50% of its stock has that subject designated as its major category.

BOOK REVIEW MEDIA STATISTICS

NUMBER OF BOOKS REVIEWED BY MAJOR BOOK-REVIEWING PUBLICATIONS, 1978 AND 1979

	Adult 1978	Adult 1979	Juvenile 1978	Juvenile 1979	Young Adult 1978	Young Adult 1979	Total 1978	Total 1979
Booklist[a]	3,524	2,900	1,075	1,280	401	1,243	5,490	5,812
Bookviews[b]	2,160	—	240	—	—	—	2,400	—
Bulletin of the Center for Children's Books	—	—	453	452	399	398	852	850
Choice[c]	6,683	6,814	—	—	—	—	6,683	6,814
Horn Book	6	23	420	334	44	119	470	476
Kirkus Services	3,451	3,938	1,250	904	—	—	4,701	4,842
Library Journal	5,800	6,014	—	—	—	—	5,800	6,014
New York Review of Books[d]	500	550	—	—	—	—	500	550
New York Times Sunday Book Review	1,974	2,000	319	300	—	—	2,293	2,300
Publishers Weekly[e]	4,453	4,336	562	545	—	—	5,015	4,881
School Library Journal	—	—	2,085	2,249	311	272	2,396	2,521
Washington Post Book World	1,644	1,856	137	128	—	—	1,781	1,984
West Coast Review of Books	1,922	2,500	78	75	—	—	2,000	2,575

[a] All figures are for a 12-month period from September 1 to August 31, e.g., 1979 figures are for September 1, 1978–August 31, 1979. Totals include reference and subscription books. In addition, *Booklist* published reviews of nonprint materials: 1,906 in 1978; 1,534 in 1979.

[b] *Bookviews* ceased publication in 1978.

[c] All figures are for a 12-month period beginning in March and ending in February, e.g., 1979 figures are for March 1979–February 1980.

[d] Figures for 1978 given in *Bowker Annual, 1979* have been revised.

[e] Includes reviews of paperback originals and reprints.

Part 5
International Reports and Statistical Analyses

International Reports

FRANKFURT BOOK FAIR, 1979

Herbert R. Lottman
International Correspondent, *Publishers Weekly*

"In Frankfurt you have to separate agitation from activity," a publisher—Jean-Manuel Bourgois of the French Bordas group—was heard to say during a *Kaffee* break at the thirty-first Frankfurt Book Fair (October 10-15). Bourgois was actually repeating a remark that had been made to him, for one of the regular features of any working day at the fair is the spectacle of publishers taking each other's pulses. He himself found the fair "tranquil" but "good for business," a typical reaction of book people from the leading publishing nations. Worldwide recession—with pockets of strength? Areas of weakness—in an otherwise flourishing market? Both views were heard. But everyone agreed this was a "serious" fair, with less hysteria about blockbuster projects (real or imaginary) than in most recent Frankfurt years. Opinions differ as to whether there had been an overall reduction in the number of people staffing each stand. But for every comment that the fair seemed less crowded, that some familiar faces were absent, there was always someone else ready to swear that everybody anybody would want to see was available to be seen.

Prior to the opening of the fair its management had put out word that the event had attained a plateau, with the number of exhibiting imprints down from last year (5,045 to the previous year's 5,098). Close examination of the data showed that in fact there were more individual stands than before (3,533 to last year's 3,319); the drop was in the number of imprints represented on collective stands (1,512 versus 1,779), confirming what fair director Peter Weidhaas called qualitative growth. (There were 3,730 foreign exhibitors, 1,266 from West Germany, 49 from East Germany.) The fair administration was putting the emphasis on stability in an attempt to defuse the emphasis in the German press on growth. According to Weidhaas the present and temporary balance—"temporary because we must always allow for the unforeseeable and therefore proceed pragmatically"—conforms to a decision of the book fair's board of directors to hold exhibition space to present dimensions. This year 150 houses that had requested extra space were turned down (and thus DM 260,000 in revenues was forfeited), while 35 publishers couldn't be accommodated at all because of late application, lack of space. The total display area covered 753,200 square feet, with rack space for 280,000 books. Eighty nations were represented, but the circle of significant publishing and bookselling nations did not seem to have widened.

The fair was open to the book trade (admission DM 2.50, or DM 5 for the run of the fair) from October 10 to 14, from 9 A.M. to 6:30 P.M., 9 A.M. to 2 P.M. on October 15, and to the general public (same entrance fees) from October 10 to 14, from 2 to 6:30

Note: Reprinted from *Publishers Weekly*, November 12, 1979, where the article was entitled "Frankfurt 1979—Book Fair Diagnosis: Stable, Tranquil and a Most Desirable Serious Condition."

P.M. No direct sales were permitted, although, as usual, professionals were able to buy single copies from each other, often at a decent discount, in the final hours.

What director Weidhaas calls "the international working fair" takes place primarily in Exhibition Halls 5 and 5a (the latter for sci-tech books); the German public is concentrated in Halls 6 and 8 (German trade books, children's and art books in 6; religious, educational, and reference books in 8). Upon this "delicate construction" —interdependent spheres, two tracks—the planners have superimposed a network of special-interest centers for the book trade: an exhibitors' center and restaurant, a German booksellers' center, and the international booksellers' center, now combined with a librarians' center, offering a message desk, a lounge and lunch area, reference materials, and lockers. A much-used literary agents' center smack in the middle of International Hall 5 supplemented the increasing number of booths rented by individual agents.

Two publishers used the fair in an unusual way: by boycotting it. Switzerland's literary imprint Diogenes told the world that it didn't think Frankfurt was worthwhile, and then laid siege to the fair, operating out of a hotel, setting its editors loose in the exhibition halls, taking a front cover ad in *Börsenblatt* to advertise its "Fair special" program, which consisted of author appearances in downtown coffeeshops and department stores, a panel discussion at the university, the premiere of a film by house author Federico Fellini. Paul Hamlyn also worked from his hotel, thanks to having 5,000 publishers within hearing distance.

The fair administration took the boycott as harmless fun. Weidhaas underlined the role of the fair as a domestic German event, a sales and promotion fair a la ABA for the German bookbuyer; the visitor tripped over television camera cables as usual in German Halle 6. It's a German fair *before* being an international one. And Weidhaas believes that such an international event can be significant only if there is a strong home market to support it.

HOTEL AVAILABILITY DECRIED

"The real story this year is the hotel situation," observed Peter Czerwonka, press chief of the German book trade organization. For the fair had been registering visitors' complaints of arbitrary, often brutal treatment—more even than in past years. In addition to cancelling room reservations at the last minute, hotels had a new practice of demanding payment for rooms up to six months in advance. Publishers reported being expelled from hotels they had been using for a dozen or more years because they didn't spend enough money (e.g., by throwing parties).

The book fair had been trying to deal with this through the city's mayor, whose leverage is tax law and exemptions, but also via the press. Fair director Weidhaas estimated there were 24,000 foreign visitors to this year's fair, for 13,000 hotel beds in the city, and so hotels as far away as Heidelberg, 50 miles distant, and bedrooms in private homes in the Frankfurt area, were being tapped. *PW* also talked to the management of a favorite fairtime hotel, the Intercontinental. Fred G. Peelen, regional vice-president for operations of Inter-Continental Hotels in Germany, led off with the observation that if Frankfurt had enough hotels to take care of visitors during the 50 days of the year when there is a trade fair in town, the hotels would operate at a loss all the rest of the year. Peelen puts the number of first-class rooms in Frankfurt at 15,000 (22,000 beds). The last hotel opened here was a Holiday Inn (in January 1978); the only promise of relief is an additional 250 to 300 rooms in a Kempinski hotel now being built just outside of town.

Peelen felt that the absence of temporary ship hotels moored along the Main River was proof that the situation was not as bad as all that. (In fact the fair did bring one such ship to town, and quickly filled it up.) The hotels admit that they accord preference to companies that give them year-round business, and blame fair participants for aggravating the situation by booking in more than one hotel in order to be sure to have rooms. The solution this year was to require deposits, a guarantee for hotel and guest.

Longer term solutions? The Intercontinental's resident manager Clement J. Barter noted that rapid connections with nearby towns make it possible to travel by train to the fair nearly as fast as one can get to it from outlying parts of the Frankfurt area. Finally, Peelen denied the persistent story that his hotel raised its rates during the fair. (They were asking DM 200 for a single room, DM 16 for breakfast, with the dollar at DM 1.70 to 1.75.) "We're ready to open our books. As the largest international chain, we couldn't afford to do anything like that."

Back on the fairgrounds there seemed to be no complaints about the organization of this year's exhibition. American publishers had their usual territory at one end of giant Hall 5. Many of the largest publishers and groups, and a lot of smaller ones, had stands of their own, staffed by heads of houses, editors, and rights managers and interpreters. Some 40 companies chose to exhibit with their exporter Feffer & Simons, but most of these also brought people from home in addition to the Feffer & Simons team of 15 headed by Paul Feffer. Nearby, Combined Book Exhibit hosted 20 individual stands and over 80 additional imprints in a collective display. CBE had also mounted a periodical exhibition in adjacent Hall 5a, and the feeling was that foreign periodicals would become an important feature of future fairs, with other countries following the lead of the Americans into Hall 5a (at present they often included journals in their book exhibits—which they are not supposed to do).

Ruth Gottstein of Independent Publishers Services (formerly Schanhaar/Gottstein) tended a flock of small and medium-sized houses, many of them West Coast imprints, provided space for agents too (like Frankfurt veteran Sally Wecksler). Gottstein was doing more agenting than ever (and found results more than satisfactory because "America is now the bargain of the publishing world"). Academia Book Exhibits, run by Emmy Jacobius (now with husband Arnold, following his retirement from the Library of Congress), represented 18 U.S. houses for rights and sales. Many American paperback houses, even when they brought top people along, exhibited with their regional distributors in large collective areas.

Some 400 British publishers were present with stands or in collective exhibitions (there was the usual government subsidy for stand rental). The Canadians had half a dozen individual stands, and most other significant Canadian imprints were represented on a large central stand staffed by the country's two publishers' associations. But Quebec took a booth of its own and demanded and got space in the French-language area of Hall 5. Of course all major nations came with national exhibitions as well as individual stands, but often the dimensions and decoration of the former had little to do with the importance of the country's publishing vitality.

For the second year a daily *Börsenblatt* was published in English and French as well as German, thanks to Macmillan, Inc., and its Berlitz linguists; Macmillan's international man Fred Kobrak served as occasional reporter as well as publisher, with a team working out of the Canadian Pacific Plaza hotel just opposite the fairgrounds. There was a print run of 10,000 for each of the five publication days, the magazine accepting ads up to 4 P.M. on the day preceding publication; it was delivered free to stands and to other strategic places before 9 A.M. each morning. Perhaps there was more promotion than news, but that may be in the nature of book fairs, and the magazine promised to be back next year.

PRINCESS DAISY THE HIGHLIGHT

The big book at Frankfurt wasn't quite a surprise, for Judith Krantz's *Princess Daisy* had been making headlines long before the fair opened with the record $3.2 million Bantam purchase of paperback rights (*PW*, The Week, September 24). Bantam went on to engineer acquisition by its British affiliate Corgi of the balance of English-language rights for $450,000, which purchased hardcover and serial rights as well as softcover, and protected the U.S. company's investment. Then, on the eve of the fair, Vienna's Fritz Molden broke another record with his offer for German rights—DM 865,000—winning an auction over Bantam's German owner Bertelsmann. Molden told *PW* he was getting his money back from a German book club (DM 550,000) and reprint publisher (DM 300,000), with another DM 300,000 expected for first serial. From Bertelsmann's point of view Molden's warning that he'd top any bid had led to a "ridiculous" situation, and Molden had the advantage of being able to spread the cost over two books, for he was also going to publish the same author's *Scruples*. Bertelsmann said it was also worried about the psychological effect of a widely reported high advance on the rest of its authors; other foreign publishers in the bidding shared this concern. And some wondered how the 15 percent Bantam royalty would affect the future of trading in reprint rights.

Auctions for foreign rights for *Princess Daisy* were being handled by Allan Eady, Crown's international sales and foreign rights manager, whose familiarity with the topography and folklore of Frankfurt came from his years with Feffer & Simons. At this fair Eady seemed omnipresent. He was taking bids at midnight rendezvous in hotel bars, striding the aisles of Hall 5 to relay new floors, extend new deadlines. One thought one heard the roll of drums as Eady turned a corner to confront a publisher anxiously waiting for the verdict. Eady discovered that sometimes he had to be a detective as well as a diplomat, for each country had its own way of negotiating, and in at least one the publishers had banded together, like dealers at an antiques auction, to keep the bids low.

Here a Talleyrand, there an Avenger, Allan Eady knocked down one national record after another. In Italy Mondadori got the book, in Spain Plaza y Janés acquired Spanish rights without Latin America (Plaza is now affiliated with Bertelsmann). Brazil's Record took world Portuguese. Then Dutch book club ECI, 65 percent Bertelsmann-owned, bought volume as well as club rights for that country. Otava got it for Finland. Virtually at closing time, Albin Michel (which already owned French rights for *Scruples*) got the book. Eady would be pursuing the rest of the literate world immediately after the fair, packing the auction figures in his briefcase like a U.S. presidential assistant carrying the nuclear code for the traveling president.

The only book that could compete with *Princess Daisy* was another American product—*Thy Neighbor's Wife*. The Gay Talese manuscript about sex in America (in the form of a reduced and bound photocopy) had arrived in midfair in the luggage of Doubleday's Sam Vaughan; it had some help in the form of the news about the record $2.5 million sale of movie rights to United Artists. Big spender Fritz Molden snapped it up for $250,000.

Albin Michel, winning bidder on a number of international hot properties, had a contender of its own in the memoirs of the Shah of Iran. Without a manuscript to show, the house's rights manager Béatrix Blavier was registering options, principally for serial rights.

An only-in-Frankfurt story was the experience of a small Canadian imprint, Lester & Orpen Dennys, in handling English-language and world rights to Graham Greene's literary autobiography, *Trial and Execution*, due next spring. The firm's Louise Dennys, a niece of the author, had been editing the manuscript (consisting of prefaces and other writing about writing) when Greene decided to give world rights to the firm to encourage independent Canadian publishing. (He was also pleased with what the house was doing with *The Bass Saxophone*, a novel by his Toronto-based friend Josef Skvorecky.)

Agent Roslyn Targ was offering *Call the Darkness Light* by Nancy Zaroulis, the novel edited by Jacqueline Onassis and already published by Doubleday with a half-million-dollar sale to NAL. Hamlyn, which had British rights, threw a Frankfurt party for Zaroulis's publishers present and potential. Israeli-based agent Barbara Rogan also carried around a first novel, her own, entitled *Zara*, encouraged by an early sale of Hebrew rights to Asher Weil's Edanim; Lois Wallace was offering the book in New York.

One dummy on a Frankfurt stand was insured for $100,000 and kept locked in a hotel safe at night: the original artwork by graphic designer Ivan Chermayeff for a Kurt Vonnegut, Jr., Nativity story, *Sun, Moon, Star*, to be published by Harper & Row a year hence. Chermayeff had done the cutout illustrations first, and Vonnegut added a text, shifting the order of the Matisse-like abstracts as suited him; at Frankfurt, Vonnegut's friend and advisor Frank Platt reinforced the sales force at the Harper booth.

But for the German reading public, the 1979 Frankfurt fair was Henry Kissinger's. There were virtually simultaneous launchings of *White House Years* in a dozen countries, and in Germany Bertelsmann and newsweekly *Der Spiegel* had paid handsomely for the right to be the ones to do it. Bertelsmann printed 100,000 copies of this first volume of memoirs at a DM 56 list price (close to $33 versus Little, Brown's $22.50, a reflection of the price levels in northern Europe today); 78,000 copies had been placed prior to publication day.

Kissinger was brought to town in a Bertelsmann jet after a visit to German Chancellor Helmut Schmidt to present a copy of the book. For security reasons, Kissinger did not go out to the fairgrounds, but he met 250 reporters, photographers, and cameras in a salon of the Frankfurter Hof hotel, then moved into another room for a reception for his publishers around the world, finally into a third room for a more intimate lunch. During the fair and just before it, German television viewers discovered not only that Kissinger spoke decent German but that he was willing to. (Kissinger had always said that his was an adolescent's German; he told the press at the Frankfurter Hof that he spoke no language without an accent.) To the surprise and delight of top people at Bertelsmann their author turned into a German TV personality, projecting an image most bookbuyers might understand and even like; the publisher immediately upped its projection of sales. In addition to Bertelsmann publisher Olaf Paeschke, Kissinger publishers present at the reception were Arthur Thornhill of Little, Brown; George Weidenfeld; French Fayard's Alex Grall; Swedish Norstedt's Lasse Bergström; and Norwegian Cappelen's Sigmund Strømme.

Recession or no, it was a fair of memorable parties. Such as Bertelsmann's, where the food never ran out, and decent food at that. The morning after, guests were still wondering aloud how much the party must have cost, and some suspected that Bertelsmann had hoped that guests would be asking each other that question.

For its seventieth anniversary Kodansha held a simpatico reception, the hosts in ceremonial costume, emcee Tom Mori leading cheers and chants, and Japanese specialties including raw fish and sake. Norway's Cappelen celebrated its one hundred and fiftieth anniversary with a party, and Sweden's Askild & Kärnekull feted its tenth with a dinner during which Timo Kärnekull greeted representatives of eight nationalities in their languages, and recipes from his company's recently published Swedish cookbook were used—and abused—by the hotel chefs.

Macmillan again held a champagne breakfast in a convenient ballroom opposite the fairgrounds where useful contacts could be made in morning light, and Reader's Digest Condensed Books staged its traditional Saturday night at the Hessischer Hof (no American publishers invited). A party was hosted by the fast-moving Kluwer group of the Netherlands; Springer-Verlag received one morning and Piper Verlag one evening; and the now traditional Gustav Lübbe banquet in an elegant Frankfurter Hof dining room seated guests at "theme" tables, where Lübbe books on these themes were scattered among flowers and glasses.

One party was used for hard sell, the product being Xaviera Hollander's first novel, *Sandra;* she and her French publisher Jean-Claude Lattès (holder of world rights) invited likely prospects for drinks and a tease—i.e., author Hollander's description of her racy manuscript, 50 pages of which remained to be written.

All this merriment may have contributed to confusion as to what was actually happening on the floor of Halle Fünf. "Boring," an American rights manager complained. "No new ideas," "A lively fair—still irreplaceable," said a Latin American. "Very satisfactory," put in an international copublishing expert (who happened to be Alfred van der Marck, general manager of McGraw-Hill's copublishing division). A British packager (in the words of Mitchell Beazley's newest employee, David Campbell, until recently with France's Gallimard) was having "an incredible fair." "The lack of brilliance, of flashy promotions, is a sign the fair is a truer reflection of what publishing is all about: a painstaking, not always rewarding activity," said Spain's Manuel Aguilar, a veteran international fairgoer who after this fair was leaving his family company to become an independent publisher with the new Altalena imprint in Madrid. "The more relaxed tempo," Aguilar went on, "is in harmony with the worldwide economic situation in the trade. But we've been through worse times."

"One year it's political crisis, another year terrorism, and now it's economic crisis," Doubleday's Sam Vaughan summed it up. "Publishers have to worry about something. But publishers are also incorrigible optimists, or they wouldn't be in this business. It depends, of course, on what books you have." (Vaughan was talking to *PW* as his foreign rights manager Jacqueline Everly was handing out another set of proofs of *Thy Neighbor's Wife* to a publisher, admonishing: "Twenty-four hours, please!"

While publishers were pondering the big picture, book fair authorities were dealing with nuts and bolts. There was a crackdown on stealing; publishers were asked to increase their own precautions on the theory that a lot of thefts were the work of exhibitors robbing thy neighbors' stands, often at the end of the working day. And stealing did seem to be down this year.

One problem the Frankfurt fair does not have is censorship; there simply aren't any restrictive rules. The era of hard-core porn which followed the student/intellectual revolt of the late 1960s is over. One persistent problem is pro-Nazi propaganda from a handful of extremist publishers. "We'd all like to exclude them," fair director Weidhaas explained, "but where would we begin and where stop?" At a fairground meeting, German authors protested the presence of the Nazis, but Weidhaas told them the alternative would be to exclude all extremists—left wing as well as right wing. Still, there was a feeling that Germany couldn't afford to be broadminded after the Nazi form of extremism. When the fair banned a pro-Nazi publisher seven years ago he went to court and got a mandate forcing the fair to accept his presence on the ground that the Frankfurt fair is a monopoly and could not discriminate.

A few American publishers displayed books bearing a red-letter streamer: "This Book Banned at the '79 Moscow Book Fair," and on the stand of William Morrow, whose president Lawrence Hughes chairs the AAP's International Freedom to Publish Committee, there was a selection of such books from several houses. Elsewhere the streamers were not very apparent, and they did not interfere (nor were they allowed to interfere) with negotiations with the Soviet copyright agency VAAP, which had fielded a team of eight headed by vice-chairman Vassily N. Sitnikov.

The third "anti-Fair" was held in a hall on the other side of the Main, to show the underground press in an atmosphere of singing and discussions. It was more of a cultural happening than a fair, but the term "anti" helped attract visitors. Outside the gates of the genuine book fair, and even within, gypsy exhibitors set up tables to show more underground press items, but also sold junk toys and other goods. How they were smuggled in each day remained a mystery to fair authorities, who decided to let them stay as long as they created no disturbance. Many took up positions beneath the overhang that connected Hall 5 and Hall 6 as a protection against rain; it served mainly this year as a protection against warm sunshine.

STM FOCUSES ON SCHOOLS

The presence in Frankfurt of leading elements of the book trade from every part of the world always facilitates a multitude of off-campus activities. Each year the morning before the opening of the fair is the occasion for a general assembly of the International Group of Scientific, Technical and Medical Publishers (STM). This time, to commemorate the organization's tenth anniversary, the assembly was combined with a symposium on Regional Influences in International Publishing. The premise was that publishers for secondary schools and colleges do better with multinational rather than international programs—i.e., adaptation to each local language and syllabus, using local authors when possible. Introduced by outgoing STM chairman Per Saugman of Blackwell Scientific Publications, the symposium heard John T. Owens of London's Macmillan Press, Manuel Aguilar, and Elsevier/NDU's Engelbart van Tongeren on developing books for a local market in the publisher's original language or in translation. The same activity seen from inside the consumer countries was dealt with by Simon Wratten of Oxford University Press (India and West Africa), Edgard Blücher of Editôra Edgard Blücher in Brazil, and Carlos Noriega Milera of Editorial Limusa in Mexico, with discussions led by Sayed El Gabri of Egypt's Al Ahram and Robert H. Craven of F. A. Davis in Philadelphia, W. Gordon Graham of Butterworth summing up.

STM's annual report, submitted by the Group Executive but marked by the wry wit of Paul Nijhoff Asser, led off with a complaint about the proliferation of international meetings on information transfer, posing problems "of duplication of effort and predatory cultivation of available resources: speakers, panel members, organizing bodies." STM announced that half its membership had already adhered to the recommended permissions guidelines for use of published materials in other works for professional purposes. In the morning business meeting, STM, which now has 134 member companies in 19 nations (32 in the United Kingdom, 28 in the United States, 18 in Germany, 8 in the Netherlands), elected new officers: Dr. Günther Hauff of Stuttgart's Thieme replacing Per Saugman as chairman, Robert Craven of F. A. Davis as vice-chairman (and if tradition holds he will be chairman in two years' time); Engelbart van Tongeren was reelected to the treasury.

The International Publishers Association (IPA) held meetings of its copyright, freedom to publish, electronic publishing, national secretaries, inter-American executive, and international committees. During this last meeting, Manuel Salvat of Barcelona's Salvat was elected IPA president for a four-year term starting next July 1, and Mexico City was chosen (after heated debate—and against Brazil) as site of the 1984 International Publishers Congress, which will be the first to be held in Latin America.

The international and inter-American committees took up the problem of book piracy, made plans to expedite the inquiry into such practices in Latin America. There was discussion of the Moscow Book Fair, with no recommendation, except the consensus that participants should avoid resorting to self-censorship. And a warm welcome was being readied for China, should that country set up a publishers association and sign bilateral agreements for respect of copyright.

CZECH WRITER MAKES APPEARANCE

The freedom to publish committee (no connection with AAP's international freedom to publish committee) heard Czech writer Pavel Kohout, who a few days earlier had been stripped of his citizenship as he attempted to return to Czechoslovakia from a stay abroad; committee members Per Sjögren (president of IPA), Ian Chapman of Collins, and Brikt Jensen of Norway's Gyldendal were joined by Harper & Row's Winthrop Knowlton, chairman of the committee. Sjögren read into the minutes an account of self-publishing by Czechoslovakian authors denied access to normal channels by their government.

IPA's executive committee took up the matter of publishing by intergovernmental agencies, such as UNESCO, on such activities as publishing for developing nations. Other international agencies were encouraging developing countries to set up government publishing instead of encouraging private initiative, largely because civil servants find it easier to deal with other civil servants.

For its Stockholm congress next May, IPA had already signed up 500 publishers (and 300 accompanying persons); the break-even figure is about 1,000, and 500 more than that would be welcome.

Each year at Frankfurt fair time Ernst Klett Verlag sponsors an international meeting of educational publishers, its subject often betraying worries about declining school population and the need to diversify. This year the theme was "The Video Disc: Challenge and Opportunity for Publishers." Held at the fair-side Plaza over coffee and cake, the meeting drew representatives of most leading U.S. and European educational houses. After greetings by Michael Klett, participants heard Klett's Dr. Bruno Oehring affirm that audiovision was not dead, "in spite of all the disappointments experienced by very many publishers." Indeed, a mass audience was developing for video recorders (425,000 sets sold in the United States in 1978, 85,000 in West Germany, with Japan's 1979 production rising to 1.8 million sets). Klett and the Netherlands' Wolters-Noordhoff were engaged in a joint venture to market Philips video discs, to become available in Europe in 1981. So Oehring and the Wolters-Noordhoff and Philips people shared the platform to demonstrate that their product was worth waiting for. "We are simultaneously colleagues and competitors," Wolters-Noordhoff's Dr. Frans Krips told the audience, reviewing the failure of international cooperation in this area since the earliest attempts to achieve it, 13 years ago. "Publishers have power even though they are reluctant to use it." In this area he felt that joint efforts were "absolutely essential." The discs demonstrated looked like ordinary 12-inch long-playing records, and could carry up to 60 minutes of programming on each side.

There was a Sunday breakfast of the Motovun group, whose summer cruise in the southern Adriatic was described by Edward E. Booher (*PW*, September 10). In an atmosphere of alumni reunion Booher and the group's guiding spirits Nebojša Tomašević and Ljubo Stefanović outlined plans for next summer's publishers conference-cruise, but also a spring trip to China. In this connection, Hideo Aoki of the Japan Uni Agency delivered a report on a Japanese publishing seminar in China during which the publishers found the Chinese seriously interested in membership in the Universal Copyright Convention. The Chinese promised to write their own legislation to make adhesion possible; this, Aoki felt, could take five to six years. Meanwhile the Chinese were ready to coproduce with foreign products, and it was likely that a number of projects would be initiated during the Motovun group's spring journey.

Forty specialists in education as well as librarians, publishers and booksellers from the United States, the United Kingdom, and continental Europe met in the town hall of Gutenberg's city of Mainz on October 12, as guests of the German Reading Association (Deutsche Lesegesellschaft), the British National Bibliography Research Fund of the British Library, and the U.K. National Book League; Grolier's Theodore Waller chaired. Delegates spoke to the problem of inadequate book information in an era otherwise characterized by information overkill. Participants included publishers, such as Colin Eccleshare of John Wiley, Kurt Fromberg of Copenhagen's Gyldendal, Martyn Goff of the National Book League, Carol Nemeyer of the Library of Congress, and Dick Ouwehand of the Netherlands' Collective Book Promotion. Rolf Zitzlsperger, who runs the Deutsche Lesegesellschaft, urged the setting up of clearinghouse in Germany to deal with book information; Goff and Peter Stockham asked for a similar program for their country via the National Book League.

The book fair itself sponsored a number of events, notably an opening night beerfest in a downtown theater, and the awarding of the German Book Trade's peace prize to Yehudi Menuhin in the traditional Sunday morning ceremony in the Paulskirche. Earlier, the formal opening of the fair at the Kongresshalle on the town side of the fairgrounds was distinguished by the remarks of French political scientist Alfred Grosser, who addressed himself to the issue of freedom of speech. An uncompromising civil libertarian, Grosser saw dangers not only in Iran's book burning but also in the tendency of French and German courts to restrict the publications of extremists in a desire to protect democracy or to prevent the spread of race hate. He felt "uneasy" when a German court allowed publication of Hitler's *Mein Kampf* with the qualification that it should not be used to change the social order. "My uneasiness turns to rejection every time that we, the free Europeans, use terms that belong more to the vocabulary of those who would deny freedom than to that of those whose world view is based on freedom." He warned that the German law against terrorism "signals real danger for literary freedom" and noted the West Berlin prosecutions of the printers of tracts.

Next year's fair (October 8–13, 1980) will once again have a theme: "Africa—Continent on the Way to Self-Discovery," to be illustrated through book exhibits, readings by African authors, panel discussions, a literary prize, and other first-time events. The previous biennial theme was "The Child and the Book" (1978); in 1982 it will be "Small Countries, Great Literature," to focus on eight minor language areas.

INTERNATIONAL LIBRARIANSHIP

Naimuddin Qureshi

*City Librarian, Bell Public Library,
Los Angeles County Public Library System*

During the past decades there has been a remarkable growth of interest and activity in international librarianship, a term not frequently used in library literature. The more commonly used term is comparative librarianship, which Chase Dane defined as "a study of library science in many countries to discover what factors are common to those countries and which are unique to one."[1] A more comprehensive definition was given by Dorothy Collings:

> Comparative librarianship may be defined as the systematic analysis of library development, practices, or problems as they occur under different circumstances (most usually in different countries), considered in the content of the relevant historical, geographic, political, economic, social, cultural, and other determinant background factors found in the situations under study. Essentially it constitutes an important approach to the search for cause and effect in library development, and to the understanding of library problems.[2]

Richard Krzys, from the University of Pittsburgh, used the term international and comparative study in librarianship, which he defined as:

> the generic term encompassing investigation into library phenomena in their intranational, cross-national, or cross-cultural contents for the proximate purpose of deepening library science through explanation, prediction, and control of library phenomena, and for the ultimate purpose of improving librarianship through comparison of variants of library practice throughout the world.[3]

To a significant extent, the accelerated development in this field of study may be traced to such factors as increased international cooperation in librarianship through UNESCO, International Federation of Library Associations and Institutions, International Federation for Documentation and other agencies, the emergence of new and developing countries desiring an effective library system as soon as possible, the aid programs and consultant services provided by governments and foundations, the international activities of some of the national library associations, and the many opportunities available to librarians to travel, study, or work in other countries.

SUPPORT FROM INTERNATIONAL ORGANIZATIONS

Leadership in promoting and supporting modern international librarianship has come from UNESCO, which has become a major force in world library affairs since its foundation. Through its worldwide library programs, its technical assistance for operational activities through experts, technicians, seminars, and field studies, UNESCO contributes to the emergence of library systems in developing countries. UNESCO's ongoing association with international nongovernmental organizations such as the International Federation of Library Associations (IFLA), the International Federation for Documentation (FID), and the International Council on Archives (ICA) has enabled the organization to extend its programs of activities with the support of the human and technical resources of these organizations. Member countries need help in the planning of national documentation and library and archives services. Planning in turn demands systematic studies of the country's social and economic situation, development trends, and other vital questions, which can only be carried out by people with proper professional and academic qualifications. By providing qualified consultants, UNESCO has assisted member countries.

The International Federation of Library Associations has made significant contributions in the field of international and comparative librarianship. Its newly defined purposes reflect the widening of IFLA's professional scope: to promote international understanding, cooperation, discussion, and research and development in all fields of library activity, including bibliography, information sciences, and the education of personnel, and to provide a body through which librarianship can be represented in matters of international interest. In February 1975 the executive board of IFLA agreed to establish an office for international lending to be located at the British Library Lending Division. One of the first activities undertaken was to collect basic information that would aid libraries all over the world in their international loan transactions.[4]

The International Council on Archives has revised its constitution and dues structure, extended its membership geographically, established regional branches and professional committees, and implemented a number of projects and publications designed to assist archival development throughout the world.

Other international organizations that have made significant contributions include International Association of Agricultural Librarians and Documentalists (IAALD), International Association of Law Libraries (IALL), International Association of Orientalist Librarians (IAOL), International Association of School Librarianship (IASL), International Association of Technological University Libraries (IATUL), and International Association of Metropolitan City Libraries (INTAMEL).

NATIONAL SUPPORT

For years the Council on Library Resources has been providing financial support to individuals, institutions, libraries, and other agencies for the improvement of library and information services in the United States. The council has also provided funds to various international library organizations and agencies for the development of their programs.

From 1967 to 1972 the International Relations Office of the American Library Association (ALA) published a regular newsletter: *Libraries in International Development*. Every issue of the newsletter contained useful articles about the development of library and information services in other countries. The International Relations Round Table of ALA also publishes a newsletter that covers significant developments in international librarianship.

In 1967 the British Library Association established an International and Comparative Librarianship Group (ICLG). In addition to organizing meetings, the group also started the publication of *Focus on International and Comparative Librarianship*.

NATIONAL INFORMATION SYSTEMS

The Intergovernmental Conference on the Planning of National Documentation, Library and Archives Infrastructures, organized by UNESCO in cooperation with the International Federation for Documentation, the International Federation of Library Associations, and the International Council on Archives, met in Paris from September 23 to 27, 1974, and unanimously adopted recommendations supporting the concept and objectives of a national information system (NATIS), encompassing all services involved in the provision of information for all sectors of the community and for all categories of users. The concept of NATIS was formulated on the basis of (1) the need for systematic planning of information infrastructures so as fully to utilize the information accumulated at the national level and to be able to participate in and benefit from existing and future world information systems; and (2) the need for coordinated planning of information resources so as to achieve greater efficiency, to improve indigenous capabilities, and to create new ones.[5] In 1976, UNESCO published a useful booklet, *Design and Planning of National Information System (NATIS)*,[6] which is intended to encourage governments convinced of the need to develop national information systems as an indispensable tool for their country's economic, cultural, and social well-being to create the mechanism that could pursue that goal.

The importance of information has lead many governments to plan their national information systems systematically to ensure, through coordination of the various individual elements, maximum use of the available information resources and facilities. The success of any such plans, however, depends on the necessary legislative action being taken at the earliest possible stage. *Establishing a Legislative Framework for the Implementation of NATIS*, published by UNESCO in 1976, gives special attention to the drafting of such legislation.[7] The U.S. National Committee for the UNESCO General Program, established in 1977, serves as the central coordinating body of the U.S. national information community and is responsible for representing and promoting the program's needs, interests, and views.

UNIVERSAL BIBLIOGRAPHIC CONTROL

A successful system of Universal Bibliographic Control (UBC), a natural extension of national bibliographic control, requires that each nation assume the responsibility for preparing and making available bibliographic records of its own publications following accepted standards in their preparation to ensure that the records can be readily used in manual and machine-readable systems throughout the world. The UBC office functions as a catalyst and coordinator of practical activities designed to achieve this ambitious goal. It serves as a secretariat to working groups and individuals engaged in special bibliographic projects, collects and disseminates information related to bibliographic standards, coordinates meetings of national and international cataloging and bibliographic organizations, and edits and issues a variety of publications on standards and other bibliographic matters. The office was also heavily involved in an international bibliographic data network feasibility study funded by a group of national libraries.

The UBC office spends a substantial amount of time in activities connected with the promulgation, publication, and monitoring of use of the numerous International Standard Bibliographic Descriptions (ISBD). The function of an ISBD is to provide a standard description for library materials. Its primary purpose is to aid international communication of bibliographic information by (1) making records from different sources interchangeable so that records produced in one country can be easily accepted in library catalogs or other bibliographic lists in any other country; (2) assisting in the interpretation of records across language barriers so that records produced for users of one language can be interpreted by users of another language; and (3) assisting in the conversion of bibliographic records to machine-readable form.[8] Another purpose of ISBD is to facilitate the compilation and production of integrated catalogs and bibliographic lists. Instead of the cumbersome and confusing practice of maintaining separate catalogs for different types of materials, the user will be able to gain access to a collection through an integrated catalog in which all entries share the same structure.

LIBRARY LITERATURE

The primary sources of data for the study of international and comparative librarianship include annual reports of libraries, library legislation, library statistics, government reports, conference proceedings, and working papers of seminars and meetings. Secondary sources include an increasing number of monographs and journal articles. But there seems to be general agreement that the literature in this field is inadequate both in quantity and quality. In 1970 Simsova and Mackee published a useful book, *A Handbook of Comparative Librarianship*,[9] which contains several chapters dealing with various aspects of comparative librarianship, as well as extensive bibliographies on library development in many countries. The second edition of the book was published in 1974. For her doctoral dissertation, Beverly Brewster studied the efforts of American library experts in assisting other countries. Later the study was published under the title *American Overseas Library Technical Assistance, 1940-1970*.[10] J. P. Danton's *The Dimensions of Comparative Librarianship* is a useful study.[11] A. M. Abdul Huq and Mohammed M. Aman did an excellent job of compiling a much needed source, *Librarianship and the Third World*,[12] which is an annotated bibliography on developing countries. Anis Khurshid studied the training facilities for librarians in four Asian countries and developed standards that were published under the title *Standards for Library Education in Burma, Ceylon, India, and Pakistan*.[13] Under the directorship of Anis Khurshid, the Department of Library Science at the University of Karachi in Pakistan collected data on librarianship in Islamic countries, which were published in *Fact Sheet on Libraries in Islamic Countries*.[14]

Other useful contributions have been made by Campbell,[15] Danton,[16] Harrison,[17] Harvey,[18] Jackson,[19] Kaser,[20] and Munthe.[21]

Among periodicals, the *UNESCO Bulletin for Libraries* has provided leadership in this area. First published in April 1947, the *Bulletin* presents original studies and reports of research in the fields of documentation, libraries, and archives from all over the world. It provides an international forum for the exchange of ideas in the development of more efficient information systems. Other useful journals in the field are *International Library Review* and *Libri*.

THE INTERNATIONAL LIBRARY INFORMATION CENTER, PITTSBURGH

Realizing the need to collect material on international and comparative librarianship in one place, the Graduate School of Library and Information Sciences (GSLIS), University of Pittsburgh, established the International Library Information Center (ILIC) in 1964. The center was to serve two major functions: (1) to act as a clearinghouse for data on library development, documentation, book production, and distribution, with regard to both U.S. and overseas resources; and (2) to serve as a training and research center in the field of international librarianship.[22] The center collects material on library and information science from all over the world. Beside supporting the educational program of GSLIS, ILIC also provides material to researchers within the United States and abroad. The collection includes primary source materials, such as papers and proceedings of library and documentation conferences, as well as newspaper and journal articles and dissertations. The center has assisted various governmental, intergovernmental, and private agencies in the preparation of study plans and itineraries for visiting librarians from various countries.

NOTES

1. Chase Dane, "The Benefits of Comparative Librarianship," *The Australian Library Journal* 3 (July 1954): 89.
2. Dorothy G. Collings, "Comparative Librarianship," in *Encyclopedia of Library and Information Science*, vol. 5 (New York: Dekker, 1971), p. 497.
3. Richard A. Krzys, "International and Comparative Study in Librarianship, Research Methodology," in *Encyclopedia of Library and Information Science*, vol. 12 (New York: Dekker, 1974), p. 328.
4. Rosamond Kerr and Tom C. Clarks, "The Development of International Standard Bibliographic Description (ISBD) and some Problems for Non-Roman Scripts," *UNESCO Bulletin for Libraries* 31 (July–August 1977): 211.
5. C. R. Sahaer, "National Information Systems and UNESCO," in *Bowker Annual of Library and Book Trade Information* (New York: R. R. Bowker, 1975), p. 336.
6. *Design and Planning of National Information Systems (NATIS)* (Paris: UNESCO, 1976).
7. Philip Sowell, A. W. Mabbs, and E. M. Broone, *Establishing a Legislative Frame Work for the Implementation of NATIS* (Paris: UNESCO, 1976).
8. Rosamond Kerr and Tom C. Clarks, "The Development of International Standard Bibliographic Description (ISBD) and Some Problems for Non-Roman Scripts," *UNESCO Bulletin for Libraries* 31 (July–August 1977): 210.
9. S. Simsova and M. Mackee, *A Handbook of Comparative Librarianship* (London: Clive Bingley, 1970).
10. Beverly J. Brewster, *American Overseas Library Technical Assistance, 1940–1970* (Metuchen, NJ: Scarecrow, 1976).
11. J. Periam Danton, *The Dimensions of Comparative Librarianship* (Chicago: American Library Association, 1973).
12. A. M. Abdul Huq and Mohammed M. Aman, comps., *Librarianship and the Third World: An Annotated Bibliography of Selected Literature on Developing Nations, 1960–1975* (New York: Garland, 1977).
13. Anis Khurshid, "Standards for Library Education in Burma, Ceylon, India and Pakistan" (Ph.D. diss., University of Pittsburgh, 1969).
14. Anis Khurshid, et al., comps., *Fact Sheet on Libraries in Islamic Countries* (Karachi: Islamic Library Information Center, Department of Library Science, University of Karachi).
15. H. C. Campbell, *Metropolitan Public Library Planning throughout the World* (London: Pergamon, 1967).
16. J. Periam Danton, *Book Selection and Collection: A Comparison of German and American University Libraries* (New York: Columbia University Press, 1963).
17. K. C. Harrison, *Libraries in Scandinavia* (London: Deutsch, 1969).
18. John F. Harvey, ed., *Comparative and International Library Science* (Metuchen, NJ: Scarecrow, 1977).
19. W. V. Jackson, *Aspects of Librarianship in Latin America* (Champaign, IL: Illinois Union Book Store, 1962).
20. David Kaser, Walter C. Stone, and Cecil K. Byrd, *Library Development in Eight Asian Countries* (Metuchen, NJ: Scarecrow, 1969).
21. Wilhelm Munthe, *American Librarianship from a European Angle* (Chicago: American Library Association, 1939).
22. Richard Krzys, "The International Library Information Center of the University of Pittsburgh," in *Encyclopedia of Library and Information Science*, vol. 12 (New York: Dekker, 1974), p. 414.

INTERNATIONAL PUBLISHERS ASSOCIATION

3 av. de Miremont, 1206 Geneva, Switzerland

J. A. Koutchoumow

Secretary-General

The International Publishers Association (IPA) was founded under the name of International Publishers Congress in 1896, when at the invitation of the French Publishers Association a first congress was held in Paris. Thirteen countries were represented, including the United States and Russia. Every three or four years thereafter publishers gathered in various places of the world, mainly in Europe. [The program of the 1980 congress in Stockholm is included later in this article—*Ed.*]

Today IPA is a group of 42 member countries. It is an international professional organization of national publishers associations fully representative of the publishers in their country. It aims to be of service to the world publishing trade, with its main objective being to proclaim and defend the publisher's right to publish and to distribute the products of the human mind, without hindrance or restrictions being imposed on these creative works. At the same time IPA takes part in the campaign to end illiteracy by encouraging the ever wider circulation of books and other published works and by encouraging the creativity of new writers and publishers in every country in the world.

Two of the most important concerns of IPA are international copyright protection and the free flow of the products of the mind across international borders unrestricted by economic barriers. IPA looks after the interests of publishers by taking an active participation in all meetings dealing with international treaties, conventions, protocols and regulations concerning copyright, and the free flow of books and related materials. IPA representation at meetings ensures the expression of publishers' interests at the intergovernmental level. Through meetings and congresses, IPA provides a forum for publishers to discuss their problems at an international level.

Sections, groups, and committees within IPA look after the varied interests of members:

Music Section (handles the music publishers' specific problems)

International STM Group (an affiliated member that deals with the affairs of scientific publishers)

International Association of Scholarly Publishers

Regional groups (in Asia, Latin America, and Europe)

Specialist committees (Copyright, Education, Information, New Media, Freedom to Publish, Financial and Administration)

SERVICES TO THE WORLD PUBLISHING TRADE

IPA helps its members operate effectively by providing essential background information on what is going on in the publishing trade at an international level. It keeps its members informed on events related to the trade. The IPA secretariat circulates a monthly newsletter, *IPA Publishing News*, which deals with general trade questions on an international scale. The *Geneva Newsletter* and the *Annual Report* give regular information on IPA activities. IPA also publishes a yearly World Book Fairs Calendar.

Regular liaison is maintained with international organizations affecting international copyright laws or international trade relations: United Nations Educational,

Scientific and Cultural Organization (UNESCO), World Intellectual Property Organization (WIPO), United Nations Conference for Trade and Development (UNCTAD), Universal Postal Union (UPU), International Booksellers Association (IBA), International Federation of Library Associations (IFLA), International Confederation of Societies of Authors and Composers (CISAC), International Literary and Artistic Association (ALAI), International Community of Museums (ICOM), International Standardization Organization (ISO), International Federation of Documentation (IFD), and many others. All meetings of concern to publishers held by these organizations are attended by IPA, which voices the interest of publishers or fulfills a watchdog function.

COPYRIGHT

The protection of copyright is to publishing what the protection of patents and trademarks is to industry, and it follows that the evolution of copyright legislation, nationally and internationally, is of particular concern to IPA. IPA is actively assisting in the establishment of internationally recognized rules and norms on the basic, crucial copyright problems of the Gutenberg and post-Gutenberg eras. Among the priorities in the IPA program are:

Enforcement of national and international copyright laws

Wide acceptance of international copyright conventions

Reprography and information communication systems

Information to members of the legal problems arising from the use of videocassettes and audiovisual discs, computers, satellites, etc.

Information on the relations between industrialized countries and developing countries with regard to foreign rights

ORGANIZATION AND MEMBERSHIP

The International Committee is the supreme body of IPA. IPA's basic policies are established by the International Committee, in which each member country has two delegates. The International Committee meets at least once a year, usually during the Frankfurt Book Fair. The International Committee appoints 14 of its members to constitute the Executive Committee.

Officers

The president of IPA (Per A. Sjögren, Rabén and Sjögren, Stockholm, July 1976–June 1980; Manuel Salvat, Spain, July 1980–June 1984) is elected by the International Committee for a period of four years. The president officially represents IPA at international events of importance to the trade, such as world book fairs, diplomatic conferences, etc. The president presides at meetings of the International Committee and the Executive Committee.

The Executive Committee assists the president with the preparatory work on the policy to be discussed and voted on by the International Committee.

A full-time secretary-general (J. A. Koutchoumow) serves as the chief operating officer at IPA headquarters in Geneva and is responsible for managing IPA's secretariat within the framework of basic policies established by the International Committee. The secretary-general is the spokesman for IPA at international meetings. He ensures a regular liaison with member associations, international organizations, and the world publishing community.

Membership

IPA's membership is made up of national publishers associations. IPA wishes to be as widely representative of the world's publishing community as possible. Through member associations, thousands of publishers are members of IPA.

Member countries include Argentina, Australia, Austria, Belgium (Antwerp/ Brussels), Bolivia, Brazil, Canada (Montreal/Toronto), Chile, Colombia, Denmark, Finland, France, Germany (Federal Republic of), Greece, Iceland, India, Indonesia, Ireland, Israel, Italy, Japan, Korea, Malaysia, Mexico, Netherlands, Nigeria, Norway, Pakistan, Peru, Philippines, Portugal, Singapore, Spain (Barcelona/Madrid), Sri Lanka, Sweden, Switzerland (Lausanne/Zurich), Thailand, United Kingdom, United States (New York/Washington), Uruguay, Venezuela, and Yugoslavia. There are two regional offices of IPA: one in New Delhi and one in Kuala Lumpur.

IPA CONGRESSES

To implement its programs, IPA organizes a congress every three to four years. One of the principal aims of an IPA congress is to offer a platform for full and open discussions among publishers from all over the world on basic industry problems. IPA cordially invites all publishers to take part in these congresses. The next IPA congress will be held in Mexico City, Mexico, in 1984. The 1965 congress was held in Washington, D.C., and the 1976 Congress in Kyoto-Tokyo. The program of the Stockholm Congress, held May 18–22, 1980, gives a clear idea of the variety of activities of IPA.

Session 1: State influence on the book trade
  a. State support of literature:
     S. Strömme, Cappelens Forlag, Norway
     C. Bourgois, Presses de la Cité, France
     K. Wilder, W. Collins Publishers, Ltd., Australia
  b. Taxation policies for book publishing:
     J. H. Verleur, Elsevier-NDU, Netherlands
  c. State-owned book publishing houses:
     G. A. Alawode, Nigerian Publishers' Association, Nigeria
     O. P. Ghai, Federation of Indian Publishers, India

Session 2: Copyright questions
  a. Report by M. Harris, chairman of the IPA Copyright Committee, United States
  b. Reprography. Collective arrangements as a solution:
     M. Harris, John Wiley, United States
  c. The problem of piracy:
     L. N. Albert, Prentice-Hall, United States
     C. Noriega, Editorial Limusa, Mexico
     N. Kumar, India

Session 3: The book trade in developing countries
  a. Transfer of rights. The need for better conditions in developing countries:
     D. N. Malhotra, India
     I. Hadad, Indonesian Publishers' Association, Indonesia
  b. Book publishing training in developing countries:
     R. E. Baensch, Harper & Row, United States
     Speakers from Latin America, Asia, and Africa

Session 4: Authors and book publishers
  a. Standard contracts and trade agreements:
     H. Friedrich, Deutscher Taschenbuch Verlag, Germany
     A. Ferm, Bokförlags AB Tiden, Sweden
     M. Znidersic, Cankarjeva Zalozba, Yugoslavia
  b. Subsidiary rights:
     M. Marmur, Random House, United States
     Speaker from France
  c. The role of literary agents with regard to book publishers:
     O. Lindhardt, Lindhardt & Ringhof, Denmark
     E. Linder, Agenzia Letteraria Internationale, Italy
     M. Spagnol, Rizzoli, Italy

Session 5: Modern media and the book trade
  a. The challenge of the modern media:
     R. E. M. van den Brink, Elsevier-NDU NV, Netherlands
  b. Scientific information:
     J.-P. Blesbois, Syndicat National de l'Edition, France
  c. Professional and educational information:
     C. Bradley, The Publishers' Association, United Kingdom
  d. The development of the modern media in Japan:
     Shogakukan, Japan
  e. The development of the modern media in the USA:
     G. Eisenberger, Charles Merrill, United States

Session 6: Schoolbooks
  a. The potential available to authorities to influence the composition and contents of schoolbooks:
     H. Hladej, Jugend und Volk Verlagsgesellschaft, Austria
     O. Storm, Föreningen Svenska Läromedelsproducenter, Sweden
  b. Possibilities for pressure groups to influence the composition and contents of schoolbooks:
     V. Hempel, United States
     G. N. Pivano, Italy
  c. The part played by educational publishers—who is to decide on the composition and contents of schoolbooks?:
     K. Pinnock, J. Murray, Ltd., United Kingdom
     E. Martinez, Santillana SA, Spain
     M. Santos, National Association of Textbooks Publishers, Spain
     D. Worlock, T. Nelson & Sons, Ltd., United Kingdom

Session 7: Marketing and distribution of books, I
  a. Traditional bookstores, other kinds of retail trade, direct mail, door-to-door, book clubs—complements or internal competition?:
     H. E. Reenpää, Otava, Finland
     Speaker from Doubleday, United States
  b. Price as a competitive means. Fixed and free book prices:
     A. Grund, Edition Grund, France
     H. Altenheim, Luchterhand Verlag, Germany

c. Our future markets:
   Creation and marketing of special books projects in the future:
   J. Mitchell, Mitchell Beazley, Ltd., United Kingdom
   Future of fiction:
   P. I. Gedin, AB Wahlström & Widstrand, Sweden

Session 8: Marketing and distribution of books, II
   a. Reports about successful marketing projects and ideas in publishing:
      P. Hamlyn, Octopus Books, United Kingdom
   b. Marketing trends and the information industry:
      J. F. Magee, A. D. Little, United States

Session 9: Technological development
   a. Technological development in printing:
      G. Broggi, Istituto Geografico de Agostini, Italy
      Speaker from Japan
   b. Computerization in the book trade:
      E. Winther, Gyldendal, Denmark
      J. Ehlers, E. Klett Publishers and Printers, Germany

Session 10: Multinational problems in publishing
   a. National publishing companies versus major foreign publishers as local competitors:
      Speaker from Brazil
      T. Rix, Longman Group, United Kingdom
      M. Lester, Lester & Orpen Dennys, Ltd., Canada
   b. Language barriers:
      I. Boldizsar, The New Hungarian Quarterly, Hungary
      Speaker from Israel

Second plenary session
   One hour free debate, chairman, P. A. Sjögren, president of IPA, Sweden

Panel discussion, "Freedom to Publish," chairman, B. Jensen, Gyldendal Norsk Forlag, Norway; panel members, A. Brink, South Africa; P. Wästberg, president of International PEN; and others

Conclusion of Congress: Recommendations

PRESEMINARS IN FINLAND, NORWAY, AND SWEDEN

In connection with the twenty-first IPA Congress in Stockholm, special seminars were planned in Finland, Norway, and Sweden, May 14-16, 1980.

Helsinki, Finland (Congress Center)

Subject: Marketing of books

1. Distribution channels of books. The relative proportions of the various channels used and their importance, as well as developments for the future.
2. Marketing of books via bookstores. The reasons for the apparent decrease in the market share of the traditional outlets for books and the influence of recent events from the viewpoint of publishers, authors, retailers, and readers.
3. Installment sales of large works. Various forms of installment selling by pub-

lishers and the importance of such sales channels for publishing and culture—now and in the future.
4. Direct mail and book clubs. A summary of the latest developments and a forecast for the future.

Oslo, Norway (Grand Hotel)

Subjects: Use of new technology in publishing: How will new procedures affect practical editorial work? New technology in publishing and its effect on structure and marketing strategy in the 1980s.

New technology and methods.
1. Survey of latest EDB equipment
2. Simple and inexpensive equipment for writing and editing
3. Better methods and equipment for maintaining and retrieving catalog information in connection with reference books
4. New communication possibilities via telelines
5. New presentation possibilities, new media

New borderlines for the publisher's field of operation.
1. Communication between publisher and writer
2. Relationship of publisher and printer
3. Maintaining and utilizing information banks
4. New fields of work

Effects on publishers' working routines.
1. New aids for editing and correction
2. New follow-up aids in production
3. New possibilities in connection with reference work
4. New markets in connection with new media
5. Changes of internal organization structures

Kungälv, Sweden (Frs Hatt Hotel)

Subject: Managing the future of educational publishing.
1. Teaching aids of the future. What kind of teaching aids can we expect in the future? How much educational planning and method will there be in future teaching aid material? Will specially produced teaching aids replace "ordinary" books, magazines, etc., or will current types of textbooks still be used in the future?
2. New media. How will new media influence the composition of future teaching material? Can multimedia systems produced by publishers be adapted to a freer view of instruction, in which teachers and pupils themselves do the planning?
3. Coproduction and copublishing. What can be achieved on the international rather than on the national level? How can we exchange information about each other's projects and publishing planning? And, if that exchange is possible, what is the most appropriate time to start such cooperation? How can we achieve a satisfactory balance between the national and the international, the specific and the general (customs, attitudes, etc.)? To what extent can the teaching aid supply problems of the developing countries be solved by means of coproduction and copublishing?

4. Textbooks for immigrants. How can we supply suitable textbooks for instruction in the various native languages? What kinds of teaching materials should we produce for instruction in the language of the immigrant's new country? What requirements should there be for editorial content with regard to values, attitudes, cultural heritage, etc.?

INTERGOVERNMENTAL MEETINGS

During 1979 IPA was also able to express the views of the publishing trade and defend its interests in various governmental and intergovernmental meetings on diverse topics, including the following: copyright (Executive Committee meeting of the Berne Union, Intergovernmental Committee meeting of the UCC); protection and support to authors and artists; avoidance of double taxation of copyright royalties; postal rates on the international level (UPU congress in Rio de Janeiro, Brazil; access of the blind to protected materials; book and record piracy; training courses for developing countries trainees.

LIBRARY AND INFORMATION SERVICES IN EGYPT, 1979

Mohamed M. El Hadi

Professor and Chairman, Department of Information Systems and Computers, National Institute of Management Development, Cairo, Arab Republic of Egypt

The Arab Republic of Egypt comprises a land area of 1 million square kilometers and has a population of 41 million inhabitants, who tend to concentrate in the Nile Valley, which is about 4 percent of the total area of Egypt. According to the present constitution of 1971, Egypt is a presidential republic with a central government and 26 governates. The president is the supreme authority and is elected every six years. The country has one house of representatives (the People's Council) elected every five years. Arabic is the official language and is used in education, literature, and the mass media. English, French, and German are considered the leading foreign languages in the country.

The educational system extends from primary schools to university levels, which all are free (primary schools are compulsory). The total school and university population reaches more than 8 million, of which 600,000 are in higher educational institutions. In spite of all efforts of formal and adult education campaigns, the percentage of illiterates in the census of 1976 was 43.2. The country is engaged in a national program to mobilize and develop its resources for extensive growth. Already the development growth rate in the year of 1979 was 9 percent.

The needs and demands for library and information services at all levels of education, research, government, business, and society generally are greater than ever before and can be expected to increase substantially in the future. Up to now, the development of library and information services emphasizes the quantity of services rather than the quality, coordination, networking, and adoption of new information technologies, which are not yet utilized in the different types of library and information services.

THE NATIONAL LIBRARY SERVICES

The Egyptian National Library, which was founded in 1870, has been developed as an important center for scholarship and culture in Egyptian literary life. In 1971, the library was incorporated in the General Egyptian Book Organization (GEBO), an autonomous corporation under the auspices of the Ministry of Culture. In 1979, the library moved to a new building complex facing the River Nile. This huge new building houses, in addition to the National Library, the National Archives, and the five centers for Editing and Publishing Arab Manuscripts, for Bibliography and Scientific computation, for Restoration and Preservation of Materials, for Documentation of contemporary Egyptian History, and for Arab Book Development, as well as the Publishing House and the Extensive Printing Press.

For a long time, the National Library has pursued the policy of creating branches for public library services in the districts of Cairo. To date there are a total of 14 branches. The Egyptian National Library assumes the double responsibility of being both a national library and offering public library services through its public library branches.

Also, the National Library is considered the national depository of the legal deposit law No. 354 of 1954. Under the copyright regulations, the library receives ten copies of every publication issued in the country. Since 1956, the library has been issuing the *Egyptian National Bibliography*. In 1978, total book production in Egypt as listed in this national bibliography was 253 foreign books and 3,127 Arabic books, of which 280 titles were translations.

In recent years the growth of the library collections has been particularly rapid. In 1952, there were 110,000 books, by 1962, the number had grown to 658,000, and in 1970, it was over 1 million. Noteworthy among the library collections is the Oriental collection, which totals 70,000 volumes in Arabic, Persian, and Turkish languages, among them 3,000 volumes written on papyri and 500 volumes on parchment or leather.

Also, the use of the library has shown a remarkable increase in recent years. As related to technical processing, a complete revision of the national library catalog has started since 1968 to ensure uniformity of cataloging styles and format and to reclassify the whole collection according to the Dewey decimal classification. A one-hundred year (1870-1969) catalog of the library's holdings is to be issued by means of computer. The card catalog of the library is maintained for the collections from 1970 onward.

In addition to the public library services offered by the National Library and its district branches for the capital city, the Ministry of Culture and the local governates provide public library services also. Numerous cultural centers, cultural caravans, bookmobiles, and library collections in mosques and churches have been assembled and organized throughout the country in recent years, but these are limited economically and professionally.

SCHOOL LIBRARY SERVICES

The Department of School Libraries of the Ministry of Education was established in 1955, with the responsibility of establishing and developing school libraries, providing them with appropriate library materials and qualified personnel, proposing budgets, planning training programs, and offering guidance and supervision for school libraries of all levels and types. The department issues book lists approved for school libraries at the various levels. The first list, issued in 1977, comprised 220 books and the second list, which appeared in March 1978, comprised 253 books.

In 1955-1956 there were only 17 libraries and 5 librarians serving the secondary school level. By the academic year 1979-1980 all the 867 secondary schools and the 1,868 elementary schools possessed libraries. All types and levels of school libraries are being served by 3,178 school librarians and 173 school library supervisors. In spite of the growth of school libraries, we find that their services have been hindered because instruction is still based fundamentally upon textbooks.

UNIVERSITY LIBRARY SERVICES

Although the University of Al-Azhar is over 1,000 years old, the first modern university, that is, Cairo University, was established in 1908. The University of Al-Azhar itself has recently been modernized to include, in addition to the old religious faculties, science, medicine, engineering, agriculture, education, commerce, etc. The Library of Al-Azhar University for Islamic Studies carries traces of medieval Islamic studies. On the other hand, the newly established libraries for the university faculties have been organized with a basis in modern library practice. Collections are classified according to the Dewey decimal classification and card catalogs are maintained.

Academic libraries in Egypt can be traced to as early as the nineteenth century with the establishment of schools of medicine in 1828 and of engineering in 1839. In 1908, the first Egyptian modern university was established as a private institution, which later became (in 1925), the first state university—Cairo University. The technical services of the university's central library were organized by Italian professionals along the lines of the Vatican Library. A central catalog was started and foreign library materials were organized according to Dewey decimal classification. Recently, the Central Library has been endeavoring to reclassify its collections on the model of the Library of Congress's classification scheme and to centralize the acquisition of all foreign serials for all the faculty libraries of the university.

The university libraries in Egypt still stress decentralization of acquisition, processing, administration, and services. All these trends are prevailing with the establishment of academic libraries in the newly established universities spread all over the country, i.e., the universities of Ain Shams, Alexandria, Assiut, Tanta, Al-Mansoura, Zagazig, Helwan, Qanal, Al-Menia, and Al-Monoufiyah. Almost all university libraries in Egypt lack academic status and recognition. Also, they have inherited serious problems in connection with the shortage of professional manpower, adequate materials, and sufficient funds.

SPECIAL LIBRARY SERVICES

Government departments, research centers, banks, public enterprises, professional societies, and other public and private organizations possess special libraries with sizable collections. Many of these libraries try to serve the specialized needs of their parent organizations. It appears that the majority of special libraries in Egypt do not state clearly their objectives, the types of materials to be collected, and the subject limitation of their collections. A certain amount of contradiction and confusion exists in relation to coverage, services, and dissemination of data. Professional standards and technical tools are lacking to guide the organization and services of special librarianship in Egypt. Also, coordination and cooperation are lacking to prevent the waste of the limited human and physical resources.

INFORMATION SERVICES

Some specialized organizations have established documentation and information organs that offer information activities such as bibliographies, indexing, abstracting, photocopying and microfilming, current awareness services, publishing, translation, and inquiry services.

The National Information and Documentation Center (NIDOC) of the Academy of Scientific Research, which was founded in 1953, has comprehensive scientific and technical information resources of 26,000 monograph titles and 3,600 periodicals currently received. NIDOC offers reference and inquiry services and bibliographical services, publishes indexes, abstracts, and directories, and provides microfilming, translations, and services to the scientific and technical personnel in the National Research Center, the Egyptian universities, scientific institutions, and enterprises.

The Documentation and Information Agency attached to the National Educational Research Center of the Ministry of Education, which was established in 1956, has proven its vitality in Egyptian educational circles. The agency offers current information awareness services, undertakes information projects and research, issues indexes, bibliographies, abstracts, directories, and reports, and organizes professional training programs.

An example of the efforts to introduce computerized bibliography in the country is associated with the National Bibliographical and Data Processing Center of the General Egyptian Book Organization, Ministry of Culture, which was established in 1972. The center possesses a computer model ICL 1900, Data General, Nova 3/D of a capacity 96 k.b., which is utilized for the National Library Arabic Catalog.
Catalog.

In recent years, Egypt has witnessed the development of regional Arab information and documentation services attached to the Arab League Secretariat and its specialized organizations such as the Arab Organization of Administrative Sciences, the Arab League Educational, Cultural and Scientific Organization, and the Industrial Development Center for Arab States. All these information centers still function in Cairo despite the move of their parent Arab organizations outside Egypt.

A recent trend in Egypt has been the establishment of microfilm information centers in governmental, industrial, and business organizations such as the Ministry of Finance, the presidency, the Cabinet of Ministers, the People's Council, the General Industrial Organization, the Iron and Steel Complex, the General Electricity Authority, Ain Shams University, Cairo University, etc. A sizable number of private and public microfilming consultancy services recently founded in Egypt offer advisory microform information services pertaining to software and hardware configuration. Noteworthy among these services is Al-Ahram Organization and Microfilm Center attached to the famous Al-Ahram Newspaper Organization. This center, beside providing consultancy services for establishing new microfilm libraries, offers national commercial documentation services in the form of the Al-Ahram Index and abstracts of academic theses submitted to Egyptian universities.

BIBLIOGRAPHICAL SERVICES

Bibliography in Egypt has always been the concern of a few highly esteemed individuals. Among the most noted are Ahmed Taymour and Ahmed Zaki. The Egyptian National Library issues the *Egyptian National Bibliography* in quarterly issues and an annual cumulative index since 1956; *Egyptian Books in Print* in January of every year for distribution during the Cairo International Book Fair since 1973; and many other catalogs and bibliographies for serials, manuscripts, and specialized subject collections. A computerized catalog of Arabic holdings from 1870 to 1969 is to be issued by the library in 1980.

From time to time university libraries in Egypt issue catalogs and accession lists of their holdings but not on a regular basis. Noteworthy among these bibliographical services are the catalog of Al-Azhar University library, which appeared in six volumes from 1943 to 1950, and the union list of periodical holdings in Cairo University libraries, which is a computerized printout of 5,000 periodical titles in the Latin alphabet possessed by the university libraries as of 1974.

Special libraries and information or documentation centers in Egypt issue numerous kinds and types of bibliographies, mostly on an ad-hoc basis and unrelated with each other.

PROFESSIONAL ASSOCIATIONS

The Cairo Library Association, established in 1945, and the Alexandria Library Association, established in 1952, were merged into the Egyptian Library Association (ELA) in 1953. Thus ELA, which opened its membership to any person interested in librarianship, played a very active role in fostering the profession and library education in Egypt until it suspended its activities in 1959. The Egyptian Library and Archives Association (ELAA), established in 1954, has restricted its membership to graduates of library schools, especially those graduated from the undergraduate library and archives program of Cairo University. The ELAA has successfully represented the interests of Egyptian librarians in connection with job classification, grading, status, and development of the profession. However, the activities of the association have been seriously limited in recent years. Egyptian school librarians working in the Ministry of Education established the School Library Association in the late 1960s. The association has been very active in fostering school librarianship and in disseminating professional literature.

In the area of publishing, the Egyptian publishers and book dealers organized the Association of Egyptian Publishers in 1965. The association has established requirements for membership. Its aims are to organize the profession and enhance cooperation among its members and with outside publishers and associations.

LIBRARY EDUCATION AND THE PROFESSION

The establishment of the Department of Librarianship and Archives at the Faculty of Arts of Cairo University marked a new era in the history of professional librarianship in Egypt. The department offers a four-year undergraduate general library and archival instruction program. In addition it offers a postgraduate program leading to a M.A. and Ph.D. for its graduates. The low number of graduates from this department, their lack of specialized knowledge, and their unfamiliarity with new technologies led many organizations to offer numerous ad hoc training programs. Among these training courses are those offered by the National Institute of Management Development in connection with information systems, documentation, records management, and library and information management. Also, the Ministry of Education, the Egyptian National Library, and many other types of libraries and documentation centers offer different sorts of training programs for their professional personnel.

In terms of professional writing, the profession is still far behind in this area. Arabic professional writings are still scarce. In-depth studies, standards, tools, and apparatus are mostly unavailable. However, in recent years the profession has witnessed the issuance of several articles, papers, reports, and monographs. The *Bibliographical Guide to Arabic Literature in Librarianship and Documentation,* issued by the Arab League Educational, Cultural and Scientific Organization in 1976, lists more than 4,000 items written in Arabic and in other languages and mostly produced by Egyptian professionals.

CONCLUSION

In spite of the growth of the Egyptian library and information services in the past two decades, the profession is faced with major problems:

Most Egyptian libraries are crowded with duplicate materials, understaffed with qualified professionals, critically short of money, and unable to keep pace with service demands.

The level of library and information services in Egypt is still below any given accepted standards. The majority of the Egyptian population are still inadequately served.

Libraries and information services tend to drift toward incompatible systems. Public school, university, and special libraries have no national standards to follow.

Public relations with potential users is poor. The public still regards librarians as keepers and custodians of books.

Most Egyptian libraries and information services are unable to afford the cost of acquiring all books and materials needed for their users.

Library development in Egypt is still hindered by the lack of appropriate personnel development training programs and the shortage of qualified professional manpower.

Libraries and information services are without any kind of a master development plan. Their growth and services are uneven and uncohesive.

Egyptian library and information services still have a long way to go before they will be able to provide the information needed for national development and modernization. There is an urgent need to develop new means and ways to cope with the serious problems facing the country. Libraries and information services must be reorganized in the future, bearing in mind the following principles:

Sharing of resources and services and good communication channels are required for good services.

Libraries should work in close cooperation and coordination with each other because they cannot afford to be isolated entities.

Network organization for library and information services is an efficient means needed to cope with scarce resources, shortage of qualified manpower, lack of funding, and few professional standards. Also, networking could enhance the utilization of new technologies in mobilizing and transmitting library and information services.

The implementation of these principles would assist in making information more uniformly available and in changing the Egyptian library's image from that of a store of books to an active and dynamic information organism.

THE PARLIAMENTARY LIBRARY: PRESENT AND FUTURE

Erik J. Spicer

Parliamentary Librarian, Library of Parliament, Ottawa, Canada

Parliamentary libraries do not exist in all countries. And many times when they do exist, they do so in name only and do not provide the services necessary to serve democratic legislatures of the developed Western model. The important national parliamentary libraries are few in number in comparison with the number of independent states represented in the United Nations, for example. But I believe that the more developed ones indicate the future development for libraries of all kinds that hope to survive in the modern age.

In the front rank we see the Library of Congress and particularly its Congressional Research Service, which has long been a model for parliamentary libraries in countries where the role of legislators is truly important. I do not believe it is enough to bring legislators into session for less than a dozen days a year and "tell them all they need to know." In the democratic process with which North Americans are most familiar, strong intellectual support is required to ensure that legislative responses to needs are based on adequate, timely, and accurate information well arranged and, on occasion, carefully explained. If parliamentary errors are made, or appear to be made, they should be political errors rather than information errors.

Though many parliaments separate the research services from the library, I feel strongly that such a separation is seldom administratively sound or sufficiently effective in practice to justify the divisive competition that separation encourages. I do not suggest that an integrated service is the only possible service or necessarily the best possible service for all countries, but it is most likely to be, and where it has been established, it has worked well. Following the American model of research integrated with library service, Australia, Canada, and Great Britain added research elements to their library services in the early 1960s. In Japan, of course, the National Diet Library, modeled after the Library of Congress, also has research service as part of its operations.

THE FUNCTIONS OF THE PARLIAMENTARY LIBRARY

But what can a good, modern, well-supported parliamentary library be expected to do? What in particular does it do that other libraries seldom or never do? This has been partially indicated by my emphasis on research service to parliaments. Few other libraries can afford to give the concentrated support to their clients that parliamentary libraries can give. Few other libraries can hope to be as well supported or as physically close to their clients as can parliamentary libraries. Although there are many different degrees of service given in parliamentary libraries, depending on the country in which they exist, most libraries are located within or very close to the legislative chamber and the offices of the members themselves. In Rome, the Chamber of Deputies and the Senate, which are in separate buildings some distance apart, each has its own large library but the services given are somewhat unequal. In Paris, too, the Senate and the National Assembly are housed in separate palaces and their large libraries are housed with them, both giving different services but presumably what their members are prepared to authorize. In London, also, the House of Lords has a library separate from that of the House of Commons and this system seems to work well for them.

I believe, however, that in addition to the traditional library services given by all parliamentary libraries those more advanced are showing the way to the future for all libraries. It is not enough to be a traditional library. And as parliamentary libraries cannot effectively be too highly specialized, as members and parliaments are interested in everything, careful selection rather than comprehensiveness is essential. The days of large, forever-expanding collections are past, particularly as the modern member expects to have transcripts or recordings of radio programs and television films.

Parliamentarians are under more pressure than any other citizens—pressures of time, pressures of being expected to have an informed opinion on virtually any subject, and pressures from constituents for assistance that often cannot be readily given. Parliamentarians cannot be invited to come in and "help themselves." Parliamentary libraries cannot be effective if they are perceived as supermarket operations like large public and university libraries. It is true that the parliamentary library in Helsinki, now in a splendid new building attached directly to the parliament buildings, is also the Finnish National Library for Law and the Social Sciences but only 10 percent of its work is done for the parliament. The parliamentary library in Hungary, in the magnificent old parliamentary buildings, is also a national library. But as its parliamentary sessions are much shorter than in Finland, its parliamentary usage is probably less significant.

Though parliamentary libraries give substantial reference service, maintain clipping files and extensive indexing, as well as providing reading rooms with books, newspapers, periodicals, and microforms, many of them also handle the parliamentary archives.

STATE/PROVINCIAL AND INTERNATIONAL COOPERATION

The number of parliamentary libraries in the sense in which I am speaking is relatively small at the national level, however there is a multiplication of parliamentary libraries at the state, provincial, or länder level in federal states, and many of these are as large in size and staff and give the same quality of service as given in some of the smaller national parliaments. In addition, in Australia, Canada, and West Germany there is close cooperation between all these parliamentary/legislative libraries, and Canada has the Association of Parliamentary Librarians in Canada, which was formally established in 1975.

In addition to the individual national and state/provincial parliamentary libraries, there are international connections as well. The parliamentary librarians of the Nordic countries—Denmark, Finland, Norway, and Sweden—have met regularly for many years. The International Federation of Library Associations has had a section on parliamentary libraries since 1935. The Inter-Parliamentary Union in Geneva has an International Centre for Parliamentary Documentation and in 1973 held an important symposium on "The Member of Parliament: His Requirements for Information in the Modern World." At the symposium a handful of parliamentary librarians from Australia, Canada, and Denmark met with members of Parliament, senators, and other representatives of national parliaments to discuss means of improving international cooperation to facilitate improved information services to parliamentarians. The proceedings have been published and a short paper, "International Co-operation on Information for Parliament," jointly authored by the Canadian Parliamentary Librarian and the director of research for the Swedish Ricksdag, also resulted. Finally, on the international scene there is also a Parliamentary Information and Reference Centre within the Commonwealth at the headquarters of the Commonwealth Parliamentary Association in Westminster.

For emerging nations, parliamentary libraries and some form of research service are increasingly seen as a desirable evidence of democracy and this is encouraged by both the Inter-Parliamentary Union in Geneva and the Commonwealth Parliamentary Association in London. Experts have been sent to Africa and elsewhere to assist and students have been sent to Canada and elsewhere to learn and practice. A parliamentary library now helps to legitimize an emerging democracy.

THE FUTURE OUTLOOK

The future for parliamentary libraries consists not only of helping to develop parliamentary material in machine-readable form and accessing nonparliamentary material through computer terminals but also in providing informed research assistance: service to parliamentary committees; the briefing of members on pertinent subjects before trips abroad, to the constituency, or into the chamber itself; the digesting of briefs, reports, and other information that are far too voluminous to permit even the most determined and dedicated member to do himself. Increasingly, for many parliamentary libraries, the days of warehousing large collections have gone—except for the maintenance of files of parliamentary papers—and the day of interpretation for specific problems with particular viewpoints has arrived.

I suggest that, if other libraries are to survive, similar services will have to be provided for their customers as well, if they demand quality service. The cliche that knowledge is power is only true if it is in the hands of those who hold positions that permit the exercise of power. In democratic states this may, in theory, be the electorate—including those who neglect to vote—but, in fact, it is in the hands of the legislators and the executive. And if we wish to have reasonable amelioration to our difficulties—not solutions, for there are no solutions—then we must ensure that we have the best quality of intellectual service in parliamentary libraries. This means improved funding, improved education, and a greater acceptance of responsibility to select information carefully, to ensure that it is presented accurately and usefully, and to ensure that it is up to date. Few other libraries can manage this, or even attempt it, but if our parliamentary/congressional libraries fail to do so, we will all suffer more severely than if any other library fails to do its job. I suggest, therefore, that any request for interlibrary loan (or for any other assistance) from your parliamentary library be treated as a matter of concern to all. It is. If parliamentary libraries, with their extraordinarily high staff/public ratio, can demonstrate satisfactorily to a nation's leaders what effective library service can be, these leaders can help convince persons in their constituencies to support good service locally.

International Statistics

AMERICAN EXPORTS AND IMPORTS AND INTERNATIONAL TITLE OUTPUT

Chandler B. Grannis

Contributing Editor, *Publishers Weekly*

In 1978, exports from the United States increased in dollar value by almost 18%, compared with 1977, according to unpublished figures made available to *PW* by the U.S. Department of Commerce. The category of general books ("not elsewhere classified and pamphlets") accounted for over half of the revenues and for the greater part of the increase. Declines were shown in export receipts for text materials and dictionaries.

While the dollar receipts for foreign sales of general books increased more than 31%, the numbers of units sold in that category rose not quite 17%—an impressive increase, but not in line with the dollar rise.

A similar trend is to be seen in comparisons of dollar sales with unit sales of technical, scientific, and professional books; of religious books; of dictionaries; and of encyclopedias. Price inflation and declines in the overseas value of the dollar are showing their effects.

Total sales to Canada stayed about the same in overall dollars as in 1977, but sales by category showed no consistent trends. Canada's share of the U.S. export market remained great—39%; but in 1977 it had been 46%, and in 1976 it was over 48%.

Imports, meanwhile, have been rising at a faster rate than exports. Dollar values of imports rose in 1978 in every group, especially the dominant general books category, where payments were up 45%. While the dollars paid were rising, the numbers of units imported were either dropping or increasing to a lesser extent than the money paid.

Once again we must call attention to the line "Shipments valued at $250 or more *only*," in the headings of Tables 1 and 2. In this regard, the government's statistics are incomplete. Book industry estimates of foreign trade suggest that these omissions from the Commerce report may amount, very roughly, to 10% of the totals printed here; so totals shown in these tables should perhaps be increased by about 10% to approximate the true totals.

Whether this deficiency in the Commerce reporting can be corrected is still to be seen. Equally important would be a reevaluation of the big catchall categories of exports ("not elsewhere classified") and imports ("other books"); such broadly miscellaneous groupings are not very informative. *PW* understands, however, that changes in this area might involve changes in legislation.

Note: Reprinted from *Publishers Weekly*, September 7, 1979.

Editor's Note: For average prices of British, German, and Latin American books, see "Prices of U.S. and Foreign Published Materials" in the Book Trade Research and Statistics section of Part 4.

TABLE 1 U.S. BOOK EXPORTS, 1976–1978
Shipments Valued at $250 or More ONLY

	Dollar Values			% Chg. 1977-1978	Exports to Canada only			Units to All Countries			% Chg. 1977-1978
	1976	1977	1978		1976	1977	1978	1976	1977	1978	
Textbooks, Workbooks and Standardized Tests (8921110)	$70,356,151	$72,060,134	$70,297,302	−2.4	$38,062,047	$39,135,076	$33,387,418	—	—	—	—
Books, Technical, Scientific and Professional (8921120)	47,061,626	45,302,922	49,479,329	+9.2	14,971,059	12,959,201	9,843,843	16,020,031	16,173,862	16,024,867	−0.9
Bibles, Testaments and Other Religious Books (8921130)	15,339,390	18,385,933	20,728,789	+12.7	5,624,764	6,550,579	6,313,640	35,526,433	39,731,193	42,153,722	+6.0
Dictionaries (8921140)	4,454,530	6,123,398	3,965,864	−35.2	1,281,679	1,203,844	914,692	1,323,859	1,749,640	1,040,744	−40.5
Encyclopedias (8921150)	28,580,665	24,586,694	32,294,083	+31.3	8,795,246	5,405,254	6,231,693	9,320,853	8,047,975	9,879,858	+22.7
Children's Picture and Painting Books (8921200)	6,857,082	5,296,324	6,404,411	+21.0	4,682,279	4,511,016	2,562,161	17,394,057	16,340,550	—	—
Books Not Elsewhere Classified & Pamphlets (8921170)	126,131,250	142,397,340	187,450,445	+31.6	70,177,174	79,221,421	87,244,510	130,445,810	134,975,663	157,759,062	+16.9
Total Domestic Merchandise—Omitting Shipments under $250	$298,780,694	$314,152,745	$370,620,223	+17.9	$143,594,248	$148,988,391	$146,597,956	—	—	—	—

Source: Extracted from U.S. Department of Commerce quarterly, *Printing and Publishing*, issues of April 1977 and 1978; heretofore unpublished 1978 data supplied to *PW* by *P&P* editors.

TABLE 2 U.S. BOOK IMPORTS, 1976–1978
Shipments Valued at $250 or More ONLY

	Dollar Values				Units			
	1976	1977	1978	% Chg. 1977-78	1976	1977	1978	% Chg. 1977-78
Bibles and Prayerbooks (2702520)	$6,109,233	$8,490,189	$8,781,188	+3.4	5,416,054	7,274,172	3,995,295	−45.1
Books Foreign Language (2702540)	19,624,085	22,170,970	25,177,094	+13.6	15,226,817	14,832,412	14,507,863	−2.2
Other Books, not specially provided for, wholly or in part the work of an author who is a U.S. national or domiciliary (2701560)	3,753,357	3,799,617	4,678,542	+23.1	2,392,853	2,694,209	2,244,604	−16.7
Other Books (2702580)	120,927,651	132,284,454	191,808,521	+45.0	146,408,941	117,836,144	159,326,315	+35.2
Toy Books and Coloring Books (7375200)	1,035,915	1,735,420	1,880,580	+8.3	—	—	—	—
Total Imports— Omitting Shipments under $250	$157,949,973	$168,480,630	$232,325,925	+37.9	—	—	—	—

Source: Extracted from U.S. Department of Commerce quarterly, *Printing and Publishing*, issues of April 1977 and 1978; heretofore unpublished 1978 data supplied to *PW* by *P&P* editors.

TABLE 3 / TITLE OUTPUT, PRINCIPAL BOOK-PRODUCING COUNTRIES

	1974	1975	1976		1974	1975	1976
	AFRICA				**EUROPE**		
Egypt	—	—	—	Austria	5,519	5,636	6,336
Nigeria	1,337	1,324	—	Belgium	—	5,848	6,414
South Africa	3,849	—	—	Bulgaria	3,863	3,669	3,813

	NORTH AMERICA			
Canada	6,834	6,735	Czechoslovakia	9,883	10,372	9,457
Mexico	5,733	5,822	Denmark	6,822	7,068	6,783
U.S.A.*	81,023	85,287	Finland	4,245	4,558	4,589
			France	28,245	—	29,371
	SOUTH AMERICA		Germany (E.)	5,546	5,800	5,792
Argentina	4,795	5,141	Germany (W.)	48,034	40,616	44,477
Brazil	—	—	Greece	2,920	2,613	3,935
Colombia	—	1,272	Hungary	8,050	8,603	9,393
Peru	1,322	1,090	Italy	9,443	9,187	9,463
			Netherlands	11,440	12,028	12,557
	ASIA		Norway	6,520	4,855	5,723
Burma	1,164	—	Poland	10,749	10,277	11,418
Hong Kong	936	880	Portugal	7,326	5,943	5,668
India	11,647	12,708	Romania	11,258	7,860	6,556
Indonesia	1,917	2,187	Spain	24,085	23,527	24,584
Iraq	143	595	Sweden	9,014	9,012	7,988
Israel	1,866	1,907	Switzerland	9,310	9,928	9,989
Japan	32,378	34,490	United Kingdom	32,133	35,526	34,340
Rep. Korea	—	10,921	Yugoslavia	13,063	11,239	9,054
Malaysia	1,237	1,445				
Pakistan	—	1,081		OCEANIA		
Philippines	—	1,609	Australia	1,761	1,761	2,325
Singapore	510	577	New Zealand	1,598	1,887	1,835
Sri Lanka	1,442	1,153	U.S.S.R.	—	78,697	84,304
Thailand	2,323	2,419	Byeloruss S.S.R.	3,766	2,941	2,489
Turkey			Ukraine S.S.R.	8,814	8,731	9,110

Source: Section 11.2 of *UNESCO Statistical Yearbook, 1977*, published 1979.

*Includes U.S. government publications (in 1974, 9,406; in 1975, 15,750; in 1976, 16,931); university theses (in 1974, 31,111; in 1975, 31,478; in 1976, 34,709); and children's fiction titles (in 1974, 2,433; in 1975, 2,292; in 1976, 2,210) not classified by subject. Not included in the U.S. figures are publications of state and local government units, publications of many institutions, and many reports, proceedings, lab manuals, and workbooks.

Table 3 shows title output by the principal book-producing countries and comes from UNESCO's *Statistical Yearbook, 1977*, just published. The yearbook does not provide any new translation figures, however; the latest were cited in *PW*, September 19, 1977.

As pointed out in earlier *PW* reports on UNESCO, the output figures still do not include the probably massive output of the People's Republic of China and of Taiwan.

BRITISH BOOK PRODUCTION, 1979

In 1979 publishers in Britain issued a total of 41,940 titles, of which 32,854 were new books and 9,086 reprints and new editions. The output of new books and new editions according to category is given in detail in Table 1. The figures have been compiled from the booklists that have appeared week by week in *The Bookseller*.

This record total of 41,940 represents an advance of 3,174 titles, or 8.2 percent, on last year's overall total of 38,766. That was itself a record, as indeed was the 1977 total of 36,322. The 1979 rise in new books is especially remarkable: the 9,086 reprints were a decrease of 150 on last year, so that the new book increase of 3,224 titles was an advance of almost 11 percent. (See Table 2.)

It is indeed interesting to see the relative decline of reprints and new editions —although this figure includes the vigorous paperback market—since in 1970 they represented almost 30 percent of British publishers' total output. At the end of the decade they represent less than 22 percent.

While the output trend is clearly upwards, despite all the well-publicized difficulties which publishers currently confront, a comment a year ago in *The Bookseller's* examination of the 1978 figures may provide one reason for the sharpness of this year's increase: "Production delays have bedevilled publishing programmes even more than usual: it is possible that, had a proportion of the titles planned for this year and now delayed until next appeared as scheduled, then the 1978 output figure might have topped 40,000." And it seems probable, too, that another contributory factor in the increased total is a larger number of English-language imported books handled through British distributors. Table 3 shows recorded output in 1979, 1974, and 1969 of ten trade houses, chosen at random, and suggests that special factors may indeed have been at work.

Inevitably, the main category comparisons in Table 4 show increases, with the exceptions only of art, chemistry and physics, and sociology, which experienced small declines. Encouragingly, children's books, up in 1977 and 1978, again showed an advance, this year by 6.8 percent. No less encouraging is the reversal of last year's fiction results: then there was a 2.4 percent fall, but 1979 has seen a rise of nearly 4 percent to 4,551 titles.

Note: Adapted from *The Bookseller* (12 Dyott St., London, England WC1A 1DF), January 5, 1980, where the article was entitled "UK's New Title Output Sharply Ahead."

TABLE 1 BOOK TITLE OUTPUT, 1979

Classification	December 1979 Total	December 1979 Reprints and New Editions	December 1979 Trans.	December 1979 Limited Editions	January–December 1979 Total	January–December 1979 Reprints and New Editions	January–December 1979 Trans.	January–December 1979 Limited Editions
Aeronautics	15	1	—	—	182	38	2	—
Agriculture and forestry	44	9	1	—	481	79	4	—
Architecture	26	4	—	—	432	101	7	1
Art	128	38	5	—	1,226	179	43	5
Astronomy	16	4	—	—	147	32	1	—
Bibliography and library economy	78	12	1	—	723	107	3	—
Biography	80	25	6	—	1,236	335	61	6
Chemistry and physics	79	15	—	—	684	102	20	—
Children's books	147	45	11	—	3,214	494	133	—
Commerce	106	25	—	—	1,073	259	1	—
Customs, costumes, folklore	12	2	2	—	128	27	7	—
Domestic science	44	13	1	1	713	131	14	1
Education	193	25	1	—	1,024	174	4	—
Engineering	139	30	1	—	1,334	263	12	—
Entertainment	63	12	1	—	559	134	9	—
Fiction	274	107	9	—	4,551	1,683	179	2
General	32	6	—	—	377	73	4	—
Geography and archaeology	43	9	2	—	362	91	5	—
Geology and meteorology	32	6	1	—	271	38	1	—
History	145	28	6	—	1,421	314	57	2
Humor	6	—	—	—	126	26	1	—
Industry	63	21	—	—	488	112	8	2
Language	67	9	1	—	633	95	8	—
Law and public administration	151	49	6	1	1,404	374	18	9
Literature	161	40	6	—	1,161	223	59	—
Mathematics	62	11	—	—	561	109	18	—
Medical science	381	110	1	—	2,510	421	17	—
Military science	15	2	—	1	173	25	1	—
Music	41	8	—	—	389	96	8	1
Natural sciences	132	30	1	—	1,157	174	21	1

TABLE 1 BOOK TITLE OUTPUT, 1979 (cont.)

Classification	December 1979				January–December 1979			
	Total	Reprints and New Editions	Trans.	Limited Editions	Total	Reprints and New Editions	Trans.	Limited Editions
Occultism	29	10	1	—	253	77	18	1
Philosophy	56	15	7	—	469	145	49	—
Photography	19	1	2	—	224	30	14	—
Plays	37	12	9	—	336	62	53	—
Poetry	72	5	4	7	788	121	59	53
Political science and economy	417	64	7	—	3,364	608	130	—
Psychology	72	11	—	—	654	123	18	—
Religion and theology	127	30	13	—	1,509	426	152	1
School textbooks	181	45	—	—	2,144	405	5	—
Science, general	6	1	1	—	82	7	1	—
Sociology	111	18	2	—	964	156	20	—
Sports and outdoor games	52	15	3	—	620	120	16	4
Stockbreeding	38	4	—	—	297	68	4	—
Trade	65	18	—	—	563	149	1	—
Travel and guidebooks	94	55	1	—	674	231	13	2
Wireless and television	42	14	—	—	259	49	4	—
Total	4,193	1,014	107	10	41,940	9,086	1,283	91

Note: This table shows the books recorded in December and the total for January–December with the numbers of new editions, translations and limited editions.

TABLE 2 GROWTH IN TITLE OUTPUT, 1947-1979

Year	Total	Reprints and New Editions
1947	13,046	2,441
1948	14,686	3,924
1949	17,034	5,110
1950	17,072	5,334
1951	18,066	4,938
1952	18,741	5,428
1953	18,257	5,523
1954	18,188	4,846
1955	19,962	5,770
1956	19,107	5,302
1957	20,719	5,921
1958	22,143	5,971
1959	20,690	5,522
1960	23,783	4,989
1961	24,893	6,406
1962	25,079	6,104
1963	26,023	5,656
1964	26,154	5,260
1965	26,358	5,313
1966	28,883	5,919
1967	29,619	7,060
1968	31,470	8,778
1969	32,393	9,106
1970	33,489	9,977
1971	32,538	8,975
1972	33,140	8,486
1973	35,254	9,556
1974	32,194	7,852
1975	35,608	8,361
1976	34,434	8,227
1977	36,322	8,638
1978	38,766	9,236
1979	41,940	9,086

TABLE 3   BOOK TITLE OUTPUT, BY PUBLISHER, 1969, 1974, AND 1979

	1979 New	1979 New Editions	1979 Total	1974 New	1974 New Editions	1974 Total	1969 New	1969 New Editions	1969 Total
Blackwell Scientific	19	21	40	5	7	12	13	10	23
Cape	40	5	45	55	2	57	55	17	72
Collins	186	40	226	348	195	543	162	74	236
Constable	24	2	26	31	4	35	27	1	28
Deutsch	57	1	58	47	5	52	50	5	55
Faber	59	31	90	77	26	103	116	46	162
M. Joseph	45	3	48	50	3	53	69	9	78
OUP	222	122	344	243	78	321	294	137	431
Routledge	116	17	133	85	29	114	126	20	146
Thames & Hudson	61	7	68	70	4	74	68	10	78
Total	829	249	1,078	1,011	353	1,364	980	329	1,309

TABLE 4   COMPARISON OF PRODUCTION BY SUBJECT, 1978 AND 1979

	1978	1979	+ or −
Art	1,304	1,226	−78
Biography	1,202	1,236	+34
Chemistry and physics	701	684	−17
Children's books	3,010	3,214	+204
Commerce	852	1,073	+221
Education	968	1,024	+56
Engineering	1,262	1,334	+72
Fiction	4,379	4,551	+172
History	1,293	1,421	+128
Industry	438	448	+50
Law and public administration	1,146	1,404	+258
Literature	1,055	1,161	+106
Medical science	2,305	2,510	+205
Natural sciences	1,146	1,157	+11
Political science	2,955	3,364	+409
Religion	1,294	1,509	+215
School textbooks	1,923	2,144	+221
Sociology	991	964	−27
Travel and guidebooks	609	674	+65

Part 6
Reference Information

Bibliographies

THE LIBRARIAN'S BOOKSHELF

Carol S. Nielsen
*Library Science Librarian,
University of North Carolina, Chapel Hill*

This bibliography is intended as a buying and reading guide for individual librarians and library collections. Some of the titles listed are core titles that any staff development collection might contain, others may be of more current interest only. Bibliographic tools that most libraries are likely to have for day-to-day operations have been excluded from this list.

BOOKS

General Works

The ALA Yearbook: A Review of Library Events, 1979. Chicago: American Library Association, 1979. $30.

American Library Directory, 1978–1979. 32nd ed. New York: R. R. Bowker, 1979. $49.95.

American Library Laws. 4th ed. Chicago: American Library Association, 1973. $40. 1st supplement, 1973–1974. 1975. $10. 2nd supplement, 1975–1976. 1977. $12.50.

American Library Association. Headquarters Library. *A.L.A. Publications Checklist, 1979.* Chicago, 1979. $3.

A Biographical Directory of Librarians in the United States and Canada. 5th ed. Chicago: American Library Association, 1970. $45.

Bowker Annual of Library and Book Trade Information 1979. 24th ed. New York: R. R. Bowker, 1979. $24.95.

Cole, John Y. *For Congress and the Nation: A Chronological History of the Library of Congress.* Washington, DC: U.S. Govt. Printing Office, 1979. $8.

Cole, John Y., ed. *The Library of Congress in Perspective: A Volume Based on the Reports of the Librarian's Task Force and Advisory Groups.* New York: R. R. Bowker, 1978. $21.50.

Directory of Special Libraries and Information Centers. 5th ed. Detroit: Gale Research Co., 1979. Vols. 1–3. Vol. 1 $90; Vol. 2 $70; Vol. 3 $80.

Encyclopedia of Library and Information Science. New York: Marcel Dekker, 1968–1979. Vols. 1–27. $55 per vol.

Estabrook, Leigh, ed. *Libraries in Post-Industrial Society.* Phoenix, AZ: Oryx Press, 1977. $13.95.

Fang, Josephine Riss, and Songe, Alice H. *International Guide to Library, Archival, and Information Science Associations.* New York: R. R. Bowker, 1976. $17.50.

Garrison, Dee. *Apostles of Culture.* New York: Macmillan Information, 1979. $14.50.

Harris, Michael, ed. *Advances in Librarianship.* New York: Academic Press, 1970–   Vol. 9, 1979. $21.

Harrod, L. M., comp. *The Librarians' Glossary and Reference Book.* 4th rev. ed. Boulder, CO: Westview, 1977. $30.

Lee, Joel, and Hamilton, Beth, eds. *As Much to Learn as to Teach.* Hamden, CT: Linnet, 1979. $12.50.

Matthews, Virginia. *Libraries for Today and Tomorrow.* New York: Doubleday, 1976. $3.95.

Shera, Jesse H. *Introduction to Library Science: Basic Elements of Library Service.* Littleton, CO: Libraries Unlimited, 1976. $10.

──────, Bobinski, George, and Wynar, Bohdan, eds. *Dictionary of American Library Biography.* Littleton, CO: Libraries Unlimited, 1977. $65.

Steele, Colin R. *Major Libraries of the World: A Selective Guide.* New York: R. R. Bowker, 1976. $22.50.

Weibel, Kathleen, and Heim, Kathleen M. *The Role of Women in Librarianship 1876-1976: The Entry, Advancement, and Struggle for Equalization in One Profession.* Phoenix, AZ: Oryx Press, 1979. $14.95.

Winckler, Paul A. *Reader in the History of Books and Printing.* Englewood, CO: Information Handling Services, 1978. $22.

Administration

Breivik, Patricia, and Gibson, E. Burr. *Funding Alternatives for Libraries.* Chicago: American Library Association, 1979. $9.95.

Find Out Who Your Friends Are: A Practical Manual for the Formation of Library Support Groups, ed. by H. Barrett Pennell, Jr. Philadelphia: Friends of the Free Library of Philadelphia, 1978. $5.

Hennepin County Library. *Friends of the Hennepin County Library: A Manual of Suggestions and Procedures for Librarians and Friends Organizations.* Edina, MN, 1978. $5.

Kemper, Robert E., and Ostrander, Richard E. *Directorship by Objectives.* Littleton, CO: Libraries Unlimited, 1977. $8.

Lancaster, F. W. *The Measurement and Evaluation of Library Services.* Washington, DC: Information Resources Press, 1977. $27.50.

Lee, Sul H., ed. *Library Budgeting: Critical Challenge for the Future.* Ann Arbor, MI: Pierian Press, 1977. $10.

──────. *Emerging Trends in Library Organization: What Influences Change.* Ann Arbor, MI: Pierian Press, 1978. $11.95.

Personnel Manual: An Outline for Libraries. Chicago: American Library Association, 1977. $3.

Prentice, Ann E. *Strategies for Survival: Library Financial Management Today.* Library Journal Special Report No. 7. New York: R. R. Bowker, 1978. $5.

Prepare! The Library Public Relations Recipe Book. Prepared by Public Relations Section, Library Administration and Management Association, American Library Association. Chicago, 1978. $4.

Staff Development in Libraries: A Directory of Organizations and Activities with a Staff Development Bibliography. Prepared by the Staff Development Committee of the Personnel Administration Section of the Library Administration Division of the American Library Association. Chicago: American Library Association, 1978. $2.

Archives, Conservation, and Manuscripts

Baker, John P., and Soroka, Marguerite C. *Library Conservation: Preservation in Perspective.* Stroudsburg, PA: Dowden, Hutchinson, and Ross, 1978. $45.

Berkeley, Edmund, Jr., et al., eds. *Autographs and Manuscripts: A Collector's Manual.* New York: Scribner's, 1978. $24.95.

Brichford, Maynard J. *Appraisal and Accessioning.* SAA Basic Manual Series. Chicago: Society of American Archivists, 1977. $3 for members, $4 for nonmembers.

Falco, Nicholas. *Manual for the Organization of Manuscripts.* New York: Queensborough Public Library, 1978. $7.

Fleckner, John A. *Surveys.* SAA Basic

Manual Series. Chicago: Society of American Archivists, 1977. $3 for members, $4 for nonmembers.

Gracy II, David B. *Arrangement and Description.* SAA Basic Manual Series. Chicago: Society of American Archivists, 1977. $3 for members, $4 for nonmembers.

Holbert, Sue E. *Reference and Access.* SAA Basic Manual Series. Chicago: Society of American Archivists, 1977. $3 for members, $4 for nonmembers.

Kemp, Edward C. *Manuscript Solicitation for Libraries, Special Collections, Museums, and Archives.* Littleton, CO: Libraries Unlimited, 1978. $18.50.

Thompson, Enid T. *Local History Collections: A Manual for Librarians.* Nashville, TN: American Association for State and Local History, 1978. $5.75.

Walch, Timothy. *Security.* SAA Basic Manual Series. Chicago: Society of American Archivists, 1977. $3 for members, $4 for nonmembers.

Williams, John C., ed. *Preservation of Paper and Textiles of Historic and Artistic Value.* Washington, DC: American Chemical Society, 1977. $41.75.

Audiovisual

Audiovisual Market Place, 1980: A Multimedia Guide. 10th ed. New York: R. R. Bowker, 1980. $23.95.

Audio-Visual Equipment Directory 1979/80. 24th ed. Fairfax, VA: National Audio-Visual Association, 1979. $28.50.

Boyle, Deirdre, ed. *Expanding Media.* Phoenix, AZ: Oryx Press, 1977. $13.95.

Brown, James W., ed. *Educational Media Yearbook 1978.* New York: R. R. Bowker, 1978. $25.

Cabeceiras, James. *The Multimedia Library: Materials Selection and Use.* New York: Academic Press, 1978. $15.

Nadler, Myra, ed. *How to Start an Audiovisual Collection.* Metuchen, NJ: Scarecrow Press, 1978. $7.

Sive, Mary Robinson. *Selecting Instructional Media: A Guide to Audiovisual and Other Instructional Media Lists.* Littleton, CO: Libraries Unlimited, 1978. $13.50.

Automation and Information Retrieval

Annual Review of Information Science and Technology. Washington, DC: American Society for Information Science. White Plains, NY: Knowledge Industry Publications. Vols. 3–5 (1968–1970) and Vols. 7–9 (1972–1974). $22 per vol. Vol. 10 (1975). $27.50. Vols. 12–14. 1977–1979. $35 per vol.

Atherton, Pauline, and Christian, Roger W. *Librarians and Online Services.* White Plains, NY: Knowledge Industry Publications, 1977. $24.

Bahr, Alice H. *Automated Library Circulation Systems, 1979–1980.* White Plains, NY: Knowledge Industry Publications, 1979. $24.50.

Butler, Brett, and Martin, Susan K., eds., *Library Automation: The State of the Art II.* Chicago: American Library Association, 1975. $7.50.

Buying New Technology. Library Journal Special Report No. 4. New York: R. R. Bowker, 1978. $3.95 prepaid.

Clinic on Library Applications of Data Processing. University of Illinois Proceedings. Champaign, IL: University of Illinois, Graduate School of Library Science, Publications Office, 1963–1979 vol. $9.

Gough, Chet, and Srikantaiah, Taverekere. *Systems Analysis in Libraries: A Question and Answer Approach.* Hamden, CT: Linnet, 1978. $9.50.

Grosch, Audrey N. *Minicomputers in Libraries 1979–80.* White Plains, NY: Knowledge Industry Publications, 1979. $24.50.

Hayes, Robert M., and Becker, Joseph. *Handbook of Data Processing for Libraries.* 2nd ed. New York: Wiley, 1974. $23.75.

International On-Line Information Meeting, First, London, 1977. Oxford: Learned Information, 1978. $30.

International On-Line Information Meeting, Second, London, 1978. Oxford: Learned Information, 1979. $30.

Kent, Allen, and Galvin, Thomas J., eds. *The On-Line Revolution in Libraries.* New York: Marcel Dekker, 1978. $29.75.

King, Donald W. *Key Papers in the Design and Evaluation of Information Systems* (American Society for Information Science). White Plains, NY: Knowledge Industry Publications, 1978. $19.95.

Lancaster, F. Wilfrid, and Gallup, Emily F. *Information Retrieval On-Line.* New York: Wiley, 1973. $20.

Martin, Susan K. *Library Networks, 1978-79.* White Plains, NY: Knowledge Industry Publications, 1978. $24.50.

Report on the Conference on Cataloging and Information Services for Machine-Readable Data Files, March 29-31, 1978. NTIS No. PB-298 496/1WL. Washington, DC: NTIS, 1978. $6.50.

Salton, Gerald. *Dynamic Information and Library Processing.* Englewood Cliffs, NJ: Prentice-Hall, 1975. $19.95.

Watson, Peter G. *On-Line Bibliographic Services—Where We're Going.* Chicago: American Library Association, 1977. $10.50.

_____, ed. *Charging for Computer-Based Reference Services.* Chicago: American Library Association, 1978. $4.

White, Howard. *Reader in Machine-Readable Social Data.* Englewood, CO: Information Handling Services, 1978. $19.

Buildings, Furniture, Equipment

An Architectural Strategy for Change: Remodeling and Expanding for Contemporary Public Library Needs. Chicago: American Library Association, 1976. $12.50.

Bahr, Alice H. *Book Theft and Library Security Systems, 1978-79.* White Plains, NY: Knowledge Industry Publications, 1978. $24.50.

Cohen, Aaron, and Cohen, Elaine. *Designing and Space Planning for Libraries: A Behavioral Guide.* New York: R. R. Bowker, 1979. $24.95.

Hannigan, Jane A., and Estes, Glenn E. *Media Center Facilities Design.* Chicago: American Library Association, 1978. $10.50.

Library Space Planning. Library Journal Special Report No. 1. New York: R. R. Bowker, 1977. $3.95 prepaid.

Lushington, Nolan, and Mills, Willis N., Jr. *Libraries Designed for Users.* Syracuse, NY: Gaylord Professional Publications, 1979. $20.

Merrill, Irving Rodgers, and Drob, Harold A. *Criteria for Planning the College and University Learning Resources Center,* ed. by Clint Wallington. Washington, DC: Association for Educational Communications and Technology, 1977. $5.95.

Myers, Gerald E. *Insurance Manuals for Libraries.* Chicago: American Library Association, 1977. $5.

Novak, Gloria, ed. *Running Out of Space—What Are the Alternatives?* Chicago: American Library Association, 1978. $14.

Nyren, Karl. *New Public Library Buildings. Library Journal* Special Report No. 8. New York: R. R. Bowker, 1979. $5.

Pollett, Dorothy, and Haskell, Peter C. *Sign Systems for Libraries.* New York: R. R. Bowker, 1979. $24.95.

Schell, Hal B., ed. *Reader on the Library Building.* Englewood, CO: Information Handling Services, 1975. $19.

Sourcebook of Library Technology: A Cumulative Edition of Library Technology Reports 1965-1975. Chicago: American Library Association, 1976. $75. $30 with current subscription to *Library Technology Reports.* On microfiche.

Thompson, Godfrey. *Planning and Design of Library Buildings.* 2nd ed. New York: Nichols Publishing, 1977. $25.

Children's and Young Adults' Services and Materials

Baskin, Barbara H., and Harris, Karen H. *Notes from a Different Drummer: A Guide to Juvenile Fiction Portraying the Handicapped.* New York: R. R. Bowker, 1977. $15.95.

Bernstein, Joanne E. *Books to Help Children Cope with Separation and Loss.* New York: R.R. Bowker, 1977. $13.95.

Braverman, Miriam. *Youth, Society and the Public Library.* Chicago: American Library Association, 1979. $15.

Broderick, Dorothy M. *Library Work with Children.* New York: H. W. Wilson, 1977. $10.

Children's Media Market Place, ed. by Deirdre Boyle and Stephen Calvert. Syracuse, NY: Gaylord Professional Publications, 1978. $15.95.

deWitt, Dorothy. *Children's Faces Looking Up.* Chicago: American Library Association, 1979. $11.

Directions for Library Service to Young Adults. Prepared by Young Adult Services Division, Services Statement Development Committee, American Library Association. Chicago: American Library Association, 1977. $2.50.

Dreyer, Sharon. *The Bookfinder: A Guide to Children's Literature about the Needs and Problems of Youth.* Minneapolis, MN: American Guidance Service, 1977. $25.

Duke, Judith S. *Children's Books and Magazines: A Market Study.* White Plains, NY: Knowledge Industry Publications, 1979. $24.95.

Fader, Daniel. *The New Hooked on Books.* New York: Putnam, 1977. $8.95.

Foster, Joan, ed. *Reader in Children's Librarianship.* Englewood, CO: Information Handling Services, 1978. $20.

Gillis, Ruth J. *Children's Books for Times of Stress: An Annotated Bibliography.* Bloomington, IN: Indiana University Press, 1978. $12.50.

Graves, Michael, et al. *Easy Reading: Book Series and Periodicals for the Less Able Reader.* Newark, DE: International Reading Association, 1979. $3.

Haviland, Virginia, ed. *Children's Literature: A Guide to Reference Sources.* Washington, DC: Library of Congress, 1966. $5.45. 1st supplement, 1972. $5.50. 2nd supplement, 1978. $7.75.

Heins, Paul, ed. *Crosscurrents of Criticism: Horn Book Essays 1968–1977.* Boston: The Horn Book, 1977. $12.50.

Huck, Charlotte S. *Children's Literature in the Elementary School.* 3rd ed. New York: Holt, Rinehart and Winston, 1976. $13.95.

Illustrators of Children's Books 1967–1976, comp. by Lee Kingman, Grace Allen Hogarth, and Harriet Quimby. Boston: The Horn Book, 1978. $32.50.

Kirkpatrick, D. L., ed. *Twentieth Century Children's Writers.* London: Macmillan, 1978. $40.

Martin, Betty, and Carson, Ben. *The Principal's Handbook on the School Library Media Center.* Syracuse, NY: Gaylord Professional Publications, 1978. $8.95.

Meacham, Mary. *Information Sources in Children's Literature: A Practical Reference Guide for Children's Librarians, Elementary School Teachers, and Students of Children's Literature.* Westport, CT: Greenwood Press, 1978. $18.95.

Richardson, Selma K., ed. *Children's Services of Public Libraries.* Allerton Park Institutes Series No. 23. Champaign, IL: University of Illinois Graduate School of Library Science, Publications Office, 1978. $8.

Rogers, JoAnn V., ed. *Libraries and Young Adults.* Littleton, CO: Libraries Unlimited, 1979. $15.

Sutherland, Zena, and Arbuthnot, May

Hill. *Children and Books.* 5th ed. Glenview, IL: Scott, Foresman, 1977. $13.95.

Turow, Joseph. *Getting Books to Children.* Chicago: American Library Association, 1978. $8.50.

College and University Libraries

Association of College and Research Libraries. *New Horizons for Academic Libraries.* Papers Presented at the ACRL 1978 National Conference. New York: K. G. Saur, 1979. $25.

Gore, Daniel, ed. *Farewell to Alexandria: Solutions to Space, Growth, and Performance Problems of Libraries.* Westport, CT: Greenwood Press, 1976. $12.50.

Josey, E. J., ed. *New Dimensions for Academic Library Service.* Metuchen, NJ: Scarecrow Press, 1975. $12.50.

Kent, Allen, ed. *Use of Library Materials: The University of Pittsburgh Study.* New York: Marcel Dekker, 1979. $25.

Lathem, Edward C., ed. *American Libraries as Centers of Scholarship.* Hanover, NH: Dartmouth College Library, 1978. Free.

Lyle, Guy R. *The Administration of the College Library.* 4th ed. New York: H. W. Wilson, 1974. $9.

Martin, Murray S. *Budgetary Control in Academic Libraries.* Greenwich, CT: JAI Press, 1978. $21.

Osburn, Charles. *Academic Research and Library Resources: Changing Patterns in America.* Westport, CT: Greenwood Press, 1979. $18.95.

Roger, Rutherford D., and Weber, David C. *University Library Administration.* New York: H. W. Wilson, 1970. $20.

SPEC Kits. Washington, DC: Association of Research Libraries. 1973–1978. Nos. 1–46. $7.50 for members, $15 for nonmembers. (Recent kits have been on such topics as Cost Studies and Fiscal Planning, Performance Appraisal, Internal Communication, and External Communication.)

Wilkinson, Billy R. *Reader in Undergraduate Libraries.* Englewood, CO: Information Handling Services, 1978. $20.

Comparative and International Librarianship

Atherton, Pauline. *Handbook for Information Systems and Services.* New York: Unipub, 1977. $17.25.

Avicenne, Paul, ed. *Bibliographical Services throughout the World.* New York: Unipub, 1978. $20.

Foskett, D. J., ed. *Reader in Comparative Librarianship.* Englewood, CO: Information Handling Services, 1976. $19.

Harvey, John F., ed. *Comparative and International Library Science.* Metuchen, NJ: Scarecrow Press, 1977. $12.

Huq, A. A. Abdul, and Aman, Mohammed M. *Librarianship and the Third World: An Annotated Bibliography of Selected Literature on Developing Nations, 1960–1975.* New York: Garland, 1977. $32.

Penna. C. V., Foskett, D. J., and Sewell, P. H. *National Library and Information Services: A Handbook for Planners.* London: Butterworths, 1977. $16.95.

Copyright

Association for Educational Communications and Technology. *Copyright and Educational Media.* Washington, DC: AECT, 1977. $3.95.

Johnston, Donald. *Copyright Handbook.* New York: R. R. Bowker, 1978. $14.95.

The Librarian's Copyright Kit: What You Must Know Now. Chicago: American Library Association, 1978. $7.

White, Herbert S. *The Copyright Dilemma: Proceedings of a Conference....* Chicago: American Library Association, 1978. $8.50.

Education for Librarianship

Bidlack, Russell E. *The ALA Accreditation Process, 1973–1976: A Survey of Library Schools Whose Programs Were*

Evaluated under the 1972 Standards. Chicago: American Library Association, 1977. $5.

Borko, Harold, ed. *Targets for Research in Library Education.* Chicago: American Library Association, 1973. $10.

Conroy, Barbara. *Library Staff Development and Continuing Education: Principles and Practices.* Littleton, CO: Libraries Unlimited, 1977. $17.50.

Conroy, Barbara. *Library Staff Development Profile Pages: A Guide and Workbook for Library Self Assessment and Planning.* Available from the author, Box 502, Tabernash, CO, 1979. $12.

Continuing Library Education Network and Exchange. *Directory of Continuing Education Opportunities for Library, Information, Media Personnel.* Washington, DC: CLENE, 1977. $15.

Financial Assistance for Library Education: Academic Year 1979–80. Chicago: American Library Association, 1978. 50¢.

Library Education and Personnel Utilization: A Statement of Policy Adopted by the Council of the American Library Association, June 30, 1970. Rev. for terminology, 1976. Chicago: American Library Association, 1976. Free.

Shera, Jese H. *The Foundations of Education for Librarianship.* New York: Wiley, 1972. $17.75.

Information and Society

Adkinson, Burton W. *Two Centuries of Federal Information.* Stroudsburg, PA: Dowden, Hutchinson, & Ross, 1978. $15.

Compaine, Benjamin. *The Book Industry in Transition.* White Plains, NY: Knowledge Industry Publications, 1978. $24.50.

Giuliano, Vincent, et al. *Into the Information Age: A Perspective for Federal Action on Information.* Chicago: American Library Association, 1978. $7.50.

Information Industry Association. *Membership Directory, 1978–79.* Bethesda, MD: Information Industry Association, 1978.

Information Market Place, 1978–79: An International Directory of Information Products and Services, ed. by Eusidic and James B. Sanders. New York: R. R. Bowker, 1978. $21.50.

Machlup, Fritz, and Leeson, Kenneth. *Information through the Printed Word.* 3 vols. New York: Praeger, 1978. $69.85.

U.S. National Commission on Libraries and Information Science. *National Inventory of Library Needs, 1975.* Washington, DC, 1977. $3.60.

Warnken, Kelly. *Directory of Fee Based Information Services: 1978/79.* Woodstock, NY: Information Alternative, 1978. $5.

Intellectual Freedom

Busha, C. H. *An Intellectual Freedom Primer.* Littleton, CO: Libraries Unlimited, 1977. $17.50.

Intellectual Freedom Manual. Chicago: American Library Association, 1975. $5.

Library History

Gates, Jean Key. *Introduction to Librarianship.* 2nd ed. New York: McGraw-Hill, 1976. $11.95.

Goldstein, Harold, ed. *Milestones to the Present: Papers from Library History Seminar V.* Syracuse, NY: Gaylord, 1978. $15.

Harris, Michael H., and Davis, Donald G., Jr. *American Library History: A Bibliography.* Austin, TX: University of Texas Press, 1978. $18.

Jackson, Sidney L. *A Brief History of Libraries and Librarianship in the West.* New York: McGraw-Hill, 1974. $20.

———, et al., eds. *A Century of Service: Librarianship in the United States and Canada.* Chicago: American Library Association, 1976. $25.

Johnson, Elmer D., and Harris, Michael

H. *A History of Libraries in the Western World*. 3rd ed. Metuchen, NJ: Scarecrow Press, 1976. $10.

Thomison, Dennis. *A History of the American Library Association, 1876–1972*. Chicago: American Library Association, 1978. $30.

Winger, Howard W., ed. *American Library History, 1876–1976*. Library Trends, July 1976. Champaign, IL: University of Illinois, Graduate School of Library Science, Publications Office, 1977. $8.

Materials Selection

Broadus, Robert N. *Selecting Materials for Libraries*. New York: H. W. Wilson, 1973. $12.

Carter, Mary D., et al. *Building Library Collections*. Metuchen, NJ: Scarecrow Press, 1974. $9.

Evans, G. Edward. *Developing Library Collections*. Littleton, CO: Libraries Unlimited, 1979. $15.

———, and Hill, Donna. *The Picture File. A Manual and a Curriculum Related Subject Heading List*. Hamden, CT: Linnet, 1978. $18.

Miller, Shirley. *The Vertical File and Its Satellites*. Littleton, CO: Libraries Unlimited, 1979. $20.

Microforms and Computer Output Microforms

Bahr, Alice H. *Microforms: The Librarians' View, 1978–79*. 2nd ed. White Plains, NY: Knowledge Industry Publications, 1978. $24.50.

Catalog Use Committee, Reference and Adult Services Division, American Library Association. *Commercial COM Catalogs: How to Choose, When to Buy*. Chicago, 1978. $2.50.

Diaz, Albert J. *Microforms and Library Catalogs: A Reader*. Westport, CT: Microform Review, 1977. $20.95.

Fundamentals of Computer Output Microfilm. Silver Spring, MD: National Micrographics Association, 1974. $2.

Gaddy, Dale. *A Microform Handbook*. Silver Spring, MD: National Micrographics Association, 1974. $6.

Saffady, William. *Computer-Output Microfilm: Its Library Applications*. Chicago: American Library Association, 1978. $10.50.

———. *Micrographics*. Littleton, CO: Libraries Unlimited, 1978. $16.

Teague, Sydney. *Microform Librarianship*. 2nd ed. Boston: Butterworths, 1979. $15.95.

Veaner, Allen B. *Studies in Micropublishing, 1853–1976*. Westport, CT: Microform Review, 1977. $24.50.

Networks and Interlibrary Cooperation

Getting into Networking: Guidelines for Special Libraries. Prepared by the Guidelines Subcommittee, SLA Networking Committee. New York: Special Libraries Association, 1977. $6.

Giuliano, Vincent. *A New Governance Structure for OCLC: Principles and Recommendations*. Metuchen, NJ: Scarecrow Press, 1978. $8.

Hamilton, Beth A., and Ernst, William B., Jr. *Multitype Library Cooperation*. New York: R. R. Bowker, 1977. $19.95.

Kent, Allen, and Galvin, Thomas J., eds. *Library Resource Sharing: Proceedings of the 1976 Conference on Resource Sharing in Libraries*. New York: Marcel Dekker, 1977. $29.75.

———. *The Structure and Governance of Library Networks*. New York: Marcel Dekker, 1979. $43.75.

The Role of the Library of Congress in the Evolving National Network. Washington, DC: U.S. Govt. Printing Office, 1978. $3.25.

Periodicals and Serials

Davinson, Donald. *The Periodicals Collection*. Rev. and enl. ed. London: Andre Deutsch, 1978. $16.25.

Guidelines for Handling Library Orders for Serials and Periodicals. Chicago: American Library Association, 1974. $1.95.

Katz, Bill. *Magazine Selection: How to Build a Community-Oriented Collection.* New York: R. R. Bowker, 1971. $12.95.

———, and Gellatly, Peter. *Guide to Magazine and Serial Agents.* New York: R. R. Bowker, 1975. $17.50.

Osborn, Andrew D. *Serial Publications: Their Place and Treatment in Libraries.* 2nd ed. Chicago: American Library Association, 1973. $15.50.

Public Libraries

Altman, Ellen, et al. *A Data Gathering and Instructional Manual for Performance Measures in Libraries.* Chicago: Celadon Press, 1976. $10.

Book Reading and Library Usage: A Study of Habits and Perceptions. Conducted for ALA. Princeton, NJ: The Gallup Organization, 1978. Available from ALA. $60.

Geddes, Andrew. *Fiscal Responsibility and the Small Public Library.* Small Libraries Publications No. 3. Chicago: American Library Association, 1978. $1.

Guidelines for Audiovisual Materials and Services for Large Public Libraries. Chicago: American Library Association, 1975. $2.95.

Hanna, Patricia B. *People Make It Happen: The Possibilities of Outreach in Every Phase of Public Library Service.* Metuchen, NJ: Scarecrow Press, 1978. $7.

Howard, Edward N. *Local Power and the Community Library.* Public Library Reporter No. 18. Chicago: American Library Association, 1978. $4.50.

Performance Measures for Public Libraries. Chicago: American Library Association, 1973. $3.50.

Prentice, Ann. *Public Library Finance.* Chicago: American Library Association, 1977. $7.

Price, Paxton, P. *Future of the Main Urban Library: Report of a Conference, October 26–27, 1978.* Las Cruces, NM: Urban Libraries Council, 1978. $7.95.

Public Library Association. *The Public Library Mission Statement and Its Imperatives for Service.* Chicago: American Library Association, 1979. $1.50.

Recommendations for Audiovisual Materials and Services for Small and Medium-Sized Public Libraries. Chicago: American Library Association, 1975. $2.95.

Shearer, Kenneth D., ed. *The Collection and Use of Public Library Statistics by State Agencies; A Compilation of Forms.* Chicago: American Library Association. Library Administration and Management Association, 1978. $13.50.

Sinclair, Dorothy. *Administration of the Small Public Library.* Chicago: American Library Association, 1979. $10.

Turick, Dorothy. *Community Information Services in Libraries.* Library Journal Special Report No. 5. New York: R. R. Bowker, 1978. $5.

Reference Services

Bloomberg, Marty. *Introduction to Public Services for Library Technicians.* 2nd ed. Littleton, CO: Libraries Unlimited, 1977. $11.50.

Fjallbrant, Nancy, and Stevenson, Malcolm. *User Education in Libraries.* Hamden, CT: Linnet, 1978. $12.50.

Katz, William A. *An Introduction to Reference Work.* 3rd rev. ed. New York: McGraw-Hill, 1978. 2 vols. Vol. 1 $14.95. Vol. 2 $13.95.

———, and Tarr, Andrea. *Reference and Information Services: A Reader.* Metuchen, NJ: Scarecrow Press, 1978. $12.50.

Lockwood, Deborah. *Library Instruction: A Bibliography.* Westport, CT: Greenwood Press, 1979. $16.50.

Lubans, John, ed. *Educating the Library User.* New York: R. R. Bowker, 1974. $15.95.

———. *Progress in Educating the Library User.* New York: R. R. Bowker, 1978. $15.95.

Morehead, Joe. *Introduction to United States Public Documents.* 2nd ed. Littleton, CO: Libraries Unlimited, 1978. $17.50.

Morgan, Candace, ed. *The Purposes of Reference Measurement.* Chicago: American Library Association, 1978. $2.

Murfin, Marjorie, and Wynar, Lubomyr. *Reference Service: An Annotated Bibliographic Guide.* Littleton, CO: Libraries Unlimited, 1977. $15.

Rader, Hannelore B., ed. *Library Instruction in the Seventies: State of the Art.* Ann Arbor, MI: Pierian Press, 1977. $8.50.

Sheehy, Eugene P. *Guide to Reference Books.* 9th ed. Chicago: American Library Association, 1976. $30.

Research

Bundy, Mary Lee, and Wasserman, Paul, eds. *Reader in Research Methods in Librarianship.* Englewood, CO: Microcard Editions Books, 1970. $14.

Carpenter, Ray L. *Statistical Methods for Librarians.* Chicago: American Library Association, 1978. $12.50.

Chen, Ching-Chih, ed. *Quantitative Measurement and Dynamic Library Service.* Phoenix, AZ: Oryx Press, 1978. $16.50.

Srikantaiah, Taverekere, and Huffman, Herbert H. *Introduction to Quantitative Research Methods for Librarians.* 2nd ed. Newport Beach, CA: Headway Publications, 1977. $8.

School Libraries

Bell, Irene. *Basic Media Skills through Games.* Littleton, CO: Libraries Unlimited, 1979. $13.50.

Cole, John Y., ed. *Television, the Book, and the Classroom.* Washington, DC: Library of Congress, 1978. $4.95.

Davies, Ruth Ann. *School Library Media Program: Instructional Force for Excellence.* 3rd ed. New York: R. R. Bowker, 1979. $16.95.

Galey, Minaruth, and Grady, William F. *Guidelines for Certification of Media Specialists.* Washington, DC: Association for Educational Communications and Technology, 1977. $3.95.

Gillespie, John T., and Spirt, Diana L. *Creating a School Media Program.* New York: R. R. Bowker, 1973. $14.95.

Hart, Thomas L., ed. *Instruction in School Media Use.* Chicago: American Library Association, 1978. $8.50.

Liesener, James W. *Systematic Process for Planning Media Programs.* Chicago: American Library Association, 1976. $7.

Media Programs: District and School. Joint Committee of ALA American Association of School Librarians and Association for Educational Communications and Technology. Chicago: American Library Association, 1975. $2.95.

Nickel, Mildred L. *Steps to Service: A Handbook of Procedures for the School Library Media Center.* Chicago: American Library Association, 1975. $4.50.

Shapiro, Lillian L. *Service Youth: Communication and Commitment in the High School Library.* New York: R. R. Bowker, 1975. $14.95.

Services for Special Groups

Brown, Eleanor F. *Bibliotherapy and Its Widening Applications.* Metuchen, NJ: Scarecrow Press, 1975. $12.50.

Cylke, Frank K. *Library Service for the Blind and Physically Handicapped: An International Approach.* New York: K. G. Saur, 1978. $18.

Rubin, Rhea Joyce, ed. *Bibliotherapy Sourcebook.* Phoenix, AZ: Oryx Press, 1978. $14.95.

———. *Using Bibliotherapy: A Guide to Theory and Technique.* Phoenix, AZ: Oryx Press, 1978. $10.95.

Schauder, Donald E., and Gram, Malcolm. *Libraries for the Blind: An International Study of Policies and Practices.* Steverage, Herts., England: Peter Peregrinas, 1979. $21.50.

Strom, Maryalls G., ed. *Library Services to the Blind and Physically Handicapped.* Metuchen, NJ: Scarecrow Press, 1977. $12.

Velleman, Ruth A. *Serving Physically Disabled People: An Information Handbook for All Libraries.* New York: R. R. Bowker, 1979. $17.50.

Wright, Keith. *Library and Information Services for Handicapped Individuals.* Littleton, CO: Libraries Unlimited, 1979. $15.

Special Libraries

Drazniowsky, Roman, comp. *Map Librarianship: Readings.* Metuchen, NJ: Scarecrow Press, 1975. $20.

Larsgaard, Mary. *Map Librarianship.* Littleton, CO: Libraries Unlimited, 1978. $18.50.

Reams, Bernard D., ed. *Reader in Law Librarianship.* Englewood, CO: Information Handling Services, 1976. $19.

Rowley, J. E. *The Dissemination of Information.* London: Andre Deutsch, 1978. $19.25.

Strable, Edward G. *Special Libraries: A Guide for Management.* Rev. ed. New York: Special Libraries Association, 1975. $8.

Strauss, Lucille J., Shreve, Irene M., and Brown, Alberta L. *Scientific and Technical Libraries: Their Organization and Administration.* 2nd ed. New York: Wiley, 1972. $19.25.

State Libraries

The ASLA Report on Interlibrary Cooperation. 2nd ed. Chicago: ALA Association of State Library Agencies, 1978. $15.

Simpson, Donald B. *The State Library Agencies: A Survey Project Report, 1979.* 4th ed. Chicago: Association of State Library Agencies (ALA), 1979. $15.

Technical Services

Bloomberg, Marty, and Evans, G. Edward. *Introduction to Technical Services for Library Technicians.* 3rd ed. Littleton, CO: Libraries Unlimited, 1976. $8.50.

Magrill, Rose Mary, and Rinehart, Constance, comps. *Library Technical Services: A Selected Annotated Bibliography.* Westport, CT: Greenwood Press, 1977. $14.95.

Technical Services: Acquisitions

American Library Association. Bookdealer-Library Relations Committee. *Guidelines for Handling Library Orders for Microforms.* Chicago, 1977. $1.95.

Grieder, Ted. *Acquisitions: Where, What and How.* Westport, CT: Greenwood Press, 1978. $18.95.

Orne, Jerrold. *The Language of the Foreign Book Trade.* 3rd ed. Chicago: American Library Association, 1976. $15.

Technical Services: Cataloging and Classification

Chan, Lois Mai. *Library of Congress Subject Headings: Principles and Applications.* Littleton, CO: Libraries Unlimited, 1978. $17.50.

The Future of Card Catalogs: Report of a Program Sponsored by the Association of Research Libraries, January 5, 1975. Washington, DC: Association of Research Libraries, 1975. Available from ERIC (ED107-210) or by writing the Association of Research Libraries. $3.

Gore, Daniel, ed. *Requiem for the Card Catalog: Management Issues in Auto-*

mated Cataloging. Westport, CT: Greenwood Press, 1979. $17.50.

Gorman, Michael, and Winkler, Paul W., eds. *Anglo-American Cataloging Rules.* 2nd ed. Chicago: American Library Association, 1978. $15.

Hewitt, Joe A. *OCLC: Impact and Use—A Study of the Charter Members of the Ohio College Library Center.* Columbus, OH: Ohio State University Libraries, 1977. $8.95.

Smith, Lynn S. *A Practical Approach to Serials Cataloging.* Greenwich, CT: JAI Press, 1978. $27.50.

Wellisch, Hans H. *The PRECIS Index System: Principles, Applications, and Prospects.* New York: H. W. Wilson, 1977. $12.50.

PERIODICALS

The journals listed below are titles that might normally be purchased as part of a continuing education program in a library or as subscriptions for individual librarians. Titles used primarily for selection have been excluded.

ALA Washington Newsletter
American Libraries
American Society for Information Science Bulletin
College and Research Libraries
Conservation Administration Review
Drexel Library Quarterly
IFLA Journal
International Cataloguing
International Classification
International Library Review
Journal of Academic Librarianship
Journal of Education for Librarianship
Journal of Library Automation
Journal of Library History
Library Journal
Library of Congress Information Bulletin
Library Quarterly
Library Resources and Technical Services
Library Trends
Libri
Medical Library Association Bulletin
Newsletter on Intellectual Freedom
OnLine
Public Library Quarterly
RQ
RSR (Reference Services Review)
School Library Journal
School Media Quarterly
Serials Librarian
Serials Review
Special Libraries
Top of the News
U* N* A* B* A* S* H* E* D* Librarian
UNESCO Bulletin for Libraries
VOYA: Voice of Youth Advocates
Wilson Library Bulletin

BASIC PUBLICATIONS FOR THE PUBLISHER AND THE BOOK TRADE

Jean R. Peters

Librarian, R. R. Bowker Company

BIBLIOGRAPHIES OF BOOKS ABOUT BOOKS AND THE BOOK TRADE

These six books contain extensive bibliographies.

Gottlieb, Robin. *Publishing Children's Books in America, 1919–1976: An Annotated Bibliography.* New York: Children's Book Council, 1978. $15.

Lee, Marshall. *Bookmaking: The Illustrated Guide to Design and Production.* 2nd ed. New York: R. R. Bowker, 1979.

$25. Bibliography is divided into four parts: Part I covers books, and includes a general bibliography as well as extensive coverage of books on all technical aspects of bookmaking; Part 2 lists periodicals; Part 3 lists films, filmstrips, etc.; Part 4 lists other sources.

Lehmann-Haupt, Hellmut, Wroth, Lawrence C., and Silver, Rollo. *The Book in America.* 2nd ed. New York: R. R. Bowker, 1951. o.p. Bibliography covers cultural history, bibliography, printing and bookmaking, book illustration, bookselling, and publishing.

Melcher, Daniel, and Larrick, Nancy. *Printing and Promotion Handbook.* 3rd ed. New York: McGraw-Hill, 1966. $24.95. Bibliography covers general reference, advertising, artwork, book publishing, color, copyright, copywriting, direct mail, displays, editing and proofreading, layout and design, lettering, magazine publishing, newspaper publishing, packaging, paper, photography, printing, publicity, radio and TV, shipping, typography, and visual aids.

The Reader's Adviser: A Layman's Guide to Literature. 12th ed. 3 vols. New York: R. R. Bowker, 1974–1977. $69.95 (3-vol. set); $27.50 (ea. vol.). Vol. 1. *The Best in American and British Fiction, Poetry, Essays, Literary Biography, Bibliography, and Reference,* ed. by Sarah L. Prakken. 1974. Chapters on "Books about Books" and "Bibliography" cover history of publishing and bookselling, practice of publishing, bookmaking, rare book collecting, trade and specialized bibliographies, book selection tools, best books, etc. Vol. 2. *The Best in American and British Drama and World Literature in English Translation,* ed. by F. J. Sypher. 1977. Vol. 3. *The Best in the Reference Literature of the World,* ed. by Jack A. Clarke. 1977.

Tanselle, G. Thomas. *Guide to the Study of United States Imprints.* 2 vols. Cambridge, MA: Belknap Press of Harvard University Press, 1971. $40. Includes sections on general studies of American printing and publishing as well as studies of individual printers and publishers.

TRADE BIBLIOGRAPHIES

American Book Publishing Record Cumulative, 1950–1977: An American National Bibliography. 15 vols. New York: R. R. Bowker, 1978. $1,500.

American Book Publishing Record Five-Year Cumulatives. New York: R. R. Bowker. 1960–1964 Cumulative. 4 vols. $110. 1965–1969 Cumulative. 5 vols. $110. 1970–1974 Cumulative. 4 vols. $110. Annual vols.: 1965–1969, $45 each; 1970, o.p.; 1971, o.p.; 1972, o.p.; 1973, o.p.; 1974, $45; 1975, $45; 1976, $45; 1977, $45; 1978, $49.50.

Book Publishers Directory: An Information Service Covering New and Established, Private and Special Interest, Avant-Garde and Alternative, Organization and Association, Government and Institution Presses, ed. by Elizabeth Geiser and Annie Brewer. Detroit: Gale, 1978. $85.

Books in Print. 4 vols. New York: R. R. Bowker, ann. $99.50.

Books in Print Supplement. New York: R. R. Bowker, ann. $49.50.

Books in Series in the United States. 2nd ed. New York: R. R. Bowker, 1979. $57.50.

British Books in Print: The Reference Catalog of Current Literature. New York: R. R. Bowker, 1979. $115. (plus duty where applicable).

Canadian Books in Print, ed. by Martha Pluscauskas. Toronto: University of Toronto Press, ann. $35.

Canadian Books in Print: Subject Index, ed. by Martha Pluscauskas. Toronto: University of Toronto Press, ann. $30.

Cumulative Book Index. New York: H. W. Wilson. Monthly with bound semiannual and larger cumulations. Service basis.

El-Hi Textbooks in Print. New York: R. R. Bowker, ann. $32.50.

Forthcoming Books. New York: R. R. Bowker. $29.75 a year. $7.50 single copy. Bimonthly supplement to *Books in Print.*

Large Type Books in Print. 2nd ed. New York: R. R. Bowker, 1978. $17.50.

Paperbound Books in Print. New York: R. R. Bowker. 2 vols. per year. $67.50.

Publishers' Trade List Annual. New York: R. R. Bowker, ann. 6 vols. $54.50.

Robert, Reginald, and Burgess, M. R. *Cumulative Paperback Index, 1939–59.* Detroit: Gale, 1973. $35.

Small Press Record of Books in Print, ed. by Len Fulton. Paradise, CA: Dustbooks, 1979. $11.95.

Subject Guide to Books in Print. 2 vols. New York: R. R. Bowker, ann. $72.50.

Subject Guide to Forthcoming Books. $27.50 a year. $42 in combination with *Forthcoming Books.*

Turner, Mary C., ed. *Libros en Venta.* New York: R. R. Bowker, 1974. $57.50. Supplement, 1974. 1976. $32.50. Supplement, 1975. 1978. $32.50. Supplement, 1976–77. 1979. $55. A Spanish-language "Books in Print/Subject Guide."

BOOK PUBLISHING

Altbach, Philip G., and McVey, Sheila, eds. *Perspectives on Publishing.* Lexington, MA: Lexington Books, 1976. $22.

ANSI Standards Committee Z-39. *American National Standard for Compiling Book Publishing Statistics. Z-39.8.* New York: American National Standards Institute, 1968. $2.75.

Bailey, Herbert S., Jr. *The Art and Science of Book Publishing.* New York: Harper & Row, 1970. $10.

Benjamin, Curtis G. *A Candid Critique of Book Publishing.* New York: R. R. Bowker, 1977. $15.

Bingley, Clive. *The Business of Book Publishing.* New York: British Book Center, 1972. $17.

Bohne, Harald, and Van Ierssel, Harry. *Publishing: The Creative Business.* Toronto: University of Toronto Press, 1973. pap. $7.50.

Bowker Annual of Library and Book Trade Information. New York: R. R. Bowker, ann. $24.95.

Bowker. *Lectures on Book Publishing.* New York: R. R. Bowker, 1957. o.p.

Briggs, Asa, ed. *Essays in the History of Publishing; in Celebration of the 250th Anniversary of the House of Longman, 1724–1974.* New York: Longman, 1974. $15.

The Business of Publishing: A PW Anthology. New York: R. R. Bowker, 1976. $12.95.

Canfield, Cass. *Up and Down and Around: A Publisher Recollects the Time of His Life.* New York: Harper's Magazine Press, 1971. $10.

Cerf, Bennett. *At Random: The Reminiscences of Bennett Cerf.* New York: Random House, 1977. $12.95.

Cheney, O. H. *Economic Survey of the Book Industry, 1930–31.* The Cheney Report. Reprinted. New York: R. R. Bowker, 1960. o.p.

Dessauer, John P. *Book Publishing: What It Is, What It Does.* New York: R. R. Bowker, 1974. $12.50. pap. $6.95.

Gedin, Per. *Literature in the Marketplace,* trans. by George Bisset. Woodstock, NY: Overlook, 1977. $12.95.

Grannis, Chandler B., ed. *What Happens in Book Publishing.* 2nd ed. New York: Columbia University Press, 1967. $17.50.

Greenfeld, Howard. *Books: From Writer to Reader.* New York: Crown, 1976. $8.95.

Harman, Eleanor, and Montagnes, Ian, eds. *The Thesis and the Book.* Toronto: University of Toronto Press, 1976. $10. pap. $5.

Haydn, Hiram. *Words & Faces.* New York: Harcourt Brace Jovanovich, 1974. $8.95.

Hodges, Sheila. *Golancz: The Story of a Publishing House.* London: Golancz, 1978. £7.50.

Jennison, Peter S., and Sheridan, Robert, eds. *The Future of General Adult Books and Reading in America.* Chicago: American Library Association, 1971. $9.

Kujoth, Jean Spealman. *Book Publishing: Inside Views.* Metuchen, NJ: Scarecrow, 1971. $14.50.

Kurian, George. *Directory of American Book Publishing: From Founding Fathers to Today's Conglomerates.* New York: Monarch, 1975. $25.

Lehmann-Haupt, Hellmut. *The Book in America.* 2nd ed. New York: R. R. Bowker, 1951. o.p.

McWhirter, Norris. *Guinness Book of World Records, 1980.* New York: Sterling. $9.89. Bantam. pap. $2.50. Section on "The Written Word."

Madison, Charles. *Irving to Irving: Author-Publisher Relations: 1800–1974.* New York: R. R. Bowker, 1974. $12.95.

Mumby, Frank A., and Norrie, Ian. *Publishing and Bookselling: A History from the Earliest Times to the Present Day.* New York: R. R. Bowker, 1974. $39.95.

Nemeyer, Carol A. *Scholarly Reprint Publishing in the United States.* New York: R. R. Bowker, 1972. $15.95.

Peters, Jean, ed. *Bookman's Glossary.* 5th ed. New York: R. R. Bowker, 1975. $11.50.

Regnery, Henry. *Memoirs of a Dissident Publisher.* New York: Harcourt Brace Jovanovich, 1979. $12.95.

Reynolds, Paul R. *The Middle Man: The Adventures of a Literary Agent.* New York: Morrow, 1972. $6.95.

Smith, Datus C., Jr. *A Guide to Book Publishing.* New York: R. R. Bowker, 1966. $12.95.

Smith, Roger H., ed. *The American Reading Public: A Symposium.* New York: R. R. Bowker, 1964. o.p.

Stern, Madeleine B. *Books and Book People in 19th-Century America.* New York: R. R. Bowker, 1978. $25.

Targ, William. *Indecent Pleasures.* New York: Macmillan, 1975. $14.95.

Tebbel, John. *A History of Book Publishing in the United States.* 3 vols. Vol. 1. *The Creation of an Industry, 1630–1865;* Vol. 2. *The Expansion of an Industry, 1865–1919;* Vol. 3. *The Golden Age between Two Wars, 1920–1940.* New York: R. R. Bowker, 1972, 1975, 1978. Vols. 1 & 2, $29.95 each; Vol. 3, $32.50.

To Be a Publisher: A Handbook on Some Principles and Programs in Publishing Education. Prepared by the Association of American Publishers Education for Publishing Program. New York: Association of American Publishers, 1979. $10.

Industry Surveys

Compaine, Benjamin. *Book Distribution and Marketing 1976–1980.* White Plains, NY: Knowledge Industry Publications, 1975. $450.

———. *The Book Industry in Transition: An Economic Study of Book Distribution and Marketing.* White Plains, NY: Knowledge Industry Publications, 1978. $24.95.

Dessauer, John P. *Association of American Publishers 1978 Industry Statistics.* New York: Association of American Publishers, 1979. Nonmemb. $220.

———, Doebler, Paul D., Noble, J. Kendrick, Jr., and Nordberg, E. Wayne. *Book Industry Trends—1979.* Darien, CT: Book Industry Study Group, 1979. $300, libraries $175, free to BISG members.

Machlup, Fritz, and Leeson, Kenneth W. *Information Through the Printed Word: The Dissemination of Scholarly, Scientific, and Intellectual Knowledge.* 3 vols. Vol. 1. *Book Publishing;* Vol. 2. *Journals;* Vol. 3. *Libraries.* New York: Praeger, 1978. Vol. 1, $22.95; Vol. 2, $24.95; Vol. 3, $20.95.

Morton Research Corporation. *The Book Publishing Industry: An Economic, Marketing and Financial Investigation.* Merrick, NY: Morton, 1976. $195.

Nordberg, E. Wayne, and Hasan, Kazi. *Paper Availability Study.* Darien, CT: Book Industry Study Group, 1977. $300.

Yankelovich, Skelly, and White, Inc. *The 1978 Consumer Research Study on Reading and Book Purchasing.* Darien, CT: Book Industry Study Group, 1978. $1,500. To library members of BISG, $50.

Special Fields of Publishing Interest

Association of American University Presses. *One Book—Five Ways: The Publishing Procedures of Five University Presses.* Los Altos, CA: William Kaufmann, 1978. $18.75. pap. $9.75.

Berg, A. Scott. *Max Perkins: Editor of Genius.* New York: Dutton, 1978. $15.

Commins, Dorothy Berliner. *What Is an Editor?* Chicago: University of Chicago Press, 1978. $10.

Hackett, Alice Payne, and Burke, Henry James. *Eighty Years of Best Sellers, 1895–1975.* New York: R. R. Bowker, 1977. $14.95.

Literary and Library Prizes. 10th ed. New York: R. R. Bowker, 1980. $24.95.

Madison, Charles. *Jewish Publishing in America.* New York: Hebrew Publishing Co., 1976. $11.95.

Mott, Frank Luther. *Golden Multitudes: The Story of Best Sellers in the United States (1662–1945).* Reprint ed. New York: R. R. Bowker, 1960. o.p.

Schick, Frank L. *The Paperbound Book in America: The History of Paperbacks and Their European Background.* New York: R. R. Bowker, 1958. o.p.

Smith, Roger H. *Paperback Parnassus: The Birth, the Development, the Pending Crises of the Modern American Paperbound Book.* Boulder, CO: Westview, 1976. $13.50.

Taubert, Sigfred. *Bibliopola: Pictures and Texts about the Book Trade.* 2 vols. New York: R. R. Bowker, 1966. $75.

BOOK DESIGN AND PRODUCTION

Grannis, Chandler B. *The Heritage of the Graphic Arts.* New York: R. R. Bowker, 1972. $19.95.

Lee, Marshall. *Bookmaking: The Illustrated Guide to Design and Production.* 2nd ed. New York: R. R. Bowker, 1979. $25.

Rice, Stanley. *Book Design: Systematic Aspects.* New York: R. R. Bowker, 1978. $17.50.

_____. *Book Design: Text Format Models.* New York: R. R. Bowker, 1978. $17.50.

Strauss, Victor. *The Printing Industry: An Introduction to Its Many Branches, Processes and Products.* New York: R. R. Bowker, 1967. $32.50.

White, Jan. *Editing by Design.* New York: R. R. Bowker, 1974. $18.50.

Wilson, Adrian. *The Design of Books.* Layton, UT: Peregrine Smith, 1974. pap. $9.95.

BOOKSELLING

Anderson, Charles B., ed. *Bookselling in America and the World: A Souvenir Book Celebrating the 75th Anniversary of the American Booksellers Association.* New York: Times Books, 1975. $9.50.

_____, Smith, G. Roysce, and Cobb, Sanford, eds. *Manual on Bookselling: How to Open and Run Your Own Bookstore.* New York: American Booksellers Association, 1974. Distributed by Harmony Books. $10.95. pap. $4.95.

Bliven, Bruce. *Book Traveller.* New York: Dodd, Mead, 1975. $4.95.

Magee, David. *Infinite Riches: The Adventures of a Rare Book Dealer.* Middlebury, VT: Paul S. Eriksson, 1973. $8.95.

CENSORSHIP

de Grazia, Edward, comp. *Censorship Landmarks.* New York: R. R. Bowker, 1969. $25.

Ernst, Morris L., and Schwartz, Alan U. *Censorship.* New York: Macmillan, 1964. $6.95.

Haight, Anne Lyon. *Banned Books.* 4th ed. updated and enlarged by Chandler B. Grannis. New York: R. R. Bowker, 1978. $13.95.

Moon, Eric, ed. *Book Selection and Censorship in the Sixties.* New York: R. R. Bowker, 1969. $14.95.

COPYRIGHT

Bogsch, Arpad. *The Law of Copyright under the Universal Convention.* 3rd ed. New York: R. R. Bowker, 1969. o.p.

Cambridge Research Institute. *Omnibus Copyright Revision: Comparative Analysis of the Issues.* Washington, DC: American Society for Information Science, 1973. $48.

Copyright Revision Act of 1976: Law, Explanation, Committee Reports. Chicago: Commerce Clearing House, 1976. $12.50.

Johnston, Donald F. *Copyright Handbook.* New York: R. R. Bowker, 1978. $14.95.

Wittenberg, Philip. *Protection of Literary Property.* Boston: The Writer, Inc., 1978. $12.95.

BOOK TRADE DIRECTORIES AND YEARBOOKS

American and Canadian

American Book Trade Directory, 1979. 25th ed. New York: R. R. Bowker, ann. $49.95.

The Book Trade in Canada: Directory. Toronto: Ampersand Publishing Services, 1978. $18.

Chernofsky, Jacob L., ed. *AB Bookman's Yearbook.* 2 vols. Clifton, NJ: AB Bookman's Weekly, ann. $10; free to subscribers to *AB Bookman's Weekly.*

Congrat-Butlar, Stefan, ed. *Translation & Translators: An International Directory and Guide.* New York: R. R. Bowker, 1979. $35.

Kim, Ung Chon. *Policies of Publishers.* Metuchen, NJ: Scarecrow, 1978. pap. $8.50.

Literary Market Place, 1980, with Names & Numbers. New York: R. R. Bowker, ann. $26.95. The business directory of American book publishing.

Publishers and Distributors of the United States: A Directory. New York: R. R. Bowker, 1979. $7.50.

U.S. Book Publishing Yearbook and Directory, 1979–80. White Plains, NY: Knowledge Industry Publications, 1979. $35.

Foreign and International

International Literary Market Place 1979–1980. New York: R. R. Bowker, 1979. $27.50.

Publishers' International Directory. 8th ed. New York: K. G. Saur, 1979. $99.

Taubert, Sigfred, ed. *The Book Trade of the World.* Vol. I. *Europe and International Sections;* Vol. II. *U.S.A., Canada, Central and South America, Australia and New Zealand;* Vol. III. *Africa, Asia.* New York: R. R. Bowker. Vol. I, 1972, $42.50; Vol. II, 1976, $42.50; Vol. III, 1978, $42.50.

Turner, Mary C., ed. *La Empresa del Libro en America Latina.* Buenos Aires: Bowker Editores, 1974. $19.95. A "Literary Market Place" for Latin America.

UNESCO Statistical Yearbook, 1977. New York: Unipub, 1977. $67.50.

Writers and Artists Yearbook. Boston:

The Writer, Inc., 1979. $10. Covers the British book world.

Newspapers and Periodicals

Directory of Newspapers and Periodicals. Philadelphia: N. W. Ayer, ann. $59.

Editor and Publisher International Year Book. New York: Editor and Publisher, ann. $60.

Irregular Serials and Annuals: An International Directory. New York: R. R. Bowker, 1978. $55.

Magazine Industry Market Place: The Directory of American Periodical Publishing. New York: R. R. Bowker, 1979. $24.50.

New Serial Titles 1950–1970. New York: R. R. Bowker, 1973. 4 vols. o.p. Available on microfilm, $100; or xerographic reprint, $250.

New Serial Titles 1950–1970, Subject Guide. New York: R. R. Bowker, 1975. 2 vols. $138.50.

Sources of Serials: An International Publisher and Corporate Author Directory to Ulrich's and Irregular Serials. New York: R. R. Bowker, 1977. $52.50.

Ulrich's International Periodicals Directory. 18th ed. New York: R. R. Bowker, 1979. $64.50.

Working Press of the Nation: Newspapers, Magazines, Radio and TV, and Internal Publications. Chicago: National Research Bureau, ann. 5 vols. $198.

EDITING

Barzun, Jacques. *Simple and Direct: A Rhetoric for Writers.* New York: Harper & Row, 1976. $10.

Bernstein, Theodore. *The Careful Writer.* New York: Atheneum, 1965. $14.95.

Colby, Jean P. *Writing, Illustrating and Editing Children's Books.* New York: Hastings House, 1974. pap. $4.95.

Fowler, H. W. *Directory of Modern English Usage.* 2nd rev. ed. New York: Oxford University Press, 1965. $12.50.

Jordan, Lewis. *The New York Times Manual of Style and Usage.* New York: Times Books, 1976. $10.

A Manual of Style. 12th rev. ed. Chicago: University of Chicago Press, 1969. $15.

Skillin, Marjorie E., and Gay, Robert M. *Words into Type.* Rev. ed. Englewood Cliffs, NJ: Prentice-Hall, 1974. $17.95.

Strunk, William, Jr., and White, E. B. *Elements of Style.* 3rd ed. New York: Macmillan, 1978. $4.95.

Zinsser, William. *On Writing Well: An Informal Guide to Writing Nonfiction.* New York: Harper & Row, 1976. $9.95.

PERIODICALS

AB Bookman's Weekly (weekly including Yearbook). Clifton, NJ: AB Bookman's Weekly. $35.

American Book Publishing Record (monthly). New York: R. R. Bowker. $23.

BP Report: On the Business of Book Publishing (weekly). White Plains, NY: Knowledge Industry Publications. $110.

Printing and Publishing: Quarterly Industry Report. Washington, DC: U.S. Department of Commerce. $5.

Publishers Weekly. New York: R. R. Bowker. $33.

Scholarly Publishing: A Journal for Authors & Publishers (quarterly). Toronto: University of Toronto Press. $17.50.

Weekly Record. New York: R. R. Bowker. $15. A weekly listing of current American book publications, providing complete cataloging information.

For a list of periodicals reviewing books, see *Literary Market Place.*

Distinguished Books

LITERARY PRIZES, 1979

ASCAP-Deems Taylor Awards—$500. *Offered by:* American Society of Composers, Authors, and Publishers. *Winners:* Warren Babb, trans., and Claude V. Palisca, ed., for *Hucbald, Guido and John on Music: Three Medieval Treatises* (Yale Univ. Press); Paul F. Berliner for *The Soul of Moira* (Univ. of California Press); Mercer Ellington and Stanley Dance for *Duke Ellington in Person* (Houghton Mifflin); James Haskins and Kathleen Benson for *Scott Joplin: The Man Who Made Ragtime* (Doubleday); Richard H. Hoppin for *Medieval Music* (Norton); H. C. Robbins Landon for *Haydn: Chronicle and Works, Vol. II* (Indiana Univ. Press); Arnold Shaw for *Honkers and Shouters* (Macmillan).

Academy of American Poets Fellowship—$10,000. For distinguished poetic achievement. *Winner:* Mark Strand.

Jane Addams Children's Book Award. For a book promoting the cause of peace, social justice, and world community. *Offered by:* Women's International League for Peace and Freedom and the Jane Addams Peace Association. *Winner:* Jamake Highwater for *Many Smokes, Many Moons* (Harper & Row).

American Academy and Institute of Arts and Letters Awards in Literature—$3,000 each. *Offered by:* American Academy and Institute of Arts and Letters. *Winners:* Arlene Croce, Barry Hannah, James McConkey, Robert M. Pirsig, Richard Poirier, John N. Morris, Philip Schultz, Dave Smith.

American Academy in Rome Fellowship in Creative Writing—$7,180. *Offered by:* American Academy and Institute of Arts and Letters. *Winner:* Joseph Caldwell.

Anisfield-Wolf Award—$1,500. For a scholarly book in the field of race relations. *Offered by:* Cleveland Foundation. *Winner:* Philip V. Tobias, ed., for *The Bushmen: San Hunters and Herders of Southern Africa* (Human & Rousseau, Cape Town, South Africa).

Association of Jewish Libraries Book Awards. For outstanding contributions in the field of Jewish literature for children. *Winners:* Doris Orgel for *The Devil in Vienna* (Dial); (posthumous body of work award) Sydney Taylor for *All of a Kind Family Books* (Follett).

James Baldwin Prize. For a new or previously unrecognized black writer of talent. *Offered by:* Dial Press. *Winner:* Raymond Andrews for *Appalachee Red* (Dial).

Bancroft Prize—$4,000 each. *Offered by:* Columbia University. For books of exceptional merit and distinction in American history, American diplomacy, and the international relations of the United States. *Winners:* Christopher Thorne for *Allies of a Kind: The United States, Britain, and the War against Japan, 1941-1945* (Oxford Univ. Press); Anthony F. C. Wallace for *Rockdale: The*

Note: For additional information on the prizes included in this list, or for information on prizes not included, see the tenth edition of *Literary and Library Prizes* (Bowker, 1980).

Growth of an American Village in the Early Industrial Revolution (Knopf).

Mildred L. Batchelder Award—citation. Intended to encourage the translation and publication in the United States of outstanding books originally written in languages other than English. *Offered by:* ALA Library Service to Children. *Winners:* Harcourt Brace Jovanovich, Inc., for *Rabbit Island* by Jörg Steiner, trans. by Ann Conrad Lammers; Franklin Watts, Inc., for *Konrad* by Christine Nostlinger, trans. by Anthea Bell.

Curtis G. Benjamin Award. For creative publishing. *Winner:* C. Stuart Brewster.

Gerard and Ella Berman Award—$500. For a book of Jewish history. *Offered by:* Jewish Book Council. *Winner:* Salo Baron for cumulative work (Columbia Univ. Press and Jewish Publication Society).

Jessie Bernard Award. *Offered by:* American Sociological Association. *Winner:* Nancy Chodorow for *The Reproduction of Mothering: Psychoanalysis and the Sociology of Gender* (Univ. of California Press).

Stuart L. Bernath Prize. *Offered by:* Society for Historians of American Foreign Relations. *Winner:* Phillip J. Baram for *The Department of State in the Middle East: 1919–1945* (Univ. of Pennsylvania Press).

Irma Simonton Black Award—scroll. For the author and illustrator of an outstanding book for young children. *Offered by:* Bank Street College of Education, New York. *Winner:* Larry Bograd for *Felix in the Attic* (Harvey House).

James Tait Black Memorial Prizes—£400 each. *Winners:* (biography) Robert Gittings for *The Older Hardy* (Heinemann); (novel) Maurice Gee for *Plumb* (Faber).

Bologna Children's Book Fair. Graphic Arts Prizes. *Winners:* (children's graphics) *Histoire du Petit Stephan Girard* (Gallimard, France); (young people's graphics) *Aurora* (Dalla Parte delle Bambine, Italy); (budding critics) *Ein Tag im Leben der Dorothea Wutz* (Diogenes Verlag, Switzerland).

Books in Canada Award. *Winner:* Joan Barfoot for *Abra* (McGraw-Hill).

Booker Prize for Fiction—£5,000. *Winner:* Penelope Fitzgerald for *Offshore* (Collins).

Boston Globe-Horn Book Awards—$200 each. For excellence in children's literature. *Winners:* (fiction) Sid Fleischman for *Humbug Mountain* (Atlantic-Little); (nonfiction) David Kheridian for *The Road from Home: The Story of an Armenian Girl* (Greenwillow); (illustration) Raymond Briggs for *The Snowman* (Random House).

John Nicholas Brown Prize. *Offered by:* Mediaeval Academy of America. *Winner:* Claiborne W. Thompson for *Studies in Upplandic Runography* (Univ. of Texas Press).

Caldecott Medal. For the most outstanding picture book for children. *Offered by:* ALA Library Service to Children. *Medal contributed by:* Daniel Melcher. *Winner:* Paul Goble for *The Girl Who Loved Wild Horses* (Bradbury).

John W. Campbell Memorial Award. *Winner:* Michael Moorcock for *Gloriana* (Avon).

Canadian Library Association Book of the Year for Children Award. *Offered by:* Canadian Association of Children's Librarians. *Winner:* Kevin Major for *Hold Fast* (Clarke, Irwin).

Melville Cane Award—$500. *Offered by:* Poetry Society of America. *Winner:* Andrew Welsh for *Roots of Lyric: Primitive Poetry and Modern Poetics* (Princeton Univ. Press).

Carey-Thomas Award. For a distinguished project of book publishing. *Offered by:* R. R. Bowker. *Winner:* Pushcart Press for *The Pushcart Prize, III: Best of the Small Presses,* ed. by Bill Henderson; (honor citation) Johns Hopkins University Press for *The American Railroad*

Passenger Car by John W. White, Jr.; (special citations) David R. Godine for Nonpareil Books and Dial Press for *American Gold* by Ernest Seeman.

Carnegie Medal. For the outstanding book for children written in English and first published in the United Kingdom. *Offered by:* British Library Association. *Winner:* David Rees for *The Exeter Blitz* (Hamish Hamilton).

Chastain Award. *Winner:* David J. Garrow for *Protest at Selma: Martin Luther King, Jr., and the Voting Rights Act of 1965* (Yale Univ. Press).

Chicago Folklore Prize Competition. *Winners:* Hoyt Alverson for *Mind in the Hear of Darkness: Value and Self-Identity Among the Tswana of Southern Africa* (Yale Univ. Press); Betty Messenger for *Picking Up the Linen Threads* (Univ. of Texas Press).

Child Study Children's Book Committee at Bank Street College Award. *Winner:* Doris Orgel for *The Devil in Vienna* (Dial).

Children's Book Guild Nonfiction Award. *Winner:* Jean Fritz.

Children's Reading Round Table Award. *Offered by:* ALA Children's Reading Round Table. *Winner:* Dorothy Haas.

Children's Science Book Award of the New York Academy of Sciences. *Winners:* (younger category) Lucia Anderson, author, and Leigh Grant, illustrator, for *The Smallest Life Around Us* (Crown); (older category) Herman Schneider, author, and Radu Vero, illustrator, for *Laser Light* (McGraw-Hill); (special award) Viking Press for "an outstanding series of books on engineering and technology."

Gilbert Chinard Prize. *Winner:* Jay Higginbotham for *Old Mobile: Fort Louis de la Louisiane, 1702-1711* (Rockwell Publications).

Cholmondeley Award for Poets—£500 each. For the benefit and encouragement of poets of any age, sex, or nationality. *Offered by:* Society of Authors (UK). *Winners:* Alan Brownjohn, Andrew Motion, Charles Tomlinson.

Christopher Awards. For books distinguished for their "affirmation of the highest values of the human spirit." *Winners:* (adult books) Robert C. Alberts for *Benjamin West: A Biography* (Houghton Mifflin); Tim Severin for *The Brendan Voyage* (McGraw-Hill); Gordon Parks for *Flavio* (Norton); Pierre-Jakez Helias for *The Horse of Pride: Life in a Breton Village* (Yale Univ. Press); Josephine Whitney Duveneck for *Life on Two Levels* (Wm. Kaufmann); Barry Holstun Lopez for *Of Wolves and Men* (Scribner's); Josh Greenfeld for *A Place for Noah* (Holt); Ivan Doig for *This House of Sky: Landscapes of a Western Mind* (Harcourt); Malcolm Muggeridge for *A Twentieth Century Testament* (Nelson); Robert Coles and Jane Hallowell Coles for *Women of Crisis: Lives of Struggle and Hope* (Delacorte Press/Seymour Lawrence); (children's books) Barbara Williams for *Chester Chipmunk's Thanksgiving* (Dutton); M. E. Kerr for *Gentlehands* (Harper & Row); Katherine Paterson for *The Great Gilly Hopkins* (Crowell); Rosalie Seidler for *Panda Cake* (Parents' Magazine).

Frank and Ethel S. Cohen Award—$500. For an outstanding book dealing with an aspect of Jewish thought originally written in English by a U.S. or Canadian resident. *Offered by:* Jewish Book Council of National Jewish Welfare Board. *Winner:* Robert Gordis for *Love and Sex: A Modern Jewish Perspective* (Farrar, Straus & Giroux).

Carr P. Collins Award for Nonfiction. *Offered by:* Texas Institute of Letters. *Winner:* J. Lon Tinkle for *An American Original: The Life of J. Frank Dobbie* (Little, Brown).

Commonwealth Poetry Prize—£250. For a first published book by a poet who comes from a Commonwealth country other than Great Britain. *Winners:* Gabriel Okara (Nigeria) for *The Fisherman's Invocation* (Heinemann); Brian Turner (New Zealand) for *Ladders of Rain* (McIndoe).

Duff Cooper Memorial Prize. For a literary work published in English or French. *Winner:* Geoffrey Hill for *Tenebrae* (Andre Deutsch).

Dartmouth Medal. *Offered by:* ALA Reference and Adult Services Division. *Winner: The Encyclopedia of Bioethics,* ed. by Warren T. Reich (Free Press).

Del Duca Prize (France). *Winner:* Paul Fournel for *Les Petites Filles Respirant le Meme Air que Nous* (Gallimard); *Little Girls Breathe the Same Air as We Do* (Braziller).

Ralph Waldo Emerson Award. *Offered by:* Phi Beta Kappa. *Winner:* Elizabeth Lewisohn Eisenstein for *The Printing Press as an Agent of Change, Vols. I and II* (Cambridge Univ. Press).

Emerson-Thoreau Medal. *Offered by:* American Academy of Arts and Sciences. *Winner:* James T. Farrell.

English Language Book of the Year Medal. *See* Canadian Library Association.

William and Janice Epstein Award—$500. To encourage fictional writing on Jewish themes. *Offered by:* Jewish Book Council of the National Jewish Welfare Board. *Winner:* Gloria Goldreich for *Leah's Journey* (Harcourt).

Christopher Ewart-Biggs Memorial Prize (Great Britain). *Winner:* Dervla Murphy for *A Place Apart* (John Murray/Devin-Adair).

Explicator Award. *Winner:* Cleanth Brooks for *William Faulkner: Toward Yoknapatawpha and Beyond* (Yale Univ. Press).

Eleanor Farjeon Award. For distinguished services to children's books. *Offered by:* Children's Book Circle (Great Britain). *Winner:* Joy Whitby.

Dorothy Canfield Fisher Award—scroll. For a book selected by children of Vermont. *Offered by:* Vermont State PTA and Vermont State Department of Libraries. *Winner:* Susan Beth Pfeffer for *Kid Power* (Watts).

E. M. Forster Award. *Winner:* Bruce Chatwin.

George Freedley Memorial Book Award. *Offered by:* Theatre Library Association. *Winner:* Richard D. Atlick for *The Shaws of London: A Panorama History, 1600-1862* (Harvard Univ. Press).

Rabbi Jacob Freedman Award. *Winner:* William M. Brinner, trans., for *Elegant Composition Concerning Relief After Adversity* by Nissim ben Jacob Ibn Shahin (Yale Univ. Press).

R. T. French Tastemaker Awards. *Winners:* (top cookbook and basic/general) Julia Child for *Julia Child and Company* (Knopf); (American/regional) Editors of Time-Life Books for *The Time-Life American-Regional Cookbook* (Little, Brown); (foreign) Marcella Hazan for *More Classic Italian Cookery* (Knopf); (specialty) Ann Seranne for *The Joy of Giving Homemade Food* (McKay); (single subject) Craig Claiborne and Pierre Franey for *Veal Cookery* (Harper & Row); (natural foods) Marion Burros for *Pure and Simple: Delicious Recipes for Additive-Free Cooking* (Morrow); (special diet) Barbara Gibbons for *The International Slim Gourmet Cookbook* (Harper & Row); (original softcover) Editors of Sunset Books and Sunset Magazine for *Cooking for Two . . . Or Just for You* (Lane).

Friends of American Writers Awards— $1,000. For natives or residents of the Middle West or books with midwestern locale, for young readers. *Winners:* (adult) Bette Howland for *Blue in Chicago* (Harper & Row); (memorial) Julie McDonald for *Petra* (Iowa Univ. Press); (juvenile) Gloria Whenlan for *A Clearing in the Forest* (Putnam).

Friends of the Dallas Public Library Award. *Winner:* Walt W. Rostow for

The World Economy: History and Prospect (Univ. of Texas Press).

Christian Gauss Award. *Offered by:* Phi Beta Kappa. *Winner:* Robert Bechtold Heilman for *The Ways of the World: Comedy and Society* (Univ. of Washington Press).

Gavel Award. *Offered by:* American Bar Association. *Winner:* A. Leon Higginbotham, Jr. for *In the Matter of Color: Race and the American Legal Process* (Oxford Univ. Press); (children's book) *Our Legal Heritage* (Silver Burdett).

Georgia Children's Book Award. *Winner:* Bill Peet for *Big Bad Bruce* (Houghton Mifflin).

Gibson Literary Awards (Canada). *Winner:* Joan Barfoot for *Abra* (McGraw-Hill).

Tony Godwin Memorial Award—six weeks at a host publisher in the United Kingdom/United States. For the encouragement of talented editors on both sides of the Atlantic. *Offered by:* Tony Godwin Memorial Trust. *Winner:* Lee Goerner (Knopf); name of UK winner not available.

Goethe House-PEN Translation Prize—$500. For the best translation from German to English. *Winner:* Leila Vennewitz for *"And Never Said a Word" and Other Works* by Heinrich Bokk (McGraw-Hill).

Golden Spur Awards. *Offered by:* Western Writers of America. *Winners:* (novel) Norman Zollinger for *Riders to Cibola* (Museum of New Mexico Press); (nonfiction) Janet Lecompte for *Pueblo, Hardscrabble, Greenhorn* (Univ. of Oklahoma Press); (young adult) Sonia Levitin for *The No-Return Trail* (Harcourt).

Eric Gregory Awards—£200–£750. For poetry or belles-lettres by writers under 30 years of age. *Offered by:* Society of Authors (UK). *Winners:* Stuart Henson, Alan Hollinghurst, Michael Jenkins, Peter Thabit Jones, James Lindesay, Brian Moses, Sean O'Brien, Walter Perrie.

Kate Greenaway Medal. *Offered by:* British Library Association. *Winner:* Janet Ahlberg for *Each Peach Pear Plum* (Penguin/Kestrel).

Guardian Children's Fiction Award—£100. *Winner:* Andrew Davies for *Conrad's War* (Blackie).

Guardian Fiction Prize—£210. For a new work of originality and promise by a British or Commonwealth writer. *Offered by:* The *Guardian*. *Winners:* Neil Jordan for *Night in Tunisia* (Writers & Readers); Dambudzo Marechera for *The House of Hunger* (Heinemann Educational).

Calouste Gulbenkian-PEN Translation Prize. *Offered by:* PEN American Center. *Winner:* Helen R. Lane for *The Three Marias: New Portuguese Letters* by Maria Isabel Barreno, Maria Teres Horta, and Maria Velho DaCosta (Doubleday).

Hawthornden Prize—£100 and silver medal. To an English writer under 41 years of age for the best work of imaginative literature. *Offered by:* Society of Authors (U.K.). *Winner:* David Cook for *Walter* (Secker & Warburg).

Heinemann Award. For the encouragement of genuine contributions to literature, particularly those unlikely to command large sales. *Offered by:* Royal Society of Literature. *Winners:* Robert Ginnings for *The Older Hardy* (Heinemann); Frank Tuohy for *Live Bait* (Macmillan).

Ernest Hemingway Foundation Award—$6,000. For the best first book of fiction by an American writer. *Offered by:* PEN American Center. *Winner:* Reuben Bercovitch for *Hasen* (Knopf).

Herskovits Award. *Winner:* Hoyt Alverson for *Mind in the Heart of Darkness: Value and Self-Identity Among the Tswana of Southern Africa* (Yale Univ. Press).

Amelia Frances Howard-Gibbon Medal. For outstanding illustration of a children's book published in Canada. *Offered by:* Canadian Library Association. *Winner:* Ann Blades for *A Salmon for Simon* by Betty Waterton (Douglas and McIntyre).

Hugo Award. For best science fiction novel. *Offered by:* World Science Fiction Convention. *Winners:* (novel) Vonda N. McIntyre for *Dreamsnake* (Houghton Mifflin); (novella) John Varley for *The Persistence of Vision* (Magazine of Fantasy and Science Fiction); (novelette) Poul Anderson for *Hunter's Moon* (Analog).

International Book Award. *Winner:* Leopold S. Senghor.

International Reading Association Children's Book Award. *Winner:* Alison Smith for *Reserved for Mark Anthony Crowder* (Dutton).

Iowa School of Letters Award for Short Fiction—$1,000. For a book-length collection of short stories. *Winner:* Mary Hedin for *Fly Away Home* (Univ. of Iowa Press).

Japan-U.S. Friendship Commission and Japan Society Translation Awards. *Winners:* Robert Epp for *Poems by Kinoshita Yuji* (Univ. of California Press, Los Angeles); Ian Hideo Levy for *The Ten Thousand Leaves* (Princeton Univ. Press).

Jerusalem Prize—$3,000. For an author who has contributed to the world's understanding of "the freedom of the individual in society." *Winner:* Sir Isaiah Berlin.

Leon Jolson Award—$500. For the best book on the Nazi holocaust. *Offered by:* Jewish Book Council of the National Jewish Welfare Board. *Winner:* Michael Selzer for *Deliverance Day* (Lippincott).

Jesse H. Jones Award. *Offered by:* Texas Institute of Letters. *Winner:* Shelby Hearon for *A Prince of a Fellow* (Doubleday).

Juniper Prize—$1,000. *Offered by:* University of Massachusetts Press. *Winner:* Eleanor Wilner for *Maya* (Univ. of Massachusetts Press).

Janet Heidinger Kafka Prize in Fiction by an American Woman. *Winner:* Mary Gordon for *Final Payments* (Random House).

Morris J. Kaplun Memorial Award—$500. For an outstanding book on the state of Israel. *Offered by:* Jewish Book Council of the National Jewish Welfare Board. *Winner:* Ruth Gruber for *Raquela: A Woman of Israel* (Coward, McCann).

Irwin Kerlan Award. For achievement in children's literature. *Offered by:* Kerlan Collection, University of Minnesota. *Winner:* Margot Zemach.

Coretta Scott King Award. *Offered by:* ALA Social Responsibilities Round Table. *Winners:* Ossie Davis for *Escape to Freedom* (Viking); Tom Feelings, illustrator, for *Something on My Mind* (Dial).

Harry and Florence Kovner Award—$500. For English-Jewish, Hebrew, or Yiddish poetry by American citizens or residents. *Offered by:* Jewish Book Council of the National Jewish Welfare Board. *Winner:* Moishe Steingart for *In Droisen Fun Der Velt* (Shulsinger Brothers).

Lamont Poetry Selection Award. *Offered by:* Academy of American Poets. *Winner:* Frederick Seidel for *Sunrise* (Viking).

Jules F. Landry Award—$1,000. For the best manuscript submitted to Louisiana State University Press in the fields of southern history, biography, or literature. *Winner:* William Gillette for *Retreat from Reconstruction, 1869-1879* (Louisiana State Univ. Press).

James Russell Lowell Prize—$1,000. *Offered by:* Modern Language Association of America. *Winner:* Andrew Welsh for

Roots of Lyric: Primitive Poetry and Modern Poetics (Princeton Univ. Press).

Lenore Marshall Memorial Poetry Prize—$3,500. For an outstanding book of poems published in the United States. *Offered by:* New Hope Foundation and *Saturday Review. Administered by:* Book-of-the-Month Club. *Winner:* Hayden Carruth for *Brothers, I Loved You All* (Sheep Meadow Press).

Somerset Maugham Award—£500. *Winners:* Helen Hodgman for *Jack & Jill* (Duckworth); Sara Maitland for *Daughter of Jerusalem* (Blond & Briggs).

Lucille J. Medwick Memorial Award—$500. *Offered by:* PEN American Center. *Sponsored by:* Medwick Foundation. *Winner:* Theodore Solotaroff "for his outstanding work as an editor of *New American Review* (1967-1972) and *American Review* (1973-1977)."

Frederic G. Melcher Book Award—$1,000. For the most significant contribution to religious liberalism. *Offered by:* Unitarian/Universalist General Assembly. *Winner:* Sissela Bok for *Lying: Moral Choice in Public and Private Life* (Pantheon).

Vicky Metcalf Awards. *Offered by:* Canadian Authors Association. *Winners:* (short story) Marina McDougall for "The Kingdom of Riddles"; (body of work) Cliff Faulknor.

Milton Society of American Book Awards. *Winners:* Roland Mushat Frye for *Milton's Imagery and the Visual Arts* (Princeton Univ. Press); Mary Ann Radzinowicz for *Towards Samson Agonistes* (Princeton Univ. Press).

Jan Mitchell Prize in Art History—$10,000. For the author of an outstanding book on art history. *Winners:* Martin Bullin and Evelyn Joll for *The Paintings of J. M. W. Turner* (Yale Univ. Press).

Charles Rufus Morey Book Award. *Winner:* Anne Coffin Hanson for *Manet and the Modern Tradition* (Yale Univ. Press).

Frank Luther Mott-Kappa Tau Alpha Research Award. For the best book in journalism. *Winner:* Kevin Michael McAuliffe for *The Great American Newspaper: The Rise and Fall of the Village Voice* (Scribner's).

Mystery Writers of America—Edgars. *Winners:* (best mystery novel) Ken Follett for *The Eye of the Needle* (Arbor House); (best first novel) William D. DeAndrea for *Killed in the Ratings* (Harcourt); (best paperback) Franklin Bandy for *Deceit and Deadly Lies* (Charter Books, Grosset & Dunlap); (fact crime book) Vincent Bugliosi and Ken Hurwitz for *Till Death Do Us Part* (Norton); (best critical/biographical study) Gwen Robyns for *The Mystery of Agatha Christie* (Doubleday); (grand master) Aaron Mark Stein; (raven) Alberto Tedeschi, Arnoldo Mondadori Editore, Milan, Italy; (juvenile novel) Dana Brookins for *Alone in Wolf Hollow* (Seabury).

National Arts Club Gold Medal of Honor. *Winner:* Allen Ginsberg.

National Book Awards—$1,000 each. *Winners:* (biography/autobiography) Arthur M. Schlesinger, Jr., for *Robert Kennedy and His Times* (Houghton Mifflin); (contemporary thought) Peter Matthiessen for *The Snow Leopard* (Viking); (fiction) Tim O'Brien for *Going After Cacciato* (Delacorte/Seymour Lawrence); (history) Richard Beale Davis for *Intellectual Life in the Colonial South, 1585-1763* (Univ. of Tennessee Press); (poetry) James Merrill for *Mirabell: Books of Number* (Atheneum); (translation) Clayton Eshleman and Jose Rubia Barcia for *The Complete Posthumous Poetry* by Cesar Vallejo (Univ. of California Press); (children's literature) Katherine Paterson for *The Great Gilly Hopkins* (Crowell).

National Book Critics Circle Awards. *Winners:* (fiction) John Cheever for *The Stories of John Cheever* (Knopf);

(poetry) Peter Davison, ed., for *Hello Darkness: The Collected Poems of L. E. Sissman* (Atlantic/Little); (criticism) Meyer Schapiro for *Modern Art: 19th and 20th Centuries—Selected Papers by Meyer Schapiro* (Braziller); (general fiction) Maureen Howard for *Facts of Life* (Little, Brown) and Garry Wills for *Inventing America: Jefferson's Declaration of Independence* (Doubleday).

National Historical Society Book Prize. *Winner:* Daniel J. Kevles for *The Physicists* (Knopf).

National Religious Book Awards. To honor outstanding religious book publishing and to stimulate reading of religious books. *Offered by:* Catholic Press Association and Associated Church Press. *Winners:* (inspirational) Joseph G. Donders for *Jesus the Stranger: Reflections on the Gospels* (Orbis); (scholarly) Albert J. Raboteau for *Slave Religion* (Oxford Univ. Press); (community life/social awareness) Donald B. Kraybill for *The Upside Down Kingdom* (Herald Press); (children/youth) Walter Wangerin, Jr., for *The Book of the Dun Cow* (Harper & Row).

Nebula Awards. For excellence in the field of science fiction. *Offered by:* Science Fiction Writers of America. *Winners:* (novel) Vonda N. McIntyre for *Dreamsnake* (Houghton Mifflin); (novella) John Varley for *The Persistence of Vision* (Magazine of Fantasy and Science Fiction); (novelette) Charles L. Grant for *A Glow of Candles, a Unicorn's Eye* (Nelson); (grand master award) L. Sprague de Camp "for a career contribution to the science field."

Nene Award. *Winner:* Beverly Cleary for *Ramona and Her Father* (Morrow).

New Jersey Library Association Garden State Children's Book Awards. *Winners:* (easy-to-read) Dick Gackenbach for *Hattie Rabbit* (Harper & Row); Ellen Weiss, illustrator, and Leatie Weiss, author, for *Heather's Feathers* (Watts); (younger fiction) Hila Colman for *Nobody Has to Be a Kid Forever* (Crown); (younger nonfiction) Jill Krementz, photographer and author, for *A Very Young Dancer* (Knopf).

New York Academy of Sciences Children's Science Book Awards. *See* Children's Science Book Awards of the New York Academy of Sciences.

New York Library Association Award. *Winner:* Leonard Everett Fisher for "the versatility and excellence of his work."

New York Times Best Illustrated Children's Book Awards. *Winners:* Chris Van Allsburg and Houghton Mifflin for *The Garden of Abdul Gasazi*; Barbara Cooney and Viking for *Ox-Cart Man*; Ray Smith, Catriona Smith, and Atheneum for *The Long Dive;* Klaus Ensikat and Chatto & Windus/Merrimack Book Service for *The Tale of Fancy Nancy*; Faith Jaques, Margaret K. McElderry and Atheneum for *Tilly's House*; Uri Shulevitz and Farrar, Straus & Giroux for *The Treasure*; Janina Domanska and Greenwillow for *King Krakus and the Dragon*.

Newbery Medal. For the most distinguished contribution to literature for children. *Donor:* ALA Library Service to Children. *Medal contributed by:* Daniel Melcher. *Winner:* Ellen Raskin for *The Westing Game* (Dutton).

Nobel Prize for Literature—about $130,000. For high achievement in the field of literature. *Offered by:* Swedish Academy, Stockholm. *Winner:* Odysseus Elytis.

PEN Translation Prize—$1,000. For the best book-length translation into English. *Donor:* Book-of-the-Month Club. *Winner:* Charles Wright for *The Storm and Other Poems* by Eugenio Montale (Oberlin Field Translation Series).

Phi Beta Kappa Science Award. *Offered by:* Phi Beta Kappa. *Winner:* John Imbrie and Katherine Palmer Imbrie for *Ice Ages: Solving the Mystery* (Enslow Publishers).

Prix Femina. *Winner:* Pierre Moinot for *Le Guetteur d'Ombre* (Gallimard).

Prix Goncourt. *Winner:* Antonine Maillet for *Pelagie la Charrette* (Grassett).

Prix Interallié. *Winner:* François Cavanna for *Les Russkoffs* (Pierre Belfond).

Prix Medicis. *Winner:* Claude Durand for *La Nuit Zoologique* (Grasset).

Prix Medicis Etranger. *Winner:* Alejo Carpentier for *La Harpa y la Sombra* (Gallimard).

Premio Mondello. *Winner:* Joseph Brodsky.

Prix Renaudot. *Winner:* Jean-Marc Roberts for *Les Affaires Etrangères* (Seuil).

Pulitzer Prizes—$1,000 each. *Offered by:* Trustees of Columbia University on the recommendation of the Advisory Board on the Pulitzer Prizes. *Winners:* (fiction) John Cheever for *The Stories of John Cheever* (Knopf); (history) Don E. Fehrenbacher for *The Dred Scott Case* (Oxford Univ. Press); (biography) Leonard Baker for *Days of Sorrow and Pain: Leo Baeck and the Berlin Jews* (Macmillan); (poetry) Robert Penn Warren for *Now and Then* (Random House); (general nonfiction) Edward O. Wilson for *On Human Nature* (Harvard Univ. Press).

Regina Medal. For distinguished contribution to children's literature. *Offered by:* Catholic Library Association. *Winner:* Morton Schindel.

John Llewellyn Rhys Memorial Prize—£100. For a memorable book by a British Commonwealth writer under 30. *Offered by:* John Llewellyn Rhys Memorial Trust/National Book League. *Winner:* Peter Boardman for *The Shining Mountain* (Hodder & Stoughton).

Richard and Hinda Rosenthal Foundation Award—$2,000. For a work of fiction that is a considerable literary achievement though not necessarily a commercial success. *Offered by:* American Academy and Institute of Arts and Letters. *Winner:* Diane Johnson.

Rutgers Award. For a distinguished contribution to children's literature. *Offered by:* Rutgers University. *Winner:* Dorothy Shuttlesworth.

Charles and Bertie G. Schwartz Award for Jewish Juvenile Literature. *Offered by:* National Jewish Book Awards. *Winner:* Irena Narell for *Joshua: Fighter for Bar Kochba* (Akiba Press).

Scott-Moncrieff Prize (Great Britain). *Winners:* John and Doreen Weightman for *L'Origine des Manières de Table* by Claude Levi-Strauss (Plon/Jonathan Cape); Richard Mayne for *Memoires by Jean Monnet* (Fayard/Collins).

Seal Books Novel Award—$50,000. *Offered by:* Seal Books (Canada). *Winner:* William Deverell for *Needles* (McClelland & Stewart).

Sequoyah Children's Book Award. *Winner:* Wilson Rawls for *Summer of the Monkeys* (Doubleday).

Lillian Smith Book Awards. *Offered by:* Southern Regional Council. *Winners:* (nonfiction) Marion A. Wright and Arnold Shankman for *Human Rights Odyssey* (Moore); (fiction) Ernest J. Gaines for *In My Father's House* (Knopf).

W. H. Smith Literary Award—£1,000. To the author of a book, written in English and published in the United Kingdom, which makes the most significant contribution to literature. *Offered by:* W. H. Smith & Son, Ltd. *Winner:* Mark Girouard for *Life in the English Country House* (Yale Univ. Press).

John Ben Snow Prize. *Winner:* Carleton Mabee for *Black Education in New York State: From Colonial to Modern Times* (Syracuse Univ. Press).

Society of Midland Authors Awards. *Winners:* (biography) Bernard J. Brommel for *Eugene V. Debs: Spokesman for Labor and Socialism* (Charles H. Kerr); (fiction) John Cristgau for *Spoon* (Viking); (history) Walter Blair and Hamlin Hill for *American Humor from Poor Richard to Doonesbury* (Oxford Univ. Press); (nonfiction) Stephen Z. Cohen and Bruce Michael Gans for *The Other*

Generation Gap (Follett); (poetry) Lucien Stryk, ed. and trans., for *Penguin Book of Zen Poetry* (Swallow); John Bennett for *Echoes from the Peaceable Kingdom* (Eerdmans); (children's books) Stella Pevsner for *And You Give Me a Pain, Elaine* (Seabury); Berniece Rabe for *The Orphan* (Dutton).

Southern California Council on Literature for Children Awards. *Winners:* (fiction) Dana Brookins for *Alone in Wolf Hollow* (Seabury); (illustration) Diane Goode for *Dream Eater* (Bradbury); (body of work) Jane Curry.

TSM Award—R. R. Hawkins Award. For outstanding publishing in the field of medicine, and the outstanding book of the year in the TSM Division. *Offered by:* Technical, Scientific and Medical Division, Association of American Publishers. *Winners:* (technical) Addison-Wesley for *The Network Nation: Human Communication via Computer* by Starr Hiltz and Murray Turnoff; (scientific) McGraw-Hill for *Handbook of Optics* by Optical Society of America; (medical) Little, Brown for *Pediatric Kidney Disease* by Chester M. Edelmann, Jr.; (business) Johns Hopkins Univ. Press for *The Productivity Dilemma: Roadblock to Innovation in the Automotive Industry* by William J. Abernathy; (journal) Plenum Press for *Grants Magazine*, ed. by Virginia White.

Theatre Library Association Award. For the outstanding book on recorded performance, including motion pictures and television. *Winner:* Kevin Brownlow for *The War, the West and the Wilderness* (Knopf).

University of Southern Mississippi Medallion for Distinguished Service in Children's Literature. *Winner:* Leonard Everett Fisher.

Irita Van Doren Award—silver bowl. For outstanding contributions to the cause of books and reading. *Offered by:* American Booksellers Association, Publishers Ad Club, and Publishers Publicity Association. *Winner:* Louis Epstein.

Harold D. Vursell Award. *Offered by:* American Academy and Institute of Arts and Letters. *Winner:* Wallace Fowlie.

Marjorie Peabody Waite Award. *Offered by:* American Academy and Institute of Arts and Letters. *Winner:* James Still.

Patrick White Award. *Winner:* Randolph Stow for *The Girl Green as Elderflower* (Viking).

William Allen White Children's Book Award—medal. For a children's book chosen by Kansas schoolchildren. *Winner:* Wilson Rawls for *Summer of the Monkeys* (Doubleday).

Walt Whitman Award—$1,000. To an unpublished poet. *Offered by:* Academy of American Poets and the Copernicus Society of America. *Winner:* David Bottoms for *Shooting Rats at the Bibb County Dump* (Morrow).

World Fantasy Awards. *Winners:* (fiction) Michael Moorcock for *Gloriana* (Avon); (short fiction) Avram Davidson for "Naples" from *Shadows* (Doubleday); (collection/anthology) Charles L. Grant, ed., for *Shadows* (Doubleday).

Yale Series of Younger Poets. For a first volume of poetry by a promising young American poet. *Offered by:* Yale University Press. *Winner:* William Virgil David for *One Way to Reconstruct the Scene* (Yale Univ. Press).

Yorkshire Arts Association Awards. *Winners:* (Premier Award) R. C. Scriven for *Edge of Darkness, Edge of Light* (Souvenir); (Established Writers Awards) Elizabeth North for *Everything in the Garden* (Gollancz); Elizabeth Gunn for *Ella's Dream* (Hamilton); (Best First Novel Award) Brian Thompson for *Buddy Boy* (Gollancz); (Special Award) George Moor for *Fox Gold* (Calder).

Morton Dauwen Zabel Award—$2,500. For a poet of progressive, original, and experimental tendencies. *Offered by:* American Academy and Institute of Arts and Letters. *Winner:* Richard Gilman.

NOTABLE BOOKS OF 1979

This is the thirty-third year in which this list of distinguished books has been issued by the Notable Books Council of the Reference and Adult Services Division of the American Library Association.

Adams, Alice. *Beautiful Girl.* Knopf.

Blythe, Ronald. *The View in Winter: Reflections on Old Age.* Harcourt.

Conot, Robert. *A Streak of Luck: The Life and Legend of Thomas Alva Edison.* Seaview.

Drucker, Peter. *Adventures of a Bystander.* Harper.

Edel, Leon. *Bloomsbury: A House of Lions.* Lippincott.

Energy Future: Report of the Energy Project at the Harvard Business School. Random.

Epstein, Helen. *Children of the Holocaust: Conversations with Sons and Daughters of Survivors.* Putnam.

Epstein, Leslie. *King of the Jews.* Coward.

Ferlinghetti, Lawrence. *Landscapes of Living & Dying.* New Directions.

Fraser, Antonia. *Royal Charles: Charles II and the Restoration.* Knopf.

Harvard Guide to Contemporary American Writing. Harvard University Press.

Haviaras, Stratis. *When the Tree Sings.* Simon & Schuster.

Hendricks, Gordon. *The Life and Work of Winslow Homer.* Abrams.

Hoagland, Edward. *African Calliope: A Journey to the Sudan.* Random.

Hoffman, Alice. *The Drowning Season.* Dutton.

Kendall, Elizabeth. *Where She Danced.* Knopf.

Keneally, Thomas. *Passenger.* Harcourt.

Kunitz, Stanley. *The Poems of Stanley Kunitz, 1928–1978.* Atlantic/Little.

Lasch, Christopher. *The Culture of Narcissism: American Life in an Age of Diminishing Expectations.* Norton.

Le Roy Ladurie, Emmanuel. *Carnival in Romans.* Braziller.

Levine, Philip. *Seven Years from Somewhere.* Atheneum.

Lewis, Norman. *Naples '44.* Pantheon.

Litwack, Leon. *Been in the Storm So Long: The Aftermath of Slavery.* Knopf.

Lorenz, Konrad. *The Year of the Greylag Goose.* Harcourt.

Lottman, Herbert. *Albert Camus: A Biography.* Doubleday.

Mailer, Norman. *The Executioner's Song.* Little, Brown.

Malamud, Bernard. *Dubin's Lives.* Farrar.

Morgan, Dan. *Merchants of Grain.* Viking.

Morowitz, Harold J. *The Wine of Life and Other Essays on Societies, Energy, and Living Things.* St. Martin's.

Morris, Edmund. *The Rise of Theodore Roosevelt.* Coward.

Munro, Alice. *The Beggar Maid: Stories of Flo and Rose.* Knopf.

Oates, Joyce Carol. *Unholy Loves.* Vanguard.

O'Connor, Flannery. *The Habit of Being: Letters Selected and Edited by Sally Fitzgerald.* Farrar.

Pearson, John. *The Sitwells: A Family's Biography.* Harcourt.

Pritchett, V. S. *The Myth Makers: Literary Essays.* Random.

Puig, Manuel. *Kiss of the Spider Woman.* Knopf.

Roth, Philip. *The Ghost Writer.* Farrar.

Ryan, Cornelius, and Kathryn Morgan Ryan. *A Private Battle.* Simon & Schuster.

Shawcross, William. *Sideshow.* Simon & Schuster.

Spencer, Scott. *Endless Love: A Novel.* Knopf.

Steinfels, Peter. *The Neoconservatives: The Men Who Are Changing America's Politics.* Simon & Schuster.

Tafel, Edgar. *Apprentice to Genius: Years with Frank Lloyd Wright.* McGraw.

Thomas, Gordon, and Max Morgan-Witts. *The Day the Bubble Burst: A Social History of the Wall Street Crash of 1929.* Doubleday.

Updike, John. *The Coup.* Knopf.

Updike, John. *Problems and Other Stories.* Knopf.

Vonnegut, Kurt. *Jailbird.* Delacorte.

Walcott, Derek. *The Star-Apple Kingdom.* Farrar.

Wolfe, Tom. *The Right Stuff.* Farrar.

BEST YOUNG ADULT BOOKS OF 1979

Each year a committee of the Young Adult Services Division of the American Library Association compiles a list of best books for young adults selected on the basis of young adult appeal. These titles must meet acceptable standards of literary merit and provide a variety of subjects for different tastes and a broad range of reading levels. *School Library Journal (SLJ)* also provides a list of best books for young adults. This year the list was compiled by Rose Moorachian and *SLJ's* Greater Boston Area Committee of Public and School Library YA Specialists and published in the January 1980 issue of *SLJ*. The following list combines the titles selected for both lists. The notation ALA or *SLJ* following the price indicates from which list each title was taken.

Allen, George N. *Ri.* Prentice-Hall. $7.95. SLJ.

Anderson, Poul. *The Merman's Children.* Berkley (dist. by Putnam). $11.95. SLJ.

Ashworth, William. *The Carson Factor.* Hawthorn. $10.95. SLJ.

Asimov, Isaac. *Extra-Terrestrial Civilizations.* Crown. $10. SLJ.

Bachman, Richard. *The Long Walk.* Signet (NAL). pap. $1.95. ALA.

Baker, Scott. *Night Child.* Berkley (dist. by Putnam). $10.95. SLJ.

Bridgers, Sue Ellen. *All Together Now.* Knopf. $6.95. ALA.

Comfort, Alex, and Jane Comfort. *The Facts of Love.* Crown. $10. ALA.

Cormier, Robert. *After the First Death.* Pantheon. $7.95. ALA.

Craig, John. *Chappie and Me.* Dodd. $8.95. ALA.

Culin, Charlotte. *Cages of Glass, Flowers of Time.* Bradbury. $8.95. ALA.

Davis, Terry. *Vision Quest.* Viking. $8.95. ALA.

Dickinson, Peter. *Tulku.* Dutton. $8.95. ALA.

Dickinson, Peter, and Wayne Anderson. *The Flight of Dragons.* Harper. $17.50. ALA.

Duncan, Julia C. *Halfway Home.* St. Martin's. $10.95. SLJ.

Edwards, Christopher. *Crazy for God.* Prentice-Hall. $8.95. SLJ.

Epstein, Jacob. *Wild Oats.* Little, Brown. $9.95. SLJ.

Forman, James. *A Ballad for Hogskin Hill.* Farrar. $9.95. ALA.

Fox, Ray E. *Angela Ambrosia.* Knopf. $7.95. SLJ.

Fuller, John G. *The Airmen Who Would Not Die.* Putnam. $10.95. SLJ.

Girion, Barbara, *A Tangle of Roots.* Scribner's. $7.95. ALA.

Guy, Rosa. *The Disappearance.* Delacorte. $8.95. ALA.

Haldeman, Linda. *Lastborn of Elvinwood.* Doubleday. $7.95. ALA.

Hanckel, Frances, and John Cunningham. *A Way of Love, a Way of Life.* Lothrop. $7.95. ALA.

Hard, T. W. *Sum VII.* Harper. $8.95. *SLJ.*

Hartman, David, and Bernard Asbell. *White Coat, White Cane.* Playboy Press/Simon & Schuster. $8.95. ALA.

Helms, Tom. *Against All Odds.* Crowell. $9.95. Warner. pap. $2.50. ALA.

Hinton, S. E. *Tex.* Delacorte. $7.95. ALA.

Ipswitch, Elaine. *Scott Was Here.* Delacorte. $8.95. ALA.

Jenkins, Peter. *A Walk Across America.* Morrow. $12.95. ALA, *SLJ.*

Kaplan, Helen. *Making Sense of Sex.* Simon & Schuster. $10.95. ALA.

Keane, John. *Sherlock Bones.* Lippincott. $8.95. ALA.

Leffland, Ella. *Rumors of Peace.* Harper. $10.95. ALA.

LeGuin, Ursula K. *Malafrena.* Putnam. $11.95. *SLJ.*

LeRoy, Gen. *Cold Feet.* Harper. $7.95. ALA.

Lifton, Betty Jean. *Lost and Found: The Adoption Experience.* Dial. $9.95. *SLJ.*

Macaulay, David. *Motel of the Mysteries.* Houghton. $10, pap. $4.95. ALA.

McCoy, Kathy, and Charles Wibbelsman. *The Teenage Body Book.* Pocket Books. pap. $5.95. ALA.

Marsh, Dave. *Born to Run: The Bruce Springsteen Story.* Doubleday. pap. $7.95. ALA.

Mazer, Harry. *The Last Mission.* Delacorte. $7.95. ALA.

Mazer, Norma Fox. *Up in Seth's Room.* Delacorte. $7.95. ALA.

Meyer, Carolyn. *The Center.* Atheneum. $8.95. ALA.

Meyers, Walter Dean. *The Young Landlords.* Viking. $8.95. ALA.

Nichol, C. W. *The White Shaman.* Little, Brown. $8.95. ALA.

Pascal, Francine. *My First Love and Other Disasters.* Viking. $8.95. ALA.

Peyton, K. M. *Prove Yourself a Hero.* Collins. $6.95. ALA.

Phillips, John Aristotle, and David Michaelis. *Mushroom: The Story of the A-Bomb Kid.* Morrow. $8.95. *SLJ.*

Rabinsky, Leatrice, and Gertrude Mann. *Journey of Conscience.* Collins. $2.95. *SLJ.*

Reed, Kit. *Ballad of T. Rantula.* Little, Brown. $8.95. ALA.

Richardson, Jim. *High School: U.S.A.* St. Martin's. $19.95, pap. $8.95. *SLJ.*

Sandler, Martin. *Story of American Photography: An Illustrated History for Young People.* Little, Brown. $16.95. ALA.

Say, Allen. *Ink-Keeper's Apprentice.* Harper. $7.95. ALA.

Sebestyen, Ouida. *Words by Heart.* Little, Brown. $7.95. ALA.

Seed, Suzanne. *Fine Trades.* Follett. $7.95. ALA.

Shange, Ntozake. *Nappy Edges.* St. Martin's. $7.95. Bantam. pap. $2.50. *SLJ.*

Southerland, Ellease. *Let the Lion Eat Straw.* Scribner's. $7.95. ALA, *SLJ.*

Sterling, Dorothy. *Black Foremothers.* Feminist Press. pap. $4.95. *SLJ.*

Summers, Ian. *Tomorrow and Beyond: Masterpieces of Science Fiction.* Workman. pap. $9.95. ALA.

Thompson, Estelle. *Hunter in the Dark.* Walker. $7.95. ALA.

Torchia, Joseph. *The Kryptonite Kid.* Holt. $7.95. ALA.

Van Leeuwen, Jean. *Seems Like This Road Goes on Forever.* Dial. $7.95. ALA.

Vonnegut, Kurt. *Jailbird.* Delacorte. $9.95. ALA, *SLJ.*

Westall, Robert. *Devil on the Road.* Greenwillow. $7.95. ALA.

Wharton, William. *Birdy.* Knopf. $8.95. ALA, *SLJ.*

Winthrop, Elizabeth. *Knock, Knock, Who's There?* Holiday. $7.95. ALA.

BEST CHILDREN'S BOOKS OF 1979

A list of notable children's books is selected each year by the Notable Children's Books Committee of the Association for Library Service to Children of the American Library Association. The committee is aided by suggestions from school and public children's librarians throughout the United States. The book review editors of *School Library Journal (SLJ)* also compile a list each year, with full annotations, of best books for children. The following list is a combination of ALA's "Notable Children's Books of 1979" and *SLJ's* selection of "Best Books 1979," published in the January 1980 issue of *SLJ.* The source of each selection is indicated by the notation ALA or *SLJ* following the price. [See the article "Literary Prizes" for Newbery, Caldecott, and other award winners—Ed.]

Adoff, Arnold. *Eats: Poems.* Lothrop. $6.95. ALA.

Ahlberg, Janet, and Allan Ahlberg. *Each Peach Pear Plum: An "I Spy" Story.* Viking. $8.95. ALA.

Allison, Linda, and Stella Allison. *Rags: Making a Little Something Out of Almost Nothing.* Potter (dist. by Crown). $14.95, pap. $6.95. *SLJ.*

Ancona, George. *It'a a Baby!* Dutton. $7.95. ALA.

Anno, Mitsumasa. *The King's Flower.* Collins. $7.95. ALA.

Aruego, Jose, and Ariane Dewey. *We Hide, You Seek.* Greenwillow. $7.95. ALA.

Asch, Frank. *Sand Cake.* Parents' Magazine Press. $4.95. *SLJ.*

Avi. *Night Journeys.* Pantheon. $6.95. *SLJ.*

Bawden, Nina. *The Robbers.* Lothrop. $6.95. ALA, *SLJ.*

Bierhorst, John. *A Cry from the Earth: Music of the North American Indians.* Four Winds. $8.95. ALA.

Blos, Joan W. *A Gathering of Days: A New England Girl's Journal, 1830-32.* Scribner's. $8.95. ALA, *SLJ.*

Blegvad, Erik. *Self-Portrait.* Addison-Wesley. $7.95. ALA.

Bosse, Malcolm J. *The 79 Squares.* Crowell. $7.95. ALA.

Bowden, Joan Chase. *Why the Tides Ebb and Flow.* Houghton. $6.95. ALA.

Bridgers, Sue Ellen. *All Together Now.* Knopf. $6.95. ALA.

Bulla, Clyde Robert. *Daniel's Duck.* Harper. $5.95. ALA.

Chess, Victoria. *Alfred's Alphabet Walk.* Greenwillow. $7.95. *SLJ.*

Christian, Mary Blount. *The Lucky Man.* Macmillan. $6.95. *SLJ.*

Cleary, Beverly. *Ramona and Her Mother.* Morrow. $6.75. ALA, *SLJ.*

Cleaver, Vera, and Bill Cleaver. *A Little Destiny.* Lothrop. $7.95. *SLJ.*

Cole, Brock. *The King at the Door.* Doubleday. $7.95. *SLJ.*

Cormier, Robert. *After the First Death.* Pantheon. $7.95. *SLJ.*

de Paola, Tomie. *Big Anthony and the Magic Ring.* Harcourt. pap. $3.95. ALA.

de Wit, Dorothy. *Tales and Legends.* Greenwillow. $8.95. ALA.

Dickinson, Peter. *Tulku*. Dutton. $8.95. *SLJ*.

Dowden, Anne Ophelia. *This Noble Harvest: A Chronicle of Herbs*. Collins. $10.95. *SLJ*.

Elliott, Donald. *Frogs and the Ballet*. Gambit. $9.95. *SLJ*.

Feder, Jane. *Beany*. Pantheon. $4.95. ALA.

Fleischman, Sid. *The Hey Hey Man*. Atlantic/Little. $7.95. *SLJ*.

Fritz, Jean. *Stonewall*. Putnam. $7.95, pap. $3.95. ALA, *SLJ*.

Garfield, Leon. *The Night of the Comet: A Comedy of Courtship Featuring Bostock and Harris*. Delacorte. $7.95. *SLJ*.

Garner, Alan. *The Stone Book*. Collins. $6.95. ALA.

Geras, Adele. *The Girls in the Velvet Frame*. Atheneum. $6.95. ALA.

Gibbons, Gail. *Clocks and How They Go*. Crowell. $6.95. *SLJ*.

Gipson, Fred. *Curly and the Wild Boar*. Harper. $5.95. *SLJ*.

Greenfeld, Howard. *Rosh Hashanah and Yom Kippur*. Holt. $5.95. ALA.

Hall, Donald. *Ox-Cart Man*. Viking. $8.95. ALA, *SLJ*.

Hannam, Charles. *Almost an Englishman*. Deutsch (dist. by Elsevier-Dutton). $7.50. *SLJ*.

Hewett, Joan. *Watching Them Grow: Inside a Zoo Nursery*. Little. $7.95. ALA.

Hinton, S. E. *Tex*. Delacorte. $7.95. *SLJ*.

Horwitz, Johanna. *New Neighbors for Nora*. Morrow. $5.95. ALA.

Howe, Deborah, and James Howe. *Bunnicula: A Rabbit-Tale of Mystery*. Atheneum. $7.95. ALA.

Isadora, Rachel. *Ben's Trumpet*. Greenwillow. $6.95. ALA.

Kalan, Robert. *Blue Sea*. Greenwillow. $6.95. ALA.

Kherdian, David. *The Road from Home: The Story of an Armenian Girl*. Greenwillow. $8.95. ALA.

King, Clive. *Me and My Million*. Crowell. $7.95. *SLJ*.

Konigsburg, E. L. *Throwing Shadows*. Atheneum. $8.95. ALA, *SLJ*.

Krasilovsky, Phyllis. *The Many Who Tried to Save Time*. Doubleday. $4.95. *SLJ*.

Krementz, Jill. *A Very Young Circus Flyer*. Knopf. $9.95. ALA, *SLJ*.

Lasker, David. *The Boy Who Loved Music*. Viking. $9.95. ALA.

Lauber, Patricia. *What's Hatching Out of That Egg?* Crown. $7.95. ALA.

Lawson, Don. *FDR's New Deal*. Crowell. $7.95. ALA.

Lobel, Arnold. *Days with Frog and Toad*. Harper. $5.95. ALA.

———. *A Treeful of Pigs*. Greenwillow. $7.95. ALA.

Lowry, Lois. *Anastasia Krupnik*. Houghton. $6.95. ALA.

McNeill, Janet. *Wait for It and Other Stories*. Faber. pap. $2.95. *SLJ*.

McNulty, Faith. *How to Dig a Hole to the Other Side of the World*. Harper. $6.95. *SLJ*.

Mangurian, David. *Children of the Incas*. Four Winds/Scholastic. $8.95. *SLJ*.

Mark, Jan. *Thunder and Lightnings*. Crowell. $7.95. ALA.

Marshall, James. *Mother Goose*. Farrar. $7.95. ALA.

Massie, Diane Redfield. *Chameleon Was a Spy*. Crowell. $6.95. *SLJ*.

Modell, Frank. *Tooley! Tooley!* Greenwillow. $6.95. *SLJ*.

Myers, Walter Dean. *The Young Landlords*. Viking. $8.95. ALA.

Peyton, K. M. *A Midsummer Night's Death*. Collins. $6.95. ALA.

———. *The Right-Hand Man*. Oxford Univ. Press. $7.95. *SLJ*.

Rice, Eve. *Once in a Wood*. Greenwillow. $5.95. *SLJ*.

Robe, Rosebud Yellow. *Tonweya and the Eagles and Other Lakota Indian Tales.* Dial. $7.95. ALA.

Rockwell, Anne. *The Old Woman and Her Pig & 10 Other Stories.* Crowell. $10.95. ALA, *SLJ.*

Roever, J. M. *Snake Secrets.* Walker. $7.95. ALA.

Sandler, Martin W. *The Story of American Photography.* Little. $16.95. ALA, *SLJ.*

Say, Allen. *The Ink-Keeper's Apprentice.* Harper. $7.95. ALA.

Sebestyen, Ouida. *Words by Heart.* Atlantic/Little. $7.95. ALA, *SLJ.*

Seixas, Judith S. *Living with a Parent Who Drinks Too Much.* Greenwillow. $6.95. ALA.

Shreve, Susan. *Family Secrets: Five Very Important Stories.* Knopf. $5.95. ALA.

Shub, Elizabeth. *Seeing Is Believing.* Greenwillow. $5.95. ALA.

Shulevitz, Uri. *The Treasure.* Farrar. $7.95. ALA.

Simon, Seymour. *The Long View into Space.* Crown. $7.95. ALA, *SLJ.*

Stevenson, James. *Fast Friends: Two Stories.* Greenwillow. $5.95. ALA.

———. *Monty.* Greenwillow. $7.95. *SLJ.*

Stiles, David. *The Tree House Book.* Avon. pap. $3.95. ALA.

Sutcliff, Rosemary. *Song for a Dark Queen.* Crowell. $7.95. ALA.

Thrasher, Crystal. *Between Dark and Daylight.* Atheneum. $8.95. *SLJ.*

Van Allsburg, Chris. *The Garden of Abdul Gasazi.* Houghton. $8.95. ALA, *SLJ.*

Van Leeuwen, Jean. *Tales of Oliver Pig.* Dial. LB $5.89, pap. $1.95. *SLJ.*

Von Canon, Claudia. *The Moonclock.* Houghton. $6.95. ALA.

Walker, Barbara M. *The Little House Cookbook.* Harper. $8.95. ALA, *SLJ.*

Watanabe, Shigeo. *How Do I Put It On?* Collins. $6.95. ALA.

Westall, Robert. *The Devil on the Road.* Greenwillow. $6.95. *SLJ.*

Willard, Nancy. *The Island of the Grass King: The Further Adventures of Anatole.* Harcourt. $7.95. *SLJ.*

Wolkstein, Diane. *White Wave: A Chinese Tale.* Crowell. $7.95. ALA.

Zhitkov, Boris. *How I Hunted Little Fellows.* Trans. by Djemma Bider. Illus. by Paul O. Zelinsky. Dodd. $6.95. ALA, *SLJ.*

BEST SELLERS OF 1979: HARDCOVER FICTION AND NONFICTION

Daisy Maryles

Associate Editor, *Publishers Weekly*

A look at the 1979 annual best seller lists supports a number of claims heard along publishers' row in the last few months:

The best selling novels of 1979 sold at a lower rate than top novels have moved at in previous years. Indeed, the combined sales of just the top two 1978 fiction titles—*Chesapeake* and *War and Remembrance*—totaled more than the combined sales of the top six best sellers of 1979.

Note: Reprinted from *Publishers Weekly,* February 22, 1980, where the article was entitled "Hardcover Bestsellers."

Only fiction by well-known writers with proven track records seemed to sell in significant quantities in hardcover during 1979. In fact, 12 of the top 15 novelists are veterans of *PW*'s annual lists, as are 7 of the 10 runners-up.

Unit sales of top-selling nonfiction remained high in 1979: 10 of the top 15 sold over 200,000 copies apiece, with the top four selling over 400,000 copies and numbers 1 and 2 well over 600,000.

High sales were spread over a broader range of titles this year. Unit sales for the top 25 novels set a new high, with 21 books reaching sales of over 100,000 copies and 24 going above 96,000 copies. The nonfiction list of the top 25 bottomed out in the high 90,000s, and several books selling over 90,000 did not make the list.

Some trends—new and not so new—can also be spotted in the list of hardcover best sellers. Traditional first novels—books with fast-moving plots and large dollops of suspense and/or sex that are released with much fanfare and notable word of mouth—are absent from the 1979 lineup. But two "first novels" of a different ilk—*Third World War: August 1985* and *Hanta Yo*—are represented, indicating that novels that read like nonfiction because of the extensive research on which the plots are based are becoming increasingly popular. The themes running through nonfiction best sellers are repeaters. How-to (missing from the 1978 top books) returns with two books on managing one's diet and body and two others on managing assets. Humor and government also continue to be popular nonfiction themes.

GATHERING THE SALES FIGURES

The books listed in the top 15 and among the fiction and nonfiction runners-up are ranked according to sales figures supplied by the publishers. All figures, they claim, reflect only 1979 U.S. trade sales—that is, sales to bookstores, wholesalers, and libraries—and omit any book club and overseas and direct-mail transactions. However, some books appear in the listings without their copy-sales figure or, as in the case of Doubleday, with approximate numbers (e.g., 12,000+). Missing or more specific figures in such cases were submitted to *PW* in confidence, for use only in placing titles in their correct positions on a specific list.

It is important to keep in mind that the word "sales" as used here refers to copies a publisher shipped and billed. In many cases, the 1979 sales figures include books still on bookstore and wholesaler shelves at the end of the year. While publishers may expect or hope that these books will eventually be sold to consumers, many of them may wend their way back as returns, since publishers don't yet have a complete accounting of post-Christmas returns on their books and since the last quarter of the year is when they ship the largest quantities of books to retailers and wholesalers across the country.

Some publishers continued to question the veracity of figures that their colleagues might quote for these lists, noting that sales figures in some houses are exaggerated to get an author on an annual list. Although devising a foolproof method for collecting sales figures for best seller lists remains an unmet challenge, *PW* thought it might be interesting to share with its readers the B. Dalton chain's 1979 best sellers, derived from sales to book customers in 410 Dalton outlets across the country between January 1, 1979 and December 31, 1979.

A quick comparison of the *PW* and Dalton lists shows that although titles attained different positions on these lists, a number of the same books appear on both lists. In fact, the same 13 fiction and 12 nonfiction titles enjoy spots among the top 15 of both lists.

TOP FICTION BEST SELLERS

Heading the 1979 fiction list is Robert Ludlum with 250,000 copies of his latest espionage thriller, *The Matarese Circle*, sold last year. This makes him the second author of this genre to head an annual list; in 1964, John le Carré made it to first place with *The Spy Who Came in from the Cold*, which thus became the first thriller to head an annual list. Ludlum is no stranger to these annual lists. He appeared in the number 8 position in both 1973 and 1978 with *The Matlock Paper* and *The Holcroft Covenant*, respectively.

Le Carré makes one of his return appearances on an annual list with his latest thriller, *Smiley's People*, which enjoyed a fast sale of 157,000 copies in the last month of the year, making it the number 10 best seller in 1979. His books have made the annual lists several times since 1964. Le Carré has claimed the number 4 spot four times in recent years—in 1965 with *The Looking Glass War*, in 1968 with *A Small Town in Germany*, in 1974 with *Tinker, Tailor, Soldier, Spy*, and in 1977 with *The Honourable Schoolboy*.

William Styron's *Sophie's Choice* is the number 2 fiction best seller in 1979, with sales of 203,000 copies. It is the only novel besides Ludlum's that sold more than 200,000 copies last year. Styron's earlier best selling novel, *The Confessions of Nat Turner*—about a slave insurrection in the South in 1831—tied for second place on the 1967 annual list and won the author a Pulitzer Prize.

The two first novels among the top 15 sellers—*The Third World War: August 1985* and *Hanta Yo*—point to a growing popularity for the fiction category called *faction*, which blends fiction and fact and, in the case of these two titles, had many booksellers reporting the books as nonfiction best sellers. With sales of 165,000 copies, *Third World War* placed number 9 on this year's list. Writing in the style of documentary history, the unlikely authors included General Sir John Hackett, former deputy chief of the general staff and commander-in-chief of the British Army of the Rhine, and a team of NATO military experts. For *Hanta Yo*, which has sales of over 130,000 copies, author Ruth Beebe Hill spent 25 years studying the Dakota Indians on whom the saga is based.

In the sixth spot, with 175,000 copies sold, is *The Dead Zone* by Stephen King. This is King's first time on an annual list, but he is no newcomer to weekly best seller lists, especially of paperbacks: a King novel, *The Stand*, currently leads *PW*'s weekly mass market list.

Aside from the three new names, all the rest of the top 15 novels are by seasoned pros who have made several appearances on these annual lists. They include Arthur Hailey, Harold Robbins, Kurt Vonnegut, Mary Stewart, Richard Bach, and Peter Benchley.

In the number 3 spot is Hailey with *Overload*, a novel about an energy crisis that could result in a permanent blackout, that sold over 187,000 copies in 1979. In his other appearances on these lists Hailey captured the number 1 spot in 1968 with *Airport* and was number 1 again in 1971 with *Wheels*. Harold Robbins, whose *Memories of Another Day* is number 4 on this list, with sales of 187,000 copies, first appeared on an annual list in 1961 when *The Carpetbaggers* was number 5, with sales of 108,000 copies; his most recent reappearance was in 1977, in the number 6 spot with *Dreams Die First*.

Kurt Vonnegut's latest, *Jailbird*, led *PW*'s weekly best seller list from the end of October through the busy Christmas buying season and racked up 184,031 sales by the end of the year to become the number 5 fiction best seller in 1979. In 1973 Vonnegut's *Breakfast of Champions* hit the number 3 spot on an annual list, and in 1976 *Slapstick or Lonesome No More* made it to number 7.

Mary Stewart fans continue to remain faithful, and her final volume in the

Arthurian saga, *The Last Enchantment*, sold enough copies to secure the number 7 spot. Beginning with 1964, every third year has seen a new Stewart novel on an annual list; most recently, *The Hollow Hills*, which was number 6 in 1973, and *Touch Not the Cat*, number 9 in 1976.

While Richard Bach makes it to the number 13 spot with sales of 147,399 copies of *There's No Such Place as Far Away*, this is a far cry from the incredible success attained by his first two books. Bach's *Jonathan Livingston Seagull* is among the few titles to hit the number 1 spot two years in a row—in 1972 with sales of more than 1.8 million and in 1973 with sales of 500,000. Bach's second book, *Illusions*, also enjoyed two seccessive years on annual lists—it was number 3 in 1977 with sales of 300,000 copies and number 7 in 1978 with sales of 162,688 more.

Sales of more than 130,000 copies of Peter Benchley's *The Island* make it number 14; it's the author's third novel with a seagoing background. His first two, *Jaws* and *The Deep*, floated to the number 3 and number 5 spots in 1974 and 1976, respectively.

Howard Fast, Ken Follett, and Joseph Heller make their second appearances on an annual list. Fast finished off his trilogy about California with *The Establishment*, which sold 168,665 copies in 1979 to garner the number 8 spot; the middle installment, *Second Generation*, was number 9 in 1978. Follett's thriller *Triple* made it to the number 11 spot a year after his *Eye of the Needle* secured the number 10 spot on an annual list. Heller's third novel, *Good as Gold*, sold 151,000 copies in 1979, enough to get the number 12 spot this year. In 1974 his *Something Happened* hit number 5 with sales of 143,000 copies.

THE FICTION RUNNERS-UP

Only three novelists are among the 10 fiction runners-up who have never made it to an annual list or a runner-up position before—Rona Jaffe, Len Deighton, and Peter Straub. One repeat from last year is Herman Wouk's *War and Remembrance*, which was the number 2 fiction leader in 1978 and remained on *PW*'s weekly list during all of 1979, capturing the lead position for the first three months of that year. Norman Mailer's latest—a true-life novel of the life and death of Gary Gilmore, executed in Utah for murder—was yet another example of the growing popularity of faction.

In ranked order, the 10 fiction runners-up are *Shibumi* by Trevanian (Crown, published 5/14/79; 129,533 copies sold); *Class Reunion* by Rona Jaffe (Delacorte, 5/14/79; 113,296); *Shadow of the Moon* by M. M. Kaye (St. Martin's, 9/21/79; 109,214); *War and Remembrance* by Herman Wouk (Little, Brown, 10/17/78); *SS-GB* by Len Deighton (Knopf, 2/16/79; 106,000); *The Top of the Hill* by Irwin Shaw (Delacorte, 11/12/79; 104,217); *The Green Ripper* by John D. MacDonald (Lippincott, 10/17/79; 98,547); *The Executioner's Song* by Norman Mailer (Little, Brown, 10/15/79); *Ghost Story* by Peter Straub (Coward, McCann & Geoghegan, 4/5/79; 96,000); and *Day of Judgment* by Jack Higgins (Holt, Rinehart and Winston, 3/26/79; 85,000).

THE NONFICTION BEST SELLERS

Humor was welcomed to top spots on the 1979 nonfiction best seller chart. The ever-popular funny lady, Erma Bombeck, again landed first on *PW*'s annual list, with sales of 692,000 copies of her latest *Aunt Erma's Cope Book*, a parody of self-help manuals. In 1978 Bombeck also was NF number 1, with sales of about 700,000 copies for *If Life Is a Bowl of Cherries—What Am I Doing in the Pits?* Her *The Grass Is Always Greener Over the Septic Tank* enjoyed the number 6 position in 1976 and the number 9 spot in 1977. The "wild and crazy" comedian, Steve Martin, found at least 450,000 fans for his book of satire, *Cruel Shoes*, which earned the number 4 spot on this year's list and includes chapters on "How to Fold Soup" and "What to Say When the Duck Shows Up."

When not laughing, Americans were interested in keeping trim. Two diet books dominated weekly best seller charts for a good part of 1979. The second nonfiction leader, *The Complete Scarsdale Diet*, first appeared on *PW*'s weekly best seller list on January 22 and held the number 1 position from the end of March through November 19, selling 642,500 copies during that time. In the number 5 place this year is *The Pritikin Program for Diet and Exercise*, which sold about 319,000 copies in 1979; it has been on weekly *PW* lists from early May through the end of the year, often in the number 2 or number 3 position.

Another area of general concern seemed to be money, with readers interested in learning how to keep ahead of inflation. One book that was on the weekly best seller lists for almost 11 months in 1979 was *How to Prosper during the Coming Bad Years*. Subtitled *A Crash Course in Personal and Financial Survival*, it hit the number 3 spot on the annual list with sales of 450,000 copies. In the number 12 position, yet another best selling financial how-to is *How to Become Financially Independent by Investing in Real Estate*, which sold 184,000 copies in 1979. First published in November 1977, the book had sold about 90,000 copies by the end of 1978. After the author insisted that his book could be a national best seller, publisher Simon & Schuster redistributed it in May 1979 with a hefty advertising budget (*PW*, Jan. 18) and a new marketing program. It made national best seller lists in early fall.

Interest in government continued in 1979, and the first installment of Kissinger's memoirs, *The White House Years*, became an immediate best seller, selling well enough to ease into the number 6 spot this year. Booksellers seemed surprised that its high price —$22.95—resulted in almost no consumer price resistance.

Another surprise for booksellers was the early availability of *The Brethren: Inside the Supreme Court*, coauthored by the best selling Watergate chronicler Bob Woodward and Scott Armstrong (*PW*, Dec. 25, 1979, and Feb. 8). Expected in January, the book was shipped in early December shortly after the authors appeared on "60 Minutes." It seemed to be the title that everyone wanted to buy, and keeping it in stock became the major problem during the Christmas sales period. The 250,000 copies the publisher was able to ship in time for Christmas shopping secured it the number 8 spot on the 1979 list. It is the current nonfiction leader on weekly national best seller charts.

In the number 7 spot is *Lauren Bacall by Myself*, which enjoyed brisk sales in the early part of the year when it perched on top of hardcover national best seller charts. By the end of 1979 the autobiographical memoir had sold 281,000 copies in hardcover and even made it to the top of the weekly mass market paperback list.

Every few years a major sports book sells to enough fans to make it to the top of an annual list: this year the controversy that ensued after the publication of *The Bronx Zoo*, an inside look at the New York Yankees by a former team player (later traded to the Texas Rangers), sold 193,000 copies, placing number 11 on this list.

A familiar cookbook got a complete rehaul, courtesy of a new publisher: *The Fannie Farmer Cookbook* appeared in a new, twelfth edition by Knopf. Not only were all the recipes retested, but the book was rewritten and redesigned. It sold 165,000 copies in the last quarter of the year, enough to get the number 14 spot on the list.

The rest of the 1979 nonfiction best sellers are by writers who are also familiar to end-of-the-year best seller charts. In ninth position with sales of 227,071 is Robert Ringer's *Restoring the American Dream*, in which he criticizes excessive regulation by government of day-to-day life. Two earlier Ringer books—*Winning through Intimida-*

tion and *Looking Out for #1*—placed number 2 in 1975 and 1977, their respective years of publication.

Charles Paul Conn scores again this year with sales of 210,000 copies of *The Winner's Circle*, which offers more information on the Amway Corporation. His first book on Amway, *The Possible Dream*, was the number 6 best seller in 1977, with sales of over 211,000 copies.

James Herriot, the well-known British veterinarian whose animal tales have been the subject of several best sellers, takes his readers through the Yorkshire countryside, the same setting as that of his earlier books. Selling 165,000 copies, *James Herriot's Yorkshire* takes the number 13 spot on the list.

Rounding off the top 15 is David Halberstam's *The Powers That Be*, a study of the growing clout of four media giants (Time Inc., CBS, the *Los Angeles Times*, and the *Washington Post*). This sold 160,000 copies in 1979. It is the author's first book since his Vietnam best seller, *The Best and the Brightest*, which sold over 107,000 copies in 1972—enough to make it a lead title among that year's runners-up.

THE NONFICTION RUNNERS-UP

The list of nonfiction runners-up comprises new books by best selling authors Lewis Thomas, Carl Sagan, Thomas Thompson, and Sylvia Porter. The slate also includes Tom Wolfe's eighth and most popular book, dealing with the first seven astronauts; a collaboration on Sophia Loren by A. E. Hotchner, who also worked with Doris Day on her revealing memoirs; a treatise on the death of elegance by Stanley Marcus, former chairman of Neiman-Marcus; a how-to by a pediatrician showing that both illness and behavior problems in children can be helped by proper diet; and Abrams's latest illustrated book of fey characters, *Giants* (which failed to achieve the success of such earlier books as *Gnomes* and *Faeries*). The last nonfiction runner-up proves that Watergate can still entice readers; here U.S. District Court Judge Sirica presents his views on the subject.

In ranked order, the 10 nonfiction runners-up are *The Medusa and the Snail: More Notes of a Biology Watcher* by Lewis Thomas (Viking, published 5/21/79; 158,000 copies sold); *The Right Stuff* by Tom Wolfe (Farrar, Straus & Giroux, 9/27/79; 144,140); *Broca's Brain: Reflections on the Romance of Science* by Carl Sagan (Random House, 5/31/79; 134,000); *Serpentine* by Thomas Thompson (Doubleday, 10/12/79; 120,000+); *Sophia, Living and Loving: Her Own Story* by A. E. Hotchner (Morrow, 2/26/79); *Sylvia Porter's New Money Book for the 80's* by Sylvia Porter (Doubleday, 9/21/79; 105,000+); *Quest for the Best* by Stanley Marcus (Viking, 8/79; 105,000); *Feed Your Kids Right* by Dr. Lendon Smith (McGraw-Hill, 4/30/79; 103,000); *Giants* illustrated by Carolyn Scrace, Juan Wijngaard and Julek Heller and devised by David Larkin (Abrams, 10/79); and *To Set the Record Straight* by John J. Sirica (Norton, 4/23/79).

Each year a number of new hardcover Better Homes and Gardens books sell in sufficient quantities to appear on these annual best seller lists, but they are excluded because of their lower prices. In 1979, BH&G had three such contenders: *Favorite American Wines and How to Enjoy Them* sold 135,712 copies during the year; *Food Processor Cook Book* sold 129,538; and *Fix It Fast Cook Book* sold 102,006.

New American Library's hardcover *Weight Watchers New Program Cookbook*, a heavily revised edition published October 1978, sold approximately 300,000 copies in 1979; 1978 sales were 220,000 copies.

HARDCOVER TOP SELLERS*

Fiction

1. *The Matarese Circle* by Robert Ludlum (March 14, 1979) Richard Marek (Putnam, dist.)
2. *Sophie's Choice* by William Styron (June 11, 1979) Random House
3. *Overload* by Arthur Hailey (January 5, 1979) Doubleday
4. *Memories of Another Day* by Harold Robbins (November 9, 1979) Simon & Schuster
5. *Jailbird* by Kurt Vonnegut (September 11, 1979) Delacorte Press/Seymour Lawrence
6. *The Dead Zone* by Stephen King (August 30, 1979) Viking
7. *The Last Enchantment* by Mary Stewart (July 20, 1979) Morrow
8. *The Establishment* by Howard Fast (October 5, 1979) Houghton Mifflin
9. *The Third World War: August 1985* by General Sir John Hackett, et al. (February 28, 1979) Macmillan
10. *Smiley's People* by John le Carré (January 2, 1980; shipped early to reach bookstores in early December) Knopf
11. *Triple* by Ken Follett (October 22, 1979) Arbor House
12. *Good as Gold* by Joseph Heller (March 23, 1979) Simon & Schuster
13. *There's No Such Place as Far Away* by Richard Bach (April 27, 1979) Delacorte
14. *The Island* by Peter Benchley (May 4, 1979) Doubleday
15. *Hanta Yo* by Ruth Beebe Hill (February 9, 1979) Doubleday

Nonfiction

1. *Aunt Erma's Cope Book* by Erma Bombeck (November 14, 1979) McGraw-Hill
2. *The Complete Scarsdale Medical Diet* by Herman Tarnower, M.D., and Samm Sinclair Baker (January 1, 1979) Rawson, Wade
3. *How to Prosper during the Coming Bad Years* by Howard J. Ruff (January 23, 1979) Times Books
4. *Cruel Shoes* by Steve Martin (June 15, 1979) Putnam
5. *The Pritikin Program for Diet and Exercise* by Nathan Pritikin and Patrick McGrady, Jr. (April 2, 1979) Grosset & Dunlap
6. *White House Years* by Henry Kissinger (October 23, 1979) Little, Brown
7. *Laren Bacall by Myself* by Lauren Bacall (January 10, 1979) Knopf
8. *The Brethren: Inside the Supreme Court* by Bob Woodward and Scott Armstrong (January 1980; shipped in early December) Simon & Schuster
9. *Restoring the American Dream* by Robert J. Ringer (August 20, 1979) QED (Harper & Row, dist.)
10. *The Winner's Circle* by Charles Paul Conn (May 14, 1979) Revell
11. *The Bronx Zoo* by Sparky Lyle and Peter Golenbock (April 20, 1979) Crown
12. *How to Become Financially Independent by Investing in Real Estate* by Albert J. Lowry (November 1977; redistributed in February 1979 and marketed as a new title) Simon & Schuster
13. *James Herriot's Yorkshire* by James Herriot (October 30, 1979) St. Martin's
14. *The Fannie Farmer Cookbook* by Marion Cunningham (August 1979) Knopf
15. *The Powers That Be* by David Halberstam (May 7, 1979) Knopf

*Rankings on this list are determined by sales figures provided by the publishers; the numbers reflect reports of copies "shipped and billed" only and should not be regarded as net sales figures since publishers do not yet know what their final returns will be.

Part 7
Directory of Organizations

Directory of Library and Related Organizations

NATIONAL LIBRARY AND INFORMATION-INDUSTRY ASSOCIATIONS, UNITED STATES AND CANADA

AMERICAN ASSOCIATION OF LAW LIBRARIES
53 W. Jackson Blvd., Chicago, IL 60604
312-939-4764

OBJECT

"To promote librarianship, to develop and increase the usefulness of law libraries, to cultivate the science of law librarianship and to foster a spirit of cooperation among members of the profession." Established 1906. Memb. 2,850. Dues (Inst.) $80–400; (Indiv.) $40. Year. June 1 to May 31.

MEMBERSHIP

Persons officially connected with a law library or with a law section of a state or general library, separately maintained; and institutions. Associate membership available for others.

OFFICERS (JUNE 1979–JUNE 1980)

Pres. C. E. Bolden, Washington State Law Lib., Temple of Justice, Olympia, WA 98504; *V.P. & Pres.-Elect.* Francis Gates, Columbia Univ. Law Lib., 435 W. 116 St., New York, NY 10027; *Secy.* Cameron Allen, Rutgers, The State Univ., School of Law Lib., 15 Washington St., Newark, NJ 07102; *Treas.* Joyce Malden, Municipal Reference Lib., 1004 City Hall, Chicago, IL 60602; *Past Pres.* J. Myron Jacobstein, Stanford Univ., Law Lib., Stanford, CA 94305.

EXECUTIVE BOARD

Officers; Sue Dyer; Mary Fisher; Lorraine A. Kulpa; Stanley Pearce; Kathie Price; Carol West.

COMMITTEE CHAIRPERSONS

(Address correspondence to national headquarters.)

Audiovisual. Randall T. Peterson.
Cataloging and Classification. Phyllis C. Marion.
Certification Board. Iris Wildman.
CONELL. Velvet Glass.
Constitution & Bylaws. Marian Boner.
Copyright. Julius Marke.
Education. Sarah K. Wiant.
Elections. Rita Dermody.
Exchange of Duplicates. Merle J. Slyhoff.
Foreign, Comparative and International Law. Suzy Lee.
Index to Foreign Legal Periodicals. Zuhair Jwaideh.
Indexing of Periodical Literature. Marlene C. McGuirl.
Joseph L. Andrews Bibliographic Award. Mortimer D. Schwartz.
Law Library Journal. Patrick E. Kehoe.
Legislation and Legal Developments. Roger Jacobs.
Membership. Barbara White.

Memorials. George Skinner.
Nominations. Bernard Reams.
Placement. Albert Brecht.
Public Relations. Dianne Witkowski.
Publications. Richard L. Beer.
Recruitment. Robin Mills.
Relations with Publishers and Dealers. Jacquelyn Jurkins.
Scholarships. Nancy J. Kitchen.
Standards. Patricia A. Wyatt.

SPECIAL INTEREST SECTION CHAIRPERSONS

Automation & Scientific Development. Thomas R. Heitz, British Columbia Law Lib. Foundation, Vancouver Lib., Courthouse, 800 W. Georgia St., Vancouver, B.C. V6C 1P6, Canada.

Contemporary Social Problems. David S. Yen, Southwestern Univ., School of Law Lib., 675 S. Westmoreland Ave., Los Angeles, CA 90005.

Government Documents. Kamla King, Wilkinson, Cragun & Barker, 1735 New York Ave. N.W., Washington, DC 20006.

Law Library Service to Institutional Residents. Cossette Sun, Alameda County Law Lib., Court House, Oakland, CA 94612.

O.C.L.C.-Law Libraries. Diane Hillmann, Cornell Univ., Law Lib., Myron Taylor Hall, Ithaca, NY 14853.

Private Law Libraries. Marie Wallace, Kindel & Anderson, 555 S. Flower St., Los Angeles, Ca 90071.

Readers' Services. Janet Wishinsky, De Paul Univ., Law Lib., 25 E. Jackson Blvd., Chicago, IL 60604.

State, Court and County Law Libraries. John Sigel, California Supreme Court Lib., Rm. 4241, State Bldg. Annex, San Francisco, CA 94102.

Technical Services. Phyllis C. Marion, Univ. of Minnesota Law Lib., Rm. 140-B, Minneapolis, MN 55455.

REPRESENTATIVES

ABA (American Bar Association) Package Plan. William Powers.

ABA Section on Administrative Law. Mary Oliver.

ABA Section on Economics of Law Practice. Mary Oliver.

ABA Section on Science and Technology. Mary Oliver.

ABA Section on Legal Education and Admission to the Bar. Mary Oliver.

American Correctional Association. D. A. Divilbiss.

American Library Association. Librarian Administration Division. Statistics Coordinating Committee. David Thomas.

American National Standards Institute. Committee PH-5. Larry Wenger.

American National Standards Institute. Committee Z-39. Robert L. Oakley.

American Society for Information Science. Signe Larson.

Association of American Law Schools. Betty LeBus.

British-Irish Association of Law Libraries. O. James Werner.

Canadian Association of Law Libraries. Thomas R. Heitz.

Council of National Library Associations. Al Coco; Jane Hammond.

Council of National Library Associations. Ad Hoc Committee on Copyright. Julius Marke.

International Association of Law Libraries. Anita K. Head.

International Federation of Library Associations. Helena Von Pfeil.

Joint Committee on Union List of Serials. Pat Piper.

Library of Congress. Carleton Kenyon.

Special Libraries Association. Jack Ellenberger.

Universal Serials & Book Exchange. Lawrence L. Kiefer.

U.S. Copyright Office. Ellen Mahar.

AMERICAN LIBRARY ASSOCIATION
Executive Director, Robert Wedgeworth
50 E. Huron St., Chicago, IL 60611
312-944-6780

OBJECT

The American Library Association is an organization for librarians and libraries with the overarching objective of promoting and improving library service and librarianship. Memb. (Indiv.) 35,798; (Inst.) 3,075. Dues (Indiv.) $50; (Nonsalaried Librarians) $15; (Trustee & Lay Members) $20; (Student) $10; (Foreign Indiv.) $30; (Inst.) $50 & up (depending upon operating expenses of institution).

MEMBERSHIP

Any person, library, or other oganization interested in library service and librarianship.

OFFICERS

Pres. Thomas J. Galvin, School of Lib. & Info. Science, Univ. of Pittsburgh, Pittsburgh, PA 15260; *V.P. & Pres.-Elect.* Peggy A. Sullivan, Chicago Public Lib., 425 N. Michigan, Chicago, IL 60611; *Treas.* William Chait, 38 Deer Run La., Hilton Head Island, SC 29928 (1980); *Exec. Dir.* (ex officio). Robert Wedgeworth. (Address general correspondence to the executive director.)

EXECUTIVE BOARD

The officers and immediate past pres.; Russell Shank (1980); Brooke E. Sheldon (1980); R. Kathleen Molz (1980); Norman Horrocks (1981); Donald Trottier (1981); Connie R. Dunlap (1982); Grace Slocum (1982); E. J. Josey (1983); Ella Gaines Yates (1983).

ENDOWMENT TRUSTEES

William V. Jackson (1980); John Juergensmeyer (1981); John Velde, Jr. (1982).

DIVISIONS

See the separate entries that follow: American Assn. of School Libns., American Lib. Trustee Assn., Assn. for Lib. Service to Children, Assn. of College and Research Libs., Assn. of Specialized and Cooperative Lib. Agencies, Lib. Admin. and Management Assn., Lib. and Info. Technology Assn., Public Lib. Assn., Reference and Adult Services Div., Resources and Technical Services Div., Young Adult Services Div.

PUBLICATIONS

American Libraries (11 issues; memb.).
ALA Handbook of Organization, 1979–1980 (ann.; personal memb.).
ALA Membership Directory (ann.; $10).
ALA Yearbook (ann.; $35).
Booklist (23 issues; $32).
Choice (11 issues; $40).

ROUND TABLE CHAIRPERSONS

(ALA staff liaison is given in parentheses.)

Exhibits. Jean Mester, H. W. Wilson Co., 950 University Ave., Bronx, NY 10452 (Chris Hoy).

Federal Librarians. Beth Fodor, U.S. Fish & Wildlife Service, One Gateway Center, Newton Center, MA 02158 (James Lockwood).

Government Documents. Francis J. Buckley, Detroit Public Lib., 5201 Wood-

Note: For a report on ALA activities during 1979, see the National Associations section of Part 1—*Ed.*

ward Ave., Detroit, MI 48202 (Bill Drewett).

Intellectual Freedom. Clara Jackson, 424 E. Summit St., Kent, OH 44240 (Roger L. Funk).

International Relations. Donald F. Jay, Humanities and Social Science Research Center, New York Public Lib., New York, NY 10018 (Jane Wilson).

Junior Members. Beth Bingham, E. Baton Rouge Parish Lib., 5511 Goodwood Blvd., Baton Rouge, LA 70806 (Robert Wedgeworth).

Library History. Donald E. Oehlerts, Miami Univ. Lib., Oxford, OH 45056 (Joel M. Lee).

Library Instruction. Jon Lindgren, Owen D. Young Lib., St. Lawrence Univ., Canton, NY 13617 (Jeniece Guy).

Library Research. Jerome Yavarkovsky, Columbia Univ. Lib., 535 W. 114 St., New York, NY 10027 (Mary Jo Lynch).

Social Responsibilities. Marjorie Joramo, Hennepin County Lib., Brooklyn Center, Edina, MN 55429 (Jean E. Coleman).

Staff Organization. Sharon Adley, Lake County Public Lib., 1919 W. Lincoln Hwy., Merrillville, IN 46410 (John Katzenberger).

COMMITTEE CHAIRPERSONS

Accreditation. Charles D. Churchwell, Dean of Lib. Services, Washington Univ., St. Louis, MO 63130 (Elinor Yungmeyer).

"American Libraries," Editorial Advisory Committee for. John Lubans, Asst. Libn. for Public Services, Univ. of Houston, One Main St., Houston, TX 77002 (Arthur Plotnik).

Awards. Marilyn Hinshaw, Assoc. Dir., Daniel Boone Regional Lib., 100 W. Broadway, Box 1267, Columbia, MO 65205 (Ann M. Cunniff).

Chapter Relations (Standing). Dadie Perlov, Exec. Dir., New York Lib. Assn., Suite 1242, 60 E. 42 St., New York, NY 10017 (to be appointed).

Conference Program (Standing). New York, 1980 Conference. Thomas J. Galvin, Dean, School of Lib. & Info. Science, Univ. of Pittsburgh, Pittsburgh, PA 15260. San Francisco, 1981 Conference. Peggy A. Sullivan, Asst. Commissioner, Chicago Public Lib., 425 N. Michigan Ave., Chicago, IL 60611 (Ruth R. Frame).

Constitution and Bylaws (Standing). Susanna Alexander, Missouri State Lib., 308 E. High St., Jefferson City, MO 65101 (Miriam L. Hornback).

Council Orientation (Special). Patricia B. Pond, Assoc. Dean, School of Lib. & Info. Science, Univ. of Pittsburgh, Pittsburgh, PA 15260 (Miriam L. Hornback).

Disadvantaged, Office for Library Service to the (Standing, Advisory). Doreitha R. Madden, Lib. Outreach Service, New Jersey State Lib., Trenton, NJ 08625 (Jean E. Coleman).

Equal Rights Amendment (Task Force). Kay Cassell, Bethlehem Public Lib., 451 Delaware Ave., Delmar, NY 12054; Alice B. Ihrig, 9322 S. 53 Ave., Oak Lawn, IL 60453 (Peggy O'Donnell).

Instruction in the Use of Libraries (Standing). Joseph A. Boisse, Samuel Paley Lib., Temple Univ., Philadelphia, PA 19122 (Andrew M. Hansen).

Intellectual Freedom (Standing, Council). Frances C. Dean, Montgomery County Public Schools, Rockville, MD 20850 (Judith F. Krug).

International Relations (Standing Council). Jean E. Lowrie, School of Libnshp., Western Michigan Univ., Kalamazoo, MI 49001 (Jane Wilson).

Legal Counsel for Replevin, Advisory Committee to (Ad Hoc). Mattie U. Russell, Curator of Manuscripts, Duke Univ., Durham, NC 27706 (Robert Wedgeworth).

Legislation (Standing Council). Ella G. Yates, Public Lib., 10 Pryor St. S.W., Atlanta, GA 30303 (Eileen D. Cooke).

Library Education (Standing, Council). Annette Phinazee, School of Lib. Science, North Carolina Central Univ., Durham, NC 27707 (Margaret Myers).

Library Personnel Resources, Office for (Standing, Advisory). David Dowell, Duke Univ. Lib., Durham, NC 27706 (Margaret Myers).

Mediation, Arbitration, and Inquiry, Staff Committee on (Standing). Robert Wedgeworth, ALA Headquarters, 50 E. Huron St., Chicago, IL 60611.

Membership (Standing). Samuel Simon, Finklestein Memorial Lib., 19 S. Madison Ave., Spring Valley, NY 10977 (Peggy Barber).

National Library Week (Standing). Sue Fontaine, Info. Officer, Washington State Lib., Olympia, WA 98504 (Peggy Barber).

Organization (Standing, Council). Arthur Curley, Public Lib., 5201 Woodward Ave., Detroit, MI 48202 (Ruth R. Frame).

Planning (Standing, Council). Juanita Doares, Public Lib., 42 St. and Fifth Ave., Rm. 112A, New York, NY 10018 (Ruth R. Frame).

Professional Ethics (Standing, Council). Barbara Rollock, Public Lib., 8 E. 40 St., New York, NY 10016 (Judith F. Krug).

Program Assessment Processes, Review (Special). Edward G. Holley, Dean, School of Lib. Science, Univ. of North Carolina, Chapel Hill, NC 27514.

Program Evaluation and Support (Standing, Council). Gerald Shields, Assoc. Dean, School of Info. & Lib. Studies, State Univ. of New York, Amherst, NY 14260 (Sheldon Landman).

Publishing (Standing, Council). Glenn E. Estes, Assoc. Prof., Grad. School of Lib. & Info. Science, Univ. of Tennessee, Knoxville, TN 37916 (Donald E. Stewart).

Reference and Subscription Books Review (Standing). Robert M. Pierson, Special Collections Div., Univ. of Maryland, College Park, MD 20742 (Helen K. Wright).

Research (Standing). John A. McCrossan, Grad. Dept. of Lib. Media & Info. Studies, Univ. of Southern Florida, Tampa, FL 33620 (Mary Jo Lynch).

Resolutions (Standing, Council). Jane Anne Hannigan, Prof., School of Lib. Service, Columbia Univ., New York, NY 10027 (Miriam L. Hornback).

Standards (Standing). Jaspar G. Schad, Box 68, Wichita State Univ., Wichita, KS 67208 (Ruth R. Frame).

Women in Librarianship, Status of (Standing, Council). Patricia Rom, 74 Seventh St., Edison, NJ 08817 (Margaret Myers).

JOINT COMMITTEE CHAIRPERSONS

American Correctional Association-ASCLA Committee on Institution Libraries. Robert F. Ensley, Senior Consultant, Lib. Development Group, Illinois State Lib., Centennial Bldg., Springfield, IL 62756.

American Federation of Labor/Congress of Industrial Organizations-ALA, Library Service to Labor Groups, RASD. Gladys E. Siegel, Head Libn., American Petroleum Inst., Washington, DC 20037.

American School Counselor Association-AASL. ALA Co-Chpn. Estelle B. Williamson, State Dept. of Educ., Div. of Lib. Development & Service, Baltimore, MD 21210; ASCA Co-Chpn. Walter M. Kearney, 116 Colesbery Dr., Penn Acres New Castle, DE 19720.

American Vocational Association-AASL. Jack Hall, Greater Lowell Regional Vocational Tech. School Dist., Pawtucket Blvd., Tyngsboro, MA 01879.

"Anglo-American Cataloguing Rules" Common Revision Fund. Donald E. Stewart, ALA headquarters.

Association of American Publishers-ALA. Thomas J. Galvin, School of Lib. & Info. Science, Univ. of Pittsburgh, Pittsburgh, PA 15260.

Association of American Publishers-RTSD. ALA Co-Chpn. Joan Seligman, 18 Stuyvesant Oval, New York, NY 10009; AAP Co-Chpn. Lucille Gordon, McGraw-Hill Book Co., 1221 Ave. of the Americas, New York, NY 10020.

Children's Book Council-ALA. ALA Co-Chpn. Geraldine Clark, School Lib.

568 / DIRECTORY OF LIBRARY AND RELATED ORGANIZATIONS

Service, Bd. of Educ., Brooklyn, NY 11201; CBC Co-Chpn. Ann Durrell, E. P. Dutton Co., New York, NY 10016.

National Council of Teachers of English–AASL. AASL Co-Chpn. Elfrieda McCauley, Public Schools, Greenwich, CT 06830; NCTA Co-Chpn. Judith Rosenfeld, Tolland, CT 06084.

National Council of Teachers of Mathematics–AASL (Ad Hoc). AASL Co-Chpn. Eloise Brown, Public School Libs., Washington, DC 20004; NCTM Co-Chpn. Doris Quander, NCTM, 1906 Association Dr., Reston, VA 22091.

Nonbook Materials, Joint Advisory Committee on. Nancy Williamson, Faculty of Lib. Science, Univ. of Toronto, 140 St. George St., Toronto, Ont. M5S 1A1, Canada.

Society of American Archivists–ALA Joint Committee on Library-Archives Relationships. Evert Volkhersz, Dept. of Special Collections Lib., State Univ. of New York at Stony Brook, Stony Brook, NY 11794.

U.S. National Park Service/ALSC Joint Committee. ALA Co-Chpn. Nancy Cummings, Clark County Lib., Las Vegas, NV 89109; U.S. National Park Service Co-Chpn. Patricia M. Stanek, Cowpens Memorial Battlefield, Chesnee, SC 29323.

AMERICAN LIBRARY ASSOCIATION
AMERICAN ASSOCIATION OF SCHOOL LIBRARIANS
Executive Secretary, Alice E. Fite
Professional Assistant, Ruth E. Feathers
50 E. Huron St., Chicago, IL 60611
312-944-6780

OBJECT

The American Association of School Librarians is interested in the general improvement and extension of library media services for children and young people. AASL has specific responsibility for planning programs of study and service for the improvement and extension of library media services in elementary and secondary schools as a means of strengthening the educational program; evaluation, selection, interpretation, and utilization of media as they are used in the context of the school program; stimulation of continuous study and research in the library field and to establish criteria of evaluation; synthesis of the activities of all units of the American Library Association in areas of mutual concern; representation and interpretation of the need for the function of school libraries to other educational and lay groups; stimulation of professional growth, improvement of the status of school librarians, and encouragement of participation by members in appropriate type-of-activity divisions; and conduct activities and projects beyond the scope of type-of-activity divisions, after specific approval by the ALA Council. Established in 1951 as a separate division of ALA. Memb. 7,000.

MEMBERSHIP

Open to all libraries, school library media specialists, interested individuals and business firms with requisite membership in the ALA.

OFFICERS

Pres. Rebecca T. Bingham, Jefferson County Public Schools, Louisville, KY 40211; *1st V.P.-Pres.-Elect.* D. Philip Baker, 195 Hillandale Ave., Stamford, CT 06902; *2nd V.P.* Anne C. Ansley; *Rec. Secy.* Betty Jo Buckingham; *Past Pres.* Anna Mary Lowrey; *Exec. Secy.* Alice E. Fite.

DIRECTORS

Patricia E. Jensen, Region I (1982); Mildred L. Younger, Region II (1980); Diane A. Ball, Region III (1981); Ruth A. Moline, Region IV (1982); Shirley L. Aaron, Region V (1981); Jean R. Ballintine, Region VI (1980); Genevieve K. Craig, Region VII (1982); *Regional Dirs. from Affiliate Assembly.* Ollie E. Bissmeyer, Jr. (1980); Marilyn Goodrich (1980); Albert Sale (1981); *NPSS Chpn.* Pauline Anderson; *SS Chpn.* David R. Bender; *Ex Officio Ed. School Media Quarterly.* Jack R. Luskay.

PUBLICATION

School Media Quarterly (q.; memb.; nonmemb. $15). *Ed.* Jack R. Luskay, School of Lib. Science, Clarion State College, Clarion, PA 16214.

NONPUBLIC SCHOOLS SECTION COMMITTEES

Executive. Pauline Anderson, Choate Secondary School, Choate Rosemary Hall, Wallingford, CT 06492 (1980).

Bylaws. Stephen Matthews, Currier Lib., Foxcroft School, Middleburg, VA 22117.

Nominating. Walter Frankel, Taft School, Watertown, CT 06795.

Program. James P. Godfrey. Rye Country Day School, Rye, NY 10580.

SUPERVISORS SECTION COMMITTEES

Executive. David R. Bender, Special Libs. Assn., 235 Park Ave. S., New York, NY 10003.

Bylaws. Dale W. Brown, Educational Media Center, Alexandria City Public Schools, 3801 W. Braddock Rd., Alexandria, VA 22302 (1980).

Nominating—1980 Election. Donald C. Adcock, Glen Ellyn Public Schools, Dist. No. 41, 793 Main St., Glen Ellyn, IL 60137 (1981).

Program—New York, 1980. Jacqueline Morris, Div. of Instructional Media, State Dept. of Public Instruction, Indianapolis, IN 46204.

Publication. Dawn H. Heller, 516 S. Ashland, La Grange, IL 60525.

DISCUSSION GROUPS

Critical Issues Facing School Library Media Supervisors. Sandra W. Ulm, 275 John Know Rd., K204, Tallahassee, FL 32303.

Networking and the Role of the School Library Supervisor. Richard J. Sorensen, 215 N. Jefferson St., Verona, WI 53593.

COMMITTEE CHAIRPERSONS

Program Coordinating. Anna Mary Lowrey, School of Info. and Lib. Studies, State Univ. of New York at Buffalo, Bell Hall, Amherst, NY 14260.

Unit Group I—Organizational Maintenance

Unit Head. Marie V. Haley, Sioux City Community Schools, 1221 Pierce St., Sioux City, IA 51105.

Bylaws. Dorothy W. Blake, 1930 Forrest Hill Dr. S.W., Atlanta, GA 30315.

Conference Program Planning—New York, 1980. Theresa M. Fredericka, 1401 Raven Crest, Frankfort, KY 40601.

Local Arrangements—New York, 1980. Lucille C. Thomas, Center for Lib. Media and Telecommunications, New York City Bd. of Educ., 131 Livingston St., Brooklyn, NY 11201 (1980).

Nominating—1980 Election. Phyllis B. Williamson, Great Falls Public Schools, Box 2428, Great Falls, MT 59403 (1980).

Resolutions. Anne C. Ansley, 139 Osner Dr., Atlanta, GA 30342 (1980).

Unit Group II—Organizational Relationships

Unit Head. Bernice L. Yesner, 16 Sunbrook Rd., Woodbridge, CT 06525.

American School Counselor Association—AASL (Joint). Estelle B. Williamson, State Dept. of Educ., Div. of Lib.

Development & Service, Baltimore, MD 21210.

American University Press Services, Inc. (Advisory). Dolores E. Victorian, Walt Whitman H.S., Bethesda, MD 20034.

American Vocational Association—AASL (Joint). Jack Hall, Greater Lowell Regional Vocational Technical School Dist., Pawtucket Blvd., Tyngsboro, MA 01879.

Association for Childhood Education International—AASL (Joint). Dorothy S. Heald, Box 1074, Tallahassee, FL 32302.

National Council of Teachers of English—AASL (Joint). Elfrieda McCauley, Public Schools, Greenwich, CT 06830.

National Council of Teachers of Mathematics (Ad Hoc/Joint). Eloise Brown, Public Schools Libs., Washington, DC 20004.

Unit Group III—Media Personnel Development

Unit Head. Frances S. Hatfield, School Bd. of Broward County, Ft. Lauderdale, FL 33312.

Library Education. Kay E. Vandergrift, School of Lib. Service, Columbia Univ., New York, NY 10027.

Networking—Interconnection of Learning Resources (Ad Hoc). Richard J. Sorenson, Dept. of Public Instruction, Madison, WI 53702.

Professional Development. Thomas L. Hart, School of Lib. Science, Florida State Univ., Tallahassee, FL 32306.

Research. Shirley L. Aaron, School of Lib. Science, Florida State Univ., Tallahassee, FL 32306.

Video Communications. Carolyn Markuson, 56 Dellwood Ave., Chatham, NJ 07928.

Unit Group IV—Media Program Development

Unit Head. Lucille C. Thomas, Center for Lib. Media and Telecommunications, New York City Bd. of Educ., 131 Livingston St., Brooklyn, NY 11201.

Early Childhood Education. Wanna M. Ernst, 16 Brisbane Dr., Charleston, SC 29407.

Evaluation of School Media Programs. Jack R. Luskay, School of Lib. Media & Info. Science, Clarion State College, Clarion, PA 16214.

Facilities, Media Center. Ruth C. McMartin, Dist. Office, Fargo Public Schools, 1104 Second Ave., South Fargo, ND 58102.

School Library Media Services to Children with Special Needs. Rosa L. Presberry, 704 Country Village Dr., No. 2C, Bel Air, MD 21014.

Standards Program and Implementation. Robert D. Little, Dept of Lib. Science, Indiana State Univ., Reeve Hall 334, Terre Haute, IN 47809.

Student Involvement in the Media Center Program. Gerald Hodges, Univ. of North Carolina-Greensboro, School of Educ., 47 McNutt Bldg., Greensboro, NC 27412.

Unit Group V—Public Information

Unit Head. Doris A. Hicks, City School Dist., Dept. of Learning Resources, Rochester, NY 14610.

Distinguished Library Service Award for School Administrators. Elizabeth M. Stephens, School Bd. of Pinellas County, 1960 E. Druid Rd., Clearwater, FL 33518 (1980).

Excellence in Curriculum Related Films. John A. Baker, 4650 Ingersoll, Houston, TX 77027 (1980); Lewis Bias, Div. of Instructional Materials, Montgomery County Public Schools, 850 Hungerford Dr., Rockville, MD 20850 (1980).

Intellectual Freedom Representation and Information. Darlene Hunter, 2541 Vernal Dr., Grove City, OH 43123.

International Relations. Esther R. Dyer, Grad. School of Lib. & Info. Science, Rutgers Univ., 4 Huntington St., New Brunswick, NJ 08903.

Legislation. Johanna S. Wood, 2631 Moreland Pl. N.W., Washington, DC 20015.

President's Award Selection, AASL/

Baker & Taylor. Frances Hatfield, Dept. of Learning Resources, School Bd. of Broward County, 1320 S.W. Fourth St., Ft. Lauderdale, FL 33312.

School Library Media Program of the Year Award Selection, AASL/EB. E. Louise Dial, 6938 E. Orme, Wichita, KS 67207.

COMMITTEES (SPECIAL)

Publications Advisory. Glenn Estes, Grad. School of Lib. & Info. Science, Univ. of Tennessee, 804 Volunteer Blvd., Knoxville, TN 37916.

AASL General Conference Planning. Jack R. Luskay, School of Lib. Media & Info. Science, Clarion State College, Clarion, PA 16214.

Resource Development. Antoinette Negro, 10022 Stedwick Rd., No. 302, Gaithersburg, MD 20760.

REPRESENTATIVES

ALA Legislation Assembly. Johanna S. Wood.

ALA Membership Promotion Task Force. Vicki Sower.

Associated Organizations for Teacher Education. Kay E. Vandergrift.

Continuing Library Education Network Exchange. Dianne T. Williams.

Education U.S.A. Advisory Board. Alice E. Fite.

Educational Media Council. Alice E. Fite.

Freedom to Read Foundation. Darlene Hunter.

Library Education Assembly. Kay E. Vandergrift.

National Council of Organizations for Children and Youth. Alice E. Fite.

RTSD/CSD/AASL Cataloging of Children's Materials. Winifred E. Duncan.

AFFILIATE ASSEMBLY

The Affiliate Assembly is composed of the representatives and delegates of the organizations affiliated with the American Association of School Librarians. The specific purpose of this assembly is to provide a channel for communication for reporting concerns of the affiliate organizations and their membership and for reporting the actions of the American Association of School Librarians to the affiliates.

Executive Committee

Marie V. Haley, Community School Dist., 1221 Pierce St., Sioux City, IA 51105.

Nominating Committee—1980 Election

M. Maggie Rogers, 1943 S.E. Locust, Portland, OR 97214.

Affiliates

Region I. Connecticut Educational Media Assn.; Massachusetts Assn. for Educational Media; Maine Educational Media Assn.; New England Educational Media Assn.; Rhode Island Educational Media Assn.; Vermont Educational Media Assn.

Region II. Delaware Learning Resources Assn.; District of Columbia Assn. of School Libns.; Maryland Educational Media Organization; Educational Media Assn. of New Jersey; Pennsylvania School Libns. Assn.; School Lib. Media Sec., New York Lib. Assn.

Region III. Assn. for Indiana Media Educators; Illinois Assn. for Media in Education; Iowa Educational Media Assn.; Michigan Assn. for Media in Education; Minnesota Educational Media Organization; Missouri Assn. of School Libns.; Ohio Educational Lib. Media Assn.; Wisconsin School Lib. Media Assn.; School Div., Michigan Lib. Assn.

Region IV. Mountain Plains Lib. Assn., Children's & School Sec.; Colorado Educational Media Assn.; Kansas Assn. of School Libns.; North Dakota Assn. of School Libns.; South Dakota School Lib./Media Assn.; Wyoming School Lib. Media Assn.

Region V. Alabama Instructional Media Assn.; Children & School Libns. Div.,

Alabama Lib. Assn.; Florida Assn. for Media in Education, Inc.; Georgia Lib. Media Dept.; School and Children's Sec., Georgia Lib. Assn.; Kentucky School Media Dept.; North Carolina Assn. of School Libns.; School & Children's Sec.; Southeastern Lib. Assn.; South Carolina Assn. of School Libns.; School Lib. Sec., Tennessee Education Assn.; Virginia Educational Media Assn.

Region VI. Louisiana Assn. of School Libns.; School Libs., Children, Young Adult Services, New Mexico Lib. Assn.; Oklahoma Assn. of School Lib. Media Specialists; School Libs. Div., Arizona State Lib. Assn.; School Libs. Div., Arkansas Lib. Assn.; Texas Assn. of School Libs.

Region VII. California Media & Lib. Educators Assn.; Hawaii Assn. of School Libs.; Idaho Educational Media Assn.; Oregon Educational Media Assn.; School Lib. Div., Idaho Lib. Assn.; School Lib./Media Div., Montana Lib. Assn.; Washington State Assn. of School Libns.

AMERICAN LIBRARY ASSOCIATION
AMERICAN LIBRARY TRUSTEE ASSOCIATION
ALTA Program Officer, Sharon L. Jordan
50 E. Huron St., Chicago, IL 60611
312-944-6780

OBJECT

The development of effective library service for all people in all types of communities and in all types of libraries; it follows that its members are concerned as policymakers with organizational patterns of service, with the development of competent personnel, the provision of adequate financing, the passage of suitable legislation, and the encouragement of citizen support for libraries. Open to all interested persons and organizations. Organized 1890. Became an ALA division 1961. Memb. 1710. (For dues and membership year, see ALA entry.)

OFFICERS (1979–1980)

Pres. James A. Hess, 91 Farms Road Circle, East Brunswick, NJ 08816; *1st V.P. & Pres.-Elect.* Jeanne Davies, Box 159, Deer Trail, CO 80105; *2nd V.P.* Nancy Stiegemeyer, 215 Camellia Dr., Cape Girardeau, MO 63701; *Secy.* Katie Wright.

BOARD OF DIRECTORS

The officers; *Council Administrators.* Albert I. Mayer; Marlys E. Mlady; David H. Werdine; M. Don Surratt; Sondrea Messing. *Reg. V.Ps.* John T. Short; Barbara Steigerwalt; Arthur S. Kirschenbaum; Barbara D. Cooper; Lila Milford; Paulette Holahan; Russell Hansen; Allan Kahn; Alex Sergienko; *Past Pres.* Barbara S. Prentice; *PLA Past Pres. Ex Officio.* Genevieve M. Casey; *Ed. The Public Library Trustee.* Robert L. Faherty.

PUBLICATION

Public Library Trustee. Ed. Robert L. Faherty, 6908 Lamp Post La., Alexandria, VA 22306.

COMMITTEE CHAIRPERSONS

Action Development. Donald C. Earnshaw, 226 S. Douglas St., Lee's Summit, MO 64063.

ALTA Foundation Committee. Ann Prentice, Grad. School of Lib. and Info. Science, Univ. of Tennessee, Knoxville, TN 37916.

Awards. John T. Short, Box E, Avon, CT 06001.

Budget. Jeanne Davies, Box 159, Deer Trail, CO 80105.

Conference Program and Evaluation.

Co-Chpn. M. Don Surratt, 440 Ames, Libertyville, IL 60048; Nell Henry, 109 N. Olive St., Searcy, AR 72148.

Education of Trustees. Jeanne Davies, Box 159, Deer Trail, CO 80105.

Task Force on Identity. Daniel Casey, 202 Scarboro Dr., Syracuse, NY 13209.

Intellectual Freedom. Norma J. Buzan, 3057 Betsy Ross Dr., Bloomfield Hills, MI 48013.

Legislation. Deborah Miller, 840 Rosedale La., Hoffman Estates, IL 60195.

Task Force on Liaison with Leagues of Municipalities. Norma L. Mihalevich, Box 287, Crocker, MO 65452.

Task Force on Literacy Programs. Marguerite W. Yates, 190 Windemere Rd., Lockport, NY 14094.

Task Force on Membership. Barbara S. Prentice, 1933 E. Third St., Tucson, AZ 85719.

Nominating. Maxine Scoville, 7720 Oakland Ave., Kansas City, KS 66112.

Task Force on Personnel Policies and Practices. Martin D. Phelan, 2524 Lorton Ave., Davenport, IA 52803.

Publications. Betty Simpson, 208 E. Second St., Mackinaw, IL 61735.

Publicity. Joanne C. Wisener, 860 19 Pl., Yuma, AZ 85364.

Task Force on Serving the Unserved. Fred K. Darragh, Box 86, Little Rock, AR 72203.

Speakers Bureau. Jo Anne Thorbeck, 2100 Irving S., Minneapolis, MN 55405.

State Associations. Nancy Stiegemeyer, 215 Camellia Dr., Cape Girardeau, MO 63701.

Jury on Trustee Citations. John Velde, Jr., 2003 La Brea Terrace, Hollywood, CA 90046.

White House Conference (Ad Hoc). Co-Chpn. Charles E. Reid, 620 West Dr., Paramus, NJ 07652; Virginia Young, 10 E. Parkway Dr., Columbia, MO 65201.

AMERICAN LIBRARY ASSOCIATION
ASSOCIATION FOR LIBRARY SERVICE TO CHILDREN
Executive Secretary, Mary Jane Anderson
50 E. Huron St., Chicago, IL 60611
312-944-6780

OBJECT

"Interested in the improvement and extension of library services to children in all types of libraries. Responsible for the evaluation and selection of book and nonbook materials for, and the improvement of techniques of, library services to children from preschool through the eighth grade or junior high school age, when such materials or techniques are intended for use in more than one type of library." Founded 1900. Memb. 4,978. (For information on dues see ALA entry.)

MEMBERSHIP

Open to anyone interested in library services to children.

OFFICERS (JULY 1979–JULY 1980)

Pres. Marilyn L. Miller, Assoc. Prof., School of Lib. Science, Univ. of North Carolina, Chapel Hill, NC 27514; *V.P.* Amy Kellman, 211 Castlegate Rd., Pittsburgh, PA 15221; *Past Pres.* Lillian N. Gerhardt, *School Library Journal,* R. R. Bowker Co., 1180 Ave. of the Americas, New York, NY 10036. *(Address general correspondence to the executive secretary.)*

DIRECTORS

The officers; Susan Collier; Carolyn Field; Suzanne Glazer; Beth Greggs; Barbara Miller (ALA Councilor); Harriet Quimby; Gail M. Sage; Zena B. Sutherland; Diana D. Young.

PUBLICATIONS

ALSC Newsletter (q.; memb.).
Top of the News (q.; memb.; $15 nonmemb.).

COMMITTEE CHAIRPERSONS

Priority Group I—Child Advocacy

Coord. Phillis M. Wilson, Rochester Public Lib., Broadway at First St. S.E., Rochester, MN 55901.

Boy Scouts of America (Advisory). Frances V. Sedney, Hartford County Lib., 100 Pennsylvania Ave., Bel Air, MD 21014.

Legislation. Jean St. Clair, 109-36 172 St., Jamaica, NY 11433.

Mass Media (Liaison with). Elizabeth Huntoon, 2046 Clifton, Chicago, IL 60614.

Organizations Serving the Child (Liaison with). Helen M. Mullen, Office of Work with Children, Free Lib. of Philadelphia, Logan Sq., Philadelphia, PA 19103.

U.S. National Park Service/ALSC (Joint). Nancy Cummings, Clark County Lib., 1401 E. Flamingo, Las Vegas, NV 89198.

Priority Group II—Evaluation of Media

Coord. Gertrude B. Herman, 1425 Skyline Dr., Madison, WI 53705.

Mildred L. Batchelder Award Selection—1980. Anne Boegen, 305 S.W. 43 Ave., Miami, FL 33134.

Mildred L. Batchelder Award Selection—1981. Virginia McKee, 33 E. Hendrickson Ave., Morrisville, PA 19067.

Caldecott Award. Charlotte Huck, Ohio State Univ., 200 Ramseyer Hall, 29 W. Woodruff, Columbus, OH 43210.

Film Evaluation. Martha Barnes, Westchester Lib. System, 280 N. Central Ave., Hartsdale, NY 10530.

Filmstrip Evaluation. Nancy Silcox, Arlington County Public Lib., 2700 S. Arlington Mill Dr., Arlington, VA 22206.

Newbery Award. Ginny M. Kruse, 1708 Regent St., Madison, WI 53705.

Notable Children's Books. Ruth Gordon, 609 North St., Susanville, CA 96130.

Notable Children's Books Reevaluation, 1971-1975 (Ad Hoc). Susan Collier, 76 Whitman Dr., New Providence, NJ 07974.

Print and Poster Evaluation. Patricia Patrick, Upper Hudson Lib. Federation, 161 Washington Ave., Albany, NY 12210.

Recording Evaluation. Kathleen Burgess, Gary Public Lib., 220 W. Fifth Ave., Gary, IN 46402.

Reference Review Task Force. Mary Ploshnick, Detroit Public Lib., 5201 Woodward Ave., Detroit, MI 48202.

Selection of Foreign Children's Books. Grace Ruth, 859 42 Ave., San Francisco, CA 94121.

Toys, Games and Realia Evaluation. Nancy Elsom, Racine Public Lib., 75 Seventh St., Racine, WI 53403.

Laura Ingalls Wilder Award—1983. Spencer Shaw, School of Libnshp., Suzzallo Lib., FM-30, Univ. of Washington, Seattle, WA 98195.

Priority Group III—People Power

Coord. Betty J. Peltola, 4109 N. Ardmore, Milwaukee, WI 53211.

Arbuthnot Honor Lecture. Dudley B. Carlson, Princeton Public Lib., 65 Witherspoon St., Princeton, NJ 08540.

Arbuthnot Honor Lecture Evaluation (Ad Hoc). John Donovan, Children's Book Council, 67 Irving Pl., New York, NY 10003.

Continuing Education. Barbara Miller, 215 N. 46 St., Louisville, KY 40212.

Media Evaluation: The Group Process, Implementation (Ad Hoc). Bridget L. Lamont, Illinois State Lib., Development Group, Centennial Bldg., Rm. 011, Springfield, IL 62756.

Melcher Scholarship. Harriet Quimby, Div. of Lib. and Info. Science, St. John's Univ., Jamaica, NY 11439.

Charles Scribner Award Selection. Catherine Romanelli, 2060 Cameron Ave., Merrick, NY 11566.

State and Regional Leadership (Discussion Group). Margaret Gillespie, Hennepin County Public Lib., 7009 York Ave. S., Edina, MN 55435.

Teachers of Children's Literature (Discussion Group). Ramona Mahood, Brisler Lib., Rm. 201, Dept. of Lib. Science, Memphis State Univ., Memphis, TN 38152; Bernice Yesner, 16 Sunbrook Rd., Woodbridge, CT 06525.

Priority Group IV—Social Responsibilities

Coord. Margaret Bush, 319 Tenth St. S.E., Apt. 2, Washington, DC 20003.

Children with Special Needs (Library Services to). Eliza T. Dresang, 440 Virginia Terrace, Madison, WI 53705.

Disadvantaged Child (Library Services to the—Discussion Group). Lynn Russell, 540 W. Briar, 4M, Chicago, IL 60657.

Intellectual Freedom. Edythe Cawthorne, Prince George's County Memorial Lib., 6532 Adelphi Rd., Hyattsville, MD 20782.

International Relations. Elizabeth B. Murphy, 4811 43 Place, Washington, DC 20016.

Preschool Services and Parent Education. Susan Galloway, Arthur Ct., Apt 222 B-2, Salisbury, MD 21801.

Program Support Publications (Ad Hoc). Beth Babikow, Baltimore County Public Lib., 320 York Rd., Towson, MD 21204.

Social Issues in Relation to Library Materials and Services for Children (Discussion Group). Anitra Steele, Mid-Continent Public Lib., 15616 E. 24 Hwy., Independence, MO 64050.

Priority Group V—Planning, Research, and Development

Coord. Margaret Poarch, South Hills Apts., No. 23, South St., Geneseo, NY 14454.

Collections of Children's Books for Adult Research (Discussion Group). Henrietta Smith, 1202 N.W. Second St., Delray Beach, FL 33444.

Local Arrangements—New York City 1980. Barbara Rollock, New York Public Lib., 8 E. 40 St., New York, NY 10016.

Membership. Marilyn W. Greenberg, 1345 Ave. de Cortez, Pacific Palisades, NY 90272.

Nominating—1979. Jane McGregor, 34 Greenmeadow Ct., Jackson, OH 45640.

Organization and Bylaws. Linda A. Fein, Northwest Regional Lib., Chelten Ave. & Greene St., Philadelphia, PA 19144.

Performance Evaluation (Ad Hoc). Phillis M. Wilson, Rochester Public Lib., Broadway at First St. S.E., Rochester, MN 55901.

Program Evaluation and Support. Amy Kellman, 211 Castlegate Rd., Pittsburgh, PA 15221.

Program—New York 1980. Martha Barnes, Westchester Lib. System, 280 N. Central Ave., Hartsdale, NY 10530.

Research and Development. Adele Fasick, 4351 Bloor St. W., Unit 40, Etobicoke, Ont. M9C 2A4, Canada.

Special Collections (National Planning of). Barbara Maxwell, Apt. 809A, Alden Park Manor, Wissahickon & Chelten Aves., Philadelphia, PA 19144.

"Top of the News" (Joint ALSC/YASD Editorial). Audrey Eaglen, Cuyahoga County Public Lib., 4510 Memphis Ave., Cleveland, OH 44144.

REPRESENTATIVES

AFL/CIO-ALA Committee on Library Service to Labor Groups. To be appointed.

ALA Appointments. Amy Kellman.

ALA Budget Assembly. Amy Kellman.

ALA Legislative Assembly. Jean St. Clair.

ALA Library Education Assembly. Barbara Miller.

ALA San Francisco Conference (1981) Program. Amy Kellman.

ALA New York Conference (1980) Program. Marilyn Miller.

ALA Membership Promotion Task Force. Marilyn Greenberg.

Caroline M. Hewins Scholarship. To be appointed.

International Board on Books for Young People, U.S. Section, Executive Board. Marilyn Miller; Mary Jane Anderson; Elizabeth B. Murphy; Barbara Elleman.

RTSD/CCS Cataloging of Children's Materials. To be appointed.

LIAISON WITH OTHER NATIONAL ORGANIZATIONS

American Association for Gifted Children. Naomi Noyes.
American National Red Cross. Red Cross Youth. Barbara Shumer.
Big Brothers and Big Sisters of America. Helen Mullen.
Boys Clubs of America. Jane Kunstler.
Camp Fire Girls. Anitra Steele.
Carnegie Council on Children. Effie Lee Morris.
Child Development Associates Consortium. Mary Jane Anderson.
Child Study Association of America. Augusta Baker.
Child Welfare League of America. Ethel Ambrose.
Children's Theatre Association. Amy E. Spaulding.
Coalition for Children and Youth. Mary Jane Anderson.
Day Care and Child Development Council of America. Margaret Bush.
Girls Clubs of America. Karen Breen.
National Association for the Education of Young Children. Theresa Chekon.
National Story League. Linda Hansford.
Parents without Partners. To be appointed.
Puppeteers of America. Darrell Hildebrandt.
Salvation Army. Margaret Malm.
Society of American Magicians. Marion Peck.

AMERICAN LIBRARY ASSOCIATION
ASSOCIATION OF COLLEGE AND RESEARCH LIBRARIES
Executive Secretary, Julie A. Carroll Virgo
50 E. Huron St., Chicago, IL 60611
312-944-6780

OBJECT

"Represents research and special libraries and libraries in institutions of post-secondary education, including those of community and junior colleges, colleges, and universities." Founded 1938. Memb. 9,000. (For information on dues see ALA entry.)

OFFICERS (JULY 1979–JUNE 1980)

Pres. Le Moyne W. Anderson, Colorado State Univ., Ft. Collins, CO 80521; *V.P. & Pres.-Elect.* Millicent D. Abell, Univ. of California, San Diego, La Jolla, CA 92093; *Past Pres.* Evan Ira Farber, Earlham College, Richmond, IN 47374.

BOARD OF DIRECTORS

The officers and the section chairs and vice-chairs; *Directors-at-Large.* Pauline Atherton (1980); Jane G. Flener (1980); William J. Studer (1981); Billy R. Wilkinson (1981). *Ex Officio.* Julie A. Carroll Virgo. *Note:* Future Board will be composed of the officers, 6 members elected at large from sections, 1 member elected at large from the Chapters Council, the ACRL Councillor, and 2 ex-offico members: the chairperson of the ACRL Budget and Finance Committee and the ACRL executive secretary.

PUBLICATIONS

ACRL Nonprint Media Publications (irreg.). *Ed.* Dwight Burlingame, Bowling Green State Univ., Bowling Green, OH 43402.

ACRL Publications in Librarianship (irreg.). *Ed.* Joe W. Kraus, Illinois State Univ., Normal, IL 61761.

Choice (11 issues; $40); *Choice Reviews on Cards* ($120). *Ed.* Jay M. Poole, 100 Riverview Center, Middletown, CT 06457.

College & Research Libraries (6 issues; memb.; nonmemb. $25). *Ed.* Richard D. Johnson, State Univ. College, Oneonta, NY 13820.

College & Research Libraries News (11 issues; memb.; nonmemb. $5). *Ed.* Jeffrey T. Schwedes, ACRL, Chicago, IL 60611.

SECTION CHAIRPERSONS

Anthropology. Anne K. Beaubien, Univ. of Michigan, Ann Arbor, MI 48109; *V. Chair & Chair-Elect.* Patricia White, Michigan State Univ., Lansing, MI 48824.

Art. Jane Anne Snider, Herron School of Art of Indiana Univ., Indianapolis, IN 46202; *V. Chair & Chair-Elect.* Jane Anne Snider.

Asian and African. Yen-Tsai Feng, Wellesley College, Wellesley, MA 02181; *V. Chair & Chair-Elect.* E. Christian Filstrup, Oriental Div., New York Public Lib., New York, NY 10018.

Bibliographic Instruction. Sharon Anne Hogan, Univ. of Michigan, Ann Arbor, MI 48109; *V. Chair & Chair-Elect.* Sharon Rogers, Univ. of Toledo, Toledo, OH 43606.

College Libraries. Carla J. Stoffle, Univ. of Wisconsin-Parkside, Kenosha, WI 53141; *V. Chair & Chair-Elect.* Willis M. Hubbard, Stephens College, Columbia, MO 65201.

Community and Junior College Libraries. James O. Wallace, San Antonio College, San Antonio, TX 78284; *V. Chair & Chair-Elect.* Barbara Collinsworth, Macomb County Community College, Warren, MI 48093.

Education and Behaviorial Sciences. Theodore C. Hines, Univ. of North Carolina at Greensboro, Greensboro, NC 27410; *V. Chair & Chair-Elect.* Eva L. Kiewitt, Indiana Univ., Bloomington, IN 47401.

Law and Political Science. Tillie Krieger, Boys Town Center for the Study of Youth Development, Boys Town, NE 68010; *V. Chair & Chair-Elect.* Frances H. Hall, North Carolina Supreme Court Lib., Raleigh, NC 27611.

Rare Books and Manuscripts. Peter E. Hanff, Univ. of California, Berkeley, CA 94720; *V. Chair & Chair-Elect.* Kenneth E. Carpenter, Harvard Business School, Boston, MA 02159.

Science and Technology. Leila Moran, National Agricultural Lib., Beltsville, MD 20705; *V. Chair & Chair-Elect.* Thomas G. Kirk, Univ. of Wisconsin-Parkside, Kenosha, WI 53140.

Slavic and East European. Edward Kasinec, Harvard Univ., Cambridge, MA 02138; *V. Chair & Chair-Elect.* Wojcieck Zalewski, Stanford Univ., Stanford, CA 94305.

University Libraries. Jean Boyer Hamlin, Rutgers Univ., Newark, NJ 17102; *V. Chair & Chair-Elect.* Pearce S. Grove, Western Illinois Univ., Macomb, IL 61455.

Western European Specialists (Pro Tem). Martin Faigel, Univ. of Alabama, University, AL 35486.

DISCUSSION GROUPS

Alternatives to the Card Catalog. James Thompson, Johns Hopkins Univ., Baltimore, MD 21218.

Cinema Librarians. Eileen Sheahan, Memphis Public Lib., Memphis, TN 38104.

Librarians of Library Science Collections. Eva Kiewitt, Indiana Univ., Bloomington, IN 47401.

Personnel Officer of Research. Elsi Mauro, Stanford Univ., Stanford, CA 94305.

Staff Development in Academic Research Libraries. Beth Marshall, Univ. of Chicago, Chicago, IL 60637.

Undergraduate Librarians. Mary Reichel, State Univ. of New York at Buffalo, Buffalo, NY 14261.

COMMITTEE CHAIRPERSONS

"ACRL Nonprint Publications" Editorial Board. Dwight Burlingame, Bowling Green State Univ., Bowling Green, OH 43402.

"ACRL Publications in Librarianship" Editorial Board. Joe W. Kraus, Illinois State Univ., Normal, IL 61761.

ACRL Academic or Research Librarian of the Year Award. James T. Dodson, Univ. of Texas at Dallas, Richardson, TX 75080.

Academic Status. Lynn F. Marko, Univ. of Michigan, Ann Arbor, MI 48109.

Appointments and Nominations. Russell Shank, Univ. of California, Los Angeles, CA 02159.

Audiovisual. David B. Walch, State Univ. College at Buffalo, Buffalo, NY 14222.

Budget and Finance. Currently vacant.

Chapters. Cleo Treadway, Tusculum College, Greeneville, TN 37743.

Chapters Council (Pro Tem). Cleo Treadway, Tusculum College, Greeneville, TN 37743.

"Choice" Editorial Board. Allan J. Dyson, Univ. of California, Berkeley, CA 94720.

Conference Executive-ACRL National Conference, Minneapolis 1981. Virgil F. Massman, J. J. Hill Reference Lib., St. Paul, MN 55102.

Conference Program Planning—New York 1980. Le Moyne Anderson, Colorado State Univ., Ft. Collins, CO 80521.

Conference Program Planning—San Francisco 1981. Millicent D. Abell, Univ. of California, San Diego, La Jolla, CA 92093.

Constitution and Bylaws. Mary W. George, Univ. of Michigan, Ann Arbor, MI 48109.

Continuing Education. Gretchen Redfield, BCR, Denver, CO 80218.

Copyright Committee (Ad Hoc). Meredith Butler, State Univ. of New York at Brockport, Brockport, NY 14420.

Developing Guidelines for Marking Rare Books for Security Purposes Committee (Ad Hoc). Terry Belanger, Columbia Univ., New York, NY 10027.

Legislation. Keith W. Russell, Univ. of Texas at Austin, Austin, TX 78712.

Membership. J. Daniel Vann III, State Univ. of New York at Buffalo, Buffalo, NY 14214.

Planning. Millicent D. Abell, Univ. of California, San Diego, La Jolla, CA 92093.

Publications. Mary Frances Collins, Univ. of Illinois, Champaign-Urbana, Urbana, IL 61801.

Publications—"College & Research Libraries," Ed. Search Subcommittee (Ad Hoc). Barbara Brown, Princeton Univ., Princeton, NJ 08540.

Standards and Accreditation. James T. Dodson, Univ. of Texas at Dallas, Box 643, Richardson, TX 75080.

"Standards for College Libraries" Revision (Ad Hoc). Arthur Monke, Bowdoin College, Brunswick, ME 04011.

Supplemental Funds. Edward Wall, Univ. of Michigan, Dearborn, MI 48128.

White House Conference and State Library Conferences (Ad Hoc). Joseph A. Boisse, Temple Univ., Philadelphia, PA 19122.

REPRESENTATIVES

American Association for the Advancement of Science. Thomas G. Kirk.

American Council on Education. Dale M. Bentz.

ALA Association of Specialized and Cooperative Library Agencies Standards for the Library Functions at the State Level Subcommittee (Ad Hoc). Jasper G. Schad.

ALA Budget and Planning Assembly. Millicent D. Abell.

ALA Committee on Appointments. Millicent D. Abell.

ALA Conference Program Committee (New York 1980). Le Moyne W. Anderson.

ALA Conference Program Committee (San Francisco 1981). Millicent D. Abell.

ALA Legislation Assembly. Keith W. Russell.

ALA Membership Promotion Task Force. J. Daniel Vann III.

AMERICAN LIBRARY ASSOCIATION
ASSOCIATION OF SPECIALIZED AND COOPERATIVE LIBRARY AGENCIES
(Formerly Association of State Library Agencies and Health and Rehabilitative Library Services Division)
Executive Secretary, Sandra M. Cooper
50 E. Huron St., Chicago, IL 60611
312-944-6780

OBJECT

To represent state library agencies, specialized library agencies, and multitype library cooperatives. Within the interests of these types of library organizations, the Association of Specialized and Cooperative Library Agencies has specific responsibility for:

1. Development and evaluation of goals and plans for state library agencies, specialized library agencies, and multitype library cooperatives to facilitate the implementation, improvement, and extension of library activities designed to foster improved user services, coordinating such activities with other appropriate ALA units.

2. Representation and interpretation of the role, functions, and services of state library agencies, specialized libraries and library cooperatives within and outside the profession, including contact with national organizations and government agencies.

3. Development of policies, studies, and activities in matters affecting state library agencies, specialized library agencies, and multitype library cooperatives relating to (a) state and local library legislation, (b) state grants-in-aid and appropriations, and (c) relationships among state, federal, regional, and local governments, coordinating such activities with other appropriate ALA units.

4. Establishment, evaluation, and promotion of standards and service guidelines relating to the concerns of this association.

5. Identifying the interests and needs of all persons, encouraging the creation of services to meet these needs within the areas of concern of the association, and promoting the use of these services provided by state library agencies, specialized library agencies, and multitype library cooperatives.

6. Stimulating the professional growth and promoting the specialized training and continuing education of library personnel at all levels in the areas of concern of this association and encouraging membership participation in appropriate type-of-activity divisions within ALA.

7. Assisting in the coordination of activities of other units within ALA that have a bearing on the concerns of this association.

8. Granting recognition for outstanding library service within the areas of concern of this association.

9. Acting as a clearinghouse for the

exchange of information and encouraging the development of materials, publications, and research within the areas of concern of this association.

BOARD OF DIRECTORS

Pres. Edward Seidenberg, Lib. Development Div., Texas State Lib., Box 12927, Capitol Sta., Austin, TX 78711; *V.P. & Pres.-Elect.* Carmela M. Ruby, California State Lib., Box 2037, Sacramento, CA 95809; *Past Co-Pres.* Phyliss I. Dalton, Robert R. McClarren. *Div. Councillor.* Susan M. Haskin (1981). *Directors at-Large.* Lee B. Brawner (1980); Susan B. Madden (1980); Robert A. Drescher. *Sec. Reps.* Stephen S. Prine, LSBPH Chpn. (1980); Sherry Ann Hokanson, LSIES Chpn. (1980); John K. Lohrstorfer, LSPS Chpn. (1980); Ruth L. Tighe, MLCS Chpn. (1980); Bridget L. Lamont, SLAS Chpn. (1980). *Ex Officio (Nonvoting). Interface ed.* Linda Howard Mielke; *Planning, Organization and Bylaws Committee Chpn.* Lorraine D. Schaeffer; *HCLS Steering Committee Chpn.* Joanne L. Crispen; *LSDS Steering Committee Chpn.* Molly Raphael; *Exec. Secy.*

PUBLICATION

Interface (q.; memb.; no subscriptions). *Ed.* Linda Howard Mielke, Special Community Service, Maryland State Dept. of Educ., Div. of Lib. Development and Service, Box 8717, Baltimore-Washington Airport, Baltimore, MD 21240.

COMMITTEE CHAIRPERSONS

American Correctional Association-ASCLA Committee on Institution Libraries (Joint). Robert F. Ensley, Lib. Development Group, Illinois State Lib., Centennial Bldg., Springfield, IL 62756.

Audiovisual. Leon L. Drolet, Jr., Dir., Suburban Audio Visual Service, 125 Tower Dr., Burr Ridge, IL 60521.

Awards. Richard T. Miller, Jr., Coord. for Development of Special Lib. Services, Missouri State Lib., 308 E. High St., Jefferson City, MO 65102.

Awards—Exceptional Service Award Jury. Beverly Daffern Papai, 52268 Country Acres Dr., Elkhart, IN 46514.

Bibliotherapy. Arleen M. Hynes, Libn., Circulating Lib., St. Elizabeth's Hospital, Washington, DC 20032.

Conference Program—New York 1980 (Ad Hoc). Kay Stansbery, Tarrant County Jr. College, 828 Harwood Rd., Hurst, TX 76053; Peter Paulson, New York State Educ. Dept., Cultural Education Center, Empire State Plaza, Albany, NY 12230.

Continuing Education. James A. Nelson, Univ. of Wisconsin Extension, 610 Langdon St., Madison, WI 53706; Dottie R. Hiebing, Continuing Education, Div. for Lib. Services, 126 Langdon St., Madison, WI 53702.

Grantsmanship (Ad Hoc). Lesley C. Loke, Massachusetts Bd. of Lib. Commissioners, 648 Beacon St., Boston, MA 02215.

Health Education (Ad Hoc). Mary A. Shopa, Chief, Lib. Services, Veterans Admin. Hospital, Northport, NY 11768.

"Interface" Editorial Policy (Ad Hoc). Chpn., four members to be appointed; *Ed.* Linda Howard Mielke; *Asst. ed.* Barbara A. Webb; *Exec. Secy.*

International Relations. Spencer G. Shaw, School of Libnshp., Suzzalo Lib., Univ. of Washington, Seattle, WA 98195.

Legislation. William T. DeJohn, Dir., Pacific Northwest Bibliographic Center, Univ. of Washington Lib., Seattle, WA 98195.

Manual on Library Service to Shut-Ins (Ad Hoc). Jan L. Ames, Washington Regional Lib. for the Blind and Physically Handicapped, 811 Harrison St., Seattle, WA 98129.

Membership Promotion. Robert A. Drescher, Illinois Valley Lib. System, 845 Brenkman Dr., Pekin, IL 61554.

Nominating. Barratt Wilkins, State Libn., State Lib. of Florida, R. A. Gray

Bldg., Tallahassee, FL 32304; Marcia Lowell, State Libn., Oregon State Lib., Salem, OR 97310.

Planning, Organization and Bylaws. Lorraine D. Schaeffer, State Lib. of Florida, R. A. Gray Bldg., Tallahassee, FL 32304.

Publications. Sally B. Roberts, Exec. Dir., New England Library Board, 231 Capitol Ave., Hartford, CT 06115.

Research. Mary R. Power, NCLIS, K St. N.W., Washington, DC 20036; Galen E. Rike, Dept. of Lib. Science, Ball State Univ., Muncie, IN 47306.

Standards. W. Lyle Everhart, Wisconsin Dept. of Public Instruction, Div. for Lib. Service, 126 Langdon St., Madison, WI 53702.

Standards for Library Functions at the State Level (Ad Hoc, Subcommittee). W. Lyle Everhart, Wisconsin Dept. of Public Instruction, Div. for Lib. Service, 126 Langdon St., Madison, WI 53702.

Standards for Library Service to the Blind and Physically Handicapped (Ad Hoc, Subcommittee). Katherine Prescott, 3617 Meadowbrook Blvd., Cleveland, OH 44118; Katherine M. Jackson, Head, Reference Div., Texas A&M Univ. Libs., College Station, TX 77843.

Standards for Library Service to the Deaf (Ad Hoc, Subcommittee). Lethene Parks, Pierce County Lib., 2356 Tacoma Ave. S., Tacoma, WA 98402.

Standards for Library Service to Patients (Ad Hoc, Subcommittee). Kathleen O. Mayo, Libn., Florida State Hospital, Chattahoochee, FL 32324; Kathleen O. Mayo, State Lib. of Florida, R. A. Gray Bldg., Tallahassee, FL 32304.

REPRESENTATIVES

ALA Government Documents Round Table (GODORT). Allan S. Quinn (1981).

ALA International Relations Committee. Spencer G. Shaw (1980).

ALA Legislation Assembly. William T. DeJohn (1980).

ALA Legislation Committee, Copyright Subcommittee. F. William Summers (1980).

ALA Library Education Assembly. Dottie R. Hiebing (1980).

ALA Membership Promotion Task Force. Robert A. Drescher (1980).

ALA/LAMA/BES. Robert F. Ensley (1980).

ALA/LAMA/SS Statistics for State Libraries Committee. C. Edwin Dowlin (1980).

ALA/LITA/ISAD Technical Standards for Automation Committee. Jay Cunningham (1980).

ALA/RASD Interlibrary Loan Committee. Jeanne H. Larsen (1980).

ALA/RTSD/CCS Cataloging: Description and Access Committee. Elizabeth Ann Breedlove (1981).

American Correctional Association (ACA). Robert F. Ensley.

Chief Officers of State Library Agencies (COSLA). Exec. Secy.

Continuing Library Education Network and Exchange (CLENE). Lesta N. B. Burt (1980).

Freedom to Read Foundation. To be appointed.

Interagency Council on Library Resources for Nursing. Frederick Pattison; Mary A. Shopa.

Urban Libraries Council. Nettie Barcroft Taylor (1980).

SECTION CHAIRPERSONS

Health Care Libraries (HCLS). Joanne L. Crispen, Dir., Lutheran General Hospital Lib., 1775 Dempster St., Park Ridge, IL 60068.

Library Service to Prisoners (LSPS). John K. Lohrstorfer, DuPage Lib. System, Box 268, Geneve, IL 60134.

Library Service to the Blind and Physically Handicapped (LSBPH). Donald John Weber, Regional Lib. for the Blind and Physically Handicapped, Box 2299, Daytona Beach, FL 32015; Stephen

S. Prine, Jr., Regional Lib. for the Blind and Physically Handicapped, Box 2299, Daytona Beach, FL 32015.

Library Service to the Deaf. Molly Raphael, Div. Chief, Public Lib., 901 G St. N.W., Washington, DC 20001.

Library Service to the Impaired Elderly (LSIES). John B. Balkema, National Council on Aging, 1828 L St. N.W., Washington, DC 20036; Sherry Ann Hokanson, Field Service Lib., Florida Regional Lib., Box 2299, Daytona Beach, FL 32015.

Multitype Library Cooperation Section (MLCS). Nancy Wareham, Cleveland Area Metropolitan Lib. System, 11000 Euclid Ave., Cleveland, OH 44106; Ruth L. Tighe, NCLIS, 1717 K St. N.W., Washington, DC 20036.

State Library Agency (SLAS). Andrea Hawkins, Washington State Lib., Olympia, WA 98504; Bridget Later Lamont, Assoc. Dir., Lib. Development, Illinois State Lib., Centennial Bldg., Springfield, IL 62756.

AMERICAN LIBRARY ASSOCIATION
LIBRARY ADMINISTRATION AND MANAGEMENT ASSOCIATION
Executive Secretary, Roger H. Parent
50 E. Huron St., Chicago, IL 60611
312-944-6780

OBJECT

"The Library Administration and Management Association provides an organizational framework for encouraging the study of administrative theory, for improving the practice of administration in libraries, and for identifying and fostering administrative skill. Toward these ends, the division is responsible for all elements of general administration which are common to more than one type of library. These may include organizational structure, financial administration, personnel management and training, buildings and equipment, and public relations. LAMA meets this responsibility in the following ways:

1. Study and review of activities assigned to the division with due regard for changing developments in these activities.

2. Initiating and overseeing activities and projects appropriate to the division, including activities involving bibliography compilation, publication, study, and review of professional literature within the scope of the division.

3. Synthesis of those activities of other ALA units which have a bearing upon the responsibilities or work of the division.

4. Representation and interpretation of library administrative activities in contacts outside the library profession.

5. Aiding the professional development of librarians engaged in administration and encouragement of their participation in appropriate type-of-library divisions.

6. Planning and development of those programs of study and research in library administrative problems which are most needed by the profession." Established 1957.

OFFICERS

Pres. Dale B. Canelas, Stanford Univ. Lib., Stanford, CA 94305; *V.P. & Pres.-Elect.* Mary A. Hall, Prince George's County Memorial Lib., 6532 Adelphi Rd., Hyattsville, MD 20782; *Exec. Secy.* Roger H. Parent. (Address correspondence to the executive secretary.)

DIRECTORS

The officers, the past president, section chairpersons, and vice-chairpersons; *Ex Officio*. Exec. Secy.; and *LAMA Newsletter* ed.

PUBLICATIONS

Friends of the Library National Notebook (q.). *Ed.* Sandy Dolnick, 4909 N. Ardmore Ave., Milwaukee, WI 53217.
LAMA Newsletter (q.; memb.). *Ed.* Ross G. Stephen, Univ. of Wisconsin-Oshkosh, 800 Algoma Blvd., Oshkosh, WI 54901.

DIVISION COMMITTEE CHAIRPERSONS

Nominating. Ernest Di Mattia, Jr., Ferguson Lib., 96 Broad St., Stamford, CT 06901.
Organization. Carolyn Snyder, Indiana Univ. Lib., Bloomington, IN 47401.
Orientation Programs. Elsi Goering, Stanford Univ. Lib., Stanford, CA 94305.
Program. Donald E. Wright, Public Lib., 1703 Orrington Ave., Evanston, IL 60201.
Publications. Committee to be appointed.
Small Libraries Publications. Regina Minudri, Public Lib., 2090 Kittredge St., Berkeley, CA 94704.

DISCUSSION GROUP CHAIRPERSONS

Middle Management. Ronald Leach, Assoc. Dir. of Libs., Central Michigan University Lib., Mt. Pleasant, MI 48859.

Network/Systems Administration Planning. Committee to be appointed.
Women Administrators. Carolyn Schwartz, Dir., Public Lib., 268 Bloomfield Ave., Caldwell, NJ 07006; Joanne R. Euster, Loyola Univ., New Orleans, LA 70118.

SECTION CHAIRPERSONS

Buildings and Equipment Section. Nancy R. McAdams, 2607 Great Oaks Pkwy., Austin, TX 78756.
Circulation Services Section. Hugh C. Atkinson, Univ. of Illinois Lib., Urbana, IL 61801.
Library Organization and Management Section. Katherine T. Emerson, Univ. of Massachusetts Lib., Amherst, MA 01003.
Personnel Administration Section. Dallas Shaffer, Prince George's County Memorial Lib., 6532 Adelphi Rd., Hyattsville, MD 20782.
Public Relations Section. Kathleen Rummel, 521 W. Roscoe, Chicago, IL 60657.
Statistics Section. Eugene T. Neely, Univ. of Missouri General Lib., Kansas City, MI 64110.

LAMA REPRESENTATIVES

ALA Legislation Assembly. Olive James.
ALA Membership Committee. Esther Perica.
Freedom to Read Foundation (FTRF). Laurence Miller.
Representative from Medical Library Association. Doris Bolef.

AMERICAN LIBRARY ASSOCIATION
LIBRARY AND INFORMATION TECHNOLOGY ASSOCIATION
Executive Secretary, Donald P. Hammer
50 E. Huron St., Chicago, IL 60611
312-944-6780

"The Library and Information Technology Association provides its members and, to a lesser extent, the information dissemination field as a whole, with a forum for discussion, an environment for learning, and a program for action on all phases of the development and application of automated and technological systems in the library and information sciences. Since its activities and interests are derived as responses to the needs and demands of its members, its program is flexible, varied, and encompasses many aspects of the field. Its primary concern is the design, development, and implementation of technological systems in the library and information science fields. Within that general precept, the interests of the division include such varied activities as systems development, electronic data processing, mechanized information retrieval, operations research, standards development, telecommunications, networks and collaborative efforts, management techniques, information technology and other aspects of audiovisual and video cable communications activities, and hardware applications related to all of these areas. Although it has no facilities to carry out research, it attempts to encourage its members in that activity as much as possible.

Information about all of these activities is disseminated through the division's publishing program, seminars and institutes, exhibits, conference programs, and committee work. The division provides an advisory and consultative function when called upon to do so.

It regards continuing education as one of its major responsibilities and through the above channels it attempts to inform its members of current activities and trends, and it also provides retrospective information for those new to the field."

OFFICERS

Pres. Barbara E. Markuson, Dir., INCOLSA, 1000 W. 42 St., Indianapolis, IN 46208; *V.P. & Pres.-Elect.* S. Michael Malinconico, Chief, Technical Service, Public Lib., Branch Lib., New York, NY 10016; *Past Pres.* Susan K. Martin, Libn., Lib., Johns Hopkins Univ., Baltimore, MD 21218; *Exec. Secy.* Donald P. Hammer. (Address general correspondence to the executive secretary.)

DIRECTORS

The officers; Mary A. Madden (1980); Jerome K. Miller (1980); Robert Miller (1980); Kenneth J. Bierman (1981); Kandy B. Brandt (1982); *Councilor.* Ronald F. Miller (1981); *Ex Officio. Bylaws and Organization Committee Chpn.* Loreta Tiemann (1980); *Ed. of JOLA.* To be appointed.

PUBLICATIONS

Journal of Library Automation (JOLA) (q.; memb.; nonmemb. $15). *Ed.* To be appointed. *Communications Ed.* Mary A. Madden, 1605 S.W. Upland Dr., Portland, OR 97221; *Book Review Ed.* Katherine King, American Banking Assn., 1120 Connecticut Ave. N.W., Washington, DC 20036; *Advertising Ed.* Judith Schmidt, Copyright Div., Lib. of Congress, Washington, DC 20540.

LITA Newsletter (bi-ann.; memb.). *Ed.*, Patricia Barkalow, Head, Systems, Univ. Lib., Univ. of Tennessee, Knoxville, TN 37916.

COMMITTEE CHAIRPERSONS

Awards. Stephen R. Salmon, Asst. V.P., Lib. Plans and Policies, Univ. of California, 650 Univ. Hall, Berkeley, CA 94720.

Bylaws and Organization. Loreta Tiemann, Lincoln City Libs., 14 & N Sts., Lincoln, NE 68508.

Editorial Board. To be appointed. Information available from the Library and Information Technology Association.

Education. Brigitte Kenney, IPB, Solar Energy Research Institute, 1536 Cole, Golden, CO 80401.

Legislation and Regulation. Ruth Tighe, NCLIS, 1717 K St. N.W., Suite 601, Washington, DC 20036.

LITA Staffing (Ad Hoc). Barbara E. Markuson, Dir., INCOLSA, 1000 W. 42 St., Indianapolis, IN 46208.

Membership. Blanche Woolls, Asst. Prof., Univ. of Pittsburgh Lib. School, Pittsburgh, PA 15261.

Nominating. Richard W. Meyer, Assoc. Dir., Robert Muldrow Cooper Lib., Clemson Univ., Clemson, SC 29631.

Program Planning. Kaye Gapen, Asst. Dir., Technical Services, 168 Library, Iowa State Univ., Ames, IA 50011.

Representation in Machine Readable Form of Bibliographic Information, RTSD/LITA/RASD (MARBI). Eleanor Montague, Univ. of California, Riverside, CA 92507.

Telecommunications. To be appointed. Information available from the Library and Information Technology Association.

DISCUSSION GROUP CHAIRPERSONS

Library Automation (COLA). Patricia H. Earnest, Lib. Automation Specialist, Brodart, Inc., Western Div., 1236 S. Hatcher St., City of Industry, CA 91748.

MARC Users. William Mathews, Information Systems, Jockey Club, New York, NY. Send mail to 73 E. Linden Ave., Englewood, NJ 07631.

SECTION CHAIRPERSONS

Audio-Visual. Ronald F. Sigler, School of Lib. Science, Univ. of Wisconsin, Milwaukee, WI 53201.

Information Science and Automation. Mary A. Madden, Independent Consultant, 1605 S.W. Upland Dr., Portland, OR 97221.

Video Cable and Communications. Robert Miller, Memphis/Shelby County Public Lib. and Info. Center, Memphis, TN. Send mail to 4146 Tarrywood Dr., Memphis, TN 38118.

AMERICAN LIBRARY ASSOCIATION
PUBLIC LIBRARY ASSOCIATION
Executive Secretary, Shirley C. Mills
50 E. Huron St., Chicago, IL 60611
312-944-6780

OBJECT

To advance the development, effectiveness, and financial support of public library service to the American people; to speak for the library profession at the national level on matters pertaining to public libraries; and to enrich the professional competence and opportunities of public librarians. In order to accomplish this mission, the Public Library Association has adopted the following goals:

1. Conducting and sponsoring research about how the public library can respond to changing social needs and technological developments.

2. Developing and disseminating materials useful to public libraries in interpreting public library services and needs.

3. Conducting continuing education for public librarians by programming at national and regional conferences, by publications such as the newsletter, and by other delivery methods.

4. Establishing, evaluating, and promoting goals, guidelines, and standards for public libraries.

5. Maintaining liaison with relevant national agencies and organizations engaged in public administration and human services such as National Association of Counties, Municipal League, Commission on Post-Secondary Education.

6. Maintaining liaison with other divisions and units of ALA and other library organizations such as the Association of American Library Schools and the Urban Libraries Council.

7. Define the role of the public library in service to a wide range of user and potential user groups.

8. Promoting and interpreting the public library to a changing society through legislative programs and other appropriate means.

9. Identifying legislation to improve and to equalize support of public libraries. Organized 1951. Memb. 4,238.

MEMBERSHIP

Open to all ALA members interested in the improvement and expansion of public library services to all ages in various types of communities.

OFFICERS (1979–1980)

Pres. Ronald A. Dubberly, Public Lib., Seattle, WA 98104; *V.P. & Pres.-Elect.* Robert H. Rohlf, Hennepin County Lib., Edina, MN 55435; *Past Pres.* Genevieve M. Casey, Div. of Lib. Science, Wayne State Univ., Detroit, MI 48202.

BOARD OF DIRECTORS (1979–1980)

The officers; Marie A. Davis; Edward A. Howard; Jacqueline E. Miller; Ervin J. Gaines; Agnes M. Griffen; Patricia Woodrum; Nancy Doyle Bolt; Mildred K. Smock; *Sec. Reps. AEPS Pres.* Jacqueline E. Thresher; *AEPS Dir.* Patricia A. Gaven; *AFLS Pres.* Louise Nyce; *MLS Pres.* Joel C. Rosenfeld; *PLSS Pres.* James B. Nelson; *SMLS Pres.* Jo Wills; *Ex Officio: Public Libraries Ed.* Kenneth Shearer, Jr. *PLA-ALA Membership Rep.* Deborah J. Spiller; *Past Pres. ALTA.* Barbara S. Prentice; *Exec. Secy.* Shirley C. Mills; *Councilor.* Emily C. Payne.

PUBLICATIONS

Public Libraries (q.; memb.). *Ed.* Kenneth D. Shearer, Jr., 1205 LeClair St., Chapel Hill, NC 27514.

Public Library Reporter (occasional). Editor varies. Standing orders or single orders available from Order Dept., ALA, 50 Huron St., Chicago, IL 60611.

SECTION HEADS

Alternative Education Programs (AEPS). Jacquelyn E. Thresher.

Armed Forces Librarians (AFLS). Louise Nyce.

Metropolitan Libraries (MLS). Joel C. Rosenfeld.

Public Library Systems (PLSS). James B. Nelson.

Small and Medium-Sized Libraries (SMLS). Jo Wills.

COMMITTEE CHAIRPERSONS

Audiovisual. Leon L. Drolet, Jr., Suburban Audiovisual Service, 920 Barnsdale Rd., La Grange Park, IL 60525.

Bylaws. Glenn Miller, Orlando Public Lib., 10 N. Rosalind, Orlando, FL 32801.

Cataloging Needs of Public Libraries. Mary Kaye Donahue, 700 Sunset Drive, No. 103, McAllen, TX 78501.

Children, Service to. Robert N. Case, Lancaster County Lib., 125 N. Duke, Lancaster, PA 17602.

Conference Coordinating—New York 1980. Edward L. Whittaker, 311 Rues La., East Brunswick, NJ 08816.

Education of Public Librarians. Peter Hiatt, 19324 Eighth Ave. N.W., Seattle, WA 98177.

Goals, Guidelines, and Standards for Public Libraries. Charles W. Robinson, Baltimore County Lib., 320 York Rd., Towson, MD 21204.

Human Services. Beverly Daffern Papai, 52268 Country Acres Dr., Elkart, IN 46514.

Information and Referral Services. Carolyn A. Anthony, Baltimore County Lib., Towson, MD 21204.

Interlibrary Cooperation. To be appointed.

Legislation. Donald J. Sager, Chicago Public Lib., 425 N. Michigan Ave., Chicago, IL 60611.

Allie Beth Martin Award. Elizabeth Fannon, Cleveland Public Lib., Cleveland, OH 44114.

Membership. Deborah J. Spiller, Chicago Public Lib., 425 N. Michigan Ave., Chicago, IL 60611.

Multilingual Library Service. Yolanda Cuesta, 911 Pierce St., Albany, CA 94706.

Nominating. Ernest DiMattia, Ferguson Lib., 96 Broad St., Stamford, CT 06901.

Organization. Alexander C. Crosman, Peoria Public Lib., 107 N.E. Monroe, Peoria, IL 61602.

Orientation. Agnes M. Griffen, Tucson Public Lib., Box 27470, Tucson, AZ 85726.

"Public Libraries" Editorial. Kenneth D. Shearer, Jr., 1205 LeClair St., Chapel Hill, NC 27514.

"Public Library Reporter." Betty J. Turock, Monroe County Lib., 115 South Ave., Rochester, NY 14604.

Publications. Larry D. Black, Public Lib. of Columbus and Franklin County, 96 S. Grant Ave., Columbus, OH 43215.

Research. W. Bernard Lukenbill, Box 7576, U.T. Sta., Austin, TX 78712.

Role of the Public Library in Providing Consumer Information (Ad Hoc). Carolyn A. Anthony, Baltimore County Lib., Towson, MD 21204.

Starter List for New Branch Collections. Constance E. Koehn, Cleveland Public Lib., 325 Superior Ave., Cleveland, OH 44114.

University Press Books for Public Libraries. Claudya B. Muller, Worcester County Public Lib., Snow Hill, MD 21863.

AMERICAN LIBRARY ASSOCIATION
REFERENCE AND ADULT SERVICES DIVISION
Executive Secretary, Andrew M. Hansen
50 E. Huron St., Chicago, IL 60611
312-944-6780

OBJECT

The Reference and Adult Services Division is responsible for stimulating and supporting in every type of library the delivery of reference/information services to all groups, regardless of age, and of general library services and materials to adults. This involves facilitating the development and conduct of direct service to library users, the development of programs and guidelines for service to meet the needs of these users, and assisting libraries in reaching potential users.

The specific responsibilities of RASD are:

1. Conduct of activities and projects within the division's areas of responsibility.
2. Encouragement of the development of librarians engaged in these activities, and stimulation of participation by members of appropriate type-of-library divisions.
3. Synthesis of the activities of all units within the American Library Association that have a bearing on the type of activities represented by the division.
4. Representation and interpretation of the division's activities in contacts outside the profession.
5. Planning and development of programs of study and research in these areas for the total profession.
6. Continuous study and review of the division's activities.

Formed by merger of Adult Services Division and Reference Services Division, 1972. Memb. 5,496. (For information on dues, see ALA entry.)

OFFICERS (1979-1980)

Pres. Nancy H. Marshall, Univ. of Wisconsin, 372 D Memorial Lib., Madison, WI 53706; *V.P./Pres.-Elect.* H. Joanne Harrar, Univ. of Maryland, College Park, MD 20742; *Secy.* Donald R. Brown, State Lib. of Pennsylvania, Box 1601, Harrisburg, PA 17126.

DIRECTORS

The officers; Florence E. Blakely; Dorothy Nyren; Thomas A. Childers; Patrick O'Brien; Charles A. Bunge; *Past Pres.* Larry Earl Bone; *Ex Officio, History Sec. Chair.* Ellen H. Brow; *Machine-Assisted Reference Sec. Chair.* Danuta A. Nitecki; *Ed. RQ.* Helen B. Josephine; *Council of State and Regional Groups Chair.* Virginia Manbeck, Sunset Park Branch, Brooklyn Public Lib., 5108 Fourth Ave., Brooklyn, NY 11220; *Exec. Secy.* Andrew M. Hansen. (Address general correspondence to the executive secretary.)

PUBLICATION

RQ (q.; memb.; nonmemb. $15). *Ed.* Helen B. Josephine, Box 246, Berkeley, CA 94701.

SECTION CHAIRPERSONS

History. Ellen H. Brow, Box 684, Lawrence, KS 66044.

Machine-Assisted Reference Services (MARS). Danuta A. Nitecki, 804 S. Lincoln Ave., Urbana, IL 61801.

COMMITTEE CHAIRPERSONS

Adult Library Materials. Della L. Giblon, Leon County Public Lib., 1940 N. Monroe St., Suite 81, Tallahassee, FL 32303.

Adults, Services to. Peggy Glover, Free Lib. of Philadelphia, Logan Sq., Philadelphia, PA 19103.

AFL/CIO-ALA, Library Service to Labor Groups. Gladys E. Siegel, American Petroleum Institute, 2101 L St. N.W., Washington, DC 20037.

Aging Population, Library Service to. Kenneth L. Ferstl, Box 13256, North Texas Sta., Denton, TX 76203.

American Indian Materials and Services. Mary Alice Tsosie, Native American Center, Student Services Bldg., No. 206, Univ. of Wisconsin, Stevens Point, WI 54481.

Bibliography. Janet M. Gilligan, Colorado State Univ. Libs., Ft. Collins, CO 80523.

Budget. H. Joanne Harrar, Univ. of Maryland, College Park, MD 20742.

Business Reference Services. Jean M. Scanlan, Price, Waterhouse & Co., One Federal St., Boston, MA 02110.

Catalog Use. Ilene F. Rockman, 2480 Coburn La., No. 2, Pismo Beach, CA 93449.

Conference Program—New York 1980. Andrea C. Honebrink, MINITEX, 30 Wilson Lib., Univ. of Minnesota, 309 19 Ave. S., Minneapolis, MN 55455.

Cooperative Reference Services. Andrea C. Honebrink, MINITEX, 30 Wilson Lib., Univ. of Minnesota, 309 19 Ave. S., Minneapolis, MN 55455.

Dartmouth Medal. Rose M. Caruso. 2219 College Lib., 600 N. Park St., Madison, WI 53706.

Facts on File Award. Virginia E. Parker, Port Washington Public Lib., 245 Main St., Port Washington, NY 11050.

Goals and Objectives for Planning. Gary Purcell, Univ. of Tennessee, Knoxville, TN 37916.

Interlibrary Loan. H. Rebecca Kroll, State Univ. of New York Lib., Buffalo, NY 14260.

Membership. Ronald P. Naylor, Rte. 1, W. Panorama Loop, Waxahatchie, TX 75165.

Isadore Gilbert Mudge Citation. Donald G. Davis, Jr., Univ. of Texas, Box 7576, Univ. Sta., Austin, TX 78712.

Nominating. H. Lynn Wishart, Washington & Lee Univ. Law Lib., Lexington, VA 24450.

Notable Books Council. Robert A. Silver, 3729 Meadowbrook Blvd., University Heights, OH 44118.

Notable Books Publicity (Ad Hoc). Virginia H. Mathews, 17 Overshore Dr. W., Madison, CT 06443.

Organization. Dorothy Nyren, Brooklyn Public Lib., Grand Army Plaza, Brooklyn, NY 11238.

Outstanding Reference Sources. Jovian Lang, OFM, 37 S. Ocean Ave., Freeport, NY 11520.

Professional Development. Eleanore R. Ficke, CLENE, 620 Michigan Ave. N.E., Washington, DC 20064.

Prototype Workshop on Performance Improvement for Reference Librarians (Ad Hoc). Tina Roose, North Suburban Lib. System, 5215 Oakton, Skokie, IL 60076.

Publications. Nancy E. Gwinn, Council on Library Resources, Inc., One Dupont Circle, Suite 620, Washington, DC 20036.

Spanish-speaking, Library Services to. Albert J. Milo, Box 832, Anaheim, CA 92805.

Standards. Elaine Z. Jennerich, Baylor Univ. Lib., Box 6307, Waco, TX 76706.

Wilson Indexes. Wayne Gossage, Bank Street College of Education Lib., 610 W. 112 St., New York, NY 10025.

DISCUSSION GROUP CHAIRPERSONS

Library Service to an Aging Population. Elliott E. Kanner, North Suburban Lib. System, 200 W. Dundee Rd., Wheeling, IL 60090; Marcia Piotrowski, 138 N. Humphrey, Apt. 3 E., Oak Park, IL 60302.

Interlibrary Loan. Marilyn H. Boria, Chicago Public Lib., Chicago, IL 60611; Elaine M. Albright, Lincoln Trail Lib. System, Champaign, IL 61820.

Reference Services in Large Research Libraries. Linda Beaupré, Univ. of Texas, General Libs., Austin, TX 78712.

Reference Services in Medium-sized Research Libraries. John M. Meador, Univ. of Houston Lib., Houston, TX 77004.

Women's Materials and Women Library Users. Helen B. Josephine, Box 246, Berkeley, CA 94701.

REPRESENTATIVES

ALA Legislation Assembly. John A. McCrossan, Dept. of Lib., Media and Info. Studies, Univ. of South Florida, Tampa, FL 33620.

ALA Legislation Committee (Ad Hoc Copyright Subcommittee). Mary U. Hardin, Oklahoma Dept. of Libs., 200 N.E. 18 St., Oklahoma City, OK 73105.

ALA Membership Promotion Task Force. Patricia M. Hogan, North Suburban Lib. System, 200 W. Dundee, Wheeling, IL 60090.

Coalition of Adult Education Organization. Eleanore R. Ficke, CLENE, 620 Michigan Ave. N.E., Washington, DC 20064; Andrew M. Hansen, ALA, 50 E. Huron St., Chicago, IL 60611.

Freedom to Read Foundation. Sylvia Glasser, Brooklyn Public Lib., Sheepshead Bay Branch, 2636 E. 14 St., Brooklyn, NY 11235.

AMERICAN LIBRARY ASSOCIATION
RESOURCES AND TECHNICAL SERVICES DIVISION
Executive Secretary, William I. Bunnell
50 E. Huron St., Chicago, IL 60611
312-944-6780

OBJECT

"Responsible for the following activities: acquisition, identification, cataloging, classification, reproduction, and preservation of library materials; the development and coordination of the country's library resources; and those areas of selection and evaluation involved in the acquisition of library materials and pertinent to the development of library resources. Any member of the American Library Association may elect membership in this division according to the provisions of the bylaws." Established 1957. Memb. 6,164. (For information on dues see ALA entry.)

OFFICERS (JUNE 1979–JUNE 1980)

Pres. William A. Gosling, 4339 Berini Dr., Durham, NC 27705; *V.P.* Karen Horny, 1915 Sherman Ave., Evanston, IL 60201; *Chpn. Council of Regional Groups.* Barbara Gates, 77 Pitman, Apt. 216, Providence, RI 02906; *RTSD Councilor.* Elizabeth Herman, 701 Tigertail Rd., Los Angeles, CA 90049; *Past Pres.* Norman Dudley, 425 Kelton Ave., Los Angeles, CA 90024. (Address correspondence to the executive secretary.)

DIRECTORS

The officers; section chairpersons; LITA Rep.; RTSD Planning Committee Chpn.; RTSD Rep. to ALA Legislation Assembly; *LRTS* Ed.: *RTSD Newsletter* Ed.; David Grey Remington, 201 I St. S.W., No. 121, Washington, DC 20024 (Council of Regional Groups V.-Chpn.); Joseph Howard, Dir., Processing Dept., Lib. of Congress, Washington, DC 20540 (Lib. of Congress liaison); S. Michael Malinconico (1980); Ann Eastman, 716 Burruss Dr. N.W., Blackburg, VA 24060; Alfred Lane, 19 Barrow St., New York, NY 10014 (parliamentarian).

PUBLICATIONS

Library Resources & Technical Services (q.; memb. or $15). *Ed.* Elizabeth Tate, 11415 Farmland Dr., Rockville, MD 20852. *RTSD Newsletter* (q.; memb. or *LRTS* subscription only). *Ed.* Arnold Hirshon, Duke Sta., Box 9184, Durham, NC 27706.

SECTION CHAIRPERSONS

Cataloging and Classification. Julieann V. Nilson, 411 E. University Ave., Bloomington, IN 47401.
Reproduction of Library Materials. Jeffrey Heynen, Congressional Info. Service, 7101 Wisconsin Ave., Washington, DC 20014.
Resources. Jean Hamlin, John Cotton Dana Lib., Rutgers Univ., 185 University Ave., Newark, NJ 07102.
Serials. Dorothy Pearson, 838 Mt. Lucas Rd., Princeton, NJ 08540.

COMMITTEE CHAIRPERSONS

Association of American Publishers/ RTSD Joint Committee. Joan Seligman, 18 Stuyvesant Oval, New York, NY 10009; Lucille Gordon, McGraw-Hill, 1221 Ave. of the Americas, New York, NY 10020 (1980).
Audiovisual. J. Randolph Call, OCLC, Inc., 1125 Kinnear Rd., Columbus, OH 43212 (1980).
Book Catalogs. Dorothy McGarry, Box 5803, Sherman Oaks, CA 91413 (1979).
Bylaws. Arnold Hirshon, Duke Univ., Perkins Lib., Cataloging Dept., Durham, NC 27707 (1979).
Commercial Processing Services (Ad Hoc). Dallas R. Shawkey, Coord., Cataloging, Technical Services Center, Brooklyn Public Lib., 109 Montgomery St., Brooklyn, NY 11225.
Conference Program. William A. Gosling, 4339 Berini Dr., Durham, NC 27705 (1980).
Education. William J. Myrick, Brooklyn College Lib., CUNY, Bedford Ave. and Ave. H, Brooklyn, NY 11210 (1980).
Filing (Ad Hoc). Joseph Rosenthal, 245 General Lib., Univ. of California, Berkeley, CA 94720.
International Cataloging Consultation (Special). John D. Byrum, Chief, Descriptive Cataloging Div., Processing Dept., Lib. of Congress, Washington, DC 20540.

Membership. Murray S. Martin, Pennsylvania State Univ., Esos Pattee Lib., University Park, PA 16802 (1980).

Nominating. Susan Brynteson, Indiana Univ. Libs., Bloomington, IN 47401 (1980).

Organization. Norman Dudley, 425 Kelton Ave., Los Angeles, CA 90024 (1979).

Esther J. Piercy Award Jury. Joseph Z. Nitecki, Polk Lib., 800 Algoma Bldg., Univ. of Wisconsin-Oshkosh, Oshkosh, WI 54901 (1979).

Planning. Susan H. Vita, 3711 Taylor St., Chevy Chase, MD 20015.

Preservation of Library Materials. Robin Gay Walker, Preservation and Preparations Dept., Yale Univ. Lib., 120 High St., New Haven, CT 06520 (1979).

RTSD/LITA/RASD (MARBI). Eleanor Montague, 5062 Tophill Place, Riverside, CA 92507.

Program Evaluation and Support. William A. Gosling, 4339 Berini Dr., Durham, NC 27705 (1979).

Public Documents RASD/RTSD/ASLA. Gail M. Nichols, 1087 Harbor Way, Rodeo, CA 94572.

Representation in Machine-Readable Form of Bibliographic Information, RTSD/LITA/RASD (MARBI). Eleanor Montague, 5062 Tophill Pl., Riverside, CA 92507.

Technical Services Costs. Mary Fischer Ghikas, Dir., Technical Processes, Chicago Public Lib., 425 N. Michigan Ave., Chicago, IL 60611 (1979).

REPRESENTATIVES

ALA Freedom to Read Foundation. Paul Cors (1981).

ALA Legislation Assembly. Ann Heidbreder Eastman (1981).

ALA Library and Information Technology Association. John W. Aubry (1979).

ALA Membership Promotion Task Force. Murray Mantin (1980).

American National Standards Institute, Inc. (ANSI), Standards Committee Z39 on Library Work, Documentation and Related Publishing Practices. Susan H. Vita (1979). Alternate to be appointed.

CONSER Advisory Group. Paul Fasana (ALA Rep. 1975-1979); Karin A. Trainer (MARBI Rep. 1977-1979).

Continuing Library Education Network and Exchange. William J. Myrick (1979).

Joint Advisory Committee on Nonbook Materials. Peter Deekle (1980); Vivian Schrader (1980).

Joint Steering Committee for Revision of AACR. Frances Hinton.

Universal Serials and Book Exchange, Inc. Alfred Lane (1980).

AMERICAN LIBRARY ASSOCIATION YOUNG ADULT SERVICES DIVISION
Executive Secretary, Evelyn Shaevel
50 E. Huron St., Chicago, IL 60611
312-944-6780

OBJECT

"Interested in the improvement and extension of services to young people in all types of libraries; has specific responsibility for the evaluation, selection, interrelation and use of books and nonbook materials for young adults except when such materials are intended for only one type of library." Established 1957. Memb. 4,000. (For information on dues see ALA entry.)

MEMBERSHIP

Open to anyone interested in library services to young adults.

OFFICERS (JULY 1979–JULY 1980)

Pres. Eleanor K. Pourron, Young Adult Services, Arlington County Public Lib., 1015 Quincy St., Arlington, VA 22201; *V.P./Pres.-Elect.* Audrey Eaglen, Cuyahoga County Public Lib., 4510 Memphis Ave., Cleveland, OH 44144; *Past Pres.* Bruce Daniels, Dept. of State Lib. Services, 95 Davis St., Providence, RI 02908.

DIRECTORS

Donald B. Reynolds; Thomas Wm. Downen; Susan Tait; Evie Wilson; Barbara Newmark; Patty Campbell.

COMMITTEE CHAIRPERSONS

Activities. Maria Pedak-Kari, Prince George's County Memorial Lib. System, Hyattsville, MD. Mailing address: 19102 Stedwick Dr., Gaithersburg, MD 20760.

Best Books for Young Adults Committee. Joni Bodart, School of Lib. Science, Texas Woman's Univ., Denton, TX 76201.

Education Committee. Gerald G. Hodges, Div. of Lib. Science/Educational Technology, Univ. of North Carolina, Greensboro, NC 27412.

High-Interest/Low-Literacy Level Materials Evaluation Committee. Ellen Libretto, Supervising Libn., Head, YA Div., Queens Borough Public Lib., 89-11 Merrick Blvd., Jamaica, NY 11432.

Intellectual Freedom Committee. Mary K. Chelton, Grad. School of Lib. and Info. Services, Rutgers Univ., New Brunswick, NJ. Mailing address: 10 Landing La., New Brunswick, NJ 08901.

Legislation Committee. Evie Wilson, YA Services Specialist, Tampa-Hillsborough County Public Lib. System, Tampa, FL. Mailing address: 8602 Champlain Ct., Apt. 85, Tampa, FL 33614.

Library of Congress, Advisory Committee to Collection (Talking Books). Eileen McMurrer, Shirlington Branch Lib., 2700 S. Arlington Mill Dr., Arlington, VA 22206.

Library Service to Young Adults in Institutions. Linda Robinson, Queens Borough Public Lib., 89-11 Merrick Blvd., Jamaica, NY 11432.

Library Services for Spanish-Speaking Youth. John W. Cunningham, YA Coord.-Northwest Regional Lib., Free Lib. of Philadelphia. Mailing address: 979 N. Fifth St., Philadelphia, PA 19133.

Local Arrangements—New York 1980. Lillian Morrison, Coord., YA Services, New York Public Lib., 8 E. 40 St., New York, NY 10016.

Media Selection and Usage Committee. Rosemary Kneale, South Euclid Branch, Cuyahoga County Lib., Cleveland, OH. Mailing address: 7020 Hunting La., Chagrin Falls, OH 44022.

Membership Promotion Committee. Barbara Newmark, Mayfield Regional Lib., 6080 Wilson Mills Rd., Mayfield Village, OH 44143.

National Organizations Serving the Young Adult Liaison. Linda Miller-Syfert, Arlington County Public Lib., Arlington, VA. Mailing address: 303 Summers Dr., Alexandria, VA 22301.

Nominating Committee—1981 Election. Alice Sedgwick, F. L. Weyenberg Lib., 11345 N. Cedarburg Rd., Mequon, WI 53092.

Organization Committee. Roberta Gellert, Lewis Rd., Irvington, NY 10533.

Outstanding Biographies for the College Bound Revision Committee. Marion Hargrove, Prince George's County Lib. System, Bowie Branch. Mailing address: 61 St. Andrews Rd., Severna Park, MD 21146.

Outstanding Books on the Performing Arts Committee. Carolyn Hale, Chestnut Hill Lib., 8711 Germantown Ave., Philadelphia, PA 19118.

Outstanding Fiction for the College Bound Revision Committee. Suzanne Sullivan, J. F. K. Lib., California State Univ.-Los Angeles, 5151 State University Dr., Los Angeles, CA 90032.

Publishers Liaison Committee. Charles

B. Davis, Dir. of Sales Promotion, Simon & Schuster, 1230 Ave. of the Americas, New York, NY 10020.
Research Committee. Shirley Fitzgibbons, College of Lib. Services, Univ. of Maryland, College Park, MD 20742.
Selected Films for Young Adults. Donna Rae Meyers, Fairview Park Regional Lib., Cuyahoga County Lib. System. Mailing address: 23691 Delmere Dr., No. 226C, North Olmstead, OH 44070.
Television Committee. Joanne Nykiel, 2521 N. Burling, Chicago, IL 60614.
Top of the News Editorial Committee. Audrey Eaglen, Head, Order Div., Cuyahoga County Public Lib., 4510 Memphis Ave., Cleveland, OH 44144.

AMERICAN MERCHANT MARINE LIBRARY ASSOCIATION
(Affiliated with United Seamen's Service)
Executive Director, Mace Mavroleon
One World Trade Center, Suite 2601, New York, NY 10048

OBJECT

Provides ship and shore library service for American-flag merchant vessels, the Military Sealift Command, the Coast Guard, and other waterborne operations of the U.S. government.

OFFICERS

Chmn. of the Bd. James C. Kellogg III; *Pres.* Mrs. George Emlen Roosevelt; *V.P.* Mel Barisic; *Treas.* James J. Hayes; *Secy.* Franklin K. Riley, Jr.

TRUSTEES

Edith Augenti; Ralph R. Bagley; H. A. Downing; John I. Dugan; Charles Francis; Arthur Friedberg; Richard I. Gulick; Robert E. Hart; Thomas A. King; J. R. Kuykendall; Carolyn McKinley; Thomas J. Patterson, Jr., Andrew Rich; George J. Ryan; S. Fraser Sammis; Philip Steinberg; Paul E. Trimble, Edward Turner; C. E. Whitcomb; Adrian P. Spidle; Jeannette Spidle; Samuel Thompson.

AMERICAN SOCIETY FOR INFORMATION SCIENCE
Executive Director, Samuel B. Beatty
1010 16 St. N.W., Washington, DC 20036
202-659-3644

OBJECT

"The American Society for Information Science provides a forum for the discussion, publication, and critical analysis of work dealing with the design, management, and use of information systems and technology." Memb. (Indiv.) 4,264; (Student) 370; (Inst.) 101. Dues. (Indiv.) $45; (Student) $15; (Inst.) $250; (Sustaining Sponsor) $500.

OFFICERS

Pres. Herbert Landau, Solar Energy Research Institute, 1617 Cole Blvd., Golden, CO 80401; *Pres. Elect.* Mary C. Berger, Cuadra Associates, 1523 Sixth St., Santa Monica, CA 90401; *Treas.* John E. Creps, Jr., Engineering Index, Inc., 345 E. 47 St., New York, NY 10017; *Past Pres.* James M. Cretsos, Merrell National Labs, 2110 E. Galbraith Rd., Cincinnati, OH

45215. (Address correspondence to the executive director.)

COUNCIL

The officers; *Chapter Assembly Councillor.* Joe Ann Clifton; *SIG Cabinet Councillor.* Bonnie C. Talmi; *Councillors-at-Large.* Toni Carbo Bearman; Charles H. Davis; Jan Krcmar; Gerard O. Platau; Edmond J. Sawyer; Julie Karroll Virgo.

PUBLICATIONS

Note: Unless otherwise indicated, publications are available from Knowledge Industry Publications, 2 Corporate Park Dr., White Plains, NY 10604.

Annual Review of Information Science and Technology (vol. 3, 1968–vol. 5, 1970 and vol. 7, 1972–vol. 9, 1974, $22 ea., memb. $17.60; vol. 10, 1975, $27.50, memb. $22; vol. 12, 1977–vol. 14, 1979, $35, memb. $28).

Bulletin of the American Society for Information Science (6 per year; memb. or $27.50 domestic, $35 foreign). Available directly from ASIS.

Collective Index to the Journal of the American Society for Information Science (vol. 1, 1950–vol. 25, 1974, $60 ea., memb. $42). Available from John Wiley & Sons, 605 Third Ave., New York, NY 10016.

Computer-Readable Data Bases: A Directory and Data Sourcebook 1979 ($95, memb. $76).

Cumulative Index to the Annual Review of Information Science and Technology (vols. 1–10, $27.50 ea., memb. $22).

Journal of the American Society for Information Science; formerly *American Documentation* (bi-mo.; memb. or $45 domestic, $50 foreign). Available from John Wiley & Sons, 605 Third Ave., New York, NY 10016.

Key Papers in the Design and Evaluation of Information Systems. Ed. by Donald W. King ($19.95, memb. $15.96).

Library and Reference Facilities in the Area of the District of Columbia (10th ed., 1979, $19.50, memb. $15.60).

Proceedings of the ASIS Annual Meetings (vol. 5, 1968–vol. 9, 1972, $15 ea., memb. $12; vol. 10, 1973–vol. 16, 1979, $19.50 ea., memb. $15.60).

COMMITTEE CHAIRPERSONS

Awards and Honors. Jerome T. Maddock, Solar Energy Research Institute, 1617 Cole Blvd., Golden, CO 80401.

Budget and Finance. John E. Creps, Jr., Engineering Index, Inc., New York, NY 10017.

Conferences and Meetings. Stephanie Normann, Solar Energy Research Institute, 1617 Cole Blvd., Golden, CO 80401.

Constitution and Bylaws. Frank Slater, University of Pittsburgh, PA 15101.

Education. Trudi Bellardo, International House of Philadelphia, 3701 Chestnut St., Philadelphia, PA 19104.

Executive. Herbert Landau, Solar Energy Research Institute, 1617 Cole Blvd., Golden, CO 80401.

International Relations. Irene Farkas-Conn, Arthur L. Conn & Associates, Inc., 1469 E. Park Pl., Chicago, IL 60637.

Inter-Society Cooperation. W. T. Brandhorst, ERIC Process & Reference Facility, 4833 Rugby Ave., Bethesda, MD 20014.

Marketing. Donald W. King, King Research, Inc., 6000 Executive Blvd., Rockville, MD 20852.

Membership. Sharon R. Pyrce, Standard Oil of Indiana, Chicago, IL 60601.

Networking. Ward E. Shaw, Colorado Alliance of Research Libs., 2045 S. Clarkson, Denver, CO 80210.

Nominations. James M. Cretsos, Merrell National Labs, 2110 E. Galbraith Rd., Cincinnati, OH 45215.

Public Affairs. Joseph Caponio, National Technical Information Service, 5285 Port Royale Rd., Springfield, VA 22161.

Publications. Robert A. Kennedy, Bell Labs, Murray Hill, NJ 08974.

Standards. Margaret Park, Computer Center, Univ. of Georgia, Athens, GA 30602.

AMERICAN THEOLOGICAL LIBRARY ASSOCIATION
Executive Secretary, Rev. David J. Wartluft
Lutheran Theological Seminary, 7301 Germantown Ave.,
Philadelphia, PA 19119

OBJECT

"To bring its members into closer working relationships with each other, to support theological and religious librarianship, to improve theological libraries, and to interpret the role of such libraries in theological education, developing and implementing standards of library service, promoting research and experimental projects, encouraging cooperative programs that make resources more available, publishing and disseminating literature and research tools and aids, cooperating with organizations having similar aims and otherwise supporting and aiding theological education." Founded 1947. Memb. (Inst.) 150; (Indiv.) 460. Dues (Inst.) $50-$300, based on total library expenditure; (Indiv.) $10-$55, based on salary scale. Year. May 1-April 30.

ATLA is a member of the Council of National Library and Information Associations.

MEMBERSHIP

Persons engaged in professional library or bibliographical work in theological or religious fields and others who are interested in the work of theological librarianship.

OFFICERS (JUNE 1979-JUNE 1980)

Pres. Simeon Daly, St. Meinrad School of Theology, St. Meinrad, IN 47577; *Recording Secy.* Vacant; *Treas.* Robert A. Olsen, Jr., Libn., Brite Divinity School, Texas Christian Univ., Ft. Worth, TX 76129; *Newsletter Ed.* Donn Michael Farris, Divinity School Lib., Duke Univ., Durham, NC 27706.

BOARD OF DIRECTORS

John Batsel; Jerry Campbell; Norman Kansfield; Harriet V. Leonard; Sarah Lyons; Stephen L. Peterson; Elmer O'Brien; Kenneth Rowe; *ATS Rep.* David Schuller.

PUBLICATIONS

Newsletter (q.; memb. or $6).
Proceedings (ann.; memb. or $10).
Religion Index One (formerly *Index to Religious Periodical Literature,* 1949-date).
Religion Index Two: Multi-Author Works.

COMMITTEE CHAIRPERSONS

ATLA Newsletter. Donn Michael Farris, Ed., Divinity School Lib., Duke Univ., Durham, NC 27706.

ATLA Representative to ANSI Z39. H. Eugene McLeod, Box 752, Southeastern Baptist Theological Seminary, Wake Forest, NC 27587.

ATLA Representative to the Council of National Library and Information Associations. James Irvine, Princeton Theological Seminary, Box 111, Princeton, NJ 08540.

ATLA Representative to the Universal Serials and Book Exchange. USBE liaison now assigned to Library Materials Exchange Committee.

Annual Conferences. Harold Booher, Episcopal Theological Seminary of the Southwest, Box 2247, Austin, TX 78768.

Archivist. Gerald W. Gillette, Presbyterian Historical Society, 425 Lombard St., Philadelphia, PA 19147.

Bibliographic Systems. Winifred Campbell, Andover-Harvard Theological Lib., 45 Francis Ave., Cambridge, MA 02138.

Clearinghouse on Personnel. David J. Wartluft, Lutheran Theological Seminary, 7301 Germantown Ave., Philadelphia, PA 19119.

Collection Evaluation and Develop-

ment. William Zimpfer, Boston Univ. School of Theology, 745 Commonwealth Ave., Boston, MA 02215.

Contacts with Foundations. John Batsel, Grad. Theological Union Lib., 2451 Ridge Rd., Berkeley, CA 94709.

Library Consultation Service. John B. Trotti, Union Theological Seminary, 3401 Brook Rd., Richmond, VA 23227.

Library Materials Exchange (formerly Periodical Exchange). Irene Owens, Howard Univ. School of Religion, 1240 Randolph St. N.E., Washington, DC 20017.

Membership. Donald Meredith, Harding Grad. School of Religion, 1000 Cherry Rd., Memphis, TN 38117.

Microtext Reproduction Board. Charles Willard, Exec. Secy., Princeton Theological Seminary, Princeton, NJ 08540; Maria Grossmann, Andover-Harvard Lib., 45 Francis Ave., Cambridge, MA 02138.

Nominating. Ellis O'Neal, Andover Newton Theological School, 210 Herrick Rd., Newton Centre, MA 02159.

Periodical Indexing Board. R. Grant Bracewell, Emmanual College Lib., 75 Queen's Pk., Toronto, Ont. M5S 1K7, Canada.

Preservation of Theological Materials, (Ad Hoc). Andrew Scrimgeour, BTI Lib., Development Office, 45 Francis Ave., Cambridge, MA 02138.

Publication. Peter DeKlerk, Calvin Theological Seminary, 3233 Burton St., S.E., Grand Rapids, MI 49506.

Reader Services. Sara Mobley, Pitts Theological Lib., Emory Univ., Atlanta, GA 30322.

Serials Control (Ad Hoc). Dorothy Parks, Divinity Lib., Joint Univ. Libs., Nashville, TN 37203.

Statistician and Liaison with ALA Statistics Coordinating Committee. David Green, Grad. Theological Union, 2451 Ridge Rd., Berkeley, CA 94709.

Systems and Standards. Doralyn Hickey, Reporter, School of Lib. and Info. Sciences, North Texas State Univ., Denton, TX 76203.

ART LIBRARIES SOCIETY OF NORTH AMERICA (ARLIS/NA)
Suite 4444, 7735 Old Georgetown Rd., Washington, DC 20014
202-656-2160

OBJECT

"To promote art librarianship, particularly by acting as a forum for the interchange of information and materials on the visual arts." Established 1972. Memb. 1,200. Dues. (Inst.) $50; (Personal) $25; (Student, Lib. Asst.) $10; (Retired, Unemployed) $8.50; (Sustaining) $150; (Sponsoring) $500. Year. Jan. 1–Dec. 31.

MEMBERSHIP

Open and encouraged for all those interested in visual librarianship, whether they be professional librarians, students, library assistants, art book publishers, art book dealers, art historians, archivists, architects, slide and photograph curators, or retired associates in these fields.

OFFICERS (JAN. 1980–JAN. 1981)

Chpn. Wolfgang Freitag, Harvard Univ., Fogg Art Museum Lib., Cambridge, MA 02138; *Secy.* Clive Philpott, Museum of Modern Art Lib., 21 W. 53 St., New York, NY 10019.

COMMITTEES

(Direct correspondence to headquarters.)

Art Book Publishing Awards.
Cataloging Advisory Committee.
Education.

Exhibition Catalogs.
Iconography.
Nominating Committee.
Standards.
George Wittenborn Memorial Award.

EXECUTIVE BOARD

The chairperson, past chairperson, chairperson-elect, secretary, treasurer, and four regional representatives (East, Midwest, West, and Canada).

PUBLICATIONS

ARLIS/NA Newsletter (bi-mo.; memb.).

Directory of Art Libraries and Art Librarians in North America (bienn.).
Directory of Members (memb.).
Guide to Primitive Art Slide Collections from Boston to Washington, DC ($3.50).
NH Classification for Photography: An Alternative to TR ($1).

CHAPTERS

Allegheny; Arizona; DC-Maryland-Virginia; Georgia; Indiana-Illinois; Kansas-Missouri; Kentucky-Tennessee; Michigan; New England; New Jersey; New York; Northern California; Ohio; Southeast; Southern California; Texas; Twin Cities; Western New York.

ASSOCIATED INFORMATION MANAGERS
Program Coordinator, Helena M. Strauch
316 Pennsylvania Ave. S.E., Suite 502
Washington, DC 20003
202-544-1969

OBJECT

To maintain a forum for emerging information managers, linking them to information sources and to other managers; to create an awareness of the value of information and its potential for increased productivity; and to improve career opportunities for information managers.

MEMBERSHIP

Information managers in industry, government, academia, or individual consultants concerned with information management. Employees of firms that market information products and/or services are also eligible for membership.

DIRECTOR

James G. Kollegger, Pres., Environmental Info. Center, Inc.

EXECUTIVE COMMITTEE

Herbert R. Brinberg, Pres., Aspen Systems Corp.; Andrew P. Garvin, Chmn. & Chief Exec., FIND/SVP; Forrest W. Horton, Info. Consultant; Sarah T. Kadec, Deputy Dir., Office of Administration, The White House; Joseph H. Kuney, V.P., Informatics, Inc.; Michael D. Majcher, Mgr., Info. Resources, Xerox Corp.

PUBLICATIONS

AIM Network (bi-weekly), newsletter.
AIM Membership Roster, annual directory.
So You Want to Be an Information Manager, Resource Kit.
Information Sources (IIA Membership Directory), a directory of information products and services.

COMMITTEES

Education. Robert S. Taylor.
Membership. John W. Gross.
Regional Programs. Michael D. Majcher.

MEETINGS

AIM Caucus, the annual business meeting of AIM. Held each spring in conjunction with the National Information Conference & Exposition (sponsored by Information Industry Association). Other regional meetings or one-day seminars are scheduled to meet member needs.

ASSOCIATION OF ACADEMIC HEALTH SCIENCES LIBRARY DIRECTORS
Secretary, Peter Stangl, Director, Lane Library, Stanford University Medical Center, Stanford, CA 94305

OBJECT

"To promote, in cooperation with educational institutions, other educational associations, government agencies, and other non-profit organizations, the common interests of academic health sciences libraries located in the United States and elsewhere, through publications, research, and discussion of problems of mutual interest and concern, and to advance the efficient and effective operation of academic health sciences libraries for the benefit of faculty, students, administrators, and practitioners."

MEMBERSHIP

Regular membership is available to nonprofit educational institutions operating a school of health sciences that has full or provisional accreditation by the Association of American Medical Colleges. Annual dues $50. Regular members shall be represented by the chief administrative officer of the member institution's health sciences library.

Associate membership (and nonvoting representation) is available to organizations having an interest in the purposes and activities of the association.

OFFICERS (JUNE 1979–JUNE 1980)

Pres. Samuel Hitt, Health Sciences Lib., Univ. of North Carolina, Chapel Hill, NC 27514; *V.P.* C. Robin Lesueur, Francis A. Countway Lib. of Medicine, 10 Shattuck St., Boston, MA 02115; *Past Pres.* Gerald J. Oppenheimer, Health Sciences Lib., Univ. of Washington, SB-55, Seattle, WA 98195; *Secy.-Treas.* Peter Stangl, Dir., Lane Lib., Stanford Univ. Medical Center, Stanford, CA 94305.

BOARD OF DIRECTORS (JUNE 1979–JUNE 1980)

Officers; Glenn L. Brudvig, Bio-Medical Lib., Univ. of Minnesota, Diehl Hall, Minneapolis, MN 55455; Marcia Davidoff, Bio-Medical Lib., Univ. of South Alabama, Mobile, AL 36688; Nina W. Matheson, Paul Himmelfarb Health Sciences Lib., George Washington Univ. Medical Center, 2300 I St. N.W., Washington, DC 20037.

COMMITTEE CHAIRPERSONS

Committee on Annual Statistics for Medical School Libraries. Richard A. Lyders.
Bylaws Committee. Richard A. Lyders.
Committee on Information Control and Technology. James F. Williams II.
Committee on Medical Education. Erich Meyerhoff.
Nominating Committee. T. Mark Hodges.
Program Committee. Yvonne Wulff.
Committee on Standards and Guidelines. Nelson Gilman.

MEETINGS

An annual business meeting is held in conjunction with the annual meeting of the Medical Library Association in June. Annual membership meeting and program is held in conjunction with the annual meeting of the Association of American Medical Colleges in October.

ASSOCIATION OF AMERICAN LIBRARY SCHOOLS
Executive Secretary, Janet Phillips
471 Park La., State College, PA 16801
814-238-0254

OBJECT

"To advance education for librarianship." Founded 1915. Memb. 790. Dues (Inst.) $125; (Assoc. Inst.) $75; (Indiv.) $15; (Assoc. Indiv.) $12. Year. Sept. 1979–Aug. 1980.

MEMBERSHIP

Any library school with a program accredited by the ALA Committee on Accreditation may become an institutional member; any educator who is employed full time for a full academic year in a library school with an accredited program may become a personal member.

Any school that offers a graduate degree in librarianship or a cognate field but whose program is not accredited by the ALA Committee on Accreditation may become an associate institutional member; any part-time faculty member or doctoral student of a library school with an accredited program or any full-time faculty member employed for a full academic year at other schools that offer graduate degrees in librarianship or cognate fields may become an associate personal member.

OFFICERS
(FEBRUARY 1980–JANUARY 1981)

Pres. Charles Bunge, Lib. School, Univ. of Wisconsin, Madison, WI 53706; *Past Pres.* Genevieve Casey, Prof., Div. of Lib. Science, Wayne State Univ., Detroit, MI 48202. (Address correspondence to the executive secretary.)

DIRECTORS

Rose Mary Magrill (Univ. of Michigan); John Clemons (Emory); Jane R. Carter (Louisiana State).

PUBLICATION

Journal of Education for Librarianship (5 times per year; $18).

COMMITTEE CHAIRPERSONS

Conference. Marcy Murphy, Assoc. Prof., School of Libnshp., Western Michigan Univ., Kalamazoo, MI 49008.

Continuing Education. Vivian Sessions, Dir., Grad. School of Lib. Science, McGill Univ., Montreal, P.Q. H3A 1Y1, Canada.

Editorial Board. Charles D. Patterson, Prof., Grad. School of Lib. Science, Louisiana State Univ., Baton Rouge, LA 70803.

Legislation. Herbert S. White, Prof., Grad. Lib. School, Indiana Univ., Bloomington, IN 47401.

Nominating. Bernard Schlessinger, Dean, Grad. Lib. School, Univ. of Rhode Island, Kingston, RI 02881.

Research. Pauline Wilson, Assoc. Prof., Grad. School of Lib. and Info. Science, Univ. of Tennessee, Knoxville, TN 37916.

REPRESENTATIVES

ALA SCOLE. Gary Purcell (Tennessee).

Council of Communication Societies. Guy Garrison (Drexel).

IFLA. Genevieve Casey (Wayne); Josephine Fang (Simmons).

Organization of American States. Margaret Goggin (Denver).

ASSOCIATION OF JEWISH LIBRARIES
c/o National Foundation for Jewish Culture
122 E. 42 St., Rm. 408, New York, NY 10017

OBJECT

"To promote and improve library services and professional standards in all Jewish libraries and collections of Judaica; to serve as a center of dissemination of Jewish library information and guidance; to encourage the establishment of Jewish libraries and collections of Judaica; to promote publication of literature which will be of assistance to Jewish librarianship; to encourage people to enter the field of librarianship." Organized 1966 from the merger of the Jewish Librarians Association and the Jewish Library Association. Memb. 450. Dues. (Inst.) $15; (Indiv.) $10. Year. Calendar.

OFFICERS (JUNE 1978–JUNE 1980)

Pres. Harvey P. Horowitz, Hebrew Union College-JIR, 3077 University Mall, Los Angeles, CA 90007; *V.P./Pres. Elect.* Barbara Leff, Stephen S. Wise Temple, 15500 Stephen S. Wise Dr., Los Angeles, CA 90025; *Treas.* Ruth M. Abelow, Temple Emanu-El and Lehrman Day School, 4585 N. Meridian Ave., Miami Beach, FL 33140; *Corres. Secy.* Stephanie M. Stern, Leo Baeck Institute, 129 E. 73 St., New York, NY 10021; *Rec. Secy.* Theodore Wiener, Subject Cataloging Div., Lib. of Congress, 1701 N. Kent St., Arlington, VA 22209.

PUBLICATIONS

AJL *Bulletin* (bienn.). *Ed.* Irene S. Levin, 48 Georgia St., Valley Stream, NY 11580.
Membership Kit.
Proceedings.

DIVISIONS

Research and Special Libraries. Sheldon R. Brunswick, Univ. of California Lib., Berkeley, CA 94720.
Synagogue School and Center Libraries. Susanna R. Friedman, Congregation Beth Israel, 5600 N. Braeswood Blvd., Houston, TX 77096.

ASSOCIATION OF RESEARCH LIBRARIES
Executive Director, Ralph E. McCoy
1527 New Hampshire Ave. N.W., Washington, DC 20036
202-232-2466

OBJECT

"To initiate and develop plans for strengthening research library resources and services in support of higher education and research." Established 1932 by the chief librarians of 43 research libraries. Memb. (Inst.) 105. Dues (ann.) $2,500. Year. Jan.–Dec.

MEMBERSHIP

Membership is institutional.

OFFICERS (OCT. 1979–OCT. 1980)

Pres. Connie Dunlap, Libn., Duke Univ. Libs., Durham, NC 27706; *V.P.* Jay K. Lucker, Dir., Massachusetts Institute of

Note: For a five-year review of ARL activities, see the article by John G. Lorenz in the National Associations section of Part 1—*Ed.*

Technology Libs., Cambridge, MA 02139; *Past Pres.* Le Moyne W. Anderson, Dir., Colorado State Univ. Lib., Ft. Collins, CO 80521; *Exec. Dir. (Interim).* Ralph E. McCoy. (Address general correspondence to the executive director.)

BOARD OF DIRECTORS

Millicent D. Abell, Univ. of California, San Diego; Charles Churchwell, Washington Univ.; Richard Dougherty, Univ. of Michigan; Frank Grisham, Vanderbilt Univ.; Irene B. Hoadley, Texas A&M Univ.; Margot B. McBurney, Queen's Univ.; Eldred Smith, Univ. of Minnesota; James F. Wyatt, Univ. of Alabama.

PUBLICATIONS

ARL Annual Salary Survey (ann.; memb. or $5).

ARL Library Statistics (ann.; memb. or $5).

ARL Minutes (s.-ann.; memb. or $7.50 ea.).

ARL Newsletter (approx. 6 per year; memb. or $12).

Foreign Acquisitions Newsletter (s.-ann.; memb. or $5 ea.).

76 United Statesiana. Seventy-six works of American scholarship relating to America as published during two centuries from the Revolutionary era of the United States through the nation's bicentennial year. Ed. by Edward C. Lathem ($7.50; $5.75 paper to nonmembs.).

13 Colonial Americana. Ed. by Edward C. Lathem ($7.50).

(The above two titles are distributed by the Univ. of Virginia Press.)

Our Cultural Heritage: Whence Salvation? Louis B. Wright; *The Uses of the Past,* Gordan N. Ray: remarks to the eighty-ninth membership meeting of the association ($2).

COMMITTEE CHAIRPERSONS

Access to Manuscripts and Rare Books. Leslie Dunlap, Univ. of Iowa Libs., Iowa City, IA 52240.

African Acquisitions. Hans Panofsky, Northwestern Univ. Lib., Evanston, Il 60210.

ARL/ACRL Joint Committee on University Library Standards. Eldred Smith, Univ. of Minnesota Libs., Minneapolis, MN 55455.

Center for Chinese Research Materials. Philip McNiff, Boston Public Lib., Boston, MA 02117.

East Asian Acquisitions. Warren Tsuneishi, Lib. of Congress, Washington, DC 20540.

Foreign Newspapers on Microfilm. Joseph E. Jeffs, Georgetown Univ. Lib., Washington, DC 20007.

Interlibrary Loan. Jay Lucker, Massachusetts Institute of Technology Libs., Cambridge, MA 02139.

Latin American Acquisitions. Carl W. Deal, Univ. of Illinois Lib., Urbana, IL 61803.

Middle Eastern Acquisitions. David Partington, Harvard Univ. Lib., Cambridge, MA 02138.

National Periodicals System. James Schmidt, Brown Univ. Lib., Providence, RI 02912.

Nominations. ARL Vice-President.

Office of Management Studies. Irene Hoadley, Texas A&M Univ. Lib., College Station, TX 77843.

Preservation of Research Library Materials. David Stam, New York Public Lib., New York, NY 10018.

South Asia Acquisitions. Louis Jacob, Lib. of Congress, Washington, DC 20540.

Southeast Asia Acquisitions. Charles Bryant, Yale Univ. Lib., New Haven, CT 06520.

Western European Acquisitions. Howard Sullivan, Wayne State Univ. Lib., Detroit, MI 48202.

TASK FORCE CHAIRPERSONS

ARL Membership Criteria. Jay Lucker, Massachusetts Institute of Technology Libs., Cambridge, MA 02139.

ARL Statistics. Richard Talbot, Univ.

of Massachusetts Libs., Amherst, MA 01002.
Bibliographic Control. James Govan, Univ. of North Carolina Libs., Chapel Hill, NC 27515.
National Library Network Development. Richard Dougherty, Dir., Univ. of Michigan Libs., Ann Arbor, MI 48109.

ARL MEMBERSHIP 1979

Nonuniversity Libraries

Boston Public Lib., Center for Research Libs., John Crerar Lib., Lib. of Congress, Linda Hall Lib., National Agricultural Lib., National Lib. of Canada, National Lib. of Medicine, New York Public Lib., New York State Lib., Newberry Lib., Smithsonian Institution Libs.

University Libraries

Alabama, Alberta, Arizona, Arizona State, Boston, Brigham Young, British Columbia, Brown, California (Berkeley), California (Davis), California (Los Angeles), California (Riverside), California (San Diego), California (Santa Barbara), Case Western Reserve, Chicago, Cincinnati, Colorado, Colorado State, Columbia, Connecticut, Cornell, Dartmouth, Duke, Emory, Florida, Florida State, Georgetown, Georgia, Guelph, Harvard, Hawaii, Houston, Howard, Illinois, Indiana, Iowa, Iowa State, Johns Hopkins, Kansas, Kent State, Kentucky, Louisiana State, McGill, McMaster, Maryland, Massachusetts, Massachusetts Institute of Technology, Miami, Michigan, Michigan State, Minnesota, Missouri, Nebraska, New Mexico, New York, North Carolina, Northwestern, Notre Dame, Ohio State, Oklahoma, Oklahoma State, Oregon, Pennsylvania, Pennsylvania State, Pittsburgh, Princeton, Purdue, Queen's (Kingston, Canada), Rice, Rochester, Rutgers, South Carolina, Southern California, Southern Illinois, Stanford, SUNY (Albany), SUNY (Buffalo), SUNY (Stony Brook), Syracuse, Temple, Tennessee, Texas, Texas A&M, Toronto, Tulane, Utah, Vanderbilt, Virginia, Virginia Polytechnic, Washington, Washington (St. Louis), Washington State, Wayne State, Western Ontario, Wisconsin, Yale, York.

ASSOCIATION OF VISUAL SCIENCE LIBRARIANS
c/o Nancy Gatlin, Southern College of Optometry,
1245 Madison Ave., Memphis, TN 38104

OBJECT

"To foster collective and individual acquisition and dissemination of visual science information, to improve services for all persons seeking such information, and to develop standards for libraries to which members are attached." Founded 1968. Memb. (U.S.) 31; (foreign) 11. Annual meeting held in December in connection with the American Academy of Optometry; Boston, MA (1978); Long Beach, CA (1979); Chicago, IL (1980).

OFFICER

Chpn. Nancy Gatlin, Libn., Southern College of Optometry, 1245 Madison Ave., Memphis, TN 38104.

PUBLICATIONS

PhD Theses in Physiological Optics (irreg.).
Standards for Vision Science Libraries.
Vision Union List of Serials (irreg.).

BETA PHI MU
(International Library Science Honor Society)
Executive Secretary, Frank B. Sessa
School of Library and Information Sciences,
University of Pittsburgh, Pittsburgh, PA 15260

OBJECT

"To recognize high scholarship in the study of librarianship, and to sponsor appropriate professional and scholarly projects." Founded at the University of Illinois in 1948. Memb. 17,000.

MEMBERSHIP

Open to graduates of library school programs accredited by the American Library Association who fulfill the following requirements: complete the course requirements leading to a fifth-year or other advanced degree in librarianship with a scholastic average of A− (e.g., 4.75 where A equals 5 points, 3.75 where A equals 4 points, etc.)—this provision shall also apply to planned programs of advanced study beyond the fifth year that do not culminate in a degree but that require full-time study for one or more academic years; receive a letter of recommendation from their respective library schools attesting to their demonstrated fitness of successful professional careers. Former graduates of accredited library schools are also eligible on the same basis.

OFFICERS (1979-1980)

Pres. George M. Bailey, Assoc. Dir. of Libs., Claremont Colleges, Claremont, CA 91711; *V.P./Pres.-Elect.* Mary Alice Hunt, Assoc. Prof., School of Lib. Science, Florida State Univ., Tallahassee, FL 32306; *Past Pres.* Blanche Woolls, Assoc. Prof., School of Lib. and Info. Science, Univ. of Pittsburgh, Pittsburgh, PA 15260; *Treas.* Marilyn P. Whitmore, Univ. Archivist, Hillman Lib., Univ. of Pittsburgh, Pittsburgh, PA 15260; *Exec. Secy.* Frank B. Sessa, Prof., School of Lib. and Info. Science, Univ. of Pittsburgh, Pittsburgh, PA 15260; *Admin. Secy.* Mary Y. Tomaino, School of Lib. and Info. Science, Univ. of Pittsburgh, Pittsburgh, PA 15260.

DIRECTORS

Harriet Miller Clem, 13484 Louisville St. N.E., Paris, OH 44669 (Rho Chapter—Kent State Univ./1980); Hazel Marie Johnson, Social Sciences Bibliographer, Hillman Lib., Univ. of Pittsburgh, Pittsburgh, PA 15260 (Pi Chapter—Univ. of Pittsburgh/1980); George L. Hebben, 2925 B Ave. W., Plainwell, MI 49080 (Kappa Chapter—Western Michigan Univ./1981); Arnulfo D. Trejo, Grad. Lib. School, Univ. of Arizona, Tucson, AZ 85721 (Beta Pi Chapter—Univ. of Arizona/1981); Marion L. Mullen, 124 Pattison St., Syracuse, NY 13203 (Pi Lambda Sigma Chapter—Syracuse Univ./1982); Catherine S. Franklin, Grad. School of Lib. Science, Univ. of Texas at Austin, Austin, TX 78712 (Beta Eta Chapter—Univ. of Texas at Austin/1982).

PUBLICATIONS

Newsletter (bienn.).

Beta Phi Mu sponsors a modern Chapbook series. These small volumes, issued in limited editions, are intended to create a beautiful combination of text and format in the interest of the graphic arts and are available to members only. In December 1978, the thirteenth in the Chapbook series was published by the society: *The History of a Hoax,* by Wayne A. Wiegand.

CHAPTERS

Alpha. Univ. of Illinois, Grad. School of Lib. Science, Urbana, IL 61801; *Beta.*

Univ. of Southern California, School of Lib. Science, University Park, Los Angeles, CA 90007; *Gamma.* Florida State Univ., School of Lib. Science, Tallahassee, FL 32306; *Delta* (Inactive). Loughborough College of Further Education, School of Libnshp., Loughborough, England; *Epsilon.* Univ. of North Carolina, School of Lib. Science, Chapel Hill, NC 27514; *Zeta.* Atlanta Univ., School of Lib. and Info. Studies, Atlanta, GA 30314; *Theta.* Pratt Institute, Grad. School of Lib. and Info. Science, Brooklyn, NY 11205; *Iota.* Catholic Univ. of America, Grad. Dept. of Lib. and Info. Science, Washington, DC 20064; and Univ. of Maryland, College of Lib. and Info. Services, College Park, MD 20742; *Kappa.* Western Michigan Univ., School of Libnshp., Kalamazoo, MI 49008; *Lambda.* Univ. of Oklahoma, School of Lib. Science, Norman, OK 73019; *Mu.* Univ. of Michigan, School of Lib. Science, Ann Arbor, MI 48109; *Nu.* Columbia Univ., School of Lib. Service, New York, NY 10027; *Xi.* Univ. of Hawaii, Grad. School of Lib. Studies, Honolulu, HI 96822; *Omicron.* Rutgers Univ., Grad. School of Lib. and Info. Studies, New Brunswick, NJ 08903; *Pi.* Univ. of Pittsburgh, School of Lib. and Info. Science, Pittsburgh, PA 15260; *Rho.* Kent State Univ., School of Lib. Science, Kent, OH 44242; *Sigma.* Drexel Univ., School of Lib. and Info. Science, Philadelphia, PA 19104; *Tau.* State Univ. of New York at Geneseo, School of Lib. and Info. Science, College of Arts and Science, Geneseo, NY 14454; *Upsilon.* Univ. of Kentucky, College of Lib. Science, Lexington, KY 40506; *Phi.* Univ. of Denver, Grad. School of Libnshp., Denver, CO 80208; *Pi Lambda Sigma.* Syracuse Univ., School of Info. Studies, Syracuse, NY 13210; *Chi.* Indiana Univ., Grad. Lib. School, Bloomington, IN 47401; *Psi.* Univ. of Missouri, Columbia, School of Lib. and Info. Science, Columbia, MO 65211; *Omega.* San Jose State Univ., Div. of Lib. Science, San Jose, CA 95192; *Beta Alpha.* Queens College, City College of New York, Grad. School of Lib. and Info. Studies, Flushing, NY 11367; *Beta Beta.* Simmons College, School of Lib. Science, Boston, MA 02115; *Beta Gamma.* Univ. of Oregon (school closed); *Beta Delta.* State Univ. of New York at Buffalo, School of Info. and Lib. Studies, Buffalo, NY 14260; *Beta Epsilon.* Emporia State Univ., School of Lib. Science, Emporia, KS 66801; *Beta Zeta.* Louisiana State Univ., Grad. School of Lib. Science, Baton Rouge, LA 70803; *Beta Eta.* Univ. of Texas at Austin, Grad. School of Lib. Science, Austin, TX 78712; *Beta Theta.* Brigham Young Univ., School of Lib. and Info. Science, Provo, UT 84602; *Beta Iota.* Univ. of Rhode Island, Grad. Lib. School, Kingston, RI 02881; *Beta Kappa.* Univ. of Alabama, Grad. School of Lib. Service, University, AL 35486; *Beta Lambda.* North Texas State Univ., School of Lib. and Info. Science, Denton, TX 76203, and Texas Woman's Univ., School of Lib. Science, Denton, TX 76204; *Beta Mu.* Long Island Univ., Palmer Grad. Lib. School, C. W. Post Center, Greenvale, NY 11548; *Beta Nu.* St. John's Univ., Div. of Lib. and Info. Science, Jamaica, NY 11439 (installed March 30, 1977); *Beta Xi.* North Carolina Central Univ., School of Lib. Science, Durham, NC 27707 (installed October 8, 1976); *Beta Omicron.* Univ. of Tennessee, Knoxville, Grad. School of Lib. and Info. Science, Knoxville, TN 37916 (installed September 29, 1977); *Beta Pi.* Univ. of Arizona, Grad. Lib. School, Tucson, AZ 85721 (installed November 5, 1977); *Beta Rho.* Univ. of Wisconsin-Milwaukee, School of Lib. Science, Milwaukee, WI 53201 (installed May 21, 1978); *Beta Sigma.* Clarion State College, School of Lib. Science, Clarion, PA 16214 (to be installed); *Beta Tau.* Wayne State Univ., Div. of Lib. Science, Detroit, MI 48202 (installed June 5, 1979).

BIBLIOGRAPHICAL SOCIETY OF AMERICA
Executive Secretary, Caroline F. Schimmel
Box 397, Grand Central Sta., New York, NY 10017

OBJECT
"To promote bibliographical research and to issue bibliographical publications." Organized 1904. Memb. 1,500. Dues. $20. Year. Calendar.

OFFICERS (JAN. 1980–JAN. 1982)
Pres. Marcus A. McCorison, American Antiquarian Society, Salisbury St. & Park Ave., Worcester, MA 01609; *1st V.P.* G. Thomas Tanselle, Guggenheim Memorial Foundation, 96 Park Ave., New York, NY 10016; *2nd V.P.* William B. Todd, Parlin Hall 110, Univ. of Texas, Austin, TX 78712; *Treas.* Frank S. Streeter, 141 E. 72 St., New York, NY 10021; *Secy.* James M. Wells, Newberry Lib., 60 W. Walton Place, Chicago, IL 60610.

COUNCIL
The officers; Katharine Pantzer; Charles A. Ryscamp; P. W. Filby; William B. Todd; Andrew B. Myers; and Lola L. Szladits.

PUBLICATION
Papers (q.; memb.). *Ed.* William B. Todd, Parlin Hall, Univ. of Texas, Austin, TX 78712. *Book Review Ed.* Kenneth Carpenter, Baker Lib., Harvard Univ., Cambridge, MA 02163.

COMMITTEE CHAIRPERSON
Publications. Stephen R. Parks, Yale Univ. Lib., New Haven, CT 06520.

CANADIAN ASSOCIATION FOR INFORMATION SCIENCE (ASSOCIATION CANADIENNE DES SCIENCES DE L'INFORMATION)
Secretariat/Secrétariat, Box 776, Sta. G, Calgary,
Alta. T3A 2G6, Canada

OBJECT
Brings together individuals and organizations concerned with the production, manipulation, storage, retrieval, and dissemination of information with emphasis on the application of modern technologies in these areas. CAIS is dedicated to enhancing the activity of the information transfer process, utilizing the vehicles of research, development, application, and education, and serves as a forum for dialogue and exchange of ideas concerned with the theory and practice of all factors involved in the communication of information. Dues (Inst.) $75; (Regular) $25; (Student) $10.

MEMBERSHIP
Institutions and all individuals interested in information science and who are involved in the gathering, the organization, and the dissemination of information (computer scientists, documentalists, information scientists, librarians, journalists, sociologists, psychologists, linguists, administrators, etc.) can become members of the Canadian Association for Information Science.

OFFICERS
Pres. A. MacDonald; *1st V.P.* Carol Bregaint; *Secy.-Treas.* L. Nugent. (Address correspondence to the secretariat.)

Note: Other Canadian library associations are listed under "Foreign Library Associations" later in Part 7—*Ed.*

DIRECTORS

F. Dolan; F. Groen; *Past Pres.* E. Clyde.

PUBLICATIONS

CAIS Bulletin (q.; free with membership).

The Canadian Conference of Information Science: Proceedings (ann.; 8th ann., 1980, $16.50).

The Canadian Journal of Information Science (ann.; nonmemb. $12).

CANADIAN LIBRARY ASSOCIATION
Executive Director, Paul Kitchen
151 Sparks St., Ottawa, Ont. K1P 5E3, Canada
613-232-9625

OBJECT

To develop high standards of librarianship and of library and information service. CLA develops standards for public, university, school, and college libraries and library technician programs; offers library school scholarships and book awards; carries on international liaison with other library associations; and makes representation to government and official commissions. Founded in Hamilton in 1946, CLA is a nonprofit voluntary organization governed by an elected council and board of directors. Memb. (Indiv.) 3,800; (Inst.) 1,000. Dues. (Indiv.) $36.50-$57.50, depending on salary; (Inst.) $36.50-up, depending on budget. Year. July 1-June 30.

MEMBERSHIP

Open to individuals, institutions, and groups interested in librarianship and in library and information services.

OFFICERS (1979-1980)

Pres. Erik Spicer, Parliamentary Libn., Lib. of Parliament, Ottawa, Ont. K1A 0A9; *1st V.P./Pres.-Elect.* Alan MacDonald, Dir. of Libs., Univ. of Calgary, Calgary, Alta. T2N 1N4; *2nd V.P.* Norman Horrocks, Dir., School of Lib. Service, Dalhousie Univ., Halifax, N.S. B3H 4H8; *Treas.* Françoise Hébert, Dir. of Lib. Services, Canadian National Institute for the Blind, 1929 Bayview Ave., Toronto, Ont. M4G 3E8.; *Past Pres.* Ronald Yeo, Chief Libn., Regina Public Lib., 2311 12 Ave., Regina, Sask. S4P 0N3. (Address general correspondence to the executive director.)

BOARD OF DIRECTORS

The officers and division presidents.

COUNCIL

The officers, division presidents, and councillors, including representatives of ASTED and provincial/regional library associations.

COUNCILLORS-AT-LARGE

To June 30, 1980. Barbara Clubb; Anne Woodsworth.

To June 30, 1981. Penelope Marshall; Pat Noonan.

To June 30, 1982. Sheila Laidlaw; Ken Haycock.

PUBLICATIONS

Canadian Library Journal (6 issues; memb. or nonmemb. subscribers, Canada $14, US $15, international $17).

Canadian Materials (4 times a year. A reviewing periodical of material in all media formats produced in Canada for elementary and secondary schools. $15 subscription).

Canadian Periodical Index (11 mo. issues; ann. cumulation; price on request). (CLA microfilms early Canadian newspapers and documents of historical importance.)

DIVISION CHAIRPERSONS (1980–1981)

Canadian Association of College and University Libraries. Hans Möller, Area Libn., Undergrad. Lib., McGill Univ., Montreal, P.Q. H3A 1V1.

Canadian Association of Public Libraries. Heather Harbord, Chief Libn., Coquitlam Public Lib., 901 Lougheed Hwy., Coquitlam, B.C. V3K 3T3.

Canadian Association of Special Libraries and Information Services. Vivienne Monty, Government Documents/Microtext Lib., York Univ., 4700 Keele St., Downsview, Ont. M3J 2R6.

Canadian Library Trustees' Association. Bob McDonald, Trustee, Edmonton Public Lib. Bd., 8411 177 St., Edmonton, Alta. T5T 0P1.

Canadian School Library Association. Pauline Fennell, Education Officer, Ontario Ministry of Educ., 17 fl., Mowat Block, Queen's Park, Toronto, Ont. M7A 1L2.

PROVINCIAL/REGIONAL ASSOCIATION REPRESENTATIVES

Association pour l'Avancement des Sciences et des Techniques de la Documentation (ASTED). Arthur Boudrias, Dir.-Gen., ASTED, 360 R. Le Moyne, Montreal, P.Q. H2Y 1Y3.

Atlantic Provinces Library Association. Lorraine McQueen, 5250 Spring Garden Rd., Apt. 804, Halifax, N.S. B3J 1E8.

British Columbia Library Association. James Scott, Box 46378, Sta. G, Vancouver, B.C. V6R 4G6.

Library Association of Alberta. Robert M. Block, Chief Libn., Medicine Hat Public Lib., 414 First St., Medicine Hat, Alta. T1A 0A6.

Manitoba Library Association. Carolynne Scott, St. Vital Public Lib., 6 Fermor Ave., Winnipeg, Man. R2M 0Y2.

Ontario Library Association. Kenneth R. Frost, 64 Bedle Ave., Willowdale, Ont. M2H 1K8.

Quebec Library Association. Diana Frye, c/o Dawson College Lib., 1001 Sherbrooke St. E., Montreal, P.Q. H2L 1L3.

Saskatchewan Library Association. Gordon L. Ray, Saskatoon Public Lib., 311 23 St. E., Saskatoon, Sask. S7K 0J6.

CATHOLIC LIBRARY ASSOCIATION
Executive Director, Matthew R. Wilt
461 W. Lancaster Ave., Haverford, PA 19041
215-649-5250

OBJECT

"The promotion and encouragement of Catholic literature and library work through cooperation, publications, education and information." Founded 1921. Memb. 3,280. Dues $20–$500. Year. July 1979–June 1980.

OFFICERS (APRIL 1979–APRIL 1981)

Pres. Sister Franx Lang, OP, Barry College Lib., Miami, FL 33161; *V.P.* Kelly Fitzpatrick, Mt. St. Mary's College, Emmitsburg, MD 21727; *Past Pres.* Sister Mary Arthur Hoagland, IHM, Office of the Superintendent of Schools, Philadelphia, PA 19103. (Address general correspondence to the executive director.)

EXECUTIVE BOARD

The officers; Rev. Robert P. Cawley, Central Assn. of the Miraculous Medal, Philadelphia, PA 19144; Brother DeSales Pergola, OSF, St. Francis Prep School,

Fresh Meadows, NY 11363; Mary A. Grant, Nazareth H.S. Media Center, Brooklyn, NY 11203; Brother Emmett Corry, OSF, St. John's Univ., Jamaica, NY 11439; Sister Teresa Rigel, CSJ, 700 Lincoln, Blue Rapids, KS 66411; Irma C. Godfrey, 6247 Westway Place, St. Louis, MO 63109.

PUBLICATIONS

Catholic Library World (10 issues; memb. or $20).

The Catholic Periodical and Literature Index (subscription).

COMMITTEE CHAIRPERSONS

Advisory Council. Kelly Fitzpatrick, Mt. St. Mary's College, Emmitsburg, MD 21727.

AASL Standards Committee. Sister Mary Arthur Hoagland, IHM, Office of the Superintendent of Schools, Philadelphia, PA 19103.

ANSI-Z39. Richard A. Davis, Rosary College, River Forest, IL 60305.

Catholic Health Association of the U.S. Pamela Kay Drayson, St. Mary's Hospital, Kansas City, MO 64108.

Catholic Library World Editorial. Sister Marie Melton, RSM, St. John's Univ., Jamaica, NY 11439.

The Catholic Periodical and Literature Index. Arnold M. Rzepecki, Sacred Heart Seminary College Lib., Detroit, MI 48206.

Catholic Press Association. John T. Corrigan, CFX, CLA Headquarters, 461 W. Lancaster Ave., Haverford, PA 19041.

Constitution and Bylaws. Sister Margaret Huyck, CSJ, St. Joseph Academy, New Orleans, LA 70122.

Continuing Education. Sister Mary Dennis Lynch, SHCJ, Rosemont College, Rosemont, PA 19010.

Continuing Library Education Network Exchange (CLENE). Sister Mary Dennis Lynch, SHCJ, Rosemont College, Rosemont, PA 19010.

Council of National Library and Information Association (CNLIA). Matthew R. Wilt, Exec. Dir., CLA Headquarters, 461 W. Lancaster Ave., Haverford, PA 19041; Brother Emmett Corry, OSF, St. John's Univ., Jamaica, NY 11439.

Elections. Mary Mountain, LaSalle College H.S., Philadelphia, PA 19118.

Finance. Arnold M. Rzepecki, Sacred Heart Seminary College Lib., Detroit, MI 48206.

Membership/Unit Coordinator. Jane F. Hindman, CLA Headquarters, 461 W. Lancaster Ave., Haverford, PA 19041.

Nominations. James C. Cox, Loyola Univ. Medical Center Lib., Maywood, IL 60153.

Program Coordinator. John T. Corrigan, CFX, CLA Headquarters, 461 W. Lancaster Ave., Haverford, PA 19041.

Public Relations. Sister Mary Margaret Cribben, RSM, Villanova College, Villanova, PA 19085.

Publications. Sister Mary Field, OP, Rosary College Lib., River Forest, IL 60305.

Regina Medal. Sister Barbara Anne Kilpatrick, St. Aloysius School, Bessemer, AL 35020.

Scholarship. Sister Jane Marie Barbour, CDP, Our Lady of the Lake Univ. of San Antonio, San Antonio, TX 78285.

Special Libraries Association. Mary-Jo DiMuccio, Sunnyvale Public Lib., Sunnyvale, CA 94087.

Universal Serials and Book Exchange (USBE). Sister Therese Marie Gaudreau, SND, Trinity College, Washington, DC 20017.

SECTION CHAIRPERSONS

Archives. Rev. John B. DeMayo, St. Charles Seminary Lib., Overbrook, Philadelphia, PA 19151.

Children's Libraries. Sally Anne Thompson, 7015 E. San Miguel, Paradise Valley, AZ 85253.

College, University, Seminary Libraries. Sister Therese Marie Gaudreau, SND, Trinity College, Washington, DC 20017.

High School Libraries. Reverend Timothy Buyansky, OSB, Benedictine H.S. Lib., Cleveland, OH 44104.

Library Education. Reverend Jovian P. Lang, OFM, St. John's Univ., Jamaica, NY 11439.

Parish/Community Libraries. Reverend Ralph J. Monteiro, OSA, Our Mother of Consolation, Philadelphia, PA 19118.

Public Libraries. Margaret Long, Public Lib. of Cincinnati, Cincinnati, OH 45202.

ROUND TABLE CHAIRPERSONS

Cataloging and Classification Roundtable. Tina-Karen Weiner, La Salle College, Philadelphia, PA 19141.

Health Sciences Roundtable. Sister Victoria Crescente, RSM, Gwynedd Mercy Academy, Gwynedd Valley, PA 19437.

CHIEF OFFICERS OF STATE LIBRARY AGENCIES
Anthony W. Miele, Director, Alabama Public Library Service
6030 Monticello Dr., Montgomery, AL 36109

OBJECT

The object of COSLA is to provide "a means for cooperative action among its state and territorial members to strengthen the work of the respective state and territorial agencies. Its purpose is to provide a continuing mechanism for dealing with the problems faced by the heads of these agencies which are responsible for state and territorial library development."

MEMBERSHIP

The Chief Officers of State Library Agencies is an independent organization of the men and women who head the state and territorial agencies responsible for library development. Its membership consists solely of the top library officers of the 50 states and one territory, variously designated as state librarian, director, commissioner, or executive secretary.

OFFICERS (NOV. 1978-NOV. 1980)

Chpn. William G. Asp, Dir., Office of Public Libs. & Interlib. Cooperation, Minnesota Dept. of Educ., 301 Hanover Bldg., St. Paul, MN 55101; *V. Chpn.* W. Lyle Eberhart, Administrator, Wisconsin Dept. of Public Instruction, 126 Langdon St., Madison, WI 53702; *Secy.* Anthony W. Miele, Dir., Alabama Public Lib. Service, 6030 Monticello Dr., Montgomery, AL 36109; *Treas.* Carlton J. Thaxton, Dir., Div. of Public Lib. Services, 156 Trinity Ave. S.W., Atlanta, GA 30303; *ALA Affiliation.* Sandra Cooper of ALA, Exec. Secy.; Donald Simpson, ASLA, Pres. (Address correspondence to the secretary.)

DIRECTORS

The officers, immediate past chairperson, and two elected members: Patricia E. Klinck, Vermont State Libn.; Russell L. Davis, Dir., Utah Lib. Commission; *Past Chpn.* Joseph F. Shubert, New York State Libn.

COMMITTEE CHAIRPERSONS

Continuing Education. Patricia Klinck, State Libn., Vermont State Lib.

Legislation. Robert Clark, Jr., Oklahoma Dept. of Libs.

Liaison with ALA and ASLA. Joe Forsee, State Libn., Mississippi Lib. Commission.

Liaison with the Librarian of Congress. Ethel Crocket, State Libn., California State Lib.

Liaison with Library of Congress, Division for the Blind and Physically Handicapped. Russell L. Davis, Utah State Lib. Commission.

Liaison with the National Commission on Libraries and Information Science. Lyle Eberhart, Wisconsin Dept. of Public Instruction.

Liaison with the U.S. Office of Education & Statistics. Joe Shubert, New York State Lib.
State Library Organization in State Government. Gary Nichols, Maine State Lib.
Statewide Planning and Network Development. Pat Broderick, Acting Dir., Pennsylvania State Lib.
Committee for Federal Documents and Liaison with Public Printer. Anthony W. Miele, Dir., Alabama Public Lib. Service.

CHINESE-AMERICAN LIBRARIANS ASSOCIATION
Executive Director, Tze-chung Li
Rosary College Graduate School of Library Science
River Forest, IL 60305

OBJECT

"(1) To facilitate better communication among Chinese-American librarians; (2) to serve as a forum for the discussion of mutual problems and professional concerns among Chinese-American librarians; (3) to promote the development of Chinese and American librarianship." Founded 1973. CALA is affiliated with the Chinese Professional Association, the Chinese Language Computer Society, and the American Library Association.

MEMBERSHIP

Membership is open to everyone who is interested in the association's goals and activities. Memb. 230. Dues. (Regular) $15; (Student and Nonsalaried) $7.50; (Inst.) $45; (Permanent) $150.

OFFICERS (JUNE 1979–JUNE 1980)

Pres. John Yung-Hsiang Lai, Libn., Harvard-Yenching Lib., Cambridge, MA 02138; *V.P./Pres.-Elect.* Lee-Hsia Ting, Prof., Western Illinois Univ., Macomb, IL 61455; *2nd V.P.* David T. Liu, Dir., Pharr Memorial Lib., Pharr, TX 78577; *Treas.* Theresa Hwa, Libn., De Paul Univ. Lib., Chicago, IL 60604; *Secy.* Carol Ku, Libn., Eastern Illinois Univ. Lib., Charleston, IL 61920; *Exec. Dir.* Tze-chung Li, Prof., Rosary College, River Forest, IL 60305.

PUBLICATIONS

Directory of Chinese American Librarians in the United States, 1976 (memb. $2.50 or $5).
Journal of Library and Information Science (2 per year; memb. or $10).
Newsletter (3 per year; memb.).

COMMITTEE CHAIRPERSONS

Annual Program. Lee-Hsia Ting, Western Illinois Univ., Macomb, IL 61455.
Awards. Henry C. Chang, State Lib., Virgin Islands 00801.
Membership. Sally C. Tseng, Univ. of Nebraska, Lincoln, NE 68508.
Nominating. Hwa-wei Lee, Ohio Univ. Libs., Athens, OH 45701.
Publications. John Yung-hsiang Lai, Harvard-Yenching Lib., Cambridge, MA 02138.

CHAPTER CHAIRPERSONS

Mid-West. Roy Chang, Western Illinois Univ. Lib., Macomb, IL 61455.
Northwest. Hong-chan Li, Univ. of Connecticut Lib., West Hartford, CT 06117.
Southwest. William Wan, Texas Woman's Univ. Lib., Denton, TX 76201.

JOURNAL OFFICERS

Margaret Fung, National Taiwan Normal Univ., Taipei, Taiwan; Chen-ku Wang, National Central Lib., Taipei, Taiwan; Tze-chung Li, Rosary College, River Forest, IL 60305; *Copy Ed.* Theodore Spahn, Rosary College, River Forest, IL 60305.

CHURCH AND SYNAGOGUE LIBRARY ASSOCIATION
Executive Secretary, Dorothy J. Rodda
Box 1130, Bryn Mawr, PA 19010

OBJECT

"To act as a unifying core for the many existing church and synagogue libraries; to provide the opportunity for a mutual sharing of practices and problems; to inspire and encourage a sense of purpose and mission among church and synagogue librarians; to study and guide the development of church and synagogue librarianship toward recognition as a formal branch of the library profession." Founded 1967. Memb. 1,300. Dues (Contributing) $100; (Inst.) $50; (Affiliated) $25; (Active Church or Synagogue) $15; (Active Indiv.) $7.50. Year. July 1979–June 1980.

OFFICERS (JULY 1979–JUNE 1980)

Pres. Alma V. Lowance, 1717 Bellevue Ave., A-826, Richmond, VA 23227; *1st V.P.* Robert Dvorak, 8 Porter Meadow, Topsfield, MA 01983; *2nd V.P.* Ruth A. Turney, 16 Windaway Rd., Bethel, CT 06801; *Treas.* Bruce B. Brown, 114 Breenwood Ave., Bloomington, IL 61701; *Past Pres.* Maryann J. Dotts, 2514 Blair Blvd., Nashville, TN 37212; *Publications Dir. and Bulletin Ed.* William H. Gentz, 300 E. 34 St., Apt. 9C, New York, NY 10016.

EXECUTIVE BOARD

The officers and committee chairpersons.

PUBLICATIONS

Church and Synagogue Libraries (bimo.; memb. or $10, Can. $12). *Ed.* William H. Gentz. Book reviews, ads, $100 for full-page, camera-ready ad, one-time rate.

CSLA Guide No. 1. Setting Up a Library: How to Begin or Begin Again ($2.50).

CSLA Guide No. 2, rev. 2nd ed. *Promotion Planning All Year 'Round* ($4.50).

CSLA Guide No. 3, rev. ed. *Workshop Planning* ($6.50).

CSLA Guide No. 4, rev. ed. *Selecting Library Materials* ($2.50).

CSLA Guide No. 5. Cataloging Books Step by Step ($2.50).

CSLA Guide No. 6. Standards for Church and Synagogue Libraries ($3.75).

CSLA Guide No. 7. Classifying Church or Synagogue Library Materials ($2.50).

CSLA Guide No. 8. Subject Headings for Church or Synagogue Libraries ($3.50).

CSLA Guide No. 9. A Policy and Procedure Manual for Church and Synagogue Libraries ($3.75).

Church and Synagogue Library Resources: Annotated Bibliography ($2.50).

A Basic Book List for Church Libraries: Annotated Bibliography ($1.75).

Helping Children Through Books: Annotated Bibliography ($3.75).

The Family Uses the Library. Leaflet (5¢; $3.75/100).

The Teacher and the Library—Partners in Religious Education. Leaflet (10¢; $7/100).

Promotion and Publicity for a Congregational Library. Sound slide set ($75; rental fee $10).

COMMITTEE CHAIRPERSONS

Awards. Judy McAdams.
Chapters. Fay W. Grosse.
Continuing Education. Elsie E. Lehman.
Finance. Austin Turney.
Fund Raising. Arthur W. Swarthout.
Library Services. Rachel D. Kohl.
Membership. Patricia W. Tabler.
Nominations and Elections. Bernard E. Deitrick.
Public Relations. Maryann J. Dotts.
Religious World Liaison. Suzanne Woodard.
Sites. Sherry D. Fleet.

CONTINUING LIBRARY EDUCATION NETWORK AND EXCHANGE (CLENE), INC.
Executive Director, Eleanore R. Ficke
620 Michigan Ave. N.E., Washington, DC 20064
202-635-5825

OBJECT

The basic missions of CLENE, Inc., are (1) to provide equal access to continuing education opportunities, available in sufficient quantity and quality over a substantial period of time to ensure library and information science personnel and organizations the competency to deliver quality library and information services to all; (2) to create an awareness and a sense of need for continuing education of library personnel on the part of employers and individuals as a means of responding to societal and technological change. Founded 1975. Memb. 390. Dues (Indiv.) $15; (Inst./Assoc.) $35-$100; (State Agency) $750-$3,000 according to population. Year. Twelve months from date of entry.

MEMBERSHIP

CLENE, Inc., welcomes as members: institutions—libraries, information centers, data banks, schools and departments of library, media, and information science—any organization concerned with continuing education; professional associations in library, media, information science, and allied disciplines; local, state, regional and national associations; individuals; state library and educational agencies; consortia.

OFFICERS (JUNE 1979–JUNE 1980)

Pres. James A. Nelson, Univ. of Wisconsin Extension, Madison, WI 53706; *Pres.-Elect.* Suzanne H. Mahmoodi, OPLIC, St. Paul, MN 55101; *Secy.* Anne Mathews, Univ. of Denver, Denver, CO 80208; *Treas.* Julie Blume, Chicago, IL 60615; *Past Pres.* Peggy O'Donnell, ALA, Chicago, IL 60611; Margaret Knox Goggin, Gainesville, FL 32601; Marcia Lowell, Oregon State Lib., Salem, OR 97310; Margaret Myers, ALA, Chicago, IL 60611; Joseph F. Shubert, State Lib. of New York, Albany, NY 12234; Garland Strother, St. Charles Parish Lib., Luling, LA 70070; Celia C. Suarez, Miami-Dade Community College, Miami, FL 33167; Dan Tonkery, Univ. of California, Los Angeles, CA 90024; Susan S. Whittle, State Lib. of Florida, Tallahassee, FL 32301.

PUBLICATIONS

CLENExchange (6/yr.). Newsletter. $4 to nonmembers.
Continuing Education Communicator (mo.). $10 (Indiv.); $15 (Institutions).
Proceedings of CLENE Assembly I: Self-Assessment (January 1976). $4.25 (memb.); $5 (nonmemb.).
Proceedings of CLENE Assembly II: Updating and Skills for Ourselves (July 1976).
Proceedings of CLENE Assembly III. (February 1977).
Directory of Continuing Education Opportunities (1979) (ann.). $22.80.
Model Continuing Education Recognition System in Library and Information Science 1979 (June) $29.80.
Who's Who in Continuing Education: Human Resources in Continuing Library, Information, Media Education (September 1979). $30.

Concept Papers

#1 *Developing CE Learning Materials.* Sheldon and Woolls (1977). $4.25 (memb.); $5 (nonmemb.).
#2 *Guide to Planning and Teaching CE Courses.* Washtien (1975). $4.25 (memb.); $5 (nonmemb.).
#3 *Planning & Evaluating Library Training Programs.* Sheldon (1976). $4.25 (memb.); $5 (nonmemb.).

#4 *Helping Adults to Learn.* Knox (1976) (out of print).
#5 *Continuing Library Education: Needs Assessment & Model Programs.* Virgo, Dunkel, Angione (1977). $10.20 (memb.); $12 (nonmemb.).
#6 *Recognition for Your Continuing Education Accomplishments.* James Nelson (June 1979).
Annotated Bibliography of Recent Continuing Education Literature (1976). $4.25 (memb.); $5 (nonmemb.).
Continuing Education Resource Book (1977). $2.55 (memb.); $3 (nonmemb.).
Continuing Education Planning Inventory: A Self-Evaluation Checklist (1977). $1.70 (memb.); $2 (nonmemb.).
Guidelines for Relevant Groups Involved in Home Study Programs (1977). $4.25 (memb.); $5 (nonmemb.).

COMMITTEES

Assembly Planning Committee.
By-laws Committee.
Committee on Committees.
Finance Committee.
Long-Range Planning Committee.
Membership Committee.
Nominating Committee.
Project Development Committee.
Publications Committee.
Task Force on the Recognition System.

COUNCIL FOR COMPUTERIZED LIBRARY NETWORKS
President, Glyn T. Evans
State University of New York Central Administration,
State University Plaza, Albany, NY 12246
518-474-1430

OBJECT

"CCLN serves several purposes. It disseminates information concerning on-line library networks; collates information provided by members; and organizes and coordinates professional development activities. In addition, it acts as a change agent by promoting dialogue within the library profession and among professional groups working in allied fields; participating in planning of the national network; informing the private sector of members' problems with existing technology and needs for new solutions; and making research and development recommendations to the federal government and foundations to facilitate support of state, regional, national, and international networking efforts."

MEMBERSHIP

CCLN has two types of membership: Network Members and Associate Members. Network Members represent on-line computerized library networks that provide services on a nonprofit basis to administratively independent libraries for a state, region, or multistate area in North America. New applicants are admitted to membership upon a two-thirds vote of current Network Members. Each Network Member has one representative with one vote at business meetings who is eligible to serve on the Executive Committee, and be appointed a program officer. Each Network Member represents its local and regional library members.

Associate Members represent individual libraries using services provided by a CCLN Network Member.

Two other types of CCLN membership are being reviewed: Affiliate Members and Educational Members. The former would include those suppliers of services, systems, or data bases that are of use or interest to Network Members. Educational Members

Note: For additional information on the Council for Computerized Library Networks, see the report from CCLN in the National Associations section of Part 1—*Ed.*

would include accredited institutions offering advanced degrees in library or information science.

OFFICERS

Pres. Glyn T. Evans (1979–1980), Dir. of Lib. Services, State Univ. of New York, Central Admin., State University Plaza, Albany, NY 12246; *V.P./Pres.-Elect.* Robin J. Braithwaite (1980–1981), Mgr. of Marketing, Univ. of Toronto Lib. Automation Systems, 130 S. St. George St., Suite 8003, Toronto, Ont. M5S 1A5, Canada; *Secy.* James G. Schoenung (1979–1981), Exec. Dir., PALINET/ULC, 3420 Walnut St., Philadelphia, PA 19104; *Treas.* John Aubry (1979–1981), Exec. Dir., Michigan Lib. Consortium (Aubry resigned his duties in late 1979; Peter J. Paulson, Dir., New York State Interlibrary Loan Network—NYSILL, New York State Lib., Cultural Education Center, Albany, NY 12238, will complete Aubry's year of service. (Address correspondence to the president.)

PUBLICATIONS

CCLN News (q.; memb.).
News Flash Current Awareness Service (irreg.; memb.).

Network Technology Reports (planned).
Resource Surveys (planned).

CCLN MEMBERSHIP 1979–1980

AMIGOS Bibliographic Council, Bibliographic Center for Research (BCR), California Lib. Authority for Systems and Services (CLASS), Cooperative College Lib. Center (CCLC), Five Associated Univ. Libs. (FAUL), Illinois Lib. and Info. Network (ILLINET), Indiana Cooperative Lib. Services Authority (INCOLSA), Michigan Lib. Consortium (MLC), Midwest Region Lib. Network (MIDLNET), Minnesota Interlibrary Telecommunications Exchange (MINITEX), New England Lib. Info. Network (NELINET), New York State Interlibrary Loan Network (NYSILL), OCLC, Inc., OHIONET, PALINET and Union Lib. Catalogue of Pennsylvania (PALINET/ULC), Pittsburgh Regional Lib. Center (PRLC), Research Libs. Group (RLG), Southeastern Lib. Network (SOLINET), State Univ. of New York (SUNY), Univ. of Toronto Lib. Automation Systems (UTLAS), Washington Lib. Network (WLN), Wisconsin Lib. Consortium (WLC).

COUNCIL OF NATIONAL LIBRARY AND INFORMATION ASSOCIATIONS, INC.
461 W. Lancaster Ave., Haverford, PA 19041

OBJECT

To provide a central agency for cooperation among library associations and other professional organizations of the United States and Canada in promoting matters of common interest.

MEMBERSHIP

Open to national library associations and organizations with related interests of the United States and Canada. American Assn. of Law Libs., American Lib. Assn., American Society of Indexers, American Theological Lib. Assn., Art Libs. Society/North America, Assn. of Jewish Libs., Catholic Lib. Assn., Church and Synagogue Lib. Assn., Council of Planning Libns., Lib. Binding Institute, Lib. Public Relations Council, Lutheran Lib. Assn., Medical Lib. Assn., Music Lib. Assn., National Federation of Abstracting and Indexing Services, Society of American Archivists, Special Libs. Assn., Theatre Lib. Assn.

OFFICERS (JULY 1979–JUNE 1980)

Chmn. Jane L. Hammond, Law Lib., Myron Taylor Hall, Cornell Univ., Ithaca, NY 14853; *V. Chmn.* Richard M. Buck, PARC, New York Public Lib., 111 Amsterdam Ave., New York, NY 10023; *Past Chmn.* Theodore Wiener, 1701 N. Kent St., Arlington, VA 22209; *Secy.-Treas.* Barbara Preschel, 400 E. 56 St., New York, NY 10022. (Address correspondence to chairman at 461 W. Lancaster Ave., Haverford, PA 19041.)

DIRECTORS

Morris L. Cohen, Harvard Law School Lib., Langdell Hall, Cambridge, MA 02138 (July 1977–June 1980); Mary M. Cope, City College Lib., City Univ. of New York, 135 St. and Convent Ave., New York, NY 10031 (July 1978–June 1981); Vivian Hewitt, Carnegie Endowment for International Peace, 30 Rockefeller Plaza, New York, NY 10020 (July 1979–June 1982).

COUNCIL OF PLANNING LIBRARIANS, PUBLICATIONS OFFICE
1313 E. 60 St., Chicago, IL 60637

OBJECT

To provide a special interest group in the field of city and regional planning for libraries and librarians, faculty, professional planners, university, government, and private planning organizations; to provide an opportunity for exchange among those interested in problems of library organization and research and in the dissemination of information about city and regional planning; to sponsor programs of service to the planning profession and librarianship; to advise on library organization for new planning programs; to aid and support administrators, faculty, and librarians in their efforts to educate the public and their appointed or elected representatives to the necessity for strong library programs in support of planning. Founded 1960. Memb. 200. Dues. $35 (Inst.); $10 (Indiv.). Year. July 1–June 30.

MEMBERSHIP

Open to any individual or institution that supports the purpose of the council upon written application and payment of dues to the treasurer.

OFFICERS (1979–1980)

Pres. Margaret DePopolo, Libn., Rotch Lib. of Architecture and Planning, No. 7-238, Massachusetts Institute of Technology, Cambridge, MA 02139; *V.P.* Patricia Coatsworth, Libn., Merriam Center Lib., 1313 E. 60 St., Chicago, IL 60637; *Secy.* Chris Hail, Frances Loeb Lib., Gund Hall, Harvard Univ., Cambridge, MA 02138; *Treas.* Gary Scales, RR 2, Box 293, Louisville, TN 37777; *Member-at-Large.* Jon S. Greene, Libn., School of Architecture and Urban Planning, Univ. of California, Los Angeles, CA 90024; *Editor Publications Program.* Jean Gottlieb, 1313 E. 60 St., Chicago, IL 60637.

PUBLICATIONS

CPL Bibliographies (20 numbers published to Jan. 1980; approx. 30 bibliographies per year). May be purchased on standing order subscription or by individual issue. Subscription rates on request.

Nos. 1–3. *Comprehensive Index to Exchange Bibliographies,* No. 1-1565, 3-vol. set ($25). Subject Index (119 pp., $12). Author Index (100 pp., $10). Numerical Index (89 pp., $9).

No. 4. *Planning Principles for Transportation Systems,* Dominick Gatto (16 pp., $3.50).
No. 5. *Futures Planning in Management,* Roger Evered (52 pp., $7).
No. 6. *Effects of Environmental Regulations on Housing Costs,* David E. Dowall and Jesse Mingilton (67 pp., $7).
No. 7. *Land Banking,* Claudia Michniewicz (13 pp., $3.50).
No. 8. *Opposition to Volunteerism,* Doris B. Gold (21 pp., $3.50).
No. 9. *Tax Incremental Financing,* Debra L. Allen and Jack R. Huddleston (13 pp., $3.50).
No. 10. *Primary Source Materials on Environmental Impact Studies,* Catharine Askow (23 pp., $3.50).
No. 11. *Historic Preservation in the Pacific Northwest: A Bibliography of Sources 1947–1978,* Lawrence N. Crumb (63 pp., $7).
No. 12. *Community Goals and Goal Formulation: A Reference,* George E. Bowen (29 pp., $3.50).
No. 13. *Discrimination in Housing,* Robert E. Ansley, Jr. (75 pp., $10).
No. 14. *Urban Recreation Planning: A Selected Bibliography,* Seymour M. Gold (15 pp., $3.50).
No. 15. *Interracial Housing Since 1970: From Activism to Affirmative Marketing,* Dudley Onderdonk III (30 pp., $3.50).
No. 16. *Wind Energy Planning: A Bibliography,* Toru Otawa (31 pp., $3.50).
No. 17. *German City Planning History: 1871–1945,* John R. Mullin (43 pp., $7).
No. 18. *Government Regulations and the Cost of Housing: A Partially Annotated Bibliography,* Anne McGowan (13 pp., $3.50).
No. 19. *Methods of Handling Complaints against the Police,* Edwana D. Collins (32 pp., $5).
No. 20. *Mobile Home Resource List,* Carol B. Meeks (24 pp., $3.50).

COUNCIL ON LIBRARY RESOURCES, INC.
One Dupont Circle, Suite 620, Washington, DC 20036
202-296-4757

OBJECT

A private operating foundation, the council seeks to assist in finding solutions to the problems of libraries, particularly academic and research libraries. In pursuit of this aim, the council makes grants to and contracts with other organizations and individuals. The Ford Foundation established CLR in 1956 and has since contributed $31.5 million to its support. CLR receives support from other foundations as well; the Andrew W. Mellon Foundation and the Carnegie Corporation of New York granted $1.5 million to CLR in 1977. The council's current program interests include establishment of a computerized system of national bibliographic control, library management and institutional development, professional education, collection building, and analysis and planning.

MEMBERSHIP

Members constitute the council's board of directors. Limited to 20.

OFFICERS

Chpn. Whitney North Seymour, Sr., Simpson, Thacher & Bartlett, One Battery Park Plaza, New York, NY 10004; *V. Chpn.* Louis B. Wright, 3702 Leland St., Chevy Chase, MD 20015; *Pres.* Warren J. Haas, Council on Lib. Resources; *Secy.-Treas.* Mary Agnes Thompson, Council on Lib. Resources.

PUBLICATIONS

Annual Report.
CLR Recent Developments.

EDUCATIONAL FILM LIBRARY ASSOCIATION
Executive Director, Nadine Covert
43 W. 61 St., New York, NY 10023
212-246-4533

OBJECT

"To promote the production, distribution and utilization of educational films and other audio-visual materials." Incorporated 1943. Memb. 1,800. Dues. (Inst.) $65–$150; (Commercial Organizations) $175; (Indiv.) $15. Year. July–June.

OFFICERS

Pres. William Murray (1978–1981) Dir., Media Services, Aurora Public Schools, 1085 Peoria St., Aurora, CO 80011; *Pres.-Elect.* Gerald Rogers (1977–1980) Editorial Service Center-Region XVII, 700 Texas Commerce Bank Bldg., Lubbock, TX 79401; *Treas.* Nadine Covert (Ex Officio) Exec. Dir., EFLA, 43 W. 61 St., New York, NY 10023; *Secy.* Jerry Hostetler (1978–1981) Asst. Dir., Media Learning Resources Service, Southern Illinois Univ., Carbondale, IL 62901.

BOARD OF DIRECTORS

The officers; Helen Cyr (1979–1982), Audio-Visual Dept., Enoch Pratt Free Lib., 400 Cathedral St., Baltimore, MD 21201; Frances Dean (1979–1982), Dir., Instructional Materials Div., Montgomery County Public Schools, 850 Hungerford Dr., Rockville, MD 20850; Robyn Foreman (1977–1980), Washington Regional Lib. for the Blind and Physically Handicapped, 811 Harrison St., Seattle, WA 98129; Stephen Hess (1979–1982), Dir., Educational Media Center, Univ. of Utah, 207 Milton Bennion Hall, Salt Lake City, UT 84112; Lillian Katz (1979–1981), Port Washington Public Lib., 245 Main St., Port Washington, NY 11050; Sister Gilmary Speirs, IHM (1979–1980), Learning Resources Center, Marywood College Lib., Scranton, PA 18509.

PUBLICATIONS

EFLA Bulletin (q.).
EFLA Evaluations.
Film Evaluation Guide (supplemented when funds permit).
Independent Film/Video Guide (q.).
Sightlines (q.). Ed. Nadine Covert.
Write for list of other books and pamphlets.

FEDERAL LIBRARY COMMITTEE
Library of Congress, Washington, DC 20540
202-287-6055

OBJECT

"For the purpose of concentrating the intellectual resources present in the federal library and library related information community: To achieve better utilization of library resources and facilities; to provide more effective planning, development, and operation of federal libraries; to promote an optimum exchange of experience, skill, and resources. Secretariat efforts and the work groups are organized to: Consider policies and problems relating to federal libraries; evaluate existing federal library programs and resources; determine priorities among library issues requiring attention; examine the organization and policies for acquiring, preserving, and making information available; study the need for a potential of technological innovation in library practices; and study library budgeting and staffing problems, including the recruiting, education, training, and remuneration of librarians." Founded 1965. Memb. (Federal Libs.) 2,600; (Federal Libns.) 4,000. Year. Oct. 1–Sept. 30.

MEMBERSHIP

Libn. of Congress, Dir. of the National Agricultural Lib., Dir. of the National Lib. of Medicine, representatives from each of the other executive departments, and delegates from the National Aeronautics and Space Admin., the National Science Foundation, the Smithsonian Institution, the Supreme Court of the United States, International Communication Agency, the Veterans Admin., and the Office of Presidential Libs. Six members will be selected on a rotation basis by the permanent members of the committee from independent agencies, boards, committees, and commissions. These rotating members will serve two-year terms. Ten regional members shall be selected on a rotating basis by the permanent members of the committee to represent federal libraries following the geographic pattern developed by the Federal Regional Councils. These rotating regional members will serve two-year terms. The ten regional members, one from each of the ten federal regions, shall be voting members. In addition to the permanent representative from DOD, one nonvoting member shall be selected from each of the three services (U.S. Army, U.S. Navy, U.S. Air Force). These service members, who will serve for two years, will be selected by the permanent Department of Defense member from a slate provided by the Federal Library Committee. The membership in each service shall be rotated equitably among the special service technical, and academic and school libraries in that service. DOD shall continue to have one voting member in the committee. The DOD representative may poll the three service members for their opinions before reaching a decision concerning the vote. A representative of the Office of Management and Budget, designated by the budget director and others appointed by the chairperson, will meet with the committee as observers.

OFFICERS

Chpn. Carol Nemeyer, Assoc. Libn. for National Programs, Lib. of Congress, Washington, DC 20540.
Exec. Dir. James P. Riley.

PUBLICATIONS

Annual Report (Oct.).
FLC Newsletter (irreg.).

INFORMATION INDUSTRY ASSOCIATION
President, Paul G. Zurkowski
316 Pennsylvania Ave. S.E., Suite 502, Washington, DC 20003
202-544-1969

MEMBERSHIP

For details on membership and dues, write to the association headquarters. Memb. Over 150.

STAFF

Pres. Paul G. Zurkowski; *V.P., Government Relations.* Robert S. Willard; *Communications Dir. and AIM Coord.* Helena

Note: For a report on the 1979 activities of IIA, see the National Associations section of Part 1. Also see the report by Robert S. Willard on 1979 legislation affecting the information industry in Part 2—*Ed.*

M. Strauch; *Dir. of Admin.* Dorothy E. Jackson; *Dir. of Member Services.* Jennifer M. Pawlikowski. (Address all correspondence to headquarters.)

BOARD OF DIRECTORS

Chmn. of the Bd. Robert F. Asleson, Information Handling Services; *V. Chmn.* Thomas A. Grogan, McGraw-Hill Information Systems Co.; *Secy.* Roy K. Campbell, Dun & Bradstreet, Inc.; *Treas.* Robert H. Riley, Chase Manhattan Bank, N.A.; *Past Chmn.* Herbert R. Brinberg, Aspen Systems Corp.; and J. Christopher Burns, Washington Post Co.; Carlos A. Cuadra, Cuadra Associates, Inc.; Haines B. Gaffner, LINK; Andrew P. Garvin, FIND/SVP; James G. Kollegger, Environment Information Center, Inc.; Edward M. Lee, Information Handling Services; John Rothman, New York Times Co.; Roger K. Summit, Lockheed Information Systems; Loene Trubkin, Data Currier, Inc.; Norman M. Wellen, Business International, Inc.

PUBLICATIONS

Information Sources (third ed., 1979).
The Information Resource: Policy, Background, and Issues—An Infostructure Handbook (1979).

COMMITTEE CHAIRPERSONS

Associated Information Managers. Helena M. Strauch, IIA.
Awards. Ronald Henderson, Information and Publishing Systems.
Education and Marketing. Herbert R. Brinberg, Aspen Systems Corp.
Government Relations. Jim Adler, Congressional Information Service.
Information Industry Survey. Phil Nielsen, A. C. Nielsen Co.
International. Norman M. Wellen, Business International, Inc.
Conference (1980). Tom Collins, SDC Search Service.
NICE Conference (1980). Roberta Gardner, Dun & Bradstreet, Inc.
Proprietary Rights. Peyton Neal, Bureau of National Affairs.
Salary Survey. Jim Peterson, Aspen Systems Corp.
West Coast. Bill Burgess, SDC Search Service.

LIAISONS WITH OTHER ORGANIZATIONS

AIM. James G. Kollegger, Environment Information Center, Inc.
Library of Congress Network Advisory Committee. Robert S. Willard, IIA.
National Council of Professional Service Organizations. Bill Creager, Capital Systems Group, and Herb Brinberg, Aspen Systems Corp.

LUTHERAN CHURCH LIBRARY ASSOCIATION
122 W. Franklin Ave., Minneapolis, MN 55404
612-870-3623
Executive Secretary, E. T. (Wilma) Jensen
(Home address: 3620 Fairlawn Dr., Minnetonka, MN 55404
612-473-5965)

OBJECT

"To promote the growth of church libraries by publishing a quarterly journal, *Lutheran Libraries;* furnishing booklists; assisting member libraries with technical problems; providing meetings for mutual encouragement, assistance, and exchange of ideas among members." Founded 1958. Memb. 1,750. Dues. $8, $15, $25, $100, $500, $1,000. Year. Jan.–Jan.

OFFICERS (JAN. 1980–JAN. 1981)

Pres. Mrs. Lloyd (Betty) LeDell, Libn., Grace Lutheran of Deephaven, 15800 Sunset Rd., Minnetonka, MN 55343; *V.P.* Esther Damkoehler, Libn., Hope Lutheran Lib., Milwaukee, WI (7822 Eagle St., Wauwatosa, WI 53213); *Secy.* Margaret Horn, Libn., Concordia Lutheran College, 275 North Syndicate, St. Paul, MN 55104; *Treas.* Mrs. G. Frank (Jane) Johnson, 2930 S. Hwy. 101, Wayzata, MN 55391; *Past Pres.* Marcella von Goertz, Libn., First Lutheran Lib., 2545 London Rd., Duluth, MN 44812. (Address correspondence to the executive secretary.)

EXECUTIVE BOARD

Mary Egdahl, Astrid Wang, Maryls Johnson, Larraine Pike, Solveig Bartz, Daniel Brumm.

ADVISORY BOARD

Chpn. Gary Klammer; Rev. Rolf Aaseng; Mrs. H. O. Egertson; Mrs. Donald Gauerke; Mrs. Harold Groff; Rev. James Gunther; Rev. A. B. Hanson; Malvin Lundeen; Rev. A. C. Paul; Don Rosenberg; Stanley Sandberg; Les Schmidt; Aron Valleskey.

PUBLICATION

Lutheran Libraries (q.; memb., nonmembs. $8). *Ed.* Erwin E. John, 6450 Warren St., Minneapolis, MN 55435.

COMMITTEE CHAIRPERSONS

Budget. Rev. Carl Manfred, Normandale Lutheran Church, 6100 Normandale Rd., Minneapolis, MN 55436.
Finance. Alida Storaasli, Dir. of Education, American Lutheran Church Women, 422 S. Fifth St., Minneapolis, MN 55415.
Library Services Board. Mrs. Forrest (Juanita) Carpenter, Libn., Rte. 1, Prior Lake, MN 55372.
Publications Board. Rev. Carl Weller, Augsburg Publishing House, 426 S. Fifth St., Minneapolis, MN 55415.

MEDICAL LIBRARY ASSOCIATION
Executive Director, Shirley Echelman
919 N. Michigan Ave., Chicago, IL 60611
312-266-2456

OBJECT

Founded in 1898 and incorporated in 1934, its major purpose is to foster medical and allied scientific libraries, to promote the educational and professional growth of health sciences librarians, and to exchange medical literature among the members. Through its programs and publications, MLA encourages professional development of its membership, whose foremost concern is for the dissemination of health sciences information for those in research, education, and patient care. Memb. (Inst.) 1,350. (Indiv.) 3,680. Dues. (Inst.) Subscriptions up to 199 $75, 200–299 $100, 300–599 $125, 600–999 $150, 1,000+ $175; (Indiv.) $45. Year. From month of payment.

MEMBERSHIP

Open to those working in or interested in medical libraries.

OFFICERS

Pres. Lois Ann Colaianni, Health Sciences Info. Center, Cedars-Sinai Medical Center, Los Angeles, CA 90048; *Past Pres.* Erika Love, Medical Center Lib., Univ. of New Mexico, Albuquerque, NM 87131; *Pres.-Elect.* Gertrude Lamb, Health Science Libs., Hartford Hospital, Hartford

CT 06115. (Address general correspondence to the executive director.)

DIRECTORS

Nina W. Matheson, Phyllis S. Mirsky, Jean K. Miller, Beatrix Robinow, John A. Timour, Naomi C. Broering, Arlee May.

PUBLICATIONS

Bulletin (q.; $45).
Index to Audiovisual Serials in the Health Sciences (4 per year; $18).
Current Catalog Proof Sheets (Option A, w., $45); (Option B, mo., $39).
MLA News (mo.; $15 per year).
Vital Notes (3 per year; $20).

STANDING COMMITTEE CHAIRPERSONS

Audiovisual Standards and Practices. Gloria H. Hurwitz, Coord. of Learning Resource Facilities, MCV Box 62, Richmond, VA 23298.
Bibliographic and Information Services Assessment. Dick R. Miller, Northeastern Ohio Univs. College of Medicine Lib., Rootstown, OH 44272.
"Bulletin" Consulting Editors Panel. Gloria Werner, Biomedical Lib., Center for the Health Sciences, Univ. of California, Los Angeles, CA 90024.
Bylaws. Emil F. Frey, Univ. of Texas, Medical Branch Lib., Galveston, TX 77550.
Certification Appeals Panel. Phyllis S. Mirsky, Reference Sec., National Lib. of Medicine, 8600 Rockville Pike, Bethesda, MD 20209.
Certification Eligibility. Pauline M. Vaillancourt, School of Lib. and Info. Science, State Univ. of New York, Albany, NY 12222.
Certification Examination Review. Lois O. Clark, Long Beach Community Hospital Lib., 1720 Termino Ave., Long Beach, CA 90801.
Committee on Committees. Gertrude Lamb, Health Science Lib., Hartford Hospital, Hartford, CT 06115.

Continuing Education. Anthony R. Aguirre, Univ. of Connecticut Health Center, Lyman Maynard Stowe Lib., Farmington, CT 06032.
Copyright. Dean Schmidt, Medical Lib., Univ. of Missouri, M-210 Medical Center, Columbia, MO 65212.
Editorial Committee for the "Bulletin." Patti K. Corbett, Ciocco Lib., 102 Parran Hall, Univ. of Pittsburgh, Pittsburgh, PA 15261.
Editorial Committee for the "MLA News." Ellen Gartenfeld, Mt. Auburn Hospital, Community Health Education Dept., 330 Mt. Auburn St., Cambridge, MA 02138.
Elections. Gertrude Lamb, Health Science Libs., Hartford Hospital, Hartford, CT 06115.
Exchange. Betsey S. Beamish, Biomedical Lib.-PSRMLS, Center for the Health Sciences, Univ. of Calif., Los Angeles, CA 90024.
Executive. Lois Ann Colaianni, Health Sciences Info. Center, Cedars-Sinai Medical Center, Los Angeles, CA 90048.
Finance. Jean K. Miller, Univ. of Texas, Health Science Center at Dallas Lib., 5323 Harry Hines Blvd., Dallas, TX 75235.
Health Sciences Library Technicians. Janet S. Fisher, College of Medicine Lib., East Tennessee State Univ., Johnson City, TN 37601.
Honors and Awards. Faith Meakin, Biomedical Lib., C-075B, Univ. of California, San Diego, La Jolla, CA 92093; *Eliot Prize Subcommittee.* Katherine M. Markee, Purdue Univ. Lib., West Lafayette, IN 47907; *Gottlieb Prize Subcommittee.* Marjorie Fuller, Mead Johnson and Co. Lib., Evansville, IN 47721; *Janet Doe Lectureship Subcommittee.* William K. Beatty, Northwestern Univ. Medical School, 303 E. Chicago Ave., Chicago, IL 60611; *Rittenhouse Award Subcommittee.* Faith A. Meakin, Biomedical Lib., C-075-B, Univ. of California, San Diego, La Jolla, CA 92093.
Hospital Library Standards and Practices. Sara I. Hill, St. Luke's Hospital, Medical Lib., Kansas City, MO 64111.

Interlibrary Loan and Resource Sharing Standards and Practices. Michelle d. O'Connell, Veterans Admin. Medical Center Lib., 3495 Bailey Ave., Buffalo, NY 14215.
International Cooperation. Carol D. Kasses, Health Sciences Lib., Columbia Univ., 701 W. 168 St., New York, NY 10032.
Legislation. Mary M. Horres, Health Sciences Lib., 223-H, Univ. of North Carolina, Chapel Hill, NC 27514.
Library Standards and Practices. James E. Raper, Jr., Medical Lib. Center of New York, 17 E. 102 St., New York, NY 10029.
MLA/NLM Liaison. Nina W. Matheson, George Washington Univ. Medical Center, Paul Himmelfarb Health Sciences Lib., Washington, DC 20037.
Membership. C. William Fraser, British Columbia Medical Lib. Service, 1807 W. 10 Ave., Vancouver V6J 2A9, B.C., Canada.
1980 National Program Committee. Nina W. Matheson, George Washington Univ. Medical Center, Paul Himmelfarb Health Science Lib., Washington, DC 20037.
Nominating. Gertrude Lamb, Health Science Libs., Hartford Hospital, Hartford, CT 06115.
Oral History. Carol Jane Fenichel, College of Lib. Science, Univ. of Kentucky, Lexington, KY 40506.
Program and Convention. Robert M. Braude, Leon S. McGoogan Lib. of Medicine, Univ. of Nebraska Medical Center, Omaha, NE 68105.
Publication Panel. Samuel Hitt, Health Sciences Lib., Univ. of North Carolina, 223-H, Chapel Hill, NC 27514.
Recertification. Winifred Sewell, 6513 76 Pl., Cabin John, MD 20731.
Scholarship. Michael Homan, Corporate Technical Lib., Upjohn Co., Kalamazoo, MI 49001.
Status and Economic Interests of Health Sciences Library Personnel. Richard Lyders, Houston Academy of Medicine, Texas Medical Center Lib., Jesse H. Jones Lib. Bldg., Houston, TX 77030.

Surveys and Statistics. Phyllis C. Self, Univ. of Illinois, Lib. of the Health Sciences, Urbana, IL 61801.
"Vital Notes" Participatory Panel. Donald L. Potts, Medical Lib. Center of New York, New York, NY 10029.

AD HOC COMMITTEES

On MLA Group Structure Implementation. Ursula H. Poland, Schaffer Lib. of Health Sciences, Albany Medical College, Albany, NY 12208.
On White House Conference on Library and Information Services. Lynn Kasner, New York and New Jersey Regional Medical Lib., New York Academy of Medicine, New York, NY 10029.
To Develop Criteria for Hospital Library Consultants. Judith Messerle, St. Joseph Hospital Lib., Alton, IL 62002.
To Develop a Statement of Goals of the Medical Library Association. Virginia H. Holtz, Middleton Health Sciences Lib., Univ. of Wisconsin, Madison, WI 53706.
To Establish an Inter-Association Representatives Panel. Ann E. Kerker, 237 Sheetz St., West Lafayette, IN 47906.
To Evaluate the "Bulletin." Phyllis S. Mirsky, Reference Sec., National Lib. of Medicine, 8600 Rockville Pike, Bethesda, MD 20209.
To Examine the Certification and Recertification Process. Beatrix Robinow, McMaster Univ., Hamilton, Ont. L8S 4J9, Canada.
To Prepare a Constitution. Elliott H. Morse, College of Physicians of Philadelphia Lib., Philadelphia, PA 19103.
"Handbook" Consultants Panel. Louise Darling, Biomedical Lib., Univ. of California, Los Angeles, CA 90024.
To Study International Exchange and Redistribution of Library Materials. C. K. Huang, Health Sciences Lib., State Univ. of New York, Buffalo, NY 14214.
To Study MLA's Role in Library Related Research. Nancy M. Lorenzi, Medical Center Lib., Univ. of Cincinnati, Cincinnati, OH 45267.

MUSIC LIBRARY ASSOCIATION
2017 Walnut St., Philadelphia, PA 19103
215-569-3948

OBJECT

"To promote the establishment, growth, and use of music libraries; to encourage the collection of music and musical literature in libraries; to further studies in musical bibliography; to increase efficiency in music library service and administration." Founded 1931. Memb. ca. 1,700. Dues. (Inst.) $31; (Indiv.) $24; (Student) $12. Year. Sept. 1–Aug. 31.

OFFICERS

Pres. Ruth Watanabe, Sibley Music Lib., Eastman School of Music, Rochester, NY 14604; *V.P./Pres.-Elect.* Donald W. Krummel, Graduate Lib. School, Univ. of Illinois, Urbana, IL 61801; *Secy.* George R. Hill, Music Dept., Baruch College/CUNY, 17 Lexington Ave., New York, NY 10010; *Treas.* Shirley Emanuel, 522 10 St. N.W., Washington, DC 20002; *Ed. of "Notes."* William McClellan, Music Lib., Music Bldg., Univ. of Illinois, Urbana, IL 61801.

DIRECTORS

The officers; Garrett H. Bowles; Stephen M. Fry; Gerald D. Gibson; Kathryn Logan; Kathleen J. Moretto; John W. Tanno.

PUBLICATIONS

Music Cataloging Bulletin (mo.; $8).

MLA Index Series (irreg.; price varies according to size).

MLA Newsletter (q.; free to memb.).

MLA Technical Reports (irreg.; price varies according to size.)

Notes (q.; inst. subscription $31; non-memb. subscription $21).

COMMITTEE CHAIRPERSONS

Audio-Visual. Arne J. Arneson, Music Lib., Univ. of Colorado, Boulder, CO 80302.

Automation. Garrett H. Bowles, Music Lib., Univ. of California at San Diego, La Jolla, CA 92093.

Cataloging and Classification. Judith Kaufman, Music Lib., State Univ. of New York, Stony Brook, NY 11794.

Constitutional Revision. Geraldine Ostrove, Lib., New England Conservatory of Music, Boston, MA 02115.

Education. Kathryn P. Logan, Music Lib., Univ. of North Carolina, Chapel Hill, NC 27514.

Legislation. Susan T. Sommer, Music Div., New York Public Lib., 111 Amsterdam Ave., New York, NY 10023.

MLA Prize. Donald P. Thompson, Univ. of Puerto Rico, Rio Pedras, PR 00931.

Microforms. Stuart Milligan, Sibley Music Lib., Eastman School of Music, Rochester, NY 14604.

Music Library Administration. Brenda Chasen Goldman, Music Lib., Tufts Univ., Medford, MA 02155.

Public Library. Cheryl E. Osborn, Greater Victoria Public Lib., 794 Yates St., Victoria, B.C., Canada.

Publications. Linda Solow, Music Lib., Massachusetts Institute of Technology, Cambridge, MA 02139.

Selection and Acquisition. Katherine Holum, Music Lib., Univ. of Minnesota, Minneapolis, MN 55455.

NATIONAL LIBRARIANS ASSOCIATION
President, June Stratton
Box 1204, South Bend, IN 46624

OBJECT

"To promote librarianship, to develop and increase the usefulness of libraries, to cultivate the science of librarianship, to protect the interest of professionally qualified librarians, and to perform other functions necessary for the betterment of the profession of librarianship. It functions as an association of librarians, rather than as an association of libraries." Established 1975. Memb. 500. Dues. $15 per year; $25 for 2 years; (Students and Retired and Unemployed Librarians) $7.50. Year. July 1–June 30.

MEMBERSHIP

Any person interested in librarianship and libraries who holds a graduate degree in library science may become a member upon election by the executive board and payment of the annual dues. The executive board may authorize exceptions to the degree requirements to applicants who present evidence of outstanding contributions to the profession. Student membership is available to those graduate students enrolled full time at any accredited library school.

OFFICERS (JULY 1, 1979–JUNE 30, 1980)

Pres. June Stratton, Box 1204, South Bend, IN 46624; *V.P./Pres.-Elect.* Norman Tanis, California State Univ. at Northridge, Northridge, CA 91330; *Immed. Past Pres.* Peter Dollard, Alma College Lib., Alma, MI 48801; *Secy.* Frank Hopkins, Franklin and Marshall College Lib., Lancaster, PA 17604; *Treas.* Mary-Elinor Kennedy, Methuen Public Lib., Methuen, MA 01844. (Address all correspondence to Box 586, Alma, MI 48801.)

EXECUTIVE BOARD (1979–1980)

The officers; Julio Martinez; Bonnie Jackson.

PUBLICATION

NLA Newsletter: The National Librarian (q.; 1 year $12, 2 years $22, 3 years $30).

COMMITTEE CHAIRPERSONS

Certification Standards. David Perkins, California State Univ., Northridge, CA 91330.

Professional Education. John Colson, 813 Somonauk St., Sycamore, IL 60178.

Professional Welfare. Julio A. Martinez, San Diego State Univ. Lib., San Diego, CA 92182.

Note: For further information on the National Librarians Association, see the article on NLA in the National Associations section of Part 1—*Ed.*

NATIONAL MICROGRAPHICS ASSOCIATION
Executive Director, O. Gordon Banks
8719 Colesville Rd., Silver Spring, MD 20910
301-587-8202

OBJECT

The National Micrographics Association (NMA) is the trade and professional association that represents the manufacturers, vendors, and professional users of micrographic equipment and software. The purpose of the association is to promote the lawful interests of the micrographic industry in the direction of good business ethics; the liberal discussion of subjects pertaining to the industry and its relationship to other information management technologies, technological improvement, and research; standardization; the methods of manufacturing and marketing; and the education of the consumer in the use of information management systems. Founded 1943. Memb. 10,000. Dues. (Indiv.) $48. Year. July 1, 1979–June 30, 1980.

OFFICERS

Pres. Truett E. Airhart, Zytron Corp., 4203 Gardendale, Suite C-214, San Antonio, TX 78229; *V.P.* B. J. Cassin, 3000 Sand Hill, Suite 210, Bldg. 3, Menlo Park, CA 94025; *Treas.* John C. Marken, Bell & Howell Co., Micro Photo Div., Drawer E, Old Mansfield Rd., Wooster, OH 44691. (Address general correspondence to the executive director.)

PUBLICATIONS

Buyer's Guide to Micrographic Equipment, Supplies and Services (ann.; free to membs. and nonmembs.). *Ed.* Denise L. Harlow. Ads accepted.

Journal of Micrographics (bi-mo.; memb. and subscriptions). *Ed.* Ellen T. Meyer. Book reviews included; product review included. Ads accepted.

Micrographics Today (mo.; memb.). *Ed.* Jean W. Farmer. New publication announcements, calendar of events. No product review or advertising accepted.

Other publications available. For information, contact Publications Department.

CHAPTER PRESIDENTS

Blackhawk. Ted Spencer, Beloit Corp., One St. Lawrence Ave., Beloit, WI 53511.

Blue Mountain. Tom Haley, Office of Admin. BMS, 906 Health and Welfare Bldg., Harrisburg, PA 17120.

Central Arizona. Richard Martinez, Central Microfilming Service, 20 E. Jefferson St., Phoenix, AZ 85004.

Chicago. Stuart Soll, Zenith Radio Corp., 1000 Milwaukee Ave., Glenview, IL 60025.

Columbia. Grant Linquist, Linco Enterprises, 407 S.E. Pine, Portland, OR 97214.

Connecticut Valley. Dave Henderson, Eastman Kodak Co., 111 Founders Plaza, East Hartford, CT 06108.

Cornhusker. Steve Kemble, Box 94921, Lincoln, NE 68509.

Garden State. Mickey Zirrith, Merck & Co., Box 2000, Rahway, NJ 07065.

Golden Gate. Marsha Adams, DYAD, 2506 Park Rd., Redwood City, CA 94062.

Greater Kansas City. Merrill F. Toms, Plaza Branch Lib., 4801 Main St., Kansas City, MO 64112.

Gulf Coast. Claud Fristoe, Eastman Kodak Co., 666 Poydras, New Orleans, LA 70130.

Hoosier. John Berg, Meridian Insurance Co., 2955 N. Meridian, Indianapolis, IN 46207.

Intermountain. Herbert White, The Genealogical Society, 50 E.N. Temple, Salt Lake City, UT 84150.

Kentucky. David Ruffra, 3M Co., 10101 Linn Station Rd., Louisville, KY 40223.

Long Island. Ken Sjogren, Grumman, 176 Tredwell Ave., St. James, NY 11780.

Maryland. Edward Sweeney, American Health & Life Insurance Co., 300 St. Paul Pl., Baltimore, MD 21202.

Metropolitan New York. Hanley Riess, Burns & Roe, Inc., 46 Wilder Rd., Monsey, NY 10952.

Michigan. Don Fergle, 21460 Van K, Grosse Pointe Woods, MI 48236.

Midwest. Roy E. Johnson, Grinnell Mutual Reinsurance Co., I-80 at Hwy. 146, Grinnell, IA 50112.

Minnesota. George Franklin, Northwest Microfilm, Inc., 15 S. Ninth St., Minneapolis, MN 55402.

National Capitol. James E. McBride, Raven System & Research, 500 E St. S.W., Washington, DC 20024.

New England. John Cardello, Honeywell Information Systems, 300 Concord Rd., Billerica, MA 01821.

Northwest. Dick Patten, Microfilm Service Co., 13540 Lake City Way N.E., Seattle, WA 98125.

Ohio. Dianne Komminsk, Micro Foto File, W. Monroe St., New Breman, OH 45869.

Old Dominion. Russell Sheahan, County of Henrico, Box 27032, Richmond, VA 23273.

Orange County. Sue K. Bolton, 3M Business Products, 601 Park Center Dr., Santa Ana, CA 92701.

Puerto Rico. Jose Morales, 3M Puerto Rico, Inc., Box M, San Juan, PR 00936.

Red River. Lloyd Parker, Southland Life Insurance, Box 2220, Dallas, TX 75221.

Rocky Mountain. Alberta Leake, Air Force Reserve Personnel Center, 10395 W. 17 Pl., Lakewood, CO 80215.

Sacramento. Betty Godfrey, A. B. Dick/Systems, 3325 Long View Dr., North Highland, CA 95660.

San Diego. Cathy Horrall, 6779 Caminito del Greco, San Diego, CA 92120.

Santa Clara. Carlos Buhk, AMDAHL Corp., 1250 E. Arques, Sunnyvale, CA 84086.

SCMA Chapter. Carolee Gennerelli, Tosco Corp., 10100 Santa Monica Blvd., Los Angeles, CA 90067.

Southeastern. John Sinclair, Oce Industries, Inc., 3300 N.E. Expressway, Atlanta, GA 30341.

Southwest. Don Boone, Brown & Root, Inc., Box 3 1 Bsmt., Houston, TX 77001.

St. Louis. Pete Gallagher, Central Microfilm, 1601 Washington, St. Louis, MO 63103.

Sunshine. James Baldwin, Independent Life Insurance, One Independent Dr., Jacksonville, FL 32276.

Tarheel. Jeff Rothman, Western Electric Co., Box 26000, Greensboro, NC 27420.

Tennessee Valley. James Baker, Metropolitan Government of Nashville, 700 Second Ave. S., Nashville, TN 37210.

Westchester. Peter F. Hovell, Connecticut Micrographics, 137 Rowayton Ave., Rowayton, CT 06853.

Western New York. Michael D. Majcher, Xerox Corp., 800 Phillips Rd., 105, Webster, NY 14580.

William Penn. John P. Campbell, Sperry Univac, Box 500, Blue Bell, PA 19424.

Wisconsin. Sybille Hamilton, NW Mutual Life, 720 East Wisconsin Ave., Milwaukee, WI 53202.

Okie. Betty Griesel, State Dept. Corrections Microfilming, Newcastle, OK 73065.

Central Texas. Barbara Broberg, Texas State Lib., Box 12927 Capital Sta., Austin, TX 78711.

Greater Alamo. To be appointed.

SOCIETY OF AMERICAN ARCHIVISTS
Executive Director, Ann M. Campbell
330 S. Wells, Suite 810, Chicago, IL 60606

OBJECT

"To promote sound principles of archival economy and to facilitate cooperation among archivists and archival agencies." Founded 1936. Memb. 3,700. Dues. (Indiv.) $20–$60, graduated according to salary; (Student) $15; (Inst.) $35, $45 effective July 1980; (Sustaining) $100.

OFFICERS (OCT. 1979–OCT. 1980)

Pres. Maynard J. Brichford, Univ. of Illinois, Urbana, IL 61801; *V.P./Pres.-Elect.* Ruth W. Helmuth, Case Western Reserve Univ., Cleveland, OH 44106; *Treas.* Mary Lynn McCree, Univ. of Illinois—Chicago Circle, Box 4348, Chicago, IL 60680. (Address general correspondence to the executive director.)

COUNCIL

Edmund Berkeley, Jr.; Frank G. Burke; Lynn Bonfield Donovan; Shonnie Finnegan; Meyer H. Fishbein; David B. Gracy II; Richard Lytle; Paul McCarthy, Jr.

STAFF

Ed. The American Archivist. Virginia C. Purdy, National Archives and Records Service, NN, Washington, DC 20408; *Dir. Administrative Services.* Joyce E. Gianatasio, 330 S. Wells, Suite 810, Chicago, IL 60606; *Membership Asst.* Bernice Brack, 330 S. Wells St., Suite 810, Chicago, IL 60606; *Bookkeeper.* Andrea Gianatasio, 330 S. Wells St., Suite 810, Chicago, IL 60606; *Publications Asst.* Mary Alice Henry, 330 S. Wells St., Suite 810, Chicago, IL 60606; *Program Officer.* Thomas C. Pardo, 330 S. Wells St., Suite 810, Chicago, IL 60606; *Newsletter Ed. and Program Officer.* Deborah Risteen, 330 S. Wells St., Suite 810, Chicago, IL 60606.

PUBLICATIONS

The American Archivist (q.; $25). *Ed.* Virginia C. Purdy, National Archives and Records Service, NN, Washington, DC 20408. Book reviews and related correspondence should be addressed to the editor. Rates for B/W ads: full page, $200; half page, $125; outside back cover, $300; half-page minimum insertion; discount = 10% for 4 consecutive insertions; 15% agency commission.

SAA Newsletter (6 issues per year; memb.). *Ed.* Deborah Risteen, SAA, 330 S. Wells St., Suite 810, Chicago, IL 60606. No ads.

PROFESSIONAL AFFINITY GROUPS (PAGs) AND CHAIRS

Acquisition. Charles Schultz, Texas A&M Univ., Lib., College Station, TX 77843 (Risteen).

Aural and Graphic Records. James W. Moore, National Archives and Records Service, Washington, DC 20408 (Risteen).

Business Archives. Douglas A. Bakken, Ford Archives, Henry Ford Museum, Dearborn, MI 48121 (Risteen).

College and University Archives. Helen Slotkin, Institute Archives, 14N-118, Massachusetts Institute of Technology, Cambridge, MA 02139 (Pardo).

Contemporary Theme Collections. Francis X. Blouin, Bentley Historical Lib., Univ. of Michigan, Ann Arbor, MI 48103 (Gianatasio).

Description. Eleanor McKay, Mississippi Valley Collection, Memphis State Univ., Memphis, TN 38152 (Pardo).

Government Records. Sue E. Holbert, Minnesota Historical Society, 1500 Mississippi St., St. Paul, MN 55101 (Gianatasio).

Manuscript Repositories. Eva Moseley,

Schlesinger Lib., Radcliffe College, Cambridge, MA 02139 (Gianatasio).

Preservation. Mary Lynn Ritzenthaler, Univ. of Illinois-Chicago Circle, Lib., Box 8198, Chicago, IL 60680. (Gianatasio).

Reference, Access & Outreach. Karyl Winn, Suzzallo Lib., FM-25, Univ. of Washington, Seattle, WA 98195 (Pardo).

Religious Archives. Sister M. Felicitas Powers, Sisters of Mercy of the Union, Office of Archives, 10000 Kentsdale Dr., Potomac, MD 20854 (Risteen).

SPECIAL LIBRARIES ASSOCIATION
Executive Director, David R. Bender
235 Park Ave. S., New York, NY 10003
212-477-9250

OBJECT

"To provide an association of individuals and organizations having a professional, scientific or technical interest in library and information science, especially as these are applied in the recording, retrieval and dissemination of knowledge and information in areas such as the physical, biological, technical and social sciences and the humanities; and to promote and improve the communication, dissemination and use of such information and knowledge for the benefit of libraries or other educational organizations." Organized 1909. Memb. 11,000. Dues. (Sustaining) $200; (Indiv.) $40; (Student) $8. Year. Jan.–Dec. and July–June.

OFFICERS (JUNE 1979–JUNE 1980)

Pres. Joseph M. Dagnese, Purdue Univ., Lib., West Lafayette, IN 47907; *Pres.-Elect.* James B. Dodd, Georgia Inst. of Technology, Price Gilbert Memorial Lib., Atlanta, GA 30332; *Div. Cabinet Chpn.* Patricia Marshall, AIAA Technical Info. Service, 555 W. 57 St., New York, NY 10019; *Div. Cabinet Chpn.-Elect.* Ruth S. Smith, Inst. for Defense Analyses, Technical Info. Services, 400 Army-Navy Dr., Arlington, VA 22202; *Chapter Cabinet Chpn.* Fred W. Roper, School of Lib. Science, 026-A, Univ. of North Carolina, Chapel Hill, NC 27514; *Chapter Cabinet Chpn.-Elect.* Didi Pancake, Univ. of Virginia, Sci/Tech Info. Center, Clark Hall, Charlottesville, VA 22901; *Treas.* Dorothy Kasman, Coopers & Lybrand, Lib., 1251 Ave. of the Americas, New York, NY 10020; *Past Pres.* Vivian D. Hewitt, Carnegie Endowment for International Peace, 30 Rockefeller Plaza, 54 fl., New York, NY 10020.

DIRECTORS

Floyd Henderson (1977–1980); Doris Lee Schild (1977–1980); Beryl L. Anderson (1978–1981); Pat Molholt (1978–1981); Jack Leister (1979–1982); Mary Vasilakis (1979–1982).

PUBLICATION

Special Libraries (11 issues; $26; add $3.50 postage outside U.S.). *Ed.* Nancy M. Viggiano.

COMMITTEE CHAIRPERSONS

Awards. Miriam Tees, McGill Univ., Grad. School of Lib. Science, 3459 McTavish St., Montreal P.Q. H3A 1Y1, Canada.

Consultation Service. Johanna E. Tallman, California Institute of Technology, Robert A. Millikan Memorial Lib., Pasadena, CA 91125.

Note: For a report on SLA activities from 1977 to 1980, see the National Associations section of Part 1—*Ed.*

Copyright. Efren Gonzalez, Bristol-Myers Products, Research Quality Compliance, 1350 Liberty Ave., Hillside, NJ 07207.
Education. Laura N. Gasaway, Univ. of Oklahoma, Law Lib., 300 Timberdell, Norman, OK 73019.
Government Information Services. Paula M. Strain, Mitre Corp., 1820 Dolley Madison Blvd., McLean, VA 22102.
Networking. James Webster, State Univ. of New York at Buffalo, Science and Engineering Lib., Buffalo, NY 14260.
Nominating Committee for Spring 1980 Elections. M. Jims Murphy, U.S. Dept. of the Army, Army Materials Mechanics Research Center, Technical Info. Office, Watertown, MA 02172.
Positive Action Program for Minority Groups. S. Rita Sparks, 522 Magnolia Ave., Royal Oak, MI 48073.
Publisher Relations. James B. Poteat, Television Info. Office, Lib., 745 Fifth Ave., New York, NY 10022.
Research. Lucille Whalen, State Univ. of New York at Albany, School of Lib. and Info. Science, 1400 Washington Ave., Albany, NY 12222.
SLA Scholarship. Barbara Sanduleak, Gould, Inc., Gould Info. Center, 540 E. 105 St., Cleveland, OH 44108.
Standards. Leroy Linder, Ford Aerospace & Communications Corp., Technical Info. Services, Ford Rd., Newport Beach, CA 92663.
Statistics. Scott Kennedy, Univ. of California, Physical Sciences Lib., Davis, CA 95616.
Student Relations Officer. Raymond E. Durrance, Univ. of Michigan, School of Lib. Science, Ann Arbor, MI 48109.
H. W. Wilson Company Award. Betty Jenkins, Columbia Univ., Teachers College, Lib., New York, NY 10027.

THEATRE LIBRARY ASSOCIATION
Secretary-Treasurer, Richard M. Buck
111 Amsterdam Ave., New York, NY 10023

OBJECT

"To further the interests of collecting, preserving, and using theatre, cinema, and performing arts materials in libraries, museums, and private collections." Founded 1937. Memb. 500. Dues. (Indiv.) $15; (Inst.) $20. Year. Jan. 1–Dec. 31, 1980.

OFFICERS (1979–1980)

Pres. Brooks McNamara, Grad. Drama Dept., School of the Arts, New York Univ., 61 W. Fourth St., Rm. 300, New York, NY 10012; *V.P.* Louis A. Rachow, Walter Hampden-Edwin Booth Theatre Collection and Lib., The Players, 16 Gramercy Pk., New York, NY 10003; *Secy.-Treas.* Richard M. Buck, Asst. to the Chief, Performing Arts Research Center, New York Public Lib. at Lincoln Center, 111 Amsterdam Ave., New York, NY 10023; *Rec. Secy.* Geraldine Duclow, Libn.-in-Charge, Theatre Arts Collection, Free Lib. of Philadelphia, Logan Sq., Philadelphia, PA 19103. (Address correspondence, except *Broadside*, to the secretary-treasurer. Address *Broadside* correspondence to V.P. Louis A. Rachow, ed.)

EXECUTIVE BOARD

The officers; William Appleton; Mary Ashe; Tino Balio; Laraine Correll; Babette Craven; Geraldine Duclow; Robert C. Eason, Jr.; Alfred S. Golding; Brigitte Kueppers; Frank C. P. McGlinn; Sally Thomas Pavetti; Betty Wharton; *Ex Officio.* Lee Ash; Mary C. Henderson; Dorothy L. Swerdlove; Don B. Wilmeth; *Honorary.* Rosamond Gilder.

COMMITTEE CHAIRPERSONS

Awards. Don P. Wilmeth.
Nominations. Dorothy L. Swerdlove.
Program and Special Events. Richard M. Buck.
Publications. Louis A. Rachow.

PUBLICATIONS

Broadside (q.; memb.).
Performing Arts Resources (ann.; memb.).

UNIVERSAL SERIALS AND BOOK EXCHANGE, INC.
Executive Director, Alice Dulany Ball
3335 V. St. N.E., Washington, DC 20018
202-529-2555

OBJECT

"To promote the distribution and interchange of books, periodicals, and other scholarly materials among libraries and other educational and scientific institutions of the United States, and between them and libraries and institutions of other countries." Organized 1948. Memb. year—libraries: Jan. 1–Dec. 31 or July 1–June 30. Memb. year—associations: Jan. 1–Dec. 31.

MEMBERSHIP

Membership in USBE is open to any library that serves a constituency and is an institution or part of an institution or organization. The USBE corporation includes a representative from each member library and from each of a group of sponsoring organizations listed below.

OFFICERS

Pres. Ralph H. Hopp, Dir., Institute of Technology Libs., Univ. of Minnesota, Minneapolis, MN 55455; *V.P./Pres.-Elect.* Margaret A. Otto, Libn. of the College, Dartmouth College, Hanover, NH 03755; *Secy.* Nina W. Matheson, Dir., Paul Himmelfarb Health Sciences Lib., George Washington Univ., 2300 I St. N.W., Washington, DC 20037; *Treas.* William A. Gosling, Asst. Univ. Libn., Technical Services, William R. Perkins Lib., Duke Univ., Durham, NC 27706; *Past Pres.* LeMoyne W. Anderson, Dir. of Libs., Colorado State Univ., Fort Collins, CO 80523.

MEMBERS OF THE BOARD

The executive director; Virginia Boucher, Head, Interlib. Cooperation, Univ. of Colorado at Boulder, Boulder, CO 80309; Henry C. Campbell, Dir., Urban Libs. Study Project, Toronto Public Libs., Box 624, Station K, Toronto, Ont. M4P 2H1, Canada; Nathan Einhorn, Chief, Exchange and Gift Div., Lib. of Congress, Washington, DC 20540; H. Joanne Harrar, Dir. of Libs., Univ. of Maryland, College Park, MD 20742; C. Lee Jones, Program Officer, Council on Lib. Resources, Inc., One Dupont Cirlce N.W., Washington, DC 20036; Jay K. Lucker, Dir. of Libs., Massachusetts Institute of Technology, Cambridge, MA 02139.

SPONSORING MEMBERS

Alabama Lib. Assn., Alaska Lib. Assn., American Assn. of Law Libs., American Council of Learned Societies, American Society for Info. Science, American Lib. Assn., American Theological Lib. Assn., Arizona State Lib. Assn., Assn. of American Lib. Schools, Assn. of Jewish Libs., Assn. of Research Libs., Assn. of Special Libs. of the Philippines, Associazione Italiana Biblioteche, British Columbia Lib.

Assn., California Lib. Assn., Catholic Lib. Assn., Colorado Lib. Assn., Dist. of Columbia Lib. Assn., Ethiopian Lib. Assn., Federal Lib. Committee, Federation of Indian Lib. Assns., Florida Lib. Assn., Idaho Lib. Assn., Interamerican Assn. of Agricultural Libns. and Documentalists, Jordan Lib. Assn., Kenya Lib. Assn., Lib. of Congress, Maryland Lib. Assn., Medical Lib. Assn., Michigan Lib. Assn., Music Lib. Assn., National Academy of Sciences, National Agricultural Lib., National Lib. of Medicine, New Jersey Lib. Assn., North Carolina Lib. Assn., Pennsylvania Lib. Assn., Philippine Lib. Assn., Smithsonian Institution, Social Science Research Council, South African Lib. Assn., Southeastern Lib. Assn., Special Libs. Assn., Special Libs. Assn. of Japan, Theatre Lib. Assn., Uganda Lib. Assn., Vereinigung Osterreichischer Bibliothekare.

STATE, PROVINCIAL, AND REGIONAL LIBRARY ASSOCIATIONS

The associations in this section are organized under three headings: United States, Canada, and Regional Associations. Both the United States and Canada are represented under Regional Associations. Unless otherwise specified, correspondence is to be addressed to the secretary or executive secretary named in the library association entry.

UNITED STATES

Alabama

Memb. 1,143. Founded 1904. Term of Office Apr. 1980–Apr. 1981. Publication. *The Alabama Librarian* (6 per year). *Ed.* Neil Snider, Sta. 12, Livingston 35470.

Pres. William Highfill, Dir., Auburn Univ. Libs., 809 Heard Ave., Auburn 36830. *1st V.P.* Dallas Baillio, Dir., Mobile Public Lib., 701 Government St., Mobile 36602; *2nd V.P.* Gerard Wingertsahn, Dir., Anniston Public Libs., Box 308, Anniston 36202; *Secy.* Alice Stephens, 620 E. Edgemont Ave., Montgomery 36111; *Treas.* Exir Brennan, 308 Main Lib., University 35486; *ALA Chapter Councillor.* To be elected.

Address correspondence to the executive secretary, Alabama Lib. Assn., Box BY, University 35486.

Alaska

Memb. (Indiv.) 276; (Inst.) 27. Term of Office. Mar. 1979–Mar. 1980. Publication, *Sourdough* (bi-mo.).

Pres. Phyllis K. Davis, Harborview School, Box 465, Juneau 99802; *V.P./Pres.-Elect.* Sharon West, Elmer Rasmuson Lib., Univ. of Alaska, Fairbanks 99701; *Secy.* Ila Jean Reiersen, Anchorage Municipal Libs., 427 F St., Anchorage 99501; *Treas.* Judy Monroe, Alaska State Lib., 650 International Airport Rd., Anchorage 99502.

Arizona

Memb. 967. Term of Office. Oct. 1, 1979–Oct. 1, 1980. Publication. *ASLA Newsletter* (mo.). *Ed.* Jane Goldman, 2467 N. Fremont, Tucson 85719.

Pres. Donald C. Dickinson, Grad. Lib.

School, 1515 E. First, Tucson 85719; *Pres.-Elect.* William Morris, 1336 E. Lawrence La., Phoenix 85020; *Secy.* Cynthia Yee, 503 N. San Jose Circle, Mesa 85201; *Treas.* Marge Goble, 6418 W. Colter St., Glendale 85301.

Arkansas

Memb. 1,150. Term of Office. Oct.-Sept. Publication. *Arkansas Libraries* (q.).
Pres. Neil K. Barnhard, Rte. 1, Box 1-B, Roland 72135; *V.P./Pres.-Elect.* Phyllis Burkett, 1006 W. Arch, Searcy 72143; *Secy.* Kathy Wright, 501 E. Fourth St., Fordyce 71742; *Treas.* Corliss Howard, 1209 E. Twin Lakes Dr., Little Rock 72205; *ALA Councillor.* Richard Reid, Univ. of Arkansas, Box 2434, Fayetteville 72701; *Exec. Secy.* Jo Jones, Box 2275, Little Rock 72203.

California

Memb. (Indiv.) 3,000; (Inst.) 178; (Business) 70. Term of Office. Jan. 1-Dec. 31, 1980. Publication. *The CLA Newsletter* (mo.).
Pres. Barbara J. Campbell, Santa Clara County Lib., 1095 N. Seventh St., San Jose 95112; *V.P./Pres.-Elect.* Regina Minudri, Berkeley Public Lib., 2090 Kittredge St., Berkeley 94704; *Treas.* William F. McCoy, Univ. of California, Lib., Davis 95616; *ALA Chapter Councillor.* Gilbert W. McNamee, San Francisco Public Lib., Business Branch, 530 Kearny St., San Francisco 94108.

Address correspondence to Stefan B. Moses, Exec. Dir., California Lib. Assn., 717 K St., Suite 300, Sacramento 95814.

Colorado

Term of Office. Oct. 1979-Oct. 1980. Publication. *Colorado Libraries* (q.). *Ed.* Janet Naumer, Grad. School of Libnshp., Univ. of Denver, Denver 80208; *Ad Mgr.* Robert Wick, Auraria Libs., Eleventh and Lawrence, Denver 80204.
Pres. Pamela Nissler, Bemis Public Lib., 6014 S. Datura, Littleton 80120; *Exec.* *Secy.* Milinda Walker, 3920 S. Truckee Ct., Aurora 80013.

Connecticut

Memb. 1,000. Term of Office. July 1, 1979-1980. Publications. *CLA MEMO* (newsletter, 10 per year); *Ed.* John Hammond, Ledyard Public Libs., Box 225, Ledyard 06339. *Connecticut Libraries* (q.). *Ed.* Frank Ferro, New Britain Public Lib., 20 High St., New Britain 06050; *Adv. Mgr.* Andy Bacon, North Haven Lib., 17 Elm St., North Haven 06473.
Pres. Jody Newmyer, J. E. Smith Lib., Eastern Connecticut State College, Willimantic 06226; *V.P./Pres.-Elect.* Nancy Kline, Univ. of Connecticut Lib., L.O.I.S., U-5H, Storrs 06268; *Treas.* Ellen Barata, Ferguson Lib., 96 Broad St., Stamford 06901; *Secy.* Pat Bandolin, Connecticut Lib. Assn., 12 Daycoeton Place, Torrington 06790.

Delaware

Memb. (Indiv.) 224; (Inst.) 22. Term of Office. May 1979-May 1980. Publication. *DLA Bulletin* (4 per year).
Pres. Patricia Scarry, Dept. of Libs., Courthouse, Georgetown 19947; *V.P.* Jean Trumbore, Morris Lib., Univ. of Delaware, Newark 19711; *Secy.* Mary Byrne, Delaware Technical & Community College, Terry Campus, Dover 19901; *Treas.* Mark Titus, New Castle County Dept. of Libs., Processing Center, Tenth and Market Sts., Wilmington 19801.

Address correspondence to the Delaware Lib. Assn., Box 1843, Wilmington 19899.

District of Columbia

Memb. 950. Term of Office. Aug. 1979-July 1980. Publication. *Intercom. Ed.* Mary Feldman, U.S. Dept. of Transportation, Lib. Services Div., 400 Seventh St. S.W., Washington DC 20540.
Pres. Nancy Gwinn, Council on Lib. Resources, One Dupont Circle N.W., Washington, DC 20036. *Pres.-Elect.* Mur-

ray Howder, National Clearinghouse for Bi-lingual Education, 1300 Wilson Blvd., Suite B2-11, Rosslyn, VA 22209; *Secy.* Judith A. Sessions, Dir., Mount Vernon College Lib., 2100 Foxhall Rd., Washington, DC 20007; *Treas.* Caroline Backlund, National Gallery of Art, Constitution Ave. at Sixth St. N.W., Washington, DC 20565.

Florida

Memb. (Indiv.) 1,190; (In-state inst.) 57; (Out-of-state inst.) 102. Term of Office. May 1979–May 1980.

Pres. Bernadette Storck, Head, Subject Depts., Central Lib., Tampa-Hillsborough County Public Lib. System, 900 N. Ashley St., Tampa 33602; *V.P./Pres.-Elect.* Samuel Morrison, Broward County Public Lib. System, Box 5463, Fort Lauderdale 33310; *Secy.* Laurie Hodge Linsley, Univ. of Central Florida Lib., Alafaya Trail, Box 25000, Orlando 32816; *Treas.* Mable Shaw, Tallahassee Community College Lib., 444 Appleyard Dr., Tallahassee 32304.

Georgia

Memb. 1,200. Term of Office. Oct. 1979–Oct. 1981. Publication. *Georgia Librarian* (q.). *Ed.* Wanda Calhoun, Augusta/Richmond County Public Lib., Augusta 30902.

Pres. Carlton J. Thaxton, Box 833, Tucker 30084; *1st V.P./Pres.-Elect.* Charles E. Beard, Dir. of Libs., West Georgia College, Carrollton 30117; *2nd V.P.* Anne C. Ansley, Consultant, Media Field Services, State Dept. of Educ., 156 Trinity Ave. S.W., Atlanta 30303; *Treas.* Frank R. Lewis, Libn., LaGrange College, LaGrange 30240; *Secy.* Marjorie J. Clark, Head Libn., North Georgia College, Dahlonega 30533; *Exec. Secy.* Ann W. Morton, Box 833, Tucker 30084.

Hawaii

Memb. 483. Term of Office. Mar. 1979–Mar. 1980. Publications. *Hawaii Library Association Journal* (bienn.); *Hawaii Library Association Newsletter* (5 per year); *HLA Membership Directory* (ann.); *Directory of Libraries & Information Sources in Hawaii & the Pacific Islands* (irreg.); *Index to Periodicals of Hawaii; Hawaii Legends Index.*

Pres. Katherine Goodhue, Branch Libn., Kailua Lib., Kailua 96734; *V.P./Pres.-Elect.* Lucretia Fudge, Program Coord., Maui Regional Lib., Wailuku, Maui 96793; *Secy.* Caroline Spencer, Branch Libn., Kalihi-Palama Lib., Honolulu 96819; *Treas.* May Suzuki, Univ. of Hawaii, Hamilton Lib., Honolulu 96822.

Address correspondence to Hawaii Lib. Assn., Box 4441, Honolulu 96813.

Idaho

Memb. 353. Term of Office. June 1, 1979–May 31, 1980. Publication. *The Idaho Librarian* (q.). *Ed.* David Green.

Pres. Geraldine Jacobs, Madison County Lib., Rexburg 83440; *V.P./Pres.-Elect.* Helen Rambo, Northwest Nazarene College Riley Lib., Nampa 83651; *Secy.* Erna Sellers, Trustee, Madison County Lib., Rexburg 83440; *Treas.* Alice Havens, Rte. 5, Box 98, Blackfoot 83221.

Illinois

Memb. 3,470. Term of Office. Oct. 1979–Dec. 1980. Publications. *ILA Reporter* (bi-ann.); *Q* (newsletter; 6 per year).

Pres. Betty Simpson, 208 E. Second St., Mackinaw 61755; *V.P./Pres.-Elect.* Robert R. McClarren, 1560 Oakwood Pl., Deerfield 60015; *Exec. Dir.* Alfred L. Woods, 425 N. Michigan Ave., Suite 1304, Chicago 60611; *Treas.* Michael J. Madden, Head Libn., Schaumburg Township Public Lib., 32 W. Library La., Schaumburg 60194; *Treas.-Elect.* Stanley D. Moreo, 104 King Arthur Ct., Apt. 3, Collinsville 62234.

Indiana

Memb. (Life) 90; (Indiv.) 1,147; (Inst.) 225. Term of Office. Nov. 1979–Nov. 1980.

Publication. *Focus on Indiana Libraries* (6 per year; $6). *Ed.* Elbert L. Watson.
Pres. Raymond Gnat, Indianapolis-Marion County Public Lib., 40 E. St. Clair, Indianapolis 46204; *V.P./Pres.-Elect.* Mary Bishop, Crawfordsville Public Lib., 222 S. Washington, Crawfordsville 47933; *Secy.* Martha Catt, Eastern Indiana ALSA, R.R. 1, Box 76A, Daleville 47334; *Treas.* Leslie R. Galbraith, Christian Theological Seminary, 1000 W. 42 St., Indianapolis 46208; *Exec. Dir.* Elbert L. Watson, Indiana Lib. Assn., 1100 W. 42 St., Indianapolis 46208.

Address correspondence to the executive director.

Iowa

Memb. 1,540. Term of Office. Jan. 1980–Jan. 1981. Publication. *The Catalyst* (bi-mo.). *Ed.* Naomi Stovall, 817 Insurance Exchange Bldg., Des Moines 50309.
Pres. Beverly Lind, Admin., Northeastern Iowa Regional Lib. System, Waterloo 50703.

Kansas

Memb. 950. Term of Office. July 1979–June 1980. Publications. *KLA Newsletter* (ann.); *KLA Membership Directory* (ann.).
Pres. Brian Beattie, Bradford Memorial Lib., El Dorado 67042; *V.P./Pres.-Elect.* Dan Masoni, Emporia Public Lib., 118 E. Sixth Ave., Emporia 66801; *Secy.* Carldon Broadbent, 930 S. Fifth, Salina 67401.

Kentucky

Memb. 1,250. Term of Office. Jan.–Dec. Publication. *Kentucky Library Association Bulletin* (q.).
Pres. Louise Bedford, Mt. Sterling Bd. of Educ., Mt. Sterling 40337; *V.P.* Sara Leech, Medical Center Lib., Univ. of Kentucky, Lexington 40506; *Secy.* June Martin, John Crabbe Lib., Eastern Kentucky Univ., Richmond 40475.

Louisiana

Memb. (Indiv.) 1,404; (Inst.) 84. Term of Office. July 1979–June 1980. Publication. *LLA Bulletin* (q.).

Pres. Coleen Salley, 5830 Vicksburg St., New Orleans 70124; *1st V.P./Pres.-Elect.* F. Landon Greaves, Box 302, SLU Sta., Hammond 70402; *2nd V.P.* Yvonne Koch, Box 1252, New Iberia 70560; *Secy.* Roland Simon, Box 52846, Lafayette 70505; *Treas.* No longer elected office, handled by the exec. dir. *Exec. Dir.* Chris Thomas, Box 131, Baton Rouge 70821; *Parliamentarian.* Charles Harrington, 309 Watson Dr., Natchitoches 71457.

Address correspondence to the executive director.

Maine

Memb. 600. Term of Office. (*Pres. & V.P.*). Spring 1978–Spring 1980. Publication. *Downeast Libraries* (4 per year). *Monthly Memo* (12 per year).
Pres. Benita Davis, Bangor Public Lib., 145 Harlow St., Bangor 04401; *V.P.* Carolyn Nolin, Maine State Lib., Augusta 04333; *Secy.* Richard Sibley, Waterville Public Lib., Waterville 04901; *Treas.* Jonathan Burns, Portland Public Lib., 619 Congress St., Portland 04101.

Address correspondence to Maine Lib. Assn., c/o Maine Municipal Assn., Local Government Center, Community Dr., Augusta 04330.

Maryland

Memb. Approx. 900. Term of Office. May 1, 1979–Apr. 30, 1980.
Pres. Katharine C. Hurrey, Dir., Southern Maryland Regional Lib. Assn., Box 1069, La Plata 20646; *1st V.P.* Dallas Shaffer, Prince George's County Memorial Lib., 6532 Adelphi Rd., Hyattsville 20782; *2nd V.P.* Beth Babikow, Baltimore County Public Lib., 320 York Rd., Towson 21204; *Treas.* Robert Greenfield, Baltimore County Public Lib., Rosedale Branch, 6105 Kenwood Ave., Baltimore 21237.

Address correspondence to Jeannette Dutcher, Exec. Secy., 115 W. Franklin St., Baltimore 21201.

Massachusetts

Memb. (Indiv.) 1,500; (Inst.) 200. Term of Office. July 1979–June 1981. Publication. *Bay State Librarian* (3 per year). *Ed.* Philip Fragasso, Wakefield Public Lib., Wakefield 01880.

Pres. Bruce Baker, Western Regional Public Lib. System, Springfield 01103; *V.P.* Helen Lowenthal, Sudbury Public Lib., Sudbury 01776; *Rec. Secy.* Helen Harding, Gale Free Lib., Holden 01520; *Treas.* Thomas Jewell, Waltham Public Lib., Waltham 02154; *Exec. Secy.* Patricia Demit, Massachusetts Lib. Assn., Box 7, Nahant 01908.

Address correspondence to the executive secretary.

Michigan

Memb. (Indiv.) 2,200; (Inst.) 100. Term of Office. Nov. 1, 1979–Oct. 31, 1980. Publications. *Michigan Librarian* (2 per year); *Michigan Librarian Newsletter* (8 per year).

Pres. Carolyn J. McMillen, Box 1495, East Lansing 48823; *V.P./Pres.-Elect.* Howard Lipton, 22504 Statler, St. Clair Shores 48081; *2nd V.P.* Lois Kuntz, 495 Furnace St., Manchester 48158; *Exec. Dir.* Frances H. Pletz, 226 W. Washtenaw, Lansing 48933; *Treas.* Marlene Thayer, Public Lib. Consultant, Dept. of Educ., Lib. Services, 735 E. Michigan Ave., Lansing 48915.

Minnesota

Memb. 850. Term of Office. *Pres. and V.P.* Nov. 1979–Nov. 1980; *Secy.* Nov. 1978–Nov. 1980; *Treas.* Oct. 1979–Nov. 1981. Publication. *MLA Newsletter* (11 per year).

Pres. Jerry Young, Anoka County Lib., 707 Hwy. 10, Blaine 55434; *V.P./Pres.-Elect.* Patricia Harpole, Minnesota Historical Society, 690 Cedar St., St. Paul 55101; *Secy.* Donald Pearce, Univ. of Minnesota-Duluth, Lib., Duluth 55812; *Treas.* Charles Richardson, Goodhue County National Bank, Red Wing 55066; *Exec. Dir.* Adele Morris, 16491 Fishing Ave., Rosemount 55068.

Address correspondence to the executive director.

Mississippi

Memb. 1,250. Term of Office. Jan. 1980–Dec. 1980. Publications. *Mississippi Libraries* (q.).

Pres. Lelia G. Rhodes, H. T. Sampson Lib., Jackson State Univ., Jackson 39217; *V.P./Pres.-Elect.* Savan Tynes, Biloxi Public Schools, 213 Miramar Ave., Biloxi 39530; *Secy.* Mirian Green, Coahoma Jr. College Lib., Rte. 1, Box 612, Clarksdale 38614; *Treas.* David Juergens, Rowland Medical Lib., 2037 First Ave., Jackson 39209; *Exec. Secy.* Kay Mitchell, Box 4710, Jackson 39216.

Address correspondence to the executive secretary.

Missouri

Memb. 1,234. Term of Office. Sept. 30, 1979–Sept. 30, 1980. Publication. *Missouri Library Association Newsletter* (6 per year).

Pres. Marilyn Stone, 1501 Joann, Columbia 65201; *V.P./Pres.-Elect.* Philip Tompkins, UMKC Lib., 5100 Rockhill Rd., Kansas City 64110; *Treas.* Betty Schramm, St. Louis County Lib., 1640 S. Lindbergh Blvd., St. Louis 63131; *Secy.* Virginia Terry, 1436 Santa Anna, St. Charles 63301.

Montana

Memb. 560. Term of Office. June 1979–June 1980. Publication. *MLA President's Newsletter* (4 per year).

Pres. Edna Berg, Libn., Bozeman Senior High, Bozeman 59715; *V.P./Pres.-Elect.* Richard Gercken, Dir., Great Falls Public Lib., Great Falls 59401; *Secy.* Mary Schmiedeskamp, Parmly Billings Lib., Billings 59101.

Nebraska

Memb. 985. Term of Office. Oct. 1979–Oct. 1980. Publication. *NLA Quarterly.* *Ed.* Delores DeJonge, 165 Wedgewood, Lincoln 68510.

Pres. Shirley Flack, Scottsbluff Public Lib., Scottsbluff 69361; *Exec. Secy.* Delores DeJonge, 165 Wedgewood, Lincoln 68510.

Nevada

Memb. 250. Term of Office. Jan. 1, 1980–Dec. 31, 1980. Publication. *Highroller* (6 per year).

Pres. Joan Kerschner, Nevada State Lib., Capitol Complex, 401 N. Carson St., Carson City 89710; *V.P./Pres.-Elect.* Martha Gould, Washoe County Lib., Box 2151, Reno 89505; *Exec. Secy.* Joyce Lee, Nevada State Lib., Capitol Complex, 401 N. Carson St., Carson City 89710; *Treas.* Cecil Nabors, Nevada State Lib., Capitol Complex, 401 N. Carson St., Carson City 89710.

New Hampshire

Memb. 348. Term of Office. May 1979–May 1980. Publications. *Granite State Libraries* (q.); *NHLA Newsletter* (mo.).

Pres. Kendall Wiggin, Merrimack Public Lib., Merrimack 03054; *1st V.P.* Benette Pizzimenti, Concord Public Lib., Concord 03031; *2nd V.P.* John Hallahan, Manchester City Lib., 405 Pine St., Manchester 03104; *Secy.* Anna Kjoss, Wadleigh Memorial Lib., Nashua St., Milford 03055; *Treas.* Joe Considine, New England College Lib., Henniker 03242.

New Jersey

Memb. 2,000. Term of Office. May 1979–May 1980. Publication. *New Jersey Libraries* (8 per year).

Pres. Drew Burns, Dir., Wayne Public Lib., 475 Valley Rd., Wayne 07470; *V.P./Pres.-Elect.* Dorothy Jones, Dir., East Orange Public Lib., 21 S. Arlington, East Orange 07018; *2nd V.P.* John Abram, Head of Reference, Newark Public Lib., 5 Washington St., Newark 07102; *Past Pres.* Mary Joyce Doyle, Dir., Bergenfield Public Lib., 50 W. Clinton Ave., Bergenfield 07621; *Admin. Secy.* Pauline A. Schear, New Jersey Lib. Assn., 221 Boulevard, Passaic 07055; *Rec. Secy.* Alyce Bowers, Dir., Rockaway Township Public Lib., Green Pond Rd., Hibernia 07842; *Corresponding Secy.* Lorraine Jackson, Dir., South Brunswick Public Lib., Kingston La., Monmouth Junction 08852; *Treas.* David I. Lance, Dir., Linden Public Lib., 31 E. Henry St., Linden 07036.

Address correspondence to the administrative secretary.

New Mexico

Memb. 500. Term of Office. Apr. 1979–Apr. 1980. Publication. *New Mexico Library Association Newsletter. Ed.* Laurel Drew, Albuquerque Public Lib., 501 Copper N.W., Albuquerque 87102.

Pres. Mary Penland, Barranca Mesa Elementary School, Los Alamos 87544; *1st V.P./Pres.-Elect.* Sarah Garrett, New Mexico State Univ. Lib., Box 3475, Las Cruces 88003; *2nd V.P.* Joseph D. Sabatini, Albuquerque Public Lib., 501 Copper N.W., Albuquerque 87102; *Secy.* Lucy Cruz, Taos Public Schools, Taos 87571; *Treas.* Cecil Clotfelter, Golden Lib., Eastern New Mexico Univ., Portales 88130.

New York

Memb. 4,500. Term of Office. Oct. 1979–Oct. 1980. Publication. *NYLA Bulletin* (10 per year, Sept.–June). *Ed.* Diana J. Dean.

Pres. Jane R. Moore, Grad. School and Univ. Center, City Univ. of New York, 33 W. 42 St., New York 10036; *1st V.P.* Patricia Mautino, Curriculum Resource Center, Oswego County BOCES, Mexico 13114; *2nd V.P.* Frances D. Clark, Cornwall Central School Dist., 122 Main St., Cornwall 12518; *Exec. Dir.* Dadie Perlov, CAE, New York Lib. Assn., 60 E. 42 St., Suite 1242, New York 10017.

Address correspondence to the executive director.

North Carolina

Memb. 2,500. Term of Office. Oct. 1979–Sept. 1981. Publication. *North Carolina Libraries* ($10; q.). *Ed.* Jonathan A. Lindsey, Carlyle Campbell Lib., Meredith College, Raleigh 27611.

Pres. H. William O'Shea, Dir., Wake

County Public Libs., 104 Fayetteville St., Raleigh 27601; *1st V.P./Pres.-Elect.* Mertys W. Bell, Dean of Learning Resources, Guilford Technical Institute, Box 309, Jamestown 27282; *2nd V.P.* Philip W. Ritter, Dir., Central North Carolina Regional Lib., 342 S. Spring St., Burlington 27215; *Secy.* David Harrington, Educational Materials Coord., Rowan County Schools, Box 1348, Salisbury, 28144; *Treas.* W. Robert Pollard, Head of Reference, D. H. Hill Lib., North Carolina State Univ., Raleigh 27607; *Dir. 1.* Carol A. Southerland, Libn., Williamston H.S., Rte. 2, Box 70, Williamston 27892; *Dir. 2.* Emily S. Boyce, Prof., Dept. of Lib. Science, East Carolina Univ., Greenville 27834.

North Dakota

Memb. (Indiv.) 350; (Inst.) 30. Term of Office. *Pres., V.P., and Pres.-Elect.* Oct. 1979–Oct. 1981. Publication. *The Good Stuff* (q.). *Ed.* Janet Crawford, Mandan Public Lib., Mandan 58554.

Pres. Tom Jones, Dir., Veterans Memorial Public Lib., 520 Ave. A E., Bismarck 58501; *V.P./Pres.-Elect.* Ron Rudser, Minot State College Lib., Minot 58701; *Secy.* Marilyn Guttromson, North Dakota Legislative Council Lib., Capitol, Bismarck 58505; *Treas.* Cheryl Bailey, Mary College Lib., Bismarck 58501.

Ohio

Memb. (Indiv.) 1,933; (Inst.) 189. Term of Office. Oct. 1979–Oct. 1980. Publications. *Ohio Library Association Bulletin* (q.); *Ohio Libraries: Newsletter of the Ohio Library Association* (8 per year).

Pres. A. Robert Rogers, Kent State Univ. School of Lib. Science, Kent 44242; *V.P./Pres.-Elect.* Nancy Wareham, Cleveland Area Metropolitan Lib. System, Cleveland 44124; *Secy.* Linda Blaha, Cuyahoga County Public Lib., Parma Regional Branch, Cleveland 44129; *Exec. Dir.* A. Chapman Parsons, 40 S. Third St., Suite 409, Columbus 43215.

Address correspondence to the executive director.

Oklahoma

Memb. (Indiv.) 925; (Inst.) 32. Term of Office. July 1, 1979–June 30, 1980. Publications. *Oklahoma Librarian* (q.); *President's Newsletter* (irreg.).

Pres. Polly Clarke, Northeastern Oklahoma State Univ., Tahlequah 74464; *V.P./Pres.-Elect.* Aarone Corwin, 9217 Nawassa, Midwest City 73130; *Secy.* Mary Sherman, Pioneer Multi-County Lib. System, 225 N. Webster, Norman 73069; *Treas.* Norman Nelson, Oklahoma State Univ. Lib., Stillwater 74074; *Exec. Secy.* Peggy Augustine, Tulsa City-County Lib., 400 Civic Center, Tulsa 74103.

Address correspondence to the executive secretary.

Oregon

Memb. (Indiv.) 730; (Inst.) 50. Term of Office. Apr. 1979–Apr. 1980. Publication. *Oregon Library News* (mo.). *Ed.* Nadine Purcell, Lib. Processing Center, 1915 Hazel St., Medford 97501.

Pres. Martha Julaphongs, Multnomah County Lib., 801 S.W. Tenth Ave., Portland 97205; *V.P./Pres.-Elect.* James Meeks, Eugene Public Lib., 100 W. 13 Ave., Eugene 97401; *Secy.* Marybeth Arbuckle, Deschutes County Lib., 507 N.W. Wall St., Bend 97701; *Treas.* Martin Stephenson, Corvallis Public Lib., 645 N.W. Monroe, Corvallis 97330.

Pennsylvania

Memb. 2,900. Term of Office. Oct. 1979–Oct. 1980. Publication. *PLA Bulletin* (mo.).

Pres. Stuart Forth, Pattee Lib., Pennsylvania State Univ., University Park 16802; *Exec. Dir.* Nancy L. Blundon, Pennsylvania Lib. Assn., 100 Woodland Rd., Pittsburgh 15232.

Puerto Rico

Memb. 259. Term of Office. Jan.–Dec. 1980. Publications. *Boletín* (s. ann.);

Cuadernos Bibliotecológicos (irreg.); *Informa* (mo.); *Cuadernos Bibliográficos* (irreg.).
Pres. Carmencita León; *V.P.* Jorge Encarnación; *Secy.* Belsie I. Cappas de Piñero; *Treas.* Digna Escalera.
Address correspondence to the Sociedad de Bibliotecarios de Puerto Rico, Apdo. 22898, U.P.R. Sta., Rio Piedras 00931.

Rhode Island

Memb. (Indiv.) 560; (Inst.) 33. Term of Office. Nov. 1979–Oct. 1980. Publication. *Rhode Island Library Association Bulletin* (mo.). *Ed.* Judith Plotz.
Pres. Louise Dolan, Barrington Public Lib., Barrington 02806; *V.P.* Beth Perry, Rhode Island College Lib., Providence 02908; *Secy.* Elliot Chesebrough, Providence Public Lib., Providence 02903; *Treas.* Elizabeth Bourne, Cranston Public Lib., Cranston 02905; *Member-at-Large.* Thomas Suprenant, Univ. of Rhode Island Grad. Lib. School, Kingston 02881.

St. Croix

Memb. 29. Term of Office. Apr. 1979–May 1980. Publications. *SCLA Newsletter* (q.); *Studies in Virgin Islands Librarianship* (irreg.).
Pres. Bonnie Isman, Box 2765, Frederiksted 00840; *V.P.* Carole Gooden, 3 Tide Village, Christiansted 00820; *Treas.* Patricia Oliver, Box 6760, Sunny Isle 00820; *Secy.* Joan Cobb, Box 2893, Christiansted 00820; *Bd. Members.* Ena Henderson; Julie Horine; Ada Anderson.

South Carolina

Memb. 920. Term of Office. Jan.–Dec. 1980. Publication. *The South Carolina Librarian* (s. ann.). *Ed.* Laurance Mitlin, Dacus Lib., Winthrop College, Rock Hill 29733; *News and Views of South Carolina Library Association* (mo.). *Ed.* John Sukovich, Wessels Lib., Newberry College, Newberry 29108.
Pres. John H. Landrum, South Carolina State Lib., Box 11469, Columbia 29211; *V.P./Pres.-Elect.* F. William Summers, College of Librarianship, Univ. of South Carolina, Columbia 29208; *2nd V.P.* Penny E. Albright, Kershaw County Lib., 1304 Broad St., Camden 29020; *Treas.* Thomas A. Marcil, Thomas Cooper Lib., Univ. of South Carolina, Columbia 29208; *Secy.* Jan Buvinger, Charleston County Lib., 404 King St., Charleston 29043; *Exec. Secy.* Louise Whitmore, Rte. 3, 160 Irwin Rd., Lexington 29072.

South Dakota

Memb. (Indiv.) 469; (Inst.) 88. Term of Office. Oct. 1979–Oct. 1980. Publications. *Book Mark* (bi-mo.); *Newsletter.* *Ed.* Phil Brown, H. M. Briggs Lib., South Dakota State Univ., Brookings 57006.
Pres. Bob Carmack, Dean of Lib. Services, Univ. of South Dakota, Vermillion 57783; *Pres.-Elect.* Dora Ann Jones, E. Y. Berry Lib., Black Hills State College, Spearfish 57783; *Secy.* Susan Sandness, Minnehaha County Lib., Hartford 57033; *Treas.* John Castleman, Brookings Public Lib., Brookings 57006.
Address correspondence to the president.

Tennessee

Memb. 1,365. Term of Office. May 1979–May 1980. Publication. *Tennessee Librarian* (q.).
Pres. Keith Cottam, Asst./Dir., Public Services-Employee Relations, Vanderbilt Univ., Lib., Nashville 37203; *V.P./Pres.-Elect.* Wilma L. Tice, Lib. Consultant, Metropolitan Public Schools, Nashville 37204; *Treas.* Joyce W. McLeary, Trustee, Jackson-Madison County Lib. Bd., Jackson 38301; *Exec. Secy.* Betty Nance, Box 120085, Nashville 37212.

Texas

Term of Office. Apr. 1979–Apr. 1980.
Pres. Annie May Gilbert, Chief Materials Processing, Dallas Public Lib., 1954

Commerce, Dallas 75201; *Pres.-Elect.* Ray C. Janeway, Dir., Texas Tech Univ. Lib., Lubbock 79409; *Continuing Exec. Dir.*, Jerre Hetherington TLA Office, 8989 Westheimer, Suite 108, Houston 77063.

Utah

Memb. 650. Term of Office. *Pres. & V.Ps.* Mar. 1980–Mar. 1981. Publications. *Utah Libraries* (bienn.); *ULA Newsletter* (irreg.).

Pres. J. Dennis Day, Dir., Salt Lake City Public Lib., 205 E. Fifth St., Salt Lake City 84111; *1st V.P.* Blaine Hall, Brigham Young Univ., Provo 84602; *2nd V.P.* Jane Peterson, Office of Legislative Research, Utah State Capitol Bldg., Salt Lake City 84111; *Exec. Secy.* Gerald A. Buttars, Utah State Lib. Commission, 2150 S. 300 W., Salt Lake City 84115; *ALA Chapter Councillor.* Nathan Smith, Lib. School, Brigham Young Univ., Provo 84602.

Vermont

Memb. 490. Term of Office. Jan.–Dec. 1980. Publication. *VLA News.*

Pres. Connell Gallagher, Univ. of Vermont, Baily Lib., Burlington 05401; *V.P./Pres.-Elect.* Edward Scott, Castleton State College Lib., Castleton 05735; *Secy.* Linda Hay, Springfield Town Lib., Springfield 05156; *Treas.* Marjorie Zunder, Head, Technical Processes, Vermont Dept. of Libs., Montpelier 05602.

Virginia

Memb. 1,067. Term of Office. Nov. 1979–Dec. 1980. Publication. *Virginia Librarian Newsletter* (5 per year).

Pres. Lelia Saunders, Arlington County Dept. of Libs., 1015 N. Quincy St., Arlington 22201; *V.P./Pres.-Elect.* Betty Ragsdale, Blue Ridge Regional Lib., Martinsville 24112; *Treas.* Donald J. Kenney, Virginia Polytechnic Institute and State Univ., Blacksburg 24061; *Secy.* Mary Haban, James Madison Univ., Harrisonburg 22801.

Washington

Memb. (Indiv.) 940; (Inst.) 31. Term of Office. Aug. 1979–July 1981. Publications. *Highlights* (bi-mo.); *Password* (bi-mo.).

Pres. Verda R. Hansberry, Seattle Public Lib., Seattle 98104; *1st V.P./Pres.-Elect.* Anthony M. Wilson, Highline Community College, Midway 98031; *2nd V.P.* June Pinnell, Bellingham Public Lib., Bellingham 98225; *Secy.* Zay Pribble Washington Regional Lib. for the Blind and Physically Handicapped, 811 Harrison St., Seattle 98129; *Treas.* Marion J. Otteraaen, Longview Public Lib., Longview 98632.

West Virginia

Memb. (Indiv.) 994; (Inst.) 76. Term of Office. Dec. 1979–Nov. 1980. Publication. *West Virginia Libraries* (q.).

Pres. David M. Gillespie, Glenville State College, 200 High St., Glenville 26351; *1st V.P./Pres.-Elect.* Judy Rule, Cabell County Public Lib., Huntington 25701; *2nd V.P.* S. Fred Natale, Weir Public Lib., Weirton 26062; *Secy.* Pamela Gorson, Clarksburg-Harrison Public Lib., Clarksburg 26301; *Treas.* Dave Childers, West Virginia Lib. Commission, Science & Culture Center, Charleston 25305; *ALA Councillor.* Jo Ellen Flagg, Kanawha County Public Lib., 123 Capital St., Charleston 25301.

Wisconsin

Memb. 2,000. Term of Office. Jan.–Dec. Publication. *WLA Newsletter* (bi-mo.).

Pres. Ramon Hernandez, McMillan Memorial Lib., 490 E. Grand Ave., Wisconsin Rapids 54494; *V.P.* John J. Jax, Univ. of Wisconsin-Stout, Pierce Lib., Menomonie 54751; *Admin. Secy.* Bonnie Lynne Robinson, 201 W. Mifflin St., Madison 53703.

Wyoming

Memb. (Indiv.) 383; (Inst.) 12; (Sub.) 8. Term of Office. May 1979–May 1980.

Publication. *Wyoming Library Roundup* (q.). *Ed.* Ruth Aubuchon, Wyoming State Lib., Cheyenne 82002.

Pres. Ruth Preuit, Box 546, Wheatland 32201; *V.P./Pres.-Elect.* Lisa Kinney, Albany County Public Lib., Laramie 82070; *Exec. Secy.* Irene Nakako, Rock Springs Public Lib., Rock Springs 82901.

CANADA

Alberta

Memb. (Indiv.) 309; (Inst.) 79; (Trustee) 36. Term of Office. May 1979–May 1980. Publication. *Letter of the L.A.A.* (mo.).

Pres. R. M. Block, Dir., Medicine Hat Lib., 414 First St. S.E., Medicine Hat T1A 0A8; *1st V.P.* Heather-Belle Dowling, Dir., Co. Strathcona Municipal Lib., 2001 Sherwood Dr., Sherwood Park T8A 3J4; *2nd V.P.* Joyce Tomie, Asst. Dir., Central Services, Calgary Lib., 616 Macleod Trail S.E., Calgary T2G 2M2; *Treas.* S. Dubrule, Head Libn., Extension Lib., Rutherford S., Univ. of Alberta, Edmonton T6G 2J4; *Hon. Secy.* Donna Gordon, Public Services Lib., Energy and Natural Resources, 9th fl., Petroleum Plaza S., 9915-108 St., Edmonton T5K 2C9.

Address correspondence to the president, Box 3063, Sta. A, Edmonton T5J 2G6.

British Columbia

Memb. 550. Term of Office. June 1, 1979–May 31, 1980. Publication. *The Reporter* (6 per year). *Ed.* John Black.

Pres. Jim Scott; *V.P.* Mary Beth MacDonald; *Treas.* Ann Dodd; *Secy.* Maureen Willison.

Address correspondence to BCLA, Box 46378 Sta. G, Vancouver V6R 4G6.

Manitoba

Memb. 300. Term of Office. Sept. 1979–Sept. 1980. Publication. *Manitoba Library Association Bulletin* (q.).

Pres. Carolynne Scott, St. Vital Public Lib., 6 Fermor Ave., St. Vital R2M 0Y2; *1st V.P.* Wm. Birdsall, No. 33, 125 Allegheny Dr., Winnipeg R3T 3A1; *2nd V.P.* Nancy Brydges, 16 Kingston Row, Winnipeg R2M 0S6; *Treas.* Hugh Larimer, 605 Kilkenny Dr., Winnipeg R3T 3E2; *Corres. Secy.* Donna Breyfogle, 514 McMillan Ave., Winnipeg R3G 0N5; *Rec. Secy.* Roy Bonnin, 195 Braemar Ave., Winnipeg R2H 2K8.

Address correspondence to Manitoba Lib. Assn., c/o E. MacMillan, 6 Fermor Ave., Winnipeg R2M 0Y2.

Ontario

Memb. 2,400. Term of Office. Jan. 1–Dec. 31, 1980. Publications. *Focus* (bi-mo.). *Ed.* Karen Smith; *Expression* (bi-mo.). *Ed.* Larry Moore; *The Reviewing Librarian* (q.). *Ed.* Fay Blostein; *The Revolting Librarian* (q.). *Ed.* Elizabeth Bream.

Pres. Kenneth R. Frost, Info. Metasystems, Inc., 64 Bedle Ave., Willowdale M2H 1K8; *V.P.* Jean Orpwood, North York Public Lib., 35 Fairview Mall Dr., Willowdale M2J 4S4; *Treas.* Jane Moore, Kenner Collegiate, Monaghan Rd. S., Peterborough K9H 4E9; *Secy.* Shirley Edgar, Fanshawe College, 1460 Oxford St. E., London N5V 1W2; *Exec. Secy.* Virginia Tayler, Ontario Lib. Assn., 73 Richmond St. W., Suite 402, Toronto M6S 1N6.

Quebec

Memb. (Indiv.) 182; (Inst.) 79; (Commercial) 11. Term of Office. May 1979–May 1980. Publication. *ABO/OLA Bulletin.*

Pres. Diana Frye, St. George's School of Montreal, 3100 The Boulevard, Montreal; *V.P.* Marie-Louise Simon, Reginald J. P. Dawson Lib., 1967 Graham Blvd., Mount Royal; *Treas.* Françoise Brais, Editions Héritage, 300 r. Arran, St. Lambert; *English Secy.* Sharon Huffman, Reginald J. P. Dawson Lib., 1967 Graham Blvd., Mount Royal; *French Secy.* Madeleine Fink, Bibliothéque municipale, 490 r. Mercille, St. Lambert J4P 2L5.

Saskatchewan

Memb. 270. Term of Office. July 1, 1979–June 30, 1980. Publications. *Saskatchewan Library* (s. ann.); *Saskatchewan Library Forum* (5 per year).

Pres. Gordon Ray, Saskatoon Public Lib., 311 23 St. E., Saskatoon; *V.P.* Karen Labuik, Wapiti Regional Lib., 145 12 St. E., Prince Albert S6V 1B7; *Secy.* Betty Taman, Saskatoon Public Lib., 311 23 St. E., Saskatoon S7K 0J6; *Treas.* Catherine McAuley, Regina Public Lib., 2311 12 Ave., Regina S4P 0N3.

Address correspondence to the secretary, Box 3388, Regina S4P 3H1.

REGIONAL

Atlantic Provinces: N.B., Nfld., N.S., P.E.I.

Memb. (Indiv.) 310; (Inst.) 185. Term of Office. May 1979–Apr. 1980. Publication. *APLA Bulletin* (bi-mo.).

Pres. Lorraine McQueen; *Pres.-Elect.* Ann Neville; *V.P. Nova Scotia.* Iain Bates; *V.P. Prince Edward Island.* Pam Forsyth; *V.P. Newfoundland.* Barbara Eddy; *V.P. New Brunswick.* Claude Potvin; *Treas.* Betty Sutherland; *Secy.* Susan Whiteside.

Address correspondence to Atlantic Provinces Lib. Assn., c/o School of Lib. Service, Dalhousie Univ. Halifax B3H 4H8, Nova Scotia.

Middle Atlantic; DE, MD, NJ, PA, WV

Term of Office. Jan. 1980–Jan. 1981.

Pres. Nicholas Winowick, Kanawha County Public Lib., 123 Capitol St., Charleston, WV 25301; *V.P.* Thomas Schear, Dir., Passaic Public Lib., Passaic, NJ 07055; *Secy.-Treas.* Richard Parsons, Baltimore County Public Lib., 320 York Rd., Towson, MD 21204.

Midwest: IL, IN, IA, MI, MN, OH, WI

Term of Office. Oct. 1979–Oct. 1983.

Pres. Robert H. Donahugh, Dir., Public Lib. of Youngstown and Mahoning County, 305 Wick Ave., Youngstown, OH 44503; *V.P.* Walter D. Morrill, Box 287, Duggan Lib., Hanover College, Hanover, IN 47243; *Secy.* Joseph Kimbrough, Dir., Minneapolis Public Lib. & Info. Center, 300 Nicollet Mall, Minneapolis, MN 55401; *Treas.* Frances Pletz, Michigan Lib. Assn., 226 W. Washtenaw, Lansing, MI 48933.

Address correspondence to the president, Midwest Federation of Lib. Assns.

Mountain Plains: CO, KS, NE, NV, ND, SD, UT, WY

Publication. *MPLA Newsletter* (bi-mo.).

Pres. Joe Anderson, State Libn., Nevada State Lib., Carson City, NV 89701; *V.P./Pres.-Elect.* Jane Kolbe, Dir., Sioux Falls College Lib., Sioux Falls, SD 57101; *Secy.* Amy Owen, Utah State Lib. Commission, 2150 S. 300 West, Salt Lake City, UT 84115; *Exec. Secy.* Joe Edelen, Head, Technical Services, Univ. of South Dakota Lib., Vermillion, SD 57069.

New England: CT, MA, ME, NH, RI, VT

Memb. 1,600. Term of Office. Oct. 1979–Oct. 1980. Publications. *NELA Newsletter* (6 per year). *Ed.* Brenda Claflin, Faxon Lib., 1073 New Britain Ave., West Hartford, CT 06110; *A Guide to Newspaper Indexes in New England.*

Pres. Edward Chenevert, Portland Public Lib., 5 Monument Sq., Portland, ME 04101; *V.P./Pres.-Elect.* Norma Creaghe, Geisel Lib., St. Anselm's College, Manchester, NH 03102; *Treas.* Clifton Giles, Univ. of Southern Maine, Gorham, ME 04038; *Secy.* Amy Howlett, Southeast Regional Lib., R.F.D. 1, Brattleboro, VT 05301; *Dirs.* Stanley Brown, Dartmouth College Lib., Hanover, NH 03755; John Jackson, Mary Cheney Lib.,

Manchester, CT 06040; *Past Pres.* Virginia Tashjian, Newton Free Lib., Newton, MA 02158.

Pacific Northwest: AK, ID, MT, OR, WA, Alta., B.C.

Memb. 1,027 (active); 327 (subscribers). Term of Office. *Pres., 1st V.P., and 2nd V.P.* 1979–1980. Publication. *PNLA Quarterly. Ed.* Daniel Newberry, Portland State Univ. Lib., Box 1151, Portland, OR 97207.

Pres. Irene Heninger, 924 Shorewood Dr., Bremerton, WA 98310; *1st V.P.* William F. Hayes, Boise Public Lib., 715 Capitol Blvd., Boise, ID 83702; *2nd V.P.* Donna Selle, Washington County Cooperative Lib. Services, Box 5129, Aloha, OR 97005; *Secy.* Joy Scudamore, Greater Vancouver Lib. Federation, 1105 Commercial Dr., Vancouver, B.C. V5L 3X3; *Treas.* Kay Salmon, Corvallis Public Lib., Corvallis, OR 97103.

Southeastern: AL, FL, GA, KY, MS, NC, SC, TN, VA, WV

Memb. 2,900. Term of Office. Oct. 1978–Nov. 1980. Publication. *The Southeastern Librarian* (q.).

Pres. Helen D. Lockhart, Coord., Community Relations and Adult Programs, Memphis/Shelby County Public Lib. and Info. Center, Memphis, TN 38104; *V.P./Pres.-Elect.* Paul H. Spence, Univ. College Libn., Univ. of Alabama in Birmingham, Birmingham, AL 35294; *Secy.* Mary Frances Griffin, Lib. Consultant, State Dept. of Educ., Columbia, SC 29201; *Treas.* John E. Scott, Dir. of Lib. Resources, West Virginia State College, Institute, WV 25112; *Exec. Secy.* Ann W. Morton, Box 987, Tucker, GA 30084.

Address correspondence to the executive secretary.

Southwestern: AZ, AR, LA, NM, OK, TX

Memb. (Indiv.) 1,658; (Inst.) 231. Term of Office. Oct. 1978–Nov. 1980. Publication. *SWLA Newsletter* (bi-mo.).

Pres. Sam A. Dyson, Dir., Louisiana Tech Univ., Prescott Memorial Lib., Ruston, LA 71270; *V.P./Pres.-Elect.* Robert L. Clark, Jr., Dir., Oklahoma Dept. of Libs., 200 N.E. 18 St., Oklahoma City, OK 73150; *Past Pres.* John F. Anderson, Dir., Tucson Public Lib., Box 27470, Tucson, AZ 85726; *Rep.-at-Large.* Sandra Coleman, Head, Reference Dept., General Lib., Univ. of New Mexico, Albuquerque, NM 87131; *Exec. Dir.* Susan K. Schmidt, Box 23713, TWU Sta., Denton, TX 76204.

STATE LIBRARY AGENCIES

The state library administrative agency in each of the states will have the latest information on state plans for the use of federal funds under the Library Services and Construction Act. The directors, addresses, and telephone numbers of these state agencies are listed below.

Alabama

Anthony Miele, Dir., Alabama Public Lib. Service, Montgomery 36130. Tel: 205-277-7330.

Alaska

Richard Engen, Dir., Libs. & Museums, Dept. of Educ., Pouch G., State Office Bldg., Juneau 99811. Tel: 907-465-2910.

Arizona

Sharon Womack, Acting Dir., Dept. of Lib., Archives and Public Records, 3rd fl. Capitol, Phoenix 85007. Tel: 602-271-3701.

Arkansas

Frances Nix, State Libn., Arkansas State Lib., One Capitol Mall, Little Rock 72201. Tel: 501-371-1526.

California

Ethel S. Crockett, State Libn., California State Lib., Box 2037, Sacramento 95809. Tel: 916-445-2585 or 4027.

Colorado

Anne Marie Falsone, Deputy State Libn., Colorado State Lib., 1326 Lincoln St., Denver 80203. Tel: 303-839-3695.

Connecticut

Charles Funk, State Libn., Connecticut State Lib., 231 Capitol Ave., Hartford 06115. Tel: 203-566-4192 or 4301.

Delaware

Sylvia Short, Dir., Div. of Lib. Development, Dept. of Community Affairs and Economic Development, Box 635, Dover 19901. Tel: 302-678-4748.

District of Columbia

Hardy R. Franklin, Dir., Martin Luther King Lib., 901 G St., N.W., Washington 20001. Tel: 202-727-1101.

Florida

Barratt Wilkins, State Libn., State Lib. of Florida, R. A. Gray Bldg., Tallahassee 32304. Tel: 904-487-2651.

Georgia

Carlton J. Thaxton, Dir., Div. of Public Lib. Services, 156 Trinity Ave. S.W., Atlanta 30303. Tel: 404-656-2461.

Hawaii

Ruth Itamura, State Libn., Div. of Lib. Services, Dept. of Educ., Box 2360, Honolulu 96804. Tel: 808-548-2430.

Idaho

Helen M. Miller, State Libn., Idaho State Lib., 325 W. State St., Boise 83702. Tel: 208-384-2150.

Illinois

Kathryn Gesterfield, Dir., Illinois State Lib., Centennial Memorial Bldg., Springfield 62706. Tel: 217-782-2994.

Indiana

C. Ray Ewick, Dir., Indiana State Lib., 140 N. Senate Ave., Indianapolis 46204. Tel: 317-633-4912.

Iowa

Barry Porter, Dir., State Lib. Commission of Iowa, Des Moines 50319. Tel: 515-281-4113.

Kansas

Ernestine Gilliland, Kansas State Lib., 535 Kansas Ave., Topeka 66601. Tel: 913-296-3296.

Kentucky

Barbara M. Williams, State Libn. and Archivist, Kentucky Dept. of Lib. and Archives, Box 537, Frankfort 40601. Tel: 502-564-7910.

Louisiana

Thomas Jacques, Louisiana State Lib., Box 131, Baton Rouge 70800. Tel: 504-342-4923.

Maine

Gary Nichols, State Libn., State Lib., Augusta 04330. Tel: 207-289-3561.

Maryland

Nettie B. Taylor, Asst. State Superintendent for Libs., Div. of Lib. Development and Services, State Dept. of Educ., Box 8717, Baltimore 21240. Tel: 301-796-8300, ext 284 or 285.

Massachusetts

David L. Reich, Dir., Massachusetts Bd. of Lib., Commissioners, 648 Beacon St., Boston 02215. Tel: 617-267-9400.

Michigan

Francis X. Scannell, State Libn., Michigan State Lib., 735 E. Michigan Ave., Lansing 48913. Tel: 517-373-1580.

Minnesota

William Asp, Dir., Lib. Div., Dept. of Educ., 301 Hanover Bldg., 480 Cedar St., St. Paul 55101. Tel: 612-296-2821.

Mississippi

Joe B. Forsee, Dir., Mississippi Lib. Commission, 1100 State Office Bldg., Box 3260, Jackson 39201. Tel: 601-354-6369.

Missouri

Charles O'Halloran, State Libn., Missouri State Lib., State Office Bldg., Jefferson City 65102. Tel: 314-751-2751.

Montana

Alma Jacobs, State Libn., Montana State Lib., 930 E. Lyndale Ave., Helena 59601. Tel: 406-449-3004.

Nebraska

John Kopischke, Dir., Nebraska Lib. Commission, Lincoln 68509. Tel. 402-471-2045.

Nevada

Joseph J. Anderson, State Libn., Nevada State Lib., Carson City 89701. Tel: 702-885-5130.

New Hampshire

Avis Duckworth, State Libn., New Hampshire State Lib., 20 Park St., Concord 03302. Tel: 603-271-2392.

New Jersey

Barbara F. Weaver, Asst. Commissioner of Education, Div. of State Lib. Archives and History, State St., Trenton 08625. Tel: 609-292-6200.

New Mexico

Clifford Lange, Dir., New Mexico State Lib., 300 Don Gasper St., Santa Fe 87501. Tel: 505-827-2033.

New York

Joseph F. Shubert, State Libn./Asst. Commissioner for Libs., Cultural Education Center, Rm. 10B41, Empire State Plaza, Albany 12230. Tel: 518-474-5930.

North Carolina

David Neil McKay, Dir./State Libn., Dept. of Cultural Resources, Div. of State Lib., 109 E. Jones St., Raleigh 27611. Tel: 919-733-2570.

North Dakota

Richard Wolfert, State Libn., North Dakota State Lib., Bismarck 58505. Tel: 701-224-2492.

Ohio

Richard Cheski, Dir., Ohio State Lib., State Office Bldg., Columbus 43215. Tel: 614-466-2693 or 2694.

Oklahoma

Robert L. Clark, Jr., Dir., Oklahoma Dept. of Libs., 200 N.E. 18 St., Oklahoma City 73105. Tel: 405-521-2502.

Oregon

Marcia Lowell, State Libn., Oregon State Lib., Salem 97310. Tel: 503-378-4367.

Pennsylvania

Patricia M. Broderick, Acting State Libn., Pennsylvania State Lib., Box 1601, Harrisburg 17126. Tel: 717-787-2646.

Rhode Island

Jewel Drickamer, Dir., Dept. of State Lib. Services, 95 Davis St., Providence 02902. Tel: 401-277-2726.

South Carolina

Betty E. Callaham, State Libn., South Carolina State Lib., 1500 Senate St., Box 11469, Columbia 29201. Tel: 803-758-3181.

South Dakota

Herschel V. Anderson, State Libn., South Dakota State Lib., State Lib. Bldg., Pierre 57501. Tel: 605-773-3131.

Tennessee

Katheryn C. Culbertson, State Libn. and Archivist, Tennessee State Lib. and Archives, 403 Seventh Ave. N., Nashville 37219. Tel: 615-741-2451.

Texas

Dorman H. Winfrey, Dir.-Libn., Texas State Lib., Box 12927, Capitol Sta., Austin 78711. Tel: 512-475-2166.

Utah

Russell L. Davis, Dir., Utah State Lib., Suite 16, 2150 S. 200 West, Salt Lake City 84115. Tel: 801-533-5875.

Vermont

Patricia Klinck, State Libn., State of Vermont, Dept. of Libs., Montpelier 05601. Tel: 802-828-3261, ext. 3265.

Virginia

Donald R. Haynes, State Libn., Virginia State Lib., Richmond 23219. Tel: 804-786-2332.

Washington

Roderick Swartz, State Libn., Washington State Lib., Olympia 98501. Tel: 206-753-5592.

West Virginia

Frederic J. Glazer, Exec. Sec., Science and Cultural Center, West Virginia Lib. Commission, Charleston 25305. Tel: 304-348-2041.

Wisconsin

W. Lyle Eberhart, Administrator, Div. of Lib. Services, Dept. of Public Instruction, Wisconsin Hall, Madison 53703. Tel: 608-266-2205.

Wyoming

Wayne H. Johnson, State Libn., Wyoming State Lib., Barnett Bldg., Cheyenne 82002. Tel: 307-777-7281.

American Samoa

Linette A. Hunter, Program Dir., Office of Lib. Services, Dept. of Educ., Box 1329, Pago Pago 96799. Tel: 633-5869 (through overseas operator).

Guam

Magdalena S. Taitano, Libn., Nieves M. Flores Memorial Lib., Box 652, Agana 96910. Tel: 472-6417 (through overseas operator).

Pacific Islands (Trust Territory of)

Augustine C. Castro, Dir. of Lib. Services, Commonwealth of the Northern Mariana Islands, Saipan, Northern Mariana Islands 96950. Tel: 6534 (through overseas operator).

Puerto Rico

Rivera de Ponce, Dir., Public Lib. Div., Dept. of Educ., Hato Rey 00919. Tel. 809-753-9191 (through overseas operator).

Virgin Islands

Henry C. Chang, Dir., Libs. and Museums, Dept. of Conservation and Cultural Affairs, Government of the Virgin Islands, Box 390, Charlotte Amalie, St. Thomas 00801. Tel: 809-774-3407.

STATE SCHOOL LIBRARY AND MEDIA ASSOCIATIONS

Alabama

Alabama Lib. Assn., Div. of Children's and School Libns. Memb. 480. Term of Office. Apr. 1979–Apr. 1980. Publication. *ALACS.*

Chpn. Doris Killingsworth, 1011 Second Ave. N.E., Fayette 35555.

Alaska

[See entry under State, Provincial, and Regional Library Associations—*Ed.*]

Arizona

School Lib. Div., Arizona State Lib. Assn. Memb. 520. Term of Office. Sept. 1979–Sept. 1980. Publication. *ASLA Newsletter.*

Pres. Alice Johnson, Box 492, Florence 85232; *Pres.-Elect.* Karen Whitney, 8247 W. Vale Dr., Phoenix 85033; *Secy.* Sally Abbott, 4114 W. Keim Dr., Phoenix 85019; *Treas.* Jane Cox, 4628 E. Calle Tuberia, Phoenix 85018.

Arkansas

School Lib. Div., Arkansas Lib. Assn. Memb. 294. Term of Office. Jan.–Dec. 1980.

Chpn. Mary Kay Sturgeon, 6607 Japonica Dr., Little Rock 72204.

California

California Media and Lib. Educators Assn. (CMLEA), Suite 204, 1575 Old Bayshore Hwy., Burlingame, CA 94010. Memb. 1,500. Term of Office. June 1979–May 1980. Publication. *CMLEA Journal* (s. ann.).

Pres. Lucille Brown, Mt. Diablo Unified School Dist., 1936 Carlotta Dr., Concord, CA 94519; *Pres.-Elect.* Curtis May, San Mateo County Schools, 333 Main St., Redwood City, CA 94063; *Past Pres.* Bettie Day, Santa Barbara County Schools, 4400 Cathedral Oaks Rd., Santa Barbara, CA 93111; *Secy.* Paul Cole, Walter Colton Jr. H.S., Monterey Peninsula Unified School Dist., Box 1031, Monterey, CA 93940; *Treas.* Kathy Pabst, San Diego H.S., 1405 Park Blvd., San Diego, CA 92101.

Colorado

Colorado Educational Media Assn. Memb. 680. Term of Office. Feb. 1980–Feb. 1981. Publication. *The Medium* (mo.).

Pres. Janice Smith, Adams County School District No. 12, 10290 N. Huron, Northglenn 80221.

Connecticut

Connecticut Educational Media Assn. Term of Office. May 1979–May 1980. Publications. *Looking Ahead to the Next Decade,* Bulletin No. 4 ($4 prepaid). *Your CEMA Professional Rights and Responsibilities* (free with the above).

Officers to be elected. Address correspondence to Admin. Secy., Anne Weimann, 25 Elmwood Ave., Trumbull 06611.

Delaware

Delaware School Lib. Media Assn. Memb. 104. Term of Office. Sept. 1979–Sept. 1980. Publication. *DSLMA Newsletter.*

Pres. Janet Dove, Educational Resource Center, Willard Hall, Univ. of Delaware, Newark 19711; *V.P.* Alice Thornton, Ogletown Middle School, Brennan Dr., Newark 19713; *Secy.* Beth Isaacs, Laurel Senior H.S. Lib., 1133 S. Central Ave., Laurel 19956; *Treas.* Carole M. Hastings, Milford Senior H.S. Lib., 1019 N. Walnut St., Milford 19963.

District of Columbia

D.C. Assn. of School Libns. Memb. 150. Term of Office. Aug. 1979–Aug. 1980. Publication. *Newsletter* (3 per year).

Pres. Edna Becton, Randall H.S., Eye St. and Delaware Ave. S.W., Washington 20024; *V.P. & Pres.-Elect.* Janice Spencer, Shepherd Elementary School, 14 St. & Kalmia Rd. N.W., Washington 20012; *Secy.* Marie Harris, Harris Elementary School, 53 & C Sts. S.E., Washington 20019; *Treas.* Jacqueline Moore, Shaed Elementary School, Third & Douglas Sts., Washington 20002; *Immed. Past Pres.* Marilyn E. Moser, Amidon Elementary School, Fourth and I Sts., S.W., Washington 20024.

Florida

Florida Assn. for Media in Education, Inc. Memb. 1,400. Term of Office. Oct. 1979–Oct. 1980. Publication. *Florida Media Quarterly* (q.).

Pres. Patricia S. Deniston, Dir. of Learning Resources, Polk Community College, 999 Ave. H.N.E., Winter Haven 33660; *V.P.* Ronald F. Johnson, Central Processing Lib., 1795 E. Wabash St., Bartow 33830; *Pres.-Elect.* Shirley Aaron, School of Lib. Science, Florida State Univ., Tallahassee 32306; *Secy.* Mary Jane Todd, Key West H.S., 2100 Flagler Ave., Key West 33040; *Treas.* Diane M. Johnson, Pinellas Park Sr. H.S., 6305 118 Ave. N., Largo 33543.

Georgia

School and Children's Lib. Div. of the Georgia Lib. Assn. Term of Office. Oct. 1979–Oct. 1981.

Chpn. Kathy Brock, Rte. 1, Box 130A, Bremen 30110.

Hawaii

Hawaii Assn. of School Libns. Memb. 240. Term of Office. Apr. 1979–Apr. 1980. Publication. *The Golden Key* (biann.).

Pres. Glenn Kawatachi, Makakilo Elementary School, 92-675 Anipeahi, Ewa Beach 96706; *V.P.* Penny Boyne, Mid-Pacific Institute, 2445 Kaala St., Honolulu 96822.

Idaho

School Libs. Div. of the Idaho Lib. Assn. Term of Office. May 1980–May 1981. Publication. Column in *The Idaho Librarian* (q.).

Chpn. Virginia Moberly, Libn., Middleton Elementary Lib., Box 66, Middleton 93644.

Illinois

Illinois Assn. for Media in Education (IAME). (Formerly Illinois Assn. of School Libns.) Memb. 750. Term of Office. Nov. 1979–Jan. 1, 1981. Publication. *IAME News for You* (q.). *Ed.* Charles Rusiewski, 207 E. Chester, Nashville 62263.

Pres. Sarah Doerner, Media Specialist, DuQuoin Community Unit Dist. DuQuoin 62832; *V.P.* Carolyn Rohrer, 324 Carmelhead La., Palatine 60193.

Indiana

Assn. for Indiana Media Educators. Memb. 950. Term of Office (Pres.). Apr. 24, 1979–Apr. 30, 1980. Publication. *Indiana Media Journal.*

Pres. Roger Whaley, New Albany 47150; *Exec. Secy.* James Thompson, Indiana State Univ., STW 1205, Terre Haute, IN 47809.

Iowa

Iowa Educational Media Assn. Memb. 700. Term of Office. Apr. 1980–Apr. 1981. Publication. *Iowa Media Message.*

Pres. Bill Oglesby, C215 East Hall, Univ. of Iowa, Iowa City 52242.

Kansas

Kansas Assn. of School Libns. Memb. 800. Term of Office. June 1979–July 1980. Publication. *KASL Newsletter* (s. ann.).

Pres. Marilyn Goodrich, R.R. 2, Box 82, Olathe 66061.

Kentucky

Kentucky School Media Assn. Memb. 625. Term of Office. Nov. 1979–Nov. 1980. Publication. *KSMA Wave Lengths*.

Pres. Janet Sue Tackett, 240 Breckinridge Sq., Louisville 40220; *Pres.-Elect.* Patricia J. Mize, Rte. 1, Calhoun 42327; *Secy.* Sara A. Brady, 1302 Bluffsprings Ct., Louisville 40223; *Treas.* Betty L. Everman, 141 Grace Ct., Apt. 2, Ft. Mitchell 41017.

Louisiana

Louisiana Assn. of School Libns., c/o Louisiana Lib. Assn., Box 131, Baton Rouge 70821. Memb. 432. Term of Office. July 1, 1979–June 30, 1980.

Pres. Louise Greeson, 5978 Chandler Dr., Baton Rouge 70808; *1st V.P. & Pres.-Elect.* Alex Kropog, Rte. 1, Box 173, Holden 70744; *2nd V.P.* Vivian Hurst, 404 Parent St., New Roads 70760; *Secy.* Genevieve M. Wheeler, 4525 E. Meadow La., Lake Charles 70605; *Treas.* Ina Sarkies, Rte. 3, Box 498, New Iberia 70560.

Maine

Maine Educational Media Assn. Memb. 160. Term of Office. Oct. 1978–Sept. 1980. Publication. *Mediacy* (q.).

Pres. Ralph Taylor, Dir., International Media Center, Univ. of Maine, Farmington 04938; *Pres.-Elect.* Marcia Thompson, Instructional Media Center, Univ. of Maine, Farmington 04938; *V.P.* Sue Daniels, Libn., Gray-New Gloucester H.S., Gray 04039; *Secy.* Linda J. Lachance, Libn., Greely H.S. Lib., Cumberland Center 04021; *Treas.* Edna Mae Bayliss, Dir., Project Lodestone, Calais 04619; *Ed.* Marcia McGee, Deer Isle-Stonington H.S., Deer Isle 04627.

Maryland

Maryland Educational Media Organization. Memb. 600. Term of Office. Oct. 1979–Oct. 1980. Publication. *MEMO-Random* (newsletter, q.).

Pres. Jane Love, George Fox Middle School, Outing Ave., Pasadena 21122; *Pres.-Elect.* Harry Bock, Prince Georges County Public School, Palmer Park Service, 8437 Landover Rd., Landover 20785; *Secy.* Mary Rollins, Arnold Elementary School, Arnold 21012; *Treas.* Margaret Denman, Western Maryland College, Westminster 21157.

Massachusetts

Massachusetts Assn. for Educational Media. Memb. 600. Term of Office. June 1, 1979–May 31, 1980. Publication. *Media Forum* (5 per year).

Pres. Janet A. Sprague, 22 Neptune Rd., Worcester 01605; *Pres.-Elect.* James M. Donovan, 9 Eel River Circle, Plymouth 02360; *Secy.* Marie T. Brady, 55 Grace Rd., Medford 02155; *Treas.* Annetta R. Freedman, 4 Suncrest Rd., Andover 01810.

Michigan

Michigan Assn. for Media in Education (MAME), Bur. of School Services, Univ. of Michigan, 401 S. Fourth St., Ann Arbor 48109. Memb. 1,250. Term of Office. 1 year. Publication. *Media Spectrum* (q.).

Pres. Edward Howard, 14861 18 Ave., Marne 49435; *Pres.-Elect.* Ruth Fitzgerald, 4151 Louis Dr., Flint 48507; *V.P.* Mary Ann Paulin, 1205 Joliet, Marquette 49855; *Treas.* Les Hotchkiss, 15426 Bealfred, Fenton 48430; *Secy.* Charles St. Louis, 3565 Green St., Muskegon 49444.

Minnesota

Minnesota Educational Media Organization. Memb. 1,200. Term of Office. May 1980–May 1981. Publication. *Minnesota Media*.

Pres. Don E. Overlie, Owatonna H.S., Owatonna 55060; *Past Pres.* John See, 17870 Italy Path, Lakeville 55044.

Mississippi

Mississippi Assn. of Media Educators. Memb. 200. Term of Office. Mar. 1979–Mar. 1980. Publication. *MAME* (newsletter, bi-ann.).

Pres. Paul Peloquin, Media Dir., Delta State Univ., Cleveland 38732.

Missouri

Missouri Assn. of School Libns., c/o MLA Exec. Office, 402 S. Fifth St., Columbia 65201. Memb. 600. Term of Office. Sept. 1, 1979–Aug. 31, 1980. Publication. *MASL Newsletter* (4 per year).

Pres. Dorothy Smith.

Address correspondence to the Missouri Lib. Assn. Exec. Office as given above.

Montana

Montana School Lib./Media, Div. of Montana Lib. Assn. Memb. 170. Term of Office. May 1979–May 1980. Publication. *Newsletter* (q.).

Chpn. Raenelle Lees, Rattlesnake School, Missoula 59801.

Address general correspondence to MSL/MA, c/o Montana Lib. Assn., Montana State Lib., 930 E. Lyndale Ave., Helena 59601.

Nebraska

Nebraska Educational Media Assn. Memb. 400. Term of Office. July 1–June 30. Publication. *NEMA Newsletter* (4 per year).

Pres. Barbara J. Brownell, Henderson Public Schools, Box 626, Henderson 68371; *Pres.-Elect.* Jim Titterington, Univ. of Nebraska-Lincoln, 421 Nebraska Hall, Lincoln 68588; *Ed. NEMA Newsletter.* Cliff Lowell, Box 485, Holdrege 68949.

Nevada

Nevada Assn. of School Libns. Memb. 55. Term of Office. Jan. 1, 1979–Dec. 31, 1980.

Chpn. Richard Pressley, Box 535, Indian Springs, 89018; *Chpn.-Elect.* Lynn Ossolinski, Box 5049, Incline Village 89450; *Councilors.* Beverly Palmer, 408 W. Sixth St., Carson City 89701; Merilyn Grosshans, 7129 Grasswood, Las Vegas 89117.

New Hampshire

New Hampshire Educational Media Assn. Memb. 140. Term of Office. Apr. 1979–Apr. 1980. Publication. *On-Line* (irreg.).

Pres. David Johnson, Dist. Media Services, Keene School Dept., 34 W. St., Keene 03431; *1st V.P.* Barbara Broderick, Sommersworth H.S., Sommersworth 03878; *2nd V.P.* Carol Shelton, Cardigan Mountain School, Canaan 03741; *Treas.* Germaine Schmanska, Lebanon H.S., Lebanon 03766; *Rec. Secy.* Nancy Cantar, Woodland Heights Elementary School, Laconia 03246; *Corresp. Secy.* Toni Ann Oster, Jonathan Daniels Elementary School, Maple Ave., Keene 03431.

New Jersey

Educational Media Assn. of New Jersey (EMAnj). (Organized Apr. 1977 through merger of New Jersey School Media Assn. and New Jersey Assn. of Educational Communication Technology.) Memb. 1,200. Term of Office. May 1979–Apr. 1980. Publications. *Signal Tab* (newsletter, mo.); *Emanations* (journal, q.).

Pres. Carolyn Markuson, 56 Dellwood Ave., Chatham 07928; *Pres.-Elect.* Anne Ida King, 3-25 Dorothy St., Fairlawn 07410; *V.P.* Ethel Kutteroff, R.R. 1, M56, Chester 07930; *Rec. Secy.* Sally Young, 8 Townsend Rd., Mendham 07945; *Corres. Secy.* Marian McKillop, RD 2, Spring Valley Rd., Blairstown 07825; *Treas.* Robert Bonardi, 2284 Alpine St., Union 07083.

New Mexico

New Mexico Media Assn. (Formed in 1977 as a merger of the New Mexico School Media Assn. and the New Mexico Assn. for Educational Communications and Technology.) Memb. 100. Term of Office. Oct. 1979–Oct. 1980. Publication. *New Mexico Media News* (bi-mo.).

Pres. Katherine E. Braman, Career Enrichment Center, 807 Mountain Rd. N.E., Albuquerque 87102; *Interim V.P.* Jay Johnstone, New Mexico State Lib., Box 1629, Santa Fe 87503; *Secy.* Patricia Martin, Tularosa Jr. H.S., Tularosa 88352; *Treas.* J. Harold Washington, Albuquerque Technical/Vocational Institute, 525 Buena Vista S.E., Albuquerque 87106.

North Carolina

North Carolina Assn. of School Libns. Memb. 800. Term of Office. Oct. 1979–Oct. 1981.

Chpn. Arabelle Shockley, Coord. of School Media Services, Winston-Salem/ Forsyth County Schools, Winston-Salem 27102; *Chpn.-Elect.* Paula Williams, Dir. of Media Services, Chapel Hill-Carrboro City Schools, Chapel Hill 27514; *Secy.-Treas.* Jeanette Smith, Dir. of Media Services, Forsyth County Day School, Lewisville 27023.

New York

School Lib. Media Sec., New York Lib. Assn., 60 E. 42 St., Suite 1242, New York 10017. Memb. 945. Term of Office. Nov. 1979–Nov. 1980. Publications. Participates in *NYLA Bulletin* (mo. except July and Aug.); *SLMS Gram.*

Pres. Evelyn Daniel, School of Info. Studies, Syracuse Univ., Syracuse 13210; *1st V.P. & Pres.-Elect.* Carol Kearney, Dir. of School Libs., Buffalo City School System, Buffalo 14202; *2nd V.P.* Frances Selip, Dir., Lib. Media Services, Pittsford Central Schools, Pittsford 14534; *Past Pres.* Caren Donnelly, Coord., Lib. Media Services, Hauppauge Public Schools, Hauppauge 11787; *Secy.* Carol Lewis, Lib. Media Specialist, Woodlawn Middle School, Schenectady 12304; *Treas.* Barbara Jones, Project Dir., School Lib. System, BOCES, Mexico 13114; *Ed SLMS Publications,* Frances Selip, Pittsford Central Schools, Pittsford 14534.

North Dakota

North Dakota Lib. Assn., School Sec. Memb. 84. Term of Office. 1 year. Publication. *North Dakota Media Newsletter* (q.).

Pres. Alvina Skogen, Harvey H.S., Harvey 58341.

Ohio

Ohio Educational Lib. Media Assn. Memb. 1,625. Term of Office. Nov. 1979–Nov. 1980. Publication. *Ohio Media Spectrum* (q.).

Pres. Hugh Durbin, Dept. of School Libs., 889 E. 17 Ave., Columbus 43211; *1st V.P.* Betty Wolford, 255 Highgrove Ct., Cincinnati 45239; *Secy.* Myra Thompson, 237 Harbel Dr., St. Clairsville 43950; *Treas.* Betty J. Carter, 9562 Friar Tuck Dr., West Chester 45069.

Oklahoma

Oklahoma Assn. of School Lib. Media Specialists. Memb. 350. Term of Office. July 1, 1979–June 30, 1980. Publications. "School Library News" column in *Oklahoma Librarian* (q.); "Library Resources" section in *Oklahoma Educator* (mo.).

Chpn. Ann Henderson, Stigler H.S., Stigler 74462; *V. Chpn. & Chpn.-Elect.* Judy Tirey, Will Rogers Elementary, Edmond 73034; *Secy.* Fran Grant, Rte. 1, Box 225, Vinita 74301; *Treas.* Dolores Loudermilk, Rte. 1, Box ST7, McLoud 74851.

Oregon

Oregon Educational Media Assn. Memb. 800. Term of Office. Oct. 1, 1979–Sept. 30, 1980. Publication. *Interchange.*

Pres. Jerry Deats, IMC Dir., Bend School Dist., 515 N.W. Bond St., Bend 97701; *Pres.-Elect.* Phil Corsow, Dist. Media Coord., N. Clackamas School Dist. No. 12, 11250 S.E. 27, Milwaukie 97222.

Pennsylvania

Pennsylvania School Libns. Assn. Memb. 1,300. Term of Office. July 1, 1978–June 30, 1980. Publications. *Learning and Media* (4 per year); *027.8* (5 per year).

Pres. Celeste DiCarlo, 327 Ridge Point Circle, A-23, Bridgeville 15017; *V.P.* Sue A. Walker, 6065 Parkridge Dr., East Petersburg 17520; *Secy.* Ruth N. Kolarik, 1314 Hoffman Rd., Ambler 19002; *Treas.*

Dorothy F. Lawley, 19 E. Dartmouth Circle, Media 19063.

Rhode Island

Rhode Island Educational Media Assn. Memb. 275. Term of Office. June 1979–June 1981. Publication. *Media News* (4 per year). All correspondence c/o RIEMA, 5 Whitwell Pl., Newport 02840.

Pres. Robert Callahan; *Pres.-Elect.* Rita Stein; *Secy.* Lillian Desrosiers; *Treas.* Tom Supprenant.

South Carolina

South Carolina Assn. of School Libns. Memb. 600. Term of Office. 1 year. Publication. *Media Messenger* (5 per year).

Pres. Clara Cooper, Moncks Corner 29461.

South Dakota

South Dakota School Libn. Media Assn., Sec. of the South Dakota Lib. Assn. and South Dakota Education Assn. Term of Office. Oct. 1979–Oct. 1980.

Pres. Judy Johnson, Central H.S., 433 N. Eighth, Rapid City 57701; *Pres.-Elect.* Pat Cook, Vermillion Middle School, Vermillion 57069; *Secy.* Margaret Brown, Pierre Jr., H.S., Pierre 57501; *Treas.* Donna Duenwald, Box 493, Platte 57369.

Tennessee

Tennessee Education Assn., School Lib. Sec., 598 James Robertson Pkwy., Nashville 37219. Term of Office. Mar. 1979–Mar. 1980.

Chpn. Betty Latture, 156-4001 Anderson Rd., Nashville 37217; *V. Chpn.* Margaret Lewis, 709 Holly Ave., South Pittsburg 37380.

Texas

Texas Assn. of School Libns. Memb. 2,000. Tern of Office. July 1979–June 1980. Publication. *Media Matters* (3 per year).

Chpn. Diantha Dawkins, 501 W. Louisiana, No. 203, Midland 79701; *Chpn.-Elect.* Linda Garrett, 725 Winifred, Garland 70541; *Secy.* Kathryn Meharg, 2631 Pittsburg, Houston 77005; *Treas.* Judy Thomas, Box 724, Abilene 79605.

Utah

Utah Lib. Assn., School Sec. Memb. 130. Term of Office. Mar. 1979–Mar. 1980. Publications. *Horsefeathers* (newsletter, mo.); *Utah Libraries* (journal, q.).

Chpn. Dona B. Walker, 6241 S. 515 E., Murray 84107; *V. Chpn.* Margaret P. Sargent, 6822 Pine View Circle, Salt Lake City 84121; *Secy.-Treas.* Mary Jensen, 1125 North University, Provo 84601.

Vermont

Vermont Educational Media Assn. Memb. 135. Term of Office. May 1979–May 1980. Publication. *VEMA News* (q.).

Pres. Marjorie H. Kneeland, South Burlington Community Lib., South Burlington 05401; *V.P. & Pres.-Elect.* William Bugbee, Barre Town Elementary School, Barre 05641; *Secy.* Susan Sutherland H.S., Wilmington 05363; *Treas.* Richard Hurd, Barre City School, Barre 05641.

Virginia

Virginia Educational Media Assn. (VEMA).

Pres. Stanley A. Huffman, Jr., Dir., Learning Resource Center, Virginia Polytechnic Institute and State Univ., Blacksburg 24060; *Pres.-Elect.* Barbara Booker, Dir., Media Services, Charlottesville City Schools, Rte. 6, Box 267, Charlottesville 22901.

Washington

Washington Lib. Media Assn. Memb. 700. Term of Office. Jan. 1, 1980–Dec. 31, 1980. Publication. *The Medium* (q.); *The Newsletter* (occasional).

Pres. Robert L. Irvine, 2766 S.W. 167, Seattle 98166; *Pres.-Elect.* Hester Davidson, 3818 N.E. 178, Seattle 98155; *V.P.*

Don Riecks, 21221 Fifth Ave. S., Seattle 98148; *Secy.* Rex Davis, 2814 Fir St., Longview 98632; *Treas.* Bruce J. Eyer, 212 S. 29 Ave., Yakima 98902.

West Virginia

School Libns. Dept., West Virginia Education Assn. Memb. 6. Term of Office. Nov. 1979–Nov. 1981. Publication. *Newsletter WVSL* (ann.).
Pres. Marilyn Jean Moellendick, 3315 Smith St., Parkersburg 26101; *Pres.-Elect.* Barbara G. Ball, 1010 Kilgore Ave., Culloden 25510; *Secy.-Treas.* Linda Adkins, Box 33, Comfort 25049.

Wisconsin

Wisconsin School Lib. Media Assn. Div. of Wisconsin Library Assn. Term of Office. Jan. 1980–Dec. 1980. Publications. *WSLMA Communique* (Jan., May, Sept.).
Pres. Carol Diehl, School Dist. of New London, 103 N. Water St., New London 54961; *V.P. & Pres.-Elect.* Marjorie Doering, Oshkosh West H.S., 375 N. Eagle St., Oshkosh 54901; *Secy.* Jim Klein, Appleton Area School Dist., Box 2019, Appleton 54913; *Financial Advisor.* Glenn Thompson, UW-Eau Claire, Eau Claire 54701; *Communique Ed.* Carolyn Cain, LaFollette H.S., Madison 53711; *Past-Pres.* Virginia Bell, Great Rivers Teacher Center, Rte. 5, Box 342, Sparta 54656.

Wyoming

Wyoming School Lib. Media Assn. Memb. 25. Term of Office. May 1979–Apr. 1980.
Chpn. Linda Goolsby, 1228 Ritter, Rawlins 82301; *Chpn. Elect.* Debbie Proctor, 359 Foothills, Gillette 82716; *Secy.* Vickie Hoff, 511½ 13 St., Rawlins 82301.

STATE SUPERVISORS OF SCHOOL LIBRARY/MEDIA SERVICES

Alabama

Ruth Johnson, Education Specialist, Lib. Media Services, Univ. of North Alabama, Florence 35630. Tel: 205-766-4100, ext. 226.

W. Raymond Jones, Education Specialist, Lib. Media Services, 111 Coliseum Blvd., Montgomery 36109. Tel: 205-832-3161.

Hallie A. Jordan, Education Specialist, Lib. Media Services, 111 Coliseum Blvd., Montgomery 36109. Tel: 205-832-3161.

Alaska

Peggy Cummings, Special Services Libn. (A/V), Alaska State Lib., Pouch G, Juneau 99811. Tel: 907-465-2919.

Arizona

Mary Choncoff, Libs. and Learning Resources, Arizona Dept. of Educ., 1535 W. Jefferson, Phoenix 85007. Tel: 602-255-5271.

Arkansas

Betty J. Morgan, Specialist in Lib. Services, State Dept. of Educ., Arch Ford Bldg., Capitol Grounds, Little Rock 72201. Tel: 501-371-1861.

California

Gerald W. Hamrin, ESEA Title IV-B Program Administrator, State Dept. of Educ., 721 Capitol Mall, Sacramento 95814. Tel: 916-445-7456.

Colorado

Richard De Fore, Supv., ESEA Title IV-B, Colorado State Dept. of Educ., 201 E. Colfax, Denver 80203. Tel: 303-839-2234.

Connecticut

John R. Billard, Dir. of Instructional Media, Box U-1, Univ. of Connecticut, Storrs 06268. Tel: 203-486-2530.

Betty V. Billman, Educational Service Specialist, State Dept. of Educ., Box 2219, Hartford 06115. Tel: 203-566-5754.

Delaware

Richard L. Krueger, Supv., Lib./Media Services and ESEA Title IV-B, State Dept. of Public Instruction, John G. Townsend Bldg., Box 1402, Dover 19901. Tel: 302-678-4667.

District of Columbia

Olive De Bruler, Dir., Dept. of Lib. Science, Public Schools of the District of Columbia, 801 Seventh St. S.W., Washington 20024. Tel: 202-724-4952.

Florida

Eloise T. Groover, Administrator, School Lib. Media Services, State Dept. of Educ., Knott Bldg., Tallahassee 32301. Tel: 904-488-0095.

Georgia

Nancy P. Hove, Coord., Media Field Services, Georgia Dept. of Educ., 156 Trinity Ave. S.W., Atlanta 30303. Tel: 404-656-2418.

Hawaii

Patsy Izumo, Dir., Multimedia Services Branch, State Dept. of Educ., 641 18 Ave., Honolulu 96816. Tel: 808-732-5535.

Idaho

Agatha TeMaat, Consultant, Educational Media (Instructional TV), Idaho State Dept. of Educ., Len B. Jordan Bldg., Boise 83720. Tel: 208-384-2113.

Illinois

Marie Rose Sivak, Education Consultant, Lib./Media Services, State Bd. of Educ., 100 N. First St., Springfield 62777. Tel: 217-782-2826.

Indiana

Phyllis Land, Dir., Div. of Instructional Media, State Dept. of Public Instruction, Indianapolis 46204. Tel: 317-927-0296.

Iowa

Betty Jo Buckingham, Consultant, Education Media, State Dept. of Public Instruction, Des Moines 50319. Tel: 515-281-3707.

Kansas

Position vacant as of March 1980. Write to Kansas State Dept. of Educ., 120 E. Tenth, Topeka 66612. Tel: 913-296-3434.

Kentucky

Judy L. Cooper and Theresa M. Fredericka, Consultants, School Media Services, Kentucky Dept. of Educ., Frankfort 40601. Tel: 502-564-4507.

Louisiana

James S. Cookston, State Supv. of School Libs., State Dept. of Educ., Rm. 602 Education Bldg., Box 44064, Baton Rouge 70804. Tel: 504-342-3399.

Maine

John W. Boynton, Coord., Media Services, Maine State Lib., LMA Bldg., State House Station 64, Augusta 04333. Tel: 207-289-2956.

Maryland

Paula Montgomery, Branch Chief, Div. of Lib. Development and Services, State Dept. of Educ., Box 8717, Baltimore-Washington International Airport, Baltimore 21240. Tel: 301-796-8300, ext. 264.

Massachusetts

Raymond L. Gehling, Jr., Coord., Lib. and Learning Resources, ESEA Title IV-B, Curriculum Services, Dept. of Educ., 31 St. James Ave., Boston 02116. Tel: 617-727-5742.

Michigan

Mary Ann Hanna, Dir., School Lib./Media Program and Coord. ESEA Title IV-B, Michigan Dept. of Educ., State Lib. Services, Box 30007, Lansing 48909. Tel: 517-374-9630.

Minnesota

Robert H. Miller, Supv., Educational Media Unit, State Dept. of Educ., Capitol Square Bldg., St. Paul 55101. Tel: 612-296-6114.

Mississippi

Yvonne C. Dyson, State Dept. of Educ., Educational Media Services, Box 771, Jackson 39205. Tel: 601-354-6864.

Missouri

Jo Albers, Lib. Supv., Dept. of Elementary and Secondary Educ., Box 480, Jefferson City 65102. Tel: 314-751-4445.

Montana

Bruce MacIntyre, Lib. Media Consultant, State Dept. of Public Instruction, Helena 59601. Tel: 406-449-3861.

Nebraska

John Courtney, Media Consultant, ESEA Title IV, State Dept. of Educ., Box 94987, 301 Centennial Mall S., Lincoln 68509. Tel: 402-471-2481.

Nevada

William F. Arensdorf, Chmn., Instructional Materials and Equipment, State Dept. of Educ., Capitol Complex, Carson City 89710. Tel: 702-885-5700, ext. 235.

New Hampshire

Reginald A. Comeau, Consultant, Educ. Media Services, Libs. and Learning Resources, Div. of Instruction, 64 N. Main St., Concord 03301. Tel: 603-271-2401.

New Jersey

Anne Voss, Coord. of School and College Media Services, State Dept. of Educ., Trenton 08625. Tel: 609-292-6256.

New Mexico

Dolores Dietz, Coord. Title IV-B, Libs. and Learning Resources, State Dept. of Educ., Santa Fe 87503. Tel: 505-827-5441.

New York

Lore Scurrah, Chief, Bur. of School Libs. and Coord. of ESEA Title IV-B, Bur. of School Libs., State Educ. Dept., Albany 12234. Tel: 518-474-2468.

North Carolina

Elsie L. Brumback, Dir., Div. of Educational Media, State Dept. of Public Instruction, Raleigh 27611. Tel: 919-733-3193.

North Dakota

Patricia Herbel, Lib. Services and Elementary Curriculum Coord., Dept. of Public Instruction, Bismarck 58505. Tel: 701-224-2281.

Ohio

Dorothy Ann Ellis, Consultant, School Media Programs, State Dept. of Educ., Ohio Depts. Bldg., 65 S. Front, Rm. 1016, Columbus 43215. Tel: 614-466-5830.

Oklahoma

Clarice Roads and Barbara Spriestersbach, Coords., Lib. and Learning Resources Div., State Dept. of Educ., Oklahoma City 73105. Tel: 405-521-2956.

Oregon

Lyle Wirtanen, Consultant, School Lib. Resources, ESEA Title IV-B, State Dept. of Educ., Salem 97310. Tel: 503-378-5600.

Pennsylvania

Joan P. Diana, Chief, Div. of School Lib. Media Services, Bur. of Instructional Support Service, State Dept. of Educ., Box 911, Harrisburg 17126. Tel: 717-783-1185.

Rhode Island

Rita Stein, Consultant, ESEA Title IV-B and School Lib. Resources, Rhode Island State Dept. of Educ., 235 Promenade St., Providence 02908. Tel: 401-277-2617.

South Carolina

Margaret W. Ehrhardt, Consultant, Lib. Services, State Dept. of Educ., Rutledge Bldg., Rm. 706, Columbia 29201. Tel: 803-758-3696.

South Dakota

James O. Hansen, Ed.D., State Superintendent, Div. of Elementary and Secondary Education, Richard F. Kneip Bldg., Pierre 57501. Tel: 605-773-3243.

Tennessee

Christine Brown, Program Mgr., School Lib. Services, 115 Cordell Hull Bldg., Nashville 37219. Tel: 615-741-1896.

Texas

Mary R. Boyvey, Learning Resources Program Dir., Instructional Resources Div., Texas Education Agency, Austin 78701. Tel: 512-475-6465.

Utah

Leroy R. Lindeman, Administrator, Curriculum and Instruction Div., State Office of Educ., 250 E. Fifth S., Salt Lake City 84111. Tel: 801-533-5550.

Vermont

Jean D. Battey, School Lib./Media Consultant, ESEA Title IV-B, Div. of Federal Assistance, State Dept. of Educ., Montpelier 05602. Tel: 802-828-3124.

Virginia

Mary Stuart Mason, Supv., School Libs. and Textbooks, Virginia Dept. of Educ., Box 6Q, Richmond 23216. Tel: 804-786-7705.

Washington

Nancy Motomatsu, Supv., Learning Resources Services, Office of State Superintendent of Public Instruction, Olympia 98504. Tel: 206-753-6723.

West Virginia

Carolyn R. Skidmore, Coord., and Susannah G. Dunn, Supv., Libs. and Learning Resources, 1900 Washington St., Rm. 346, Charleston 25305. Tel: 304-348-3925.

Wisconsin

Dianne McAfee Williams, Dir., Bur. of Instructional Media Programs, State Dept. of Public Instruction, Madison 53702. Tel: 608-266-1965.

Wyoming

Jack Prince, Coord. for Instructional Resources, State Dept. of Educ., Hathaway Bldg., Cheyenne 82002. Tel: 307-777-7411.

American Samoa

Linette Alapa Hunter, Program Dir. of Lib. Services, Office of Lib. Services, Dept. of Educ., Pago Pago 96799.

The Pacific Islands (Trust Territory of)

Tomokichy Aisek, Supv. of Lib. Services, Dept. of Educ., Truk, Caroline Islands 96942.

Augustine Castro, Supv. of Lib. Services, Dept. of Educ., Saipan, Mariana Islands 96950.

Tamar Jordan, Supv. of Lib. Services, Dept. of Educ., Majuor, Marshall Islands 96960.

Puerto Rico

Blanca N. Rivera de Ponce, Dir., Public Lib. Div., Dept. of Educ., Hato Rey 00919. Tel: 809-753-9191; 754-0750.

Virgin Islands

Beulah Harrigan, Acting Dir., L.S.I.M. Dept. of Educ., St. Thomas 00801.

INTERNATIONAL LIBRARY ASSOCIATIONS

INTER-AMERICAN ASSOCIATION OF AGRICULTURAL LIBRARIANS AND DOCUMENTALISTS
IICA-CIDIA, Turrialba, Costa Rica

OBJECT

"To serve as liaison among the agricultural librarians and documentalists of the Americas and other parts of the world; to promote the exchange of information and experiences through technical publications and meetings; to promote the improvement of library services in the field of agriculture and related sciences; to encourage the improvement of the professional level of the librarians and documentalists in the field of agriculture in Latin America."

OFFICERS

Pres. Fernando Monge, Centro Internacional de Agricultura Tropical, Cali, Colombia; *V.P.* Yone Chastinet, BINAGRI (Biblioteca Nacional de Agricultura), Brasília, DF, Brazil; *Exec. Secy.* Ana Maria Paz de Erickson, IICA-CIDIA, Turrialba, Costa Rica. (Address correspondence to the executive secretary.)

PUBLICATIONS

Boletín Informativo (q.).
Boletín Especial (irreg.).
Revista AIBDA (2 per year).
Proceedings. Tercera Reunión Interamericana de Bibliotecarios y Documentalistas Agrícolas, Buenos Aires, Argentina, April 10-14, 1972 (U.S. price: $10 including postage).
Proceedings. Cuarta Reunión Interamericana de Bibliotecarios y Documentalistas Agrícolas. Mexico, D.F., April 8-11, 1975 (U.S. price: Memb. $5 including postage; nonmemb. $10 including postage).
Proceedings. Quinta Reunión Interamericana de Bibliotecarios y Documentalistas Agrícolas, San Jose, Costa Rica, April 10-14, 1978 (U.S. price: Memb. $10 plus postage; nonmemb. $15 plus postage).

INTERNATIONAL ASSOCIATION OF AGRICULTURAL LIBRARIANS AND DOCUMENTALISTS
MAFF, Central Veterinary Laboratory, New Haw, Weybridge, Surrey KT15 3NB, England

OBJECT

"The Association shall, internationally and nationally, promote agricultural library science and documentation as well as the professional interest of agricultural librarians and documentalists." Founded 1955. Memb. 525. Dues. (Inst.) $26; (Indiv.) $13.

OFFICERS (1975-1980)

Pres. P. Aries, France; *V.Ps.* H. Haendler, Germany, M.S. Malugani, Costa Rica; *Secy.-Treas.* D. E. Gray, UK; *Ed.* R. Farley, USA.

EXECUTIVE COMMITTEE

H. Buntrock, Luxembourg; S. Contour, France; G. de Bruyn, Netherlands; A. L. Geisendorf, Switzerland; K. Harada, Italy; F. C. Hirst, UK; M. J. MacIntosh, Canada; J. C. Sisan, Philippines; A. T. Yaikova, USSR; representatives of National Assns. of Agricultural Libns. and Documentalists.

PUBLICATIONS

Quarterly Bulletin of the IAALD (memb.).

AMERICAN MEMBERSHIP

By individuals or institutions.

INTERNATIONAL ASSOCIATION OF LAW LIBRARIES
Vanderbilt Law Library, Nashville, TN 37203, USA

OBJECT

"To promote on a cooperative, non-profit, and fraternal basis the work of individuals, libraries, and other institutions and agencies concerned with the acquisition and bibliographic processing of legal materials collected on a multinational basis, and to facilitate the research and other uses of such materials on a worldwide basis." Founded 1959. Memb. 550 in 60 countries.

OFFICERS

Pres. Igor I. Kavass, USA; *1st V.P.* William A. F. P. Steiner, England; *2nd V.P.* Jacob D. Korevaar, Switzerland; *Secy.-Treas.* Arno Liivak, USA.

ELECTED AND APPOINTED MEMBERS

Gerhard Dahlmanns, Germany; Myrna Feliciano, Philippines; Edwin J. Glasson, Australia; Ryohei Hayashi, Japan; Klaus Menzinger, Germany; Lajos Nagy, Hungary; N. Anthony Ogbeide, Nigeria; Adolf Sprudzs, USA.

SERVICES

1. The dissemination of professional information through the *International Journal of Law Libraries*, the *IALL Newsletter*, through continuous contacts with the affiliated national groups of law librarians, and through work within other international organizations, such as IFLA and FID.
2. Continuing education through the one-week IALL Seminars in International Law Librarianship annually.
3. The preparation of special literature for law librarians, such as the *European Law Libraries Guide*, and of introductions to basic foreign legal literature.
4. Direct personal contacts and exchanges between IALL members.

IALL REPRESENTATIVES

A liaison between the law librarians of their regions and the IALL administration is being appointed for every country or major area.

PUBLICATION

International Journal of Law Libraries (formally *IALL Bulletin*) appears three times a year since 1972. *Ed.-in-Chief* Klaus Menzinger, Juristisches Seminar, Werthmannplatz, D-78 Frieburg, Fed. Rep. of Germany; *Assoc. Ed.-in-Chief* Ivan Sipkov, Law Lib., Lib. of Congress, Washington, DC 20540, USA.

INTERNATIONAL ASSOCIATION OF METROPOLITAN CITY LIBRARIES
c/o Friedrich Andrae, Dir., Hamburger Öffentliche Bücherhallen, Gertrudenkirchhof 9, D-2000 Hamburg 1, Federal Republic of Germany

OBJECT

"The Association was founded to assist the worldwide flow of information and knowledge by promoting practical collaboration in the exchange of books, exhibitions, staff, and information." Memb. 97.

OFFICERS

Pres. Jürgen Eyssen, Stadtbüchereien Hildesheimestr. 12, D-3000 Hannover 1, Germany; *Secy.-Treas.* Friedrich Andrae, Hamburger Öffentliche Bücherhallen, Gertrudenkirchhof 9, D-2000 Hamburg 1, Germany; *Past. Pres.* Keith Doms, Free Lib. of Philadelphia, Logan Sq., Philadelphia, PA 19103. (Address correspondence to the secretary-treasurer.)

PROGRAM

A research team and correspondents are engaged in drawing up a practical code of recommended practice in international city library cooperation and in formulating objectives, standards, and performance measures for metropolitan city libraries.

PUBLICATIONS

Review of the Three Year Research and Exchange Programme 1968-1971.
Annual International Statistics of City Libraries (INTAMEL).

INTERNATIONAL ASSOCIATION OF MUSIC LIBRARIES
Svenskt musikhistoriskt arkiv, Sibyllegatan 2, S-11451 Stockholm, Sweden

OBJECT

"To constitute a representative international organization charged with stimulating and coordinating all the activities, national and international, of music libraries, archives, and documentation centers, and to study and facilitate the realization of all projects dealing with music bibliography and music library science." Memb. 1,700.

OFFICERS (SEPT. 1977–AUG. 1980)

Pres. Barry S. Brook, City Univ. of New York, 33 W. 42 St., New York, NY 10036, USA; *V.Ps.* Israel Adler, Jerusalem, Israel; Karl Heinz Köhler, Berlin-DDR; Brian Redfern, London, England; Hans Steinbeck, Zurich, Switzerland; *Secy.* Anders Lönn, Svenskt musikhistoriskt arkiv, Sibyllegatan 2, S-11451 Stockholm, Sweden; *Treas.* Wolfgang Rehm, Heinrich-Schütz-Allee 29, D-3500 Kassel-Wilhelmshöhe, Fed. Rep. of Germany. (Address general correspondence to the secretary.)

PUBLICATION

Fontes Artis Musicae (4 per year, memb.).

COMMISSION CHAIRPERSONS

Bibliographical Research. François Lesure, Dépt. de la Musique, Bibliothèque Nationale, 2 r. Louvois, F-75002 Paris, France.
Broadcasting Music Libraries. Bengt Kyhlberg, Sveriges Radio, S-10510 Stockholm, Sweden.
Cataloging. Brian Redfern, School of Libnshp., Polytechnic of North London, 207-225 Essex Rd., London N1 3PN, England.
Education and Training. Don L. Roberts, Music Lib., Northwestern Univ., Evanston, IL 60201.
International Inventory of Musical Sources. Kurt von Fischer, Laubholzstr. 46, CH-8703 Erlebach ZH, Switzerland.
International Repertory of Music Literature. Barry S. Brook, RILM Center, City Univ. of New York, 33 W. 42 St., New York, NY 10036.

International Repertory of Musical Iconography. Barry S. Brook, Research Center for Musical Iconography, City Univ. of New York, 33 W. 42 St., New York, NY 10036.
Libraries of Conservatories and Colleges of Music. Anthony Hodges, Royal Northern College of Music, 124 Oxford Rd., Manchester M13 9RD, England.
Music Information Centers. Anna van Steenbergen, CeBeDeM, r. de l'Hôpital 31 bte 2, B-1000 Brussels, Belgium.
Public Music Libraries. Eric Cooper, London Borough of Enfield, Music Dept., Town Hall, Green Lanes, Palmers Green, London N13 4XD, England.
Record Libraries. Claes Cnattingius, Sveriges Radio, Grammofonarkivet, S-10510 Stockholm, Sweden.
Research Music Libraries. Rudolf Elvers, Westendallee 65, D-1000 Berlin 19, Fed. Rep. of Germany.

US BRANCH

Pres. Harold E. Samuel, Music Lib., Yale Univ., 98 Wall St., New Haven, CT 06520; *Secy.-Treas.* Don L. Roberts, Music Lib., Northwestern Univ., Evanston, IL 60201.

UK BRANCH

Pres. Miriam Miller, BBC Music Lib., Yalding House, 152-156 Gt. Portland St., London W1N 6AJ; *Hon. Secy.* Susan M. Clegg, Birmingham School of Music, Paradise Circle, Birmingham B3 3HG; *Hon. Treas.* Ruth Davies, The Library, CCAT, Collier Rd., Cambridge CB1 2AJ.

PUBLICATION

BRIO. Eds. Clifford Bartlett, BBC Music Lib., Yalding House, London W1N 6AJ, and Malcolm Jones, Birmingham Public Lib., 2020 Seventh Ave. N., Birmingham, AL 35203 (2 per year; memb.).

INTERNATIONAL ASSOCIATION OF SOUND ARCHIVES
c/o David Lance, Keeper, Dept. of Sound Records,
Imperial War Museum, Lambeth Rd., London SE1 6HZ, England

OBJECT

IASA is a UNESCO-affiliated organization that functions as a medium for international cooperation between archives and other institutions that preserve recorded sound documents. The association is involved in such fields as the preservation, organization, and use of sound recordings; techniques of recording and methods of reproducing sound; the international exchange of literature and information; and in all subjects relating to professional sound archive work.

MEMBERSHIP

Open to all categories of archives, institutions, and individuals who preserve sound recordings or have a serious interest in the purposes or welfare of IASA.

OFFICERS (1978–1981)

Pres. Rolf Schuursma, Stichting Film en Wetenschap, Hengereldstr. 29, Utrecht, Netherlands. *V. Ps.* Marie-France Calas, Phonothèque Nationale, 19 r. Richelieu, 75084 Paris Cedex, France. Tor Kummen, Norsk RikskringKasting, Bjornstjerne Bjornsons, Plass 1, Oslo 3, Norway. Dietrich Schüller, Phonogrammarchiv der Österreichischen Akademie der Wissenschaften, Liebiggasse 5, A-1010 Vienna, Austria. *Ed.* Ann Briegleb, Ethnomusicology Archive, Music Dept., Univ. of California, Los Angeles, CA 90024, USA. *Assoc. Ed.* Frank Gillis, Archives of Traditional Music, Indiana Univ., Bloomington, IN 47401, USA. *Secy.* David Lance, Dept. of Sound Records, Imperial War Museum, Lambeth Rd., London SE1 6HZ, England. *Treas.* Ulf Scharlau, Süddentscher Rundfunk, Postfach 837, 7000 Stuttgart 1, Fed. Rep. of Germany.

PUBLICATIONS

An Archive Approach to Oral History.
Directory of IASA Member Archives.
Phonographic Bulletin (3 per year; memb. or subscription).

INTERNATIONAL COUNCIL ON ARCHIVES
Secretariat, 60 r. des Francs-Bourgeois
F-75003 Paris, France

OBJECT

"To establish, maintain, and strengthen relations among archivists of all lands, and among all professional and other agencies or institutions concerned with the custody, organization, or administration of archives, public or private, wheresoever located." Established 1948. Dues. (Indiv.) $25; (Inst.) $40; (Archives Assns.) $100; (Central Archives Directorates) $150 minimum, computed on the basis of GNP and GNO per capita.

PUBLICATIONS

Archivium (ann.; memb. or subscription to Verlag Dokumentation München, Possenbacher Str. 2, Postfach 71 1009, D-8 Munich 71, Fed. Rep. of Germany).

ICA Bulletin (s. ann.; memb., or U.S. $3).

Microfilm Bulletin (subscriptions to Centro Nacional de Microfilm, Serrano 15, Madrid 6, Spain).

ADPA—Archives and Automation (ann. £3 memb.; subscriptions to L. Bell, Public Record Office, Chancery La., London WC2A 1LR, England).

Guides to the Sources of the History of Nations (Latin American Series, 11 vols. pub.; African Series, 6 vols. pub., 2 vols. in prep.; Asian Series, 1 vol. pub.).

Archival Handbooks (6 vols. pub.).

INTERNATIONAL COUNCIL OF THEOLOGICAL LIBRARY ASSOCIATIONS
Doddendaal 20, 6511 DG Nijmegen, Netherlands

OBJECT

"The Council aims at furthering cooperation among its members, at serving their interests on an international level, and in general, at participating to the best of its ability in helping forward theological libraries, even those not affiliated with participating associations, especially those situated in developing countries. The Council pursues its ends by organizing reciprocal exchange of information among members, by undertaking special studies and common duties, and by representing externally the mutual interests of its members." After a ten-year initial period, in 1972 the council was constituted as an association in legal form, with headquarters in Nijmegen, Netherlands.

MEMBERSHIP

Ordinary membership is open to associations of libraries or library directors provided the associations aim at promoting the interests of libraries devoted to theology either primarily or to an important degree. *Extraordinary* members may be natural or juridical persons devoting themselves to furthering theological librarianship at an international level.

OFFICERS

Pres. Herman Morlion, Heverlee, Belgium; *V.P.* Paul C.-J. Mech, Paris, France; *Secy.-Treas.* Rudolph Th. M. van Dijk, Doddendaal 20, 6511 DG Nijmegen, Netherlands. (Address all correspondence to the secretary.)

SERVICES

From its early beginnings, the council has had a stimulating influence on participating associations seeking to extend the scope of their services for the benefit of libraries so as to make them internationally useful. The following services are in operation all over the world:

1. The furtherance of a worldwide flow of religious and theological literature through the corporation World Library Service, a center that functions as a worldwide intermediary of theological and related books and periodicals from all over the world. Address: Faber Str. 7, Box 9005, 6500 GE Nijmegen, Netherlands. Correspondence may be in any Germanic or Romance language.

2. The exchange of book duplicates through *TEOL* (*Theologici Exquisiti Oblatique Libri*). Approximately ten times a year a list of *Opera Desiderata and Opera Oblata* is circulated among subscribing libraries. Circulation is so arranged that equal opportunities are offered to far distant as well as to nearby libraries. Address: L'Epiphanie, av. du Général de Gaulle, 91450 Soisy-sur-Seine, France.

3. The exchange of review duplicates through *ZEIKO* (*Zeitschriftenkomplettierungstelle*). *ZEIKO* receives offers and requirements and collates the former with the latter. Each time a given title appears in both categories, *ZEIKO* brings the libraries concerned into direct contact with each other. Address: Hörsterplatz 5, 4400 Münster, Fed. Rep. of Germany.

4. The indexing of theological literature through *CERDIC* (Centre de Recherche et de Documentation des Institutions Chrétiennes). Each volume (the first covered both 1966 and 1967) of its annual publication *RIC* (*Répertoire bibliographique des institutions chrétiennes*) presents a working tool that arranges under 2,000 key words and indexes in five languages (French, English, German, Spanish, Italian) the analytical elements of some 7,000 books and articles. Each volume is published in 25 or more countries. Address: Palais universitaire, pl. de l'Université, 67000 Strasbourg, France.

INTERNATIONAL FEDERATION FOR DOCUMENTATION
Box 30115, 2500 GC The Hague, Netherlands

OBJECT

To group internationally organizations and individuals interested in the problems of documentation and to coordinate their efforts; to promote the study, organization, and practice of documentation in all its forms, and to contribute to the creation of an international network of information systems.

PROGRAM

The program of the federation includes activities for which the following committees have been established: Central Classification Committee (for UDC); Research on the Theoretical Basis of Information; Linguistics in Documentation; Information for Industry; Education and Training; Classification Research; Terminology of Information and Documentation; Patent Information and Documentation; Social Sciences Documentation. It also includes the BSO Panel (Broad System of Ordering).

OFFICERS

Pres. H. Arntz, Deutsches FID-Komitee, 534 Bad Honnef/Rhein, Fed. Rep.

of Germany; *V.Ps.* Ricardo A. Gietz, CAICYT, Moreno 431/33, 1091 Buenos Aires, Argentina; Peter J. Judge, CSIRO, Box 255, Dickson, ACT 2602, Australia; Peter Lázár, OMKDK, Box 12, 1428 Budapest, Hungary; *Treas.* Herbert S. White, Grad. Lib. School, Indiana Univ., Bloomington, IN 47401, USA; *Councillors.* V. Ammundsen, Lyngby, Denmark; M. Brandreth, Ottawa, Canada; G. Carrión R., Mexico City, Mexico; E. Currás, Madrid, Spain; S. Fujiwara, Tokyo, Japan; M. W. Hill, London, UK; C. Keren, Tel Aviv, Israel; J. Michel, Paris, France; A. I. Mikhailov, Moscow, USSR; A. Sinai, Tehran, Iran; V. Stefanik, Bratislava, Czechoslovakia; L. Perez Tapanes, Havana, Cuba; *Belgian Member.* J. de Keersmaecker, Brussels, Belgium; *Secy.-Gen.* K. R. Brown, The Hague, Netherlands; *Pres. of FID/CLA,* J. Arias Ordoñez, Bogata, Colombia; *Pres. of FID/CAO.* Doo-hong Kim, Seoul, Rep. of Korea. (Address correspondence to the secretary-general.)

PUBLICATIONS

FID News Bulletin (mo.) with supplements on document reproduction (q.).

Newsletter on Education and Training Programmes for Specialized Information Personnel (q.).
International Forum on Information and Documentation (q.).
R & D Projects in Documentation and Librarianship (bi-mo.).
FID Directory (bienn.).
FID Publications (ann.).
FID Annual Report (ann.).

Proceedings of congresses; Universal Decimal Classification editions; manuals; directories; bibliographies on information science, documentation, reproduction, mechanization, linquistics, training, and classification.

MEMBERSHIP

Approved by the FID Council; ratification by the FID General Assembly.

AMERICAN MEMBERSHIP

National Academy of Sciences–National Research Council.

INTERNATIONAL FEDERATION OF FILM ARCHIVES
Secretariat, Coudenberg 70, B-1000 Brussels, Belgium

OBJECT

"To facilitate communication and cooperation between its members, and to promote the exchange of films and information; to maintain a code of archive practice calculated to satisfy all national film industries, and to encourage industries to assist in the work of the Federation's members; to advise its members on all matters of interest to them, especially the preservation and study of films; to give every possible assistance and encouragement to new film archives and to those interested in creating them." Founded in Paris, 1938. 64 members in 45 countries.

EXECUTIVE COMMITTEE
(JUNE 1979–JUNE 1981)

Pres. Wolfgang Klaue, DDR; *V.Ps.* Eileen Bowser, USA; David Francis, UK; Vladimir Pogacic, Yugoslavia; *Secy.-Gen.* Robert Daudelin, Canada; *Treas.* Jan de Vaal, Netherlands. (Address correspondence to B. Van der Elst, executive secretary, at headquarters address.)

COMMITTEE MEMBERS

Cosme Alves-Netto, Brazil; Todor Andreykov, Bulgaria; Raymond Borde, France; Freddy Buache, Switzerland; Jon Stenklev, Norway.

PUBLICATIONS

Film Preservation (available in English, French, and German).
The Preservation and Restoration of Colour and Sound in Films.
Film Cataloging.
Study on the Usage of Computers for Film Cataloguing.
Handbook for Film Archives.
International Index to Film and Television Periodicals (cards service).
International Index to Film Periodicals (cumulative volumes).
Preservation of Film Posters.
Guidelines for Describing Unpublished Script Materials.
Annual Bibliography of FIAF Members' Publications.
Proceedings of the FIAF Varna Symposium—1977: L'Influence du Cinema Sovietique Muet Sur le Cinema Mondial/ The Influence of Silent Soviet Cinema on World Cinema.

INTERNATIONAL FEDERATION OF LIBRARY ASSOCIATIONS AND INSTITUTIONS (IFLA)
Netherlands Congress Bldg., Box 82128,
2508 EC The Hague, Netherlands

OBJECT

"To promote international understanding, cooperation, discussion, research, and development in all fields of library activity, including bibliography, information services, and the education of library personnel, and to provide a body through which librarianship can be represented in matters of international interest." Founded 1927. Memb. (Lib. Assns.) 160; (Inst.) 740; (Aff.) 97; in 109 countries.

OFFICERS AND EXECUTIVE BOARD

Pres. Else Granheim, Dir., Norwegian Directorate for Public and School Libs., Oslo, Norway; *1st V.P.* G. Pflug, Dir.-Gen., Deutsche Bibliothek, Frankfurt/Main, Fed. Rep. of Germany; *2nd V.P.* Ludmilla Gvishiani, Dir., State Lib. of Foreign Literature, Moscow, USSR; *Treas.* Marie-Louise Bossuat, Dir., Bibliographical Centre of the National Library, Paris, France; *Exec. Bd.* G. Rückl, Dir., Central Lib. Institute, Berlin, DDR; E. R. S. Fifoot, Bodley's Libn., Bodleian Lib., Oxford, UK; Jean Lowrie, Dir., School of Libnshp., Western Michigan Univ., Kalamazoo, Michigan, USA; J. S. Soosai, Rubber Research Institute of Malaysia, Kuala Lumpur, Malaysia; *Ex Officio Member.* H. P. Geh, Chmn., Professional Bd., Dir., Württembergische Landesbibliothek, Stuttgart, Fed. Rep. of Germany; *Secy.-Gen.* Margreet Wijnstroom, IFLA headquarters; *Dir., IFLA International Office for Universal Bibliographic Control:* D. Anderson, c/o Reference Div., British Lib., London, UK; *Dir., IFLA Office for International Lending:* M. B. Line, c/o British Lib. Lending Div., Boston Spa, Wetherby, West Yorkshire, UK; *Publications Officer:* W. R. H. Koops, Univ. Libn., Groningen, Netherlands; *Professional Coordinator:* A. L. van Wesemael, IFLA headquarters.

PUBLICATIONS

IFLA Annual.
IFLA Journal (q.).
IFLA Directory (ann.).
IFLA Publications Series.
International Cataloguing (q.).

AMERICAN MEMBERSHIP

American Assn. of Law Libs.; American Lib. Assn.; Art Libs. Society of North America; Assn. of American Lib. Schools; Assn. of Research Libs.; Assn. of Music Libs.; International Assn. of Law Libs.; International Assn. of Orientalist Libns.; International Assn. of School Libns.; Medical Lib. Assn.; Special Libs. Assn. *Institutional Members:* There are 130 libraries and related institutions that are institutional members or affiliates of IFLA in the United States (out of a total of 900), and 40 Personal Affiliates (out of a total of 97).

INTERNATIONAL INSTITUTE FOR CHILDREN'S LITERATURE AND READING RESEARCH
Mayerhofg. 6, A-1040 Vienna, Austria

OBJECT

"To create an international center of work and coordination; to take over the tasks of a documentations center of juvenile literature and reading education; to meditate between the individual countries and circles dealing with children's books and reading." Established Apr. 7, 1965. Dues. Austrian schillings 250 (with a subscription to *Bookbird*); Austrian schillings 320 (with a subscription to *Bookbird* and *Jugend und Buch*).

PROGRAM

Promotion of international research in field and collection and evaluation of results of such research; international bibliography of technical literature on juvenile reading; meetings and exhibitions; compilation and publication of recommendation lists; advisory service; concrete studies on juvenile literature; collaboration with publishers; reading research.

OFFICERS

Pres. Adolf März; *Hon. Pres.* Josef Stummvoll; *V.P.* Wilhelmine Lussnig; *Dir.* Richard Bamberger; *V.-Dir.* Otwald Kropatsch. (Address all inquiries to director at headquarters address.)

PUBLICATIONS

Bookbird (q.; memb. or Austrian schillings 250 [approx. $14]).

Jugend und Buch (memb. or Austrian schillings 90 [approx. $7]).

Schriften zur Jugendlektüre (series of books and brochures dealing with questions on juvenile literature and literary education in German).

INTERNATIONAL ORGANIZATION FOR STANDARDIZATION
ISO Central Secretariat
1 r. de Varembé, Case postale 56, CH-1211 Geneva 20, Switzerland

OBJECT

To promote the development of standards in the world in order to facilitate the international exchange of goods and services and to develop mutual cooperation in the spheres of intellectual, scientific, technological, and economic activity.

Note: For a report on recent activities of ISO TC 46, see the joint report from ANSC Z39 and ISO TC 46 in the National Associations section of Part 1—*Ed.*

OFFICERS

Pres. Henri-Durand, France; *V.P.* Ralph Hennessy, Canada; *Secy.-Gen.* Olle Sturen, Sweden.

TECHNICAL WORK

The technical work of ISO is carried out by over 160 technical committees. These include:

TC 46—Documentation (Secretariat, DIN Deutsches Institut für Normung, 4-10, Burggrafenstr., Postfach 1107, D-1000 Berlin 30, Germany). Scope: Standardization of practices relating to libraries, documentation and information centers, indexing and abstracting services, archives, information science, and publishing.

TC 37—Terminology (*Principles & Coordination*) (Secretariat, Osterreichisches Normungsinstitut, Leopoldgasse 4, A-1020 Vienna, Austria). Scope: Standardization of methods for setting up and coordinating national and international standardized terminologies.

TC 97—Computers & Information Processing (Secretariat, American National Standards Institute ANSI, 1430 Broadway, New York, NY 10018, USA). Scope: Standardization in the area of computers and associated information processing systems and peripheral equipment, devices, and media related thereto.

PUBLICATIONS

Catalogue (ann.).
Memento (ann.).
Annual Review.
Bulletin (mo.).
Liaisons.
Member Bodies.

INTERNATIONAL YOUTH LIBRARY
Kaulbachstr. 11a, D-8 Munich 22, Federal Republic of Germany

OBJECT

To develop and maintain an international reference library and clearinghouse for both primary and secondary children's literature; to organize exhibitions of children's books in Munich and for travel throughout the world; to maintain a lending library for children in eight languages (English, French, German, Italian, Spanish, Dutch, Greek, and Japanese) and to provide activities allied with the lending library, such as book discussions; to promote international cooperation and understanding through the development of mutual exchange in the field of children's literature among the various countries; to provide study opportunities for children's book specialists from other countries by making available a three-month scholarship (eight per year), not only to engage in research but to assist in the further development of their country's collection at the IYL; to cooperate with the section for children's libraries of IFLA and with UNESCO (IYL is an associated project). Founded 1948 by Jella Lepman.

PUBLICATIONS

Children's Prize Books: A Catalog from the International Youth Library Concerning 67 Prizes (the leading national children's book awards from various countries). *Ed.* Walter Scherf, Verlag Dokumentation, Munich, Fed. Rep. of Germany; R. R. Bowker, New York, NY.

Catalogs from the Internationale Jugendbibliothek (18 vols.), G. K. Hall & Co., Boston, MA; comprising five catalogs; alphabetical, by language, classified, title, illustrator.

Quarterly Program; announcement of activities (International Youth Lib., Munich, Fed. Rep. of Germany).

The Best of the Best: Picture, chil-

dren's and youth books from 108 countries or languages. *Ed.* Walter Scherf, Verlag Dokumentation, Munich, Fed. Rep. of Germany; R. R. Bowker, New York, NY.
Basic Catalogues of Children's Books from South Europe, nos. 1–12. *Ed.* Walter Scherf, Verlag Dokumentation, Munich, Fed. Rep. of Germany.
Papers and Information Materials, New Series, nos. 1–11.
Bewältigung der Gengenwart? (*How to Overcome the Present? Emancipation and Social Criticism in Children's and Youth Literature*). *Ed.* Elisabeth Scherf, Verlag Dokumentation, Munich, Fed. Rep. of Germany.
Das Porträt der Frau in der zeitgenössischen Jugendliteratur (*How Women Are Portrayed in Current Youth Literature*). *Ed.* Gerda Neumann, Verlag Dokumentation, Munich, Fed. Rep. of Germany.

FOREIGN LIBRARY ASSOCIATIONS

The following list of regional and national foreign library associations is a selective one. For a more complete list with detailed information, see *International Guide to Library, Archival, and Information Science Associations* by Josephine Riss Fang and Alice H. Songe (R. R. Bowker, 1976). The *Guide* also provides information on international associations, some of which are described in detail in the article on "International Library Associatons" that appears earlier in Part 6 of this volume. A more complete list of foreign and international library associations also can be found in *International Literary Market Place* (R. R. Bowker), an annual publication.

REGIONAL

Africa

International Assn. for the Development of Documentation, Libs. and Archives in Africa, Secy. Zacheus S. Ali (Nigeria), Box 375, Dakar, Senegal.

Standing Conference of African Lib. Schools, c/o School of Libns., Archivists and Documentalists, Univ. of Dakar, B.P. 3252, Dakar, Senegal.

Standing Conference of African Univ. Libs. (SCAUL), c/o Ed. E. Bejide Bankole, Univ. Libn., Univ. of Lagos, Yaba, Lagos, Nigeria; Convener-Secy. John Ndegwa, Univ. Libn., Univ. of Nairobi, Kenya.

Standing Conference of Eastern African Libns., c/o Tanzania Lib. Assn., Box 2645, Dar-es-Salaam, Tanzania.

The Americas

Assn. of Caribbean Univ., Research and Institutional Libs. (Asociación de Bibliotecas Universitarias, de Investigación e Institucionales del Caribe), Gen. Secy. Oneida R. Ortiz, Apdo. Postal S, Estación de la Universidad, San Juan, PR 00931.

Latin American Assn. of Schools of Lib. and Info. Science (Asociación Latinoamericana de Escuelas de Bibliotecología y Ciencias de la Información), Colegio de Bibliotecología, Universidad Nacional Autónoma de México, México 20, D.F., Mexico.

Seminar on the Acquisition of Latin American Lib. Materials, SALALM Secretariat, Benson Latin American Collection, Univ. of Texas at Austin, SHR 1-108, Austin, TX 78712.

Asia

Congress of Southeast Asian Libns. IV (CONSAL IV), Chpn. Maenmas Chavalit, c/o National Lib., Samsen Rd., Bangkok 3, Thailand.

British Commonwealth of Nations

Commonwealth Lib. Assn., Exec. Secy., Box 534, Kingston 10, Jamaica, West Indies.

Standing Conference on Lib. Materials on Africa, c/o Institute of Commonwealth Studies, 27 Russell Sq., London WC1B 5DS, England.

Europe

LIBER (Ligue des Bibliothèques Européennes de Recherche), Assn. of European Research Libs., c/o K. W. Humphreys, European Univ. Institute, Badia Fiesolana, Via dei Roccettini 5, San Domenico di Fiesole, Florence, Italy.

Scandinavian Assn. of Research Libns. (Nordiska Vetenskapliga Bibliotekariefōbundet), c/o Wilhelm Odelberg, Royal Swedish Academy of Sciences, S-10405 Stockholm, Sweden.

NATIONAL

Afghanistan

Afghanistan Lib. Assn. (Anjuman Kitab-Khana 1), Box 3142, Kabul.

Argentina

Argentine Assn. of Libs. and Scientific and Technical Info. Centers (Asociación Argentina de Bibliotecas y Centros de Información Científicos y Técnicos), Santa Fe 1145, Buenos Aires. Exec. Secy. Olga E. Veronelli.

Australia

Australian School Lib. Assn., Exec. Secy. John Ward, Box 118, Carlton 3053.

Lib. Assn. of Australia, Science Centre, Exec. Dir. Gordon Bower, 35 Clarence St., Sydney, N.S.W. 2000.

Lib. Automated Systems Info. Exchange (LASIE), Box 581, Brookvale, N.W.S. 2100.

School Lib. Assn. of New South Wales, c/o Guri Mackinnon, Box 80, Balmain, N.S.W. 2041.

School Lib. Assn. of Queensland, c/o Secy., Box 429, Redcliffe, Qld. 4020.

State Libns. Council, Chpn. K. A. R. Horn, Lib. Council of Victoria, 328 Swanston St., Melbourne, Vic. 3000.

Austria

Assn. of Austrian Libs. and Libns. (Verband Österr. Volsbüchereien und Volksbibliothekare), Langegasse 37, A-1080 Vienna.

Belgium

Assn. of Libns. and Documentalists of the State Institute of Social Studies (Association des Bibliothécaires—Documentalistes de l'Institut d'Etudes Sociales de l'Etat), Secy. Claire Gerard, 26 r. de l'Abbaye, B-1050 Brussels.

Assn. of Theological Libns. (Vereniging van Religieus-Wetenschappelijke Bibliothécarissen), Minderbroederstr. 5, B-3800 St. Truiden, Exec. Secy. K. Van de Casteele, Elsbos 16, B-2520 Edegem.

Belgian Assn. of Archivists and Libns. (Association des Archivistes et des Bibliothécaires de Belgique/Vereniging van Archivarissen en Bibliothecarissen van Belgie), Gen. Secy. Raphaël de Smedt, Bibliothèque Royale Albert I, 4 bd. de l'Empereur, B-1000 Brussels.

National Assn. of French-Speaking Libns. (Association nationale des Bibliothécaires d'Expression française), Exec. Secy. J. Peraux, 56 r. de la Station, B-5370 Havelange.

National Council of Hospital Libs. (Conseil national des Bibliothèques d'Hôpitaux), Exec. Secy. F. Delsemme, 98 chaussee de Vleurgat, B-1050 Brussels.

Bolivia

Bolivian Lib. Assn. (Asociación Boliviana de Bibliotecarios), Casilla 992, Cochabamba.

Brazil

Assn. of Brazilian Archivists (Associação dos Arquivis tas Brasileiros), Praia de Botafogo, 186, Sala B-217, Rio de Janeiro.

Brazilian Federation of Lib. Assns. (Federação Brasileira de Associações de Bibliotecários), Rua Avanhandava, 40, Conj. 110, São Paulo, SP.

Lib. Assn. of Paraná (Associação Bibliotecária do Paraná), Rua Cândido Lopes, Box 8796, Curitiba, Paraná 80.000.

Library Assn. of São Paulo (Associação Paulista de Bibliotecários), Rua 13 de Maio 1100, Conj. 32, CP 343, São Paulo, SP.

Bulgaria

Lib. Sec. at the Trade Union of the Workers in the Polygraphic Industry and Cultural Institutions (Biblioteĉna Sekcjica pri Zentralnija Komitet na Profsãjuza na Rabotnicite ot Poligraficeskata Promišlenost i Kulturnite Instituti), Pres. Nikola Tschervenkov, Sofia Gdanov 7.

Canada

Bibliographical Society of Canada (La Société Bibliographique du Canada), Secy.-Treas. Marion D. Cameron, Box 1878, Guelph, Ont. N1H 7A1.

Canadian Assn. of Law Libs. (Association Canadienne des Bibliothèques de Droit), Exec. Secy., Box 220, Adelaide St. Postal Sta., Toronto, Ont. M5C 2J1.

Canadian Assn. of Lib. Schools (Association Canadienne des Écoles des Bibliothécaires), Pres. Gerald Prodrick, School of Lib. and Info. Science, Univ. of Western Ontario, London, Ont. N6A 5B9.

Canadian Council of Lib. Schools (Conseil Canadienne des Écoles Bibliothécaires), Pres. Daniel Reicher, Dir., Ecole de bibliotheconomie, Univ. de Montreal, Montreal, PQ H3C 3J7.

Canadian Lib. Assn., Exec. Dir. Paul Kitchen, 151 Sparks St., Ottawa, Ont. K1P 5E3. (For detailed information on the Canadian Lib. Assn. and its divisions, see "National Library and Information Industry Associations, U.S. and Canada"; for information on the library associations of the provinces of Canada, see "State, Provincial, and Regional Library Associations.")

Chile

Chilean Lib. Assn. (Colegio de Bibliotecarios de Chile), Casilla 3741, Santiago.

Colombia

Assn. of Colombian Libns. (Colegio de Bibliotecarios Colombianos), Apdo. Aéreo 3212, Bogotá.

Colombian Lib. Assn. (Asociación Colombiana de Bibliotecarios), Apdo. Aéreo 30883, Bogotá.

Costa Rica

Assn. of Costa Rican Libns. (Asociación Costarricense de Bibliotecarios), Apdo. Postal 3308, San José.

Cyprus

Lib. Assn. of Cyprus (Kypriakos Synthesmos Bibliothicarion), Box 1039, Nicosia.

Czechoslovakia

Assn. of Slovak Libns. and Documentalists (Zväz slovenských knihovníkov a informatikov), Pres. Vít Rak; Exec. Secy. Štefan Kimlička, Michalská 1, 885 17 Bratislava.

Central Lib. Council of the Czechoslovak Socialist Republic (Ústřední knihovnická rada CSSR), Secy. Jaroslav Lipovsky, Karmelitská 7, Prague 1.

Denmark

The Archives Society (Arkivforeningen), Exec. Secy. Steen U. Zangenberg, Rigsarkivet, Rigsdagsgården 9, DK-1218 Copenhagen.

Assn. of Danish Research Libs. (Danmarks Forskningsbiblioteks-forening), c/o Rigsbibliotekarembedet, Christians Brygge 8, DK-1219 Copenhagen K.

Assn. of Danish School Libs. (Danmarks Skolebiblioteksforening), Exec. Secy. Niels Jacobsen, Vejlemosevej 21, DK-2840 Holte.

Danish Assn. of Music Libs., Danish Sec. of AIBM (Dansk Musikbiblioteksforening, Dansk sektion of AIBM), Secy., Royal Lib., Music Dept., Christians Brygge 8, DK-1219 Copenhagen K.

Danish Lib. Assn. (Danmarks Biblioteksforening), Trekronergade 15, DK-2500 Valby-Copenhagen.

Dominican Republic

Dominican Lib. Assn. (Asociación Dominicana de Bibliotecarios/ASOD-OBI), c/o Biblioteca Nacional, Plaza de la Cultura, Santo Domingo, Pres. Prospero J. Mella Chavier; Secy.-Gen. Veronica Regus de Tosca.

Egypt

See United Arab Republic.

El Salvador

El Salvador Lib. Assn. (Asociación de Bibliotecarios de El Salvador), c/o Biblioteca Nacional, 8a Av. Norte y C. Delgado, San Salvador.

Ethiopia

Ethiopian Lib. Assn. (Ye Ethiopia Betemetsahft Serategnot Mahber), Exec. Secy. Yitateku Negga, Box 30530, Addis Ababa.

Finland

Assn. of Research and Univ. Libns. (Tieteellisten Kirjastojen Virkailijat-Vetenskapliga Bibliotekens Tjänstemannaförening R.Y.), Exec. Secy. Anneli Arjasto, Lib. of the Institute for Cultural Relations between Finland and Soviet Union, Armfeltintie 10, SF-00150 Helsinki 15.

Finnish Assn. for Documentation (Suomen Kirjallisuuspalvelun Seura-Samfundet för Litteraturjänst i Finland), Pres. Saima Wiklund, Kuusankoski Kymi Kymmene Oy.

Finnish Libns. Assn. (Suomen Kirjastonhoitajat-Finlands Bibliotekarier R.Y.), Exec. Secy. Anneli Putkönen, Cygnaeuksenkatu 4B11, SF-00100 Helsinki 10.

Finnish Lib. Assn. (Suomen Kirjastoseura), Exec. Secy. Hilkka M. Kauppi, Museokatu 18, SF-00100 Helsinki 10.

France

Assn. of French Archivists (Association des archivistes français), 60 r. des Francs-Bourgeois, F-75141 Paris, Cedex 03.

Assn. of French Info. Scientists and Special Libns. (Association Francaise des Documentalistes et des Bibliotécaires Specialisés), Exec. Secy. Y. Rosenfeld, 5, av. Franco russe, 75007 Paris.

Assn of French Libns. (Association des Bibliothécaires Français), Exec. Secy. Marcelle Beaudiquez, 65 r. de Richelieu, F-75002 Paris.

Assn. of French Theological Libs. (Association des Bibliothéques ecclésiastiques de France), Exec. Secy. Paul-Marie Guillaume, 13 r. Dhavernas, F-80000 Amiens.

German Democratic Republic

Lib. Assn. of the German Democratic Republic (Bibliotheksverband der Deutschen Demokratischen Republik), Hermann-Matern-Str. 57, DDR-1040 Berlin.

Germany (Federal Republic of)

German Assn. for Documentation (Deutsche Gesellschaft für Dokumentation, e.V.), Westendstr. 19, D-6000 Frankfurt am Main 1.

Assn. for Libnshp. and Documentation in Agriculture (Gesellschaft für Bibliotekswesen und Dokumentation des Landbaues), Paracelsusstr. 2, D-7000 Stuttgart 70.

Assn. of Archives and Libns. in the Evangelical Church (Arbeitsgemeinschaft der Archive und Bibliotheken in der evangelischen Kirche), Pres. Helmut Baier, Veilhofstr. 28, D-8500 Nurnberg.

Assn. of Art Libs. (Arbeitsgemeinschaft der Kunst- und Museumsbibliothek), Exec. Secy. Albert Schug, Kattenbug 18, D-5000 Cologne 1.

Assn. of Certified Libns. at Research Libs. (Verein der Diplom-Bibliothekare an wissenschaftlichen Bibliotheken, e.V.), Universitatsbibliothek, Postfach 102148, D-4630, Bochum 1.

Assn. of Church Lib. Assns. (Arbeitsgemeinschaft der Kirchlichen Büchereiverbände Deutschlands), Exec. Secy. Erich Hodick, Wittelsbacherring 9, D-5300 Bonne 1.

Assn. of German Archivists (Verein deutscher Archivare), Hessisches Staatsarchiv, Schloss, D-6100 Darmstadt.

Assn. of German Libns. (Verein deutscher Bibliothekare, e.V.), Pres. Joseph Daum, Universitätsbibliothek der Technischen Universität, Pockelsstr. 13, D-3300 Braunschweig.

Assn. of Libns. in Public Libs. (Verein der Bibliothekare an Öffentlichen Bibliotheken, e.V.), Pres. Karl-Heinz Pröve, Roonstr. 57, D-28, Bremen 1.

Assn. of Libs. for Law and Documentation (Arbeitsgemeinschaft für juristisches Bibliotheks- und Dokumentationswesen), Chpn. Renate Bellmann, Juristisches Seminar der Universität, Neue Aula, D-7400 Tübingen.

Assn. of Libs. of the Catholic Church (Bundesarbeitsgemeinschaft der Katholisch-Kirchlichen Büchereiarbeit), Exec. Secy. Erich Hodick, Wittelsbacherring 9, D-5300 Bonn 1.

Assn. of Medical Libs. (Arbeitsgemeinschaft für Medizinisches Bibliothekswesen), c/o Joseph-Stelzmann-Str. 9, D-5000 Cologne-Lindenthal.

Assn. of Protestant Libs. (Deutscher Verband Evangelischer Büchereien), Bürgerstr. 2, D-3400 Göttingen.

Assn. of Regional Libs. (Arbeitsgemeinschaft der Regionalbibliotheken), Staats- und Stadtbibliothek Schaezlerstr. 25, D-8900 Augsburg.

Assn. of Special Libs. (Arbeitsgemeinschaft der Spezialbibliotheken, e.V.), c/o Senckenbergische Bibliothek, Bockenheimer Landstr. 134-138, D-6 Frankfurt am Main.

Assn. of Univ. Libs. (Arbeitsgemeinschaft der Hochschulbibliotheken), Olshausenstr. 29, D-2300 Kiel.

Ghana

Ghana Lib. Assn., Box M.430, Accra.

Greece

Greek Lib. Assn. (Enosis Ellenon Bibliothakarion), Amerikis 11, Athens 134.

Guatemala

Lib. Assn. of Guatemala (Asociación Bibliotecológica Guatemalteca), Dir., Biblioteca Nacional de Guatemala, 5a Av. 7-26, Zona 1, Guatemala City.

Guyana

Guyana Lib. Assn., Asst. Secy. P. E. Dos Ramos, c/o National Lib., 76/77 Main St., Box 110, Georgetown.

Honduras

Assn. of Libns. and Archivists of Honduras (Asociación de Bibliotecarios y Archivistas de Honduras), Secy. Gen. Juan Angel Ayes R., 3 Av. 4 y 5 C., no. 416, Comayagüela, DC, Tegucigalpa.

Hungary

Assn. of Hungarian Libns. (Magyar Könyvtárosok Egyesülete), Secy. D. Kovács, Box 486, H-1827 Budapest.

Info. Science Society (Tajekoztatási Tudományos Társaság), c/o Pál Gágyor, Kossuth ter 6–8, Budapest 1055.

Iceland

Icelandic Lib. Assn. (Bókavarðafélag Íslands), Pres. & Exec. Secy. Th. Thorvaldsdóttir, Box 7050, 127 Reykjavík.

India

Indian Assn. of Special Libs. and Info. Centres (IASLIC), P-291 CIT Scheme 6M, Kankurgachi Calcutta 700054.

Indian Lib. Assn., Delhi Public Lib., S. P. Mukerji Marg, Delhi 110006.

Punjab Lib. Assn., 233 Model Town, Jullundur City-3.

Indonesia

Indonesian Lib. Assn. (Ikatan Pustakawan Indonesia), Pres. Soekarman Kartosedono; Secy.-Gen. John P. Rompas, Jalan Merdeka Selatan 11, Jakarta, Pusat.

Iran

Iranian Lib. Assn., Exec. Secy. M. Niknam Vazifeh, Box 11-1391, Tehran.

Iraq

Iraq Lib. Assn., Central Lib., Univ. of Baghdad, Box 12, Baghdad.

Ireland (Republic of)

Irish Assn. for Documentation and Info. Services, Exec. Secy. Alf MacLochlainn, National Lib. of Ireland, Dublin 2.

Irish Assn. of School Libns. (Cumann Leabharlannaithe Scoile-CLS), Headquarters: The Lib., Univ. College, Dublin 4, Exec. Secy. Sister Monaghan, Loreto College, Foxrock, Co. Dublin.

Lib. Assn. of Ireland (Cumann Leabharlann Na h-Éireann), Pres. W. D. Linton; Hon. Secy. N. Hardiman, Thomas Prior House, Merrion Rd., Dublin 4.

Israel

Israel Lib. Assn. (Irgun Safrane Israel), Chpn. I. Steinberg; V. Chpn. A. Marbach; Exec. Secy. S. Goldberg, Box 303 Tel Aviv.

Italy

Federation of Italian Public Libs. (Federazione Italiana delle Biblioteche Popolari), c/o la Società Umanitaria, Via Davario 7, Cap. N., I-20122 Milan.

Italian Libs. Assn. (Associazione Italiana Biblioteche), Via Milano 76, c/o Istituto di Patologia del Libro, I-00184 Rome.

National Assn. for Public and Academic Libs. (Ente Nazionale per le Biblioteche Popolari e Scholastiche), Via Michele Mercati 4, I-00197 Rome.

National Assn. of Italian Archivists (Associazione Nazionale Archivistica Italiana), Viale Trastevere 215, I-00153 Rome.

Ivory Coast

Assn. for the Development of Documentation, Libs. and Archives of the Ivory Coast (Association pour le Développement de la Documentation, des Bibliothèques et Archives de la Côte d'Ivoire), c/o Bibliothèque Nationale, B.P. V-180, Abidjan.

Jamaica

Jamaica Lib. Assn., Box 58, Kingston 5.

Japan

Japan Assn. of Agricultural Libns. and Documentalists (Nippon Nogaku Tosyokan Kyogikai), Taiyoseimei Bldg., 2-17-2 Shibuya, Shibuya-ku, Tokyo 150.

Japan Documentation Society (Nippon Dokumentêsyon Kyôkai), Sasaki Bldg., 5-7 Koisikawa 2-chome, Bunkyô-ku, Tokyo.

Japan Lib. Assn. (Nippon Toshokan Kyôkai), Secy-Gen. Hitoshi Kurihara, 1-10 1-chome, Taishido, Setagaya-ku, Tokyo 154.

Japan Pharmaceutical Lib. Assn. (Nippon Yakugaku Toshokan Kyôgikai), c/o Lib., Faculty of Pharmaceutical Sciences, Univ. of Tokyo, Hongô 7-3-1 Bunkyô-ku, Tokyo.

Japan Special Lib. Assn. (Senmon Toshokan Kyôgikai), Exec. Dir. Yasunosuke Morita, c/o National Diet Lib., 1-10-1 Nagata-cho, Chiyoda-ku, Tokyo 100.

Jordan

Jordan Lib. Assn., Pres. Mahmoud el-Akhras; Secy. Yousef Qandil; Treas. Izzat Zahidah, Box 6289, Amman.

Korea (Democratic People's Republic of)

Lib. Assn. of the Democratic People's Republic of Korea, Secy. Li Geug, Central Lib., Pyongyang.

Korea (Republic of)

Korean Lib. Assn. (Hanguk Tosogwan Hyophoe), Exec. Dir. Dae Kwon Park, 100–177, 1-Ka, Hoehyun-dong, Choong-ku, Box 2041, Seoul.

Laos

Laos Lib. Assn. (Association des Bibliothécaires Laotiens), Direction de la Bibliothèque nationale, Ministry of Education, Box 704, Vientiane.

Lebanon

Lebanese Lib. Assn., National Lib., p. de l'Etoile, Beirut.

Malaysia

Lib. Assn. of Malaysia (Persatuan Perpustakaan Malaysia), Box 2545, Kuala Lumpur.

Mauritania

International Assn. for the Development of Documentation, Libs. and Archives in Africa, Mauritanian Branch (Section Mauritanienne de l'Association Internationale pour le Développement de la Documentation, des Bibliothèques et des Archives en Afrique), La Bibliothèque Nationale, Box 20, Nouakchott.

Mexico

Assn. of Libns. of Higher Education and Research Institutions (Asociación de Bibliotecarios de instituciones de Ensenãnza Superior e Investigación), Pres. Elsa Barberena, Apdo. Postal 5-611, México 5, D.F.

Mexican Assn. of Libns. (Asociación Mexicana de Bibliotecarios, A.C.), Apdo. 27-132, México 7, D.F.

Netherlands

Assn. of Archivists in the Netherlands (Vereniging van Archivarissen in Nederlan), ter Pelkwÿckpark 21, Zwolle.

Assn. of Theological Libns. (Vereniging voor het Theologisch Bibliothecariaat), Secy., Box 289, NL-6500 A9 Nijmegen.

Assn. of Univ. Libs. and the Royal Lib. (UKB-Samenwerkingsverband van de Universiteits- en Hogeschoolbibliotheken en de Koninklijke Bibliotheek), Exec. Secy. J. L. M. van Dijk, Universiteitsbibliotheek, Postbus 616, 6200 MD Maastricht.

Dutch Lib. Assn. (Nederlandse Vereniging van Bibliothecarissen, Documentalisten en Literatuuronderzoekers, 'NVB'), Secy. G. van Dijk, c/o Provinciale Bibliotheek van Zeeland, Abdij 9, Middelburg.

Netherlands Assn. of Business Archivists (Nederlandse Vereniging van Bedrijfsarchivarissen), Secy. C. L. Groenland, Aalsburg 25–26, 6602 WD Wijchen.

New Zealand

New Zealand Lib. Assn., 10 Park St., Box 12-212, Wellington 1.

Nicaragua

Assn. of Univ. and Special Libs. of Nicaragua (Asociación de Bibliotecas Universitarias y Especializadas de Nicaragua/ABUEN), Apdo. 2252, Banco Central de Nicaragua, Managua.

Nigeria

Nigerian Lib. Assn., c/o E. O. Ejiko, Hon. Secy., Kashim Ibrahim Lib., Ahmadu Bello Univ., Zaria.

Norway

Assn. of Archivists (Arkivarforeningen), Riksarkivet, postboks 10 Kringsjå, Oslo 8.

Assn. of Norwegian Research Libns. (Norske Forskningebibliotekarers Forening), Malerhaugveien 20, Oslo 6.

The Norwegian Lib. Assn. (Norsk Bibliotekforening), Malerhaugveien 20, Oslo 6.

Pakistan

Pakistan Lib. Assn., Box 1284, Islamabad.

Society for the Promotion and Improvement of Libs., Al-Majeed, Hamdard Centre, Nazimabad, Karachi 18.

Panama

Asociación Panameña de Bibliotecarios, c/o Inés Maria Herrera, Apdo. 3435, Panama City.

Papua New Guinea

Papua New Guinea Lib. Assn., Box 5368, Boroko, P.N.G.

Paraguay

Paraguayan Assn. of Univ. Libns. (Asociación de Bibliotecarios Universitarios del Paraguay), c/o Yoshiko M. de Freundorfer, Head, Esceula de Bibliotecologia, Universidad Nacional de Asunción, Asunción.

Peru

Assn. of Peruvian Archivists (Asociación Peruana de Archiveros), Archivo General de la Nación, C. Manuel Cuadros S/N, Palacio de Justicia, Apdo. 1802, Lima.

Assn. of Peruvian Libns. (Asociación Peruana de Bibliotecarios), Apdo. 3760, Lima.

Lib. Group for the Integration of Socio-Economic Info. (Agrupación de Bibliotecas para la Integración del la Información Socio-Económica), Apdo. 2874, Lima 100.

Philippines

Assn. of Special Libs. of the Philippines (ASLP), Pres. Susima Lazo Gonzales, Box 4118, Manila.

Philippine Lib. Assn. Inc., Pres. Juvenal Y. Catajoy, Rm. 301, National Lib. Bldg., T. M. Kalaw St., Ermita, Manila.

Poland

Polish Libns. Assn. (Stowarzyszenie Bibliotekarzy, Polskich), Chmn. Witold Stankiewicz; Secy.-Gen. Leon Łoś, ul. Konopczynskiego 5/7, 00-953 Warsaw.

Portugal

Portuguese Assn. of Libns., Archivists, and Documentalists (Associação Portuguesa de Bibliotecarios Arquivistas e Documentalistas), Edificio da Biblioteca Nacional, Campo Grande 83, 1700 Lisbon.

Rhodesia

Rhodesia Lib. Assn., Box 3133, Salisbury.

Scotland

See United Kingdom.

Senegal

Senegal Assn. for the Development of Documentation, Libs., Archives and Museums (Commission des Bibliothèques de l'ASDBAM, Association Sénégalaise pour le Développement de la Documentation, des Bibliothèques, des Archives et des Musées), B.P. 375, Dakar.

Sierra Leone

Sierra Leone Lib. Assn., c/o Secy., High Court Lib., Siaka Stevens St., Freetown.

Singapore

Lib. Assn. of Singapore, c/o National Lib., Stamford Rd., Singapore 0617.

South Africa

South African Lib. Assn. (Suid-Afrikaanse Biblioteekvereniging), c/o Ferdinand Postma Lib., Potchefstroom Univ., Potchefstroom.

Spain

National Assn. of Libns., Archivists and Archeologists (Asociación Nacional de Bibliotecarios, Archiveros, Arquelogos, y Documentalistas), Paseo de Calvo Sotelo 22, Apdo. 14281, Madrid 1.

Sri Lanka (Ceylon)

Sri Lanka Lib. Assn., c/o Lib., Univ. of Sri Lanka, Colombo Campus, Box 1698, Colombo 3.

Sudan

Sudan Lib. Assn., Box 1361, Khartoum.

Sweden

Assn. of Special Research Libs. (Sveriges Vetenskapliga Specialbiblioteks Förening), Pres. W. Odelberg, Kungl. Vetenskapsakademiens bibliotek, Fack, 104 05 Stockholm.

Swedish Assn. of Archivists (Svenska Arkivsamfundet), Rikjsarkivet, Fack, S-10026 Stockholm.

Swedish Assn. of Univ. and Research Libs. (Svenska Bibliotekariesamfundet), Sveriges lantbruksuniversitets bibliotek, Ultunabiblioteket, S-750 07 Uppsala.

Swedish Council of Research Libs. (Forskningsbiblioteksradet), Exec. Secy. Karin Melin-Fravolini, Box 6404, S-113 82 Stockholm 6.

Swedish Lib. Assn. (Sveriges Allmänna Biblioteksförening), Tornavägen 9, Box 1706, S-221 01 Lund.

Swedish Society for Technical Documentation (Tekniska Litteratursällskapet), Secy. Birgitta Levin, Box 5073, S-10242 Stockholm 5.

Union of Univ. and Research Libs. (Vetenskapliga Bibliotekens Tjänstemannaförening), Pres. Bo Strenstrom, Box 36, S-13101 Nacka.

Switzerland

Assn. of Swiss Archivists (Vereinigung Schweizerischer Archivare), c/o Schweiz Bundesarchiv, Archivstr. 24, CH-3003 Bern.

Assn. of Swiss Hospital Libs. (Association Suisse des Bibliothèques d'Hôpitaux/ Vereinigung Schweizerischer Krankenhausbibliotheken), Exec. Dir. J. Schmid-Schädelin, Hirschengraben 22, CH-8001 Zurich.

Assn. of Swiss Libns. (Vereinigung Schweizerischer Bibliothekare/Association des Bibliothécaires Suisses/Associazione dei Bibliotecari Svizzeri), Exec. Secy. W. Treichler, Schweizerische Landebibliothek, CH-3003 Bern.

Swiss Assn. of Documentation (Schweizerische Vereinigung für Dokumentation/ Association Suisse de Documentation), Secy. K. Zumstein, Postfach A-158, CH-8032 Zurich.

Tanzania

Tanzania Lib. Assn., Box 2645, Dar-es-Salaam.

Trinidad and Tobago

Lib. Assn. of Trinidad and Tobago, Box 1177, Port of Spain, Trinidad.

Tunisia

Tunisian Assn. of Documentalists, Libns. and Archivists (Association tunisienne des Documentalistes, Bibliothécaires et Archivistes), BP 575, Institut Ali Bach Hawba, 2 r. de Champagne, Tunis.

Uganda

Uganda Lib. Assn., Exec. Secy. I. M. N. Kigongo-Bukenya, Dip. Lib., D.P.A. (Mak), Box 5894, Kampala.

Uganda Schools Lib. Assn., Box 7014, Kampala.

Union of Soviet Socialist Republics

USSR Lib. Council, Pres. N. S. Kartashov, Lenin State Lib., 3 Prospect Kalinina, 101 000 Moscow.

United Arab Republic

Egyptian Assn. for Archives and Libnshp., Exec. Secy. Ahmed M. Monsour,

Lib. of Fine Arts, 24 El-Matbâa, Al-Ahlia, Boulaq, Cairo.
Egyptian School Lib. Assn., 35 Algalaa St., Cairo.

United Kingdom

Aslib, Dir.-Gen. Basil Saunders, 3 Belgrave Sq., London SW1X 8PL.
Assn. of British Theological and Philosophical Libs., Hon. Secy. Mary Elliott, King's College Lib., Strand, London WC2R 2LS.
Bibliographical Society, Joint Secys. M. M. Foot and R. J. Roberts, The Rooms of the British Academy, Burlington House, Piccadilly, London W1V 0NS.
British and Irish Assn. of Law Libns., Secy. D. M. Blake, Libn., Harding Law Lib., Univ. of Birmingham, Box 363, Birmingham, B15 2TT.
The Lib. Assn., Exec. Secy. Keith Lawrey, 7 Ridgmount St., London WC1E 7AE.
Private Libs. Assn., Exec. Secy. Frank Broomhead, Ravelston, South View Rd., Pinner, Middlesex.
School Lib. Assn., Chpn. Don H. Rogers, Victoria House, 29-31 George St., Oxford OX1 2AY.
Scottish Lib. Assn., Dept. of Libnshp., Robert Gordon's Institute of Technology, St. Andrew St., Aberdeen AB1 1HG, Scotland.
Society of Archivists, Hon. Secy. Mrs. C. M. Short, South Yorkshire County Record Office, Cultural Activities Centre, Ellin St., Sheffield, S1 4PL.
The Standing Conference of National and Univ. Libs., Exec. Secy. A. J. Loveday, 102 Euston St., London NW1 2HA.
Welsh Lib. Assn., Hon. Secy. Geoffrey Thomas, Gwynedd Lib. Service, Maesincla, Caernarfon, North Wales.

Uruguay

Lib. and Archive Science Assn. of Uruguay (Agrupación Bibliotecológica del Uruguay), Exec. Pres. Luis Alberto Musso Ambrosi, Cerro Largo 1666, Montevideo.

Venezuela

Assn. of Venezuelan Libns. and Archivists (Colegio de Bibliotecólogos y Archivólogos de Venezuela), Apdo. 6283, Caracas 101.

Wales

See United Kingdom.

Yugoslavia

Croatian Lib. Assn. (Hrvatsko bibliotekarsko društvo), Pres. Vera Mudri-Škunca; Secy. Nada Gomerčić, Marulicev trg 21, 41000 Zagreb.
Lib. Assn. of Bosnia and Herzegovina (Društvo Bibliotekara Bosne i Hercegovine), Obala 42, Sarajevo 71000.
Society of Libns. in Slovenia (Društvo bibliotekarjev Slovenije), Exec. Secy. Majda Armeni, Turjaška 1, YU-61000 Ljubljana.
Society of Libns. of Macedonia (Društvo na bibliotekarite na Makedonija), Kliment Ohridski Narodna i Univerzitetska Biblioteka, YU-91000 Skopje.
Union of Lib. Workers of Serbia (Savez Bibliotečkih Radnika Srbije), Secy. Branka Popović, Skerlićeva 1, YU-11000 Belgrade.
Union of Libns. Assns. of Yugoslavia (Sveza društev bibliotekarjev Jugoslavije), Exec. Sec. Božika Zdravković, Ramiz Sadiku b b, 38000 Priština.

Zaire

Zairian Assn. of Archivists, Libns. and Documentalists (Association Zaïroise des Archivistes, Bibliothécaires et Documentalistes), Exec. Secy. Mulamba Mukunya, B.P. 805, Kinshasa XI.

Zambia

Zambia Lib. Assn., Box 2839, Lusaka.

Directory of Book Trade and Related Organizations

BOOK TRADE ASSOCIATIONS, UNITED STATES AND CANADA

For more extensive information on the associations listed in this section, see the annual issues of the *Literary Market Place* (Bowker).

Advertising Typographers Assn. of America, Inc., 461 Eighth Ave., New York, NY 10001. 212-594-0685.

American Booksellers Assn., Inc., 122 E. 42 St., New York, NY 10017. 212-867-9060. *Pres.* Charles S. Haslam; *Exec. Dir.* G. Royce Smith.

American Institute of Graphic Arts, 1059 Third Ave., near 63 St., New York, NY 10021. 212-752-0813. *Pres.* James K. Fogleman; *Exec. Dir.* Caroline W. Hightower.

American Medical Publishers Assn. *Pres.* Judith M. Kennedy, Little, Brown & Co., 34 Beacon St., Boston, MA 02106. 617-227-0730. *Secy.-Treas.* G. James Gallagher, Williams & Wilkins Co., Baltimore, MD 21202. 301-528-4211.

American Printing History Assn., Box 4922, Grand Central Sta., New York, NY 10017. *Pres. & Ed. of APHA Newsletter,* Catherine T. Brody, New York City Community College Lib., 300 Jay St., Brooklyn, NY 11201. 212-643-5323; *V. Ps.* Jack Golden, Philip Grushkin, E. H. "Pat" Taylor; *Secy.* Jean Peters; *Treas.* Philip Sperling; *Ed. of Printing History.* Susan Thompson. (Address correspondence to APHA, Box 4922, except Newsletter matters, which go directly to Catherine Brody.)

American Society for Information Science (ASIS), 1010 16 St. N.W., Washington, DC 20036. 202-659-3644.

American Society of Indexers, 235 Park Ave. S., 8 fl., New York, NY 10003. *Pres.* Bernice Heller, C511 Arbor House, 7901 Henry Ave., Philadelphia, PA 19128. 215-482-8566.

American Society of Journalists & Authors, 1501 Broadway, New York, NY 10036. 212-586-5650.

American Society of Magazine Photographers (ASMP), 205 Lexington Ave., New York, NY 10016. 212-889-9144. *Dir.* Stuart Kahan.

American Society of Picture Professionals, Inc., Box 5283, Grand Central Sta., New York, NY 10017. *Pres.* Margaret Matthews. 212-972-6396; *Secy.* Alice Lundoff. 212-888-3595.

American Translators Assn., Box 129, Croton-on-Hudson, NY 10520. 914-271-3260. *Pres.* Thomas R. Bauman; *Staff Admin.* Rosemary Malia.

Antiquarian Booksellers Assn. of America, Inc., 50 Rockefeller Plaza, New York, NY 10020. 212-757-9395. *Pres.* Laurence

Note: See the reports from the American Booksellers Association and the Association of American Publishers in the National Associations section of Part 1, and the report from the Book Industry Study Group, Inc., in the Book Trade Research and Statistics section of Part 4—*Ed.*

Witten; *V.P.* John H. Jenkins; *Admin. Asst.* Janice M. Farina; *Secy.* Elisabeth Woodburn Robertson; *Treas.* Harvey W. Brewer.

Assn. of American Publishers, One Park Ave., New York, NY 10016. 212-689-8920. *Pres.* Townsend Hoopes; *V.Ps.* Thomas D. McKee, Henry R. Kaufman; *Staff Dirs.* Phyllis Ball, Gregory Gore, Parker B. Ladd, Mary E. McNulty, Patricia A. McLaughlin. *Washington Office.* 1707 L St. N.W., Washington, DC 20036. 202-293-2585. *V.P.s* Richard P. Kleeman, Robert Rasmussen; *Staff Dirs.* Roy H. Millenson, Diane G. Rennert, Carol A. Risher; *Chmn.* Alexander C. Hoffman, Doubleday & Co.; *V. Chmn.* Leo N. Albert, Prentice-Hall; *Secy.* Gordon R. Hjalmarson, Scott Foresman & Co.; *Treas.* Alexander J. Burke, Jr., McGraw-Hill Book Co.

Assn. of American University Presses, One Park Ave., New York, NY 10016. 212-889-6040. *Pres.* J. G. Goellner, Dir., Johns Hopkins University Press, Baltimore, MD 21218. 301-338-7871; *Exec. Dir.* John B. Putnam.

Assn. of Canadian Publishers, 70 The Esplanade E., Toronto, Ont. M5E 1R2 Canada. 416-361-1408. *Pres.* Patricia Aldana; *V.P.* Malcolm Lester; *Treas.* Harry van Ierssel; *Exec Dir.* Arden Ford.

Assn. of Jewish Book Publishers, House of Living Judaism, 838 Fifth Ave., New York, NY 10021. *Pres.* Jacob Steinberg, Bobbs-Merrill Co., One Pennsylvania Plaza, New York, NY 10001. 212-947-2540. (Address correspondence to the president.)

Bibliographical Society of America. See the preceding section, Directory of Library Organizations, under National Library Associations, United States and Canada, for detailed information.

Book Industry Study Group, Inc., Box 2062, Darien, CT 06820. 203-655-2473. *Chmn.* Andrew H. Neilly, Jr.; *Treas.* DeWitt C. Baker; *Secy.* JoAnn McGreevy; *Managing Agent.* John P. Dessauer, Inc.

Book League of New York. *Pres.* Richard J. Cloonan, George Braziller Co., One Park Ave., New York, NY 10016. 212-889-0909; *Treas.* A. C. Frasca, Jr., Freshet Press, Inc., 90 Hamilton Rd., Rockville Centre, NY 11570. 516-766-3011.

Book Manufacturers Institute, 111 Prospect St., Stamford, CT 06901. 203-324-9670. *Pres.* George G. Nichols, National Publishing Co., Box 8386, Philadelphia, PA 19101; *Exec. V.P.* Douglas E. Horner.

Book Publicists of Southern California, 9255 Sunset Blvd., Suite 515, W. Hollywood, CA 90069. 213-858-7112. *Pres.* Irwin Zucker; *V.P.* Steve Fiske; *Secy.* Nancy Sayles; *Treas.* Bruce Merrin.

Book Week Headquarters, The Children's Book Council, Inc., 67 Irving Place, New York, NY 10003. 212-254-2666. *Exec. Dir.* John Donovan; *Chpn. of the 1980 Book Week Comm.* Margery Cuyler, Holiday House, 18 E. 53 St., New York, NY 10022. 212-688-0085.

The Bookbinders' Guild of New York, c/o *Secy.* Sam Greene, Murray Printing Co., 60 E. 42 St., New York, NY 10017. 212-490-8703. *Pres.* Robert C. Pedersen; *V.P.* Alice Sanchez; *Treas.* Gene Sanchez, William Morrow & Co., 105 Madison Ave., New York, NY 10016; *Asst. Secy.* Steve Davidson, Rae Publishing Co., 282 Grove Ave., Cedar Grove, NJ 07009.

Bookbuilders of Boston, c/o *Pres.* Stephen Wright, Lindenmeyer Paper Co., 35 Mt. Washington Ave., Boston, MA 02107. 617-268-9280. *1st V.P.* Terry McGarry, Houghton Mifflin Co., One Beacon St., Boston, MA 02108. 617-725-5000.

Bookbuilders of Southern California, 5225 Wilshire Blvd., Suite 316, Los Angeles, CA 90036. *Pres.* Casimira Kostecki, Goodyear Publishing Co.,

1640 Fifth St., Santa Monica, CA 90401; *V.P.* Bob Ryerson, Griffin Printing, 554 W. Colorado St., Glendale, CA 91204; *Secy.* Sally Kostal, Goodyear Publishing Co., 1640 Fifth St., Santa Monica, CA 90401.

Bookbuilders West, 170 Ninth St., San Francisco, CA 94103. *Pres.* Roy A. Wallace, Maple-Vail Book Manufacturing Group, 1615 Bonanza St., Walnut Creek, CA 94596. 415-934-1440; *V.P.* Eva Strock, Harper & Row, 1700 Montgomery St., San Francisco, CA 94111. 415-989-9000; *Secy.* Ruth Cole, Wadsworth, 10 Davis Dr., Belmont, CA 94002. 415-595-2350; *Treas.* Bill Ketron, Times-Mirror Press, Box 157, Los Altos, CA 94022. 415-948-7015.

Booksellers Assn. of Philadelphia, c/o The Catholic Lib. Assn., 461 W. Lancaster Ave., Haverford, PA 19041. 215-649-5250. *Pres.* Barbara Bates, Westminster Press, 902 Witherspoon Bldg., Philadelphia, PA 19107. 215-893-4424; *V.P.* Alan Glass, New Jersey Monthly, 1101 State Rd., Bldg. I, Princeton, NJ 08540. 609-921-7576; *Secy.* Nancy Evoy, Gladwyne Public Lib., Gladwyne, PA 19330. 215-642-3957; *Treas.* Matthew R. Wilt, Catholic Lib. Assn., 461 W. Lancaster Ave., Haverford, PA 19041. 215-649-5250.

Brotherhood of Book Travelers, c/o *Pres.* Bebe Cole, 101 Second St., Garden City, NY 11530. *Treas.* Dick Clunan, George Braziller; *Secy.* Lou Cohen, St. Martin's.

Canadian Book Publishers' Council, 45 Charles St. E., Suite 701, Toronto, Ont. M4Y 1S2, Canada. 416-964-7231. *Pres.* Robert H. Ross, D. C. Heath Canada, Ltd.; *1st V.P.* Peter J. Waldock, Penguin Books Canada, Ltd.; *2nd V.P.* Ronald D. Besse, Gage Publishing, Ltd.; *Exec. Dir.* Jacqueline Nestmann-Hushion; *Member organizations.* The School Group, The College Group, The Trade Group, The Paperback Group.

Canadian Booksellers Assn., 56 The Esplanade, Suite 400, Toronto, Ont. M5E 1A7, Canada. 416-361-1529.

Chicago Book Clinic, 54 E. Erie St., Chicago, IL 60611. 312-787-6261. *Pres.* S. A. Ferrara, Nelson-Hall Publishers; *Exec. V.P.* Richard Congdon, Northern Illinois Univ. Press; *Treas.* Dorothy Anderson, Nelson-Hall Publishers.

Chicago Publishers Assn., c/o *Pres.* Robbert J. R. Follett, Follett Publishing Co., 1010 W. Washington Blvd., Chicago, IL 60607. 312-666-5858. *V.P.* John B. Saunders, Science Research Assocs., Inc., 155 N. Wacker Dr., Chicago, IL 60606. 312-984-2198.

The Children's Book Council, 67 Irving Pl., New York, NY 10003. 212-254-2566. *Exec. Dir.* John Donovan; *Assoc. Dir.* Paula Quint; *Asst. Dir.* Peter Dews; *Pres.* Dorothy Briley, *V.P. & Ed.-in-Chief,* Lothrop, Lee & Shepard Co., 105 Madison Ave., New York, NY 10016. 212-889-3050.

Christian Booksellers Assn., Box 200, 2620 Venetucci Blvd., Colorado Springs, CO 80901. 303-576-7880. *Exec. V.P.* John T. Bass.

Connecticut Book Publishers Assn., c/o *Pres.* Alex M. Yudkin, Associated Booksellers, 147 McKinley Ave., Bridgeport, CO 06606. *V.P.* Lawrence Hill, Lawrence Hill & Co., 24 Burr Farms Rd., Westport, CT 06880; *Treas.* Henry Ferguson, Inter Culture Assocs., Box 277, Quaddick Rd., Thompson, CT 06277. 203-923-9494.

Conseil Supérieur du Livre, 1151 Alexandre DeSève, Montreal, P.Q. H2L 2T7, Canada. 514-524-7528. *Exec. Dir.* Thomas Déri; Assn. des éditeurs canadiens. *Pres.* Yves Dubé; Assn. des libraries du Québec. *Pres.* Louise R. Fortier; Société canadienne française de protection du droit d'auteur. *Pres.* Pierre Tisseyre; Société des éditeurs de manuels scolaires du Québec. *Pres.* André Préfontaine.

The Copyright Society of the U.S.A., New York Univ. School of Law, 40 Washington Sq. S., New York, NY 10012. 212-598-2280/2210. *Pres.* David Goldberg; *Secy.* Eugene H. Winick; *Exec. Dir.* Alan Latman; *Asst.* Kate McKay.

Council on Interracial Books for Children, Inc., 1841 Broadway, New York, NY 10023. 212-757-5339. *Dir.* Bradford Chambers; *Pres.* Beryle Banfield; *V.P.s* Irma Garcia, Albert V. Schwartz; *Managing Ed., CIBC Bulletin.* Ruth Charnes; *Bk. Review Coord.* Lyla Hoffman; *Dir., CIBC Racism & Sexism Resource Center for Educators.* Robert B. Moore; *American Lib. Assn. Liaison.* Harriett Brown; *Contest Dir.* Katie M. Cumbo; *West Coast.* Antonia Pérez, Byron Williams.

Edition Bookbinders of New York, Inc., 375 North St., Teterboro, NJ 07608. 201-489-7484. *Exec. Secy.* Morton Windman; *Pres.* Sam Goldman, Publishers Book Bindery; *V.P.* Robert G. Luburg, Tapley-Rutter Co.; *Treas.* Martin Blumberg, American Book-Stratford Press.

Educational Paperback Assn., c/o *Pres.* Allan Hartley, H.P. Koppelmann, 140 Van Block Ave., Hartford, CT 06101. *Exec. Secy.* Sandra Topolski.

Evangelical Christian Publishers Assn., Box 35, La Habra, CA 90631. 213-947-3819. *Exec. Dir.* Donald C. Brandenburgh.

Fourth Avenue Booksellers. *Perm. Secy.* Stanley Gilman, 237 E. Ninth St., New York, NY 10003.

Graphic Artists Guild, 30 E. 20 St., Rm. 405, New York, NY 10003. 212-982-9298. *Pres.* Gerald McConnell.

Guild of Book Workers, 633 Fifth Ave., New York, NY 10022. 212-757-6454. *Pres.* Mary C. Schlosser.

Information Industry Assn. See "National Library and Information-Industry Associations" earlier in Part 7—*Ed.*

International Assn. of Book Publishing Consultants, c/o Joseph Marks, 485 Fifth Ave., New York, NY 10017. 212-867-6341.

International Assn. of Printing House Craftsmen, Inc., 7599 Kenwood Rd., Cincinnati, OH 45236. 513-891-0611. *Pres.* Thomas L. Stockwell; *Exec. V.P.* John A. Davies.

International Copyright Information Center (INCINC), Assn. of American Publishers, 1707 L. St. N.W., Suite 480, Washington, DC 20036. 202-293-2585. *Dir.* Carol A. Risher.

International Standard Book Numbering Agency (ISBN), 1180 Ave. of the Americas, New York, NY 10036. 212-764-3384. *Exec. Dir.* Emery I. Koltay. *Officers.* Beatrice Jacobson, Leigh C. Yuster.

JWB Jewish Book Council, 15 E. 26th St., New York, NY 10010. 212-532-4949. *Pres.* Sidney B. Hoenig.

Library Binding Institute, 50 Congress St., Suite 633, Boston, MA 02109. 617-227-7450. *Exec. Dir.* Dudley A. Weiss; *Public Relations Dir.* Beverly Adamonis.

Literary Publishers of Southern California. *See* Western Independent Publishers (WIP).

Magazine & Paperback Marketing Institute (MPMI), 344 Main St., Suite 205, Mt. Kisco, NY 10549. 914-666-6788. *Exec. V.P.* Woodford Bankson, Jr.

Metropolitan Lithographers Assn., 123 E. 62 St., New York, NY 10021. 212-759-0966. *Pres.* Ralph Mazzocco; *Exec. Dir.* Albert N. Greco.

Midwest Book Travelers Assn., *Pres.* William Holland, HP Books, Box 5367, Tucson, AZ 85703; *V.P.* Paul Dimmitt, Harcourt Brace Jovanovich; *Treas.* John Stromayer, Holt, Rinehart and Winston; *Secy.* Ted Heinecken, Heinecken Associates.

Minnesota Book Publishers Roundtable, c/o *Pres.* William F. Kosfeld, Motorbooks International, Box 2, Osceola, WI 54020. 715-294-3345; 800-826-6600. *V.P.* John N. Dwyer, Liturgical Press, Collegeville, MN 56321; *Secy.-Treas.* Diana Hestwood, The Math Group, 396 E. 79 St., Minneapolis, MN 55420.

National Assn. of College Stores, 528 E. Lorain St., Oberlin, OH 44074. 216-775-1561. *Pres.* David Cooper, Students Book Corp., N.E. 700 Thatuna, Pullman, WA 99163. 509-332-2537; *Gen. Mgr.* Russell Reynolds.

National Council of Churches of Christ in the U.S.A., Div. of Education and Ministry, 475 Riverside Dr., New York, NY 10027. 212-870-2271 or 870-2272. *Assoc. Gen. Secy.* Emily V. Gibbes.

National Micrographics Assn. For detailed information, see National Library and Information-Industry Associations, United States and Canada, earlier in Part 7—*Ed.*

New England Small Press Assn. (NESPA), 45 Hillcrest Pl., Amherst, MA 01002. *Dirs.* William R. Darling, Diane Kruchkow.

New Mexico Book League, 8632 Horacio Pl. N.E., Albuquerque, NM 87111. 505-299-8940. *Exec. Dir.* Dwight A. Myers; *Pres.* James Dyke; *V.P.* Norman Zollinger; *Treas.* Frank N. Skinner; *Ed.* Carol A. Myers.

New York Rights & Permissions Group, *Chmn.* Dorothy McKittrick Harris, Doubleday & Co., 245 Park Ave., New York, NY 10017. 212-953-4420.

New York State Small Press Assn., c/o The Promise of Learnings, Inc., Box 1264, Radio City Sta., New York, NY 10019. 212-586-4235. *Exec. Dir.* Janey Tannenbaum; *Gen. Mgr.* Jim Mele.

Northern California Booksellers Assn., c/o *Pres.* Sonya Blackman, Books Unlimited, 1975 Shattuck Ave., Berkeley, CA 97404. 415-845-6288.

Periodical & Book Association of America, Inc., 205 E. 42 St., New York, NY 10017. 212-486-9777. *Exec. Dir.* Joseph Greco.

Periodical Distributors of Canada. *Pres.* Gerald Benjamin, 425 Guy St., Montreal, P.Q. H3J 1T1, Canada. 514-931-4221; *Secy.* Jim Neill, 120 Sinnott Rd., Scarborough, Ont., Canada. 416-752-8720.

Philadelphia Book Clinic. *Secy-Treas.* Thomas Colaiezzi, Lea & Febiger, 600 Washington Sq., Philadelphia, PA 19106. 215-925-8700.

Pi Beta Alpha (formerly Professional Bookmen of America, Inc., 1215 Farwell Dr., Madison, WI 53704. *Pres.* B. B. Akert; *Exec. Sec.* Charles L. Schmalbach.

Printing Industries of America, Inc., 1730 N. Lynn St., Arlington, VA 22209. 703-841-8100. *Pres.* Rodney L. Borum.

Printing Industries of Metropolitan New York, Inc., 461 Eighth Ave., New York, NY 10001. 212-760-1729. *Pres.* Paul Noble; *Dir. Pub. Rel.* Daniel Soskin.

Proofreaders Club of New York, c/o *Pres.* Allan Treshan, 38-15 149 St., Flushing, NY 11354. 212-461-8509.

Publishers' Ad Club, c/o *Sec.* Bridget Marmion, Farrar, Straus & Giroux, 19 Union Sq. W., New York, NY 10003. 212-741-6900. *Pres.* Sherrie Murphy, Rizzoli International Publications, 712 Fifth Ave., New York, NY 10019. 212-397-3721; *V.P.* Fran Keegan, Book-of-the-Month Club, 485 Lexington Ave., New York, NY 10017. 212-867-4300; *Treas.* Les Turner, Los Angeles Times, 711 Third Ave., New York, NY 10017. 212-697-6200.

Publishers' Alliance, Box 3, Glen Ridge, NJ 07028. 201-429-8757. *Exec. Secy.* Linda P. Grant.

Publishers' Library Promotion Group, *Pres.* Gail Schlegel, Dodd, Mead, 79 Madison Ave., New York, NY 10016. 212-685-6464; *V.P.* Beverly Horowitz, Dell Publishing, 245 E. 47 St., New

York, NY 10017. 212-832-7300; *Treas.* Neal Porter, Farrar, Straus & Giroux, 19 Union Sq. W., New York, NY 10003. 212-741-6916; *Corres. Secy.* Paula Silberberg, Bradbury Press, 2 Overhill Rd., Scarsdale, NY 10583. 914-472-5100; *Rec. Secy.* Hilda Dworkin, Pocket Books, 1230 Ave. of the Americas, New York, NY 10020. 212-246-2121. (Address general correspondence to the president.)

Publishers' Publicity Assn., Inc. *Pres.* Barbara J. Hendra, Barbara Hendra Assocs., 140 Sterling Pl., Brooklyn, NY 11217. 212-783-6759; *V.P.* Diane O'Connor, Avon Books, 959 Eighth Ave., New York, NY 10019. 212-262-6255; *Secy.* Selden Sutton, Little, Brown & Co., 747 Third Ave., New York, NY 10017. 212-688-8380; *Treas.* Eileen Prescott, Eileen Prescott Co., 733 Third Ave., New York, NY 10017. 212-682-2268.

The Religion Publishing Group, c/o Eve F. Roshevsky, Doubleday & Co., 245 Park Ave., New York 10017. 212-953-4673. *Pres.* William Griffin, Macmillan Publishing Co., 866 Third Ave., New York, NY 10022; *Secy-Treas.* Eve F. Roshevsky.

Research and Engineering Council of the Graphic Arts Industry, Inc., 1340 Old Chain Bridge Rd., McLean, VA 22101. *Pres.* Harold A. Molz; *1st V.P., Finance and Membership.* Gilbert Bachman; *2nd V.P. and Secy.* Donald H. Laux; *Managing Dir.* Deforest D. Choha.

Society of Authors' Representatives, Inc., 40 E. 49 St., New York, NY 10017. 212-548-6333. *Pres.* Peter Shepherd; *Exec. Secy.* Jeanne Boose.

Society of Photographer & Artist Representatives, Inc. (SPAR), Box 845, New York, NY 10022. 212-832-3123. *Exec. Dir.* Jim York.

Society of Photographers in Communication. *See* American Society of Magazine Photographers (ASMP).

Southern California Booksellers Assn., c/o *Pres.* Miriam Bass, Vroman's Book Store, 695 E. Colorado, Pasadena, CA 91101. 213-449-5320. *V.P.* Jack Dawley, Simon & Schuster, 5751 Valley Oak Dr., Los Angeles, CA 90068; *Secy.* Roberta Whitehead, Northridge Books, Northridge, CA 91324. 213-349-5484; *Treas.* Joe Chevalier, Chevalier's Books, 126 N. Larchmont, Los Angeles, CA 90004. 213-465-1334.

Standard Address Number (SAN) Agency. *See* International Standard Book Numbering Agency.

Technical Assn. of the Pulp & Paper Industry (TAPPI), One Dunwoody Pk., Atlanta, GA 30338. 404-394-6130. *Pres.* W. O. Kroeschell; *V.P.* Sherwood G. Holt; *Exec. Dir.* Philip E. Nethercut; *Treas.* W. L. Cullison.

Translation Research Institute, 5914 Pulaski Ave., Philadelphia, PA 19144. 215-848-7084. *Dir.* Charles Parsons.

West Coast Bookmen's Assn., 27 McNear Dr., San Rafael, CA 94901. *Pres.* George Corey, 464 Park Ave., Apt. E, Laguna Beach, CA 92651; *Secy-Treas.* Phillip R. Ventura, 1521 Verde Vista Dr., Monterey Park, CA 91754.

Western Book Publishers Assn., c/o George Young, Box 558, Corte Madera, CA 94925. 415-595-1142.

Western College Bookstore Assn. *Pres.* Peter Paskill, Portland State Univ. Bookstore, 531 S.W. Hall, Portland, OR 97201. 503-226-2631; *Secy.-Treas.* A. H. Smith, Oregon State Univ. Bookstore, Memorial Place at Jefferson St., Box 489, Corvallis, OR 97330. 503-754-4323.

Western Independent Publishers (WIP), Box 216, Rte. 1, Winters, CA 95694. 916-662-3364. *Pres.* Noel Peattie; *Treas.* Gail Schlachter.

Women's National Book Assn. c/o *Natl. Pres.* Ann Heidbreder Eastman, 716 Burruss Dr. N.W., Blacksburg, VA 24060. 703-951-4770 (home). *Dir.* of

Public Affairs Programs, College of Arts and Sciences, Virginia Polytechnic Institute and State University, Blacksburg, VA 24061. 703-961-6390 (office); *V.P./Pres.-Elect.* Mary Glenn Hearne, 3838 Granny White Pike, Nashville, TN 37204. 615-244-4700 (lib.). 615-383-8969 (home); *Review Ed.* Mary V. Gaver, 300 Virginia Ave., Danville, VA 24541. 804-799-6746; *Corres. Memb. Chmn.* Anne J. Richter, 55 N. Mountain Ave., Apt. A2, Montclair, NJ 07042, 201-746-5166; *Editor, "The Bookwoman."* Kerry Tucker, 25 W. 16 St., New York, NY 10011. 212-679-7300. CHAPTER PRESIDENTS: *Binghamton.* L. Jeanette Clarke Lee, 8 Pine St., Binghamton, NY 13901. 607-723-6626; *Boston.* Frances Mulchay, 39 Leavitt St., Hingham, MA 02043; *Cleveland.* Kathalee Grant, Independence Public Lib., 7121 Valley View Dr., Independence, OH 44131. 216-447-2060; *Detroit.* Olga Pobutsky, 16815 Parkside, Detroit, MI 48221. 313-863-1389; *Grand Rapids.* Celene Idema, 2501 Leonard N.W., Grand Rapids, MI 49504. 616-543-0344; *Los Angeles.* Carole Garland, 2405 Roscemare Rd. Apt. 7, Los Angeles, CA 90024 (home). Pinnacle Books, Inc., 1 Century Plaza, 2029 Century Park E., Los Angeles, CA 90067. 213-552-9111 (office); *Nashville.* Janice Sanford, Nolensville, TN 37135. 615-776-2428 (home). 615-784-3040 (lib.); *New York.* Margaret Klee Lichtenberg, Wanderer Books, Simon & Schuster, 1230 Avenue of the Americas, New York, NY 10020. 212-245-6400, ext. 1433 (office). 712 Washington St., New York, NY 10014. 212-929-1355 (home); *Pittsburgh.* Linda Marcus, 1228 Bennington Ave., Pittsburgh, PA 15217. 412-682-6397; *San Francisco.* Adele Horowitz, Presidio Press, 31 Pamaron Way, Novato, CA 94947. 415-457-5850 (office). 45 De Sota, San Francisco, CA 94127 (home); *Washington, DC/ Baltimore.* Susan Bistline, President, Bistline Associates, 1629 K St. N.W., Suite 401, Washington, DC 20006. 202-223-4490.

INTERNATIONAL AND FOREIGN BOOK TRADE ASSOCIATIONS

For Canadian book trade associations, see the preceding section on Book Trade Associations, United States and Canada. For a more extensive list of book trade organizations outside the United States and Canada, with more detailed information, consult *International Literary Market Place* (R. R. Bowker). An annual publication, it also provides extensive lists of major bookstores and publishers in each country.

INTERNATIONAL

Antiquarian Booksellers Assn. (International), 154 Buckingham Palace Rd., London SW1W 9TZ, England.

International Booksellers Federation (IBF), Grünangergasse 4, A-1010 Vienna 1, Austria. *Secy.-Gen.* Gerhard Prosser.

International League of Antiquarian Booksellers, 5 Bloomsbury St., London WC1B 3QE, England. *Pres.* Stanley Crowe.

International Publishers Assn., 3 av. de Miremont, CH-1206 Geneva, Switzerland. *Secy.-Gen.* J. Alexis Koutchoumow.

NATIONAL

Argentina

Cámara Argentina de Editores de Libros (Council of Argentine Book Publishers), Talcahuano 374, p. 3, Of. 7, Buenos Aires 1013.

Cámara Argentina de Publicaciones (Argentine Publications Assn.), Reconquista 1011, p. 6, 1003 Buenos Aires. *Pres.* Modesto Ederra.

Cámara Argentina del Libro (Argentine Book Assn.), Av. Belgrano 1580, p. 6, 1093 Buenos Aires. *Pres.* Eustasio A. Garcia.

Federación Argentina de Librerías, Papelerías y Actividades Afines (Federation of Bookstores, Stationers and Related Activities), España 848, Losario, Santa Fé.

Australia

Assn. of Australian Univ. Presses, c/o Australian National Univ. Press, Box 4, Canberra, A.C.T. *Pres.* Brian Clouston.

Australian Book Publishers Assn., 163 Clarence St., Sydney, N.S.W. 2000.

Australian Booksellers Assn., Box 3254, Sydney, N.S.W. 2001.

Wholesale Booksellers Assn. of Australia, c/o Book Supplies Pty. Ltd., 55 York St., Sydney, N.S.W. 2000. *Secy.* David Joel.

Austria

Hauptverband der graphischen Unternehmungen Österreichs (Austrian Graphical Assn.), Grünangergasse 4, A-1010 Vienna 1.

Hauptverband des österreichischen Buchhandels (Austrian Publishers and Booksellers Assn.), Grünangergasse 4, A-1010 Vienna. *Secy.* Gerhard Prosser.

Osterreichischer Verlegerverband (Assn. of Austrian Publishers), Grünangergasse 4, A-1010 Vienna. *Secy.* Gerhard Prosser.

Verband der Antiquare Österreichs (Austrian Antiquarian Booksellers Assn.), Grünangergasse 4, A-1010 Vienna. *Secy.* Gerhard Prosser.

Belgium

Cercle Belge de la Librairie (Belgian Booksellers Assn.), Rue du Luxembourg 5, bte. 1, B-1040 Brussels. *Admin. Secy.* R. Mertens.

Fédération des Editeurs Belges (Belgian Publishers Assn.), 111 av. du Parc, B-1060 Brussels. *Dir.* J. De Raeymaeker.

Syndicat Belge de la Librairie Ancienne et Moderne (Belgian Assn. of Antiquarian and Modern Booksellers), r. du Chêne 21, B-1000 Brussels.

Vereniging ter Bevordering van het Vlaamse Boekwezen (Assn. for the Promotion of Flemish Books), Frankrijklei 93, B-2000 Antwerp. *Secy.* A. Wouters. Member organizations: Algemene Vlaamse Boekverkopersbond; Uitgeversbond-Vereniging van Uitgevers van Nederlandstalige Boeken at the same address; and Bond-Alleenverkopers van Nederlandstalige Boeken (book importers), De Smethlaan 4, B-1980 Tervuren. *Secy.* J. van den Berg.

Bolivia

Cámara Boliviana del Libro (Bolivian Booksellers Assn.), Librería Los Amigos del Libro, Box 682, La Paz. *Secy.* Peter Lewy S.

Brazil

Associação Brasileira de Livreiors Antiquarios (Brazilian Assn. of Antiquarian Booksellers), Rua Cosme Vehlo 800, Rio de Janeiro.

Associação Brasileira do Livro (Brazilian Booksellers Assn.), Av. 13 de Maio 23, andar 16, Rio de Janeiro.

Camara Brasileira do Livro (Brazilian Book Assn.), Av. Ipiranga 1267, andar 10, São Paulo. *Secy.* Jose Gorayeb.

Sindicato Nacional dos Editôres de Livros (Brazilian Book Publishers Assn.), Av. Rio Branco 37, andar 15, Rio de Janeiro. *Exec. Secy.* Maria Helena Geordane.

Bulgaria

Drzavno Obedinenie Bulgarska Kniga (State Bulgarian Book Assn.), pl. Slavejkov 11, Sofia.

Soyuz Knigoizdatelite i Knizharite (Union of Publishers and Booksellers), vu Solum 4, Sofia.

Burma

Burmese Publishers Union, 146 Bogyoke Market, Rangoon.

Chile

Cámara Chilena del Libro, Casilla 2787, Santiago.

Colombia

Cámara Colombiana de la Industria Editorial (Colombian Publishers Council), Cr. 7a, No. 17-51, Of. 409-410, Apdo. áereo 8998, Bogotá. *Exec. Secy.* Hipólito Hincapié.

Czechoslovakia

Ministerstvo Kultury CSR, Odbor Knižni Kultury (Ministry of Culture CSR, Dept. for Publishing and Book Trade), Staré Mésto, námesti Pěrstýně 1, 117 65 Prague 1.

Slovak Center for Publishing and Booktrade, c/o SLOVART, Foreign Trade Co. Ltd., Gottwaldovo námesti 6, 805 32 Bratislava. *Deputy Gen. Mgr.* Pavol Holéczy.

Denmark

Den Danske Antikvarboghandlerforening (Danish Antiquarian Booksellers Assn.), Silkegade 11, DK-1113 Copenhagen.

Danske Boghandleres Bogimport A/S (Danish Booksellers Bookimport Ltd.), Herlev Hovedgade 199, Box 546, DK-2730 Herlev. *Dir.* Hans Pedersen.

Den Danske Boghandlerforening (Danish Booksellers Assn.), Boghandlernes Hus, Siljangade 6, DK-2300 Copenhagen S. *Secy.* Elisabeth Brodersen.

Den Danske Forlaeggerforening (Danish Publishers Assn.), Købmagergade 11, DK-1150 Copenhagen K. *Dir.* Erik V. Krustrup.

Ecuador

Sociedad de Libreros del Ecuador (Booksellers Society of Ecuador), C. Bolivar 268 y Venezuela, Of. 501, p. 5, Quito. *Secy.* Eduardo Ruiz G.

Finland

Kirja-ja Paperikauppojen Liittory (Finnish Booksellers and Stationers Assn.), Pieni Roobertinkatu 13 B 26, SF-00130 Helsinki 13. *Secy.* Pentti Kuopio.

Suomen Antikvariaattiyhdistys Finska Antikvariatföreningen (Finnish Antiquarian Booksellers Assn.), P. Makasiininkatu 6, Helsinki 13.

Suomen Kustannusyhdistys (Publishers Assn. of Finland), Bulevardi 6A 10, SF-00120 Helsinki 12. *Secy.-Gen.* Unto Lappi.

France

Cercle de la Librairie (Booksellers Circle), 117 bd. St.-Germain, F-75279 Paris, Cedex 06.

Fédération française des Syndicats de Libraires (French Booksellers Assn.), 117 bd. St.-Germain, F-75279 Paris, Cedex 06.

Office de Promotion de l'Edition Française (Promotion Office of French Publishing), 117 bd. St.-Germain, F-75279, Paris, Cedex 06. *Asst. Dir.* Marc Franconie.

Syndicat National de l'Edition (French Publishers Assn.), 117 bd. St.-Germain, F-75279 Paris, Cedex 06. *Secy.* Pierre Fredet.

Syndicat National de la Librairie ancienne et moderne (Assn. of Antiquarian and Modern Booksellers), 117 bd. St.-Germain, F-75279 Paris, Cedex 06. *Secy.* G. Fleury.

Syndicat National des Importateurs et Exportateurs de Livres (National French Assn. of Book Importers and Exporters), 117 bd. St.-Germain, F-75279 Paris, Cedex 06.

Germany (Democratic Republic of)

Börsenverein der Deutschen Buchhandler zu Leipzig (Assn. of GDR Publishers and Booksellers in Leipzig), Gerichtweg 26, 701 Leipzig.

Germany (Federal Republic of)

Börsenverein des deutschen Buchhändels (German Publishers and Booksellers Assn.), Grosser Hirschgraben 17-21, Box 2404, D-6000 Frankfurt am Main 1. *Secy.* Hans-Karl von Kupsch.

Bundesverein der deutschen Versandbuchhändler e.V. (National Federation of German Mail-Order Booksellers), Rheinstr. 30/32, D-6200 Wiesbaden.

Landesverband der Buchhändler und Verleger in Niedersachsen e.V. (Provincial Federation of Booksellers and Publishers in Lower Saxony), Hausmannstr. 2, D-3000 Hannover 1. *Managing Dir.* Wolfgang Grimpe.

Verband Bayerischer Verlage und Buchhandlungen e.V. (Bavarian Publishers & Booksellers Federation), Thierschstr. 17, D-8000 Munich 22. *Secy.* F. Nosske.

Verband der Verlage und Buchhandlungen in Baden-Württemberg (Federation of Publishers & Booksellers in Baden-Württemberg), Leonhardsplatz 28, D-7000 Stuttgart.

Verband deutscher Antiquare e.V. (German Antiquarian Booksellers Assn.), Leonhardsplatz 28, D-7000 Stuttgart 1.

Verband Deutscher Bahnhofsbuchhändler e.V. (Federation of German Station Booksellers), Grosser Hirschgraben 19H, D-6000 Frankfurt am Main 1.

Verband Deutscher Buch-, Zeitungs- und Zeitschriften-Grossisten e.V. (Federation of German Wholesalers of Books, Newspapers and Periodicals), Classen-Kappelmann-Str. 24, D-5000 Cologne 41.

Verband deutscher Bühnenverleger e.V. (Federation of German Theatrical Publishers), Bundesallee 23, D-1000 Berlin 31.

Verband deutscher Schulbuchhändler e.V. (Federation of German Textbook Sellers), Marienstr. 41, D-4, Düsseldorf.

Vereinigung evangelischer Buchhändler (Assn. of Protestant Booksellers), Lehenstr. 31, D-7000 Stuttgart 1.

Ghana

Ghana Booksellers Assn., Box 7869, Accra.

Great Britain

See United Kingdom.

Greece

Syllogos Ekdoton kai Vivliopolon Athinon (Assn. of Publishers and Booksellers of Athens), Stadiou 40, Athens.

Syllogos Ekdoton Vivliopolon (Greek Publishers Assn.), 22-24 Har. Trikoupi St., Athens.

Hong Kong

Hong Kong Booksellers & Stationers Assn., Man Wah House, Kowloon.

Hungary

Magyar Könyvkiadók és Könyvterjesztök Egyesülése (Assn. of Hungarian Publishers and Booksellers), Vörösmarty tér 1, 1051 Budapest. *Pres.* György Bernát.

Iceland

Booksellers Assn. of Iceland, Skólavördustíg 2, Reykjavik.

Iceland Publishers Assn., Laufasvegi 12, 101 Reykjavik. *Pres.* Arnbjorn Kristinsson, Freyjugötu 14, 101 Reykjavik.

India

All-India Booksellers and Publishers Assn., 17L Connaught Pl., New Delhi 1. *Pres.* Mohan Lal Choudary.

All-India Hindi Publishers Assns., 3625 Subhash Marg, 110 002 New Delhi.

Bombay Booksellers & Publishers Assn., c/o Bhadkamkar Marg, Navjivan Cooperative Housing Society, Bldg. 3, Sixth fl., Office 25, Bombay 400 008.

Booksellers & Publishers Assn. of South India, c/o Higginbothams Ltd., Mount Rd., 600 002 Madras.

Delhi State Booksellers & Publishers Assn., c/o The Students' Stores, Box 1511, 110 006 Delhi. *Secy.* Devendra Sharma.

Educational Publishers Assn., 4c Daryaganj, New Delhi.

Federation of Indian Publishers, M-138, Connaught Circus, New Delhi 110 001. *Pres.* G. A. Vazirani; *Exec. Secy.* M. C. Minocha.

Indian Assn. of Univ. Presses, Calcutta Univ. Press, Calcutta. *Secy.* S. Kanjilal.

Publishers Assn. of India, 14-18 Calicut St., Ballard Estate, Bombay 400 038. *Chmn.* P. S. Jayasinghe.

Indonesia

Ikatan Penerbit Indonesia (IKAPI) (Assn. of Indonesian Book Publishers), Jalan Pengarengan 32, Jakarta Pusat III/4. *Pres.* Ismid Hadad. P.T. Indira, Jalan Sam Ratulangie 37, Box 181, Jakarta Pusat. *Managing Dir.* Wahyudi D.

Iran

Iranian Publishers Assn., Box 1030, Tehran.

Ireland (Republic of)

Book Assn. of Ireland, 21 Shaw St., Dublin 2. *Secy.* Eoin O'Keeffe.

CLE/Irish Book Publishers Assn., 7-8 Lower Abbey St., Dublin 1. *Secy.* Hilary Kennedy.

Israel

Book & Printing Center of the Israel Export Institute, Box 29732, 47 Nahlat Benyamin St., Tel Aviv. *Dir.* Shlomo Erel.

Book Publishers Assn. of Israel, Box 20123, 29 Carlebach St., Tel Aviv. *Exec. Dir.* Benjamin Sella; *International Promotion and Literary Rights Dept. Dir.* Lorna Soifer.

Israel Book Importers Assn., c/o Emanuel Brown, 35 Allenby Rd., Tel Aviv.

Italy

Associazione Italiana degli Editori di Musica (Italian Assn. of Music Publishers) Piazza del Liberty 2, I-20121 Milan.

Associazione Italiana Editori (Italian Publishers Assn.), Via delle Erbe 2, I-20121 Milan. *Secy.* Archille Ormezzano.

Associazione Librai Antiquari d'Italia (Antiquarian Booksellers Assn. of Italy), Via Jacopo Nardi 6, I-50132 Florence. *Pres.* Renzo Rizzi.

Associazione Librai Italiani (Italian Booksellers Assn.), Piazza G. G. Belli 2, I-00153 Rome.

Jamaica

Booksellers Assn. of Jamaica, c/o Sangster's Book Stores, Ltd., Box 366, 97 Harbour St., Kingston.

Japan

Antiquarian Booksellers Assn. of Japan, 29 San-ei-cho, Shinjuku-ku, Tokyo 160.

Books-on-Japan-in-English Club, Shinnichibo Bldg., 2-1 Sarugaku-cho 1-chome, Chiyoda-ku, Tokyo 101.

Japan Book Importers Assn., Rm. 302, Aizawa Bldg., 20-3 Nihonbashi, 1-chome, Chuoku, Tokyo 103. *Secy.* Kazushige Terakubo.

Japan Book Publishers Assn., 6 Fukuromachi, Shinjuku-ku, Tokyo 162. *Secy.* S. Sasaki.

Japan Booksellers Federation, 1-2 Surugadai, Kanda, Chiyoda-ku, Tokyo 101.

Textbook Publishers Assn. of Japan (Kyokasho Kyokai), 20-2 Honshiocho Shinjuku-ku, Tokyo 160. *Secy.* Masae Kusaka.

Kenya

Kenya Publishers Assn., Box 72532, Nairobi.

Korea (Republic of)

Korean Publishers Assn., 105-2 Sagandong, Chongno-ku, Seoul 110. *Secy.* Kyung-hoon Lee.

Luxembourg

Fédération des Commerçants–Groupe Papetiers-Libraires (Federation of Retailers, Group for Stationers and Booksellers), 21 Allée Scheffer, Luxembourg. *Pres.* Jean-Pierre Krippler; *Secy.* Victor Delcourt.

Malaysia

Malaysian Book Publishers Assn., Box 335, Kuala Lumpur 01-02. *Hon. Secy.* J. B. Ho.

Mexico

Cámara Nacional de la Industria Editorial (Mexican Publishers Assn.), Vallarta 21, p. 3, México 4, D.F. *Secy.* Rafael Servin Arroyo.

Instituto Mexicano del Libro A.C. (Mexican Book Institute), Paseo de la Reforma 95, Dept. 1024, México 7, D.F. *Secy.-Gen.* Isabel Ruiz González.

Morocco

Association des Libraires du Maroc (Assn. of Booksellers of Morocco), 67 r. de Foucauld, Casablanca.

Netherlands

Koninklijke Nederlandse Uitgeversbond (Royal Dutch Publishers Assn.), Nieuwe Zijds Voorburgwal 44, 1012 SB Amsterdam. *Secy.* R. M. Vrij; *Managing Dir.* A. Th. Hulskamp.

Nederlandsche Vereeniging van Antiquaren (Antiquarian Booksellers Assn. of the Netherlands), Nieuwe Spiegelstra. 40, 1017-DG Amsterdam. *Pres.* A. Gerits.

Nederlandse Boekverkopersbond (Booksellers Assn. of the Netherlands), Waalsdorperweg 119, 2597-HS The Hague. *Secy.* Y. C. van Straaler.

Vereeniging ter bevordering van de belangen des Boekhandels (Dutch Book Trade Assn.), Lassusstraat 9, Amsterdam-Z. *Secy.* M. van Vollenhoven-Nagel.

New Zealand

Book Promotions (N.Z.) Ltd., Box 11-377, Wellington. *Secy.* K. Fortune.

Book Publishers Assn. of New Zealand, Box 78071, Grey Lynn, Auckland 2. *Pres.* D. J. Heap. *Dir.* Gerard Reid.

Book Tokens (N.Z.) Ltd., Box 11-377, Wellington. *Secy.* K. Fortune.

Booksellers Assn. of New Zealand, Inc., Box 11-377, Wellington. *Dir.* Harold T. White.

Nigeria

Nigerian Publishers Assn., c/o P.M.B. 5164, Ibadan.

Univ. Booksellers Assn. of Nigeria, c/o Univ. of Ife Bookshop, Ltd., Univ. of Ife, Ile-Ife.

Norway

Norsk Antikvarbokhandlerforening (Norwegian Antiquarian Booksellers Assn.), Ullevalsveien 1, Oslo 1.

Den norske Bokhandlerforening (Norwegian Booksellers Assn.), Øvre Vollgate 15, Oslo 1.

Norsk Bokhandler-Medhjelper-Forening (Norwegian Book Trade Employees Assn.), Øvre Volgate 15, Oslo 1.

Den norske Forleggerforening (Norwegian Publishers Assn.), Øvre Vollgate 15, Oslo 1. *Dir.* Tor Solumsmoen.

Norsk Musikkforleggerforening (Norwegian Music Publishers Assn.), Box 1499 Vika, Oslo 1.

Pakistan

The Pakistan Publishers and Booksellers Assn., YMCA Bldg., Shahra-e-Quaid-e-Azam, Lahore.

Paraguay

Cámara Paraguaya del Libro (Paraguayan Publishers Assn.), Librería Internacional, Estrella 380, Asuncion.

Peru

Cámara Peruana del Libro (Peruvian Publishers Assn.), Apdo. 10253, Lima.

Philippines

Philippine Book Dealers Assn., c/o Philippine Education Co., Quezon Ave., corner Banawe, Metro Manila. *Pres.* Jose C. Benedicto.

Philippine Educational Publishers Assn., 927 Quezon Ave., Quezon City 3008, Metro Manila. *Pres.* Jesus Ernesto R. Sibal.

Poland

Polskie Towarzystwo Wydawców Ksiaźek (Polish Publishers Assn.), ul. Mazowiecka 2/4, 00-048 Warsaw.

Stowarzyszenie Księgarzy Polskich Zarząd Główny (Assn. of Polish Booksellers), ul. Mokotowska 4/6, 00-641 Warsaw. *Pres.* Tadeusz Hussak.

Portugal

Associação Portuguesa dos Editores e Livreiros (Portuguese Assn. of Publishers and Booksellers), Largo de Andaluz 16, 1, Esq., Lisbon 1.

Rhodesia

Advertising Media Assn., c/o Associated Chambers of Commerce of Zimbabwe Rhodesia, Box 1934, Salisbury.

Booksellers Assn. of Rhodesia, Box 1934, Salisbury. *Hon. Secy.* L. Craven.

Romania

Centrala editorială (Romanian Publishing Center), Piața Scînteii 1, R-71341 Bucharest. *Gen. Dir.* Gheorghe Trandafir.

Singapore

Singapore Book Publishers Assn., Box 846, Colombo Court Post Office, Singapore 0617. *Secy.* Lena U Wen Lim.

Singapore Booksellers Assn., 428-429 Katong Shopping Center, Singapore 15. *Pres.* N. T. S. Chopra.

South Africa (Republic of)

Associated Booksellers of Southern Africa, One Meerendal, Nightingale Way, Pinelands 7405. *Secy.* P. G. van Rooyen.

Book Trade Assn. of South Africa, Box 337, Bergvlei 2012.

Overseas Publishers Representatives Assn. of South Africa, Box 8879, Johannesburg. *Secy.* P. Hardingham.

South African Publishers Assn., Box 123, Kenwyn 7790. *Secy.* P. G. van Rooyen.

Spain

Federación de Gremios de Editores de España (Spanish Federation of Publishers Assns.), General Pardiñas 29, Madrid 1. *1st V.P.* Francisco Pérez González.

Gremi d'Editors de Catalunya (Assn. of Catalonian Publishers), Mallorca, 272-274, Barcelona 37. *Pres.* Antoni Comas Baldellou.

Gremio Nacional de Libreros (Assn. of Spanish Booksellers), Fernandez de la Hoz 12, Madrid 4.

Gremio Sindical de Libreros de Barcelona (Assn. of Barcelona Booksellers), C. Mallorca 272-276, Barcelona 9.

Instituto Nacional del Libro Español (Spanish Publishers and Booksellers Institute), Santiago Rusiñol 8-10, Madrid 3. *Secy.* Eduardo Nolla López.

Sri Lanka

Booksellers Assn. of Sri Lanka, Box 244, Colombo 2. *Secy.* W. L. Mendis.

Sri Lanka Publishers Assn., 61 Sangaraja Mawatha, Colombo 10. *Secy.-Gen.* Eamon Kariyakarawana.

Sweden

Svenska Antikvariatföreningen, c/o Rönnells, Birger Jarlsgatan 32, S-11429 Stockholm.

Svenska Bokförläggareföreningen (Swedish Publishers Assn.), Srearägen 52, S-111 34 Stockholm. *Managing Dir.* Jonas Modig.

Svenska Bokhandlareföreningen, Div. of Bok-, Pappers- och Kontorsvaruförbundet (Swedish Booksellers Assn., Div. of Book, Stationery and Office Supply Dealers), Skeppargatan 27, S-114 52 Stockholm. *Secy.* Per Nordenson.

Svenska Musikförläggareföreningen (Swedish Music Publishers Assn.), Drottninggt 81A, S-11160 Stockholm.

Svenska Tryckeriföreningen (Swedish Printing Industries Federation), Blasieholmsgatan 4A, Box 16383, S-10327 Stockholm. *Managing Dir.* Per Gålmark.

Switzerland

Schweizerischer Buchhändler- und Verleger-Verband (Swiss German-Language Booksellers and Publishers Assn.), Bellerivestr. 3, CH-8008 Zurich. *Managing Dir.* Peter Oprecht.

Società Editori della Svizzera Italiana (Assn. of Publishers for Italian-Speaking Switzerland), Viale Portone 4, CP 282, CH-6501 Bellinzona.

Societě des Libraires et Editeurs de la Suisse Romande (Assn. of Swiss French-Language Booksellers and Publishers), 2 av. Agassiz, CH-1001 Lausanne. *Secy.* Robert Junod.

Vereinigung der Buchantiquare und Kupferstichhändler der Schweiz (Assn. of Swiss Antiquarians and Print Dealers), c/o Markus Krebser, Bälliz 64, CH-3601 Thun.

Thailand

Publishers and Booksellers Assn. of Thailand, c/o *Secy.* Plearnpit Praepanich Praepittaya L.P., 115/10 Soi Asoke, Sukhumvit Rd., Bangkok.

Tunisia

Syndicat des Libraires de Tunisie (Tunisian Booksellers Assn.), 10 av. de France, Tunis.

Turkey

Editörler Derneği (Publishers Assn.), Ankara Caddesi 60, Istanbul.

United Kingdom

Assn. of Learned and Professional Society Publishers, R. J. Millson, c/o Institution of Mechanical Engineers, 1 Birdcage Walk, London SW1H 9JJ.

Booksellers Assn. of Great Britain & Ireland, 154 Buckingham Palace Rd., London SW1W 9TZ. *Dir.* G. R. Davies.

The Educational Publishers Council, 19 Bedford Sq., London WC1B 3HJ. *Dir.* John R. M. Davies.

National Book League, Book House, East Hill, London SW18. *Dir.* Martyn Goff, O.B.E.

National Federation of Retail Newsagents, 2 Bridewell Pl., London EC4V 6AR.

The Publishers Assn., 19 Bedford Sq., London WC1B 3HJ. *Secy. & Chief Exec.* Clive Bradley.

Uruguay

Asociación de Libreros del Uruguay (Uruguayan Booksellers Assn.), Av. Uruguay 1325, Montevideo.

Cámara Uruguaya del Libro (Uruguayan Publishing Council), Carlos Roxlo 1446, p. 1, Apdo. 2, Montevideo. *Secy.* Arnaldo Medone.

Yugoslavia

Assn. of Yugoslav Publishers and Booksellers, Kneza Miloša Str. 25/I, Box 883, Belgrade. *Pres.* Jelenko Bućevac.

Zambia

Booksellers Assn. of Zambia, Box 139, Ndola.

U.S. BOOK DISTRIBUTION AND EXCHANGE PROGRAMS

THE ASIA FOUNDATION
550 Kearny St., San Francisco, CA 94108

OBJECTIVE

A publicly supported nonprofit philanthropic organization founded in 1954 and incorporated in the state of California, the Asia Foundation's main office is in San Francisco. It has a branch office in Washington, D.C., with resident offices and programs in 12 countries from Korea through Southeast Asia to Afghanistan.

The purpose of Books for Asia, a project of the Asia Foundation, is to send American books and professional journals quickly and efficiently to people in Asia who need them urgently. The Asia Foundation's field offices keep the San Francisco staff informed about specific book requirements. Regular shipments are made based on this information.

ACTIVITIES

Under the Asia Foundation's program, textbooks, general literature, reference works, and specialized books and journals are donated by individuals, volunteer civic and campus groups, public institutions, school districts, and publishing houses.

Books are sent to Asia not only for student use but for businesspeople, people in the professions, scholars, government administrators, civic leaders, and libraries for the general public. During the past 24 years, it has shipped more than 16 million books and journals to Asia.

Funds for shipping, as well as donations of books, are needed. Cash contributions for Books for Asia made to the Asia Foundation are tax deductible. Donations of books and journals are also deductible under special provisions of the tax laws. Address inquiries to Carlton Lowenberg, Dir., Books for Asia, 451 Sixth St., San Francisco, CA 94103. 415-982-4640.

BOARD OF TRUSTEES

The Asia Foundation is governed by a board of trustees of private citizens broadly representative of the American interest in assisting Asians in the further growth and development of their own societies. The president is Haydn Williams. The chairman of the board of trustees is Russell G. Smith. Other board members are Barry Bingham, Sr., Ellsworth Bunker, Mrs. John Sherman Cooper, Herbert C. Cornuelle, R. G. Follis, R. Allen Griffin, Caryl P. Haskins, Charles J. Hitch, Stuart T. K. Ho, Ernest M. Howell, George F. Jewett, Jr., Grayson Kirk, Robert Huntington Knight, Turner H. McBaine, George C. McGhee, Robbins Milbank, Mrs. Maurice T. Moore, George R. Packard, Mrs. Charles H. Percy, Rudolph A. Peterson, Lucian W. Pye, Madeleine Haas Russell, and Brayton Wilbur, Jr.

DARIEN BOOK AID PLAN, INC.
1926 Post Rd., Darien, CT 06820
203-655-2777

OBJECTIVE

A nonprofit volunteer women's organization formed in 1949 by a group of residents of Darien, Conn. The bylaws state: "The purpose of this Association shall be to build a foundation of peace, understanding and friendship by the free distribution of books and selected magazines." Book Aid has been a pioneer in recycling, as its motto is "Make Your Books Do Double Duty."

ACTIVITIES

Now in its thirtieth year, the organization has sent over 1,100 tons of free material to more than 100 foreign countries and within the United States. Reading material is sent only on request. Letters are received from libraries, colleges, schools, hospitals, and Peace Corps and Vista volunteers. All are considered and order slips are prepared for those Book Aid is able to fill. This past year 35.8 tons of books were sent to 60 countries and 18 states. Book Aid is now the principal source of books for Peace Corps volunteers.

Since 1970 free reading material has been sent via Vista volunteers in the United States to teenage and community centers, Indian reservations, correctional institutions, schools, and to other organized groups that have a real need.

EXCHANGE OF BOOKS

The lobby of the workshop at 1926 Post Rd., Darien, Connecticut, is always open to receive donations of reading material in good condition. Contributions of books from individuals, schools, libraries, and publishers are always greatly appreciated. Book contributions are deductible for tax purposes but donors must make their own appraisal of value.

Every book received is screened for good print, good condition, and good content. Except for classics, the policy is to send only up-to-date, good to excellent hardcover and paperback educational and recreational books, both fiction and nonfiction. Yellowed, marked, or torn pages, broken or dirty bindings, too fine print, or out-of-date or unsuitable content are reasons for elimination of material. It is helpful if contributors screen their books according to these criteria before sending them to Book Aid.

All material must be sent prepaid. No collect shipments can be accepted. Anyone planning to donate a very large amount of material should contact Book Aid in advance, as storage space is limited.

Request letters should include complete address, name, size, and age level of group; categories of subjects; number of multiple copies needed; and any other information that would aid the volunteer in filling the order. Representatives of accredited groups may choose books at the workshop. If large amounts are desired, the representatives should contact Book Aid before coming to select material.

THE ENGLISH-SPEAKING UNION OF THE UNITED STATES
16 E. 69 St., New York, NY 10021
212-879-6800

OBJECTIVE

In an effort to foster understanding, mutual trust, and friendship between the people of the United States of America and the rest of the English-speaking world, the English-Speaking Union (E-SU) sponsors two international book programs. In 1947, the Books-Across-the-Sea (BAS) activity was invited to become a part of the national education and information program of the English-Speaking Unions of the United States and the Commonwealth, and in 1961, the Commonwealth Schoolbook Fund was initiated as a volunteer program of the New York branch. Information concerning the programs may be obtained from the coordinator of the BAS program, Mary Ellen Moll, and from Susan Fried, founder of the Commonwealth Schoolbook Fund.

E-SU OFFICERS

The chairperson of the English-Speaking Union is the Honorable Anne Armstrong, former ambassador to the Court of St. James's. The president is John I. B. McCulloch, CBE.

BOOKS-ACROSS-THE-SEA

The Books-Across-the-Sea program, started as an activity of the Outpost—a society of Americans in war-torn Britain—to help interpret contemporary American life, promotes the exchange of books between the Commonwealth and the United States. The collection, originally housed by the R. R. Bowker Co., Columbia University, and the New York branch of E-SU, now comprises a unique Commonwealth Library of over 8,600 books at E-SU's national headquarters in New York City, and has been expanded to include books from Australia, Canada, India, and New Zealand. These books are available for use as loan collections by the E-SU's 85 branches and by schools and other institutions. The library at national headquarters welcomes reference use by scholars and others interested in Commonwealth research, primarily in the fields of the humanities and social sciences.

American books sent to the Commonwealth countries aim to present life and thought in America. Generally they are books that are not widely printed outside the United States. Adult and juvenile panels, composed of prominent men and women from the book world, meet regularly to select from books submitted by publishers those that best fulfill the purpose of the program. These selections are carefully annotated and the resulting lists are widely distributed to libraries, colleges, and individuals. The largest collection is housed in the Page Library at Dartmouth House, London, where it is available to universities, schools, and other institutions. Smaller but growing collections are also available in Australia, Canada, India, and New Zealand.

The books from the Commonwealth are chosen abroad in the same manner and become part of the library at the national headquarters in New York.

COMMONWEALTH SCHOOLBOOK FUND

The Commonwealth Schoolbook Fund is a volunteer program started in 1961 to enable local government-approved schools in developing countries of the Commonwealth to purchase much needed schoolbooks, both in English and in the native tongue.

The administrators of this program work closely with government officials, United Nations missions, and consulates of the countries involved. To date, students in 354 schools have benefited.

FREEDOM HOUSE/BOOKS USA
20 W. 40 St., New York, NY 10018

OBJECTIVE AND ACTIVITIES

A nonprofit, educational program of Freedom House created to distribute American books to potential leaders of the developing nations in Asia, Africa, and Latin America. Some schools, libraries, and other institutions, particularly those not supported by a government, are also sent book collections.

The titles are selected by a committee of prominent authors. Overseas representatives of some 40 American voluntary agencies select the recipients. Volunteers with the Peace Corps overseas also assist in the distribution.

The books are selected to share the American cultural heritage and provide a picture of the United States that will counteract misconceptions about it abroad.

Support for Freedom House/Books USA comes exclusively from the American public on a voluntary basis.

The present operation is the result of a merger in 1967 of the Freedom House Bookshelf and Books USA, Inc. The Bookshelf is in its twenty-first year, while Books USA was created 17 years ago by Edward R. Murrow when he headed the U.S. Information Agency.

There is currently a backlog of thousands of unfilled requests for book packets with additional requests arriving daily. As Mr. Murrow stated, "The hunger of people abroad for books is insatiable."

OFFICERS

The president of Freedom House/Books USA is John Richardson, Jr.; treasurer is Leon Levy; and secretary is Philip van Slyck. Other board members include Roscoe Drummond, columnist; Helen Meyer, president, Dell Publishing Co.; Steuart L. Pittman, attorney; John T. Sargent, president, Doubleday and Co.; Frank E. Taylor, publisher; and Mrs. George C. Vietheer, director, League of Women Voters of New York City. Leonard R. Sussman, executive director of Freedom House, is also the supervisor of the book distribution program.

LAUBACH LITERACY INTERNATIONAL
Box 131, Syracuse, NY 13210
315-422-9121

OBJECTIVE

A nonprofit organization founded in 1955 to motivate and support the voluntary teaching of the 800 million adults in the world who lack the ability to read their native language. Laubach Literacy's goal is that each student achieve a level of reading, writing, language, and basic computation skill that enables him or her to function effectively in those activities of society that normally require literacy skills.

OFFICERS AND TRUSTEES

The principal executives who have responsibility for publishing are Robert S. Laubach, president; Edward H. Pitts, executive vice-president; Alfred J. Morris, managing director, New Readers Press; and Robert F. Caswell, director of educational programs and international publishing.

Trustees of the corporation are Kathy Brodsky, John C. Cairns, Charles A. Chappell, Jr., Jean Coleman, Mrs. J. Foster Collins, David C. Cook III, David Crosson, Russell B. French, David E. Hostetler, Robert S. Laubach, Albert Longden, Gloria Rasberry, Robert Sieber, Betty A. Ward, and Frank T. Wood, Jr. Principal staff members or liaison persons in each country where publishing is underway are H. Amid Mamnoon (Afghanistan), Elizabeth Vencio (Brazil), Maria G. de Rentería (Mexico), Luis Oscar Londono and Hector Piedrahita (Colombia), A. K. John (India), Roberto Batista (Panama), and Ed Mukwereza (Rhodesia).

ACTIVITIES

The support activities of Laubach Literacy are principally development and publishing of books and other learning materials; training volunteers; technical assistance; and administration and funding of international literacy programs. Motivational activities include recruiting volunteers; creating public awareness of the problem of illiteracy; and requesting voluntary donations for program support.

Laubach Literacy's publishing operations focus on the writing, field testing, producing, and distribution of literacy primers and follow-up readers that are written for use by volunteer tutors and adult learners. The publications are designed to teach basic communication skills, including reading and writing, while helping adult learners to identify and implement solutions to their problems. Easy-to-read newspapers and audiovisual aids are used as supplementary materials to help the newly literate develop the problem-solving skills they need to realize their potential. Programs to produce these materials are operating presently in the United States, Panama, Colombia, India, Mexico, and Rhodesia.

The largest Laubach Literacy publishing operation is carried on in the United States by its New Readers Press Division. New Readers Press publishes materials for use by the Laubach volunteer program (National Affiliation for Literacy Advance) in the 50 states and Canada, and for public school programs of adult basic education and special education.

The basic reading "primer" is the five-volume New Streamlined English series, with teacher's guide and many helps. A wide selection of follow-up readers is published in such areas as family life education, health and drugs, jobs and work, religion, social studies and history, consumer information, and other coping skills. *News for You*, a weekly newspaper for adult readers, is published in two easy-to-read levels.

An exemplary program in the international field is being carried on in Colombia, but Laubach-style teaching materials are used in many countries other than those in which this organization is currently involved. Frank C. Laubach, the late founder, was instrumental in developing literacy materials in 103 countries and 312 languages.

Calendar, 1980-1981: Association Meetings and Promotional Events

The list below contains information regarding place and date of association meetings or promotional events that are national or international in scope. Information is as of January 1980. For further details, contact the association directly. Addresses of library associations and book trade associations are listed in Part 7 of this *Bowker Annual*. For additional information on book trade and promotional events, see the *1980 Exhibits Directory*, published by the Association of American Publishers; *Chase's Calendar of Annual Events*, published by the Apple Tree Press, Box 1012, Flint, Mich. 49501; *Literary Market Place* and *International Literary Market Place*, published by R. R. Bowker; *Publishers Weekly* "Calendar," appearing in each issue; and *Library Journal's* "Calendar" feature, appearing in each semimonthly issue.

1980

May

5-9	International Reading Association	St. Louis, MO
8-11	Association of American Publishers	Colorado Springs, CO
9-14	International Book Festival	Nice, France
12-16	Associated Church Press	Nashville, TN
15-16	Association of Research Libraries	Salt Lake City, UT
15-18	The Booksellers Association of Great Britain and Ireland	Bristol, England
18-22	International Publishers Association	Stockholm, Sweden
19-22	National Computer Conference	Anaheim, CA
21-26	International Book Fair	Warsaw, Poland
22-27	International Book Fair	Quebec, Canada
27-30	Information Industry Association	Washington, DC
*	American Society for Information Science	Pittsburgh, PA

June

7-10	American Booksellers Association	Chicago, IL
7-12	Special Libraries Association (conference)	Washington, DC
12-18	Canadian Library Association	Vancouver, B.C.
14-19	Medical Library Association	Washington, DC
16-20	American Theological Library Association	Denver, CO
22-25	American Association of Law Libraries	St. Louis, MO
22-25	Association of American University Presses	Hershey, PA
6/29-7/1	Church and Synagogue Library Association	Hartford, CT

*To be announced.

6/29-7/4	Association of College and Research Libraries	New York, NY
6/29-7/5	American Library Association	New York, NY
6/29-7/5	Theatre Library Association	New York, NY (with ALA)

July

1-6	National Education Association	Los Angeles, CA
20-24	Christian Booksellers Association	Dallas, TX
26-29	Canadian Booksellers Association	*

August

3-7	International Association of Printing House Craftsmen	Las Vegas, NV
12-15	Theatre Library Association	New York, NY (with ATA)
*	Associated Booksellers of Southern Africa, Ltd.	Johannesburg, South Africa

September

*	International Micrographic Congress	Hong Kong
18-23	International Board on Books for Young People	*

October

2-5	Antiquarian Booksellers Association of America	New York, NY
5-7	London Book Fair	London, England
5-10	American Society for Information Science	Anaheim, CA
6-8	Face to Face: The Annual Publishing Conference and Exposition	New York, NY
7-10	Information Industry Assn. Conference	San Francisco, CA
8-13	Frankfurt Book Fair	Frankfurt, Germany
9-11	National Science Teachers Association	Cleveland, Ohio
10-12	Boston Globe Book Festival	Boston, MA
15-16	Association of Research Libraries	Washington, DC
19-22	Association of Records Managers and Administrators	Boston, MA
26-29	Book Manufacturers Institute	Las Palmas, CA
*	Interuniversity Communications Council (EDUCOM)	*
*	Special Libraries Association (meeting)	New York, NY

November

12-14	National Micrographics Association	Phoenix, AZ
19-23	National Council for the Social Studies	New Orleans, LA
21-24	National Association for the Education of Young Children	San Francisco, CA
21-26	National Council of Teachers of English	Cincinnati, OH

*To be announced.

December

27-30	American Historical Association	Washington, DC
27-30	Modern Language Association	Houston, TX

1981

January

27-30	Special Libraries Association (meeting)	Portland, OR

February

1-7	American Library Association	Washington, DC
13-16	American Association of School Administrators	Atlanta, GA
*	Music Library Association	New Haven, CT

March

15-22	Leipzig Book Fair	Leipzig, Poland

April

2-5	National Science Teachers Association	New York, NY
4-8	National Association of Elementary School Principals	Anaheim, CA
5-10	Association for Educational Communication and Technology	Philadelphia, PA
5-10	Jerusalem International Book Fair	Jerusalem, Israel
10-16	National Art Education Association	Chicago, IL
11-13	Association of California School Administrators	San Francisco, CA
12-16	National Home Study Council	San Antonio, TX
12-17	Association for Childhood Education	Little Rock, AR
13-16	American Educational Research Association	Chicago, IL
19-22	American Association of Community and Junior Colleges	Washington, DC
19-24	National Association of College Stores	Atlanta, GA
20-23	Catholic Library Association	New York, NY
22-25	Music Educators	Minneapolis, MN
22-25	National Council of Teachers of Math	St. Louis, MO
4/27-5/1	International Reading Association	New Orleans, LA

May

4-7	National Computer Conference	Chicago, IL
7-8	Association of Research Libraries	New York, NY
11-13	Association of American Publishers	Bermuda
23-26	American Booksellers Association	Atlanta, GA
5/29-6/4	Medical Library Association	Montreal, Canada

*To be announced.

June

14-18	Special Libraries Association (conference)	Atlanta, GA
6/28-7/1	American Association of Law Libraries	Washington, DC
6/28-7/4	American Library Association	San Francisco, CA
6/28-7/4	Theatre Library Association	San Francisco, CA (with ALA)
*	American Theological Library Association	St. Louis, MO
*	Church and Synagogue Library Association	St. Louis, MO

July

2-7	National Education Association	Minneapolis, MN

October

25-28	Book Manufacturers Institute	Marco Island, FL
25-30	American Society for Information Science	Washington, DC
28-29	Association of Research Libraries	Washington, DC
*	Special Libraries Association (meeting)	New York, NY

December

27-30	Modern Language Association	New York, NY

*To be announced.

Index

A

AACR2, see *Anglo-American Cataloging Rules*
AAHPER, see American Alliance for Health, Physical Education and Recreation
AALL, see American Association of Law Libraries
AAP, see Association of American Publishers
AAP Newsletter, 133, 139
AASL, see American Library Association, American Association of School Librarians
AAUP, see Association of American University Presses
ABA, see American Booksellers Association
ABA Basic Book List, 113
ABA Book Buyer's Handbook, 112
ABA Newswire, 112-113
ABA Sidelines Directory, 113
ACRL, see American Library Association, Association of College and Research Libraries
AGRICOLA, 111
AGRICOLA Users Guide, 111
AIBDA, see Inter-American Association of Agricultural Librarians and Documentalists
AIM, see Associated Information Managers
AIM Career Clearinghouse, 152
AIM Membership Roster, 152
AIM Network, 152
AJL, see Association of Jewish Libraries
ALA, see American Library Association
ALA-AASL-Scholastic Magazines National Poster Contest, 123
"ALA Satellite Seminar on Copyright," 117
ALA's for ERA, 118
ALSC, see American Library Association, Association for Library Service to Children
ALTA, see American Library Association, American Library Trustee Association

ANSC, see American National Standards Committee Z39
ANSI, see American National Standards Institute
AOI, see Accent on Information
ARL, see Association of Research Libraries
ARL Newsletter, 143
ARLIS/NA, see Art Libraries Society of North America
ASCLA, see American Library Association, Association of Specialized and Cooperative Agencies
ASIS, see American Society for Information Science
ATLA, see American Theological Library Association
Abdul Huq, A. M., 493
"About Books," 124
Abstracts: Strengthening Research Library Resources Program, 242
Academic Library Development Program, 266
Academic Library Management Intern Program, 268
Academic Library Program, 266-267
Academic Research and Library Resources, 362
Accent on Information, 63
Action, placement services, 318
Adult Illiteracy in the United States, 362
Affirmative Action Register, placement services, 317
"Agricultural Information Users and Their Needs," 110
Agriculture of the American Indian: A Selected Bibliography, 111
Allyn & Bacon, sues Wiley, 42
Aman, Mohammed M., 493
"America through American Eyes," 135
American Alliance for Health, Physical Education and Recreation, research and information center, 63
American Association of Junior Colleges Career Staffing Center, placement services, 316-317
American Association of Law Libraries, 563-564
placement services, 309

699

American Association of Law Libraries (Cont.)
  Special Interest Sections, 402
American Association of School Librarians, see American Library Association, American Association of School Librarians
American Book Awards, 39, 113, 132, 136
American Bookseller, 112
American Booksellers Association, 112-114
  annual meeting, 39
  BISG support, 443
  Booksellers School, see Booksellers School
American Chemical Society, placement services, 309
American Folklife Center, 96
American Foundation for the Blind, Commission on Standards of Accreditation of Services for the Blind, see Commission on Standards of Accreditation of Services for the Blind
American Libraries, 117
  placement services, 309
American Library Association, 115-124, 565-568
  American Association of School Librarians, 119, 568-572
    national conferences, 34
    Promotion and Recognition of Secondary School Media Programs Committee, 119
  American Library Trustee Association, 119-120, 572-573
    annual conference, 1979, 116-117, 121
  Association for Library Service to Children, 120, 573-576
    Symposium on "Books and Broadcasting for Children," 28-29
    WHCOLIS resolution, 34
  Association of College and Research Libraries, 120, 576-579
    national conference, 120
    placement services, 309
  Association of Specialized and Cooperative Library Agencies, 120-121, 579-582
    background history, 58-59
    grant from OE, 120
    Library Service to the Deaf Section, 59
  Black Caucus, placement service, 310, 319
  Committee on Accreditation, 119
  Freedom to Read Foundation, 27, 118
  grant from Kellogg Foundation, 116
  grant from NEH, 116
  International Relations Office, 491
  International Relations Round Table, program on IFLA activities, 115
  Library Administration and Management Association, 121, 582-583
    Committee on Sexism and Racism Awareness, 121
    publications, 121
    Statistics Coordinating Committee, 363
    Statistics Section, 121, 364-366
  Library and Information Technology Association, 121, 583-585
    Video Cable Communications Section, 121
  Library History Round Table, 122
  midwinter meeting, 1980, 32-33, 117
  Office for Intellectual Freedom, 118-119
  Office for Library Personnel Resources, 123
  Office for Library Service to the Disadvantaged, 123
    grant from Lilly Endowment, 123
    Library Service for American Indian People, 123
  placement services, 309
  Public Information Office, 123-124
  Public Library Association, 121-122, 585-587
  Publishing Services, 117-118
  Reference and Adult Services Division, 122, 587-589
    History Section, Local History Committee, 122
  Resources and Technical Services Division, 122, 589-591
    Resources Section, Library Materials Price Index Committee, 455
  services for the handicapped, 58-59
  Social Responsibilities Round Table, R.I. Affiliate, placement services, 310
  statistical activities, 363-366
  Statistics Coordinating Project, 363
  Young Adults Services Division, 122, 591-593
    miniconferences, 35
    support of youth's rights, 35
  youth services divisions, 34

American Library History Round Table, see American Library Association, Library History Round Table
American Library Trustee Association, see American Library Association, American Library Trustee Association
American Merchant Marine Library Association, 593
American National Standards Committee X12, Business Data Interchange, liaison with ANSC Z39, 127
American National Standards Committee Z39, 124–132, 266, 369–370
 annual meeting, 127
 funding, 127–128
 international activities, 129–132
 officers and subcommittees, 128–129
 standards approved, 125
 Subcommittee 20, Standard for Price Indexes for Library Materials, 370
American National Standards Institute, standards for building adaptation, 56
American Overseas Library Technical Assistance, 493
American Printing House for the Blind, materials for the blind, 61
American Society for Information Science, 593–594
 placement services, 310
American Theological Library Association, 595–596
 placement services, 310
America's Library of Classics, 40
Anglo-American Cataloging Rules, 15, 122, 265, 360–361
Aquaculture and Hydroponics: A Bibliography, 111
Architectural and Transportation Barriers Compliance Board, 54, 56
Archives, 259–263
 documentary materials, preservation, 260
  see also Library materials, conservation and preservation
 manuscript donations, 185
 see also International Council on Archives; International Federation of Film Archives; National Historical Publications and Records Commission; Society of American Archivists
Art Libraries Society of North America, 596–597
 placement services, 310
Ashley Books, sues CBS, 42
Asia Foundation, 689–690
Associated Information Managers, 597–598
Association for Educational Communication & Technology, placement services, 310
Association for Library Service to Children, see American Library Association, Association for Library Service to Children
Association of Academic Health Sciences Library Directors, 598
Association of American Library Schools, 599
Association of American Publishers, 132–140
 annual meeting, 39
 BISG support, 443
 Book Distribution Task Force, 135
 College Division, 137
 Communications Task Force, 135–136
 cooperation with other associations, 139
 Education for Publishing Committee, 133
 Education for Publishing Program, 135
 Freedom to Read Committee, 134
 General Publishing Division, 136
 International Division, 138–139
 International Freedom to Publish Committee, 134–135
 Management Audit Team, technology watch, 133
 Mass Market Paperback Division, Rack Clearance Center, 136–137
 Postal Committee, 114, 134–135
 Professional and Scholarly Publishing Division, 137–138
 School Division, 138
 small publishers conference, 39
 Smaller Publishers Group, 133
 Technical, Scientific and Medical Division, see under Professional and Scholarly Publishing Division
Association of American University Presses
 annual convention, 39
 BISG support, 443
Association of College and Research Libraries, see American Library Association, Association of College and Research Libraries

Association of Jewish Libraries, 600
Association of Research Libraries, 140–145, 600–602
  Center for Chinese Research Materials, 144
  Office of Management Studies, 144
    Academic Library Program, *see* Academic Library Program
    Collections Analysis Project, *see* Collections Analysis Project
    Lilly Endowment support, 144
  programs and projects, 143–144
  Task Force on Statistics, 143
Association of Specialized and Cooperative Library Agencies, *see* American Library Association, Association of Specialized and Cooperative Library Agencies
Association of Visual Science Librarians, 602
Associations, book trade, *see* Book trade associations
Associations, library, *see* Library associations
Associations, publishers, *see* Book trade associations
Audiovisual materials
  bibliography, 523
  fair use of broadcast works, 185
  off-air taping, 71–72
  off-air videotaping, 192
    copyright, 200
  videocassettes, 117
  see also American Library Association, Library and Information Technology Association, Video Cable Communications Section; Microforms; Videodisc technology
Audiovisual Resources in Food and Nutrition, 110
Auel, Jean, 41
Awards, library, 349–355
  see also Grants, library; Scholarships; *also* names of specific awards and grants
Awards, literary, 539–548
  see also Books, best books; Best sellers; *also* names of specific awards

B

BISG, *see* Book Industry Study Group
BISG Bulletin, 445

BLA, see *Bibliographies and Literature of Agriculture*
BMI, *see* Book Manufacturers Institute
BOCES, *see* Board of Cooperative Educational Services
BRS, *see* Bibliographic Retrieval Services
BSDP, *see* Council on Library Resources, Bibliographic Service Development Program
Bender, David R., 167
Benjamin, Curtis G., Award for Creative Publishing, 139
Best sellers, 554–560
Beta Phi Mu, 603–604
Betamax case, 72
Bibliographic control
  standards, 265–266
  see also Universal Bibliographic Control
Bibliographic data bases
  AAP concerns, 135
  linking, 265
  national, 82
  special education materials, 61
  see also Data bases; *also* names of bases, e.g., MEDLARS
Bibliographic Retrieval Services, 66, 67
Bibliographic Society of America, 605
Bibliographies and Literature of Agriculture, 111
Bibliography of Bibliographies, 122
Bibliography of Humanistic Reading for Grade Levels 1–8, 123
Bibliography on Professionalism (NLA), 160
Blume, Judy, 32
Board of Cooperative Educational Services, 30
Bock, D. Joleen, 441
Bologna Children's Fair, 40
Book clubs, 139
Book exports, 510–514
Book fairs, 40
  dates, 695–698 passim
Book imports, 449, 510–514
Book Industries Study Alert, 445
Book Industry Distributions Systems Alert, 445
Book Industry Study Group, 443–446
Book Industry Trends, 444, 445, 475
Book Manufacturers Institute, BISG support, 443
Book outlets, *see* Bookstores
Book programs, 689–694
  see also names of programs

INDEX / 703

Book publishing, *see* Publishing
Book review media, 477
Book sales, 37
  direct marketing, 139
  statistics, 471
  wholesale, 476
  see also Books, consumer expenditures
Book stores, *see* Bookstores
Book trade
  bibliography, 444-445, 532-538
  directories and yearbooks, 537
  international, 40, 138-139
  statistics, *see* Book exports; Book imports; Book sales; Books, consumer expenditures; Books, prices and price indexes; Publishing statistics
  surveys, 443-446
    bibliography, 535-536
Book trade associations, 39-40
  foreign, 682-689
  international, 682-689
  meetings, 114, 695-698
  U.S. and Canada, 676-682
  see also names of specific associations
Bookmobiles, 11
Books
  automatic ordering, 37
  best books, 549-550
    juvenile, 552-554
    young adults, 550-552
    see also Awards, literary; Best sellers
  consumer expenditures, 473-475
  design and production, 536
  distribution, *see* Publishing, distribution of books
  prices and price indexes, 446-453, 458, 459, 460
    British, 463, 464
    German, 455, 465
    Latin American, 454, 466
    see also Library materials, prices and price indexes; Paperback books, prices and price indexes
  sales, *see* Book sales
  title output, *see* Publishing statistics, title output
  translations, 449
  see also Paperback books; Textbooks
"Books and Broadcasting for Children," symposium, 28-29, 120
Booksellers, continuing education, 113
Booksellers School, 113
Bookselling
  backlists, 37
  bibliography, 536-537

  college, AAP concerns, 137
  cost ratios, 37
  expenditures, *see* Books, consumer expenditures
  financial problems, 114-115
  number of, 476-477
Bookstores
  college, AAP concerns, 137
  expenditures, *see* Books, consumer expenditures
  number of, 476-477
Boonin, J. M., 455
Börsenblatt, 483
Boss, Richard, 361
Bowe, Frank, 55
Braunagel, Judith S., 363
British Library Association, International and Comparative Librarianship Group, 491
Broadcasting stations, *see* Telecommunications, broadcasting stations
Brother, Shirley A., 204
Burke, Theresa M., Employment Agency, 307
Business Week, Information Processing Department, 155

C

CAIS, *see* Canadian Association for Information Science
CALA, *see* Chinese-American Librarians Association
CALS, *see* Current Awareness Literature Service
CATLINE, 106
CCC, *see* Copyright Clearance Center
CCLN, *see* Council for Computerized Library Networks
CCRM, *see* Association of Research Libraries, Center for Chinese Research Materials
CETA, *see* Comprehensive Employment and Training Act
CHEMLINE, 107
CLA, *see* Canadian Library Association; Catholic Library Association
CLENE, *see* Continuing Library Education Network and Exchange
CLR, *see* Council on Library Resources
COM, *see* Computer Output Microform
COMSEARCH Printouts, 276
COMSTAC, *see* Commission on Standards of Accreditation of Services for the Blind

CONSER, *see* Conversion of Serials
CONTU, *see* National Commission on New Technological Uses of Copyrighted Works
COSLA, *see* Chief Officers of State Library Agencies
CPL, *see* Council of Planning Librarians
CSLA, *see* Church and Synagogue Library Association
Cable television, *see* Telecommunications, cable television
California Library Association, 7
Call the Darkness Light, 485
"Campus Paperback Best-Seller List," 137
Canadian Association for Information Science, 605-606
Canadian Library Association, 606-607
  Intellectual Freedom Fund, 32
Capital Letter, 139
Carrie, 32
Cataloging and classification, 15-16
  bibliography, 531-532
  costs of catalogs, 361
  OCLC catalogs, 166
  on-line OCLC system, 165, 166
  see also Bibliographic control; CATLINE; Libraries, computerized functions; Library of Congress, catalog closing; Library of Congress, cataloging; Library of Congress, Cataloging in Publication program
Catalyst, placement services, 317
Catholic Library Association, 607-609
Censorship, *see* Intellectual freedom
Center for the Book, 95, 190
Cheatham, Bertha M., 28
Chen, Ching-Chih, 360
Chermayeff, Ivan, 485
Chief Officers of State Library Agencies, 609-610
Children's books, *see* Books, best books, juvenile
"Child's Place," 30
Chinese-American Librarians Association, 610
Chronicle of Higher Education, placement services, 316
Church and Synagogue Library Association, 611
"Citizen Information Seeking Patterns: A New England Study," 360
Clan of the Cave Bear, 41
Clearinghouse Memorandum, 63
Cline, Hugh, 361

Closer Look, 61
Cohen, Nathan M., 204
Collections Analysis Project, 144, 266
College and university libraries
  acquisitions, 9-10
    CLR support, 267
    expenditures, 378-379
  additions and renovations, 432, 435, 436-437, 438
  bibliography, 526
  construction, 431-440
  Egypt, 503
  expenditures, 378-379
  HEA support, 221-223
  personnel, training, 268
  services for the handicapped, 62
  statistics, *see* Library statistics, college and university libraries
  use of resources, 236
  see also Research libraries; Two-year college libraries
College bookstores, *see* Bookstores, college
College Guide for Students with Disabilities, 62
Commerce Information Retrieval Service, 153
Commission on Standards of Accreditation of Services for the Blind, 104
Communications Act of 1934, revision, 201
Comparative Evaluation of Alternative Systems for the Provision of Effective Access to Periodical Literature, 81-82
Competition Review Act, 1979, 192
Comprehensive Employment and Training Act, 20
Computer Output Microform, 16
Congdon and Lattes, 41
Congressional Chatauqua on Information, 153
Conservation of library materials, *see* Library materials, conservation and preservation
Consortium of Rhode Island Academic and Research Libraries, 14
Consumer Research Study on Reading and Book Purchasing, 444
Continuing Library Education Network and Exchange, 19, 612-613
Conversion of Serials, 266
Cooke, Eileen D., 175
Cooperation, library, *see* Library cooperation

INDEX / 705

Cooperative College Register, placement services, 317
Copyright, 13-14, 70-73, 185
  AAP activities, 134
  bibliography, 526, 537
  fair use, 71-72
  IPA concerns, 496
  international, 72
  legislation, 72
  off-air videotaping, 192
  see also Off-Air Taping Conference; Photocopying
Copyright Clearance Center, 14
  distribution of royalties, 42
  IIA participation, 154
Copyright Revision Act, 140
Council for Computerized Library Networks, 145-149, 613-614
Council for International Exchange of Scholars, placement services, 318
Council of Library/Media Technical Assistants, placement services, 310
Council of National Library and Information Associations, 614-615
Council of Planning Librarians, 615-616
Council on Library Resources, 81, 264-271, 616
  Academic Library Management Intern Program, see Academic Library Management Intern Program
  Bibliographic Service Development Program, 265-266
    Joint Committee on Bibliographic Standards, 265
  fellowship program, 269
  support to international organizations, 491
Current Awareness Literature Service, 110
Cylke, Frank Kurt, 99

D

Danton, J. P., 493
Darien Book Aid Plan, Inc., 690-691
Data bases
  commercial searching, 66-67
  copyright protection, 200
  FIC, 75
  machine-readable, government, 85-86
  microforms, 143
  NTIS, 85
  national, for archives and mss., 261
  on-line searching, 67
  research, 252
  special education materials, 60-61
  toxicology, 107
  see also Bibliographic data bases; Foundation Center, data bases; Libraries, computerized functions; also names of bases, e.g., RTECS
Debons, Anthony, 362, 370
Definitions for Library Statistics, 363
Design and Planning of National Information System, 492
Design Criteria: New Public Building Accessibility, 56
Dessauer, John P., 443, 444, 467, 473
Dial-a-Reg, 76
Dimensions of Comparative Librarianship, 493
Directory of Archives and Manuscript Repositories in the United States, 259, 261
Directory of Fee-Based Information Services, 69
Directory of Library Research and Demonstration Projects, 232
Directory of Literacy and Adult Learning Programs, 123
Documentary material, see Archives
Doebler, Paul D., 443, 444
Dog Day Afternoon, 31
Dollard, Peter, 156
Dougherty, Richard M., 268
Drennan, Henry T., 232
Dunlap, Leslie, 259

E

ECER data base, 61
EFLA, see Educational Film Library Association
ELA, see Egyptian Library Association
ERA, see Equal Rights Amendment
ERIC, see Educational Resources Information Center
ESEA, see Elementary and Secondary Education Act
E-SU, see English-Speaking Union of the United States
Editing, bibliography, 538
Edles, Nadine, 371
Education and Human Development, Inc., 233
Education for All Handicapped Children Act, 54
Education for librarianship
  bibliography, 526-527

Education for librarianship (Cont.)
  CLR concerns, 268-269
  Egypt, 505-506
  training in service to the handicapped, 64-65
  see also Higher Education Act, Title II-B; Library personnel, continuing education; Library personnel, trainee programs; Library schools
Educational Film Library Association, 617
Educational Information Service, placement services, 317, 318
Educational Paperback Association, 39
Educational Resources Information Center Clearinghouse on Handicapped and Gifted Children, 61
Egyptian Books in Print, 504
Egyptian Library Association, 505
Egyptian National Bibliography, 504
Egyptian National Library, 502
El Hadi, Mohamed M., 501
Elementary and Secondary Education Act
  Title IV-B, Instructional Materials and School Library Resources, 189, 190, 218-220
    allotments by state, 219
    band instruments, 187
    high-cost children allotments, 220
    program purpose allotments, 220
  Title IV-D, Guidance, Counseling and Testing, 31
Emergency Building Temperature Restrictions Regulations, 185-186
Emerson, Katherine, 364
Energy conservation, *see* Libraries, energy conservation
English-Speaking Union of the United States, 691-692
Equal Access, 120
Equal Rights Amendment, 21, 118
  ALA support, 32-33
  SLA and non-ratifying states, 170
"Essentials or Desiderata of the Bibliographic Record as Discovered by Research," 361
Establishing a Legislative Framework for the Implementation of NATIS, 492
Exceptional Child Education Resources, 61

F

FAMULUS, 110
FIC, *see* Federal Information Centers
FID, *see* International Federation for Documentation
FLA, *see* Federal Library Committee
FNIC, *see* Food and Nutrition Information Center
FTRF, *see* American Library Association, Freedom to Read Foundation
Fact Sheet on Libraries in Islamic Countries, 493
Farkas, Eugene M., 109
Federal Computer Systems Protection Act, 200
Federal Government Printing and Publishing Policy Issues, 197
Federal Information Centers, 73-79
  list, 76-79
Federal Information Centers Act, 74
Federal libraries, employment, 315-316
Federal Library Committee, 617-618
Federal Libraries and Information Services, pre-White House Conference, 44, 45
Federal Programs for Libraries, 213
Federal Register, 76, 239
Federal Research Service, placement services, 317
Federal Software Exchange Center, 86
Fellowships, *see* Council on Library Resources, fellowship program; Grants, library; Information science research, grants; Scholarships
"First Amendment Implications of Secondary Information Services," 155
Fisher, Sheldon Z., 221
Foglestrom, Clarence, 204
Folklife and Fieldwork, 96
"Folk-Songs of America," 96
Food and Nutrition Information Center, 110
Foreign library associations, *see* Library associations, foreign
Forever, 32
Foundation Center, 271-276
  data bases, 277-278
  field offices and cooperating libraries, 272-275
  publications, 276
Fox, Bette-Lee, 410, 431
Frankfurt Book Fair, 40, 481-489
  meeting of education specialists, 489
Frase, Robert W., 124
Freedom House/Books, USA, 692-693
Freedom of speech, *see* Intellectual freedom

Freedom to publish, *see* Intellectual freedom
Freedom to read, *see* Intellectual freedom
Freedom to Read Foundation, *see* American Library Association, Freedom to Read Foundation
Friends of Libraries, USA, 121

G

GPD, *see* Association of American Publishers, General Publishing Division
GRA&I, see *Government Reports Announcements & Index*
GRS, *see* General Revenue Sharing
Galvin, Thomas J., 115
Garrison, Guy, 359
Garrison, William, 86
Geddes, Andrew, 120
Gell, Marilyn K., 43, 46
General Revenue Sharing
  statistics, 243–245
  support for libraries, 242–245
German Book Trade Peace Prize, 489
Give-a-Book Certificate programs, 113
Goldhor, Herbert, 392
Goldwater, Barry, 40
Goudy, Frank Wm., 242
Government Inventions for Licensing, 85
Government Printing Reorganization Act, 191
Government Publications: Their Role in the National Program for Library and Information Services, 83
Government Reports Announcements & Index, 85
Grannis, Chandler B., 37, 446, 510
Grant proposals
  foundation grants, 282–284
  HEA, Title II-C, 240
  information science research, 254
  NHPRC, 260–261
Grants, information science, *see* Information science research, grants
Grants, library
  CLR, 270–271
  FTRF, 119
  foundation, 277–285
    computer analysis, 278–285
    list, 285–303
  HEA, 140–141, 221–222, 239–242
  NEH, 246–251

NHPRC, 259–261, 262–263
NLM, 109
  statistics, 279–282, 283, 284–285
  see also Grant proposals; Library funding; Scholarships
Green, Joseph, 380
Green Thumb, 91
Greenaway, Emerson, 59
Greene, Graham, 485
Griffin, Richard E., 167
Grosser, Alfred, 489
Grosset & Dunlap, sues Stratenmeyer Syndicate and S & S, 42
Guide to Archives and Manuscripts in the United States, 259
Guide to Manuscripts in the National Agricultural Library, 111
Guidelines for Collection Development, 122
"Guidelines for Selection of Representatives to International Conferences, Meetings, and Assignments," 115
Gwinn, Nancy E., 264

H

HEA, *see* Higher Education Act
Hafter, Ruth F., 361
Hagemeyer, Alice, 58
Handbook of Comparative Librarianship, 493
Handbook of Standard Terminology for Reporting Information about Libraries, 364
Handicapped people, *see* Library services for the handicapped
Handicapping America: Barriers to Disabled People, 55–56
Harman, David, 362
Hasan, Kazi, 444
Heim, Kathleen M., 334
Henderson, Carol C., 175
Hepatitis Knowledge Base, 108
Hess, James A., 120
"High Interest/Low Reading Level Information Packet," 122
Higher Education Act
  H.R. 5192, HEA extension, 177, 182
  Title I, Education Outreach Program, 177
  Title II, College and Research Library Assistance, 189

Higher Education Act (Cont.)
  Title II, Library Training and Research, 189
  Title II-A, College Library Resources, 176, 177, 189, 221-223
  Title II-B, Library Education, 223-232
  Title II-B, Library Research and Demonstration Program, 176, 177, 232-238, 359, 360
    funded projects, 238
    grants by category, 234
    sponsoring organizations, 237
    see also Education for librarianship
  Title II-C, Strengthening Research Library Resources, 140-141, 176, 177, 189, 239-242
  Title II-D, National Periodicals Center, 81, 142-143, 189-190, 191, 198
  Title VII, Construction, Reconstruction and Renovation of Academic Facilities, 177-178
  Title XI, Urban Grant University Program, 182
Hill, G. R., 455
Hirschberg, Vera, 43
Historical records, see Archives
Home Country Employment Registry, placement services, 318
Horton, Forest, 151
How to Build Your Writing Skills, 137
How to Comply with the Emergency Building Temperature Restrictions, 186
How to Get the Most out of a College Education, 137
How to Get the Most out of Your Textbook, 137
How to Prepare Successfully for Examinations, 137
Hughey, Elizabeth H., 204
Hunter, Carmen St. John, 362
Huntoon, Elizabeth, 28

I

IAALD, see International Association of Agricultural Librarians and Documentalists
IALL, see International Association of Law Libraries
IASA, see International Association of Sound Archives
ICA, see International Council on Archives
ICLG, see British Library Association, International and Comparative Librarianship Group
IESMP, see Information Exchange System for Minority Personnel
IFLA, see International Federation of Library Associations and Institutions
IIA, see Information Industry Association
ILIC, see International Library Information Center
INMARSAT, see International Maritime Satellite Organization
INTAMEL, see International Association of Metropolitan City Libraries
IPA, see International Publishers Association
IPA Publishing News, 495
ISBN, see International Standard Book Numbers
ISO, see International Organization for Standardization
ISO/TC 46, see International Organization for Standardization, Technical Committee 46
IST, see National Science Foundation, Division of Information Science and Technology
ITU, see International Telecommunication Union
IYC, see International Year of the Child
Ihrig, Alice B., 47
In Pursuit of American History, 259
Index Medicus, 105
Inexpensive Book Distribution Program, see Reading Is FUNdamental, Inexpensive Book Distribution Program
Information, scientific and technical, see Scientific and technical information
"Information Agenda for the 1980's," 116
"Information and the American Citizen," 116
Information brokers, 12, 66-69
  rates, 68-69
  regional networks, 13
Information centers, federal, see Federal Information Centers
Information Exchange System for Minority Personnel, placement services, 310
Information Industry Association, 39, 149-155, 618-619
  annual conference, 1980, 154-155
  Associated Information Managers, 152

INDEX / 709

committees, 153-155
Hall of Fame Award, 151
programs and projects, 151-153
Information Industry Market Place, 69
Information Manager, 155
Information Needs of Urban Residents, 236
Information Resource: Policy, Background and Issues, 151
Information science research
 data bases, 252
 grants, 251-258
  awarded, 255-258
 infometrics, 253
 information processing, 252-253
 NTIA grants, 89
 standards and measures, 252
 technology, 253-254
Information services
 bibliography, 69, 523-524, 527
 CLR services, 265-266
 citizen-to-government flow, 202
 citizen's needs, 236
 and civil rights, 202
 document delivery, 198
 Egypt, 503-504
 exporting, 198-199
 for the blind, 101
 government competition, 197-200
 grants, *see* Information science research, grants
 international, 154, 202-203, 490-494
 legislation, *see* Legislation affecting information industry
 management uses, 68
 occupational surveys, 362-363
 on-demand, 66-69
 personnel
  job openings, 152
  salaries, 151
  surveys, 370
  training programs, 225-227
 surveys, 151
 see also Bibliographic Retrieval Services; Council for Computerized Library Networks; Information Industry Association; Library cooperation; U.S., Information clearinghouses
Information Sources, 151
Information technology
 NTIA policies, 90-91
 viewdata, 91
Information World, 155
Informer, 63

Inside Our Home, outside Our Windows, 96
Institute for Telecommunications Sciences, *see* National Telecommunications and Information Administration, Institute for Telecommunications Sciences
Intellectual freedom, 27, 31-32, 41-42
 Alfred Grosser address, 489
 bibliography, 527, 537
 see also American Library Association, Office for Intellectual Freedom; Association of American Publishers, Freedom to Read Committee; Association of American Publishers, International Freedom to Publish Committee
Interagency Committee on Telecommunications Applications, 89
Inter-American Association of Agricultural Librarians and Documentalists, 656
Intergovernmental Conference on the Planning of Documentation, Library and Archives Infrastructures, 491-492
Interlibrary loan, 30
 international, 144
 NLM, 106
 NYSILL subsystem, 13
 OCLC services, 166
 see also Libraries, automated circulation systems; Library cooperation
International Association of Agricultural Librarians and Documentalists, 656-657
International Association of Law Libraries, 657
International Association of Metropolitan City Libraries, 657-658
International Association of Music Libraries, 658-659
International Association of School Librarianship, placement services, 318
International Association of Sound Archives, 659-660
International Council of Theological Library Associations, 660-661
International Council on Archives, 490, 491, 660
International Development Cooperation Act, 203
International Federation for Documentation, 661-662

International Federation of Film Archives, 662–663
International Federation of Library Associations and Institutions, 663–664
　CLR grants, 267
　contributions to comparative librarianship, 490, 491
　Council meeting, 45th, 115
　Parliamentary Library Section, 508
　Special Libraries Division, 171
International Group of Scientific, Technical and Medical Publishers, general assembly, 487–488
International Institute for Children's Literature and Reading Research, 664
International library associations, see Library associations, international
International Library Information Center, Pittsburgh, 493
International Maritime Satellite Organization, 88
International Organization for Standardization, 664–665
　Technical Committee 46, 129–132
　　plenary assembly, 130
　　steering committees, 130–131
　　Z39 review of standards, 131–132
International Publishers Association, 495–501
　committee meetings, 487–488
　congress, Stockholm, 488, 497–499
　Freedom to Publish Committee, 488
　organization and membership, 486–497
International Relations Round Table, see American Library Association, International Relations Round Table
International School Services, placement services, 318
International Standard Book Numbers, 445
International Symposium on Animal Health and Disease Data Banks: Proceedings, 111
International Telecommunication Union, 90
International Year of Disabled Persons, 53
International Year of the Child, 28–30
International Youth Library, 665–666
Inter-Parliamentary Union, International Centre for Parliamentary Documentation, 508
Island Trees, N.Y., 31, 119

Issues and Resolutions: A Summary of Pre-Conference Activities, 48, 360
"Issues for Delegate Consideration," 169

J

JCP, see Joint Committee on Printing
Jahoda, Gerald, 360
Jarvis-Ganns Initiative, see Proposition 13
Jerusalem Book Fair, 40
"Job Mobility of Men and Women Librarians and How It Affects Career Advancement," 363
Joint Committee on Printing, 83, 183–184, 197
Junior colleges, see Two-year college libraries

K

Kacena, Carolyn, 334
Keller, Helen, Center, 63
Kennedy, John F., Center for the Performing Arts, see Library of Congress, Performing Arts Library
Kent, Allen, 361
Kettel, Dorothy A., 204
King, Stephen, 32
King Associates, Inc., 48
King Research, Inc., 48
Kissinger, Henry, 485
Klett, Ernest, Verlag, 488
Klor, Robert M., 277
Knenlein, Donald R., 73
Kohout, Pavel, 488
Koutchoumow, J. A., 495
Krantz, Judith, 41, 484
Ku Klux Klan, 32
Küng, Hans, 42
Kurzweil Reading Machines, 23–24, 35

L

LAMA, see American Library Association, Library Administration and Management Association
LC, see Library of Congress
LHRT, see American Library Association, Library History Round Table
LIBGIS, see Library General Information Surveys

LITA, *see* American Library Association, Library and Information Technology Association
LMRU, *see* Library Management Research Unit
LRC, *see* School library/media services; Two-year college libraries
LSCA, *see* Library Services and Construction Act
LTR, *see Library Technology Reports*
Laboratory Animal Data Bank, 107
Laubach Literacy International, 693–694
Law libraries
　bibliography, 402, 403
　construction, 440
　statistics, *see* Library statistics, law libraries
　see also Library services and programs, access to law material
Learmont, Carol L., 321
Learning resource centers, *see* School library/media services; Two-year college libraries
Legislation affecting information industry, 195–203
　Congressional action, 197–203
　H.R. 4392, Appropriations for Departments of State, Justice, Commerce, the Judiciary, and Related Agencies, 198
　PL 96-39, 199
　S. 918, 199–200
　U.S. Executive Branch action, 196–197
Legislation affecting libraries, 175–187
　federal, 5
　research libraries, 140–141
　see also Library services for the handicapped, legislation; Library statistics, legislation
Legislation affecting publishing, 187–195
Leonard, Lawrence E., 204
Levy, Alix C., 66
Lewis, Alfred J., 401
Librarians
　certification, 161
　continuing education, 19–20
　　see also Library personnel, continuing education
　demand and supply, 324
　employment, 17–18
　　grievances, 160
　　nonlibrary, 319–320
　　overseas, 317–319
　exchange programs, 319
　international concerns, *see* Libraries, international concerns
　job lines, 307–309
　occupational surveys, 362–363
　placement services, 307–320
　placements, *see* Library schools, placements
　rehabilitation services, 62–64
　salaries, 169, 321, 324–325, 328
　　beginning, 342
　see also Library directors; Library personnel; *also* subdivision personnel under types of libraries
"Librarians and Their Stereotype," 362
Librarianship and the Third World, 493
Libraries
　acquisitions, 9–10, 378
　　bibliography, 531
　　see also subdivision acquisitions under types of libraries
　automated circulation systems, 16–17
　　see also Libraries, computerized functions
　building regulations for the handicapped, 56–57
　California, 6–7
　computerized functions, 14–15, 104
　　bibliography, 523–524
　construction, *see* subdivision construction under types of libraries
　energy conservation, 10–11
　equipment, furniture, buildings, etc., bibliography, 524–525
　expenditures, under LSCA Title III, 217
　　see also subdivision expenditures under types of libraries; *also* Library materials, library expenditures
　fines, 25, 33
　history, bibliography, 527–528
　　see also American Library Association, Library History Round Table
　international concerns, 490–494
　Iran, 27
　legislation, *see* Legislation affecting libraries
　national, *see* National libraries
　number of, U.S. and Canada, 373–374
　OCLC users, 164, 166
　public relations, 23
　reference services, bibliography, 529–530
　security, 25–27
　statistics, *see* Library statistics

Libraries (Cont.)
  technical services, bibliography, 531–532
  users, 361–362
  see also College and university libraries; Law libraries; Medical libraries; Parliamentary libraries; Public libraries; School library/media services; Special libraries; Two-year college libraries
Libraries in International Development, 491
Library Acquisitions: A Look into the Future, 444
Library administration, see Library management
Library Administration and Management Association, see American Library Association, Library Administration and Management Association
Library agencies, state, see State library agencies
Library and Information Technology Association, see American Library Association, Library and Information Technology Association
Library Association of Australia, biennial conference, 115
Library Association Record, 454
Library associations
  Canada, see Library associations, national; Library associations, provincial; Library associations, regional; *also* names of library associations in Canada
  continuing education programs, 19
  Egypt, 505
  foreign, 666–675
  international, 490–491, 656–666
  meetings, 695–698
    SLA involvement, 170
  national, 563–631
  placement services, 309–311, 312
    see also subdivision state and regional, below
  provincial, 640–641
  regional, U.S. and Canada, 641–642
  SLA student groups, 168–169
  state, 631–640
  state and regional, placement services, 312
  see also School library/media associations, state
Library awards, see Grants, library; Scholarships

Library Bill of Rights, 27, 34–35, 49
Library cooperation
  bibliography, 528
  international, 4, 21–22, 508
    SLA participation, 171
  LSCA support, 216–217
  multitype systems, 14
  school/public libraries, 30–31
  U.S. national libraries, 106
  WHCOLIS pre-conferences, 51
  see also Interlibrary loan; Networks
Library Cost Model Project, 143
Library directors
  salaries and sex, 337–341, 343
  sex and per capita support, 336, 338, 339
  see also Association of Academic Health Sciences Library Directors
Library funding, 7–9, 32–33, 204–217
  additions and renovations costs, 422–427
  Carter budget, 188–189
  construction costs, 411–421
  federal, 4, 5–6, 20, 178–179
  local, 6
  matching funds, 204
  public libraries, 10, 204, 334–337, 385–386, 387–389, 390–391
  state, 6, 381–382
  see also ESEA; General Revenue Sharing; HEA; LSCA
Library General Information Surveys, 364
  current status, 366–367
  Public School Library Media, 395–400
  Survey of Special Libraries in State Governments, 392–395
Library History Round Table, see American Library Association, Library History Round Table
"Library in American Society," 117
"Library Is Filled with Success Stories," 123
Library literature
  bibliography, 521–532, 532–533, 533–534
  comparative and international, 493
  vacancy notices, 307
Library management, 18
  bibliography, 522
  CLS intern program, 266
  health science libraries, 268–269
  see also Library directors; Library trustees
Library Management Research Unit, 454

Library materials
  bibliography, 528
  conservation and preservation, 26–27, 98
    bibliography, 522–523
    CLR support, 267–268
    temperature controls, 186
  for the deaf, 58
  funding, per capita, 385–386, 387–389, 390–391
  library expenditures, 375–379, 381–382
  prices and price indexes, 454–466
  standards, 370
  school library/media services, 396, 397
  special libraries, 392–393, 394
  see also Audiovisual materials; Microforms; Periodicals; Serial publications
Library Materials Price Index Committee, see American Library Association, Resources and Technical Services Division, Resources Section, Library Materials Price Index Committee
Library of Congress, 94–99
  acquisitions, 97
  American Folklife Center, see American Folklife Center
  budget, 96–97
  catalog closing, 15
  cataloging, 97–98
  Cataloging in Publication program, ANSC standards, 127
  Center for the Book, see Center for the Book
  Congressional Research Service, 96, 97, 507
  exhibits, 98–99
  HEA funding, 177
  James Madison Memorial Building, 94
  merit selection system, 316
  Motion Picture, Broadcasting and Recorded Sound Division, 97
  as National Bibliographic Center, 143
  as national library, 4
  National Library Service for the Blind and Physically Handicapped, 57, 64, 99
  National Referral Center, 95–96
  Performing Arts Library, 94
  publications, 98–99
  Rosenwald, Lessing J., Collection, 97
Library personnel
  continuing education, 19–20, 169

  HEA Institute Program, 223–224, 227, 228–232
    see also Librarians, continuing education; Library associations, continuing education programs
  employment, see Librarians, employment
  salaries and sex, 334–344
  surveys, 370
  trainee programs, HEA support, 223–224
  volunteers, 20
  NLS, 101
  see also American Library Association, Office for Library Personnel Resources; also subdivision personnel under types of libraries
Library Photocopying and the U.S. Copyright Law of 1976, 170
Library research and development, 359–363
  bibliography, 530
  HEA support, 232–238
  NEH support, 248
  NLS, 102
Library scholarships, see Scholarships
Library schools, 18–19
  accredited, 345–347
  job-hunting seminars and courses, 314–315
  placement services, 312–315
  placements, 321–333
  programs, 18–20
  programs in service to the handicapped, 64–65
  see also Association of American Library Schools
Library Services and Construction Act, 204–217
  acquisitions funding, 10
  Title I, Library Services, 189, 204, 205–213
    budget, 176
  Title III, Public Library Construction, 213–216
    budget, 176
Library services and programs, 24–25
  access, 4
  access to law material, 24
  access to medical literature, 24
  Egypt, 501–506
  fees, 15, 34
  humanities programs, 22–23, 36
  LSCA and matching funds, 206–207
  LSCA support, 33–34

Library services and programs (Cont.)
  literacy programs, 233, 362
  NEH support, 246-251
  outreach programs, 22-23
  rural development, 235
  special libraries, 392, 394
  see also Association of Research Libraries, programs and projects; Information services; National Librarians Association, programs and projects; Public libraries, reference services
Library Services for American Indian people, OLSD activities, 123
Library services for children and young adults, 34-35, 35-36
  bibliography, 525-526
  IYC programs, 28-30
  Iran, 29
  OCLC services, 167
  see also American Library Association, Association for Library Service to Children; American Library Association, Young Adults Services Division
Library services for minority groups, 23
Library services for persons of limited English-speaking ability, LSCA support, 210-211
Library services for special groups, bibliography, 530-531
Library services for the aging, LSCA support, 211-212
Library services for the blind, 23-24, 61, 99-105
  LSCA support, 209-210
  NLS regional libraries, 102-105
  see also Information services, for the blind
Library services for the deaf, 24, 58
  ALA support, 58-59
  LSCA funding, 58
  school programs, 61-62
Library services for the disadvantaged
  LSCA support, 207, 208
  see also American Library Association, Office for Library Service to the Disadvantaged; Library services and programs, outreach programs; Library services for minority groups
Library services for the handicapped, 23-24, 53-66, 99-105
  ALA support, 58-59
  college library services, 62
  HEA support, 233, 234
  handicapped person defined, 55
  LSCA and state support, 204
  LSCA support, 209-210
  legislation, 54-55
  school library/media services, 60-62
  see also Librarians, rehabilitation services; Library schools, programs in service to the handicapped; Library services for the blind; Library services for the deaf
Library services for the institutionalized
  LSCA and state support, 204
  LSCA support, 208-209
Library statistics, 363-371
  college and university libraries, 378-379, 431-440
  federal surveys, 366, 367
    see also Library General Information Surveys
  foundation grants, 278-282, 283, 284-285
  law libraries, 401-409, 440
  legislation, 178-181
  NLM, 107
  placement figures, 322-323, 326-328, 320
  public libraries, 375-379, 380-391, 410-430
  research libraries, 143, 268
  salaries, 330, 332-333
  school library/media services, 395-400
  special libraries, 392-395
  standard terminology, 368-369
  standards, 368-369
  two-year college libraries, 441-442
  see also American Library Association, Library Administration and Management Association, Statistics Section; American Library Association, Statistics Coordinating Project; Association of Research Libraries, Task Force on Statistics; also ESEA; HEA; LSCA; Libraries, number of; Library funding; U.S., population served by libraries
Library Technology Reports, 118
Library trainees, HEA support, 223-224
Library trustees
  legal liability, 18
  training, 18
Linden Press, 41
Lister Hill National Center for Biomedical Communications, 108

construction completed, 105
Literacy, *see* Library services and programs, literacy programs
"Literacy, Libraries Can Make It Happen," 123
Literary Classics of the U.S., 40
Little, Arthur D., report, 81, 395
Livingston, Barbara, 410, 431
Lobby legislation, *see* Regulation of Lobbying Act
Local Government Records: An Introduction to Their Management, Preservation and Use, 260
Lockheed, 66, 67
  Dialorder Service, 67
London Book Review, 41
Lorenz, John G., 140
Lottman, Herbert R., 481
Lovejoy, Eunice, 58, 99
Lutheran Church Library Association, 619–620
Lynch, Mary Jo, 359

M

MEDLARS, 105–106
MEDLINE, 106
MLA, *see* Medical Library Association; Music Library Association
McClung, James W., 94
McClure, Charles, 362
McKenna, Frank E., 168, 170
McNulty, Mary, 132
Madison, James, Memorial Building, *see* Library of Congress, James Madison Memorial Building
Male and Female under 18, 27
Management Review and Analysis Program, CLR support, 266
Mann, Patrick, 31
Manual on Bookselling, 113
Manuscript donations, tax credit, 185
Manuscripts, *see* Archives
Martin, Allie Beth, Award, 122
Maryland Regional Planning Council, 236
Media Programs: District and School, 396
Medical libraries
  funding, federal, 189
  see also Library services and programs, access to medical literature; National Library of Medicine
Medical Library Assistance Act, 109, 176
Medical Library Association, 620–622
  placement services, 310–311

Medical Literature Analysis and Retrieval System, *see* MEDLARS
Mehnert, Robert B., 105
"Member of Parliament: His Requirements for Information," 508
Menuhin, Yehudi, 489
Mergers and acquisitions, 38–39
Metropolitan libraries, *see* Public libraries; Research libraries
Microforms
  agricultural literature, 111
  bibliography, 528
  documentary material, 259
  machine-readable data bases, 143
  NPC as competition, 198
  prices and price indexes, 462
  see also Selected Research in Microfiche
Minorities, *see* American Library Association, Black Caucus; Telecommunications, broadcasting stations, minority ownership
Mitchell, Gwen Davis, 42
Montreal Book Fair, 40
Moscow Book Fair, 40, 133
Motovun Group, 488–489
Music Library Association, 623
  placement services, 311
Music materials, NLS collection, 101
Myers, Margaret, 307

N

NACS, *see* National Association of College Stores
NAL, *see* Technical Information Systems/National Agricultural Library
NARIC, *see* National Rehabilitation Information Center
NATIS, *see* National Information System
NCES, *see* National Center for Education Statistics
NCHEMS, *see* National Center for Higher Education Management Systems
NCHEMS Handbook of Standard Terminology, 368–369
NCLIS, *see* National Commission on Libraries and Information Science
NEH, *see* National Endowment for the Humanities
NHPRC, *see* National Historical Publications and Records Commission
NICE, *see* National Information Conference and Exposition
NLA, *see* National Librarians Association

NLA Newsletter, 159
NLM, *see* National Library of Medicine
NLS, *see* Library of Congress, National Library Service for the Blind and Physically Handicapped
NLW, *see* National Library Week
NMA, *see* National Micrographics Association
NPA, *see* National Publications Agency
NPC, *see* National Periodicals Center (proposed)
NPSAC, *see* National Periodicals System, Advisory Committee
NSF, *see* National Science Foundation
NTIA, *see* National Telecommunications and Information Administration
NTIS, *see* National Technical Information Service
NTP, *see* National Toxicology Program
National Agricultural Library, *see* Technical Information Systems/National Agricultural Library
National Association of College Stores
  annual meeting, 39
  BISG support, 403
National Book Awards
  final ceremonies, 39, 139
  replaced by TABA, 132
National Center for a Barrier Free Environment, report, 56
National Center for Education Statistics, Learning Resources Branch, 364
  Library Personnel Resources Survey (proposed), 370
  see also Library General Information Surveys
National Center for Higher Education Management Systems, 368–369
National Center on Educational Media and Materials for the Handicapped, data base, 61
National Citizens Emergency Committee to Save Our Public Libraries, 183
National Commission on Libraries and Information Science, 80–83
  Task Force on Public/Private Sector Relations, 82
  IIA participation, 154
  WHCOLIS planning, 44–45
National Commission on New Technological Uses of Copyrighted Works, 200
National Diet Library (Japan), 507
National Endowment for the Arts, reauthorization, 187

National Endowment for the Humanities
  Cultural Institutions Program, 247
  Fellowship Support for Advanced Study, 247
  grant to ARL, 143
  grant to OMS, 266
  humanities projects, 36, 246–247
  reauthorization, 187
  Research Resources Program, 247–248
  support for libraries, 246–251
National Enquiry on Scholarly Communication, 361
National Historical Publications and Records Commission, 258–263
  legislation, 184–185
  publications program, 259–260
  Records Grant Program, 260
National Information Conference and Exposition, 152–153
National Information System, 152–153
National Institute of Handicapped Research, 63
  established, 54–55
National Librarians Association, 156–162, 624
  Grievance Referrals Committee, 160
  Professional Welfare Committee, 161
  programs and projects, 158–159
National libraries
  Egypt, 502
  Japan, 507
  see also Federal libraries; Parliamentary libraries; *also* names of national libraries
National Library Act, 183, 190
National Library Network (proposed), 30
National Library of Medicine, 105–109
  card catalog closing, 106
  funding, federal, 189
  HEA funding, 177
  Knowledge Base Program, 108
  Lister Hill National Center for Biomedical Communications, *see* Lister Hill National Center for Biomedical Communications
  National Medical Audiovisual Center, 108–109
  Regional Medical Library Program, 109
  Toxicology Information Program, 107–108
National Library Service for the Blind and Physically Handicapped, *see* Library of Congress, National Library Service for the Blind and Physically Handicapped

INDEX / 717

National Library Week, 123–124
National Medical Audiovisual Center, *see* National Library of Medicine, National Medical Audiovisual Center
National Micrographics Association, 625–626
National Periodicals Center (proposed), 4, 12, 81, 82, 153, 177, 182, 190, 191–192, 198, 199
   ARL concerns, 141–143
National Periodicals Center: Technical Development Plan, 81, 267–268
National Periodicals System, 81
   Advisory Committee, 81
National Preservation Report, 98
National Publications Act of 1979, 183–184, 191
National Publications Agency, 184, 198
National Publications Committee, 183–184
National Referral Center, *see* Library of Congress, National Referral Center
National Registry for Librarians, 307
National Rehabilitation Information Center, 63–64
"National Reporting on Reference Transactions," 364
National Science Foundation
   Division of Information Science and Technology, 251–252
   grant to University of Pittsburgh, 370
   support for information science research, 251–258
National Technical Information Service, 83–86, 127
   Advisory Committee, 154
   Federal Software Exchange Center, *see* Federal Software Exchange Center
National Telecommunications and Information Administration, 86–91
   Institute for Telecommunications Sciences, 87
   Office of Federal Systems and Spectrum Analysis, 87
   Office of Policy Analysis and Development, 87
   Office of Telecommunications Applications, 87
National Toxicology Program, 107–108
Neely, Eugene T., 363
Neff, Evaline B., 204
Network brokers, *see* Information brokers
Networks, 11–12
   bibliography, 528
   electronic mail, 110
   LC activities, 98
   Library services for the blind, 102–105
   national, 11
   school library/media services, 82
   see also National Library Network (proposed)
   parliamentary libraries, 509
   regional, 13–14, 30
   on-line users of OCLC, 163, 164
   third party access, 13
   see also Bibliographic control; Council for Computerized Library Networks; Information services; Library cooperation; *also* names of specific networks
New American Library, hardcover editions, 41
"New York Is Book Country," 40
Newbery/Caldecott Award banquet, 35
Newspapers
   bibliography, 538
   rates and index values, 455, 462
   searches of offices, 188, 202
   vacancy notices, 307
Nielsen, Carol S., 521
Noble, J. Kendrick Jr., 445
Nordberg, E. Wayne, 443, 444
Norwood, Babetta, 223
Nyren, Karl, 410, 431

O

OCLC, *see* Ohio College Library Center
OE, *see* U.S., Office of Education
OIF, *see* American Library Association, Office for Intellectual Freedom
OLPR, *see* American Library Association, Office for Library Personnel Resources
OLSD, *see* American Library Association, Office for Library Service to the Disadvantaged
OMB, *see* U.S., Office of Management and Budget
OMS, *see* Association of Research Libraries, Office of Management Studies
Oak Ridge National Laboratory, Toxicology Information Response Center, 107
Obscenity, *see* Pornography and obscenity

Office for Library Personnel Resources, *see* American Library Association, Office for Library Personnel Resources
Office for Library Service to the Disadvantaged, *see* American Library Association, Office for Library Service to the Disadvantaged
Off-Air Taping Conference, 185
Ohio College Library Center, 11, 12-13, 162-167
  HEA support, 236
  interlibrary loan subsystem, 166
Ohio Libraries Reach Out, 58
Olympia Press, 40
On-Line, Inc., conference, 155
Organizational Case Studies of Collection Development Policies and Practices, 361
Osburn, Charles, 362
Ospry, Bernard, 4

P

P.E.N. American Center, survey of writers, 37
PIO, *see* American Library Association, Public Information Office
PLA, *see* American Library Association, Public Library Association
Palmour, Gene, 361
Paper Availability Study, 444
Paperback books
  AAP concerns, 136-137
  growth in output, 37
  prices and price indexes, 452-453, 459, 460
  title output, 448
  see also Association of American Publishers, Mass Market Paperback Division
Paperwork and Redtape Reduction Act, 202
Papier, Lawrence W., 233
Parents as Reading Partners, 30
Parliamentary libraries, 507-509
  see also Library of Congress
Paul, Sandra K., 445
"Perceived Values of Information Sources for Library Decision-Making," 362
Performance of Card Catalogs: A Review of Research, 361
Perigord Press, 40
Periodicals
  access, 81

  bibliography, 528-529, 532, 538
  for the blind, 101
  prices and price indexes, 456
  see also National Periodicals Center (proposed); Serial publications
Perspective on Libraries, 116
Peters, Jean R., 445, 532
Peters, Marybeth, 70
Photocopying, 5-year copyright review, 185, 192
Photocopying by Academic, Public and Non-Profit Research Libraries, 134
Physical Disability: A Psychological Approach, 55
Pioneer Valley Union List of Serials, 216
"Planning Process for Public Libraries," 121
Plotnik, Arthur, 117
Pornography and obscenity, legislation, 188
Postal rates
  classification, 194-195
  Court of Appeals Case, 194
  fourth class, 193
  increases, 42, 114
  legislation, 184, 193-195
  parcel post discounts, 194
  special rate fourth class, 193, 194
  uniform rates, 194
  see also U.S., Postal Rate Commission; U.S., Postal Service
Postal Reform Act, 201
Postal Reorganization Act, 114, 194
Postal service, private carriers, 193-194
Postal Service Act of 1979, 184, 193
Preservation of library materials, *see* Library materials, conservation and preservation
Price, Richard, 31
"Price Index for Legal Publications," 455
"Price Indexes, Foreign and Domestic Music," 455
Princess Daisy, 41, 484
Printed materials, copyright of graphic designs, 185
Prizes, *see* Awards; Grants, library; Information science research, grants; Scholarships
Problems of Bibliographic Access to Nonprint Media, 82
Progress Report on the Occupational Survey of Information Professionals, 362
Project Mediabase, 82
Proposition 13, 6-7, 33

Public Health Service Act, Title III-J, Medical Libraries, 189
Public Information Office, see American Library Association, Public Information Office
Public libraries
  acquisitions, 376–377
  additions and renovations, 422–427
  bibliography, 529
  Canada, construction, 429
  circulation statistics, 383–384, 385–386, 387–389, 390–391
  construction, 410–430
    LSCA support, 213–216
  construction costs, 428–429
  expenditures, 381–382
  personnel
    number of, 383–384
    work load, 385–386, 387–389, 390–391
  reference services, 383–384
  statistics, see Library statistics, public libraries
  support and sex, 334–344
  see also Research libraries
Public Library Association, see American Library Association, Public Library Association
"Public Library Service to Physically Handicapped Persons," 360
Public Telecommunications Facilities Program, 87
Publication of American Historical Manuscripts, 259
Publishers
  continuing education, 133, 135
    seminars overseas, 499–501
  imprints, 40
  international meeting of educational publishers, 488
  sales, see Book sales
Publishers associations, 676–689
  see also Book trade associations
Publishing, 37–42
  bibliography, 534–536
  distribution of books, BISG study, 445, 475
  IPA services, 495–496
  international cooperation, 133
  legislation, see Legislation affecting publishing
  pirated editions, 40
  small publishers, 136
    see also Association of American Publishers, Small Publishers Group

  subsidiary rights, 37
  see also Editing
Publishing statistics, 467–473
  title output, 446–453, 512–513
    British, 514–518
    international, 510–514
  see also Book exports; Book imports; Book sales; Books, consumer expenditures; Books, prices and price indexes

Q

Qureshi, Naimuddin, 490

R

RASD, see American Library Association, Reference and Adult Services Division
RLG, see Research Libraries Group
RLIN, see Research Libraries Information Network/Washington Library Network
RML, see National Library of Medicine, Regional Medical Library Program
RTECS, 107
RTSD, see American Library Association, Resources and Technical Services Division
Rack Clearance Center, see Association of American Publishers, Mass Market Paperback Division, Rack Clearance Center
Radio stations, see Telecommunications, broadcasting stations
"Read More about It," 36, 41, 95
Reading in America, 1978, 95
Reading Is Fun Day, 190
Reading Is FUNdamental, Inexpensive Book Distribution Program, federal funding, 189
Reading, Writing and Other Communication Aids for the Handicapped, 57
"Recent Studies in Measurement for Better Decisions and Service in Public Libraries," 121
Reference and Adult Services Division, see American Library Association, Reference and Adult Services Division
Reference Works for Small and Medium-Sized Libraries, 122

Reforma, placement services, 311
Register of Copyrights, see U.S., Register of Copyrights
Registry of Toxic Effects of Chemical Substances, see RTECS
Regulation of Lobbying Act, 192–193
Rehabilitation Act of 1973, 54, 56, 63
  amendments of 1978, 54–55
Report on Book Industry Information Needs, 443
"Report on the Study of Library Use at Pitt," 361
Research, library, see Library research and development
Research in information science, see Information science research
Research libraries
  HEA support, 140–141, 239–242
  LSCA support, 212–213
  legislation, see Legislation affecting libraries, research libraries
  statistics, see Library statistics, research libraries; *also* Association of Research Libraries, Task Force on Statistics
  see also Association of Research Libraries
Research Libraries Group, 12–13
Research Libraries Information Network/Washington Library Network, 11, 12, 13
Resources and Technical Services Division, see American Library Association, Resources and Technical Services Division
Revenue sharing, see General Revenue Sharing
Rhodes, Sarah N., 251
Right to Financial Privacy Act, 202
Robert, William H., 32
Rogan, Barbara, 485
Role of Publishers in the National Library Network, 135
Role of the School Library Media Program in Networking, 82
Rundell, Walter Jr., 259
Ryerson, Ted, 83

S

SAA, see Society of American Archivists
SAMANTHA, 111
SAN, see Standard Address Numbering
SBDC, see Small Business Development Center Act
SDC, see Systems Development Corporation
SLA, see Special Libraries Association
"SLA Salary Survey Report," 169
SLD, see International Federation of Library Associations and Institutions, Special Libraries Division
SRIM, see Selected Research in Microfiche
STM, see International Group of Scientific, Technical and Medical Publishers
Savage, Noël, 3
Schick, Renée, 66
Schieber, Philip, 162
Schoenung, James G., 145
Scholarly Communication, 37, 361
Scholarships
  CLR, 269
  HEA, 223–224, 225–227
  NEH, 247
  recipients, 349–356 passim
  sources, 347–349
  Stephen Greene Fund, 133
  see also Grants, library
School library/media associations, state, 646–652
School library/media services
  bibliography, 530
  Egypt, 502–503
  expenditures, 396, 398, 399
  funding, 31
  see also ESEA
  network participation, 30, 82
  personnel, 399, 400
  job opportunities, 316
  rural communities, 235
  services for the handicapped, 60–62
  state supervisors, 652–655
  statistics, see Library statistics, school library/media services
"School Media Centers: Focus on Issues and Trends," 119
Scientific and technical information
  licensable technology, 85
  NTIS collections, 84
Scott, B., 455
Securing a New Library Director, 120
Selected Research in Microfiche, 85
Serial publications
  bibliography, 528–529
  prices and price indexes, 457

Serving Physically Disabled People: An Information Handbook for All Libraries, 60
"Sexism: Monitor Awareness—Review Thinking Sessions," 121
Seymour, Whitney North Jr., 4
Shah of Iran, memoirs, 484
Shelley, Fred, 259–260
Short Title Catalogue of Eighteenth Century Printed Books in the National Library of Medicine, 106–107
Simmons, Beatrice, 218
Sinnot, Lorraine, 361
Slanker, Barbara O., 443
Small Business Administration, hearing, 153
Small Business Development Center Act, 199
Smardo, Frances, 29
Smith, G. Roysce, 112
Smith, Linda C., 392
Society for Scholarly Publishing, meeting, 39
Society of American Archivists, 627–628
Soviet-American Library Seminar, 1st, 21, 115
Speaker, 27
Special libraries
 bibliography, 531
 CLR training activities, 268–269
 Egypt, 503
 expenditures, 394, 395
 personnel, 169, 393, 394
 serving state government agencies, 392–395
 statistics, *see* Library statistics, special libraries
 see also Law libraries; Medical libraries
Special Libraries Association, 167–172, 628–629
 annual conferences, 170–171
 boycotts non-ERA states, 33
 China fund, 171
 placement services, 311
 Professional Development Department, 169
 services to members, 171–172
 see also Library associations, SLA student groups
Spicer, Erik J., 507
Standard Address Numbering, 37
"Standards for Accreditation, 1972," 119
Standards of Librarianship in Burma, Ceylon, India and Pakistan, 493
Standards of Services for the Library of Congress Networks of Libraries for the Blind and Physically Handicapped, 120
State and Local Fiscal Assistance Act, 242
State libraries, bibliographies, 531
State library agencies, 642–645
 LSCA support, 212
 placement services, 311–312
 political pressures, 6
 support of resource libraries, 205
 WHCOLIS pre-conferences, 6, 44, 47–53
 see also American Library Association, Association of Specialized and Cooperative Library Agencies; Chief Officers of State Library Agencies
State Library Agencies: A Survey Project Report, 120
State library associations, *see* Library associations, state
State school library/media associations, *see* School library/media associations, state
State University of New York at Albany, library research program, 236
Statistical surveys, *see* Library statistics
Stevens, Frank A., 221, 223, 239
Sun, Moon, Star, 485
Systems Development Corporation, 66, 67
 Electronic Mailbox, 67

T

TABA, *see* American Book Awards
TIS/NAL, *see* Technical Information Systems/National Agricultural Library
TLA, *see* Theatre Library Association
TOXLINE, 107
TRIC, 63
TSM, *see* Association of American Publishers, Technical, Scientific and Medical Division
Talese, Gay, 484
Tape recordings, *see* Audiovisual materials
"Technical Economic Analysis of Alternatives for Access to Periodical Literature," 142
Technical information, *see* Scientific and technical information
Technical Information Systems/National Agricultural Library, 109–111
 funding, federal, to NAL, 189

Telecommunications
  broadcasting stations
    assignment of frequencies, 90
    land mobile radio, 88
    minority ownership, 88
    programming choices, 87–88
  cable television, deregulation, 88
  eavesdropping, 90
  government use, 87, 89–90
  international, 87, 88
  international spectrum management, 90
  public service agencies users, 89
  rural services, 88–89
  systems reviews, 90
Telephone directories, blue pages, 76
Teletext, 91
Television stations, see Telecommunications, broadcasting stations
Television, the Book and the Classroom, 95
Textbooks, 37
  AAP concerns, 138
  college, 137
  LC, Center for the Book conference, 190
  marketing, 137
Theatre Library Association, 629–630
Thomas, John, 156
Thy Neighbor's Wife, 484, 486
Time to Heal, 42
Touching, 42
Toward a National Program for Library and Information Services: Goals for Action, 80
Toxicology Data Bank, 107
Toxicology Information Response Center, see Oak Ridge National Laboratory, Toxicology Information Response Center
"Trends in Public Library Research in the 1970's," 359
Trezza, Alphonse F., 80
Trial and Execution, 485
Troiano, Richard, 321
Truett, Cecily, 29
Two-year college libraries, construction, 441–442

U

UAP, see Universal Availability of Publications
UBC, see Universal Bibliographic Control
UNESCO, library programs, worldwide, 490
UNESCO Bulletin for Libraries, 493
UPC, see Universal Product Code
USBE, see Universal Serials and Book Exchange
Unions, 20–21
U.S.
  Census of Manufactures, 467, 468
  Code revision, Title 44, Government Printing and Document Distribution, 183–184, 191, 197–198
  Congress
    budget process and libraries, 175–176
    Joint Committee on Printing, see Joint Committee on Printing
  Copyright Office, 70–73, 185
    5-year review, see Photocopying, 5-year copyright review
  criminal code, 187–188
  Department of Agriculture, TIS/NAL, see Technical Information Systems/National Agricultural Library
  Department of Commerce
    National Technical Information Service, see National Telecommunications and Information Administration
    "Standards Information Center," 199
  Department of Defense, placement services, 318
  Department of Education, 183
  General Services Information, Office of External Affairs, Office of Consumer Affairs, see Federal Information Centers
  information clearinghouses, 92–93
  International Communication Agency, placement services, 318
  Office of Education
    Bureau of Education of the Handicapped, 61
    grant to ASCLA, 120
  Office of Management and Budget, FIC studies, 74
  Office of Personnel Management, Librarian's Register, 315
  population served by libraries, 371–372
  Postal Rate Commission, 114, 194
    see also Postal rates
  Postal Service
    electronic mail, 201–202
    subsidies, 42

see also Association of American Publishers, Postal Committee
President
Committee on Employment of the Handicapped, Library Committee, 59
messages on information policy, 196–197
Register of Copyrights, 70, 71, 185
Senate, Education Subcommittee hearings on basic skills, 190
Weather Bureau, Green Thumb, 91
Universal Availability of Publications, 82
Universal Bibliographic Control, 492
Universal City Studios, Inc., v. *Sony Corporation of America*, 71–72
Universal Product Code, 39
Universal Serials and Book Exchange, 630–631
University of California, Berkeley, CLR grant, 268
University of California, Los Angeles, on-line microfiche catalog, 236
University of North Carolina, Greensboro, access to school media material, 236
Urban libraries, *see* Public libraries; Research libraries
Use of Library Materials: The University of Pittsburgh Study, 361

V

Velleman, Ruth A., 53, 60
"Video Disc: Challenge and Opportunity for Publishers," 488
Videocassettes, *see* Audiovisual materials, videocassettes
Videodisc technology, biomedical uses, 108
Videotape, *see* Audiovisual materials, off-air videotaping; Audiovisual materials, videocassettes
Visual Artists Moral Rights Amendments, 1979, 200
VOICE of Z39, 127
Vonnegut, Kurt Jr., 485

W

WARC, *see* World Administrative Radio Conference
WHCOLIS, *see* White House Conference on Library and Information Services
WHO, *see* World Health Organization
WITS, *see* Worldwide Information and Trade System
Wanderers, 31, 32
Washington Book Fair, 40
Washington State Library, computer simulation for network planners, 236
Wedgeworth, Robert, 115
Weiderkehr, Bob, 361
Weidhaas, Peter, 481, 482
Weintraub, Kathryn, 361
"What Americans Are Reading," 124
"Where to Turn for Help in Folklore and Folklife," 96
White House Conference on Library and Information Services, 3–5, 38, 43–47, 47–48
AAP concerns, 136
ALA concerns, 116
Conference Information Center, 45
delegates, 44–45
discussion group categories, 50–51
Information Community Advisory Committee, 154
library research support, 360
preconference resolutions, 48–49
pre-conferences, *see* State library agencies, WHCOLIS pre-conferences
President Carter's address, 45–46
Resolution on Library Statistical Surveys by the Federal Government, 368
resolutions, 4–5, 46–47, 80–81, 186, 190
SLA activities, 169
theme groups, 3–4, 45
White House Years, 485
Willard, Robert S., 195
Williams, Sally F., 454
Wilson, Pauline, 362
Winnick, Pauline, 204
Witkins, Janis, 277
Women in Scholarly Publishing, 39
Wood, James L., 124
World Administrative Radio Conference, 90
World Health Organization, NLM assistance, 106
Worldwide Conference on Special Libraries, 1st, SLA participation, 171
Worldwide Information and Trade System, 153, 198, 199

"Worldwide Information Sources," 171
Wright, Beatrice, 55
Writings on American History, 259

Y

YASD, *see* American Library Association, Young Adult Services Division

Z

Z39, *see* American National Standards Committee Z39
Zara, 485
Zaroulis, Nancy, 485
Zurcher v. *Stanford Daily*, 188, 202
Zurkowski, Paul G., 149

DIRECTORY OF U.S. AND CANADIAN LIBRARIES

This directory has been compiled for ready reference. For libraries not listed, see the *American Library Directory* (R. R. Bowker, 1979).

UNITED STATES

Univ. of Alabama
Amelia Gayle Gorgas Library, Box S, University, AL 35486
Tel: 205-348-5298

Alameda County Library
224 W. Winton Ave., Hayward, CA 94544
Tel: 415-881-6337

Annapolis & Anne Arundel County Public Library
5 Harry S. Truman Pkwy., Annapolis, MD 21401
Tel: 301-224-7371

Arizona State Univ. Library
Tempe, AZ 85281
Tel: 602-965-3415

Atlanta Public Library
10 Pryor St. S.W., Atlanta, GA 30303
Tel: 404-688-4636

Baltimore County Public Library
320 York Rd., Towson, MD 21204
Tel: 301-296-8500

Boston Athenaeum
10½ Beacon St., Boston, MA 02118
Tel: 617-227-0270

Boston Public Library
666 Boylston St., Box 286, Boston, MA 02117
Tel: 617-536-5400

Boston Univ. Libraries
Mugar Memorial Library, 771 Commonwealth Ave., Boston, MA 02215
Tel: 617-353-3710

Brigham Young Univ.
Harold B. Lee Library, University Hill, Provo, UT 84602
Tel: 801-374-1211

Brooklyn Public Library
Grand Army Plaza, Brooklyn, NY 11238
Tel: 212-636-3111

Broward County Libraries
Box 5463, Fort Lauderdale, FL 33310
Tel: 305-972-1100

Brown Univ. Libraries
John D. Rockefeller, Jr. Library, Providence, RI 02912
Tel: 401-863-2162

Buffalo and Erie County Public Library
Lafayette Sq., Buffalo, NY 14203
Tel: 716-856-7525

Univ. of California, Berkeley
University Library, Berkeley, CA 94720
Tel: 415-642-3773

Univ. of California, Davis
General Library, Davis, CA 95616
Tel: 916-752-2110

Univ. of California, Los Angeles
University Library, 405 Hilgard Ave., Los Angeles, CA 90024
Tel: 213-825-1201

Univ. of California, San Diego
University Libraries, Mail Code C-075, La Jolla, CA 92093
Tel: 714-452-3336

Univ. of California, Santa Barbara
Campus Library, Santa Barbara, CA 93106
Tel: 805-961-2741

Carnegie Library of Pittsburgh
4400 Forbes Ave., Pittsburgh, PA 15213
Tel: 412-622-3100

Case Western Reserve
University Libraries, 11161 E. Blvd., Cleveland, OH 44106
Tel: 216-368-3506

Univ. of Chicago
Joseph Regenstein Library, 1100 E. 57 St., Chicago, IL 60637
Tel: 312-753-2977

Chicago Public Library
425 N. Michigan Ave., Chicago, IL 60611
Tel: 312-269-2900

Univ. of Cincinnati
Main Library, University & Woodside, Cincinnati, OH 45221
Tel: 513-475-2535

Cincinnati-Hamilton County Public Library
800 Vine St., Cincinnati, OH 45202
Tel: 513-369-6000

Cleveland Public Library
325 Superior Ave., Cleveland, OH 44114
Tel: 216-623-2800

Univ. of Colorado at Boulder
University Libraries, Norlin Library, M450, Boulder, CO 80309
Tel: 303-492-7511

Colorado State Univ.
William E. Morgan Library, Fort Collins, CO 80523
Tel: 303-491-5911

Columbia Univ. Libraries
535 W. 114 St., New York, NY 10027
Tel: 212-280-2241

Univ. of Connecticut Library
Storrs, CT 06268
Tel: 203-486-2219

Contra Costa County Library System
1750 Oak Park Blvd., Pleasant Hill, CA 94523
Tel: 415-944-3423

Cornell Univ. Libraries
Ithaca, NY 14853
Tel: 607-256-4144

Cuyahoga County Public Library
4510 Memphis Ave., Cleveland, OH 44144
Tel: 216-398-1800

John Crerar Library
35 W. 33 St., Chicago, IL 60616
Tel: 312-225-2526

Dallas Public Library
1954 Commerce, Dallas, TX 75201
Tel: 214-748-9071

Dartmouth College
Baker Memorial Library, Hanover, NH 03755
Tel: 603-646-2235

Dayton-Montgomery County Public Library
215 E. Third St., Dayton, OH 45402
Tel: 513-224-1651

Denver Public Library
1357 Broadway, Denver, CO 80203
Tel: 303-573-5152, ext. 271

Detroit Public Library
5201 Woodward Ave., Detroit, MI 48202
Tel: 313-833-1000

District of Columbia Public Library
901 G St. N.W., Washington, DC 20001
Tel: 202-727-1101

Duke Univ.
William R. Perkins Library, Durham, NC 27706
Tel: 919-684-2034

Emory Univ. Libraries
Atlanta, GA 30322
Tel: 404-329-6861

Enoch Pratt Free Library
400 Cathedral St., Baltimore, MD 21201
Tel: 301-396-5430

Fairfax County Public Library
5502 Port Royal Rd., Springfield, VA 22151
Tel: 703-321-9810

Univ. of Florida Libraries
Gainesville, FL 32611
Tel: 904-392-0341

Florida State Univ.
Robert Manning Strozier Library, Tallahassee, FL 32306
Tel: 904-644-2706

Fort Worth Public Library
300 Taylor St., Fort Worth, TX 76102
Tel: 817-870-7700

Fresno County Public Library
2420 Mariposa St., Fresno, CA 93721
Tel: 209-488-3191

Georgetown Univ.
Joseph Mark Lauinger Library, 37 and O Sts. N.W., Washington, DC 20057
Tel: 202-625-4095

Univ. of Georgia Libraries
Athens, GA 30602
Tel: 404-542-2716

Harvard Univ. Library
Cambridge, MA 02138
Tel: 617-495-2401

Univ. of Hawaii Library
2550 The Mall, Honolulu, HI 96822
Tel: 808-948-7205

Hennepin County Library System
York Ave. S. at 70, Edina, MN 55435
Tel: 612-830-4944

Univ. of Houston
M. D. Anderson Memorial Library, 4800 Calhoun Blvd., Houston, TX 77004
Tel: 713-749-4241

Houston Public Library
500 McKinney Ave., Houston, TX 77002
Tel: 713-224-5441

Howard Univ. Libraries
Founders Library, 500 Howard Pl. N.W., Washington, DC 20059
Tel: 202-636-7234

Univ. of Illinois at Urbana-Champaign
University Library, Wright St., 230 Library, Urbana, IL 61801
Tel: 217-333-0790

Indiana Univ. Libraries
Tenth St. and Jordan Ave., Bloomington, IN 47401
Tel: 812-337-3403

Indianapolis-Marion County Public Library
40 E. St. Clair St., Box 211, Indianapolis, IN 46206
Tel: 317-635-5662

Univ. of Iowa Libraries
Iowa City, IA 52242
Tel: 319-353-4450

Iowa State Univ. Library
Ames, IA 50011
Tel: 515-294-1442

Jacksonville Public Library System
Haydon Burns Library, 122 N. Ocean St., Jacksonville, FL 32202
Tel: 904-633-6870

Jefferson Parish Library
3420 North Causeway Blvd. at Melvin Dewey Dr., Box 7490, Metairie, LA 70010
Tel: 504-834-5850

Johns Hopkins Univ.
Milton S. Eisenhower Library, Baltimore, MD 21218
Tel: 301-338-8325

Joint Univ. Libraries
419 21 Ave. S., Nashville, TN 37203
Tel: 615-322-2834

Kansas City Public Library
311 E. 12 St., Kansas City, MO 64106
Tel: 816-221-2685

Univ. of Kansas Libraries
Watson Memorial Library, Lawrence, KS 66045
Tel: 913-864-3601

Kent State Univ. Libraries
Kent, OH 44242
Tel: 216-672-2962

Univ. of Kentucky
Margaret I. King Library, Lexington, KY 40506
Tel: 606-257-3801

King County Library System
300 Eighth Ave. N., Seattle, WA 98109
Tel: 206-344-7465

Library of Congress
Washington, DC 20540
Tel: 202-287-5000

Los Angeles County Public Library System
320 W. Temple St., Box 111, Los Angeles, CA 90053
Tel: 213-974-6501

Los Angeles Public Library
630 W. Fifth St., Los Angeles, CA 90071
Tel: 213-626-7555

Louisiana State Univ. Library
Baton Rouge, LA 70803
Tel: 504-388-2217

Maricopa County Library
3375 W. Durango, Phoenix, AZ 85009
Tel: 602-269-2535

Univ. of Maryland at College Park
University Libraries, College Park, MD 20742
Tel: 301-454-3011

Univ. of Massachusetts at Amherst
University Library, Amherst, MA 01002
Tel: 413-545-0284

Massachusetts Institute of Technology Libraries
Rm. 14 S-216, Cambridge, MA 02139
Tel: 617-253-5651

Memphis-Shelby County Public Library
1850 Peabody Ave., Memphis, TN 38104
Tel: 901-528-2950

Univ. of Miami
Otto G. Richter Library, Memorial Dr., Box 248214, Coral Gables, FL 33124
Tel: 305-284-3551

Miami-Dade Public Library System
One Biscayne Blvd., Miami, FL 33132
Tel: 305-579-5001

Univ. of Michigan Library
Ann Arbor, MI 48109
Tel: 313-764-9356

Michigan State Univ. Library
East Lansing, MI 48824
Tel: 517-355-2344

Milwaukee Public Library
814 W. Wisconsin Ave., Milwaukee, WI 53233
Tel: 414-278-3000

Minneapolis Public Library
300 Nicollet Mall, Minneapolis, MN 55401
Tel: 612-372-6500

Univ. of Minnesota
O. Meredith Wilson Library, Minneapolis, MN 55455
Tel: 612-373-3097

Univ. of Missouri-Kansas City
General Library, 5100 Rockhill Rd., Kansas City, MO 64110
Tel: 816-276-1531

Montgomery County Department of Public Libraries
99 Maryland Ave., Rockville, MD 20850
Tel: 301-279-1401

Nassau Library System
900 Jerusalem Ave., Uniondale, NY 11553
Tel: 516-292-8920

National Agricultural Library
U.S. Department of Agriculture, 110301 Baltimore Blvd., Beltsville, MD 20705
Tel: 301-344-3778

National Library of Medicine
8600 Rockville Pike, Bethesda, MD 20014
Tel: 301-496-6308

Univ. of Nebraska-Lincoln
Don L. Love Memorial Library, Lincoln, NE 68588
Tel: 402-472-2526

State Univ. of New York at Albany
University Library, 1400 Washington Ave., Albany, NY 12222
Tel: 518-457-8551

State Univ. of New York at Buffalo
Lockwood Memorial Library, 3435 Main St., Buffalo, NY 14214
Tel: 716-831-2502

State Univ. of New York at Stony Brook
Frank Melville Jr. Memorial Library, Stony Brook, NY 11794
Tel: 516-246-5650

New York Public Library
Astor, Lenox and Tilden Foundations Library, Fifth Ave. and 42 St., New York, NY 10018
Tel: 212-790-6262

New York Univ.
Elmer Holmes Bobst Library, 70 Washington Sq. S., New York, NY 10012
Tel: 212-598-2484

Newberry Library
60 W. Walton St., Chicago, IL 60610
Tel: 312-943-9090

Univ. of North Carolina at Greensboro
Walter Clinton Jackson Library, 1000 Spring Garden St., Greensboro, NC 27412
Tel: 919-379-5880

Northwestern Univ. Library
1935 Sheridan Rd., Evanston, IL 60201
Tel: 312-492-7658

Univ. of Notre Dame
University Libraries, Notre Dame, IN 46556
Tel: 219-283-7317

Ohio State Univ.
William Oxley Thompson Memorial Library, 1858 Neil Ave. Mall, Columbus, OH 43210
Tel: 614-422-6151

Univ. of Oklahoma
William Bennett Bizzell Memorial Library, 401 W. Brooke, Norman, OK 73019
Tel: 405-325-2611

Oklahoma State Univ. Library
Stillwater, OK 74074
Tel: 405-624-6313

Omaha Public Library
212 S. 15 St., Omaha, NE 68102
Tel: 402-444-4800

Orange County Public Library
431 City Drive S., Orange, CA 92668
Tel: 714-634-7841

Univ. of Oregon Library
Eugene, OR 97403
Tel: 503-686-3111

Univ. of Pennsylvania Libraries
3420 Walnut St., Philadelphia, PA 19174
Tel: 215-243-7091

Pennsylvania State Univ.
Fred Lewis Pattee Library, University Park, PA 16802
Tel: 814-865-0401

Free Library of Philadelphia
Logan Sq., Philadelphia, PA 19103
Tel: 215-686-5322

Phoenix Public Library
12 E. McDowell Rd., Phoenix, AZ 85004
Tel: 602-262-6451

Univ. of Pittsburgh
Hillman Library, Pittsburgh, PA 15260
Tel: 412-624-4400

Prince George's County Memorial Library
6532 Adelphi Rd., Hyattsville, MD 20782
Tel: 301-699-3500

Princeton Univ. Library
Princeton, NJ 08540
Tel: 609-452-3180

Purdue Univ. Libraries
Stewart Center, West Lafayette, IN 47907
Tel: 317-749-2571

Queens Borough Public Library
89-11 Merrick Blvd., Jamaica, NY 11432
Tel: 212-990-0700

Rice Univ.
Fondren Library, 6100 S. Main, Box 1892, Houston, TX 77001
Tel: 713-528-4141

Univ. of Rochester
Rush Rhees Library, Rochester, NY 14627
Tel: 716-275-4461

Rutgers Univ. Libraries
College Ave., New Brunswick, NJ 08901
Tel: 201-932-7507

Sacramento Public Library
7000 Franklin Blvd., Suite 540, Sacramento, CA 95823
Tel: 916-440-5926

Saint Louis County Public Library
1640 S. Lindbergh Blvd., Saint Louis, MO 63131
Tel: 314-994-3300

Saint Louis Public Library
1301 Olive St., St. Louis, MO 63103
Tel: 314-241-2288

San Antonio Public Library
203 S. St. Mary's, San Antonio, TX 78205
Tel: 512-223-6851, ext. 31

San Bernardino County Free Library
104 W. Fourth St., San Bernardino, CA 92415
Tel: 714-383-1734

San Diego County Public Library
5555 Overland Ave., Bldg. 15, San Diego, CA 92123
Tel: 714-565-5100

San Diego Public Library
820 East St., San Diego, CA 92101
Tel: 714-236-5800

San Francisco Public Library
Civic Center, San Francisco, CA 94102
Tel: 415-558-4235

San Jose Public Library
180 W. San Carlos St., San Jose, CA 95113
Tel: 408-277-4822

San Mateo County Public Library
25 Tower Rd., Belmont, CA 94002
Tel: 415-573-2056

Seattle Public Library
1000 Fourth Ave., Seattle, WA 98104
Tel: 206-625-2665

Smithsonian Institution Libraries
Constitution Ave. at Tenth St. N.W.,
    Washington, DC 20560
Tel: 202-381-5496

Univ. of South Carolina
Thomas Cooper Library, 1600 Sumter St.,
    Columbia, SC 29208
Tel: 803-777-3142

Univ. of Southern California
Edward L. Doheny Memorial Library,
    University Park, Los Angeles, CA 90007
Tel: 213-746-6050

Stanford Univ.
University and Coordinate Libraries, Stanford,
    CA 94305
Tel: 415-497-2016

Syracuse Univ. Libraries
Ernst S. Bird Library, 222 Waverly Ave.,
    Syracuse, NY 13210
Tel: 315-423-2575

Tampa-Hillsborough County Public Library System
900 N. Ashley, Tampa, FL 33602
Tel: 813-223-8947

Temple Univ.
Samuel Paley Library, Berks and 13 Sts.,
    Philadelphia, PA 19122
Tel: 215-787-8231

Univ. of Tennessee, Knoxville
James O. Hoskins Library, Knoxville, TN
    37916
Tel: 615-974-0111

Univ. of Texas
Mirabeau B. Lamar Library, Box P, Austin,
    TX 78712
Tel: 512-471-3811

Texas A & M Univ. Libraries
College Station, TX 77843
Tel: 713-845-6111

Tulane Univ. of Louisiana
Howard-Tilton Memorial Library, New
    Orleans, LA 70118
Tel: 504-865-5131

Tulsa City-County Public Library
400 Civic Center, Tulsa, OK 74103
Tel: 918-581-5221

Univ. of Utah
Marriott Library, Salt Lake City, UT 84112
Tel: 801-581-8558

Univ. of Virginia
Alderman Library, Charlottesville, VA 22901
Tel: 804-924-3026

Virginia Polytechnic Institute
Carol M. Newman Library, Blacksburg, VA
    24061
Tel: 703-951-8712

Univ. of Washington Libraries
FM-25, Seattle, WA 98195
Tel: 206-543-1760

Washington State Univ. Library
Pullman, WA 99163
Tel: 509-335-4577

Washington Univ. Libraries
Skinner and Lindell Blvds., St. Louis, MO
    63130
Tel: 314-889-5400

Wayne State Univ. Libraries
5210 Second St., Detroit, MI 48202
Tel: 313-577-4050

Univ. of Wisconsin—Milwaukee
University Library, 2311 E. Hartford Ave.,
    Milwaukee, WI 53201
Tel: 414-963-4785

Yale Univ.
Sterling Memorial Library, 120 Hight St., Box
    1603A, Yale Sta., New Haven, CT 06520
Tel: 203-436-8335

CANADA

Univ. of Alberta Libraries
Edmonton, Alta. T6G 2J8
Tel: 403-432-3790

Bibliothèque Municipale de Québec
37 rue Ste-Angele, Quebec, P.Q. G1R 4G5
Tel: 418-694-6356

Univ. of British Columbia Library
2075 Wesbrook Mall, Vancouver, B.C. V6T 1W5
Tel: 604-228-3871

Etobicoke Public Library
Box 501, Etobicoke, Ont. M9C 4V5
Tel: 416-248-5681

London Public Library & Art Museum
304 Queens Ave., London, Ont. N6B 3L7
Tel: 519-432-7166

McGill Univ. Libraries
3459 McTavish St., Montreal, P.Q. H3A 1Y1
Tel: 514-392-4948

McMaster Univ.
Mills Memorial Library, 1280 Main St. W., Hamilton, Ont. L8S 4L6
Tel: 416-525-9140

Montreal City Library
1210 Sherbrooke E., Montreal, P.Q. H2L 1L9
Tel: 514-872-2908

National Library of Canada
Library Documentation Center, 395 Wellington St., Ottawa, Ont. K1A 0N4
Tel: 613-966-1623

Queen's Univ. at Kingston
Douglas Library, Kingston, Ont. K7L 5C4
Tel: 613-547-5950

Regina Public Library
2311 12 Ave., Regina, Sask. S4P 0N3
Tel: 306-569-7615

St. Catharines Public Library
59 Church St., St. Catharines, Ont. L2R 7K2
Tel: 416-688-6103

Saskatoon Public Library
311 23 St. E., Saskatoon, Sask. S7K 056
Tel: 306-652-7313

Scarborough Public Library
1076 Ellesmere Rd., Scarborough, Ont. M1P 4P4
Tel: 416-291-1991

Toronto Public Library
40 Orchard View Blvd., Toronto, Ont. M4R 1B9
Tel: 416-484-8015

Univ. of Toronto Library
Toronto, Ont. M5S 1A5
Tel: 416-978-2294

Univ. of Western Ontario
University Library, 1151 Richmond St. N., London, Ont. N6A 3K7
Tel: 519-679-6191

Windsor Public Library
850 Ouellette Ave., Windsor, Ont. N9A 4M9
Tel: 519-258-8111